P9-BJR-559

Contemporary
Literary Criticism

Guide to Gale Literary Criticism Series

For criticism on	Consult these Gale series
Authors now living or who died after December 31, 1959	*CONTEMPORARY LITERARY CRITICISM (CLC)*
Authors who died between 1900 and 1959	*TWENTIETH-CENTURY LITERARY CRITICISM (TCLC)*
Authors who died between 1800 and 1899	*NINETEENTH-CENTURY LITERATURE CRITICISM (NCLC)*
Authors who died between 1400 and 1799	*LITERATURE CRITICISM FROM 1400 TO 1800 (LC)* *SHAKESPEAREAN CRITICISM (SC)*
Authors who died before 1400	*CLASSICAL AND MEDIEVAL LITERATURE CRITICISM (CMLC)*
Black writers of the past two hundred years	*BLACK LITERATURE CRITICISM (BLC)*
Authors of books for children and young adults	*CHILDREN'S LITERATURE REVIEW (CLR)*
Dramatists	*DRAMA CRITICISM (DC)*
Hispanic writers of the late nineteenth and twentieth centuries	*HISPANIC LITERATURE CRITICISM (HLC)*
Native North American writers and orators of the eighteenth, nineteenth, and twentieth centuries	*NATIVE NORTH AMERICAN LITERATURE (NNAL)*
Poets	*POETRY CRITICISM (PC)*
Short story writers	*SHORT STORY CRITICISM (SSC)*
Major authors from the Renaissance to the present	*WORLD LITERATURE CRITICISM, 1500 TO THE PRESENT (WLC)*

ISSN 0091-3421

Volume 93

Contemporary Literary Criticism

Excerpts from Criticism of the Works
of Today's Novelists, Poets, Playwrights,
Short Story Writers, Scriptwriters, and
Other Creative Writers

Brigham Narins
Deborah A. Stanley
EDITORS

George H. Blair
Jeff Chapman
Pamela S. Dear
Daniel Jones
John D. Jorgenson
Aarti D. Stephens
Polly A. Vedder
Thomas Wiloch
Kathleen Wilson
Janet Witalec
ASSOCIATE EDITORS

GALE

DETROIT • NEW YORK • TORONTO • LONDON

STAFF

...igham Narins and Deborah A. Stanley, *Editors*

...n, Pamela S. Dear, John D. Jorgenson, Aarti D. Stephens,
...en Wilson, and Janet Witalec, *Contributing Editors*

George H. Blair, Daniel Jones, Polly A. Vedder, and Thomas Wiloch, *Associate Editors*

Christopher Giroux, John P. Daniel, Linda Quigley, and John Stanley, *Assistant Editors*

Marlene S. Hurst, *Permissions Manager*
Margaret A. Chamberlain, Maria Franklin, *Permissions Specialists*

Diane Cooper, Michele Lonoconus, Maureen Puhl, Susan Salas,
Shalice Shah, Kimberly F. Smilay, *Permissions Associates*

Sarah Chesney, Edna Hedblad, Rita Velazquez, *Permissions Assistants*

Victoria B. Cariappa, *Research Manager*

Tamara C. Nott, Michele P. Pica, Tracie A. Richardson, Norma Sawaya, *Research Associates*

Alicia Noel Biggers, Julia C. Daniel, *Research Associates*

Mary Beth Trimper, *Production Director*
Deborah L. Milliken, *Production Assistant*

Sherrell Hobbs, *Macintosh Artist*
Randy Bassett, *Image Database Supervisor*
Robert Duncan, *Scanner Operator*
Pamela Hayes, *Photography Coordinator*

Library of Congress Catalog Card Number 76-46132
ISBN 0-8103-9271-2
ISSN 0276-8178

Printed in the United States of America
10 9 8 7 6 5 4 3 2 1

Contents

Preface   vii

Acknowledgments   xi

Preface

A Comprehensive Information Source on Contemporary Literature

Named "one of the twenty-five most distinguished reference titles published during the past twenty-five years" by *Reference Quarterly,* the *Contemporary Literary Criticism (CLC)* series provides readers with critical commentary and general information on more than 2,000 authors now living or who died after December 31, 1959. Previous to the publication of the first volume of *CLC* in 1973, there was no ongoing digest monitoring scholarly and popular sources of critical opinion and explication of modern literature. *CLC,* therefore, has fulfilled an essential need, particularly since the complexity and variety of contemporary literature makes the function of criticism especially important to today's reader.

Scope of the Series

CLC presents significant passages from published criticism of works by creative writers. Since many of the authors covered by *CLC* inspire continual critical commentary, writers are often represented in more than one volume. There is, of course, no duplication of reprinted criticism.

Authors are selected for inclusion for a variety of reasons, among them the publication or dramatic production of a critically acclaimed new work, the reception of a major literary award, revival of interest in past writings, or the adaptation of a literary work to film or television.

Attention is also given to several other groups of writers-authors of considerable public interest—about whose work criticism is often difficult to locate. These include mystery and science fiction writers, literary and social critics, foreign writers, and authors who represent particular ethnic groups within the United States.

Format of the Book

Each *CLC* volume contains about 500 individual excerpts taken from hundreds of book review periodicals, general magazines, scholarly journals, monographs, and books. Entries include critical evaluations spanning from the beginning of an author's career to the most current commentary. Interviews, feature articles, and other published writings that offer insight into the author's works are also presented. Students, teachers, librarians, and researchers will find that the generous excerpts and supplementary material in *CLC* provide them with vital information required to write a term paper, analyze a poem, or lead a book discussion group. In addition, complete bibliographical citations note the original source and all of the information necessary for a term paper footnote or bibliography.

Features

A *CLC* author entry consists of the following elements:

- The **Author Heading** cites the author's name in the form under which the author has most commonly published, followed by birth date, and death date when applicable. Uncertainty as to a birth or death date is indicated by a question mark.

- A **Portrait** of the author is included when available.

- A brief **Biographical and Critical Introduction** to the author and his or her work precedes the excerpted criticism. The first line of the introduction provides the author's full name, pseudonyms (if applicable), nationality, and a listing of genres in which the author has written. To provide users with easier access to information, the biographical and critical essay included in each author entry is divided into four categories: "Introduction," "Biographical Information," "Major Works," and "Critical Reception." The introductions to single-work entries—entries that focus on well known and frequently studied books, short stories, and poems—are similarly organized to quickly provide readers with information on the plot and major characters of the work being discussed, its major themes, and its critical reception. Previous volumes of *CLC* in which the author has been featured are also listed in the introduction.

- A list of **Principal Works** notes the most important writings by the author. When foreign-language works have been translated into English, the English-language version of the title follows in brackets.

- The **Excerpted Criticism** represents various kinds of critical writing, ranging in form from the brief review to the scholarly exegesis. Essays are selected by the editors to reflect the spectrum of opinion about a specific work or about an author's literary career in general. The excerpts are presented chronologically, adding a useful perspective to the entry. All titles by the author featured in the entry are printed in boldface type, which enables the reader to easily identify the works being discussed. Publication information (such as publisher names and book prices) and parenthetical numerical references (such as footnotes or page and line references to specific editions of a work) have been deleted at the editor's discretion to provide smoother reading of the text.

- Critical essays are prefaced by **Explanatory Notes** as an additional aid to readers. These notes may provide several types of valuable information, including: the reputation of the critic, the importance of the work of criticism, the commentator's approach to the author's work, the purpose of the criticism, and changes in critical trends regarding the author.

- A complete **Bibliographical Citation** designed to help the user find the original essay or book precedes each excerpt.

- Whenever possible, a recent, previously unpublished **Author Interview** accompanies each entry.

- A concise **Further Reading** section appears at the end of entries on authors for whom a significant amount of criticism exists in addition to the pieces reprinted in *CLC*. Each citation in this section is accompanied by a descriptive annotation describing the content of that article. Materials included in this section are grouped under various headings (e.g., Biography, Bibliography, Criticism, and Interviews) to aid users in their search for additional information. Cross-references to other useful sources published by Gale Research in which the author has appeared are also included: *Authors in the News, Black Writers, Children's Literature Review, Contemporary Authors, Dictionary of Literary Biography, DISCovering Authors, Drama Criticism, Hispanic Literature Criticism, Hispanic Writers, Native North American Literature, Poetry Criticism, Something about the Author, Short Story Criticism, Contemporary Authors Autobiography Series,* and *Something about the Author Autobiography Series.*

Other Features

CLC also includes the following features:

- An **Acknowledgments** section lists the copyright holders who have granted permission to reprint material in this volume of *CLC*. It does not, however, list every book or periodical reprinted or consulted during the preparation of the volume.

- Each new volume of *CLC* includes a **Cumulative Topic Index,** which lists all literary topics treated in *CLC, NCLC, TCLC,* and *LC 1400-1800.*

- A **Cumulative Author Index** lists all the authors who have appeared in the various literary criticism series published by Gale Research, with cross-references to Gale's biographical and autobiographical series. A full listing of the series referenced there appears on the first page of the indexes of this volume. Readers will welcome this cumulated author index as a useful tool for locating an author within the various series. The index, which lists birth and death dates when available, will be particularly valuable for those authors who are identified with a certain period but whose death dates cause them to be placed in another, or for those authors whose careers span two periods. For example, Ernest Hemingway is found in *CLC,* yet F. Scott Fitzgerald, a writer often associated with him, is found in *Twentieth-Century Literary Criticism.*

- A **Cumulative Nationality Index** alphabetically lists all authors featured in *CLC* by nationality, followed by numbers corresponding to the volumes in which the authors appear.

- An alphabetical **Title Index** accompanies each volume of *CLC*. Listings are followed by the author's name and the corresponding page numbers where the titles are discussed. English translations of foreign titles and variations of titles are cross-referenced to the title under which a work was originally published. Titles of novels, novellas, dramas, films, record albums, and poetry, short story, and essay collections are printed in italics, while all individual poems, short stories, essays, and songs are printed in roman type within quotation marks; when published separately (e.g., T. S. Eliot's poem *The Waste Land),* the titles of long poems are printed in italics.

- In response to numerous suggestions from librarians, Gale has also produced a **Special Paperbound Edition** of the *CLC* title index. This annual cumulation, which alphabetically lists all titles reviewed in the series, is available to all customers and is typically published with every fifth volume of *CLC*. Additional copies of the index are available upon request. Librarians and patrons will welcome this separate index: it saves shelf space, is easy to use, and is recyclable upon receipt of the next edition.

Citing *Contemporary Literary Criticism*

When writing papers, students who quote directly from any volume in the Literary Criticism Series may use the following general forms to footnote reprinted criticism. The first example pertains to material drawn from periodicals, the second to material reprinted in books:

[1]Alfred Cismaru, "Making the Best of It," *The New Republic,* 207, No. 24, (December 7, 1992), 30, 32; excerpted and reprinted in *Contemporary Literary Criticism,* Vol. 85, ed. Christopher Giroux (Detroit: Gale Research, 1995), pp. 73-4.

[2]Yvor Winters, *The Post-Symbolist Methods* (Allen Swallow, 1967); excerpted and reprinted in *Contemporary Literary Criticism,* Vol. 85, ed. Christopher Giroux (Detroit: Gale Research, 1995), pp. 223-26.

Suggestions Are Welcome

The editors hope that readers will find *CLC* a useful reference tool and welcome comments about the work. Send comments and suggestions to: Editors, *Contemporary Literary Criticism,* Gale Research, Penobscot Building, Detroit, MI 48226-4094.

Acknowledgments

The editors wish to thank the copyright holders of the excerpted criticism included in this volume and the permissions managers of many book and magazine publishing companies for assisting us in securing reprint rights. We are also grateful to the staffs of the Detroit Public Library, the Library of Congress, the University of Detroit Library, Wayne State University Purdy/Kresge Library Complex, and the University of Michigan Libraries for making their resources available to us. Following is a list of the copyright holders who have granted us permission to reprint material in this volume of *CLC*. Every effort has been made to trace copyright, but if omissions have been made, please let us know.

COPYRIGHTED EXCERPTS IN *CLC*, VOLUME 93, WERE REPRINTED FROM THE FOLLOWING PERIODICALS:

The American Book Review, v. 14, August-September, 1992; v. 14, December, 1992-January, 1993. © 1992 by *The American Book Review.* Both reprinted by permission of the publisher.—*American Indian Culture and Research Journal,* v. 4, 1980 for "The Uses of Oral Tradition in Six Contemporary Native American Poets" by James Ruppert. Copyright © 1980 James Ruppert. Reprinted by permission of the author.—*The Americas Review,* v. 19, Winter, 1991. Copyright © 1991 *The Americas Review.* Reprinted by permission of the publisher, Arte Público Press--University of Houston.—*The Atlantic Monthly,* v. 233, February, 1974 for "A True Inheritor" by Katie Louchheim. Copyright 1974 by The Atlantic Monthly Company, Boston, MA./ v. 201, May, 1958 for "Where Men Are the Men" by Edward Weeks. Copyright 1958, renewed 1979, by The Atlantic Monthly Company, Boston, MA. Reprinted by permission of the Literary Estate of Edward Weeks./ v. 190, October, 1952 for "At War with Texas" by Phoebe Lou Adams. Copyright 1952 by The Atlantic Monthly Company, Boston, MA. Reprinted by permission of the author.—*Belles Lettres: A Review of Books By Women,* v. IV, Summer, 1991; v. 10, Spring, 1995. Both reprinted by permission of the publisher.—*The Bloomsbury Review,* v. 13, January-February, 1993 for an interview with Elizabeth Cook-Lynn by Jamie Sullivan. Copyright © by Owaissa Communications Company, Inc., 1993. Reprinted by permission of Elizabeth Cook-Lynn and Jamie Sullivan.—*Book World--The Washington Post,* v. XVII, April 10, 1988; v. XXI, August 25, 1991; v. XXII, June 13, 1993; v. XXV, July 9, 1995. © 1988, 1991, 1993, 1995, Washington Post Book World Service/Washington Post Writers Group. All reprinted with permission. —*Booklist,* v. 90, September 1, 1993. Copyright © 1993 by the American Library Association. Reprinted by permission of the publisher.—*Boston Review,* v. XX, Summer, 1995 for a review of "Galatea 2.2." by Paul Gediman. Copyright © 1995 by the Boston Critic, Inc. Reprinted by permission of the author.—*Cahiers Victoriens & Edouardiens,* n. 22, October, 1985. All rights reserved. Reprinted by permission of the publisher.—*Chicago Review,* v. 13, Autumn, 1959. Copyright © 1959, renewed 1987 by *Chicago Review.* Reprinted by permission of the publisher.—*Chicago Tribune--Books,* May 23, 1993 for "Fate of the Innocent" by Sven Birkerts. © copyrighted 1993, Chicago Tribune Company. All rights reserved. Reprinted by permission of the author.—*The Christian Century,* v. LXXXI, April 22, 1964. Copyright 1964 Christian Century Foundation. Reprinted by permission from *The Christian Century.*—*The Christian Science Monitor,* v. 85, September 3, 1993 for "A Brave Woman's Saga of Survival Continues" by Gretchen M. Bataille. © 1993 The Christian Science Publishing Society. All rights reserved. Reprinted by permission of the author.—*Commonweal,* v. CXIX, April 10, 1992. Copyright © 1992 Commonweal Publishing Co., Inc. Reprinted by permission of Commonweal Foundation.—*Contemporary Psychology,* v. 39, February, 1994 for "The Best of Us Did Not Return" by Dan P. McAdams. Copyright © 1994 by the American Psychological Association. Reprinted by permission of the publisher and the author.—*Cross Currents,* v. 4, 1985 for "Jaroslav Seifert--The Good Old Drinking Poet" by Josef Skvorecky. Reprinted by permission of the author.—*The Hudson Review,* v. XXIX, Spring, 1986; v. XL, Spring, 1987. Copyright © 1986, 1987 by The Hudson Review Inc. Both reprinted by permission of the publisher.—*Human Behavior,* v. 6, July, 1977 for "The Frankl Meaning" by David Cohen. Copyright © 1977 Human Behavior Magazine. Reprinted by permission of Watson, Little Ltd., for the author.—*Hungry Mind Review,* n. 32, Winter, 1994. Reprinted by permission of the publisher.—*Index on Censorship,* v. 14, April, 1985. Copyright Writers & Scholars International Ltd., 1985. Reprinted by permission of the publisher.—*Indian Literature,* v. XIII, 1970 for a review of "Morning Face" by Saros Cowasjee. Reprinted by permission of the author.—*The International Fiction Review,* v. 4, January, 1977 for "Mulk Raj Anand's Confession

Bogan. Reprinted by permission of Ruth Limmer.—Bowles, Gloria. From *Louise Bogan's Aesthetic of Limitation.* Indiana University Press, 1987. © 1987 by Gloria Bowles. All rights reserved. Reprinted by permission of the publisher.—Braendlin, Bonnie Hoover. From "The Prostitute as Scapegoat: Mildred Rogers in Somerset Maugham's 'Of Human Bondage'," in *The Image of the Prostitute in Modern Literature.* Edited by Pierre L. Horn and Mary Beth Pringle. Ungar, 1984. Copyright © 1984 by Frederick Ungar Publishing Co., Inc. Reprinted by permission of the publisher.—Brave Bird, Mary, with Richard Erdoes. From *Ohitika Woman.* Grove Press, 1993. Copyright © 1993 by Mary Brave Bird and Richard Erdoes. Reprinted by permission of Grove Press, Inc.—Bruchac, Joseph. From an interview in *Survival This Way: Interviews with American Indian Poets.* Sun Tracks,The University of Arizona Press, 1987. Copyright © 1987 The Arizona Board of Regents. All rights reserved. Reprinted by permission of the publisher.—Burt, Forrest D. From *W. Somerset Maugham.* Twayne Publishers, 1985. Copyright © 1985 by G. K. Hall & Co. All rights reserved. Reprinted with the permission of Twayne Publishers, an imprint of Simon & Schuster Macmillan.—Cook-Lynn, Elizabeth. From "You May Consider Speaking about Your Art...," in *I Tell You Now: Autobiographical Essays by Native American Writers.* Edited by Brian Swann and Arnold Krupat. Copyright © 1987 by the University of Nebraska Press. All rights reserved. Reprinted by permission of the publisher.—Cowasjee, Saros. From "Mulk Raj Anand: The Fusion of History and Fiction," in *Subjects Worthy Fame: Essays on Commonwealth Literature in Honour of H. H. Anniah Gowda.* Edited by A. L. McLeod. Sterling Publishers Private Ltd., 1989. © 1989, A. L. McLeod. Reprinted by permission of A. L. McLeod.—Farrar, John. From *The Literary Spotlight.* George H. Doran Company, 1924. Copyright, 1924, by George H. Doran Company. Renewed 1951 by John Chipman Farrar.—Frank, Elizabeth. From *Louise Bogan: A Portrait.* Alfred A. Knopf, 1985. Copyright © 1985 by Elizabeth Frank. All rights reserved under International and Pan-American Copyright Conventions. Reprinted by permission of Alfred A. Knopf, Inc.—Harrex, S. C. From "Western Ideology and Eastern Forms of Fiction: The Case of Mulk Raj Anand," in *Asian and Western Writers in Dialogue: New Cultural Identities.* Edited by Guy Amirthanayagam. The Macmillan Press Ltd., 1982. © Guy Amirthanayagam 1982. All rights reserved. Reprinted by permission of Macmillan, London and Basingstoke.—Loss, Archie K. From *Of Human Bondage: Coming of Age in the Novel.* Twayne Publishers, 1990. Copyright ©1990 by G. K. Hall & Co. All rights reserved. Reprinted with the permission of Twayne Publishers, an imprint of Simon & Schuster Macmillan.—Moore, Patrick. From "Symbol, Mask, and Meter in the Poetry of Louise Bogan," in *Gender and Literary Voice.* Edited by Janet Todd. Holmes & Meier, 1980. Copyright © 1980 by Raul Hilberg. All rights reserved. Reprinted by permission of the publisher.—Naik, M. K. From *W. Somerset Maugham.* University of Oklahoma Press, 1966. Copyright 1966 by the University of Oklahoma Press. Reprinted by permission of the publisher.—Osers, Ewald. From *An Umbrella From Piccadilly.* By Jaroslav Seifert, translated by Ewald Osers. London Magazine Editions, 1983. © Translation Ewald Osers. Reprinted by permission of the publisher.—Pallan, Rajesh K. From "Encounter with the Self: A Study of the Confessional Mode in Mulk Raj Anand's 'The Bubble'," in *The New Indian Novel in English: A Study of the 1980s.* Edited by Viney Kirpal. Allied Publishers Limited, 1990. Reprinted by permission of the author.—Parrott, Cecil. From *The Plaque Column.* By Jaroslav Seifert, translated by Ewald Osers. Terra Nova Editions, 1979. English translation © Ewald Osers. Introduction © Sir Cecil Parrott. Reprinted by permission of John Johnson Ltd.—Reed, John R. From *Old School Ties: The Public Schools in British Literature.* Syracuse University Press, 1964. Copyright © 1964, renewed 1992, by Syracuse University Press. All rights reserved. Reprinted by permission of the publisher.—Seifert, Jaroslav. From *Les Prix Nobel.* Nobel Prize Foundation, 1985. Copyright © by the Nobel Foundation 1985. Reprinted by permission of the publisher.

PERMISSION TO REPRODUCE PHOTOGRAPHS APPEARING IN *CLC*, VOLUME 93, WAS RECEIVED FROM THE FOLLOWING SOURCES:

Eichner, Sara. Alvarez, Julia, photograph. Reproduced by permission of William Eichner: **p. 1;** Anand, Mulk Raj, photograph by Marilyn Stafford: **p. 21;** Victor, Thomas. Bogan, Louise, photograph. Reproduced by permission: **p. 59;** Erdoes, Richard. Brave Bird, Mary, photograph. Reproduced by permission of Richard Erdoes: **p. 108;** Cook-Lynn, Elizabeth, photograph. Reproduced by permission: **p. 114;** Halsman, Philippe. Ferber, Edna, later years, photograph. © Halsman Estate. Reproduced by permission: **p. 133;** Vesely, Katharina. Frankl, Viktor, photograph. © Katharina Vesely. Reproduced by permission: **p. 192;** Maugham, W. Somerset, 1935 photograph. AP/Wide World Photos. Reproduced by permission: **p. 225;** Bauer, Jerry. Powers, Richard, photograph. © Jerry Bauer. Reproduced by permission: **p. 274;** Zivkovic, Lagorka. Seifert, Jaroslav, photograph. © Lutfi Ozkok. Reproduced by permission: **p. 303.**

Julia Alvarez

1950-

Dominican-American novelist and poet.

The following entry provides an overview of Alvarez's career through 1995.

INTRODUCTION

Best known for her first novel, *How the García Girls Lost Their Accents* (1991), Alvarez is noted for portrayals of familial relationships, the Hispanic immigrant experience, and for insights into such issues as acculturation, alienation, and prejudice. Alvarez frequently blurs the lines between poetry and fiction and uses circular rather than chronological narrative structures. Writing about *How the García Girls Lost Their Accents,* Jason Zappe has stated that "Alvarez speaks for many families and brings to light the challenges faced by many immigrants. She shows how the tensions of successes and failures don't have to tear families apart."

Biographical Information

Born in New York City, Alvarez was raised in the Dominican Republic until the age of ten. She was encouraged by her parents, especially her mother, to consider herself American and therefore different from the rest of their extended family. In 1960 Alvarez and her family fled the Dominican Republic because of her father's involvement in a plot to overthrow the dictator Rafael Trujillo, who had ruled the country for nearly thirty years and was ultimately assassinated in 1961. The family moved back to New York City, and Alvarez grew up in the Bronx, where her father established a medical practice. Alvarez has noted that her subsequent feelings of alienation "caused a radical change in me. It made me an introverted little girl." She immersed herself in books and eventually began to write. Alvarez went on to earn undergraduate and graduate degrees in literature and writing and became an English professor at Middlebury College in Vermont. Her first collection of poetry, *Homecoming,* was published in 1984. Alvarez has since earned numerous awards and grants, including a National Endowment for the Arts grant, an Ingram Merrill Foundation grant, and the PEN Oakland/Josephine Miles Award for excellence in multicultural literature.

Major Works

Critics note that in *Homecoming* Alvarez uses simple, eloquent language and a wide range of narrative techniques to address such themes as family ties and love. *How the García Girls Lost Their Accents,* while often called a novel, is a series of fifteen short stories interwoven to tell one tale in reverse chronological order. Spanning the years from 1956 to 1989, this work chronicles the lives of the García

sisters—Carla, Sandra, Yolonda, and Sopía—from their upbringing in the Dominican Republic to their escape to the United States. Largely autobiographical, the work explores such issues as acculturation, coming of age, and social status. Alvarez's next novel, *In the Time of the Butterflies* (1994), is set in the Dominican Republic and relates in fictional form the true story of the four Mirabal sisters, the Butterflies, or *Las Mariposas.* As active opponents of Trujillo, three of the four sisters were murdered by the government in 1960. In arguing for the importance of the part they played in Dominican history and consciousness, Alvarez also explores more universal themes of history, tyranny, freedom, and survival. Her bilingual collection of poetry, *The Other Side/El Otro Lado* (1995), addresses immigrant life, self-identity, and the contradictions that arise when memories of childhood impinge on adult realities.

Critical Reception

The critical reaction to Alvarez's works has been generally positive, with most critics praising her sympathetic and personal portraits of families and the immigrant experience. However, some have faulted her unconventional narrative structures, particularly in *How the García Girls Lost Their Accents* and *In the Time of the Butterflies,* and her uneven characterizations. Commenting on *How the García Girls Lost Their Accents,* Ilan Stavans has stated: "Alvarez has an acute eye for the secret complexities that permeate family life. Although once in a while she sets into melodrama, her descriptions are full of pathos." Similarly, Stavans states that *In the Time of the Butterflies* is "full of pathos and passion, with beautifully crafted anecdotes interstitched to create a patchwork quilt of meaning and ideology."

PRINCIPAL WORKS

Homecoming (poetry) 1984
How the García Girls Lost Their Accents (novel) 1991
In the Time of Butterflies (novel) 1994
The Other Side/El Otro Lado (poetry) 1995

CRITICISM

Fred Muratori (review date Winter 1986)

SOURCE: A review of *Homecoming,* in *New England Review and Bread Loaf Quarterly,* Vol. IX, No. 2, Winter, 1986, pp. 231-32.

[*In the following excerpt, Muratori praises the poems in* Homecoming.]

The sonnet lives . . . in a first book by poet and fiction writer Julia Alvarez. . . . "33," a sequence of forty-one sonnets that takes its title from the poet's age, fills half the volume [*Homecoming*]. It's a diary-like assemblage of meditations, stories, and confessions, of which the following is fairly typical:

> Ever have an older lover say: God!
> I once thought I used to love so and so
> so much, but now that I love you, I know
> that wasn't love! Even though it feels good
> at our age to be flattered with being
> the first woman a man has ever loved,
> it burns my blood thinking of those I loved
> with my whole soul (small as it was back then)
> quibble if what they felt for me was love
> now that they've had a taste of the real stuff.
> I say, Don't trust those men with better,
> bigger versions of love if they refuse
> the small shabby sample they gave others
> the tribute of believing it was true.

The poem rhymes, or half rhymes, somewhat modestly, but its decasyllabic lines are consistent and again we find a *volta* four lines from the end. The everyday language of the poem, with its plethora of monosyllabics, its conversational expressions, and its parenthetical aside, flows rapidly within a highly controlled enclosure. The poem springs from a feeling of betrayal and outrage (tempered with a

bit of savvy irony), and its final admonishment has a bitter edge. But again the sonnet form encourages a surprise reversal as the poet, in a moment of resolve, understands that a profession of "real love" may be true and false at the same instant, that the defining of love is an ongoing process of revision and comparison, and that a belief in one's feelings at the moment they're felt is the least one can demand of another. The poem's exasperation is all the stronger for its containment; the piece demonstrates how effectively formal limitations and direct, "natural" language can work together. It specifies a place where emotions and the intellect can meet on common ground. This is diary verse with a difference.

Cecilia Rodríguez Milanés (review date July 1991)

SOURCE: "No Place Like Home," in *The Women's Review of Books,* Vol. 8, Nos. 10-11, July, 1991, p. 39.

[*In the following review, Milanés calls* How the García Girls Lost Their Accents *a portrait of "its protagonists' precarious coming of age."*]

As so many immigrants and exiles know, you can never go back home. It's never the same—or rather *we* are not the same. In Julia Alvarez' novel the sisters Carla, Sandra, Yolanda and Sofía lose their island accents, life and ways, but *How the Garcia Girls Lost Their Accents* is not simply about adjustment and acculturation. It is about its protagonists' precarious coming of age as Latinas in the United States and gringas in Santo Domingo.

On the first anniversary of the family's life in the US, Carla makes a clearly unrealizable wish:

> What do you wish for on the first celebration of the day you lost everything? Carla wondered. Everyone else around the table had their eyes closed as if they had no trouble deciding. Carla closed her eyes too. She should make an effort and not wish for what she always wished for in her homesickness. But just this last time, she would let herself. "Dear God," she began. She could not get used to this American wish-making without bringing God into it. "Let us please go back home, please," she half prayed and half wished.

Chucha, the voodoo-practicing servant, predicts what the reader is made aware of through the separate but interrelated stories that make up the chapters:

> I feel their losses pile up like dirt thrown on a box after it has been lowered into the earth. I see their future, the troublesome life ahead. They will be haunted by what they do and don't remember. But they have spirit in them. They will invent what they need to survive.

They do indeed survive, and when one compares their lives with that of their island counterparts—pampered queens sheltered in a complex of family houses barricaded by a high stone wall against the violence, poverty and danger of the Dominican Republic, saddled with philandering husbands, with little more to anticipate but the next cousin's wedding—the sisters' somewhat haunted life is preferable. They are, in fact, their own women, standing up to boyfriends, husbands, lovers and parents—even the island family when it comes down to it.

Back home the girls had art lessons and learned to ride horseback. There were trips abroad and chauffeurs awaiting them in the driveway of the lush family compound. Their native Spanish is a protective garment wrapped around them, but in the US English defrocks Spanish: there are Catholic schools, redneck neighborhoods, identical suburban houses and, later, a great deal of typical American teenage life.

Donna Rifkind   (review date 6 October 1991)

SOURCE: "Speaking American," in *The New York Times Book Review,* October 6, 1991, p. 14.

[*Rifkind is an American critic. In the following review, she provides a mixed assessment of* How the García Girls Lost Their Accents, *stating that in this work Alvarez "has not yet quite found a voice."*]

To speak without an accent is the ultimate goal of the immigrant, yet the literature of immigration requires an accent to lend it authenticity and flair. This threshold— between accent and native speech, alienation and assimilation—is the golden door through which the Dominican-American writer Julia Alvarez sails with *How the Garcia Girls Lost Their Accents,* her first collection of interwoven stories. It is a threshold that, in our multicultural era, many other American writers have recently crossed, including such best-selling authors as Oscar Hijuelos, Jamaica Kincaid and Amy Tan. Yet stories about this experience are at least as old as the classical image of Aeneas, his son by his side and his father on his back, venturing to a profoundly foreign new world.

Julia Alvarez's Garcia girls—Carla, Sandra, Yolanda, Sofia—are steeped in longstanding traditions of their own. They share a noble Spanish ancestry dating back to the *conquistadores.* In their homeland, the Dominican Republic, their prodigious family is wealthy and influential, occupying a Kennedyesque compound of opulent homes. But when their father, the gracious, cultured Dr. Garcia, joins in a botched attempt to oust the dictator Rafael Trujillo, the family is forced to escape to New York.

The Americanization of these grammar school girls means fighting for a distinctiveness they have never known. Back at the island compound, they lived among a multitude of aunts, uncles, cousins (Dr. Garcia himself is the youngest of 35 children, 25 of them legitimate). Every experience was a group activity: when one cousin caught the measles, all the children were quarantined together to insure a collective immunity.

With the Garcia girls' new-world individuality comes the pain of discrimination, the greenhorn's terror. Their characters are forged amid the taunts of schoolmates, who raise questions about identity in a language they barely understand. "Here they were trying to fit into America among Americans; they needed help figuring out who they were, why the Irish kids whose grandparents had been micks were calling them spics. Why had they come to this country in the first place?"

Their parents can't be counted on to answer these questions. Dr. Garcia, who after years in the United States still cringes at the sight of uniforms and black Volkswagens (the car of the secret police back home), stubbornly clings to the memories and accents of the old world. Mrs. Garcia, whose clothes and shoes match just a bit too perfectly and whose malaprops ("It takes two to tangle, you know") are an embarrassment, is a good enough mother for indulged and overprotected island girls, but for emancipated New York teen-agers she's "a terrible girlfriend parent, a real failure of a Mom."

Despite the lack of guidance, though, all four girls are determined to assimilate. Their tour through an American adolescence and young adulthood includes some familiar baggage: anorexia, experimental drugs and sex (this is the late 1960's), failed relationships, nervous breakdowns, psychiatrists, and, ultimately, the American dream of every junior Ms.: professional success harmoniously balanced with marriage and children.

Julia Alvarez, who teaches English at Middlebury College in Vermont, devotes nearly half of her stories to the mature discontents of the Garcia girls. But because their adult preoccupations are by now such cliches—the staples of women's magazines and pop fiction—these chapters are by far the book's weaker half. Much more powerful are the rich descriptions of island life and the poignant stories detailing the Garcias' first year in the United States. These come at the end of the book, curiously, for Julia Alvarez has chosen to tell her tale backwards: the first section of five stories dates from 1989 to 1972, the middle five stories from 1970 to 1960 and the last five from 1960 to 1956.

While this seems at first to be an unnecessary bit of gimmickry, it is in fact a shrewd idea: by locating the best stories last, Ms. Alvarez has made this a better book than it might otherwise have been. She has, to her great credit, beautifully captured the threshold experience of the new immigrant, where the past is not yet a memory and the future remains an anxious dream. Her second and more ambitious goal, however, that of translating her characters' voices into an unhackneyed American idiom, has gone unrealized. The Garcia girls may indeed have lost their accents, but in her first book of fiction Julia Alvarez has not yet quite found a voice.

Jason Zappe   (review date Winter 1991)

SOURCE: A review of *How the García Girls Lost Their Accents,* in *The Americas Review,* Vol. XIX, Nos. 3-4, Winter, 1991, pp. 150-52.

[*In the following review, Zappe offers a positive summation of* How the García Girls Lost Their Accents, *stating Alvarez "shows how the tensions of successes and failures don't have to tear families apart."*]

When the *conquistadores,* the first immigrants to the New World, landed in the Caribbean they weren't forced to adopt to new ways. They retained the privileged position of conqueror and did not have to learn a new language, or a new culture or to endure endless and merciless racial abuse.

But when the Garcias, who were direct descendants of the original *conquistadores,* came to the United States they were forced to learn new ways. The Garcias are the central players in Julia Alvarez's novel ***How the Garcia Girls Lost Their Accents***. The family fled its home in the Dominican Republic to begin a new life in the United States and went from being part of an upper echelon to the challenging status of immigrant.

Alvarez centers on the Garcia family and its struggles to assimilate in the United States. Alvarez, like Sandra Cisneros, began as a poet before turning to fiction, and with the publication of her first book, she displays a talent for portraying the immigrant experience with sensitivity and light-heartedness. Alvarez never once allows the reader to think growing up in a foreign culture, especially the United States, is ever easy.

Alvarez's narrative explores the Garcias and how the four daughters come of age in the United States. The reader discovers the Garcia family—Papi, Mami, Yolanda, Carla, Sofia and Sandra—as the novel unfolds backward, the way a dying person might remember her life.

The Garcias come to the United States as political exiles after a failed coup attempt on the Dominican dictator Rafael Trujillo. Papi was one of the coup leaders. The Garcias are aided by a CIA agent with an affection for little girls. Alvarez makes another reference to this type of molestation when she tells of the time Carla was walking home from school in the Bronx and was accosted by a man in a car.

Alvarez's predominant theme with the context of assimilation is culture clash. It can be seen back on the Island between the young and the old, in the United States between the girls and the other kids and between the girls and their parents. Culture clash becomes the fundamental antagonist in Alvarez's story as each and every one of the Garcias must face up to it.

The reader is introduced first to Yolanda, the poet, as she returns to the Island in 1989 after a five-year absence. She confesses she would like to return forever because she never really felt at home in the States, even though she also discovers how Americanized she has become. Yolanda, who becomes Joe in the States, witnesses at once the charm of the Island and how foreign it has become to her liberated modern way of life.

As the tale of the Garcias in the new world progresses, each of the family members, mostly the girls, recount the troubles and obstacles they overcame. All four had to deal with the pressures of having Old World parents. This weighed heavily on the girls since it occurred when young people in the States were undergoing a cultural revolution. They had to balance living up to Papi's expectations and the anticipations of their new Anglo boyfriends.

All four daughters like life in the Bronx, where Papi has set up his medical practice, and all want more from this New World. Papi and Mami never thought the four girls would adapt so well or want so much from the States.

During their high school years, they discovered that most of what their Old World parents had told them was bad,

turned out to be fun. Soon this new teenage life was in and "Island was old hat, man. Island was the hair-and-nails crowd, chaperons, and icky boys with all their macho strutting and unbuttoned shirts and hairy chests with gold chains and teensy gold crucifixes."

All through their school years the girls returned to the Island during the summers. Mami insisted they go, even if they did not want to, feeling she was making sure they never forgot where they had come from.

It was on the Island that they behaved as "alta sociedad" ladies did. They would behave like they had "never been to the States or read Simone de Beauvoir." When they began college, the trips back to the Island stopped.

Mostly the girls saw the trips as punishment. They truly wanted to become Americanized and forget the ways of the past. Most descendants of European immigrants have successfully adapted to life in the United States at the expense of the ways of the Old World, but today's immigrants from other lands still struggle to fuse the ways of the two. And this conflict pervades the lives of the Garcias.

All four of the Garcia girls were willing to trade the safety and tradition of the Old World for the freedoms and choices in the new. And as illicit love letters, bags of pot and birth control devices are found by Mami and Papi, it becomes apparent to them that their girls have become fully Americanized. But the assimilation process does not always rely on how radical chic one can become. In the case of Yolanda, her Americanization is realized as she wrote her ninth-grade valedictorian speech and finally sounded like herself in English.

As the girls come of age and find their own paths in their new homeland, the reader comes to understand how a family must grapple with the intricacies of assimilation in its attempts to determine its place in a new culture. The Garcias manage to stay together through all the conflicts, both inner and outer. Alvarez suggests that a family with strong devotion and love can conquer a new world and not have to disappear as the younger generation assimilates.

Alvarez speaks for many families and brings to light the challenges faced by immigrants. She shows how the tensions of successes and failures don't have to tear families apart; indeed, she suggests the opposite is possible. The Garcias pull together when trouble arrives. The family unit never breaks down in Alvarez's story even as the Garcia girls grow to be independent in a new land.

Julia Alvarez with Catherine Wiley   (interview date March 1992)

SOURCE: An interview, in *The Bloomsbury Review,* Vol. 12, No. 2, March, 1992, pp. 9-10.

[*Wiley is an American educator and critic who has written works on feminism and drama. In the following interview, Alvarez discusses such subjects as her identity as a Latina, the Women's movement, and her family.*]

[*Wiley*]: *You've said that maybe what we are doing is mov-*

ing forward in a circle, in reference to women's issues, I think.

[Alvarez]: About plot and about how we tell stories, about how women are [supposed to be] relational instead of directional. We think of others, of the whole network and how, in the traditional household, everyone's being taken care of, so we think relationally. I was talking about the plot as a quilt, which is a way that I think a lot of women experience plot, as opposed to the hero directed on his adventures and conquering things and getting a prize, at all odds doing what he needs to do.

When I was teaching Louise Erdrich's *Love Medicine,* I remember one of the reviews said this is just a collection of stories, which it is in part. Rayna Green, who edited *That's What She Said: Contemporary Poetry & Fiction by Native American Women* came and talked to my class when I was in Washington, D.C., and she was saying how Native American people experience the truth. It is something you get at, that's right there, but the truth is all the points around the truth, around the circle. Each little perspective somehow is what the truth is, and that, therefore, Louise Erdrich, in a way, was picking up plot that was out of her experience. It's that sense of moving in a circle.

You still moved from A to B in **The Garcia Girls,** *but it's not necessarily one direction.*

Yes, it's not one direction. We found this our in the women's movement: you don't just move forward. All of a sudden, women of color were saying, this is a middle-class movement. Then you have to fix up your business here, between each other. It wasn't just a forward directed thing, it was more moving in a circle, and it's not as quick probably.

But at least you sound optimistic when you say moving forward.

Well, I hope so. Some of the stuff happening now with the supreme court and abortion programs, you wonder where we're going.

That's true. In terms of the women's movement, I remember there was a theme in your novel when the sisters gang up to save Fifi from the macho Dominican boyfriend. At one point they are promoting women's rights, and they said they had given up with the various aunts and cousins because there wasn't any point in discussing those things down there. Do you feel like that's changing at all for women in the Dominican Republic?

Oh yes. One of the things that I've discovered going back now on my own, not to visit family, is that there's a whole world out there beyond my family and my cousins and their orientation. One member of my family is a little bit of a maverick there and was involved with a center for women that's very active in all of Central America but based in the Dominican Republic. They were giving seminars and had women from all over Central America and other Caribbean countries. I took a seminar and I realized, "Hey, there's another world here." I've become very close with one of the writers there, Chiqui Viceoso. She's in *Breaking Boundaries,* that book on Latino writing. It's criticism and testimonials, as they call them, on Latino

writers. Chiqui has a testimonial in there. Anyhow, she is a writer there, and she's also very active politically, and through her also I've been thrown into another world that doesn't have anything to do with my family.

And so that must be an issue of class as well?

It's an issue of class, but not completely. There are some women there who had privileged backgrounds, but they just changed their orientation and made other choices from the ones their families had made for them—I'm thinking of my maverick cousin who really has made other choices too. But it does have to do with class somewhat too, that's really true. There is another organization of campesinos (rural workers) that is very much a grassroots kind of thing coming out of the Dominican Republic. It's a little country that's going to really break loose one of these days.

Break loose from . . . ?

Well, we had this President who's been there forever—I think he's eighty-four or eighty-six. He's spent this last term mostly obsessed with the idea of [celebrating] Columbus, spending all this money on buildings and doing construction mostly for tourists, internal imperialism in a way, getting the country all spiffed up for foreigners. So I think his term is going to be up, he's going to die soon, and what happens in terms of leadership will really be interesting.

Do you think that women will play a more active role in national politics?

Yes, absolutely. At least, I hope so.

I guess you have to be hopeful. I loaned **The Garcia Girls** *to a Puerto Rican friend of mine. She read it and liked it very much, but she said, "You know it's strange, this doesn't feel really Latina to me." And I said, "Well it's the Dominican Republic, it's not Puerto Rico." And she said it's very strange because she didn't relate to it as a Latina. Do you feel like the label, Latina writer, is . . . ?*

Inaccurate? I don't know. I think when I write, I write out of who I am and the questions I need to figure out. A lot of what I have worked through has had to do with coming to this country and losing a homeland and a culture, as a way of making sense, and also it has to do with the sisterhood of my sisters and myself. They were the only people I really had as models. We were moving in a circle, because none of us knew any more than the other one but all we had was each other, not feeling part of this world and not really feeling part of the old world either.

It reminds me of my students in ethnic literature, who [sometimes] complain, why do we have to label, why do we have to say African American woman writer, why do you have to say Chicana lesbian writer. Why can't you just say writer or American writer? I'm never really sure how to respond. On the one hand, that specificity is important in terms of this person, writing as a Latina and about those kinds of tensions in a culture. On the other hand, everybody should just be allowed to be a writer.

I think part of my experience has been that for a lot of my professional life, I haven't been part of the community. I have two sisters who live in the Boston area, and they work in Latino communities. Their work is there, their friends are there, they speak Spanish with their friends, and I always feel a yearning when I'm with them. I live in Vermont, where I don't have that kind of connection at all. I always feel like I don't have that context. When I met Sandra Cisneros, I felt like she's got her country here, she's got a community in San Antonio that I've never experienced living in this country. There was a conference in New York [on women writers]. Some Dominicanas and a woman who does ethnic literature called me up after it. Someone had shown them a poem by Julia Alvarez, who was teaching out in Illinois. They called me up and said, "Julia, who are you?"

"Where have you been?"

So the next conference they had, I went. I felt . . . I didn't know you all were [out there]. I've been reading American Latina writers, but I hadn't had the interchange, the dialogue. That I really miss.

Like a home away from home. In your poetry, were you writing self-consciously as a Latina, as an immigrant in the way the novel is addressing those kinds of issues?

Not at all. It's really funny because when the poet Marilyn Haphern read my book of poems, **Homecoming,** she said, "You know I read that book, and, except for the first poem, 'Homecoming,' I wouldn't know that you were a Latina." It was interesting and made me think about a couple of things. First of all, that book is very much finding a voice as a woman. That was the primary thing that I was addressing, because when I first went to college I didn't have any writing sisters and most of my teachers were males. The two female authors that I read were Jane Austen and Emily Dickinson in a survey course.

We all have that in common.

So when I got out of grad school, the writing program, and was starting to write, I was really blocked because I was trying to sound like those guys, and I didn't have anything to say like them. I was at Yaddo, the writing colony, and I could hear all the typewriters going when I was having the worst writer's block because I was getting ready to write my great work, and I didn't hear those voices. What happened was that I went outside my study room—you're not supposed to bother anybody until dinner—and the only people around were all the maids. There was somebody vacuuming the big mansion, and the cook was making our lunches. So I went downstairs and sat on the stool and talked to the cook and paged through her cookbook. I started writing down lists of words about cooking and started talking to her about cooking. And I started writing what became the whole first section of the book of poems, the housekeeping poems. I went back to the voices that I did hear—my mother, my aunts, maids, all talking about cooking and making beds and ironing and all that stuff—and used those as my metaphors. What I think I was trying to do in that book was to validate that this was something I could write about. I was so blocked, I didn't think that that was literature.

I didn't either, I don't think.

So I wasn't writing a lot about the Dominican Republic, and I think the other thing was that when I started to write more and more about that experience, it came out in narrative rather than lyric.

Why did you switch genres?

"Homecoming" is a narrative poem, longer than the others. It's almost as if it's the beginning of a story. Well, I started writing stories, thinking that I would just write a few.

In terms of teaching, we're always trying to impress on our students the idea of difference and, despite the women's movement, the differences between women are as important as the differences between women and men. There are, for example, different Latina voices . . .

It's interesting. I find that true, in terms of being a Latina writer and being compared especially to Sandra Cisneros, whose book came out at a different time. At the same time, I guess I want to see a real cohesiveness happen, a real dialogue happen among Latinas and Latina writers. Yesterday, in Iowa, this Chicana who runs the women's center there started talking about how there are certain words that you just can't say in English because it doesn't get to what it is you have to say, and we started talking about what some of those words were. That dialogue was so amazing. I hadn't thought about that, but it's true.

Do you ever write in Spanish?

Not at all. I consider Spanish my childhood language, a language that stayed static at ten. I use it with my parents, and I use it with the family. Now, I do want to study more and get back into it because of Chiqui and my friends in the Dominican Republic. Some of them are writers.

I was thinking as I was reading, would this be something you'd like to see translated into Spanish?

They sold the Spanish rights.

Did you have a good translator?

I don't know. The publisher chooses the translator, and I guess you only have veto power if you don't like it. My friend Chiqui tried to translate a group of my poems into Spanish, and she is a poet too, so they just sound wonderful in Spanish. But I had somebody translate a story of mine into Spanish for a critical article, and it just didn't sound right. Mostly because she translated it into what I felt was good Spanish.

Proper Spanish, you mean?

Yes, Castillian Spanish instead of what I'm used to speaking.

One thing I really liked in the novel were the different voices, especially near the end where you had the two guardia and the Haitian maid.

Chucha.

Yes, I thought that was great. Was that hard to do, especially the two men who are sort of the enemies and obviously there's a huge class difference between them. Even though they're threatening the family, they're really doing it from a position of not being empowered themselves?

Yes, yes. That story, **"Blood of the Conquistadores,"** was one that I really had to write because I have no memories of our last day on the island. I think it's the pivotal day of my life, and I can't remember anything that happened.

I did an experiment. I wrote the story, and I wanted to get all the points around the circle, to build that day as it might have happened, doing it with a fictional family instead of the real family. Afterwards I wrote every member of my family and asked them if they would write to me their memory of the last day. All my sisters, my parents, wrote me a little page of memory, and then I sent them the story. There is the issue about writing out of autobiography, that people will think it's true or that you're lying. So what I did was I showed them that what each had come up with was different from what I had done in the story.

> I think when I write, I write out of who I
> am and the questions I need to figure out.
> A lot of what I have worked through has
> got to do with coming to this country and
> losing a home land and a culture, as a way
> of making sense.
>
> —*Julia Alvarez*

And yet it was one experience.

Yes, and also that I didn't remember anything. That's why I had made it up. It isn't that I was using something that had happened, but that I was recreating it. One sister insisted that her memory was that we had all rolled the car out of the driveway so that the secret police wouldn't hear it, instead of turning on the motor. Then, because I compared notes with everyone, I told my older sister that that was Teeta's memory, and she said, that didn't happen at all, that was from *The Sound of Music*. So, what came out of all this was memory, and it's very tricky. I mean, memory is already the story you made up about the past.

But for the voices that weren't in your family, that was pure fiction on your part, wasn't it?

Yes, but also identification, just imagining from people I knew growing up. One of the reasons I don't speak "good" Spanish is that I learned it from the maids. They're the people I spent time with when we were little. My sisters talk about where their [current political involvement] comes from, given some of our cousins in the Dominican Republic and their concerns. Part of it is that our mother was very removed and didn't do a lot of mothering and parenting. The ones who we were close to, who hung out with us, fed us, were the maids, and that's where we have the emotional connection.

It sounds like the nineteenth-century in this country. Many Whites had closer emotional ties to their Black nannies, and of course, literally you had Black women who had to nurse White kids and to leave their own children. It sounds similar.

Yes, in some ways. I think that we all feel a connection and a real tension in conflict. For instance, two sisters find it very hard to go back.

I bet.

They don't have connection to some of the aunts and cousins; you just connect out of something so old. When I've been down there recently, I lived in a village. I didn't live with family. That's the next thing I'm writing about. It was a real education for me. Also, it made me think about what my choices are in the future. I don't think I want to keep on for the rest of my life teaching at Middlebury College. Part of it is that Bill, the guy I married, is part of a project called Volunteer Eye Surgeons International. They go to third world countries and volunteer time. He's been to the Dominican Republic several times, and there's a clinic set up, kind of an outreach clinic. What we're thinking of is living part of the time there and maybe starting some sort of project.

Has your family given you a hard time about the novel?

Let's put it this way, the person that I thought would give me the hardest time—my father—not at all. He called up after he read it, weeping, saying that he was so proud of me. My sisters were a little taken aback. I think it's really hard to read something that is close enough to the truth, but has been reworked and remade and recast, and not feel somehow exposed. We all went through a real rebellious phase when we came and were suddenly exposed to the sixties and war protests and drugs and sex. We'd been raised in such a tight little controlled family. But the things that happened in the story aren't things that necessarily happened to us, though those issues did come up, so that feels like an exposure. But each one reacted differently, and they all have come around. One of them said that it was really hard for her, but she really felt that it was for her to deal with. But they're also very proud of me and feeling kind of mixed. The one is my mother, it's still, oh dear . . .

Has she read the whole thing?

I think so. It reminds me very much of one of the things I teach in minority women's literature—how strong the mandate of silence is. The grandmother of all these books is Maxine Kingston's *The Woman Warrior;* it starts out with "My mother told me never ever to repeat this story." [This] is even stronger, I think, for immigrant and minority populations where it feels like it's a betrayal of the group to go outside of the group somehow, to tell the story.

It's interesting that your father really liked it. As I was reading, I kept getting a sense of how the father in the book is a little Trujillo, all of the metaphors of control and benevolence with a twist. The daughters sort of resent him and yet feel that they need that kind of person. It's a great metaphor for how these dictators get there in the first place.

I think it also points to how the fictional family is also different from the real family. In some ways, I feel that my real mother has been a muse, but it's been much more complicated.

The mother in the book seems to act as sort of a buffer between the daughters and the father.

Yes, and some of that has happened in my real family, but the mother wants her daughters to flourish and do things and so forth. She herself has caught the bug of wanting to be her own woman, that kind of thing.

Oh, yes. I was going back to what you had said earlier on about feeling that in this country you're also part of the other country even though, for example, your Spanish was cut off. But in terms of writing, you've found some kind of a balance between the tradition of the family and all of those Dominican aspects of your life that are really important but which you had to change to be an American.

Sometimes it hits me that I think I write out of feeling that it doesn't quite balance and that I need to figure it out. For instance, what I'm working on now—I don't know if it will come to anything, you never do until it comes to something—is how people become politicized. How does that happen? Let's say someone living in this country goes back to the Dominican Republic and encounters a whole world of people who are very politically involved, very leftist, very radical, have made some choices about their lives and given up a lot of ways of thinking out of a real sense of commitment. When I went back there and lived in this village, I went down to write. All of sudden, I was getting involved in different things happening in the village, including that there was no school, and why wasn't there a school, and then trying to get the village kids involved in raising money for a school by doing an art project. It took a lot of time, and the NEA was ticking away, and I wasn't getting any writing done. Then the resort across from this village fenced off their land, so to get to work the villagers had to go way around the peninsula, and nobody has a car, and it takes an hour and a half, etc. So I got involved in going to the managers and talking, and going to a lawyer, and all of a sudden, my life as a writer . . . I saw that if I lived there, I don't know that I would continue as a writer.

Ilan Stavans   (review date 10 April 1992)

SOURCE: "Daughters of Invention," in *The Commonweal,* Vol. CXIX, No. 7, April 10, 1992, pp. 23-5.

[*Stavans is an American novelist and critic. In the following review, he calls* How the Garcá Girls Lost Their Accents *"a brilliant debut."*]

In the mood for a Dominican author writing in English? You are likely to find only one: Julia Alvarez, who left her country at ten and now lives and teaches at Middlebury College. Besides a book of poetry published in 1986 (intriguingly titled **Homecoming**), she is the writer of this delightful novel, a tour de force that holds a unique place in the context of the ethnic literature from which it emerges. In the age of affirmative action in life and literature, those looking for themes like drug addiction, poverty, and Hispanic stereotypes are in for a surprise. Much in the tradi-

tion of nineteenth-century Russian realism, and in the line of the genuine "porcelain" narrative creations of Nina Berberova, **How the García Girls Lost Their Accents** has as its protagonist the García de la Torre, a rich family in Santo Domingo and its surroundings whose genealogical tree reaches back to the Spanish *conquistadores.* Through the García family's sorrow and happiness, through the spiritual and quotidian search that leads to their voluntary exile in the United States, the dramatic changes of an entire era are recorded. Energetic, curious, and bellicose, their collective plight is a struggle to keep up with the times, and also, an adjustment to a culture that isn't theirs.

The plot focuses on the relationship of four sisters: Carla, Sandra (Sandi), Yolanda (Yo, Yoyo, or Joe), and Sofia (Fifi). Their aristocratic upbringing as S.A.P. s—Spanish American Princessés—takes them from their "savage Caribbean island" to prestigious schools in New England and from there to an existence as middle-class citizens in the Bronx. They undergo discrimination and suffer from linguistic misunderstandings. They iron their hair according to the latest fashion and buy bell-bottom-pants with fringe. As women in difficult marriages and troubled breakups, theirs is the customary rite of passage of immigrants assimilating into another reality. Their rejection of the native background, nevertheless, is told with humor and has a sense of unrecoverable loss because, for as much as the García sisters want to become American, they remain conscious of the advantages of their Dominican selves. Hence, Alvarez's is a chronicle of the ambivalence with which Hispanics adapt to Anglo-Saxon idiosyncracies.

Made of fifteen self-contained chapters collected in three symmetrical parts, more than a novel the volume ought to be read as a collection of interrelated stories. Each segment reads as an independent unit, with the same set of characters recurring time and again in different epochs and places. As a whole, the narrative spans three decades, the first chapter beginning in 1988 and the last reaching as far back as 1956. Similar to some plots by the Cuban musicologist Alejo Carpentier and the British playwright Harold Pinter, the García girls, as if on a journey back to the source, navigate from maturity to adolescence, from knowledge to naïveté, from light to darkness—that is, their lives are perceived in reverse. In the process, the characters slowly deconstruct their personalities and reflect upon their Catholic education at home in the hands of a "respectable," highly schematic father. In his 1982 autobiography *Hunger for Memory,* Richard Rodriguez, while attacking bilingual education, discussed the impairment of the native tongue and the acquisition of the "father" tongue, English. Because Alvarez is uninterested in such meditations, her book, in spite of the title, isn't about language. Here and there the narrative does offer insightful reflections on the transition from an ancestral vehicle of communication to an active, convenient one. Yet the idea of "losing" one's accent is nothing but a metaphor: a symbol of cultural abandonment.

A secondary leitmotif also colors the plot—that of the coming of age of a candid female writer and her indomitable need to describe, in literary terms, her feelings and immediate milieu. Yoyo, the author's alter ego, is a sensible, extroverted adolescent who loves to write poetry. In **"Daughter of Invention,"** perhaps the volume's best story and one recalling Ralph Ellison's first chapter of *Invisible Man,* she is asked to deliver a commencement speech. Her mother helps her out. In search of inspiration, Yoyo finds Whitman's *Leaves of Grass,* in particular "Song of Myself," and writes a speech celebrating her egotism, her excessive self-interest. The theme infuriates her father. In a rage of anger, he tears up the manuscript. But the mother's support encourages the girl to deliver the speech, which she does quite successfully. She is praised by her own repentant father with a gift of a personal typewriter.

Obviously, as a whole *How the García Girls Lost Their Accents* is Yoyo's product. Although its content is told by shifting narrators, she is the soul inside the text. She contrasts and ponders. She is puzzled and flabbergasted by the circumstances around her. The world gains and loses its coherence in her mind. In an illuminating segment about Pila, a bizarre maid with voodoo powers who inspired nightmares, Yoyo writes about her first discovery of things Dominican. Hers is a story of wonder and disbelief. Accustomed to a certain climate of order and to the rules set forth by her parents, she is disoriented by the behavior of the maid. After a series of mishaps that involve a cat and strange tales by a grandmother, the section concludes:

> [After those experiences] we moved to the United States. . . . I saw snow. I solved the riddle of an outdoors made mostly of concrete in New York. My grandmother grew so old she could not remember who she was. I went away to school. I read books. You understand I am collapsing all time now so that it fits what's left in the hollow of my story? I began to write, the story of Pila, the story of my grandmother . . . . I grew up, a curious woman, a woman of story ghosts and story devils, a woman prone to bad dreams and bad insomnia. There are still times I wake up at three o'clock in the morning and peer into the darkness. At that hour and in that loneliness, I hear [Pila], a black furred thing lurking in the corners of my life, her magenta mouth opening, wailing over some violation that lies at the center of my art.

The entire volume is a gathering of memories, a literary attempt to make sense of the past. Alvarez has an acute eye for the secret complexities that permeate family life. Although once in a while she steps into melodrama, her descriptions are full of pathos. The political reality in the Dominican Republic, although never at center stage, marks the background. The repressive thirty-year-long Trujillo dictatorship, which culminated with the leader's assassination in 1961, makes the Garcías happy but complicates their lives. The democratic elections that brought Juan Bosch into power bring a period of tranquillity, interrupted by the 1965 civil war that brought the U.S. intervention and ended in the election, supervised by the Organization of American States, of Joaquín Balaguer. The family is pushed to an exile that makes its religious faith stumble and its traditions collapse. Yet *How the García Girls Lost Their Accents,* unlike scores of narratives from south of the Rio Grande, is free from an anti-American message: in Tennessee Williams's terms, its primary concern is a minuscule glass menagerie, the fragile life of a group of individuals swept by epic events they constantly fight to ignore.

While imperfect and at times unbalanced, this is a brilliant debut—an important addition to the canon of Hispanic letters in the U.S. By chosing to write for an English-speaking audience, Alvarez is confessing her own loyalty: albeit reluctantly, she is in the process of losing her accent. Still, the accent refuses to die.

Bruce-Novoa   (review date Summer 1992)

SOURCE: A review of *How the García Girls Lost Their Accents,* in *World Literature Today,* Vol. 66, No. 3, Summer, 1992, p. 516.

[*Juan D. Bruce-Novoa, who frequently writes under his surname only, is a Costa Rican-born American critic and educator. In the following positive review, he discusses the narrative structure of* How the García Girls Lost Their Accents.]

U.S. Latino literature is dominated by male Chicanos, Puerto Ricans, and Cuban Americans. It may therefore surprise readers to discover that possibly the best novel in this category during 1991 comes from a Dominican American woman. However, the U.S.'s long involvement in Dominican internal affairs has produced a steady stream of immigrants. New York City contains the largest urban concentration of Dominicans in the world. U.S. Dominican literature was bound to appear.

Legitimately surprising are the maturity and technical polish of Julia Álvarez's first novel, *How the García Girls Lost Their Accents*. Granted, the author is no novice, having a Ph.D. in literature, a decade of experience teaching writing, and a book of poetry (*Homecoming,*) to her credit. Nevertheless, common wisdom about ethnic literatures claims that each group must crawl before it walks, and so Álvarez's sprint out of the narrative starting blocks demands theoretical rethinking of ethnic literary development.

Álvarez utilizes a standard immigration motif: her narrative charts family history both to trace adjustments to the changing cultural environment and to recover its roots in the land of origin. During the voyage the reason necessitating immigration is found, the essential catalyst in transforming citizens of one nation into immigrants who eventually become ethnic residents of a new country. The paradigm, however, has been dominated by patriarchal codes, the conflict within the acculturation family often being portrayed as the disintegration of the father's position as head of the family and a shift of focus to the mother. *García Girls* both appropriates and violates this pattern. The García family experiences a sometimes painful liberation from patriarchy, but the search for roots, instead of nostalgically confirming the old chauvinist system, debunks it.

Álvarez structures the narrative in temporally receding subsections, from 1989 to 1956, shifting the perspective among four sisters to create multiple points of view and an air of a family project. From the start the search motif emerges, with one of the sisters back on the island visiting her family and hoping she has finally found a real home after twenty-nine years of unsettled life. When she goes out on her own, however, she is disoriented by the mixture of her U.S. openness (unbecoming an island woman of the upper class), forgotten cultural codes, and the desire to retrieve island pleasures. She never does reach the familial estate where, as a child, she was taught to ride English style. Instead she is caught in a sign of racial, class, and national conflict, which, ironically, turns out to be the real roots she is hunting for—though readers only understand the full import of the discovery in the final chapters. In the end not only is patriarchy debunked but a matrilineal line of mixed blood and class is affirmed, albeit as a repressed contributor to origins. A most entertaining, significant contribution to U.S. Latino literature.

Alvarez on her childhood in The Dominican Republic:

Although I was raised in the Dominican Republic by Dominican parents in an extended Dominican family, mine was an American childhood. Technically, I am American, for I was born in New York City and lived there for three weeks before my parents returned "home," their first emigration having failed owing to my mother's homesickness. That technicality of birth, however, would not have amounted to anything but paper citizenship if it hadn't been backed up by a sense of the honor and privilege the certificate conferred on me. "Just remember," my father explained to my older sister and me. "You could become president. You were born there." My mother referred to her first two daughters as her *Americanitas* and to the last two as *criollas* (homemade). My cousins would often ask me what I remembered about living in that magic land. I'd claim to recall a great many things from those first three weeks. Only once did my memory fail me, when I said that snow came in several colors.

When my parents returned to the Dominican Republic right after I was born, they moved into a house on my grandparents' property, where the extended family lived—grandparents, uncles, aunts, a band of cousins—all of us fans of the Americans. My mother's family had had money for a while, and in the last three generations—what with half-a-dozen revolutions, changes of governments, as well as hurricanes, droughts, earthquakes, and several American marine occupations—they had learned that a good education is the best investment. The sons and daughters were sent off to the United States to boarding schools. Upon graduation, the girls were brought home because too much schooling might spoil them for marriage. The sons went on to good colleges—Cornell, Yale, Brown.

Julia Alvarez, in The American Scholar, *Winter, 1987.*

Elizabeth Starcevic   (review date August-September 1992)

SOURCE: "Talking about Language," in *The American*

Book Review, Vol. 14, No. 3, August-September, 1992, p. 15.

[*Starcevic is a critic and professor of Spanish. In the following review, she praises Alvarez's portrayal of the family in* How the García Girls Lost Their Accents *but faults her for not having "consistently developed voices."*]

[In *How the García Girls Lost Their Accents*], it is the voices of the García girls, the four lovely daughters of Mami and Papi García, who singly and in chorus offer the shifting choral poem that recounts their life as "strangers in a strange land." (Julia Alvarez left the Domincan Republic when she was ten years old. She published *Homecoming,* her first book of poetry, in 1986.) Privileged children of a privileged Dominican upper-class family, they are forced to leave their idyllic family compound to come and live in New York. Their father, Carlos García, one of thirty-three children, is a well-established professional in his country. Their mother, Laura de la Torre, traces her heritage back to the conquistadors and never forgets to mention a Swedish grandmother among her ancestors. Her father, a representative from the Dominican Republic to the United Nations, is involved in national politics, but with a difficult and complex relationship to the reigning dictator Rafael Trujillo. Carlos García and many of his relatives and friends become involved in an attempt to overthrow Trujillo that is at first supported and then abandoned by the United States. García is aided in his flight from his homeland by one of the Americans who implement this policy of fluctuating imperialism.

The threads of politics, race, and class surface often in this circular depiction of the García family's life in the United States. Beginning and ending in the Dominican Republic, in a quest to perhaps go home again, the stories unfurl from the present to the past, from 1989 to 1959. They are grouped in three sections with five stories each. Weaving together the life "before" and the life "after," these histories of immigrant experience are filled with humor, love, and intimate detail.

The shock felt by the girls when they abruptly change their life circumstances seems unbearable at first. Initially in limbo and wishing to return to their home, the girls experience racism, sexism, perversion, and a poverty that they were totally unused to. Isolated by language, they bond together within their already clannish patriachal family, which is also being bombarded by the demands of the new world. Traditional roles are challenged, and upheaval permeates their interactions.

Although Carlos García is drawn as the patriarch and all the girls seek his approval, it is Laura de la Torre who plays the significant role as a mediator between two cultures. Educated in the United States, she merges the self-confidence of her wealthy background with a receptivity toward the new challenges. Energetic and intelligent, she is always thinking of new inventions. Her creativity is stymied, yet she finds other outlets in the activities of her children and her husband. She is a vivid, alive character whose contributions to the necessary adjustments of her new life are both critiqued and appreciated by her daughters. Through her stories about them we discover their accomplishments and their defeats, their adventures and professional advances. When Mami tells their story, each girl feels herself to be the favorite.

Carla, Yolanda, Sandra, and Sofía García grow up in a tumultuous period in the United States. This is the time of the Vietnam War, the sexual revolution, drugs, and feminism. While trying to negotiate the strict limits imposed on them by their parents, the sisters develop as a group and individually. "The four girls," as they are called, constantly see themselves as part of a similarly dressed collective, understanding only later that this made their mother's life easier while making them miserable. Their parents, while appreciated and loved, were not really able to guide them in their new tasks. Indeed, the cultures often seem to war against each other as the girls are told to be good, Catholic, respectful, unsullied virgins in an atmosphere that pushes for new mores and individualistic attitudes. They are sent to prep school in Boston and later go on to college. Marriages, divorces, breakdowns, and careers all form part of the adjustment. At least one, Yolanda, the poet, the writer whose voice is perhaps the strongest throughout the novel, decides as an adult to consider spending some time in the Dominican Republic and perhaps discovering at last her real home. There is overlay, however, in the cultural clashes. On one of their visits, these "American" sisters, who no longer fit as Dominicans, unite to rescue Sofía, the youngest. Having fallen in love and become emptyheaded almost simultaneously, she is ready to go off to a motel with her macho cousin, who believes that using condoms is an offense to his manhood.

In these visits and in their memories of their birthplace, we learn of the prejudices toward Haitians and darker-skinned country girls who are both needed and looked down upon. The portrayal of Chucha, the ancient Haitian servant, who is feared for her temper, her voodoo spells, and her practice of sleeping in a coffin, offers a glimpse into the historical complexity of the relationships of the two countries that share the island of Hispaniola. Comfort and ease that are taken for granted are provided by a series of servants who may spend their entire lives in the compound. Their livelihood depends on the whims of the employer, and one of the Garcías' maids is abruptly dismissed for having one of the children's toys in her possession even though Carla had given it to her as a gift.

The class privilege that was abruptly disturbed by the failed coup attempt does not disappear completely in the new world. Carlos García obtains a job immediately through his American benefactor Dr. Fanning. Little by little he is able to establish a practice and to provide ever greater comfort for his family. The Garcías are helped as well by Mrs. García's father. It is on a special evening out with the Fannings that we see the problematic relationship of U.S. neocolonialism replayed and that Sandi learns the power of emotional blackmail.

Scenes of pain and hardship but also of great humor are found throughout the novel. We listen to Laura García describe finding her husband and Carla in the bathroom painting white sneakers red with nail polish. Or, shades of magical realism, we watch Sandi discover one of the island's famous sculptors, naked and chained, in a shed strewn with giant figures in wood. Eventually she sees that he has sculpted her face on the statue of the virgin for the annual nativity crèche. Banding together, the sisters play on the names of their family in Santo Domingo, translating them literally so that they sound silly in English.

Language is a central feature of the book, beginning with the title. From Mrs. García's "mixed-up idioms that showed she was green behind the ears," to Yolanda's poetry, to the author, the girls, the mother and the father, all the aunts who want them to speak Spanish, the nuns and the police who want them to speak English, all the characters talk about language.

These are stories about relationships. Women are at the center, and we see the world through their eyes but also hear of it through their mouths. These are people of an oral tradition, and even though they have moved on to a writing stage, the power of the voice is what carries them. The book is uneven, and its organization into individual stories highlights this. The author has not really found consistently developed voices. Nevertheless, as we are pulled backward toward the moment when these Dominicans will become immigrants, we are pulled into the world of this family, we are drawn into their hopes and their dreams and their strategies for living, and we are glad. We enjoy what we learn, we enjoy the music of this chorus, we feel included in their lively, passionate world, and we want more.

Julia Alvarez   (essay date February 1993)

SOURCE: "Black behind the Ears," in *Essence,* Vol. 23, No. 10, February, 1993, pp. 42, 129, 132.

[*In the following essay, Alvarez discusses issues of color in relationship to the Dominican immigrant experience.*]

When [*How the Garcia Girls Lost Their Accents*] came out last year, invitations streamed in to speak at gatherings as one of a new wave of Latina writers, "a woman of color" who had made a splash on the mainstream shore. I didn't know if anyone had seen my picture on the back cover, or even read my book, but I was worried that I'd get to the gathering and disappoint everyone by turning out to be the wrong kind of Latina, a sorry white one.

One invitation I accepted was to a public school in New York City with a large population of Dominican kids. I would be a role model of what one of their own could achieve in this country. After my talk, my agent told me about a conversation she had overheard. Two sugar-cane-brown Dominican girls had been waiting eagerly for me to enter the classroom. When I did, one turned to the other and said, "What she got to say to us? She's a white girl."

"But by the time you were through talking," my agent assured me, "they were laughing with you."

Later, at a conference on Dominicans in the United States, I confided to my friend Sergio what had happened. "The thing is," I argued, as if the girls might hear me, "I've got family their color. My own *abuelita* [grandmother] looks pretty dark in her photos."

"And I've got cousins who could make you look tanned!" Sergio smiled. His own rich brown skin belied the New York winter outside and glowed with tropical warmth. My olive color had waned into a white blah.

"Dominicans learn that kind of talk here," Sergio continued. "That idea of *us,* the Blacks, and *them,* the whites, isn't a Dominican discourse in the D.R." He reminded me that ours is a racially mixed society: Black, white, mulatto, with whatever diluted bit is left of the Taino Indians. Almost every family has a variety of shades. "You know how the saying goes?"

We laughed and then, in unison in Spanish, we repeated it, "We all have a little black behind the ears."

Perhaps because of what that saying affirmed, I had never thought of myself as the wrong color Latina. I was just one of a rainbow coalition of colors in my large extended family.

Or so I had convinced myself, wanting to submerge completely the issue of race in ethnicity. But incidents such as the one in the public school got me thinking. Had I been unconscious of racism until we came to the United States? If we were a rainbow-coalition family of different shades, why was the black shade relegated to behind the ears, like dirt that wasn't supposed to show? Wasn't it clear that the pot of gold was clearly toward the lighter end of that rainbow?

Growing up in the Dominican Republic, my cousins and I were always encouraged to stay out of the sun so we wouldn't "look like Haitians." At family gatherings, when features were declined down to which great-aunt gave us our noses or pairs of eyes, dark coloring was ascribed to someone's "not thinking ahead." As we girls grew up, we had endless bedroom comparison sessions of your good hair versus my bad hair, my fine nose versus your flared one, your light shade of *café con leche* versus a potential boyfriend's heavy-duty, full-strength *cafecito* color.

All of us aspired to be on the lighter side of the spectrum. Don't get me wrong. None of us wanted to be white-white like those pale, limphaired *gringos,* whites who looked as if they'd been soaked in a bucket of bleach. The whiter ones of us sat out in the sun to get a little *color indio,* while others stayed indoors rubbing Nivea on their darker skin to lighten it up!

During one of my summer visits, I fell in mad, passionate love with a dark-skinned cousin; my *primo* was far enough removed that our kids wouldn't come out funny. "Just dark," an aunt teased, but there was no real prohibition in the remark. Albertico, or Tico as I nicknamed him, came from *una familia muy buena,* a family with money and prestige. Color cut across class lines. As another Dominican saying goes: A rich Black is a mulatto; a rich mulatto is a white man. I would be making good match.

And so would he, I learned. Besides my dowry of coming from a good family myself, I had white genes to bring into Tico's family pool. His mother courted me, sending over desserts: poufy macaroons, a flan swimming in sugar syrup, a white frosted production that looked like a trial run on a wedding cake. "Why?" I asked.

"She likes you." Tico smiled, his nostrils flaring.

"She doesn't even know me," I argued. I had talked to Doña Mercedes maybe twice.

"She likes what she sees."

That was long ago, but during a recent trip "home," I witnessed an instance of racism I didn't like seeing. The incident gave me some insight into the roots of the Dominican racism I had grown up with.

I was visiting La Romana where Haitian sugarcane workers flood the market on Saturdays to shop. Two equally Black men were arguing in loud voices over some mistake in an exchange of pesos. One insulted the other, *"Negro maldito!"* Cursed Black!

"Aren't they both Black?" I asked the Dominican friend who was with me.

"Oh no," he explained. "The Haitian one is Black, the other one is Dominican."

A week after my return from my trip, I finally reached my friend Sergio on the phone. *"Ven acá!"* —Come here! —I confronted him. "You told me that racism is a discourse Dominicans learn in the States." I related my recent thoughts about growing up thinking light is right, as well as the incident I had witnessed on the street.

"I didn't say we didn't have racism," Sergio responded. "I said we didn't think of ourselves as Blacks and whites, *them* and *us.* See, Dominicans see the real Blacks as the Haitians, the real whites as the Americans. It's the old house-slave mentality, a little above the dark field hands but below the white masters."

"What's going to change that kind of attitude?" I asked him.

"What they call here 'role models,' " Sergio answered.

"Black ones?" I asked in a small voice, fearing I'd be canceled out.

"And white ones with all that black behind the ears getting onto the piece of paper," he said, laughing that bubbly Creole laughter I would have identified as Dominican anywhere. I was laughing, too, thinking of my olive-skinned Papi and my dark *abuelita* and my white *prima* and my *india* niece—claiming them all.

Ilan Stavans (review date 7 November 1994)

SOURCE: "Las Mariposas," in *The Nation,* New York, Vol. 259, No. 15, November 7, 1994, pp. 552, 554-56.

[*In the following mixed review, Stavans calls* In the Time of the Butterflies *"simultaneously invigorating and curiously disappointing."*]

Not long ago, I heard Julia Alvarez call attention to an intriguing linguistic tic in her native Dominican culture: When you ask somebody what's up and no easy reply can be found, people are likely to say, *Entre Lucas y Juan Mejía.* "Between the devil and the deep blue sea" isn't the right equivalent in English, Alvarez added, "because you aren't describing the sensation of being caught between a pair of bad alternatives."

> "So-so" isn't the meaning either, because the Dominican expression isn't at all meant to suggest bland stasis, mediocrity. It's much more intriguing than that. "How are you doing?" "I'm between Lucas and Juan Mejía." And who are these guys? . . . The very story that inspired the saying is gone. So . . . you have to go on and tell the tale of why you feel the way you do. What are the forces you're caught between? How did you get there? And how does it feel to be there?

Alvarez's *oeuvre* is precisely about this type of crisis—the identity of the in-betweens—and about why she feels the way she does in somebody else's country and language (she immigrated to the United States with her family when she was 10). Although this subject is ubiquitous in ethnic literature in general, her pen lends it an authenticity and sense of urgency seldom found elsewhere. In fact, in the current wave of Latina novelists she strikes me as among the least theatrical and vociferous, the one listening most closely to the subtleties of her own artistic call. She stands apart stylistically, a psychological novelist who uses language skillfully to depict complex inner lives for her fictional creations.

Alvarez's journey from Spanish into English, from Santo Domingo to New York City, from Lucas to Juan Mejía, was the topic of ***How the García Girls Lost Their Accents,*** a set of loosely connected autobiographical stories published in book form in 1991, about well-off Dominican sisters exiled in *el norte*. The critical reception was mixed, though readers wholeheartedly embraced the book as charming and compassionate—a sort of minor echo of Laura Esquivel's *Like Water for Chocolate*—and it was welcomed with the type of jubilation often granted works by suddenly emergent minorities. After all, Dominican literature, in Spanish or English, is hardly represented in bookstores and college courses here. Indeed, not since the early twentieth-century larger-than-life scholar and essayist Pedro Henríquez Ureña delivered the Charles Eliot Norton lectures at Harvard University in 1940-41, on the topic of literary currents in Hispanic America, had a writer from the Dominican Republic been the target of such admiration here.

In spite of Alvarez's fairly conservative, yet semi-experimental approach to literature, what makes her a peculiar, nontraditional Dominican writer is her divided identity. "I am a Dominican, hyphen, American," she once said. "As a fiction writer, I find that the most exciting things happen in the realm of that hyphen—the place where two worlds collide or blend together."

Alvarez's novelistic debut evidenced a writer whose control of her craft was sharp but less than complete—some of the autonomous segments of ***García Girls*** were not knit together well, for example, leaving the reader holding several frustratingly loose ends. Now, three years later, such shortcomings have been largely erased, as her haunting second novel easily surpasses her earlier achievement. And while this vista of the political turmoil left behind by émigrés like the García girls still may not be proportional

to her talents, it is extraordinary in that it exhibits quick, solid maturing as an artist. In spite of its title, ***In the Time of the Butterflies*** is not crowded with magic realist scenes à la Gabriel García Márquez and Isabel Allende. Instead, it's a fictional study of a tragic event in Dominican history, when, on November 25, 1960, three outspoken Mirabal sisters, active opponents of the dictatorship of Rafael Leónidas Trujillo, were found dead near their wrecked Jeep, at the bottom of a 150-foot cliff in the northern part of the country. Today the Mirabals are known throughout the Caribbean as The Butterflies—*Las Mariposas*. Alvarez uses her novel to explore their tragic odyssey and, metaphorically, bring them back to life.

The novel's 300-plus pages are full of pathos and passion, with beautifully crafted anecdotes interstitched to create a patchwork quilt of memory and ideology. We see the sisters as teens, fighting with Papá, marrying, leading double lives, commenting on the Cuban revolution, becoming rebels themselves, going on to bury husbands and sons. The organization is symmetrical: The book's major parts are laid out in four sections, one devoted to each of the three murdered sisters and one to the fourth sister, who escaped their fate. We have thus a quatrain of novellas, only one of which doesn't end in tragedy. Here's how Alvarez has Dedé, the surviving Mirabal sister, remark on the assassination:

> It seems that at first the Jeep was following the truck up the mountain. Then as the truck slowed for the grade, the Jeep passed and sped away, around some curves, out of sight. Then it seems that the truck came upon the ambush. A blue-and-white Austin had blocked part of the road; the Jeep had been forced to a stop; the women were being led away peaceably, so the truck driver said, *peaceably* to the car.

While the Mirabal incident might seem a bit obscure to American readers (most of Dominican history, perhaps even the U.S. invasion, does), it offers an amazing array of creative opportunities to reflect on the labyrinthine paths of the Hispanic psyche. Others in the Dominican Republic have used this historical episode as a springboard to reflect on freedom and ideology, among them Pedro Mir in his poem "Amén de Mariposas" and Ramón Alberto Ferreras in his book *Las Mirabal*. Alvarez takes a decidedly unique approach: She examines the martyrdom of these three Dominican women as a gender battlefield—three brave, subversive wives crushed by a phallocentric regime. In an openly misogynistic society, the Mirabals are initially dealt with by the government in a delicate, somewhat condescending fashion, which of course doesn't exclude the oppressive power from annihilating them in the end.

The official newspaper of the Trujillo regime, *El Caribe*, treated the deaths of Minerva, Patria and María Teresa Mirabal and their driver, Rufino de la Cruz, all between 25 and 37 years of age, as an accident. Not only did it report the incident without much explanation, it failed to mention the sisters' anti-Trujillo activities. Nor did it acknowledge that a fourth sister wasn't among the victims and had thus survived. Assuming her role as historian and

> I am a Dominican, hyphen, American. As a fiction writer, I find that the most exciting things happen in the realm of that hyphen—the place where two worlds collide or blend together.
>
> —*Julia Alvarez*

marionetteer, Alvarez fills in the gaps. She didn't know the sisters personally and she laments at the end of her volume that the reluctance of people in the Dominican Republic to speak out or open up to strangers, as well as the chaotic state of affairs in the nation's libraries and research centers, made it difficult for her to gather historical data. But her task was hardly biographical. "I wanted to immerse my readers in an epoch in the life of the Dominican Republic that I believe can only finally be understood by fiction, only finally be redeemed by the imagination," she writes. "A novel is not, after all, a historical document, but a way to travel through the human heart."

Alvarez writes, for instance, that Trujillo himself had a crush on Minerva, who responded publicly by slapping him in the face. She also analyzes the religious education María Teresa received and later metamorphosed into antiauthoritarian animosity. Much in the *Butterflies* novel resembles *How the García Girls Lost Their Accents*: Hispanic domesticity is at center stage, analyzed in light of the intricate partnerships and rivalries of the four sisters. The male chauvinism that dominates the Hispanic family is meant to mirror and complement Trujillo's own machismo, with home and country approached as micro- and macrocosms. The style is deliberately fragmentary and openly Faulknerian. Alvarez's pages made me think, time and again, of the Israeli writer A.B. Yehoshua: By intertwining disparate literary forms (journals, first-person accounts, correspondence, drawings, etc.) Alvarez allows each Mirabal to acquire her own voice. Pasted together, their voices provide a sense that Truth, capital "T," is a collective invention.

Unlike many Latino writers of her generation, Alvarez abandons the United States in theme and scenario to analyze the role of women under dictatorships in the Southern Hemisphere. Trujillo's presence is felt from afar, as an overwhelming shadow controlling and destroying human happiness—so overarching is the dictator, in fact, that it seems to me he becomes the central character. The Mirabal sisters fight *el líder* as both a real and a ghostlike figure. Their opposition is also an attack against phallocentrism as an accepted way of life in Hispanic societies. In this respect, *In the Time of Butterflies* ought to be equated with a number of Latin American works about dictators (known in Spanish as *novelas del dictador*), including Miguel Angel Asturias's *El Señnar Presidente* and Augusto Roa Bastos's *I, the Supreme*. And it is a first-rate addition to the shelf of works by Latina literary artists who write about chauvinism, from Delmira Agustini to Rosario Ferré. In her Postscript, Alvarez writes:

> During [Trujillo's] terrifying thirty-one-year regime, any hint of disagreement ultimately resulted in death for the dissenter and often for members of his or her family. Yet the Mirabals had risked their lives. I kept asking myself, What gave them that special courage? It was to understand that question that I began this story.

Fiction as an instrument to decodify a tyranny's hidden and manifest tentacles. Fiction as a tool of journalism and vice versa. Fiction as a device to reclaim a stolen aspect of history. Ironically, it is precisely at this level that Alvarez's volume is simultaneously invigorating and curiously disappointing. The author herself appears at the beginning of the plot: It is 1994 and, as an American woman with broken Spanish, she is eager to interview Dedé. Dedé offers much data about her sisters' journey, from their convent education to their first love affairs and subsequent marriages to high-profile activists in the fifties. Indeed, Dedé serves as the backbone to the entire story. But Alvarez leaves reaction to the Mirabals' assassination to a twenty-page epilogue, in which we find out about public outrage and the spectacular, media-oriented trial of their murderers, which took place a year after Trujillo was killed in 1961. Interleaving news clips, court testimony, interviews and other paraphernalia throughout her narrative might have helped—anything, to insert the Mirabals more firmly in the flux of Dominican memory.

Notwithstanding this structural handicap, *In the Time of the Butterflies* is enchanting, a novel only a female, English-speaking Hispanic could have written. By inserting herself in the cast as *la gringa norteamericana,* Alvarez links the old and the new. At a time when many Latino writers seem so easily satisfied exploring the ghetto, in fictional terms, of drugs, crime and videotape, Alvarez, a writer on a different kind of edge, calls attention to the Latin American foundations of Hispanic fiction in English and dares once again to turn the novel into a political artifact. The inside covers of her book are illustrated with typography listing women and men assassinated by Trujillo. Recalling the Vietnam Memorial in Washington, D.C., the names seem endless, an homage to patriotic anonymity. Alvarez pays tribute to only three of these names, but the rest are also evoked in her lucid pages. Her novel is a wonderful examination of how it feels to be a survivor, how it feels to come from a society where justice and freedom are unwelcome and where the answer to the question "How are you?" often has to be, *Entre Lucas y Juan Mejía.*

Dwight Garner   (review date Winter 1994)

SOURCE: "A Writer's Revolution," in *Hungry Mind Review,* No. 32, Winter, 1994, p. 23.

[*In the following review, Garner finds* In the Time of the Butterflies *"a worthy novel with a mixed palette of human emotions, but Alvarez has sketched too frequently with pastels."*]

Julia Alvarez is a dreamboat of a writer. Her language is fresh and economical. She zeros right in on piquant details. Best of all, her feeling for the complex chemistry between Latin American women (primarily groups of daughters) is a joy to behold. Her two novels—*How the García Girls Lost Their Accents,* and now, *In the Time of the Butterflies*—sit lightly on the lap. They're never less than bright and engaging.

Perversely enough, though, Alvarez's new novel is wonderful in ways that occasionally blunt its emotional impact. Based loosely on a true story, *In the Time of the Butterflies* is about four middle-class sisters of the Dominican Republic who, along with their husbands, helped overthrow the corrupt and violent dictatorship of Rafael Leonidas Trujillo. The revered Mirabal sisters were known by their code name, Las Mariposas—the Butterflies—and their politics cost them their lives. Three were assassinated in 1960, shortly before Trujillo's fall.

In the novel's postscript, Alvarez writes of her desire to humanize the Mirabals, who are "wrapped in superlatives" and have "ascended into myth" in the Dominican Republic. At this, she succeeds splendidly. The sisters—Patria, Minerva, Dede, and Maria Teresa—are each brought vividly to life. Alvarez tells their stories individually, in monologues and journal entries, and their voices are happily idiosyncratic.

Alvarez is a dreamboat of a writer. Her language is fresh and economical. She zeros right in on piquant details.

—Dwight Garner

The Mirabal house may be a place where, as Minerva notes, the young girls "had to ask permission for everything: to walk to the fields to see the tobacco filling out; to go the lagoon and dip our feet on a hot day; to stand in front of the store and pet the horses as the men loaded up their wagons with supplies." But it's also a house that brims with food and warmth and games, and as the girls grow they learn how much better their lives are than most people's under Trujillo's regime.

The girls' political and sexual awakenings, as often happens, coincide. There's a stunning scene in which Patria, while praying, finds her intense religious feelings crossing over into earthier regions: "My mouth, for instance, craved sweets, figs in their heavy syrup, coconut candy, soft golden flans. When those young men whose surnames have been appropriated for years by my mooning girlfriends came to the store and drummed their big hands on the counter, I wanted to take each finger in my mouth and feel their calluses with my tongue."

It's in this first half of *In the Time of the Butterflies* that the book seems most confident. Alvarez writes compellingly about growing up under a brutal political regime that squashed dissent and encouraged citizens to spy on their neighbors. (Alvarez's own family fled the Dominican Republic when she was ten.) It's only later, when the

Mirabal sisters themselves become political, that the book sometimes seems less convincing.

When several of the sisters begin dating men with ties to the country's leftist resistance movements, they themselves get drawn in. Before long, the sisters are hiding weapons shipments, making homemade bombs, and "the whole family walked around in fear" of being found out.

These scenes are well sketched, but Alvarez doesn't provide enough background (factual or emotional) for them. Although we learn about the horrors of Trujillo's regime, the country's politics are not discussed in any depth. Worse, you get no clear sense of what attracts the girls to radical politics, beyond glamour and simple reactionary anger. One minute they are kissing boys behind shrubs; the next, they're whipping up Molotov cocktails.

Alvarez's prose is almost too willfully deft and playful to impart a sense of gravity and drama to these proceedings. You're let down emotionally, because you never quite *feel* the danger the sisters are in. The bad guys rarely seem more than self-important stooges, the equivalent of Keystone Cops, and the sisters' encounters with them feel almost like games. Later in the book, when the sisters and their husbands are imprisoned and treated badly, this problem is only exacerbated. Prison seems merely like a particularly shabby summer camp.

It's an old, creaky literary game, knocking a novelist for being too "writerly"—somehow too good at what she does. And Alvarez is far more than an air-dancing acrobat, shedding bright bits of fluff. On the basis of her first two books, she's shown a remarkable ability to climb inside the heads of her characters and distill complicated emotions into a sharp sentence or two. She's among America's finest young writers.

Hers is a language of abundance; she sings hymns to the outsized joys and sorrows of quotidian existence. In *In the Time of the Butterflies,* however, her exuberance betrays her somewhat. This is a worthy novel with a mixed palette of human emotion, but Alvarez has sketched too frequently with pastels.

Roberto González Echevarría (review date 18 December 1994)

SOURCE: "Sisters in Death," in *The New York Times Book Review,* December 18, 1994, p. 28.

[*Echevarría teaches Hispanic and comparative literature. In the following mixed review, he comments on character, plot, and theme in* In the Time of the Butterflies.]

Hispanic writers in the United States have published several novels of unquestionable merit, the most recent success being Cristina Garcia's *Dreaming in Cuban.* Most deal with the pains and pleasures of growing up in a culture and a language outside the mainstream. If becoming an adult is a trying process under ordinary circumstances, doing so within varying and often conflicting expectations can be even more bewildering and alienating. It makes growing up, which is by its very nature self-absorbing, doubly so. A person can emerge not a harmonious blend, but simultaneously two (or more) selves in conflict. This predicament is much more dramatic when people speak two or more languages, for the inner life can be like a United Nations debate, complete with simultaneous translations and awkward compromises.

All this is, of course, the stuff of literature, which is why it has become the central concern of Hispanic writers in this country. It was the explicit theme of Julia Alvarez's delightful first novel, *How the Garcia Girls Lost Their Accents,* and it is the subtext of her second. *In the Time of the Butterflies*. But by dealing with real historical figures in this novel, Ms. Alvarez has been much more ambitious than she was in her first, as if she needed to have her American self learn what it was really like in her native land, the Dominican Republic.

On the night of Nov. 25, 1960, Patria, Minerva and Maria Teresa Mirabal—three sisters returning from a visit to their husbands, political prisoners of the dictator Rafael Leonidas Trujillo—were murdered by Trujillo's henchmen. This was one of those appalling atrocities that galvanize opposition to a murderous regime and signal the beginning of its demise. Indeed, Trujillo was slain six months later, and the Dominican Republic began a tortuous and tortured attempt at democracy. The Mirabal sisters, already admired for their resistance to the Trujillo regime before they were murdered, became part of the mythology of the Dominicans' struggle for social and political justice, and the day of their death is observed in many parts of Latin America today.

In an epilogue, Ms. Alvarez, who was 10 years old when her family came to the United States in the year the Mirabal sisters were assassinated, runs through the usual commonplaces about the freedom of the historical novelist in the handling of facts, and expresses her desire to do more than merely add to the deification of the Mirabals. In fictionalizing their story she has availed herself of the liberties of the creative writer, to be sure, but alas, I am afraid she did not escape the temptation to monumentalize.

Ms. Alvarez's plan is flawless. As she proved in her first novel, she is skilled at narrative construction, though she lacks a compelling style and her English is sometimes marred by Hispanisms. (Once we accept the idea of English-speaking Mirabals, there is no reason for them to have accents.)

In the Time of the Butterflies opens with a thinly disguised version of Ms. Alvarez, an Americanized Dominican woman who wants to write something about the Mirabals and is looking for information. She visits the family home, now a kind of shrine, run by Dedé, the surviving fourth sister, who had remained at home that night, and who, expectedly, is tortured by guilt and haunted by the burden of memory. Dedé's recollections and musings open and close the novel, nicely framing the action.

The core of the book is made up of chronological reminiscences by the murdered sisters from childhood to the time of their brutal demise. Because we know their fate in advance, everything is colored by sadness and anger. The Mirabals are a traditional provincial Dominican family, portrayed in clichéd fashion—a middle-class rural clan

anchored by the inevitably philandering but supportive patriarch and the warm, caring and wise mother. Happy, bourgeois families like the Mirabals were, for many years, the heart of the Trujillo dictatorship's support.

As Ms. Alvarez tells their story, the Mirabal sisters are drawn into politics by Trujillo's intolerable wickedness rather than by any deeply felt or intellectually justified commitment. The sisters appear, on the whole, to be reactive and passive. Their education in religious schools, and their chaste and rather naïve development into womanhood, take up too many tedious pages. Probably to heighten the evil import of Trujillo's deeds, the Mirabals are portrayed as earnestly innocent and vulnerable, but that diminishes their political stature and fictional complexity.

Ms. Alvarez clutters her novel with far too many misdeeds and misfortunes: rape, harassment, miscarriage, separation, abuse, breast cancer. Are the sisters victims of fate, Latin American machismo, American imperialism or only the particularly diabolical nature of Trujillo's dictatorship? Eulogy turns into melodrama and history becomes hagiography. There is a touch of the maudlin even in the title—the Mirabals were affectionately known in their lifetime as the *mariposas,* the butterflies. There is indeed much too much crying in this novel.

Hispanic Americans today have "old countries" that are neither old nor remote. Even those born here often travel to their parents' homeland, and constantly face a flow of friends and relatives from "home" who keep the culture current. This constant cross fertilization makes assimilation a more complicated process for them than for other minority groups. This "living origin" is a determining factor for Hispanic writers in the United States, as William Luis, a professor of Latin American literature at Vanderbilt University and the leading authority on this phenomenon, has pointed out. This is why the most convincing parts of *In the Time of the Butterflies* have to do with Dedé, the survivor, and her anguished role as memorialist, which in turn becomes Ms. Alvarez's role. It is here that we best understand the depths of Ms. Alvarez's despair and the authenticity of her effort to represent the inner drama of her conversion to an American self.

There is for Hispanic writers in the United States the added burden of a very active, popular literary tradition in Spanish, including some of the most distinguished names in contemporary world literature. Carlos Fuentes, Mario Vargas Llosa, Gabriel Garcia Marquez and Octavio Paz. In its concern with history and dictatorship, *In the Time of the Butterflies* seems to be echoing Garcia Marquez, and the emphasis on a clannish rural family is reminiscent not only of that modern master but also of his disciple Isabel Allende.

But the actual history in *In the Time of the Butterflies* is very blurry. I find no connection between the specific dates Ms. Alvarez gives to mark periods in the Mirabals' lives and either Dominican or broader Latin American history. Serious historical fiction establishes links between individual destiny and pivotal political events. It shows either the disconnection between the individual and the larger flow of sociopolitical movements or, on the contrary, the individual as a pawn of history. In either case there is irony, but in this novel the reader is not made aware of a broader, more encompassing political world.

In the Time of the Butterflies reads like the project the Americanized Dominican woman at the beginning of the novel ("a *gringa dominicana* in a rented car with a road map asking for street names") would have come up with after pondering the fate of the Mirabal sisters from her perspective as a teacher on a United States college campus today. Had Julia Alvarez concentrated more on her dialogue with Dedé she would have produced a better book. It would have had the touch of irony provided by the realization that the *gringa dominicana* would never really be able to understand the other woman, much less translate her.

Janet Jones Hampton (review date Spring 1995)

SOURCE: "The Time of the Tyrants," in *Belles Lettres: A Review of Books by Women,* Vol. 10, No. 2, Spring, 1995, pp. 6-7.

[*Hampton is a professor of Spanish. In the following review, she applauds* In the Time of the Butterflies.]

Julia Alvarez came to the United States from the Dominican Republic in 1960 with her family to escape the tyranny of the Trujillo regime. Shortly after their escape, the Mirabal sisters, who were part of Alvarez's father's resistance group, were murdered by the regime, becoming martyrs. Intrigued by the courage of these sisters, Alvarez, the highly acclaimed author of *How the García Girls Lost Their Accents,* decided to write a fictional version of their story. *In the Time of the Butterflies* is the result.

The novel relates the lives of the three Mirabal sisters—Patria, Minerva, and María Teresa—in their own words and as recalled by Dedé, their surviving sibling. Spanning the period from 1938 to the present, the novel focuses on the era of the Trujillo dictatorship, from 1930 to 1961. It reveals how each of the sisters, known together as the "mariposas" (butterflies), becomes a dissenter and ultimately a martyr.

The life of the Mirabal family was fairly normal until Trujillo tried to seduce Minerva, who spurned him. Like her namesake of Greek mythology, Minerva proves to be a warrior committed to defend both home and country from enemies. Until that time, the Mirabals, who operated a rural store, enjoyed a growing business, were respected in their community, were involved in their church, and had the opportunity to educate their daughters. Through education, the daughters grow aware of the possibility of a free society and eventually commit themselves to making it a reality. In spite of the need to be wary in both speech and action, the Mirabals' family life is marked by both hilarity and personal sadness. As the regime increasingly squeezes them, they eschew material acquisitions and further embrace one another. This solidarity, coupled with their resistance to Trujillo, makes the Mirabals enemies of the regime but heroes to their people.

The story is related through first-person accounts of each sister, resulting in multiple perspectives of central events.

It is embellished with María Teresa's diary entries and sketches, as well as bits of poetry and song. Alvarez not only opens a window on the remarkable daily life of that period, but also provides a chilling view into the heart of Trujillo's darkness. Alvarez states: "I wanted to immerse my readers in an epoch in the life of the Dominican Republic that I believe can only finally be understood by fiction, only finally be redeemed by the imagination." She indeed realizes this goal. . . .

Alvarez's grasp of metaphor and humor will delight the enthusiasts of Barbara Kingsolver's prose.

When the final pages of [this book] turned, I think that the reader will agree with the words of Julia Alvarez: "A novel is not, after all, a historical document, but a way to travel through the human heart."

Rochelle Ratner (review date 15 April 1995)

SOURCE: A review of *The Other Side/El Otro Lado,* in *Library Journal,* Vol. 120, No. 7, April 15, 1995, p. 80.

[*In the following review, Ratner praises* The Other Side/El Otro Lado.]

Alvarez (author of . . . *How the Garcia Girls Lost Their Accents*) writes poems as impressive as her fiction. In the opening sequence [of *The Other Side/El Otro Lado*] writing of a loving maid and governess, she portrays with graceful simplicity the world of haves and have nots suggested in the duality we find in the title. Whereas poets from similar backgrounds—uprooted, mocked—write bitterly of the past and ambivalently of the future, Alvarez optimistically sets about **"Making Up the Past."** As the poems move from childhood memories to adult realities, they become less succinct, less headed toward closure. Lines stretch out. Anger enters. The setting of the long title sequence is ironic: at an artist's colony not far from her native town, the author suffers in the midst of a lengthy writer's block as she is joined by a lover she's not sure she loves. Yet she reaches out, in the final poem, not to all the people she might have been but toward the mute girl.

Publishers Weekly (review date 24 April 1995)

SOURCE: A review of *The Other Side/El Otro Lado,* in *Publishers Weekly,* Vol. 241, No. 17, April 24, 1995, p. 65.

[*In the following review, the critic lauds* The Other Side/El Otro Lado *as a "meticulous examination of self-evolution."*]

Widely known for her novels, *How the Garcia Girls Lost Their Accents* and *In the Time of the Butterflies,* Latina author Alvarez claims her authority as a poet with this collection. Tracing a lyrical journey through the landscape of immigrant life, these direct, reflective and often sensuous poems are grouped into five sections which, like the points of a star, indicate a circle. Alvarez begins with **"Bilingual Sestina,"** a meditation on leaving her native Dominican Republic for an alien land and strange language. She ends with the title poem **"The Other Side / El**

Otro Lado," a long, multipart narrative recounting her return to her homeland as a woman transformed—translated—by the years she has lived in America from native to guest. The speaker may claim "There is nothing left to cry for, / nothing left but the story / of our family's grand adventure / from one language to another," but this poetry resonates precisely because that story embodies larger questions about self-identity. A meticulous examination of self-evolution, Alvarez's assured collection reveals that change can take us across borders so slowly that only on reaching the other side can we see the distances we've come.

Ruth Behar   (review date May 1995)

SOURCE: "Revolutions of the Heart," in *The Women's Review of Books,* Vol. XII, No. 8, May, 1995, pp. 6-7.

[*In the following review, Behar contextualizes* In the Time of the Butterflies *as a historical novel about Latina women and revolution.*]

So often I have wondered: Where are the women among those gigantic looming shadows of the male liberators, tyrants, generals, colonels and revolutionaries who have ruled the countries of Latin America and the Caribbean for the past century? Did women not fight alongside Simón Bolívar and José Martí? Have women not shared beds with revolutionaries like Emiliano Zapata and Pancho Villa, or dictators like Batista and Duvalier? Were there no women in the Sierra Maestra with Fidel Castro? The history textbooks tell the story of Spanish America's bloody national struggles for independence, decolonization and freedom as if women were never there, as if women had no place in the nation and in history. Is there really no story for those women other than the romance?

Latina fiction writers in the United States have lately begun to seek answers to these questions. They increasingly cross the border into Latin America, claiming its history as their own and translating it into English for North American readers. The Chicana writer Sandra Cisneros has a short story, "Eyes of Zapata," in her recent collection *Woman Hollering Creek,* in which a mistress who has known him since childhood imagines the Mexican revolutionary as sadly tender and vulnerable. Cristina García, the Cuban American writer, creates a feisty protagonist in her novel *Dreaming in Cuban,* based on her own grandmother who stayed behind on the island; this Cuban grandmother, her ears decorated with drop-pearls, single-handedly watches over the northern coast to prevent *yanqui* invasions that might topple Fidel Castro, who she imagines will one day thank her personally for her heroic patriotism.

In her engaging new novel [*In the Time of the Butterflies*], the Dominican American poet and writer Julia Alvarez joins these Latina writers in the feminist quest to bring Latin American women into the nation and into history as agents, out from under the shadows of those larger-than-life men who, too often, have treated the countries under their rule as personal fiefdoms. Yet Alvarez goes further: she explores the sly ways dictators plant pieces of themselves "inside everyone of us." This point comes to

life in a brilliant scene in which the Mirabal family, haplessly trying to stay on the good side of the Dominican dictator, attends a party at Trujillo's mansion. There, Minerva, the Mirabal daughter most committed to the struggle to topple the regime, is surprised by her disappointment when Trujillo doesn't immediately ask her to dance. As she sagely observes, "This regime is seductive. How else would a whole nation fall prey to this little man?" When Trujillo finally asks her to dance, she catches herself, as they make small talk, lying to protect a friend: "Instantly, I feel ashamed of myself. I see now how easily it happens. You give in on little things, and soon you're serving in his government, marching in his parades, sleeping in his bed." Women's resistance to dictators, Alvarez shows us, is fraught with problems, not the least being their susceptibility to the erotic power of charismatic male leaders.

Widely known as the "little Caesar of the Caribbean," Rafael Leonidas Trujillo was the Dominican Republic's brutal dictator for 31 years, from 1930 to 1961. In August of 1960, during the last year of his rule, Julia Alvarez fled to the United States with her parents and three sisters; her father had participated in an underground plot to overthrow Trujillo which the secret police had uncovered. In her first novel, *How the García Girls Lost Their Accents,* she chronicled her upper-class family's life in exile in New York City, alternating between the voices of four sisters as they came of age.

Though only ten years old when her family went into exile, Alvarez was haunted throughout her childhood by the story of another four girls, the Mirabal sisters, who stayed behind in the Dominican Republic and suffered a cruel fate in Trujillo's final hour. Their story, an eerie shadow biography and counterpoint to the story of the García girls, is the subject of this new novel. Returning home through steep mountains on the night of November 25, 1960—they had been to see their husbands, jailed as political prisoners—three of the sisters, Patria (aged 36), Minerva (34) and María Teresa (25), were murdered by Trujillo's henchmen. The sisters, members of the same underground as Alvarez' father, had once been harassed and jailed themselves for speaking out against the regime, but they refused, in the spirit of their code name Las Mariposas—the Butterflies—to clip their wings. Less than a year later, Trujillo was assassinated.

The fourth sister, Dedé, to whom Alvarez dedicates her novel, is introduced in the opening pages. In 1994 Dedé is 66 years old. She is inspired to look back again at her memories of the events leading to the night of her sisters' murders by the visit of an inquisitive *gringa dominicana* who speaks an uneasy Spanish, an obvious alias for Alvarez. Ironically, it is Dedé, the sister who was ambivalent about participating in the underground and remained home on that night, who tells the story of her sisters and oversees their transformation (in real life and in the novel) into national and even international heroines. (Today in Latin America, November 25th is the International Day Against Violence Toward Women.)

The revolution against Trujillo Alvarez depicts is the individual revolution taking place in the hearts of each of the Mirabal sisters, who at different times, for different reasons and in different ways, join in the common struggle to liberate their nation and their psyches from the power of dictators. Reproducing the structure of her first novel, Alvarez crafts separate voices and personas for them as they come of age and define themselves as daughters, sisters, wives, mothers and, most wrenchingly, citizens of a fatherland that sacrifices its women when they become too strong.

Patria, the eldest, is devoutly Catholic and comes to the underground resistance against Trujillo through her religious thirst for justice. Yearning for redemption, she views the struggle in terms of a need for trust and national reconciliation:

> "I wanted to start believing in my fellow Dominicans again. Once the goat was a bad memory in our past, that would be the real revolution we would have to fight: forgiving each other for what we had all let come to pass." Minerva, the most fearless and earnest revolutionary of the four, questions every form of patriarchal authority, and even dares to slap Trujillo as they dance at his mansion when he rams his groin into her dress. María Teresa, the youngest and most naive, is presented through her diaries and drawings, preciously full of exclamation points and bubbling emotions. While her child's voice is irritatingly cute, her adult voice is more subtle, particularly when she questions Minerva's unwavering passion for the revolution. "For me love goes deeper than the struggle," María Teresa admits, "or maybe what I mean is, love is the deeper struggle. I would never be able to give up Leandro to some higher ideal the way I feel Minerva and Manolo would each other if they had to make the supreme sacrifice."

Finally there is Dedé, the survivor, who never completely signs on to the resistance. After the nightmare of the Trujillo dictatorship she belatedly but firmly develops the courage to make her own choices: to divorce her husband (for her, the revolution is about a feminist rethinking of home rather than of nation) and to bring up her sisters' children without resentment, even at the cost of sheltering them from the full weight of their own history.

This is a historical novel in which forgetting wins out over remembering. Alvarez offers us a paradox: her novel bears witness to the urgency of her quest for memory, but for her characters healing comes only through forgetting. By the end of the novel Fela, the former black servant of the Mirabal family who has become a spirit medium, announces that the dead sisters are at peace and no longer clamor to speak through her body. In turn, Minou, Minerva's daughter, announces that she and her husband hope to build a house "up north in those beautiful mountains"—where her parents happen to have been murdered. Dedé decides that Minou's obliviousness to history is the forgiveness that brings forth a different future: "She's not haunted and full of hate. She claims it, this beautiful country with its beautiful mountains and splendid beaches—all the copy we read in the tourist brochures." But life in the Dominican Republic in a post-Trujillo, post-revolutionary time is chillingly carefree, with "Free Zones going up everywhere, the coast a clutter of clubs and resorts." Dedé

notes that "We are now the playground of the Caribbean, who were once its killing fields. The cemetery is beginning to flower." Yet she can't help asking herself: "Was it for this, the sacrifice of the butterflies?"

As in a Greek tragedy, we know from the beginning the destiny that awaits the Mirabal sisters. It is the development of their characters rather than the unfolding of the plot that carries the narrative forward. And yet, as with any well-told tragic tale, we expect to be devastated by their deaths when we finally get to them. Although the last 150 pages of the book read quickly, as the story pushes past the slow-moving girlhood stories to the metamorphosis of the sisters into The Butterflies, the narrative edges closer and closer to tragedy, yet never quite hits the mark. Alvarez chooses to scrunch up time at the end of the novel, letting the assassination of the sisters unfold in a twenty-page epilogue told in Dedé's voice.

To be sure, it is exquisitely written. In a touchingly banal detail, a store-owner recalls that, just before starting up the mountain, the youngest of the sisters wanted ten cents' worth of cinnamon, yellow and green Chiclets. "He dug around in the jar but he couldn't find any cinnamon ones. He will never forgive himself that he couldn't find any cinnamon ones. His wife wept for the little things that could have made the girls' last minutes happier." But to crush the reader's heart with the full impact of the murders, Alvarez needed to keep us longer with the sisters—to expand not shrink time as they climb the mountains to their death.

As a Cuban-born Latina, I read with special interest the many allusions Alvarez makes to Fidel Castro and the Cuban revolution. For Latin American and Caribbean leftists in the 1950s who dreamed of undoing the legacy of poverty, inequality and racism and struggled against nearly impossible odds to overthrow dictators, it was difficult not to be swept off your feet by the young *guerrilleros* Fidel Castro and Ernesto "Che" Guevara. For the Mirabal sisters of Alvarez' novel, Fidel and Che become models of young revolutionary manhood, forming a stark contrast to the power-hungry, lecherous, aging figure of the dictator Trujillo. Patria imagines that the Lord himself has directed her to name her youngest son Raúl Ernesto, Che for short. Minerva takes to reciting the famous words Castro uttered after serving time in jail for his revolutionary actions: "*Condemn me, it does not matter. History will absolve me!*"

In the Time of the Butterflies demonstrates that history has more than absolved the Mirabal sisters. Whether history can absolve revolutionaries who become dictators is a question I would have liked to see Julia Alvarez pose, if only because it is a burning one for those of us who still want to believe in the possibility of revolutions for the Caribbean that don't turn sour. Had Alvarez developed the voice of her alias, the *gringa dominicana* who returns to her abandoned homeland to learn about The Butterflies from the history-weary Dedé, she might have been able to offer a more nuanced view of what revolutions look like the morning after. But rather than explore the limits of recovering and reclaiming the past, she chooses to downplay the role of the novelist bearing witness to history. She forfeits a golden opportunity, I think, to add depth to her story and break with the predictable four-voice narrative. In a brief "real life" postscript, Alvarez claims that only through fiction's transformations is it possible to understand a history as complex as that surrounding the Mirabal sisters. The notion is tantalizing but unsatisfying: why did she not weave the story of that transformation into the novel itself?

Yet despite these criticisms, I am in debt to Julia Alvarez for her creative ambition, which she largely fulfils: for showing that although revolutions turn sour, they matter. And for showing that when they turn sour for women, they must be remembered even more adamantly. For the history of any nation rightly belongs not to women who forgive and forget but to those who forgive even as they remember.

Further Reading

Criticism

Review of *How the García Girls Lost Their Accents,* by Julia Alvarez. *The Antioch Review* 49, No. 3 (Summer 1991): 474-75.

Brief plot summary of the novel.

Cain, Michael S. Review of *How the García Girls Lost Their Accents,* by Julia Alvarez. *Multicultural Review* 1, No. 1 (January 1992): 42.

Praises Alvarez's insights into family dynamics but notes that she sometimes leaves "frustrating gaps in the story of this family's journey between cultures."

Gambone, Philip. Review of *The Other Side/El Otro Lado,* by Julia Alvarez. *The New York Times Book Review,* No. 29 (16 July 1995): 20.

Notes that *The Other Side/El Otro Lado* continues the bicultural themes of Alvarez's previous works.

Miller, Susan. "Caught Between Two Cultures." *Newsweek* 119, No. 16 (20 April 1992): 78-9.

Compares *How the García Girls Lost Their Accents* to other Latino writing, including Cristina Garcia's *Dreaming in Cuban* and Victor Villasenor's *Rain of Gold.*

———"Family Spats, Urgent Prayers." *Newsweek* 124, No. 16 (17 October 1994): 77-8.

Praises *In the Time of the Butterflies* for its portrayal of Latina women.

Oliver, Bill. "From Tangents to Trespasses." *New England Review* 15, No. 3 (Summer 1993): 208-12.

Lauds *How the García Girls Lost Their Accents* for its thematic depth and portrayal of family relations.

Omang, Julia. "For This They Died?" *The Los Angeles Times Book Review* (26 February 1995): 8.

Praises *In the Time of the Butterflies* for its revealing portrayal of Dominican history.

Powers, Katherine A. "A Tale of Tragedy on a Caribbean Island." *The Christian Science Monitor* (17 October 1994): 13.

Praises *In the Time of the Butterflies* for its depiction of male/female and sororal relationships.

Walsh, Elsa. "Arms and the Women." *Book World—The Washington Post* (27 November 1994): 7.

Laudatory review of *In the Time of the Butterflies* in which Walsh states that the work is "at once personal and political, both sweet and sweeping in scale."

Wiley, Catherine. Review of *How the García Girls Lost Their Accents,* by Julia Alvarez. *The Bloomsbury Review* 12, No. 2 (March 1992): 9.

Praises *How the García Girls Lost Their Accents* for its "plurality of voices."

Additional coverage of Alvarez's life and career is contained in the following source published by Gale Research: *Contemporary Authors,* Vol. 147.

Mulk Raj Anand

1905-

Indian novelist, short story writer, autobiographer, essayist, and nonfiction writer.

The following entry provides an overview of Anand's career through 1992. For further information on his life and works, see *CLC,* Volume 23.

INTRODUCTION

Along with R. K. Narayan and Raja Rao, Anand is credited with establishing the basic forms and themes of modern Indian literature written in English. At the core of his writing is a humanist philosophy that incorporates elements of socialist political and economic theory. Critics argue that his socially conscious works have shed keen insights on Indian affairs and enriched his country's literary heritage.

Biographical Information

Born in Peshawar, India, Anand began his formal education at a time when the Indian educational system emphasized proficiency in English. The author has since criticized the education he received in Indian primary and secondary schools and at the University of Punjab for neglecting Indian and European culture and leaving students ill-prepared for adult life. Anand attended University College and Cambridge University in England, where he studied English literature and forged friendships with members of the Bloomsbury Group, including E. M. Forster and Virginia Woolf. After receiving his doctorate in English in 1929, Anand spent several years in Europe before returning to India to join Mohandas K. Gandhi's crusade for national independence from British rule. Anand's first novel, *Untouchable,* was published in 1935 and included an introduction by Forster. Anand has held several teaching positions, including the first Tagore Professorship of Fine Arts at the University of Punjab from 1963 to 1966, and has served as editor of the Indian arts quarterly *Marg* since 1946. He has been recognized with a number of awards, including the Sahitya Academy Award in 1947, the World Peace Council Prize in 1952, and the Padma Bhushan Award in 1968.

Major Works

His personal experiences and the reform of India's political, social, and cultural institutions are major elements in Anand's writings. Such early fictional works as *Untouchable, The Coolie* (1936), and *Two Leaves and a Bud* (1937) dramatize the cruelties inherent in the caste system and the suffering induced by poverty. *Untouchable,* for example, was inspired by the author's childhood memory of a low-caste sweeper boy who carried him home after he'd been injured; the boy was, however, beaten by Anand's

mother for touching her higher-caste son. The book was a revelation to readers unaware of the circumstances of life in a caste society and sparked extensive critical debate. Anand's interest in social themes continued in *The Coolie* and *Two Leaves and a Bud,* which relate the tribulations of working-class life in India. Critics assert that in his early work Anand employed a markedly polemical style when attributing India's social problems to the caste system, British rule, and capitalism. His style and thematic focus shifted to more psychological and humanistic interpretations in such later works as *The Private Life of an Indian Prince* (1953)—which explores the emotional and mental deterioration of a young royal who neglects his duties in pursuit of an affair with a peasant woman—and in the autobiographical novels comprising his "Seven Ages of Man" series, in which he relates the events of his life through the character Krishan Chander. The first volume in the series, *Seven Summers* (1951), spans the first seven years of the author's life and explores the interplay of reality and imagination unique to childhood. In *Morning Face* (1968), Anand recounts the inadequacy of his early education and the cruel treatment he and other students endured at the hands of their schoolmasters, memories that led the author in later years to campaign for educational reform in India. *Confession of a Lover* (1984) explores the pain of a lost love during the author's college years. *The Bubble* (1984), which covers his life as a student and young writer in London, includes much discussion of his involvement with the Bloomsbury Group writers.

Critical Reception

For his realistic portrayals of the social and economic problems suffered by Indians because of the caste system and British colonial rule, Anand is considered by many critics to be one of India's best writers. The value of his novels, according to Margaret Berry, "is the witness they offer of India's agonizing attempt to break out of massive stagnation and create a society in which men and women are free and equal." Although Anand's early works were faulted by some critics for stereotypical characterization, didacticism, and melodrama, critics have noted a restraint in later novels that enhances the persuasiveness of his appeals. Krishna Nandan Sinha has remarked: "While the later novels retain the passion for social justice, they sound greater emotional depths."

PRINCIPAL WORKS

Apology for Heroism: A Brief Autobiography of Ideas (autobiography) 1934
Untouchable (novel) 1935; revised edition, 1970
The Coolie (novel) 1936; revised edition, 1972
Two Leaves and a Bud (novel) 1937
The Village (novel) 1939
Across the Black Waters (novel) 1940
The Sword and the Sickle (novel) 1942
The Big Heart (novel) 1945
*Seven Summers: The Story of an Indian Childhood (novel) 1951
The Private Life of an Indian Prince (novel) 1953; revised edition, 1970
The Road (novel) 1961
*Morning Face (novel) 1968
Between Tears and Laughter (short stories) 1973
Conversations in Bloomsbury (essays) 1981
*Confession of a Lover (novel) 1984
*The Bubble (novel) 1984

*These works comprise the first volumes in a projected seven-volume series known as the "Seven Ages of Man."

CRITICISM

Ronald Dewsbury (review date Autumn 1936)

SOURCE: A review of *The Coolie,* in *Life and Letters To-Day,* London, Vol. 15, No. 4, Autumn, 1936, pp. 208, 210.

[*In the following review, Dewsbury praises* The Coolie *as a realistic depiction of India.*]

Mr. Anand, in a series of novels, is presenting the panorama of the real contemporary India. **The Coolie** is a frightening picture, and the author has achieved his purpose by making us wonder what on earth can be done to "save" his country. It is obvious that present evils must be corrected—evils of exploitation and graft. But the book goes much further by showing the inhumanity of man to man, proletarian to proletarian, bourgeois to bourgeois. When class meets class, why should we expect them to love one another who cannot love themselves? Remove existing evils—and the problem of human nature remains. And here the author offers no help.

He might retort that he has shown how the Indian working man is devitalised by improper feeding, by a handful of rice and chapatis. But the bourgeois has been eating for years and years, and look what it has done for him! Indeed it would have been pleasant if the East could have shown us that eating is just another bourgeois dope, like religion. Only the other day there was a story in the newspapers of an invalid who had consulted a Yogi and had been advised to live entirely on salt and water. For sixty-seven years the salt-and-water drinker had lived a splendidly healthy life! But it must be recorded that the author writes with admirable ease, although he is occasionally defeated by his own excellence. The smirking hysteria about small matters, which he has so cleverly depicted, tends to nullify climaxes. Because of its theme—the life of an ordinary domestic servant and factory-hand—the book does not present the opportunities for drama offered by the author's previous work, **The Untouchable.** Yet it should be read by everyone who is interested in "the social scene," because only this skilful Indian author could have made accessible this real material, and because Mulk Raj Anand does show that under the present system India is at its worst.

Kate O'Brien (review date 28 April 1939)

SOURCE: A review of *The Village,* in *The Spectator,* Vol. 162, No. 5783, April 28, 1939, p. 730.

[*O'Brien was an Irish novelist and playwright. In the following excerpt, she extols the universality of the theme of* The Village.]

The Village is a slow and informative narrative of peasant life in a remote community of the Punjab in the years just before the War of 1914-1918. Accumulatively and without sensationalism, it gives a vivid picture of a life that is poor and terrible, but in many aspects extremely dignified, and which is made complicated and alarming by ritualistic fears, regulations and traditions which, though novel, can of course be paralleled by similar evolutions and excesses in any old and self-conscious race. The interesting thing, indeed, about this story is that, closely localised as it is, its theme is universal, not to say commonplace. For it tells of the growth of a sensitive boy in uneasy revolt against the inflexible way of life of his family and of his caste in general. A subject which must have produced thousands of novels in all languages and which will continue to produce them.

[Lalu] Singh is the youngest son of an ageing, impoverished farmer in the village of Nandpur. He likes his farm-work and is good at it; he has moods of great feeling for his harassed, sensitive and rather moody father, as also for his affectionate, fussy mother. These characters are well done, as they persuade us of their truth to themselves, yet are also clear-cut presentations of the eternal parent, male and female. Lalu desires to please them, but he has done well at school, speaks English and has glimpses in his soul of a free and reasonable life, stripped of the excessive superstitions of the Sikh faith, and of taboos of dress and custom which make for discomfort and disease. He does not wish to be betrothed against his will when he is fifteen; he gets his hair cut short at a village fair; he speaks his mind to the pompous village money-lender of whom his father and everyone else goes in terror. Altogether, though affectionate and willing to please, he is compelled repeatedly to shock his people, and he gives trouble in the village until at last he has to run away from home and enlist in a Sikh regiment. In the last chapter he is sailing from Karachi, homesick and uncertain, in September, 1914.

He is an attractive boy, and his mild, adolescent problems are sufficiently interesting in themselves, because of the good sense and restraint with which they are stated, and also because they bring us into easy contact with the day-to-day life of an Indian village, still practically untouched, in its routine at least, by the remotely suggested, almost mystical civilisation of the *angrezi,* the English. There is no bitterness in the book; indeed its tone is tender and gentle, and there is plenty of humour in the character-drawing. There is much to be learnt from it of the patience, dignity and gaiety of certain hard and desolate ways of life, and it is a novel which promotes understanding between peoples.

G. L. Anderson   (review date October-December 1951)

SOURCE: A review of *The Indian Theatre,* in *Journal of American Folklore,* Vol. 64, No. 254, October-December, 1951, p. 439.

[*In the following review, Anderson asserts that "Anand sees the theatre as a potent instrument for social reform."*]

This attractively printed and illustrated volume [*The Indian Theatre*] is at once a somewhat partisan history of the theatre in India today and an essay on the persistence and value of the folk tradition in the theatre. The author sketches first the origin of folk drama—a subject which does not readily admit of such compression as it receives here—and then surveys the theatre in each of the great provinces of India. The book is of value in presenting compactly the extensive and varied use of folk institutions and themes in the drama of a politically awakened India. In Bengal where the influence of the Tagore household has been considerable Mulk Raj Anand finds a satisfactory professional theatre, but he believes that the future of the Indian theatre lies with such groups as Shankar and his dance troupe in Andhra and the Indian People's Theatre Association with its use of bardic recitals and folk songs and semi-dramatic folk materials as well as real folk plays. The successful middle and upper class Parsi theatre of Bombay and the Europeanized drama of the centers of former British influence the author condemns as vulgarly commercial and decadent. The chief contribution of the west has been the theatre building.

Most of the material here is available elsewhere but less conveniently, and the folklorist who is concerned with the use of folk materials for reviving regional culture interest and for political propaganda will find much that is stimulating. One is vividly reminded, however, of the proletariat drama phase in both Russia and the United States in the author's critical attitude. Aside from folk plays, "good" plays are plays which have to do with the great famine of Bengal, the plight of the factory workers in Bombay, and the inherent viciousness of the aristocratic society of old India. That such burning issues should predominate in a new and experimental drama is only natural, but an analogy with *The Lower Depths* and also with the Chinese Communists' use of the ancient Yangko dance of the peasants as the basis for a drama of political indoctrination is clear. Mulk Raj Anand sees the theatre as a potent instrument for social reform. This makes him underemphasize the possibility of giving new life to the Indian theatre generally by the methods of more "literary" innovators like Tagore, and he would blame the lack of success of the professional drama largely on a failure of the dramatist to have his roots in a strong folk tradition, for which good western style lighting is no substitute.

But the Indian theatre even in Calcutta has not yet got good western style lighting, scenery, acting techniques, or direction, and there is no reason to suspect that a renaissance in the Indian drama would not see on a conventional stage the successful adaptation of materials from classical Indian literature as well as from folk sources or that it would necessarily exclude a combination of eastern and western elements. The attempts toward this so far are inconclusive, as several more conservative students of the Indian theatre have pointed out.

Saros Cowasjee   (essay date July 1968)

SOURCE: "Mulk Raj Anand: Princes and Proletarians," in *Journal of Commonwealth Literature,* July, 1968, pp. 52-64.

[*An Indian-born Canadian educator, novelist, screenwriter, and critic, Cowasjee is the author of* So Many Freedoms: A Study of the Major Fiction of Mulk Raj Anand *(1977) and* The Last of the Maharajas *(1980), a screenplay based on Anand's* The Private Life of an Indian Prince. *In the following essay, Cowasjee examines* The Private Life of an Indian Prince, *focusing on the novel's characters and structure.*]

Six years after writing a confession of over two thousand pages, which publishers would not touch, Mulk Raj Anand gained recognition in 1932 with a cookery book, ***Curries and Other Indian Dishes.*** The confessions were inspired by the daughter of a scientific philosopher in a North Wales university, and doggedly pursued in the assurance that she would marry him if he could find a publisher. The first volume of the confessions, ***Seven Summers,*** did not appear till 1951. The Welsh girl had found a husband in 1932 and Anand had married Kathleen Van Gelder in 1938. It was good for Anand's 'prolificacy' and 'versatility' not to have opened his literary career with **Seven Summers,** which the *Times Literary Supplement* found 'generally uninteresting'. With **Curries and Other Indian Dishes** no reviewer had any complaints. The *Times Literary Supplement* gave more space to, and spoke more enthusiastically of Anand's recipes than it did about Anand's **The Golden Breath: Studies in Five Poets of the New India**.

[In *Indian Writing in English,* 1962,] Srinivasa Iyengar writes that Anand chose 'the hazardous profession of letters, probably more by accident than design'. This is not so. He had begun his confessions in 1926, he was writing notes on books for T. S. Eliot's *Criterion* during 1928-29 and had established contact with Professor Bonamy Dobrée, Herbert Read, Laurence Binyon, D. H. Lawrence, Aldous Huxley and Middleton Murry. In 1930 he visited the Lawrences in France and published his first brief study, **Persian Paintings.** By the time his first two (and most characteristic) novels, **Untouchable** (1935) and **Coolie** (1936) appeared, Anand had already published six books.

Untouchable was written in Gandhiji's Sabramati Ashram in a week in 1932 and substantially revised in 1933. Nineteen publishers turned it down, and Anand contemplated suicide but was saved by the poet Oswell Blakeston, who persuaded Wishart's to accept it. The novel is not only a powerful social tract but also a remarkable technical feat. The action takes place within the compass of a single day, but the author manages to build round his hero Bakha (a sweeper lad of eighteen who cleans latrines) a spiritual crisis of such breadth that it seems to embrace the whole of India. There is no better appreciation of the novel than E. M. Forster's Preface:

> Is it a clean book or a dirty one? Some readers, especially those who consider themselves all-white, will go purple in the face with rage before they have finished a dozen pages, and will exclaim that they cannot trust themselves to speak. I cannot trust myself either, though for a different reason: the book seems to me indescribably clean and I hesitate for words in which this can be conveyed. Avoiding rhetoric and circumlocution, it has gone straight to the heart of its subject and purified it.

Coolie was written in three months, and shares with **Untouchable** not only Anand's social angers, but its immense popularity (these two novels have been translated into over thirty languages). There are no classical unities in **Coolie,** the exigencies of plot are swiftly dismissed, the canvas is much wider and the characters more varied. **Coolie** is a study in destitution; its hero, Munoo, not strictly an untouchable, is a young hillboy who is dragged into the plains in the false joy of going to work and seeing the world. The first contact with reality shatters his dreams. Arriving in the house of a bank clerk, he falls foul of a shrewish and vindictive housewife, and before he flees from his employers' frenzied rage he has relieved himself at their door and thereby lowered their prestige. Munoo next arrives in a primitive pickle factory from which desti-

ny uproots him and sends him as one of the proletariat of the cotton industry to Bombay, and finally as the servant of an Anglo-Indian woman to Simla. He dies of tuberculosis, watching the peaceful hills and valleys he had originally deserted.

The novel relates a series of adventures in picaresque manner, but here the hero is no rogue but himself the victim of the world's rogueries. Munoo is beaten from pillar to post as millions are beaten even today; if his caste is not questioned it is because cash has become the only human relationship. Munoo is a most attractive character, with his warm-heartedness, his love, and comradeship, his irrepressible curiosity and zest for life. When he dies, nothing of real value seems lost (except his own lust for life), yet such is the force of the author's pity that much good appears to have gone to waste.

In the trilogy **The Village** (1939), **Across the Black Waters** (1940) and **The Sword and the Sickle** (1942) Anand traces the maturing of a North Indian peasant lad, Lal Singh. The first volume deals with the hero's struggle with a society rotten with superstitions and taboos, and stagnant with hopelessness; the second volume with the part played by Indian troops in the First World War, and Lal Singh's disillusion with the actuality of Europe; the final volume brings Lal Singh back to India where he grasps for reality among his own people awakening to a new political consciousness. Though the road is long, there is the glimmer of a free, unified India. With **The Big Heart** (1945), which like his first novel chronicles the events of a single day, Anand carries the themes of the trilogy into our present-day urban society. The struggle here is between the hereditary coppersmiths (Anand's own father came from a family of coppersmiths) and the capitalists who own the factory. Ananta, the leader of the coppersmiths, is killed and the machines win, but Ananta's idea of a Trade Union survives and will be realized.

In 1945 Anand left England for India, and after a few months in the Punjab settled in Bombay. Arriving at a time when the British at last seemed serious about leaving India, Anand wondered what a free India peppered with over five hundred feudal states would be like. In his novels he had castigated the British Imperialists; could the princes be allowed to go scot free? Meanwhile Anand had met a Singhalese woman, and on her advice had initiated an art magazine, *Marg.* In 1948 he went back to England to get a divorce but on his return to Bombay with the divorce papers, found that the person whom he had hoped to marry had fallen in love with someone else. He had a nervous breakdown and was nursed by the wife of a foreign consul who advised him to write the anguish out of his system. The result was **Private Life of an Indian Prince,** which, says Anand [in a letter to the critic dated 18 November 1967], 'rushed out of me in one month'. It was put aside and not published till 1953. A useful comparison can be sustained between this novel and Manohar Malgonkar's *The Princes;* indeed in the handling of several incidents Malgonkar gives evidence of having been influenced by **Private Life of an Indian Prince**. Through their respective heroes both novels are concerned with the fate of the five-hundred-odd princes who vanished with Indian

Independence in 1947; both expose the prejudices and customs of the princely class; both present the same ignorance, bigotry, false pride and total inability to come to grips with facts. There are also the conventional themes associated with princely life—tiger shoots, arranged marriages, concubines, the rightful Maharani relegated to obscurity after giving birth to an heir-apparent and the favourite mistress angling for the throne for her illegitimate son, the blind and inexplicable love of the ignorant few for their 'Divine' ruler. The narrator in Anand's novel is the personal physician of Maharaja Ashok Kumar, in Malgonkar's the heir-apparent Abhayraj. Both these characters represent the voice of sanity, pitted against the reactionary and medieval attitudes of the rulers themselves. Here, unfortunately for Malgonkar, the comparison between the two works ends. Anand's *Private Life of an Indian Prince* is a Dostoevskian novel on the grand scale, while Malgonkar's *The Princes,* tailored for the Western reader, is overtly concerned with the princes' plight in 1947.

Though the immediate impulse was to provide therapy for his own illness ('written from the white heat of a tremendous crisis' [letter from Anand to the critic dated 22 November 1967]), Anand was thoroughly prepared for the task. He had thought about a novel with a prince as the central character some time before World War II, when a prince he had taught in Simla in the twenties finished up in an asylum, just as his hero does. He had observed the princes carefully, not only as people interesting in their own right but also because of their impact on the common man. Above all, there was Anand's own inclination, as [in a letter to the critic] he himself explains:

> My knowledge of Indian life at various levels had always convinced me that I should do a *comédie humaine*. In this the poor, the lowly and the untouchables were only one kind of outcasts. The middle sections and the nabobs and rajas were also to be included as a species of untouchables. Unfortunately, there has not been time to show the poor-rich of our country, who deserve pity more than contempt.

The material he required was all there. In his treatment and handling of it he was influenced by Tolstoy and Dostoevsky, authors whose works he had read with delight. One can also detect some influence of André Gide, and André Malraux's *Man's Fate,* which, says Anand [in a letter to the critic], 'was very much in my mind for ten years before I wrote *Private Life*'.

Anand's narrator is Dr Hari Shankar, and Anand in the 'Author's Note' to the novel is at some pains to impress on us that the neutral 'I' has become a character in his own right and should 'not be mistaken for the author'. One may ask why an explanation was ever necessary unless there is something in the book which creates a different impression. On a few occasions the narrator certainly speaks for the author. But Anand is right in insisting that he should not be confused with the narrator, for Dr Shankar is more often than not the disembodied voice of reason and sanity. He is actually modelled on a man of liberal mind, Lalla Man Mohan, who was private secretary to the late Maharaja of Patiala. But a more important reason for the author to dissociate himself from the narrator is that Anand has caricatured some aspects of his own emotional life in the person of Maharaja Ashok Kumar; one must not forget the circumstances which induced Anand to write this novel. It may not be generally known that Anand at this period was unjustly declared a decadent by the Bombay group of the Progressive Writers' Association. There is as much of Anand in his Prince as in his narrator, and this partly accounts for the penetrating psychoanalysis of the Prince's character. Dr Shankar is the rational side of the author analysing the irrational side as seen in the Prince.

The Private Life of an Indian Prince is a Dostoevskian novel on the grand scale.

—*Saros Cowasjee*

Private Life of an Indian Prince opens with a public scandal. And what a scandal it is! Maharaja Ashok Kumar, better known as Vicky or Victor to his friends, has taken Bunti Russell to the *khuds* (ravines) 'for the obvious purpose', and there is as much tension in the Russell household as there is anxiety in the Maharaja's lodge. 'I have found no evidence of rape, but there has been an attempt at penetration', announces Colonel Jevons of the Civil Hospital in Simla after examining Bunti. And he wants to see the Prince:

> 'Tell him to go to his mother's!' His Highness roared. 'Who does he think he is! *Sala!* Monkey-face! Doesn't he realize who I am? Ask him to get out of my house . . . Get out! Get out! . . .'
> And now he was hysterical, his voice rising to a shrill querulous height, his face livid and tense and contorted into an ugly expression, his lithe, bony body waving like that of a viper.
>
> We all rushed towards him, whispering hoarsely:
>
> 'Highness! Highness!'
>
> He lay down frothing and struggling, his eyes looking upwards with a look which was distant and forbidding.

There is a scuffle with Captain Russell, which the Prince wins with the aid of his coarse and vulgar A.D.C., Captain Pratap Singh, a giant Sikh 'with nothing in his head except a little white matter under the bun of his long black hair'. Regal rage is now at its pitch, and so continuous is the monologue and so persuasive the campaign of denunciation that even the keen-witted and sceptical Dr Hari Shankar is inveigled into accepting the Prince's plan to lodge an official complaint with the Deputy Commissioner against Captain Russell for laying hands upon the sacred person of the Maharaja. But the Deputy Commissioner refuses to see His Highness, and on the trip back Vicky sees the need for a drastic remedy:

As we drove away from the Deputy Commissioner's bungalow it impressed itself upon His Highness, in the quiet cool of the evening, that things had gone very wrong, that he would have to do something very drastic to mend the situation into which he had got himself. For he asked his rickshaw coolies to come abreast of the rickshaw in which I was riding and told me, with more pathos than he had brought to his voice before in uttering the same truth, 'I am a rat in a hole.'

Anand is a master of the mock-heroic and the anti-climax. The passage just quoted reveals two of his chief characteristics: first, his sense of pity, not diffused and clotted, but tempered with an irony which bites an incident into the memory; second, the lyrical element, which shows its full brightness when the author settles down to a clinical analysis of his character.

In the intervals of the Bunti-Vicky episode, we get to know more of the complex character of the Prince. He is a clever, spoilt womanizer on the brink of political and personal disaster. A febrile romantic, proud of his ancestry, he has inherited more of the vices than virtues of his order; one who indulges in broad gestures, melodramatic speeches, and strange histrionics to avert the inevitable disaster. Dr Shankar edges the thermometer into his mouth, but knows that the real malady of his patient lies elsewhere:

> For his intelligence seemed to have run riot through the large gaps in his education and experience . . . So it was touching to see the clashes between the poetry and prose of his life, the contradictions that arose from his reflection of the feudal, aristocratic idea that all excellence is inheritance, and the sense of direction which dictates integration through the discovery of values in the new society. The spirits of his dead ancestors were pulling him towards the old virtues, prowess, splendour, firmness, dexterity, generosity, heroism in battle and the other duties of the high-caste, superior, *kshattriya* prince, while a number of new demons, the fashions of the hour, were pulling him into another direction, on account of the shameless schooling through which his childhood in his father's zenana, and his boyhood and youth in the hands of the Angrezi Sarkar, had put him. For he had learnt all the filth that his retinue of servants in the palace could teach him, and been spoiled by his doting mother, always anxious to save his life against the homicidal fury of his father's concubines . . . All the old values and the new demons had been increasingly at war with each other in his soul. And there was no knowing where they would take him, since the will through which alone such powers could be harnessed had been sedulously crushed by the Angrezi Sarkar and his own parents a long time ago. He had few resources left after these two heredities had done their work. Except that he had an uncanny gift of perception, an almost convalescent abjectness, which was the opposite of his extraordinary cruelty, and a violent energy for voicing his fads and fancies, whether they took the form of naive outbursts, mere flippancy, or the more balanced rationalizations of poetry, which was always like someone else's confirmation of his own complaints. All his scandalous behaviour, therefore, was due to the incongruity of the various strains in him that were trying to unite and become one person, but only made him a kind of montage man, a pathetic creature, a spoilt child.

Anand's craftsmanship is demonstrated from the way he organizes and unravels his material. He opens the novel (which is divided into four parts) with the scandal, then tells us enough about Vicky to arouse our curiosity. What is Vicky doing in Simla when the fate of his State is in the balance? What are conditions like back home? Who is Ganga Dasi from whose grip the Prince cannot free himself? All this information Anand divulges to the reader during the royal party's return to the State, a journey which has become necessary because of the scandal, the exhortations of the Prime Minister, and the compulsions of Vicky's mistress, Ganga Dasi. Had Anand opened his novel with the tangled history of the Prince's life and that of his State, the reader might have lost interest in the story. Anand wisely defers it till the homeward journey begins.

In the train Dr Shankar recapitulates Vicky's past to see if anything can be done to give him a fresh start. Anand spreads (and deliberately confuses) Vicky's history over fifteen pages, but we come to learn the essentials. After sifting the mass of machinations and intrigues we learn that the Tikyali Rani (his third wife) has given him a male heir whom Vicky is afraid to acknowledge as he is completely within the power of his nymphomaniacal mistress Ganga Dasi, who also has a son by him. Unable to get the States Department in Delhi to recognize Ganga Dasi's son, Vicky attempts to feed his mistress's greed for wealth by tyrannizing over his subjects and extorting money from them. The Tikyali Rani has sent several appeals to the States Department and Vicky's position is precarious. To add to his troubles the people in the State are on the point of rebelling, and the Congress Government is insisting that he sign the Instrument of Accession. There is a way out of this morass, but one that Vicky can only talk about, not take.

Part Two is almost twice as long as the other parts together. Like a Greek play, the novel moves steadily towards its catastrophe. Simla with its scandal was a paradise compared to what Vicky has to face in Sham Pur. There are two powerful forces working against him: the first is Ganga, whose emotional hold he realizes as acutely as his inability to free himself from it; the second is the public, and here his intuitive political sagacity is circumscribed by his environment, upbringing, temperament, and misplaced confidence in himself. The first force impinges on the second, with devastating consequences for Vicky and his State. Dr Shankar, seeking to reach and reveal the wellspring of human actions, never quite succeeds in summing up either Ganga Dasi or Vicky as concisely as they do each other. Vicky describes Ganga as a 'bitch' and a 'consummate actress', while she describes Vicky as 'very clever', 'very cruel', and 'very jealous'.

Ganga Dasi is brilliantly portrayed as an illiterate but powerful hill-woman. The daughter of an unhappy alliance, she grew up as a lonely and secretive child and was enjoyed by several villagers even before she was fourteen. Abused by others, she began to exploit her physical charms and moved from one lover to another, till she finally came to Sham Pur and cast her spell on Vicky. Vicky knows all this and more, and Dr Shankar is surprised that in spite of this knowledge he should trust her and live with her. Vicky's reasons are as credible as the passions themselves are perilous:

> 'I had behaved badly to my wives, and she had been bad. . . . So I thought that two bad people might make a good pair. . . . She understands me in a strange kind of way. And sex . . .'

> 'I feel that all this emotional insecurity is a heavy price to pay for brief moments of pleasure.'

> 'I must not be unfair to her, Dr Shankar. You see, I can't tell you of the happiness she gave me when she first came to me. You will laugh at this. But I felt that someone had come into my life, someone who knew the life of a town like Lahore amidst all these yokels, someone to cling to in the midst of all the artificiality of the state where I was a kind of tin god. To have a private life with someone devoted to you after all the ballyhoo of pomp and splendour! And she was a lovely companion and gave me such assurance. I could work ten times harder because I had a satisfactory personal life. She used to bath me with her own hands and fuss after me a good deal in the beginning. And so I surrendered to her more completely than I have ever surrendered to any other woman. She told me all the secrets of her affairs and wished that she had met me first when she was nearly a virgin . . .'

In spite of the fact that he felt no security in Gangi [in a footnote, Cowasjee notes that "Gangi is a familiar form of Ganga"], he found in her general amiability and charm, consolations such as he could not get from the company of his chaste, rather too proper wife. And while he suffered the agonies of hell from the ups and downs of Gangi's incalculable temperament, he was fascinated by the challenge of her moods, by the excitement and thrills of those changing colours, of which her vanities, frailties, ficklenesses and cruelties were the secondary hues as against the lush splendour of the primary colours of her lusts and passions. It was really the call of one chameleon to another, for they had both emerged, with similar temperaments, from the orbits of their respective affairs and mistaken their fatigue for the urgent need of each other. In the aura of the atmosphere that prevailed between them through the long-drawn miseries of days, the nights were relieved by the high-powered love-making and the reaching out to an insouciance where both of them felt calm and assured, having touched the ultimate limits of sex which held them both prisoners of each other . . . The complex of his present position was, however, too intricate to admit of any simplification, and in the game of hide-and-seek which he and Gangi played they were approximating towards desires and impulses in themselves and each other which were wild and boundless and inchoate, the urgings of capacities which had been perverted and thwarted by the unreality of their lives, by the substitution in their careers of 'felt wants' for 'real wants'.

This explains much, but not all, and nobody is more conscious of that than Dr Shankar himself. Later in the novel he makes fewer attempts to dissect their relationship, and prefers terms such as 'sadist', 'masochist', and 'split personality' to sum up Ganga Dasi. After all, these terms are accurate and safe, and in spite of their generality as near the mark as any clinical psycho-analysis.

If the relationship between the two defies complete scrutiny, its effects on Vicky are only too palpable. The more Ganga indulges in promiscuity (her victims include the Prime Minister Popatlal J. Shah, the journalist Kurt Landauer, and the Political Secretary Bool Chand) the greater is Vicky's rage, which generally culminates in bursts of uncontrollable sobbing. The irony, however, is that Ganga seems to profit from her aberrations: the more she turns to other men for sex the greater is her hold on Vicky. Failing to get her son in line for the throne, she forces Vicky to bestow money and jewellery on her, and this he does by exacting huge fees from his starving peasants. Thus Ganga's greed brings Vicky into a dangerous conflict, and at a most inopportune time, with his subjects. His personal impulses and his passion for his mistress prevent him from looking into the larger social issues that are involved. If he meets Ganga's challenge with hysterical tears, he meets the political challenge from his people and the Government of India with melodramatic gestures. Needless to say he loses both contests.

On the political plane Vicky has to contend with the Sardars, some of them his close cousins. They so hate him that they have joined with the Communist guerillas to topple his administration. He is also opposed by the Praja Mandal in the capital (who are secretly encouraged by the Congress Party to agitate for democratic rule) and the States Department (which is prepared to use the public unrest to force the Prince to sign the Instrument of Accession). But the real protagonist in this drama is the people, and everything that Vicky does, personal or social, has a direct bearing on them. Though the centre of attraction is Vicky, the public looms large on the canvas and its power and presence are never forgotten. Here is Dr Shankar ruminating in the hunting lodge:

> The culminative effect of the whole noisy evening, with the opposing wills, was to produce in me a repeated sense of the doom that was imminent in it all: the cruel, ugly inevitability of the disruption that was in store for us, the main actors in the drama, both individually and collectively. For impinging on my consciousness was the pressure of the people of Sham Pur, who, though absent from this scene, were yet perhaps the most powerful actors in the drama, the invisible mass lying in wait to ambush the intriguing, agonized, decadent prince and his courtiers, and ready to wipe out the whole putrescent order with a ruthless determination to clean up the Augean stables of the feudalist oligarchy.

Vicky meets this challenge with his foolish boastings and

self-deluding lies: he talks of the friends he has among the other princes, his ability to cope with the intrigues of his enemies, his desire to 'renew in the people the belief that I have their interests at heart'. In his hypocrisy he even quotes Shri Ram Chandra, King of Ayodhya: 'There shall be no pain in my heart in having to resign for the sake of pleasing my subjects; every tie of affection, every feeling of compassion, every happiness, even the idol of my heart, my wife . . .' At other moments he talks about his genius which nobody understands: 'But I shall make you understand. I shall make everyone understand! I shall show you the stuff I am made of! I . . . I . . . I . . .'

The practical measures to defend his State take the shape of army manoeuvres near the Indian border, which he himself supervises, wearing the uniform of an Honorary Major-General. Instead of impressing the peasants, the manoeuvres anger them for tanks and jeeps roll over their crops. He organizes a shoot for Mr Peter Watkins ('nearly the Ambassador'!) of the American Embassy in Delhi in the futile hope of seeking American intervention. The whole thing is a fiasco. The net results are that his mistress gets a chance to sleep with Kurt Landauer, and Sardar Vallabhai Patel, Union Minister for States, orders Vicky to report immediately to Delhi.

The scene that follows is perhaps the best in the novel. In Delhi Vicky is asked to wait indefinitely, and this alone brings down his pride several notches. At last, while Vicky sits in a brothel shedding sentimental tears over a song, and thinking of his Ganga, he is informed that the interview will take place at five o'clock the next morning.

The business of the next day is brief. With a scowl Patel addresses Vicky as Raja (a title inferior by one degree) and he is soon reduced to less than his normal size. The Minister chides him for maladministration, ruthless suppression, and corruption, and before Vicky has had a chance to say one-tenth of what he had rehearsed while waiting, he has signed on the dotted line and the destiny of Sham Pur has mingled with that of the Indian Republic. There is little exaggeration in Anand's epigrammatic summary: 'Sardar Vallabhai (Wishmarck) Patel growled, like a big angry bull, twice or thrice from the rostrum in Delhi. And most of the sons of Suns and Moons fell into line as children of the earth.'

Vicky returns to Sham Pur musing: 'Now, I shall be more or less in the same position as Gangi, one of the disinherited! Maybe, this will bring us closer together.' In the meantime Ganga has fled with the Political Secretary, Bool Chand, a snorting *bania,* and the privation and humiliation weigh more heavily on Vicky's mind than the loss of his kingdom. A search is organized, but there is no trace of Ganga; nor a limit to Vicky's obsession with her. The new Prime Minister, Pundit Gobind Das (the leader of the Praja Mandal), comes to seek Vicky's help against the Communists who are marching towards the capital Vicky gives glimpses of his political acumen, but his last words to the Prime Minister are 'to dismiss Bool Chand and extort some information about my wife's [mistress's] whereabouts'.

Anand could have finished his novel here, for it would

have been as easy to take Vicky to a lunatic asylum now as later. The last two parts of the novel deal with Vicky's brief exile in London and his mental collapse, and here Anand goes as far as possible to extract from the situation what he terms the Yoke of Pity—the 'compassionate understanding of the dignity of weakness, of negative, broken down people who struggle so hard to survive at some human level and sometimes surpass themselves by doing things least expected of them, such as the ultimate love of Vicky for Ganga Dasi for whom he has her paramour murdered and ends up by losing his mind' [letter from Anand to the critic].

To prevent the story from lapsing into sentimentality, Anand introduces the amusing episode of Vicky seducing the shop-girl, June Withers. This the Prince achieves with all the finesse he is capable of, and even his dim-witted A.D.C. shows gumption by announcing aloud Vicky's title to the beholders just as Vicky is about to panic. The campaign to seduce June Withers is better conducted than the one to preserve his State. On one flank June is attacked with temptations such as a Rolls Royce, cocktails, dresses, dinners; on the other by the Prince's manoeuvres, which range from reading Miss Withers's palms to confessions such as 'I have lost my throne . . . But that wouldn't have mattered. Only, only, the woman I loved also left me . . .' However, Vicky's passion for Ganga is genuine and June cannot replace her. He has Ganga's lover Bool Chand murdered through his agents, and loses his mind at the shock of realizing what he has done.

The Prince's madness is deftly handled; here is a scene that takes place in the plane on the homeward journey:

> 'How do you do, Doctor Shankar! I am Maharaja Ashok Kumar of Sham Pur. Don't you understand, you swine?—I am a prince! Why, why do you hold me like that? Let me go, let me go, rape-mother! . . . Let me go! . . . I shall allow no one to come near me, not even the Viceroy . . . Why did that dhobi touch me? I am a king. Do you not understand? I am the Maharaja Ashok Kumar, spoiler of my salt! . . .'
>
> 'Come, come, Victor, you are not a little boy any more,' I rebuked him in a firm voice. 'Don't be a fool!'
>
> This seemed to sober him. And, with a cunning candour imprinted on his face, he said:
>
> 'Why am I ill?'
>
> 'You must calm down,' I said.
>
> But by this time the lucidity had gone and he was shouting at the top of his voice:
>
> '*Khabardar! Khabardar!* The thieves are coming! Look out, folk, the robbers! the bandits!'
>
> 'Try and sing,' I suggested again, smacking my lips sympathetically.
>
> 'Try and sing,' he repeated my words, and mimicked me by smacking his lips sympathetically.
>
> I held his left hand and pressed it warmly.
>
> 'Sing,' I said.

And he burst out with the raucous lilt of a First
World War Sikh soldier's song:

'Han ni, may I buy you, may I buy you
Black slippers, with high heels,
What is the use of Indian style shoes,
Ni, Harnam Kauré! . . .'

Shankar leads his Prince to the portals of the lunatic asylum in Poona and, having got his royal patient admitted,
begins a lengthy self-analysis.

Anand is still writing vigorously and since 1953 has published several novels and short stories. Fine as these later
works are, they do not possess the energy and sweep of
Private Life of an Indian Prince. It is not easy for Anand
to surpass himself. He may. But even if he does not, it will
not matter—his reputation is secure. He is the first Indian
writer in English to dispel the myth built around the Indian character: the myth about 'contentment' in the midst
of poverty, 'mystical silence', 'spiritual attainments'. In
his novels, for the first time the Indian masses have been
clearly and intimately described with pitiless realism and
deep understanding, and the exploiters—whether imperialists or feudalists—savagely denounced. Since the publication of **Untouchable** and **Coolie,** many Indian writers
have followed the lead given by him yet none has so far
surpassed him. In his own country, his only serious rival
in the art of fiction is R. K. Narayan. But to compare
Narayan with Anand is as futile as to compare Jane Austen with Tolstoy. The difference between the two is of that
order.

Saros Cowasjee   (review date 1970)

SOURCE: A review of *Morning Face*, in *Indian Literature*, Vol. XIII, No. 1, 1970, pp. 147-49.

[*In the following review, Cowasjee compares Anand to Tolstoy and praises Anand's depiction of the protagonist's
philosophical transformation.*]

Morning Face is a worthy sequel to **Seven Summers**
(1951); the two volumes being a part of a much larger
work called *The Seven Ages of Man,* which is still in the
process of being written. Very few writers apart from Trollope, Sir Edmund Gosse, Goethe and Tolstoy, have been
able to recapture childhood effectively. Among these,
Anand is closest to Tolstoy, and for his literary model he
takes Tolstoy's *Childhood, Boyhood* and *Youth*. Like Tolstoy, Anand has a remarkable capacity to enter childhood,
the capacity for wonder which one also finds in Pushkin.

The comparison with Tolstoy does not end here. The two
writers are among the first in their countries to describe
the life of a child from within, from the child's point of
view. With them it is the child itself which expresses its
childish feelings, and it does this as if to compel the reader
to judge full-grown people from the child's angle of vision.
So close indeed is the identity that no sooner they speak
of children, they become children themselves. Also common between the two writers are their vivid impressions
of childhood, the carefully worked out narrative details,
and the leisurely manner of narration. But Anand's is perhaps a little too leisurely: **Morning Face** is longer than

Tolstoy's three volumes taken together. The work would
have been better had Anand exercised a little more selec-
tivity: it is not necessary to record every joy and every woe
that visits a child. Spelling mistakes and a careless use of
ellipses do further injury to an otherwise well conceived
and well written book.

The book is more than the blurb or the author's 'Dedication' purports it to be. Growth from innocence to experience is only one of its themes, and the hero's journey
through the 'torments of the Hindu hell' would be hell itself were it not for the rich comedy that permeates the
work. Krishan Chander is a Freudian boy if ever there was
one. But to his contemporaries he is 'Chooia', 'Pilpili
Sahib', 'Bijoo'; one who recites 'twinkle, twinkle, little
stars' at the least persuasion: be it for the benefit of the
Head Master or for the Inspector of Schools—Mr. Marsden. Beaten and bullied by boys older than himself, he
manages to hold his own. Only twice does he lose nerve:
once when the homosexual master invites him to sit on his
lap, and the second time when he reaches puberty while
riding a mare! His horror at finding his pajamas sodden
are matched by his aunt's casual attempt to comfort him:
'Go, there is nothing to worry about! All that has happened to you is that you have become a man—Now you
can no longer sleep with your arms around my neck . . .
You will have to get a little wife of your own . . . I will
write a postcard to your father and tell him.'

Two aspects of the work deserve to be noted. The first is
the needle sharp observations with which the book
abounds, and the author's ability to probe into the many
subsidiary motives (by-products, if you wish) which accompany the central issue. The visit of the English doctor
to examine his cousin Kaushalya is reminiscent of the finest scene in **Coolie,** where Mr. W. P. England visits Babu
Nathoo Ram's home for tea. This is how Anand describes
it:

> The gloom into which our household was
> plunged was lifted again for a while by our
> brother Harish bringing with him Colonel Bar-
> rie, the Inspector General of Jails, who was also
> a doctor. The mere coming into our lane of a
> white face, and a physician so exalted, filled the
> family with pride, especially as the Angrezi
> speech in which he talked to father and Harish
> seemed to our neighbours in the lanes to promise
> an almost certain cure of Kaushalya's tuberculo-
> sis.

The second aspect is the gradual and wholly convincing
transformation of [the] hero into a revolutionary and an
agnostic. Since the elders can provide no answers to his
searching queries, he formulates his own conclusions. The
philosophic speculations are of a type in which a young
boy may well indulge. Young Krishan Chander toys with
the idea of death, and concludes: 'But then, I argued, I was
in love with life and was it not a great feat to do away with
oneself because one could not be really free.' Later in the
book he falls in love with his brother's mistress, Mumtaz,
and reasons: 'Nothing was right or wrong. Only there was
love or no love. All those who despised others were unhappy in their own hearts.' In Anand's simple deductions
there is an indescribable power.

Anthony Trollope once said that 'it is dangerous to write from the point of "I". The reader is unconsciously taught to feel that the writer is glorifying himself, and rebels against self-praise. Or otherwise the "I" is pretentiously humble, and offends from exactly the other point of view.' Anand has so far escaped both these pitfalls. This is partly because he has exercised objectivity to an exceptional degree, and partly because little that is dramatic in relation to his own self has yet taken place. But the third volume, which is still to be published, may prove the most difficult. It will obviously deal with the author as 'Lover' (Anand is strictly following the order of the 'seven ages' as established by Jacques in *As You Like It,* and the third stage deals with 'the lover / Sighing like a furnace'). Here it may not be easy to steer clear of self-pity and self-praise. Also, the total lack of inhibition which has marked the first two volumes of the autobiography may bring about its own debacle: the 'loves' could appear imaginary as they sometimes do in Rousseau's *Confessions,* or they may smack of exhibitionism as in Frank Harris's *My Life and Loves.*

But all this may be premature foreboding. What can be said with perfect justice is that in writing ***Morning Face*** Anand has made doubly sure that he will live—both as author and character.

Suresht Renjen Bald (essay date October 1974)

SOURCE: "Politics of a Revolutionary Elite: A Study of Mulk Raj Anand's Novels," in *Modern Asian Studies,* Vol. 8, No. 4, October, 1974, pp. 473-89.

[*In the following excerpt, Bald identifies traits common to all of Anand's novels, including a protagonist who highlights social injustice and a hero who espouses revolution.*]

Mulk Raj's novels follow an identical pattern: each describes a principal figure who brings into focus the injustices of society; his abortive and misdirected attempts for a better life in the existing unjust state; and the appearance of the revolutionary hero, who shows him that realization of a good life is only possible *after* the destruction of the present order. The novels end on a note of hope in the anticipated Revolution. Though the *milieu* of the novels differs, the character of the message and of the messenger remains remarkably consistent.

The objective of initial failure is to sharpen the profile of the true revolutionaries, the messiahs. The false prophets or imposters come under the labels 'Terrorists' or 'Spontaneous Revolutionists', Gandhi the 'bourgeois saint', and those who offer religion as the Truth. [In a footnote, Bald adds: "see the role played by Kanwar Rampal Singh's gang in ***The Sword and the Sickle,*** Gandhi in *ibid.,* and ***The Untouchable,*** and Colonel Hutchinson in ***The Untouchable.***"] They tempt the main characters by advocating *'wrong'* action and raising false hopes.

The characterization of the messiah figures in all the novels is similar: virtues of traditional Hindu heroes appear combined with those of a Leninist hero. [In a footnote, Bald states that the virtues of traditional Hindu heroes are "self-control, asceticism, non-attachment to worldly goods and family ties, and an unmitigated devotion to the

Truth."] The two types merge smoothly. Mohan (*Coolie*) is respected and admired by the rikshaw pullers because of his renunciation of the comfortable life: 'Rumor goes that . . . he has been to Vilayat (England) and is such a learned man . . . He comes from a high class family . . . He had an easy life in his childhood and youth. And now he is doing a sort of penance for his sins.' In contrast, Onkarnath, the Congressite trade unionist in *Coolie,* is a 'prim well-groomed man, dressed in a homespun *silk* tunic and *silk* dhoti . . . his eyes and brow wrinkled darkly near the edges of the *expensive* tortoise shell glasses. His lower lip is twisted into a sardonic contempt for everything but himself . . .' He lacks the simplicity of Mohan, the true revolutionary; unlike Mohan, he is a poor speaker, unable to evoke enthusiasm amongst the mill-hands for the Gandhian faith in negotiation with the mill-owners.

What Lallu (***The Sword and the Sickle***) notices about the revolutionary leader Sarshar is his asceticism: in contrast to Kanwar Rampal Singh's gang of pseudo-revolutionaries, who smoke the best cigarettes and drink imported liquor, Sarshar austerely smokes the cheap *bidis.* He possesses a 'demoniac devotion' akin to the Hindu ideal of *bhakti.* Sarshar radiates an aura of dedication, sincerity, self-sacrifice and austerity. Rampal Singh's group, on the other hand, is characterized by a light-hearted tomfoolery. Rampal Singh himself is described as an 'easygoing, loosely dressed, quick witted buffoon,' as if to describe his thought processes.

Mahatma Gandhi, seen through the eyes of Lallu, 'seemed to be full of himself, of his own spiritual struggles. And Lallu felt himself lapsing into listlessness, as if he were being suffocated by the deliberately exalted simplicity of this egoistic, confessional talk of self-perfection. He wanted to bring the Mahatma to a concrete decision. But the aroma of moral grandeur, purity, and simplicity that surrounded this place [Gandhi's quarters at *Anand Bhavan*] made him feel as if he were a huge uncouth figure with large legs and big paws in a glass palace.'

Puran Singh (***The Big Heart***) is called *Bhagat* by his followers, a traditional title for the devoted one. He is depicted as full of 'unselfishness and spirit of sacrifice . . . though he has renounced religion.' Revolution is his new 'religion'. Thus a pattern emerges: the advocates of Revolution are all men who come from the top, the privileged classes, they do not rise from the ranks. However, they 'renounce' their privileges to identify with the underprivileged, to devote themselves to the Cause and to spread the gospel of revolt among the masses. They are the politically active *sannyasis* (ascetics), and it is because they embody the virtues of the traditional leader that the masses hold them in high regard. One may well ask if the masses accept the leadership of Mulk Raj's messiahs because they fit the pattern of the ideal leader in the context of Hindu political culture or because of the nature of their message.

The Leninist vanguard theory of Revolution to which Mulk Raj Anand subscribed intensified the elitism of the Hindu 'superior born' leader. The result is disastrous. Anand's revolutionaries, though trying hard to be one with the people, cannot help emerging as superior human beings: they profess faith in Man and commitment to Man's integrity; however, *they* decide what is 'good' for man. In *The Big Heart,* Puran Singh declares '. . . a great deal of my belief in truth arises from my love and respect for man as such. . . . I believe in a restoration of man's integrity if he is to control machinery at the present time. I believe, in fact, if we can have any religious faith, morality or code at all today, it must arise from the reassertion of man's dignity, reverence for his name.' Yet he feels no betrayal of his beliefs when he agrees with his protégé, Ananta, that the coppersmiths are 'like children and . . . lack confidence. . . . They haven't been able to make up their minds, whether they hate machines too much to take jobs in the factories or whether they are really looking for jobs there. And *we ought to make up their minds for them.*' In *Coolie,* Mohan tries to identify himself with the rikshaw pullers by becoming a rikshaw man himself, but talks to the coolies as a superior; 'You fool,' he rebukes an indifferent coolie, 'You will let them [the exploiters, the landlords] kill you. You are all ignorant slaves. How can I drill any sense into your heads?' Sauda, the Trade Unionist, likewise uses abusive language to stir the workers in the cotton mills to strike:

> Stand up for your rights, you *roofless wretches,* stand up for justice! Stand up you *frightened swine.* Stand up and fight! Stand up and be the men you were meant to be and don't crawl back into the factories like the *worms* that you are! Stand up for life, or they will crush you and destroy you altogether! Stand up and *follow me!* From tomorrow you go on strike and we will pay you to fight your battle with the employers! Now stand up and recite with me the chapter of your demands. (italics mine)

The charter is drawn up by the leaders without any consultation with the aggrieved parties. The workers are shamed into following the Trade Unionists. Sauda appeals to their feudal notion of *izzat* (honor), and their manliness: 'Would you let anyone throw away the turbans off your head? . . . Then where is your idea of *izzat* gone?' asks Sauda, 'Where is your sense of dignity? Where is your manhood?' Mutual respect between the leader and the led is entirely absent. One detects a contempt for the lowly and the under-privileged, a lack of confidence in the Revolution of the 'people'. The elites are dedicated to the revolutionary cause, they 'know' that Revolution is necessary and their job is to convince the ignorant masses of its necessity. Looking down on the masses does not produce any emotional or spiritual conflict in their minds.

Revolt against authority is the central theme of Mulk Raj's novels; it was also the theme of his relationship with his father, the symbol of authority in the household. He was fascinated by revolt, and treated it sometimes as an end rather than a means. However, along with this fascination for revolt is a preoccupation with authority leading him to replace existing father figures with the dictatorship of the Revolutionary leader, the messiah who would lead the 'people' to consciousness and revolt, speak *for* the poor and the downtrodden, and set up a 'paternalist State', to give tractors and fertilizers to the peasants, retaining the power to give or withhold.

Lallu, the central figure in Mulk Raj Anand's trilogy, accepts Revolution as a creed only after a series of rebellions in the village. As an adolescent [in *The Village*] he defies the mores of his Sikh village community by shaving his long hair, eating meat cooked by a Muslim, and flirting with the landlord's daughter. On being severely punished for his deviant behavior by the headman of the village, his father and his elder brothers, Lallu rejects familial and communal discipline. He runs away from home to seek liberation in the Army. Yet the Army is merely a replacement for the close-knit village community with its authoritarian superiors, which Lallu had rejected. After discharge from the Army he seeks commitment to authority in the elitism of Revolution.

Though the peasants of Nasirabad rebel against the landlord's insistence on forced labor, they derive courage to do so from the leadership of Kanwar Rampal Singh, a declassed landlord [in *The Sword and the Sickle*]. The peasants respect authority too much; and they accept it in the traditional manner of *mai-bapism.* They cannot repudiate one *mai-bap* (mother-father) without the security of another. Their mode of address for Rampal Singh is *Maharaj* (ruler), *Huzoor* (lord), or *Sarkar,* all servile in their connotations.

Lallu wants the state to 'redivide the land, create Sarkari (state) farms, and give every village a tractor or two, as Kanwar Sahib says they are doing in Roos' [*The Sword and the Sickle*]. Munnu (*Coolie*) wonders why 'the *Angrezi Sarkar* had not razed the old city and built (modern) shops and houses, and decorated them with tables and chairs'. Both assume that it is the duty of the state to do so. When, as a World War I sepoy, Lallu visits France, he is impressed by the French farmers' use of chemical fertilizers. Instinctively he exclaims [in *Across the Black Waters*], 'The Sarkar ought to invent [fertilizers] in Hind', and distribute them among the Indian peasants.

Puran Singh (*The Big Heart*) believes in 'bhakti, devotion . . . working for others'. After becoming an enlightened revolutionary, Lallu (*The Sword and the Sickle*) believes: 'as the *bhagats,* the devoted ones in the past practiced the "at your service" ideal of our religion, so we [revolutionaries] have to give, give, give of ourselves'. To both of them it is important to *serve* the poor, for 'he who gives himself to the service of others is blessed, is enriched'. This deep-seated belief in authority and paternalism is not only in keeping with traditional Indian political culture but also with the workings of the British Raj. Paternalist authority of the state is not questioned; what is questioned is the character of the men who wield it.

Mulk Raj's treatment of industrialism, though influenced by Marxism, possesses uniquely Indian ingredients. Industrialism itself is good; the machine is a hero except under capitalism, when it becomes a villain. Puran Singh points out [in *The Big Heart*]: 'If you [the workers] have the *controlling switch* [power] in your hand, you can make the machine your slave rather than your master. . . . It is that switch or *destruction*.' Destruction involves loss of 'their *manhood,* the *dignity* of their place in the brotherhood, their *sense of community*'.

Mulk Raj points out how a sense of brotherhood existed in precapitalist India. It is present in his *thathair* community before the advent of the factory, in the village that both Mannu and Lallu leave, and even among the untouchables of Bakka's world. The coppersmiths address each other as 'brothers', and the severest and most effective punishment for the *thathair* turned factory owners and responsible for unemployment among the artisans, is social boycott of their household by the community [*sic*]. This proves especially effective at the time of weddings, when people refuse to contract marriage with a family thus boycotted. Ananta stresses to his coppersmith brethren: 'If we belong to hunger and suffering we belong to it together'. The sense of community of the coppersmiths is preserved by their living in the same *Mohalla* (area) of the town. Both Munnu and Lallu come from a close-knit village community. In the city for the first time oprhan Munnu [from *Coolie*] felt lonely; after taking the plunge of running away from home Lallu 'recognized himself, a pitiful figure, walking along the dusty highway alone, in the oppressive muzzy windless solitude of the land' [*The Village*].

It was to regain this feeling of community which was being threatened by the introduction of the concept of 'Mine' and 'Thine', that Mulk Raj launched his propaganda of the Revolution [in *The Sword and the Sickle*]: 'For Revolution is a need for togetherness, Comrade, the need to curb malice among men, the need for men to stand together as brothers . . .'. However, the community Mulk Raj was seeking was the recapture of an emotional security lost by the peasant-turned-laborer, or by the breakdown of the artisan caste brotherhood. It was not the Marxian philosophical community of the self with its creative essence, from which union followed the Marxist harmony between men. [In a footnote, Bald states: "Here I accept Robert C. Tucker's thesis (see his *Philosophy and Myth in Karl Marx*) that the only community Marx was concerned with was the community of the self: man with his external and internal human nature; this split of man's human nature was evident in the material world by the splitting of collective man into classes—the exploiter and the exploited. To Marx, self change, or Revolution, was to be the work of the fully alienated worker, the proletariat: 'emancipation of the workers contains universal emancipation' (Marx, *Manuscripts of 1844*)."] In spite of his apocalyptic tone and revolutionary zeal, Mulk Raj wanted to make a heretical transition, in the Marxian context, from the collectivism of the caste and village to the harmony of the revolutionary utopia. His revolutionary messiahs preach Revolution not to the wholly alienated proletariat, but to the unemployed artisans of *The Big Heart* who have never worked for the 'capitalists', the unskilled laborers of *Coolie*, and the peasantry of *The Sword and the Sickle*.

Somehow a Revolution was to solve everything: Mulk Raj's message is the urgency of effecting such a Revolution; his visions, the resurrection of man the day after the Revolution: ' . . . let us make another effort to destroy those who do not love us'. 'Now is the time to live in and through the struggle. . . . Now is the time to change the world, to fight for Life and Happiness . . .' [*The Sword and the Sickle*] for 'Life makes a fresh start with every

great change and overturning. And those who have lost faith and been degraded, disfigured and mutilated, become aware of their *manhood,* and rise to the full heights of their dignity, become men and learn to stand erect with their turbans on their heads . . .' [*The Big Heart*]. By one blow, overnight, the Revolution was to create new men who are whole individuals.

In the tradition of Marxist Revolutionists, Mulk Raj externalized the 'solitary, poor, brutish, nasty' Hobbesian man, placing him in the objective reality of institutional life or private property. Destruction of the corrupting institutions was to lead simultaneously to the emergence of tenderness, brotherliness and creativity in man: ' . . . a "Revolution" after which men would find a new way of living in which they would discover a new brotherhood, away from the pettiness created by the miseries of the present, by the need of profit makers and the lust for power of the Sarkar . . .' [*The Big Heart*].

'Brotherhood' and 'manhood' are linked in Mulk Raj's post-revolutionary era; 'pettiness' and 'greed' with the present 'capitalist' age of profiteering. After the Revolution, Man realizes his essence as collective man in 'togetherness'; profit, greed, and egoistic need make man less human by placing barriers between man and man.

Saros Cowasjee (essay date January 1977)

SOURCE: "Mulk Raj Anand's *Confession of a Lover*," in *The International Fiction Review,* Vol. 4, No. 1, January, 1977, pp. 18-22.

[*In the following essay, Cowasjee discusses theme and character in* Confession of a Lover.]

Anand's latest novel [*Confession of a Lover*] has its roots in the "confession" that he wrote at the behest of Irene, the beautiful daughter of a scientific philosopher, whom he had met soon after arriving in England in 1925 to study philosophy at University College, London. Irene was impressed by Anand's gift of storytelling and encouraged him to write about himself and his family. Anand's narrative soon ran into 2,000 pages, but no publisher could be found to publish the whole or even part of the work. It did not, however, go to waste: the narrative became a source of many of Anand's novels and short stories, and finally the basis of his most ambitious work—the projected story of his life in seven volumes under the general caption *Seven Ages of Man*. Of these, only three volumes have so far appeared: *Seven Summers* (1951), *Morning Face* (1968) and *Confession of a Lover* (1976).

A month after the publication of *Confession of a Lover,* Mulk Raj Anand—conscious that I had criticized him for carelessness and verbosity—wrote to me [in a letter dated March 9, 1976]: "You will find the *Confession* fairly well printed—also better proof correction: and I have cut thirty pages in page proofs to make it compact even at the risk of eliminating certain phases of consciousness of a morbid youth." Nevertheless, this book of four hundred odd pages is much too long for what it has to say, and the errors in printing and spelling are as numerous as in *Morning Face*. The name of the German philosopher Nietzsche appears several times in the book and is spelt differently on different occasions, but it is not once spelt correctly. Anand, who has adopted the fictional name Krishan Chander, tells us in one place that he had read Shakespeare's *Julius Caesar* "several times" and was asked on one occasion by his college principal to read aloud Mark Antony's speech on the death of Caesar. But both names, Antony and Caesar, are misspelled. A work full of such mistakes cannot be rated very highly, and it is a sad reflection on present-day critical attitudes that a reviewer [L. N. Gupta in *The Sunday Hitavada* (7 March 1976)] should call this book "the best Indo-Anglian novel published so far." Still, the book is not without its strong points.

Confession of a Lover deals with Krishan Chander's life at Khalsa College, Amritsar, from 1921 to 1925. The book opens with the hero in homespun Indian clothing and a sola topee on his head bicycling breezily to college, and ends with his taking a train to Bombay—en route to England—sad and disillusioned. Between these two events much happens to him. Small in build, but with an enormous ego, he is bullied by boys bigger than himself. Along with his favorite aunt, Devaki, he is excommunicated for dining with a Muslim family. He comes under the influence of Gandhi; he writes poetry, encouraged by the poet Dr. Muhammad Iqbal, and by his professors. He falls in love with the Muslim Yasmin, the sister-in-law of his closest friend Noor Muhammad and for once a woman of his own age. He learns of Yasmin's betrothal to Gul Muhammad, a railway guard, and flees to Bombay, but not before he has been arrested and jailed in Lahore as a suspected terrorist. In Bombay he cultivates the friendship of the journalist B. G. Horniman, Executive Editor Mr. Brelvi of the *Bombay Chronicle,* and Mr. Marmaduke Pickthal—an Englishman who has embraced the Muslim faith. On his father's advice he returns to Amritsar to complete his studies. The relative peace of college life is disturbed by an address given to the students by Dr. Annie Beasant, followed by the suspension of three professors for holding nationalistic views. The students organize a *dharna*—a sit-down strike. Krishan Chander is arrested, beaten, and jailed by the police. On his release he is suspected by a section of the student body of having betrayed their interest to the college authorities, and in turn is beaten by them. While he is recovering in hospital, Yasmin visits him and they decide on an excursion to an *ashram* on the River Beas. A few weeks later he learns that Yasmin is carrying his baby. His plans to elope with her are foiled by her death (she is presumably murdered by her suspicious husband). Krishan, mad with grief, contemplates suicide, or becoming a sadhu, or writing a long elegy on the death of his beloved. But he learns of his success in the B.A. examination and elects instead to go for higher studies abroad.

The book's theme is Anand's many loves: his love of political and social freedoms, his love of Gandhi, his love of poetry, and most of all his love for Yasmin. Of these, only his love for Yasmin captivates the reader, and that best when Anand settles down to a clinical analysis of Krishan's psyche and motives. It is well known that Anand, in his youth, was absorbed in the political struggle, and that he had great respect for Gandhi; but unfortunately the political passages make some of the most boring pages

in the book. The reason for this is that Anand has nothing new to offer: the political and social arguments are a rehash of what he has already said in his novels and in **Morning Face**. The only change we do notice is that nearly all the characters—Indian and English—are in favor of Indian freedom.

Many of the characters in **Confession of a Lover** lack complexity, and the hero's long discourses with them (especially with Professor Henry—a theosophist and a transcendentalist) on the Vedas, the Gita, God, *karma,* consciousness, the universe, man-woman relationship, body-soul, Gandhi, self, the nature of reality, and so on, make tedious reading. The characters speak alike, and in their long speeches there is something unreal, something stilted and pretentious. When Krishan Chander first meets Dr. Iqbal, the poet advises him: "Knowledge . . . experience of that knowledge and reverence for all who give knowledge, even if you don't agree with them. These things are important. Read, read, everything that comes your way. Read the Sufis, Rumi, Attar, Kabir, Nanak, read Nietchze [*sic*], *Thus Spake Zarathustra.* You can grow. Everyone can. There is no special tribe of Brahmins. Every man can become Superman. Man is God. Only life, life and more life!" Reverend Thomas Williams (a chance acquaintance who paid Krishan's fare to Bombay), Mr. B. G. Horniman, and Mr. Marmaduke Pickthal speak in the same lofty manner, and what any one of them says can be assigned to another with no injury to their respective personalities. The fact is that they are not individuals but the author's mouthpieces. Reverend Thomas Williams blames his compatriots in words that remind us of John de la Havre's diatribes in **Two Leaves and a Bud:** "I tell you, the White Sahibs have done nothing. Only imposed the machine civilisation on people with the sword. Money is the white man's god. Exploitation is his religion! They have sapped the energy of the people everywhere! Climate does the rest!" When Krishan tells Mr. Horniman and Mr. Pickthal how he was caned for breaking a curfew in Amritsar, Horniman exclaims: "Shabash!—I apologise, boy, for British bad behaviour . . . Not all Englishmen are like Dyer. Mrs. Besant, Andrews, myself and many others are on the side of Gandhi." And this is what Pickthal says: "Anyone who opposes General and Sir Michael O'Dyer is my friend. I want to go to Amritsar and apologise to the people there for the bad behavior of my countrymen. I want to assure them that all of us are not murderers!" In Anand's previous novels the English characters, with one or two exceptions, showed little sympathy for Indian aspirations. We are now presented with a work in which every English character (there are some five or six of them in the book) stands for Indian freedom. We cannot help suspecting that Anand is building up a case against Britain by showing that every thinking Englishman was against British rule in India.

The principal Indian characters in the book are portrayed with sophistication. There is the saintly and uncomplaining Noor, whose love of religion has not blinded him to his love of man, and who has in his heart a place for the rigorous teachings of the Koran as well as the erratic behavior of his agnostic friend, Krishan. He helps bring Krishan and Yasmin together at considerable risk to himself, and later when Krishan is leaving for England he conveys his sense of loss with remarkable restraint: "I am happy for you, brother—but . . . I shall be left alone." [In an endnote, Cowasjee adds: "Noor was Anand's closest friend during his college days and became the subject of his long short story **'Lament on the Death of a Master of Arts,'** published by Naya Sansar (Lucknow) in book form in 1938. The story deals with a series of memories that pass through the mind of Noor as he lies dying of consumption. The character Azad is Anand himself, and it is worth noting how closely Krishan of **Confession of a Lover** resembles Azad of **'Lament on the Death of a Master of Arts.'** The story, which I find uninteresting, is among the author's favorite (see *Author to Critic: The Letters of Mulk Raj Anand to Saros Cowasjee,* Calcutta: Writers Workshop. 1973)."]

There is Yasmin, delineated in fine detail and easily the most memorable female character in all of Anand's fiction. Married against her will to a man much older than herself, she gives every atom of her love to Krishan with an abandon which belongs only to those who have one goal, one passion, one dream. A more sensitive poet than Krishan, she answers his histrionic outpourings in verse with a couplet of her own:

> I hear the cry of pain from your heart,
> As though it is the shriek of my first child.

We have Krishan's mother, simple and affectionate as of old, who meets the new challenge of her son's growing arrogance with undying devotion. When Krishan is pining at the death of Yasmin, the mother, who has never known what it is to fall in love, ventures to soothe her boy's pain with a promise to get him a lovely bride! However misdirected, against such love there is no reproof.

Among the lesser characters we meet the illiterate Prabha (who figured in **Coolie**), wise in what Anand would call "the wisdom of the heart." When Krishan is justly angry with his mother, Prabha reminds him in his humble manner: "But mother is mother after all. . . . There is a mysterious connection between the mother and child." And we are equally impressed, though in quite a different way, by the colorful Professor of Persian Maulana Murtaza Hussain, whose one handicap is that he does not know English. When a student praises Professor K. M. Mitra for his notes in English of the Persian poet Sa'di's *Gulistán* and *Bústán,* the Maulana bursts out: "Aré, salé! —I also know Professor Kay Em Mitra . . . Thousands of Kay Em Mitras have issued from the drops of my urine!" Having routed his adversary, he intones in his mellifluous voice:

> I may tell you the Truth
> If you do not mind. O Brahmin cold!—
> The idols in your worship-place
> Have become old . . .

The students thump the tables in approbation, and we readily endorse their acclamation.

In **Confession of a Lover,** Anand occasionally succumbs to the perils of self-glorification when speaking of Krishan's love of freedom and poetry. Some of Krishan's blusterings—such as "Rebellion and freedom! . . . It is only through rebellion against everything false that I have written poetry"—might be forgiven as the impetuousness of a vain and egoistic young man, but it is difficult to condone the praises heaped upon him by the literary and political personages in the book. Professor Henry tells Krishan that he is "potentially a young god"; the poet Iqbal prophesies "both disaster and glory" for him; and Mr. Horniman, after hearing Krishan read one of his compositions, bursts out in ecstacy: "Superb! Boy! Superb opening! . . . The repetitions!—You are a poet alright! . . . We shall correct the English here and there: Your fault is exuberance! But it was also Shakespeare's fault! We shall print it. It is terrible and beautiful!" What is even more distressing than the eulogy is the discovery that the lines that Anand gets Horniman to applaud are essentially a repetition of the opening lines of the book, the phrase "walking along" being now substituted for the original "cycling along" of the opening. In a circuitous way, Anand is getting an English character in this autobiographical novel to praise his prose style. And he asks for no modest praise, either!

Despite self-praise and self-deception, the book reflects Anand's genius in exploring the human mind, showing the fears, horror, and selfishness that accompany man's most persistent goals. The story on one level may be looked upon as a dramatization of Julia's lament in Byron's *Don Juan:*

> Man's love is of man's life a thing apart,
> Tis woman's whole existence . . .
>
> > (Canto cxciv)

In the loves of Krishan and Yasmin for each other, there is a difference. For Yasmin there is no turning back, nowhere to go should Krishan fail her. For Krishan there is refuge in poetry, politics, and in the dreams which make up so much of his life.

The story of a modern Radha and Krishna is played out, not in the glades of Bindraban as in the legend, but in the city of Lahore and on the banks of the River Beas. Innocence gives way to experience as the two make love. Love itself becomes a frightened thing as the lovers fear detection by the elders of their respective communities. What would the world say of a married Muslim woman with a child giving herself up to a *kafir?* And that is not the end of Yasmin's dilemma. Would Krishan accept her daughter along with her? "You would love her," she pleads with Krishan as waves of jealousy possess him. And to comfort him, she adds: "The little one is more mine than his [her husband's]." The woman in love is also a mother, and she loves Krishan with the dual force of a mother and a beloved. "You are a baby," she tells him. "My baby—like my other little one." Not long after, she is carrying his baby.

Yasmin's predicament cries out for help. Krishan, who had earlier felt that poetry cannot be a substitute for life and that it was Yasmin he wanted, now feels that his love for her was only in his imagination, and that he had used it "for the purpose of poetry, like all the Urdu bards." When he is congratulated by Noor's wife on "becoming a potential father," his courage fails him. Elopement, which he himself had once suggested, appears a crude and prosaic proposition to him, yet he is prepared to go through with it because "the poetry of action" is demanded of him now. In the face of the realities, the poet sheds some of his poetry and honestly explores the nature of his feelings: "I had the corroding doubt that I really wanted the pleasure of physical love. Perhaps, awful thought, I still loved myself and my pleasures more than I loved Yasmin. I was a megalomaniac. I wanted the experience of making love, but did not want the burden of her." As he waits in Kashmir for her to arrive, a telegram announces her death. Here, at last, is the moment of poetry, and what poet would deride it? Freed of the responsibility of having to take care of her, he can now turn back and rail at a malevolent God and recall his immense loss. Krishan's self-dramatization—a blending of genuine grief with playacting—is the finest thing in the book. With Yasmin's death a whole fictive world of possibilities open[s] up before him:

> Perhaps, the only way out would be to do away with myself before my parents arrived. And then if there was any truth in the idea of an after life, I would be united with Yasmin.

> The drama of this thought elated me for a few moments. Soon, however, it occured [*sic*] to me, that I did not believe in life after death at all. And if I was going to commit suicide, it would be because my desires had not been fulfilled. Also, I would be doing so, because of my fear of the scandal that would soon ensue and out of the terror of my father's contempt, and my mother's everready tears. . . .

> I shook myself out of my torpor. I felt humiliated in my own eyes that I had forgotten the joys of belonging to Yasmin so quickly. Was my love really fading? Why was I not suffering, but dramatising everything? How could love change? It would be better to steal out to her; go to Lahore, dig out the dead body and embrace her. Then I could dash my brains out on the stone of her grave and lie there by her. Someone, like the poet Iqbal, who understood the love of Majnun for Laila, might suggest that I be buried next to Yasmin. And that would be a more glorious end to this miserable life than suicide in my hovel.

No poet kills himself until he has wrenched out the last bit of resolution and catharsis from life. Krishan decides to live. He thinks of becoming a sadhu and seeing strange visions; he envisages writing an elegy like Tennyson's *In Memoriam*. That he does neither is the correct finale to the book. The poet moves on to conquer other worlds, leaving death and dismay behind him.

Anand is presently working on the fourth volume of the autobiographical novel, which he has tentatively entitled *The Bubble* and which deal[s] with his first five years in England. It could easily prove to be a memorable work (considering the new and rich material he will have on hand), if he bears in mind what he has told us all along in his best novels—that heroism often lies in the realization of the unheroic in oneself.

Kate Kellaway   (review date 1 January 1982)

SOURCE: A review of *Conversations in Bloomsbury,* in *New Statesman,* Vol. 103, No. 2650, January 1, 1982, p. 21.

[*In the review below, Kellaway comments on Anand's recollections of the Bloomsbury Group.*]

When T.S. Eliot, Leonard and Virginia Woolf, Arthur Waley, E.M. Forster, Clive Bell and others met Mulk Raj Anand, they little realised they were being committed to memory. Memory seems to have been a quirky editor: these conversations, recalled from the Thirties, are spare and stilted. Sometimes only the small-talk seems to have survived; sometimes a conversation about Hindu philosophy or modern art is embarked upon with unnerving speed almost before the tea has reached the table.

Mulk Raj Anand, Indian novelist and philosopher, was ambitious to discuss and contemplate, and Bloomsbury must frequently have been a disappointment to him. It is easy to sympathise both with Mulk and with T.S. Eliot when they met. Mulk Raj Anand wants to talk about *The Waste Land*. Eliot wants to talk about the weather. When at last Mulk Raj Anand succeeds in making Eliot talk, the dialogue is surprising.

> 'What shall we do tomorrow?' Eliot quoted from his own poem when the caramel custard came.

> 'The hot water at ten', I added brightly.

In another conversation, Clive Bell disgraces himself by talking rudely and impatiently about 'significant form' in art. Virginia Woolf is alluring but aloof during a shadowy conversation at the Hogarth Press. Lytton Strachey is friendly and provocative: 'We are here to have unusual sensations.' Arthur Waley is shy and learned.

Each conversation is punctuated by food and drink—glasses of sherry, Dundee cake, China tea. These details are carefully recorded. Mulk had a great enthusiasm for crumpets which, sadly, like many of his other enthusiasms, he felt at the time should be suppressed.

Conversations in Bloomsbury contains many remarks almost made and then withheld. Mulk Raj Anand strictly edited his own conversation. He felt that his exuberance was naive and a sign of foreignness. He was an outsider longing to be included. The result is an odd reversal: it is the Bloomsbury people who seem foreign and unfamiliar. E.M. Forster is quoted as saying: 'One thing about India, it makes you feel natural.'

The opposite was true for Mulk Raj Anand in England. In the tube people looked at him as if he was a criminal because he wore a garish tie. The typical Englishman he nicknamed 'the melancholy gentleman' in contrast to the meaning of his own name, 'King of the Country of Happiness.

Govind N. Sharma   (essay date Summer 1982)

SOURCE: "Anand's Englishmen: The British Presence in the Novels of Mulk Raj Anand," in *World Literature*

Written in English, Vol. 21, No. 2, Summer, 1982, pp. 336-41.

[*Sharma is an Indian-born Canadian critic. In the following essay, he examines Anand's portrayal of British characters in his novels.*]

The British presence in the novels of Anand is persistent, pronounced, and pervasive. It is there from the first novel, **Untouchable** (1935), to the most recent one, **Confessions of a Lover** (1977). The British are in the novels not simply as background, a part of the social tapestry, but rather as figures in the forefront, sometimes occupying the centre of the social stage and dominating the action, as in **Two Leaves and a Bud,** at other times impinging directly on the moral consciousness of the leading characters.

The circumstances of Anand's birth and upbringing made it inevitable that the British presence should be a compelling element in his consciousness. The years of his growth and maturity were those of India's struggle for freedom from British rule. Anand's home province the Punjab, was one of the active centres of this struggle; the Jallianwalla Bagh massacre in 1919, in which the British officer Colonel Dyer shot down 378 unarmed Indian men, women and children, seriously injuring one thousand others, took place in his hometown, Amritsar. In the disturbances that followed the massacre Anand himself had the distinction of being arrested and beaten by the police, receiving severe stripes on his back in addition to much abuse.

For a writer whose own life history constitutes the main source material of his work, it was natural that Anand should write about the British. But the British presence is there for other reasons too. Anand, besides being a social critic, is also a writer with a satiric vision, taking special delight in pointing out the discrepancy between appearance and reality. He has a particular fondness for mischief, and nothing gives him greater delight than to unmask the pretensions of the righteous and respectable, to show that Pandit Kali Nath, the venerable custodian of orthodox Hinduism, is little better than a lecherous old man, that the arrogant and blustering sahibs on the tea plantations are cowards, scared by the phantoms of their own brains. So insistent is this urge that he does not spare even his own father. Babu Ram Chand, the character based on Anand's father in **Morning Face,** is a respectable man of the world, "the Shadow Colonel of the Regiment," but he has no compunction in exploiting his widowed sister-in-law Devaki.

It seems unavoidable, then, that Anand should derive a peculiar satisfaction in exploding the myths which had been so sedulously fostered by the British in order to justify their subjugation of India. The most powerful of these was that the British had brought order in place of anarchy, justice in place of injustice. British liberals even believed that they had taught Indians the meaning of human dignity.

Anand demonstrates, in **Two Leaves,** that the order established by the British was based on terror and the ruthless suppression of the weak by the strong. In this work, the British, who never tire of preaching the sacredness of the law of contract, have no hesitation in reducing the plantation workers to the position of serfs. It is possible that these planters are an extreme case, not typical of the British rulers in India. Although such men may not be perceived by members of their own race as altogether virtuous, there can be no doubt that the entire official machinery stood solidly behind them. Their politics appear to have the full approval of the government, as is indicated by the Viceroy's acceptance of an invitation for a shoot. The dispatch of army units and airforce planes by the authorities, in response to a false alarm by the planters, shows how the higher officers of the government itself share the planters' state of mind.

This is the state of funk, of the nervous fear from which all tyrants suffer. The planters, in spite of their luxurious style of living and the conviction of their own superiority to all Indians, are frightened men who wear steel plates under their waistcoats and carry revolvers in their pockets. Indeed, the plantation is in many ways a microcosm of the whole country under imperial rule. Anand's tragedy is the tragedy of empire: how the free British set forth to enslave others and how, once this enslavement is begun, they become more and more the victims of their own fear and delusions, prisoners of the past who see in every request for redress of grievances an incipient mutiny such as had occurred in 1857. The main objective of the empire, according to Anand, was economic exploitation; it was for economic gain that it became essential for the British to maintain the myth of the white man's superiority, what the planters refer to as their "prestige." Reggie Hunt's bearer, Afzal, is allowed to play polo because of the shortage of players, and because he is a good horseman. However, he cannot be allowed to score a goal; that would make him, in his prowess, the equal of white men and thus explode the myth of their superiority.

One assumes, then, as far as Anand is concerned, that the myth of British superiority is directly related to the myth that sees the British presence so essentially concerned with the imposition of order. In their anxiety to sustain a condition of both superiority and order, the whites become comical and ridiculous, all their heroics being little better than histrionics. Anand portrays them as not so much wicked as stupid, not so much knaves as fools. Some—Reggie Hunt, for example—are even worse. He has been criticized as a melodramatic villain, a maniac obsessed with sex. The problem that he represents, however, did exist. It was a matter of common knowledge that the British planters in India, like their counterparts in the American South, indulged in sexual exploitation of female labourers. Like Anand, Raja Rao in his description of the Skeffington coffee estate in *Kanthapura* draws attention to this abuse. Anand's point is that a system which permits its members both to exploit and degrade others without fear of consequent punishment must be rotten to the core. It ruined the lives not only of poor Indians like Gangu, but also of noble and sensitive Englishmen like de la Havre and Barbara Macara. Anand's recognition that persons like these did exist among the Englishmen in India suggests his objectivity and freedom from racial bias. *Two Leaves* itself is dedicated to an English friend, Montagu Slater.

But the British presence in the fiction of Anand is not just a part of the social reality, representing colonial domination and exploitation, racial arrogance and bigotry, and generating social and political tensions. He also draws attention to the fact that it has become an important element in the moral consciousness of the middle-class Indian, perhaps every Indian, symbolizing to him a new style of life, one more intelligent, alert, better organized, and therefore superior. Awareness of this lifestyle has created a deep cleft in the Indian psyche, a sharp fissure, as a result of its being pulled in different directions. The Indian shares with other colonials an awed admiration for the ruling race's way of life, and a swelling contempt for his own. However, as a member of an ancient race, he has grown up in a deeply rooted culture, and forces at work in the world around him are reminders of its essential sanity and wisdom, once rid of the corruptions which had crept into it.

Bakha, in **Untouchable,** is the first Anand character to show an awareness of this inner conflict born out of the pull of two differing ways of life. He is portrayed as a votary of "fashun" who would rather shiver in his thin and worn-out blanket than wrap himself in a heavy Indian-style quilt. He starts with the simple notion that putting on clothes like those of the white sahibs would make him, too, a sahib. The clothes, however, have a symbolic significance: the Western shirt and shorts, hat, boots, and blanket, being neatly cut, snug and smart, indicate order and discipline; the Indian *dhoti,* turban, and quilt, being loose and sloppy, denote the sloveliness and flabbiness of the Indian way of life. Bakha finds even the Indian manner of performing ablutions—all the hawking, gargling, and spitting—disgusting, for he knows that the "Tommies" dislike it.

The case for Indian culture and civilization in the novel is put by the poet Iqbal Nath Sarshar. However, this whole episode hangs like an appendage to the main story. It does not form an integral part of its structure, neither does it have much impact on Bakha's consciousness beyond creating a slight tremor in his mind.

The theme of conflict between two cultures is taken up in real earnest and with greater sophistication in the two autobiographical novels, **Seven Summers** and **Morning Face.** They are in the tradition of the *bildungsroman,* depicting the hero's growth and his quest for identity. Krishan's consciousness is torn between the two polarities of the West and the East, represented at the simplest level by the father and mother. The father, not English himself, is a worshipper of the English. He is head clerk of the Thirty-eighth Dogra Regiment, a faithful servant of the Angrezi Sarkar, the British raj in India, and hates the nationalists as troublemakers. As the son of this head clerk, Krishan is brought up in the cantonments at Nowshera and Mian Mir. Here, he sees the sahibs living in their beautiful bungalows with lush green lawns, neatly trimmed hedges, and fierce dogs to guard them from any intrusion by the natives. Krishan is struck with awc whcn he sees these heavenly beings, and has infinite respect for his father because he associates with them.

The climax of this first youthful phase is reached when he gets an idea of the power and glory of the Angrezi Sarkar through the pomp and pageantry of the Delhi Durbar of 1911. Shortly after this, he visits his mother's village, Daska, and is introduced to his grandfather, Nihal Singh. Meeting with this handsome, dignified and proud old man, a veteran of the Sikh wars against the British, suggests to him the viability of another way of life, based on a different set of values. He realizes on his return from the village that the armed camp of the cantonment is really a prison, full of meanness and sordidness, in which "the hardened sepoys were all struggling to guard their skins against a court-martial, and were hourly seeking to ingratiate themselves with inflexible, inscrutable, superior white Sahibs" [**Seven Summers**].

There are other introductions, too, leading to fresh discoveries: to his uncle Sardar Singh, whose superb musical rendering of "the anguished refrains of the poet Waris Shah" instil in his little soul, "finally and forever," love for his own Punjabi speech; to the Dutt brothers in Amritsar, who tell him of the heroes of the freedom movement, trying to inspire him with pride in the Hindu tradition.

However, Krishan's longing to become a sahib is too insistent. The high point of this infatuation is reached when the shocking spectacle of the bania boy, Mohkam Chand, being kicked by Marsden Sahib, Inspector of Schools, fails to arouse resentment in him. Instead, the Englishman's exhortation that he and his classmates should be like English schoolboys works as an "echoaugury." Krishan tries to suppress the weakness of indulging in the realms of poetry and vague speculation, and tries to cultivate the ideal of speaking English like an Englishman, of playing cricket and of wearing clothes like an Etonian, "which I imagined was the perfect type of little Englishmen, destined to rule Indians and kick 'natu' fellows like Mohkam Chand, because they would not conform to the rules and regulations laid down" [**Morning Face**].

Krishan does later overcome this infatuation with things English, and he experiences the romance of awakening to the apperception of being an Indian. Perhaps the flogging he received in the wake of the Jallianwalla Bagh massacre hastened his liberation, acting like a baptism of fire following a new birth. But the struggle itself is significant. Krishan has been described by Anand as a modern Krishna, an incarnation of the Yadu hero, the great warrior who fought against tyranny and injustice, the transcendant poet-prophet who unravelled to man new realms of poetry and imagination, showing him the way to intellectual, moral, and spiritual fulfilment. Krishan's quest for identity is thus not unique, but typical. The only way for an Indian of the Iron Age (Kaliyug) to find himself is not through blind imitation of the Englishman's lifestyle, "imitation Sahibhood," discarding the entire Indian tradition as moribund and defunct. The struggle for him does not have to be between tradition and modernity, as critics like M.K. Naik [in his *Mulk Raj Anand,* 1973] would have us believe. No, the real choice must be between a living tradition and a dead tradition, between what is life affirming and life denying. Anand's vision sees the English as catalytic agents who, by encouraging Indians to fashion themselves in the British image, in fact oblige them to go out in search of their lost souls. Indeed, the British presence in the fiction of Anand is itself a basic principle of structure, an indispensable instrument for embodying his philosophical and moral concerns.

S. C. Harrex   (essay date 1982)

SOURCE: "Western Ideology and Eastern Forms of Fiction: The Case of Mulk Raj Anand," in *Asian and Western Writers in Dialogue: New Cultural Identities,* edited by Guy Amirthanayagam, The Macmillan Press, 1982, pp. 142-58.

[*In the following essay, Harrex focuses on theme and structure in Anand's fiction, noting a close relationship between form and moral-social ideology.*]

Any discussion of the formal and technical aspects of Mulk Raj Anand's fiction necessitates consideration of Anand's intentions, attitudes and themes. Anand explores aspects of the human condition, mainly Indian, from the point of view of certain assumptions; his stories, characters and themes evolve out of the interactions of these assumptions with mirror images of 'real life'; his dramatisations of these interactions constitute a quest for a coherent world view. I would further postulate a close correlation between this quest for ideological structure and his quest for the fictional form most compatible with his instincts and prejudices as a writer.

Whether the ideological pursuit initiates, or takes precedence over, the formal pursuit (or vice versa) is difficult to determine, though I suspect that in most of his novels Anand has taken the view that form should be subservient to content. Investigation of Anand's philosophical ideas, both in his fiction and non-fictional prose, including letters, prompts me to offer the theory (and the present essay is based on it) that for Anand the Marxist-socialist pursuit of the proper (i.e. humanist) social structure and his own fictional pursuit of the appropriate verbal structure, if not virtually one and the same, are complementary aspects of a single purpose.

Anand is a serious and moral writer because he sees the salvation of mankind as dependent on the humane, compassionate, loving, lasting fulfilment of this single purpose. His viewpoint, or ethical base, is cosmopolitan—Indian, anti-Brahmin, *this* rather than *other* world-oriented. Perhaps the ultimate form of fiction which he has attempted to write might be described as the socio-political messianic novel.

The close correlation between formal narrative problems and moral-social questions to which I have alluded is clearly illustrated in the structure of Anand's first novel, *Untouchable.* Here, the initial problem of the writer, in the context of literary technique, and that of the reformer, in the social context, are identical: how to perceive experience from the untouchable's point of view, how to enter such an alien individual and caste consciousness? At this level, then, the writer and social worker are as one; both are 'committed', though for many writers this type of commitment may be a largely subconscious process. In Anand's case the commitment is quite conscious, and I see nothing counter-art in it, providing story is not turned into

diatribe, nor propaganda promoted under a veneer of literary method. A conscientious desire not to succumb to these pitfalls of commitment, it is fair to say, has been a motivating element in Anand's quest for structures.

This quest, however, has been influenced not simply by Anand's belief that the twentieth-century novelist should be a responsibly committed writer, but by a complex of factors, included among which are the following: Anand's philosophy of Marxist Humanism; his conception of the authorial self as a dual personality combining the social observer's detachment with the revolutionary zeal of the romantic prophet figure; his technique of self-projection (notably through the invention of characters who act as spokesmen for his own ideas) whereby the objective social-realist form can accommodate much of his own 'felt experience', the subjective life of dream, the autobiographical moment; his effort to define form and technique in terms of idiosyncratic concepts like 'Indian expressionism', 'the desire image', 'neorealism', 'poetic realism', 'new myth versus old myth', and 'the body-soul drama'; and, lastly, his attempt to fuse the Western realist tradition of the novel with the Indian tradition of the moral fable.

An analysis of Anand's formal and technical achievement, accordingly, may logically begin with the Anand terminology and philosophical background, out of which Anand's fictions have evolved and taken shape. A reading of *Apology for Heroism,* which Anand describes as an 'Autobiography of Ideas', indicates that Anand's stories are, but not exclusively, dramatisations of these mainly Marxist-humanist ideas. In *Apology,* Anand makes clear his own sense of identification with the 1930s criteria of commitment, particularly social responsibility, humanistic idealism and a requirement that the novel change man and thereby society—though he was also conscious that too inflexible a commitment to the 'age of concern' could dehumanise literature:

> . . . in the Thirties social problems tended to supersede the problem of the individual in literature. The old 'Fates', 'God', 'Evil in man' and 'Nature', almost gave place to the new 'Fates', 'Economics' and 'Politics' as they affected the 'Common Man', though . . . the intellectual concept tended to dominate imaginative literature and made for abstractions in poetry and fiction. (*Apology for Heroism*)

Here Anand hints at one of the problems he himself faced in seeking a fictional form which would enable him to convey his ideas about the situation of the common person (Bakha, Munoo, Ganga, Lal Singh, Ananta, Gauri) without turning that person into an intellectual abstraction.

Relevant to this problem, as recorded in *Apology for Heroism,* was Anand's experience of a crisis of belief and identity which was to become one of the dominant motives or themes of Indo-Anglian literature, a conflict between the traditional self and the modern ego, between the Indian Absolutist interpretation of the cosmos and the relativist interpretation of scientific Marxism, between ideals of submission and social justice:

> This negative tradition tended to pull all my newly-acquired ideas askew . . . apparently, a

man who docilely accepted his position within the framework of traditional Hindu caste society, however low and humiliating that position, was a good citizen, whereas those who consciously questioned tradition and suffered unwillingly were moral lepers. Everyone was born to his position and had to accept his lot through the cycle of birth to rebirth. Except, of course, that you had the right to ask the eternal questions and to see yourself as part of Reality, even though you could not alter your position in the every-day world of appearances. So that you remained a frantically agitated, impetuous, fictional being trying to realize that you were capable of being filled with God and thus seeking to become one with the omnipotent, omniscient, all-pervading free spirit, the Absolute above, but really consigned to the iniquities of hell on earth, without a hope of bettering yourself. So this was man!

This view, resulting from the attempt to resolve the tension of personal identities through 'a rediscovery of Indian ideals' (*Apology*), had its correlative in Anand the writer as he sought a fusion of Indian and Western forms of creative expression to match the philosophy he wanted to advocate. He named his form 'poetic realism', and we can legitimately name his philosophy Socialist Humanism.

The line of argument can be better understood if we dovetail into it further statements from *Apology for Heroism*. Thus:

> The problem then, that I tried to face as a writer was not strictly a private, but a private-public problem . . . the introduction into creative narrative of whole new peoples who have seldom entered the realms of literature in India. And experience becomes an attempt at poetry even though the result is a somewhat ragged rhythm . . . there is a great deal to be said for this approach, which I may call the flight of winged facts, to poetic realism.

Anand saw his 'poetic realism' as a 'synthesis' of 'bifurcated' Western schools of literature, namely subjective formalism and 'social realism', neither of which singly could engage and portray the 'whole man'. Thus:

> Though I believe in realism, I am, as I have said, for a poetic realism. I would like, for instance, to stress the importance of the desire image, or the romantic will, in writing, and I stand altogether for art against literary photography. And just as I found myself on a synthesis of the values so far bifurcated in Europe, just as I desired . . . a view of the whole man, in order that a new kind of revolutionary human may arise, so I have been inclined to stress the need for a truly humanist art commensurate with the needs of our time. (*Apology*)

Anand proceeds to argue that the artist, by emphasising the 'revolutionary aspect of art' (*Apology*), improves or intensifies life through ' "creative myth", so as to change life in the deeper centres of other people's experience' (*Apology*):

> Only, there is a living myth and a dead myth,

and the desire image, which is the basis of revolutionary romanticism, must be really creative and must help men to integrate in society and not provide a formula for escape. (*Apology*)

Here we see in summary, by way of extrapolation, Anand constructing a dialectic involving subjective form and objective realism, the old myth of Vedanta and the new myth of Marxian 'individuation', which is to culminate in a poetry of revolutionary humanism. This connection between form and ideology bears the impress of much Marxist literary theory that was current in the 1930s, and particularly as expounded by Christopher Caudwell in *Illusion and Reality* (1937):

> The full understanding of the mutual interpenetration of reflexive movement of men and nature, mediated by the necessary and developing relations known as society, is the *recognition* of necessity, not only in Nature but in ourselves and therefore also in society. Viewed objectively this active subject-object relation is science, viewed subjectively it is art. . . .
>
> *Proletarian* art in realising itself will become *communist* art. This process is simply a parallel in the sphere of ideology to what will take place in the sphere of material economy.

For Anand, too, the literary expression and the ideological theory are complementary aspects of a single purpose. Anand would seem to require that he be judged as a writer according to how successfully he fulfils the Marxist requirements of the artist. His romanticism (or desire image) is equivalent to the species of Utopianism whereby Marxists idealise the deterministic end-product of the socio-economic dialectic: the image of a just society in which the state will wither away. Or, as Anand puts it, the new myth of love (brotherhood) and the ethic of a new humanism ('revolutionary romanticism') will fulfil both the corporate and individual dream as a result of a 'struggle for the deepest socialism and the deepest human personality' (*Apology*). Some years after making this statement Anand continues to assert:

> I would like to prove that a new contemporary myth (of growth to awareness) of the whole potential man is possible, as against the myths of *Ramayana* and *Mahabharata* . . . it is possible to have a contemporary myth. (*Author to Critic: The Letters of Mulk Raj Anand*, ed. with an Introduction and Notes by Saros Cowasjee, 1973)

What I have tried to demonstrate, to this point, is that Anand's theory of fiction was influenced by his exposure to Western ideas. The subject of his fiction, however, is not intellectual cross-currents in Europe, but India as experienced by the Indian. Because he saw the core problem of India to be the crushing weight of the allegedly 'dead myth' of 'neo-Hinduism' and Vedantic Absolutism, he reacted at first by expressing himself in a fictional form derived from Western literary theory rather than traditional Indian sources. As such, understandably, Anand gained a reputation as a social realist; but it was a reputation he was to become increasingly unhappy with. First, because he felt the Indian quality of both his work and sensibility was undervalued or neglected; second, because he sought a balance between Western and Indian structures of expression, especially as the identity crisis could not be resolved through the adoption of an extreme position, either Anglophile or Eastern, and moreover his increasing recognition of the deficiencies of Western societies coincided with a revived sense of positive values within the Indian tradition; third, because in aiming at balance through a fusion of Indian fable and European realist novel, Anand, I believe, was coming to terms with a tendency to contradiction within himself (ambivalent responses to East and West, tradition and modernity) despite the fact that the primary pattern of his worldview remained anti-traditional and Marxist-humanist.

This last development includes various announcements that his commitment involved a crucial element of romanticism in his vision, and was strengthened by the presence of an indigenous Indian response to life, which he refers to as 'the body-soul drama'. Thus:

> Critics around me conceive literary realism as the description of the world as it is. I was born a Hindu and, therefore, I have never taken appearances for reality . . . I wished to write about human beings who were not known or recognised as human at all, or admitted into society— such as the outcastes . . . by going below the surface to the various hells made by man for man with an occasional glimpse of heaven as the 'desire image'. I have never been objective, as the realists claim to be. And my aim is not negative, merely to shock but to stimulate consciousness at all levels.

> There was no tradition in the Indian novel for this. And being of the thirties, I was mistaken for a proletarian writer, a social realist. This is nonsense . . . I do not believe in the scientific novel or documentary. I never abandoned human beings in order to pursue a theory . . . I admit that this has led to a certain formlessness, but look for the fantasies in the labyrinthine depths of degradation and you will find them there. Perhaps much better than in Kipling. . . I wanted to create in *Coolie* a boy in all his humaneness, as against the fantastic Kim. (*Author to Critic*)

> I rely on my subconscious life a good deal . . . and allow my fantasy to play havoc with facts. I believe all of us Indians are expressionists, that is to say, we enact a body-soul drama in everything we write . . . (*Author to Critic*)

> I do not like naturalism. I have consciously, and unconsciously, written as an Indian *expressionist;* this expressionism is traditional with us, imaginative dramatisation . . . at the risk of exaggeration . . . The problems of machine exploitation, Victimhood, unfulfilled potentiality, are tackled in defence of *innocence* against the evils of the profit system of the west, in the spirit of William Morris and Ruskin and Gandhi. Romanticism is here as in Rimbaud more prophecy than acceptance—the desire image is important. (Letter to S. C. Harrex, 23 Oct. 1965)

These and similar statements reveal Anand fiercely defending his authorial self-image, but I am not sure that he has done himself justice in some of his reactions to what

he regards as inaccurate criticism. Perhaps as a result of over-reacting in spur-of-the-moment statements to charges that his novels are largely didactic documents, and given that he is both an energetic thinker and talker as well as a prolific writer, he has understandably enough been unable to maintain an entirely consistent position. Thus, for instance, in one letter to Saros Cowasjee, he comments 'I believe the old myth lingers in the form of romanticism' (*Author to Critic*), thereby contradicting his usually approving use of the term 'romanticism', as when he maintains that the 'success' of 'humanism' 'lies in the implied romanticism.' On the whole, such discrepancies are unimportant, superficial.

Anand's theory of fiction was influenced by his exposure to Western ideas. The subject of his fiction, however, is not intellectual cross-currents in Europe, but India as experienced by the Indian.

—*S. C. Harrex*

When, however, we examine Anand's doctrine 'body-soul drama', on the basis of which (as we have seen) he defines himself as an Indian expressionist, not a social realist, we discover that Anand's expressionism is not exclusively Indian; that in fact it has evolved out of the Marxist argument, as becomes apparent if you compare the following statement by Anand with that previously quoted from Caudwell:

> The body is mind, the mind body. There is no god. And the dialectical connections in almost all human activity result both in the *knowledge* we have of the world and the *insights* we occasionally derive. The world of knowledge is the sphere of philosophy and science. The world of insight belongs to literature and the creative arts, especially to poetry. The compulsion of curiosity, the desire for communication, and the necessary expression, are derived from the same source in both books of knowledge and books of passion. But while factual truth eliminates metaphor more and more, the creative truth depends more and more on the imagination which likens one thing to another . . . there is a deeper meaning in my theory of knowledge and metaphysics, and there is a coherence in the psycho-physical or psycho-social use of the terms 'body' and 'soul'. The dialectic is just popularly called drama. (*Author to Critic*)

Here, then, is evidence that in his quest for form Anand has Indianised a Western materialist structure derived largely from Marx (perhaps via Caudwell), and has tried to find for this structure, applied to Indian conditions, an alternative to the social-realist mode of expression which, in the West, has been the dominant methodology of fiction. This may explain why, even as early as *Untouchable,* Anand sought to heighten or intensify his representation of Indian life by setting it within a literary structure which was a version of moral fable.

At this stage of the argument, I offer two points on Anand's behalf. First, that to trust entirely the teller who maintains 'I would not consider myself a social realist because I have never professed a doctrine of that kind' (Letter to S. C. Harrex, 24 June 1965), and not the tale (e.g. *Untouchable, Seven Summers, The Sword and the Sickle*), is to diminish one of Anand's considerable achievements in Indian fiction. Accusations like 'communist' and 'propagandist', which have caused Anand to think of Naturalist and Realist as pejorative terms, are reduced to irrelevance by the fact that Anand, using conventional techniques of realism, has opened up a vast subject area of Indian life which had been neglected in literature prior to Anand's 1930s fiction.

My second proposition in defence of Anand is that the charge of didacticism levelled against him often ignores a difference, or disparity of cultural assumptions, underlying Indian and English canons of criticism; a disparity indeed which has culminated in the ironic spectacle of the Eastward-looking Marxist critic seeking to reverse the anti-didactic tradition of his Western critical heritage, at the same time as the Indian critic is revolting against the native tradition of didactic aesthetics. If, then, it can be shown that Anand adapted the Indian tradition of fable (which assumes that art and didacticism are not incompatible), I fail to see that this experiment in itself is aesthetically or technically objectionable. Deficiencies of execution, examples of which are to be found in Anand's writing, are another matter.

As this first half of my argument is a theoretical prelude to a discussion of Anand's technique of structuring his vision within individual novels, I believe it appropriate to conclude this section of the essay with two statements from Anand which reveal his strengthening conviction that his story-teller role was fabulist and folk-oriented:

> . . . 'expressionism', by which I mean the typically Indian creative attitude of staging the body-soul drama as in the folk-literature . . . My 'realism' is only superficially like that of the West-European. Deep underneath, all the characters search for their human destiny in the manner of the heroes of our forest books. (*Author to Critic*)

> . . . while accepting the form of the folk tale, specially in its fabulous character, I took in the individual and group psychology of the European *conte* and tried to synthesise the two styles. And thus I sought to create a new kind of fable which extends the old Indian story form into a new age, without the overt moral lessons of the ancient Indian story, but embodying its verve and vitality and including the psychological understanding of the contemporary period. (Preface, *Selected Stories*, 1955)

. . . . .

In his first novel, *Untouchable* (1935), Anand created a formal model which went further towards realising the type of structure his philosophical disposition required

than he was perhaps capable of appreciating at the time. Obviously, the circumstances in which the novel came to be written are relevant to his attempt to produce a form appropriate to his ideas and feelings as projected into the largely fictionalised situation of the largely fictional protagonist, Bakha.

Anand had previously written a two-thousand page 'confession' which, by all accounts, was amorphous in form. This confession was the embryo of the 'seven ages of man' sequence of autobiographical novels beginning with *Seven Summers,* a sequence which, given the style of *Morning Face,* encapsulates personal history in a sort of free-verse prose stream that externalises the recollection process. *Untouchable,* too, grew out of segments of the original 'confession', and Anand was conscious that, if he was to communicate the novel's social issues effectively, he needed a tighter structure than was permitted by a linguistic 'expressionism' which operated like a whirlpool or expanding gyre. I admit that Anand has taken the view that the writer may have to sacrifice formal effectiveness in the interests of 'soul drama':

> The novel is a form too amorphous to be controlled precisely. The relative merits of a book, from an author's point of view, may lie in his feeling of how much he was able to express of the soul drama, and at how many levels. Perhaps, in this point of view I would consider *Untouchable* to be a more intense work than the others. (*Author to Critic*)

Despite this assumption, in writing *Untouchable* Anand engaged in 'the intolerable wrestle' with amorphousness, presumably in the belief that, whereas the fluid form was appropriate in novels of purely subjective experience, when an objective interpretation of reality was to be attempted a formal balance of private and impersonal elements was necessary. The result was that in *Untouchable,* and later in *The Big Heart,* Anand reverted to a classical model: a prose-fiction structure shaped by the use of the 'three unities' technique. In thus facing the literary technical problem, Anand was simultaneously confronting the caste problem, the central subject in *Untouchable*. That is to say, he had an intuitive sense that the novel medium was amorphous in the same sense, correlatively speaking, that pre-Marxist society was chaotic. By 'imaging' reality in terms of the dramatic-unities technique, and by providing 'desire images' of change as well as a climax suggesting a potential structure to be adopted by society, Anand tackled the formal and ideological problems simultaneously and as one.

A further correlation in *Untouchable* between the formal discipline and the social theme, in the context of relating fact to fiction in accordance with the theory of commitment, derives from Anand's reliance on autobiographical experience, and his effort to incorporate it in the narrative data from the social environment. In **'The Story of my Experiment with a White Lie'** (*Indian Literature,* Vol. X, No. 3, 1967), Anand informs us that Bakha is modelled on a boy he knew, and that the novel's compassionate viewpoint arose in part out of an incident when the untouchable carried me home when I had been hit by a stone . . . without caring about what my mother would say about his having polluted me by his touch . . . I developed a guilt about him which compelled appeasement.

The episode is dramatically utilised in **Untouchable** and reappears in **Seven Summers**. Anand also reveals in the same article that, in order to acquire the right perspective on untouchability, he went to Gandhi's *ashram* to learn first-hand the Mahatma's *'harijan'* philosophy of reform. The Mahatma apparently advised him to put himself in the Untouchable's place. Thus Anand cleaned latrines, while learning from Gandhi how to relate the self-discipline of Hindu idealism to social purpose. Perhaps this experience helped Anand resolve some of his formal difficulties as a budding novelist.

Whatever the cause, however, Anand succeeded in formulating a structure which satisfied his own idea of what he wanted to reveal and how. This structure, as I said earlier, involved the problem of defining the personality, consciousness, being, of the protagonist from the joint point of view of character presentation and social theme. At the beginning of the day of the novel, Bakha is natural man; the caste system has not as yet inculcated vice into his character. He is portrayed at work in the latrines, and the scene illustrates two concepts: the Gandhian principle that all work is ennobling, and a 'drama' of contrast between the 'body-soul' splendour of the youth and the unpalatable nature of his work. This work, though, is not to be despised because of its menial, sensory, natural characteristics, but because of the pernicious doctrine of caste with its vicious-circle identification of the work role—cleaning up dung—and the state of the outcaste's soul. Filth is to filth.

Out of this situation, Anand evolves a narrative pattern which combines the moral-fable form and the principle of 'interplay, indeed interpenetration, of situation and character', which Anand saw as the 'significant feature of the Western short story' (**Indian Short Stories,** edited by Mulk Raj Anand and Iqbal Singh, 1946). Present in Bakha's character is the pathetic incongruity of natural vitality sapped by conditioned docility. Then in the epiphany-like main 'touching' scene we see the interplay of character and incident producing the germ of a new consciousness in Bakha, beginning with a realisation of his social identity. The birth of this consciousness conforms to Gandhi's psychological approach to the problem of untouchability, whereby the outcast is encouraged to develop self-esteem in place of self-abasement. From this point on, the narrative development—involving as it does Bakha's increasing enlightenment regarding work, social discrimination, poverty and the doctrine of pollution—fulfils the requirement of the moral fable: the evil of the social system has been exposed, and the novel concludes with a 'desire image' suggesting how the evil should be eradicated.

Bakha experiences the 'shock' of self-recognition: 'It illuminated the inner chambers of his mind. . . . A shock . . . had passed through his perceptions, previously numb and torpid' (**Untouchable**). After this experience Bakha is developed into something of a fable figure, and

is endowed with an elementary visionary quality. He has the ability to contrast the familiar with the unknown and this is described in terms of 'the impulse which tries to create a new harmony':

> . . . he had grown out of his native shoes into the ammunition boots he had secured as a gift. And with this and other strange and exotic items of dress, he had built up a new world, which was commendable, if for nothing else, because it represented a change from the old ossified order . . . He was a pioneer in his own way . . .

Having thus far opposed the two elements ('ossified order', 'impulse . . . to create a new harmony') in the dialectical narrative structure, Anand employs two devices to bring Bakha to the brink of a personal and social Hegelian synthesis. The first device is the 'desire image'. As Anand has pointed out, the ending of **Untouchable** is conceived as a 'prophecy' 'suggesting a choice of possibilities' (Christ, Gandhi, Marx, the machine) because of his belief that the writer who does not have a romantic as well as realistic point of view will not see the whole of life and will be in danger of affirming only 'the negation of life':

> The novel of revolutionary romanticism . . . seeks the desire image, that is to say to suggest what the writer would like life to be like, by implication, as against what it is . . . (**'The Story of my Experiment with a White Lie'**)

The second device Anand uses to promote his social vision is the spokesman figure, the young poet, who is introduced in the final scene and explains the 'choice of possibilities' to a section of the crowd that includes the receptive Bakha. The poet reveres Gandhi as 'the greatest liberating force of our age', but suggests that India 'has suffered for not accepting the machine'. If **Untouchable** can develop a consciousness of self-respect and India adopts the flush-system, then untouchability may be eradicated. Structurally, this conclusion is reached through a coalescence of *desire image* and *spokesman* devices.

The device of the spokesman, discussed above, was for Anand a means of satisfying two distinct inner urges; thus he projected into the novel an image of the desired reality and an imagined connection between himself as the reformist spokesman-author and the underprivileged on whose behalf he was writing fiction. The device is reincarnated in the final scenes of **Coolie** (1936) in the person of Mohan, a revolutionary intellectual, who says 'come with me and we shall kill the landlord one day, and get your land', and who at the end clutches the dying Munoo's hand thereby signifying that, despite the tragedy of the past, its victim dies briefly united to a potentially regenerate future. In Anand's third novel, **Two Leaves and A Bud** (1937), the Mohan figure has become a major character (De la Havre), indicating that in this work Anand regarded the fable element as equally important as the portrayal of the peasantry and the exposé of corrupt imperialism.

The 'desire image' and self-projection techniques are most completely synthesised in **The Big Heart** (1945), in which the spokesman figure is again a poet, and undoubtedly Anand's ideal of himself. The hero of the novel, Ananta, is a spontaneous roguish Adam whose generous character is evident in his favourite saying: 'There is no talk of money, brother; one must have a big heart'. The poet sees in Ananta the foundation of the new modern man. However, it is the poet who articulates the humanism which the hero enacts:

> I believe in the restoration of man's in-
> tegrity . . . the reassertion of man's dignity, rev-
> erence for his name, and a pure love for man in
> all his strength and weakness, a limitless com-
> passion for man, an unbounded love especially
> for the poor and downtrodden . . .

Thus Ananta embodies those qualities of the heart and the poet those of the head which in combination will create the new Adam of Anand's future society. The poet's discourses at the end of *The Big Heart* are not merely a choric comment on the tragic action: they are intended to leave the reader with the image of a desirable social form for which Ananta is a noble sacrificial prelude.

A new variation of the body-soul or character-author drama occurs in *Private Life of an Indian Prince* (1953), in which Anand projects himself into the Shankar role while modelling Victor on a Prince from real life and infusing into the portrait of Victor traumatic psychological experiences which Anand himself had undergone prior to writing the novel. *Private Life,* considered as a narrative structure, is Anand's most ambitious experiment with 'point of view'. Regarding this aspect of form, Anand has offered the following account of his intention and practice:

> . . . the neutral character Dr. Shankar was in-
> vented to become Shiva's third eye and to burn
> out the dross, confusion and the chaos of emo-
> tions in order to achieve a certain balance. . . .
> If there is any alliance between myself and a
> character, it is with the narrator. But, always in
> my novels, the characters take charge. The nov-
> elist should try to become the great god, Brah-
> ma, who creates mankind, but is not responsible
> for it, that is to say, does not determine their des-
> tiny. Distance is very important in art, because
> art though like life, and reflecting it, is not life.
> (*Author to Critic*)

Shankar has clearly defined roles as character and narrator, and through him Anand attempts to achieve 'distance' by adopting from psychiatry the technique of clinical detachment. Thus when the doctor refers to Victor as 'an important case history for my files' he is speaking both as character and narrator. Shankar's prismatic analysis of Victor's condition is a point of view which combines Freudian and sociological techniques of analysis, further illustrating my contention that Anand in his fiction is constantly seeking a form in which literary and social models are subsumed into a single structure. Clinically, Shankar dwells on the unconscious, biological, sexual, Oedipal origins of Victor's neurosis. Sociologically, he diagnoses Victor as the product of historical circumstances in which princely tradition and modern morality were a destructive combination. Anand brings off some dark, dramatic effects by contriving Shankar as a kind of Poe narrator, who is custodian of a haunted psychotic's soul and witness to its Empedoclean disintegration. There is also in this 'se-cret sharer' situation an echo of the Conradian technique of narrative.

Shankar's fragmentary discourses, which at the end of the novel fill the narrative vacuum created by Victor's retreat into madness, are mainly reiterations of some of the main assertions in *Apology for Heroism*. Shankar advocates Anand's doctrine of humanistic vitalism and revolution—believed to be a product of historical necessity—as a therapeutic solution both to Victor's and society's afflictions. Shankar's criticism of non-attachment and mysticism, his dismissal of the crude distinction between a spiritual East and a materialistic West, his plea for 'the recognition of our responsibilities', his belief in man, in man as a homogeneity, not a 'bifurcation' of body and soul, in man as 'the final fact of the universe', are all attitudes which parallel exactly, at times even in phrasing, statements in *Apology for Heroism*.

An analysis of Anand's quest for structure, then, may fittingly conclude that Anand's fictional forms are allegorical representations (sometimes simple moral fables, sometimes mythic conceptions) of his social theories and philosophical ideas. Anand's trilogy—*The Village* (1939), *Across the Black Waters* (1940), *The Sword and the Sickle* (1942)—is his most comprehensive attempt to define through allegory, myth, fable and 'poetic realism' the meaning for India of the modern historical process. The hero of the trilogy, Lal Singh, evolves out of the world of traditional myth, of religious ritual and metaphysical powers, into the relativist universe of Anand's modern myths: the people, humanism, revolution, reason, human love.

In *The Sword and the Sickle* this new mythos replaces the ancient mythos which had provided a dance of death, Kali-Kalyug symbolic framework for *Across the Black Waters*. Quite early in *The Sword and the Sickle* Anand describes the 'new Fate' which replaced the 'old Fate' yet was equally 'cruel':

> It was a Fate which seemed to him to have been
> working before the war . . . which had something
> to do with the school he went to, with the maca-
> damised roads which had connected the village
> to the town for movement and transport, with
> miles of railways . . . with telephones without
> wires, and the war . . . it seemed to have been
> hidden behind the illusions to which he had as-
> pired, behind the mirage of picturesque Vilayati
> farms and Sahibhood. But now from the corrod-
> ed hearts of the people at home and his own baf-
> flement, he had vague glimmerings of this new,
> inexorable Deity in the Pantheon of Indian
> Gods. It was disguised in the din and bustle of
> the cities . . . and in his own despair . . . he
> would know it and seek to master it.

The new Fate then is historical process according to Marx, and the new Kali is a hybrid Indo-British, bourgeois-capitalist, imperialist-landlord ogre. Anand's mythos has archetypal manifestations and values. Its classic incarnation, referred to reverentially, is the Russian Revolution; Marx, Lenin, Gandhi and Nehru are its epic avatars; it reveals with mythic certitude and folk simplicity the division between rich and poor; and it chants the poetry of humanism, proclaiming that 'love and understanding', not 'murder', is the 'way' to the 'imagined utopia'.

Lal Singh faces the classic modern choice of standing apart or being part of a cause, and as a protagonist in the abyss between past and present he is modern India personified, if not mythologised. He confronts the new world as Outsider, faces the choice of becoming an iconoclastic anti-hero or fulfilling the *dharma* of Self by losing self in the Absolute of the Marxist *nirvana*. Resolution is in favour of the latter, of what in fact is a modern transfiguration of the traditional Vedantic motive.

And finally, in this ultimate image of Lal Singh about to serve his stint in gaol, assured that the iron bars of illusion do not a prison of Reality make, absorbed into a consciousness greater than self, Anand defines how, in his quest for structures, he has Indianised literary and political models derived from the West, and Westernised traditional Indian values.

Shyam M. Asnani   (review date Spring 1983)

SOURCE: A review of *Conversations in Bloomsbury,* in *World Literature Today,* Vol. 57, No. 2, Spring, 1983, p. 348.

[*Below, Asnani comments favorably on* Conversations in Bloomsbury.]

Mulk Raj Anand is a multidimensional phenomenon on the contemporary Indian literary scene. Besides being a major Indian novelist, he is well known as a founder of *Marg,* a professor of art and literature, a maker of short films and the author of the pioneering book *The Hindu View of Art* (1933) as well as works on a wide variety of subjects such as art, painting, education, theatre, criticism, poetry, Indian cuisine, female beauty and Indian culture and civilization. Though Anand turned seventy-seven last December, with his characteristic energy he is actively engaged in the task of reconstructing a new India as cultural adviser to the Prime Minister and as the moving spirit behind several national and international cultural associations, university seminars and conferences. These days he is active in helping the rural populace build roads, open new schools and raise standards of hygiene. While his richly variegated personality is difficult to appraise, a brief cataloguing of some of his significant achievements can only give a hint of his profuse output. Those who know Anand personally often wonder wherein lies the source of his bewildering stamina—creative as well as social.

Part of his indefatigable exuberance and almost inexhaustive imagination has been captured in *Conversations in Bloomsbury*. Soon after a brief jail term during the Gandhi movement in the early twenties, Anand went to London to study philosophy and came in contact with several great writers and artists there. In addition to preparing the draft of his first confessional novel, Anand corrected proofs for the Hogarth Press in the basement of the Woolfs' house, wrote short reviews for T. S. Eliot's *Criterion* and conversed frequently and informally in pubs, bookshops and coffeehouses with such members of the legend-ary Bloomsbury group as E. M. Forster, Leonard and Virginia Woolf, Aldous Huxley, H. Read and B. Dobree.

Anand's aim here is not merely to reveal the obsessions and prejudices of literary personalities whom he met, but instead, through his recollection of these conversations, to explore his own personality. We see Anand emerging as an "electric, miscellaneous and unconventional romantic in his concentration of the human predicament." The talks conjure up before us some of those lovable, liberal English intellectuals with their freethinking attitudes which counterbalanced Kipling's contempt for the "lesser breeds." The book is rich in anecdotal detail and interspersed with humorous, sparkling repartee and scintillating dialogues. Much of the talk centers on the arts, religions, politics, literatures, cultures, philosophies and ethnologies of India, and the book assumes great significance in that the author here acts as a genuine cultural emissary of his country. Not only does he correct the ingrained prejudices of the British intellectuals against India, but he also helps them understand and appreciate its rich cultural heritage.

The image Anand deliberately foists on his reader is that of an intelligent and inquisitive young Indian gifted with "rich and varied sensibility," imbibing new ideas, asking pointed questions, itching always for confrontations with the British intellectuals, discovering his own roots. He appears by turns nebulous and labored, shy and garrulous, embarrassingly gauche and formidably egocentric, taut and taciturn. Constructed from notes, diary entries and memory (as he recently assured me), Anand's *Conversations* offers highly useful biographical insight into the early years of his life as well as into his personality and literary creed.

Mulk Raj Anand   (essay date 1983)

SOURCE: "The Sources of Protest in My Novels," in *The Literary Criterion,* Vol. XVIII, No. 4, 1983, pp. 1-12.

[*In the following essay, Anand discusses the artistic principles that informed his novels and the relationship between his life and writings.*]

Various studies of my novels by scholars have, in recent years, confirmed what I tried to show in the autobiography of my ideas, *Apology for Heroism,* as also in the autobiographical novels, that there has always been an emergent connection between my life and my writings, throughout my creative career.

Of course, some critics have interpreted my obsession with truthful presentation of the realities of life as ideological. Quite a few members of our academic intellegentsia are addicted to terms like classicism, romanticism, realism, and naturalism, which make for abstract analysis of novels. They often ignore the pressure of human life, the compulsion of which on the writer's conscience, may be through miscellaneous inspirations in the novel specially in evolving characters, and tracing their motivations from the reservoir of faiths and individual diversities. The anarchy of feelings is indistinct in nature. Emotions are woven into the texture of a fictional narrative, from uncontrolled impulses. Each novel might, therefore, compel internalist interpretation.

Not from external standards, of principles of criticism, built on the traditions of the novel, which arose in the West from the 18th Century downwards should our own fictions be judged. Our interpreters have to sense the collective unconscious of our own people, from the inherited oral cultures, in decay or renewal. In this way, the critics may be able to judge our fictional works, more creatively as they would then go to the sources of our insights into the concrete human situations rather than through abstract theories which don't yield novels.

There have been pioneering critiques of this kind from the study of sources of creations of novelists and poets, in the West, like those by Edmund Wilson in *The Wound and the Bow,* by D. H. Lawrence in his *Studies in Classic American Fiction,* by John Middleton Murry in his *Son of Woman,* by George Lukacs in his essays on Thomas Mann, and by Edward Thompson in *Rabindranath Tagore.* These examples have been lost on our commentators. Our critics unconsciously belong to the category, described by Jean Paul Sartre, as always in unhappy relationships with their wives who have to wait for them to come to dinner, because they can't tear themselves away from reading classics and evolving categories to define each mood, feeling and idea. Most of the critics, who have written about my novels, have not noticed that my fictions arose from the compulsion of life, which have been reenacted by me, again and again. They treat my fictional works according to the dates of publications, in chronological order in the dominant English manner, where *text is all.* And if the text reveals men and women in dirty clothes, soiled hands and perspiring faces, they are unsavoury. Said Edward Garnett: 'We English don't like characters in rags to come into our drawing rooms'. And the Brown Sahibs feel the same way about novels which deal, as E. M. Forster once said, 'with the seedy side of life'.

I made my first conscious protest as a writer, when I came away from Bloomsbury after hearing the critic, Edward Sackville West, declare: 'There can be no tragic writing about the poor! They are only fit for comedy, as in Dickens: The canine can't go into literature'.

I was just then writing **Untouchable**. I left London and went to Gandhi's Sabarmati Ashram in 1927. There I learnt some sincerity, truthfulness and simplicity. And as the Mahatma sent me to the people, before I should write any more novels, from that time onwards my protests about the human predicament under the Empire, and in the atmosphere of our own decay, became self-conscious. I persistently examined my own conscience. I had intimate experience of villages, small town people, big town grandies, experience of life's little ironies, tragedies and struggles.

All experience then became the reservoir from which I wrote my fictions, hoping to transform the raw material of life freely into communicable forms, rather than accept the mould of the rigid objective form of Flaubert. Personal as my novels are, based on my experiences, they are written by an 'I' at some distance from myself and the charac-

ters. The resulting fictions may have sometimes seemed amorphous. Much as the novelist may try to control people's lives, the imperceptible feelings of characters, and their emotions tend to overflow, as in Balzac, Tolstoy and Proust.

My novels were intended to be different from others, departure from the upper and middle section fictions of Tagore. I wished to recreate the folk, whom I knew intimately, from the lower depths, the lumpens and the suppressed, oppressed, repressed, those who had seldom appeared in our literatures, except in Sarat Chatterji, Prem Chand and Bibhuti, Tarashankar and Maneck Bannerji.

I had realised after my stay in Sabaramati Ashram, that I could not stand alone, always looking at the heaven's where the Gods live, because they were now hidden behind the twilight. I was, however, face to face with humans, specially the hollow cheeked men with dazed eyes, the women who grew old from drudgery and forced childbearing before they were young, naked children with distended bellies and big eyes, beggars whining for alms, my widowed aunts, my drunkard uncles, stalwart sepoys, Pathan frontiermen frightened of the Ferungies and carrying guns, in fact men and women in a world reduced to slavery. Daridvanarayan, or the God incarnate, were the flesh and blood for me to worship. And in the struggle for emergence of which they were part, each contact brought the sense of a certain sacredness. A new kind of religion was then, emergent in my novels, a religion of love for people. Worship of each character, became a passion behind the writing. I accepted all the strengths and weaknesses of the people. Maybe empathy for human beings, makes for a tennous relationship, enabling the novelist to remain within himself, and yet be with others, a pervasive relationship of Leviathanic complexities.

As the relationship between the author and others revealed the horrors of the inequalities through which those above have perpetrated cruelties on those below, generation after generation, either through caste discrimination, or the power of the Rajas over the Ryots, or priests with the rigid ritualistic prejudices, I allied myself with the urges of men to free themselves through whispers of discontent, or sighs in half-sleep, or in violent and nonviolent actions. In this way, I sensed the pain of life, which the more privileged took out of the weaker members of the flock. I knew the patriarchs who enslaved women by imposing conventions which curtailed their freedom, behind the prison of purdah or semi-purdah. I was aware of the ignorance of the underprivileged, who expiated their own miseries, by celebrating ritual murders. I was aware of the miseries of the rich who were always in fear of losing their worldly wealth. I was aware of the Imperial state with its Gods and goddesses, George Panjim and Mallika Mary. I gave up the systems of philosophy. Unable to sleep easily, I woke up every morning to see how men and women dreaded other men and women, how they bowed before the White Sahibs, the Bania moneylenders, and the officers. There were millions of the disinherited who ate only one meal a day. If I could not physically 'wipe every tear from every eye' as Gandhiji said we must do, I felt I could utter a thousand cries to wake up people, free them from the weight of slumber. As every prayer of the folk was to an idol of a past dead myth, I felt I could create myself, and others, who had become bundles of infantile disorders, suffering in the various seasons of hell, under the reign of Yama, by looking into other people's eyes, to see 'the light in smiles'. Only insights and outsights into the anarchic world, might bring inner maturation to human beings. The terror of one's self, may be got over, by asking everyday, as in *Brihdaranyaka Upanishad*: 'who am I?', 'where do I come from?', 'And where am I going?'. I would have to recognise my identity, as an Indian, not subservient to the white rulers. And I would have to be a man without the help of an anthropomorphic God. I knew it would be difficult to be free men from all the fears. But I had hunches about freeing myself and others *into* our passions for breaking out of uncertainties.

My novels were intended to be different from others. I wished to recreate the folk, whom I knew intimately, from the lower depths, the lumpens and the suppressed, oppressed, repressed, those who had seldom appeared in our literatures.

—*Mulk Raj Anand*

As I felt many inchoate urges in the days of my growth, I came to awareness of things beyond the fixtures of *dastur,* custom through daily experience of human misery and the pain of life.

I saw the mandala of Gods of my mother, on which stood images of Guru Nanak, Krishna, Aga Khan, Yessuh Messaih and a snake engraved on metal. I asked questions about them. They were not answered, until my father, a fashionable Arya Samajist told me that our ancestors had made thunder and lightening into Indra, the sky into Varuna, and the Sun into Surya. Gone was this exalted cosmic view in our time. But in spite of explanations about the origin of Gods, the God with a big beard, sitting in top of the sky, which most people believed in, lingered in my fear-haunted imagination. So when a young cousin of mine died at the age of nine of T.B. I wrote a letter of protest to the God in heaven asking Him how He could take away the little innocent who had committed no fault.

I noticed that, among my playmates, were boys and girls, who were considered superior, if they were the children of parents in big houses, and inferiors if they were the children of parents in small shabby hutments. And our parents asked us to have a bath after playing with children from the hutments, because we may have touched untouchables. I early realised that, as we were of the Kshatriya caste, we were superior, with Brahmins above us, and Vaishya shop-keepers slightly inferior to us, and all outcastes far far below us. The cruelty of this God-made order came home to me, when Bakha, a sweeper boy, brought me home bruised in the head by an accidental

stone. My mother abused him for carrying me and touching me. And she bathed me even though I was bleeding. This little incident was to remain in my conscious-unconscious, and became a passion for justice against the old old fixtures of non-human discrimination against untouchables. And this passion became the protest implicit in my first published novel *Untouchable* which has been called the proto-type of the protest novel in the new world, now emergent from the dead systems, supposedly ordained by the supreme God. The opposition of the superior and inferior became an obsession with me long before I read Marx.

I became early aware of the anomalies of our family. My father belonged to a coppersmith brotherhood of Amritsar, who had worked for generations on the Golden Temple, and made utensils. He went to a Christian School. And, on passing Matric, he joined the British-Indian army as a clerk. He observed the customs of the Coppersmith brotherhood, even when he presided over the local Arya Samaj. On the other hand, as a 'servent of the Sahibs', he had become a 'Shadow Colonel', and adopted George V as God Almighty, *Andaata,* giver of bread. Although read in advanced literature of the West, he agreed to arrange marriages, dowries for his two elder sons, which cut short their studies, and forced them to become part of the order of Babus, used by the alien Sarkar for the routine work of the empire.

The ceremonies of weddings were performed by Brahmins according to Vedic rites, burning good ghee to banish evil spirits. Prayers were pronounced in a language, which not even the priests understood. Infinite repetition of high sounding words was necessary. The aim of the recitations was not to evoke thoughts, but to perpetuate the supremacy of worship, *pujapath.*

I once fainted as a boy, when I saw a goat being butchered in the temple of Kali, where my mother used to take me in our hometown. I never got over the revulsion from this murder. And it is from my tenderness for living things that my indignation against the mumbo jumbo of ritual arose. I began to feel that living words of creative writing are inspired, not by rhetorical repetition, but from maturing of insights, through experience of pain, and may take warmth from sympathy.

The incident which upset my own childlike admiration of the Pink Sahibs was insignificant enough. I salammed the Adjutant Sahab of my father's regiment and started at him out of curiosity. He hit me with a cane and I went crying to my father, who did not say anything, but accepted the punishment I got for the crime of looking up to the Sahib.

Later in April 1919, when Police Raj was declared by the alien Sarkar in Amritsar, to stop the protests against the Rowlatt Act, forbidding gatherings of four people, I went out of home to see what the curfew was about—I was caught by the police and kept chained to many others all night. Next morning I was given seven stripes of the cane by an Indian policeman, under orders of the Anglo-Indian Superintendent of Police. I shrieked at the punishment. My mother came and rescued me, tearing her hair in anger against the red-faced Afsar. I could never forget her helpless rage against the police. And when my father refused to notice the bruises on my body, I was confirmed in my dim feelings of rebellion against him and the Sarkar. I realised that the army and the police and the law were the Indian instruments of the Ferungi, instruments of the King Emperor, himself an instrument of a big machine which devoured human beings in the empire.

I began to listen to the terrorists, who wanted to abolish those who made war on people, by throwing bombs on the oppressors.

Later, being too weak for such heroism, I listened to the message of non-violence of Gandhi. The Mahatma was talking of a bloodless sacrifice, of accepting lathi blows against the bloodshed by the ruling power. I felt the vast oppression from behind an invisible wall, which prevented Gods in Whitehall from listening to the Mahatma's still small voice. In between there were the preachers of Christian ethics. But the rulers were stuffed up dummies of automatic power, hollow inside while the abstract Sarkar was an organised oppression, with bayonets and machine guns, which were to ensure the carrying of the white man's burden of responsibility of Kipling's Indian native, 'half-savage half-child'. And most of the natives accepted the hollowmen, as masters, so long as they got the paltry silver coins at the end of every month.

The primitivist expression, including the use of ugly words, epithets and staccato phrases, in my novels of the lost Utopia of childhood, shows that people had retained some sense of honour, as they felt that the rape of mother and sister was an insult.

So the alienation of my principal characters with their hopeless ventures in freedom, was presented in tragedies, which are not realistic, but expressionist dramas of struggle between the poetic ambition of heroes to emerge from the depths of degradation, to recover their human inheritance. Only my new heroes-antiheroes were not deliberately uplifted into a classical world, and presented in allegory. They were kept within the framework of personal experience in a time-bound world. They may become symbols of struggle and may later appear as new mythical figures, representing youth as urging towards freedom. Against the idea that their fate has been determined before their birth, but they are angels struggling in the dawn.

My novels, then, to me are whirlpools where I have been able to meet individuals in the chaos, in relative distinction from each other, in the midst of indistinction. I have returned, in each fiction to recognise some people in the undifferentiated mass. And in the recognition, from alliance, has been a kind of expiation of my burning conscience about the sufferings of men and women. The writing of each novel has been an effort to be with others, while remaining myself, in the area of freedom, which is love. If the life of each individual is in kinship with other lives and yet a unique mystery, into which we can only have glimpses, every human being is a god or a goddess. And every insult, every humiliation, every deprivation, every lowering of dignity, must be protested. Because only by the love we give to others can we be human, only in the defence of the divine status of human beings, have we the

opportunity to end the alienation of men and women from each other, brought by fear, petty differences, and the confusions of dark-mindedness, which swarm around to ghosts and demons of the night.

The yoke of pity has been carried by some of the most sensitive men in every generation in our land. It has relieved every age. As pity is in essence, love, I have tried to rescue this love, which becomes love of life in every form, against hatred, which is the death of love. In this sense, love takes the place of God. And as the defiance of all those offences, injuries, deceits, lies and murders of the body-soul, becomes holy anger, my protests are expressions of my holy anger.

As love is the core of human relations, the very first need of men and women, from which comes procreation, family, the social group, and the state we have to see how, in the evolution of life, the old primitivist tokens, totems and taboos have survived and been accepted as eternal inspirations in the name of tradition. So much so that the cautionary words and images, which were to sanctify and preserve human relations as sacred, have been perverted, and life has often been sacrificed in the name of religion. That is why the poet Iqbal cried out from the depths of our degradation, in the early years of our century:

> 'To tell the truth Oh Brahmin old,
> The idols in thy temple have grown cold'.

In my novels, therefore, which seek to recreate living human relations, in all their intricacies, I have been compelled to be concrete (realistic if you like to put it that way), I have tried and looked at the realities of life, hoping that each day be a new day of happiness with a new Sun, a new moon, with new people who may inherit the good things of the past, but may look to the future. This may have meant wandering through the labyrinths, but one can recognise one's own face, and the faces of others, not by servitude to fixed images, but by living experience of men and women only, through a religion based on love.

My characters were not meant to be revised versions of old mythical symbols of the epics. I think that human beings change, in a changing universe, even if ever so little. So old mythical characters like Sita, or Savitri, or Rama, are not eternal types, who must be repeated in new incarnations. My characters are conceived as human beings of a different historical age which is not the changeless samsara of tradition. They struggle in this life, on earth, in the here and the now, even as their struggles end in failures. Or they grope in the dark, and then emerge here and there, through our new contemplations and reveal the contours of the still mysterious universe, defined in the past through fear, but now being revealed through adventures in the heavens and on earth.

My new myths also aspire to some certainties in the religion of man. Every happenstance can lead to fresh realisation of Space-time continuance. The writer and the artist are ever in search of new myths to escape fixations. Many old certainties dissolve. Some, which are relevant, are assimilated. But changes of style in art and literature, are due to the crisis of creation, when men and women renounce the old dead symbols to create new myths, in search of the freedom to grow and renew the jaded personality. Renewal is eternal. Otherwise men remain dead-in-life. Renaissance is the cue for all human passions in the freedom to grow over to higher consciousness.

Apart from the essentiality of metaphorphical protest about the human predicament in a time in which the Gods have failed, mine is the willed extroversion of hope against despair, perchance the monolithic state may break down, through its own mechanical failures.

I feel that war is the ultimate sacrifice of victims, offered up by men of power, in which both victors and vanquished, face death, which is the arbiter of human destiny.

The dehumanisation of man reaches its apotheosis in the armed subjection of people. The cruelty and barbarism of absolute power, sanctified by past Rajas of one kind or other, may not be acceptable to the awakening erstwhile slaves. The sacrifice of humanness may not go on forever.

I admit that few men have risen to become Gods in our transitional age. Humanity in the mass faces the institutionalised violence of the modern state, omnipotent even when it professes participation of peoples. And every new Spartacus fails, because the state refuses to wither away. The old authoritarianism of the Egyptians, the Romans, the Chinese and Indian feudalists, comes back. The fascist slogan commands like the ancient patriarchs 'to believe, to obey, and to fight'. The new Dictators put up enemy dummys and announce 'Laser war' against their enemies. Bloody sacrifice of one mass against another is asked for by the new incarnations of Caesars. Only war can confer on the barbarian conqueror, the title of God. Never mind the cost in the possible death of all.

The failure of the neo-idealists is that they are too refined to look at the gift horses in the mouth, and to protest, because they rediscover themselves in a frozen art. They do not wish to include human cause (which includes political, social and psychopathic alienations), in polite fiction.

To be sure, creative arts reflect life in a mirror. But the concave mirror is also a mirror. And one does not always talk with one's own face in the mirror. The mirror is other people. The love of Narcissus for himself makes him feel he is a God: Others are not admitted as his kin. He alone is himself, his higher self, which means he has become God Almighty. Therefore he is no more human.

The novels about human beings need the author, and others, men and women and children in the whirlpool, where there are contrary impulses, clashing trends, doubts, misgivings, making life a river which flows sometimes caught in whirlpools and then rushing in waves towards the ocean. Each human being, as an individual, brings his own repressed culture and inner wishes, to express himself, through signs, broken speech and attitudes. His or her personal myth is born of facts and fantasies. In a novel there are elements which are indeterminate, particular and concrete. The contrary impulses reflect confusions. If the novelist liberates his characters, and they take charge of their own destinies, fiction may release their inner sentiments and feelings and action, remove the taboos of religion, or the state, and reveal their predicaments, which by themselves lift the burden of pain off the consciousness and make for transcendence, which is ecstasy.

The reader often says, then, on reading a genuine novel: 'Oh I too feel like Dostoevsky's Idiot, or Tolstoy's Natasha, or Prem Chand's Hori'.

The emptiness of ritualistic rhetoric has already given place to the sense of humanity in the significant novels of our age, through the liberation of love of life against death. The humanist novel speaks, in living speech, often in passionate frenzies, from the uprush of spirit to express itself. The new novel thus exorcises the monsters and terrors of dissolution from the hell on earth, made by people for each other. Sartre was right when he spoke, figuratively that 'Hell is other people'.

The novel is for the world's continuance. It is urged to express itself in uneasy syntax, in dim perspectives, and from the dim urges of those, who seek to break the shackles of serfdom imposed by the past. It is inspired by the urges for many freedoms, baulked [*sic*] by the demons of power. It is against the insults, injuries, deceits, lies, hypocrisies, the mortifications and murders, brought by the oppressors of the world.

The protest novel is the source of renewal of the human person.

Saros Cowasjee (essay date 1989)

SOURCE: "Mulk Raj Anand: The Fusion of History and Fiction," in *Subjects Worthy Fame: Essays on Commonwealth Literature in Honour of H. H. Anniah Gowda,* edited by A. L. McLeod, Sterling Publishers Private Ltd., 1989, pp. 17-26.

[*In the following essay, Cowasjee argues that Anand's presentation of Indian life and politics in the early to mid-twentieth century is both accurate and insightful.*]

No Indian writer of fiction in English comes anywhere near Mulk Raj Anand in providing a social and political portrait of India from the time of the Delhi Durbar of 1911 to the demise of the Indian princes following Indian independence in 1947. Historical personages such as Gandhi, Nehru, and Vallabhbhai Patel walk the pages of his novels, and political events (such as the Kisan Sabha Movement in *The Sword and the Sickle*) are intricately woven into their designs.

Anand is an expositor, a political novelist, one who sees his characters and their actions in relation to the social, economic, and political upheavals of his time. In this study I shall limit myself to a discussion of the following three topics as they figure in his novels: first, a social problem—the evils of untouchability; second, a political personality—the person and legend of Gandhi; and third, an historical event—the demise of the Indian princes.

Untouchability, "an excrescence of Hinduism" as Gandhi called it, has occupied Anand from his early youth and was the subject of his first novel, *Untouchable* (1935), and a much later work, *The Road* (1961). It also figures prominently in his fictionalised autobiographies and many of his short stories. There is a moving chapter devoted to Bakha (the hero of *Untouchable*) in his latest autobiographical work, *Pipali Sahab: Story of a Childhood Under the Raj* (1985).

Anand's interest in the plight of the untouchables dates back to a childhood experience. To put it in his own words [from a letter to the critic dated 7 November 1985]:

> I had known the untouchables in the squalid followers' lanes of the cantonments, where my father's regiment was stationed. Being much despised for the dirty work they did for the caste Hindu sepoys, one of the sweeper boys, a handsome young man called Bakha, had saved my life when I was accidentally hit by a stone on the head during a boys' quarrel. My mother had abused him for polluting me by carrying me home.
>
> This episode had left an indelible mark on my naive child's mind. And Bakha had endeared himself to me by the fact that he was a shining hero to us boys, a good hockey player . . . who sang Punjabi songs in a melodious voice. One day he was insulted by an upper-caste Hindu as he was walking in the bazaar to go and clean latrines. He had accidentally touched a caste Hindu, who slapped him on the face. He told us boys this story that day and I had wept to see him sad and crying. And I wrote this story of the insult to Bakha.

The novel *Untouchable* has all the above facts. However, it is not the facts that make the novel memorable, but what Henry James calls "the power to guess the unseen from the seen." And here Anand was particularly aided by his visit to Gandhi's Sabarmati Ashram, arranged through the good offices of the Irish poet and mystic George Russell. The thrice-a-week discussion with Gandhiji and the symbolic cleaning of latrines enriched his perception. (Gandhi himself first cleaned a latrine in the Calcutta Congress of 1901 and records the event in his autobiography.) The love and warmth that emanated from Gandhi found its way into the hero's personality. But what most helped Anand was Gandhi's going through the manuscript and suggesting substantial excision. "Untouchables don't talk in such big words," said Gandhi [according to Anand], "nor in long sentences. In fact, they don't say much. They are so suppressed, they only mumble, and meekly join hands."

This advice Anand certainly took to heart. In his almost physical inability to revolt, his submission, his habitual subservience to superiors who insult him, Bakha is one with the vast majority of the outcastes. It is this fidelity to character that makes *Untouchable* a major novel without depriving it of its social importance. Still, one may ask whether Anand could not have filled in some more of the historical details pertaining to the emergence of this "fifth class", which had no sanction in *Varnashramu Dharma,* the divinely ordained division of society into four groups: Brahmin, Kshatriya, Vaishya, and Sudhra. The present-day untouchables were originally aborigines who came under the sway of the advancing Aryans and were given the task of carrying corpses and cremating them. Also, as

Swami Vivekananda declared, the old priestcraft was entirely responsible for this fiendish segregation—a point which could well have been brought into the novel. And the opportunity was all there: instead of the much-confused talk about *Vedas* and *Upanishads,* maya and nirvana with which the novel ends, a little confused talk on the origins of untouchability would have been more to the point.

Though there were other social reformers (such as Ram Mohan Roy, Dayananda Saraswati, Ramakrishna, and Swami Vivekananda), it was Gandhi who made the cause of the untouchable his own as no one had ever done. He made his first strong public statement on untouchability on his assumption of leadership of the Indian National Congress in 1920, and from then on he kept the cause in the public eye through his passionate oratory and vivid imagery. By the time he died he had spoken and written more on untouchability than on any other subject. It is completely appropriate that the highlight of the novel should be Gandhi's address on untouchability.

Adroitly, Anand fashions the person of Gandhi as many of us remember him: the little man swathed in a white shawl, with his bag, protruding ears, his long nose bridged by a pair of glasses, and a quixotic smile. But more than these details is the mass appeal of Gandhi that Anand has been able to convey: the surging crowd, the myriad voices, the rush of eager feet, the spontaneous cry, "Mahatma Gandhi ki jai" that drowns every other sound. There is, as the author says, "terror in this devotion, half-expressed, half-suppressed". It is worth noting that Anand had not witnessed a Gandhi meeting on the untouchables prior to writing this novel, and that the actual meeting at which Gandhi delivered this speech was, in real life, a disappointment to Gandhi. "Gandhi," so the press reports [in *The Collected Works of Mahatma Gandhi, Vol. 19, 1920-21,* 1961], "regretted in the beginning the small attendance and said that incidents such as the present took away what little faith he had in conferences as an effective agency of social reform." Anand in his novel ignores Gandhi's complaint: he is concerned with the long-range truth of history which may differ from the everyday occurrences of history.

Gandhi's speech is carefully drawn from a speech he gave at the Suppressed Classes Conference in Ahmedabad on 13 April 1921. Anand has shortened the speech, keeping only those exhortations of Gandhi to which Bakha could easily relate his day's experiences. The concluding lines of the speech ("Two of the strongest desires that keep me in flesh and bone are the emancipation of the untouchables and the protection of the cow. When these two desires are fulfilled, there is swaraj, and therein lies my own Moksha [salvation]") show the dual role of Gandhi as Mahatma and politician in Indian life. To bracket a social evil like untouchability with an accepted religious practice like the protection of the cow is to make untouchability a very serious issue.

Gandhi's speech is also important, as it sets the date of the action of the novel—the year 1921. The fate of the untouchables improved over the years, and in November 1948, nine months after the death of Gandhi, the Constit-

uent Assembly of India passed a provision legally abolishing untouchability. But matters of "conscience" and "customs" are difficult to legislate out of existence. As early as
June 1927 Gandhi had said in *Young India:* "The removal
of untouchability is not to be brought about by any legal
enactment. It will be brought about only when the Hindu
conscience is roused to action and of its own accord *re-
moves* the shame" [quoted from *The Essential Gandhi,* edited by Louis Fischer, 1962]. Gandhi was right, and
Anand wrote **The Road** in 1961 to prove to Jawaharlal
Nehru that untouchability was very much prevalent despite the legislation. So, indeed, it was; but you don't write
a novel to prove a point.

The Road, though based on an actual incident that Anand
had witnessed in the early fifties in Gurgaon district (caste
Hindus refusing to quarry stones touched by untouchables), is in essence a rehash of the observations already
made in **Untouchable.** Once again we have the caste Hindus tyrannizing their outcaste brethren; we meet the hypocritical and lecherous priest of old; even the incident of the
slap that Bakha earned for touching a caste Hindu is there,
though in a somewhat different form: but what was in **Untouchable** a highly dramatic situation is now reduced to
a mere contrivance. **The Road** remains a slight work, and
Anand's insistence that he breaks new ground in the
novel—his outcastes are now prepared to fight back
against injustices—does not add to its attraction. The flaw
in the novel lies deep: it is in the artistry (the writing is undistinguished and the characterisation weak), and what is
artistically a failure cannot be historically a success.

Anand claims that the single strongest influence on him
has been that of Mahatma Gandhi. Gandhi is referred to
with reverence in his fictional autobiographies; Gandhi's
name crops up in **Coolie** (1936), **The Big Heart** (1945),
and **Private Life of an Indian Prince** (1953); and he appears in person as a character in **Untouchable** and **The
Sword and the Sickle.** In the latter the portrayal of Gandhi is so severe that I was inclined to ask Anand how he
viewed Gandhi then. This is what he said [in a letter to the
critic dated 14 January 1986]:

> The important thing about the Mahatma was, in
> the first instance, after Jallianwalla Bagh, his
> general legend. . . . The mass contact campaign
> of Gandhi took us to the villages and small
> towns. Often Nehru took me with him. So, many
> of the characters in the novels are the human be-
> ings I lived with, ate with, and worked with in
> the freedom struggle. If the hero of **The Sword
> and the Sickle** is disrespectful to Gandhi, it is
> not because I was myself irrelevant, but I did
> share, to some extent, the protest of the left
> against the Mahatma's belief in his doctrine of
> trusteeship of the poor by the rich.

Few would question that the legend of Gandhi was as potent a force as the man himself. In **Untouchable** Anand
highlights the legend: he devotes twice as many pages to
the frenzy of the audience and to the Gandhi legend—"no
sword could cut his body, no bullet could pierce his skin,
nor fire could scorch him!"—as to the speech itself. In **The
Sword and the Sickle** Anand sets out to destroy the legend
of Gandhi, and this he does principally through his hero,

Lalu—a demobilised young man who is trying to organise
a peasant revolt against the landlords. Lalu meets Gandhi
and some of his irreverent remarks, such as "The man is
a physical deformity", may be pardoned as revealing the
spleen of a disappointed and hot-headed young man. But
we have to take seriously the comments coming from
Anand in his role as author omniscient. Anand describes
Gandhi as "a little lop-eared, toothless man with a shaven
head, which shone clean like a raw purple turnip" dictating an article on the "conservation of the cattlewealth of
India" and the "adulteration of ghee". The words dictated
by Gandhi are all taken from his writings in *Harijan,* but
whereas in **Untouchable** Anand had given coherence to
Gandhi's speech through careful selection, he now makes
it deliberately disjointed. Finally, Gandhi turns to Lalu
and speaks to him about soul-force, non-violence, untouchability, the spinning wheel, self-perfection, and the
sublimation of sexual urges—subjects dear to Gandhi but
out of context in the present circumstances.

The impression that Gandhi leaves—and there can be no
mistake that this is the impression the author wishes to
convey—is that his mind wanders, that he is an "inveter-
ate non-stop talker", showing "evident pleasure in hearing
his own voice", and that his humility is exaggerated and
false. Anand, however, concedes that Gandhi is sincere
and honest, and has a "genius of joining issue with authority". Through Count Rampal Singh (modelled on Kanwar
Brajesh Singh of Kalakankar, who later became famous
for his liaison with Stalin's daughter Svetlana Alliluyeva),
we are grudgingly told of Gandhi's Champaran campaign.
In Champaran (Bihar) Gandhi (at considerable risk to his
person) forced the British Government to inquire into the
grievances of the peasants against the English indigo
planters. It was here, as Gandhi's biographer D. G.
Tendulkar observes [in *Mahatma, Vol. 1, 1869-1920,*
1951], that "Gandhi realised the mission of his life and
forged a weapon 'by which India could be made free'."
But the novel offers no such deductions.

Anand's disillusionment with Gandhi at this period stems
from various factors. Anand was at this time, as Louis
MacNeice observes in his unfinished autobiography *The
Strings Are False* (1965), "a crusader for the Indian Left".
And the view of the Indian Left, as indeed of the Comin-
tern, was determined by the Communist M. N. Roy's
equating Gandhi with the feudal elements in India, calling
him "the acutest and most desperate manifestation of the
forces of reaction." But what most irked Anand, who had
witnessed the British coal miners' strike in 1926 and had
himself fought on the Republican side in the Spanish Civil
War, was Gandhi's "doctrine of trusteeship of the poor by
the rich". (This seemed to strike at the very root of organised labour's campaign to combat capitalistic exploitation.) To this may be added Gandhi's pacifism at a time
when the democratic world was engaged in a life-and-
death struggle against Hitler and the forces of fascism.

Anand's view of Gandhi changed dramatically when Gandhi launched the Quit India movement in 1942, and since
then the Mahatma has risen steadily in his estimation.
When I asked Anand in January 1986 what his present as-

sessment of Gandhi was, he insisted that I pick up pen and paper and write down:

> Seldom in the history of mankind has there been a man who allied himself with the lowest of the low and the highest of the high to bring them together and demand the moral right of all subject people to be free and enjoy human rights.

This may be so, but such a man has never entered his fiction, and in all likelihood never will. Anand's great gift lies in depicting man struggling in all his weakness, and the Gandhi he now visualises has proportions too heroic for him to accommodate.

After a stay of twenty-five years in England, Anand returned to India in 1946 to witness the country win independence and the 500-odd princely states merge into the Indian Union. In 1948 he wrote *Private Life of an Indian Prince* (published 1953), not so much to show the demise of the princely order as to provide a therapy for his own illness. (Anand had suffered a nervous breakdown over an affair with a hill-woman and had been advised to write the anguish out of his system.) Of course, his knowledge of the princes and their administration was there to give his fictional episodes the detail and immediacy of a painfully reconstructed past. He had been a tutor to the Rana of Bhuji, a tiny principality in the Simla Hills, for two summers (1923 and 1924), and he had known the Patiala court through Lala Man Mohan, ex-private secretary to the late Maharaja. He was also familiar with the All India States Peoples' Movement (known as the Praja Mandal) and the insurrectionary tactics used by the Indian Congress to destabilise the princely states in order to establish their own influence.

Anand's novel invites comparison with Manohar Malgonkar's *The Princes* (1963). Both novels, through their respective heroes, concern themselves with the fate of the princes who vanished with Indian independence; both are peppered with the prejudices and customs of the princely class; both expose the same ignorance, bigotry, false pride, and total inability to come to grips with facts. The narrator in Anand's novel is the personal physician to Maharaja Ashok Kumar (better known as Vicky); the narrator in Malgonkar's novel is the heir-apparent, Abharaj; and both these characters represent the voice of sanity, which speaks out against the reactionary and medieval attitude of the rulers themselves.

The differences between the two novels are equally marked. Anand's *Private Life of an Indian Prince,* as the title suggests, is the personal saga of one prince—though that does not prevent him from being a prime representative of his order. Malgonkar's title, *The Princes,* clearly indicates that he is writing of the princes as a collective body. Moreover, Malgonkar's purpose is to provide an accurate history of the princes, and he shows every evidence of having studied documents pertaining to the subject. Events such as the princes contemplating a third force as a counterweight to the Muslim League and the Indian Congress, Lord Mountbatten's address to the Chamber of Princes on 25 July 1947, and the merger of the Chhatisgarh and Orissa states into the neighbouring provinces all accord with history. In Anand's novel historical exacti-

tude is secondary. When I pointed out to him certain inconsistencies in *Private Life of an Indian Prince,* he hurled back at me defiantly: "I am not writing history, or even historical novels, but about the collective unconscious of various human beings in the novel form" [letter to the critic dated 17 April 1986].

In design, too, *The Prince* reveals Malgonkar's urge for a comprehensive historical portrayal. The novel opens with a prologue, Queen Victoria's celebrated pledge to the princes of 1 November 1858, that "We shall respect the right, dignity, and honour of the native princes as our own". (The blind trust of the princes in this pledge contributed much to their undoing.) It concludes with a press release on 1 November 1958 on the opening ceremony of a hydroelectric dam in what was once the state of Begwad. Within this framework the action is narrowed to twenty-five years: from the early 1920s to the merger of the states in 1949. In Anand's *Private Life of an Indian Prince,* the period covered is only a few months. The novel opens soon after 15 August 1947—the date of Indian independence. By then all but three princes (the rulers of Kashmir, Hyderabad, and Junagadh) had signed the Instrument of Accession. This story is about a fourth (the ruler of Sham Pur—a fictitious state) who holds out against the Union. In this he is encouraged by his nymphomaniacal mistress Ganga Dasi, a powerful and illiterate hill-woman whose spell holds him in a grip beyond all counsel. Needless to say, he loses both his state and his mistress.

Antony Copley, in a recent article "The Politics of Illusion: Paul Scott's *The Raj Quartet*", poses some awkward choices of focus for the reader when assessing an historical novel. "Should he simply comment on how faithful the novel is to the history, measuring the novelist's powers as historian against those of the professional historian? Should he, alternatively, ask how plausibly 'historical' the fictional events are? Or should he strike a mean between these two positions and ask why the novelist has chosen these years and these events as the subject of his novels?"

Antony Copley, himself an historian, poses these questions as an historian. But what criteria must a literary critic apply in evaluating an historical work? There is no quick answer to this, but I think Anand in *Private Life of an Indian Prince* has produced a great historical novel by freeing himself from the shackles of history. Some of the episodes are based on real events but are transformed to suit the demands of characterisation. The Maharaja firing a rifle into the air to disperse a mob has its origin in the Rana of Dhami (ruler of one of the Simla states) firing on a group of cultivators who had come to present their grievances. This was in 1939, and it is reported that four people were killed. However, in Anand's novel the Maharaja scares only the pigeons and doves from their niches in the palace gateway. The part played by the Praja Mandal in the fall of the Maharaja has its parallel in events in several states, and it also forms an important part of Malgonkar's novel.

Anand makes creative use of history: the events, when they are not real, are completely plausible. One such event, and the finest in the novel, is Vicky's interview with Sardar Vallabhbhai Patel, Union Minister of States, at five o'clock in the morning. (Nehru had once casually remarked to Anand that the Sardar interviews princes at all hours of day.) The hour chosen by Anand is significant: it shows not only the Sardar's bullying nature but also his power and astuteness. The prince, already smarting from the humiliation at having to wait for an appointment, is scolded like a schoolboy for maladministration, suppression, and corruption. Before he has had a chance to say anything in his own defense (not that there is much the prince can say), Patel has got him to sign on the dotted line and the destiny of Sham Pur has mingled with that of the Indian Union. There is no exaggeration in Anand's epigrammatic summary: "Sardar Vallabhbhai (Wishmarck) Patel growled, like a big angry bull, twice or thrice from the rostrum in Delhi. And most of the sons of Suns and Moons fell into line as children of the earth."

What gives stature to *Private Life of an Indian Prince* is Anand's deft handling of his characters. Pervasive as the history is, he never allows the historical background to obtrude itself upon his portrayal of the prince, just as the prince never allows his political ambitions to determine his emotional life. After signing away his state, Vicky returns to Sham Pur, musing, "Now I shall be more or less in the same position as Gangi, one of the disinherited. Maybe this will bring us close together." The discovery that his mistress has deserted him weighs more heavily upon him than the loss of his kingdom. Later, when exiled in London, he lays bare his heart to a shop-girl whom he has seduced: "I have lost my throne," he tells her. "But that wouldn't have mattered. Only, only the woman whom I loved also left me."

Unlike Malgonkar's *The Princes,* Anand's novel ends not with what happened to the state but with what happened to the man. The prince goes mad. But in dissecting and revealing the process of insanity, the author recovered from the nervous breakdown he had himself suffered. The conjoining of a personal crisis and clear political vision helps make *Private Life of an Indian Prince* into a great historical novel that is at the same time a work of art.

Rajesh K. Pallan   (essay date 1990)

SOURCE: "Encounter with the Self: A Study of the Confessional Mode in Mulk Raj Anand's *The Bubble,*" in *The New Indian Novel in English: A Study of the 1980s,* edited by Viney Kirpal, Allied Publishers Limited, 1990, pp. 11-23.

[*In the following essay, Pallan discusses the quest of "being" and "becoming" as presented in* The Bubble.]

Mulk Raj Anand believes that it is not the consciousness of men that determines their existence, but, it is their social existence that determines their consciousness. The life of an individual is undergoing various changes, transformations, metamorphoses through various struggles against the slavery of mind and body. And this confrontation of opposites compels human beings to renew themselves in order to evolve to the higher degrees of consciousness:

Consciousness becomes the highest ideal of the

awakening individual. The renewal is not an obvious or predetermined Karmic process. It is the kind of dialectic of conflicts, oppositions and labyrinthine rhythmic interplay of echoes and immediate feelings and may possibly result in some kind of fusion through experience of life at different levels, in different situations. ["**Reflections on the Novel,**" *Commonwealth Literature,* edited by C. D. Narasimhaiah, 1981]

And this "labyrinthine rhythmic interplay of echoes" results in a fusion through the multiple experiences and praxes in Anand's autobiographical novel, *The Bubble* of the "Seven Ages of Man" series. Manifesting his moral vision to an intense and powerful degree, *The Bubble* is a ruthlessly frank analysis of Krishan Chander Azad's life in London, the variegated influences that left their indelible impressions on his sensitive mind, the usual depravities, hypocrisies and cruelties that make up our society. The novel, while enacting the body-soul drama, is an apogee of human development from *being* to *becoming.* The present study purports to attempt an analysis of how Krishan encounters his self from all the convexities and concavities of the mirror of experiences, how he discovers the "wisdom of the heart," and how he recovers himself from the ravages of illusions.

In this autobiographical novel, Anand is attempting to forge a new metaphor in his anti-hero, Krishan, who struggles and strives to relate with the cosmos. By delineating the patriarchal influences, the idiosyncrasies, the predilections, the prejudices and the proclivities in the character of Krishan Chander, Anand lays bare the shimmeriness of life, its direct, naked realities, double-think, the deception of men and women, their dreams, aspirations, hopes, fears and failures and their clash with outer forces in order to come to terms with the whole of objective reality. How the life-process of an individual is "baulked [*sic*] by the hangovers of the past prohibitions and the imposition of new inhibitions" [**"Reflections on the Novel"**], how life becomes a heap of broken images, how the self encounters the brave new world, how it is forced to work within a set of parameters—a grammar of life attitudes, formalised by a grammar of interests and motives, only to "conduct" the self, and the self-actualization, the personal and the impersonal, the subjective element with the equilibrium of objective reality.

Shorn of verbosity, pompousness and pedantry, *The Bubble* is an account of "ruthless self-examination," where, in its battery of intellect, there is an effacement of the self, an extinction of the ego, signifying [to Saros Cowasjee in *So Many Freedoms*] that "heroism often lies in the realization of the unheroic in oneself."

It is not a tale of two cities but of two continents. The anti-hero hero, Krishan Chander, goes to London to do a doctorate in philosophy under the guidance of Prof. Dicks (Dawes Hicks) and gets "a grounding in Greek and Modern Thought." Gauche in manners and dogged by memories of Yasmin and Aunt Devaki, the scents and sounds of the "city of nectar", his letters to his friend, Noor, bear the stamp of nostalgia. His Indian friends in London include a Bengali fixer of jobs, a straight-laced Sardar, Tochi (Tarlochan Singh), a notorious philanderer, Madan

Mohan Mehta, and a Yoga teacher. Carrying with him the cargo of his own heritage Krishan Chander falls in love with Evelyn, Lucy, Irene, and feels "involved in a new drama of conflicting emotions, Faust, tempted to surrender his soul to the Devil." Krishan is "impetuous" and desires "to grow, to expand, to absorb everything—and quickly."

Cutting himself off from the "ocean of nectar", he launches on a "philosophical quest", experiences "ghooanmaaon", which is a churning not of oceans but of the spirit. Encountering for the millionth time the reality of experience and forging in the smithy of his soul the uncreated conscience of his race, Krishan Chander feels "like a falcon who can fly and conquer the world." The focus of the novel centres on the relationship between Krishan and Irene (the Irish girl), at whose behest, he writes his confession. And the various contraries, ambiguities, vacillations and vicissitudes of their friendship are chronicled in the novel with an authentic and poignant note of experience at first hand.

Keeping in view the political climate of pre-independence days, Krishan's vision becomes bifocal and the "to-ing and fro-ing" between two continents becomes integral to his student days in England till he realizes the efficacy of the saying of a Chinese sage, "Going on means going far. And going far means returning." Krishan resolves to return to India while his beloved, Irene, languishes in a Dublin jail after joining the Irish freedom movement. The whole story revolves round Krishan's "quest of knowledge", his discovery of the self, his odyssey from innocence to experience, from *being* to *becoming,* "a falcon born to soar."

In the novel, the name of the hero is certainly reminiscent of the Krishna of the Yadus. But Krishan Chander is a new human Krishna, an anti-hero hero, living in action in the terrible decay of the tragic twentieth century, unable to rise to the stature of the old God of Brindaban. [According to Anand in a letter to the critic dated 28 June 1984, the] whole subversion is deliberate as the novelist's intention has been

> to create, from the concrete human situations, a possible man, who is resilient enough to evolve in spite of all the odds, from a street urchin brought up among the poor untouchable, through the slave period of foreign rule to make some kind of self from the many broken selves— the broken bundle of mirrors, into a montage man, now and then aware of the need to be a whole man.

In fact, Krishan Chander is a new Krishna who lives and loves and does the things which the God Krishna of the *Mahabharata* did not do. He lives and moves and "has his being in new situations in the changed world of today" [letter from Anand to the critic dated 29 May 1984]. The unmistakable message of *The Bubble* is that the Western renaissance has affected human life, and the individual can only grow, if he goes beyond Faust, to understand the secret of the self by ruthless self-examination and extirpation of all falsities, ritualistic make-beliefs and lies. "The creation of a personal myth as against the old myth of India," Anand strongly feels, "is very necessary if a con-

temporary literatue is to arise." In his "Journal to Irene", Krishan Chander avers that some of the old myths have to be accepted because they are relevant but "there have to be new myths for the future."

Krishan Chander breaks down at every stage of his life through adverse circumstances and strategies. Because the new *Mahabharata* wars are world wars and men have already destroyed the gods by accepting them as ritualistic-escape [mechanisms], Krishan Chander feels that the image is in torment while God Krishna is a happy God dancing away in Mathura-Brindaban. Krishna Chander tells Rev. Thomas in *The Bubble* that "actually we had become puritans though the injunctions of the elders and fear of our women being raped by foreign incomers and the flirtations of Krishna and Radha were frowned upon." Krishan Chander tries to "go beyond embeddedness in customary gods." He does not want to depend on ready-made formulas but desires to go on brooding, philosophising and discovering himself and makes up his mind to read a thousand books, to learn from many philosophers before he can launch on the vaulting ambition to be "himself." Even through constant and "recurring ghaoon-maoon", Krishan Chander thinks that each human being should create his own norm in himself and engage himself in the quest of his own self as he declares:

> I must always remember Iqbal's teaching, that even though in a breakdown, one can collect oneself—if one persists in self-criticism, by seeing one's reflection in the mirror. . . . I must create myself with the will. As there is no God, I must cause myself by asserting I am. As perhaps, God Himself was his own beginning. Maybe, I can be myself in the wild goose chase in this absurd world of Heisenberg.

Again, Krishan Chander expresses the same sentiment in his conversation with Maud Gonne that he "respects the old philosophy only because if the creator of the cosmos is in all bodies, then all of us are part of him—and we are all Gods! Creators!"

By employing the Yajnavalkya—Maitreyi myth in *The Serpent and the Rope,* Raja Rao tries to suggest that men and women are still united in the soul and that they need not seek union in the body even when married. In *The Bubble,* Anand suggests that the body-souls unite or have to fuse for union in the real world. The body and the soul are not antagonistic; they are complementary. The question is not of Either/Or but of Both/And. The enactment of the body-soul drama is a process and not a consequence—a process to reach the higher planes of consciousness, a voyage from the *being* to the *becoming*. The first consummation of Krishan Chander's affair with Irene is depicted intensely where their souls seem to have flowed into each other until the suppressed dreams open up new vistas. He takes Irene in his arms and leads her violently to the divan bed and, in a flash, he feels his whole world of ideas flowing into his nerves as he urges forward to his pleasure in the warmth and longings of abandon with an inchoate calm, beyond the memories of Yasmin, Evelyn and Lucy, and even beyond the restraints which the parental home imposed on him.

Krishan Chander, in his "ghaoon-maoon", realizes that he is not in relation to God, but in relation to others, not only to his situation as a human being or to his own feelings and ideas, but in relation to the being-in-this-world situation of everyone, in a unique, vague but genuinely possible connection. His jaded nerves and tensions make him ruffled:

> One does not know the undercurrents going on within one's body, not to speak of the grooves cut deep, deep inside one by heredity. . . . Is it possible that the body is soul and soul is the body?

Krishan Chander's soul expands into the broad vistas before his roving eyes and he feels like Faust who sold out to the Devil and now wishes to recant. While climbing the famous Mount Snowdon enthusiastically, Krishan feels that since childhood, his heart has been in the mountains, the sparkle in his body-soul, which is the blurred light in all persons that burns away the deadness and rekindles their *being*. He dares to abolish the opposition of passion and fact in his confession and make it the revelation of his body-mind-spirit by recovering it from the forgotten world of urges, dreams and his Raja Rasalu adventures:

> For while Beauty gives the discreet pleasure of art, Truth includes all the facts of human existence, love, hate, death, adversity and the feel of things which is the inner layer of understanding, perhaps, the evolutionary process of the body-soul itself.

The pleasure-principle of poetry and the reality-principle of philosophy are the warp and woof of Krishan's body-soul adventures. He desires to explore the body so that his soul can envelop it, occupy it and make it shine with sheer abandon. The energies in the body, Krishan feels, are, perhaps ignited by will which stirs the subterranean currents onto gestures, sounds and pantomimes, which acquire meaning through expression itself; the source of the immanent spirit is a dynamic process of comprehension. That is why, he exhorts Irene to "synchronise our rhythms":

> I must transform the spiritual thesis of the incorporeal spirit into man's independent consciousness which arises from the body to the soul, as awareness of oneself through recognition of others. . . .

This amply illustrates Anand's assertion that he "wrote from the compulsion of a morbid obsession with myself and the people who possessed me deep in my conscience." It is a sort of body-soul search which is behind his creative activities. Anand maintains that in the creative process itself, both the body and soul are involved and, as a matter of fact, the distinction between the body and soul disappears, and the creative artist sees that "the body is soul and the soul body."

In Hermann Hesse's novel *Siddhartha,* Siddhartha tells Govinda that "love is the most important thing in the world." It is in the same spirit of love, admiration and respect that Krishan Chander treats Irene, and she becomes, like Kamala in *Siddhartha,* a symbol of illumination, self-exploration and enlightenment. It is through Irene that

Krishan discovers himself. He categorically explains it to Irene:

> I believe we make ourselves by unmaking ourselves, by constant self-examination. There is no outside fate! . . . Maybe someone's light illumines our small selves. . . .
>
> Your eyes for instance. . . .

Krishan Chander, in his new-fangled faith, observes that he must not allow his curiosity to become slavery to the thoughts of others and must live in this concrete world, face all its decay accepting the dynamism of the people. Shunning the fear of talking of his passions, he desires to be spontaneous, liberate himself from every moral laceration, exonerate every weakness, crush every prejudice and perceive every nuance of the secrets of his body-soul by recalling his actual experiences:

> Whoever decides to go on a quest must persist, even through the ugly topsy-turvy world of surrealism, tortuous and horrible as it may be, to discover the frightful chaos beneath the glitter on the surface.

In his endeavour to renew himself, Krishan Chander resolves to discover a way of life by which he can live with others, discard the images and illusions in which he does not believe, destroy the shams and get rid of hypocrisies. In the process, even his casual effrontery in pursuing multiple experiences seems to enrich his confession by discovering for him how unpredictable impulses and coincidences are found in one's *being*. He decides to write more intensely in his "confession about the poor in spite of the dictum of Edward Sackville West." He likes to concretize his aspiration for freedom and mature his realization of the self. Only in writing his confession does he find "the only escape from unhappiness of life." He wants to see the growth of his *being* in the joys of childhood, boyhood and youth accepting the miseries as mere obstacles to growing-up. He musters up the courage to become a revolutionary, a "rebel", thus freeing himself from the corrosions "behind the facade of the Hindoo in me." After seeking so many freedoms, Krishan understands that life is not for personal salvation; but to live in and through others as the revolutionaries lived. That is why, he decides to write about Bakha, the sweeper boy, as a new kind of hero of India, who makes the effort to come up from the labyrinths.

The tension of trying to *see* beyond *looking* grows all the more intense in his *being*. He resolves to pour out in his confession all his liquid feelings and show how all are fragmented. This exercise might fragment Krishan further but he firmly believes that by giving vent to "miscellaneous hunches about myself", by showing how we have fallen, he would be in a position to lift all to the stars. He thinks of the "rough hands of Ananta, Rallia and Ali", hardened by wielding the hammer, or stoking fires into furnaces, or polishing brass. He ventures into the sense of the rough edges of the world, beyond the heavenly order. Learning a good deal about himself by writing his confession, he realizes that facing up to oneself constantly is important. He also feels that one can be more truthful if one can find words for both the outsights and the flotsam and jetsam that lurk beneath one's mind. *The Bubble* proves to be a kind of recognition of personal identity from among his many selves. While entering the intimacies of inner feelings, writing in the confessional mode becomes a fire which not only destroys the falsities but also lights up the mind:

> I feel that the confessional novel which Irene inspired me to write has certainly increased my capacity for apperceptions. In a novel, one can begin to see one's soul. It is a kind of self-creation. Seeing oneself in the mirror. And connect the various selves I am trying to link up. . . . I have been able to expose many of the myths by which we Indians live. I have dissipated some of the lies we all inherit.

Without succumbing to the habit of name-dropping and without indulging in self-praise, Anand, with deft strokes of Dickensian sympathies, reels out Krishan's encounters with E. M. Forster, W. B. Yeats, Maud Gonne, Leonard Woolf, Virginia Woolf, Palme Dutt, Eric Gill, Gertrude Stein, T. E. Lawrence, the Russels, Paedor O'Donnell, Walter Sickert and a host of others; indeed, a whole gallery of famous names comes alive in flesh and blood walking through the narrative, pouring out cups of tea, guzzling liquor, discussing and debating on important issues and, all in all, behaving like normal *homo sapiens*. The novel is a long discourse on philosophers and poets.

While Krishan's nationalistic temper is honed by the Gandhian influence, and as a Panjabi, he has Iqbal as his mentor, later on, he is graduated into atomism as the basic metaphysic of the realists of the twenties and thirties. While writing his doctorate, he learns that the imagination is the basis of belief in Hume's theory of knowledge in which the building blocks are impressions. In addition to Russel's and Hume's philosophy, Krishan embraces the philosophies of Hegel, Gandhi, Nietzsche, Schopenhauer, Rimbaud and Krishnamurthy. But he is properly groomed by Hume's philosophy that there can be no memory without a self, and no self without memory. Like Hume, one of Krishan's central problems is that of personal identity.

Now, what was the bubble of which the title speaks? Krishan explains to Irene,

> I had always been interested in my various bubbling selves. . . . Now I want to prick all the bubbles. And poke my tongue out against all the patriarchs, lamenters, the professors and the clever phrasemongers. I feel our lives may have a meaning, on this earth, in the flesh and the blood, in the here-now.

His inspiration for doing so is Rimbaud in whose poem, the magician says, "we live inside a bubble, as in a womb. And in this we grow. But at times, we can see ourselves in it. . ." In *The Bubble,* a tramp, blowing bubbles from a clay pipe, comes to Krishan and Irene in a cafe, and cheekily blows the bubbles onto their table. Krishan and Irene purchase the pipe and start blowing bubbles but while doing so, Krishan has all the uncanny feelings about bubbles forming and dissolving. When the flask of liquid soap is exhausted, they put the pipes away and look into

each other's eyes "as though to search for our love, beyond the bubbles." In one of his conversations with Krishan, Professor Rhys says,

> The bubble opens at birth and then seals the child. With each perception, the bubble opens and shuts, urged from within. After birth, life in the bubble tries to grow and move. In the transparent glass, the moves are reflected. . . . Something like this happens all the time.

Participating in the discussion, Krishan says that Shakespeare also talks of the bubble in Jacques's speech to which Professor Rhys replies, "Bubbles always burst!" The metaphor has multiple meanings—the bubble of desire, the "explosion" of love when two bubbles meet, the bubble of self-complacency and above all, the sense of transience and uncertainty of human life, but many coloured as the rainbow hues which bubbles often reflect. These bubbles may be likened to the "pipedreams" which Eugene O'Neill's characters nurture in his plays. The title is apposite as the many bubbling selves of the anti-hero hero, Krishan Chander, are depicted, dissolved and decimated, and, again, like the phoenix, rise, resurrect and renew themselves from their ashes. In the attempt, Krishan Chander strengthens his will "to be more than myself", to seek an escape from illusions in order to recognize the polarity between illusion and reality, between the serpent and the rope, between "the mirror and the lamp" (to borrow W. B. Yeat's impressive analogy).

Running right from *Seven Summers* to *The Bubble,* the journey motif is inextricably integrated in the four volumes of the "Seven Ages of Man" series in order to present Krishan Chander's instinctive urge for the discovery of the self. In *Seven Summers,* Part I, entitled "The River," the anonymous excerpt, in fact, presents the essence of Anand's fictional art:

> I love roads . . . I love to walk, walk, walk, for it is an opportunity for thought developing into a clear process, often leading to self-illumination and discovery. . . .

In the beginning of the first section, Krishan stands for a long while with his thumb in his mouth "wondering where the road comes from and where it goes." Almost in each one of his later novels, the road or a long walk or a journey appears to signify the quest motif. Again, the laying of the road is the central theme of the novel, *The Road.* In Part II of *Seven Summers,* entitled "The River", the anonymous excerpt speaks of the river that "breaks down all landmarks, destroys habitations and crops and human beings in the torrential course, carving out other channels. . . ." In the dedicatory note appended to *Morning Face,* Anand writes:

> And life is everywhere. It is the measureless movement towards light against darkness. It is the refreshing river which sweeps the bones and ashes and much of history along in its mysterious course towards the ocean.

In Part I of *Morning Face* entitled "City of Dreadful Nights", the journey motif is patently clear as Krishan Chander travels by train to Amritsar, "the engine puff-puffed as the railway train chuck-chucked, and . . . the trees on the long, straight road sped past, in the opposite direction to which we were going. . . ." *Confession of a Lover,* too, is structured around movement. Even actual journeys to Lahore to Bombay, finally, to another country are undertaken in the novel. The opening paragraph of *Confession of a Lover* captures Krishan's rhythms, their incessant flow and his natural excitement:

> As I cycled along towards Lohgarh gate as I cycled along, pressing the pedal hard . . . I was full of the naive enthusiasm of a young heart-squanderer, ready to love everyone and everything. . . .

In *The Bubble,* the journey motif is manifest as Krishan Chander rides on his Triumph motor cycle in Dolgelly village roads. While climbing up to Mount Snowdon, the memories of Kangra and the lower Himalayas come crowding into his mind and make the alien mountains a part of his *being,* of his primaeval emotions of wonder, admiration and love:

> I asked myself why I had gone away from the main road. The answer came that somehow, I wanted to go into bylanes to penetrate the jungle . . . and then ultimately to climb up to Mount Snowdon . . . one day I will take it all in my stride and get to the peak.

Getting to the peak of Mount Snowdon describes the symbolic ascent of the body and mind in growth. The "hills", the "road", the "trees", "seeds", "plants", "flowers" all become significant symbols and images of ascent, growth, evolution, "poetry" and "courage" which recur in *The Bubble.* Krishan Chander wants his inward journey to become his outer adventure, and endeavours to get to "the source of my exuberance, from which I may pour myself out in words." For him, there is no end of the road; the inner landscapes he spans all his life through a dark night, weary and bruised by the hardships on the way, "tormented by the demons of hatred, jealousy and spite."

Krishan's incessant longings to search new stars, scale new heights, recurring in the four volumes of the "Seven Ages of Man" series, assume a new dimension in *The Bubble.* In our over-crowded planet, modern man feels suffocated in our cash-nexus society and aspires to search for new sources of food for the mind and body. Not without reason did the ancients call the thorny path of human progress a road towards the stars. Probing the skies is the essence of Krishan's progress; what was a spontaneous striving at the start of *Seven Summers,* grows into a conscious quest—"the Himalayas of aspiration" in *The Bubble.* Recalling the echo of his mentor Iqbal's voice: "We live by creation of ends. We shine by the light of desire", Krishan Chander desires to hold his head high, and "looks at the stars" because there are always "the stars to look at when the earth hides the Sun at the end of the day." In the promised three parts of the "Seven Ages of Man" series—*And So He Played His Part, A World Too Wide* and *Last Scene*—the growth and evolution of the anti-hero hero and many other impressions which impinge on his consciousness, would be delineated.

Making an assessment of *The Bubble,* Khushwant Singh rightly believes that Anand has produced a delightful au-

tobiographical novel which is "entertaining, utterly readable and totally unpretentious." Anand has really uttered his words with the breath of life itself. It manifests Anand's fecundity of imagination, fidelity to the experience and finality of perspective as is patently clear in the relationship of Krishan and Irene which "transcends earthly copulation to attain a mystic grandeur." Towards the end of the novel, Krishan recalls the "uplook" in Irene's eyes and vows that:

> As long as I can look, I will try and see into the
>   farthest distances;
> As long as I can walk, I will move at a faster
>   pace;
> As long as I can stand I will struggle;
> And, in this geography and hope, the stars, you
>   and I will be held together by love. . . .

Unlike Marie Corelli's *Open Confession To a Man from a Woman* ("If I love thee, what is that to thee?"), *The Bubble* is not a platitudinous plot of love-affair. Nor does it smack of exhibitionism as does Frank Harris's *My Life and Loves.* Nor is it packed with crockery-breaking scenes as we find in D. H. Lawrence's novels like *Sons and Lovers.* On the contrary, it is a rare achievement on the part of Anand to fuse love with duty, the self with the patina of history by weaving his matrix with ruthless self-examination and strengthening the moral fibre of the society without ostentation and pompousness. Around and about throng, impalpably, memories, dreams and desires and all falsity and sentimentality is singed by the fire of intense suffering. Resultantly, to borrow the words of Jack Lindsay, "we touch the spring of human renewal . . . the complete harmony, the enduring liberation."

Like Stephen Daedalus of James Joyce's novel, *A Portrait of the Artist as a Young Man,* Krishan in *The Bubble,* discovers a conscience in himself when, in alien environs, he endeavours to test himself daily in the smithy of his soul, aware of his release from the Indian hangover of sobriety. In the enactment of body-soul drama, we learn how our environment constricts us, how we remain cocooned in complacency, and how many exhilarating experiences await us if we struggle a little. The enigma of arrival at the truth of Krishan's *being* is resolved towards the end of the novel as Krishan, like Ulysses, resolves to strive, to seek, to adventure, to live by trial and error in order to participate in the coming cataclysms of his country:

> . . . I shall become a human being among other human beings. I am convinced that the subject of philosophy is the human person, and not what I thought it was . . . the interminable quest for salvation only for myself.

The air of truthfulness, authenticity and maturity, with which his letter to his father is charged, bears the unmistakable impress of his assertion that "my search for faith was a search for truth." Bolstering his faith with "truth", Anand develops a social conscience in his anti-hero hero, Krishan, who challenges to change the very social fabric and strives to improve not only his personal lot but also to enrich the social awareness and thus become "the maker of ever new worlds, the dreamer of ever new dreams." The optimistic note unflinching faith in man's meaningful search for Truth is struck in Krishan's letter to Irene in which he speaks of new challenges, new situations and new difficulties:

> . . . One cannot remain fixed in the type one has become, because one ceases to be. One must awaken to fresh possibilities, latent in the winter's decay, the opening of buds into flowers and the promise of the coming of luscious fruit on the tree of happiness. . . . We have to nourish the flowers of humanity.

The Bubble carries the reader a major step forward in the "Seven Ages of Man" series. Apparently rambling in form, it has an inner structure of its own. Steering clear of the often overdone inwardness of the stream of consciousness novel, its structure—including letters, extracts from diaries, conversations with the Bloomsbury intelligentsia, other eminent literary figures and straightforward narrative—does not suffer from aesthetic over-distancing. The "laboured effects" of *Morning Face* are not palpable in *The Bubble* as, in it, Anand zeroes in on what is worth *being* rather than on what is worth *having*.

In such an autobiography, thinly veiled in the garb of fiction, Anand brilliantly eschews the hazards of exhibitionism, calls a spade a spade, and with no hush-hush commodiousness, fathoms deep into his frailties, failures and fixations, testing almost clinically, all his tumult on the anvil of Truth. Probing deep into the recesses of his subconscious mind, he does not reveal to conceal. Rather all the cogitations are communicated with such a tenacity of purpose, the definiteness of design and an awakened sense of conscience that his revelations become "holy particulars" which are "written in heart's blood to crystallise thought as a new kind of novel." The praxes of Krishan gives a jolt to the reader's self-complacency and nudge him into shrugging off the lethargy of custom, goad him to discover new "Americas", to get over the "slavery of shameful and dreary past of supine acceptance" so that hundreds of flowers may bloom in the desert of our hearts.

Marlene Fisher   (review date Summer 1992)

SOURCE: A review of *Between Tears and Laughter,* in *World Literature Today,* Vol. 66, No. 3, Summer, 1992, pp. 580-81.

[*In the following review, Fisher comments on the major themes of the stories collected in* Between Tears and Laughter.]

The 1991 edition of *Between Tears and Laughter* is a reissue of the collection of short stories that was first published, under the same title, in 1973. Four stories have been added that were not part of the 1973 volume: **"Savitri," "May the Ridge Rise," "Night Falls on Shiva's Hills,"** and **"Sati Sapni."** The twenty-one selections included in the current edition represent vintage Mulk Raj Anand.

Here, as in such collections as *The Barber's Trade Union and Other Stories,* Anand has brought the concept of a Western literary genre—that of the short story—into the Asian, Indian context. In telling the tales found in *Be-*

tween Tears and Laughter he has drawn upon both the European *conte* and the bardic recital of the Indian tradition. The tales, moreover, are truly short. The two longest, **"Between Tears and Laughter"** and **"The Sinful Life and Death of Tinkori,"** are ten and thirteen pages respectively; **"May the Ridge Rise"** is a two-page fable.

However historical their form, the stories are distinctly modern in their themes. They deal with violence; they deal with cruelty; they deal with caste, particularly untouchability; and they deal with the kind of manipulative, bureaucratic, postindependence "democracy" that Anand, tongue in cheek, presents as part of the fabric of village India.

The tales in this slim volume indeed veer between tears and laughter. The tears are those of anguish, of horror, sometimes of sentimentality. The laughter is, in turn, wry, sardonic, charming. In the title story [**"Between Tears and Laughter"**] the space between tears and laughter is obliterated. Savitri's anxiety and hunger, her poverty and abandonment, cause tears and laughter to become indistinguishable from each other. They merge in pain and madness.

The short opening tale, **"Savitri,"** is a powerful and moving account, from within the young widow's own consciousness, of the terror of sati, certainly for the woman so doomed. The final story, **"Sati Sapni,"** is a cynical mockery of the same theme. The cynicism is evident in the effort on the part of two low-caste characters to become wealthy in a most unusual and contemptuously sly way. They force a male snake to die by fire, lure its "wife" into the committing of sati, and then establish what they expect will be a profitable shrine at the site. By the end of the story, pilgrimages have already begun.

Cruelty to animals, cruelty exercised by families toward their own members, inter- and intracaste cruelty, cruelty of the young toward the old and of the old toward the young—it is all there in *Between Tears and Laughter.* And as always, Anand is wonderful at getting inside the skin of young people. Also as always, he has written with the consciousness and self-consciousness of the spinner of tales. Even the witch in the story of that same title, an old woman who chants, mantralike, to her daughter-in-law, to her son, to her grandchildren "May they die," is loved by the little one "because she told him tales."

It is through the art of literature, in this instance the art of the short story, that Anand makes his points and engages his readers. It is through this vehicle that we come to feel and to understand some of the realities of Indian village life, in all their starkness and in their occasional humor.

FURTHER READING

Biography

Pontes, Hilda. "The Education of a Rebel: Mulk Raj

Anand." *The Literary Half-Yearly* XXVII, No. 2 (July 1986): 105-23.

Documents Anand's experiences as a student in India.

Criticism

Cowasjee, Saros. "Mulk Raj Anand's *Untouchable:* An Appraisal." *Literature East and West* XVII, Nos. 2-4 (June-September-December 1973): 199-211.

In-depth discussion of *Untouchable*'s plot, characters, and themes.

Mukherjee, Arun P. "The Exclusions of Postcolonial Theory and Mulk Raj Anand's 'Untouchable': A Case Study." *Ariel* 22, No. 3 (July 1991): 27-48.

Examines *Untouchable* in the context of postcolonial literature.

Nasimi, Reza Ahmad. "Anand's Language of Compassionate Objectivity." In *The Language of Mulk Raj Anand, Raja Rao and R. K. Narayan,* pp. 5-28. Delhi: Capital Publishing House, 1989.

Identifies characteristic traits in Anand's writing, including the author's use of narrative structures and imagery.

Pontes, Hilda. "Anand's *Untouchable:* A Classic in Experimentation of Theme and Technique." In *Studies in Indian Fiction in English,* edited by G. S. Balarama Gupta, pp. 128-41. Gulbarga, India: JIWE Publications, 1987.

Gives an analysis of *Untouchable,* more than fifty years after its publication, and discusses critics' changing assessments of the novel and its author.

Sharma, Ambuj Kumar. *The Theme of Exploitation in the Novels of Mulk Raj Anand.* New Delhi: H. K. Publishers & Distributors, 1990, 162 p.

Analyzes the theme of exploitation in Anand's fiction from various angles. Sharma also includes a bibliography of primary and secondary sources.

Interview

Fisher, Marlene. "Interview with Mulk Raj Anand." *World Literature Written in English* 13, No. 1 (April 1974): 109-22.

Interview conducted on May 19, 1973, in which Anand discusses his influences, other Indian writers, and the future of Indian writing in English.

Louise Bogan

1897-1970

American poet, critic, editor, and translator.

The following entry provides an overview of Bogan's career. For further information on her life and works, see *CLC*, Volumes 4, 39, and 46.

INTRODUCTION

A major American lyric poet whose darkly romantic verse is characterized by traditional poetic structures, concise language, and vivid description, Bogan is known particularly for her honest and austere rendering of emotion. Douglas L. Peterson noted that she wrote "mainly of highly personal and painful experience—of personal losses suffered through death and the betrayal of intimate and deeply valued personal relationships, of time passing and of her acute awareness of the fragility of all things caught in time." Bogan's work is often compared with the short lyrics of such seventeenth-century poets as Thomas Campion, John Dryden, and Ben Jonson, and she shares with these writers an emphasis on musicality and craftsmanship as well as a subdued sense of grief and despair. Also a distinguished critic who served as a poetry editor for the *New Yorker* from 1931 to 1970 and authored numerous works of literary criticism, Bogan is known for her exacting standards and her penetrating analyses of many of the major poets of the twentieth century.

Biographical Information

Born in Livermore Falls, Maine, Bogan's early life was marked by turbulence and instability. Her mother was prone to unpredictable and often violent behavior and would periodically abandon her family, sometimes to engage in extramarital affairs. By age eight Bogan had become what she once described as "the semblance of a girl, in which some desires and illusions had been early assassinated: shot dead." Bogan's father eventually moved the family to Boston, where she attended Girls' Latin School and was trained in Greek, Latin, and classical verse. She went on to attend Boston University, but left in 1916, after only one year, to marry a young soldier. Bogan entered this marriage in part to escape her unstable home life, but the relationship ended shortly after the birth of a daughter, Mathilde, in 1917; a 1925 marriage to Raymond Holden, managing editor of the *New Yorker,* also failed. Bogan went to New York City in 1919, where she became friends with such writers as William Carlos Williams, Margaret Mead, and Edmund Wilson. Her poems were first published in *Poetry* in 1921, and in 1923 her first collection, *Body of This Death,* was released. Throughout the 1920s and 1930s, Bogan experienced severe depression, for which she underwent psychoanalysis and was voluntarily institutionalized more than once. During this time she also began to experiment with prose, producing an autobi-

ographical trilogy and writing stories and reviews for the *New Yorker.* Bogan won numerous awards during her lifetime, including a Guggenheim Foundation grant in 1933, the Bollingen Prize for poetry in 1955, and the Creative Award from Brandeis University in 1962. She died in 1970. Extolling the significance of Bogan's verse at a memorial tribute, W. H. Auden stated: "What, aside from their technical excellence, is most impressive about her poems is the unflinching courage with which she faced her problems, her determination never to surrender to self-pity, but to wrest beauty and joy out of dark places."

Major Works

Bogan's first poetry collection, *Body of This Death,* concerns such themes as family, betrayal, the limitations of time and beauty, and the psychology of sexual conflict. In "Medusa," for example, Bogan describes the emotional and psychological impact of a traumatic childhood incident: "This is a dead scene forever now. / Nothing will ever stir. / The end will never brighten it more than this, / Nor the rain blur." *Dark Summer* (1929) gathers the most significant poems from Bogan's first book as well as several new poems. Progressing toward a more purely lyrical mode, the new pieces expand upon her concerns with love, betrayal, passion, and wisdom. Included among the new poems are "The Mark," "Come Break with Time," and "Seasonal Autumnal," works which Yvor Winters once stated would "demand . . . comparison with the best songs of the sixteenth and seventeenth centuries." The collection *The Sleeping Fury* (1937), Bogan's last whole book of original verse, contains some of her most highly regarded and frequently anthologized poems, including "Italian Morning," "Roman Fountain," and "Kept." Cheryl Walker has noted that *The Sleeping Fury* is "a volume in which [Bogan's] several conceptions of mind—as psyche, as intellect, and intuition—come together." *Poems and New Poems* (1941) comprises works gathered from Bogan's three previous books and a selection of sixteen new pieces in which she occasionally experiments with meter and rhyme. Bogan's most successful writing from her previous volumes appears with several new poems in *Collected Poems, 1923-1953* (1954). The last volume of poetry Bogan published during her lifetime, *The Blue Estuaries: Poems, 1923-1968* (1968), adds twelve pieces to *Collected Poems*. In addition to her poetry, Bogan published numerous volumes of literary criticism, including *Achievement in American Poetry* (1951), *Selected Criticism* (1955), and *A Poet's Alphabet* (1970); a collection of letters, *What the Woman Lived* (1973); and an autobiography, *Journey around My Room* (1980).

Critical Reception

Early in her career, Bogan received attention primarily for the technical expertise of her verse. In 1937 Allen Tate stated: "In addition to distinguished diction and a fine ear for the phrase-rhythm she has mastered a prosody that permits her to get the greatest effect out of the slightest variation of stress." Most critics have observed that later in her career Bogan expressed an increased concern with weighty psychological and emotional issues, particularly in an attempt to confront difficult personal themes relating to inner conflict. Bogan's verse is not identified with any particular poetic school or movement, and for this reason some commentators have asserted that she has received less extensive critical appraisal than she would have otherwise. Recent criticism has tended to focus on Bogan's poetic voice, her contributions to the development of feminine verse, and the complexity of her themes. Cheryl Walker has stated that "all we can state with certainty is that Louise Bogan succeeded in creating some superb lyrics. She never prostituted her talent and what she has left us has a granitic edge. If her opus is small, it is also durable." Reaction to Bogan's critical works has been favorable, with reviewers praising her knowledge, clarity, and comprehensiveness. One review of *Achievement in American Poetry* stated that "like all Miss Bogan's criticism, this book is full of acute, spirited, and authoritative judgements of writers and works, expressed with grace and wit." Bogan's collection of letters and autobiography, although posthumously published, were also well received, with critics noting they provide invaluable insights into Bogan's life and writings. Writing about *Journey around My Room*, William Pritchard has stated: "Louise Bogan wanted her poetry to stand alone, free from the facts of her biography though deeply informed by them. But this mosaic, in some of its juxtapositions of prose and poems, helped me to a sharper sense of how good a poet she could be."

PRINCIPAL WORKS

Body of This Death   (poetry)   1923
Dark Summer   (poetry)   1929
The Sleeping Fury   (poetry)   1937
Poems and New Poems   (poetry)   1941
Achievement in American Poetry, 1900-1950   (criticism) 1951
Collected Poems, 1923-1953   (poetry)   1954
Selected Criticism: Prose, Poetry   (criticism)   1955
The Golden Journey: Poems for Young People [editor with William Jay Smith]   (poetry)   1965
The Blue Estuaries: Poems, 1923-68   (poetry)   1968
A Poet's Alphabet: Reflections on the Literary Art and Vocation   (essays)   1970
What the Woman Lived: Selected Letters of Louise Bogan (letters)   1973
Journey around My Room: The Autobiography of Bogan, a Mosaic   (autobiography)   1980

CRITICISM

Allen Tate   (review date Summer 1937)

SOURCE: A review of *The Sleeping Fury*, in *The Southern Review*, Louisiana State University, Vol. 3, No. 1, Summer, 1937, pp. 190-92.

[*Tate was an influential American critic who was closely associated with two critical movements, the Agrarians and the New Critics. In the following excerpt, he remarks favorably on* The Sleeping Fury, *commenting in particular on Bogan's poetic control and craftsmanship.*]

Miss Louise Bogan has published three books, and with each book she has been getting a little better, until now, in the three or four best poems of *The Sleeping Fury,* she has no superior within her purpose and range: among the women poets of our time she has a single peer, Miss Léonie Adams. Neither Miss Bogan nor Miss Adams will ever have the popular following of Miss [Edna St. Vincent] Millay or even of the late Elinor Wylie. I do not mean to detract from these latter poets; they are technically proficient, they are serious, and they deserve their reputations. Miss Bogan and Miss Adams deserve still greater reputations, but they will not get them in our time because they are "purer" poets than Miss Millay and Mrs. Wylie. They are purer because their work is less involved in the moral and stylistic fashions of the age, and they efface themselves; whereas Miss Millay never lets us forget her "advanced" point of view, nor Mrs. Wylie her interesting personality.

This refusal to take advantage of the traditional privilege of her sex must in part explain Miss Bogan's small production and the concentrated attention that she gives to the detail of her work. Women, I suppose, are fastidious, but many women poets are fastidious in their verse only as a way of being finical about themselves. But Miss Bogan is a craftsman in the masculine mode.

In addition to distinguished diction and a fine ear for the phrase-rhythm she has mastered a prosody that permits her to get the greatest effect out of the slightest variation of stress.

> In the cold heart, as on a page,
> Spell out the gentle syllable
> That puts short limit to your rage
> And curdles the straight fire of hell,
> Compassing all, so all is well.

There is nothing flashy about it; it is finely modulated; and I think one needs only to contrast Miss Bogan's control of her imagery in this stanza, the toning down of the metaphor to the simple last line, with the metaphorical juggernaut to which Miss Field's muse has tied herself, to see the fundamental difference between mastery of an artistic medium and mere undisciplined talent. Miss Bogan reaches the height of her talent in **"Hence-forth, from the Mind,"** surely one of the finest lyrics of our time. The "idea" of the poem is the gradual fading away of earthly joy upon the approach of age—one of the stock themes of English poetry; and Miss Bogan presents it with all the freshness of an Elizabethan lyricist. I quote the two last stanzas:

> Henceforth, from the shell,
> Wherein you heard, and wondered
> At oceans like a bell
> So far from ocean sundered—
> A smothered sound that sleeps
> Long lost within lost deeps,
> Will chime you change and hours,
> The shadow of increase,
> Will sound you flowers
> Born under troubled peace—
> Henceforth, henceforth
> Will echo sea and earth.

This poem represents the best phase of Miss Bogan's work: it goes back to an early piece that has been neglected by readers and reviewers alike—**"The Mark"**—and these two poems would alone entitle Miss Bogan to the consideration of the coming age.

But there is an unsatisfactory side to Miss Bogan's verse, and it may be briefly indicated by pointing out that the peculiar merits of **"The Mark"** and **"Henceforth, from the Mind"** seem to lie in a strict observance of certain limitations: in these poems and of course in others, Miss Bogan is impersonal and dramatic. In **"The Sleeping Fury"** she is philosophical and divinatory; in **"Hypocrite Swift"** she merely adumbrates an obscure dramatic situation in a half lyrical, half eighteenth-century, satirical style. Neither of these poems is successful, and the failure can be traced to all levels of the performances; for example, to the prosody, which has little relation to the development of the matter and which merely offers us a few clever local effects.

Louise Bogan with Ruth Limmer   (interview date Fall 1939)

SOURCE: "The Situation in American Writing: Seven Questions," in *Critical Essays on Louise Bogan,* edited by Martha Collins, G. K. Hall & Co., 1984, pp. 49-53.

[*Limmer is an editor who compiled Bogan's* A Poet's Alphabet *and* What the Woman Lived: Selected Letters of Louise Bogan, 1920-1970. *The following is Bogan's response to a questionnaire that was submitted to a number of American writers; it was originally published in the* Partisan Review *in Fall 1939. Bogan comments on her writing, literary criticism, and American society.*]

[*Limmer*]: *Are you conscious, in your own writing, of the existence of a "usable past"? Is this mostly American? What figures would you designate as elements in it? Would you say, for example, that Henry James's work is more relevant to the present and future of American writing than Walt Whitman's?*

[Bogan]: Because what education I received came from New England schools, before 1916, my usable past has more of a classic basis than it would have today, even in the same background. The courses in English Literature which I encountered during my secondary education and one year of college were not very nutritious. But my "classical" education was severe, and I read Latin prose and poetry and Xenophon and the Iliad, during my adolescence. Arthur Symons' *The Symbolist Movement,* and the French poets read at its suggestion, were strong influences experienced before I was twenty. The English metaphysicals (disinterred after 1912 and a literary fashion during my twenties) provided another literary pattern, and. Yeats influenced my writing from 1916, when I first read *Responsibilities.* —The American writers to whom I return are Poe (the Tales), Thoreau, E. Dickinson and Henry James. Whitman, read at sixteen, with much enthusiasm, I do not return to, and I never drew any refreshment from his "thought." Henry James I discovered late, and I read him for the first time with the usual prejudices against him, absorbed from the inadequate criticism he has generally received. It was not until I had developed some independent critical judgment that I recognized him as a great and subtle artist. If civilization and great art mean complexity rather than simplification, and if the humane can be defined as the well understood because the well-explored, James' work is certainly more relevant to American writing, present and future, than the naive vigor and sentimental "thinking" of Whitman.

Do you think of yourself as writing for a definite audience? If so, how would you describe this audience? Would you say that the audience for serious American writing has grown or contracted in the last ten years?

I have seldom thought about a definite "audience" for my poetry, and I certainly have never believed that the wider the audience, the better the poetry. Poetry had a fairly

> I have never been able to make a living by writing poetry and it has never entered my mind that I could do so. I think the place in our present American set-up for the honest and detached professional writer is both small and cold.
>
> —*Louise Bogan*

wide audience during what was roughly known as the "American poetic renaissance." It has been borne in upon me, in the last ten years, that there are only a few people capable of the aesthetic experience, and that, in this group, some persons who are able to appreciate "form" in the graphic arts, cannot recognize it in writing, just as there are writers who cannot "hear" music, or "see" painting. This small element in the population remains, it seems to me, more or less constant, and penetrates class distinctions. People may be led up to the threshold of the aesthetic experience, and taught its elements and its value, but I have never seen a person in whom the gift was not native actually experience the "shock of recognition" which a poem (or any work of art) gives its appreciator. And it is individuals to whom the aesthetic experience is closed, or those who know what it is, but wish to load it with a misplaced weight of "meaning" (and it seems incredible that such people as the last named exist; it is one of the horrors of life that they do)—it is such people who think that this experience can be "used." —Certainly the audience for the disinterested and the gratuitous in writing was never very large, in America. The layer of American "culture" has always been extremely thin. And it has not deepened in itself, but has been subject to fashions hastily imposed upon it. And the American "cultural" background is thick with ideas of "success" and "morality." So a piece of writing which is worth nothing, and means nothing (but itself) is, to readers at large, silly and somewhat immoral. "Serious writing" has come to mean, to the public, the pompous or thinly documentary. The truly serious piece of work, where a situation is explored at all levels, disinterestedly, for its own sake, is outlawed.

Do you place much value on the criticism your work has received? Would you agree that the corruption of the literary supplements by advertising—in the case of the newspapers—and political pressures—in the case of the liberal weeklies—has made serious literary criticism an isolated cult?

No. —The corruption of the literary supplements is nearly complete, but who would expect it to be otherwise, when publishers admit that they are selling packaged goods, for the most part: that their products, on the whole, stand on the same level as cigarettes and whiskey, as sedatives and pain-killers? —I have written criticism for liberal weeklies and can testify that in the case of one of them, no pressure of any kind has ever been put upon me. I have also been left perfectly free by a magazine which makes no claim to be anything but amusing. . . . Serious criticism is, now in

America, seriously hampered by the extraordinarily silly, but really (on the sentimental public at large), amazingly effective under-cover methods of certain pressure groups. But if there is no one who has the good sense to see the difference between warmed-over party tracts and actual analysis—if the public swallows such stuff whole— perhaps that is what the public deserves. Perhaps there is a biological bourgeoisie, thick headed and without sensibilities, thrown up into every generation, as well as an economic one. I discovered, long ago, that there are human attributes the gods themselves, as some one has said, cannot war against, and some of them are stupidity, greed, vanity, and arrogance.

Have you found it possible to make a living by writing the sort of thing you want to, and without the aid of such crutches as teaching and editorial work? Do you think there is any place in our present economic system for literature as a profession?

I have never been able to make a living by writing poetry and it has never entered my mind that I could do so. I think the place in our present American set-up for the honest and detached professional writer is both small and cold. (But then, it was both small and cold for. . . . Flaubert, in 19th century France.)

Do you find, in retrospect, that your writing reveals any allegiance to any group, class, organization, region, religion, or system of thought, or do you conceive of it as mainly the expression of yourself as an individual?

My writing reveals some "allegiances" (if this term means certain marks made upon it by circumstance). I was brought up in the Roman Catholic Church, and was exposed to real liturgy, instead of the dreary "services" and the dreadful hymnody of the Protestant churches. There was a Celtic gift for language, and talent in the form of a remarkable excess of energy, on the maternal side of my family. And I was handed out, as I have said, a thorough secondary classical education, from the age of twelve through the age of seventeen, in the public schools of Boston. I did not know I was a member of a class until I was twenty-one; but I knew I was a member of a racial and religious minority, from an early age. One of the great shocks of my life came when I discovered that bigotry existed not only among the Catholics, but among the Protestants, whom I had thought would be tolerant and civilized (since their pretentions were always in that direction). It was borne in upon me, all during my adolescence, that I was a "Mick," no matter what my other faults or virtues might be. It took me a long time to take this fact easily, and to understand the situation which gave rise to the minor persecutions I endured at the hands of supposedly educated and humane people. —I came from the white-collar class and it was difficult to erase the dangerous tendencies—the impulse to "rise" and respect "nice people"—of this class. These tendencies I have wrung out of my spiritual constitution with a great deal of success, I am proud to say. —Beyond these basic influences, I think of my writing as the expression of my own development as an individual.

How would you describe the political tendency of American

writing as a whole since 1930? How do you feel about it yourself? Are you sympathetic to the current tendency towards what may be called "literary nationalism"—a renewed emphasis, largely uncritical, on the specifically "American elements in our culture?

The political tendency of American writing since 1930 is, I believe, more symptomatic of a spiritual *malaise* than is generally supposed. Granted that the economic crisis became grave; it is nevertheless peculiar and highly symptomatic that intellectuals having discovered that "freedom" is not enough, and does not automatically lead to depth of insight and peace of mind, threw over *every scrap of their former enthusiasms,* as though there were something sinful in them. The economic crisis occurred when that generation of young people was entering the thirties; and, instead of fighting out the personal ills attendant upon the transition from youth to middle age, they took refuge in closed systems of belief, and automatically (many of them) committed creative suicide. . . . "Literary nationalism" has valuable elements in it; it opened the eyes of writers, superficially at least, to conditions which had surrounded them from childhood, but which they had spent much effort "escaping." But when this nationalism took a fixed form (when it became more fashionable to examine the situation of the share-cropper, for example, than the situation of slum-dwellers in Chelsea, Massachusetts, or Newark, New Jersey) its value dwindled. And the closing of one foreign culture after another, to the critical and appreciative examination of students, is one deplorable result of thinking in purely political terms. Any purely chauvinistic enthusiasm is, of course, always ridiculous.

This is the place, perhaps, to state my belief that the true sincerity and compassion which humane detachment alone can give, are necessary before the writer can pass judgment upon the ills of his time. To sink oneself into a party is fatal, no matter how noble the tenets of that party may be. For all tenets tend to harden into dogma, and all dogma breeds hatred and bigotry, and is therefore stultifying. And the condescension of the political party toward the artist is always clear, however well disguised. The artist will be "given" his freedom; as though it were not the artist who "gives" freedom to the world, and not only "gives" it, but is the only person capable of enduring it, or of understanding what it costs. The artists who remain exemplars have often, it is true, become entangled in politics, but it is not their political work which we remember. Nonsense concerning the function of the arts has been tossed about for centuries. Art has been asked, again, as the wind changed, to be "romantic," "filled with sensibility," "classic," "useful," "uplifting" and whatnot. The true artist will instinctively reject "burning questions" and all "crude oppositions" which can cloud his vision or block his ability to deal with his world. All this has been fought through before now: . . . . Turgenev showed up the pretentions of the political critic Belinsky; Flaubert fought the battle against "usefulness" all his life; Yeats wrote the most superb anti-political poetry ever written. Flaubert wrote, in the midst of one bad political period: "Let us [as writers] remain the river and turn the mill."

Have you considered the question of your attitude towards

the possible entry of the United States into the next world war? What do you think the responsibilities of writers in general are when and if war comes?

In the event of another war, I plan to oppose it with every means in my power. The responsibilities of writers in general, I should think, lie in such active opposition.

An excerpt from *Journey around My Room*

What makes a writer? Is it the love of, and devotion to, the actual act of writing that makes a writer? I should say, from my own experience, No. Some of the most untalented people *adore* writing: some have elaborate set-ups for the ritual: enormous desks, boxes of various kinds of paper; paper clips; pencil-sharpeners; several sorts of pen; erasers, ink, and what-not. In the midst of all this they sit and write interminably. I suppose they *could* be called writers; but they should not be.

Is it intellectual power? Yes, I suppose so: of a kind. But it is sometimes the kind of intellect that is not fitted to pass examinations. It need not include, for example, the kind of photographic memory that produces a school career of straight A's. It is certainly not intellectual power functioning in an abstract way.

A writer's power is based on what we have come to call *talent,* which the dictionary describes first off as "a special natural ability or aptitude." Later on in this definition, talent is described as a *gift.* It is as a gift that I prefer to think of it. The ancients personified the giver of the gift as the Muse—or the Muses: the Daughters of Memory. The French use the word *souffle* figuratively for what passes between the Muse and the artist or writer—*le souffle du génie*—the breath of inspiration; and any writer worth his salt has felt this breath. It comes and goes; it cannot be forced and it can very rarely be summoned up by the conscious will. . . .

Talent and technique: the basic needs of a writer. For, as the talent, the gift, grows, it begins to absorb the other more usually human attributes. It draws intuition, intellect, curiosity, observation to itself; and it begins to absorb emotion as well. For a writer's power is based not upon his intellect so much as upon his intuition and his emotions. All art, in spite of the struggles of some critics to prove otherwise, is based on emotion and projects emotion.

Louise Bogan, in Journey around My Room: The Autobiography of Louise Bogan, A Mosaic, *Viking, 1980.*

Robert E. Spiller   (review date March 1953)

SOURCE: A review of *Achievement in American Poetry, 1900-1950,* in *American Literature,* Vol. XXV, No. 1, March, 1953, pp. 117-18.

[*Spiller was an American educator, editor, and critic whose works included* Four Makers of the American Mind: Emerson, Thoreau, Whitman, and Melville *(1976). In the review below, he provides a mixed assessment of* Achievement in American Poetry.]

This brief survey of twentieth-century poetry in America [*Achievement in American Poetry, 1900-1950*] is one of six books which together attempt to review and evaluate American literature by types during the first half of the century. This book differs from some of the others in that Miss Bogan is herself a poet and critic of note rather than an academic scholar, and her book is a personal essay rather than a work of historical objectivity. It also differs in that the author devotes a substantial number of her few pages to French, Irish, Spanish, and British poets who have been influential in America at a sacrifice of careful analysis of the work of poets who have been native and resident in this country. The result is an essay on modern poetry rather than on American poetry, in which Rilke receives almost as much attention as Frost, Auden rather more than either of them, and the team of Pound and Eliot approximately as much as all other individual American poets put together. The book therefore cannot be taken seriously as a history of twentieth-century American poetry.

It can, however, be taken seriously as an essay written to a well-defined and rather generally accepted thesis: that T. S. Eliot discovered an aesthetic which successfully resolved the confusions of modern industrial man and made his experience once more available to poetic insight. Pound, according to this view, prepared the way for the master by his ubiquitous experimentation and protest; and Wallace Stevens, W. C. Williams, and Marianne Moore learned enough of the new way to write distinguished if not great poetry. Other poets like Frost, Sandburg, Hart Crane, and younger poets like Karl Shapiro are measured according to their relative distances from the central light. In Eliot, the new freedoms become the new discipline of interpretation. His own achievement in *The Waste Land* and *Four Quartets* adequately meets the requirements of his critical theory and provides fixed poles of reference for all lines of poetic development in the period.

This statement is something of an oversimplification of what is itself a vast oversimplification of the facts. But it is the essential gospel of an increasingly articulate group of contemporary poets and critics of poetry. In attempting to give it historical validity, Miss Bogan has indulged in many pages of generalizations about cultural facts and movements and parallel developments in other arts and in the arts of other countries. Most of these have at least some of their roots in facts, but they are offered so generously that they can be defended neither logically nor chronologically. Her method can be accepted only if her book is taken as a provocative essay by a sensitive and exciting imagination. Keen insights, stimulated rather than supported by wide and eclectic reading, have produced a book which should open its subject up to further study and perhaps to sounder historical analysis.

Richard Eberhart (review date 30 May 1954)

SOURCE: "Common Charms from Deep Sources," in *The New York Times Book Review,* May 30, 1954, p. 6.

[*Eberhart was an American poet, playwright, and educator. In the following review of* Collected Poems, 1923-53, *he praises the depth and forceful emotion of Bogan's work.*]

Louise Bogan's poems adhere to the center of English with a dark lyrical force. What she has to say is important. How she says it is pleasing. She is a compulsive poet first, a stylist second. When compulsion and style meet we have a strong, inimitable Bogan poem.

There is relatively little technical innovation in her poems. She writes mainly in traditional verse forms, handled with adroitness and economy. The originality is in the forceful emotion and how this becomes caught in elegant tensions of perfected forms. She has delved in antique mysteries and brought up universal charms from deep sources, from a knowledge of suffering and from full understanding of the lot of man.

Some of her short lyrics have been known for a long time. To these she adds an arsenal of profound and beautiful poems: [*Collected Poems, 1923-53*]. Her struggle is to throw off the nonessential, to confront naked realities at their source. Her poems are rich in passionate realizations, expressing in turn irony, bitterness, love and joy.

Her attitudes come down to a deep sincerity, the result of her strongly searching quality. A profundity of psychological knowledge works in the poems. One feels that truths of life, death and love have been confronted and uncompromising answers given.

Miss Bogan writes portrait poems like **"The Romantic"** and satirical poems like **"At a Party."** There is a small body of sententia, **"To an Artist to Take Heart."** She has a group of story or parable poems, such as **"The Crossed Apple," "Medusa," "Cartography"** and **"Evening in the Sanitarium."** I made a list of what I call her universal poems. This was quite long, including **"My Voice Not Being Proud," "The Alchemist," "Men Loved Wholly Beyond Wisdom," "Memory"** and **"Cassandra."**

This is a rich vein. I also made a list I called pure lyrics, a long list including **"Song for a Slight Voice," "I Saw Eternity," "Old Countryside," "Exhortation," "Man Alone," "To My Brother," "Spirit's Song," "Heard by a Girl"** and **"The Dream."** Her finest work is also in this vein.

Miss Bogan, who reviews poetry for *The New Yorker,* has year to year devoted careful thought to other poets, presenting their work in review with precise commentaries. She has developed these to a fine point of critical interest and sagacity. One had the notion that she wrote sparingly herself. This book is most welcome in giving the reader for the first time the full dimension of her poetic talent. The feeling is of somber strength, of a strong nature controlling powerful emotions by highly conscious art. There is marked skill in her restraint. Her best poems read as if time would not be likely to break them down.

There are many poems one would like to quote. Here is the last part of one, **"Sub Contra."**

> Let there sound from music's
> root
> One note rage can understand,

A fine noise of riven things.
Build there some thick chord
  of wonder;
Then, for every passion's
  sake,
Beat upon it till it break.

Perhaps that will indicate Miss Bogan's depth.

Jean Starr Untermeyer   (review date 24 December 1955)

SOURCE: "A Seasoning of Wit," in *The Saturday Review,* Vol. XXXVIII, No. 52, December 24, 1955, p. 24.

[*Untermeyer was an American poet. In the review below, she lauds* Selected Criticism.]

When one has read through Louise Bogan's **Selected Criticism,** seventy essays written over a period of twenty-five years and ranging through the whole of the contemporary literary terrain, with an occasional salute to the past (as in the case of Goethe's 200th birthday celebration), one feels this author possessed not so much of a point of view as a point of vantage—at the living center of the culture she has inherited and cherished and to which she has contributed. Secure, here, she has exposed her own sensibility to the sensibility of each personality under consideration, and this juxtaposition must have yielded rewards to Miss Bogan as it does to her readers.

Throughout—but especially with the major figures—one feels that the urge of the female Eros toward relatedness has not been hampered, and therefore the reading which preceded these writings comes through as a shared experience and not as a professional chore. Miss Bogan is a mistress of concision and the salience she can pack into a page and a half speaks for discipline as well as taste. One editorial device is as praiseworthy as it is practical: this is the device of grouping critiques of one author, written at different periods, into what amounts to a condensed and multifaceted summation of his or her chief qualities. Would this device had been used consistently instead of only occasionally. As it is, the collected papers on Eliot, Hopkins, Rilke, James, and Edith Sitwell, to name a few, are excellent, all the more for the moral as well as the technical standpoint implied.

The analogies to painting and particularly to music are apt and enriching. How right Miss Bogan is about the hazards of translation and the interpretative role that the musical settings by Schubert and Hugo Wolf play in respect to Goethe's poems. While this reviewer does not see eye to eye with Miss Bogan at all points—for instance, the relative importance of Robert Frost and R. M. Rilke, whom Miss Bogan docs not, however, compare—there is assent in the main to the judgments here so sensitively set forth.

Of Miss Bogan's wit it has been spoken; I would liken it less to a sword thrust (not an endearing feminine exercise) but rather to a seasoning. Reversing the common saying: she has taken it in and she can dish it out. The flavor is sweet and pungent.

Paul Ramsey   (essay date Summer 1970)

SOURCE: "Louise Bogan," in *The Iowa Review,* Vol. 1, No. 3, Summer, 1970, pp. 116-24.

[*Ramsey is an American educator, poet, critic, and novelist. In the following essay, he lauds Bogan's achievements as a lyric poet, stating "to say that some of her lyrics will last as long as English is spoken is to say too little."*]

Louise Bogan is a great lyric poet.

Greatness in poetry is hard to discuss, especially in the lyric. It is comparatively easy to show that Bogan is a very good poet: powerful in feeling, surprising and chaste in diction, strong in structure, masterly in imagery and rhythm, important in themes; but greatness in the lyric is impact and profundity and so simple as almost to defy scrutiny. The thing happens; the note is struck; in Bogan's own language the "terrible . . . / Music in the granite hill" sounds, and there we are, where her poems arrive time and again.

Lyrics are to be judged by depth and perfecting, not range, yet the reach of her work is more than its slightness in quantity might suggest. She writes mostly on the traditional lyric subjects, themselves comprising no small range, of love, time, passion, grief, nature, death, music, stoicism, limitation, art (not overmuch), memory, dreams. She also has done some very fine light verse with its own special quartz wryness, and manages to have something to say of psychiatrists, malevolent cocktail parties, Jonathan Swift, St. Christopher.

It is the saint who is most the stranger. He is tough and able (arrived from a fresco), an infrequent sort of visitor to her poems. Religion is almost wholly lacking in her work, except in hints, including the brilliant but puzzling hints of the near light verse of **"I Saw Eternity,"** and the spirits who do appear (**"Spirit's Song," "The Daemon"**) are dark ones. Perhaps the lack is an ingredient in the grief which persistently and profoundly underdwells her poems.

Her unique talent is ending poems. I know no other poet who ends so many poems so well. Her endings startle and compose, in most of the poems I discuss, and in at least these others: **"Betrothed," "Come Break with Time," "The Frightened Man," "Kept," "Late," "The Romantic," "To Be Sung on the Water,"** and **"Winter Swan."**

Her rhythms are brilliant, unique, and work in a variety of kinds: the short-line free verse of **"The Dragonfly";** the free verse, varied in line length, often near or in rising rhythm, of **"Summer Wish";** the mostly rising rhythm with five strong stresses of **"Didactic Piece,"** one of her best poems; the long-line free verse, quite different in the two poems, of **"Baroque Comment"** and **"After the Persian";** the special falling rhythms of **"Train Tune";** and her **"Poem in Prose,"** mostly, despite its title, in rising rhythm with some counterposing with falling rhythms.

These poems, all done well, show a very unusual range of metrical accomplishment, but it is no accident that her most powerful poems are work in which, in Theodore Roethke's words about these poems, the "ground beat of the great tradition can be heard." The great tradition in English verse since the late sixteenth century is accentual-syllabics, primarily iambics, and Roethke's words are well chosen: some of her best poems are accentual-syllabic, and some are near, near enough for her pulsing variations (especially the pressure of grouped, strong accents) to be heard as changes from the norm.

The tradition is heard in other ways than metrical, in diction, image, and thought, yet always heard afresh. She does not violate the dignity of the commonplace by self-indulgent attitudes or freakish privacies, yet has something distinct to say.

She can even write greatly about emotion, a rare achievement, as in the superb **"Men Loved Wholly Beyond Wisdom"**:

> Men loved wholly beyond wisdom
> Have the staff without the banner.
> Like a fire in a dry thicket
> Rising within women's eyes
> Is the love men must return.
> Heart, so subtle now, and trembling,
> What a marvel to be wise,
> To love never in this manner!
> To be quiet in the fern
> Like a thing gone dead and still,
> Listening to the prisoned cricket
> Shake its terrible, dissembling
> Music in the granite hill.

The poem says that passion is destructive and frustration terrible and fearful. These are known truths, yet only in Shakespeare's sonnets known with fiercer precision than here. The precision is reached by the images and the rhythms. The visions and tensions tell us what is felt; what is felt is the subject of the poem. Thus the poem is new knowledge of a very important kind. Of the images the staff without the banner is just and potent, requiring a moment's reflection. The other images have an immediately seen propriety yet lead to far reaches of feeling: fire, dry thickets, fern, prison, granite.

The poem is, in logical shape, a dilemma. A disjunction is offered, this or that, each alternative leading to the tragic. The poem does not say or imply whether other alternatives exist, but surely means—and says in its profound sense of closure, of completeness—there tragedy exists in any resolution of human sexuality, a truth of great moral importance.

Metrically the poem is magnificent, as are several of her poems. It is the one poem I shall discuss in some metrical detail. The principles involved apply to other poems of hers which are near traditional norms. This poem stays within hearing distance of the accentual-syllabic and turns to iambics in the last verse. The variations are more than would occur in more traditional meters but still are heard as variations. To move further from those expectancies, as much modern near-iambic free verse does, is to lose strength, the strength of vibrancy across the norm. The pattern of the poem is rising trimeter, and the following verses scan traditionally: vv. 2, 3, 4, 5, 7, 9, 10, 13. The first line scans as trochee trochee iamb trochee, but the effect is not of a falling line, because of the comparative

strength of "loved" and because an iambic substitution breaks a trochaic pattern much more than a trochaic substitution breaks an iambic pattern. Shifting back and forth from rising to falling rhythm, and grouping strong stresses together often in unusual ways, are the two means by which she most frequently varies from the standard procedures of accentual-syllabic. The bacchiac (light followed by two strongs), a most unusual foot in English verse, occurs often enough in her poetry to be a singular feature. Several times in her poems the bacchiac is correct in the scansion, and the grouping more often occurs when some other scansion would apply. It occurs in verse eight, of which the best scansion is bacchiac iamb iamb feminine ending (others, acceptable foot by foot, would violate the trimeter pattern).

The sixth line scans as trochees, with iambic movement between the commas; the next to last verse scans as straight trochees, with rocking rhythm after the comma. The last verse begins falling but turns back to resolving iambs; its shape, iambic with trochee in the first place, is traditional. The struggle against the norm subsides; what is sounded, sounds.

Such rhythms are empowered by a control that subtilizes intense feeling, by passion that extends and renews form, and bear a real analogy to the subject of the poem; the contrast of, the struggle between, restraint and passion. The subject appears directly or indirectly in a number of her poems. **"Ad Castitatem"** deals directly with the theme. It is a good poem, well structured (parallel invocations with nice distinctions and some narrative progress) and beautiful in imagery, especially in the unforgettable "a breeze of flame." The rhythms are delicate but comparatively lax, mixing short-line free verse and iambics without achieving the intensities the kinds separately can have.

"The Alchemist" is about the passion of the mind in struggle with the passion of the flesh. The poem is in strict iambic tetrameter, except for some truncated lines, truncated iambic tetrameter being itself an important traditional measure; and once again the rhythmical changes are intense, perhaps too intensely mimetic in "ceased its sudden thresh." The poem is about the failure of the will to govern passion, yet displays, in opposition to that theme, will governing passion to a single majestic continued poetic metaphor which is the poem. Most poems—they are legion nowadays—about the impossibility of the control or understanding of our experience are, with more consistency than Bogan's poem displays, written in lax and disordered styles and rhythms, but are for the same reason much inferior to Bogan's poems.

The view of the poem is stoic, anti-rational, pessimistic, and at least approaches physicalism. If "flesh" is not the sole reality, it is the controlling one, and the mind submits. Since I believe that all four of these views have something seriously wrong with them, my admiration needs explaining. It will not do to separate aesthetics and belief, since one responds to, is moved by, the attitudes expressed in and through the forms, nor will it (simply) do to appeal to "imaginative patterns of experience" or the like as against belief, since, for one thing, some imaginative patterns of experience are more moving and more in accord with reality than others, that is, imaginative patterns themselves can be judged as better and worse. For a second thing, to insist that we are moved in poems by imaginative patterns of experience under or across beliefs is to imply that such patterns are more valid than the beliefs and that to be consistent one should reject the beliefs. Tolerance becomes a monism, and there are logical problems in belief which neither politeness nor rhetoric can dissolve.

What validates the poem is its truth, partial but relevant, and deeply seen. Passion is powerful; not all can be controlled; reasonings fail; experience can be grim and must be met honestly. That is not all there is to say; but there is that much to say, as this poem and other of her poems beautifully show.

Nor is she here offering, or necessarily exemplifying, a general truth. The alchemist in the poem is one (one individual) who seeks a passion of the mind and finds unmysterious flesh. Others may successfully go beyond the submission to passion, for instance the speaker in **"Knowledge,"** who knows the limits of passion and its treasures, seeks to learn beyond passion and finds in the poem's success an experience which goes beyond the self.

"Knowledge" is over-structured, each verse paralleling the corresponding verse in the other stanza, but the parallelism does strengthen the impact of the last two verses "Trees make a long shadow / And a light sound." In these verses the richness of quantity and the curious grouping of accent (the simplest scansion of the next-to-last verse is trochee bacchiac feminine ending) abet the creation of the physical, literal, perfected ending which is the knowledge the poem speaks of and seeks.

"Henceforth, From the Mind" turns from the perception of nature to the strangeness of the mind's reflection of the world. It is one of her best known poems, and remains one of my favorites despite the poor second stanza. Poor writing is very rare in Bogan's work; in fact she is one of the most consistent poets in this respect since Campion and Herrick; but the second stanza of the poem is crudely written and has a bad confusion caused by syntax. In "joy you thought" the joy from the tongue is in meaning other than the powerful joy of youth—the difference is the point of the stanza—but the syntax identifies them, and the confusion damages the comparison. Shakespeare at times says more in his syntactical thickets than simple syntax could obtain; and in Bogan's **"Didactic Piece"** the syntax of the first stanza, especially of the last verse in it, is dislocated or else very clumsy, yet does not for me damage the emotional force of the passage. Here the syntax does harm, because Bogan says something less and more confused than she meant. The last three verses of the stanza are heavy-handed clichés, with some overstressed alliteration.

The first stanza, however, is well written and of high generalizing power, and the last two stanzas are one of the most perfectly modulated analogies in English poetry. The image is not phenomenological, though it could have been pushed that way easily enough, since what one hears in a shell is one's blood, not the sea; but the poem has no hint of that. The mind's view of experience is strange, distant, and modified by emotion and memory, but the line to real-

ity is still there; the echo is of truth. What is true is truly loved, even at a distance.

Love moves in grief and dreams, deeply, darkly, in many of her poems; her themes mix there. "I said out of sleeping," says **"Second Song,"** as less explicitly say her poems often. What comes from or descends to sleeping is lucid and other. **"Second Song"** is a delicate farewell to passion whose delicacy is crossed by the "Black salt, black provender." The phrase may be vaginal, or anal, or for all I know or can prove neither; but to say so is not to explain the force of the phrase, since (presumably) many phrases share such sources; the power of the phrase remains literally incalculable. Its force in the poem comes in some part from its unexpectedness in context, as though she were applying her own rule in **"Sub Contra"** that notes should be "delicate and involute" but "Let there sound from music's root / One note rage can understand."

She asks of wine in **"To Wine."** to offer "All that is worth / Grief. Give that beat again." Grief is in the strength of her dreams. Dreams open on reality that the day does not reckon, reality of the mind and, as she hints once in a while, perhaps beyond. In her criticism she is sometimes for the untrammeled in art or sexuality, celebrating modernism for its freeing of the unconscious; but in her verse she never loses touch with mind's and form's lucidities even when sounding the murmurous kingdom of the undernotes. A touch of severe conscience, a passion for truth without pretension, a vested memory (I like to think) of the rockscape of her native Maine, keep her to a center where extremes meet and irradiate each other.

"Come, Sleep . . ." (spaced periods hers) is about dreaming. It describes, in magnificently fresh and concise phrases, bee, ant, whale, palm, flower, grass; asks whether they dream; replies:

> Surely, whispers in the glassy corridor
> Never trouble their dream.
> Never, for them, the dark turreted house reflects
>   itself
> In the depthless stream.

The stream is of the mind's depth and it may be deeper. Since the stream is depth-less, not to be measured, we cannot say how far it goes in or beyond the mind. The shades of voice are haunted utterance, reflective of their meaning; yet the house of the poem is well built.

Two of her best known poems, **"The Dream"** and **"The Sleeping Fury,"** are imagined accounts of dreams, and **"Medusa"** is a retold myth, very like a dream. **"The Dream"** and **"The Sleeping Fury,"** though very well done, are less successful and less dreamlike for me than other poems in which dreams flash in or cross. Perhaps the clarity of narrative development, the conscious visibility of Freudian meanings, or the not quite persuasively earned reversals get in those poems' way, or in mine.

"Medusa" perfects its motion in stillness, becoming image and example of her lyrics. Good lyrics are active objects, Bogan's especially so, steadier in shape and livelier in motion than most. She, like Medusa, fixes motion; unlike Medusa, she does not stop motion. If one fixes motion so that it stops, one has not fixed *motion;* one has usurped its place. Zeno's arrow does not fly. **"Medusa,"** which is about the startlingness of stopped motion, is itself active and changeless, each note struck, and heard. The tipped bell does make its sound.

What the poem is about, beyond the legend, is not made clear. The legend is retold, not as allegory, although it sounds allegorical, but as private experience. One may apply analogies, to death, eternity, time, the past, the paralysis of fear, a moment of trance, but such are analogies, not given meanings, and the poem provides no bridge to any of them. Analogies are subclasses of a larger class; and subclasses are not each other's meanings, except when intentionally made so by signals. Nor are the poem's psychic sources its meaning in the way that psychic sources are part of the meaning within **"The Dream"** and **"The Sleeping Fury."** Sources and analogies help to empower the poem; but the poem does not say them. It happens; and it stops.

"Old Countryside" is of the most etched yet suggestive lyrics in the language. Its sensuous description is firm as eye can hold; what is unsaid, painfully unheard, is the silence. The impression of clarity is so final that it is startling to find surface difficulties which make the obscure silence even stranger.

The "we" is unidentified, perhaps generic: it could refer to friends, lovers, brother and sister. The time sequence is elusive. "All has come to proof" since the day remembered of the attic in the country house on a stormy day. The third stanza refers to a time between the time of the memory in stanzas one and two and the present time; since the present is "long since" that nearer time, the first time must be long long since. "Far back" from the time of the third stanza occurs the fourth stanza. The "far back" suggests space, as though the last severe images were in a place that endured "in the stillest of the year" and the stillness stops time and space, in vision. Chronologically the fourth stanza, which has snow, occurs at least one winter before the "winter of dry leaves" and could be much earlier. One cannot tell the relation between the time of the fourth and first stanzas, except that the first stanza seems earlier. It does not matter. Memory makes time past irremediably far and contemporary, as does the poem.

One detail puzzles, either an odd ellipsis or a shift to the godlike, the *we* pulling down oak leaves in a winter of dry leaves, as though they were the agents of the change. The detail in general is simply the finest I know in a lyric poem, total in the clarity of what is seen and in the integrity of what is felt: "The summer thunder, like a wooden bell, / Rang in the storm . . . ," the "mirror cast the cloudy day along / The attic floor . . . ," ". . . we heard the cock / Shout its unplaceable cry, the axe's sound / Delay a moment after the axe's stroke," and then the perfection of love and clear pain of the last stanza:

> Far back, we saw, in the stillest of the year,
> The scrawled vine shudder, and the rose-branch
>   show
> Red to the thorns, and, sharp as sight can bear,
> The thin hound's body arched against the snow.

The rhythms are uniquely hers; the meter is conventional

without variation. The poem is in the form called "the heroic quatrain." Except for four anapests, anapestic substitution being normal in much nineteenth- and twentieth-century iambics, and the graceful trimeter in stanza two, no variation occurs that one could not find in Dryden's heroic quatrains. The quatrain is traditionally used for narrative, generalizing, and explicit meditation (Dryden's *Annus Mirabilis* and Gray's *Elegy Written in a Country Churchyard*); here it is used for particularizing, and implicit meditation. Its "narration" is the narrating and relating of memories. Like much in Gray and Dryden, it focuses motion and stillness in quietly echoing tones; and it achieves a sharpness of definition unique in the examples I know of the form, either historical or modern.

In **"Song for the Last Act,"** perhaps her greatest poem and certainly the one I find most moving, her powerfully controlled energies throb with a different resonance. Of all her poems it has the most visible frame (a variation of the refrain verse is repeated at both the beginning and end of each of the three stanzas) and the most radical wildness of meaning and image.

> Now that I have your face by heart, I look
> Less at its features than its darkening frame
> Where quince and melon, yellow as young
>   flame,
> Lie with quilled dahlias and the shepherd's
>   crook.
> Beyond, a garden. There, in insolent ease
> The lead and marble figures watch the show
> Of yet another summer loath to go
> Although the scythes hang in the apple trees.
>
> Now that I have your face by heart, I look.
>
> Now that I have your voice by heart, I read
> In the black chords upon a dulling page
> Music that is not meant for music's cage,
> Whose emblems mix with words that shake and
>   bleed.
> The staves are shuttled over with a stark
> Unprinted silence. In a double dream
> I must spell out the storm, the running stream.
> The beat's too swift. The notes shift in the dark.
>
> Now that I have your voice by heart, I read.
>
> Now that I have your heart by heart, I see
> The wharves with their great ships and archi-
>   traves;
> The rigging and the cargo and the slaves
> On a strange beach under a broken sky.
> O not departure, but a voyage done!
> The bales stand on the stone; the anchor weeps
> Its red rust downward, and the long vine creeps
> Beside the salt herb, in the lengthening sun.
>
> Now that I have your heart by heart, I see.

The first stanza is mellow description with seemingly firm shapes, yet the firmness is in a way only a seeming. Art and nature share the passage, and one cannot exactly visualize the relation of parts. A face is a face in a portrait whose frame is darkened by time and itself painted with flowers, by a window which gives on an actual garden; *or* the face is framed by a garden behind which is another garden. Neither statement quite reaches, and the small sur-rationality prepares for the second stanza.

The metaphor in the opening of the first stanza is general, "Now that I have your face by heart, I look," varied to the musical and self-inconsistent in the second stanza: "Now that I have your voice by heart, I read (the music)." To have music by heart is precisely not to read it. The music in the second stanza breaks loose beyond itself and statable meaning and returns, storming the silence of its passion. To paraphrase one needs to repeat the metaphors: the music read on the page is not for music's cage; the emblems mix with words, shake and bleed; the staves are shuttled over with silence. The general meaning, however, is in its tending clear: understanding the person addressed is like knowing musical notes and what in music reaches through and beyond the notes into love and pain and passion. To understand is to relate the formulable knowledge and the mystery, as the stanza does, in subject and feeling. The "double dream" includes the music and the silence. (The shift to the image of the stream was probably influenced by two lines from "Secret Treasure" from Sara Teasdale's book *Strange Victory,* a book praised by Bogan in *Achievement in Modern Poetry.* The lines are "Fear not that my music seems / Like water locked in winter streams." The first stanza, even more certainly, echoes some details from "In a Darkening Garden" in the same book.)

In the third and last stanza, the poem moves away from the shifting of meaning to an abundantly clear and plangent image of a port, the sea's edge as an image of oncoming death. It is a traditional image, realized with greatness, with as much beauty and regret as the first stanza's, as much strangeness of pain as the second stanza's, and as much control of the exact measure of sound touched in image on shaded meaning and feeling as that of any poem in our heritage:

> . . . the anchor weeps
> Its red rust downward, and the long vine creeps
> Beside the salt herb, in the lengthening sun.
>
> Now that I have your heart by heart, I see.

It is a great poem, and substantial to my argument. For the case for poetic greatness is always, finally, the poems. To say that some of her lyrics will last as long as English is spoken is to say too little. For since value inheres in eternity, the worth of her poems is not finally to be measured by the length of enduring. To have written **"Song for the Last Act," "Old Countryside," "Men Loved Wholly beyond Wisdom," "Didactic Piece," "Medusa," "Henceforth, from the Mind," "The Alchemist," "Second Song," "Night,"** and some dozens of other poems of very nearly comparable excellence is to have wrought one of the high achievements of the human spirit, and to deserve our celebration and our love.

Thomas Lask   (review date 31 October 1970)

SOURCE: "The Poet as Critical Reader," in *The New York Times,* October 31, 1970, p. 27.

[*In the review below, Lask praises* A Poet's Alphabet, *stating that "for a book of criticism, [Bogan's] volume is unusual in the amount of sheer reading pleasure it provides."*]

Louise Bogan's critical pieces [in *A Poet's Alphabet*] come to us almost as from another age. Not that her subjects are dated. The list of poets reviewed could not be more contemporary. But her tone of civilized inquiry, her judgment that was both detached and involved, the complete absence of trivia and small talk and her desire only to engage the work at hand make her appear a sport in these days of ego-bruising and assertive journalism. She is kind but sharp eyed, soft spoken but penetrating, sympathetic but not fooled. Though her tastes and values are stamped on every page, she never intrudes in person—remarkable in a book of this length. I cannot imagine any poet no matter how severely handled (Peter Viereck for example), grumbling at her criticism, for she is so obviously concerned with the art and craft of the maker.

As a critic, Miss Bogan, who died this year, took a median position between the New Criticism at one end and sociological (or Marxian) criticism at the other. She refused to identify the poet with the historical processes of his age, though she did admit that such narrow readings had their validity. On the other hand, she was not willing to strip the work down to its formal elements only, as if the poet was a disembodied muse living in no fixed time or place and without those idiosyncrasies that made him what he was and no other. There is also little poking around in myth or in depth psychology.

But she was minutely aware of the poet's relation to the poetic currents of his time: what he had learned from others, how much he was alike, how he differed from them. She was automatically conscious of the technical finish of the poetry she was reading. Above all she was attuned to the emotional climate in which the poet wrote and the impact he made on the reader. A distinguished poet herself, she was rare in that she participated in the esthetic experience from the other end as a reader, a perceiver. Not so profound perhaps as other critics, she was most useful to that man, who, not without resources of his own, still needed some indication as to where to begin.

Her manner was so quiet, her style so unemphatic that they sometimes obscured the force of her judgments, I doubt whether a more pithy statement of Auden's spiritual development (up to that time) could have been framed than the one she penned in 1944. In a brief piece written in 1957, she pointed out how so much experimental writing 'becomes formula ridden and a victim of its own conventions. A book could be written (and perhaps already has) on her obiter dictum that Yeats and Pound achieved modernity but that Eliot was modern from the start. And in dealing with the French poet Paul Eluard, who was esthetically a surrealist and politically a communist, she touched the exposed nerve of a whole generation of writers who embraced a dogma that was completely inimical to their poetic faith.

She could be wrong and she could be disappointing in her pieces, which is to say that she was mortal. An exquisite and scrupulous craftsman with a leaning to order, she had a natural tendency to respond to formal workmanship, and though she was always fair, she was not always cordial to those who liked to call William Carlos Williams and Charles Olson master. Thus I think she missed the boat in evaluating Donald Allen's significant anthology *The New American Poetry, 1945-1960,* which was at once a survey of the situation in poetry and a rallying cry to the young.

Offended by the raucous element in the book and by a quality that was raw and unfinished, she felt that the "art of language" could easily disappear under the onslaughts of the untutored, and therefore failed to understand the great appeal such poetry had for many youngsters. Since she herself had no trouble in recognizing what was quick and alive in formal writing, she could not understand the distaste of those who saw academic verse as a wasteland of dried-out forms and brittle language.

And because in writing for magazines, her reviews had to be short, they sometimes raised expectations she did not fulfill. Her succinct piece on John Berryman's *77 Dream Songs* had the poet all set up for a devastating knockout punch, when lo! the review ended.

If this notice has concentrated on her poetry reviews, it is due in part to personal preference, in part to the amount of space they occupy in the book. However, she brought the same qualities of knowledge and insight to her reviews of fiction and criticism. The shortcomings and strengths of R. P. Blackmur, for example, are summed up precisely and accurately in the smallest possible space. Her longer pieces on Dorothy Richardson and Flaubert's *L'Education sentimentale* must have restored those books and authors to a new generation. Her comments on French writing throughout shows her deep understanding of that nation's culture.

For a book of criticism, her volume is unusual in the amount of sheer reading pleasure it provides.

Harry Morris   (review date Autumn 1972)

SOURCE: A review of *A Poet's Alphabet,* in *The Sewanee Review,* Vol. LXXX, No. 4, Autumn, 1972, pp. 627-29.

[*In the following positive review of* A Poet's Alphabet, *Morris states that in this critical work Bogan "finds the strengths of her writers and emphasizes these in deft, bright, compact, and perceptive analyses."*]

Louise Bogan is a poet who generates affectionate approval. Somewhat the same as for Caroline Gordon among the novelists, the feeling pervades that Miss Bogan never received the recognition due her work; and those who write about her verse go extra weight to correct the imbalance. I think especially of Paul Ramsey's loving essay which begins, "Louise Bogan is a great lyric poet," and ends, "To say that some of her lyrics will last as long as English is spoken is to say too little." On the face of it, Mr. Ramsey would seem to have gone too far, and I believe he has; but I am willing to make the same mistake about her reviews and criticism.

A Poet's Alphabet is a delight to read. The arrangement takes us from Auden to Yeats, from American Literature

to the Yale Series of Younger Poets. The dates of composition take us from 1923 to 1969, the year before Miss Bogan's death in February, 1970. The chief experience one undergoes in *A Poet's Alphabet* is admiration for Miss Bogan's generosity, which however is bestowed never at the expense of truth. Miss Bogan finds the strengths of her writers and emphasizes these in deft, bright, compact, and perceptive analyses. It is instructive to any critic or reviewer that Miss Bogan, in assessing the work of over 120 authors, approves (my count was casual) a round 100. Therefore it is easier to list the writers who come short. Max Eastman, Louis Untermeyer, John Berryman, Peter Viereck, Robinson Jeffers, Archibald MacLeish, Horace Gregory, Randall Jarrell, Karl Shapiro, Stephen Spender, Sandra Hochman, Edith Wharton, Katherine Hoskins, John Ashbery, and John Hollander come in for greater or lesser disapproval, although, in her kindness, Miss Bogan almost never is negative completely. Some of these censured are admired elsewhere in her reviews (often as translators).

The alphabetic arrangement of the book has its great advantage for the reader who prefers to use it as a guide to the poets of his interest; but for the reader who would learn something of Louise Bogan, it has its drawbacks. To submit to alphabet is to neglect chronology. We cannot follow Miss Bogan's changing tastes when essays under A are often those written in the 'forties,' fifties, and 'sixties, whereas her first piece (1923) does not appear until L. To get her next ten pieces in order disorders the alphabet as follows: SCPCAHEJOS.

It may be a mistake also (of the editors, not of Miss Bogan) that Miss Bogan's obituary is reprinted from the *New Yorker,* where we learn that the reviewer's first piece in that magazine appeared March 21, 1931, and her last December 28, 1968; for the reader will look in vain for a piece from either of those years. In general, the scholarship of the editors is casual. We wonder which pieces come from the *New Yorker* and which from other sources; nor does the acknowledgments page help, for it fails to account for several essays, most notably the last piece she wrote: the essay on Pablo Neruda (1969). Nevertheless, the book is handsomely printed and generally well-edited for a trade edition.

If we take the trouble to read through a second time, following the years rather than the alphabet, we can discover Miss Bogan's development well enough. Evidence of a certain conservatism is found frequently in the early materials: "the experimental side of literature must adjust itself to 'reality' and to the changes in the human situation. Without abolishing a continued 'openness' toward experiment, writers must not insist upon a stubborn avant-gardism when no real need for a further restless forward movement any longer exists" (1950). In her reviews of the 'fifties and 'sixties, Miss Bogan appears to have come to some terms with the experimentalists and vers librists, whom for a long time she held off: "Here, watching a cultivated sense of tradition through modern attitudes and techniques, we sense the possibility of a new reconciliation in modern verse, for so long filled with division and dissent" (1954). Yet her need of form dies hard. One of the longer essays in her book is a defense of formal poetry under the guise of espousing its delights: "formal art—art in which the great tradition is still alive and by which it functions—is as modern as this moment. . . . This is the formal art fragments of which we should not only as readers 'shore against our ruins,' but keep as a directing influence in whatever we manage to build—to create" (1953).

Of the very great writers, Miss Bogan calls Yeats (during his lifetime) "the greatest poet writing in English" and says of Eliot that "The *Collected Poems* are more than a work of poetic creation; they are a work of poetic regeneration" (1936). On Frost Miss Bogan gives balanced and honorable judgment of considerable perception, recognizing the poet as self-limited, but within those limits capable of a "masterful ordering of experience" when well into his old age, years in which so many poets decline. On Pound Miss Bogan arrived in 1955 where so many of us have wound up more recently: "The actual form of the *Cantos* . . . now seems slightly fossilized—worthy of note as origin and process but with no truly invigorating aspects."

Perhaps the service that Miss Bogan has done for letters during her life is discernible best in her constant approval of the significant literary movements on the continent and her vigorous support of translation as a means of making available, no matter how imperfectly, the thought of the influential cultures of France, Germany, Spain, and to a lesser extent of modern Greece and the Orient.

Katie Louchheim　(review date February 1974)

SOURCE: "A True Inheritor," in *The Atlantic Monthly,* Vol. 233, No. 2, February, 1974, pp. 90-2.

[*Louchheim was an American poet, nonfiction writer, and critic. In the following positive review of* What the Woman Lived, *she comments on Bogan's life and works.*]

In a letter dated 1939, Louise Bogan expands an argument about Boswell and Johnson into a few epithets on life: "Aloneness is peculiar-making, to some extent, but not any more so . . . than lots of Togetherness I've seen."

Miss Bogan's aloneness was never peculiar, and always deliberate. A good deal of her seclusion was spent in carrying out one of her own dicta: "The least we can do, is to give a phrase to the post."

In the more than four hundred letters collected and edited by Ruth Limmer in **What the Woman Lived,** Miss Bogan managed to give us a stylish, clear, and entertaining literary history of the fifty years from 1920 to 1970.

Besides her addiction to aloneness, Miss Bogan practiced public reticence. She used many disguises, the chief of which was wit. In response to her publisher's (John Hall Wheelock of Scribner's) request for biographical material, she wrote: "I have a job reviewing books of poetry for *The New Yorker* [a position she held for thirty-eight years], I won a Guggenheim in 1933. I am wild about music, and I read everything but books on Grover Cleveland and novels called *O Genteel Lady.*"

In a letter never mailed, she added irony: "My dislike of telling future research students anything about myself is intense and profound. If they know everything to begin with, how in hell can they go on eating up their tidy little fellowships researching?" Under the questionnaire's heading "Literary and social preferences," she wrote: "My social preferences range from truck and taxi drivers who make me laugh, locomotive engineers, when they are good-looking and flirtatious, delivery boys, and touching old people. . . ." She also lists a few dislikes: "dirty finger-nails . . . well-bred accents . . . the professional literati of all ages, other women poets (jealousy!), other men poets, English accents, Yale graduates and bad writing and bad writers."

The facts of the matter were that Louise Bogan's first book of poetry was published in 1923 and her first critical review, on D. H. Lawrence, came out in the same year. And except for a brief period when she worked as an assistant in the St. Mark's Place public library (Marianne Moore was a member of the staff), filed index cards at Columbia University (a job found for her by Margaret Mead), and clerked in Brentano's, she gave her life to creating and commenting upon literature. All told there were six books of poetry (the final collection, still in print, is called *The Blue Estuaries*), three books of criticism (the last, *A Poet's Alphabet,* appeared posthumously in 1970), four volumes of prose translations, an anthology of poetry for young people, even a bibliography of English belles lettres during World War II, which she compiled while she was consultant in poetry to the Library of Congress.

A sizable body of work, and all of it of the highest quality, but how does one celebrate poetry which does not create philosophic structures, does not shock or shriek, does not break new technical trails? Her poetry is simply *there.* Existing within the long line of the English lyric, it speaks to demonstrate that time and fashion do not alter ultimate human concerns.

She would not kick up her heels to the rhythms of the Roaring Twenties, nor would she later lead parades for or against economic injustice, fascism, democracy, racial inequalities. That is not what poetry is about. As she said time and again—and she was the most gracefully lucid, learned, and unprogrammatic critic of her generation—poetry is sound, is rhythm, is memorable language.

Miss Bogan's talent was formidable. Her poetry alone would have more than satisfied anyone else's need for creative expression. The letters, one must assume, were written for her own entertainment, as well as that of friends. Impetuous, never restrained or cautious, full of capricious and diverting images, plus exhilarating cerebral pyrotechnics, they make for first-class theater.

"Get all the *bear* into your work!" she advised author May Sarton. "Get all the bitterness, too. That's the place for it"—advice she practiced with a fine flourish. She was not given to hedging. Virginia Woolf is accused of having "a very inhuman side . . . Her feminism was bound up with her fears." Ellen Glasgow is described as "a lending-library set-up." The G. Am. public (Great American public: the letters are sprinkled with abbreviations) "likes pompous spinsters to tell them what life is really like." Jane Austen is "the only English novelist that a poet can respect. She's clean and onto it all and witty."

Henry James constantly reappears until by the end of the book we have read through everything he ever wrote, along with Miss B's perceptive comments. He is at once described as "superb . . . I am enchanted by the absolute sureness in method" and attacked as "both impotent and afraid." Of Archibald MacLeish she said: "He has real talent, without any doubt, but he has been too friendly with Conrad Aiken, T. S. Eliot, etc.; his ear is too good."

When Isherwood and Auden came to this country in 1940, she refused to meet them. Their politics bothered and their talents were not yet proven. By 1941, however, she wrote: "Auden is a swell person, complicatedness and all." In later years she liked to quote what Auden told her: "We should talk back to God; this is a kind of prayer." (When she died in 1970, Auden gave the eulogy at the American Academy of Arts and Letters.)

Miss Bogan could be tender. After an argument with a close friend, Rolfe Humphries (poet, classicist, and translator), she assuaged him: "At least you leave the most important part of me alone. We never quarrel about poetry, which after all . . . is a region of the mind; it just happens that it is the region wherein, at our best, we both live."

Besides her reticence, her delight in wounding wit, the pleasure she took in arguing, the notion that it was vulgar to sell herself, there was her very distinct Irish paranoia. The Irish, and she was very Irish, are "really forest dwellers," she wrote to Rufina McCarthy Helmer in 1937, "with all the forest-dweller's instincts, and . . . since, or when, the Irish forests disappeared, they all developed such a terrible neurosis, from being forced to be out in the open so much." In a letter to Edmund Wilson, she further elaborated the idea: "Good God, what a country this is! It's not a country, it's a neurosis. Never come here, when you are apt, or liable, to ideas of reference, or to other paranoid symptoms."

Miss Bogan's susceptibility to "ideas of reference" may have begun with "an extraordinary childhood and an unfortunate early marriage into which last state I had rushed to escape the first." Her second marriage, to Raymond Holden (minor poet and novelist), was a stormy one: "I was a demon of jealousy and a demon of fidelity too, morbid fidelity." Her struggles with recurrent depressions (several bouts in sanatoriums) led her to a philosophical conclusion: "No one is let be, we are all forced in some way. Only the truly miserable, the truly forlorn are not forced, they are left alone by a God who has forgotten them."

Miss Bogan was never forlorn, perhaps because she was severe with herself. In a letter to Rolfe Humphries she wrote: "We are all self-lovers to an almost complete degree. So—act only enough to get yourself a little something to eat, and a bed to sleep on, and a drink, and a bunch of flowers. Act only enough to get yourself a little bit of love."

Miss Bogan came upon love after her first bout of depres-

sion. To Harriet Monroe, founder and editor of *Poetry* magazine, she wrote: "I feel at once renewed and disinherited. Different people say different things. My doctor insists that I love; Robert Frost . . . recommends fear and hatred." She chose love. In a later letter to Edmund Wilson, she claimed to have been "made to bloom . . . by the enormous lovemaking of a cross between a Brandenburger and a Pomeranian, one Theodore Roethke. . . . He is very, very large and he writes very very small lyrics." Roethke was twenty-six and she was thirty-eight.

Their correspondence lasted more than thirty years. The letters illustrate vividly the enormous encouragement, advice, and help that Miss Bogan gave the struggling poet: "You will have to *look* at things until you don't know whether you are they or they are you." Roethke also suffered from recurrent depressions. She writes to him that loss of face is the worst thing that can happen to anyone: "I know, because I have lost mine, not once, but many times. And believe me, the only way to get it back is to put your back against the wall and fight for it. You can't brood or sulk or smash around in a drunken frenzy . . . if you smash yourself dead, they won't give a damn . . . it's the self that must do it. You Ted Roethke, for Ted Roethke. I Louise Bogan, for Louise Bogan."

Other love affairs are hinted at but in many of the letters she refers to her lifelong conviction that for her "work was the only panacea." In various forms, she rephrases this belief. To Morton Zabel, assistant editor of *Poetry* magazine, she wrote: "The one thing to remember is that intellectual curiosity and the life of the mind are man's hope."

The more than seventy letters to Zabel are full of carefully chosen details that illuminate the dailiness of place, people, and problems, as well as a record of the imaginative interchanges between two scholarly human beings. They are also a study of the tests and strengths of friendship— Miss B quarreled with Zabel when, rightfully, she suspected him of collecting her letters for possible posthumous use. In 1941 she wrote: "I think we ought to come right down to cases, and clear up a few matters, before either renewed friendship, or eternal silence. . . . I have finally come to realize that you are not treating the letters as a gay correspondence between friends, but as *a collection* . . . everything I write you is being put into a kind of coffin. . . . This realization must, of course, break my correspondence with you. . . . I'll write to people who think of me as a human being, and not as a museum piece."

What is important about Miss Bogan is all in the letters: her humanness, her intellectual powers, her depressions, her taste for the good life ("I do love tables, chairs, libraries, silk underwear, clean sheets, food cooked to order, paper and pencil and music"), her incorruptibility, her conspiratorial heritage. Her praise of Marianne Moore most nearly resembles a self-portrait: "A fine, firm, human and tough point of standing."

In the early sixties, she wrote to William Maxwell (a *New Yorker* editor): "The nearer one comes to *vanishing*, the stranger it seems." In a later letter, written from a sanatorium, she observed: "One evening, with a gibbous moon hanging over the city (such *visions* as we have!), like a piece of red cantaloupe, and automobiles showing red danger signals . . . I thought I had reached the edge of eternity, and *wept* and *wept.*"

She had mastered terror, climbed over mountains of difficulties, and come out with her laughter intact. Her laughter could be diabolic. In one of the last letters she speaks of her inability to get going on the *New Yorker* piece. "I have decided, however, to mention the fact . . . that Anne Sexton is the first woman in history to have written a hymn to her uterus."

This was the woman both admired and feared. The Bogan tone in the letters, as in the poetry, is unmistakable. She seduces the ear.

As Theodore Roethke said, "Bogan is one of the true inheritors . . . and the best work will stay in the language as long as the language survives."

One suspects that Miss Bogan would have scoffed at the title **What the Woman Lived.** What the Woman Lived Through would at least have been accurate and she might have preferred it.

William Maxwell   (review date 29 November 1980)

SOURCE: "A Life of Poetry and Suffering," in *The New Republic,* Vol. 183, No. 22, November 29, 1980, pp. 38-40.

[*Maxwell was an American novelist, short story writer, and editor. In the following review of* Journey around My Room, *a volume edited by Ruth Limmer, he calls Limmer's work "a labor of love" and comments on Bogan's life and career.*]

At two different periods in her life Louise Bogan kept a journal, most of which was published in the *New Yorker,* in the issue of January 30, 1980. Drawing on this, and on her letters, poems, stories, literary criticism, and conversation, Ruth Limmer has made a narrative mosaic that she calls the autobiography of Louise Bogan [*Journey Around My Room*]. Autobiography presupposes the writer in the driver's seat. It is a handling over, by the writer, of his or her life, and it stands or falls by its candor, which is felt in a personal way. If the handing over is done by someone else, then it is a different literary form—in this instance a species of anthologizing.

In her introduction Miss Limmer admits **Journey Around My Room** is not the autobiography Louise Bogan would have written had she chosen to.

> A stage manager, not the playwright, has decided on the scenes and acts and on how to arrange and light the script. These are not her choices of prose or poetry, not her sequences, not her chapter divisions. But the book *always* speaks in her voice and is true to her experience as she revealed it.

A better analogy would have been the dramatization of a novel; one recognizes the action and often stretches of dialogue, but the shaping hand is the dramatist's and the nature of the work is inevitably altered when it is lifted from the printed page and given to actors to speak.

Miss Bogan's poetry, her criticism, her journal, and the best of her very few short stories all have an identifying quality. They are formal, crystalline, without self-indulgence or self-pity, and well beyond the small, the merely personal. They have arrived at a kind of perfection, and I do not think time will separate them from it. Her journal appears to have been written not for publication but as a way of dealing with certain abiding emotional conflicts, which she approaches again and again and turns aside from just as she is about to clear the hurdle. It is not a failure: the thing she failed to say, the story she could not bring herself to tell, is somehow there in that tense preparation and turning aside at the last moment. It is an extremely moving document.

Miss Limmer's collage has been done with the utmost care, and is clearly a labor of love. It is made up almost entirely of wonderful writing not easily come by. Such as: "In their cage at evening, in the zoo, one hippopotamus, with his great low hanging ponderous face, nuzzled the side of another. What if tenderness should be lost everywhere else, and left only in these creatures?" And:

> As I remember my bewilderment, my judgment can do nothing even now to make things clear. The child has nothing to which it can compare the situation. And everything that then was strange is even stranger in retrospect. The sum has been added up wrong and this faulty conclusion has long ago been accepted and approved. There is nothing to be done about it now.

And "The dreadful thing about north rooms: not that there is no sunlight in them now, but that there has never been sun in them . . . like the minds of stupid people: that have been stupid from the beginning and will be stupid forever." And "Above these objects hangs a Japanese print, depicting Russian sailors afflicted by an angry ocean, searchlights, a burning ship, and a boatload of raging Japanese." It is enough to make an ordinary writer wring his hands.

The title of Miss Limmer's book is the title of Louise Bogan's most remarkable short story, which is in turn borrowed from the *"Voyage autour de ma chambre"* of Xavier de Maistre. The editor has broken up the story into six parts that are placed, in italics, at the beginning and end and elsewhere in the book. It may not occur to many readers to read the italicized paragraphs continuously, and so discover the masterpiece of story-telling they are confronted with. For that reason, I wish the story had not been broken up.

When the notes specify rearrangement I have been led, out of curiosity, to see what the rearrangements are. In themselves they are usually slight: the beginning of a sentence altered by two or three words for the sake of a transition; or a paragraph transposed or inserted into the middle of another paragraph, in a slightly different context. It is occasionally disconcerting to find that items follow one another sometimes with no white space or printer's symbol to warn the reader that the source has shifted. In two instances material from the journal is misdated. Passages are sometimes identified not by a phrase taken from the text, as is customary, but by the subject under consideration, with the result that identification becomes uncertain. And a note like "Except as noted, the remainder of this chapter, mostly written between 1932 and 1937, comes from *Antaeus, JOAP*" ["**Journal of a Poet,**" the title given to the selections from the journal that were published in the *New Yorker*], and the LB papers" is perhaps a bit slapdash. More serious than any of these things, however, is that the journal has been tightened up, made continually "relevant" to a theme that the editor is interested in presenting. The result is that the natural and always mysterious and, in the case of a poet, important association of ideas has been tampered with. For example, in the book the statement

> The poet represses the outright narrative of his life. He absorbs it, along with life itself. The repressed becomes the poem. Actually, I have written down my experiences in the closest detail. But the rough and vulgar facts are not there.

stands by itself with a printer's decoration separating it from the preceding material. In the journal it is part of an entry that begins "Terrible dreams!" and goes on to describe a morning of wind and rain, the tail end of a hurricane. And the paragraph in question is followed by a sentence from Chekhov: "And all things are forgiven and it would be strange not to forgive." It seems to me that there has been a loss, intellectually and emotionally.

A case for editing can always be made, but the simple truth is that you cannot rearrange any writer's work without in some way altering the effect, and if it is a writer of the first quality, is it yours to rearrange, morally speaking? On the other hand, would any publisher have been willing to publish, in the year 1980, a small volume of the fragmented and not very voluminous journal of a first-rate but never wildly popular poet? The answer to this question, I am afraid, is no.

In a chronology at the beginning of the book, and by means of entries here and there, some if not all of the rough and vulgar facts of Louise Bogan's life are made known. She was born in Livermore Falls, Maine, in 1897. Her father found it hard to make a living, and moved his family from one ugly decaying Massachusetts mill town to another. They lived sometimes in a house of their own, more often in shabby hotels and boardinghouses. It was a world teetering on the edge of nightmare. Of her mother she says,

> Secrecy was bound up in her nature. She could not go from one room to another without the intense purpose that must cover itself with stealth. She closed the door as though she had said goodbye to me and to truth and to the lamp she had cleaned that morning and to the table soon to be laid for supper. . . . When she stood in front of the mirror adjusting her veil, it could mean she was going to church or downtown, but it could also be that she was going to the city, to her other world; it could mean trouble.

After witnessing a violent scene between her mother and father that she was too young to understand, she was gathered up in her mother's arms and when she woke the next morning she and her mother and another woman were in a wooden summerhouse on a lawn in front of a house she had never seen before. Once her mother was gone for weeks and they had no idea where she was or with whom. "A terrible, unhappy, lost, spoiled, bad-tempered child. A tender, contrite woman, with, somewhere in her blood, the rake's recklessness, the baffled artist's despair" is her summing up of this central figure of her childhood. And again, speaking of her mother:

> I never truly feared her. Her tenderness was the other side of her terror. Perhaps, by this time, I had already become what I was for half my life: the semblance of a girl, in which some desires and illusions had been early assassinated: shot dead.

She was lucky in her schooling, and quick to educate herself. She began writing poetry in her early teens. After a year at Boston University she was offered a scholarship at Radcliffe and instead of taking it she married Curt Alexander, a corporal in the Army. He was, by her own description, a beautiful man and she was in love with him, but she also wanted to escape from her mother. When her husband was transferred to the Canal Zone she followed him, four months pregnant and so seasick when she arrived that she was taken off the boat on a stretcher. The unchanging tropical landscape struck her as hostile, and the marriage was a mistake. ("All we had in common was sex. Nothing to talk about. We played cards.") She left him twice, the second time permanently, and he died at 32. She supported herself and her infant daughter by workings as a clerk in Brentano's and then as an assistant in various branches of the New York Public Library. Marianne Moore was working in one of them, but shyness prevented the younger woman from introducing herself. In 1922 Harriet Monroe took five of her poems for *Poetry,* and she went abroad on her widow's pension, to study the piano in Vienna. Her first published criticism was a review of D. H. Lawrence's "Birds, Beasts, and Flowers" for *The New Republic,* two years later. That same year her first book of poems was published by Robert M. McBride and Company. She married the poet Raymond Holden in 1925, and in 1931 had her first breakdown. ("I refused to fall apart, so I had to be taken apart, like a watch.") In 1933 she got a Guggenheim fellowship and went abroad for several months. While she was gone, her husband had an affair, which she found out about and could not forgive. She continued to live with him for a few months and then left him, though she was still deeply in love with him. According to John Hall Wheelock, who was her editor at Scribner's and her friend, the poet was damaged as well as the woman. She wrote very few poems from then until the very end of her life and even that recovery amounted to a handful of marvelous poems, not an outpouring. She supported herself by reviewing, by spells of teaching here and there, and by public readings. She had a lifelong fear that the squalor of her childhood would overtake her in old age. It did not. She was given many awards and honors. In 1965 she had a third breakdown, and recovered, and on the 4th of February, 1970, died alone in her apartment on West 169th Street, almost in the shadow of the George Washington Bridge.

It is a life equally full of accomplishment and suffering.

The suffering was of a particularly terrible kind, but madness did not prevail. "It is not possible," she said,

> for a poet, writing in any language, to protect himself from the tragic elements in human life. . . . These are the subjects that the poet must speak of nearly from the first moment that he begins to speak.

Robert B. Shaw   (review date 27 December 1980)

SOURCE: " 'The Life-Saving Process,' " in *The Nation*, New York, Vol. 231, No. 22, December 27, 1980, pp. 710-12.

[*Shaw is an American poet, educator, and editor whose works include* The Wonder of Seeing Double *(1988). Below, he provides an overview of* Journey around My Room, *discussing in particular Bogan's difficult life.*]

Every part of the subtitle of this book [***Journey Around My Room: The Autobiography of Louise Bogan, A Mosaic by Ruth Limmer***] deserves comment. Louise Bogan, the well-known poet and critic who died at age 72 in 1970, never completed what in conventional terms could be called an autobiography. "Mosaic" is an apt word for this assemblage by Ruth Limmer, Bogan's literary executor, of widely disparate writings of a personal bent—journals and notebooks, short stories, articles, letters and poems (including a few not before published). In Limmer's imaginative but unobtrusive arrangement, these fragments fuse in a greater unity than one would have thought possible. Gaps, some of them considerable, remain; this is not a full self-portrait but a revealing sketch for one. As a much-anthologized poet and *The New Yorker*'s regular reviewer of verse, Bogan could have sought the public eye as assiduously as some of her contemporaries—Edna St. Vincent Millay, for example. Privacy remained her passion, however; she met life with the wariness of one who was her own sole protector. Given her intense reticence and the traumatic quality of the past that was hers to remember, it is remarkable that she got as much on paper as she did.

As a record of events, the book is by no means sunny reading. Although Bogan had that talent often observed in Irish lapsed Catholics for taking things hard, much that happened to her would have been hard on anyone. Her greatly loved elder brother was killed in World War I. She had two bad marriages. The first, briefer one was to an army officer whom she wedded at 19 in a spirit of rebellious escape, and with whom it soon became apparent she had nothing in common. The second marriage, longer and more emotionally destructive, was to Raymond Holden, a now forgotten lyric poet whose talent did not begin to approach hers. She lived through phases of near-alcoholism, and was hospitalized several times for psychic strain. As with most writers, she struggled during her life to stay solvent, and often found it a losing battle.

In her last years she wrote little verse and found it harder to withstand, even with the help of drugs, the waves of depression that increasingly engulfed her. Some of these agonies come clear only in Limmer's introduction and table of chronology. Except for a tense account of the breakup of her marriage to Holden, Bogan's treatment of cheerless adult experiences is oblique and elliptical. What she writes of more amply is the unhappy childhood that lay behind and no doubt determined some of these later events. It was those earliest wounds—which people may at length grow used to, but can never in a lifetime outgrow—that she felt compelled to uncover.

Bogan's parents were antithetical personalities who could not finally break away from each other; the household was a place of continual strife. "I must have experienced violence from birth," she writes. "But I remember it, at first, as only bound up with *flight*." She sets down a typical scene:

> It is in lamplight, with strong shadows, and an open trunk is the center of it. The curved lid of the trunk is thrown back, and my mother is bending over the trunk, and packing things into it. She is crying and she screams. My father, somewhere in the shadows, groans as though he has been hurt. . . . And then my mother sweeps me into her arms and carries me out of the room.

Separations were followed by reconciliations, equally doomed. The child effaced as much of this as she could from consciousness: once, for two days, she went blind. "I remember my sight coming back, by seeing the flat forked light of the gas flame, in its etched glass shade, suddenly appearing beside the bureau. What had I seen? I shall never know."

The father remains a dim figure, always, dogged in his attempt to live with a woman he could not understand. From scattered details one gets a vivid impression of the mother's volatile character, her beauty and recklessness, her alternate fits of boredom with domesticity and of guilty conscience which brought her home from bouts of infidelity. From childhood on, Bogan's feelings about her mother were hopelessly ambivalent. Contradictions bristle forth when she attempts to write about her.

> I never truly feared her. Her tenderness was the other side of her terror. Perhaps, by this time, I had already become what I was for half my life: the semblance of a girl, in which some desires and illusions had been early assassinated: shot dead.

It seems likely that Bogan's continued bafflement by her parents was one major reason for the memoir's remaining unfinished. She was too scrupulous to fool herself into believing that she could adequately explain them. And even if she had been able, it seems unlikely that she would have cared to document their misfortunes in a clinical fashion. She had little liking for the confessional style in poetry that was coming into vogue late in her career. "The poet represses the outright narrative of his life. He absorbs it, along with life itself. The repressed becomes the poem. Actually, I have written down my experience in the closest detail. But the rough and vulgar facts are not there." As it is in her poetry, so it is here, in the best of her prose. Facts, whether beautiful or terrible, are not flatly denoted but powerfully intimated in Bogan's rendering of the landscapes and interiors of her childhood: the depressed New

England mill towns and the seedy neighborhoods in Boston where she grew up.

Her sharpness of eye and fineness of phrasing are especially apparent in her writing about Ballardville, the small town in Massachusetts where the family lived from her seventh through her twelfth year. She describes the weather of the place, the autumn days when "half the town would lie in the shadow of a long cloud and half the town would stand shining bright, the weather vanes almost as still in a strong blast coming from one quarter as in no wind at all, the paint sparkling on the clapboards." She writes with affection and longing of her neighbor Mrs. Gardner's household, where, in flight from the strain and instability of her own, she first discovered "the beauty of a spare but planned life, in which everything was used." With fervor and a wealth of detail, she catalogues the everyday objects of this house: the piano, the painted china, the "silver card-receiver on the table in the hall." One comes to feel that she is not merely indulging in comfortable nostalgia but re-creating a vision of order that was to express itself in her poetry. "*One of everything* and everything ordered and complete"—it was with this kind of New England thrift that she ordered the lineaments of her poems, few of which go beyond a page, most of which give an impression of amplitude surprisingly at odds with their brevity.

When she learned to read, comparatively late, it seemed to her that "the door had opened, and I had begun to be free." She remembers:

> The stove in the dining room stood out from the wall, and behind it, on the floor, with an old imitation astrakhan cape of my mother's beneath me (as a rug to discourage drafts), I began to read everything in the house. . . . The coal in the stove burns steadily, behind the mica door; I remember the feel of the ingrain carpet against the palms of my hands, and the grain of the covers of the books, the softness of the woolen cape against my knees.

Later, she notes, her escape was completed as she began to write poetry while attending Girls' Latin School in Boston:

> I began to write verse from about fourteen on. The life-saving process then began. By the age of 18 I had a thick pile of manuscript, in a drawer in the dining room—and had learned every essential of my trade.

"She did not like books with no weather in them. Or paintings in which the objects cast no shadows," Bogan writes of herself in a stray note. No observant reader of this book or of her poetry needs to be told this. She loved to chronicle changes in light; in the poems the shadow is an image of transience, a token of mortality and of the inward and outward obscurities that attend our lives. It could be said that she remains partly in shadow throughout this book. But the image serves to suggest something more than tragic foreboding: a depth and substantiality, we might say, without which existence would be impoverished. A balance, exact and unfalsifying, of darkness and light, of pas-

sion and intelligence, was what Bogan sought to capture in her writing.

Bogan's correspondence, edited by Ruth Limmer in 1973 as *What the Woman Lived,* displayed her devotion to craft and her ample, sometimes savage humor. It traced her friendships with Edmund Wilson, Theodore Roethke and other writers, which did much to bring her through hard times. Her habit in letters was to keep her troubles in the background. This new volume, austere and fragmentary though it is, deepens the reader's sense of her character by sounding its more somber notes. It makes evident the vulnerabilities with which she struggled and which she successfully transformed to strengths in her art.

None of her poems are badly written, many are memorable, and a few—**"Henceforth, From the Mind," "Song for the Last Act," "To My Brother," "Roman Fountain"**—stand among the best in English in this century. Her career was a triumph of courage and modesty. As she said, having received an honor for her writing late in her life, "Not bad for the little Irish girl from Roxbury." Not bad at all.

William Pritchard   (review date 4 January 1981)

SOURCE: "Pieces of Private Feeling," in *The New York Times Book Review,* January 4, 1981, pp. 4, 24.

[*Pritchard is an American critic, educator, and editor. In the following positive review of* Journey around My Room, *he states that "this mosaic. . . helped me to a sharper sense of how good a poet [Bogan] could be."*]

For years the name Louise Bogan meant for me an accomplished minor poet who did lots of reviewing for *The New Yorker;* then in 1973, three years after her death, her literary executor and friend, Ruth Limmer, brought out a volume of her letters, [*Journey Around My Room*] sensitively edited and introduced. No one could read these through without realizing that Bogan was an extraordinary person, altogether larger in wit, anger, passion, contempt for stupidities and proud reticence than one had gathered from the poems alone. This is exactly how she insisted that it be, for as she remarks here, "open confession for certain temperaments (certainly for my own), is not good for the soul, in any direct way." She was also suspicious of journal-keeping, in which the tendency toward "self-regarding emotion . . . can become overwhelming." It was her belief that "the poet represses the outgoing narrative of his life," and that this repressed material becomes the poem.

Given these strongly held principles, how could she have written an autobiography? The answer is that in fact she didn't, and that what Ruth Limmer has given us in this extremely interesting, often moving book, is a "mosaic" assembled by her from pieces of Louise Bogan's journals, poems, bits of criticism and letters, notebook entries and other fugitive expressions. A perilous enterprise, when the subject in question was such a finished, even austere craftsman, and my guess is that she would have been shocked, could she have read this book, into asking: Is it *me?* Is it Art? A reader will pass on the first question, but answer the second one in the affirmative. So we stand in Ruth Limmer's debt for this piece of imaginative construction.

The first (and most absorbing) part of the book consists of childhood recollections—moody, evocative renderings of growing up in Ballardville, Mass. (near Lowell). Here Bogan's voice is absorbed in remembering: "The whole town, late in October, felt the cold coming on; in bleak afternoon the lights came out early in the frame houses; lights showed clearly across the river in the chill dusk in houses and in the mill. Everyone knew what he had to face."

There is the pleasure in clearly naming the elements of Mrs. Gardner's kitchen, in a house where Louise and her parents first boarded when they moved to Ballardville: "black iron pans and black tin bread pans; a kettle; a double boiler; a roaster; a big, yellow mixing bowl; custard cups; pie tins; a cookie jar. . . . And I can taste the food: Pot roast with raisins in the sauce; hot biscuits; oatmeal with cream; sliced oranges; broiled fish with slices of lemon and cut-up parsley on top, with browned butter round it. Roast pork; fried potatoes; baked tomatoes. . . ." There are especially vivid portraits of her mother as she cuts apples, or sews, or prepares the house against a hot New England summer day: "The parlor shutters were closed; the inner blinds, behind the long loose curtains, which descended from the tops of the window to the floor (where they lay in brushed-aside folds), were pulled down tightly to the sills. All over the house, the blinds were down." One has similar memories, and Bogan's deliberate, attentive prose startles them into life.

"Why do I remember this house as the happiest of my life?" she asks, adding that she was never really happy there. But it was there that she began to read, thus both combating and deepening the isolation she felt, an isolation that pervades these reflections. For she was, in her word, a "Mick" and a Roman Catholic whose escape from the faith seems to have been prompted by the determination to live her life "without the need of philosophy" and to write poetry which "must deal with that self which man has not made, but been presented with." As much as any poet writing in this century, she had a mind that remained unviolated by ideas, of self or world reform. Like Frost, she was less interested in making the world better than in rendering it in verse, with all its evils and imperfections.

Ruth Limmer's preface is disarming in that she admits that *Journey Around My Room* is surely not the book Bogan would have written had she chosen to, pointing out further that whatever distortion there is in it lies in its relative absence of humor. One feels this absence especially on turning back to the letters (*What the Woman Lived: Selected Letters of Louise Bogan 1920-1970,* ed. Ruth Limmer), so full of tough-minded, healthily sardonic observations, such as her description of Thomas Mann at Princeton ("gives me a pain—I always said his eyes were too near together") or Anaïs Nin ("this totally humorless dame"). I do think that in dividing up the book into 15 chapters, each one headed by a line from a rather feeble Bogan poem called **"Train Song"**—"Back through clouds / Back through clearing / Back through distance / Back through silence," and so forth—the editor has stage-managed (Ruth Limmer's own term for her editorial role) her subject into an ethereal and portentous figure whom the hu-

morous Bogan, for all her depressions, would have shrunk from.

Louise Bogan wanted her poetry to stand alone, free from the facts of her biography though deeply informed by them. But this mosaic, in some of its juxtapositions of prose and poems, helped me to a sharper sense of how good a poet she could be. At one point she writes about the nostalgia connected with hearing music on the water, or band concerts, or piano music "played however inexpertly, along some city street." The editor puts next to these thoughts a lovely poem which, by virtue of its placement, I truly heard for the first time

> Beautiful, my delight,
> Pass, as we pass the wave.
> Pass, as the mottled night
> Leaves what it cannot save,
> Scattering dark and bright.
>
> Beautiful, pass and be
> Less than the guiltless shade
> To which our vows were said;
> Less than the sound of the oar
> To which our vows were made,
>
> —
>
> Less than the sound of its blade
> Dipping the stream once more.

"I STILL THINK POETRY HAS SOMETHING TO DO WITH THE IMAGINATION. I STILL THINK IT OUGHT TO BE WELL WRITTEN. I STILL THINK IT IS PRIVATE FEELING, NOT PUBLIC SPEECH," she wrote to Rolfe Humphries in 1938. In a poem such as **"To Be Sung on the Water,"** there was nothing desired or promised that she didn't perform.

An excerpt from *Journey around My Room*

"To make oneself, and to be nothing but the self that one has made—that is Existentialism's aim and end." Novels, autobiographies, and critico-philosophical dissertations can come into being through such aims, but never poetry. For poetry must deal with that self which man has not made, but has been presented with; with that mystery (by no means a totally absurd one) by which he finds himself surrounded. It is these gifts that the poet must spend his life confronting, describing, and trying to interpret. It is not possible, for a poet, writing in any language, to protect himself from the tragic elements in human life. . . . Illness, old age, and death—subjects as ancient as humanity—these are the subjects that the poet must speak of very nearly from the first moment that he begins to speak.

Poets, traditionally, historically, were those who asked basic (and unanswerable) questions. Who are we? Why do we live? Do we die forever?

Louise Bogan, in Journey around My Room: The Autobiography of Louise Bogan, A Mosaic, *Viking, 1980.*

Carol Moldaw (essay date 1984)

SOURCE: "Form, Feeling, and Nature: Aspects of Harmony in the Poetry of Louise Bogan," in *Critical Essays on Louise Bogan,* edited by Martha Collins, G.K. Hall & Co., 1984, pp. 180-94.

[*In the following essay, Moldaw examines Bogan's aesthetic principles and style.*]

Like T. S. Eliot, and unlike William Carlos Williams, in answer to whom she wrote the essay **"On the Pleasures of Formal Poetry,"** Louise Bogan believed that verse is never free. For her, the music and meaning of a poem are indissoluble, and the experience which inspires a poem must be transformed in order to become a work of art:

> "unadulterated life" *must* be transposed, although it need not be "depersonalized." Otherwise you get "self-expression" only; and that is only half of art. The other half is technical, as well as emotional, and the most poignant poems are those in which the technique takes up the burden of feeling *instantly;* and that presupposes a practised technique.

Bogan felt that her own work expressed her personal experience without betraying it; experience pervades the poems, but is disguised. As she wrote in her journal, and to an admirer, respectively:

> The poet represses the outright narrative of his life. He absorbs it, along with life itself. The repressed becomes the poem. Actually, I have written down my experience in the closest detail. But the rough and vulgar facts are not there.

> with my work . . . you are dealing with emotion under high pressure—so that *symbols* are its only release.

Autobiographical veracity does not consist of "rough and vulgar facts"—these are replaced by, or released in the form of, symbols. Furthermore, "technique takes up the burden of feeling." In a sense this is incontrovertible, for emotion is always conveyed through the textures of the surface. But Bogan's phrase also signifies that feeling is problematic, a "burden," which it is technique vital function to express successfully. She has no sympathy for technique for technique's sake: "The fake reason, the surface detail, language only—these give no joy."

To describe what, beyond technique, a poem requires to be emotionally effective, Bogan used the term "the breath of life," which connotes both vitality and the rhythmic basis of human nature. In **"The Pleasures of Formal Poetry,"** Bogan traces the pleasure of rhythmical utterance to physical activities, and finally to the human body and breath itself:

> I want to keep on emphasizing the pleasure to be found in bodily rhythm as such. . . . We think of certain tasks, the rhythm of which has become set. Sowing, reaping, threshing, washing clothes, rowing, and even milking cows goes to rhythm. . . . Hauling up sail or pulling it down; coiling rope; pulling and pushing and climbing and lifting, all went to different rhythms; and these rhythms are preserved for us, fast or slow, smooth or rough, in sailors' songs.

> How far back can we push this sense of time? . . . It certainly springs from the fact that a living man has rhythm built in to him, as it were. His heart beats. He has a pulse. . . . and man shares with the animals not only a pulse, but an attendant rhythm: his breathing.

Focusing on language as an accompaniment to and preserver of the rhythms of physical acts imparts an importance to form—sound, rhythm, rhyme—that is not dependent on words. Poetry's primary distinction here is that it combines words (descriptions, meanings) with rhythms which in themselves are firmly rooted in the human psyche.

Bogan often expresses her predilection for the rhythmical aspects of poetry through the metaphor of music. Music was one of Bogan's great loves. She once wrote, "you can have anyone who writes 'odic poems.' I'm going right back to pure music: the Christina Rossetti of our day, only not so good. My aim is to sound so pure and so liquid that travelers will take me across the desert with them. . . ." Music is the central image of many of Bogan's poems. The titles reflect this: twelve poems are called songs, and other titles include **"The Drum," "M., Singing," "To Be Sung on the Water," "Musician,"** and **"Train Tune."** Bogan also weaves sound into other images, often describing a motion along with its sound, as in **"Betrothed"**:

> But there is only the evening here,
> And the sound of willows
> Now and again dipping their long oval leaves in
>   the water.

The image of willows "dipping their leaves" creates a continuum of rhythmical motion while it refers to, and is meant to evoke, the sound which accompanies this motion. Further, the sounds of the words create the melodious sounds they invoke. In **"Old Countryside"** we experience the various seasons primarily through sounds:

> The summer thunder, like a wooden bell,
> Rang in the storm above the mansard roof,
>
>   . . . . .
> . . . wind made the clapboards creak.
>
>   . . . . .
> . . . we heard the cock
> Shout its unplaceable cry, the axe's sound
> Delay a moment after the axe's stroke.

The correlation between the rhythmical natures of the aesthetic and natural worlds and the human psyche is at the heart of Bogan's poetry. To a large extent the poems are about poetry and the aesthetic process. Many images central to the poems are of sound and rhythmical motion, two fundamental elements of poetry which also emphasize its connection with human life. The poems most expressive of spiritual peace, like **"Song for a Lyre"** and **"Night,"** are those in which images of natural rhythms dictate emotional rhythms. The awe and harmony embodied in these poems emanate from a vision of the natural and changing world, and the poems end with a declaration drawn from human experience. The appeal is to a world in which rhythms and form embody otherwise inexpressible emotions. The most peaceful world is neither rigid, with too much form, as in **"Sub Contra,"** nor chaotic, as in the beginning of **"Baroque Comment,"** but fluid, ordered to the point where patterns are discernible.

"Sub Contra," which uses as metaphors the techniques and forms of music, expresses the desire for a pattern that will fulfill passionate demands. The poem exists in an aesthetic vacuum, without a surrounding world. No person is explicitly present: the ear, brain, heart, and rage take the place of an individual. The poem asks technique to "take up the burden of feeling," but technique alone, "like mockery in a shell," is inadequate, until the emotions provide impetus and direction. **"Sub Contra"** is about the discovery that a good poem "cannot be written by technique alone. It is carved out of agony, just as a statue is carved out of marble":

> Notes on the tuned frame of strings
> Plucked or silenced under the hand
> Whimper lightly to the ear,
> Delicate and involute,
> Like the mockery in a shell.
> Lest the brain forget the thunder
> The roused heart once made it hear,—
> Rising as that clamor fell,—
> Let there sound from music's root
> One note rage can understand,
> A fine noise of riven things,
> Build there some thick chord of wonder;
> Then, for every passion's sake,
> Beat upon it till it break.

The desire for "One note rage can understand" is initially countered by a dispassionate tone and an emphasis on a controlled, contrived aspect of music. The first five lines describe the formation and reception of music's sound simply and meticulously, first deviating from exposition with "whimper," which is affective. "Whimper" usually suggests a quality of emotion emanating from the source of the sound—for instance a child whimpers to convey a need. Bogan, however, inverts this. The notes themselves do not whimper, the ear perceives the sound as such, and the passive construction of "Plucked . . . under the hand" de-emphasizes the musician's role. This inversion conveys the idea that the listener infers, or passively creates, the tremor of the emotional. The ear, "delicate and involute," appears more complex than the music.

Next, the notes are compared to "the mockery in a shell." The metaphor, predicted and supported by "involute," which suggests the shape of a shell as well as the ear, conveys both the emotionally neutral sense of being imitative, and the sense that the music is hollow, without real inspiration. The implication is that this music, like the sound of the sea heard from a shell, is not authentic.

Dissatisfied with this state of things, the poem from here on is exhortative, asking for a note, then a chord, then a rhythm, to inspire the brain in the way the heart once did. Although the music so far has been unsatisfying, the exhortation implies the heart's present inability to inspire the brain without assistance.

As the poem redefines the musical process outlined at its beginning, and shifts from "the frame of strings" to "music's root," the music evolves until it becomes adequate first to the demands of rage, and finally, "for every passion's sake." "One note" and "a fine noise of riven things" expand into "some thick chord of wonder"; and "beat," which suggests a drum, not a stringed instrument, replaces "plucked." The rhythm of the poem also becomes more insistent: the last two lines both begin and end on a strong stress. The hortatory subjunctive, "let," demanding something from no one in particular, delays the necessity of direct address until, at the poem's end, "build" and "beat" demand action from the musician, who had been portrayed as passive. Whereas the music at the beginning was only a mockery, this is meant to be emotionally authentic.

It is the demand, "Then, for every passion's sake, / Beat upon it till it break," which reinvigorates the poem and allows, finally, a cathartic release. The poem's frustration stemmed from its own inabilities—technique alone was inadequate, as was the heart. Only in combination, with directives from the emotions and ability from technique, can the poem achieve its desired resolution.

"Sub Contra" expresses the desire for an aesthetic form which will exemplify, or even create a heightened state of emotion. In contrast, **"Baroque Comment"** embraces the world and its aesthetic creations and embodies the human desire for harmony. Its theme is the already resolved coexistence of the world, form and symbolic expression.

> From loud sound and still chance;
> From mindless earth, wet with a dead million
>   leaves;
> From the forest, the empty desert, the tearing
>   beasts,
> The kelp-disordered beaches;
> Coincident with the lie, anger, lust, oppression
>   and death in many forms:
>
> Ornamental structures, continents apart, sepa-
>   rated by seas;
> Fitted marble, swung bells; fruit in garlands as
>   well as on the branch;
> The flower at last in bronze, stretched backward,
>   or curled within;
> Stone in various shapes: beyond the pyramid,
>   the contrived arch and the
>   buttress;
> The named constellations;
> Crown and vesture; palm and laurel chosen as
>   noble enduring;
> Speech proud in sound; death considered sacri-
>   fice;
> Mask, weapon, urn; the ordered strings;
> Fountains; foreheads under weather-bleached
>   hair;
> The wreath, the oar, the tool,
> The prow;
> The turned eyes and the opened mouth of love.

Unlike any other poem by Bogan, **"Baroque Comment"** has facets which recall Whitman: parallelism, long lines, and the listing of images. And, unlike many of Bogan's poems, this one contains no "I." Any emotive powers seem to emanate not from the viewer, but directly from that which is viewed.

In the first stanza the images reflect the chaotic organic

world and the human destructive forces. Immediately, with the preposition "from," the poem asserts that this organic chaos is the origin of something else, the nature of which is not yet specified. The adjectives emphasize the natural chaos and lack of proportion. Sound, not merely present, is "loud." Chance, in direct contrast, is "still"—perhaps because it is abstract and insubstantial. The earth, "mindless," cannot function as the controlling center; nor can the "tearing" beasts, or the "kelp-disordered" beaches. Both "mindless" and "disordered" are privative, pointing to the lack of control, the lack of human influence, and indirectly introducing the idea of form.

The distinctly human faculties, "the lie, anger, lust, oppression, and death in many forms," each imply a morally antithetical partner. Without the existence of truth, calmness, spiritual love, justice, and natural death, there would be no vocabulary for the other; they *are* only in the context of what they are not. The line, which begins "Coincident with," also affirms that the aesthetic, spiritual creations which follow in the second stanza neither arise from, nor exclude, the humanly created chaos.

The second and last stanza presents that which emerges from the chaos; it does not ask how the transformation, or the impulse to transform, occurs. "Ornamental structures, continents apart, separated by seas" arise as if by a natural extension of human existence. They are the expression and symbol of the ordering human.

For the poem as a whole, what must be noted, besides the absence of the "I," is that the poem does not contain a complete sentence. The presence of a verb would presume to solve the question of how aesthetic objects or symbols are derived from the chaotic earth. Its absence avoids the question, and precludes the formation of a time sequence. The earth precedes aesthetic creation, but the process may have always been, and may still be occurring. The world is not devoid of disorder; "the lie, anger, lust . . ." have not been purged even though there are "palm and laurel chosen as noble and enduring." The relationship is posited as continual, and the transformed does not replace either its antecedent or that which is antithetical. However, out of the natural disorder, as though requiring it, comes that which is distinguished by harmony and form.

Some of the aesthetic images are in fact related directly to particular images in the first stanza. "The pyramid" inhabits an otherwise "empty desert"; "the named constellations" contrast with the "kelp-disordered beaches"; the leaves, "palm and laurel chosen as noble and enduring," give "mind" to the "mindless earth, wet with a dead million leaves"; "fruit in garlands as well as on the branch" also contrasts with the leaves' decay. "Speech proud in sound" gives dignity and order to "loud sound," as "death considered sacrifice" does to both "still chance" and "death in many forms."

These images harken to a sense of reason, harmony, and fulfillment: they order, elevate, and immortalize the natural world. The flower is "at last" in bronze—safe from death, consecrated in full bloom or in bud. The phrase "at last" is the most explicit hint of the all but untraceable

tone of relief and peace which nevertheless dominates the stanza.

The images loosely follow a progression from the created objects to the implements of creation (themselves created) to the final declaration of the human, portrayed as one passionately receptive. But the nouns are generic, visually accessible only through their universality, and the adjectives and adjectival clauses do not help us see the images. Instead they stress the artifice, the difference between the humanly created and their organic counterparts. The adjectives are all participles, invoking the unmentioned creative force: "*fitted* marble," "*swung* bells," "*contrived* arch," "*named* constellations," and "*ordered* strings." Thus, while the created objects refer to the organic world, they have new symbolic connotations, as the fruit of the human impulse and ability to create, to shape objects of beauty and order.

The last five lines, shorter and more sparse, move in quick succession through the images (eight of them are nouns without qualifiers), and thus accentuate the fact that the objects are listed without explicit purpose. At the same time their simplicity de-emphasizes the baroque quality of the list and slows the pace. It is in these lines that the human figure is introduced, and the objects ("Mask, weapon, urn . . . / . . . / The wreath, the oar, the tool, / The prow") are closer to the human world. The centrality to human endeavours clarifies what the previous images only suggest: design and pattern, ordering and naming, are expressions of the human desire for harmony and for self-realization.

The ending line, "The turned eyes and the opened mouth of love," indirectly addresses the question of how the transformation from disorder to harmony occurs. As in **"Sub Contra,"** authentic expression can originate only in the emotions. Love, at once spiritual and sexual, is the apex of humanness. The most natural of the poem's images, the eyes and mouth can be seen as the essential link between the natural world and aesthetic creations. It is typical of Bogan that the sensuous image, "opened mouth," also suggests the imminent acts of speech, song, or prayer: the beginnings of expression.

"Baroque Comment" acts as an elaborate reminder. As if arguing by example, it transmits, through images and abstract ideals, a vision of harmony. Unlike **"Sub Contra,"** which arises from dissatisfaction and demands something missing from the poem, **"Baroque Comment"** posits no dissatisfaction. Lacking a verb, an explicit argument, and a specific persona, the poem affirms a world in which symbols "take up the burden of feeling instantly."

Like "the turned eyes and the opened mouth of love," many of the images which end the poems are of things caught in the midst of incipient, or endlessly recurrent, motion. This is another way that Bogan's poems convey the rhythmic and the emotional together: the motion symbolizes the point of change in both nature and the emotions; in itself it captures the essence of a situation.

"Winter Swan" and **"Old Countryside"** both end with images of arrested motion. **"Winter Swan,"** which contains the challenge, "But speak, you proud!," poses the "leaf-caught world once thought abiding" as a "dry disarray and artifice," and ends with "the long throat bent back, and the eyes in hiding." **"Old Countryside"** recounts change in the guise of prophecy "come to proof." The last image, seen "far back . . . in the stillest of the year," is "the thin hound's body arched against the snow."

Like aesthetic objects, the stilled images bring the world into focus. Each image can be thought of as stilled only by the perceptions of the poems themselves. In the reality of the past they continue—the swan to sing its death song, the hound to leap, the human being perhaps to kiss—but in memory they are caught, and become significant, in these postures of incipient motion. They are cathartic because they direct the reader to the point of change.

Whereas a sense of freedom, or eternity, results when the stilled images seem to be part of a continuum, other images seem frozen in stasis. Stasis is the result of fear, and occurs when the elements of the self and the world cannot be integrated, as in **"Medusa,"** or when the persona is stymied by her inability to perceive and feel fully, as in **"Henceforth, from the Mind."** These poems, and some of the early embittered love poems, disclose an imbalance between the elements of the self and the world—a desire to escape into a world wholly formalistic, without the dangers inherent in the chaotic physical world. The result is akin to the musical and emotional rigidity in **"Sub Contra,"** which that poem ultimately overcomes.

"A Tale," the first poem in Bogan's first, fourth, fifth, and sixth books, ends with an image of the double. It initially presents the impulse to go past the contrived signs of change ("The arrowed vane announcing weather, / The tripping racket of a clock") and then to escape from the transitory altogether ("Seeking, I think, a light that waits / Still as a lamp upon a shelf "). The last two stanzas suggest that the end of the youth's journey is to be very different from the peaceful and domestic light he seeks:

> But he will find that nothing dares
> To be enduring, save where, south
> Of hidden deserts, torn fire glares
> On beauty with a rusted mouth,—
>
> Where something dreadful and another
> Look quietly upon each other.

The language describing the landscape indicates nothing in reality, but instead a mythic, or inner landscape—the dark regions of the self. Though the double figures confront each other "quietly," it is with the quiet of terror. Stillness is not, the youth discovers, synonymous with peace.

The confrontation of the selves, inescapable and uncontrollable, can lead to spiritual death. Things are stilled, but this does not lead to an aesthetic focusing: stillness becomes their nature. Bogan returns to the double in **"Medusa," "The Sleeping Fury," "The Dream,"** and **"The Meeting."** Like **"A Tale,"** these poems do not exist in the natural world; they are part of myth, or abstract and symbolic. **"Medusa"** exemplifies the entrapment that results from confrontation with the other self. In the poem it is not, as in the myth, just the viewer who turns to stone; the entire perceived world is paralyzed:

> And I shall stand here like a shadow
> Under the great balanced day,
> My eyes on the yellow dust, that was lifting in
>   the wind,
> And does not drift away.

Only in the poems **"The Sleeping Fury"** and **"The Dream,"** where the speaker faces the double with "control and understanding," is the paralysis circumvented, and does "the terrible beast . . . put down his head in love."

"The Alchemist," "Henceforth, from the Mind," "Summer Wish," "Spirit's Song," and **"Little Lobelia's Song"** also embody the double theme. In these poems the persona is split, implicitly or explicitly, into two irreconcilable selves, usually a physical and spiritual self. **"The Alchemist"** relates the futile attempt to transmute the substance of the baser self into "A passion wholly of the mind" and finds

> . . . unmysterious flesh—
> Not the mind's avid substance—still
> Passionate beyond the will.

The rigidity in these poems stems from a denial of the natural—an asceticism or romanticism which will not, or cannot, accept the dangers perceived in the physical world. As in the beginning of **"Sub Contra,"** the persona is resigned, or even wants, to exist in a circumscribed world. In **"Henceforth, from the Mind,"** "joy, you thought, when young, / Would wring you to the bone, / Would pierce you to the heart" has as little effect as "shallow speech alone." In **"Little Lobelia's Song,"** which is written from the perspective of a spirit "not lost but abandoned," the spirit wants to, but cannot, reenter the "blood and bone."

The only double which is positive for Bogan is that which reflects and expresses the real, as an aesthetic image does. The divided self is built upon fear and depends upon emotional barriers; the aesthetic object, like the images of things caught, focuses. It comes out of the natural world but creates something more and connotes peace and permanence. In **"Division,"** the aesthetic double, the "replica," is the tree's shadow, and it is the shadow, not the tree itself, which is "woven in changeless leaves" and "clasped against the eye."

"Baroque Comment" is a full expression of the world divided into itself and its aesthetic reflection. Its underlying assumptions—that natural disorder contains the kernels of order, that the human destructive forces are akin to the creative forces, that created order referring back to the natural world epitomizes harmony—also underlie Bogan's life-affirming poems, such as **"Song for a Lyre"** and **"Night,"** which address the problem of form in experience itself.

Emotions and insights, like aesthetic objects, and like the images of things caught, focus and order the world. Conversely, the world itself can be a source of inner exhaltation and freedom. Bogan broaches this in a letter to Morton Zabel:

> concerning the heightening which comes to the
> artist when he acquires the habit of regarding life
> as mythical and typical. That's only another way

of saying that when one lets go, and *recognizes* the stream on which we move as the same stream which moves us within—that it is time and the earth floating our blood and flesh, floating its own child—and stops fighting against the kinship, the light flows in; peace arrives.

In Bogan, the desire to duplicate things through description is countered by the stronger desire to duplicate and evoke responses to the things perceived. Thus, the poems are often written in the past tense, from the specific viewpoint of memory, and the claims which the past makes upon the present are equaled by memory's reevaluation of the past. Throughout there is a tension between sensuous particulars and the abstract.

Bogan called poetry "the heart's cry" and said that "it gives reality freedom and meaning." She made these aesthetic principles her subject, and took on the double task of "going back to pure music" and expressing "what I have become and what I know."

—*Carol Moldaw*

In both **"Song for a Lyre"** and **"Night"** the speaker gathers strength from the rhythms of nature which, though not all exclusive to night, are perceived as night phenomena. Neither poem emphasizes the speaker's experience until the last stanza, but both return to the human element, with a clear sense of renewal that is caused by the *perception* of natural, continuous rhythms.

In **"Song for a Lyre"** the images of the leaves, the stream, sleep, and dream are repeated incrementally. The setting of night exists primarily on two levels—the night as present, and the night as future. The shift into the future is subtle: only the modal auxiliary "must" and the repeated adverb "soon" reveal the future tense. It is as if night is so completely imagined, and so like past nights of the same season, that it is present.

SONG FOR A LYRE

The landscape where I lie
Again from boughs sets free
Summer; all night must fly
In wind's obscurity
The thick, green leaves that made
Heavy the August shade.

Soon, in the pictured night,
Returns—as in a dream
Left after sleep's delight—
The shallow autumn stream:
Softly awake, its sound
Poured on the chilly ground.

Soon fly the leaves in throngs;
O love, though once I lay
Far from its sound, to weep,

When night divides my sleep,
When stars, the autumn stream,
Stillness, divide my dream,
Night to your voice belongs.

Here the moments of summer's passing and autumn's return revitalize both the world and the speaker. The recurrence of change is shared: the speaker "again" is in the particular landscape; summer "again," and inevitably, turns to autumn. The change cleanses and lightens the world: the "thick, green leaves" disperse; the "shallow autumn stream" awakens; the speaker is reunited with the memory of her lover.

The speaker's relation to this world is not as a participant, and not even fully as a witness, but as an *anticipant*—renewed by the signs of approaching change. Furthermore, the speaker is moved not only by the coming transformation of the earth, but by her awareness of the transformation; because the natural changes are foreseen, they occur first within the speaker's mind. Though the images refer to the landscape, they have their origin and effect almost equally in the imagination.

This imagination, however, is not severed from the world, but attuned to it; part memory, it needs only the intimation of seasonal change to infer the rest. The first inference occurs with the change from the present tense ("The landscape where I lie") to the future ("all night must fly"). The landscape is abstract to the point of being nondescriptive; suggesting only that the speaker is outdoors, it in fact encourages the idea that she is being metaphorical, and actually may be indoors. The full phrase ("Again from boughs sets free / Summer") inverts our usual conception of the relationship between the land and the season. Normally, the season is imbued with the power to affect and dominate the land; here it is the land which discards, "sets free," the season. Only with the shift to the future tense, "the thick, green leaves" which the imagination foresees, does the language become more descriptive.

The second stanza further emphasizes the description's imaginative qualities: night becomes "the pictured night," which suggests both night imagined and a night of dreams. The metaphor of the dream "left after sleep's delight" is extended to the stream, "softly awake," as if while dry it too had been asleep. As in **"Betrothed,"** it is the sound that signals the stream's movement and motivates the more visually descriptive language of the "shallow autumn stream" and the "chilly ground."

Although the poem so far indicates the imagined and remembered aspects of experience, it is the external world which has been described, and described in terms of its motion. In the last stanza, the speaker is more prominent, as the awareness of the natural world and the continued remembrance of the lover inspire her.

Many of the images in the last stanza echo images in the first two stanzas, but they are woven together, and not merely reiterative. Even the repetition of "soon" is altered, by the lack of a comma, as if what was soon to arrive had drawn nearer; and that image itself, "fly the leaves in throngs," draws us deeper into autumn than does the similar image in the first stanza. "O love, though once I lay

/ Far from its sound, to weep," echoing the poem's first line, "The landscape where I lie," introduces the emotions directly, in the past tense.

The object to which "its sound" refers may be either the autumn stream or all the sounds of night. But revealing that the speaker had wept, and in her sorrow had excluded the world, the stanza concludes by capsulizing her revelatory experience. We are first given the conditions ("When night . . ." "When stars . . .") that evoke the lover's voice, and not until the last line are we introduced to love, the catalyst that brings the speaker out of herself and allows her to experience the world.

That the effect of the repeated images in the last stanza differs from their effect in the preceding stanzas is due partially to the introduction of the lover, and partially to the interweaving of images. The freed leaves, the returning stream, the stars and stillness are integrated to create a night fuller and more real. The images of sleep and dream, metaphorical in the preceding stanza, also now inform the speaker's reality. The poem has come full circle; from an emphasis upon a reality which the speaker creates, or anticipates, it moves to a reality which is bestowed.

The sense of fullness in this stanza also results from its formal divergence from the first two. It contains one additional nonrhymed line, and a different rhyme pattern, *a b c c d d a*, rather than *a b a b c c*. "Stream" and "dream," rhymed in the second stanza, are here a couplet, accentuating their partnership, while the last line's rhyme with the first envelops the two adjacent couplets.

"Song for a Lyre," initially describing seasonal change, ends with the correlation between the perception of the elements and the vivid remembrance of the lover. As such, the poem affirms the soothing power of evocation even as it affirms the soothing power of love.

A later poem, **"Night,"** makes a similar correlation among the elements, perception and the human heart. In **"Night,"** however, the speaker is not explicitly present, and the experience of renewal is more implicit in the imagery itself. Not written in a set stanzaic form, the overall construction relies, as it does in **"Baroque Comment,"** on the suspension, finally the omission, of the main clausal verb. Like **"Song for a Lyre,"** **"Night"** makes manifest the recurrent, eternal, and healing qualities of rhythmic motion:

NIGHT

The cold remote islands
And the blue estuaries
Where what breathes, breathes
The restless wind of the inlets,
And what drinks, drinks
The incoming tide;

Where shell and weed
Wait upon the salt wash of the sea,
And the clear nights of stars
Swing their lights westward
To set behind the land;

Where the pulse clinging to the rocks
Renews itself forever;

Where, again on cloudless nights,
The water reflects
The firmament's partial setting;

—O remember
In your narrowing dark hours
That more things move
Than blood in the heart.

The first three stanzas form the beginning of a periodic sentence that is never concluded. Because the poem's substance resides in the description of ongoing motion, the missing verb (which would act definitively) becomes superfluous. The parallel construction of the adjectival clauses, connected by "where," and the unremitted use of the present tense, indicate the continuity which informs the poem's peaceful mood.

Sensuous particulars relieve the initial abstractness of the landscape; the "cold remote islands" become accessible through images signifying recurrent motion—the "restless wind" and the "incoming tide"—which form the basis for the equally rhythmical, but more detailed, images in the following stanzas. Ending a line with the repetition of "breathes" (the two "breathes," with the pause between them, occupy over half the line, and all of its metrical stress) suspends the poem's motion. The following line, particularly in its lighter sounds and its more visual image, relieves the suspension, and, by giving the verb an object, unexpectedly carries the image forward. This pattern, which recurs in the next two lines (where "drinks" echoes "breathes" and "incoming tide" echoes "wind of the inlets"), evinces a calm, rhythmical, life-imbued landscape.

The expansiveness suggested in the first stanza is reinforced now by more specific images, each of which revolves around the tide or the moving stars. The poem embodies the idea of movement: nothing is static; no motion is concluded; the scene is not limited to any specific night, but is ever-present.

The insistence upon continuing motion is emphasized by the rhymes and sounds which reverberate throughout the poem. The irregular meter rests upon iambs and anapests; many lines end on a falling rhythm (islands, estuaries, inlets, westward, forever, setting, remember), intimating the next strong beat of the iamb. Within stanzas, and from one stanza to the next, words echo each other in sound. In the second stanza, for example, *s*'s, *w*'s, and strong open vowels are repeated, and there is one internal rhyme, "nights" and "lights," in the middle of consecutive lines. The words "wash," "stars," "weed," "swing," "set," and "behind" are echoed by "water," "dark" (and "heart"), "wind," "inlets," and "tide."

By the last stanza, rhythms, sounds, and images, focused on the recurrent motions of the sea and the night sky, have cumulated to the single effect of tranquillity. With the last stanza the poem interrupts itself, breaking the adjectival clause, and the poet addresses herself.

The last stanza brings the poem, for the first time, to the human world, only to remind us that the human being is enriched and strengthened by attending to the natural world. The underlying connection between "blood in the heart," which moves, and the seascape, its essence also expressed as recurrent motion, is that all life, and in particular the salt blood of the human being, originated in the sea. In asserting that to look beyond oneself is more self-sustaining than to dwell, in one's "narrowing dark hours," on "blood in the heart," the poem also suggests that it is the life-sustaining rhythmical forces which connect us to the origins, the essences, of our lives. Implicated in this scheme is poetry; its essence also rhythmical recurrence, it too unites the human with the fundamental forces of life.

Bogan called poetry "the heart's cry" and said that it "gives reality freedom and meaning." She made these aesthetic principles her subject, and took on the double task of "going back to pure music" and expressing "what I have become and what I know." One feels that the en-

---

An excerpt from *What the Woman Lived*

March 17, 1955

Dear May [Sarton]:

—I want to write you rather fully about the problem of argument in poetry, but cannot do it properly today. Of course, everything is material for poems—even the "passive suffering" (sometimes) that Yeats deplored; but argument should be dramatized, as Yeats learned to dramatize, rather than projected straight—the dramatic monologue helps. It is impossible really to argue, in lyric poetry, because too many abstractions tend to creep in—and abstract ideas must get a coating of sensuous feeling before they become true poetic material; unless one is a born satirist. Auden argues, it is true, but with much satire involved; his use of the rhymed couplet in *N[ew] Y[ear] Letter* derives from Butler's *Hudibras* (a sturdy satirist) more than from the more waspish Pope. The element of wit has to be present; there is nothing duller or more unmalleable than serious conviction, seriously expressed. Even Eliot, in *Four Quartets,* keeps everything flexible, simple and conversational, in the more argumentative sections. —Certainly "unadulterated life" *must* be transposed, although it need not be "depersonalized." Otherwise you get "self-expression" only; and that is only half of art. The other half is technical, as well as emotional, and the most poignant poems are those in which the technique takes up the burden of the feeling *instantly;* and that presupposes a practised technique. . . . I have a pamphlet, the record of a Rede Lecture, given by C. M. Bowra, on "Poetry and Inspiration," which I'll tuck into an envelope and send you, some day soon. It has charming and fruitful examples of poets working at top speed—that speed when true fusion of thought and feeling occurs.

Love on the day of all the Patricks!

Louise

Louise Bogan, in a letter in What the Woman Lived: Selected Letters of Louise Bogan, 1920-1970, *Harcourt, Brace, Jovanovich, 1973.*

---

deavours are not separable, but become part of each other in a given poem. Through image, sound, and rhythm, the poems express the desire for and the discovery of natural and aesthetic forms that uplift human consciousness.

Donna Dorian   (review date Spring-Summer 1985)

SOURCE: "Knowledge Puffeth Up," in *Parnassus: Poetry in Review,* Vol. 12, No. 2, Spring-Summer, 1985, pp. 144-59.

[*In the following review of* The Blue Estuaries, *Dorian discusses themes of anger, fear, and womanhood in Bogan's poetry, arguing that "Bogan chose an archetypal perspective which enabled her to circumscribe the demands of narrative, to avoid the culturally accepted gestures of female identity."*]

For Louise Bogan, writing wove a lifeline, a silver cord between heaven and hell. No longer plucking self-knowledge from the tree, she reached for the branches of song. How difficult that aspiration when one considers how long women have been punished for the theft of an apple, forbidden to write by the demands of silence and mute suffering. Bogan's poetry was intricately laced with this taboo against self-revelation, which she conceived never in didactic or argumentative terms, but as song. In so doing, she broke with one tradition by keeping to another.

Theodore Roethke, in his definitive essay on Bogan, found that her poetry recalled the lyrics of Campion and Jonson, which frequently served as texts for music. Roethke's aim was to place Bogan's poems not so much as lyrics meant to accompany musical setting, but "as part of the severest lyric tradition in English." Certainly hers is a poetry that "sings," that "imitates music in effect," and not a poetry of speech. Without ever indulging in the effusions of personality, Bogan based her poetry on direct expression which repeatedly filtered the rhythms of colloquial speech into an epigrammatical diction. Her return to the Renaissance lyric—be it that of Campion or Donne—refreshed and aerated twentieth-century poetry as her very discretion seems, nonetheless, to call for accompaniment—a lute, a viol, a cello—and to echo what is felt but is left unsaid: "Pain is a furrow healed / And she may love you most. / Cry, song, cry / And hear your crying lost."

> Louise Bogan believed that all her talent came from her mother's side of the family, so that the source of psychic hurt in her life seemed to her also the source of the means of triumph over that hurt. Whatever damage Mary and Daniel Bogan inflicted on Louise's capacity to give and receive "normal" love, they never tried to suppress her gifts, which were brought to birth with the inextinguishable strength of all powers as natural as they are compensatory.

So states Elizabeth Frank, who in her recent critical biography, *Louise Bogan: A Portrait,* made much headway in unearthing the "actual occasions" which Bogan so meticulously swept out of her poems, her criticism, her public life. Bogan's letters and criticism offer only a fragmentary look at the woman, whetting as much curiosity as they satisfy. And she had difficulty with her memoirs, a task she returned to over and over without finally completing herself. She did not like to reveal.

In Frank's attempt to plait psychological motivations with the poems, she made clear that the privacy of Bogan's work served more than a literary function, that like the poetry itself, it drew its source from Bogan's relationship with her mother. The three poems discussed at length in this essay—**"Medusa," "Cassandra,"** and **"The Sleeping Fury"**—acted as drawing boards upon which Bogan transformed those complicated feelings toward her mother into a public, lyric poetry.

The daughter of a New England mill worker and a handsome but thorny woman, Louise Bogan was born on August 11, 1897, in Livermore Falls, Maine. In 1882, when Mary Murphy Shields married Daniel Bogan in Portland, Maine, she was only seventeen; for her, marriage was a matter of course and the only available means of gaining autonomy. Instead, it thwarted her desire for cultivated society, and she early lost all romantic interest in her husband. It seems symbolic of the problems that would follow that Mary Bogan would continue to grow after her youthful marriage, to tower five inches above her husband—a fact for which she never forgave him.

Mary Bogan played out her frustrations upon each member of her family. She consorted with other men, deserting home for days on end, leaving no clues to her whereabouts. Though it is difficult to know just how many times this actually occurred, it happened often enough to have broken any sense of security Louise and her younger brother Charles could have felt. On occasion, the daughter would be brought along on these trysts, to sit alone in the hall, "to see the ringed hand on the pillow. I weep by the hotel window, as she goes down the street with another. . . ."

From childhood on Bogan carried the knowledge of her mother's deception, which shamed her and led her to insulate herself from others. Revealing her mother's affairs would only have provoked her mother's anger and threatened the remaining stability of family life. So the harboring of secrets became a norm—and "truth became charged with doubleness."

> "I never truly feared her," Louise Bogan later concluded, "Her tenderness was the other side of her terror." Even so, by the age of eight, or even perhaps as early as five or six, Louise Bogan was an exile from conventional life and had become, "what I was for half of my life: the semblance of a girl, in which some desires and illusions had been early assassinated: shot dead."
>
> (Elizabeth Frank: *A Portrait*)

But Mary Bogan did not want her daughter to repeat her mistakes, and encouraged her to attend what is now Boston's Girls' Latin school. There she began to write verse, and she tells us, "By the age of eighteen, I had a thick pile of manuscript in a drawer in the dining room—and had learned every essential of my trade." But in 1916, at eighteen, and much against her parents' protests, she forfeited a scholarship from Radcliffe to marry Curt Alexander, an Army man. Within a year, in the Panama Canal Zone,

Louise Bogan gave birth to a child. But the marriage was doomed, just as the marriage of Louise's parents had been, and within a year, Bogan, daughter in arms, returned to Boston. Although the couple attempted two brief reconciliations, they separated permanently in 1919. The following year her estranged husband died of pneumonia.

The widowed Bogan moved to New York. In an unusually brief time, the twenty-two-year-old established a reputation as a literary figure. Her poems began to appear with regularity in the leading journals, and she kept frequent company with Margaret Mead, Ruth Benedict, Malcolm Cowley, Lola Ridge, and Edmund Wilson, who would encourage her career as a critic. At twenty-six, she married Raymond Holden, a writer and sometime editor at *The New Yorker*. This period hovered behind Bogan's first volume of poems, **Body of this Death,** of which she would write so eloquently to Theodore Roethke many years later:

> And let me tell you right now, the only way to get away is to get away; pack up and go. Anywhere. I had a child, from the age of 20, remember that, to hold me back, but I got up and went just the same, and I was, God help us, a woman. I took the first job that came along. Then there was a depression on, as there is now, not quite so bad, but still pretty poor, and I lived on 18 bucks a week and spent a winter in a thin suit and a muffler. But I was free. And when this time, I couldn't free myself by my own will, because my will was suffering from a disease peculiar to it, I went to the madhouse for six months, under my own steam, mind you, for no one sent me there, and I got free. —When one isn't free, one is a thing, the thing of others, and the only point in this rotten world, is to be your own, to hold the scepter and mitre over yourself, in the immortal words of Dante.
>
> (Louise Bogan: **What the Woman Lived:**
> **Selected Letters**)

During those early years in New York, perhaps as she sat at her desk, she must have thought how no woman in her family had chosen, could have chosen at twenty-two to survive on her own wits. Now as much an exile from herself as once she had been from experience, she confronted these conditions in **"A Tale,"** a poem of astute self-knowledge. Where once the futility of her family and her marriage had demanded escape, now her own unconscious called her to face something dreadful in herself. Traveling to the precipice of change, she arrived at the first moment of self-consciousness—if she was afraid of what she had seen, the poem, as poised and skillful as its hero, defied that fear. And so it was also the poet and the poem who looked "quietly upon each other."

> This youth too long has heard the break
> Of waters in a land of change.
> He goes to see what suns can make
> From soil more indurate and strange.
>
> He cuts what holds his days together
> And shuts him in, as lock on lock:
> The arrowed vane announcing weather,
> The tripping racket of a clock;

Seeking, I think, a light that waits
Still as a lamp upon a shelf,—
A land with hills like rocky gates
Where no sea leaps upon itself.

But he will find that nothing dares
To be enduring, save where, south
Of hidden deserts, torn fire glares
On beauty with a rusted mouth,—

Where something dreadful and another
Look quietly upon each other.

By dramatizing internal conflict she avoided the insipid revelations of an egotistical personality—"The lyric, if it is at all authentic, is based on emotion, on some actual occasion, some real confrontation," Bogan wrote. Later, poetic reflections would be posed in dialogue and exhortation, in the subterfuges of the mythological mask, often to be enhanced by rhythmical variations, which permitted her, paradoxically, to move out of the world of appearances into the world of the great archetypal presences, to make hers a poetry not of the individual self, but a map of the feminine sensibility.

In **"Medusa"** Bogan continues to examine the nature of fear, to find it the primary source of evil. "To decapitate = to castrate," wrote Freud in his short essay on the male castration complex, "Medusa's Head." "The terror of Medusa is a terror of castration that is linked with the sight of something—primarily the female genitals, probably those of an adult, essentially those of the mother." Freud's theory, of course, was shaped by the Greek myth, in which the attempts to destroy the Gorgon were, in effect, the efforts of men to overcome and control the threat of all libidinous female sexuality. But in Bogan's version, it is a woman who looks upon the mother. Mutated and mutating, both mother and daughter are condemned, trapped inside the self, outside time.

I had come to the house, in a cave of trees,
Facing a sheer sky.
Everything moved,—a bell hung ready to strike,
Sun and reflection wheeled by.
When the bare eyes were before me
And the hissing hair,
Held up at the window, seen through a door,
The stiff bald eyes, the serpents on the forehead
Formed in the air.
This is a dead scene forever now.
Nothing will ever stir.
The end will never brighten more than this,
Nor the rain blur.

The water will always fall, and will not fall,
And the tipped bell make no sound.
The grass will always be growing for hay
Deep on the ground.

And I shall stand here like a shadow
Under the great balanced day,
My eyes on the yellow dust, that was lifting in
        the wind,
And does not drift away.

Though Freud had begun his exploration of the family romance at the time of Bogan's **"Medusa,"** her poem was one of the first to probe the psychological complexities of the mother and daughter relationship. But the fate of Medusa has been seen for centuries as akin to Persephone's, both ravished by dark gods and forced to go among the dead: Persephone reigned as the Queen of the Underworld; Medusa was transformed into a forbidding aspect of the Queen of Death. Persephone's name, in fact, may well be derived from a pre-Hellenic word that has been given Greek form, meaning "she who was killed by Perseus." Jung and Kerényi, in *Essays on a Science of Mythology,* note the grim, repellent power of these figures:

What we conceive philosophically as the element of *non-being* in Persephone's nature appears, mythologically, as the hideous Gorgon's head. . . . It is not, of course, *pure* non-being, rather the sort of non-being from which the living shrink as from something with a *negative sign*: a monstrosity that has usurped the place of the unimaginably beautiful, the nocturnal aspect of what by day is the most beautiful of all things.

Inherent in Persephone's mystery is the unfolding of sexual desire which severs her from her mother and the idyllic world of childhood. It is the mythic, unspeakable pain of that separation—and the mother's ensuing anger, the daughter's terror—that rests at the heart of **"Medusa,"** just as it is Persephone who stands before the raging Gorgon in Bogan's poem. As the future looms dark before her, the world becomes an open door, and she is tempted out. But she cannot move; she remains in deadlock, in shadow, eclipsed. She cannot assert herself against the image of the mother any more than she can overcome the consequences of her own sexuality. To break from the past, from the all-embracing mother, from the guilt and knowledge of her "monstrous" sexuality, is an act of heresy. She becomes stone and statue, a stilled slayer of the Gorgon/Mother, acting out her trauma. "For becoming stiff means an erection," Freud continued in "Medusa's Head." "Thus in the original situation, it offers consolation to the spectator, he is still in possession of a penis, and the stiffening reassures him of the fact." In Bogan's poem the female speaker, standing as if for eternity under the great balanced day, assumes the masculine stance—in erectus; avoiding her feminine sexuality, she succumbs to non-being.

The tone of Bogan's poem suggests her submissiveness, the severity of her guilt: the uniform syntax is a kind of box, a cage. There is no hortatory voice, no banging on the walls of her prison. The sounds of the words, and not their meaning, delicately modulate from stanza to stanza: a succession of open "a" and "o" rhymes, "fall/hay," "sound/ground," "shadow/away." Bogan cuts away at the myth of motherhood mellifluously. She reverses the Pygmalion myth. The mother sculpts the living daughter into stone, "forever young," "the unravished bride of quietness." The desire for experience is uttered only as longing in the poem's music; its language dissembles.

> For Louise Bogan, writing wove a lifeline,
> a silver cord between heaven and hell. No
> longer plucking self-knowledge from the
> tree, she reached for the branches of song.
> How difficult that aspiration when one
> considers how long women have been
> punished for the theft of an apple,
> forbidden to write by the demands of
> silence and mute suffering.
>
> —*Donna Dorian*

Behind the music comes the undressing: the poet is afraid of what she has seen—and the consequences of its telling. Between the seer and the seen runs an umbilical cord: An "old barnacled umbilicus, Atlantic cable / Keeping itself in a state, it seems, of miraculous repair," wrote Sylvia Plath in her *"Medusa,"* a poem that detonated the idealized myth of motherhood. Knowledge puffeth up, it deforms us, it expands us, it changes us. Where Plath named Medusa frankly as the mother, in a voice that refused to stay sequestered in decorous language, Bogan submitted to the mother, burying herself musically in a language against which neither she nor her mother could rage. Yet Bogan's poetry made Plath's possible by initiating explorations below the conscious ego, focusing clearly on feminine psychology. As Roethke was the first to note, "the man-in-the-mother"—the mother within—was most urgent to Bogan. By internalizing conflict, she assumed moral responsibility for her subject and its masterly tone. Yet Plath and Bogan carved their demons like recalcitrant marble into poetic form as their poems nearly scorched the fabric of everyday life. Myth validated their fear, stamped it with an archetypal dye, and placed their terror in history—in the country of women. In return Plath and Bogan gave us poems—children born—Bellerophon and Chrysaor—freed from Medusa's fallen head.

The verse of contemporary female poets is marked by an abundance of poems concerned with myth. In the essay "The Thieves of Language: Women Poets and Revisionist Mythmaking," Alicia Ostriker discussed the phenomena:

> Since 1960 one can count over a dozen major works of revisionist myth published by American women. In them the old stories are changed, changed utterly by female knowledge of female experience, so that they can no longer stand as foundations of collective male fantasy. Instead they are corrections; they are representations of what women find divine and daemonic in themselves; they are retrieved images of what women have collectively and historically suffered: in some cases they are instructions for survival.

Among the "breakthrough works" appearing between 1959 and 1965, Ostriker cites Van Duyn's *Valentines to the Wide World,* H.D.' s *Helen in Egypt,* Levertov's *The Jacob's Ladder,* Rich's *Snapshots of a Daughter-in-Law,* Kizer's *Pro Femina,* Sexton's *To Bedlam and Part Way*

Back, Plath's *Ariel.* Bogan's poetry is omitted, of course, because it predates the works under discussion (*Collected Poems* appeared in 1953, including **"Medusa"** [1921], **"Cassandra"** [1926], and **"The Sleeping Fury"** [1936]). Yet, however much Bogan's poetry might be considered a precursor to the work of contemporary female poets— for all its attention to the "subterranean tradition of female self-projection and self-exploration," Bogan, even during the radical movements of the Thirties, was opposed to the politicizing of literature. Nor did she ever intend anything like destroying the "male hegemony over language." Rather, as Roethke wrote, hers was a poetry upon which "the ground beat of the great tradition can be heard, with the necessary subtle variations."

Those variations, of course, are important. Like other poets of the modernist generation, Bogan was working through problems implicit in Romantic theory and practice. Although her three mythological poems follow a Romantic tradition of "mythic revisionism" in which "the poet personally experiences forces within the self so overwhelming that they must be described as gods and goddesses, titans, demiurges and demons," in versification and attitude she held to an Elizabethan mode. A poet of disguise and discretion, she employed not only the mythological mask, but the masks of others ("he" as in **"A Tale,"** the child, the girl, the romantic), sometimes omitting reference to the poem's speaker altogether, in order to release herself from the modernist dilemma of subjectivity. Like the Renaissance lyric, her poetry, rarely if ever, dramatized "the voice speaking to itself or to nobody. It was always a directed performance." Remarkably like Eliot in his dictum that "Poetry is not an expression of personality, but an escape from personality," Bogan believed that "the poet represses the outright narrative of his life. He absorbs it, like life itself." This stance served her position as a female poet, as it enabled Bogan to speak not merely for herself, but for the many.

> To me, one silly task is like another.
> I bare the shambling tricks of lust and pride.
> This flesh will never give a child its mother,—
> Song, like a wing, tears through my breast, my
>   side,
> And madness chooses out my voice again,
> Again. I am the chosen no hand saves:
> The shrieking heaven lifted over men,
> Not the dumb earth wherein they set their
>   graves.

In **"Cassandra,"** Bogan exhorts the mixed mind she bore toward her own poetic identity as she finds the voice of the sibyl whom Christa Wolf has called, in her own *Cassandra,* "the first professional working woman in literature," she who stands "as the watchword for the condition of women." Tricked by Apollo, yet intelligent, cunning, Cassandra snatched from the god the gift of prophecy. For her betrayal, for her desire to stand close to the gods and share in their nature, she "would bare the shambling tricks of lust and pride"—like Medusa, to be condemned for hubris, for what in the Greek world held the place of sin. But it was not guilt that Cassandra felt upon her punishment, but misfortune. Nor did she know regret, for the Greeks had no conception of choice, only fate: And so she tells us:

"I am the chosen no hand saves." Torn as she is by song, "the shrieking heaven lifted over men," Bogan's Cassandra still owed herself something: "self-knowledge, detachment, cool-headedness."

In humanity's struggle to comprehend its irrational impulses, the nature of death and immortality, the seemingly impossible accomplishments of the male hero have been heralded as victories. But Cassandra's visions, miraculous in their own manner, were vehemently rejected. Victims are often attracted to magic, to psychic phenomena, as if the limitless affect of pain, if fully seen, could actually bring clairvoyance, collapse the barriers of time and space. Poet and seer often share a common ground: suffering engenders the lyric cry. For Bogan it came to awesome consequence as she sought to carve the poem out of agony, to bring the poem "to an unbearable point of crisis." Shaping as it does the beginnings of a Shakespearean sonnet, **"Cassandra"** is refused turn and resolution just as both were denied to its speaker.

One assumes Bogan truncated the sonnet because its traditional connotations were unsuited to Cassandra's character. Although the form was in common use in Bogan's day, its general lack of success in the hands of other female poets—Millay, Teasdale, and Wylie, for example—led Bogan to take up arms against it. Of the sonnet sequence she wrote:

> *Women* should not write them any more! The linked formality makes chance of discursiveness too great, and the sonnet, *as such,* is never discursive. It is dramatic; the dramatic lyric framework . . . The early sonnet sequences (Sidney's, for example) are based on a terrific concept of courtly (*demanding*) passion and *morality.* They are pointed. They are channeled. —With D.G. Rossetti, etc., the whole thing begins to dissolve.
>
> (Louise Bogan: **What the Woman Lived: Selected Letters**)

And later:

> It allows women to go on and on, either praising the lover or blaming him. It also allows shows of complete and utter subservience (women rarely write sonnets in a mood of rebellion). It allows, in fact, infinite, hair-splitting wrangling.
> (Bogan/Limmer: **Journey Around My Room**)

Bogan gets around these problems in **"Cassandra"**—and in the three complete sonnets included in **The Blue Estuaries**—by casting the poem in her "to-hell-my-love-with-you-mode," stating with customary asperity and wit "perhaps we gals are at our best on this note." Though we miss the psychological layerings of Browning's dramatic monologues, the subtle plays between narrator and listener, set in a dramatic framework, **"Cassandra"** is a soliloquy: alone, she speaks out from the stage of history into a void, into the audience of all time, all space. Bogan here is again a master of tone: although even a completed sixteen-line sonnet might seem unequal to the breath of subject, her compression of the music of terror, of anger and self-pity, revenge and victory, avoids the pitfalls of over-dramatization and heroine-worship. She concludes with the ring of epigrammatical closure—a mode which had considerable effect upon lyric poetry, and especially the sonnet, during the Renaissance:

> To 'dispel' (to undo the spell) or to dismiss is the epigrammatist's characteristic gesture. In love or hate, praise or blame, he is saying something so that he will not have to say it again. He writes a poem not when he is moved but when he ceases to be. He records the moment of mastery—not the emotion, but the attitude that conquered it.
>
> (Barbara H. Smith: *Poetic Closure*)

In the final couplet, **"Cassandra"** confirms that she is subservient to nothing but her own vision; comprehending her anguish, she conquers it, to some extent, does away with its spell. "The blood jet is poetry," Sylvia Plath wrote. "There is no stopping it." Yet, as Christa Wolf remarked. "Cassandra's prophecies have stood the test of time, and it now seems that it was only she who wholly understood herself." If vision and song are a madness, it is not only because they appear so to the world, but because song comes as a possession: it breaks from the body as Eve sprang from the rib of Adam: divine, and yet made human.

In **"The Sleeping Fury"** Bogan looks beyond anger to anger's cause, and in so doing makes peace with her demons: both mother and muse. Here is the fury, the spirit of anger and revenge, "Hands full of scourges, wreathed with your flames and adders." Avengers of parricide and perjury, the Furies pursued Orestes even after his acquittal for the murder of Clytaemnestra. In **"The Sleeping Fury"** at last they appear for a moment appeased:

> You are here now,
> Who were so loud and feared, in a symbol before me,
> Alone and asleep, and I at last look long upon you.
>
> Your hair fallen on your cheek, no longer in the semblance of serpents,
> Lifted in the gale; your mouth, that shrieked so, silent.
> You, my scourge, my sister, lie asleep, like a child,
> Who, after rage, for an hour quiet, sleeps out its tears.
>
> The days close to winter
> Rough with strong sound. We hear the sea and the forest,
> And the flames of your torches fly, lit by others,
> Ripped by the wind, in the night. The black sheep for sacrifice
> Huddle together. The milk is cold in the jars.
>
> All to no purpose, as before, the knife whetted and plunged,
> The shout raised, to match the clamor you have given them.
> You alone turn away, not appeased; unaltered, avenger.
>
> Hands full of scourges, wreathed with your flames and adders,

You alone turned away, but did not move from
    my side,
Under the broken light, when the soft nights
    took the torches.

At thin morning you showed, thick and wrong
    in that calm,
The ignoble dream and mask, sly, with slits at
    the eyes,
Pretence and half-sorrow, beneath which a cow-
    ard's hope trembled.

You uncovered at night, in the locked stillness
    of houses,
False love due the child's heart, the kissed-out
    lie, the embraces,
Made by the two who for peace tenderly turned
    to each other.
You who know what we love, but drive us to
    know it;
You with your whips and shrieks, bearer of truth
    and of solitude;
You who give, unlike men, to expiation your
    mercy.

Dropping the scourge when at last the scourged
    advances to meet it,
You, when the hunted turns, no longer remain
    the hunter
But stand silent and wait, at last returning his
    gaze.

Beautiful now as a child whose hair, wet with
    rage and tears
Clings to its face. And now I may look upon you,
Having once met your eyes. You lie in sleep and
    forget me.
Alone and strong in my peace, I look upon you
    in yours.

Here the mother, Medusa, once her daughter's captor, once captive to herself, returns from the Underworld, from non-being, "Her hair no longer in the semblance of serpents." As the Demeter Erinys she now becomes the "opener of the way," not to death, but to life, her whips and shrieks reshaped as hands, as appeals to justice, harassment now the agency of self-knowledge. Just as the Kore is at root a single entity, so the Fury is recognized in all of her aspects as one, "My scourge, my sister, a child." As actual mother and mother-within, she appears in all of her variety, whole—mending the splintered self, healing the soul's division.

And so Persephone returns, as the speaker of **"The Sleeping Fury,"** risen from her own death, from Medusa's paralyzing stare, to gaze upon her terrible mother, "beautiful now as a child." "It is the Horrible Great Mother that we must conquer in order to reach the symbolic Isis," wrote Bogan to May Sarton in 1955, referring to Erich Neumann's theories. "The symbolism was relevant in my case, I don't know about anyone else's." Seeing, as Neumann did in *The Great Mother,* the images of the terrible mother as expressions of the consuming unconscious, Bogan must have recognized them as akin to her own psychic foe. Yet the mother, in her luminous aspect, is of "the highest feminine wisdom": "vessel of transformation, blossom, the unity of Demeter, reunited with Kore, Isis, Ceres, the moon goddesses." "To enter into the figure of Demeter

means to be pursued, to be robbed, raped, to fail to understand, to rage and grieve, but then to get everything back again." And so she does in **"The Sleeping Fury,"** as daughter nurtures mother, as the mother sleeps like a child whose hair is "wet with rage and tears." From the Underworld, "where the black sheep for sacrifice huddle together," she returns "at thin morning" "no longer the hunter"—and so mother and daughter are reunited, released from the pain of their separation—Persephone risen from the dead, Cassandra from the purgatories of song. Finally fury has become as redemptive as speech. In modern dress, the poem reenacts the myth of Persephone and Demeter, to unfold the mystery of Eleusis: "For to be laid in the fire, and yet to remain alive, that is the secret of immortality."

Elizabeth Frank's careful investigative work led her to the original inspiration for the poem: "L'Erinni Addormentata," which depicts a beautiful Megaera, the jealous Erinys concerned with the punishment of sexual crimes. Bogan brought back a postcard of the image from the Museo Nazionale della Terme in Rome, from a trip made to Europe in 1933 meant as a separation from her husband whom she divorced the following year. And it is fitting that through Megaera, "a symbol before me," Bogan should make peace with "her own punishing rage against her mother's and Holden's betraying sexuality and against herself, perhaps, for wishes and acts confused and obscurely entangled with the people she loved."

For all her admiration of Rilke, Bogan knew how easily poems about art objects lapse into hackneyed statement: by removing all reference to the sculpture, she cleared the poem of all but its true subject. The poem's free verse opens toward an inner expansiveness, reinforcing the "victory of release." Bogan seldom departed from the traditional demands of prosody, believing that without rhyme and meter the poem would cave in beneath the weight of emotion, that formal control permitted the liberation of feeling. Form was responsible for the grace of emotion, for the sensuality of her statement, no matter her subject, as it objectified the poem, creating the distance necessary to look upon it as outside and other. In **"The Sleeping Fury,"** Bogan still exploits form, but in a manner more radical and original than usual. Internally cohesive, its refrain-like repetition of sounds and phrases subtly modulated, **"The Sleeping Fury"** is almost iconic in form (like many of the poems of Herbert) as the generally three-lined stanzas correspond to her three-headed muse. These many repetitions ("You alone turned away, not appeased, unaltered, avenger," "You alone turned away, but did not move from my side," "You when the hunted turns, no longer remain the hunter," and so on) pivot, return, accrue, as if in litany, until **"The Sleeping Fury"** concludes in a transformation made possible, it seems, by the alchemy of language itself.

Myth originated in Greek religion as "an attempt to regulate and control man's destiny through ritual." At least in a metaphorical sense, Bogan reenacts that religious impulse here, participating in the mystery of Eleusis through the variety of her repetitions. She "tames and placates" traditional prosody just as she overcomes the oppressive demon of mother and song.

In **"The Sleeping Fury,"** as in **"Medusa"** and **"Cassandra,"** Bogan chose an archetypal perspective which enabled her to circumscribe the demands of narrative, to avoid the culturally accepted gestures of female identity. In so doing she did not attempt to reclaim the past, but to project the present, to project emotion: "For a writer's power is based not upon his intellect so much as upon his intellect so much as upon his intuition, and his emotions. All art, in spite of the struggle of some critics to prove otherwise, is based on emotion and projects emotion." In her empathy for certain mythological symbols Bogan was transformed by the symbols themselves, to move from "savage innocence," madness, and anxiety to a poetry of mature moral consequence "based upon simple expression, deep insight, and deep joy."

Elizabeth Frank   (essay date 1985)

SOURCE: "The Leaf-Caught World," in *Louise Bogan: A Portrait,* Alfred A. Knopf, 1985, pp. 108-30.

[*In the following excerpt, Frank analyzes the poems collected in* Dark Summer.]

The poems in *Dark Summer* are arranged in a loosely chronological sequence. The first section contains poems published for the most part between 1924 and 1927, and is followed by a section devoted to **"The Flume,"** the long poem written in the summer of 1924. The third section consists of a selection of poems from *Body of This Death,* and is followed by a group of poems "in a later mood." The final section is again devoted to a single long poem, **"Summer Wish,"** which Bogan finished just before she and Holden moved into the Hillsdale house in May 1929. Between the earlier and later groups it is difficult to single out strong differences. The earlier poems emphasize change, the later ones fulfillment, but both groups have a lowering inquietude.

On the whole, *Dark Summer* is a more difficult, obscure, and satisfying book than *Body of This Death.* Natural observation gives a new freshness and vigor to Bogan's language, and signals a shift away from the earlier book's almost exclusive preoccupation with the psychology of sexual conflict.

In the very title of the book lies its core of meaning. The phrase *dark summer* is an oxymoron, a paradox of the senses, capable, as dreams are capable, of reconciling opposites in a chiaroscuro of suggestion and association. Throughout the volume both *dark* and *darkness* recur with obsessive frequency. There is the dark of the grave in **"Sonnet,"** of forgetfulness in **"If We Take All Gold,"** of renewing rest in **"Tears in Sleep,"** of shadow in **"Division," "The Mark,"** and **"The Cupola."** While each of these poems gives a particular force to its use of *dark* or *darkness,* in all of them it comes to stand for latency, concealment, and imminence, for whatever lies at a remove from will and control. Above all, it signifies the deepest layer of the unconscious, where hidden instinct gathers force and prepares to obliterate the powers of both reason and resistance by which the "vulgar upper consciousness" makes its claim to mastery.

In the first poem of the book, **"Winter Swan,"** Bogan reveals a new and fresh engagement with observation. Looking at a swan gliding across an icy pond, Bogan's speaker experiences such a moment of acute anxiety that she feels herself estranged from time. The whole poem is about this disjunction and disunity. The romantic imagination can no longer succeed in its attempts to imbue the external world with its own coloring and texture. Garden and earth, which had formerly been compliant with desire, are "hollow," although "Within the mind" and "Under the breast" the "live" and "willing" blood still burns. In the elegiac questioning of the swan's detached existence and the heart's yearning for a landscape like itself, the poem establishes two orders of time, the first being nature's time, the second being what, in **"Didactic Piece,"** Bogan calls "the heart's wearing time," which is time clocked and charted through the seasons of feeling. Swept up in the anguish of perceiving that the world and itself are not the same entity, the poem's voice cries out:

> But speak, you proud!
> Where lies the leaf-caught world once thought
>   abiding,
> Now but a dry disarray and artifice?
> Here, to the ripple cut by the cold, drifts this
> Bird, the long throat bent back, and the eyes in
>   hiding.

The labor of acknowledging and putting away the past continues in the next poem, **"If We Take All Gold,"** whose fairy-tale tropes of treasure and house give an aphoristic transparency to an otherwise complex sequence of psychological insights:

> If we take all gold
> And put all gold by,
> Lay by the treasure
> In the shelved earth's crevice,
> Under, under the deepest,
> Store sorrow's gold:
> That which we thought precious
> And guarded even in sleep
> Under the miserly pillow,
> If it be hid away
> Lost under dark heaped ground,
> Then shall we have peace,
> Sorrow's gold being taken
> From out the clean house,
> From the rifled coffers put by.

First published in *The Nation* in October 1925, three months after Louise Bogan married Raymond Holden, it represents a truce with the self, enacted after a psychic battle has taken place, the terms of which require nothing less than the dispersal of fiercely hoarded misery. From the "clean house" of the new beginning, Bogan equates "sorrow's gold" with both refuse and stolen treasure which must be "Lost under [the] dark heaped ground" of the unconscious. Only there, leaching into the soil of lost memories, can it serve the cause of "peace."

Having confronted the past in the volume's first two poems, Bogan now goes on, in **"The Drum,"** to crown her labors with triumphal joy, as passionate instinct rises up with full force. A celebration of rhythm, it is one of those poems Bogan wrote with flawless control over diction and meter. As in the earlier **"Sub Contra"** in *Body of This Death,* she interweaves consonance and assonance to great imitative effect. It is almost possible to hear the suspended silences between beats, as the poem's percussion just averts regularity and offers continual surprise. This formal gaiety and manifest delight in the pulse and sound of language are precisely the poem's point, the "answer" to the "blood refused" of neurotic suffering.

In **"Division," "The Mark,"** and **"The Cupola,"** Bogan returns to the intense *looking* of **"Winter Swan."** These are difficult poems, concerned with correspondences between perceived natural fact and intuitions about absence, isolation, time, and fate, and each abounds in more or less abstract renderings of emblematic configuration. In the first stanza of **"Division,"** for instance, the poet observes shadow with an increasing pressure of selection and compression:

> Long days and changing weather
> Put the shadow upon the door:
> Up from the ground, the duplicate
> Tree reflected in shadow;
> Out from the whole, the single
> Mirrored against the single.

And just as the speaker in **"Winter Swan"** had cried out to the silent bird in protest against the dismantled perfection of summer, so here the speaker cries out to the patterned shadow, not to question or protest, but to answer it, as it were, or recount how *seeing* imprints in the memory an image of the fleeting moment:

> Replica, turned to yourself
> Upon thinnest color and air—
> Woven in changeless leaves
> The burden of the seen
> Is clasped against the eye,
> Though assailed and undone is the green
> Upon the wall and the sky:
> Time and the tree stand there.

Had Bogan's journals and notebooks from the 1920s survived the Hillsdale fire, chances are they might have revealed a good deal about her growing interest in perception. We might well have found brief, richly observed descriptions of natural scenes: colors of earth and hills in various seasons, light at different angles and different times of day. These would have made a good deal more evident her affinities with her American Romantic forebears—Emerson, Thoreau, and Dickinson—with whose imaginations hers most certainly establishes continuity. In **"The Mark"** she writes a "Metaphysical" poem that recalls figures as disparate as Donne and Vaughan and the Surrealist painter Giorgio de Chirico (whose early paintings of piazzas transected by menacing shadow were, curiously, called "Metaphysical"):

> Where should he seek, to go away
> That shadow will not point him down?
> The spear of dark in the strong day
> Beyond the upright body thrown,
> Marking no epoch but its own.
>
> Loosed only when, at noon and night,

> The body is the shadow's prison.
> The pivot swings into the light;
> The center left, the shadow risen
> To range out into time's long treason.
>
> Stand pinned to sight, while now, unbidden,
> The apple loosens, not at call,
> Falls to the field, and lies there hidden,—
> Another and another fall
> And lie there hidden, in spite of all
>
> The diagram of whirling shade,
> The visible, that thinks to spin
> Forever webs that time has made
> Though momently time wears them thin
> And all at length are gathered in.

Throughout the poem, Bogan concentrates on the fateful indivisibility of man and shadow, capturing the dread of mortality implicit in the notion of time as a web and the urgent desire for escape that it breeds. Only at noon—the shadowless moment—is escape possible, when the eye is momentarily deceived into an illusion of timelessness. But time moves inexorably on, as the apples of late summer drop "unbidden" into the lap of mortality.

With **"The Cupola,"** Bogan gives the play of light and shade a more "realistic" treatment, one based, perhaps, on her impressions of an old house in Hillsdale. The mirror hung on the wall of a cupola, with its image of mixed oak and beech leaves, becomes "a handsbreadth of darkest reflection," with *darkest* sustaining the weight of intimation and imminence that anchors the entire book in disquietude. Yet the mystery of the poem is that the whole scene it records is quite accidental and casual: "Someone has hung the mirror here for no reason" and

> Someone has thought alike of the bough and the
>   wind
> And struck their shape to the wall. Each in its
>   season
> Spills negligent death throughout the abandoned
>   chamber.

Thus the "abandoned chamber" becomes a *camera obscura,* projecting the chance episodes of seasonal life with utmost passivity and unintentional art.

Bogan's instinct to compress her meditative and metaphysical impulses into the strict brevity of the formal lyric was sound. In **"Didactic Piece,"** which she placed in the fourth and "later" section of the book, she attempts an extended meditative poem, with largely unsuccessful results. It is impenetrable in places, and fails as a whole, despite some fine passages, particularly the opening evocation of the two orders of time, the human and the nonhuman, and the two orders of reality they command:

> The eye unacquitted by whatever it holds in alle-
>   giance;
> The trees' upcurve thought sacred, the flaked
>   air, sacred and alterable,
> The hard bud seen under the lid, not the scorned
>   leaf and the apple—
> As once in a swept space, so now with speech in
>   a house,
> We think to stand spelled forever, chained to the
>   rigid knocking

> Of a heart whose time is its own flesh, momently
>   swung and burning—
> This, in peace, as well, though we know the air
>   a combatant
> And the word of the heart's wearing time, that
>   it will not do without grief.

The poem goes on to develop what might be called the internal monologue of an enraptured visionary, cleansed of sorrow, and perhaps guilt, and newly intoxicated with the hold that the visible, natural world has over his imagination. Like a censer, "momently swung and burning—," he is consumed by joy against which he uninnocently guards himself by the warning that grief and change are also part of the nature of things:

> The limit already traced must be returned to and
>   visited,
> Touched, spanned, proclaimed, else the heart's
>   time be all:
> The small beaten disk, under the bent shell of
>   stars,
> Beside rocks in the road, dust, and the nameless
>   herbs,
> Beside rocks in the water, marked by the heeled-
>   back current,
> Seeing, in all autumns, the felled leaf betray the
>   wind.

This reversion to grief and change as a check upon joy occurs not just in the poems about perceiving the natural world, but in a number of lyrics in *Dark Summer*. "Cassandra" follows "Division," and "Girl's Song" follows "The Cupola." Both of these are dramatic and personal, and both speak of a fatality irreconcilable with any simple acceptance of natural faith. "Cassandra" is the more idiosyncratic poem, an impassioned outburst by the woman who feels the terrible burden of her gift of poetic speech. The mode is emblematic or quasi-allegorical, as it had been in "Stanza" ("No longer burn the hands that seized"), as if the poem were inscribed or engraved as a motto underneath a picture of the doomed Trojan prophetess. Warning those who pursue their own destruction, Cassandra can speak only in the accents of madness, the speech of truth but not of persuasion or belief. She is cursed by clairvoyance, cut off from the ordinary lot of her sex:

> This flesh will never give a child its mother,—
> Song, like a wing, tears through my breast, my
>   side,
> And madness chooses out my voice again,
> Again. . . .

She is the voice of fury itself, "The shrieking heaven lifted over men, / Not the dumb earth, wherein they set their graves." Her knowledge is apocalyptic, her urgency daemonic, the symbol of that part of the psyche which drives the conscious mind to recognize truths it is reluctant to accept. For Cassandra, poetry assaults and afflicts her, setting her off from humankind and rendering her the doomed and solitary witness of "the shambling tricks of lust and pride." Thus the poem serves as evidence for what Harold Bloom was the first to say: that Louise Bogan, while "usually categorized as a poet in the metaphysical tradition or meditative mode . . . is a Romantic in her

rhetoric and attitudes." From its hidden source, poetry creates speech which is profoundly *other* and *opposed* to the received notions of men.

A more conventional lyric theme can be found in the strong, simple speech of "Girl's Song." Bogan wrote it in Vienna on May 25, 1922, and its composition gave her some trouble. The first stanza originally read:

> Winter, that is a roofless room,
> Tavern to rain, was our love's home.

But she had already used the phrase, "This is a countryside of roofless houses, — / Taverns to rain, —" in "A Letter." Clearly an image based on a vivid memory of New England landscapes, it was changed to

> Winter, that is a fireless room
> In a locked house, was our love's home.

This eccentric, sad metaphor captures the bitterness and irony that Bogan sustains throughout the entire poem. She worried about its tone, asking Rolfe Humphries, who wanted to publish it in *The Measure* during his acting editorship, if it didn't sound "*too* Housman," too pastoral, melancholy, and ironic. Humphries must have reassured her, since she made no further changes.

It is one of Bogan's consummate "girl's songs," a cross between a traditional lyric on spring's return and a girl's lament for the betrayal of love and her lost innocence. This mix of genres was already familiar in the seventeenth century, where, as in Campion's "The peaceful westerne wind," irony is found in the *contrast* between spring's return and love's death. Bogan's disabused speaker, however, sees an identity, and an inevitability, in the simultaneity of the two events. Addressing her imagined rival, she prophesies the same fate she herself has suffered, speaking no more as a "girl" but as an experienced woman. Here the heart's time and nature's time beat out the same rhythm:

> Now when the scent of plants half-grown
> Is more the season's than their own
> And neither sun nor wind can stanch
> The gold forsythia's dripping branch,—
>
> Another maiden, still not I,
> Looks from some hill upon some sky,
> And, since she loves you, and she must,
> Puts her young cheek against the dust.

The three poems which conclude the first section of *Dark Summer,* "Feuer-Nacht," "Late," and "Simple Autumnal," are extraordinary, rich with complex harmonies of sound and meaning. Bogan never mentions "Late" in her letters and papers, and, to my knowledge, it has been overlooked by both reviewers and critics. Yet it is as strong and as bleak a presentation of spiritual desolation as exists in her work. Its images of a broken psyche extend as far back as the brutal desert landscape of "A Tale," as the no-longer ecstatic imagination surveys the "sterile cliff" and "cold pure sky" of its emptied visions. Thus barren, maddening, and mocking, the world stands denuded and hostile. The screaming cormorant, the "Stony wings and bleak glory" that "Battle in your dreams" appear to have walked out of some Yeatsian nightmare. Cryptic as the poem is—for we know nothing about its composition or background—its sense of desolation and derangement is unmistakable. Two poems from the later, second part of the book—**"Fiend's Weather"** and **"I Saw Eternity"**—speak of a similar mood of wild embitterment and terrible clairvoyance. In **"Fiend's Weather"** there is a windstorm of disillusionment, so that the mind now sees the world with a fierce knowledge of reality:

> In this wind to wrench the eye
> And curdle the ear,
> The church steeple rises purely to the heavens;
> The sky is clear.
>
> And even to-morrow
> Stones without disguise
> In true-colored fields
> Will glitter for your eyes,

The same mood of enraptured despair produces the equally driven and ecstatic vision of **"I Saw Eternity"**:

> O beautiful Forever!
> O grandiose Everlasting!
> Now, now, now,
> I break you into pieces,
> I feed you to the ground.
>
> O brilliant, O languishing
> Cycle of weeping light!
> The mice and birds will eat you,
> And you will spoil their stomachs
> As you have spoiled my mind.
>
> Here, mice, rats,
> Porcupines and toads,
> Moles, shrews, squirrels,
> Weasels, turtles, lizards,—
> Here's bright Everlasting!
> Here's a crumb of Forever!
> Here's a crumb of Forever!

The poem inverts the beginning of Henry Vaughan's "The World":

> I Saw Eternity the other night
> Like a great *Ring* of pure and endless light,
>   All calm, as it was bright,
> And round beneath it, Time in hours, days, years
>   Driv'n by the spheres
> Like a vast shadow mov'd.

Vaughan's poem held a deep attraction for Bogan, who was fascinated by the planetary dance. True to her contrast-loving nature, she preferred the pre-Copernican picture of the universe, yet held to her modern sense of man's diminished and dependent position within its law-governed order. It is an act of daemonic despair to break the harmonious unity of Eternity and light, and to feed its fragments to the lowly creatures of the earth.

Bogan composed **"Feuer-Nacht"** at Yaddo, in August 1926, and like **"The Alchemist,"** it charts the course of relentless passion. Figurative to the point of allegory, but built out of private metaphors, its "shuttered eye," "leaf-shaped flame," rock, sedge, and grass belong to the same rough geography, that inner New England, of Bogan's early poetic world. In German, *feuer* means "passion" as

well as "fire," and the title's "night of fire" suggests a wild, dangerous, and forbidden conflagration that burns at night, witnessed from a secret place, devouring everything in its path. Like the "fire in a dry thicket / Rising within women's eyes" of **"Men Loved Wholly Beyond Wisdom,"** this is love at its most savage and violent, strangely enhanced through being contained in the stark formality of the poem's structure.

"Simple Autumnal" follows, and it is one of the great lyrics in American poetry. The poem's long lines steadily bear the burden of unreleased, shored-up emotion in a dirgelike rhythm that moves with all the dignity of a solemn procession:

> The measured blood beats out the year's delay.
> The tearless eyes and heart, forbidden grief,
> Watch the burned, restless, but abiding leaf,
> The brighter branches arming the bright day.
>
> The cone, the curving fruit should fall away,
> The vine stem crumble, ripe grain know its sheaf.
> Bonded to time, fires should have done, be brief,
> But, serfs to sleep, they glitter and they stay.
>
> Because not last nor first, grief in its prime
> Wakes in the day, and hears of life's intent.
> Sorrow would break the seal stamped over time
> And set the baskets where the bough is bent.
>
> Full season's come, yet filled trees keep the sky
> And never scent the ground where they must lie.

This sleep, this stupor that arrests life appears as the refusal to mourn, a perverse defiance of that process Freud called "grief-work," whereby painful memories must be reexperienced, and relinquished. The tenacious avoidance of pain engenders a deeper suffering. The exhaustion of the girl in **"A Letter,"** who craves only her food "and sleep," the stone speaker of **"Medusa,"** and the stone girl with lifted heel in **"Statue and Birds,"** have all suffered this paralysis, this inability to surrender to the claims of life. Yet, according to natural law, grief exists for precisely this purpose, to awaken the sufferer to feeling and time. Its course is limited, its role "not last nor first." The delay must end, and life win out. Bogan made this point clear to herself in altering the last line. When first published in *The New Republic* in December 1926, it read: "And never scent the ground where they will lie." This she changed to "And never scent the ground where they must lie," an emendation that precisely defines the poem's conflict, being a statement of necessity, resistance to which is possible only through the narcosis of denial.

The poem is a cry for deliverance not *from* but *to* the body of this death, to the liberation of grief and integration into the seasonal cycles of ripening and decay that are the principal themes of *Dark Summer* as a whole. Behind it lies a terrible fear of sterility and estrangement from natural life. The landscape of **"Simple Autumnal"** sets forth, as no poem of Louise Bogan's had yet done, the task her poetry as a whole had assumed as early as the adolescent **"Poplar Garden"**—to seek alliance with life, through art, rather than escape, and to set the wintry, betrayed, stunned, and sleeping heart to beating.

First published in the June 1925 issue of *The Measure,* "The Flume" was included in **Dark Summer,** but then removed from all subsequent collections. It is perhaps Bogan's most openly autobiographical poem, and, considering her belief in the superiority of art detached from its source, obviously unacceptable to her. But it was an extremely useful poem for her to have written. Thinking that she was temperamentally unfit for long narratives in either prose or verse, she found that she could tell a complex story set down in long, untiring writing bouts. More important, the poem also allowed her to cut away an abundance of crystalline nuggets from the matrix of childhood memory. In a letter to John Hall Wheelock from Hillsdale on December 7, 1928, thanking him for his praise of the poem, she wrote that she had spent her childhood in mill towns and "was happy to be able to do something with that remembered noise of water." The flume reached back as far as memory could go, to Milton, where she later remembered that it "cascaded down the rocks, with bright sun sparkling on the clear, foamy water. My mother was afraid of the flume. It had voices for her; it called her and beckoned her. So I, too, began to fear it."

The woman in the poem, like Louise's mother early in the century, is married to a man who leaves every day for work. But there the resemblance between the two ends; the woman in **"The Flume"** is much closer to Louise herself, who, when she was writing the poem in the summer of 1924, was consolidating her relationship with Raymond Holden and trying hard to overcome the distrust that reached back to Milton and her betraying mother. Modeled on Viola Meynell's short stories, but composed in verse, the poem attempts to exorcise Bogan's fear by giving it distance and a separate shape blended of memory and invention.

The poem did not start out as a long narrative. At first, Bogan had wanted only to write a lyric about thunder. "Did you ever have that kind of mindless, idealess compulsion that you must do a lyric called 'Thunder' (or any other name)?" she wrote to Rolfe Humphries on July 22, 1924. Two days later she informed him that she hoped to finish the passage on lightning (which eventually became Part II) and that in it she planned to concentrate on the thunder more than the lightning, adding that "the lightning startles me merely, the thunder would wring me with fright were I a mole underground." By the end of August, the poem had become a narrative, and an exasperating one at that. She informed Humphries that she had lost all interest in its heroine, "who used to rush around the house hoping she'd be betrayed. I'm sure she's been betrayed by this time and has taken to washing dishes and having babies, like any other milky-breasted female, married to a he-man." By September 6th, the end was in sight. The lightning passage was finished and there was only one more part, out of four altogether, to compose. At what point the poem strayed from its original preoccupation with thunder to the flume itself has not come to light, despite Bogan's occasional progress reports to Humphries.

The poem's story could not be simpler. The heroine, going about her daily tasks in a fury of suspicion, searches the house for clues of her husband's infidelity. In a sudden storm she experiences her inner turmoil and the outer tumult as a single madness, hearing the sound of the flume, in the momentary stillness between roars of thunder, as a symbol of the love she cannot accept. At last, returning to her home after what appears to be an attempt to run away, she undergoes a moment of illumination that restores her to wholeness and enables her to love and accept love in return.

Throughout, the poem is studded with precisely recalled and imagined details which establish the mingled atmosphere of the simple New England house, its rootedness within the seasons, and the woman's wild emotion:

> The fields have gone to young grass, the syringa
>   hung
> Stayed by the weight of flowers in the moving
>   morning.
> The shuttered house held coolness a core against
> The hot steeped shrubs at its doors, and the blaz-
>   ing river.
> She in the house, when he had gone to the mill,
> Tried to brush from her heart the gentlest kiss
> New on her mouth. She leaned her broom to the
>   wall,
> Ran to the stairs, breathless to start the game
> Of finding agony hid in some corner,
> Tamed, perhaps, by months of pity, but still
> Alive enough to bite at her hands and throat,
> To bruise with a blue, unalterable mark
> The shoulder where she had felt his breath in
>   sleep
> Warm her with its slow measure.

She searches the rooms of the house for a letter or a ring, anything "to set her grief, / So long a rusty wheel, revolving in fury," but all she hears is

> . . . the noise of water
> Bold in the house as over the dam's flashboard,
> Water as loud as a pulse pressed into the ears,
> Steady as blood in the veins . . .

Because of the "guilt in her to be betrayed," the "terrible hope" that her husband cannot love her, she cannot sleep in peace beside him:

> At night his calm closed body lay beside her
> Beyond her will established in itself.
> Barely a moment before he had said her name,
> Giving it into sleep, had set the merciful
> Bulwark of spare young body against the dark-
>   ness.
> Her hair sweeps over his shoulder claiming him
>   hers,
> This fine and narrow strength, although her
>   hands
> Lie, shut untenderly by her own side.
> Her woman's flesh, rocking all echoes deep,
> Strains out again toward ravenous memory.
> He lies in sleep, slender, a broken seal,
> The strong wrists quick no more to the strong
>   hand,
> The intent eyes dulled, the obstinate mouth
>   kissed out.
> Outside the dam roars. He is perhaps a child,
> With a child's breath. He lies flexed like a child,
> The strong ribs and firm neck may count for
>   nothing.

She will think him a child. He is weak and he
will fail her.

In Part II the terror within is matched by the terror without. The thunder comes as she huddles against the dusty
wallpaper, sweeping her up into the whirl of her suppressed instincts—the same movement of feeling presented in **"Feuer-Nacht."** Suddenly she loves her life and
its orderly tasks in "the free still air." This stillness deeply
present within her is the stillness (as opposed to the terrible "purpose" of her obsession) of nature in its darkest,
most primitive, mysterious, and abiding form:

> —Still—still—everything quieter then
> Than the very earth escaping under the plough
> The depth beyond seed of the still and deep-
>   layered ground
> Stiller than rock; than the blackest base of rock,
> Than the central grain crushed tight within the
>   mountain.

Yet she fights this stillness, saying nothing to her husband
when he returns except what might be said casually at dinner time about a storm. Still she fights acceptance, wishing
to hurl the thunder at the growing earth and the love, the
"itching love / So much like sound," pulsing within her
like the waters over the flume.

In the final section the woman, who has run away, returns
to her house. Her husband is still at work, but there is a
good fire in the kitchen that "has turned the stove lids gol-
den-red." As she "pulls the frozen patch of veil from her
mouth / And stands, like a stranger, muffled from the
cold," her obsession—the "unsated pulse of fury"—
returns. But she soon becomes aware of the winter's deep
quiet; the flume is frozen solid, its customary roar silenced:

> And here at last the lust for betrayal breaks.
> Her blood beats on, and her love with her blood
> Beats back the staring coldness that would kill
>   her,
> Laying a palm over the ebb and return
> Of her warm throat, heard now for the first time
> Within this room. Soon he will find her,
> Still dressed for flight, quiet upon his bed,
> When he has hurried from the weighted cold
> Toward the faint lamp upstairs. She will lie there
> Hearing at last the timbre of love and silence.

On the subject of withdrawing the poem from later collected editions, Bogan wrote:

> I have never been quite sure about **"The Flume."**
> It came from the right place, and I worked hard
> on it, and it has some nice moments—the hot
> stove and the no-sound of water—which were
> actually observed and lived with, at one period
> of my life. Perhaps I have the feeling that one
> doesn't get out of that kind of obsession so easi-
> ly—the "facts" are false, at the end. When I'm
> dead, someone will gather it up and insert it in
> the *works,* I suppose. With notes!

The truth was that, in life itself, Bogan had never quite
conquered her own obsession with betrayal, and fate had
conspired with her fears. The ending *is* melodramatic and
"easy." Still, the heroine's experience of love as the onrush

of a bodily force, far from being false, was and remained
a central ideal in Bogan's faith, both as an artist and a
human being.

Not surprisingly, the poems that come after **"The Flume,"**
those Bogan gathered as the fruits of a "later" mood, are
filled with further intimations of pain and blight. The title
poem, **"Dark Summer,"** published a year after Bogan
married Holden, registers a vision of consummation from
which the speaker and her companion are unaccountably
excluded:

> Under the thunder-dark, the cicadas resound.
> The storm in the sky mounts, but is not yet
>   heard.
> The shaft and the flash wait, but are not yet
>   found.
>
> The apples that hang and swell for the late
>   comer,
> The simple spell, the rite not for our word,
> The kisses not for our mouths,—light the dark
>   summer.

Akin to the thunder section in **"The Flume,"** the poem
sketches a pastoral ceremony of erotic fulfillment within
time. But unlike the late comer, who will receive the fruit
and the kisses, the speaker and her lover seem to be caught
within a premature, unripe, and unripening love, prevented once again by some nameless obstacle from participating in the flow of natural time and love. Another kind of
sexual pessimism haunts **"Tears in Sleep":**

> All night the cocks crew, under a moon like day,
> And I, in the cage of sleep, on a stranger's breast,
> Shed tears, like a task not to be put away—
> In the false light, false grief in my happy bed,
> A labor of tears, set against joy's undoing.
> I would not wake at your word, I had tears to
>   say.
> I clung to the bars of the dream and they were
>   said,
> And pain's derisive hand had given me rest
> From the night giving off flames, and the dark
>   renewing.

Bogan has made this poem the vehicle of an extraordinarily subtle insight into one way in which neurotic grief and
suffering ultimately provide a defense against passion. In
her "cage of sleep," the speaker of the poem is separated
from the "stranger"—the other, the lover—whose presence is true, and real, and as such far more dangerous than
the "false grief" that afflicts the dreamer. And **"For a
Marriage"** stops at nothing short of sexual cynicism. Out
of a pretty trope of sentimental exchange, which might
well have a source in Sidney's "My true love hath my
heart and I have his," Bogan constructs an elaborate (and
somewhat labored) conceit of marriage as a double-edge
sword—the wife's neurotic character—which the husband
(suitor-courtier-knight) must "clasp on." In return for
girding himself with this weapon, he gets to "keep his life
awake," an ever-ready defender of his wife against herself.
At the very least, "he will know his part," have a purpose,
role, and destiny, and these in turn will shield him against
the recognition of his own weaknesses.

In such poems as **"Simple Autumnal"** and **"Tears in**

Sleep," the mode of contrast, so essential to Bogan's poetic imagination, in which public and private images forge ironic antitheses, resembles Baroque chiaroscuro, in which illuminated masses move in and out of heavy shadow. A description of Renaissance tropes as "both openly resplendent and artificially shadowed" applies equally well to Bogan's figures, with their strongly pictorial contrasts of light and dark. In yet another way her preoccupation with light and dark places her securely within the tradition of the American Renaissance. Critic Clement Greenberg has pointed out that "chiaroscuro, literally and figuratively, was the favorite vehicle of Victorian poetic meaning." Bogan, who apprenticed herself to Victorian poetry, shares the tendency of Hawthorne, Poe, Melville, Dickinson, and, later, James, to work with "oppositions which heave a retreating, inward-directed force like that of contrasts of light and shade within deep space."

Bogan's chiaroscuro took its tone and technique from seventeenth-century lyric poetry, its mixing of private and public symbols from Symbolism, and its precision from her American eye for visual fact. In the brief lyric, **"Song for a Slight Voice,"** a poem in which musical instruments serve as intricate emblems much as they do later in the magnificent **"Song for the Last Act,"** Bogan presents the figure of a heart likened to a viol "Stained with the dark of resinous blood," evoking a cluster of chiaroscuro-like impressions incapable of naturalistic analysis. In **"The Crossed Apple,"** she mixes Yankee and Baroque sensibilities to perfection, blending the traditional fairy tale with a plainly worded yet ecstatic vision of earth, and setting forth the apple as both an archetypal symbol of temptation and fall, and a matter-of-factly observed object in nature, much as Thoreau himself might have discussed it. During the Hillsdale period she was avidly reading Thoreau, and may well have encountered this paragraph in "Wild Apples":

> These apples have hung in the wind and frost and rain till they have absorbed the qualities of the weather or season, and thus are highly *seasoned*, and they *pierce* and *sting* and *permeate* us with their spirit. They must be eaten in *season*, accordingly, —that is, out-of-doors.

The speaker in **"The Crossed Apple"** makes a similar claim:

> Eat it; and you will taste more than the fruit:
> The blossom, too,
> The sun, the air, the darkness at the root,
> The rain, the dew,
>
> The earth we come to, and the time we flee,
> The fire and the breast.

The surprising end—"I claim the white part, maiden, that's for me. / You take the rest"—is gloriously mean-spirited: the speaker well knows that the red half, **"Sweet Burning,"** is full of love's poison. Such a poem comes out of the freedom to mix genres. In **"Sonnet,"** however, with its stately and solemn language, Bogan displays a sense of obedience toward convention, with somewhat uncertain results. She herself was not absolutely sure about the poem. Writing to Ruth Benedict in March 1929, she asked her friend to be *"perfectly* critical about it. Is all this bone

business just funny?" The bone business *was* funny. And there was a touch of "fine writing" of the sort Bogan was ordinarily the first to censure. The intricate meditative sonnet on high "Metaphysical" matters was not her forte, despite the recent example of Elinor Wylie's estimable results with the form. Bogan needed a core of drama, common life, and strong speech to give vitality to her work. Yet, in **"Come, Break with Time,"** she writes an extremely meditative, "Metaphysical," and at the same time *simple* lyric. Vaughan's trope of Time "in hours, days, years / Driv'n by the spheres / Like a vast shadow," echoes in it through the antiphonal language of command and defiance that prevails in **Body of This Death** but with the exception of this poem is fairly muted in **Dark Summer.** In this poem, however, Bogan offers two voices, one that exhorts and another that retorts. The exhorting voice, which belongs to the nature-hating will, counsels the defiant heart to cease commerce with change, and its insidious, soothing tones are directed at a heart both wearied and weakened by time. The besieged yet defiant heart can only utter, *"I shall break, if I will."* The exhorting voice, hearing this ambiguity, bypasses it with its own executioner's sophistry in "Break, since you must," an oracle preempting all choice and counseling only compliance with necessity. This severance from time may be death, but it is more likely the sleep of **"Simple Autumnal,"** or the paralysis of **"Medusa,"** where comfort is gained only by becoming virtually insensate.

With **"Old Countryside,"** Bogan completes the group of poems in the "later mood." Bogan later said that she saw the poem as holding to some of the Imagist precepts, primarily direct treatment of the *thing,* whether subjective or objective, and strict avoidance of any word not bearing directly on the presentation of the matter at hand. The poem is filled with such directness: the "slant shutter," "mansard roof," the mirrors in the attic (like those in **"The Cupola"**), the creaking clapboards, the "You" of the poem "braced against the wall . . . , / A shell against your cheek," the brown oak-leaves, dry trees, the "scrawled vine," the "rose-branch . . . / Red to the thorns," and "The thin hound's body arched against the snow." As the facts which demonstrate that "all has come to proof," these sharply etched images have the edited exactness of memory, the extraordinary clarity of watchful intuition marking a cycle of fulfillment:

> Long since, we pulled brown oak-leaves to the
>   ground
> In a winter of dry trees; we heard the cock
> Shout its unplaceable cry, the axe's sound
> Delay a moment after the axe's stroke.
>
> Far back, we saw, in the stillest of the year,
> The scrawled vine shudder, and the rose-branch
>   show
> Red to the thorns, and, sharp as sight can bear,
> The thin hound's body arched against the snow.

Pain edges this final vision. The rose-branch stands naked, the hound holds its body back from the snow, and the shuddering vine, in being "scrawled," suggests some indecipherable message which can only be understood in retrospect. The poem's imagery, which on one level is as public and precise as an illustration to some book of *très riches heures,* is on another level a hieroglyphics of fate.

Published in the August 1929 issue of *Scribner's Magazine,* **"Old Countryside"** is Bogan's poem of love and praise to the months she and Holden spent working on the Hillsdale house. It is Holden who braces the wall and holds the shell, the figure of stability and harmony. The two people in the poem have come full circle; they share a past of labor and of lived-out time. Thus the last two stanzas are all the more haunting. The "unplaceable" cry of the cock, the as yet indistinct possibility of betrayal, echoes at the end, and the hound's arched back remains as taut and poised as suspicion.

Harold Bloom, calling **"Summer Wish"** Louise Bogan's "most ambitious poem," believes that it marks "the crisis and mid-point of her career," but this was to come in the next decade of her life. **"Summer Wish,"** however, does sum up a period of personal and poetic fulfillment, and it is her one great poem in a major style and major mode, capable of standing alongside Yeats's "The Tower" and Stevens's "Sunday Morning" as a testament of renewal and acceptance.

In a letter to May Sarton in 1954, Bogan remarked, "The last time I lived with the full cycle of the seasons was more than 20 years ago, when Raymond and I had the little house near Hillsdale. 'Summer Wish' came out of that." It came, too, out of her obsession with sexual betrayal, which once again provides the poem with its obsessive structure of *antithesis.* She says, in her prefatory notes to the recorded reading of the poem, that its dialogue form is not strictly an imitation, although "the form of a dialogue between two voices is one often used by Yeats," and adds that the "background of the poem is New England."

The poem's roots reach deep into the history of the English lyric, as far back, in fact, as the medieval lyric, "Sumer is icumen in," which is echoed in the epigraph to **"Summer Wish,"** the opening lines of Yeats's "Shepherd and Goatherd": "That cry's from the first cuckoo of the year. / I wished before it ceased." They are spoken by the Shepherd, the affirmative voice of Yeats's poem, whose wish is objectless, a cry of pure desire simultaneous with the cry of the early cuckoo.

Yet another of Yeats's poems, "Ego Dominus Tuus," provided a model. On May 1, 1929, Bogan wrote to John Hall Wheelock that **"Summer Wish"** was "really coming to life. For a time I despaired of it; now it has its shape and sound, a climax or two and an ending that really excites me, all in the mind; one or two good intensive spurts will finish it, I trust." She added that it would take the form of "a colloquy between *This One* and *The Other,*" phrases which are translations of *Hic* and *Ille,* the voices of "Ego Dominus Tuus," who act out the Yeatsian division between the known self and its unknown other.

Within this highly formal structure, Bogan presents a meditative eclogue on the problem of despair. The two voices remain voices, not characters, although the subject matter is exactly the same as that in the versified, highly psychological short story of **"The Flume."** Each voice has its own sound, its own rhythms, diction, and tone through

which Bogan shows the power of language to create and sustain a point of view which each speaker assumes to be "objective."

Thus, in **"Summer Wish,"** Bogan's task is not to absorb the negative self within the stronger affirmative self, but simply to get the First Voice to speak the language of the Second. It is no easy goal. The First Voice perversely misinterprets everything the Second says, throwing out embittered, querulous challenges to it, in an attempt to disqualify whatever the Second Voice offers by way of affirmation or assurance. Wisely, the Second Voice quietly outmaneuvers the First by responding with *description* rather than retort. But it must work hard. The First Voice proclaims deception, concealment, and doom with consuming pessimism. Summer is not the season of renewal, but the harbinger of autumn and mortality:

> We call up the green to hide us
> This hardened month, by no means the beginning
> Of the natural year, but of the shortened span
> Of leaves upon the earth. . . .

With the knowledge that such despair devours everything offered to appease it, the Second Voice makes no counterargument, but rather mingles pure praise in a surface of pure description:

> In March the shadow
> Already falls with a look of summer, fuller
> Upon the snow, because the sun at last
> Is almost centered. Later, the sprung moss
> Is the tree's shadow; under the black spruces
> It lies where lately snow lay, bred green from the cold
> Cast down from melting branches.

Through this calm exposition, the Second Voice in effect gives a reasonable explanation for the appearances the First Voice regards with dread. It looks forward rather than back, delighting in the inflections of change. To the Second Voice the vernal equinox cannot lie: it augurs the "look of summer"; but the First Voice finds this "A wish like a hundred others," cracking open the Second's optimistic almanac as if it were a bitter nut of delusion. With fanatic resistance, the First Voice shouts out its denials:

> You cannot, as once, yearn forward. The blood now never
> Stirs hot to memory, or to the fantasy
> Of love, with which both early and late, one lies
> As with a lover.

To the first Voice, desire, volition, the capacity to make wishes are not only pure illusion, but blind egotism:

> Now do you suddenly envy
> Poor praise you told long since to keep its tongue,
> Or pride's acquired accent,—pomposity, arrogance,
> That trip in their latinity? With these at heart
> You could make a wish, crammed with the nobility
> Of error. It would be no use. You cannot
> Take yourself in.

This despairing confession forms the heart of the poem.

To wish—to be capable of desire—is, in effect, to write a poetry of praise: of what, to the resentful and cynical will, *looks like* arrogant insincerity and mere literature. Incapable of this simple rite of acceptance and faith, the First Voice bitterly acknowledges its own sense of futility. With its picture of the world stemming from its own broken, paralyzed self, it can only see the world *as* itself.

The Second Voice, evading the First's animadversions as it had at the beginning of the poem, urges it to "Count over" what exists separate from itself:

> . . . lilies
> Returned in little to an earth unready,
> To the sun not accountable;
> The hillside mazed and leafless, but through the
>   ground
> The leaf from the bulb, the unencouraged green
> Heaving the metal earth, presage of thousand
> Shapes of young leaves—lanceolate, trefoil,
> Peach, willow, plum, the lilac like a heart.

To the First Voice, this vision is neither spontaneous nor true, but made up of disguised remnants of memory and dream. Having failed to relinquish the past, the First Voice sees it concealed in every aspect of the present!

> Now must you listen again
> To your own tears, shed as a child, hold the
>   bruise
> With your hand, and weep, fallen against the
>   wall,
> And beg, *Don't, don't,* while the pitiful rage goes
>   on
> That cannot stem itself?

The First Voice now reveals itself distinctly as a *woman's,* as it continues its litany of pain and despair:

> Or, having come into woman's full estate,
> Enter the rich field, walk between the bitter
> Bowed grain, being compelled to serve,
> To heed unchecked in the heart the reckless fury
> That tears fresh day from day, destroys its
>   traces,—
> Now bear the blow too young?

Against this outburst, more a soliloquy than a reply, the Second Voice invokes the pattern and movement of the growing light of early April. It is light "there's no use for," existing purely in itself, independent of memory, desire, dream, or any form of human illusion, and "misplaced" because it affirms a world detached from the human. True to itself, the First Voice senses a snare and rejects this vision of tranquility, conjuring up, in another recapitulation of Bogan's private obsessions, the "betraying bed" and its "embrace that agony dreads but sees / Open as the love of dogs." These are eyes made not to see beauty, but the pornographic horrors of jealousy. For the First Voice, spring's arrival and sexual betrayal are identical, as they are for the speaker of **"Girl's Song."**

Persistent, assured, and transcendent, the Second Voice offers a visual parable that recalls both **"Division"** and **"The Mark,"** pointing to the human freedom to make everything, or nothing, from the visible:

> The cloud shadow flies up the bank, but does not

> Blow off like smoke. It stops at the bank's edge.
> In the field by trees two shadows come together.
> The trees and the cloud throw down their shad-
>   ow upon
> The man who walks there. Dark flows up from
>   his feet
> To his shoulders and throat, then has his face in
>   its mask,
> Then lifts.

In these lines Louise Bogan achieves mature poetic vision, mapping out a place for human life in a universe defined by mortality rather than by man's relation to himself, freeing him from solipsism only to prepare him for death. It is at this point at last that the First Voice hears what the Second has said. Questioning itself, it sees its own madness, its own unintelligibility, and its own brooding narcissism:

> Will you turn to yourself, proud beast,
> Sink to yourself, to an ingrained, pitiless
> Rejection of voice and touch not your own, press
>   sight
> Into a myth no eye can take the gist of;
> Clot up the bone of phrase with the black con-
>   flict
> That claws it back from sense?

Admitting that it perverts reality and speaks in an indecipherable private language which shuts off the possibility of shared meaning, the First Voice goes on to acknowledge its division of "the gentle self" into "a yelling fiend and a soft child." Out of this, the confrontation necessary for renewal takes place, and although its tones are still defeatist, the First Voice accepts "a vision too strong / Ever to turn away."

As if sensing that the First Voice has now reached a point of maximum openness, the Second responds with a Blakean vision of evening: "In the bright twilight children call out in the fields. / The evening takes their cry. How late it is!"

The antiphon of children and evening echoes the epigraph, with its cuckoo's cry and Shepherd's wish. Going on to present a vision of ultimate order within time, the Second Voice brings the poem to resolution:

> Fields are ploughed inward
> From edge to center; furrows squaring off
> Make dark lines far out in irregular fields,
> On hills that are builded like great clouds that
>   over them
> Rise, to depart.
> Furrow within furrow, square within a square,
> Draw to the center where the team turns last.
> Horses in half-ploughed fields
> Make earth they walk upon a changing color.

As the Shepherd's wish merges with the cry of the bird, the First Voice fits its voice to the Second's: "The year's begun; the share's again in the earth." No longer a traitor to itself, it pours out its joy, rich with the laughter of "the natural life," as Yeats's Goatherd calls it. Laughter draws the poisons, "aconite, nightshade, / Hellebore, hyssop, rue, —" and leaves freedom for the wish:

Speak it, as that man said, *as though the earth
  spoke,*
By the body of rock, shafts of heaved strata, separate,
Together.

The man referred to in these lines is Thoreau, who wrote,
on March 3, 1841:

I hear a man blowing a horn this still evening,
and it sounds like the plaint of nature in these
times. In this, which I refer to some man, there
is something greater than any man. It is as if the
earth spoke.

This human vision now overwhelms the First Voice:

Speak out the wish.
The vine we pitied is in leaf; the wild
Honeysuckle blows by the granite.

An excerpt from *Journey around My Room*

I used to think that my life would be a journey from the
particular squalor which characterized the world of my
childhood to another squalor, less clear in my mind, but
nevertheless fairly particularized in my imagination.
When I see some old building—one of those terrible
rooming houses with a milk bottle and a brown paper
bag on nearly every windowsill—being demolished, I say
to myself, in real surprise: "Why, I have outlasted it!"
For it was these old brick hotels and brownstone lodging
houses that I early chose, consciously as well as subconsciously, as the dwelling of my old age. I saw them,
moreover, as they were in my childhood, with the light
of a gas mantle making their dark green and brown interiors even more hideous; with the melancholy of their
torn and dirty lace-curtained windows intact. Before the
upper windows of some, an electric sign of an early vintage—of the kind that sported a sort of running serpent
of red or green electric bulbs—was fastened; and I often
have imagined the room behind or contingent to such a
sign: the chair by the window, lit up by this fitful and
pitiful light. Or I imagined my old age shut up in one of
those brownstone houses, which, jelled in poverty, still
stand on the upper side streets of cities. There among
varnished furniture, grotesque wicker chairs, and dusty
carpets, I would rock away my ancient days. There, if
the downward sweep of fortune's wheel caught me off
balance, I would end up; return. The old residents were
waiting, shuffling up and downstairs in felt slippers; gos-
siping on the landing. The gas ring and the cheap frying
pan, the improvised larder with its bits of food, the
chipped enamel coffeepot and the saucepan for soup—all
were there, behind some ragged curtain, waiting for me
to return—to relive, in poverty-stricken old age, my poverty-stricken youth *in Ballardvale, a small town in Massachusetts, on the Boston & Maine Railroad.* . . .

Louise Bogan, in Journey around My Room: The
Autobiography of Louise Bogan, A Mosaic, *Viking,
1980.*

At last, when the Second Voice speaks to the First, it can
guide it, confident of shared vision:

See now
Open above the field, stilled in wing-stiffened
  flight,
The stretched hawk fly.

Like the end of Stevens's "Sunday Morning," with its casual flocks of pigeons, and the bird's "sleepy cry" among
the "deepening shades" of Yeats's "The Tower," the poem
concludes with an earthly moment that makes no claims
beyond its own evanescent completeness. Though the
poem may well be Louise Bogan's "Resolution and Independence," as Harold Bloom has called it, its assent is not
to human endurance, but to nature and time as the some-
thing-more-than-human that defines, and gives an unas-
sailable dignity, to the human.

Gloria Bowles   (essay date 1987)

SOURCE: "The Authority of Male Tradition," in *Louise
Bogan's Aesthetic of Limitation,* Indiana University Press,
1987, pp. 19-33.

[*In the following excerpt, Bowles examines the influence of
the Symbolists, the Metaphysicals, W. B. Yeats, and Johann Wolfgang von Goethe on Bogan's artistic development.*]

[T]he historical sense compels a man to
write not merely with his own generation in
his bones, but with a feeling that the whole
of the literature of Europe from Homer and
within it the whole of the literature of his
own country has a simultaneous existence
and composes a simultaneous order.

　　　　　—T. S. Eliot, "Tradition and
　　　　　　　the Individual Talent"

May a poet write as a poet or must he
write as a period?

　　　　　—Laura Riding and Robert Graves,
　　　　　　　A Survey of Modernist Poetry

I have been thinking about Censors. How
visionary figures admonish us . . .

　　　　　—Virginia Woolf, *Diary*

[T]hose women artists esteemed by men are
not ones to declaim themselves women.
Neither in puzzlement or pain (like Lowell)
nor in bitterness (like Louise Bogan).

　　　　　—Florence Howe, *No More Masks!*

To think about literary influence in the case of a woman
writer is to find oneself in the midst of a special complexity. The woman writer must contend with two traditions:
that tradition which has been considered normative, universal—the male literary tradition—and that writing
which until recently was not thought of in terms of a tradition but as a kind of minor current flowing below the
mainstream—the writing of women. The work of Louise
Bogan gives us a particularly compelling opportunity to
see how these two traditions conjoin in the poetry and
thought of a distinguished woman of letters writing from

the twenties through the forties in America. It is clear, on the one hand, that the woman poet comes to the tradition of male poetry from a different route than men; and it is also clear that in one way or another she must contend both with the women writers who preceded her and those who are writing in her own time. Some women poets do not make a point of avoiding the label "woman poet"; Louise Bogan, however, began her career by publicly dissociating herself from other female poets. She made it quite clear she wanted to be placed among the poets of the mainstream (male) tradition. In 1939 Bogan agreed to respond to a *Partisan Review* questionnaire on literary influence. She had in the past declined such requests, being private both about her life and her influences. By 1939, however, she was more conscious about her image as a poet: She had published three major books and was well ensconced as the *New Yorker*'s poetry editor. The *Partisan Review* asked if she was "conscious, in your own writing, of the existence of a 'usable past,' " if that usable past was primarily American, and to what extent she thought Whitman and James were crucial to the development of an American literary tradition. It is clear from her response that Louise Bogan's idea of what poetry should be came from that canon of male poets taught in literature courses in high school and college. Her response shows she wanted to be seen in terms of that tradition. She pointed first to her classical background:

> Because what education I received came from New England schools, before 1916, my usable past has more of a classic basis than it would have today, even in the same background. The courses in English literature which I encountered during my secondary education and one year of college were very nutritious. But my "classical" education was severe, and I read Latin prose and poetry and Xenophon and the *Iliad* during my adolescence.

From this early study of the Latin poets Bogan first experienced the pleasures of formal poetry, pleasures of rhythm and control that would remain at the center of her aesthetic. Rhythm for her was bound up with human life: "So we see man, long before he has much of a 'mind,' celebrating and extending and enjoying the rhythms of his heartbeat and of his breath." And: "We think of certain tasks the rhythm of which has become set. Sowing, reaping, threshing, washing clothes . . . "

In her response to the *Partisan Review,* Bogan went on to acknowledge the modernist poets and their predecessors who in the late nineteenth and early twentieth century changed ideas of what poetry should be. It is not surprising that Bogan, who was always acutely aware of literary currents and was a self-educated literary historian, looked to these poets:

> Arthur Symons' *The Symbolist Movement,* and the French poets read at its suggestion, were strong influences experienced before I was twenty. The English metaphysicals (disinterred after 1912 and a literary fashion during my twenties) provided another literary pattern, and Yeats influenced my writing from 1916, when I first read *Responsibilities.* The American writers to whom I return are Poe (the *Tales*), Thoreau, E. Dickin-

son and Henry James. Whitman, read at sixteen, with much enthusiasm, I do not return to.

Thus, Bogan's strategy is to invoke the dominant tradition and to place herself within it. I want now to focus on the center of her response, the attribution of influence to the symbolists, the metaphysicals and Yeats, for here are the roots and the flower of modernism, that tradition in which Louise Bogan wanted her own work to find its place. I will save discussion of the only American, and the only woman in this list, Emily Dickinson, for the next chapter, and will remark upon those influences, such as Rilke, who are not mentioned in this catalogue. What Bogan leaves out of this official list is as interesting as what is put in; the list shows us her idea of the way she wished to be seen in terms of the history of poetry.

Thus, before we proceed, I want to add the complication of gender to this list of influences. Only time and distance would make it possible for Bogan to speak directly on this subject. The issues she raises in the following passage from her *Achievement in American Poetry, 1900-1950,* published in 1951, were barely under the surface as she began her literary career. As she opens her chronicle of the development of modern American poetry—after she had nearly completed her contribution to that development— Bogan puts forward the view that Edwin Arlington Robinson had restored some truth to poetry: His contribution was to bring it "from the sentimentality of the nineties toward modern veracity and psychological truth." Yet, according to Bogan, he "did little to reconstitute any revivifying warmth of feeling in the poetry of his time." In her chapter called "The Line of Truth and the Line of Feeling," Bogan then goes on to point out who did bring that "warmth of feeling" to poetry:

> This task, it is now evident, was accomplished almost entirely by women poets through methods which proved to be as strong as they seemed to be delicate. The whole involved question of woman as artist cannot be dealt with here. We can at this point only follow the facts, as they unfold from the later years of the nineteenth century to the beginning of the twentieth: these facts prove that the line of poetic intensity which wavers and fades out and often completely fails in poetry written by men, on the feminine side moves on unbroken. Women, as "intuitive" beings, are less open to the success and failures, the doubts and despair which attack reason's mechanisms. Women's feeling, at best, is closely attached to the organic heart of life. . . .

Bogan assiduously avoids "the question of the woman artist" (although in her later years she liked to quote Henry James's line about "that oddest of animals, the artist who happens to be born a woman"). She brings together those seeming opposites, strength and delicacy, as the special characteristics of women such as Lizette Woodworth Reese and Louise Imogen Guiney. Although she did not speak openly about it until the fifties, this idea of woman's gift would have a profound impact on Bogan's assessment of what was valuable in poetry and what she could use from the dominant tradition. As we look more closely at Bogan's public statement for the *Partisan Review,* let us keep in mind the limitations and problems inherent in any study of influence. For the sake of this study, I define as "influences" those poets from whom Bogan learned the lessons of craft and whose examples gave or denied her permission to express certain kinds of emotion in poetry. The earliest influences were the most crucial ones, those that carried her through her relatively brief lyric career. Ours will be an excursion into the ways in which Bogan's work differs from, and is similar to, those artists she invokes as a literary pattern; for, as we shall see, the male tradition has limited usefulness for the woman poet. It is, in fact, my contention that Bogan absorbed the stylistic lessons of modernism and then used those techniques to elaborate a necessarily different subject matter, the themes of love, madness, and art derived from her life as an American woman. Moreover, as our final chapters will show, although she learned from and used the male modernist tradition, she paradoxically made a major contribution to the development of a female tradition in poetry. In other words, as she used the male tradition, she transformed it for women.

Louise Bogan's letters and critical work contain many more references to the symbolists and to Yeats than to the metaphysicals. She read the symbolists early in her career and then in 1936 she carefully reread Baudelaire, Mallarmé, and Rimbaud. ("This morning I got down five or six notebooks, that have been gathering dust in the back closet, and discovered how v. studious I was in 1936. Pages and pages in French and English . . ." [To May Sarton, 23 May 1954]) Of the three major symbolist poets, I think only Mallarmé had any direct influence on her style, although his subject matter, as we shall see, was not open to her. She identified with Rimbaud's irreverence ("He did the only thing a poet *should* do: he shocked hell out of everyone by a series of semi-criminal acts, and then he got out, for good and all" [To Rolphe Humphries, 26 Sept. 1938]), but she did not think the "surrealist" mode suitable for women. Most of her writing about Baudelaire was occasioned by new translations of his work, including a 1947 version, which prompted her to speak of "the first poet who saw through the overweening pretensions of his time." She also noted that "the working of this stylistic machine are now outmoded. And nothing is more tiresome than the reiterated subject—so usual in the early Baudelaire—of women as puppet, as sinister idol of the alcove, or as erotic mannequin." Bogan's early understanding of what we now call "images of women" in male literature is remarkable—but what interests us most here is that Baudelaire's French rhetoric was too outdated for a modern American poet to use in any direct way. We can only say that Bogan is distantly related to Baudelaire, in the sense of a long historical line that finally produced modern poetry, since the compactness and the intensity of the modernist lyric do owe something to the author of *Les Fleurs du Mal*.

We do not always agree today with its critical judgments but Arthur Symons's *The Symbolist Movement* was important because it introduced the French poets to an English-speaking audience. For Symons, Mallarmé's art of suggestion, the evocation of emotion, the emotion itself in the poem, brought something new to the art:

"Poetry," said Mallarmé, "is the language of a state of crisis"; and all his poems are the evocation of a passing ecstasy, arrested in mid-flight. This ecstasy is never the mere instinctive cry of the heart, the simple human joy or sorrow . . . which he did not admit in poetry. It is a mental transposition of emotion or sensation, veiled with atmosphere, and becoming, as it becomes a poem, pure beauty.

In this dramatic, hyperbolic passage, we have the idea of an emotion caught by the poet, a technique Bogan imitated. Yet for her there was nothing trivial about "the cry of the heart." In fact, she once said that she could not write novels because "my talent is for the cry or the *cahier*. . ." (To Theodore Roethke, 6 Nov. 1935). For Mallarmé, as one contemporary critic has written, "the more rigidly the poetic symbol excludes the world of natural reality and the initial emotion the more closely it approximates the ideal of art." Bogan's poetry depends on this initial emotion: "Lyric poetry, if it is at all authentic . . . is based on emotion—on some real occasion, some real confrontation," she wrote (To Sister M. Angela, 20 Aug. 1966).

From Mallarmé and the modernist school that followed him Bogan learned distancing, surely. Yet it is a matter of degree; she would not move so far from the emotion as to disown it. Although his extreme attitude toward emotion in poetry was not her own, Mallarmé's technique was instructive for her. In 1954 she praised one of May Sarton's poems because it used a symbol like the center of a wheel, with spokes radiating out from, and returning to, the poem's center: "I liked 'Little Fugue,' unbreakable old symbolist that I am: a central symbol holds all together, and yet radiates. . . . This grand (in the Irish sense) method Mallarmé passed on to us. . . ." In order to make this point more concretely—and to show how Bogan carved out a poetic territory influenced by, but different from, that of her male masters—let us look closely at one of the most famous examples of a work that articulates Mallarmé's flight into a pure realm of art. "Les Fenêtres" harks back to Baudelaire and looks forward to the English symbolists. I have selected this poem for its expression of a dominant modernist theme; only later would Mallarmé develop to their fullest the new techniques these themes made necessary. There are many other poems I might have chosen to illustrate the escape into pure beauty—and its concomitant flight from life—that characterizes male poetry from the late nineteenth century through the 1920s; I have selected this one because it stands at the beginning of a poetic tradition upon which Mallarmé had enormous influence. For in "Les Fenêtres" Mallarmé imagines a dying man in a hospital, weary of flesh and material reality, who presses his pale face up against a window bathed in sunlight. There he finds a kind of Baudelairian vision of peace and beauty that provokes an overwhelming sense of disgust with the material world, represented as women and children:

Ainsi, pris du dégoût de l'homme a l'âme dure
Vautré dans le bonheur, où ses seuls appétits
Mangent, et qui s'entête à chercher cette ordure
Pour l'offrir à la femme allaitant ses petits,

(Thus, seized with a disgust of man whose hard
    soul
Wallows in happiness, where only his appetites
Eat, and who persists in searching for this filth
In order to offer it to the woman nursing her
    children,)

The dying man-poet would leap through the windows to flee the real world. Remarkably, he sees himself reborn as an angel:

Je fuis et je m'accroche à toutes les croisées
D'où l'on tourne l'épaule à la vie, et, béni,
Dans leur verre, lavé d'éternelles rosées,
Que dore le matin chaste de l'Infini

Je me mire et me vois ange! et je meurs, et j'aime
—Que la vitre soit l'art, soit la mysticité—
À renaître, portant mon rêve en diadème,
Au ciel antérieur où fleurit la Beauté!

(I flee and I hang on to all the windows
From where one turns one's shoulder away from
    life, and, blessed,
In their glass, washed by eternal dews,
Which gild the chaste morning of the Infinite,

I look at myself and I see myself as an angel! and
    I die and I love
—Whether the pane be art or whether it be mys-
    ticism—
To be reborn, wearing my dream like a diadem,
To the prior heaven where Beauty flowers!)

This would-be angel must be thrust out of reverie and returned to earth: "Mais, hélas, Ici-bas est maître" (But alas! the world below is master). Forced to live with human stupidity, still, in the final stanza his bitter self asks once again, beseechingly, whether there is a way out, an escape from this life down below.

"Les Fenêtres" is a youthful poem, marked by the excesses of youth, yet it registers the sentiments of many modernist poems written before and after it. These are the poems dedicated to an aesthetic that would take life out of art. In the years that followed "Les Fenêtres" Mallarmé succeeded more and more in achieving "total annihilation of the 'life' emotion which inspired the poem." Aspects of this aesthetic would reach into twentieth-century modernist poetry. In "Les Fenêtres" Mallarmé expresses a disgust for the physical, and in an act of hubris rare for a woman who writes and impossible to Bogan, he imagines himself escaping the Real, fleeing to a transcendent realm beyond the glass. He can even see himself as Ange. The modernist aesthetic, when it posits an absolute division between art and life, is antithetical to women's realities. First, a woman is usually in no position to choose life or the state of an angel; she must go on "allaitant ses petits," feeding her children, if not literally her children, then responding to the consuming needs of real human beings. (And if she chooses to entrust the care of her daughter to others at certain points in her life, the woman poet like Bogan or H.D. is accused of consummate selfishness.) Love and relationship is at the root of Bogan's poetry; when she cut herself off, as she did sometimes, in exhaustion, she could not write.

Bogan's conscious confrontations with the tradition forced her to define herself as a poet. She carved out her own subject matter and her own style.

—Gloria Bowles

The reader of modern poetry, then, who comes to *The Blue Estuaries* expecting the flight from life, the exclamations over the Void that we see in such poems as "Les Fenêtres," will be thrown off guard, even led to say this is not "good" poetry because it is different. The preoccupation with the Void can be traced to Baudelaire's "gouffre" poems; this is the abyss of nothingness that, for Baudelaire, the Catholic moralist, meant confrontation both with a loss of faith and a hanging on to it. The loss becomes complete among many male writers and thinkers later in the nineteenth century, and into the twentieth, which spawned great variations on this theme of the emptiness of life. The final existential attitude, we now understand, was inimical to most women, who as the guardians of life had neither the luxury nor the predilection to think about non-life. We have said that Bogan learned something about distancing from Mallarmé and the twentieth-century modernists but she never took it as far as her male precursors. Put differently, Bogan used modernist examples to rein in her powerful emotions, but she also wanted feeling and human experience in the poem. This use of modernist form distinguishes her both from the male modernists and from the legacy of female poetry that she wished to counter. In **"The Cupola"** we have both the distancing and the attachment to experience. The speaker enters a dome-shaped room, a setting inspired perhaps by Bogan's Maine birthplace which had "such a cupola and eaves made of gingerbread. . . ." She finds in this upper room a mirror that reflects nature, the outdoors. Trees and the wind appear in this mirroring:

THE CUPOLA

A mirror hangs on the wall of the draughty cu-
    pola.
Within the depths of glass mix the oak and the
    beech leaf,
Once held to the boughs' shape, but now to the
    shape of the wind.

Someone has hung the mirror here for no reason,
In the shuttered room, an eye for the drifted
    leaves,
For the oak leaf, the beech, a handsbreath of
    darkest reflection.

Someone has thought alike of the bough and the
    wind
And struck their shape to the wall. Each in its
    season
Spills negligent death throughout the abandoned
    chamber.

The poem illustrates what Bogan learned from the modernists about indirect expression; seen in the context of the other poems in this, her most "removed" volume, **Dark Summer** (1929), the setting becomes a metaphor for the human capacity for destruction. In the first stanza, there is the feeling of the room, the presence of the speaker in it, and the moving of trees reflected in a mirror. Human agency, something even a little frightening, enters in the second, for "someone" has placed the mirror in this room, seemingly for no reason. Yet it provides an "eye," even a double vision for anyone coming into this secret, shuttered place; the lovely, inspired phrase, "a handsbreath of darkest reflection," brings the suggestion that this room yields the chance for greater self-knowledge. The poem grows more violent in the third stanza, repeating the idea of human agency: There is no choice now but to see clearly the destruction that wind and bough bring in their wake. Emotional destruction of some kind; this we know both from the poem and the volume in which it appears. The atmosphere of absence in the poem is inspired by symbolist techniques as is the evocation of the effect of emotion rather than the specific emotion itself. "Peindre non la chose, mais l'effet qu'elle produit" (Paint not the thing itself but the effect it produces), wrote Mallarmé as he began his Hérodiade. For Mallarmé, the effect would have increasing importance; he would eventually try to shape poetry that was "about" nothing. For Bogan, the rendering of emotional experience was always paramount. In **"The Cupola"** she stays with the inner experience. The poem is a way of understanding experience, not an escape from it. For Bogan, then, the distancing technique operates to register tumultuous human emotion, the effects of terrible division and destruction, feelings that could get out of control in the poem (and in her life) without a contained method for expressing them.

Mallarmé's fenêtre/mirror, on the other hand, beckons toward a realm beyond material reality; Bogan's mirror functions to see human emotional experience doubly. Her sense of the interior scene is dominant: this woman poet is not looking out the window (or leaping out of it) to find transcendent reality. Rather, she is very much in the room, a space she has created. Like many women (and not because of nature but due to nature) Bogan had a strong sense of interiors. This is evident from her journals, her short story **"Journey Around My Room,"** and from her own rooms, described by May Sarton. Here she is speaking of the apartment where Bogan lived from 1937 until her death in 1970:

> I shall not ever forget walking into the apartment at 137 East 168th Street for the first time, after an all-night drive from Washington. I felt a sharp pang of nostalgia as I walked into that civilized human room, filled with the light of a sensitized, bitter, lucid mind. The impact was so great because not since I walked into Jean Dominique's two rooms above the school in Brussels had I felt so much at home in my inner self. In each instance the habitation reflected in a very special way the tone, the hidden music, as it were, of a woman, and a woman living alone, the sense of a deep loam of experience and taste expressed in the surroundings, the room a shell that reverberated with oceans and tides and

waves of the owner's past, the essence of a human life as it had lived itself into certain colors, *objets d'art,* and especially into many books. . . . Louise's word for this atmosphere was 'life-enhancing.'

Sarton's prose is richly evocative of the surroundings Bogan created for her work. Out of a sense of domestic interiors, her own emotional experience, the lessons of the modernists and the "negative" examples of her female precursors, Louise Bogan created a poem like **"The Cupola."**

To summarize, then: Although there is some Mallarmian symbolist influence in the qualities of her verse, content is another matter entirely. Mallarmé disdained the crowd; Baudelaire described life as a hospital in which each of the sick desired only to change beds. This attitude is called "the horror of life" by Roger L. Williams in his study of nineteenth-century French authors. I do not wish to dismiss the great contribution of the French tradition but rather to delineate its limitations for a poet like Louise Bogan whose subject matter came from the center of emotional experience. Not impervious to a certain measure of horror and disgust with existence, she nonetheless kept confronting this attitude and reconnecting with a more complex view of life. As we shall see in the next chapter, her sense of the female gift was inextricably linked to the "heart" that women bring to poetry. It is finally paradoxical that one who inveighed against the female tradition ultimately came to define women's talent in almost stereotypical ways and would in her later career criticize those women poets who tried out "male" modes of expression. But of course a stereotyping of female qualities and a revolt against "female" tradition go hand in hand.

The phrasing of Louise Bogan's response to the *Partisan Review* inquiry about literary influence gives us a clue about the relative importance of her of the "metaphysical" poets. Her syntax suggests they were not crucial: They were a "fashion," a "literary pattern," wedged between the larger influences, the symbolists and Yeats. It is, in fact, hard to relate Bogan to the tradition of metaphysical poetry in part because she wrote very little about it and because it is difficult to say exactly what is meant by the term. Samuel Johnson first named this seventeenth-century mode in the eighteenth, and T. S. Eliot, in an essay first published in 1921 which Bogan may have read, linked it to modernism in the twentieth. Eliot's essay focuses on the stylistic properties of the metaphysicals and on their capacity for thought. Certainly this model did not function for Bogan in the same way as it did for Eliot, that is, as a way to bring thought into poetry. Her work is more reflective than intellectual and this stance comes out of her own experience. Bogan herself had a rather specific definition of metaphysical. Writing to May Sarton, she noted, "You have a *metaphysical* bent: you desire the universal behind the apparent; you have a passion for the transcendent" (21 Oct. 1961). Bogan's later meditative poetry asserts connections between the human and the natural world, a philosophy that derives from her own experience of change and time. The "sexual realism" of some of the metaphysicals had an appeal for the moderns, says one commentator: "In its earliest manifestations, it was . . . distinguished by revolutionary and highly original attitudes toward sexual love. . . . A new kind of sexual realism, together with an interest in introspective psychological analysis . . . became an element in the metaphysical fashion." Surely the stylistic influence was most felt by Bogan, the "telescoping of images and multiplied associations," "the brief words and sudden contrasts" that Eliot notes in his essay "The Metaphysical Poets," citing Donne's

> A bracelet of bright hair about the bone.

Bogan's **"To a Dead Lover,"** published in 1922 and later suppressed, begins

> The dark is thrown
> Back from the brightness, like hair
> Cast over a shoulder.

Jeanne Kammer was one of the first to point out that women poets come to modernism by a very different route from men. She leads us to another distinction between Bogan's choice of subject matter and the province of the male poets she so admired. For Kammer, the tight, controlled poems of male modernists "represent both a dramatization of and a withdrawal from a culture fragmented, disordered, and lacking in central values and vision." Kammer writes that if women's poems reflect fragmentation, this is an "internal division . . . a private experience opposed to the public one of men." Bogan felt that those large questions of the relationship between man and civilization were not her province; only men, in her view, could write about the wasteland. This attitude is another example of her internalization of ideas of woman's role. She seemed to accept the notion that because men are the creators of civilization, because they instigate and fight its wars, they are uniquely qualified to write about this political realm. She made a distinction between the internal world and the external and she felt her subject, even the *genuine* subject, of art was the internal. In the mid-thirties, during the trauma of the Spanish Civil War and the threat of a second large European conflict, Bogan had terrific fights with her male friends about politics. For her, "politics" was the petty, egotistical fight for power among factions, all of them equally ridiculous. Her own lower middle-class origins had something to do with this attitude: The attempt of intellectuals to save the masses was faintly comic to her. Politics was subsumed under something larger, the movements of History, which had a certain inevitability: " '[H]istory' is itself a stream of energy, is 'generous inconsistency'; and . . . those who work with it succeed best when they realize this, as the artist always realizes it. It can't be pawed out of shape; it must be listened to, before being acted upon" (7 Oct. 1940). It is art that nourishes the soul: "I know, and knew, that politics are nothing but sand and gravel: it is art and life that feed us until we die. Everything else is ambition, hysteria or hatred" (To Theodore Roethke, 14 Dec. 1937). She lamented the effect of politics on the poetry of the thirties: "I still think that poetry has something to do with the imagination; I still think it ought to be well-written. I still think it is private feeling, not public speech" (8 July 1938). These attitudes separated her from many of the male poets of her generation as well as from some of the women. H.D., for example, wrote about the effects of war from a female perspective, focusing on its results for personal relationships; her later poetry would dissect patriarchy and male power. H.D. felt as connected to wars of the present and the past, as affected by them, as men. Millay was criticized by Bogan and many others for her political poetry and activism. We are just beginning to learn the extent of the female literary response to the First and Second World War; the more we know, the more Bogan's rejection of this subject matter seems a "female" response and a further example of the limits she set for her work—limits determined in part by her sense of what was possible to a woman poet of her time who wanted immortality through art.

Bogan's conscious confrontations with the tradition forced her to define herself as a poet. She carved out her own subject matter and her own style. Her emotions were so intense that they often threatened to get out of control: she used the modernist aesthetic to provide a form for her strong feelings. "You will remember, I am sure, in dealing with my work, that you are dealing with emotion under high pressure—so that symbols are its only release," she wrote to one interpreter (To Sister M. Angela, 20 Aug. 1966). If modernism was for her a formal strategy for releasing emotion through symbol and compact form, and a way of putting behind her the influences of her early apprenticeship, such as Morris and Rossetti, it did not lead to the "depersonalization" advocated by Eliot. In the fifties, she located her aesthetic between the "depersonalization" of her era and the new confessional modes. Writing to May Sarton, she pointed out that in poetry, "certainly, 'unadulterated life' must be transposed, although it need not be 'depersonalized.' Otherwise you get 'self-expression' only; and that is only half of art." The distinctions between "transpose," "adulterated," and "depersonalized" are subtle indeed and understandable only within the context of Bogan's interpretation of the "male" and "female" traditions of poetry, which we are studying here, and their relationship to her particular talent. For Bogan, emotion is central to the poem but to no avail without skill: "The other half is technical, as well as emotional, and the most poignant poems are those in which the technique takes up the burden of the feeling instantly; and that presupposes a practiced technique . . ." (To May Sarton, 17 Mar. 1955). Through the poem the poet is unburdened of that weight of emotion. This idea of the burden of emotion is delineated in a short essay called **"The Springs of Poetry,"** which Bogan published in 1923 and which we will consider in chapter 5. The idea is also strikingly similar to one held by Sara Teasdale. This is Teasdale's theory of poetry as she outlined it in 1919:

> My theory is that poems are written because of a state of emotional irritation. It may be present for some time before the poet is conscious of what is tormenting him. The emotional irritation springs, probably, from subconscious combinations of partly forgotten thoughts and feelings. Coming together, like electrical currents in a thunderstorm, they produce a poem. . . . The poem is written to free the poet from an emotional burden. Any poem not so written is only a piece of craftmanship.

Teasdale's emphasis is on the emotion; Bogan, a member of the generation after Teasdale, a modernist, underlines the companionship of craft and feeling.

Bogan, then, felt herself walking a fine line between the two traditions, the female and the male. Because it emphasizes the expression of personal feeling and experience, her work did not fit in with Eliot's pronouncements on "objective poetry"—an aesthetic position that, we should note, had a profound impact on an academic establishment that did not notice Bogan's oeuvre. By the fifties, Bogan had some perspective on other, more extreme manifestations of modern objectivity. Her review of *Auroras of Autumn,* for example, again makes her point about life in poetry. "[N]o one," she writes of Wallace Stevens, "can describe the simplicities of the natural world with more direct skill. It is a natural world strangely empty of human beings, however; Stevens' men and women are bloodless symbols." She feels that his "technique overwhelms the poem: . . . [T]here is something theatrical in much of his writing; his emotions seem to be transfixed rather than released and projected, by his extraordinary verbal improvisations. . . ." A preoccupation with technique—sometimes a way to escape feeling—prevents the release of emotion into the poem. In this review Bogan laments that many younger poets try to imitate Stevens as though they did not realize that other kinds of modern poetry tap the "transparent, overflowing and spontaneous qualities that Stevens ignores."

Her belief in a poetry based on confrontation with emotional experience would lead her eventually to Rilke. She read him late, in 1935, writing to her editor, "And I've just discovered Rilke. Why did you never tell me about Rilke? My God, the man's wonderful" (To John Hall Wheelock, 1 July 1935). She used his invention of the *Ding-Gedichte* ("thing-poems") to great advantage in her later poems. His example may have influenced the title poem of **The Sleeping Fury,** published in 1937. In that year, she wrote that Rilke was the "rare example of the poet who, 'having learned to give himself to what he trusted,' finally 'learned to give himself to what he feared'." Her collections from **The Sleeping Fury** onward took as epigraph two lines from Rilke:

> Wie ist das klein, womit wir ringen;
> was mit uns ringt, wie is das gross . . .
>
> (How small is that with which we struggle;
> how great that which struggles with us.)

Louise Bogan's lack of attraction to the more life-denying manifestations of modernism would lead her to feel a greater affinity for Yeats than for Eliot or Stevens. In fact, of all the male influences, Yeats was the most decisive in her early formative years, the only poet writing in English to make such an impact. She read his work early, in 1916, when she was only nineteen, thus four years before the publication of her first volume, **Body of This Death** (1923). Her collected criticism, **A Poet's Alphabet** (1970), includes five essays on Yeats; one dating from 1938 is entitled **"The Greatest Poet Writing in English Today."** The affinity for Yeats came on many levels. His intensity, his lyricism, his song, mirrored her ambitions for poetry. His aesthetic was hers: "a style of speech as simple as the sim-

plest prose, like the cry of the heart. It is not the business of the poet to instruct his age. His business is merely to express himself, whatever that self may be." Singing is a major theme in her work as it is in Yeats; for Bogan, music was almost as essential as breathing. Her writing on rhythm in poetry often relates the rhythm of breath and song. She played the piano and grew up in a "family of singers: my mother and my brother were constantly 'bursting into song.' And I began to study the piano at seven" (To Sister M. Angela, 5 July 1969). Like Yeats, Bogan had to pull herself away from the influences of the Pre-Raphaelites; like his, her poems could be both bitter and proud. Above all, she admired his enduring capacity for trying to understand his experiences and then transmuting them into art. Her attraction was even more profound because of her Irish roots, an identification strengthened by the immigrant's experience of discrimination: "It was borne in upon me, all during my adolescence, that I was a 'mick,' no matter what my other faults or virtues might be." There were enormous differences as well, those that can be attributed both to class and gender. Yeats had an aristocrat's education, first at home and then in private schools. His central political involvements were far from Bogan's experience. Among Bogan's essays on Yeats, her longest focuses on his role in Irish struggles for artistic and political independence; eventually she would express some impatience with the more conservative expressions of his political life. Nor did she, as a woman who internalized social stereotypes of femininity, have such grand poetic ambitions; Yeats "read a special symbolism into all his private acts and relationships," writes M. L. Rosenthal; and, as Edward Engelberg has pointed out in *The Vast Design,* he developed a complex symbolic system to image his thoughts and feelings. Bogan's aesthetic of limitation decreed that such ambitions were not appropriate to female talent. Moreover, she did not think the idea and argument common to prose was appropriate for lyric poetry. One can find echoes of the early Yeats in early Bogan, in the simplicity of passionate language, even in the melancholy tone; yet she would never use symbol in the way Yeats did in his more philosophical works of the late twenties, after he wrote *A Vision.* In **"The Cupola,"** for example, the image of the mirror insinuates itself into the poem; Yeats, on the other hand, brought to the poem an authoritative or dominant image inspired by his personal mythic system. In fact, much of the power of his later poetry derives from this assertion of a single image.

So far we have seen that the male tradition is authoritative enough that Louise Bogan claimed it and then went on to both selectively use and discard aspects of it. Before we bring to an end this journey into the authority of male influence, I wish to suggest yet another source of inspiration that Bogan did not mention in her catalogue of influences: Johann Wolfgang von Goethe. I realize we are now speaking different languages; however, the direct lyricism, the lack of interest in philosophical themes in the early poems, the "romanticism"—these qualities Bogan shared with the German poet. She read him (with the help of a dictionary and translations) early in her career and in 1924, quoting the "Wandrers Nachtlied," she wrote to a friend:

The stripped, still lyric moves me more, invariably, than any flummery ode
ever written—although, of course, Keats and
the Romantics were only partly
flummery—but

> Über allen Gipfeln
> Ist Ruh

gives me such happiness I want to cry.

(To Rolphe Humphries, 24 July 1924)

Goethe had a remarkable gift for spontaneity—his lyrics
are among the most inspired, the most direct and un-
mediated, I have read. ("Über allen Gipfeln," or so the
myth goes, was scrawled in a moment of inspiration on the
wall of a mountain hut.) This spontaneity stayed with him
all his life. Like Bogan, he was often overwhelmed by
Eros, although his love poems tend to be happier than hers
and his lyric vein lasted much longer. Bogan worked hard
on her German so that she could appreciate its poets. In
an essay on Goethe published in 1949, she noted, rightly
I think, that he is little appreciated by English-speaking
readers because the translations are so poor. For what
counts in so many of his lyrics is *sound*. Bogan suggested
that those who do not read German listen to Hugo Wolf's
songs based on Goethe's lyrics:

> Anyone who has listened to the wild longing of
> the Wolf-Goethe "Kennst du das Land" or to
> the noble and transcendent beauty of their "Pro-
> metheus" and "Ganymed" has experienced the
> only world it is important to share with any
> great poet—the world of his intense emotion and
> his piercing vision.

Late in her life, this strong affinity for Goethe led to translations of several of his prose works, which she worked on
with Elizabeth Mayer. *Elective Affinities* came out in 1963
and *The Sorrows of Young Werther* and *Novelle* in 1971.

What Bogan shares with Goethe, then, is at once a devotion to the formal qualities of art and to intense lyricism,
that is, poetry inspired by significant emotional experience. Yet both poets felt they had to learn to check their
unrestrained emotions; Goethe's early lyrics are overflowing with passion and energy, and in his middle years, he
spoke through *Faust* of the necessity to rein in emotions
that threatened to engulf him. Yet he managed to sing of
love in old age, too, in the eloquent lyrics of the *West-
östlicher Divan*. Ultimately, through Goethe, we realize
that Bogan's poetry has as much of a Romantic cast as a
modern one. Although he does not link her to Goethe,
Harold Bloom some years ago recognized this Romantic
heritage:

> Louise Bogan is usually categorized as a poet in
> the metaphysical tradition or meditative mode,
> following Donne, Emily Dickinson, and older
> contemporaries like Eliot and Ransom. Yet, like
> so many modern poets, she is a Romantic in her
> rhetoric and attitudes. . . . Miss Bogan is pure-
> ly a lyrical poet, and lacks the support of the per-
> sonal systems of Blake and Yeats, by which
> those poets were able more serenely to contem-
> plate division in the psyche. Miss Bogan is nei-
> ther a personal mythmaker, in the full Romantic

tradition, like her near contemporary Hart
Crane, nor an ironist in the manner of Tate, to
cite another poet of her generation. The honesty
and passion of her best work has about it, in consequence, a vulnerable directness.

The last line of this 1958 evaluation echoes Bogan's point
of view in her essay on the female poetic gift, **"The Heart
and the Lyre"** (1947), which I shall discuss in the next
chapter. Bloom at once underlines Bogan's specialness as
he places her within a part of the male tradition that she
did not count, whether consciously or unconsciously, as
"influence." Bloom's is one of the few critical evaluations
before the new feminist criticism that came close to an accurate assessment of Bogan's place in Anglo-American
poetry. His last line opens the way to a consideration of
gender and poetry—although Bloom is not conscious of
this possibility.

Louise Bogan manipulated the white male tradition to her
advantage: By studying and using modernism's lessons,
she put herself within the reigning tradition. This was only
half of her task; the other was to dissociate herself from
the prevailing stereotype of the woman poet, that image
of the wailing and uncontrollable poetess of the nineteenth
century. Susan Gubar and Sandra Gilbert have pointed
out that the woman artist "must confront precursors who
are almost exclusively male, and therefore significantly
different from her. . . . On the one hand, . . . the woman
writer's male precursors symbolize authority; on the other
hand, despite their authority, they fail to define the ways
in which she experiences her identity as a writer." Bogan
used what she could from the male tradition but it had its
limits for her, as it does for any woman, since the emotional experience that goes into the poem is *the experience of
a woman*.

FURTHER READING

Bibliography

Knox, Claire E. *Louise Bogan: A Reference Source.* Metuch-
en, N.J.: The Scarecrow Press Inc., 1990, 315 p.
  Annotated guide to works by and about Bogan.

Criticism

Bowles, Gloria. "Louise Bogan: To Be (or Not To Be?)
Woman Poet." *Women's Studies* 5 (1977): 131-35.
  Argues that Bogan's criticism, letters, and poetry evince
  an ambivalent and contradictory attitude toward womanhood.

Ciardi, John. "Two Nuns and a Strolling Player." *The Nation,* New York, 178, No. 21 (22 May 1954): 445-46.
  Favorably reviews Bogan's *Collected Poems, 1923-53*
  and remarks on works by Leonie Adams and Edna St.
  Vincent Millay.

Collins, Martha, ed. *Critical Essays on Louise Bogan.* Boston:
G. K. Hall & Co., 1984, 210 p.
  Reprints numerous reviews and essays on Bogan's works
  by prominent critics and scholars, including Mark Van

Doren, Kenneth Rexroth, W. H. Auden, and Marianne Moore.

Dodd, Elizabeth. "The Knife of the Perfectionist Attitude," in *The Veiled Mirror and the Woman Poet: H. D., Louise Bogan, Elizabeth Bishop, and Louise Glück,* pp. 71-103. Columbia: University of Missouri Press, 1992.

Discusses the aesthetics of Bogan's poetry. Dodd contends that Bogan considered emotion the source of poetry and combined "a personal classicism" with "elements of lyric romanticism."

Engels, Vincent. "A Memorable Poetry Year." *The Commonweal* XI, No. 2 (13 November 1929): 53-5.

Favorably reviews *Dark Summer,* praising Bogan's sparse language.

Moses, W. R. A review of *Poems and New Poems,* by Louise Bogan. *Accent* II, No. 2 (Winter 1942): 120-21.

Contends that Bogan's poetry possesses a precision and purity that sets it above the work of her contemporaries.

Muller, John. "Light and the Wisdom of the Dark: Aging and the Language of Desire in the Texts of Louise Bogan," in *Memory and Desire: Aging—Literature—Psychoanalysis,* edited by Kathleen Woodward and Murray M. Schwartz, pp. 76-96. Bloomington: Indiana University Press, 1986.

Explicates Bogan's view of human desire, relying especially on her poetry for clarification of her position. Muller contends that Bogan depicted desire as a deceptive impulse arising from narcissism and the ego and, furthermore, believed that aging can enable an individual to understand the nature of desire.

Nicholl, Louise Townsend. "Louise Bogan's Book." *The Measure: A Journal of Poetry* 32 (October 1923): 15-9.

Laudatory review of *Body of This Death.*

Rexroth, Kenneth. "Among the Best Women Poets Writing Now in America." *New York Herald Tribune Book Review* 30, No. 47 (4 July 1954): 5.

Reviews Bogan's *Collected Poems, 1923-53,* along with works by Babette Deutsch and Leonie Adams. Rexroth argues that Bogan's poetry "handles and judges life in real terms" and that her words "seize the mind."

Ridgeway, Jaqueline. *Louise Bogan.* Boston: Twayne Publishers, 1984, 146 p.

Surveys Bogan's career with individual chapters devoted to each major collection.

Upton, Lee. "The Re-Making of a Poet: Louise Bogan." *The Centennial Review* XXXVI, No. 3 (Fall 1992): 557-72.

Remarks on Bogan's critical reception and concludes that Bogan's poetry "will continue to be read—perhaps even more so as we come to recognize the ways that her poetry explores the unconscious dynamics of women's experience."

Whittemore, Reed. "The Principles of Louise Bogan and Yvor Winters." *The Sewanee Review* LXIII, No. 1 (January-March 1955): 161-68.

Compares the poetry of Bogan and Winters, concluding that "ultimately their poems' most noteworthy element is style rather than substance."

Additional coverage of Bogan's life and career is contained in the following sources published by Gale Research: *Contemporary Authors,* Vols. 73-76, 25-28 (rev. ed.); *Contemporary Authors New Revision Series,* Vol. 33; *Contemporary Literary Criticism,* Vols. 4, 39, 46; *Dictionary of Literary Biography,* Vol. 45; *Major 20th-Century Writers,* and *Poetry Criticism,* Vol. 12.

Mary Brave Bird

1953-

(Also known as Mary Crow Dog, Ohitika Win, and Brave Woman) American political activist and autobiographer.

The following entry provides an overview of Brave Bird's life and career through 1993.

INTRODUCTION

A Lakota Sioux of the Brulé, or Sichangu, tribe, Brave Bird is known for her autobiographies, *Lakota Woman* (1990) and *Ohitika Woman* (1993), both of which were written with Richard Erdoes. These works are notable for their candor and insight into the problems and challenges faced by Native American women in contemporary Native culture and American society.

Biographical Information

Brave Bird was born on the Rosebud Sioux Indian Reservation in South Dakota, where she was raised by her grandparents and educated at the St. Francis mission school. While a teenager, she became interested in the history, religion, and traditions of her people, and, in 1971, she joined the American Indian Movement (AIM). With other AIM members, Brave Bird occupied the Bureau of Indian Affairs building in Washington, D.C., in 1972 and participated in the protest and siege at Wounded Knee, South Dakota, in 1973. There she met her future husband, Leonard Crow Dog, a Sioux holy man and Indian rights activist. She later divorced Crow Dog and remarried. She is the mother of five children.

Major Works

In *Lakota Woman,* which was published under the name Mary Crow Dog, Brave Bird recounts her impoverished childhood on the Rosebud Sioux reservation, her rebellious youth, her growing awareness of her heritage, and her marriage to Crow Dog. This work, which won the American Book Award in 1991, also details Brave Bird's involvement in the 71-day siege at Wounded Knee, during which her first child, Pedro, was born. *Ohitika Woman,* published under the name Mary Brave Bird, traces the author's life from 1977 to 1992. In this work, she describes her participation in the Native American Church, her continuing struggles with poverty and alcoholism, a near-fatal car accident, and her relationship with her children and second husband Rudy.

Critical Reception

Critical reaction to *Lakota Woman* and *Ohitika Woman* has been generally favorable. Most praise Brave Bird's candor in describing the difficulties and hardships of

growing up as a Native American woman. Several critics comment on her "fierce feminism," her political activism in the American Indian Movement, and her work to preserve Indian identity, religion, and traditions. While some critics applaud her storytelling ability and accessible "kitchen-table style," a few fault the "cyclical" structure of her writing, arguing that it sometimes confuses the chronology of events and detracts from the impact of the narrative. Still, most critics agree that Brave Bird's autobiographies contribute much toward a better understanding of the cultural and social challenges faced by Native American women in contemporary American society. Gretchen M. Bataille has stated: "In her Lakota society, Brave Bird has found strength and support as well as a shared history. In spite of the poverty, alcoholism, and routine beating of women that she has witnessed and been a victim of, Brave Bird is a survivor who understands the context of her life. She is communicating her pain as well as her joys to people who see only curio shops on their trips through South Dakota."

PRINCIPAL WORKS

Lakota Woman [as Mary Crow Dog; with Richard Erdoes] (autobiography) 1990
Ohitika Woman [as Mary Brave Bird; with Richard Erdoes] (autobiography) 1993

CRITICISM

Gretchen M. Bataille   (review date 19 June 1990)

SOURCE: "Search for an Indian Self," in *The Washington Post,* June 19, 1990, p. 4.

[*Bataille is an American educator and author of several books on Native American culture. In the following favorable review of* Lakota Woman, *she praises Brave Bird's candor but suggests that the work's "cyclical" structure may be difficult for readers used to linear narratives and chronological autobiographies.*]

Mary Crow Dog's autobiography, **Lakota Woman,** is the story of one woman; however, it tells the tale of many Indian women who have faced the wrath and the pride of their own men and the brutality of government control, and benign neglect, but who have emerged strong and whole in spite of their wounds. Mary Crow Dog is a Lakota woman, and the narrative resonates with the anguish of that reality.

Hers is a harsh story of enduring the whip of Catholic nuns in boarding school and the pain of losing some of her friends in the Indian struggle for civil rights. The title reflects her final acceptance of identity: From viewing herself as a half-breed to achieving wholeness through the Sun Dance ceremony, she has accepted her role within the tribe and for herself.

The traditional power of women, based on the stories of White Buffalo Woman and celebrated by puberty ceremonies, has been eroded and Indian women have been the victims of rapes, beatings and forced sterilizations. Although Mary Crow Dog recognizes that Indian men give "great lip service to the status women hold in the tribe," women are no longer held in such high esteem as tradition would dictate.

Structurally the narrative is difficult to follow if one is accustomed to chronological life histories. But Mary Crow Dog is Indian, and the cyclical pattern so often employed in stories and reflected in ceremonies provides the framework for her narrative. The cycle began before 1890 and erupted with Wounded Knee and the massacre of Indian people by the 7th Cavalry. Eighty-three years later Mary Crow Dog has her first son during the 1973 takeover at Wounded Knee. Echoes of the past reverberate throughout the book; she recalls the "ghostly cry and lamenting of a woman and child coming out of the massacre ravine" of Wounded Knee Creek while she escapes the gunshots that strike close to her and her new baby.

Mary Crow Dog, the wife of the Sioux holy man Leonard Crow Dog, provides the reader with information about Indian history and contemporary reality as she interweaves her life story with that of her people. Although the traditional *tiyospaye,* or extended family, has been destroyed by the intervention of government regulations, boarding schools and the intrusion of social workers, in the end a different kind of extended family has emerged. She tells of her "family" during the Wounded Knee siege; even in New York, where she waited for her husband's release from prison, Mary Crow Dog found "family" to care for her. Contemporary Indian reality has bred new relationships to maintain connections to tradition and to ensure cultural continuity amid change.

Early in the narrative, she writes, "You have to make your own legends now." The full story of Wounded Knee will never be told, but Mary Crow Dog's account echoes those of others who saw the event as cruel recognition that life had not changed much for Indians in South Dakota. The deaths of Pedro Bissonette and Annie Mae Aquash are testimony to what Mary Crow Dog sees as the ongoing persecution of American Indians. In spite of the 1868 Fort Laramie Treaty and the recognition of the Sioux as an independent nation, reservations continue to be what Vine Deloria Jr. calls "dependent domestic nations."

Mary Crow Dog's narrative is an addition to a long history of Indian life stories, some written in English and others told through interpreters. The bicultural production of a text created by an Indian woman working with a white man is not unusual, yet the questions always remain—how much is Mary Crow Dog's story and how much was filtered through the lens of collaborator Richard Erdoes' knowledge of Indian life? Erdoes worked with Lame Deer

---

An excerpt from *Ohitika Woman*

Maka ke wakan—the land is sacred. These words are at the core of our being. The land is our mother, the rivers our blood. Take our land away and we die. That is, the Indian in us dies. We'd become just suntanned white men, the jetsam and flotsam of your great melting pot. The land is where even those Native Americans who live in the wasichu cities, far away from home, can come to renew themselves, where they can renew their Indianness. We have an umbilical cord binding us to the land and therefore to our ceremonies—the sun dance, the vision quest, the yuwipi. Here, the city Indians can relearn their language, talk to the elders, live for a short while on "Indian time," hear the howl of brother coyote greeting the moon, feel the prairie wind on their face, bringing with it the scent of sage and sweet grass. The white man can live disembodied within an artificial universe without ties to a particular tract of land. We cannot. We are bound to our Indian country.

It is no wonder that we love it so.

Mary Brave Bird, in her *Ohitika Woman,* Grove Press, 1993.

---

to produce his autobiography, and this story complements Lame Deer's narrative. The voices in each are different, however, suggesting that much of what has been written has been presented as Mary Crow Dog related it.

This is not the reflective story of an Indian who has lived to old age; Mary is 34 years old when the story is told. This is not an account that consciously attempts to maintain old ways or traditional stories as many autobiographies have done. More than anything, this is the story of Mary Crow Dog's growing awareness of who she is as a Sioux woman and as a political force for change for her people. The messianic movement of the Ghost Dance in 1890 brought brief promise to the Plains Indians who danced because that was the only hope they had. The founding of the American Indian Movement in 1968 rekindled that hope. In the 16 years of her life that form the basis of the book, Mary Crow Dog has learned that she is the inheritor of the memories and stories of the past. As a Lakota woman, she has learned the importance of storytelling to create and maintain identity.

Patricia Guthrie   (review date 1 July 1990)

SOURCE: A review of *Lakota Woman,* in *The New York Times Book Review,* July 1, 1990, p. 15.

[*In the following review, Guthrie assesses* Lakota Woman.]

"Two thousand came to Wounded Knee in 1973. *One stayed,*" reads the epitaph of a Sioux Indian buried at the South Dakota site. Mary Crow Dog was part of the 71-day siege of Wounded Knee's museum, church and trading post by the American Indian Movement. Seventeen years old at the time, she lost an uncle and bore a son during the takeover, which pitted the Federal Government's military might against medicine men and young men armed with old rifles. Ms. Crow Dog's *Lakota Woman,* written with Richard Erdoes, the author of *The Pueblo Indians* and *The Sun Dance People,* details how she arrived at that fateful confrontation. Raised by Sioux grandparents and a mother who refused to teach her the native language because "speaking Indian would only hold you back, turn you the wrong way," Ms. Crow Dog received her initiation into Indian traditions during the Wounded Knee siege, where she learned from the spiritual leader Leonard Crow Dog, whom she subsequently married. The story of her coming of age in the Indian civil rights movement is simply told–and, at times, simply horrifying. Throughout the book, Ms. Crow Dog's recollections seem to exemplify the Cheyenne proverb that introduces her story: "A nation is not conquered until the hearts of its women are on the ground."

Penny Skillman   (review date Summer 1991)

SOURCE: "Fleshing Out Our Story of America," in *Belles Lettres: A Review of Books by Women,* Vol. VI, No. 4, Summer, 1991, p. 5.

[*In the following excerpt, Skillman praises Brave Bird's candid portrayal of the American Indian Movement during the 1960s in* Lakota Woman.]

Mary Ellen Crow Dog tells such an entertaining story of her life in *Lakota Woman* that it is easy at times to overlook the fact that the tale is about the Native American struggle to stave off genocide. Crow Dog relates how a young hippie from New York visited the Rosebud reservation on which she lived in the late 1960s and challenged the "res" Indians: "Black people are getting it on. Indians are getting it on in St. Paul and California. How about you?"

The American Indian Movement spread like wildfire in the political vacuum that existed on the reservations, and of all the rights movements, it was a particular thorn in the government's side. Crow Dog observes about the Indian and Black struggles: "They want in. We Indians want out!"

AIM was made up predominantly of young Indians and elders who had kept to the traditional ways of living. The author does an excellent job of describing how their civil rights battles changed their thinking and catapulted her and others from a rural arena to national prominence. "We lived in a strange, narrow world of our own, suspicious of outsiders. Later, we found ourselves making speeches on campuses, in churches, and on street corners talking to prominent supporters such as Marlon Brando, Dick Gregory, and Angela Davis." From a youth of alcoholism and hoboing on and off the reservation, Crow Dog joined the 1972 cross-country march on Washington, after which the Indians occupied the Bureau of Indian Affairs building there. The BIA building occupation made what AIM leader Russell Means referred to as "a helluva smoke signal" since it represented the Indian Nation taking a significant collective action for the first time.

The second section of the book is largely taken up with the 1973 Indian occupation of Wounded Knee, the subsequent government siege to reclaim it, and later the author's marriage to and life with Lakota medicine man Leonard Crow Dog. Difficult questions, such as the presence of sexism in the Indian movement and the meaning of pervasive alcoholism on the reservation are not avoided, yet the author's analysis of these issues is not in depth. But this is a reflective, refreshingly non-defensive story told by a woman who understood its political implications. Could anyone who lived through the now glorious-seeming 1960s not enjoy this look at one of the civil rights struggles the tumult of those times produced?

Mahtowin   (review date March-April 1992)

SOURCE: "Mary Crow Dog: Real Life Hero," in *New Directions for Women,* Vol. 21, No. 2, March-April, 1992, p. 28.

[*Mahtowin is a Lakota political activist who writes about Native issues. In the following essay, she praises the positive portrayal of Native American women in* Lakota Woman.]

Being a Native woman, I think a lot about the fact that there are so few positive images of Native women in American popular culture. Chances are if you can name three historically prominent Native women, they will be Pocahontas, Sacajaweah and La Malinche, all three of whom, at best, were severely taken advantage of by the white conquerors or, at worst, betrayed their race.

Indian women, when we appear at all (and usually we don't; I'll never forget or forgive the organizers of the massive women's march on Washington in April 1989 for not including even one Native woman on the program) are portrayed as mute beasts of burden or, alternatively, lithesome and loose women who eagerly await the coming of the white man. Nowhere in American popular culture will you find the strong, resourceful, hilarious and human Native women–women whom we remember in our oral history and whom we know as our grandmothers, sisters, friends, mothers and daughters–who have been fighting side by side with Native men against colonialism since the day Columbus got lost.

Things are better at least in the realm of literature where we now have so many gifted women writers, such as Leslie Marmon Silko and Beth Brant, to name only two. If you want to find out what life is really like in Indian Country, open up a book by a Native writer.

Which brings me to **Lakota Woman,** the autobiography of Mary Crow Dog. Read it. Mary Crow Dog is a real life Native heroine. She grew up in the 1950s and 1960s, somehow managing to survive the brutality of racism and reservation poverty, boarding school and wild days of drinking and fighting. As the American Indian Movement (AIM) grew, accompanied by a resurgence in Native pride and militancy, Mary Crow Dog took part in political actions and became increasingly more traditional, less assimilated and lost. She gave birth to her first child during the AIM occupation of Wounded Knee on Pine Ridge Reservation in South Dakota in 1973. She later married the Lakota medicine man Leonard Crow Dog, who was imprisoned for his political activities.

Her story is not just hers, but the story of a whole generation and era. Crow Dog writes of such women as her friend Annie Mae Aquash, the militant Micmac who was murdered by the FBI. She vividly describes the death squads and reign of terror on Pine Ridge during the 1970s both before and after the Wounded Knee occupation. She also talks about the Native American Church, Lakota traditions and what its's like to be the wife of a leading medicine man.

Lakota Woman is narrated in an accessible, "kitchentable" style–you can just imagine Mary Crow Dog sitting across from you talking about her life. The book is funny, appalling in its depiction of racism and government oppression and painfully honest. Mary Crow Dog has lived through and participated in a lot of history in less than forty years, and I hope her story will be read by the widest possible audience.

Kirkus Reviews (review date 1 July 1993)

SOURCE: A review of *Ohitika Woman,* in *Kirkus Reviews,* Vol. LXI, No. 13, July 1, 1993, p. 827.

[*In the following review, the critic offers a mixed assessment of* Ohitika Woman, *stating that while it lacks the "excite-ment" of* Lakota Woman, *it is "a forceful presentation of Native American life today."*]

Native American activist Brave Bird—whose autobiography *Lakota Woman* (1990; written under the author's former married name of Crow Dog) will soon be released as a film directed by Jane Fonda—returns with a disturbing sequel.

Lakota Woman turned heads with its angry plea for Native American rights, its outspoken feminism—and its blatant antiwhite racism. Brave Bird has mellowed a bit, although she still makes caustic remarks about white women, especially New Agers whom she accuses of cashing in on traditional Indian religion. Sadly, her personal life seems as chaotic as ever, as she relates a horrifying story of chronic drunkenness, drug-taking, brawls, poverty, homeless shelters, and batterings by lovers. Readers willing to put up with the sordidness—which culminates in a drunk-driving crash and subsequent open-heart sur-

---

An excerpt from *Ohitika Woman*

All across the country, among all the tribes, Native Americans are angry because the whites are selling our medicine. What Native Americans are saying is that our religion and ceremonies have become fads, and a fashionable pastime among many whites seeking for something that they hope will give meaning to their empty lives. And so our medicine is sold, and hawked about, by fake, non-Indian, so-called "plastic medicine men," giving themselves fancy Indian-sounding names like "Buffalo Grazing on the Mountainside," or "Golden Eagle Soaring to the Sky," or "Free Soul Wrapped in Morning Mist." Such names would not fool a ten-year-old Rosebud kid but are very impressive to the gullible wasichu. Their numbers are growing because there is money, real big bucks, to be made in the fake medicine man (or woman) business. It is an offshoot of the New Age movement and the result of Indians being "in," and of flood of supposedly pro-Indian movies. After macrobiotics, Zen, and channeling, the "poor Vanishing Indian" is once more the subject of "deep and meaningful conversation" in the high-rises.

One white woman, who claims to have supernatural powers taught to her by a Native American holy woman, and who also says that she belongs to a sisterhood of Indian spiritual women that doesn't actually exist, puts on mass sessions of Native teachings. She hires large auditoriums in which she teaches Native wisdom and spirituality to as many as six hundred white participants who pay over three hundred dollars apiece. Members of the audience also have to buy drums and drumsticks, crystals, smudge sticks, a special cushion to sit on, and, especially, the lady's books. Take pencil and paper and figure out the profits she makes. There are some self-styled medicine people who literally make a million dollars a year by selling our medicine.

Mary Brave Bird, in Ohitika Woman, *Grove Press, 1993.*

gery for Brave Bird—will no doubt get the message: that Indians, Lakota in particular (Pine Ridge reservation is the poorest county in the nation), have been shoved to the bottom of the American barrel. Easier to digest are Brave Bird's accounts of Native American rituals, including sweat lodges, spirit communication, and sun dances (during one, Brave Bird is suspended from a tree by thongs skewered through her back). Once again, the author presents a fierce feminist brief, offering biographical tributes to a number of Native American women and celebrating her own "womb power," which brought her five kids—the last by her new husband, Rudi, a tattoo artist.

Without the intrinsic excitement of the first installment, with its firsthand history of AIM and siege at Wounded Knee; still, a forceful presentation of Native American life today.

Pat Monaghan (review date 1 September 1993)

SOURCE: A review of *Ohitika Woman,* in *Booklist,* Vol. 90, No. 1, September 1, 1993, p. 10.

[*In the following positive review of* Ohitika Woman, *Monaghan provides an overview of the book and briefly discusses its publishing history.*]

More than a decade ago and hard upon the success of *Lame Deer: Seeker of Visions,* the autobiography of a Lakota shaman that he coauthored, [Richard] Erdoes completed another manuscript. As he relates in his introduction to this volume [*Ohitika Woman*], that manuscript was rejected by his publisher. "This book is much too radical," the wise editor said. "Mysticism is in. Make her into a witch." Erdoes and Brave Bird (then Crow Dog) refused. That manuscript became the best-selling *Lakota Woman* (1990), which related Brave Bird's life as a rebellious, hard-drinking reservation girl who gave birth to her first child while a teenager on the embattled Wounded Knee reservation. *Lakota Woman* closed when Brave Bird was a partner to radical shaman Leonard Crow Dog. *Ohitika Woman* picks up Brave Bird's life from then to the present. Far from rising above all the problems of poverty and alienation on the reservation, Brave Bird eventually found herself overwhelmed by them. The book opens with Brave Bird crashing, drunk, into a power pole and ends with her "enduring," as she says. In between, we learn of the difficulties facing Native American women today: the domestic brutality, the abandonments, the assaults. But we learn as well of the medicine and rituals that strengthen women of Native American heritage. Despite the pain that courses through it, the book is ultimately hopeful, even if the hope is just that Native American women can continue to endure.

Gretchen M. Bataille (review date 3 September 1993)

SOURCE: "A Brave Woman's Saga of Survival Continues," in *The Christian Science Monitor,* Vol. 85, No. 196, September 3, 1993, p. 11.

[*In the following favorable review, Bataille examines the themes in* Ohitika Woman, *focusing on the role of women in contemporary Native American society and the cultural clash between Native and White American societies.*]

Mary Brave Bird is Ohitika Win, or Brave Woman, the name she earned as a result of her commitment to her people and her community. The badge was not won easily, as this account of a hard life shows.

Brave Bird's story up to 1977 was recounted in *Lakota Woman* (1990), and *Ohitika Woman* continues her history. She tells of her experiences through the artist and writer Richard Erdoes, who along with his wife, Jean, befriended Brave Bird and supported efforts of the American Indian Movement and tribes to gain redress for the grievances of 500 years.

That two books telling the life of one Lakota woman should be published in such a brief period, and that the first should have already received the American Book Award, is testimony to the public interest in the lives of women at the margins of mainstream society, women who are immersed in their own societies in spite of the hardships and deprivations.

In her Lakota society, Brave Bird has found strength and support as well as a shared history. In spite of the poverty, alcoholism, and routine beating of women that she has witnessed and been a victim of, Brave Bird is a survivor who understands the context of her life. She is communicating her pain as well as her joys to people who see only curio shops on their trips through South Dakota.

Ohitika Woman begins in 1991. Brave Bird has survived a near-fatal automobile accident and credits her will to live to a vision of her grandmother telling her she had to survive to care for her children. Brave Bird places herself within family and tribe, tracing her lineage and remembering past events in her life, and then comes back to the present.

As she writes this book, her life is stable: She has remarried, she has stopped drinking, she has reached a level of understanding with her mother, and she is committed to caring for her children. By the end of the book, the reader wants her to succeed and to bring other women with her.

It won't be easy, however. Brave Bird catalogs the abuses Indian women face—at the hands of their men and at the whim of federal bureaucracies, such as the Indian Health Service, and local social service agencies. She poignantly describes Indian women as "always pressing down hard to stop the bleeding of their hearts."

In addition to one woman's life story, the book provides a walk through the darkest pages of Indian-white history in the United States. This history is the backdrop for contemporary Indian reality: It explains why the Sioux have turned down money for their land and why many have rejected Christianity for traditional religions and ceremonies, such as sweat baths and the sun dance.

An increasing number of American Indians are writing about their lives and experiences, and many of them are college-trained professionals. In *The Broken Cord* (1989), Modoc writer Michael Dorris tells the devastating story of fetal alcohol syndrome; he has seen in his adopted children the results of the life Brave Bird describes. There cannot be a redeeming justification for alcoholism and crippling poverty; however, Brave Bird helps the reader understand why the conditions exist.

In a final irony, Brave Bird discusses the increased interest in Indianness, manifested in modern Indian medicine shows, crystals, channeling, and backyard sweat lodges.

None of this interest improves the lives of those Indians living in the poorest counties of the US, and "new age" enthusiasm cannot remove uranium tailings from despoiled Indian land or provide Indians with uncontaminated ground water. All the sympathy in the world will not provide jobs for Indians at the Rosebud or Pine Ridge Reservations.

Brave Bird ends her account by saying, "in the end the spirit wins out." Although it is an appropriate literary ending, changes in the conditions of native Americans will come about only when there is a change in the "spirit" of those outside of American Indian cultures.

FURTHER READING

Criticism

Adams, Phoebe-Lou. Review of *Lakota Woman*, by Mary Crow Dog. *The Atlantic Monthly* 265, No. 5 (May 1990): 133
    Favorably assesses *Lakota Woman*.

Devereaux, Elizabeth. "Two Women," in *The Village Voice Literary Supplement*, No. 100 (November 1991): 27.
    Comparative review of *Madonna Swann: A Lakota Woman's Story as Told through Mark St. Pierre* and *Lakota Woman*.

Norton, Margaret W. Review of *Ohitika Woman*, by Mary Brave Bird. *Library Journal* 118, No. 13 (August 1993): 112, 114.
    Positive review of *Ohitika Woman*.

Review of *Ohitika Woman*, by Mary Brave Bird. *Publishers Weekly* 240, No. 29 (19 July 1993): 243.
    Presents an overview of *Ohitika Woman*.

Additional coverage of Brave Bird's life and career is contained in the following source published by Gale Research: *Native North American Literature.*

Elizabeth Cook-Lynn

1930-

(Born Elizabeth Bowed Head Irving) American poet, short story writer, and novelist.

The following entry provides an overview of Cook-Lynn's career through 1993.

INTRODUCTION

Cook-Lynn is a Crow Creek Sioux writer whose works explore the tensions between twentieth-century Sioux culture and white American society. While her poetry frequently utilizes Indian myth, religion, and tradition to explore the social and cultural roots of Native Americans, her prose generally focuses on the physical and psychological hardships of contemporary Native American life. Strongly influenced by her familial and tribal past, the northern plains landscape, and the works of Kiowa writer N. Scott Momaday, Cook-Lynn often blends traditional Native American chants and tales with western poetry and prose.

Biographical Information

Cook-Lynn was born at Fort Thompson on the Crow Creek Sioux Reservation, where she grew up in a traditional extended-family atmosphere. Her father and grandfather served on the Crow Creek Tribal Council for many years, and her grandmother was a bilingual writer for Christian newspapers. In addition to being well-known figures in Sioux history, these family members had a profound influence on Cook-Lynn's writing. Cook-Lynn received a bachelor's degree in journalism and English from South Dakota State College in 1952, and, in 1970, completed a master's degree in education, psychology, and counseling at the University of South Dakota. She has also pursued graduate study at such institutions as New Mexico State University, University of Nebraska, and Stanford University. After working as a journalist and teaching at the high school level, Cook-Lynn become a professor of Native American studies at Eastern Washington University in 1971 and professor emeritus in 1993. Cook-Lynn also founded *The Wicazo Sa Review,* a journal of Native American studies. She published her first collection of poetry, *Then Badger Said This,* in 1983. Cook-Lynn has received numerous grants, including the National Endowment for the Humanities grant from Stanford University in 1978 and the Northwest Institute for Advanced Studies grant in 1986.

Major Works

In *Then Badger Said This* Cook-Lynn blends traditional stories, oral history, and modern poetic techniques to explore the relationship between contemporary Dakotas and their past. For example, in the poem "The Last Remark-

able Man," which is introduced by a photograph of a Dakota ancestor, Cook-Lynn examines the importance of knowing one's Native American roots; "The Flute Maker's Story" incorporates traditional Indian song and articulates the link between Indian culture and the land. James Ruppert has observed that "in may ways [this] book is an attempt to confirm and recreate the continuance of song, spirit, and history." The deprivations and challenges of contemporary Sioux life are the focus of the stories in *The Power of Horses, and Other Stories* (1990), which address such themes as discrimination, the failure of the English language to adequately articulate Indian sensibilities and needs, brutality against Native Americans, dysfunctional Indian family relationships, and the realities of reservation life. John Purdy has noted that "*The Power of Horses* is a collage of individual characters' experiences that draws into a specific landscape over a long period of time. We come very close to this place and the people who inhabit it." The novella *From the River's Edge* (1991), which takes place in South Dakota during the mid-1960s, continues to pursue the clash between contemporary Sioux life and white American society. The story concerns the trial of a white man who is accused of rustling cattle from John Tatekeya, a respected Sioux Indian rancher. In a bizarre miscarriage of justice, Tatekeya, the victim, is made to look like the guilty party, thus reinforcing the view that Native Americans and the white man will never be able to live together in trust, harmony, and peace.

Critical Reception

The critical response to Cook-Lynn's works has been mixed. While many critics applaud her poetic style, evocation of place, and exploration of the meaning and interpretation of history, others fault her prose for what they see as stereotypical characterizations and intrusive narrative structures. For example, writing about *From the River's Edge,* Purdy has noted that "there are moments . . . when the narrator becomes intrusive [and we] are lectured, at times, on the history of Anglo/Native American relations." Nevertheless, most critics agree that Cook-Lynn's writings are important for their valuable insights into Native American life. Concerning her work, Cook-Lynn has stated that writing is "an act of defiance born of the need to survive. It is the quintessential act of optimism born of frustration. It is an act of courage, I think. And, in the end, . . . it is an act that defies oppression."

PRINCIPAL WORKS

The Badger Said This (poetry) 1977
Seek the House of Relatives (poetry) 1985
The Power of Horses, and Other Stories (short stories) 1990
From the River's Edge (novella) 1991

CRITICISM

James Ruppert (essay date 1980)

SOURCE: "The Uses of Oral Tradition in Six Contemporary Native American Poets," in *American Indian Culture and Research Journal,* Vol. 4, No. 4, 1980, pp. 87-110.

[*Ruppert is an American educator and critic who specializes in Native American literatures. In the following essay, he discusses Cook-Lynn's use of oral tradition in the poetry collection* Then Badger Said This.]

[*Then Badger Said This*] contains purely descriptive passages as well as oral history, but like Momaday's *The Way to Rainy Mountain,* [Cook-Lynn's] approach to history is not the cold, unimaginative one of literal history, but a highly oral process where the personal and the cultural merge. Reflective of this holistic approach to Sioux culture and history, she includes old stories, contemporary poetry, oral history, song, personal narratives and art work.

For Cook-Lynn, the past is not a cold stone tablet; it is a living vital force. As she watches the changes of the present world, it becomes easier for her, and subsequently for us, to understand and believe the changes of history and legend. The personal leads to understanding and confirmation of the mythic, for they are not as separate as some would think. In her description of the flooding behind the Missouri River Project, section II, we are brought to that understanding as we see the people and the land sharing the same fate. They are tied together under the flooding of the dominant culture as they have always been tied together. Section XIII tells of a scene, timeless in location, where a woman, her child and the child's father are fixed in a confluence of the ritual and the personal. The ritual, itself timeless, patterns their perceptions as it does their movements. As the woman contemplates her past, the man and the child, she comes to the painful realization, "The past is always past as it is always present."

This requires a change in perception for those of us who look on history as the rational accumulation of facts. In her preface we are warned to open our minds, ears and eyes to the insight, clear in oral cultures, that history also consists of memory and imagination. To understand history is to imagine, but also it is to hear, to listen. . . . [Cook Lynn] proposes that literalist history is flawed because it has no sound. However indefinite sound may be, it is essential to identity and survival. Survival may depend on listening to sounds around one and this important process eventually gives one language and history. Cook-Lynn tells a variant of the story of the arrow-maker in his shelter. Swan, the young warrior, is working on his arrows while in enemy country. He hears the hoot of an owl nearby and sees the reflection of an enemy in a bowl of water. He lines his arrows up, pointing them in all directions until he surprises the enemy and slays him. The gathering of sensory detail (and attention to it) allows the warrior to survive. The Sioux would agree that the owl spoke to Swan, and "the gathering of sensory detail available to you gives the process of language." The history of the young warrior requires imagination and the memory of sensual detail on the listener's part. A literal historian would not understand where the Sioux would.

History and words are even more closely tied in the poem, **"The Last Remarkable Man,"** which starts with the photograph of one of the ancestors. This remarkable man seems to become alive as the poem continues. His words still hold power. In the Council, the words of others carefully recreate him, bring him back. If the present and the past live simultaneously, then the old man still lives or is continually reborn. With the loss of the literal sense of history we come into a richer, if more difficult world. Cook-Lynn fears that this vision of history has been lost by some contemporary Indians. While she notes that some hold out hope for all mankind because the "universal spread of the myths of men" will reintroduce the oral, she fears that the vision is being abandoned:

> We have walked away from history
> and dallied with a repetition of things
> to the end of the bar and booze
> Like a time bomb it ticks as rapidly
> for White Hawk as for Little Crow
> or me

Song plays a large role in holding this vision intact. Music and the word are always past and present, simultaneously held in a traditional relationship between land and culture. In **"Flute Maker's Story"** the song of the flute player expresses the "mythic pulse" and embodies it in the moment. These songs have power and they etch that power on the land. The flute player's song "interleafs the shadow of the past with standard lines of life and grief." As the song embodies the vision of history as present, it teaches "the word and belief." The land is charged with sound, ready to speak, and the human is taught culture and history, or at least the vision necessary for both. On the next page in section V, we find the rocks speaking to an old Sisseton woman and through them she listens and knows the past. She is able to find the body of a young boy drowned many days previously. It is as if all history still lived in the world around us, if we could but hear it speak. Unfortunately all this could be lost. The section "History of Unchi" suggests that the death of the old storyteller, and those like her, could eventually lead to the sky ceasing to talk. When all things cease to talk, history will be no more.

For Cook-Lynn, the past is not a cold stone tablet; it is a living vital force.

—*James Ruppert*

While sound and song are the life of history, they are also the strength and potency of individuals. The Sioux speak of Meadowlark who, because she is on the ground and open to predators, uses her song to build her strength and survive. Her song speaks to men of all things in the lives of mankind. Cook-Lynn tells of individuals who though they seem Westernized on the surface, still use the songs to bring them strength and identity, and help them survive. Those who can't sing, as in the poem, **"Room of God and Door to Heaven,"** are lost to continual searching and unfulfillment. The poems in this book, which at many times read like songs, give the author a sense of strength and identity. They help make history as they express it, such as in "When you talk of this," where how we speak of people and events creates a history for them.

Cook-Lynn observes that "the response to sound is evident in all Sioux art forms." The book as a whole seems to bear this out. The artwork, poems, stories and legends are all alive with sound and spirit. The two move together, as she reveals in the first poem in the book, "The spirit lives / when it moves and sings your name." The position of the listener is one of hanging by fingernails at the ridge of words. It is here we achieve spirit. The poem breaks up and is scattered throughout the book with only strategic words repeated: "it moves–and sings–your name–at the ridge of words–seedlike and shiny." By falling into words, we fall into the world of oral history, song and spirit. In many ways the book is an attempt to confirm and re-create the continuance of song, spirit and history. The compan-

ion piece to this poem is the last poem where the old uncle "sings the unreal songs" and mends the wind. The uncle seems to live in that world of spirit and song, and when others think of him, it is always in the context of the old stories. It is he who comforts the little girl, renews her in a time of sadness, by telling the old story of the Sun Gazer's death and the sunflower that sprang from the burial mound to turn its face to the eternal sun. In telling, she believes and touches spirit.

Elizabeth Cook-Lynn with Joseph Bruchac   (interview date 1987)

SOURCE: "As a Dakotah Woman: An Interview with Elizabeth Cook-Lynn," in *Survival This Way: Interviews with American Indian Poets,* Sun Tracks and The University of Arizona Press, 1987, pp. 57-72.

[*Bruchac is an Abenaki poet, short story writer, novelist, author of children's books, editor, educator, and critic. In the following interview, Cook-Lynn discusses her poem "At Dawn, Sitting in My Father's House," the development of her literary style, and the influence of Kiowa author of N. Scott Momaday on her writings.*]

Elizabeth Cook-Lynn is a writer whose voice has only begun to be heard at a time when most other writers are already well established. As she says of herself, she truly came to writing in her forties and is still hesitant to call herself a poet. A member of the Crow Creek Sioux Tribe, she was raised on the reservation and is a fluent speaker of Dakotah. Her work reflects her connection to her people and she has been described by some critics as one of the most authentic of Native American "tribal" voices. . . .

"At Dawn, Sitting in My Father's House"

I.

          I sit quietly
in the dawn; a small house in the Missouri breaks.
A coyote pads toward the timber, sleepless as I,
guilty and watchful. The birds are commenting on his
passing. Young Indian riders are here to take the old
man's gelding to be used as a pick-up horse at the
community rodeo. I feel fine. The sun rises.

II.

          I see him
from the window; almost blind, he is on his hands and
knees gardening in the pale glow. A hawk, an early riser,
hoping for a careless rodent or blow snake, hangs in the wind-
current just behind the house; a signal the world is
right with itself.

          I see him
from the days no longer new chopping at the hard-packed

earth, mindless of the dismal rain. I hold the
seeds
cupped in my hands.

III.

The sunrise nearly finished
the old man's dog stays here waiting, waiting,
whines
at the door, lonesome for the gentle man who
lived here. I
get up and go outside and we take the small foot-
path to the
flat prairie above. We may pretend.

—Elizabeth Cook-Lynn

*[Bruchac]: I like that poem. The mood you've created is
such a gentle and evocative one. The picture you give of the
relationship with your father—though you don't speak directly about that—is a very strong one.*

[Cook-Lynn]: Yes. I didn't know that for a long time,
about my relationship to my father. It just seemed to be
like all relationships are. I think that's one of the interesting things about being a poet, it leads you to discover
things. The discovery of the relationship with my father
is one of the marvelous things that has happened through
the years. He's been dead now for five years, and I wrote
this poem after his death but before I had really gone to
this place. I think the poem does say a lot of things about
my relationship with my father, who has turned out to be
quite influential. I think the poem probably does some
other things as well. You know, the Sun is, in Sioux mythology, a male figure. There are several ways to say
"Sun." You can say *tunka-shina,* which is the actual word
that you use for your blood grandfather. So, the Sun itself
becomes a kind of father figure, symbolically speaking or
metaphorically speaking—in the poem. This is one of
those poems, too, that was just so easy to write. It was all
right there. It's probably one of the poems that I've written most quickly and I don't know how to explain that,
either. It's positive poem, too. The Sun rises and so everything is all right, even though it is a poem about death.

*That is one of a number of things which strike me about
this poem: the clarity and simplicity of statement, those very
brief and direct sentences; the way the dawn comes into the
poem and the sun is rising so that even though it is a poem
about your father's death it is not pessimistic or negative.*

Yes, and that brings up, perhaps, some of the religious
matters in the poem. We are talking about the dawn, after
all, and there are many songs that one knows about *anpao
wichakpe,* which is the morning star that comes then.
There are lots of songs that are sung, religiously speaking.
I happen to be doing some translation of some songs right
now. I didn't have that in mind, I suppose, when I wrote
the poem, but it does have that quality of singing to the
dawn. Then there is kind of a finished thing, too. The sun
rises in the morning and that is the end. The sunrise is
really finished. That's something I like about it. You
know, so many times you write a poem and you're not satisfied and you just work at it and struggle with it so that
it does seem complete. This one just was completed without any effort.

*There's a philosophical direction the poem takes—an atti-
tude toward death, dying, and those who have died, which
I see in American Indian writing in general.*

Death is certainly part of life. I think this poem affirms
that cultural idea. It's not a poem that is in despair over
this death. It is a poem that rather accepts it, I think, in
that kind of way that American Indians have. It is not a
poem that is filled with grief and loss. The narrator of the
poem says, "I hold the seeds cupped in my hand." And
when the hawk rises in the wind currents behind the
house . . . there are so many things. And the sunrise itself
finishing, that's a very positive sort of thing. It's odd, I
suppose, that a Native American writer uses these kinds
of things but very seldom knows about it until later. Until
someone talks about it or pays particular attention to it.
I was talking to Ray Young Bear one time, and he and I
had just had some of our work discussed by Jim Ruppert.
It was an essay called "The Oral Tradition and Six Native
American Poets," something like that. Ray was saying, "I
really like to read that because it makes so much more
sense to me. It sort of explains to me what I'm doing and
it clarifies it for me." I don't know if I ever told Jim that.
I should have, probably. I felt the same way. I think there
are a lot of poets, however, who *know* what they are doing.
I think that Ray certainly does have a notion of many of
those things. But I think that what he was saying was that
when you talk about it, when you read some literary criticism, then it does clarify things you might not have
thought about. I have the sense that *I* know less about
what I'm doing as a poet than most people I talk to. So,
it's an interesting process.

When did you become a writer?

The question of when you did become a writer is a question that I really don't know how to answer because I still
don't consider myself a writer. Another friend of mine
who is a writer said recently, "I finally got a passport and
on it, where they asked occupation, I put down 'writer.'
So now I'm a writer. It's on my passport." I said, "Well,
I've never come to that conclusion." I think of myself in
a lot of ways. I'm a teacher. I'm a mother. I'm a wife and
a grandmother. I *am* a teacher. I do accept that. But when
I talk of myself as a writer I don't know if I am. I very
often say "I could have been a writer" (laughs). So I have
this ambivalence, but I have been writing forever. As a kid
I went to schools on the reservation, around Fort Thompson and Big Bend. When I first learned to read and write,
I used to copy poems down—before I knew what poems
were. I had these notebooks that I kept and I just copied
them exactly as they were in the book. So I have the recognition that it was always an art which interested me, before I even knew what poetry was. I didn't write a lot of
poetry when I was a child. I probably didn't write poetry
until I was in college. I wrote stories, but I didn't do much
of that until I was in college. My undergraduate degree is
in Journalism, and I got that at South Dakota State College. It was then that I became very much interested. I
wrote early things and published them then and after I
was married. They were *terrible* things, and I don't know
why anyone published them. Often quite emotional. So
that's how I began, but I really didn't like anything I wrote

until I got to be forty. Then I liked what I wrote. Then I really started publishing, and people started talking to me about what I was writing. Then I gave readings and so on. Isn't that odd?

What led you to write poetry and fiction?

I don't know. I haven't the foggiest notion about that. I just know that I have always been interested in writing and I have always been interested in language. I grew up, of course, in the midst of some very difficult times for reservation Indians. I was born and raised on the reservation. I married another Sioux from another reservation, the Cheyenne River Sioux Reservation, my first marriage. I'm sure that the whole notion of poetry and writing and those rather esoteric kinds of things were far from the influences in my life. I'm sure that becoming a college professor wasn't even in the realm of possibility. So it's very strange how I managed to write and become a college professor and the editor of a magazine and all these things. I don't really know. But I *did* have a grandmother whose name was Eliza Renville. She was from the Sisseton Wahpeton Sioux Reservation up near the Canadian, North Dakota border. She wrote. She was a woman who seldom spoke English and so she wrote in Dakota language for some of the early Christian newspapers that came out of that part of the country. I was very close to that grandmother. I was with her quite a bit. She lived probably four miles from where we lived. I used to walk back and forth and we would talk and she was a writer. She was taught by the Presbyterian missionaries. There were Presbyterian missions in both North and South Dakota, and she and her family were very much involved in that. Her father and her grandfather helped put together one of the first Dakota dictionaries. Contemporary writers don't arise out of nowhere. They don't operate in a vacuum, they come out of some kind of tradition. So, even though I wasn't sure about all of that stuff and didn't know a lot of it, I think that must have been influential. I still have a lot of those newspapers that were published then. I suppose they started publishing them in something like 1850-60, and they went through to the 1930s. So there was a long tradition in that and my grandmother, even though she was really a *traditional* woman, became involved in that. Most of the time Christians thought that only men were people of importance, that her father and her brother were the important people. But somehow Eliza—I'm named after her, too—Eliza Renville did this. I read those newspapers every now and then. Of course she wrote about religious things. She also wrote about community things. And she also wrote about traditional things because there was a kind of a combination of Christianity with the old tradition that was still going on.

So, you have both Dakota oral tradition and relatively unknown Dakota literary tradition to back yourself up with?

Yes. A lot of people don't think that there really is a Dakota literary tradition. A lot of people have no sense of that at all. But there is a kind of an interesting dual tradition there, and this was before very much work had been done concerning how to write down the language. I think she was writing at a time when people were just discovering how to do that. There's been a lot of criticism of that sort

of thing lately in that the writing syllabary is pretty much oriented toward the English language rather than finding ways to do it like the Crees have done or as the Cherokees did back in the old days, where they invented their own alphabet. That didn't occur for the Sioux.

> One of the things I worry about when I write poetry is whether I utilize the devices that one knows about poetry in the Western tradition. I think that I don't concentrate on a kind of lyric tradition that might come out of classical European poetry.
>
> —*Elizabeth Cook-Lynn*

This ties into a statement you made in Wicazo Sa Review: *"Different poets concentrate in different ways and my own individual way of concentration generally comes from what I know as a Dakota woman." Can you expand on that?*

One of the things I worry about when I write poetry is whether I utilize the devices that one knows about poetry in the Western tradition. I think that I don't concentrate on a kind of lyric tradition that might come out of classical European poetry. When you concentrate on the lyric you are interested in emotion and then you are doing certain things. I would like to be able to do that, but that's not really my concentration. So, I concentrate more on the narrative. If you're concentrating on the narrative more than the lyric, then you're interested in the story, not the emotion. Then you're interested in characters and events. I think that's what I meant. And much of what I do in that rises out of the story or history. I'm not a really terribly religious person with access to all the rituals and all of that. So, I think I'm concentrating in different ways. Does that explain it?

Yes. It also makes me think of your reference to a statement of Robert Penn Warren's: "short stories destroy poetry." Because of the way you use storytelling techniques in your poetry, I felt that you don't agree with him.

Oh, yes. I think I don't agree with him. I think that they rise from the same thing. I think that they're both there. I've written a lot of poetry that is directly related to a story I've written. The poem may say something different, but it is certainly connected to the story.

Your first book, **Then Badger Said This,** *was published in 1978 and reissued in 1981. That book's structure is very interesting. You combine poetry, personal narrative, story, and essay. How did you happen to put it together that way?*

Well, of course the influence of Scott Momaday on Indian writers is just profound. I was trying, of course, to write the Sioux version of *The Way To Rainy Mountain*. I was trying to find out what I could discover in that volume about the Sioux tradition and what I know. So I started out to do that and I will be perfectly up front and open about that. People have said that *The Way To Rainy Mountain* and **Then Badger Said This** are similar in structure and I think that Elaine Jahner even wrote an essay in which, I believe (I haven't read it), she commented on the similarity of those two works. I happen to think that Scott Momaday discovered something terribly important when he did that, for all of us of specific tribal histories. He did it for himself, for a Kiowa, but I wanted to do it for myself, as a Sioux, in some important way. I don't know if I can say much more about that. But, of course, it fell into chaos and I ended up simply ending and putting a few poems in. The reason I called it **Then Badger Said This** was because the badger is not a terribly important figure in Sioux literature but he is *always there*. He comments on what people say. He sort of keeps the plot moving. Sometimes his observations are correct and sometimes they are not. But his basic function is to keep the plot moving. That's kind of how he operates in Sioux literature. So that's what I wanted to do with that. I wanted to keep the plot moving. Actually, I think you could use the devices that Momaday chose to use in there and you could explain a lot about the Yakimas and the Dakotas and the Hopi, all sorts of tribal perspectives could come out of that.

You seem, like Momaday, to have done quite a successful job of blending various forms of narrative to produce an overall different texture and result.

Well, I don't know that it was so much a classic quest on my part, as it is in his, clearly. Then he has the prologue and the epilogue also, which explain that. The essay "The Man Made of Words" goes along to explain it even further. I don't know that I was into it to that degree. However, I wanted to find out what the past has to do with the present, what oral tradition has to do with what you're doing today in literature. Things like that interest me. I think that more Indians who really come from some kind of a traditional background ought to try to use that form that he has put so clearly in front of us. It is more the Indian novel, you see, than *House Made of Dawn*. It does what a novel does, it gives you that worldview. That's the function of a novel. So I consider that the form of the Indian novel. I think it is fantastic.

How would you describe that form?

I don't really know. I don't know that I discovered that so much when I tried to utilize it. But I'm sure that you can see the possibilities in that form by looking at **Then Badger Said This**. Let's take a look at the one that starts on page 22:

> When the Dakotapi really lived as they wished, they thought it important to possess a significant tattoo mark. This enabled them to identify themselves for the grandmothers who stood on the ghost road entering the spirit world asking, "Grandchild, where is your tattoo?" If the Dakotah could not show them his mark, they pushed that one down an abyss and he never reached the spirit land.

That, of course, is myth. That's myth that everybody knows, I suppose. I'm not making it up and I'm not saying anything original. Any Dakotah who reads this simply knows it. Then, I talk about a particular man, LaDeaux.

He dies and there is something in there that doesn't allow him to reach the spirit land. So, he has to have this ritual for that to occur. The father of the little girl sings the song, paints the man's face, and wraps him to get him ready for that journey. We never knew exactly what had happened to him. That comes from an actual death I knew as a child, I really did know Jack LaDeaux.

Were you the little girl?

Yes, I'm the little girl in the story and this is, of course, my father again. I don't want to make my father out to be a really traditional religious figure, because he wasn't. He was just an ordinary man who didn't consider himself necessarily virtuous or religious. So that story is a personal matter I have to explore. I never did know why LaDeaux died, but there was something awful about it. Then the poem, which follows the story, gives some answers to that. I wrote the poem years later. In fact, I was leaving Seattle one time to drive across Montana to South Dakota. It was Sunday morning. I looked out of the window and there was this man standing there in his long gray coat and I thought for a moment I knew him. Then when I turned around and watched him I didn't know him. But I got to thinking what a terrible thing it must be, what terrible thing happened to this man that here he is now, probably drunk for days? The most terrible crime that can be committed in Sioux culture, in Dakotah culture, is to commit a crime against one's own relatives and against one's own brother. So I make that up, you see, and that gives me an explanation for why it is that LaDeaux found himself in the position of not being accepted into the spirit world. It also says something about the significance of myth and how it impacts one's own life. That's what I wanted to do when I put those three pieces together.

Myth, then, impacts your life not just through the past but in an on-going way?

Yes, it does. Yes, indeed it does. It explains many things for you. So, that's what I wanted to do. I wanted to use myth and personal history and poetry to discover a cultural value and to say what that value was in the very beginning and to say what it is now. That's what I was trying to do when I was doing this. I was so totally moved when I saw Momaday doing this in some important sort of way that I really didn't understand fully at the time—nor do I yet, probably. But I was for years trying to explain some of these things and then, when I saw how Momaday managed that, it was extremely useful. And I think it would be useful to a lot of Indians who are still significantly connected to the past.

I'm struck, too, by the place where you've retold a story much like a story Momaday told. I'm thinking of the Sioux story of the boy in the lodge, which is very much like Momaday's now well-known parable of the arrow-maker.

Yes, it is from the Dakotah literary tradition.

But the message of your story seems a bit different from Momaday's.

In Momaday's story the enemy is recognized because he does not know the language. In your story, the owl speaks to the boy, Swan, and the connection to the natural world is the significant turning point.

Yes, I thought of that at one time, but I sort of forgot about it. What do you make of that?

It shows, to me, the way traditions cross boundaries throughout Native American cultures . . . and that there are different lessons which can be gained through almost the same stories.

Yes, I think that both of those things are probably very true. You know that the Kiowas are very closely related to the Dakotahs, culturally speaking. In fact, we have a lot of stories that talk about the Kiowas, our traditional stories. I would imagine that is true of the Kiowas. They must have taken note of the Sioux . . . traditionally speaking. (laughs) Of course, the Sioux have a tendency to think how important they are. But I do remember some stories my Grampa used to tell, and they did mention the Kiowas particularly. And they were rather familial kinds of stories, almost like the stories that one tells about the Cheyenne. There's a lot of that kind of familial relationship in Sioux tradition. So, the Kiowas aren't terribly far removed, and I think that the story itself is in all of the Northern Plains and the Southern Plains literatures. It is a very common kind of story among groups that are similar. I suppose if you went to the Northwest or if you went to the East Coast, it wouldn't be there. So there is a kind of commonality, and perhaps that is why I was so terribly emotionally moved when I read Momaday back in the '60s.

Would you regard Momaday as one of the major influences on your writing?

Definitely—and I think Momaday is one of the major influences on almost any Indian writer that I know. That's why I'm so disappointed in this new biography that's out on Momaday written by Matthias Schubnell, published by Oklahoma University Press. It says things that indicate Momaday's *real* contribution to literature is in common themes and common ground with people like Wallace Stegner and Georgia O'Keefe and five or six other western artists. Well, I think that is important to say about Momaday, that he *is* also effective in the western literary tradition. But the fact is that Momaday, almost single-handedly, made it possible for many of us to find out what it is we know and to express it.

Yes, I think that book misses the point—as have a number of other critical studies which discuss Momaday. Are there certain things special to American Indian culture which you deliberately don't write about or only refer to indirectly?

Oh, yes. I was thinking about that when I was talking about that thing from **Badger,** talking about the myths, the personal experience, and then the poem. I've got shoeboxes full of that stuff I don't publish and I feel it's an invasion—not only myself, but the people that I know, an invasion of the traditions which I don't really know that much about and I don't know that I should be talking about. So, yes, there is a lot of stuff I don't want to deal with. Sometimes I go ahead and do it anyway, but I'm not so happy about that. There is a story in **Then Badger Said**

This about the woman and the little girl. I was talking to another Dakotah friend of mine, Beatrice Medicine, and she said, "Oh, that story is really good." And I said I was worried writing about that because I don't know anything at all about that thing I refer to in the story, the Elk Society, the male society that men used to have, societies that gave them power over women. I don't know a thing about that. But the fact is that I felt all right imagining it because I'm a woman anyway and a woman isn't supposed to know anything about that. (laughs) So I felt that would be all right. And maybe the Dakotahs who read it would say, "Well, she's a woman and she doesn't know." But I think there are two ways to approach that. One is that you don't know everything you need to know to explore it. The other thing is that perhaps it shouldn't be explored at all in the literary context—written and in English language.

I'm worried about a lot of the things I write. The trouble is you're expected to know absolutely everything. You're supposed to be this expert and you're supposed to have so much authority. The fact is I'm only a poet. I'm not an historian, I'm not a linguist, I'm not all these other things. I'm just a poet, and people have to understand that. Jim Ruppert also said in an article that of all the writers he knew I was the one who functioned as a tribal historian. I was appalled when I read it and I wrote to him jokingly and said, "Jim, really this is terrible." He said, "Well, I see that in your work." And I said, "But historians are supposed to be *right* about things. They're supposed to know. And besides that, historians are not self-appointed (in Sioux culture, at least) as poets are." But I think there is that worrisome feeling, and I've talked to Ray Young Bear who also expresses the same thing. I think a number of Indian poets worry about that. Even writing about my father intimately, or my mother or my daughter or my grandparents, I feel those also are invasions. The real trouble with being a poet is that you have to let people know you. I want to be a poet but I also want to be anonymous. (laughs)

You mention the difference between men and women in Dakotah ritual life. I know some white feminist writers who—at one time, at least—would just hit the roof at the idea of women being excluded from things, at purely male ceremonials. But I sense a different feeling on your part. Can you explain that?

Oh, yes. There has always been a kind of politeness toward one another. Politeness toward men because they're men and politeness toward women because they're women. You know, even in our language there are those distinctions. Women have different endings to words. They say things, they have words, vocabulary, that men don't use. The same is true on the other side. There are male kinds of things that women don't say. So I think there has always been the recognition of a kind of respect for one another as genders. Respect of gender. People, I think, have misinterpreted that and have often said about Indian women that they are simply beasts of burden following ten paces behind carrying all the bundles. That is *not* the traditional perspective on feminine life. I think maybe after Christianity came, after the world changed, that things *have* occurred which American Indian women might want to discuss in the feminist perspective. But I grew up, perhaps in those times when Indian women were seen as inferior. I was born in 1930 when women were having very difficult times and Indians in general.

I think now that Indian women and men are going to have to become familiar with one another in a contemporary setting and discuss the things that have happened to us. You know, there are a lot of Indian women writers now with very strong voices. I think it is possible that different Indian cultures will approach these matters in different ways. Many people think that Sioux culture is very male-dominated, but I think that taking note of that traditional respect of gender is a very important thing to say. Whether or not that excludes men from women's experiences and women from men's experiences, I don't know. I tried to write about that—about an old couple that used to come and visit my grandmother and grandfather. They would come with a team and wagon and they would stay for days. They came from Standing Rock. When it was time for them to leave, she was the one who went out and caught the horses and harnessed them. Then he would get in the wagon and sit up there. She would hand him the reins and then get in the back, with her blanket or shawl over her head and sit with her back against his seat. Then they would leave. I never thought anything of that. Their children were gone, and he was old and very ill and couldn't catch the horses. She was younger than he was, his third wife, I would say. So she did it, and I think that's the way things were and I didn't think of that as being a detrimental thing to their relationship nor did I think of it as a detirmental thing to her as a woman. I tried to write about this but was not satisfied with it. However, I did not perceive Lucy as being an inferior figure. This was just the way it had to be done.

Elizabeth Cook-Lynn   (essay date 1987)

SOURCE: "You May Consider Speaking about Your Art . . . ," in *I Tell You Now: Autobiographical Essays by Native American Writers,* edited by Brian Swann and Arnold Krupat, University of Nebraska Press, 1987, pp. 56-63.

[*In the following essay, Cook-Lynn discusses the reasons she became a writer, her poetic themes, and her use of Indian myth and history in her poetry.*]

Ever since I learned to read, I have wanted to be a writer.

I was born in the Government Hospital at Fort Thompson, South Dakota, in 1930, and when I was a "child of prairie hawks" (*Seek the House of Relatives*), I lived out on the Crow Creek (a tributary of the James and the Missouri) in what anthropologists like to call "an extended family." And I loved to read.

Reading, if it is not too obvious to say so, precedes writing, though I teach college students today who are examples of an apparently opposing point of view. They have read nothing.

On the contrary, I read everything: the Sears catalog, *Faust,* Dick and Jane, *Tarzan of the Apes, The Scarlet Letter,* the First Letter to the Corinthians, *David Copperfield,*

"The Ancient Mariner," Dick Tracy, "Very Like a Whale," *Paradise Lost, True Confessions,* and much more. I went to whatever libraries were available as often as I went anywhere.

But I read nothing about the Dakotapi. Much later I took a history course at South Dakota State College called "The Westward Movement," and there was not one mention of Indian Nations! I keep the text for that course on my own library shelf as a marvelous example of scholarly ineptitude and/or racism.

Wanting to write comes out of that deprivation, though, for we eventually have to ask, what happens to a reasonably intelligent child who sees him or herself excluded from a world which is created and recreated with the obvious intent to declare him or her *persona non grata?* Silence is the first reaction. Then there comes the development of a mistrust of that world. And, eventually, anger.

That anger is what started me writing. Writing, for me, then, is an act of defiance born of the need to survive. I am me. I exist. I am a Dakotah. I write. It is the quintessential act of optimism born of frustration. It is an act of courage, I think. And, in the end, as Simon Ortiz says, it is an act that defies oppression.

In those early days, even though I had a need to write—that is, survive—I lived in a world in which the need to write was not primary. The need "to tell," however, was. And so I listened and heard about a world that existed in the flesh and in the imagination, too, and in the hearts and minds of real people. In those days I thought the world was made up of "Siouxs" and "Wasichus" [whites].

It is this dichotomous nature of the real world and the literary world and, yes, the present world that accounts for the work I do. It is the reason I call myself a Dakotah poet, however hesitantly I accept the label, however unclear the responsibilities that come with that label.

The best way to begin a philosophical discussion concerning the nature and substance of the work of a contemporary Dakotah poet is to admit, oddly enough, to a certain kind of timidity and lack of confidence and to conclude by saying that I do not speak for my people.

First of all, one must be timid because there is the consideration that poets have a tendency to think too much of themselves. It is quite possible that we poets think we are more significant, more important than we are; that the events we choose to signal as important for one reason or another are, after all, something else; that the statements and interpretations we have given to these events are mistaken and/or irrelevant.

Second, the idea that poets can speak for others, the idea that we can speak for the dispossessed, the weak, the voiceless, is indeed one of the great burdens of contemporary American Indian poets today, for it is widely believed that we "speak for our tribes." The frank truth is that I don't know very many poets who say, "I speak for my people." It is not only unwise; it is probably impossible, and it is very surely arrogant, for *We Are Self-Appointed* and the self-appointedness of what we do indicates that the responsibility is ours and ours alone.

Therein lies another dichotomy: I claim to be a Dakotah poet by disclaiming that I speak for my people.

I am not greatly surprised that this dichotomy does not exist for the "real" poets of our tribes, the men and women who sit at the drum and sing the old songs and create new ones. That is an entirely different matter, for it remains communal. Thus, when I hear the poetry of the Crown Butte Singers, the Porcupine Travelers, and the Wahpekute Singers, I have every confidence that they speak in our own language for the tribes, Oyate.

"A Poet's Lament: Concerning the Massacre of American Indians at Wounded Knee" is a good example to use to discuss and illustrate the problems that I see involved in the matter of responsibility for a poet like me, one who writes English, using contemporary forms.

This poem describes what was and is a very public event. Yet as a self-appointed poet I bring my own perceptions into this tribal event even as I am aware of the public nature of the event and the history that surrounds it. The private histories which do not rely upon the written word, research, and text are a part of that perception.

> All things considered, they said,
> Crow Dog should be removed.
> With Sitting Bull dead
> It was easier said.
>
> And so the sadly shrouded songs of poets,
> Ash-yellowed, crisp with age
> arise from drums to mark in fours
> three times the sacred ways
> that prayers are listened for; an infant girl stares
> past the night, her beaded cap of buckskin
>   brightens
> Stars and Stripes that pierce
> her mother's breast; Hokshina, innocent
> as snow birds, tells of Ate's blood as red as
>   plumes
> that later decorate the posts of death.
>
> "Avenge the slaughtered saints," beg mad-eyed
> poets everywhere as if the bloody Piemontese are
>   real
> and really care for liberty of creed; the blind
> who lead the blind will consecrate the Deed, in-
>   deed!
>
> All things considered, they said,
> Crow Dog should be removed.
> With Sitting Bull dead
> It was easier said.

In this specific case I mean to suggest that it is the responsibility of a poet like me to "consecrate" history and event, survival and joy and sorrow, the significance of ancestors and the unborn; and I use one of the most infamous crimes in all of human history, which took place against a people who did not deserve to be butchered, to make that responsibility concrete. Only recently has the mainstream of American society been confronted with the monstrous nature of this historical act and others like it, but Indians have always known it.

The ceremony I describe in the second stanza really did occur, I'm told; the people and the warriors gathered within hours after the dreadful killing, and they swept into the grounds and guarded their dead, placing twelve red-draped markers at the perimeters of the site. I don't know if this is "true." I wasn't a witness. I have not read any account of it. Surely, though, in the memories of the people, this ceremony took place in order to consecrate the event. And the poem that I write in English and in contemporary form, and the songs that continue to rise from drums in Dakota and in traditional forms a century later, recreate that consecration. That is what I mean to hold on to when I talk of responsibility in the creative process.

It is no accident that I refer to the number "twelve" to record this event in sacred terms, for that number figures prominently in sacred ritual. It is no accident that I begin and end with the names of Sitting Bull and Crow Dog, both religious leaders of the people, because I mean to deliberately place this event which is usually described in military terms into the religious context to which it speaks.

Ceremony, in literary terms, can be said to be that body of creative expression which accounts for the continued survival and development of a people, a nation. In this instance, it relies upon ancient symbols which are utilized spontaneously in a communal effort to speak with the givers of prayers, to recall the knowledge about life and death that has its origins in mythology and imagination.

> **Writing for me is an act of defiance born of the need to survive. I am me. I exist. I am a Dakotah. I write. It is the quintessential act of optimism born of frustration. It is an act of courage, I think.**
>
> **—Elizabeth Cook-Lynn**

The people who gathered to perform this ceremony a hundred years ago did so at risk of their lives. It was then and remains now an important commitment to nationhood and culture. They imagined the grief of the Unktechies who arose from the water, hundreds, perhaps thousands of years ago, to give the people a religion and then went deep into the Earth to listen for the sounds of our drums, songs, poetry, and prayers. The people wept and sang of their own grief and sorrow.

Years ago when I was twenty and I first started sending out my poems, an editor wrote on an acceptance letter a question that has haunted me for the rest of my so-called career as a poet. She asked, "WHY is Native American poetry so incredibly sad?"

Now I recognize it as a tactless question asked out of astounding ignorance. It reflects the general American attitude that American Indians should have been happy to have been robbed of their lands and murdered. I am no longer intimidated, as I once was, by that question, and

I make no excuses for the sorrow I feel in my heart concerning recent history. I do not apologize for returning to those historical themes, for that is part of the ceremonial aspect of being a Dakotah poet.

Attending to ceremonial matters as a writer does not mean, however, that I am not writing about myself. Quite the opposite is true. There is a self-absorption in my work which is inherent in my survival as a person, and my identity as a Dakotah. This self-absorption has always been a part of tradition, I think, for Dakotahs, in spite of the pervasive articulation in recent times of the idea that the Indian "self" was somehow unimportant; that Indians have been absorbed in the contemplation of the natural world, readily giving themselves up to it, mastered by it philosophically as well as physically; that submission to environment dominates American Indian life and belief.

This overstatement has been handy for the perpetuation of the longed-for nineteenth-century idea concerning the ultimate and expected disappearance of Natives and Native America from this continent. It is convenient to suggest from this imagined obsession with the natural world that the American Indian would become an artifact, too unreal and obsolete for survival in the modern world. The Indian's "journey," then, as a race of people, would be concluded.

The function of contemporary American poetry is to disavow that false notion.

One of what I consider my best poems is entitled, **"Journey,"** and it is an attempt to express that disavowal:

I. DREAM

> Wet, sickly
> smells of cattle yard silage fill the prairie air
> far beyond the timber; the nightmare only just
> begun, a blackened cloud moves past the sun
> to dim the river's glare, a malady of modern
>   times.
>   We prayed
> to the giver of prayers and traveled to the spirit
> mounds we thought were forever; awake, we
>   feared that
> hollow trees no longer hid the venerable ones we
>   were taught
> to believe in.

II. MEMORY

> Dancers with cane whistles,
> the prairie's wise and knowing kinsmen
> They trimmed their deer skins
> in red down feathers,
> made drum sticks from the gray grouse,
> metaphorically speaking, and knocked on doors
> which faced the East.
> Dancers with cane whistles,
> born under the sign of hollow stems,
> after earth and air and fire and water
> you conjure faith to clear the day.
> Stunningly, blessedly you pierce the sky
> with sound so clear each winged creature soars.
>
> In my mind Grandmothers, those old partisans
>   of faith

> who long for shrill and glowing rituals of the
>   past,
> recall the times they went on long communal
> buffalo hunts; because of this they tell the
> lithe and lissome daughters:
>   look for men who know the sacred
>   ways
>   look for men who wear the white-
> striped quill
>   look for dancers with cane whistles
>   and seek the house of relatives to
> stay the night.

III. SACRISTANS

> This journey through another world, beyond
>   bad dreams
> beyond the memories of a murdered generation,
> cartographed in captivity by bare survivors
> makes sacristans of us all.
>
> The old ones go our bail, we oblate preachers of
>   our tribes.
> Be careful, they say, don't hock the beads of
> kinship agonies; the moire-effect of unfamiliar
>   hymns
> upon our own, a change in pitch or shrillness of
>   the voice
> transforms the ways of song to words of poetry
>   or prose
> and makes distinctions
> no one recognizes.
> Surrounded and absorbed, we tread like Etrus-
>   cans
> on the edge of useless law; we pray
> to the giver of prayer, we give the cane whistle
> in ceremony, we swing the heavy silver chain
> of incense burners. Migration makes
> new citizens of Rome.

The journey theme is pervasive in contemporary Native American poetry. The oral traditions from which these expressions emerge indicate a self-absorption essential to our lives. They follow the traditions of native literatures which express as a foremost consideration the survival of the individual, thus the tribe, thus the species, a journey of continuing life and human expectancy.

The final responsibility of a writer like me, and an essential reason to move on from "wanting to be a writer" to actually writing, is to commit something to paper in the modern world which supports this inexhaustible legacy left us by our ancestors. Grey Cohoe, the Navajo poet and artist, once said to a group of Native American students we were working with: "Have confidence in what you know."

That is difficult when we ordinarily see ourselves omitted from the pages of written histories. but not impossible.

Kirkus Reviews **(review date 15 May 1990)**

SOURCE: A review of *The Power of Horses and Other Stories,* in *Kirkus Reviews,* Vol. LVIII, No. 10, May 15, 1990, pp. 670-71.

[*In the following unfavorable review of* The Power of Horses, *the critic contends that the characters are stereo-*

typical, the prose is flat, and the stories "seem more like lectures."]

This first collection of short fiction by a Native American raised on a South Dakota reservation displays all the faults and none of the strengths of much ethnic literature—it's predictable, preachy, and full of cant phrases. Characters of whatever ethnicity seem mere caricature in Cook-Lynn's flat prose.

A prologue alerts us to the theme of these 15 pieces—the importance and power of the past and its myths for the Dakotapi of the Upper Plains. Unfortunately, Cook-Lynn spends more time throughout telling us this than suggesting it in her narratives. Many of these anecdotal stories, in fact, seem more like lectures on the customs of the Sioux: **"Mahpiyato"** distinguishes the various English words for describing a blue sky from the single tribal term, with its presence of the Creator. In the title story, a young girl's father, out of respect for the mythic power of his horses, decides to set them free rather than sell them to an insensitive white man. Meanwhile, Cook-Lynn, justifiably but with a fictional heavy-handedness, demonstrates little sympathy for the various Christian missionaries who proselytize her people. **"A Visit from Reverend Tileston"** reveals the buffoonish ways of evangelicals in the Thirties; **"The Clearest Day"** proves that even a black missionary can't appreciate the transcendental ways of tribal dancing. Many of the other stories rehearse a litany of woe: Families are torn by alcoholism; returning soldiers from various wars are brutalized by fighting the white man's battles; a family is destroyed by their **"Squaw Man"** (i. e., their white father); and some are just victimized by disease. In **"A Good Chance,"** a young radical poet, back on the reservation after a year in jail, is shot dead for no apparent reason before he can consider a scholarship to the University of California.

Not quite agitprop, Cook-Lynn's fictional martyrology is of anthropological interest, but its general artlessness makes it a weak addition to the literature of outrage.

Gardner McFall   (review date 12 August 1990)

SOURCE: "Great Plains Tragedies," in *The New York Times Book Review,* August 12, 1990, p. 16.

[*In the following review of* The Power of Horses, *McFall favorably assesses Cook-Lynn's portrayal of the culture-clash between whites and Native Americans.*]

The poem that serves as a prologue to Elizabeth Cook-Lynn's first collection of short stories [*The Power of Horses*] signals a unifying thread of her fiction, which depicts the lives of her fellow Sioux in the Great Plains: "The mythology / and history of all times / remains remote / and / believable." With sympathetic characters and stylistic simplicity, Ms. Cook-Lynn reveals the endurance of a people subjected to centuries of "violent diaspora and displacement." The inadequacies of white culture and the damage it has caused within the Native American ethos are glaringly apparent here. In the first story, for example, we see how the English language fails to express Dakota experience and perception. And in the penultimate story,

the police tragically shoot a talented Indian youth before he can take advantage of a university scholarship. The Smithsonian Institution's archeological "find" of a lost Indian village near the young man's home would seem an ironic, concluding detail to the cruelty and dispossession Ms. Cook-Lynn's volume generally records. But, in fact, the final story, about a handicapped boy, ends with hopeful expectancy. However misguided and deleterious the effects of the white man, the Sioux emerge with their identity intact: their remembrance of ritual song, dance and legend, their connection to the land, contribute to the beauty, meaning and continuity of their lives as they try to bridge two disparate societies. While individually some of these 15 stories offer the merest glimpse of the Sioux heritage as it informs the present, together they amply illuminate its strengths. By turns humorous, poetic and poignant, *The Power of Horses* is a welcome addition to the growing body of Native American literature—for what it tells us about America today and about this country's past.

Publishers Weekly (review date 17 May 1991)

SOURCE: A review of *From the River's Edge,* in *Publishers Weekly,* Vol. 238, No. 22, May 17, 1991, pp. 53-4.

[*In the following review, the critic favorably assesses* From the River's Edge.]

A trial concerning stolen cattle becomes the foil to the tragic relationship between Native Americans and later arrivals in Cook-Lynn's (*The Power of Horses*) spare, poignant novel. Soon after agreeing to press charges against a young white man for the theft, Sioux John Tatekeya finds himself and his tribe, the Dakotahs, on trial. Along with other South Dakota reservations dwellers, Tatekeya has been forced to relocate in order to make way for a new dam. Accordingly, the trial seems a sad continuation of the Dakotahs' troubled history. But when a relative testifies against him, Tatekeya feels that a line has been crossed: colonialism has finally cost his people their essential value, responsibility to family. Woven throughout the courtroom proceedings are the mournful recollections of Tatekeya and his lover, Aurelia. Beautifully fusing the Northern Plains setting with her plot [in *From The River's Edge*], Cook-Lynn establishes a larger significance for the trial and, despite occasional lapses in narrative momentum—telling rather than showing salient developments—places the sorrows and frustrations of Native Americans in stark relief.

Robert Houston   (review date 8 September 1991)

SOURCE: A review of *From the River's Edge,* in *The New York Times Book Review,* September 8, 1991, p. 35.

[*In the following review of* From the River's Edge, *Houston examines Cook-Lynn's literary style and technique.*]

Elizabeth Cook-Lynn's *From the River's Edge* is a short novel both noble in intent and complex in concept. It is so heavily flawed in its execution, however, that ultimately neither intent nor concept can rescue it from its inability to maintain the "vivid and continuous dream" that the novelist John Gardner rightly named as the special reality of fiction. Ms. Cook-Lynn, a respected Native American studies scholar who has previously published a collection of stories (*The Power of Horses and Other Stories*) and two collections of poems, apparently has yet to make the leap from the language and approach of scholarly writing and polemic to the more complicated craft of novel writing.

The time is the late 1960's, a period of dislocation (in several senses) for the Dakota Sioux because of the flooding of their ancestral lands by a Federal dam project. The book's protagonist, John Tatekeya, is a Sioux cattleman in South Dakota who returns from a two-week drinking bout to discover that 42 of his cattle–nearly half his herd–have been stolen. Although at 60 years of age he has learned that "the white man's law was no more powerful than his religion," he nonetheless has no place else to turn for justice. With great misgiving, he allows himself to become involved in a trial against his white neighbor on a charge of rustling.

The trial furnishes both the controlling metaphor and the frame for the book's larger story. The defense's strategy is to put John on trial: his character, his sense of responsibility as a rancher, his intelligence are all brought into question. John is forced to bear humiliation after humiliation as his adulterous affair with a younger woman, Aurelia, comes to light, and his drinking habits and many brushes with the law are paraded before his neighbors. The defense lawyer even tries to imply that he might have stolen his own cattle.

The final blow comes when the son of John's oldest friend, Harvey Big Pipe, inexplicably testifies against him. John understands at last that by allowing himself to become an instrument of the white man's justice system, he has put on trial the whole sense of who he and his people are. Once again, the white man's justice has betrayed the Sioux, has made the victim seem the guilty one, though now something even more insidious is at work: this "justice" system has led John and his people to betray *themselves,* to put at risk their own sense of dignity and oneness.

Through flashbacks, ruminations and historical notes, we are given to understand that John's trial is emblematic of the long cycle of theft and betrayal the white man has imposed on the Indian–theft of land, of lives, of religion, of an entire way of life. In the end, no matter what the verdict, John understands that he can truly win nothing, that once again he can only prove what his ancestors learned in their time: "that life in accordance with the white man's ways was indecent." While Aurelia concludes that no one, white or Indian, can be saved from an existential aloneness by the past any longer, John, who is of a different generation, seeks what sad comfort he can in the traditions of that past.

It is a powerful notion for a story, and John and Aurelia are potentially strong characters. Ms. Cook-Lynn, however, in a failing not uncommon to new novelists (especially those who feel passionately about their material), has seriously marred both story and characters by forever getting in their way. From such basic problems as clunky transitions and confusing line breaks in dialogue to trickier ones such as an inappropriate and pedantic narrative voice, a penchant for telling instead of showing, awkward integration of background exposition, unconvincing dialogue and a heavy-handed advocacy and intrusiveness on the part of the narrator, the flaws jerk us out of the dream almost page by page.

When the author experiments by including two of her own previously published poems in the thoughts of her characters, the reader's reaction is likely to be less admiration for the poems than exasperated incredulity. And while the book's prose does in places rise to truly lovely heights, especially in its fine re-creation of the landscape, too often it descends to textbookish cliches or mere wordiness.

From the River's Edge is the work of a clearly intelligent, committed writer who has launched herself out in a craft she has not yet learned to sail.

Carol Kino (review date 18 October 1991)

SOURCE: "Old Loyalties," in *The Times Literary Supplement*, No. 4620, October 18, 1991, p. 22.

[*In the following favorable review, Kino discusses the characterizations, plot, and themes of* From the River's Edge.]

From the River's Edge tells the story of John Tatekeya, a Dakota Sioux Indian, who finds forty-two head of cattle missing from his reservation grazing lands. John seeks redress from the United States criminal justice system, only to fall victim to one of the courtroom's most hallowed abuses—discrediting the witness. During the trial, with his family present, the defence exposes his arrest record, his heavy drinking and his affair with a younger woman. Throughout, Elizabeth Cook-Lynn makes it clear that these are the workings of white man's law—which bears scant relation to John's notion of justice.

Although the novel's action follows the course of the trial, its theme is more truly betrayal—beginning with that of the Native Americans by their *nouveau* American conquerors. Mingling fictional recollection with historical sources, the author invokes the noble spectres of the vanquished nineteenth-century Sioux leaders. She also reveals that a few years before the trial (which occurs in the late 1960s), the United States government flooded the tribe's ancient grounds, by damming the river for hydropower. But when one of John's fellow tribe members volunteers as a witness against him, it grows clear that the more devastating betrayal is the Indians'—of the old loyalties, and of each other. This is wonderful material for a novel, which is let down by Cook-Lynn's uneven execution.

Intent on marshalling evidence, Cook-Lynn falls into stereotyped characterization as often as the trial's white lawyers. She also treads unsteady ground by interpolating fact into fiction. Though John's character is invented, his courtroom dialogue is lifted from an actual trial transcript. This provides a modicum of documentary truth but plays havoc with the truth of the characters.

It is the Indians who are the author's strongest suit. When they're allowed to wander by themselves, they are alluring. As John methodically strings wire on his pasture fence, or his young mistress tells stories to her dying grandfather, they are described in a simple, folkloric voice, without the glossily finished surface of much American fiction. Too often, though, the Sioux are burdened with unbelievable thoughts ("a tragicomic scene, thought John"), and lumpish dialogue and narrative. John and his brother, swigging bourbon and reminiscing, are interrupted by the narrator: "In the mnemonic retelling of that long-ago event, the brothers reconciled the reverential and historical with the comic and the absurd."

The writing is more successful in the stories collected in *The Power of Horses and Other Stories*—especially in those narratives with the restricted vision of the first-person narrator. In **"A Good Chance"**, for instance, an Indian woman returns to the reservation to tell a young Sioux poet, just released from prison, that he's been accepted into a university writing programme. But everyone she meets tries to dissuade her. He's lost "those worthless, shitty dreams" of assimilation, they say; he's found peace in Indian separatism. Still, compelled by the need to hear him speak for himself, she searches till she finds him. This simple, powerful story shows that Elizabeth Cook-Lynn has moving tales to tell; let us hope she keeps on searching for eloquence.

Georgia Jones-Davis   (review date 3 November 1991)

SOURCE: "The Rhythm of the Sioux," in *Los Angeles Times Book Review,* November 3, 1991, p. 13.

[*In the following review of* From the River's Edge *and* The Power of Horses, *Jones-Davis praises Cook-Lynn's prose style and storytelling abilities.*]

John Tatekeya "(Tah-TAY-kee-ya)," the hero of Elizabeth Cook-Lynn's novel *From the River's Edge,* notes that his lover Aurelia has "the ability to adapt the rhythm of one language to change the sound of another. And so, when she talked in English she often used the sounds of Dakotah, the cadence and tone of Dakotah speech." In this passage, Cook-Lynn, a member of the Crow Creek Sioux tribe, has described what is most distinctive and effective about her own writing voice. If you saw *Dances With Wolves,* you heard the Sioux language spoken; here you'll recognize a similar, staccato-like cadence in her wonderful prose. When Cook-Lynn slips in the occasional Dakota phrase, you will want to hear the words spoken out loud: " 'Tokiya la he?' she asked. 'Where are you going?' "

Storytelling traditionally was taken very seriously by Native Americans, as it was intimately tied to tribal belief systems. The storytellers themselves had an elevated status, and often were thought to possess special powers. They were the teachers and visionaries. They carried a grave responsibility: the complete history of a culture. Even the youngest children soon came to understand that every story, even the silliest, contained a history lesson or an illustration of values or the spiritual dimension in the lives of the people.

Cook-Lynn is a storyteller in the tradition of Native America. She is not concerned with multidimensional characterization or exciting plots. Essentially, her stories are lessons—about morality, tradition, learning to live within a culture with values counter to your own. Her briefest sketches in *The Power of Horses,* such as **"Mahpi-yato"** and **"Bennie,"** demand to be read aloud. Enigmatic, poetic, they possess a true sense of spiritual mystery.

Cook-Lynn's lean, terse voice captures the essence of contemporary Sioux reservation life in a few deliberate, delicate strokes, wasting not a word, not an image. She presents a stark picture of poverty, alcoholism, dysfunctional families, reservation towns that feel as empty as a local's wallet. Her language is as spare as a Northern Plains wintry landscape. There's no denying the power of even the simplest of her images:

> You think you see old women leaving marked trails in the tall burnt grass as they carry firewood on their backs from the river, and you think you hear the songs they sang to grandchildren, and you feel transformed into the past. But then, winter comes. The earth freezes solid. And you wish for July and the ripe plums and the sun on your eyelids.

Cook-Lynn's slender collection of elegant and powerful short stories, *The Power of Horses,* was published in 1990; her publisher, Arcade, published her new novel this past summer. *From the River's Edge* tells the story of a Dakota cattleman in the late 1960s trying to find justice within the American legal system and how this trial changes his life. Tatekeya has had about 100 head stolen and finds *himself* the one on trial.

> John's experience with the law was considerable. He had been hauled in by the police many times. The tribal police, municipal cops, the state patrol. Driving under the influence, speeding, resisting arrest, illegal parking, no license tabs, assault . . .

Now he's the one bringing the charges.

> The white man has always stolen from the Sioux, he thought. . . . First it is our land, then our way of life, our children, and finally even the laws of our ancestors. And now this white man, the son of my white neighbors, has stolen my goddamn cows.

Southern Californians may be not as knowledgeable of the recent history of the Sioux as Midwesterners. Cook-Lynn refers to but does not illuminate details about the federal water project that dammed sections of the Missouri River, flooding portions of Sioux land.

Cook-Lynn makes us see the history behind and ahead of her character John Tatekya in *From the River's Edge.*

—*Georgia Jones-Davis*

Also, deeper in the background of the novel are the federal government's termination policies in the late 1950s and early '60s that encouraged Indians to quit the reservations and find work and a new way of life in cities. What they encountered was racism, unemployment and urban poverty. Many chose to return to the reservation by the late '60s, despite terrible rural conditions. In the cities they possessed little that defined them as Sioux (or any other particular tribal identity). People sharing a diminishing cultural tie were brought back together on the reservations. They once again had the Sun Dance, sacred songs, the land their ancestors had lived and died on–all vital connections to a reawakening historical identity. In the late '60s, the American Indian Movement (AIM) was gaining a political foothold on the reservations that would eventually lead to the violent confrontation with the federal authorities at Wounded Knee. Tatekeya's experience foreshadows the tragedy of AIM.

Cook-Lynn makes us see the history behind and ahead of her character John Tatekeya. This is a ploy she uses in some of the stories in *The Power of Horses* as well, reminding us that we are in the presence of a storyteller manipulating characters for the benefit of the lessons at hand. We know that he will grow old, blind, return to the old ways. What's paramount here is *how* the trial will turn Tatekeya in the direction we know he will go. It is what unkind, uninvited events will teach Tatekeya that counts.

Juxtaposed with John is his lover, Aurelia, an independent, beautiful woman half his age, who, despite her alcoholism, has retained a connection to the ancient traditions: "The desultory telling of stories by the old people with whom she lived informed her daily life and gave meaning to the world she knew." The results of John's trial force each of these two into opposing destinies: John is led back into the supportive circle of family and tradition. Aurelia loses her tenuous connection to what had sustained her: "She now began to accept . . . that the stories of the pipestone quarries of her people were apocryphal. Like the sacred grounds of Palestine, they could no longer symbolize the final restoration in the modern world."

Anger—and irony—is evident in many of the stories, as well as in the novel. Cook-Lynn is as political as she is poetic. *Wasichus*—whites, but essentially all non-Indians—often come across as hostile and murderous (In the story **"Last Days of a Squaw Man,"** Gracie has a white father who abuses her and her siblings; at his funeral they abuse each other), pathetic, arrogant and insensitive (Youngest Daughter, in the story **"A Visit from Reverend Tileston,"** hopes that the white missionary knows about "the four blanket carriers who once helped [her uncle] find his way home from a long and difficult journey.")

The American legal system, modern technology, Christianity, scholarships, prison—none of these has an impact, finally, on the integrity of what is essentially Indian, posits the author. But, Cook-Lynn is saying, a personal peace must be made with this other, imposing world:

> The magic acts of white men don't seem to work well on Indians, I thought, and the stories they tell of our collective demise have been greatly exaggerated; or, to put it into the vernacular of the

> myth tellers of my childhood, *"Heha yela owi hake,"* this the appropriate ending to the stories which nobody was expected to believe anyway.

Believe in the stories, Elizabeth Cook-Lynn tells her audience, Indian and non-Indian. It's hard not to believe in such remarkable prose and vision.

Elizabeth Cook-Lynn with Jamie Sullivan (interview date November 1992)

SOURCE: "Acts of Survival: An Interview with Elizabeth Cook-Lynn," in *The Bloomsbury Review,* Vol. 13, No. 1, January-February, 1993, pp. 1, 6.

[*In the following interview, which was conducted during November 1992, Cook-Lynn discusses the characters, plot and Native American themes in* From the River's Edge.]

"Writing is an essential act of survival for contemporary Indians," Elizabeth Cook-Lynn says. As a teacher, essayist, poet, and more recently as a fiction writer, Cook-Lynn has made this survival her life work. A member of the Crow Creek Sioux Tribe, she was born on the reservation at Fort Thompson, South Dakota, in 1930. From 1971 until 1989 she taught English and Native American Studies at Eastern Washington University. Since returning to South Dakota to write full-time, she has published a collection of short stories, *The Power of Horses* (1990), and a novel, *From the River's Edge* (1991). This latter work tells a story few Americans outside of South Dakota know: how the building of dams on the Missouri River in the 1950s flooded Indian land, adding yet another chapter in the long history of land taken from Indians to fuel the power-hungry culture that threatens to engulf them. This interview was conducted through the mail and by telephone in November 1992.

[Cook-Lynn]: Problems. I don't know why we always have to talk about Indian "problems." But, of course, we do. And it's a "his-story" question. As the Lakota/Dakota people, mostly called by the French derivative name of Sioux, have become the film and pop-culture model for "Indio" in this America, so have we become the symbol for everything else, including resistance. It is no accident that the American Indian Movement occupation in the sixties and seventies happened on Sioux lands. It could have happened no place else. Think about it. My view is that until title to certain lands in South Dakota, in the Black Hills, is returned to Sioux, our situation will continue to be "more pronounced," as you call it. Vine Deloria is absolutely right when he says that the relationship between specific lands and the people is crucial. He says that when the people are removed from the land, there is no way for them to "do their part." It is a profoundly ethical matter, and I am, personally, deeply committed to it. America doesn't want to face that particular ethical issue concerning "the problems of Native Americans in South Dakota." Yet, the Sioux remind them of that very thing every time they look up from their busy lives and see us; so they continue to try to take care of the "poverty" in pitiful, stupid ways. I went to a meeting at Brookings not too long ago and heard an old Santee man from Flandreau say: "You know what is wrong with us. We, the Sioux

Oyate, used to hold land in common. That is what made us a nation of people. And we no longer do. And, we are pitiful." It was a statement that everybody knew was true. The treaty-protected Great Sioux Reservation was broken up into seven, eight separate reservations, and the Black Hills were stolen in the process. Few whites understand the violence of that criminal act.

[*Sullivan*]: *John Tatekeya, protagonist of* **From the River's Edge,** *is somewhat disdainful of his mother's conversion to Christianity, which he considers "less time-consuming and easier on the physical self" than "any of the Indian religious practices" he knows. Although, of course, the conversion was never complete, what was lost by those Native Americans who did convert to Christianity? Is Christianity too easy?*

Hey, Jamie, I don't want to talk about Christianity, either Gee! I'm really "full of it," huh? The question, though, makes us pit "those who did convert" against those who didn't, when the issue is what everyone lost. Tatekeya doesn't pit people against each other. At least, I don't think he does. He isn't even particularly angry with his mother. Her conversion is just a fact of their lives. You know, it's a little like the "full-blood" versus "the breed" controversy that has taken over the media, the movies, the so-called "discourse" for the last 20 years. Some writers who discuss the rise of the American Indian Movement think it was caused by such matters. Who is a breed! Who is a Christian? Others think it was caused because we didn't have flush toilets on the reservation. What those people need to look at is federal Indian policy, which removed the people from the land in the fifties and sixties and seventies—the "relocation" policy. They need to look at the flooding of Indian lands all up and down the Missouri River for the development of hydropower. It started with the Flood Control Act of 1930-something and ended with the Crow Creek Indians and everybody else all up and down the river standing knee-deep in flood water before they knew what happened to them.

You told Spokane Woman, *"My poems about men seem to say more about me than my poems about women." Does this have anything to do with your choice of John Tatekeya as the protagonist of* **From the River's Edge?** *Does he tell us anything about you?*

I think men always tell women who they are. That's not a very popular thing to say these days. But it is an unfortunate truth. And often a tragic truth. Look at Woody Allen and Mia Farrow if you want to see a tragic example! Look at Judge Thomas and Anita Hill! I could go on with this but I'd better not. It's probably little different for Indians than it is for anybody else, though there is all that discussion about matriarchy and patriarchy, stuff the social scientists get into. I would like to think that, traditionally, Sioux women were very strong and we continue to be. That does not mean, however, that our brothers and fathers weren't just as strong and influential in our lives. What Tatekeya tells you about me, I think, is that even though I recognize this truth and I could, therefore, be a bitter woman, I am not. I see Tatekeya as a man who knows how to love, and he knows who he is, and what more could you ask? About **River's Edge,** the "choice" of

protagonist was never up for grabs in this story. I've known this story a long time, could have told it 20 years ago, and it is Tatekeya's story. He is a composite of men I have known well.

John Tatekeya walks a very tight rope. He seems at times close to self-hatred. Yet in the sweat lodge near the end of the novel, he has maintained some dignity. Or at least he survives. Is he emblematic of today's Native Americans?

I would like to be the kind of fiction writer (and essayist) who neither "sits on the fence" nor "beats around the bush," to use a couple of old cliches. It is important to me that Indians tell their stories well and in accordance with their own histories and experiences.

—*Elizabeth Cook-Lynn*

This is an important question to me, yet I don't know how to discuss it very effectively. People in South Dakota often think that Sioux Indians hate themselves *for being Indian* and that's why they drink. I remember one time, when I was a young mother living in Huron, I went to the doctor's office and the nurse, during our visit, asked, "Are you Indian?" "Yes," I said. And she said, "Well, that's nothing to be ashamed of," immediately assuming that I was. She blithely launched into a long discussion about all the "good Indians" she was acquainted with. You know, of course, and so do I, that self-hatred is often the result of oppression, in this case, racial oppression, and so I suppose we might come to that conclusion. But for me it is a wrong conclusion. I remember talking to a friend of mine from Rosebud, a young man who had a terrible alcohol problem. He said, "You know, Liz, I could just see myself sitting on the curb, drunk, saying 'I'm proud to be a Lakota. . . .'" And he and I tried to talk about it. But it's hard to explain. Maybe we should explore matters of "shame" and "guilt" as they apply to oppression. Maybe somebody already has, I don't know. But as far as I'm concerned, I did not grow up with Indians who hated themselves *for being Indians*. I don't know many Indians who are like that, though there are some. So no, John does not hate himself. His fear throughout the novel is that because of what is happening to him, he may no longer be a Dakotah. He would be in a fix then because he couldn't, as Deloria has said, "do his part." He knows the songs and sings them, and the songs always say how good it is to be a Dakotah, and that one must try to know what that means. In the end, he has faith; he is a Dakotah as he has always been, and it is a positive ending, at least, in that sense. I hope people don't think this is a novel about self-hatred. It's a novel about the destruction of a river. Self-hatred probably comes more from not being loved and that happens in families, especially nowadays. One of the things about Aurelia, in this story, is that her mother has not loved her. So she does not have the spiritual life that

John has, and, though it is not self-hatred, in the end she is still questioning and has no answers.

*In **From the River's Edge**, John Tatekeya thinks often of Old Benno, his teacher, spiritual guide, and in some ways his father, in some ways his conscience. Did someone provide this guidance to you? Can young Native Americans still find this kind of cultural leader? And have you become this sort of teacher yourself?*

When I was a kid living along the Crow Creek with my grandmother, Eliza, we knew an old man whose name was Ben Oldest Child, and everyone called him Benno. He didn't have any front teeth, and so he spat on you when he talked to you. He was a great talker, just like my grandfather, Joe (Bowed Head) Irving. I suppose I modeled the character on him, though there were many people in my life like that, especially when I was very young, before those grandparents died. No one was conscious then of having a "teacher" or a "spiritual guide," and so sometimes, even in my fiction, I worry that such stuff is contrived. There's so much crap now about medicine men and "shamans," I think it is perpetuated by all those ethnographic biographies that are essentially written by white men. I don't know about "cultural leaders." That kind of thing is supposed to happen in families and, for the most part, I think it still does. Still, I wonder how much distortion there is because people are accepting the notion that so-called "cultural leaders" can function someplace other than the *tiospaye*. When I taught at a western university, I think students wanted to see me as some kind of "tribal elder," especially the students who did not come from a tribal home life. I really reject that role.

I'm just a writer and teacher of Native American studies and literature. I just try to tell a "real" story with "real" characters and not get too carried away. Writers ought not add to the confusion.

Did the observance of the 500th anniversary of Columbus' arrival in Central America stimulate any helpful discussion? It produced a massive amount of literature, two major Hollywood films, and a PBS series. Did anyone get the story right?

Interesting and timely question. I suppose there are no "right" stories nor "wrong" ones, only real ones. There are just the stories. And real stories are very powerful, no matter whose they are. No people in the world have been more successful in telling their myths and stories than Americans, from Columbus to the Pilgrims to James Fenimore Cooper to Walt Disney and Kevin Costner. These are the "national narratives" of America and they go on and on and on. People (with the exception of the Indians) believe in them! Some very successful novelist once said, "Reality does not begin to mean until it has been made art of." That treasured idea, both wonderful and awful, is particularly dangerous to Indians, because in spite of all the hype of the Quincentennial, the white man's story of colonialism is still told as a virtuous business, and Indian reality is unknown. The white man ways—alas, it is a violent story and somewhat regrettable, yet a story of courage and virtue! No one hears the stories, for example, that the Mayans tell about their revolt in the 1500s, when they decided they would kill the invaders and kill all the animals and plants brought here by colonists. Those stories fit so well with a little ridiculous story I tell in *From the River's Edge* when John and his brother get drunk, steal his wife's chickens, sell them, and go to Bismarck to the last pow-wow of the season. It's a resistance story, you see, but everyone just wants to see it as a couple of drunks doing their thing.

Few, even today, hear the stories of resistance nor the stories of survival. And that's because they don't really want to hear them. Just the other day I got a rejection slip from a publisher on a manuscript of essays that they found "well-presented and carefully documented," but they said their editors "took exception to your tone, 'far too much anger, sarcasm and cynicism,'" and they felt "that the reader could readily understand the wrongs committed without additional finger-pointing, etc. Perhaps a more objective tone would provide wider accessibility to your material?"

Indians, you see, are permitted a *little* anger, a *little* sarcasm, but too much is, of course, too much! This from a press in Minnesota that has claimed some interest in what they call "crosscultural" or "multicultural" works. There is, instead, "institutional circulation of culturally significant narratives," to use Stephan Greenblat's words, and it's a form of censorship. That kind of circulation is what these presses and the media and the schools are doing, and that's why we are seeing the film *The Last of the Mohicans* again instead of reading snotty little essays by Indian intellectuals! The kind of censorship of our works that goes on is mindboggling. The inner fear, for me, is that we will succumb, and watching AIM leaders play significant parts in the Cooper story tells me how foolish and mindless we can become if given enough encouragement.

All in all, I would like to be the kind of fiction writer (and essayist) who neither "sits on the fence" nor "beats around the bush," to use a couple of old cliches. It is important to me that Indians tell their stories well and in accordance with their own histories and experiences.

John Purdy (review date December 1992-January 1993)

SOURCE: "Bleak and Beautiful Moments," in *The American Book Review*, Vol. 14, No. 5, December, 1992-January, 1993, pp. 1, 3.

[*An American critic and educator, Purdy has written several essays on such Native American writers as James Welch, Leslie Marmon Silko, and Louise Erdrich. In the following review, he favorably assesses* The Power of Horses, and Other Stories *and* From the River's Edge.]

The Power of Horses includes some of the best stories from the anthologies, and they share the powerful voice of the more recent ones in the volume. Moreover, taken together, they reflect a very clear vision of the life of Crow Creek, as seen by Cook-Lynn. Her stories over the years have been wonderful in their sparse brevity, but now they are given a context that makes them even more compelling. Like Sherwood Anderson's *Winesburg, Ohio* or

Faulkner's *Go Down, Moses,* **The Power of Horses** is a collage of individual characters' experiences that draws one into a specific landscape over a long period of time. We come very close to this place and the people who inhabit it.

Cook-Lynn's fiction is as stark, rolling, and sometimes startling as the northern prairie she describes. Set on the reservation, these thirteen stories share a set of central historical events: the last battles against European incursion and therefore the establishment of the reservation itself; the equally damaging onslaught of Christian missionaries; the Reorganization years of the John Collier administration in the Bureau of Indian Affairs; and the damming of the Missouri River for a hydroelectric project. They are, of course, all related and they mark the ebb and flow of the Dakotah sense of self-determination, an identity based upon the people's ability to direct their own future. When the battle is lost, the ceremonial practices outlawed, the ancient, crucial places submerged under a blanket of muddy water, what is left? To her credit, Cook-Lynn shows us the effects clearly, but does not let us misconstrue her lesson. **The Power of Horses** is not a book that perpetuates the stereotypical "doomed Indian" myth; it is a tribute to survival.

The opening story, **"Mahpiyato,"** is a good example and an apt introduction to what follows. In it, an old woman and her granddaughter walk to the river to pick berries, "as they had done all their lives," and find a moment of sudden beauty as a cloud passes over the water. The woman emphasizes with "the sound of her voice that a sober and interesting phenomenon was taking place right before their very eyes." And the child, "a steadfast and modest companion of the old woman, knew from long experience about the moments when the stories came on. . . ." The woman quizzes the child and we learn that this sudden vision is called *Mahpiyato,* and it can be encompassed only in terms of Dakotah language and literature: "To say just 'blue' or 'sky' or 'cloud' in English, you see, doesn't mean much." Instead, there must be a comprehension accompanying the description: "You see, she is blue. And she is gray. *Mahpiyato* is, you see, one of the Creators. Look! Look! *Look at Mahpiyato!*" The next line, the final one of the story, is equally telling: "Her voice was low and soft and very convincing."

The story is only one-and-a-half pages long, and it says everything. Cook-Lynn faces the dilemma of every Native writer who wishes to convey a tribal point of view through the English language and euramerican written literary conventions. Her characters must speak English so that her non-Native audience can understand. Like the woman in her story, she must educate by demarcating the differences in perspective, but also by taking us inside her cultural milieu. We learn that Mahpiyato is a Creator, that the Creator is feminine, that she exists in a variety of ways simultaneously (that she may be a being of apparent oppositions and contradictions), that we can learn about her from stories, and that one can find joy and identity by witnessing her manifestations. (We also witness a fundamental linking of generations, and therefore an implied continuity of identity over time.) Finally, we are called to look

at her through the stories that follow in the collection, stories told in a voice that is "low and soft and very convincing." We have been given the aesthetic of **The Power of Horses.**

The Power of Horses **is not a book that perpetuates the stereotypical "doomed Indian" myth; it is a tribute to survival.**

—John Purdy

But Cook-Lynn does not paint a romantic human landscape. Life in this place over the last century has been hard, traumatic, and always tenuous. Characters face threats and challenges not only to their individual survival, but to the survival of their cosmos: Young Nephew returns from Vietnam to the place where explosive violence is easily justifiable and always self-destructive; Gracie faces the self-limitation—the memories and emotional scars—created by an abusive, Anglo father whose "rights," even in death, supersede hers and her siblings'; Anita loses her children in a custody battle and is powerless to recapture their love; and Magpie is gunned down in jail at a time when his future is at its brightest. Throughout the book, one cannot help but feel the pervasive sense of frustration and hopelessness that continuously threatens the fundamental unity of the Dakotah and therefore their identity as a people, yet this sense is mitigated by an equally powerful message of endurance and survival.

It is sadly ironic that **The Power of Horses** was published in a year that also gave us the immensely popular movie *Dances with Wolves.* It is ironic because both deal with tribal groups of the Sioux nation, but from very different points of view, sad because the wrong one was enjoyed by so many. *Dances* uses an Anglo hero to idealize and romanticize Native Americans (although novelist David Seals has pointed out its inadequacies, including the humor of male Sioux using the feminine form of the language); **The Power of Horses,** on the other hand, paints a compelling, realistic, detailed water color of life on the Crow Creek Reservation in this century, with all its bleak and beautiful moments, its history written in terms of human endurance. There are no Lieutenant John Dunbars or Natty Bumppos in this collection, only characters who struggle and then go on.

From the River's Edge, set against an ever-present history of appropriation, exploitation, and colonial genocidal purges, likewise records the endurance of traditional lifeways, viewpoints, and values, and affirms their veracity in modern times. In the preface to the novel, for example, we witness (from the river's edge) the initial flooding of the Missouri River by the Oahe Dam, a hydroelectric project the federal government has imposed upon the Dakota landscape and Dakotah people, but even in the face of such a radical and onerous change "it is easy to believe that this vast region continues to share its destiny with a people who have survived hard winters, invasions, migrations, and transformations unthought of and unpredicted." It is a destiny, however, that is–as all futures are, inherently–tentative.

Cook-Lynn's years of experience–on the reservation, and as a writer, historian and activist–enliven the novel. At once, it is the story of John Tatekeya (pronounced Tah-TAY-kee-yah), of a hundred years of history, of the changing landscape, and of a potentially fundamental shift in the interactions of a people. As she tells us very early on, "it takes only a small event in the life of an ordinary man to illuminate the ambiguities of an entire century." A court trial over the theft of Tatekeya's cattle provides the small event that illuminates the century for us, and at the physical and thematic center of the novel we are given the fundamental question of the work, and of the century for the Sioux: is a life of honor and community still possible in a modern, changing world?

One wonders, for as the trial progresses attention shifts from the thief and the missing cattle to John himself, and then something terrible happens: a fellow tribesman testifies against him, for personal reasons. The foundations of Sioux identity quake as John acknowledges "in his heart the uncompromising pride and courage inherent in the Dakotah way of life, and the loss of it, momentarily at least, in the behavior of everyone connected with this miserable trial." The unquestionable has been questioned, and this is "the price of the entrenchment of white civilization in his life and the lives of others." Of course, questions require answers, and Cook-Lynn provides them, but they are at once similar to, and subtly different from those of her contemporaries.

The story is set in the mid-1960s, at a time when the first vestiges of the activism that was to become the American Indian Movement appeared in cities around the country. Within a few years, the reclamation/occupation of Wounded Knee, southwest of Crow Creek Reservation, would dramatize both an outspoken idealization of "Indian," pantribal identity and the debate within and between tribes about the future of traditional lifeways and sociopolitical structures. In other words, Cook-Lynn takes us to an historical crux, a moment at which individuals assessed their situations and reacted.

Cook-Lynn composes short chapters in *From the River's Edge* that, like her short stories, are powerful in themselves. There are moments of truly wonderful insight shared with a voice clear and resonant.

—John Purdy

John Tatekeya is the embodiment of the debate. Much of the narrative is devoted to exploring his internal dilemma as he faces the "ambiguities" inherent in his situation. (The internal monologues of his lover, Aurelia, late in the novel are equally revealing and perhaps as central to the novel.) While most of this exploration is well handled, there are moments, however, when the narrator becomes too intrusive, and this is the one weak point in an otherwise useful narrative device. We are lectured, at times, on the history of Anglo/Native American relations, and while this may be new territory for some, the number of readers not sufficiently versed in that history will be minimal. These historical facts are indeed significant and noteworthy, but intrusions and redundant nonetheless. Tatekeya's personal reflections are wholly adequate to carry the history of who he is and how he came to be at this moment that may spell a distinct change in his people's lifeways, and therefore result in a very different people in the future.

Cook-Lynn's strengths are amply apparent in the novel. She composes short chapters that, like her short stories, are powerful in themselves. There are moments of truly wonderful insight shared with a voice clear and resonant. We follow Tatekeya on his associative wanderings through time as he wrestles with what is happening to him and to his community. In order to resolve his problems and answer the central question of what will happen to his people in the future, he must measure his own life in terms of Dakotah values, as Cook-Lynn explicates them and the ways that they are passed from generation to generation. Appropriately, at moments when he surveys his own experience (his internal landscape), he also surveys the physical landscape of Crow Creek, which is inseparable from his identity, and this is where we find the nondramatic revelation.

> He lifted his eyes toward the hills which spread out and away from the river, like earthen monuments of the past, forever, ophidian, resolute. . . . John Tatekeya of the Dakota prairielands and his people had forever possessed great confidence in their collective presence in their homelands. More than he thought about it, John felt it and simply held it in his heart.

Cook-Lynn offers answers and resolutions to his dilemma; as elsewhere, they are muted, understated and poignant. Unfortunately, literary critics are fond of the big splash, the loud, ponderous event. For this reason, when one reads about contemporary Native American literatures, one date is prominent: 1969. In that year N. Scott Momaday won the Pulitzer Prize for his first novel, *House Made of Dawn*, the first time a Native American won such a prestigious literary award. The publication of Cook-Lynn's first novel has not made as big a noise in literary circles, but it deserves to. It is compelling and relevant and wonderfully engaging.

David Kvernes   (review date February 1993)

SOURCE: A review of *From the River's Edge,* in *Western American Literature,* Vol. XXVII, No. 4, February, 1993, pp. 385-86.

[*In the favorable review of* From the River's Edge, *Kvernes comments on Cook-Lynn's ability to portray the Native American experience in the "white man's" world.*]

The spirit of a place, the Big Bend of the Missouri in central South Dakota, broods over . . . [*From the River's Edge*]. The river and its surrounding bluffs and bottom-lands are an enduring presence, yet the damming of the river and the flooding of tribal lands epitomize the changes that a greedy and insensitive white society have forced on the Dakotah Indians who live there.

The Indians have been encouraged to take up ranching, and John Tatekeya, a Dakotah cattleman, has succeeded where many of his people have failed. When forty-two of his horned Herefords are stolen, he reluctantly seeks in the white man's court to get them back. The trial is a frustrating and humiliating experience. John feels betrayed by the incomprehensible language and tactics of the white lawyers and even more by the damaging testimony of one of his own people. In his mind the question arises: has everything changed; have even the deepest Indian values been lost—honor, truth, and reciprocity among families? The voices of the Wise Ones, Old Benno and Gray Plume, come back at crucial times to reassure him, and his wife and neighbors are there when the climactic events threaten to overwhelm him. Vestiges of the old community do remain.

Yet the trial and its aftermath are not the whole story. A variety of scenes in the life of the Dakotah community are interspersed with trial scenes in skillfully managed counterpoint. There is wonderful low comedy in the awkward capture and sale of a roostful of chickens to finance a trip to an Indian dance gathering, and there is a love story between John and Aurelia, a complex young Dakotah woman, as deep and bittersweet as those stories ever are in life. In some of the stream-of-consciousness passages, where we hear the thoughts of John or Aurelia, the novel teeters on the edge of becoming an essay on the "brutal and exploitive" treatment of Indians by whites, but it is always brought back from that edge by the action of a well-made plot.

Those who have come to appreciate Cook-Lynn's fictional gift in *The Power of Horses and Other Stories* will welcome her move to the broader canvas of the novel.

FURTHER READING

Criticism

Jordan, Robert. Review of *From the River's Edge,* by Elizabeth Cook-Lynn. *Library Journal* 116, No. 9 (15 May 1991): 108.

> Favorably assesses *From the River's Edge.*

Steinberg, Sybil. Review of *The Power of Horses, and Other Stories,* by Elizabeth Cook-Lynn. *Publishers Weekly* 237, No. 22 (1 June 1990): 46.

> Praises Cook-Lynn's ability to present the plight of 20th-century Native Americans.

Tucker, Debbie. Review of *The Power of Horses, and Other Stories,* by Elizabeth Cook-Lynn. *Library Journal* 115, No. 8 (1 May 1990): 111.

> Applauds Cook-Lynn's ability to elucidate the culture clash between white Americans and Native Americans.

Additional coverage of Cook-Lynn's life and career is contained in the following sources published by Gale Research: *Contemporary Authors,* Vol. 133; *DISCovering Authors Modules: Multicultural Authors*; and *Native North American Literature.*

Edna Ferber

1887-1968

American novelist, short story writer, playwright, and autobiographer.

The following entry presents an overview of Ferber's career. For further information on her life and works, see *CLC*, Volume 18.

INTRODUCTION

Ferber is best known for novels and short stories featuring typically American characters, romantic and melodramatic plots, detailed descriptive passages on historical and geographical settings, and an optimistic, celebratory belief in American history and mythology. Immensely popular with readers throughout the five decades of her career, many of her works—including *Show Boat* (1926), *Cimarron* (1930), and *Giant* (1952)—were made into successful movies. The author of two autobiographies, Ferber also collaborated with George S. Kaufman on several stage plays, notably *The Royal Family* (1927) and *Dinner at Eight* (1932). Critic W. J. Stuckey wrote that "whatever the final judgment about Ferber's work, there is no doubt that her finger was always on the pulse of what many American readers felt or wanted to feel about American life."

Biographical Information

Born in Kalamazoo, Michigan, Ferber moved in 1890 with her parents and sister Fannie to Ottumwa, Iowa, where her father operated a general store. Impelled by that community's undisguised anti-Semitism, the Ferbers moved to the prosperous, liberal town of Appleton, Wisconsin. After graduating from high school, Ferber worked as a newspaper reporter for the *Appleton Daily Crescent* and the *Milwaukee Journal*. While a journalist, she began writing short stories; the first to be published was "The Homely Heroine," in *Everybody's Magazine*, November, 1910. After suffering what some commentators have called a nervous breakdown while working at the *Milwaukee Journal*, Ferber returned to her family's home in Appleton where, during her recuperation, she wrote her first novel, *Dawn O'Hara* (1911). Fully recovered, Ferber devoted all of her time to fiction writing, living a peripatetic life in which she maintained residences in New York and Chicago. Ferber first became famous for the short stories she published in such popular magazines as *Everybody's* and *American Magazine*. Her first collection, *Buttered Side Down*, was published in 1912. This was followed by collections of her very popular "Emma McChesney" stories: *Roast Beef, Medium* (1913), *Personality Plus* (1914), and *Emma McChesney and Co.* (1915). Following the critical success of her novel *The Girls* in 1921, Ferber began to concentrate on this genre and on her collaborations with Kaufman, which resulted in several successful

Broadway productions. Ferber received the Pulitzer prize for fiction in 1925 for her novel *So Big,* and went on to write many more popular works, including *Show Boat, Cimarron, Saratoga Trunk* (1941), and *Giant,* as well as two autobiographies, *A Peculiar Treasure* (1939) and *A Kind of Magic* (1963).

Major Works

Dawn O'Hara, which Ferber always dismissed as an immature effort, is set in New York City and presents the life of a young woman who falls in love with and marries a man who eventually goes mad and has to be hospitalized permanently. Emotionally damaged by this turn of events, Dawn seeks medical attention and recovers with the help of a young German doctor. Ferber's stories about Emma McChesney, a character who represented what at the time was referred to as the "new woman" in American society, are set mainly in Chicago and focus on Emma's travails as a single mother with a burgeoning career selling "T. A. Buck's Featherloom Petticoats." *The Girls,* also set in Chicago, explores the lives of three generations of spinsters, whose lives reflect the destructive influence of possessive mothers on their children. Beginning in the 1920s, Ferber collaborated with Kaufman on several plays, including *Minick* (1924), *The Royal Family, Dinner at Eight, Stage Door* (1936), *The Land is Bright* (1941), and *Bravo!* (1949). These plays typically deal with the idiosyncracies and foibles of upper-class urban life and are often set in New York City. The novel *So Big* revolves around a strong female character, Selina DeJong, a teacher who marries a farmer but is soon widowed and must raise her son and tend the family farm with little help. Inspired by the mythology of nineteenth-century American riverboat life, *Show Boat* depicts life on the *Cotton Blossom,* a floating theater and nightclub that travels along the Mississippi river. The story focuses on Magnolia Hawkes, daughter of *Cotton Blossom*'s captain, and Gaylord Ravenal, a dashing gambler. Soon after Magnolia and Gaylord marry, Gaylord deserts his young wife, who then becomes a vaudeville star in Chicago in order to support her daughter Kim. *Show Boat* served as the basis for the Jerome Kern and Oscar Hammerstein II musical as well as three movies, including the famous MGM musical version of 1951. *Cimarron* is set in the Oklahoma territory of the late nineteenth-century, at about the time of the land rush of 1889. The story focuses on the dashing, impractical, and irresponsible Yancy Cravat, his wife Sabra, and their children. After Yancy deserts his family, Sabra takes charge, transforming both the family and the farm into healthy, prosperous enterprises. Eventually Sabra becomes an important political and moral force in Oklahoma's campaign for statehood. In 1939 Ferber published the first of two autobiographies, *A Peculiar Treasure,* which chronicles her childhood and her early literary career before World War II; *A Kind of Magic* chronicles her rise to celebrity and fortune from the 1940s through the early 1960s, and includes her thoughts about her own literary style. *Saratoga Trunk* is set in Saratoga Springs, Texas, and concerns the romance between Clint Maroon, a Texas cowboy and adventurer, and Clio Dulaine, the illegitimate daughter of a New Orleans Creole family. Determined to marry for money and power, Clio eventually discovers that true love is always more important than money. *Giant,* which is also set in Texas, depicts life among the members of the Benedict family. The story unfolds on the Riatta Ranch and involves love relationships, oil interests, and the pursuit of money, power, and influence. In 1958 Ferber published her last novel *Ice Palace,* which is set in Alaska. Critics contend that Alaskan history and geography—rather than the characters—are the real focus of the story. Christine Storm is the bridge between her feuding grandfathers and their differing views on the future of Alaska. At one time they were pioneers and friends, now Czar Kennedy supports the economic exploitation of Alaska's natural resources, while Thor Storm fights to preserve Alaska's pristine wilderness. This personal struggle for control of Alaska's destiny occurs just as the territory embarks on its quest for American statehood.

Critical Reception

Critical reception of Ferber's writings has generally been favorable. Most critics recognize the appeal of her romantic, nostalgic portrayal of American history and geography, and note her ability to create colorful characters.

While many critics applaud Ferber's strong female characters—Emma McChesney, for example—most realize that her characters tend to be stereotypical, two-dimensional, and are uniquely suited to the melodramas in which they appear. Still, most critics agree that Ferber's novels and short stories are engaging and enjoyable, and are among the best examples of popular American storytelling. Stuckey has concluded: "Ferber's popularity and the critical attention she has received suggest that when the definitive study of popular taste in America is written, her novels, plays, and short stories will have to be reckoned with."

PRINCIPAL WORKS

Dawn O'Hara: The Girl Who Laughed (novel) 1911
Buttered Side Down (short stories) 1912
Roast Beef, Medium: The Business Adventures of Emma McChesney and Her Son, Jock (short stories) 1913
Personality Plus: Some Experiences of Emma McChesney and Her Son, Jock (short stories) 1914
Emma McChesney and Co. (short stories) 1915
Our Mrs. McChesney [with George V. Hobart] (drama) 1915
Fanny Herself (novel) 1917
Cheerful By Request (short stories) 1918
A Gay Old Dog (screenplay) 1919
$1200 a Year [with Newman Levy] (drama) 1920
Half Portions (short stories) 1920
The Girls (novel) 1921
Gigolo (short stories) 1922; also published as *Among Those Present,* 1923
†*Minick* [with George S. Kaufman] (drama) 1924
So Big (novel) 1924
The Eldest: A Drama of American Life (drama) 1925
‡*Show Boat* (novel) 1926
Mother Knows Best: A Fiction Book (short stories) 1927
The Royal Family [with Kaufman] (drama) 1928; also produced as *Theatre Royal,* 1935
Cimarron (novel) 1930
American Beauty (novel) 1931
Dinner at Eight [with Kaufman] (drama) 1932
They Brought Their Women (short stories) 1933
Come and Get It (novel) 1935
Stage Door [with Kaufman] (drama) 1936
Nobody's In Town (novellas) 1938
A Peculiar Treasure (autobiography) 1939
The Land Is Bright [with Kaufman] (drama) 1941
No Room at the Inn (short stories) 1941
Saratoga Trunk (novel) 1942
Great Son (novel) 1945
One Basket: Thirty-One Stories (short stories) 1947
Bravo! [with Kaufman] (drama) 1949
Giant (novel) 1952
Ice Palace (novel) 1958
A Kind of Magic (autobiography) 1963

*This work is based on Ferber's short story of the same name.

†This work is based on Ferber's short story "Old Man Minick."

‡This work served as the basis for the stage musical by Oscar Hammerstein II and Jerome Kern. Their musical was adapted for the screen in 1936 and 1951.

CRITICISM

Frederic Taber Cooper   (review date July 1911)

SOURCE: A review of *Dawn O'Hara*, in *The Bookman*, New York, Vol. XXXIII, No. 5, July, 1911, p. 534.

[*In the following slightly favorable review of* Dawn O'Hara, *Cooper praises Ferber's ability to convey her tragic story with "light-heartedness" and a "warm-hearted understanding of the things which go to make the essential joy of living."*]

Dawn O'Hara, by Edna Ferber, is a book that [offers] a problem and in a certain sense answers it in its own sub-title. The problem is this: supposing a girl, after a few months of mad happiness, finds that she is bound for life to a man who has suddenly broken down and whom the doctors pronounce incurably insane. The sub-title of the book is "The Girl Who Laughed;" and that is not a bad answer to a good many of life's most trying problems. At the opening of the story, however, Dawn is very far from being in a mood for laughter. Ten years of unrelieved strain on a New York daily paper, with the driving necessity of paying her husband's hospital bills ever at her heels, at last breaks her down; and her sister and her fairly well-to-do brother-in-law pick her up bodily and transfer her to the peace and quiet of their home somewhere not many miles from Milwaukee. At this point it is not surprising for the reviewer to discover that he has a story before him which he is simply going to spoil if he tries to retell it. Supposing, for instance, he should say bluntly: This is the story of a young woman who has no right to think of love and marriage, and to whom a perverse fate has sent the kindest, staunchest, most lovable young German doctor you can well imagine. He makes a well woman of her by the sheer magnetic force of his will to have her live. And then, when they both realise what they mean to each other and what the hopelessness of their case means to both, they try to bury themselves in hard work, he in his Milwaukee practice, she in newspaper reporting on a paper in the same city, where his influence has found an opening for her. And then, at an hour when it seems as though nothing worse could overtake them, fate does give one added twist of the screw and her husband is released from the asylum as cured and comes to Milwaukee to claim her. None of this begins to touch the real essence of the book because, although it deals in tragedy, it is a fabric woven from threads of sheer light heartedness, unquenchable courage, warm-hearted understanding of the things which go to make the essential joy of living. There are, for instance, certain chapters in the book picturing a delightful, unique, inimitable German boarding-house in Milwaukee that makes one sigh while reading them, partly from a vague nostalgia for happy bygone days in German pensions, partly also from sheer envy of the subtle touch that penned them. And then, too, there is one portrait of a broken-down sporting editor, a man whose days are numbered, a man vulgar in speech and with many sins upon his conscience, but who, nevertheless, is rich in some of the rarest gifts that human nature knows and whose final tragedy leaves a vacant spot in the heart akin to that of a personal bereavement. For these reasons it seems the part of wisdom to inscribe the name of Edna Ferber in some easily accessible part of our memory whereby there shall be no danger in the future of missing anything that may come from her pen. It would seem that she is a young woman who has gone some distance already on the road of achievement and is likely to go much further.

Hildegarde Hawthorne   (review date 20 April 1913)

SOURCE: "Everyday Folk," in *The New York Times Book Review,* April 20, 1913, p. 232.

[*In the following favorable review of* Roast Beef, Medium, *Hawthorne praises Ferber's depiction of the modern American woman.*]

"Roast beef, medium." A sane sensible order, pretty certain to result in something wholesome and satisfying. Not a food only, as Miss Ferber tells us, but a philosophy. Not a philosophy only, but an art, an art she makes delightful in this volume of stories [***Roast Beef, Medium: The Business Adventures of Emma McChesney and Her Son, Jock***], telling not about the exceptional, the lurid, or the miraculous, but just about the everyday, regular, I've-met them-a-dozen-times sort of people.

First of all, the book is human, ever so human and ever so real. The heroine, Emma McChesney, is a living creature, some one we get to know well and can't afterward do without. Even if we've only met her once, we would know her the instant we set eyes on her, and though her name might have slipped our memory, we should feel sure we weren't making a mistake in going up and recalling ourself to her notice: "I never could remember a name," we should announce, "but I know I've met you somewhere around, and I'm not going to let you get away like this."

Really, it's hard to recall that it's a book I'm writing about. And yet, with what enjoyment one returns to it, grinning a bit as one turns home, saying cheerily, "Thank goodness, I've not quite finished with Emma's adventures," and hurrying over the chores so as to settle down comfortably with the volume for the evening.

Emma is a traveling woman for the Featherloom Skirt Company, sweet, fresh, and direct as a west wind, and as feminine as her "line." Indeed, the essential woman of these stories is one of their greatest charms. They couldn't have been written by any one but a woman; what's more, they couldn't have been written by any one but a woman of to-day. For their outlook on life and the world is that of the woman who has measured both, who has met them first and not second hand. Emma knows how to take care of herself and how to rely on herself, without being a whit less the woman, without being looked upon as queer or advanced or any of those things she would have seemed to herself and others a generation ago. And that makes much of her charm, her balance, and naturalness.

The book is written in the vernacular. It's for us, right here and now! We know what is meant when Emma declares:

> I've seen matinée idols and tailors' supplies salesmen, and Julian Eltinge, but this boy had any male professional beauty I ever saw beaten, looking as handsome and dashing as a bowl of cold oatmeal.

Emma has the up-to-date way of putting things. "A woman's as old as she looks with her hair on the dresser and the bed only a few minutes away," she remarks, and that is only one out of many.

Emma has been a wife and is a mother. She has a boy of 17, only no one will believe her when she tells about him. But how she manages that lad! Read **"Chickens"** for one, and admire. And how she manages the fat man, and T. A. Buck, too, for that matter, for there is a love story, though, as Miss Ferber assures us, it's a logical one, and doesn't leave any one in any one's arms in the last paragraph.

There is nothing slipshod nor shoddy about this work of Miss Ferber's. For all its seeming slangy ease, there is good hard work behind it, close observation, untiring study. It's as American as pumpkin pie, and there isn't a character in it who is not thoroughly alive, various as these characters are. A woman doesn't knock about over the continent, living in sleepers and small town hotels week in and week out, without running into some pretty odd persons and queer happenings. And things were not always pleasant on the road. Emma McChesney has a tough time of it now and then; even the boy isn't always as considerate as he might be. She is not the cryey sort, but there are moments when the tears must have their way for a minute—tears the reader, if she is a woman, will thoroughly sympathize with; may possibly share. But her friend, Mary Cutting, who mustn't be missed either, in a world where her like are too rare, has a formula for times like these:

> It's a glorious, good old world; it's a glorious, good old world; it's a glorious, good old world. And I daren't stop a minute for fear of forgetting my lesson.

Well, it's a brave, fun-loving, human book, the best Miss Ferber has yet given us, and it arouses a distinct longing for more. And, happily, the illustrations by Mr. Flagg are more than acceptable, fitting delightfully into the stories, inspired with the same just appreciation of the American type and the American sense of humor that is so strong in the author.

The New York Times Book Review (review date 20 September 1914)

SOURCE: A review of *Personality Plus: Some Experiences of Emma McChesney and Her Son, Jock,* in *The New York Times Book Review,* September 20, 1914, p. 386.

[*In the following favorable review of* Personality Plus, *the critic discusses the "fine human quality in these stories."*]

All those who know and love Emma McChesney—to know her and to love her being one and the same thing—will be interested in the career of the son Jock whose "yellow streak," inherited from a worthless father, caused his plucky mother so many, anxious moments. In the five stories gathered together in this volume under the title of one of them, *Personality Plus,* Miss Ferber tells us what happened to Jock—and his mother—when that self-confident young man graduated from college and went into the advertising business. Jock has his ups and downs, his failures and successes, but always that sunniest and bravest of women. Mrs. McChesney, secretary of the T. A. Buck Featherloom Petticoat Company, stands behind him, as big hearted and shrewd as in the days when we first met her "representing T. A. Buck." In truth, Jock's various haps and mishaps are of interest to us principally as they affect that splendid example of the modern business woman, his mother.

As in all Miss Ferber's work there is a certain fine, human quality in these stories which makes a swift and irresistible appeal. They are all so real, so instinct with the life of "that great, big, solid, safe, spot-cash mass known as the middle-class"—the class Emma McChesney belonged to and understood so well that even though there came a time when the very up-to-date advertising company declared her methods "old fashioned" and a letter **"Dictated But Not Read"** took some of the sparkle from her eyes and some of the buoyancy from her carriage, she was justified in the end and saved the Featherloom Company "real money—and large chunks of it," to quote T. A. Buck, once junior, who reappears in this new volume, as does Fat Ed Myers, Mrs McChesney's former rival.

There is in the concluding story a hint that the author intends that it shall be our farewell to Emma McChesney, but if this is so we trust that she will reconsider and change her mind. For amid all the more or less excited talk in praise and dispraise of the modern woman it is good to have before us so fine a representative of the type as this Mrs. McChesney, who was "as motherly as she was modern," and could help and understand her son all the better because of her own personal experiences. No wonder Jock felt that one of the biggest things he could do was **"Making Good with Mother."**

The New York Times Book Review (review date 17 October 1915)

SOURCE: A review of *Emma McChesney & Company,* in *The New York Times Book Review,* October 17, 1915, pp. 390, 396.

[*In the following favorable review of* Emma McChesney & Company, *the critic praises Ferber's realistic characterization of her protagonist.*]

According to all the rules of precedent, one should by now be thoroughly tired of Emma McChesney. Miss Edna Ferber should be especially tired of her, and Emma herself should be tired of life.

But Emma has always been a defier of precedent. She was, you remember, the pioneer among traveling saleswomen, and the travelers for rival firms shook their heads gravely and prophesied a sudden termination to the career of the Buck Featherloom Petticoat Company's charming young agent. Woman's place, they said, was the home—this woman's place, especially.

Her historian has told us, however, that Emma's ingenuity and perseverance brought her victory over all her rivals, including Fat Ed Meyers. Also it has been revealed to us that her undomestic occupation did not hinder her success in an operation peculiarly domestic—that of making a man out of that somewhat unpromising subject, her son Jock.

But now [in ***Emma McChesney & Company***] comes her greatest exploit. She appears, more vivacious and attractive than ever, as the heroine of a new book—the third in which she has figured. We find her "cleaning up" Buenos Aires with the same easy power that she had been accustomed to exercise on the dry goods buyers of East St. Louis; we find her (in one of the most humorous and original love stories that has appeared for years) becoming the wife of our old friend, T. A. Buck, her employer; we see her reveling in the new-found joys of a home life undisturbed by business cares, and later, after leisure had grown irksome to her active brain, yielding to the Call of the Petticoat, and triumphantly reentering the world of commerce, and finally—amazing spectacle! —we see her in the role of an eminently practical but (of course) doting grandmother.

Now, the extraordinary thing about this series of stories is the cumulative humanness of their heroine. We have had too many series of stories about types—chorus girls, confidence men, engineers, cowboys, and the rest. As a rule the central figure of such a series is the same in the thirtieth story as he was in the first, with this important exception, that he is more of a confidence man or a cowboy, or whatever it is, and less of a personality—more of a type and less of a human being.

There is one thing which every writer of a series of type stories should get into his mind, that is that in real life, and especially in real life in the United States, there is no such thing as a type. For instance, there are no people who are, body and soul, waking and sleeping, eating, drinking and making love, traveling salesmen. There are vegetarians, Christian Scientists, Republicans, people who like Conrad, kelly-pool players, admirers of post-impressionism, of Dr. Henry van Dyke and of little neck clams with mignonette sauce, who make a living by salesmanship. But their occupation is their only bond; they must be catalogued, not primarily as salesmen, but as human beings.

This psychological fact, which has escaped the attention of many of our most industrious contributors to the magazines, has not eluded Miss Edna Ferber. The Emma whose adventures fill this entertaining volume is the same Emma who first stepped daintily into the hearts of the public from the pages of the *American Magazine*. But the years have passed, and have left their imprint on Emma as on everyone in the world. She has not remained stationary,

like most of the central figures in popular series of magazine fiction; she has grown, physically, mentally and spiritually.

That is why no one can really be tired of Emma McChesney—or Emma Buck, as we must call her now. She is too radiantly alive to be tired of life, too radiantly alive for us to be tired of her. She is made, it seems, not of paper and ink but of flesh and blood. She is not a type, she is a fallible, changeable, lovable human being. May she live to be a great-grandmother, and Edna Ferber live to tell us all about it!

The New York Times Book Review (review date 7 October 1917)

SOURCE: A review of *Fanny Herself*, in *The New York Times Book Review*, October 7, 1917, p. 380.

[*In the following mixed review of* Fanny Herself, *the critic applauds the realism of the characters and story in the first half of the novel, but faults the concluding chapters for losing the narrative's momentum.*]

In the amusing preface to her new novel, Miss Ferber declares that she would not be at all surprised if Molly Brandeis should turn out to be the real heroine of the book, instead of ***Fanny Herself***. And this is precisely what happens, although the portion of the book in which Mrs. Brandeis appears is to a great extent but an introduction to the main story, and she is presently removed from the scene, leaving the centre of the stage to Fanny. With her exit the interest of the novel sags noticeably, and from that moment steadily declines, growing less and less as the tale approaches its conclusion. For Fanny, too, is a far more attractive person in what may be fairly called the first half of the story, as the emotional little girl and the devoted daughter, than she is as the "super-woman" who galvanized into life the half-dead infants' wear department of the great Chicago mail-order house, and was able to draw cartoons so extraordinarily well that "there wasn't a woman cartoonist in the country—or man either, for that matter—who could touch" this remarkable Fanny Brandeis.

The first part of this new book is as human, as delightful, and as vividly real as anything Miss Ferber has ever done. The scene is laid in the little town of Winnebago, Wis. There Molly Brandeis came, with her incompetent husband and two children, some years before the story begins, and there he opened the general store called "Brandeis' Bazaar." It was during these years of her husband's lifetime that Molly Brandeis learned "the things one should not do in business, from watching Ferdinand Brandeis do them all." And when he died and she found herself obliged to take hold she did it vigorously, determined to wrest a living for herself and her two children out of the store that was losing money, not making it. She succeeded—succeeded by dint of the hardest kind of hard work, at a cost of nerves and energy that exhausted her before she was really old. A brave, shrewd, tolerant, intelligent woman, as big-hearted and humor-loving as her dear friend, Mrs. Emma McChesney, she quickly wins the reader's affection and respect and never loses either of them. From the moment when, with one drastic action, she settles the fate of the green-and-blue plush album, she has all our attention, and it is with a thrill of eager anxiety that we go with her on that first, all-important buying trip. The relations between the mother and the emotional, clever daughter, and of both with the small town in which they lived, are drawn deftly and with a real understanding. In the little Jewish community of Wisconsin, Molly Brandeis lost caste when she took up her husband's business. That did not worry her much, but Fanny resented it for her—resented that and a good many other things. The little Jewish community, the small town itself, are made entirely actual to us; with a touch here and a touch there we are given the very essence and flavor of Winnebago, but always the central figure is dear Molly Brandeis.

In what can be called the second part of the book, Fanny goes to Chicago, and there is an interesting account of the big Haynes-Cooper mail order establishment. Fanny has decided to live her life on a very different basis from her mother's, and begins by denying her Jewish origin. But she has the instinctive understanding of suffering and sympathy with it which she owes to her inheritance from persecuted generations, and these interfere greatly with her plans. Of course, a love affair is presently introduced; and after a regrettable bit of melodrama we leave Fanny enlightened and happy. Apart from the account of the Haynes-Cooper business, this section of the book is not any too interesting. There are several extremely long descriptions of Chicago and New York, and the hero indulges in more than one lecture. But Molly Brandeis, a woman near akin to the well-known Mrs. Emma McChesney, is at once thoroughly good and thoroughly likable. We see her dealing tactfully with her many trying customers, hearing confidences of every possible description by the big stove in her little store, reading Balzac and Zola in her few spare moments, watching with understanding eyes Fanny's struggle during the memorable Day of Atonement. A very real, not easily forgotten person, it is she who, with the little town of Winnebago, Wis., makes this story of *Fanny Herself* worth while.

The New York Times Book Review (review date 22 September 1918)

SOURCE: A review of *Cheerful—By Request*, in *The New York Times Book Review*, September 22, 1918, pp. 399, 408.

[*In the following favorable review of* Cheerful—By Request, *the critic discusses the strengths and weaknesses of the individual stories.*]

Edna Ferber's new book of short stories [*Cheerful—By Request*] is thoroughly and entirely—Edna Ferber. Which means that the tales are outwardly simple, inwardly complex stories of human nature, and especially feminine human nature. They differ in detail a good deal, these women, yet fundamentally they are all of one type—the small-town, essentially domestic type of woman, to whom mending and dishwashing and cooking and cleaning are customary and not at all distasteful tasks. And so they are in truth all akin—the lingerie buyer for the big Chicago

firm, the woman who came from the sinister "House-with-the-Closed-Shutters," the hotel housekeeper, and the actress and the shopgirl—akin to one another, and also to a certain Mrs. Emma McChesney.

Yet one of the best stories in the book—perhaps the very best—is not a woman's story, but a man's, **"The Gay Old Dog."** The hero, Jo Hertz, is "a plump and lonely bachelor" of 50, and the story tells how the demands and claims of three selfish sisters made of a man who was naturally domestic, a man who would have found complete satisfaction in a wife and children and a home, one of the type known as a "Loophound." Miss Ferber has never done better work than in her description of this household, of the man at heart a dreamer of dreams, externally "the dull, gray, commonplace brother of three well-meaning sisters." And they were well meaning; they never intended to rob him of youth and love and happiness, of the wife who should have been his and the son who should have been his, yet they did just these very things. Their story would by itself suffice to make the volume worth while.

"Cheerful—By Request," the first story in the book, is not one of the best, though there is much that is good and much that is very real in this account of the lame little woman who reigned over the storage warehouse of Hahn & Lohman, the great theatrical producing firm, and had once hoped to be a star; and of Sarah Haddon, the beautiful and triumphant, who had everything she wanted—for a while. **"The Tough Guy"** shows what the war did to "Buzz" Werner, toughest of the tough in Chippewa, Wis., and then comes a tale which ranks only a very little way below **"The Gay Old Dog,"** a woman's story, this time, the story of **"The Eldest."** There are few of us who have not met in town or country, small flat or cottage, or comfortable middle-class establishment, some one playing the part which fell to Rose's share. Her mother was ill, and so she, the eldest, took her mother's place and looked after the children and the household. Simple and commonplace enough, surely! The sort of thing girls are doing all the time. But the cost of it to the girl—that is what Miss Ferber shows us, very quietly and without sentimentality. The average writer, intent—often obliged to be intent—on filling the demand for a happy ending, would have given to this tale the obvious, rose-tinted, and entirely false conclusion. Not so Miss Ferber. She holds firmly to the truth, and so we leave Rose clearing the table and washing the dishes as she had done every night for years past, and as we know she will do every night for years to come. **"That's Marriage,"** while entertaining, is distinctly inferior both to **"The Eldest"** and to the story which follows it, **"The Woman Who Tried to Be Good."** There is in this latter tale one dreadful moment when the reader fears that Miss Ferber is about to sink into that slough of bathos which has ingulfed so many writers; the moment passes quickly, and soon one sees how unnecessary the fear has been. Blanche Devine, known all over the town, renting a little white cottage in a thoroughly respectable street—to the intense indignation of the other residents—and striving to be herself respectable and "good," is quite as pathetic a figure as the forlorn drudge, Rose.

The great mass of ordinary, workaday people—it is from

this that Miss Ferber selects her characters, characters she understands thoroughly, and so interprets as to win for them the reader's sympathy and liking. This new book of hers is by no means funny, though the author has not lost her gift for putting things humorously. In it one will find more tears than laughter, more tragedy than comedy— that tragedy of living on, which is often so much worse than simple dying; it is; however, far too brave a book to be in the least a lugubrious one.

The New York Times Book Review   (review date 9 May 1920)

SOURCE: A review of *Half Portions,* in *The New York Times Book Review,* May 9, 1920, p. 236.

[*In the following favorable review of* Half Portions, *the critic notes that Ferber's characters are similar to those of O'Henry.*]

There are times while reading Edna Ferber's stories that one thinks of O. Henry. It is not the O. Henry plot with its surprising conclusion, its snap at the end, but the O. Henry characterizations that come to mind. Miss Ferber picks her people from among the everyday persons, the man in the street, the shop girl, the farmer who is strangely out his element in the city, just the types that O. Henry found ready-made to his hand around practically every corner in New York. *Half Portions,* Miss Ferber's latest collection of short stories, emphasizes the impression she has already made. It is a book that is thoroughly enjoyable and laughable from beginning to end.

Nine stories are included in the book and each one of them, in its own way, possesses the true Ferber spirit. If one were to look for a philosophy in Miss Ferber's work one would probably reach the conclusion that all things, good and bad, should be viewed through a generous sense of humor. Miss Ferber can be serious when she chooses, but her serious moments have always a bit of humor lurking about the corner to lighten the more drab aspects. Certainly some of the characters in her stories have a hard enough struggle to get along, but the whimsical attitude of Miss Ferber presents them in such a light that the reader remembers only the happier aspects.

As a developer of character Miss Ferber carries her art a bit further than most short story writers. One of the stories in *Half Portions,* for instance, is called **"The Maternal Feminine."** The character of Aunt Sophy Decker is developed into such a rounded figure that the story stands forth as a first-class character sketch. Aunt Sophy is a spinster. She makes and sells hats to the female population of Chippewa, Wis. At 50 she has become in figure what is known as "stylish stout." Her three sisters, all of them well married, view with some frigidity the business of Aunt Sophy. But Aunt Sophy fills most efficiently her part in life. She is shrewd, kindly, hail-fellow-well-met with the millinery salesmen and a rock of refuge for her nephew and niece. When the war comes and the nephew, Eugene, is killed, it is to Sophy that the visiting Red Cross worker immediately turns, saying, "You must be a very proud woman." She had found in Sophy's eyes the flaming maternal instinct.

Among the other stories that stand out is **"April 25th, as Usual."** It describes how Mr. and Mrs. Hosea C. Brewster of Winnebago, Wis., leave their large, comfortable home at the instigation of their art-student daughter for a duplex apartment in New York. How long they last there and the reason for their return to Winnebago make up an amusing tale. Then there is **"Old Lady Mandle,"** which treats the old subject of the mother-in-law in a new and, pathetic light. **"You've Got to Be Selfish"** is the story of the rise of three celebrities in the theatrical world and is probably based upon some real facts. **"Long Distance"** and **"Un Morso Doo Pang"** are both war stories, the first named having its locale in a reconstruction hospital in England. **"Un Morso Doo Pang"** gives a new twist to the girl-left-behind theme. **"One Hundred Per Cent."** is another war story and it brings back our old friend Emma McChesney, now Mrs. T. A. Buck. In this story Emma goes on the road as a saleswoman again, doing the work of three men, so that they may be relieved for war duty. **"Farmer in the Dell"** and **"The Dancing Girls"** complete the book.

Edna Ferber has been described as a writer who goes "eavesdropping upon humanity." She does, and she catches many undercurrents that reveal life and its tangled threads.

Blanche Colton Williams   (essay date 1920)

SOURCE: "Edna Ferber," in her *Our Short Story Writers,* Dodd, Mead & Company, Inc., 1941, pp. 146-59.

[*In the following essay, which is a chapter from her book originally published in 1920, Williams discusses Ferber's short stories.*]

Few critics have accused Miss Edna Ferber of preaching a doctrine. "Me'n George Cohan," she wrote in 1912, "we jest aims to amuse." But few would deny that her stories possess qualities sane and wholesome. And the philosophy on which they are built is Work, with a capital W— Carlylean Work.

It is not remarkable that the joy of work illuminated throughout her scintillant pages has been forgotten in the display itself, as the great cause of a Fifth Avenue night-parade may be a matter of indifference to the observer who "just loves pageants and processions, anyway." The flying flags, the drum-beat of the march, the staccato tread, the calcium reds and yellows may obscure the slogan bearing banner. It is remarkable that the inciting force of Miss Ferber's triumphant march has been neglected by the student of underlying causes. There are those of us who believe it to be the significant word she has chanted to the sisters of her generation.

To one who has followed her stories from the beginning, Miss Ferber would seem to have undergone a silent communion with herself, and after asking, "What shall my writing stand for?" answered unhesitatingly, "Work!" In the Emma McChesney stories, which require three volumes—with one or two overflowing into succeeding collections, she emphasizes the beauty and joy and satisfaction that are the need of labor. And her second published story was an Emma story: **"Representing T. A. Buck"**

(*American,* March, 1911). It succeeded **"The Homely Heroine,"** her first, published in *Everybody's,* November, 1910. This fact, again, may escape the reader of her first volume, **Buttered Side Down** (March, 1912), which although it groups a number of her representative "working" characters in **"The Leading Lady," "A Bush League Hero,"** and **"The Kitchen Side of the Door"** yet presents variations of the main theme. As for example, the last-named cries aloud that the busy-folk on the kitchen side are more respectable than the tippling ladies and gentlemen (by courtesy) in front. But **Roast Beef Medium** (1913), including stories written and published before some of those in the first volume, essays to sound what becomes a trumpet call in **Emma McChesney and Co.** (1915).

Hortense of **"Blue Serge"** thinks:

> "If you're not busy, you can't be happy very long."
>
> "No," said Emma, "idleness, when you're not used to it, is misery."

And Miss Smalley of the same story:

> I've found out that work is a kind of self-oiler. If you're used to it, the minute you stop you begin to get rusty, and your hinges creak and you clog up, and the next thing you know you break down. Work that you like to do is a blessing. It keeps you young.

And the author herself (in **"Sisters Under Their Skin"**):

"In the face of the girl who works, whether she be a spindle-legged errand-girl or a ten thousand dollar a year foreign buyer, you will find both vivacity and depth of expression." . . . She begins this story by asserting: "Women who know the joys and sorrows of a pay envelope do not speak of girls who work as working girls." The whole story hangs on this thesis.

When Emma visited her son, Jock, and her daughter-in-law, Grace, and her grand-daughter, Emma McChesney, charming elderly women came to call.

They fell into two classes:

> . . . the placid, black-silk, rather vague women of middle-age, whose face has the blank look of the sheltered woman and who wrinkles early from sheer lack of sufficient activity or vital interest in life; and the wiry, well-dressed, assertive type who talked about her club work and her charities. In their eyes was that distrust of Emma which lurks in the eyes of a woman as she looks at another woman of her own age who doesn't show it.

And the volume ends with this final statement (in **"An Étude for Emma"**): ". . . there's nothing equal to the soul-filling satisfaction that you get in solo-work."

Miss Ferber has expressed sincerely her own beliefs in these and other passages, and throughout the larger structural values of her stories: in Emma's continuous struggle with the game of life, exemplified in a series of individual conflicts; in her efforts to make of Jock a man, and in her

great service to the T. A. Buck Featherloom Petticoat Company. In an article entitled **"The Joy of the Job"** (*American,* March, 1918), she says she is sorry for any woman who can play when she wishes. "Play is no treat for an idler." She works, according to her statement, three hundred and fifty mornings a year; she may play golf on the three hundred and fifty-first. It is not that she lacks desire to play, as the pink and green sweaters stream past her door. But the habit of work and the satisfaction that comes from having worked are such that she knows the eighteen holes of golf would be dull and flat once she deserted her typewriter for the links. "And that's the secret of the glory of the work habit. Once you've had to earn your play, you never again can relish it unearned."

From Kalamazoo, Michigan, where she was born August 15, 1887, Edna Ferber moved at an early age to Appleton, Wisconsin. There she went to "grade school" and to "high school," and there at seventeen years of age she began work on *The Daily Crescent,* the youngest reporter of her time. "It was a harrowing job," she admits, including as it did for her day's work "everything from the Courthouse to the Chicken Pie Supper at Odd Fellows' Hall, from St. Joseph's Monastery to the crippled flagman at the railroad crossing up in the chute, from the dry goods store to Lawrence University." Small wonder she learned humanity. When a critic suggested that her tales possessed an insight into human nature "which, if not genuine, is very well stimulated," her retort was forthcoming: "Humanity? Which of us really knows it? But take a fairly intelligent girl of seventeen, put her on a country daily newspaper, and then keep her on one paper or another, country and city, for six years, and—well, she just naturally can't help learning some things about some folks." . . . It is but logical that human interest leads all other qualities of her fiction.

Miss Ferber has told how from a hammock on her father's porch, where she spent much time at a season when she required rest—or as she phrases it, when the shop-sign read "Closed for Repairs"—she studied the passing townspeople. Life became for her a great storehouse in which at desire she may now enter, and from the shelves of which she may take down whatever she needs.

She was correspondent for two Milwaukee papers in these years of 'prenticeship and, later, for *The Chicago Tribune.* And she finished before she was twenty-four her first novel, **Dawn O'Hara,** her experience with which speaks for her artistic and literary ideals. For she threw the script into the waste-basket, whence her mother rescued it. This work, to some extent autobiographic, was published in 1911 and brought its author immediate success. After its publication she found ready market for her short stories.

Many of these first tales depend for background upon Appleton, which becomes "our town" in **"The Homely Heroine," "The Leading Lady," "Where the Car Turns at Eighteenth"**—spite of its title—and **"A Bush League Hero"** (all in **Buttered Side Down**). **"A Bush League Hero"** was written after a summer of watching the Bush League team play in Appleton, as Miss Ferber wrote the *Bookman* critic who expressed amusement over her naïveté in connection with the sport of baseball. By and by, in succeeding volumes, Appleton, Beloit, and Slatersville gave way to Chicago and New York, and even to cities of other countries. But Chicago and New York are her preferred settings, as St. Louis and New York are Fannie Hurst's.

> **Miss Ferber compensates her reader for lack of plot values by her character interest, and also by interest in immediate detail.**
>
> —*Blanche Colton Williams*

Her earlier stories, like her later ones, are about men clerks, women clerks, milliners, traveling salesmen and saleswomen, cooks, stenographers, leading ladies, household drudges, advertising specialists—the list is incomplete. No writer shows greater growth in storymaking than Miss Ferber—one need only compare *Roast Beef Medium* with any of the later McChesney stories—but she has never been "strong on plot." As she herself admits she does not know—and presumably cares less—what a plot is, she can hardly feel her confessed ignorance to be a handicap. In fact, she goes so far now and then as to twit the critic who insists upon plot as the *sine qua non* of a story. In "The Eldest" (of *Cheerful—By Request,* 1918) she makes her critic, you will remember, a Self-Complacent Young Cub, who says: "Trouble with your stuff is that it lacks plot. Your characterization's all right, and your dialogue. But your stuff lacks *raison d'être*—if you know what I mean." To which she retorts: "But people's insides are often so much more interesting than their outsides. . . ." And it is with people she succeeds best. "The Eldest," for instance, when it appeared some years ago in *McClure's,* was praised by Franklin P. Adams as the best short story of the year. Yet the plot is worn thin: a lover comes back after many years, only to marry the sister, the younger sister, of his former sweetheart. The interest lies in the character of Rose, the drudge, the slave, the living sacrifice, eternally new as eternally old. In the same volume, "The Gay Old Dog," which has been reprinted at least twice, faithfully portrays a loop-hound, as he would be known in his Windy City, the young man grown old through sacrifice, the counterpart of "The Eldest." Gallant Emma McChesney, cheerfully fighting to hold down a man-size job—knowing it requires six times as much work from a woman as from a man to draw for her the same salary—sprang into existence as the ideal of the modern business woman. She will reflect this particular age in her own particular so long as popular interest holds; after that time she will serve for the antiquarian. She is the heroine of *Roast Beef Medium,* of the five stories in *Personality Plus* (1914), of which her son is the hero, and of *Emma McChesney and Co.* (1915). From the number, or chapters, of the last-named, one may select diverting so-called stories. No reader will find fault with "Chickens," displaying the strong mother hand of this charming sales-

woman; nor with "Pink Tights and Ginghams" "featuring"—as Emma would say—her sympathy for her sex; nor with "Broadway to Buenos Aires," proving her business acumen, her boundless energy, and her zest for a fight; nor with "Thanks to Miss Morrissey," wherein after all she reverts to an old-fashioned sort of woman. But the truth is that the author is a novelist in her method. She leaves the reader with memories of her people, as novels do and should do, not with memories of a story. The individual tales of Emma's prowess dwindle in comparison with the fabric he creates out of Miss Ferber's generous distribution of scraps and his own pleasurable tedium in piecing them together. They are ultimately forgotten in the whole pattern. Mrs. McChesney has become real to her creator. In addressing a class at Columbia University, Miss Ferber said quaintly, "When Emma walks in upon me, I *must* give her my attention!"

Even the early stories of Miss Ferber emphasize for the first time in fiction a motive as old as the stomach of man: food. Pearlie Schultz, the Homely Heroine, wins her first—and doubtless her last—kiss through her noodle soup, her fried chicken, and hot biscuits; Jennie of "Maymeys from Cuba" succumbs, in her hunger, to a Scotch scone, after mouth-watering descriptions, by the author, of a corner fruit-stand and the grocery department of a big store. If you would be made ravenous, O weary of palate one! read "Maymeys from Cuba." And if you would recall the days of yore read the description (in "The Kitchen Side of the Door") "of a little world fragrant with mint, breathing of orange and lemon peel, perfumed with pineapple, redolent of cinnamon and clove, reeking of things spirituous." Of a world where "the splutter of the broiler was replaced by the hiss of the siphon, and the pop-pop of corks and the tinkle and clink of ice against glass." Perhaps after this devastating passage, the point should be made that no better temperance story has ever been published; beside it, most others look like ready-made propaganda.

Nor does the author forget the negative aspect of this food business. Emma McChesney, who first appears in "our town," dying—in her travel-weariness—for something "cool, and green, and fresh," is informed by the waitress that the menu offers "ham'n aigs, mutton chops, cold veal, cold roast"—to which Emma hopelessly interrupts, "Two, fried." Spectators at the performance of *Our Mrs. McChesney* will not forget Ethel Barrymore's winning question about the prospect for supper, the desk clerk's "Hungarian goulash!" nor Ethel's "My God!" as she departed stairward.

Keats's feast in *The Eve of St. Agnes* has long been praised by epicures, in art, if not in food. The marvel is that no one between Keats and Edna Ferber so emphasized the gustatory appeal. She continues it, with subtle discrimination, in "The Gay Old Dog." He was the kind of man who mixes his own salad dressing. "He liked to call for a bowl, some cracked ice, lemon, garlic, paprika, salt, pepper, vinegar, and oil, and make a rite of it."

So does Miss Ferber make a rite of food as her generation makes of it a ceremonial. Three titles out of six covering her stories suggest eating, the latest of which is humorously reflective, unconsciously so, perhaps, of reduced rations ensuing upon the war: *Half Portions* (1920). Or is it indicative that the author is losing her own zest in food? Some years ago she thought in terms of food comparisons. For example, to the Editor of *The New York Times,* she wrote: "I'm the sort of person who, when asked pointblank her choice of ice-cream, says, 'Chocolate, I think—no, peach! No—chocolate! Oh, I don't know.' That being true, how can you expect me to name off-hand the story which I consider the best short story in the English language?" [*The New York Times,* January 25, 1914]. It may be mentioned, in passing, that she lists Maupassant's "The String" and "The Necklace," O. Henry's "An Unfinished Story," Jesse Lynch Williams's "Stolen Story," and Neil Lyon's "Love in a Mist" among those she has preferred—at various times. In her article, **"The Joy of the Job,"** note the conditions upon which the "chicken salad is a poem, the coffee a dream, the French pastry a divine confection." Be it understood that all this is quoted in admiration.

Miss Ferber compensates her reader for lack of plot values by her character interest, as has been observed, and also by interest in immediate detail. And this is but another way of saying that she entertains by her style. She probably worked like a young fury, through newspaper training and through conscious study of word composition, to achieve her brilliant pyrotechnics. In her first collection, she is guilty of the absurd, " 'No, you don't!' hissed Gus." She had still to learn, apparently, that hissing requires a sibilant sound. Or, if she meant to burlesque faintly, her purpose is not obvious. In her first book, again, she refers too frequently to the trite, or the prevalent trick. "The short November afternoon was drawing to its close (as our best talent would put it)" . . . " 'Better bathe your eyes in *eau de cologne* or whatever it is they're always dabbing on 'em in books.' " . . . "As the novelists have it, their eyes met." . . . "As the story writers put it, he hadn't even devoured her with his gaze." . . . Her later stories have hardly outgrown this habit of jerking and calling halt to the steady march of the narrative, or these interruptions for which no contrasting cleverness and originality can compensate.

This author, like Mr. Joseph Hergesheimer, probably grew up with The Duchess. But her sardonic references to the lady leave doubt as to her opinion. She knew her Martin Chuzzlewit, her Jane Eyre, her O. Henry, and her Bible. Her admiration for George Cohan is genuine. She depreciates, by implication, the "balled-up" style of Henry James. Dickens and O. Henry are her forbears in humor, as the Holy Scriptures back her philosophy. . . .

From a sort of cavil against New York, Miss Ferber finally came to New York—no, "came on" to New York, with her heroine in **"Sun Dried."** Then, her first story in *Emma McChesney and Co.* gets away from Manhattan. Her love for travel and her journalistic ability to profit by new scenes are reflected in **"Broadway to Buenos Aires"** no less than in her own photographs and fact articles. **"The Guiding Miss Gowd"** (of *Cheerful—by Request*) testifies to an acquaintanceship with Rome, as the photograph of Miss Ferber stepping from the porch of a summer house in Hawaii is proof of her presence there. **"Ain't Nature**

Wonderful?" (*McClure's,* August, 1920) creates the certainty, as well as her photograph facing an article she wrote for *The American,* of December, 1916, that she knows the Rockies.

All her stories belong to the O. Henry school, but like her younger sister, Fannie Hurst, she has stolen away and farther on, bearing with her from the modern wizard only the trick of catching interest or the turn of a phrase. If O. Henry had never opened "Hearts and Crosses" with "Baldy Woods reached for the bottle and got it," perhaps she might not have begun *Cheerful—by Request* with "The editors paid for the lunch (as editors do)." But life has expanded in the decade and more since O. Henry's passing; it swings in arcs beyond the reach he needed to compass all of it he would. This one of his successors has widened the sweep, as the lover of New Bagdad would have done had he lived.

Half Portions is a varied assortment of new tales, as *Cheerful—by Request* gathers up old and new. The best are, as one would anticipate, stories of character, wherein the "story"—from a technical point of view—is usually negligible. **"Old Lady Mandel"** is but the summing up of the career of a professional mother. Yet **"One Hundred Per Cent,"** besides bringing Emma back, happens to be one of the first-rank patriotic stories published in the progress of the War. **"April 25th, as Usual"** marks the height of her accomplishment for 1919. After its appearance in *The Ladies' Home Journal* it was voted by the Committee from the Society of Arts and Sciences one of the best among thirty-two stories of the year, and was reprinted in the Society's annual volume—*The O. Henry Memorial Award Prize Stories.*

Miss Ferber stretches a continually expanding canvas; she is prodigally wasteful of whole novels in stories like **"The Gay Old Dog"** and **"Old Lady Mandel."** The novel, we venture to predict, is the field wherein she will ultimately "lay by" her most important work.

Louise Maunsell Field   (review date 30 October 1921)

SOURCE: A review of *The Girls,* in *The New York Times,* October 30, 1921, p. 16.

[*In the following favorable review of* The Girls, *Field praises Ferber's sense of realism.*]

Congratulations to Edna Ferber! For her new novel, *The Girls,* is not only the best, and very much the best, book she has as yet written, but it is also one of the best that has so far been produced upon its particular subject. It has a realism, a fairness, a sanity not often found, and especially rare in stories which portray, or profess to portray, the "flapper" of the present day. Those who have contended that sweeping condemnation of that young person is unfair will rejoice in the picture of "Charley"—otherwise Charlotte—Kemp, aged something over 18 and intensely modern, "who loathed cheapness, and bobbed hair, and wriggling ways, and the whole new breed of her contemporaries who were of the hard-drinking, stairway-kissing, country-club petting class." But frank-spoken Charley is neither the most notable nor the central figure in the novel.

Miss Ferber has sketched the lives of three unmarried women of different generations. First, there is Charlotte Thrift, 18 at the time of the Civil War, a woman of seventy-odd in the year 1916, when the action of the tale begins. But in going back to the lavender-scented romance of Charlotte Thrift, spinster, we go back to the Chicago of the seventies, and even a little earlier, to the days when "Chicago sidewalks were crazy wooden affairs, raised high on rickety stilts," and merino dresses and green velvet bonnets were the height of fashion. Then there comes Lottie Payson, Charlotte's namesake, the only daughter of Charlotte Thrift's only sister, Carrie. Lottie is 32 in 1916, fun-loving, intelligent, with a "fine, straight back," and an "elfish interior." She often felt 16 and irresponsible, and did not find it easy to be always well-balanced and matter-of-fact. Third and last is Charley Kemp, Lottie's niece and namesake, the only daughter of Lottie's older sister Belle. It is Lottie who is the central figure of the book, Lottie, in whom many a spinster of 32—or thereabout—will see herself and her own life reflected. "Lottie was the kind of girl who 'is needed at home,'" and Lottie had a conscience, and a strong sense of duty. "For ten years or more she had been so fully occupied in doing her duty—or what she considered her obvious duty—that she had scarcely thought of her obligations toward herself." But the years slipped swiftly by, and presently the day came when she admitted: "It seems to me I've just been running errands for the last ten years or more. Running errands up and down, while the world has gone by."

The Girls has a realism, a fairness, a sanity not often found, and especially rare in stories which portray, or profess to portray, the "flapper" of the present day

—Louise Maunsell Field

Charlotte Thrift's parents had tyrannized over her consciously and conscientiously with the best possible intentions. With the best possible intentions, and quite unconsciously, Lottie's mother tyrannized over her, ruling her through her conscience and her affections. She is a wonderfully well-drawn character, this Mrs. Carrie Payson, who in time of emergency had taken a man's place, who was so level-headed in business matters, so competent and so indomitable. "Mrs. Payson did not dream that she had blocked her daughter's chances for a career or for marital happiness. Neither did she know that she looked down upon that daughter for having failed to marry." Yet, after all, Charley the modern, Charley who had been permitted to mold her life as she chose and without parental interference, is left, when the novel comes to an end, with as little of success as Lottie, looking forward bravely enough, avowing herself "the kind that goes on," but looking forward to, at best, a marriage that will be only a makeshift, a kind of compromise. She had taken up the most modern of careers after an expensive training, only to abandon it

when the pinch came and try something different, to find that also less than satisfactory. But though very much at loose ends, she is only a little over 20 when we leave her, and the future may have much that is worth while in store for her. The war had changed Lottie's life, but she is, one feels, only on the threshold of new difficulties when the book closes, difficulties that her "brave lie" is all but certain to entail. "The Thrift Girls"—that was what people called the three Charlottes—had not worked things out. Neither Charlotte of the long-skirted riding habit and the rose, nor Lottie of the trim, sensible tailor-mades, nor Charley of the "white woolly sweater and gym pants . . . clear-eyed, remorseless, honest, fearless, terrifying."

The novel is inconclusive; for the situation, the woman's problem it presents, no conclusion has as yet been found. Charlotte, submissive and brow-beaten; Lottie, made defenseless by her sense of duty; Charley, who maintained that "There is no higher duty than that of self-expression," and who would not have tolerated for a moment that ransacking of her private papers against which her grand-aunt had not even dreamed of protesting—each represents a type and a generation, and each is a fine example of her type and generation. But it is Lottie who is the foremost figure, and her story which predominates. There are many vivid scenes in that story, scenes which linger in one's memory. The Friday night dinners, for example, to which Mrs. Payson's married daughter Belle was expected to bring her good-natured husband and rather less good-natured daughter, whether any of them wanted to come or not; Lottie's brief rebellion when Mrs. Payson's obstinacy brought on a condition of affairs which caused Lottie to reproach herself "grimly, unsparingly"; the evenings during which Lottie sat alone on the piazza of the little cottage at the Michigan lake resort, those evenings which were "terrible beyond words"; the meeting of the Reading Club, from which Lottie is "striding home" when first we see her, are all of them completely real, fragments of everyday life so placed before us that we see all their underlying drama. There are of course weaknesses in the book; the Jeannette episode, genuine enough in its beginning, loses its convincingness from the moment Jeannette enters the Payson home, while Ben Gartz, though a true enough type, is used by the author in a decidedly "fiction" way, both with Lottie and Charley. Toward the close the book drags a little, and Mrs. Payson is put out of the way a trifle too conveniently. The Mrs. Paysons of this world live long. But these are, after all, small blots upon a truthful, broad-minded and very interesting narrative, a book upon which its author, as was said in the beginning, is to be heartily congratulated.

Francis Hackett   (review date 4 January 1922)

SOURCE: A review of *The Girls,* in *The New Republic,* Vol. XXIX, No. 370, January 4, 1922, pp. 158-59.

[*In the following mixed review of* The Girls, *Hackett applauds the realistic details of the plot and characters, but faults Ferber's "underlying sentimentalism and snappy technique."*]

At one time it looked as if nothing could drag Chicago into

the focus of the novelist. It wasn't simply that Chicago didn't want to sit, in all its sprawling horror: it was also that the artist shrank from touching Chicago. Frank Norris, Theodore Dreiser, H. B. Fuller, Robert Herrick, Edith Wyatt—each of them roped the beast and yanked him forward, but there was a felt resistance and a not quite happy conquest. The sitter and the artist both remained, if not uncomfortable, certainly heroically strained.

Miss Ferber marks a difference. She is not in the least strained. Chicago to her is one of the richest, most natural, most established of themes. She doesn't feel it necessary to get the whole thing in: she knows precisely what slice of the bourgeois community she wishes to cut. At the same time she is aware of all Chicago. The city permeates her book [*The Girls*]. Not only that, it permeates the three generations of Chicagoans with whom she so buoyantly and glowingly deals. She abounds in her sense of a living community whose origins are not hidden under the innumerable transfers and liens and notations of history but are vividly exposed to anyone with a feeling for drama. She rejoices in this drama and has the clearest professional instinct as to the way to handle it. To let Prairie Avenue, and the transmogrifications of Prairie Avenue, go to waste, is a piece of negligence luckily impossible to Miss Ferber. Here, she seems to say, is History caught in the act. Here is Charlotte Thrift in 1860 kissing Jesse Dick good-bye as he marches off to war—marching off in front of the Court House steps in full sight of the Addison Canes, the Thomas Holcombs, the Lewis Fullers, the Clapps . . . And here, in 1917, is the grand-niece Charley, saying good-bye over dinner and dance at the Bismarck Gardens, (now the Marigold Gardens), saying good-bye to her own Jesse Dick. In 1860 the boy was disreputable because he was a Dick of "Hardscrabble," a poor white Dick. In 1917 he was disreputable because he was the son of Delicatessen Dick, and a poet. Disreputable, that is, in the eyes of that lower middle-class Anglo-Saxon respectability which domesticated itself on Prairie Avenue and built a brick church over its safety deposit vaults wherever possible. So Miss Ferber focusses the rich and delicious contrast in what, for the Chicagoan, must be called an historical novel.

It is done so tellingly, so appreciatively, so intelligently, that one is ready to dilate at great length on its good points. Miss Ferber does not, it is true, stand away from her Charley. She espouses Charley's generation just as warmly as she espouses Judge Emma Barton of the Girl's Court, "wise, humorous, understanding Emma Barton." Or just as warmly as she indicates a very human newspaper reporter who is Irish but is called Winnie Steppler. But in spite of this partisanship, which is really sentimental and demagogic and hampers the reader in forming his own convictions, Miss Ferber does possess a decided gift of creating character structurally. She shows this best in meeting that famous test of creative ability, the family. Her family is a living organism and its contingencies spring from their real centre, the parents' will to power.

To illustrate or dramatize that will to power, Miss Ferber does a daring thing. She telescopes life. She shows Charlotte Thrift defeated by both father and mother in her love

for the boy who goes to the Civil War. Charlotte Thrift remains a spinster, a rebel by temperament but not effectual. In contrast to her is the practical sister, Carrie Payson. This woman, who becomes the head of the Prairie Avenue household and the real estate business after her husband decamps with the family fortune, is an excellent study of the managerial philistine. With her will to power, as usually happens in novels and sometimes in life, she has cirrhosis of the imagination. What Miss Ferber sees most acutely, however, is the incompetence that goes with her tyranny. Now this woman, executive and limited, has two daughters Belle and Lottie. Belle fulfills her philistine destiny by marrying successfully, though on the South Side. She becomes interesting only when the war smashes up her husband's crockery business and when she, in turn, tries to manage her daughter, Charley, into a profitable marriage.

Chicago permeates *The Girls*. It permeates the three generations of Chicagoans with whom Ferber so buoyantly and glowingly deals.

—*Francis Hackett*

Lottie is the shy, yielding, unmarried woman of thirty, very attractive. The second of "the Girls," she is a sort of plump and well-groomed Miss Lulu Bett. Lottie totes after freedom in a dilapidated family electric, but she is really her mother's chauffeur and slave and the nearest she flies to romance is when Rutherford Hayes Adler, a most winning youth, comes courting, only to be beaten off by mother. Lottie is revealed admirably in her Chicago surroundings. The celebrated meeting of her Reading Club in which spinsterhood is brutally vivisected by Beck Schaefer is one of the most adroit chapters in the book. But the third of "the girls," Charley, is Miss Ferber's largest contribution to the history of family tyranny. She is not revoltée. She isn't hysterical. She isn't excited about "the older generation trying to curb the younger." She isn't "fresh." She isn't tough. She is, as Miss Ferber delightedly depicts her, clear-eyed, strong-willed, competent and chic. Her speech and her acts reveal an adventurous and at the same time responsible character. Whether she goes to work at Shield's (Field's) or takes up dancing, allows dozens to court her or selects her one poet for herself, she is a model of the clean-cut, self-reliant youth that now dazzles, and apparently exasperates, the middle-aged world. Miss Ferber sees her as roselike. She describes her in her boyish slang, in her athletic slimness, in her freedom, in her perfect digestion, with something a little like adoring envy. At any rate, Charley is the shell with which the older generation is torpedoed or to be torpedoed.

Certainly Mr. Ben Gartz, the war-profiteer or goulash baron, is torpedoed by Charley when he comes saying it with candy, box seats and flowers. The portrait of this gentleman, painted in oil, is extremely well done, and all the better done because it is moderate. Ben Gartz, "a fat man, in a derby, at a picnic," is really heard by Miss Ferber. Unlike Mr. Sinclair Lewis, she does not strain to make her philistines super-typical. She quotes them accurately and delicately, toasting them without burning them. And her kindly paunchy bachelor with the wet kiss who thinks he's "different from most" is not more distinctly heard than Charley or her young poet or Lottie or Beck Schaefer. The extraordinary verisimilitude of speech is never lost all through the book, except possibly with the Swedish servant. And this quickness to respond to human inflection in speech is matched by a similar quickness to respond to gait, to pace, to form.

The sadness, then, is that at the last, on the home stretch, Miss Ferber wobbles horribly. She brings in a baby, Lottie's war-baby, which Lottie accumulates while doing warwork in France, after her declaration of independence. The nice boy-poet, Jesse Dick, is killed at the front, but that permits Miss Ferber to take her curtain with a trick baby on the stage. Well, perhaps not a trick baby, but certainly one of the least likely and most irrelevant of babies, for whom the proud mother can only blurb, "I'm not excusing it. There is no excuse. They were the happiest three days of my life—and always will be."

It's a miserable mealy-mouthed speech, and out of character. Charley, in addition, is not, as she might be, shown to us in one of those situations which tests the young generation for sympathy as well as for nerve. Here, it seems to me, Miss Ferber has paid the penalty of her underlying sentimentalism and her snappy technique. But that leaves most of *The Girls* intact. It is that fascinating thing, a novel of community, viewed with an enormous command of detail and a fine observation, a real enthusiasm for theme and for the bright race of life. Such infidelity as, to my view, it exhibits is essentially serious. The story, at the end, reveals the flatness of an alloy. Yet, doctored, true metal is there.

The New York Times Book Review   (review date 5 November 1922)

SOURCE: A review of *Gigolo*, in *The New York Times Book Review*, November 5, 1922, p. 10.

[*In the following mixed review of* Gigolo, *the critic contends that while the plots and characters of the stories are realistic, Ferber at times undercuts this quality with excessive melodrama or lack of narrative pacing.*]

Every one who is at all conversant with the current magazines has by this time become well acquainted with the typical Edna Ferber short story. Eight of these short stories have been collected in the present volume, to which the least worthwhile of them gives its title, **"Gigolo."** Of the eight **"Old Man Minick"** is perhaps the best, with **"Home Girl"** and **"The Sudden Sixties"** as formidable contestants for the honor of first place. The scenes are laid in various places—Chicago, of course, New York, Hollywood, Paris, Winnebago, Wisconsin and Okoochee, Oklahoma—but the characters invariably belong to what we know as "the plain people." Some of them have a good deal of money, and others very little, but, rich or poor,

they always, or almost always, are members of the same general order—that vast order of the commonplace.

"The Afternoon of a Faun," which has the place of honor in the forefront of the book, is the not very credible tale of a young mechanic, working in a garage, adored by all the girls of his acquaintance, and very much bored thereby. "Fella don't like to have no girl chasing him all the time. Say, he likes to do the chasing himself," he presently avers. **"Old Man Minick,"** which comes next, is an admirably realistic study of an old man of seventy, who, after losing the wife who had "spoiled him outrageously" during the forty-odd years of their married life, went to live with his son and his entirely well meaning daughter-in-law. The humor and pathos, the deft characterization and perfect verisimilitude of this tale are admirable, representative, though on a smaller scale, of the best work done by the author of *The Girls*. The story, which is to some extent a companion tale to **"Old Man Minick"**—**"The Sudden Sixties"**—is not quite so good. One cannot help feeling that Hannah Winter's unselfishness is just a little overdone, yet there is much truth in the analysis of her mental attitude, and of her daughter's. There are young matrons innumerable who, like those in Marcia's set, lean heavily on their own mothers, and cannot understand why these older women who "haven't a thing to do" should not be willing and glad to take care of their grandchildren, rendering first aid at any moment without the least regard for plans or preferences of their own. There are plenty of married daughters who would do well to read **"The Sudden Sixties"** carefully and to think over it deliberately, thereby perhaps saving other women from the fate of Hannah Winter.

"Home Girl" is another excellent bit of realism, admirable in its pictures of character and of environment. There is no one of us who does not count at least one Cora in the list of her acquaintances—except the Coras themselves, who would not recognize their own type, mirrored in Miss Ferber's pages. And are there any among city dwellers who do not know such apartments as the one in which Ray and Cora lived, where "everything folded, or flapped, or doubled, or shot in, or shot out, or concealed something else, or pretended to be something it was not?" Wilson Avenue, too, is to be found in other cities besides Chicago, with its "one-room-and-kitchenette apartments" and delicatessen shops displaying "chromatic viands" at the fanciest of fancy prices. "Shylock, purchasing a paper-thin slice of pinky ham in Wilson Avenue, would know his own early Venetian transaction to have been pure philanthropy." It is an accurately detailed picture of one aspect of our modern city life, this story of **"Home Girl."**

No less modern, if not quite as good, is the story of the high-grade comedy actress, Harrietta Fuller, who went to Hollywood and found herself in what was to her a topsy-turvy world, where youth and prettiness were of utmost importance, and intelligence and craftsmanship of very little. Her experiences are amusing to read about, but at last they proved too trying to be endured, even with the aid of her highly cultivated sense of humor. **"Ain't Nature Wonderful!"** is an entertaining farce, with a good bit of truth tucked in amid the laughter. More people than a few have adopted the pose taken by Florian Sykes—and without having his various excuses for so doing. "Gigolo," though it gives a colorful picture of one effect of the war, is not convincing, besides being too long drawn out, a fault which in a lesser degree appears in several of these tales, especially the rather uninteresting **"If I Should Ever Travel!"** A gigolo, Miss Ferber explains, "generally speaking, is a man who lives off women's money. In the mad year 1922 A. D., a gigolo, definitely speaking, designated one of those incredible and pathetic creatures . . . who for 10 francs . . . would dance with any woman wishing to dance on the crowded floors of public tea rooms, dinner or supper rooms in the cafés, hotels and restaurants of France." How Gideon Gory of Winnebago, Wis., fell to these depths, lower than which "could no man fall," and how he was presently rescued therefrom, the story tells.

They are for the most part interesting tales, these of Miss Ferber's. She knows well the kind of people with whom the majority of her stories deal, knows their surroundings and the sort of lives they lead, and puts them before us vividly and well.

John Farrar   (essay date 1924)

SOURCE: "Edna Ferber," in *The Literary Spotlight*, George H. Doran Company, 1924, pp. 135-45.

[*Farrar, an American journalist, editor, and critic, founded the publishing companies Farrar and Rinehart and Farrar, Straus and Company, now known as Farrar, Straus and Giroux. In the following anecdotal essay, he discusses Ferber's evolution from journalist to short story writer and novelist.*]

At one time, Edna Ferber was in the gravest danger of letting her cleverness run away with her. It might have been her artistic undoing. She would start a short story so brilliantly that one gasped, fearful for the climax of anything so sparklingly begun. But she got over that, and she got over the O. Henry influence. There may be many who will contradict this; certainly there is justification for the opinion that she was an imitator. But she has learned to write her stories backward. She once told an editor who had praised a certain piece of work of hers, that she was certain it was going to turn out a good story because she was able to put down the last sentence before she wrote the first.

I imagine she writes all her stories that way. Turn to **"The Maternal Feminine"** in a recent collection. I would wager anything that the process she employed was the one I have uncovered. But don't spoil a great short story by reading it backward. Then look up **"The Gay Old Dog,"** if you are a man, and wince at the knowledge Edna Ferber has of the male species. How has she learned so much about us? What divination is hers, that she can read the man heart so clearly, understand the loneliness of the old bachelor, the while she also reveals the truth about the unmarried woman in one piercing sentence? It is little short of genius to put these things on paper. If Emma McChesney leaped from the page, and grasped your hand, and lived at your house all the while you read of her, there are likewise dozens of Miss Ferber's characters since those happy days who will always hold a place in your fiction friendships.

Edna Ferber came from a small town. She worked on newspapers in small towns in the middle west; and she has absorbed the people of small towns as few writers since George Ade have done. Indeed, she seems to me quite as important as that great philosopher-humorist, even though she lacks his profound observation.

It is little more than ten years since her first story appeared in *Everybody's Magazine*—one of the best bits of character drawing she has ever done, by the way. It was called **"The Homely Heroine,"** and I think it runs to not over 2,300 words. For it she received the munificent sum of $62.50. She was tickled to death—particularly with the extra fifty cents. She had broken in. The little Kalamazoo girl had arrived. What matter that the check was small? She'd show 'em.

Those who imagine editors are always trying to find ways of keeping young authors in their place, should note what followed in the case of the utterly unknown Edna Ferber. People talked of that yarn. It was passed around in editorial offices, spoken of as the most promising short story since O. Henry's earliest work. There was a mad rush to get Miss Ferber's next product. I think importunate telegrams were sent to her. But her head was not turned. She was too wise, too poised, too sensible, even at that early age. You see, when you have knocked about on newspapers in Appleton, Wisconsin, in Milwaukee and Chicago, you take flattery lightly. There are bound to be bumps ahead, for all the momentary clear sailing. But Edna Ferber was not a flash in the pan. Her next story was equally good; and *The American Magazine* got hold of her—one of the editors went west to call upon her, to see who she was, find out what she looked like, after the manner of the modern progressive hunter after fiction. He found a slip of a girl, alert, with brown eyes that glowed like live coals, an abundance of black hair which she slashed right back from a well molded forehead, and a skin like velvet on which cream has been poured. He heard a vibrant voice, that uttered terse, sharp sentences. Sometimes they were too sharp and terse; for Miss Ferber likes her own way, deny it as she will, and never hesitates to say just what she thinks, regardless of whether or not it is wise to do so. Here was a keenness of mind that was refreshing. Edna Ferber exuded health and energy; her answers were apropos, discriminating, final. There was little pose about her. She was just a normal girl with a wild ambition—though she confessed even then that she would rather be an actress than an author. I have seen her give an imitation of Bernhardt that was uncanny—she can even look like the great French tragedienne by the simple process of putting a feather boa around her neck and pulling her hair over her eyes, from which the glasses have been removed.

But the stage was not for her. She took to the pen—or the typewriter, as they all do nowadays—as a Salvation Army lassie to a tambourine; and she sailed in bravely and wrote a novel. It was called *Dawn O'Hara*. Miss Ferber herself would tell you not to read it now, she has gone so far beyond it. It was crude and forced and jerky. She was, in those days, essentially a worker in miniatures, and after the near-failure of this maiden effort, she was wise enough to revert to the writing of brief short stories on the order of **"The Homely Heroine."** They seemed to flow from her pen—typewriter, I mean; but they didn't do anything of the sort. They were the result of most assiduous work. She plugs away every morning of her life, whether she feels like it or not. When she is living in New York, at an up-town hotel, she hurries out before breakfast and gets a brisk walk around the Reservoir in Central Park, to fresh-en her brain, and think over what she shall do that day. When she is in Chicago, it is the shore of Lake Michigan that feels the patter of her rapid feet as she takes a consti-tutional around Jackson Park. She divides her time now between these two great cities, and has never been able to say which she likes the better.

Though she lives in hotels, with her mother, she is the most domestic person you can imagine, and she almost re-sents the prepared food she eats. For she loves to cook, and knows all sorts of tempting recipes. But she says she and her mother cannot be bothered with servant prob-lems; and so they go on living at comfortable apartment hotels, free to come and go as they wish.

For Miss Ferber likes to travel; but she doesn't like to pack her bags without an object in view. Therefore, whenever she decides that she wants a trip to the coast, she arranges a neat little reading tour for herself. In this way she ap-peases that never dormant desire to express herself histri-onically. And how she does read her own stories! Wom-en's clubs who have been lucky enough to capture her, have always felt more than rewarded. She knows **"The Gay Old Dog"** practically by heart. She merely puts the book on a table near her, as an orator places his notes by his plate for occasional reference, and then plunges into the story, like the true artiste she is, and gets her effects through dramatic pauses which many a professional ac-tress might do well to study and emulate. She can imitate almost any dialect; and shop-girl slang is heaven to her. I really think that the stage lost a great character actress when literature claimed Edna Ferber.

After the immense vogue of the McChesney stories, it was inevitable that they would be dramatized. George V. Ho-bart collaborated with their creator; and Ethel Barrymore played the leading rôle for two years, with enormous suc-cess. Since then, Miss Ferber has written but one play, and that again in collaboration. Newman Levy and she got an idea-of-the-moment in the small salaries paid to college professors in American universities; under the title of *$1,200 a Year* they tore off a comedy that was tried out and came to grief on the road; but it lives within the pages of a volume, and is well worth looking up. Parts of it are astonishingly clever. I think the trouble with it was that too few people, immersed as they all were in their own tragic financial difficulties, gave a hang what salaries col-lege professors were paid. It is not what might be called a burning question. And it was not an altogether actable play. Maybe it was written too hastily. It is curious how many fiction writers think that a play is an easy method of expression.

There are those who abominate Miss Ferber's cocksure-ness, her too-scintillating phrases, her measured determi-nation always to be apt and smart. I can see perfectly how certain of her stories would grate on certain people; but beyond that surface glitter and shine there is always, to me

at least, a realization of her understanding of, and sympa-thy for, the plain folk she writes about. She loves humani-ty, and is unafraid to reveal her love. A waiter, a manicure, a tired Cook's tourist, an ex-convict, a seamstress, a milli-ner—all these claim her heart; and she can put them on paper in blinding, vivid paragraphs, and cause you to ex-claim, "Why, I know a person just like that!" Sometimes she is too photographic; and then again often she slurs over some character in whom you have become greatly in-terested. For some reason he or she has not held Miss Fer-ber, and so it's out of the story for that unfortunate. I am thinking particularly of the poet, in *The Girls*. There was not nearly enough of him.

And speaking of that flaming novel of Chicago, how Miss Ferber must be chuckling at those critics of hers who have insistently reiterated that she was not big enough to write anything sustained. Oh yes, they were prompt to praise her collections under such titles as *Buttered Side Down, Half Portions, Roast Beef Medium,* and *Personality Plus*—a goodly showing, when you come to think of it, even though the titles might be found fault with by the dis-criminating and over-sensitive. Is there a little cheapness in such names of books? I have heard critics deplore her tendency to be downright common. She has played to the gallery, they contend; she is too fond of the newspaper method, too anxious to seem to know it all. "She's fresh"—and I use the word in its double sense—was the way one critic put it. All her books have gone into several editions, and there is no doubt that Miss Ferber could go on indefinitely reaching a loyal public through her short stories alone. But she is not content to remain in a groove. *The Girls* formed in her active brain as a cameo; but it got away from her, swept her off her feet after she began it, and she found page after page rustling from her machine. Then one day, having shut off the telephone for weeks, she discovered on her desk a full-fledged novel, which *The Woman's Home Companion* wanted as a serial, at a most gratifying price. And later the astute reviewers of the land hailed it as one of the finest novels of the year—Heywood Broun, F. P. A., Percy Hammond, and a host of others were loud in their praise of it.

It is so far ahead of *Fanny Herself* that one wonders where Miss Ferber will go in the next ten years. If she can travel that fast, there's no telling what broad highway she may take. For her art has ripened; and in depicting the manless household of the Thrift girls, on Chicago's South Side, she has torn down not only one wall, but all four, and allowed the whole world not to peep but to see openly those three generations of lonely women. The story mounts with every chapter; and Miss Ferber's clean-cut style, held beautiful-ly in check, exactly suits the material at her hand. She pounds in her effects, makes these "girls" walk down the streets with you, turn windy corners with you; and she causes the old Chicago to pass in a panorama before your eyes. The scene wherein the soldiers of the Civil War march away from the Lake City is tremendous—a whirl-wind of action. And all the threads are finally gathered up—as the critics all said a mere short-story writer couldn't gather them. They are not only gathered, they are tied in a deft knot, and one is left with a feeling of complete satisfaction. It is Miss Ferber's triumph that she has accomplished this *tour de force*. Yet was it artistic to cover so long a period of time in so short a compass? There are moments in **The Girls** when you feel the nervous desire of the short story writer to whittle to the bone. It might have been a greater book if she had expanded more and compressed with less anxiety.

There is no doubt that Miss Ferber could go on indefinitely reaching a loyal public through her short stories alone.

—*John Farrar*

Edna Ferber is known for her reliability in her dealings with editors. If she is asked to finish a certain piece of work by four o'clock on a Tuesday afternoon, at four o'clock on the Tuesday afternoon the completed product is on the editorial desk. She says it is just as easy to be businesslike as not. Her newspaper training, no doubt. Her letters accompanying her manuscripts are often as clever as the manuscripts themselves. Her abrupt beginnings and endings are a joy. There's never a wasted word.

She motors in Chicago as if she had done it all her life—loops around the puzzling Loop with ease and grace; and her passenger doesn't even hold his breath when she swings into throbbing Michigan Avenue and darts out to the South Side or over toward Evanston.

Like all successful authors, Miss Ferber has had innumerable offers to write directly for the screen. What captions she could do! She spent a few months in Hollywood, wrote a fine article about her impressions of that mad little colony, and incidentally sold the motion picture rights to two or three of her books. But her mother was almost killed in a motor accident on one of the boulevards, and they experienced a definite trembling of the earth; and altogether Miss Ferber felt she would be more at home in the middle west; so they packed up and shipped back to Chicago. Then they packed up and shipped on to New York, where, Miss Ferber claims, she misses Chicago. She says, very wisely, that if any of her material is suitable for screen production, there it is to purchase; but she hasn't the time nor the inclination to spend her energy on scenarios. It is the right attitude to take; when every author realizes that it is foolish to try to serve two masters, both books and motion pictures will be all the better.

Miss Ferber has many friends. I heard her say, with her usual frankness, to a good-looking young man, "You're handsome, yes—but you're stupid." Afterward he told me that he was afraid of her, but found such candor refreshing. She will dance, when she is seeking copy, in the lowest of Chicago "dives," with Carl Sandburg or Ben Hecht or Harry Hansen or young Gene Markey; and the next evening she will be at the smartest dinner, talking brilliantly with these same men, enjoying each party with equal gusto. She likes Fanny Butcher's Book Shop, and all the people in it; and when she comes east she hobnobs with

Franklin P. Adams, William Gillette, Rutger Jewett, Albert A. Boyden (when he isn't in Poland), Julian Street, Charles Hanson Towne, Alexander Woollcott, and many others who make New York the shining spot it is. But much as she cares for social life, she cares more for good honest hard work. That is why she is one of the highest priced short-story writers in the whole country to-day. She refuses to produce too much, believing that the best one is capable of cannot be written hastily to meet the needs of waiting markets. I know of one editor who, eager for her work, left a signed blank contract with her. She had but to fill in the figures and return it to him. She confesses that the temptation was great; but she did not feel that she could do her best under such conditions and so the contract went back—unsigned by her.

Do you get a picture of Edna Ferber from that little story?

Saturday Review (New York)   (review date 21 August 1926)

SOURCE: "Showing America," in *Saturday Review,* New York, Vol. 111, No. 4, August 21, 1926, pp. 49, 54.

[*In the following largely favorable review of* Show Boat, *the critic, lamenting his modern culture's lack of what he calls "local color," suggests that while Ferber's novel captures much of the feel of life on the Mississippi in the 1890s, it is perhaps too self-consciously nostalgic, "got up," to be fully satisfying.*]

Who speaks a good word for the 'nineties now? What critic celebrated the exquisite low reliefs of Mary Wilkins Freeman's short stories when last year the American Academy awarded her its gold medal a decade (as usual) too late? Who spoke a fitting word at the death of James Lane Allen, recalling that pearl of Southern sentiment, "The Kentucky Cardinal—(the toes, were they really cut off!)?" Who forgets, but who speaks, of Colonel Carter of Cartersville and his rugged cuffs, or Amos Judd, or Monsieur Beaucaire, or the whimsical creoles of George Washington Cable, or Van Bibber, or Dr. Lavendar? Outmoded now the humors of sentimental hearts and alien to the city life of an America that finds "nize" babies and hotel women and night clubs more amusing than country life, which, according to present convention, is sordid, or the small town, which exists now only to be satirized. And yet, though lacking our sophisticated superiority, what a gift that generation had! They were not writers of scope and ruthless honesty. No American accepted in the 'nineties would have had the courage, under the maternal eye of Howells, to put in *all* about the murder (and the murderer, and his sisters, and his cousins, and his aunts) as Dreiser is now applauded for doing. They were not disillusioned—life for them was full of queer corners where the saddest and most amusing things happened. They were never bored, and never bored their readers. Like the actors of that day, they were not ashamed of sure-fire appeals to the sentiment of their audiences. Tears, happy endings, mysterious great ones (a specialty of Robert Chambers), reversals, broken hearts and mended ones were common property, and even Miss Wilkins made her provincial New England grandiose in its tragedies, unlike Main Street of today, or that most undesirable house under the elms of O'Neill's New England. But what a sense for personality they had, what a feeling for character and neighborhood, how many people they created that one can still call by name!

Theirs was the art of local color, a minor art, in which the color often subdues the story to its own uses, yet an art especially congenial to a congeries of sections such as was, and to some extent still is, the United States. Was there ever a nation richer in materials for a picturesque literature in the day when a New Englander *was* a New Englander, a Southerner still unreconstructed, the West untamed, the South West still Spanish, the hill folk primitive, the Irish immigrant not yet pursy, the great rivers still alive with traffic, pioneering a fact, and such levellers as syndicates, moving pictures, *The Saturday Evening Post,* and chain stores not yet invented!

We shall regret the loss of all that color. We are already regretting it: the screen has begun to revive the old character parts and make romantic the individualism of the days before standardization; the novelists, wearying of analysis, are beginning to reconstruct.

Miss Edna Ferber's just published **Show Boat** is local color come to life again, and it is not merely because she takes for scene the Cotton Blossom river theatre floating down the Mississippi that her book is so rich in "characters" (Schultzy, Ravenal, Parthy, Captain Andy, Julie, Elly, Magnolia, the heroine herself), "characters" are at home in a local color story. There is not much plot, for the author is interested in life not in plot, there is just the river and the folk of its own that it breeds like a flora and fauna. Miss Ferber has less to go on than the writers of the 'nineties who had seen for themselves local color at its liveliest. One feels that she has "got up" the river and wide-open Chicago and even the marvelous New England school-marm Parthenia, who makes the theatre serve puritanism and thrift, got them all up with the high competence of her short stories of modern bourgeois life where nothing relevant is omitted and nothing irrelevant retained. But the getting up is good. When Kim, the granddaughter, so to speak, of the Show Boat emerges as a stage success of the modern, sophisticated variety in New York, the fabric of the story weakens and pales. The "frail and brittle" life of current New York does not lend itself to local color.

Not so the Mississippi. With the river, Miss Ferber's synthesis is a grand success. We have learned something about story telling (thanks to the high price of space) since the 'nineties, and Miss Ferber uses her experience. The narrative skips adroitly back and forward through three generations, plucking from roaring Chicago and brittle New York only what will best serve as background for the show boat where Elly and Julie perform, while Jo sings spirituals in the galley, Parthy glares over her corsets, Magnolia makes her debut and the river rushes by.

The local colorists of an earlier generation would enjoy, one guesses, **Show Boat,** while finding it (like New York) a little brittle, intellectual, "got up." They would be pleased with the "characters," quick to approve such

drama as the discovery of Julie's Negro blood, or the comedy of Gaylord's "ef he loves yuh and you love him," and if they should say that it is only local color after all, why so were theirs, so is all local color unless it is something more.

Donald Davidson   (review date 22 August 1926)

SOURCE: "Edna Ferber," in *The Spyglass: Views and Reviews, 1924-1930,* edited by John Tyree Fain, Vanderbilt University Press, 1963, pp. 70-4.

[*An American poet, literary critic, social commentator, and historian, Davidson is best known as a member of the Fugitive poets—a group of southern American writers that included John Crowe Ranson, Robert Penn Warren, and Alan Tate—and as a member of the Agrarians—a group that included many of the Fugitives and promoted the idea of agrarianism (as opposed to industrialism) in their writings on politics, social criticism, and economic theory. In the following review, originally published in the* Nashville Tennessean *on August 22, 1926, he praises the descriptive, panoramic elements of* Show Boat, *but concludes that the novel, like all of Ferber's work and, indeed, "most novels by women," lack depth.*]

Edna Ferber explained in **So Big** that cabbages are beautiful, and a multitude of readers, including the Pulitzer Prize committee, agreed with considerable exhibitions of pleasure. In **Showboat,** her new book, she tells us that the Mississippi and Ohio rivers are beautiful, or were beautiful in the days of the 1870's when floating theaters went leisurely up and down Southern rivers; that the life of people moving on or around these rivers was beautiful; that Chicago was at least partly beautiful in the bad, mad days of Gambler's Alley, and that modern theatrical New York with its cut-and-dried sophistication is rather feverishly unbeautiful.

That is to say, both **So Big** and **Showboat** are differently pointed adventures in Miss Ferber's determined search for the romantic element in American life. Selina Peake, the heroine of **So Big,** was placed by unfortunate circumstances in a dull world of cabbages and stolid Dutch farmers; she refused to be defeated, and bravely made the commonplace romantic. **Showboat** presents the obverse of the same theme. Here again Miss Ferber's people (and shall we say Miss Ferber herself) flee from dullness. They escape to the Cotton Blossom Floating Palace Theater and are removed from the boredom of a stationary existence. They enjoy the changing pageantry of river banks and river towns; they have a colorful world of their own. And Magnolia Ravenal, the heroine of **Showboat,** is the creature of this world, a flesh-and-blood symbol of the universal human yearning after the exotic, a wistful gypsy pertinaciously clinging to her own dreams. Thus while Sinclair Lewis and the Main Street school condemn American life, Miss Ferber follows the lead of those who extol it, at least in the manifestations of its immediate past. It is interesting to observe that she, like Sherwood Anderson recently, has been drawn in her new novel to the "magnet-South" significantly described by Whitman. And here again Southerners have left their own rightful and native themes to be exploited by alien hands. Decidedly, the "newness" of the novel *Showboat* is that it depicts the river life which nobody has touched since Mark Twain, and at that a phase which Mark Twain, so far as I remember, did not explore.

To describe the book more definitely I find it very handy to quote from the title page of the beautifully bound and excellently printed copy furnished me. This says:

> The Time—from the gilded age of the 1870's, through the 90's up to the present time. The Scene: The earlier parts of the story take place on the Cotton Blossom Floating Palace Theater, a showboat on the Mississippi. The background—is panoramic. Twice a year the unwieldy boat was towed up and down the mighty river and its tributaries; it was a familiar sight from New Orleans to the cities of the North, from the coal fields of Pennsylvania to St. Louis, and stirring presentations of *East Lynne, Tempest and Sunshine,* and other old dramatic favorites, by the actors and painted ladies of the Cotton Blossom troupe, are still remembered in Paducah, Evansville, Cairo, Cape Girardeau, Natchez, Vicksburg, Baton Rouge and in many other river towns and cities.

This panoramic feature gives the author a grand opportunity for descriptive work, and she makes the most of it. The novel is as much pictorial as dramatic. It evokes a mood of lazy contemplation through which scenes and people move gracefully transfigured into romantic shapes. Edna Ferber writes vividly and deftly, never too much, always just a right amount, perhaps too tastefully so. And her style has a richness and flexibility I do not remember to have observed in her work before. Episodes merge gently into each other. There is no frenzy or dash, no splashing of emotion. All is subdued, restrained, measured, carefully turned, almost retrospective. The book has structural peculiarities which may bother a few impatient readers. Miss Ferber uses very deftly the back-and-forth type of narrative which Joseph Conrad liked so much. But in her hands this device does not serve for quite as powerful ends as in Conrad's novels. And here and there one sees marks of the "serialized" novel!

Magnolia Ravenal, Miss Ferber's heroine, grows up on the showboat, a yearning, inquisitive child, and such she remains all her days. She is romantic and rather selfish, but doesn't achieve any great dignity. Even when she makes a reckless marriage with the gentlemanly gambler, runs away to lead a rocky up-and-down existence in Chicago, and narrowly escapes being sucked into the "underworld" of those days, she is still just childish, wistful, innocent. She is surpassed by her parents, two creations vastly more interesting. Captain Andy Hawks, the playboy owner of the floating theater, and that indomitable Puritan housekeeper, Parthenia Hawks, the solidest person in the book. The various minor characters, including the urbane gambler-actor, are well done, but Captain Andy and Partheny have the real stuff of life in them. Their queer mating, their odd administration of the floating theater, their opposite philosophies of life are treated in a somewhat Dickensian, almost slapstick manner. But there is an exuberance about

them that Miss Ferber does not allow her other characters. They are fun.

Edna Ferber writes vividly and deftly, never too much, always just a right amount, perhaps too tastefully so.

—*Donald Davidson*

Some major criticisms might be made. The ending of the book is quite incongruous. Miss Ferber becomes ironic and satirical in treating theatrical life in New York, with Magnolia's daughter, Kim, depicted as a successful ready-made actress. Miss Ferber does not play fair, either, in introducing at various points in the narrative certain prescient references to the Negro spirituals so popular nowadays.

It seems an illegitimate foresight, even a truckling to the mood of the moment, to equip her heroine with a perhaps unnatural admiration for "I Got Shoes," "Go Down, Moses," and "Deep River." It is a cheap trick. And Miss Ferber's pictures of Southern people, though always interesting, are generally in the conventional, sentimental vein. A more general fault is that the book seems always on the point of becoming very serious, without ever really becoming so. Miss Ferber delicately skirts the edge of tragedy, never plunging in. Just so much tears, so much pathos, so much wickedness, so much ugliness—just enough to make us faintly aware that all might not be quite as beautiful as it seems, and then, plenty of movie sunshine to dash away the clouds. It looks as if Miss Ferber had carefully mixed her ingredients for a large popular audience. And I will not question her right to that audience, and it would not make any difference if I did. *Showboat* will please lots of people, and why shouldn't it? Doubtless it will be a best seller, and who cares if it is? I'll prophesy right now that it will be chosen by the Book-of-the-Month Club.

At this point one remembers what some notable critics have said about the superiority of women novelists over men novelists in America. Didn't somebody say once that Dorothy Canfield, Willa Cather, Elinor Wylie, Edna Ferber, Ellen Glasgow, et al., had made a much better showing than any similar number of men novelists in this country? Maybe it is only the masculine ego which makes me unwilling to concede this superiority. At any rate, I for one do not see it. I certainly see the defects in the work of Theodore Dreiser, James Branch Cabell, Sinclair Lewis, John Dos Passos and others. But their writing has a substance which I do not find in the novels by women. Dreiser, for example, is as crude as an old fence post; neither he, nor any of the men except Cabell and Thomas Beer, have anything like the finesse and clear serenity of Willa Cather or Elinor Wylie. But they somehow go deep. They get down to strata that the women seldom reach. Perhaps it is too obvious a comment to say that the men have "virility," and too foolish a derogation to claim that the ladies are . . . well . . . ladies! Still I can't help wondering whether any of the women have written a novel as solid, as strong, as portentous, as Dreiser's *An American Tragedy*. I don't believe so. Shall I say, then, that the men have (convention prohibits me to use an Elizabethan term, so I choose a rural word) . . . "innards"? Maybe so, maybe not. At any rate, Edna Ferber's books, charming as they may be, have no . . . "innards."

Louis Kronenberger   (review date 22 August 1926)

SOURCE: "*Show Boat* Is High Romance," in *The New York Times Book Review*, August 22, 1926, p. 5.

[*Kronenberger was an American essayist, biographer, novelist, and educator. In the following favorable review of* Show Boat, *a portion of which was excerpted in* Contemporary Literary Criticism, *Vol. 18, he describes the novel as "little else but an irresistible story," largely due to its self-consciously romantic and nostalgic tone at a time when most "serious" literature strove for realism.*]

We need not be sentimentalists to regard the past with a romantic eye. It is the normal way of regarding it. The past is, at first hand, romantic. Disenchantment comes only when we reconstruct it laboriously with the aid of history books and contemporary documents, or when we treat it in terms of the present. Flaubert pored for many years over source-material, and *Salammbo* is not romantic. John Erskine brought Helen up to date, and *The Private Life of Helen of Troy* is not romantic. But in general the realists have considered their own age and the romanticists an earlier one.

At a time when realism is all but monopolizing literature, one experiences a sensation of delighted relief in encountering **Show Boat**. It is gorgeously romantic—not in the flamboyant and artificial manner of the historical romance which twenty-five years ago, under the titles of *Janice Meredith* and *Richard Carvel* came definitely labeled before the American public; not staggering beneath a weight of costume and local color. **Show Boat** comes as a spirited, full-breasted, tireless story, romantic because it is too alive to be what the realists call real; because it bears within itself a spirit of life which we seek rather than have; because it makes a period and mode of existence live again, not actually different from what they were, but more alluring than they could have been. **Show Boat** is romantic not because its people and events violate any principle of possibility, but because they express a principle of selection. Miss Ferber has chosen the brightest colors and let the dull ones go. She has avoided the contrasts by which the brightness would fade into the common light of day. **Show Boat** is dominated by one tone as Hergesheimer's *Balisand* is dominated by another.

After the days of Mark Twain, the Mississippi holds small place in American literature. Now it reclaims its place, happily as the scene of later days than Mark Twain's. River travel such as he described had fallen off with the coming of railroads, and Captain Andy Hawks of **Show Boat**, facing the fact in the late '70s but satisfied by no life save that of the river, compromised with buying a show boat—one of those floating theatres which moved from town to town for a one or two night stand, by day approaching the town with calliope screaming and flags flying, by night shining with hundreds of lights above the river. On board with him was his wife Parthy, a hard, gaunt New Englander who should have been a spinster; his daughter Magnolia, at first a child, later on the ingenue of his troupe; the troupe itself, all "picked" characters for the purposes of the novel; and, when the time was ripe, that most engrossing and romantic character of all—Gaylord Ravenal.

Magnolia Hawks was as much in sympathy with her spry half-Gallic little father as his wife was out of it. Parthy Hawks mistrusted the show-boat existence, though in the end her repressions conquered her and made her the show boat's worst slave. She also mistrusted Gaylord Ravenal, who came aboard it to act, only because he fell in love with Magnolia. She found out all about him, but she could not keep Magnolia from marrying him. They stole off and were married in a small river town, Ravenal paying the minister with his last $10. How enjoyable a figure he is from start to finish and how flawlessly he comes up to every requirement of his romantic part! Exiled from New Orleans for killing a man in self-defense; aristocratic and nonchalant, perfectly groomed, a cool, inveterate gambler, leading Magnolia, in after years when Andy Hawks had been drowned, to a see-saw existence in Chicago, fluctuating with his gains and losses at faro—a delightful figure from start to finish, and a delightful finish, when he leaves Magnolia $600 and goes away forever.

The third generation in Magnolia's family is her daughter Kim; and though she brings the story up to modern times, she leaves its tone of romance unimpaired. She becomes a great actress in the New York City of today, moving about in a social milieu in which appear such actual figures as Woollcott and Broun, Crowninshield and Swope, Katharine Cornell and Ethel Barrymore, all of them glimpsed fleetingly. But Miss Ferber carries her story further, makes it swing full-circle. When old Parthy dies, having made half a million with her show boat, Magnolia goes back for the funeral and feels the call of the past. She can't leave the "Cotton Blossom," and down the Mississippi, presumably in this year 1926, she goes with it, stopping on June 2 at a town called Lulu. By bringing the story of the show boat up to date Miss Ferber almost makes the cord snap; but it holds somehow, perhaps because Magnolia herself makes the last romantic gesture.

All art is a luxury in the sense that it fills a place beyond the physical necessities of life, but some art there is which is entirely ornamental, which does not reveal life, or probe character, or feed the soul. **Show Boat** is such a piece of writing—a gorgeous thing to read for the reading's sake alone. Some, perhaps, will conscientiously refer to it as a document which reanimates a part of the American scene that once existed and does no more. But this writer cannot believe it is that; rather it is a glorification of that scene, a heightening, an expression of its full romantic possibilities. There was, no doubt, a gallant Andy Hawks in the old days, and a Magnolia, and more Gaylord Ravenals than one; there was such a scene as that recorded of Julie Dozier when she was discovered to have negro blood;

there was a Parthy Hawks who ran a show boat down the river, an indomitable woman who formed an anomaly among show boat proprietors; but they were never the one group who lived on the "Cotton Blossom." Plenty of prose intermingled with the poetry of the true scene, plenty of realism with the romance. And all these things, of course, Miss Ferber knew before and while and after she wrote *Show Boat*.

But Life, here, gives way unrestrainedly to Art. And Art functions in one one tone—the romantic. Some will not submit to this, and will object to a piece of melodrama here, a wild coincidence there, an unconvincing character somewhere else. That will be an esthetic mistake. Let us accept the delightful lives these people lead. All in all, when you look back upon the story it is amazing how little that is exciting and complicated has happened; this is biography rather than "plot." Miss Ferber has told her story without stint, a long free-breathing story, safe from the careful selectiveness and lacunation of modern schools of writing. It never becomes sentimental; at times it is high romance, at times light romance, at times comedy; but it is never melancholy romance. There is no sighing after the snows of yesteryear. With *Show Boat* Miss Ferber establishes herself not as one of those who are inaugurating first-rate literature, but as one of those who are reviving first-rate story-telling. This is little else but an irresistible story; but that, surely, is enough.

The Bookman   (review date September 1926)

SOURCE: A review of *Show Boat,* in *The Bookman,* New York, September, 1926, pp. 91-2.

[*In the following review, the critic favorably assesses* Show Boat.]

Show Boat is magnificent. It is a definite advance in minor characterization and in atmospheric writing over *So Big*. The main characters are fine, too, although it is difficult to rival a Selina De Jong even with a Magnolia Ravenal, with whom Selina would have had much in common. Miss Ferber's documentation of her story of theatre days down the rivers of mid-America is admirable. This is a book particularly notable for the small scene, the memorable wave of the hand, the magnificent dress, the unforgetable gesture. Edna Ferber builds now like Dickens. Her rarest moments are still, however, her own. There will be much discussion, I fancy, of the manners of this novel, which will probably be called mannerisms. The time scheme, for one thing, is puzzling to me, but that is part of the story and it may be that Miss Ferber would not gain her effect so splendidly did she not make use of motion picture placing of scenes. The other trick is more annoying to me than to most people. She mentions by name so many living people I don't like that I am brought up against the fact that perhaps in life I shouldn't like her imaginary characters as much as she's making me like them. It would take much more than Edna Ferber's art to make Woollcott a hero to me, but then, she does mention Ethel Barrymore, which is some consolation. Anyhow, Miss Ferber has written a noteworthy book constantly interesting, amazingly colorful, a better book than *So Big*. The greatness of the Missis-

sippi is here, too—even if the main theme of her story does occasionally escape her in her absorption with glitteringly and beautifully detailed trivialities.

The Spectator   (review date 6 November 1926)

SOURCE: A review of *Show Boat,* in *The Spectator,* Vol. 137, No. 5132, November 6, 1926, p. 824.

[*In the following review, the critic favorably assesses the plot and characters of* Show Boat.]

Richly romantic, packed with incident and sentiment, this new book *Show Boat* by Edna Ferber brings back the colourful past of the Southern States of America in the 'eighties and the 'nineties. The principal characters live the varied life of the little stock theatrical companies which went up and down the big rivers and played *East Lynne* and other vanished delights to the populations of the small riverside towns and villages. Parthenia Ann Hawks—grim consort of merry Captain Andy Hawks, owner of the "Cotton Blossom Floating Palace Theatre"—rules the troop of actors, actresses, darkies, engineers and what not that make up the personnel of this wandering home of melodrama. Their daughter, Magnolia, is treated more strictly than any seminary Miss: her childhood, nevertheless, is one long pageantry which changes little, at first, when she weds an impecunious, handsome young actor who looks a gentleman and behaves like one consistently. His real profession, however, is not actor, but gambler. Magnolia and he (Gaylord Ravenal) break away at last from the iron rule of the acid old Mrs. Hawks and taste all the glories of life in Chicago. Often when his luck at faro failed, Ravenal swiftly removed his wife to cheap lodgings and spare times followed: fur coats and diamond rings vanished. Then once more the sun shone; they returned to a fashionable hotel, dined out nightly and flourished. Gradually Magnolia begins to long for the old, securer days of the river showboat, and at the end of the long and quite delightful book she finds herself back there. All the characters in this attractive story are drawn with a generous and lively hand, and despite its romantic quality *Show Boat* has a most genuine ring. It is cordially recommended for an utterly readable, rather touching, and ably managed story, all the more effective because it does succeed in recapturing something of the vanished glamour of the days of the bustle.

Louis Kronenberger   (review date 17 April 1927)

SOURCE: "Salt and Gusto in New Tales by Edna Ferber," in *The New York Times Book Review,* April 17, 1927, p. 2.

[*In the following mixed review of* Mother Knows Best, *Kronenberger contends that all of the short stories are enjoyable, but some lack originality and realism.*]

For sheer readability few writers can equal Edna Ferber. She writes so smoothly and brightly, with so much gusto, with so wide-awake a style and so clever a selection of detail that she routs all that is commonplace and casts out all that is dull. Her variety is remarkable, as any one must agree who reads the eight short stories in *Mother Knows Best*. Either she or her publishers, by the way, choose to call these stories "novelettes." It is true that most of them contain sufficient material for novelettes and even novels, but it is inescapably true also that all of them are constructed upon pure short-story principles, and three or four of them on that principle of ironic surprise which Maupassant inspired with "The Necklace" and "The Jewels" and O. Henry made popular with dozens upon dozens of his stories. Novelettes do not end as **"Our Very Best People"** and **"Blue Blood"** end: theirs is the ending of the modern American magazine story.

But naturally it is not what they are called but what they are which makes these stories important. Though all are interesting, though all are clever, though all are Edna Ferber, it seems reasonable to assert that four of the eight are really good, and that four artistically are failures. Four of these stories, at least, sacrifice something either in the way of truth or in the way of originality. In two of them the iron hand of the commercial magazine permits a hackneyed formula and a final ironic twist to rob the material of both originality and significance; **"Our Very Best People"** shows its ending almost from the start, follows a path that has long since been worn bare, and never for two seconds rings true, and **"Blue Blood"** adds to a thin main plot a hackneyed subplot only that it may end the story with a meretricious twist. The third of the unsuccessful stories, **"Holiday,"** is unsuccessful because, lacking an organic plot, the superficial realistic detail and study of character which might have saved it from complete lack of meaning are joylessly void of freshness. It is a very unusual kind of failure on Miss Ferber's part. And **"Consider the Lilies"** falls down because, ironically enough, it should have been a real novelette and not a short story. Pali should have been made a full flesh-and-blood character if her reversion to type was to ring true; instead she was hurried through forty-five years of life, hastily permitted to indulge her instincts, and then hurried back to Chicago.

In her other four stories Miss Ferber has done her jobs handsomely. They are not stories which will greatly hearten those of us who feel that the short story in America today fails to express anything of real importance or significance or basic truth. All of them are simply superficial studies in character. But the surfaces are incomparable. Physically, socially, typically, these people—the mother in **"Mother Knows Best,"** the two old ladies in **"Perfectly Independent,"** the servant in **"Every Other Thursday,"** the telephone company employee in **"Classified"**—live. They live with great clearness, with great force. They, supreme embodiments of types, are made through a wealth of skillful detail into breathing and living individuals. They have no depth, no soul, no temperament; so profoundly Miss Ferber, in thirty-odd pages apiece, can not go. But they live fully enough to make the stories they dominate interesting and vivid and real. They live fully enough to make those stories, not great works of art, but something more significant than reading matter. That is why they are the four successful stories in the book. For simply as reading matter, the other four are almost if not quite as enjoyable.

Many things contribute to make Miss Ferber so brilliantly readable. For one thing, her sense for detail is unerring. She takes the familiar, the graphic, the expressive in places and people and things and sets it before you, and the pleasure of recognition is undefeatable. She does not make the mistake of Fanny Hurst, with whom she is often rather unjustly compared; she does not dye and perfume her detail with comparisons and rhapsody and sentimentality. Her style is light and warm and salty. Her gusto is tremendous, yet she is relatively objective. Her irony is bright but never brittle. And above all, she is at once romantic and a realist. She isn't a sentimentalist, seeing things as they might have been—simply a romantic seeing as they might be at the same time the realist in her sees things as they are. A single paragraph from **"Mother Knows Best"** will illustrate her double point of view:

> Something in the sight of this awkward white-faced child transforming herself miraculously before their eyes into the tragic mask of the buxom Coghlan, or the impish grotesqueries of the clownish Hite or the impressive person of Mansfield moved the beholder to a sort of tearful laughter.

How Miss Ferber longs to make the child-actress a thundering sensation then and there! But her head, not her heart, knows best. The paragraph continues:

> Still, it cannot truthfully be said that there was anything spectacular about this, her first appearance on a professional stage. The opinion was that, while the kid was clever, she ought to be home in bed.

To those of us who are also strange mixtures of realism and romance, a method like the one above is a boon. We can have our cake and eat it, too. No one can afford to pass up such an opportunity.

Stanley Vestal   (review date 22 March 1930)

SOURCE: "Miss Ferber's Myth," in *The Saturday Review of Literature*, Vol. VI, No. 35, March 22, 1930, p. 841.

[*In the following mixed review of* Cimarron, *Vestal suggests that while the novel is historically inaccurate, it is nonetheless true to the "spirit" of the region.*]

We have long since become accustomed to the habit of English novelists, who come to this country for a brief visit and then go home and write a book about the States. But for an American novelist to apply the same methods in writing about an unfamiliar region within the States is something of a novelty. Miss Ferber has done this in her new book on Oklahoma [*Cimarron*], and done it daringly, adding American efficiency to the tried technique of her British exemplars. For she spent far less time in Oklahoma than the Englishman commonly spends in the States, and the resulting book is vastly more interesting than most which have been produced by others in this kind. Indeed, it is probable that Miss Ferber's success is due in no small degree to the shortness of her sojourn in the West, for she could hardly have remained much longer without suspecting that she was being made the victim of extravagant

Western humor. Her coming was well advertised in advance, and the hospitable natives provided her with a good show. But Miss Ferber may take comfort, if not exult, in the ire which her book has aroused in the breasts of indignant old-timers, who—rather absurdly—expect a novel to be history.

On the other hand, it must be admitted that the business of the novel is not plot, nor setting, nor incident, but the notation of the human heart. Since Miss Ferber's triumphant journalism has rather neglected this important business, she can scarcely blame those who concentrate upon the things which she has placed in the foreground and who criticize her work accordingly. In a volume wherein the tourist's notebook and photograph album so constantly obtrude, it is natural that readers who have notebooks and albums more extensive and reliable should compare notes and raise objections.

It is quite unfair, however, to complain of her use of incident or even of the falsification of dates, places, and historical events: all this is quite within the province and privilege of the novelist. When Zane Grey, for example, portrays Kit Carson as a swaggering bully, he is well within his rights, though utterly false to history. Such things may be unwise, but are thoroughly legitimate. But when the poet presents the spirit of a region or a period in a false light, we incline to think that he has violated the canons of the historical novel and deserves censure.

The really significant things in any community are the things which that community takes for granted, and these things are never mentioned, and can hardly be explained to strangers. We submit that this is the weakness of Miss Ferber's attempt to tell the story of the Run—that famous charge of a vast multitude upon the free land of Oklahoma: she was unaware of the real historical background, the mores, of the time and region. And this need not have been so, considering the wealth of authentic incident she had at her command. Willa Cather, another alien who writes of the Southwest, avoided this pitfall: she used all the liberties of the artist in fiction, freely adapting and falsifying incident and character, yet has uniformly preserved intact the spirit of the Old Southwest. Her bad men observe the mores of the type, as Miss Ferber's do not, and by this test the one book stands and the other falls. Miss Ferber's gunmen (I use the term advisedly) are presented sympathetically, humanly, but they know nothing of the code which would have made it impossible for a cowboy to shoot a man's hat off in the company of his wife, or to take pot shots at a preacher during a religious service—even one held in a gambler's tent. The grotesqueries of the Run were wild enough, but they are not the grotesqueries which Miss Ferber has invented.

The later chapters, which deal with matters observed by the author for herself, are more acceptable, but even here the feeling which underlies them has escaped her. She has done excellent reporting, has constructed a ripping yarn, has given us novel incidents, novel characters, a fresh setting, has created a strange new Sooner mythology [in a footnote, Vestal adds that a " 'Sooner' was a settler who had illegitimately found his way into Indian territory before it was thrown open for settlement. The 'Sooners' are

the Hengists and Horsas of Oklahoma"], and for this we should be grateful. Her book is a fantasy.

Judged as fantasy, it is a gorgeous piece of work, and recalls at moments the richness of startling incident, the amazing turns, the incredible adventures and persons of the *Arabian Nights*. And as fantasy her book is sound, for it has caught the essential fact about Oklahoma—the fact that there every man has the spirit of a seeker after buried treasures; every man has the fairyland faith in something for nothing, a faith justified every time he looks at the skyscrapers of Tulsa or the oil rigs of Oklahoma City. This spirit, which was not the spirit of the Run, has become the soul of Oklahoma today, and Miss Ferber's reporting eye has caught it. To her this was all unreal, fantastic, and no genius could have made her book historical. So seen, the book is genuine and worth the reading.

The New York Times Book Review (review date 23 March 1930)

SOURCE: "Miss Ferber's Vivid Tale of Oklahoma's Salting," in *The New York Times Book Review*, March 23, 1930, p. 4.

[*In the following favorable review of* Cimarron, *the critic explores the character of Yancy Cravat and applauds the portrayal of pioneer life in the Oklahoma territory.*]

The exuberance and gusto, the robust romanticism of Miss Ferber's **Cimarron** are so compelling that they almost insensitize the reader against its artistic deficiencies. For this is a tale in the same vein as Miss Ferber's **Showboat,** frankly glamourous, headlong in its story-telling fervor. She has filled in with the boldest of strokes a canvas even more colorful, more animated, than her picture of troupers' life in the old days on the Mississippi. The scene of **Cimarron** is Oklahoma, and the story is traced against one of the most spectacular backgrounds in American life. The opening up of that great territory, its overnight settlement in the Run of '89, the raw days of its mushroom growth, the fantastic scramble when oil was discovered— these are the materials upon which Miss Ferber has drawn. "Only the more fantastic and improbable events contained in this book," she says in her foreword, "are true. . . . In many cases material entirely true was discarded as unfit for use because it was so melodramatic, so absurd as to be too strange for the realm of fiction."

The story is told chiefly through the experience of Yancey Cravat and the young wife who went with him from their home in Kansas to seek their fortunes in the new territory. This Yancey Cravat is by all odds the best of Miss Ferber's creations, and one of the most picturesque figures in the whole range of American fiction. Gaylord Ravenal of **Showboat** is pale beside him. Big, hearty and handsome, with a "great buffalo head" which he had a trick of lowering when stirred to anger, with his flowery speech and his immense animal vitality, his romantically shrouded and whispered-about past, he had swept young Sabra Venable off her feet when he came to Wichita from no one knew where and launched his fiery paper, *The Wichita Wigwam.* The Venables, Mississippi gentry who had migrated to Kansas after the Civil War, could never whole-heartedly accept him. They worried about his antecedents, the gossip that said he was of Indian blood, the reports of his lawless life in the Cimarron, that stretch of No-Man's Land on the border between Texas and the Indian Territory. They had given him their daughter with strong misgivings.

There is no better scene in Miss Ferber's novel than her opening one, in which Yancey, before the assembled Venables, tells them the story, hypnotized against their will, of the great Oklahoma Run from which he had just returned:

> "Folks, there's never been anything like it since creation. Creation! Hell! That took six days. This was done in one. It was history made in an hour—and I helped make it. Thousands and thousands of people from all over this vast Commonwealth of ours" (he talked like that) "traveled hundreds of miles to get a bare piece of land for nothing. But what land! Virgin, except when the Indians had roamed it. 'Lands of lost gods and godlike men!' They came like a procession—a crazy procession—all the way to the border, covering the ground as fast as they could, by any means at hand—scrambling over the ground, pushing and shoving each other into the ditches to get there first. God knows why—for they all knew that once arrived there they'd have to wait like penned cattle for the firing of the signal shot that opened the promised land. As I got nearer the line it was like ants swarming on sugar. Over the little hills they came, and out of the scrub-oak woods and across the prairie. They came from Texas and Arkansas and Colorado and Missouri. They came on foot, by God, all the way from Iowa and Nebraska! They came in buggies and wagons and on horseback and muleback. In prairie schooners and ox carts and carriages. . . .

Yancey was on fire with enthusiasm for the new country. He was going back, he said, to have a part in its building up, and Sabra and little Cim would go with him. Sabra was eager, her family dismayed. They went, Sabra picturing herself as one of the pioneer women whom Yancey eulogized as having "made this country what it is." The rawness of the life was to be a shock to her, but Sabra belongs in the line of Miss Ferber's indomitable, executive women whom she endows with strength beyond that of their men, and Sabra is to repeat their history. Yancey becomes a force in the Oklahoma country, but a quixotic force, too restless to run his life in an appointed mold. It is Sabra who takes over the day-by-day management of the paper he founded and builds it up, Sabra who finally embarks on the political career he disdained and thrust away from him. She enters Congress and as we take our leave of her it is hinted that she may become Governor. Yancey's life, for all its glamour, runs a descending scale, his end at once heroic and pathetic. To Sabra belongs the sober triumph. There is a taint of feminist thesis about these women of Miss Ferber's which makes them somewhat synthetic and not wholly convincing.

And indeed, those who like their novels to be unerring in their psychology will find Miss Ferber unsatisfying time

and again. She is frequently illogical, free in her use of coincidence, and unsure in her handling of deep emotion, as in the scene of Yancey's death on the last page of *Cimarron*. But a book like *Cimarron* is to be read for other reasons. Read it for its vivid re-creation of the scenes through which Yancey and Sabra lived, for its splendidly kaleidoscopic view of a young American city coming into existence, with its shifting social patterns and its broad diversity of types, with its background of disinherited Indians coming at last, by an ironic turn of fate, into that bewildering wealth which oil brought to them. *Cimarron* is not the sort of book one reads again and again for beauties newly discovered; it is a book which one reads once with avidity, for a picture that remains indelible.

The Bookman   (review date July 1930)

SOURCE: A review of *Cimarron*, in *The Bookman*, New York, Vol. LXXI, No. 4, July, 1930, p. 440.

[*In the following review, the critic favorably assesses the characters and themes of* Cimarron.]

In 1889 Sabra Cravat, dressed in gray cheviot braided with elaborate curlycues, wearing a bonnet with a bird on it, and high button boots, mounted the seat of a covered wagon and drove from the comparative civilization of Wichita, Kansas, to the red wastes of the newly opened Oklahoma. In the wagon ahead was her Peer Gynt of a husband, the picturesque, mysterious Yancey Cravat. She took with her her silver spoons and cake dish, monogrammed linen, her principles and her traditions. He took with him his printing press, the six shooters that were already notched, his hatred of settled, humdrum life.

It was freedom and newness that the man wanted; the woman wanted the old order replanted upon the new soil. Together they came to the nightmare of Osage—a "city" of shanties and tents, filled with scum and heroes, with grim pioneer women and harlots. Here the man and woman started a newspaper and raised two children. But slowly Osage grew respectable, a little stale. The man could not endure it and went on to newer lands. The woman, left alone most of the time, ran the social life, the newspaper, the city, and then went to Congress. In the end Yancey dies. His life has been wandering, heroic, quixotic, a little absurd (he is too "silver-tongued" for the modern mind). Hers has been brave, successful—arid.

Miss Ferber picturesquely calls the battle which she describes so dramatically [in *Cimarron*] the battle between "the sunbonnets and the sombreros". From the first, Sabra Cravat and the other "basically conventional women were working unconsciously, yet with a quiet ferocity, towards that day when one of them would be able to say, standing in a doorway with a stiff little smile upon her face,

" 'Awfully nice of you to come'.

" 'Awfully nice of you to ask me', the other would reply." The sunbonnets triumph. Osage in forty years has become exactly the sort of place the women wanted. But what of those wild, childish, freedom-loving wearers of the sombreros? Many, like the magnificent Yancey Cravat, may today be bums and idlers, hanging about construction camps. Once there was work on an heroic scale for these American Peer Gynts to do, but now the Osages of an earlier day have become only one more Minneapolis, Louisville, Zenith City. . . . So the sunbonnet has triumphed.

Around the principal characters are grouped a rousing galaxy of lesser stars—bad men and worse women, millionaire Indians (the money comes to them through oil—my favorite detail in the book—wonderful Indians!), Venus Lodges, Culture Clubs, dance hall proprietors, a living medley of engaging humanity, including a Jewish shopkeeper who is the flower of an ancient civilization.

Some lecture on "the modern novel" might take for comparison Miss Roberts's *The Great Meadow* and Miss Ferber's *Cimarron*. Both tell a similar story of how women left security and peace for the sake of the men they loved and went out into a wilderness to found a new land. Both authors have chosen as protagonists rather average, unimaginative women. It seems to me remarkable how Miss Ferber by her native vigor avoids the pitfalls Miss Roberts sinks into, and with what enthusiasm and humor Miss Ferber plunges into bogs neatly side-stepped by the fastidious Miss Roberts. In Miss Ferber's world little coons fall into cream puddings, you get the hat shot off your head, you are cheated of your claim by a hussy in black tights. With Miss Roberts you may go by wagon from Virginia to the Blue Grass and only be molested by the hooting of a false owl. You may see your husband's mother murdered and scalped by savages and the affair fade away into a twilight of Berkeleian philosophy. Miss Ferber is closer to the heart of life and she is further from "art". Although the central story of Sabra Cravat lacks something of the charm of *Show Boat* and *So Big*, still *Cimarron* is certainly Edna Ferber at her best.

Henry Seidel Canby   (review date 17 October 1931)

SOURCE: "Gusto vs. Art," in *The Saturday Review of Literature*, Vol. VIII, No. 13, October 17, 1931, p. 201.

[*Canby was an American editor, educator, biographer, and literary critic. In the following review, he contends that while* American Beauty *is well-constructed and realistic in its surface details, it lacks the subtlety and depth of a great novel.*]

The Poles came in. They tore up the brush-grown fields of old Connecticut and forced new yield from them. They settled in those loveliest of American landscapes and, utterly oblivious of their dim beauty, saw them only as land, unused land, cheap land. They brought a peasantry on a soil that had never known a peasantry before, clucked heartily to hearty women and beat them when they needed it, gawked at the faded New Englanders who first hired and then sold to them, grasped drunkenly at the new vulgarisms of the towns, and in the second generation ran hungrily to the mills and the movies, the peasant starch in them turning sour at the first touch of industrialism. They had energy instead of a code; they were hot for undiscriminated experience, and rushed on change.

Their New England hosts, who lived in the clapboarded, green-shuttered houses, with moulding about the eave's line, remembering what they had been, looked at the present with sardonic resignation. Poverty, disorder, and drink were powerless to touch their inmost being, which was still that of a chosen people. The ill kept highway of their lives followed a row of ruined elms down through wrecked pastures until it ended in a swamp, yet never lost its essential dignity.

The Poles were not like that, nor did they resemble the Colonial ancestors of these warped New Englanders, who, though land hungry, full-blooded, and energetic also, brought with them an idea of an ample, decorous, and ordered dwelling-place, the outward and visible sign of an inward and, if not spiritual, certainly intellectual, grace:—Litchfield, Southbury, Ridgefield, the white, elm-shaded farmsteads, the great brick houses of Connecticut.

The Pole wanted to be American but he could not understand American beauty. It was unreal to him and his gusto was for reality; and indeed American beauty had become unreal. It was a shadow of a shade of the past in the great houses, like the house of the Orrange Oakes in Edna Ferber's novel [*American Beauty*], it was shrunk into ugliness in the old maid, Jude, and bloated into eccentricity in Big Bella. These women kept the strength the men of the family had lost, but it was sterile strength. Their mates, if they had any, were mated to their vices and decays, their souls were strong, but so caged by circumstances that they could not get back into what should have been their world. Men and women of their sort had gone up in the world, or down and out.

The Pole was the reality New England seemed to need. He looked it, he felt it, the old soil renewed for him, and his children raced over the acres. But though he saved the farms and propped up the decaying houses, he could not restore them to dignity and independence. And when he married with the old stock his children inherited both the tenacity of the peasant and the pessimism of the run-out race. They were, perhaps, the makings of a new people, but you could not tell. Reality, which had been so vivid in their Polish fathers, so vigorous in their English great-great grandmothers, lay only on the surface of these half breeds. What was beneath the novelist does not tell us. Her power ceased when she stopped writing of the thwarted eccentrics and the full-blooded, tangible Poles.

It is the very interesting novel of Edna Ferber called *American Beauty* I am describing, and I am trying by indirection to get at a true criticism of a writer whose vigor and sense of tangible reality are unequalled, and yet who here and elsewhere seems curiously to fail to attain her objective, no matter how brilliantly she mops up the trenches as she goes. In a sense, she is like her own Poles, full-blooded, virile, with an imagination that wrests the essential circumstances from a scene, and builds scenes which, in her novels and afterwards in the movies, captivate the American mind. And yet she has too much gusto to pause to capture the spiritual realities of her American scene. Her New England past (of which much is made in this novel of generations) has a conventional heartiness like the stories told to a child. She sees it as the Poles saw the great brick houses, as the medievals looked at the Roman ruins. Something is lost, something that was New England. No one can question the reality of her genre pictures, no woman has written more vivid and vigorous scenes than Big Bella's in this book. They shine with vigor (like her Poles), they sweat reality, but those more elusive realities with which a great novelist must equally struggle are dim or undiscovered. You get the American beauty rose, but not the aster, the gentian, not even the goldenrod.

This is a definition of what Miss Ferber has done, not an assertion that her art is necessarily limited by her gusto for the high visibility of certain kinds of living. But circumstances have not favored her art. She has been too popular. Audiences wait for her, knowing what to expect. She cannot disappoint. For them, the last Oakes descendant marries the millionaire's daughter and saves the old home—and that is the outline plot of *American Beauty* into which Miss Ferber has stuffed such vivid scenes and such compelling contacts of alien and native. For them, the ancestors are made rich and nobly mannered, for them romantic aristocracy broods over degenerate moderns. For them she is a showman for her novel, playing up romance and sentiment, writing by climaxes, twisting and inverting the order of her narrative so that her goods may be displayed to the careless millions who have to be tricked into reading. Her art is naturally primitive and objective, slapdashed in broad strokes, with little thought of a third dimension in her composing. But her craftsmanship has become too sophisticated and tricky. She dangles stock characters and stock situations before the door of the museum in which she has collected so much that is novel and vivid and well-observed in American life.

Powerful, popular writers like Edna Ferber must make the choice between the easiest and the hardest way in writing. External reality, when once you learn to capture it, is a bait for any public; but it requires eminent self-control not to play with it, not to use this power to make trite characters and stock situations sure-fire for the public taste. Books which, though not subtle, might be consistent and harmonious in composition and vigorous throughout, become patchworks of bright scenes in a stale pattern. This is Edna Ferber's danger. Her gifts can be too easily vulgarized. She should go into a retreat. She should hide away from the editors of *The Ladies Home Journal* and *The Delineator*. She should practice austerity like Willa Cather, or set herself to harmonize her rich imaginings like a Persian rug. No one wants her to be a New Englander, but she should stop playing the Pole. She should lift her reality into that higher and finer stage in which it becomes a creative element in the true but unreal world of the finest fiction.

Mary Ross (review date 18 October 1931)

SOURCE: "A Brilliant Pageant," in *New York Herald Tribune Books,* October 18, 1931, p. 3.

[*In the following review, Ross favorably assesses* American Beauty.]

Miss Ferber's title is cryptic. This story is not, as one might expect, of hothouse America, of cities and show girls and night clubs, but of the green upper valleys of Connecticut. There in the seventeenth century passed a gay procession of Cavaliers.

> You saw women a-horseback through the wild grandeur of the Connecticut landscape in fine shoes of flowered russet or red Morocco; silks and velvets and brocades fashioning the gowns under their favorite cloaks of scarlet. The men, too, in cloaks of fine red cloth, with long vests of plush in gay colors, and plush breeches.

They went onward, the more adventurous, where Western lands were richer; later the cities drained the land of its most adventurous. Behind them they left Oakes House, set proudly among the acres that Captain Orrange Oakes had bought of the Indians. As time rolled past there were left only embittered women watching the land, their lives sinking into neglect. Then there came a new race of immigrants, sunburned, broadfisted men whose wives and children plodded beside them in the tobacco fields, Polish peasants intent on the land to be had for working. The new mingled with the remnants of the old—and the country saw their hybrid sons and daughters.

Miss Ferber's *American Beauty,* if I am not mistaken, is not merely the beauty of the old house for which Christopher Wren sent the drawings or the wooded hills and stone-rimmed fields about it, but of the self-renewing cycles of life whereby Briton followed Indian, and the Slav the Briton, each destroying and building, yet leaving the imprint of living on the places through which they passed. She has taken a curious form for her story. Exiled from the cities because of his health, old True Baldwin in 1930 left the business of being a Chicago millionaire to go back with his daughter to the Connecticut farm of his boyhood, and especially to see if there still lived in the great house nearby the proud Judith Oakes who had scorned a poor boy. Judith had long since died, a tyrannical spinster; the man who lived in the lovely old house now was named Olzak. Then for an interlude which occupies most of the book there follows the story of the house through two centuries of its proud founders and their waning descendants. Miss Ferber is at her happiest when she is drawing people of action, and Orrange Oakes and his kinsmen give her a gorgeous sweep. Even in the wilderness splendor was their way of life. Even their later generations of degeneracy could not be commonplace. In the end the story again comes forward to True Baldwin and his daughter and to Orrange Oakes Olzak, the son of a Polish peasant and of Tamar, who recreated in feature and spirit the Tamar Oakes of two centuries before. Once again we are left believing the Oakes acres are to know care; the old house to be restored in its beauty; Cavalier, Pole and the humble blood (and dollars!) of millionaires will carry the cycle on the ascendant.

The first Tamar died of exhaustion when as a wayward child of fifteen she wandered from the great house on the eve of its housewarming to visit the Indians. His father could not bear the separation from his darling. Her slim body was cremated in the kiln where the bricks for the house had been burnt from the land's own clay, and her ashes were laid to rest in a jade box under the great hearthstone of the dining room of Oakes House. The last Tamar of the story, her granddaughter generations removed, lived to feel the weight of the crumbling family hanging about her and bearing her down as she slaved to keep the acres intact and to hand them and the Oakes pride down to her son, who had the features and bearing of the first Orrange. Yet that legacy of pride must have perished with her but for the crude peasant who fathered her child and the upstart Baldwin riches that kept the place from the auction block.

Whether or not features and characters will pop up unmistakably in successive generations is a problem which for present purposes we may leave to the biologists. Miss Ferber makes a glowingly credible tale of it, as vivid in the undoing of the family as in the days of its greatness. Her book is a pageant, arresting in the unashamed brilliancy of its colors, its pleasure in spirited action, and its affirmation of human vitality.

Margaret Wallace   (review date 18 October 1931)

SOURCE: "A Connecticut Pageant by Miss Ferber," in *The New York Times Book Review,* October 18, 1931, p. 7.

[*In the following mixed review, Wallace applauds the vivid characters in* American Beauty, *but faults Ferber for emphasizing pageantry over plot.*]

In her newest novel, **American Beauty,** Edna Ferber has made yet another and more ambitious excursion into the annals of American history. The pageant of Colonial settlement she attempts to portray here in the life of a single family involves the founding and growth of a civilization and its decay and replacement by a new order.

The story is told in four deftly related panels. The first, set in 1930, depicts the return of the New England farm boy, True Baldwin, to the rocky fields he had deserted years before to make his fortune in the West. The second, a flashback to 1700, is centred upon the resplendent cavalier figure of Captain Orange Oakes, who founded his manorial estate in Connecticut upon a thousand acres—a thousand beautiful, wild, fertile acres—purchased by barter from old Chief Waramaug himself. The third opens in 1890, when the Oakes family has already entered upon a slow but relentless process of disintegration, and when the State itself is divided in unequal conflict between the thin, watery, emasculate descendants of pioneer American families, and the coarse, vigorous, thrifty, land-loving and prosperous Polish immigrants. The fourth panel completes the cycle, returning to 1930 and to the purchase by True Baldwin of the Oakes farm, with Orrange Olszak, a Polish-American descendent of the original owner, as manager and overseer.

As always, Miss Ferber's interest in history is principally an interest in the revival of its pageantry and color. Captain Orrange Oakes is a splendid figure in costume.

> Though his buff coat was of dressed leather, the hand-fashioned hooks and eyes down its front were of real silver. His falling collar was of linen, but it was tied with little tassels. The feather in his hat was dark in color—brown or black—but thick as moss, and his long doeskin gloves were embroidered in gold threads and colored silks. He actually paid fourteen pounds for every pair of his handsome double-channeled boots. There was leather enough in them for six ordinary pairs of shoes.

Captain Oakes is a magnificent and slightly cinematographic personage, astride his enormous black horse, riding before his family on the way to church, or supervising the building of his great brick house—

> a proper house, such as the Oakes have always had. A house for a gentleman and a gentleman's family . . . b'gad! I'll live in no keeper's cottage sort of dwelling so that in every room in the house your nostrils tell you what's for dinner.

But of his mind, and of the motives that brought him from England to Massachusetts, and from Massachusetts to Connecticut, we catch only a slight glimpse. The real history is pretty thoroughly buried beneath the pageantry.

So it is throughout the novel. Miss Ferber creates a number of strikingly pictorial characters—the second Orrange Oakes, who returned to England to be hanged by Cromwell on Tower Hill; Judith Oakes, who, maintaining the pride and arrogance of the Oakes traditions, dried up into a stiff and slightly puckery New England spinsterhood; Amaryllis Oakes, who cast tradition aside and eloped with a wandering peddler, and Jothan Oakes, the ugly, agile little dwarf. But their background retains the two-dimensional quality of a stage setting. There is little in them of actual identification with the country whose growth they are meant to represent; little enough of the feeling tentatively expressed by Captain Orange in a letter to his good friend, Christopher Wren: "It [Connecticut] has a resemblance to our own dear Kent, but the sky looms larger, the trees grow higher, the rocks seem more grim. It has quite another kind of beauty. A kind of American beauty."

The chronicle is carried out through successive generations of the Oakes family, with very little that is definite in the way of plot, or conflict, or even incident. **American Beauty** is really a succession of individual portraits, well drawn and effectively contrasted—the thin, tight-lipped New Englanders set against the rugged, full-blooded Polish peasantry; the slight, aristocratic figure of the last Tamar Oakes set against the warm, brown, coarse figure of her farm-hand husband, Ondia Olszak. Lacking plot, as it does, there was need of a centralization upon a single character to give the book force and unity; and this centralization also is lacking. **American Beauty** falls definitely below the level of Edna Ferber's best work.

Dorothy Van Doren   (review date 28 October 1931)

SOURCE: "American Beauty Shoppe," in *The Nation,* New York, Vol. 133, No. 3460, October 28, 1931, pp. 462-63.

[*Van Doren was an esteemed American novelist, critic, and autobiographer; her husband was poet Mark Van Doren. In the following largely negative review of* American Beauty, *she laments Ferber's reliance on melodrama, a "curse," she argues, that detracts from the potential of the novel.*]

Imagine a finely designed, sturdily built New England house. There are many such in New England. Imagine the bricks neatly turned and strongly laid, the small-paned windows giving off the mauve and pale rose of old glass, the fan-light over the door a thing of delicately patterned beauty, the chimneys numerous and promising many fires within; imagine the oaks placed justly, the slope from the house covered with turf. Think of the oak sills, as firm as the day they were laid two hundred years ago, the white-oak rafters, the paneling in the great kitchen, of chestnut two feet wide; think of the brick ovens, made to receive bread laid in on an iron shovel, the cranes to swing the soup kettle on, the iron hooks for the skillets, the brass fenders, the bed-warmer for winter nights . . . . Think of such a house filled to the doors, upstairs and down, with the grossest and shiniest of Grand Rapids furniture. And weep.

It is Miss Ferber's curse that she cannot write a novel that will be read by fewer than 100,000 persons. This is not to say that a fine novel will not be read by its many thousands; it is to say that most of the novels which command large sales have in them elements of vulgarity that make them acceptable to so many different kinds of people. Miss Ferber is not the ordinary large-sale novelist. If she were, one might cheerfully lump her with the Ethel M. Dells of her generation and let her count her royalties in peace. But she is plagued by that bitter worm that will give honest writers no rest: she wants to write a great novel, about a great subject, treated greatly. If one may judge merely by what she has written in the last few years, she is furiously ambitious, and in the highest sense. Nothing less than the best will please her.

She wrote **Cimarron**. It was a large canvas, the wild, sweeping, magnificent story of a conquering people. It read like a movie, and in the movies I have no doubt it fully justified its romantic plot. She has written **American Beauty**. It is about New England, where grow the twisted roots of the tree that is now America. It is about the New England house that was built out of the exuberance of the early settlers, proudly taking their land from the Indians, entirely self-sustaining, filling their house with warmth and color and life and many children; and about that house when the builders and their children were seized with a decay that left them dwarfed and broken and bitter; and about that house again when new blood, new foreign blood, this time from the south of Europe instead of the north, came to reclaim those acres but to let the house die of dirt and neglect, while their children, in turn, left for the hat factories of Danbury and Waterbury. This is the stuff of which to make a novel! Miss Ferber must have known it or she would not have worked up her material with such pains. There have been many novels written about New England, none from exactly this angle. There was every reason for the success of this one. Not its material but its artistic success.

Every reason, that is, except for Miss Ferber's curse. She was not content to let New England tell its own story, to take a house and family and let them change and decay as they have in truth done. She must needs introduce a romantic interest, a Chicago millionaire who returns to reclaim his lost acres, with a daughter—an architect, mind you! —who will not only remodel the house but marry the last survivor of the old New England family. It is all rather a pity. But it will undoubtedly sell. Even to those persons whose roots are in New England, who like a good, rousing story about their home land, and do not object to a bit of love interest thrown in.

George D. Nickel   (review date January 1933)

SOURCE: A review of *Dinner at Eight*, in *Sociology and Social Research*, Vol. XVII, January, 1933, p. 297.

[*In the following review, Nickel favorably assesses the characters and plot of* Dinner at Eight.]

George S. Kaufman will get you if you don't watch out. He has a discerning eye that quickly penetrates the veneer of politeness and convention, and a sharp pen that delights in scratching this surface to reveal the selfish struggle within. Among his victims have been the theater in his **Royal Family,** Hollywood in *Once in a Lifetime,* national politics in *Of Thee I Sing,* and now with the aid of Edna Ferber is added the upper quartile of New York society in **Dinner at Eight**.

The theme with modification might be any dinner party. A cross section is taken of every one involved from the kitchen help to the guests of honor. On the surface all is harmony and remains so where the dinner party is concerned; fashion and convention decree it thus. But beneath the polite notes and telephone calls, beneath the genial conversation are exposed a galaxy of strains and stresses, pent up feelings, and conflicting emotions.

The doctor fights against falling in love with the wife of his friend the business giant while he clutches the secret that a patient, his host, has but a few days to live. The business giant has a threefold task. He must: (1) assist his President in assuaging the nation's economic grief; (2) secretly fleece his host out of a block of stock; and (3) learn the identity of the scoundrel who is seducing his wife. The host tolerates the business giant believing he sees in him the salvation for his own business while he conceals his illness from his family. The cook finds her toothache augmented by a love triangle among the servants which climaxes in the kitchen at serving time. The hostess overcomes her contempt for the fill-in guests while she hides her chagrin over the fact that the guests of honor left for Florida two hours before dinner. And so it goes: serenity on the outside, seething cauldrons within. No one is happy, but all pretend to be.

In addition to clear-cut character depiction and a thorough job of analysis the writers have incorporated a philosophical touch that renders the play well-balanced and stimulating to the imagination.

Desmond MacCarthy   (review date 14 January 1933)

SOURCE: "Excitement, Satire, Speed," in *The New*

Statesman and Nation, Vol. V, No. 99, January 14, 1933, pp. 41-2.

[*MacCarthy was an English essayist and critic. In the following review, he favorably assesses* Dinner at Eight, *noting its fast pace and well-drawn characters.*]

Dinner at Eight, at the Palace Theatre, by George Kaufman and Edna Ferber, both gifted authors (her novel, **Show Boat** was very superior to the popular play made from it), is an exceptionally animated performance: violent, unintermitted animation—that is the outcome and the aim of this ingenious mixture of ingredients, each of which is pungent enough to flavour for some palates the whole play. I can well imagine one playgoer declaring afterwards that **Dinner at Eight** is excruciatingly funny, and another, that it is excruciatingly painful. The fact is **Dinner at Eight** is both; it is extremely amusing *and* thoroughly remorseless; which of these aspects will predominate in your own retrospect depends upon whether you happen to be tender or tough; but while you are in the theatre, in either case, you will be swept along by its vivacious velocity.

One important point at which the transatlantic stage differs from ours is *tempo:* their pace is double ours. (Of course, I am only speaking of the tip-top American play of the moment, not of such deep plays as Eugene O'Neil's *Strange Interlude.*) Recall the rattle and flash with which *Broadway,* for example, dashed to its terminus. Now, an English audience was once content to ruminate receptively while the playwright was preparing his situations. It used to be for connoisseurs even an added pleasure to be able to observe him at it, digging with deliberation the dry trench down which the water was eventually to flow. In the well-made three-act drama the whole of the first act, and often the greater part of the second, was devoted to this steady trenching. But the modern, and especially the American-modern, temperament hates preparation and adores—surprise. Of course, there must be some preparation, or incidents won't hold together and crescendo would be impossible, but what is absolutely necessary must now be conveyed by hints and flashes; by a casual word dropped in the midst of chatter, by a gesture while the spectator's eye is on something else. No more preparation is allowed; it would be boring. The quality of attention demanded of the modern audience is therefore that which enables the driver of a racing car while swerving past a van to catch the name on a signpost as it whisks behind him. When I compare these methods with old leisurely ways of telling a story on the stage, I am reminded of that pathetic figure, the Baker, in *The Hunting of the Snark* who, by the by, had some vital information to impart. He began, you remember:

> "My father and mother were honest, though
>   poor—"
> "Skip all that," cried the Bellman in haste,
> "If it once becomes dark, there's no chance of a
>   Snark—
>   We have hardly a minute to waste."

Then, he tried again:

> "A dear uncle of mine (after whom I was
>   named)
>   Remarked when I bade him farewell—"
> "Oh skip your dear uncle," the Bellman exclaimed,
>   As he angrily tinkled his bell.

At a tip-top American play I hear perpetually the furious tinkle of that bell. Though bewildered, for I have myself a ruminating mind, I find I am often exhilarated by this speeding-up. It certainly makes me impatient afterwards of being compelled to stare at the slow evolution on the stage of a situation all-too-clear and perhaps not important. And I am sure the movie habit has quickened considerably the rapidity of the public's capacity for attention, though we orientals must still strike western playwrights and producers as very slow in the up-take. But our own are hurrying; Mr. Noel Coward was pretty brisk in his methods in *Private Lives*—and we liked them. A London audience to-day will not find **Dinner at Eight** too fast to follow, while it is so strewn with points that if, as I did, they only take one out of five, they will find nevertheless they have a mindful.

Dinner at Eight is extremely amusing *and* thoroughly remorseless; which of these aspects will predominate in your own retrospect depends upon whether you happen to be tender or tough; but while you are in the theater, in either case, you will be swept along by its vivacious velocity.

—Desmond MacCarthy

One of the tests I apply to plays, before recommending or cursing them, is the degree to which I have lost self-consciousness myself in the theatre. If I have been so riveted that I ceased to know that I was a human-being sitting between others, then, whatever on reflection I may think of its *value,* that performance goes straight into my category of good entertainments. The play and actors have passed the great, elementary, fundamental test. At the Palace Theatre from the rise to the fall of each curtain, and even during the short "blacking-out" intervals between the four scenes of which each act is composed, the performers succeeded in turning me into a mere characterless percipient attentive only to them. But, and this also is criticism of the play, I did not spend the act-intervals (though I was eager enough to get back to my seat to see what was coming) in that delicious state of gently-heaving emotion and astonished clarity of mind that fine drama produces. I did not wander about the lobby hoping to Heaven no one would speak to me; on the contrary, click, I was back again in myself, ready to talk about anything and wondering, not about the play, but if I was thirsty enough to enjoy a glass of beer and when I could get my hair cut. Well, if the reader thinks me a reliable thermometer, after those two statements he ought to know for himself where to place, roughly, ***Dinner at Eight*** as a play and, for certain, that it was exceedingly well acted. "But what was it like? Shall *I* enjoy it?" These, too, are questions, whatever reader asks them, it is my business to try to answer.

Well, it was like Peter Arno's *Parade* come to life, with an undertow of tragedy pulling through it. Does the *New Yorker* amuse you? Do you enjoy the bite of its humour, its gay toughness, its amoral moral and anti-social social satire? If you enjoyed, say, the humour of the picture of a big "butter-and-egg man" putting a detaining paw over the too-often filled champagne glass of a little "chippy" and murmuring with a leer of portentous tenderness, "Darling, don't spoil my dream"; if you have chuckled over those drawings of spoilt women and pompous men in preposterously luxurious surroundings losing all corresponding *tenu,* and collapsing into a native, yet not always unamiable, indignity; if you have relished those grotesque pictorial contrasts between pretences and realities ("Get up, you mutt, we're to be married to-day"); if you have appreciated the economy with which a laconic legend will explode the whole satire of the picture (I wish to suggest a parallel here between the snap of the dialogue and the mordant humour of the situations in ***Dinner at Eight***); if you have recognised in modern American satire of Americans—yes, through the very heyday of "bunk" and "bally-hoo" and of a snatch-as-snatch-can society—the survival of a civilised, intellectual standard as cruel and incorruptible as that of Forain and Lautrec in Paris of the 'eighties—then, you will thoroughly enjoy this play. You will appreciate, then, the acrid pathos of the male movie-beauty (all profile, no talent) whose day is over but with the help of gin pretends it is not (Mr. Basil Sydney's performance was perfect), who, on the very night he is invited as a lion to *the* dinner party, turns on the suicide's gas in his gorgeous apartments for which he can never pay. You will relish the Billingsgate back-chat spurting from the mouth of "a dainty rogue in porcelain," and staggering, like the jet from a hose, the raging impetuosity of her millionaire husband. (One claps Mr. and Mrs. Packard wildly in their tremendous matrimonial row while dressing for *the* party.) You will not miss the subtlety of the refined doctor's infatuation (he also is invited) with the aforesaid pink and silvery little slut, or the tableau she hastily prepares for him in bed with a serious book upon her knees: "not that, the big one, you nit-wit," she yells at her maid. (Kitty Packard, ex-cloak-room attendant, is an "introvert," her husband an "extrovert"; she has got hold of those tags from her lover, and on her pearly, peevish lips they suggest the whole of the doctor's amorous technique and his own self-deception.) And the hostess! The agitated social climber, Mrs. Jordan, who has no need to climb, but must be in it, in it, in it; and to whom social occasions are so pre-eminently important, that when the pivots of her party an English Lord and Lady chuck at the last moment, she astounds us—we who know that one guest has suffocated himself, that her husband has been ruined by Packard and has angina pectoris, that her maid has been seduced by her butler, that her engaged daughter is in love with the movie-star, that the Packard menage is in dissolution, that the doctor's wife is miserable and the doctor ashamed of himself—with an hysterical outburst, in the vein of, "Was ever trouble like to mine!" Miss Irene Vanbrugh's deftness, alacrity and crescendo in this part are a treat to watch. Is there a point of rest for the imagination in this rattling satire? Yes—a small one—her husband, the old-fashioned American man of business, played with dignity by Mr. Tristan Rawson.

May Lamberton Becker   (review date 7 May 1933)

SOURCE: "For Everybody Is a Story," in *The New York Herald Tribune Books,* May 7, 1933, p. 6.

[*Becker was an American journalist, critic, and author of books for children. In the following review, she favorably assesses* They Brought Their Women.]

Everybody has a story: that has been said since autobiographical novels began. Miss Ferber's new book [***They Brought Their Women***] seems based upon a sounder principal: everybody *is* a story. If it creates a person, a short story need do no more. If it reveals him in his everyday action, picked out in his group by the spotlight of creative understanding, it will do much more. If it chooses to turn on this light at a crucial moment or in some period of stress, it may have amazing possibilities in the hands of one experienced in life and in the handling of literary material.

This is why the opening **"Glamour"** is so good a story: Like most of the eight titles in the collection, this one should be pronounced with a rising inflection. To Miss Frayne, the "glamourous" actress, the word has a sardonic ring.

> Linda awoke now, not drowsily, deliciously, as one who has been deep sunk in refreshing slumber, but suddenly, with a look very like terror on her face, as though she had yielded unwillingly to sleep and resented the hours spent in its embrace. The instant she awoke her hand reached quickly under her pillow and brought forth a scuffed and dogs-eared booklet, crudely bound in heavy yellow paper and fastened with clips.

Here it is Friday, the new play opens on Wednesday in Cleveland, with three performances yet to go in a part she has played for ten months, and she not only doesn't know her lines, but like every real actress in a leading role at this stage in rehearsal she is sure she never will. Through the crowding duties of a crashing day, exercising, catching a swift morning moment with her child, rehearsing intently at the theater and at home, trying on, undergoing the unwelcome repose of the new hair-do, the "seventy-three typewritten pages of her enormous and overwhelming part," and the ever-present necessity of the cueing process, weave in and out like the principal theme of a complicated fugue. But like a fugue, the day for all its rush and clatter is orderly as a house-wife's shopping list. Like Linda's morning exercises, so crazy to watch, all her doings are "stern antics, and the disjointed sentences wise, orderly and meaningful." Somehow, one feels, the play will open on time. Her husband really does know the right words, as well as the right words to say, when he repeats: "Say, you'll knock 'em cold. You always have. You always will. . . . Listen, if you were dead sure of yourself in a new part I'd know you were through."

All this is more than photographically, phonographically accurate. It is true. It is so true in every particular it makes a "retired" actress ache all over. But what makes it more than true is that it really *is* glamour. The story does actually create in some fashion transcending its facts, the special inexplicable charm that keeps not only the Lindas but every one else with the stage in the blood in what we soberly call the theatrical profession.

Four of the eight stories go round one working-day from sleep to sleep. These naturally make the better half of the book: such a method works best within such limits. All are sharply localized, for the most part in large cities. **"Hey, Taxi!"** goes round the clock with Ernie Stewig, a gifted New York hackman of the post-war school. **"One Day in Wall Street, 1929"** dates to such a degree that it is off the track of the rest of the book. **"Keep It Holy"** keeps to places open on Sunday to a small-town girl sick with solitude in New York; this is the only one reminding a reader that there is still a flap or two left in the dead fish of the O. Henry method. Otherwise the stories are distinctively Miss Ferber's own, her world and her way of taking it—though the taxi story could do without the heigh-ho ending, it being hard to use anything again that has once been used by Katharine Brush.

The aviation story—on the outskirts of Wichita—and the one about the faithful wife who trails her husband on a Mexican trip to see that he has all the comforts of home, are more conventional treatments of the general conspiracy of women, of what we like to think is the old school, to do men good in spite of themselves. In the one about the American girl married not only to a Frenchman but to the characteristic middle-class French vision of life and its responsibilities, returning widowed with her son to a post-smash America, there is the nearest to a definite, discernible "purpose." But though something the same feeling deepens the color in **"Fraulein,"** this story, the pride of the collection, depends for its success on nothing less than the skill with which a single character, emerging from the background of a group, is brought into brilliant illumination.

It opens in a millionaire establishment to which the last necessary touch, two children, has been added. Along with this somewhat perfunctory item goes another item, the children's young German nurse—not that anybody thinks of her above-stairs as young, or thinks of her at all for six days in the week. For Fraulein functions as quietly as a perfect digestion—and on her afternoon out the household has what amounts to a community colic. On the stroke of two, Berta emerges from her uniform and steps firmly and competently into her own rich, real life. On the stroke of midnight she returns to bring magic calm to a frantic baby, to motion to a distraught mother. "Go to bed, Madam." "I wouldn't take her job if I were starving," moans the limp lady of the house. "What a life!"

It is more than a tag. What a life, indeed!

Edith H. Walton (review date 14 May 1933)

SOURCE: "Edna Ferber's Volume of Short Stories," in *The New York Times Book Review*, May 14, 1933, p. 7.

[*In the following review of* They Brought Their Women, *Walton argues that while she has the talent to write realistic and exciting short stories, "depth, subtlety, intensity are beyond Miss Ferber."*]

In a somewhat unexpected preface to this volume of tales [*They Brought Their Women*] which is her first since *Mother Knows Best*—Edna Ferber makes several generalizations about the short story.

"By its very form and brevity," she says, "it is restricted from penetrating deeply into the fundamentals of life. Profound human emotion demands a larger canvas." Lest this sound disheartening, she has, however, something to add in defense.

"It may be," she says further, "that the terrific tempo of the past fifteen years will prove to have been too much for the wind and limb of the novelist—the short story, crowded into a handful of words, may be the form which has most truly caught the kaleidoscopic picture of our generation."

Provocative as they are, it is questionable whether these remarks apply to any and all short stories. Remembering Chekhov, Katherine Mansfield, Sherwood Anderson, one is inclined to be skeptical about the necessary absence of profound emotion. There is no doubt, however, that Miss Ferber has diagnosed her own work acutely, has pointed out its weakness and its strength. Warm, alive, observant, her short stories skim the cream from the surface of modern life and preserve it in all its richness. That is all they do. Depth, subtlety, intensity are beyond Miss Ferber—and with the possible exception of **"Her Girls,"** that is as true of her novels as of her short stories.

To quote her own words, Miss Ferber's gift is, indeed, for the kaleidoscopic, for the shifting picture painted in quick, bold strokes. In *They Brought Their Women* she wisely gives this talent free play. There is the taxi-driver—"hard, tough, disillusioned, vital and engaging"—whose adventures throughout a typical Saturday one follows so absorbedly. There is the tragically lonely little country girl who attempts to fill her desolate New York Sundays with visits to the Metropolitan and the Aquarium. There is that biting account of a weary, breathless day in the life of a famous actress—who personifies glamour to an envious and admiring public. There is **"Fräulein,"** with its admirable descriptions of nursemaids chattering in the park, and there is, less successfully, **"Wall Street—'28."**

Merely because her surfaces gleam so realistically, it would be a mistake to suppose that Miss Ferber lacks understanding, or is blind to the problem of social values. It is plain, for instance, that she has a healthy distaste for the vapid, coddled life of the rich and that she is aware of the deep malaise which has increasingly come to blight the more conscious and intelligent members of the upper classes. Particularly does she detest—as her title story proves—the smug, conventional, pampered woman who is determined that her man shall not stray toward any adventurous horizons. Unfortunately, Miss Ferber lacks the savage sting and insight of a Ring Lardner. Here is an immature and superficial protest, always too simplified, too explicit. That the protest is there at all is something—but it is not enough.

Considered from the point of view of technique, Miss Ferber's obviousness is equally apparent. She scores her hits with a sledge hammer, unmistakably, so that nobody of normal intelligence could miss them. Her taxi-driver, returning to his garage in a car running with blood, makes his commentary in the ironic manner popularized by Katherine Brush's "Night Club." "The West," said Ernie, dreamily. . . . "That's the place where I'd like to go. . . . That's the life. Nothing ever happens in this town." So, too, in the other stories. Miss Ferber knows an effective ironic device when she sees one, but she forgets that a large portion of her public is equally well trained—and growing a bit sated.

By this time one may take Miss Ferber's very real merits for granted. She is rarely boring—and certainly not in this volume. She is a born story-teller. She has a kind of human warmth and raciness which may, in the unpredictable end, win her a solider place than some of her contemporaries who are now regarded with greater critical solemnity. She is, in fact, so richly endowed a writer that one is always wishing she were a better one. Again to quote her own words, there seems no foreordained reason why she should have been restricted "from penetrating deeply into the fundamentals of life."

Zona Gale (review date 24 February 1935)

SOURCE: "Edna Ferber's Roaring North Woods Tale," in *New York Herald Tribune Books*, February 24, 1935, p. 3.

[*Gale was a Pulitzer Prize-winning American dramatist, novelist, essayist, and critic. In the following favorable review of* Come and Get It, *she applauds the unrelenting pace of the novel.*]

There are two ways, there are many ways of writing fiction from fact. One is to use the method which Henry Adams employed not for writing fiction, but for imposing a mood. For permitting the reader not so much exercises in shared factual observation as in opening a door, offering a threshold. In *San Christobal de la Habana* Joseph Hergesheimer employs, again not for fiction, the same method—giving the reader no record, no sequence, but catching him up into the very air and levels of that which he has to communicate. Virginia Woolf is able to use these channels to a mood, and indeed to a record, in fiction itself; and some of the younger fiction writers are employing these ways, experimentally, or else simply and with no thought that there is any other way to write.

Such handling of material which is based on some moment of the past, may have all the fabric of tapestry, of anything woven and colored and dim. It may be like needle-point, all leafy and shadowy, with certain sudden detail of faces, etched out in petit point clear, telling, small vignettes of the chief actors in high moments. And over all there will be that somnolence which settles even on the immediate past, even on yesterday, so that yesterday's beings will be wrapped in their certain heritage—dream. All this is so handled, for example, in *Lamb in His Bosom,* life throbbing but already divined from somewhere else, seen as the moon sees it.

But now here is Edna Ferber, with a story of Wisconsin woods and Wisconsin lumber days, which records the history of Barney Glasgow as if he and his family moved beneath a make-up glass, every pore visible. The drive of her *Come and Get It* is enormous—title, talk, pages which tell how paper is made, from pulp to print, how a tree is felled from notch to crash; the camp routine, the men, the lumbertown hotel and theater—all are recorded with an unequalled power of factual observation, so that one, knowing nothing of these facts, knows too that their documentation must be minutely accurate. A great glass is laid upon them all. Voices, other sounds, phrases, gestures, resentments, angers, all are thrown large on a near screen. That mythical woodsman, Paul Bunyan, seems to have cast his spell here, and all the people loom large, loud, more. You see Gargantuan figures, definite, moving in a crash of trees, din of dishes, throb of the mill, clash of action and reaction. The book moves like wind and water and thunder, there is not a dull moment—or a still moment—in its progress. Even the inversions add to its rushing flowage: "Down the stairway of his house came Barney Glasgow," to breakfast, and with a grim intention. The characterizations, so apt, so thrusting, are threaded through with the comment of the author, as it were in person, with an immense power of witty and vital detail, pouring from the lips of the recorder. And the reader is borne from phrase to phrase, as before a rapid speaker.

The story of Barney, millionaire papermill owner, retrospectively cookee, chore boy, cruiser, is a rounded whole, done with that which one feels to be fidelity and knows to be extraordinary power. The writing of his history, the drawing of his family and of Swan, the vignette of the tragedy of the trees. Lotta Morgan escaped from the "stockades," the slow dawn of Barney's recrudescence, the pitiful waste of emptiness of the little Napoleon, intent on himself, all this is gorgeously painted, in a great slashing laying-out of facts from the shoulder, definite and driven and somehow filled with sound. Incredible talk, some of it—phrases, and accusations and a roughage, current among the "principals." Clatter, stamping, crackling, exclamation, chiding, altercation, rebellion—all the words of sound are there, very loud.

The first sixteen chapters of the book are an absorbing tale, carrying one breathlessly, remorselessly, to an authentic climax. The story of creatures, caught in the days of the denuding of the land, reaching out for wealth as once they reached for raw meat, and mentally unaware of either process. These people are hewn sharp out of their background and vanish. One is less sure of Lotta, in the pages following. Less sure whether there could be, indeed, a town in which the neighbors, through cruelty or kindness or curiosity, would not once have come to see the wife of their old friend's son; less sure that there is any authentic "society," European or American, which would have received

Lotta with no greater change in her than is recorded. But for Barney's story there can be no question. The power and the energy here communicate themselves to the reader, vital, immense. This woman, writing with the drive of her sheer power, observing, recording, communicating to you what she sees—functioning lavishly, like a maple tree, showering down characters, situations, relationships. There they are. Come and get them, as the mill-owners got the trees, as they "got" their lives. There is the picture—take it or leave it. Somehow a wide-hipped, deep-bosomed, loud-voiced picture, of those now gone, yet still beating with blind forces but the mind hardly arisen at all.

And at the end, when Barney's grandchildren stand with Swan, his own teacher, to fell their first tree, and the record goes word for word as it was given for Barney fifty years earlier, felling his first tree, you get that moment of wisdom, of a rhythm beyond their voices, beyond the purring of any dynamo, which lies within the book.

No tapestry of a past, woven and many-colored. But the record of a past, seen in hard sunlight, heard very near at hand, and without a moment dull—or still.

Fred T. Marsh   (review date 24 February 1935)

SOURCE: "Edna Ferber's *Come and Get It*," in *The New York Times Book Review*, February 24, 1935, p. 6.

[*In the following mixed review of* Come and Get It, *Marsh applauds Ferber's eye for evocative detail, but contends that the novel loses its appeal and effectiveness in the closing chapters.*]

To that great army of the American fiction-reading public who liked *The Girls* (1921), *So Big* (1924), *Show Boat* (1926), *Cimarron* (1930), *American Beauty* (1931), the short stories and the plays (with George S. Kaufman) of Edna Ferber, her new novel, *Come and Get It,* is recommended. It is of a piece with the rest.

Her publishers say of Edna Ferber that she is boxing the compass for America. She has written of New England, the old South, the Middle West and the Southwest, the cities and the farms, the past and the present in American life with equal virtuosity. Now she trains her sharp eyes and agile mind on the great Northwest country, particularly on the Wisconsin forests and paper mills, more especially on a wood pulp millionaire and his family.

The novel opens in 1907 with Barney Glasgow already the richest man in the State, one of the big millionaires of the country—the wood pulp king. Outside there is a panic; it is the era of Roosevelt, trust-busting, muckrakers. But the robber baron of the north woods is very comfortably and securely entrenched. Who is this Barney Glasgow? We go back to the early days of lumbering and paper-making in Wisconsin; to the days when Barney Glasgow was a boy in a lumber camp, through the years of his youth as a lumberjack, to the days of his early successes in business and investment deals, leading up to the time when he marries old Jed Hewitt's plain and disagreeable daughter and inherits the Hewitt fortune. We follow the history of the family, thereafter, from 1907, through the tremendous expansion of the war years, through the boom, the crash and the depression, into the present when, shorn of much of its power and wealth, the family seems to have, for the time being, come to a pause.

That is the general scheme and plan. Miss Ferber deplores the waste and greed and destruction resultant on the policy of the early and later timber barons. But she is not effective as a muckraker. She "emotes" over material, after she has gathered it; she is a story-telling reporter and she gets her story over to an American public which prefers sentiment to drama. But Miss Ferber can be an A1 reporter. However the experts may quibble over her data—and there is always room for quibbling—she collects her material in thoroughgoing fashion. Then she organizes it and injects her freshly gleaned technical knowledge, historical anecdotes, twice-told tales, into a piece of magazine-story fiction. All her novels start off bravely; but toward the end her own emotions seem to get the better of her and, after a consistent pattern, go off the deep end into what can only be called bathos. Thus she robs her people of that dignity and individuality with which, as an intelligent and sympathetic observer, however superficial, she has endowed them.

Just as *So Big,* which won the Pulitzer Prize back in 1926 and was a superior best-seller, went to pieces after the fine and moving first half, wound up with a one-armed French general and an entourage of celebrities coming down to weep over the Mother of So Big, so *Come and Get It* proceeds from a brave beginning to a linked series of heart throbs. Before Barney Glasgow, along with many of the other early characters, is destroyed physically he has been destroyed for us as the unusual and striking character we came to know in the first half of the novel.

But the device of blowing sky-high much of her impedimenta in the way of early characters in order to concentrate on the few she wishes to carry over from one generation to another, seems justified as a technical device in avoiding an awkward transition and keeping the story a continuously moving one through the years.

The latter part of the novel deals with the cosmopolitan womenfolk of the American millionaire hierarchy in New York, Paris, London and the various vacation grounds of the plutocracy during the era of prosperity.

In his fifties, Barney Glasgow had lost his heart and his head over the 18-year-old granddaughter of his old boss, Swan Bostrom. As a young lumberjack he had known her grandmother. He showers on the whole family—his old comrade Swan, Swan's daughter Karie, and the girl, Karie's daughter Lotta, all the advantages possible without rousing suspicion. But Lotta has the instinctive knowledge of her own unique physical loveliness. She is, with her mixture of Swedish, Portuguese and other racial strains, a rare, an extraordinary beauty. Even as a young girl she knows her worth, by instinct, and while she permits Barney, as an old friend of her grandfather, to shower gifts upon her, she is canny enough to realize that her best bet is Barney's son, Bernie Glasgow, sole heir to his father's millions and, what is more to the point, marriageable. Lotta is well done at this stage. It is not that she is shrewd, calculating or ungrateful. It is that she is emotionally as cool as a child and as simple, direct and egotistical as a child.

We are taken the rounds of high-powered plutocratic international society during the Twenties. Lotta, with her raving beauty and her millions, with her mother, Karie, who has the instinctive sense that her rôle is that of a homely, crude, mighty pioneer woman of the American Northwest, becomes the rage. She and her mother break down every barrier, Lotta's beauty and Karie's forthright, downright, honest vulgarity vying for chief attraction.

This part of the novel could easily be made into an operetta as fascinating and charming as **Show Boat**—given Jerome Kern's music. Indeed, it smacks of that illuminating, if theatrical, manner of catching the volatile essence of a situation which is the glory of musical romance.

Edna Ferber remains the stanch American; she both knows and loves the vast varieties of American life. Her methods and interpretations, however, suggest, rather than the realistic novelist, the social historian at one extreme and the theatre at the other.

The Commonweal   (review date 6 November 1936)

SOURCE: A review of *Stage Door*, in *The Commonweal*, Vol. XXV, No. 2, November 6, 1936, p. 51.

[*In the following review of* Stage Door, *the critic applauds all aspects of the production, but notes that the characters are "mere types."*]

Stage Door, though it is not George S. Kaufman and Edna Ferber at their best, is an amusing, well acted and skilfully staged little comedy. It has to do with the rivalry between stage and screen, and the brave fight made by Terry Randall to become a legitimate actress. Terry sees her pretty but brainless roommate become a successful Hollywood star, and her chance comes only at the end, when her roommate has failed in rehearsals for a Broadway play, and Terry gets the opportunity to take her place. But it is not the story that counts in **Stage Door**; it is the local color of the Footlights Club for girls, Mr. Kaufman's wisecracks, his direction, and the acting. We might wish that the characters were less mere types and the story had a little more importance, because we know what Mr. Kaufman and Miss Ferber accomplished in **The Royal Family** and in **Dinner at Eight**; but there is no doubt that as a good show **Stage Door** rings the bell. And the Kaufman touch in the direction is everywhere apparent. Who but Mr. Kaufman would ever have invented that delicious scene in the girls' bedroom, when they put black masks over their eyes, and then turning out the light, the room is alternately dark and brightly illuminated by an electric sign which flashes across the street? And the Kaufman wisecracks are as gay and as mordant as ever.

The acting is equally good. Miss Margaret Sullavan returns from Hollywood to play Terry, and plays it with charm, grace and naturalness. Fortunately for the stage Miss Sullavan is apparently not one of those young women we hear about during the action of **Stage Door** who sign seven-year contracts with the movies without the hope of ever getting back to Broadway! Now that she is back may

her returns be frequent. Of the host of young women in the play special mention should go to Lee Patrick for her utterance of Mr. Kaufman's more bitter reflections, to Catherine Laughlin for the girl who gets married, to Jane Buchanan and to Frances Fuller. Of the men Onslow Stevens is attractive as the movie agent, and Priestly Morrison as a human country doctor. The rest act with color and celerity. In short, **Stage Door,** despite its local mood, will probably appeal to most of the theatregoing public, and because of Miss Sullavan to many patrons of the movies.

Joseph Wood Krutch   (review date 7 November 1936)

SOURCE: "Too Good Not to Be Better," in *The Nation*, New York, Vol. 143, No. 19, November 7, 1936, pp. 557-58.

[*Krutch was an American drama, literary, and social critic who wrote esteemed studies of Samuel Johnson, Edgar Allan Poe, and Henry David Thoreau. In the following review of* Stage Door, *he attributes both the strengths and weaknesses of the play to George S. Kaufman, and laments the fact that the play itself is far less intelligent than its many witty lines and gags.*]

It is unfair, of course, but anyone as good as George S. Kaufman must pay the penalty for not being a great deal better. He has paid it before and he will have to pay it again in connection with **Stage Door** which he has written in conjunction with Edna Ferber. Since the penalty generally includes an extremely profitable run, it is perhaps not too severe, and yet Mr. Kaufman must have heard "It's enormously amusing but—" too often not to entertain very melancholy convictions on the subject of human ingratitude. The scene is a boarding-house for aspiring young actresses somewhere in the fifties, and all of the play's very good best is strictly topical in nature. Underneath is a sentimental story and a familiar sentimental moral—that the real actor would rather starve in the theater than live in luxury anywhere else, even in Hollywood—but what really counts is the succession of what would have been called in the seventeenth century "the humours of a boarding-house."

It is true that even these may not be strictly new. One could easily guess beforehand that one was going to meet the girl who could play anything if she was given a chance, the girl who thinks that men are dreadful, and the girl who goes wrong in mink. But Mr. Kaufman and Miss Ferber have hit them off with such crisp, amusing strokes that they seem quite fresh, and the whole thing moves with such perfect ease in such a perfectly calculated tempo that one is carried irresistibly forward on a ripple of laughter. All the gags, whether expressed in words or embodied in "business," are as smart as a night club which won't open till tomorrow and as quotable as what the *New Yorker* will say next week. The proletarian playwright who goes Hollywood is "one of those fellows who start off on a soap box and end in a swimming pool"; the austere young lady who is sure "Kit Cornell isn't seen at parties" gets "Yeh, Bernhardt was a home girl, too" in reply; and the bit of business in which the irreverent flapper throws the peel of a banana she has been eating in front of the top-hatted proletarian renegade and then beckons him forward with a finger deserves to win a place in the standard repertory of gags. "It's tremendously amusing but—."

The real reason that it is impossible to enjoy one of Mr. Kaufman's shows without feeling a certain undercurrent of resentment is, I think, that the lines are not only much better than the play itself but also actually upon a much higher level of intelligence. At its best his wit is pretty nearly everything which wit ought to be. It is smart and sophisticated and crisp; it is also based upon shrewd insight and a keen sense of sham even in its most modish embodiments. Why is it that the plays themselves must be fundamentally incompatible with the spirit of their dialogue, that they must be based upon hokum of the very sort which the man who writes them was born to expose? How merry he himself could make with the thesis he is preaching and with the more sentimental of the scenes through which he develops it! Or could he? Perhaps, after all, the answer is that his intelligence and his power of criticism exhaust themselves in a phrase, that the part of him which speaks in epigrams cannot make any whole of itself.

Margaret Lawrence   (essay date 1936)

SOURCE: "Go-Getters," in *The School of Femininity*, Kennikat Press, 1966, pp. 183-209.

[*In the following excerpt from a book originally published in 1936, Lawrence focuses on the role of women in Ferber's writings, discussing the historical context in which Ferber's work first appeared and noting how she reflected and promoted women's new status in society.*]

Behind the war generation and the post-war youth lay long centuries of feminine silence and economic helplessness. The ghost of it still haunted the race. Emancipation was so recent, it was confusing. The ghost appeared in the confusion. When the emotionalism of the war faded, and the excitement of the new emancipation gave way before the necessity of making some program for women, a very real problem came up. There was a generation of women left over from the war. When the war casualties were counted, and the war-wrecked men were admittedly of terrifying numbers, it was seen that a whole generation of women would have to go through the remainder of their lives without any kind of what had been previously considered normal relations to men and to family. Two possibilities faced these women. They could take the place of the men who had died, or who were shattered. If they did not, the old men would carry on far beyond their time, and the world would be worse off than ever. Or they could look upon themselves as already dead along with their male contemporaries, and get whatever relief the dead presumably get in surveying the sufferings of the living. Sexually they could have no normal future. It was celibacy, or inversion; it was a "catch as catch can" sexual relationship with the strong men left, and this of necessity likely to be shared with other women, or it was relationship with the broken men who survived, or with the unfit who had not served, or with the very young if they could be had, or the very old. Whichever way the individual woman decided,

there was no use at all in setting up once again the old romantic standard. It would be too painful. Also it would be futile.

It was fortunate, or unfortunate, whichever way we may choose to see it, that at the very time when a generation of women realized their sexual predicament, the sexual foundation of nervous disorders was broadcasted to the public. The subject of sex and all its ramifications in society became the dominating subject of contemporary thinking and writing. People had turned bitterly away from both national and international politics. There was no solution in sight. The deeper one delved into state relationships and humanity in the mass, the worse the general human situation appeared. People on the ebb from the illusionary emotion of the war accepted the hopelessness of things on a big scale. The interest in sex was in one sense a mark of a retreat from the large to the small. More than that, it was something that appeared to be new. War and social conflict were old subjects, and completely baffling to the human spirit, but men and women saw some possibility in a new attention to sex of arriving at some understanding of themselves in particular. They tackled sex with pioneering intensity. All the historic figures came up for reexamination. They were discovered to be historic neurotics. Women saw feminine history in a new light. They saw their contemporary situation in a new light. It was not a soft, flattering light. It was a light which threw into utter clarity all the difficulties before them. It convinced them of the need to revalue. It gave the revaluation the emotional purposefulness of opening up new territory. It intensified the original feminist rebellion. The little girl pals had taken one step in assuming sexual nonchalance. The go-getting women into which some of them evolved took another step in assuming a sexual determination and a corresponding determination to pull the world round into acquiescence concerning an entirely new type of femininity.

It happened at the same time that the commercial world became conscious of women. This fact made a world of difference for the go-getting female. The world was her dish. The great cosmetic firms and the great dressmaking firms sprang into commercial power almost overnight. The little girl pal had painted herself for her boy-friend. The go-getting woman painted herself for the sake of her own morale. The advertisers told her that a woman was only as old as she looked. Cosmetics, they went on to say, defeated time. The little girl pal dressed herself to remind her boy-friend that she was a good fellow. The go-getting woman dressed herself to remind herself that the world was her dish. The right clothes made a lot of difference to the woman approaching her prime. The little girl cut her hair in defiance against her elders. The go-getting woman kept her hair short because it was convenient, and also "youthifying"—a new word used by the advertisers. The little girl pal smoked because it was a shocking thing to do. The go-getter smoked because smoking was a kindly sedative, and also, so it was said, a help in the matter of fighting fat. For women had come to look upon fat as their worst enemy. Commerce helped them in that viewpoint. All kinds of contraptions appeared for women in their struggle against pelvic padding. The little girl had kept slim because it was boyish. The go-getter kept her weight down because the less she had to carry, the keener was she in the game. The little girl went pagan sexually as a gesture of contempt to her elders and their sense of propriety. The go-getting woman went after what sexual outlet she decided she needed because it was part of her equipment. No woman could afford to insult her glands.

The little girl pals looked at one another incidentally when there were no boy-friends around. The go-getters look at one another appraisingly.

The reason is obvious—the inherited sense of rivalry among women. This has been sharply intensified by the new rivalry in business and professional experience. The instinctive fear of a woman that any new woman might attract the attention of the man has added to it a new fear that every new woman may be getting along in the world better than herself. The old biological fear led women to imitate other women. If a particularly attractive woman wore her hair in a certain attractive way, the women who were subconsciously afraid of her followed the style. The old biological fear always made women examine one another interestedly. It was sound business. It was study of the competitor. The new fear has not pushed the old fear out, but has intensified and amplified it. One of the incidental, if not altogether main, reasons why women attend their own clubs and go to meetings and to social affairs is to take in the appearance of other women. It is to be seen in any public place, even upon trains and street-cars—women looking one another over. It is not seen among men. Men look at women in public places where both sexes meet. When they go to men's affairs they go in boyish good fellowship to foregather merely with their own kind. Women, except for the out-and-out declared nymphomaniac, do not in public places examine the men. Which shows that their minds are concerned with their competitors.

Men have sometimes said impatiently that women are like sheep; they do what any style leader or success leader does. This has been off the point. The point has always been respect for the dangerous competitor and her methods, and every woman who is honest with herself knows what the point has been. It is this constant watchfulness concerning competition which has made women difficult in general in their business relationships with one another. It is sound on a small scale. But it is unsound in larger issues. It tangles and complicates. It makes it hard for a woman to concentrate upon an impersonal issue, or in other words, to attend to the game for its own sake. It makes it hard for her to applaud when another woman makes a successful run. She relates that success to her own failure.

The feminists explain this tendency in their sisters as part of the inherited technique of the harem. They hope that after a few generations of feminism it will disappear. They make a rapid rationalizing twist, and point to the increased interest of women in the doings of women as a growth in their feminist appreciation. It is a very doubtful rationalization. It twists in a circle back to the old study of the competitor camouflaged.

The magazines are full of the work of enterprising women interested in this new phase of femininity. They are writing murder stories and stories of business, with possibly interrelations with the domesticity of women. They are writing history, or rather rewriting it. They are handling any kind of fiction and assignment they think an editor will tolerate. Most of them stand securely on two feet. One foot is modern and daring; the other foot is safely conventional, for the good reason that the magazines and their readers prefer conventionality. Most of them do not use characters; they use handy types. Most of them do not produce atmosphere; it is much easier to concoct a set-up. They invariably have their eyes on the screen, and when they write a story about a woman the mark of the screen star is upon her. They write with a background of a mahogany desk, a cable address, two telephones and stacks of memo sheets. They are business women making shrewd use of fiction because it is an excellent paying business once it is established.

Ahead of this go-getting fleet there are several women of definitely magnificent fiction proportions.

The first of them is Edna Ferber.

Future historians will turn to Edna Ferber for vivid first-hand reporting of the time in fiction.

—*Margaret Lawrence*

Edna Ferber appeared when women first appeared on a big scale in business and careers through the English-speaking world.

There were great candy-makers, great cosmeticians; there were great corsetières, great women dressmakers, great dieticians. There was an army of women selling insurance and real estate and all the things that women want to buy. There were lawyers and doctors and the odd female preacher. Every one of them felt joyously at the beginning of a great new era in history. They regarded themselves as pioneers.

This was the feeling of the years. It was the breath-taking decade after the war. Women drove cars and airplanes. They directed enterprises. They made money. The world was theirs. The magazines said so. If one judged by the advertising, there were no men in the world at all, or, at the most, men who were decorative appendages to such women as might still feel the need of them either in perpetuity or temporarily. It was the decade of hilarious divorcing. No woman had to stick [in] a relationship that bored her. She could make her own way. She could also make the man pay up for having had her a while. The law was on her side. It was a decade of strong women and adventurous women. It was as if all the stored-up female energy of the ages suddenly blew off.

Edna Ferber's first stories had to do with women who

pushed their way into competition in business with men. She glorified the woman commercial traveler and the woman producer. They were case histories of actual go-getting women, and she related them by her astute journalistic sense to the subconscious opinion which all women were holding of themselves. The combination was excellent for her own bank account, and excellent stimulus for the progress of feminist enterprise, and excellent also for the increase of the primary documentary sources of the feminist movement. Unquestionably, future historians will turn to Edna Ferber for the gathering of vivid first-hand reporting of the time in fiction. She is, therefore, to an almost final extent, the supreme feminist.

Whether it was out of utter feminist conviction, or out of the accidental attraction of the keen journalist for good material, only Miss Ferber herself will know. But whatever the conscious, or subconscious, motivation might have been at the beginning, she stands now as the supreme fictional annalist of careerist women in the heyday of their careers.

She has used a characteristic technique which by a lucky strike related itself to the intellectual methods of the go-getting women of the first post-war decade. It is a shunting technique.

"Shunting" is a technique which allows the story to pull forward and backward leisurely.

It was what a lot of women were doing until they got up full steam to go ahead. It is what women in the past had done with their lives. More than that, it is the way women had thought. No woman had ever taken off immediately and cleanly and clearly into a career. She shunted around for years with biological possibilities. She gathered experience and the experience had inevitably to do with the career of some man before she was convinced that she should be at her own career.

This is what makes the shunting technique popular with women and native to them.

More than that, it is a technique which belongs to the new world and to commerce. The new world was opened up by railways, and the courier of the new world was the commercial traveler. Without any exaggeration it can be said that the rhythm of the new world was the rhythm of the train shunting up and down in railway-stations. The movement of the train got into the thinking and the talking of the commercial gentlemen who sat by the hour in smoking cars and exchanged stories with their fellow travelers. When they got back home to their wives and families the rhythm was still upon them, and all that they said was said in the shunting manner of their traveling.

Women started to go upon the road. They took the primary materials of millinery and dressmaking out from the big cities to the little towns and the villages. Laces and buttons and artificial flowers. Corsets and lingerie and ribbons. A new order of women. A change in the trade. They fraternized with the traveling men on the trains. They exchanged stories with them in the small commercial hotels all over the country. They spoke the same language. It was a language of sales approach and order lists and the conditions of trade. It was these women who as fiction material first attracted Edna Ferber, and before any other author had realized the story wealth of them, she tumbled into their portraiture, telling her stories in the manner of the good fellow sitting in the smoking room with the boys, and influenced definitely in her narrative rhythm by the shunting movement of the train. She was influenced also by another train effect. The commercial traveler telling a story was under the necessity to get his story told quickly. Some of the boys would have to get off at the next station. The superimposition of brevity eliminated all the decorative literary or philosophical additions to a story, and produced an interesting technical combination of bare story detail with a shunting movement from point to point instead of a general progression of plot.

This, so far as the new world is concerned, is a fundamental story form. The story in the new world is in its origin a traveler's narrative. Travelers who met casually on the road had no community of interest for conversation, and in place of the gossip usual to people contained in a familiar small community or group, they put the story. It was invariably struck in its beginning from some accidental comment, and shunted backwards and forwards from that comment into a sequence of events which had some relation to the thing which provoked the original comment.

This peculiar technique comes out of and belongs exclusively to a country which has only recently emerged from pioneer experience, and which is unequally developed. That is, there was always some vacant land in the great stretches of the North American continent which called out the people of pioneering temperament from the already settled districts and lured them away into the primitive delight of trekking and pioneering. So it follows, because of the law of the association of ideas and emotions, that the story form most intimately connected with these people would be the traveler's narrative told in the familiar traveling rhythm. Throughout the United States and Canada there were still places to which the traveling salesman came as a messenger from the big world. He was received as minstrels formerly were received in the great castles of the old medieval world. He represented movement and news as well as commerce. When Edna Ferber's stories began to be published, the motor-car was just beginning to be popularly available. The American people were on the edge of possessing machines to gratify their inherited taste for the trek, and also on the edge of receiving new entertainment through the ether and the silver screen, but neither of these was quite ready for the popular wide market when she swung into fiction. She caught the tide of familiarity. In her technique and in her material she was altogether American. She combined the new energy of women, which was a pioneering energy, and the trekking sense of the continent, and she did it with more concentrated fidelity, with deeper sincerity and more primitive simplicity, than any other American writer.

There is nothing in her stories borrowed from Europe. There is no shadow of sophisticated weariness. Sometimes there are touches of naïveté, but these touches come from the author's sense of the zest for living, which is the breath of any new civilization.

She writes as if none of the authors of Europe existed. From the classical standpoint she has no style whatever. But from the vital standpoint of how style is associated with the emotion of time and place, she has perfect style.

Apart entirely from her fidelity to the rhythm of primitive pioneer story-telling, and apart entirely from her absorption in the current of the American scene, Edna Ferber is of towering importance to the School of Femininity. She belongs to the great procession—Austen, the Brontës and Eliot—who presented the feminist picture.

In all Edna Ferber's work there is an undercurrent of dissatisfaction with men.

—Margaret Lawrence

Serena de Jong, the heroine of her greatest book, *So Big*, belongs with Elizabeth Bennett·and Jane Eyre and Maggie Tulliver. Her other women are like the other women of Miss Austen, the Brontës and George Eliot. They are the Elizabeths and the Janes and the Maggies out in a new world on the make, selling lingerie, performing on show boats, running newspapers and raising prize asparagus, struggling with emotion and finding themselves relief in action. But there is one great difference, and it is the difference between the nineteenth-century lady and the twentieth-century woman—her women are not dependent upon men for the adequate conduct of their lives. Elizabeth Bennett, had she been disappointed in Mr. Darcy after marriage, would have been in an emotional whirlwind, and Miss Austen, had she tackled such a situation, would have been hard put to it to find a neat conclusion. Little Jane Eyre, if fate had not taken the wild and fascinating Mr. Rochester by the scruff of his unrighteous neck and handed him over to her, would have been a flattened out little mortal. Poor Maggie Tulliver had to be drowned after a purgatory of isolation because she had magnetism which she could not use to her own advantage. But Serena and all the women of Edna Ferber take erotic disappointment in their twentieth-century stride and do not expect anything from men. They say to themselves—men are like that—and find plenty to do besides looking around for another hero or getting drowned. And this in spite of the fact that they are women of deep emotions and strong passionate attachments. They observe their husbands; they mother their sons and their daughters, and expect no undue amount either of love or of great stature from any of them in return. Life to them is worth what it brings in experience. They live in the feminist era in the new world.

Serena de Jong, facing disappointment both in her husband and her son and raising the best asparagus in the State, is a symbol of the new woman. She is not a romantic figure in the old sense, yet she is a woman of new romance, courageous, real and vital.

In all Edna Ferber's work there is an undercurrent of dissatisfaction with men which is characteristic of all the general writing of the modern School of Femininity in its present phase. It may be a half-way phase. The woman of the next phase may come to the conclusion that her real work for the race is to maintain at all cost and with great creative effort the illusion of romance and greatness in men. But for the present she seems to be of the general opinion that men are weak, or that at least the men of this period are not strong enough for the women whose strength has been bred of the feminist pioneering era. Serena de Jong met no man who was as strong as herself, and this is true of all Edna Ferber's women. It is the plaint of all strong women, and women for the time are through with the nursing of an illusion. There is too much to do in the big impersonal world. It is the tragedy which Olive Schreiner foresaw when she wrote *The Story of an African Farm*. Men would inevitably be a step behind the new woman. But it is an even greater tragedy than Olive Schreiner foresaw. She believed in the race. She taught that strong women would breed strong sons. Edna Ferber shows her women disappointed in their sons; for the sons are never quite so rugged in fiber as their pioneering mothers; and the conclusion is that strength needs more than one parent. So has the feminist story reached one of its plateaux of experience, and what is to be done about it? For nature created women normally incapable of happiness in companionship with men weaker than themselves. Meanwhile there remains much of the world yet to be conquered for women, and this is the real love of the women she portrays in the height of their powers.

Isabel Currier   (review date 13 February 1938)

SOURCE: "Manhattan Summer Music," in *New York Herald Tribune Books,* February 13, 1938, p. 5.

[*In the following review, Currier favorably assesses the characterizations and plotlines of "Nobody's In Town" and "Trees Die at the Top," the two novellas in* Nobody's In Town.]

"Everybody who is anybody" leaves New York in the summertime, seeking escape from the heat. After they have gone "The Little People . . . claim the New York that is rightfully theirs." Anonymously, they continue the routine of their days to keep the city of the world fed and thirst-free and clean. The great machinery of massed life never stops, and those who keep it running are unaware that **"Nobody's In Town."** They are unaware, too, of the intergrooving of their lives to form the arteries and veins of the urban heart of America.

You see them function in the complete human circuit that is modern New York through a series of vignettes forming one of two short novels in Edna Ferber's new book [*Nobody's In Town*]. A successful young man in Wall Street is left alone in his East Side apartment when his wife goes to Europe. The individuals who insure his summer comfort appear, as in a kaleidoscope, in control of the reservoir providing water for his shower, the Washington Market in which a retailer shrewdly maneuvers to procure raspberries for his dinner, the incinerator disposing of his garbage. The links binding their personal lives to his are forged swiftly and brilliantly. In Central Park, he finds young people dancing and making love. From his East Side apartment, the colored cook hurries to Harlem to the flamboyant summer blooming of a modern jungle, out of which the folk music of a nation echoes around the world. The vitality of this hugely patterned tapestry is realized through Miss Ferber's clear focus on a section of humanity, to bring it into perspective as the entity of humanity.

Contrasts of a different, but related tempo are in **"Trees Die at the Top,"** which matches the peaks of life in America today with the peaks scaled by pioneer forefathers. The reader is taken on two journeys from the Atlantic to the Pacific. The first trip to California is with the Forty-Niners, their wives and children. It is a painful and heroic progress of eighteen miles a day, rain or shine, to complete the conquest of three thousand miles of wilderness. The second journey is in the company of descendants of the Forty-Niners. Parents, children, nurse and personal maid are on a de luxe train which is straddling the continent. In its drawing rooms they endure, with self-conscious nobility, the hardships of air-conditioning, night noises at stationstops, over-rich food and underexercise for thirty-six luxurious hours. The author's purpose is bold and bitter and brilliant. Out of the magnificent vitality of America's pioneers has come a race of pampered softies. She gives us our own generation—flabby, bloodless and frustrate.

Both stories are vividly characterized, and realized with the vigor and human awareness which make Edna Ferber a compelling storyteller.

Katherine Woods   (review date 5 February 1939)

SOURCE: "Edna Ferber and Her America," in *The New York Times Book Review,* February 5, 1939, pp. 1, 30.

[*In the following review of* A Peculiar Treasure, *Woods favorably assesses Ferber's first autobiography.*]

It was a lovable country town in Wisconsin, in the early years of the century: tree-shaded, prosperous, civilized, and stimulating as such a town is bound to be if one has the keenness and imagination really to look at it. "Just to sit on the front porch and watch the town go by is something of an education" in an open-living American community like this. And the formal education of the remarkably progressive high school offered extracurricular attractions as well: plays, debates, dances, the weekly "forum" with its sociability that was so urgently important to its participants. At 14 one sang in one's church choir. But almost every one of the girls had a beau in the male choir at the fashionable Congregational Church (where the local drayman was nevertheless one of the ushers and passed the collection box). In the "stinging cold white Winters" one skated on the river, caught bobs for rides on snowpacked roads. There was a lot of fudge made, and corn popped, in the evenings. There were elocution contests—one's heart's delight. And one always somehow found time to read, anything and everything, a book a day. In one's home there might be anxieties and sometimes sadness, but such affectionate companionship, such lively fun! One lived along happily, part of the life—so characteristi-

cally American—of the Middle Western town. Only for this girl there were some differences.

She had the alert and energized mind of the born reporter, swift, incisive, undeceived and unforgetting.

And she was a Jew.

Edna Ferber's girlhood was very happy in this small town. And in the small town her autobiography actually focuses, though it draws vivid and memorable pictures from various other parts of the world. It is an autobiography which is intensely interesting in every incident, on every page: the success story of an American girl who made good; the mercilessly hardworking—albeit glamorous—career of a popular novelist and playwright; the story of a Jew. She reminds us of this last, repeatedly; otherwise we should forget it; and she does not want us to forget. Here, then, is her dramatic story, told with wit and humor and compassion, intensity and pride, and always with brilliant reporting. Edna Ferber's success is, of course, not surprising; what is surprising is that as a young girl she had no wish to write; she never thought of it.

Her gentle, sensitive, impractical Hungarian-born father had set up a store in Kalamazoo, Mich., and there the two Ferber girls were born. But the family did not stay in that town long. And soon her high-spirited young mother, who had rather shocked the neighbors at first by her dashing Chicago clothes and independent ways, set herself to helping her rather unbusinesslike husband in his work. Next to the author, it is Julia Ferber who is this autobiography's heroine: "a humorous, gay, shrewd woman with an amazing sense of values. She belongs definitely to that race of iron women which seems to be facing extinction in today's America; hardy, indomitable." Life with her could never be dull. Nor could it be fainthearted, even though the family, like so many American middle-class families, was often harried by business worries. It was when these were at their worst that Edna Ferber's father began to go blind.

She was consumed by ambition. Later she was to write with an eager social consciousness. But it was personal success which beckoned in those early hopes. The child of a theatre-loving family, Edna was determined to be an actress. She told her parents that she was going to "elocution school," and when they said she couldn't do that because they hadn't the money, she flounced out of the house in a "white-hot rage" and got a job as a reporter on the local paper at a salary of $3 a week. So, accidentally, as she says, and "in a storm," her career began. She was 17 then; and in all the years since, she says, "I don't remember a day when I haven't been writing."

Even so, she never thought of writing fiction in those newspaper days. Her whole ambition now was to be a good reporter. She was a good reporter. In all this life-story there is nothing more arresting than the memories and reflections of the years when Edna Ferber was a good reporter, until she drifted, almost, into the writing of fiction after an illness. By that time the writing habit was fixed. "Without in the least meaning or planning it," she stepped into creative fictional work. A little later Chicago stories were "tumbling one after another" out of her typewriter, and in the far-away New York, which she never dreamed then of visiting, magazine editors were accepting all her stories and asking for more.

The novelist's eyes have seen and Ferber's mind has stored wherever she has been. And her autobiography is packed with dramatic detail, always and everywhere.

—Katherine Woods

Newspaper work had taught her to write, years of omnivorous reading had given her a vocabulary, strength of character made it natural for her to welcome struggle and turn even disappointment into a tool for progress. But observation was the gift—talent, if you like—with which she was born. In Chicago she looked for stories; her mind was trained to do that, almost unconsciously now. Yet long before that, back to some miserable years of childhood in a rough, ignorant, cruelly anti-Semitic mining town, her eyes had been wide open, her mind even then quick and vital in its grasp. She saw things that were strange, or vivid, or amusing, or horrible or, sometimes, too fantastic to write about; she writes about some of them here for the first time.

With the exception of *Fanny Herself,* Edna Ferber's fiction has never been autobiographical. She has seldom taken a character from life. She can claim the novelist's power of projecting herself into a situation, an environment, an emotion, without need for specific experience. Of the creation of "lifelike" characters, and its funny boomerangs, she has a number of amusing things to say. "The average reader seems incapable of realizing the existence of the imagination in writers," she remarks, and later, in telling the piquant tale of the writing and production of *The Royal Family,* she declares that the authors had "no particular theatrical family" in mind, and adds: "We did, however, plan to use one member of the Barrymore family—John; not as a whole, but bits of him. He was, of course, too improbable to copy from life." She did not describe any one particular house in *American Beauty.* It was not on the Mississippi that she gathered personal knowledge for *Show Boat.* But the flood in that book is a childhood memory of the Iowa River.

Farm women in Appleton, Wis., found their way into *So Big,* after that novel's chief character had been suggested by the sight of a woman in a Chicago truck market; and the paper mills of Appleton gave their grist to *Come and Get It.* The redoubtable Julia Ferber had experiences which were valuable to "Emma McChesney." A chance remark from Winthrop Ames aroused the interest from which *Show Boat* developed. A talk with Mr. and Mrs. William Allen White (themselves the type, she points out, of the best in America) was the unconscious beginning of *Cimarron.* The novelist's eyes have seen and her mind has stored wherever she has been. And her autobiography is packed with dramatic detail, always and everywhere.

Then, when she had written all these books and plays, she realized that she had really been writing chronicles of America (Rudyard Kipling in a letter stressed her "value as an historical painter"), and that that was as it should be. That was what she would choose to do. She loves all America, but especially the Middle West and the Far West stimulate and fascinate her; she loves the small towns; she loves what with poise and frankness she calls the "middle class"; she loves the freedom, the initiative, the courage and energy, the youth, the very wastefulness, of this country. She is not a jingo; she sees her country's faults and its present dangers. But she is a provincial American; a small town girl who has made good; an heir to the pioneer spirit; a passionate democrat.

To her own amazement, Edna Ferber burst into a speech in Union Square once, smashing down with hard facts and clear thinking upon an oratory which was shrieking of Russian "freedom." She has the same weapons against Nazism and anti-Semitism. But what she leaves with her readers here is something subtler and more pervasive than argument: the far stronger thing which is simple memory; not hers alone, but theirs as well. The small town which is the American background; the pioneer spirit which has been building America for 300 years—which of us has not such traditions, such pride? At its worst that spirit was ruthless and greedy; at its best it sought a real Promised Land. Pilgrim, Huguenot, Catholic, Quaker, Jew—here are our memories; here is the spirit of a nation; here is our peculiar treasure of democracy and freedom, to be guarded by us all.

Peter Quennell   (review date 24 June 1939)

SOURCE: "Impressions of a Best-Seller," in *The New Statesman and Nation,* Vol. XVII, No. 435, June 24, 1939, pp. 998, 1000.

[*Quennell was an American essayist, novelist, and critic. In the following review of* A Peculiar Treasure, *he praises Ferber as a keen observer and an honest and enthusiastic writer, rather than as a particularly accomplished novelist or insightful autobiographer.*]

From several points of view *A Peculiar Treasure* is an engaging book. It gives us a vivid sketch of an active and successful woman: it traces the outline of a busy and exciting career: it helps to explain the methods and psychology of a modern best-seller. It is readable, diffuse, slipshod, enthusiastic, entertaining, naive. Miss Ferber is not fatuously self-complacent. On the other hand, she is neither unduly self-critical nor exaggeratedly introspective and, looking back across her life, she can afford to feel satisfied. She is modestly pleased with her present position and proud of her ancestry. The peculiar treasure mentioned on the title page is the Jewish blood to which she attributes the strain of devoted diligence so apparent in her personal and literary dealings. From the same source, no doubt, she inherits her vitality, her somewhat exuberant sentimentality—relieved by a considerable degree of shrewdness—the touch of humility that appears in the narrative of her greatest triumphs. No reader is likely to begrudge her the success she enjoys. Miss Ferber's adult career began at the age of nineteen when she left her quiet Middle-Western home and started work as an early "sob-sister" on the Milwaukee *Journal*. Some of Miss Ferber's liveliest and best-written pages are concerned with her recollections of the Milwaukee background, the streets of that squalid, prosperous beer-brewing town, the fascinating world of the newspaper office, the police courts, the boarding houses, the people encountered. She was immensely overworked and exceedingly happy. In the end, over-exertion and under-feeding brought on a complete physical breakdown; Miss Ferber was obliged to retreat to Appleton and, during convalescence, she started to write a novel. *Dawn O'Hara* she admits was dreadful stuff; but it was at last published and ever since has been selling steadily. Her short stories—more meritorious and at that time even more successful—first propelled her down the slipway towards fame and fortune.

Her subsequent progress may be compared to that of some great transatlantic liner. Storms have come cannonading against the vessel's sides; there have been dark days, nasty moments, rain and thunder; but the schedule of performance has been manfully adhered to, the record preserved. Luckily for herself, she is in love with work—not necessarily with her own work, certainly with the idea of work in the abstract. Never impeded by diffidence or dilettantism, she has discovered in herself a means of diverting personal energy into creative channels, and from immediate experience producing saleable copy that both more important and less accomplished writers have often lacked. In composition, she seems to have eliminated an intermediate and—to judge by the biographies of such novelists as Flaubert, Tolstoi, Proust—uncommonly tedious and exhausting stage. Thanks, it may be, to her newspaper training, she is one of the best organised of modern novelists: no sooner has she received an impression than she is able to absorb it and, no sooner has it been absorbed, than it takes shape as a book, meaty, satisfying, solid, abounding in incident. No dismal periods of indecision and hesitation: no gloomy search for the inevitable in rhythm and epithet. Notwithstanding the hard work, it's been easy going . . .

So much for the limitations of Miss Ferber's method. There is a pleasing simplicity about her account of the circumstances through which her various stories have come to be written. For example, having just published a novel, enormously efficient and well-documented, about life in Oklahoma, she happens to be spending a week-end on Long Island. There, "walking towards us against the background of a spectacular sunset," whom should she catch sight of but a Polish market-gardener? The Poles, she learns, have ousted the old bankrupt New England families. Fifty years ago they began to arrive:

> Half of New England's Polish now. They're wonderful farmers. They live in the old New England houses that were built in the 1700's by hand . . . Well, there it was. *American Beauty.* My holiday was over. Just as when Winthrop Ames had happened to say show boat to me, starting me towards the South and the world of the Mississippi and the floating theatre, and as William Allen White . . . had given me that

first fascinating glimpse of the dramatic possibilities in Oklahoma, so now Walter Lippmann's brief comment set my imagination racing . . .

She struggled, Miss Ferber tells us, against the temptation. "I was tired; I didn't want to do that kind of book again . . . But the urge to write the New England novel was stronger than the desire to smother it. Perhaps I should have been stern about practising birth control on *American Beauty.* Conceived in careless love I hadn't meant to have it. But there it was."

No sooner has she received an impression than she is able to absorb it and, no sooner has it been absorbed, than it takes shape as a book.

—*Peter Quennell*

So a new novel popped into the world and, like every novel Miss Ferber has yet published, it was born with a substantial platinum spoon in its mouth. Nor should one feel aggrieved at its early good fortune. As Miss Ferber remarks, while apologising for the immaturity of *Dawn O'Hara,* "everything I have written, from that time to this, with the exception of the novel *Show Boat,* which is frankly romance and melodrama, has had a sound sociological basis." That, of course, is why Miss Ferber's books are so very much more readable than most English stories of equivalent rank. She has never lost her enthusiasm for the American scene. Though her characterisation is seldom profound or subtle, though her mannerisms are often journalistic, she is swept along by the dignity and breadth of her subject-matter. In Europe, the second- or third-rate novelist is usually reduced to writing of fourth-rate characters, existing in conditions of precarious gentility or dubious intellectuality, sadly circulating in some all-too-familiar squirrel's cage; while Miss Ferber can draw on the resources of a gigantic continent, stocked with a dozen different races, full of extremes of wealth and poverty, where contrasts are dramatic and obvious as the landscape is vast. Well, Miss Ferber has had the wit to grasp her advantage, and the energy and tenacity to give her observations a literary form. None of her books may be really memorable, but none is worthless. What is more, she has derived tremendous enjoyment from writing them. Her latest book is not a masterpiece of autobiography; but its qualities by far outweigh the defects that derive from them.

Rose Feld   (review date 2 November 1941)

SOURCE: "Saratoga and New Orleans—and Edna Ferber," in *New York Herald Tribune Books,* November 2, 1941, p. 5.

[*Feld was a Rumanian-born American critic and journal-*

ist. In the following favorable review, she praises the characterizations and plotline of Saratoga Trunk.]

Again Edna Ferber has taken a slice out of America's past and made it come alive. In *Saratoga Trunk,* her new novel, she has gone back to the '80's of New Orleans and Saratoga, two cities which at different poles represented the lustiness, the vitality and the romance of the period. Both scenes are admirably suited to her abilities. She has a feeling for the color and the sparkle of the robust, a relish for honesty of emotions and actions, however rooted in dishonesty; a kinship with a generation which had a deep respect for good food. *Saratoga Trunk* is certain to take its place beside her *Show Boat* which for mood and feeling it closely resembles. Not for nothing have the movies snatched up this story, written with her rare instinct for theater and her tremendous gift for investing characters with glamour.

Miss Ferber opens her story in the present when eighty-nine-year-old Clint Maroon, picturesque millionaire, with his wife, Clio Maroon, is meeting the members of the press to give them a statement about the gifts he is making to national institutions. The reporters have come to ask questions about the value of property, paintings, ships, holdings, the possessions of which the Maroons are freeing themselves. Impatiently they sweep aside the efforts of the still physically impressive octogenarian to tell them what he considers the real story they should print, the personal tale of intrigue, swindle and ruthlessness upon which his riches were made. He gives hints of his wife's oblique forebears, of a murder accusation, of his own guilt in dealing with men; but the reporters have a deadline to meet; they cannot spare the time to listen to memories which have no bearing on the front-page news they've come for.

> **One closes *Saratoga Trunk* with the feeling of having lived in a rich and exciting world, peopled by fascinating and exciting characters no less real because they are eccentric and romantic.**
>
> —*Rose Feld*

It is the story they think unimportant and insignificant which makes the novel; the tale of Clint and Clio Maroon. They met in New Orleans, she at twenty a beautiful young woman just returned to her native city after an absence of fifteen years; he at thirty a handsome Texan who had come to the languorous Creole metropolis to try his fortune at games of chance. Clio belonged in New Orleans; she was the daughter of a Creole aristocrat, Nicolas Dulaine, and of Rita Vaudreuil, famous beauty whom he had installed in his house in Rampart Street. There Rita Dulaine, as she called herself, had shot and killed Dulaine in a lovers' quarrel. The scandal had been hushed up by his family, and Rita, accompanied by her sister, Belle Piquery, the child Clio and the two servants, Kakaracou, the colored

maid, and Cupidon, her dwarf son, were shipped off to Paris. One must read the book to get the rich flavor of this fantastic group—the languishing beauty who gave all for love, the robust and lusty Aunt Belle who knew the price of favors, and the two loyal and bizarre servitors who watched over the two women and the child. So brilliantly are they portrayed that it is their consistent strangeness which gives them their quality of integrity as creatures in a demi-monde of a departed era.

With her mother's dark beauty and her aunt's practical shrewdness, Clio was determined to get out of life what each of them had missed—respectability and wealth. Clint Maroon, the handsome Texan in the white sombrero, could give her neither, she knew, but the attraction between them was too strong to deny. They became lovers with the realistic understanding that it was a temporary partnership which would end when Clio met the rich and respectable man who would become her husband.

Magnificently Miss Ferber describes the New Orleans of the early '80s, against which the two vivid characters move in an aura of increasing scandal. One gets the atmosphere of the city in her enumeration of its thrilling odors, coffee, ships, exotic fruits, old churches, which blended together became "the smell of an old and carnal city, of a worldly and fascinating city"; one becomes familiar with the romance of its conventions and customs in her description of the opera, the social castes, the markets, the early mass, the food at Hippolyte Begue.

Because of her attachment for Clint and her notoriety as the daughter of the famous places, Clio realized that New Orleans could never give her the position she craved. Fortified by money she received from the Dulaines in a ruthless blackmail scheme, she followed Clint to Saratoga, the gambling paradise of the North. Here, with her eye-opening entourage of the turbaned black maid and the uniformed dwarf, she became a sensation as Countess de Chamfret. This is straight theater on the part of Miss Ferber, not wholly convincing but admissible as part of her romantic tale. And just as she captures the feel of New Orleans down to its bones, so does she recreate the fever and flavor of the Northern city, "prim, bawdy, vulgar, sedate, flashy, substantial." This was Saratoga, and this in many ways was Clio Dulaine. It suited her with all its extravagances, not the least of which was the great wealth of Bart Van Steed, the spa's most eligible and most mother-ridden bachelor.

Readers of American history will remember the industrial ferment of the latter half of the nineteenth century, the fight for oil, for land; for railroads, for steel; the pillaging of public and private property, the swindling and brutality of the "robber barons." Miss Ferber brings enough of this into her story to explain the rise of Clint Maroon. The handsome and, at times, naïve Texan wanted no part in these activities; as he explained to Clio, he had come to Saratoga to get himself "a little honest money—cards, roulette, horses and so forth." But the fashionable United States Hotel housed financial as well as social intrigue, and before long Clint was involved in the fight between the timid Van Steed and the scheming Jay Gould over the control of the Albany & Tuscarora Railroad. The story of the battle at Binghamton over the hundred-mile road makes a bloody page in American history, and Miss Ferber uses it with excellent effect in her story. The end is clear in the beginning.

One closes *Saratoga Trunk* with the feeling of having lived in a rich and exciting world, peopled by fascinating and exciting characters no less real because they are eccentric and romantic. The secret of Miss Ferber's achievement is rooted in many things—her vitality and belief in the people she creates; her meticulous care with all details of background and characterization; her unfailing sense of drama. Possibly this adds up to genius. At any rate, *Saratoga Trunk* will be relished and remembered not alone for the love story of Clio and Clint but for Aunt Belle, for Kakaracou and Cupidon, for Mrs. Coventry Bellop, poverty stricken social leader of Saratoga, and for nostalgic evocations of a forgotten day in New Orleans and Saratoga.

Margaret Wallace   (review date 2 November 1941)

SOURCE: A review of *Saratoga Trunk*, in *The New York Times Book Review*, November 2, 1941, p. 4.

[*In the following excerpt, Wallace favorably assesses the characters and the pictorial style of* Saratoga Trunk.]

The most cautious reviewer can predict skyrocket success for *Saratoga Trunk*—and not feel that he is getting out on a limb, either. Few of Edna Ferber's vastly popular novels of the past decade have arrived on the book counters with more fanfare. In abridged form it has been serialized by a national magazine, and it will be seen on stage and screen as soon as the ponderous machinery for producing an A spectacle can begin grinding it out. *Saratoga Trunk* is what is known in a field of human endeavor only slightly less hazardous than the publishing business as a natural.

One can see without difficulty why this should be so. The pictorial qualities of Edna Ferber's costume novels are built-in. Others may write with a fuller knowledge of history or a keener sense of character analysis. But Edna Ferber is almost alone—almost, because *Gone With the Wind* has something of the same quality—in giving her reader the impression that she is actually writing in technicolor. As fundamentally dramatic as *Cimarron,* with all the lavish and eye-filling qualities of *Show Boat,* this new novel may well outstrip either of them in enduring popularity.

Certainly Clint and Clio Maroon are among the most vital and engaging figures in Edna Ferber's long and colorful gallery of heroes and heroines. We meet them in modern Saratoga, where they have been rich, respectable, and powerful—and front page news—for sixty years. The reporters and camera men are gathered again. Is it true, Mr. Maroon, that you've turned your collection of paintings over to the Metropolitan Museum? Is it true your Adirondacks estate is to be a free Summer camp for boys? Is it true you're giving away every penny of your fortune to the government after you've pensioned your old employees?

It was all true, the tall drawling old man agreed. Only that was not the story Clint Maroon wished to tell. He wanted the public to know how he stole the fortune he now proposed to give away—"stole millions from millionaires who were stealing each other blind. We skimmed a whole nation—took the cream right off the top." He wanted people to understand how it was that this could not happen today, and that America was a better and more hopeful land because of it. The reporters would not listen. Clio, white-haired and straight as a reed at 79, had warned him that they would not. A grand old man, Clint Maroon—one of America's first citizens—but his mind was clearly not what it used to be.

It all went back to New Orleans and a house on Rampart Street. Clio Dulaine was half Creole aristocrat, half a nameless member of the underworld. She was beautiful and unscrupulous, and she had resolved not to commit the sentimental follies of her mother. Rita Dulaine had known love and luxury. Clio coveted riches and respectability. She made that clear to Clint Maroon almost at once. She had picked him up in the French Market, a tall Texas cowboy with a white sombrero and a diamond stud. Inside a fortnight she was in love with him and he with her. What was more important, they understood each other perfectly.

Together they hatched the blackmail plot against the Dulaine family which financed their descent upon fashionable Saratoga. They did not go together, which would have been distinctly imprudent. Clint owned a racehorse and was better than fair at any gambling game he had ever heard of. Clio wanted a millionaire—Bart Van Steed for choice. She got off the train, attended by her fantastic colored servants and followed by a cartload of crested luggage, as the Countess de Chanfret. To cap it all she drove up to the United States Hotel in Bart Van Steed's phaeton. A telegram signed with his mother's name had brought him to the station; for young Mr. Van Steed, whose name could be conjured with, was frightened to death of his mother.

Saratoga Trunk is a flamboyant story in a setting to match. No amount of description can suggest half so well as a direct quotation the gusto with which Edna Ferber builds up her background:

> Here, in July, were gathered the worst and best of America. Here, for three months in the year, was a raffish, provincial and swaggering society; a snobbish, conservative, Victorian society; religious sects meeting in tents; gamblers and racetrack habitues swarming in hotels and paddocks and game rooms . . . Invalids in search of health; girls in search of husbands. Politicians, speculators, jockeys; dowagers, sporting men, sporting women; middle-class merchants with their plump wives and hopeful daughters; trollops, railroad tycoons, croupiers, thugs; judges, actresses, Western ranchers and cattle men. Prim, bawdy, vulgar, sedate, flashy, substantial. Saratoga.

As polished prose a passage like this may be open to criticism, but it beats into the reader's mind with irresistible energy nevertheless. And it leaves an impression behind, an impression so nervous and colorful and even dazzling that it may outlast many more sober statements.

Fairfax Downey   (review date 22 November 1941)

SOURCE: "Ferber . . . ," in *The Saturday Review of Literature,* New York, Vol. XXIV, No. 31, November 22, 1941, p. 18.

[*Downey was an American journalist, poet, and critic. In the following review, he favorably assesses* Saratoga Trunk.]

"Hi, wait a minute, fellas," broke in the tabloid reporter. "Something tells me Mr. Maroon isn't kidding. Are you, Mr. Maroon? Say listen, maybe we're missing the real story." . . .

They did miss the real story, that group of newspaper men and women interviewing Clint and Clio Maroon in their rooms in the United States Hotel, Saratoga. Of course they already had a big story: the old Colonel's announcement that he was giving away his many millions. Also they had a deadline to meet. Furthermore there was dynamite in the sensational confession the old-timer from Texas was trying so hard to make. Add to press of time and chance of libel the fact that any reporter prefers to cover one yarn at a time.

So they missed it. No matter. Miss Ferber, who was a reporter when she was seventeen, covered it for them, and did she do a job on it! The story within the "frame," the fabulous career of Clint and Clio, is her new novel, *Saratoga Trunk.* Unpacking it is absorbing entertainment. There's everything in it but the kitchen stove—no, that's in, too, and the New Orleans and Saratoga dishes cooked on it will make your mouth water. The author could hardly be expected to provide an appendix with recipes, yet there is sure to be a demand for them. Perhaps the publishers will come through with a gustatory supplement, gathering rosebuds and publicity while they may.

Miss Ferber serves up some very nice phrases, too. As for instance, in describing the *Vieux Carré* of New Orleans: "Past the old houses whose exquisitely wrought ironwork decoration was like a black lace shawl thrown across the white bosom of a Spanish *señora.*" Or of Saratoga: "A neat New England town with a veneer of temporary sophistication, like a spinster school teacher gone gay."

And there is also a theme. Colonel Maroon states it when he tells the reporters:

> This is going to be a different America . . . This country today is finer and more honest and more free and democratic than it has been since way back in Revolutionary days. For a century we big fellows could grab and run. They can't do it today. It's going to be the day of the little man. Tell them to have faith and believe that they're the best Americans in the decentest government the world has ever seen.

But none of these—theme or background or well-turned phrases—get in the way of the main business, which is the telling of a tale; they only further it and enhance it, which is as it should be. Perhaps the beginning of the *liaison* between Clint and Clio in her New Orleans house is rather too lightly sketched. Many an incident could have been developed to greater length. Indeed the book could have been half again as long without being overwritten. But

Miss Ferber has been mindful of that cardinal principle of the entertainer: Stop while they still want more. Successful playwright that she is, she knows good theater.

Saratoga Trunk, of course, is just that. Good theater. Can it be a mere coincidence? No, never! The story, it may be confidently predicted, will soon be out from between boards and on the boards. Call in Collaborator George Kaufman. Page the one and only Jerome Kern to compose the score. He hasn't had a chance like this since *Show Boat;* the book is crammed with song cues. Cast Clio, Clint, Kaka, Cupidon. What parts!

Please reserve me two on the aisle, Miss F.

Nathan L. Rothman   (review date 27 January 1945)

SOURCE: "Love-Letter to Seattle," in *The Saturday Review of Literature,* New York, Vol. XXVIII, No. 4, January 27, 1945, p. 24.

[*In the following review of* Great Son, *Rothman praises Ferber's skill as a novelist but laments the fact that she did not fully develop her story in this novel.*]

Miss Ferber is a swell writer, gifted, fertile, and imaginative. And she is unfair to book reviewers. Here she has written a lively contemporary American romance, with certain inadequacies plain upon the face of it. We are prepared to speak to her in pained and loving accents. But right before us, in nice large type, is a two-page introduction in which she has ticked off these very inadequacies, neatly, clinically, and without omission. Absolutely unfair. We hope this is not the signal for a new trend of self-reviewed novels. Probably few novelists could give so accurate an account of their own work. "This book," she says, "should have been a trilogy . . ." but the vast dimensions of her subject so baffled her that she decided to ". . . attack with a slingshot. . . . Here, in capsule form, is that which should have been a lavish and prodigal feast." This, in essence, is her own analysis of it, and it is very, very true.

Seattle is her subject, the Northwest region of which it is the hub, Rainier looming over it, the lumber and the mines, the whole sprawling history between the gold strike and the two great wars. It is a great story, and Miss Ferber has conceived for it an American family that grew along with it for four generations of time, not a device of unique effectiveness but one that would serve to bind things up. Yet instead of moving along largely and binding it together, she has telescoped it into really capsule form, and for no earthly reason save that she was averse to writing "one of those 1180 page romances . . . the awesome and bulky type of volume that is so tough on the stomach muscles when read in bed . . ." (still that introduction). But that is sheer nonsense. There is nothing wrong with 1800 page romances except that the wrong people have been writing them lately. Here exactly was the time and reason for writing a huge, exciting novel—a big theme, and a writer with the yen and the power to do it well. We should certainly like to have seen those three tomes by Edna Ferber, with all of the Northwest written into them. Instead she has squeezed four generations of national and family history, of a people sprawling across a landscape, of mining camps and city growth and moneygrabbing and love-search, into 280 pages, using all the convenient and ineffectual tricks of flashback to do it.

Of course it reads like a slingshot job, as she knew as soon as she had written it. The wonder of it is that it is readable just the same, and that is merely the wonder of her own talents, which she forgot to lay aside, her verve and enthusiasm and humor, her love of people and America. Some of this fabulous Melendy family are all-too-familiar literary characters: the crochety, dominant old matriarch, Madame Melendy; her heroic, empire-building son Vaughan, with his prim wife Emmy on the one hand, and his faithful love, a Yukon singing girl, Pansy Deleath, on the other (Miss Ferber, those names!); and even the youngest generation, Mike, gay, brave, loose-ends, then comes Pearl Harbor. All this to make it short and easy. But some of them, like Dike, Vaughan's son, and his wife, Lina Port, and a brief view of Emmy's pioneer mother, come sharply alive, when Miss Ferber takes any trouble with them. They add up, mixed in quality inside their stirring landscape, to a heartfelt love-letter to Seattle, written in haste. Next time, Miss Ferber, please write it out in longhand. We'll wait.

William Du Bois   (review date 28 January 1945)

SOURCE: "Tintypes by Ferber," in *The New York Times Book Review,* January 28, 1945, p. 5.

[*Du Bois was an American educator, novelist, poet, playwright, and critic. In the following review of* Great Son, *he argues that Ferber has failed to provide her potentially interesting characters with a suitably compelling plot.*]

First there's Exact Melendy—a great-grandame complete with Godey-book silks, medicinal rye, toy railroad, and the finest view in all Seattle. Then there's her son Vaughan—a two-fisted taker in his day. There's Emmy, his pneumatic wife, whose mother was a Mercer girl. There's his son Klondike, born of Pansy, his violet-eyed Alaskan mistress, and offered to the world as his legal offspring. Dike, despite a crumbling fullback facade, is soft at forty-odd. Could he be otherwise, after such American luxury items as "Harvard and good scotch and third-row seats and four-rib roasts and sixteen-cylinder cars?"

There's Lina, his wife—an actress and a full-time cat. There's Cliff, who writes her plays and spends his spare time burlesquing the ghost of Woollcott. There's a clutch of Japanese servants, who behave very oddly indeed as Pearl Harbor Sunday begins to rumble in the plot. Last, and most voluble, are the Young People, the Heirs of Tomorrow: great-grandson Mike (a flying fool, who knows there's nowhere to go but up), and Reggie, the simon-pure—and inevitable—refugee.

Having listed the principals in Edna Ferber's new book, the reviewer can only pause and stare blankly at the names. Any Ferber fan will recognize the ingredients for one of those bang-up romances she's been putting together so neatly for a generation now. But this time the craftsman's hand has produced a *croquis*—and nothing more. To put it as bluntly as possible, there are too many old parties ruminating on the glories of yesterday—and yawning, much too contentedly, in the cocoons of their wealth. Pearl Harbor Sunday cracks the cocoons: a flashback, now and then, pants hard to give the illusion of life. One still has the airless sensation that belongs to the diorama in a city museum. One looks back longingly to the genuine clash and bustle of *Cimarron* and *Show Boat,* back to the deep emotional grasp of *So Big.*

Miss Ferber has every right to produce a "novel of character," as the jacket blurb insists she has done. But an old hand at fiction should remember that no character is compelling until he is put in believable conflict. Ignoring this truism of her trade, she has let a well-earned public down with a bang.

Rose Feld   (review date 28 January 1945)

SOURCE: "A Rich Lusty Story of a Family and a City," in *New York Herald Tribune Weekly Book Review,* January 28, 1945, p. 3.

[*In the following mixed review of* Great Son, *Feld applauds the plotline as "a lavish and prodigious feast," but contends that the characters are not well-defined.*]

In a two-page introduction to her novel *Great Son,* Edna Ferber makes what she calls "an inadequate excuse for a slim book on a Gargantuan subject." No excuses, no apologies are necessary for this volume for, however lacking it may be in its creator's eyes, this story of Seattle comes alive with the spirit of its intention. The strokes are broad, but never wasteful; the story sprawls but never without radius from a central core.

One paragraph from Miss Ferber's foreword might well be quoted as an ideological review of the book. Here it is: "Everything in and about Seattle—its people, its scenery, its spirit, its politics, its energy, its past, its future—is larger than life. Curiously enough, there is, too, about the region a dreamlike quality baffling to the outsider. This quality, misty as Rainier itself, imparts an unreality to the whole. Romantic, robust, the people and the city have an incredible past and a future beyond imagination. The present completely escapes the chronicler. It is so vast that one cannot see it in perspective and must be content with a worm's-eye view."

Great Son is, in a way, the elaboration of the above, both in terms of a city and terms of a family. The book goes back to 1851 and it holds the present. Exact Melendy, robust, domineering nonogenarian is the matriarch of the family: Mike Melendy, her great-grandson, more at home in his airplane than in his father's house, is representative of the present generation. The years spanning the lives of these two hold the story of a city's fabulous growth.

Seattle was a wilderness when the infant Exact, named after the boat which brought her, was carried in her mother's arms to meet the father who had never seen her. Ninety-two years later, Madam Melendy looked down from her lavish home upon a city that her father would never have recognized. "It was fantastic, it was thrilling, it was absurd, it was majestic. It could have been the most beautiful city in the world—it might yet be, one day." Madam

Melendy took pride in her city and in the fact that men like her husband and her son had built it.

The story of the city and the Melendys is closely interwoven. Jotham Melendy came from Illinois to the Northwest for land and got it, grabbed it and grew rich and powerful with it. His son, Vaughan, made land poor by a panic which swept the country, heard the call of Alaska and rebuilt the family's name, and power, but young Mike, his son, was alive with the unrest of a generation that has the detached social perspective of winged creatures.

The early growth of the city was fabulous, a giant, naive and rich, stretching his limbs, adorning himself, living by his own rules. So was the early saga of the Melendys. Miss Ferber devotes the major part of her book to the story of Vaughan Melendy who, like the city, knew few rules outside of his own making.

Vaughan Melendy was married to Emmy, daughter of a Mercer girl when he set out for Alaska. In New York, in 1866, one hundred New England virgins set sail for Seattle for the purpose of acquiring husbands. The leader of this highly respectable group was a serious-minded young pioneer of the Northwest, Asa Mercer, who knew that a land without wives and mothers was a land without a future. In Seattle today, descendants of the Mercer girls are as socially important as Boston's Mayflower families.

In Alaska, Vaughan Melendy, sober and ambitious, a little confused over the staleness of his marriage with Emmy, met Pansy Derleath, daughter of a broken-down singer. The romance between these two is told in the best Ferber tradition. It is alive, honest, earthy and real. Their son, Dike, was adopted by Vaughan and house-proud Emmy, their wealth symbolized by two bags of gold. Pansy came to Seattle shortly after and Vaughan built a house for her a short distance from his own. In telling their story, Miss Ferber catches the breath and the heart-beat of the extravagant period peopled by extravagant human beings.

The other characters in the book, with the exception of Madam Melendy, are less clearly defined. Or rather, in contrast to the lusty stock that came before them, they seem soft and colorless. Much of this is deliberate, for in writing of them Miss Ferber indicates that their ineffectuality lies in their being products of a past rather than actors in a present. There is an implicit accusation against those who make no return of service to a land which had been extravagantly generous to them. She points this up in the introduction of Reggie Dresden, an eighteen-year-old German refugee girl, who knows how wonderful it is to live in this country. In Mike, also, the youngest Melendy, she sees the germination of a deep-sense of human responsibility that goes beyond the security of a family or an individual.

Going back again to Miss Ferber's introduction, she says that *Great Son* is "in capsule form . . . that which should have been a lavish and prodigious feast." Perhaps she is right but the capsule is a potent one and should drive the individual to the sources that make a feast. A novelist who achieves that achieves something to be proud of.

James Gray   (review date 1946)

SOURCE: "Edna Ferber," in his *On Second Thought,* University of Minnesota Press, 1946, pp. 154-64.

[*In the following review, Gray examines* A Peculiar Treasure, *contending that it is a forthright autobiography and reveals the particulars of Ferber's literary success.*]

Edna Ferber is an enormously gifted person. She is also a thoughtful analyst of human experience. This aspect of her intelligence she has seldom revealed in her fiction, which habitually takes a firm, possessive hold upon a heroine and leads her resolutely through a series of highly contrived incidents in a standardized siege against the citadel of success. Ironically, it is in Miss Ferber's autobiography, *A Peculiar Treasure,* that she fully reveals her talent for offering a detached and impersonal comment on the mixture of perils and pleasures in human life. Here she has made a carefully critical examination of the assets she brought to the task of writing fiction and of the high-handed use she has made of them.

"What there is to see, I'll see," was Edna Ferber's battle cry almost from the moment she was born. As a little Jewish girl she saw what there was to see in Ottumwa, Iowa, and that was plenty. It included a lynching performed at a street corner of the tough mining town in broad daylight. As a girl reporter in Appleton, Wisconsin, and in Milwaukee she saw what there was to see. And that was plenty, too, because her assignments included everything from covering murder trials to interviewing "Fighting Bob" La Follette.

As a prima donna in the world of popular letters, she saw everything in New York, Berlin, and Paris because she had not lost her curiosity and knew that everything noted with the novelist's insatiable appetite for detail might eventually come in handy in a book.

She has told all this in her autobiography, *A Peculiar Treasure,* her richest, most honest, and most searching story.

When a popular, competent craftsman turns his back upon the long years of constructing stories to satisfy the magazine audience and decides at last to tell about himself, he almost always writes a good book. All the experience of disciplining his material stands him in good stead. The dramatic instinct for finding the word, the phrase, the happening that will reveal character and light up the significance of a way of life has matured. But there is no longer any need to be sly and cunning in bringing the tale to a right conclusion. The pattern of the life exists. It has justified itself. All that is required is to chip away deftly what is irrelevant or repetitious and let the truth be shown. That is what Edna Ferber has done in this admirable autobiography.

In a curious way *A Peculiar Treasure* follows the formula of Edna Ferber's novels. It is a success story. As in *So Big* and *Show Boat,* the central character begins her life in obscurity, struggles resolutely, battles down the succession of emergencies that intervene between herself and triumph, and winds up at last in a Park Avenue penthouse.

But the difference between Edna Ferber's own story and that of the characters she has created in fiction is that nothing in her upward climb seems fortuitous or contrived. Her triumph can be completely understood when the whole record is given with candor and courage.

Miss Ferber has been tremendously successful with her audience because she had qualities which, however imperfectly she revealed them in her early work, sprang out of self-respect. She had a proper reverence for her Jewish background, for the Hungarian forebears who she could still remember had been men of substance and achievement even when the bitter loafers in an Iowa town flung the word *sheeny,* at her. She had a proper confidence in her ability to make use of the opportunities offered by the prewar America into which she had been born.

Two other habits of mind brought her success in her middle twenties. One was the fact that she used the material of her own world in her fiction. She saw her mother, a sad, high-hearted woman, turn in and run the family store when her husband's sight began to fail. Out of that experience she created, with the large help of intuition, the first American businesswoman in fiction, the triumphant Emma McChesney, whom Theodore Roosevelt liked so well that he undertook to advise the author about what the course of the character's subsequent life should be. To American readers, Emma McChesney seemed like a brilliant new creation simply because Edna Ferber had the good sense not to take her characters off the hand-me-down shelf. Today, looking back over what she has written, Edna Ferber is able to see that what she did with her material was often tricky, sentimental, and unworthy of the fine urgency of the first creative impulse. But she profited nonetheless by that original desire to write honestly about American life.

The second thing that helped her was her dramatic flair. The little girl in Appleton won prizes for declamation. The mature woman says that she is still a frustrated Bernhardt because she has never been on the stage. But the harnessed lightning of insight which makes a play move is in the best of her stories.

Yes, this is a good book, revealing and humorous. But what is for me the most interesting part is the brilliant record of the early years spent in a difficult milieu, each trial of which was faced with a gay resolution.

As a Jew Miss Ferber is concerned, eloquently and with the greatest dignity, over the plight of her fellow people in other lands.

"All my life," she says in conclusion, "I have lived, walked, talked, worked as I wished. I should refuse to live in a world in which I could no longer say this. . . . It has been my privilege . . . to have been a human being on the planet Earth; and to have been an American, a writer, a Jew. A lovely life I have found it, and thank you, sir."

Robert van Gelder (essay date 1946)

SOURCE: "An Interview with Edna Ferber," in his *Writers and Writing,* Charles Scribner's Sons, 1946, pp. 360-65.

[*In the following essay, based on a 1945 interview, Gelder examines Ferber's views on the writing process.*]

Edna Ferber waited for the publication of her new novel, *Great Son.* Her hands and her talk were restless. The talk ranged over the hard drinking of some American writers and their wives: "She was like a little girl, a child, but after the cocktails and wine at dinner, she filled a whole tumbler full of Scotch and drank it down as I'd drink water; before long she looked like an old hag." The talk reached to Russia and Communism: "It's a good system for them; sure, it is. I visited there as a tourist and I know what they want. They want oranges and shoes and wrist watches and fountain pens and little cars to drive in. We have those things. What we want is here," said Miss Ferber, pointing to her heart, "and here," pointing to her head. Speaking of hearts, said Miss Ferber, she had recently come from Washington, where she had taken the "two-step," a physical test designed for young Navy fliers. The person being tested runs up and down two steps "about forty times, and the chart that they make afterward should be," said Miss Ferber wistfully, "all regular little cones." But hadn't the test been designed for the pick of the nation, the youngest, strongest, physically most perfect? "Yes, I suppose so," Miss Ferber said. "But the chart should be all regular little cones."

Miss Ferber spoke of "all the vitality that I have," but corrected herself to say, "that I had." She gives, however, an impression of great vitality. As she talks she acts, mimics, and though her eyes, which are striking, are alert for every response, they are not wary but have the look that expects and presumes response. One has the impression, watching her, of a person who after a fairly long and very full lifetime has reached an edge looking down into uncertainty, but who has never before quite known uncertainty, who has always filled up that pit with competence and work and pride in work and success.

She said: "I want to write five plays before I die." Had she been working on one recently? "No, the last thing that George (George S. Kaufman) and I did was *Bright Land,* and that—as you probably remember—was a semi-flop. George and I haven't talked plays lately. I think I may try one alone."

She wants to write plays, she said, because there is some fun in doing them. "So much of the work on a novel is just lonely labor—the pile of manuscript that grows so very slowly as you slave through long stretches of description and narrative. But a play is all dialogue—that is, it is purely people that you are dealing with all the time. And I like to write dialogue.

"You know, it occurs to me as I speak, won't the new novels be largely dialogue? All swift pace and people? I've read that wonderful book, *A Walk in the Sun,* by Harry Brown, and it is great, it's magnificent. What a beautiful job!" She quoted lines of the dialogue spoken by a soldier who is longing for an apple, a soldier who is writing a letter in his head. "Can't you just see the boy as he says that? So young, so concentrating . . ."

> Ferber wants to write plays, she said, because there is some fun in doing them. "So much of the work on a novel is just lonely labor."
>
> —*Robert van Gelder*

The mention of youth brought more animation to her voice and manner. "The best thing we can do—that is, my crowd, my generation—is to clear out of the way, make room for the kids, the young people who are twentyish, the soldiers and their girls and sisters. My goodness," exclaimed Miss Ferber, "what books they will write! Because they are honest and their world is debunked and they see it straight and clear. They even think straight, think honestly, and they are not afraid. Out of all of the mess of the 1920's and the miseries of the 1930's these amazing young people—the greatest generation, to my mind, since the people in the covered wagons.

"My generation was afraid and so was yours. Afraid of sex and inhibitions—well, of course, I can take inhibition or leave it alone; I don't really mind an inhibition—that is, it can be useful. But, anyway, the new generation isn't for them or afraid of them. My crowd was afraid of so many things—of words and emotion, of love. We had to be shocked with love. But these people can talk about love simply, naturally, and admit they love a home, or a Mom, or a Dad. We couldn't possibly have done that without quotation marks. But their voices are quiet, and they are controlled; they say what they feel as they feel it. They are sound people.

"They are a great hope in a world that for years has been gripped by an all-pervading fear, a fear that is everywhere as though it were a great sound from the sky. It is fear that is behind the hate, intolerance, bigotry, the verbal and actual slitting of throats. You see it on the streets—a woman and child walk along and the child isn't quick enough crossing the street, so the woman shouts at it, 'Why don't you come on!'" Miss Ferber shouted (and an echoing sound in the next room indicated that her startled, white-coated houseman had dropped a plate or an ash tray) "The woman slaps the child. Now that's fear, nothing more. We all feel it, except the young people. Perhaps they can save us from terrible times."

To the question of why, as she was so conscious of this fear and of the need to exorcise it, she did not use it as a theme for a novel, Miss Ferber closed her eyes and slowly responded: "One doesn't quite know the method."

She did use that theme, she said, in her autobiography, *A Peculiar Treasure*. "Now you know—or rather, anyone who knows me knows—that if I lived to be 105 I wouldn't think it worth while to write my autobiography. I wouldn't do it. But with this theme, and feeling that I couldn't be entirely effective with the theme in a novel—because it is so vast, so overwhelming, so much our whole time—I decided to concentrate it in the story of the Jewish family that I knew best, and of course that was my own family. People like to know what is behind the scenes, they like a keyhole view, so I thought I'd give them that and this theme with it. I've had many, many readers.

"But as for themes in fiction—every one of my books has had a theme deep in it that was very important to me. I should say every book except *Show Boat,* which hadn't any theme, which was just fun. But the rest have—though I suppose not many people know it.

"They didn't know it because—I think—if you write with humor, with lightness, entertainingly, you're not counted serious. If your writing is easy and pleasant for a great many readers, a phrase comes to be used on you—a phrase that I've begun to hate with a deep, strong, almost nauseating hatred. I don't even like to say it, the silly hybrid!"

It developed that the objectionable phrase is "best-seller."

"I was going over the advance publicity for my new book and I found in there—'best-seller.' I said, 'Please! Why? Why, even by my publisher, am I dismissed as a best-seller? *Show Boat,* I said, 'was written in 1925. And this is the year 1945. *So Big* was written in 1923, and this is 1945. *Cimarron,* came along in 1928—and they all are reprinted in those wonderful little books that are sent to the soldiers—yes, the Armed Services Editions. Well, goodness,' I said. 'Do you call books best-sellers—which means out today and gone tomorrow—and is a hateful, slurring derogatory phrase—when those books are being read and reread down through more than twenty years—and are being printed in the tens of thousands right today?'

"I shouldn't tell you this, I suppose," said Miss Ferber. "I've never told anyone, not one soul, of what a man said of my work in a letter not addressed to me but that I saw. The man was an Englishman. He wrote of me—I'm embarrassed saying this; repeating this rather, because certainly I'm not saying this. I'm only quoting—that it was probable that I would not be appreciated in my country and in my time. The man who said that was Rudyard Kipling, and his letter is in the Doubleday, Doran offices. Another man, writing from England too, said the same thing. He was James M. Barrie."

Miss Ferber said that *Great Son* will be her last book in the field of historical fiction. "I want to live in today." She has been, she said, enchanted by certain phases in the development of this country, "by the figures—they were never people, but they were figures recognizable as people"—who had built the country, made it great. But now she was through with history. "I have that same feeling that I had when I finished with 'Emma McChesney.'"

"And that was?"

"Well, I wrote a good many stories about Emma McChesney. She was a good character and I was afraid to try a novel, and you know—when you write with some success you contract obligations. And Emma McChesney was so popular that she took care of my obligations. Of course, I was writing other stories along with those about her, but many of the others weren't really short stories—they were novels cut down. 'Old Man Minick' was a novel with a whole life crammed into a few thousand words. I had it in my mind that I was a short-story writer and no more. Yet my ideas were those that should go into a novel. It was as though I were taking enough clothes to fill a trunk and instead of putting them into a trunk put them into a suitcase. Then there I was sitting on the suitcase trying to close it. Ends of skirts and arms of blouses wouldn't go in, so I'd take the scissors and snip them off. That's what happens when you try to pack a novel into 5,000 words.

"Then a contract came from *Cosmopolitan* for more McChesney stories, and the line for payment was left blank. That meant that I could fill it in for any amount I wanted. Well, I knew that if I signed that contract I was a gone duck. I'd be writing Emma McChesney stories from then on. I sent back the contract unsigned and wrote *The Girls*—and became a novelist.

"What's in my novels that will last? Well, I don't know. I'm not so old yet that I reread what I've done in the past, mourning among my souvenirs. But I do know that what you are emerges; whether you are a writer or not, what you are becomes clear, and if you are a writer, then what you are is there in your writings for every one to read. As for me, if I don't last, if what I've done isn't good enough, I can't ever say I did it for the wife and kids. I've written what I wanted to write, and always the best I could do at the time."

James MacBride   (review date 16 February 1947)

SOURCE: "Thirty-One by Ferber," in *The New York Times Book Review*, February 16, 1947, p. 3.

[*In the following review of* One Basket, *MacBride praises the collection as representing Ferber "at her best."*]

Miss Ferber's short stories (her blurbist informs us solemnly) are required reading in schools and colleges. For once, it is pleasant to agree with the publicity department. Selected by the author herself from over a hundred published items, the stories in this volume will repay the closest study of the fledgling who would go and do likewise. For the confirmed novel-reader who shuns slick paper, they are vigorous examples of an author at the top of her form—a virtuoso lightness of phrasing, a shrewd ear for dialogue, plus real understanding of the standard problems Americans have faced in the past and must go on facing. Those who have found Miss Ferber's full-length output a bit cine-colored of late should take pleasure in rediscovering her at her best.

The first story in the collection was published in 1913 ("**The Woman Who Tried to Be Good**"); the last, a rather-too-sand-papered study of a career girl's heart-throbs ("**The Barn Cuts Off the View**") appeared in 1940. Most of the well-remembered, much-anthologized, well-loved yarns are in between: "**Every Other Thursday**," "**The Gay Old Dog**," "**Mother Knows Best**," "**Trees Die at the Top**," "**The Afternoon of a Faun**," "**No Room at the Inn**," and "**Old Man Minick**," which served as a spring-board for one of Miss Ferber's first plunges into Broadway. These titles alone would make the collection worth while.

Most of them have worn well with the years; all of them will repay a second reading.

As always, Miss Ferber is at her best when she stays closest to the milieu of her formative years—when she was carving out the raw material of her art as a reporter in the Middle West. Her back-street Chicago is more convincing than her Riviera romances; her prairie mornings will stay in your memory long after you've forgotten her station-wagon repartee. But even the most severely hand-tailored of her stories is much more than merely entertaining: if her matriarchs are terrifying and completely real, her star-crossed women executives, faded ingenues, and freshly lacquered adolescents are no less human under their patter. Sometimes, as in her novels, Miss Ferber's sheer, exuberant talent, her flair for the theatrical, outruns her material—with a consequent loss of realism. But even here, the emotion is honest. Her effective range is much narrower than these titles would indicate—yet every story is written from her heart.

George Jean Nathan   (review date 1949)

SOURCE: A review of *Bravo!*, in his *The Theatre Book of the Year: 1948-1949*, Alfred A. Knopf, 1949, pp. 153-62.

[*Nathan was an esteemed American journalist, playwright, author, and critic. In the following review of the 11 November 1948 Broadway production of* Bravo!, *he argues that while the play has technical, structural problems, "it contains much of the stuff on which good plays are made."*]

The advance out-of-town reports on the play [*Bravo!*] were so fiercely grim that, having often after long experience become rather cynical in such cases, I went to the New York opening in a somewhat optimistic mood and learned, as sometimes in the past, that it was not entirely ill-founded. That rewriting had been done during the try-out period and even directly afterward was more or less apparent, but there was not enough of it to keep one from speculating why it is that plays which are condemned outright on the road frequently, when we get a look at them, are discovered to be not without some commendable qualities.

The reason is not altogether elusive. Plays like this are designed primarily for metropolitan showing and find themselves astray in other surroundings. The people they deal with are people with whom many New Yorkers are familiar yet who are recognized very faintly, if at all, in the thitherward communities. The humor, as well, is what for want of a more exact phrase may be termed New York humor and depends largely for its acceptance on acquaintance with persons, places, manners, language and eccentricities of conduct which are peculiar—and peculiar is surely the word—to the American metropolis. To expect an audience in even such a city as Boston to respond to something as intimately Manhattan, despite an appearance of more general scope, as various elements and flavors in a play like this is to believe that that audience in its personal constitution is identical in cosmopolitanism, attitude and idiosyncrasy with a New York one, a belief that would take some believing. I am not reflecting on the

Boston or any other out-of-town audience any more than I am vouching for any superiority in the New York audience; I simply argue the difference between them. While a New York audience may possibly not like the play any better than such a road one, which turned out to be true in this instance, the reasons for the dislike are not always the same.

That the play, about a group of Central European theatrical refugees trying to get a foothold in America, has its serious shortcomings, no one, least of all I, will contradict. Its dramaturgy here and there is patchy; it does not follow any perceptible direct line; and it intermittently goes off on rather incommodious tangents. But it has so much incidental honest sympathetic charm, so much droll observation of character and so much understanding humor that, in my case, it makes on the whole for agreeable alternately touching and comical diversion. And two better performances than Oscar Homolka's and Lili Darvas' as the displaced Molnár-like playwright and his inamorata whom for years he has been too busy to find time to marry, I have not seen since the season started.

They say that plays are not written but rewritten. They do not but should also say that, when they are rewritten—and at the last moment, as to a degree this one has been—plays are not only rehearsed but re-rehearsed. *Bravo!* has not been re-rehearsed enough, with the consequence that some of its rewritten last act finds its actors stumbling all over themselves and many of its points garbled. It is further evident that a little additional rewriting might have helped not only that final act but the preceding acts. Nevertheless, even as it stands, the play entertains me a deal more than many another theoretically more published one. Its characters in the main are freshly drawn; there is no dusty air, so common to many of these plays about theatre folk, in a larger portion of the dialogue; and the humor, to use a now moribund adjective of the early Twenties, is civilized. It may not, in the strict critical sense, be a good play—and just for the sake of professional standing let it so be recorded in these annals—but, good or not, it contains much of the stuff on which good plays are made.

John Barkham   (review date 28 September 1952)

SOURCE: "Where It's the Biggest and Bestest," in *The New York Times Book Review*, September 28, 1952, pp. 4-5.

[*In the following favorable review of* Giant, *Barkham argues that the novel presents a scathing view of Texas, one that Texans will probably resent.*]

If you haven't read Edna Ferber's name on any new novel lately, it isn't (as you might have suspected) because she was relaxing on the royalties from *Show Boat, Cimarron, Saratoga Trunk* and other movie masterpieces made from her books. On the contrary, it was because Miss Ferber was brewing the biggest witch's broth of a book to hit the great Commonwealth of Texas since the revered Spindle blew its top. Miss Ferber makes it very clear that she doesn't like the Texas she writes about, and it's a cinch that when Texans read what she has written about them

they won't like Miss Ferber either. Almost everyone else is going to revel in these pages.

For unsophisticated Easterners, *Giant* is going to be a guided tour to an incredible land unlike any they have ever seen before. (Texans, of course, have diligently fostered such a legend for years.) It outdoes anything our material culture has ever produced. Miss Ferber's Texas is the apotheosis of the grandiose, the culmination of that biggest-and-bestest cult peculiar to this side of the Atlantic. Whether it is recognizable to anyone inside of Texas is something else again. But *Giant* makes marvelous reading—wealth piled on wealth, wonder on wonder in a stunning, splendiferous pyramid of ostentation.

Her Texas was not altogether a surprise to this reviewer. Although he has not recently dallied at the Shamrock or shopped at Neiman-Marcus, he has run across oil aristocrats in the royal suites at the Savoy in London, the Grand in Stockholm and elsewhere, and has been suitably awed. And wasn't it Bob Ruark who recently told us in *Esquire* that in Texas even the midgets stood six feet high, and that you never met anybody there but rich millionaires and poor millionaires.

This is the Texas Miss Ferber has put into her bitter, brilliant, corrosive, excoriating novel. She refuses to genuflect to the lords of the oil wells or the barons of the ranches. Her Texas is a state where the skies are clamorous with four-engined DC-6's carrying alligator jewel cases and overbred furs, "where a mere Cadillac makes a fellow no better than a Mexican." An exaggeration? Perhaps, but one which Texans have put over.

It requires courage to take all this apart as scathingly as Miss Ferber has done; and in the process of so doing she paints a memorable portrait of that new American, *Texicanus vulgaris,* which is all warts and wampum.

She does this by marrying her heroine, Leslie, an elegant Virginian, to Jordan Benedict 3d, head of the Reata Ranch, whose frontiers stretch into the middle of tomorrow. When "Bick" brings his lovely, naïve bride into his cattle empire, he also takes with him a host of curious readers whose prying eyes are to be dazzled by what they see. It's a world of its own, "all noise and heat, big men and bourbon, and elegantly dressed, shrill-voiced women who needed only three plumes to be presented as they stood at the court of St. James." Gradually Leslie becomes familiar with the gradations of Texas wealth: as cotton once snooted at the cattle rich, so now the cattle rich sneer at the oil rich—with Miss Ferber sneering at all of them.

For our author believes passionately that this glorification of wealth is a massive and dangerous symptom in our body politic. She makes Leslie say things like: "Here in Texas we have very high buildings on very broad prairies, but very little high thinking or broad concepts." Most of all she resents the treatment of the Mexican-American in his native Texas. To the monolithic men in cream-colored Stetsons and tooled boots whose daughters cost a heifer a day to keep in Swiss finishing schools, the Mexican is a sub-human to be used as a *vaquero* or ranchhand but kept out of public places meant for white folks. To point her moral she makes one of the Benedict children marry a

Mexican, and subjects one of them to a supreme insult at a four-motor party.

Admittedly, this novel presents the Texan larger and more chromatic than life, but life-size is large enough. And it's true that people in big empty places like to behave as the gods did on Olympus. As for bigness, says Miss Ferber militantly, it's time Texans stopped confusing it with greatness. "Are sunflowers necessarily better than violets?"

It's easy to spend hours debating the rights and wrongs of this red-hot novel. It all depends where you come from and what you think of Cadillac-cum-Dallas culture. But no one can deny the explosive impact of this story. For all the slickness of its writing (and Miss Ferber is a past mistress of best seller style), *Giant* carries the kind of message that seldom finds expression in such chromium-plated prose. What's more, Miss Ferber states it with a conviction that carries the ring of sincerity. All this may make it impossible for her to revisit the great Commonwealth without the law at her hip, but at least she has written a book that sets the seal on her career.

It is possible, if other novelists rush in where Miss Ferber has not feared to tread, that the Houston-Dallas axis may replace Park Avenue-Bel Air as the symbol of opulence in our fiction. In that event, *Giant*—an October Book-of-the-Month choice—will become known as the first of our A. S. (After Spindletop) classics.

Florence Haxton Bullock   (review date 28 September 1952)

SOURCE: "Edna Ferber Tells a Big-as-Life Story of Oil-and-Cattle Texas," in *New York Herald Tribune Book Review,* September 28, 1952, p. 1.

[*In the following favorable review of* Giant, *Bullock examines Ferber's themes, characterizations, and portrayal of contemporary Texas life.*]

Edna Ferber does best with a big story: Chicago in its burgeoning youth, the rugged Southwest, life on the Mississippi in show boat days, New England in her period of decline—and now, in *Giant,* she gives us this big, reluctantly loving portrait of the fabulously rich outsize state of Texas, and the Texians (as Miss Ferber's quick ear hears them calling themselves). Caught up in this very satisfying personal story is all contemporary Texas, with some of its romantic past thrown in to show what lies back of the vigorous, generous, brassily arrogant present and the good and rather different future that Miss Ferber foresees on the way.

In the foreground of *Giant* is the great Riata Ranch, growing for a hundred years to its present three and a half million acres, improving its breed, building up a more than regal hereditary empire. (In the course of *Giant* it develops that a few of the big ranches are even now in process of being cut down to common-man size.) And alongside Riata in recent years, and much too close for comfort, are the rich new oil wells pouring their molten gold into the hands of new-rich millionaires. Free and reckless as birds of prey, these oil men think nothing of flying their elegant-

ly equipped four-motored planes a thousand miles to glossy, roistering parties; while their wives and daughters solo forth in the morning in their one or two engined "little bitty" planes, their hair in curlers, to pick up a hamburger at Joe's or some needed condiment for lunch. *Giant*'s story is wide enough, too, to include the lowly vaqueros, among them the descendants of old Spanish families or Mexican Americans, some of whom were herding their own cattle on the Texas plains long before the Yanquis came in to crowd them out. Now they sell a man's courage, endurance, skill for trivial wages and a squalid shanty to house their wives and children. Even the "wet backs" have their part in this inclusive yet always highly personal Texas story.

Giant begins on a recent March day when "the vast and brassy sky, always spangled with the silver glint of airplanes, roared and glittered with celestial traffic." Everybody who was anybody in the whole length and breadth of Texas was en route to Jett Rink's party at the Conquistador. The Jordan Benedicts of Riata Ranch were going reluctantly, and taking with them their usual miscellany of house guests, including the ex-King and Queen of Sergovia. Mrs. Benedict (Leslie)—one of the smartest, best bred women in Texas—was "dressed for the air journey—blue shantung and no hat." That the Benedicts should consent to come to his party was a major triumph for that flamboyantly new-rich Johnny-come-lately scoundrel Jett Rink. Jett had, not too long ago, been one of the Riata's ranch hands, and even then was impertinent enough boldly to admire the Riata's sacrosanct mistress. At the party a dramatic, physical clash takes place which sends the novel scurrying back into the Benedicts' past to find out what has led up to this public, brutal "kneeing" of young Jordan, scion of the great Riata ranch, by his mannerless mongrel host.

Upwards of twenty years ago Leslie came, a girl of spirit and ideas, from a highly civilized Virginia background, to the great family-owned Riata, and found herself a captive bride. Captive in the sense that she was compelled by custom and her husband's prejudices to live a closely restricted life. Leslie had never dreamed that women in her exalted position were actually second-class citizens in a man's world.

Leslie was disturbed by other inequalities, too—by the poverty of her husband's ranch hands, and by the inhumane social and economic barriers existing everywhere else in Texas between the Mexicans and Spanish-Americans and the arrogantly race-proud top-dog American Texians. When all her efforts to do a little something about it were thwarted. Leslie dutifully devoted herself to building a civilized life for her husband, and children, replacing the barracks-like Big House with a beautifully managed home. But she continued to oppose her husband's and everybody else's opinions in the areas where she thought they and all Texas were wrong. So that in the end—by the time the *Giant* story reaches the here and now once more—Leslie's independent-minded children, each in his or her own highly individual, very modern way, were ready to turn to and help build a new Texas upon the feudalism, the bigotry, the abundant riches of the past.

The "ideas" in *Giant* are all deeply imbedded in its fascinating story. Round-ups, barbecues, spectacular parties and lowly "wetbacks"—all the decors of contemporary Texas life, from costumes by Neiman-Marcus to current political wrestlings between the new industrial communities financed by oil vs the big ranches—play their lively part in this big-as-life, colorful portrait of changing Texas. *Giant* is a real Edna Ferber novel!

Phoebe Lou Adams   (review date October 1952)

SOURCE: "At War with Texas," in *The Atlantic Monthly*, Vol. 190, No. 4, October, 1952, pp. 100-01.

[*Adams is an American writer and critic. In the following review of* Giant, *she favorably assesses its plot, themes, and characterizations.*]

The state of Texas is hero, heroine, villain, and supporting cast in Edna Ferber's new novel, *Giant* and at that, Miss Ferber doesn't pretend to deal with the whole state. She has settled for that portion of Texas with more than ten millions, plus its Mexican retainers. That adds up to a large number of people, but Texas overshadows all of them.

Although Miss Ferber writes to entertain, and never fails to do it with an expert mixture of action, sentiment, humor, and melodrama, two themes not usually classed as entertainment have appeared in most of her novels. One is the corrosive effect of money, and the other is the evil of group prejudices. Texas, rich and frankly anti-Mexican, was made to order as a showcase for these topics, and at times Miss Ferber seems on the verge of forgetting her plot altogether in order to pursue them. She never quite does it, though.

The plot in question has to do with Leslie Lynnton, more or less of Virginia, who marries Jordan Benedict, very decidedly of Reata Ranch, and begins a war with Texas that will last as long as she lives, to say nothing of the length of a novel. She dislikes the cooking, the lack of intellectual activity, the preoccupation with money, and the virtual disenfranchisement of citizens with Mexican ancestry. "When the hell are you going to settle down and behave like everybody else?" roars her exasperated husband, who is quite satisfied with Texas as it stands. "Never," says Leslie.

The Benedict family fracas rolls through the book, never losing the reader's interest because of the variety and picturesqueness of the life that inspires it. Although Leslie and Jordan refuse to change, Texas changes around them at astonishing speed. It seems to get bigger and more ornate with every paragraph. A vote by the assembled Benedict clansmen compels Jordan to permit oil wells on Reata, and the oil wells reduce cattle ranching, the love of his life, to the status of a rich man's toy. The children get disconcerting ideas. The feudal devotion of the Mexican ranch hands dies with the old men whose sons, back from Iwo Jima or the Coral Sea, display an unaccountable resentment of the status of second-class citizens. Cattle

millionaires, once scorned by cotton millionaires, now scorn oil millionaires. Practically everybody is a millionaire, though, with more money, brighter jewels, stronger liquor, bigger airplanes, colder air-conditioning plants, and duller conversation than anyone else on earth.

Miss Ferber makes no predictions about the future of Texas. She records her view of the state's present tartly, deftly, with a relish for bizarre detail. Uncle Bawley (a charming but tearful old gentleman who discovers after fifty years of ranching that he is allergic to cattle) draining bacon on a cow chip is a figure not easily forgotten.

Ernest Gruening   (review date 30 March 1958)

SOURCE: "Edna Ferber's Novel of Alaska's Dreams and Dramas," in *New York Herald Tribune Book Review*, March 30, 1958, p. 1.

[*Gruening, who served as governor of Alaska from 1939 to 1953 and senator from 1958 to 1969, was also a critic and author of several books about Alaska. In the following favorable review, he examines the plot, characters, and themes of* Ice Palace.]

A painting of Alaska influenced by modern abstractional tendencies would be large, sparkling, brilliant with blues—of sky and sea—gleaming with whites of mammoth glaciers and towering peaks, vivid with the warm greens of virgin forest and tundra, crowned with the gold of the Midnight Sun, shimmering with the yellows and purples of long twilights or of the wavering aurora, and flashed with the crimson and pink that suggest the bustle of vibrant human life.

Such is the arresting picture, though not abstract, that Edna Ferber, great word painter, has splashed on her book-length canvas, *Ice Palace*. The title will give Alaskans a shudder—since for ninety-one years they have sought to refute the myth that "Seward's Folly" is a scarcely habitable land of snow and ice—until they discover that the Ice Palace of the novel is not Alaska, but a fourteen-story apartment-hotel, housing every modern convenience: a super-market, shops, restaurant, beauty parlor, etc., a city under one roof. Its official name is the Kennedy Building, but its pressed glass walls have given it its accepted nickname.

It is the creation of one of the principal characters, a self-made tycoon, Zebedee Kennedy, known as "Czar Kennedy," whose prototype all Alaskans will recognize. Coming to Alaska in the gold rush days, he cannily forwent the mad prospectors' scramble, engaging instead in the more certainly remunerative supplying of their wants. In time, he erected an economic empire of motion picture theaters, apartment houses, a newspaper, a coal mine, and later, radio stations.

He is not the only fictional character drawn from reality. Alaskans will identify the Seattle fisheries magnate, Dave Husack, forty years previously an immigrant peasant boy, retaining his middle-European accent. They will see resemblances—if not likenesses—to other persons living or recently deceased.

The scene is laid in Baranof, a mythical composite city in central Alaska, which comes closer to resembling Fairbanks than any other Alaskan community—with variations, since Baranof is both buttressed by lofty mountains, and on the sea, which Fairbanks is not. The design, following the formula in Miss Ferber's Texas novel *Giant,* is an Alaskan urban common denominator.

"Every third woman you passed on Gold Street in Baranof was young, pretty, and pregnant. The men, too, were young, virile, and pregnant with purpose. Each, making his or her way along the bustling business street, seemed actually to bounce with youth and vitality."

Thus the people of today's Alaska. But also of yesterday's:

"Only an occasional sourdough relic dating back to the gold-rush days of fifty years ago, wattled and wary as a turkey cock, weaving his precarious way in and out of the frisky motor traffic, gave the humming town a piquant touch of anachronism."

Ferber, in almost documentary fashion, deals with Alaska as a whole: its character, its drama, its potentials, its basic problem, and its people.

—*Ernest Gruening*

The heroine of the story is lovely, teenage Christine Storm. Both parents died in her infancy under dramatic circumstances, peculiarly Alaskan. Her mother was the daughter of Czar Kennedy and of a Tacoma lumber heiress, who herself died of grief over the death of her daughter and son-in-law. Christine's father was the son of Thor Storm, a giant of brain and brawn, who had emigrated from Norway as a youth, came to Alaska on the same boat with Kennedy, and had struck up an association of sorts with him. The orphaned Chris—as she was called by all—had been brought up by the two doting grandfathers, with the assistance of Bridie Ballantyne, once a trained nurse, but now, in her sixties, the attractive, dynamic greeter of Baranof. The two grandfathers, linked by their love for Chris and for Alaska, differ profoundly in their outlook on life. Beneath the ties which bind them lie deep divergences. They come to light continually in the editorial conflict between Czar Kennedy's "Daily Lode" and Thor Storm's weekly "Northern Light," both published in Baranof.

It is Czar Kennedy's ambition to marry his granddaughter to Bayard Husack, playboy son of the fisheries magnate, to combine their two economic empires for the greater control of Alaska, and through their joint influences get young Husack appointed governor of Alaska. To achieve their objective, Kennedy and Husack conspire to bring Bayard to Baranof with a very beautiful siren, Dina Drake, who is acting as one of Dave Husack's secretaries, and is hoping to capture Bay, to whom she is reportedly

engaged. The design is to awaken sufficient jealousy in Chris, to kindle her affection for young Bay. The party arrives in Baranof with a retinue which includes, besides the Husacks, a just-retired general, appointed as a front for a Seattle salmon-packing concern, a fisheries lobbyist, Arne Kleet, and an official of the Department of the Interior. The Baranof Chamber of Commerce stages a welcome for these V.I.P. s, as the story opens.

The plot proceeds from there. It is a continuing struggle between the two grandfathers for control of Chris' mind and life. Interwoven, also, is the struggle between the opposing forces that would keep Alaska a territory, represented by Czar Kennedy and Dave Husack, and those who perceive its great destiny in the liberation by statehood, a cause fervently espoused by Thor and Chris Storm and Bridie Ballantyne, outspoken rebels against the economic and political forces that have, for decades, exploited Alaska, and have kept it in Colonial servitude. The action moves to Oogruk, another mythical town resembling Kotzebue, and to a "scene" in the United States Senate, when the Alaska Statehood Bill is up.

After many exciting incidents, which will make first-class motion-picture material, the story draws to a close with the death of Chris' two grandfathers.

There has been considerable book-length fiction about Alaska—Jack London's, Rex Beach's, Edison Marshall's. Their novels have dealt with different episodes and aspects of Alaska's variegated life. Edna Ferber, in almost documentary fashion, deals with Alaska as a whole; its character, its drama, its potentials, its basic problem, and its people, whom she obviously likes and admires, and with whose aspirations she clearly sympathizes. *Ice Palace* vividly and understandingly gives us glimpses of Alaska as it was, pictures it as it is—in transition—and suggests inspiringly what it may become. Thus we have the first all-Alaskan novel, of a scope befitting "the Great Land."

Elizabeth Janeway   (review date 30 March 1958)

SOURCE: "Strong Men Face to Face," in *The New York Times Book Review,* March 30, 1958, p. 4.

[*Janeway, whose husband was the noted economist Eliot Janeway, is an American novelist, educator, nonfiction writer, and critic. In the following mixed review of* Ice Palace, *she applauds the nonfictional, historical aspects of the novel, arguing that the plot is "absent-minded to the point of being ramshackle."*]

It was a maxim of my father's, quoted from a source I have unhappily forgotten, that the purpose of local color in writing is "to give artistic verisimilitude to an otherwise bald and unconvincing narrative" [in a footnote, Janeway adds that the line was "spoken by Pooh Bah in W. S. Gilbert's *The Mikado*"]. Whether Edna Ferber is familiar with this quotation I don't know, but her new novel, *Ice Palace,* is one of the most forceful illustrations of its validity that I have ever come across. A plot which is absent-minded to the point of being ramshackle, and smudged lay figures who have served as characters from the days of Robert W. Chambers if not of Ouida, are here combined with quite interesting bits of Alaskan history and atmosphere. The result is a hybrid form in which the fictional element has nearly succumbed to the nonfictional.

Actually, the local color is quite amusing, though not amusing enough to achieve its desired end. The narrative remains uncompromisingly bald. But it is evident that Miss Ferber has worked very hard. She has certainly been to Alaska, and flown all over it, and talked to hundreds of its inhabitants, and read many books on the subject. Having thus labored, she has brought forth a sort of movie script married to a survey of geography, industry and politics in our largest territorial possession. Readers, asked what *Ice Palace* is about, will reply that it is about Alaska and so it is, much more than it is about any of the characters who nominally animate its pages.

We begin with two strong men meeting face to face aboard a boat plying north from Seattle in Gold Rush days. One is good and one is bad, and one is rich and one is poor, and one is liberal and one is not. Since Miss Ferber is a passionate devotee of the "flashback," we meet them first in the present, but are soon swept off in the author's time-machine for a look at the past twenty chapters long.

The good, poor, liberal old man, Thor Storm, is the owner of a crusading newspaper. He is also (a proper Ouida touch) the descendant of Norwegian kings who fled to the new world because he did not wish to lead the artificial life required of kings' descendants. The rest of the plot, however, is more Lanny-Budding than Graustarkian, for the bad, rich, reactionary but charming old man, Czar Kennedy, is working closely with Seattle millionaires who are exploiting Alaska and preventing it from becoming a state. The two old men share a granddaughter, Christine, a black-eyed blonde and our heroine. Two young men are competing for Christine's hand—the indolent son of one of the millionaires, and a poor, good, liberal, half-Eskimo airline pilot.

Miss Ferber seems definitely more interested in the facts that her research has turned up than in the perfunctory structure she has thrown together to hang them on, for when she is faced with a choice between romance and a description of the Alaskan canned-fish industry, the cannery wins every time. A wedding breakfast is followed by no honeymoon scene, but by a survey of the housing shortage in the city the author has named Baranof.

The volume of instruction covered by a sugar-coating of fiction to make it palatable has been with us for a long time. Miss Ferber, however, has now carried the process so far that she has produced a pill of fiction with a sugar-coating of good honest research. A few old-fashioned readers with an anachronistic affection for fiction will regret that such a production should be billed as a novel.

Edward Weeks   (review date May 1958)

SOURCE: "Where Men are the Men," in *The Atlantic Monthly,* Vol. 201, No. 5, May, 1958, pp. 78, 80.

[*In the following mixed review, Weeks applauds the geographical and historical scope of* Ice Palace, *but contends that the believability of the characters and plot are compromised by Ferber's "theatricality."*]

In *The Emma McChesney Stories,* Edna Ferber staked out her claim as a delineator of American character; and in *Show Boat* she gave us one of the most appealing romances of the stage. Thereafter, in novels like *Cimarron* and *Giant,* she has written of the big operator, the limitless and often unscrupulous development of our natural resources, and the corrupting effect of power and wealth upon the individual. In *Ice Palace* she has moved her setting to Alaska, our last frontier, and again she is writing about big strapping men: Thor Storm and Czar Kennedy (the very names spell strength), Thor with his Norwegian heritage and Henry George philosophy, Czar with his Yankee shrewdness and his greed to own the whole place. They came over on the same boat, pioneered together, and for fifty years have rivaled each other. Now, as Miss Ferber puts it, they are waging "a silent persistent battle for the welfare—as they saw it—of the girl Christine." Chris is their solitary grandchild, born in the carcass of a caribou in a howling blizzard; she is twenty-five when the story opens, unmarried, black-eyed, golden-haired, hard to curb. The question is, Who will do it?

This reads to me like an old Morality. Czar's associates from Outside, the boys from Seattle—Dave Husack, Sid Kleet, and Cass Baldwin—are the very embodiment of those predatory commercial interests which have been trying to monopolize Alaska for the past half century. For reasons of profit they oppose statehood, and for the same reasons they would suppress every local spokesman with the courage to oppose their schemes. The history of Seward's Purchase, the story of the early reckless days, of the potential locked in these vast northlands have been carefully built into the novel, but the pity of it is that by her process of overenlargement, Miss Ferber makes the picture seem less than believable.

Part of the trouble is traceable to her extravagant phrasing. I am prepared to believe that everything in Alaska is larger than life, except human nature, which I suspect must be pretty much the same there as it is here. Yet in phrases like these the author does less than justice to her people: "Oscar's little eyes narrowed to slits"; "A little cold white flame of dislike shot from beneath Czar Kennedy's eyelids"; "he ruffled the silver plumes of his hair"; "tossing the amber stuff down their throats with one quick backward jerk of the head"; "Sid Kleet's steely voice cut the tension"; "Her hatless head was like a golden torch"; "His lethal gaze searched the crowd, passionless and coldly menacing as the eye of a Colt .38." Phrases like these are as subtle as brass knuckles. Apart from such theatricality, the virtue of this book is the fact that Miss Ferber cares deeply about the future both of Alaska and of mankind. As she makes clear in Thor's last statement to Chris: "What a lovely world. The loveliest. We've had it, a gift, for a million million years, and now we're throwing it away. A pity. Alaska, the arsenal. It should be free."

W. G. Rogers   (review date 8 September 1963)

SOURCE: "In the Moonlight and Magnolia the Protest

Was Lost," in *The New York Times Book Review,* September 8, 1963, p. 6.

[*Rogers was an American journalist and critic. In the following review of* A Kind of Magic, *he suggests that while "Miss Ferber bares no soul" in this autobiography, she provides insights into her career and the times in which she lived and worked.*]

Edna Ferber again, we ask ourselves? When hasn't there been Edna Ferber? About 40 years ago she gave us the Pulitzer winner, *So Big* followed by *Show Boat* and *Cimarron.* Her public, she says, extends over four generations. She keeps on like "Ol' Man River," and we're glad of it, and we're lucky.

She's lucky, too, in her parentage, in what she describes as her "declarative and purposeful" self, in her health, her drive, even her name, which is a clipped and catchy run of four syllables, easy to remember, short enough to fit the spine of a book or, in bright lights, a theater entrance.

Over the years there have been a lot of theaters, and there still are, she doesn't hesitate to remind us. She has done six plays, five in collaboration with George S. Kaufman, and also written 25 books, including this one [*A Kind of Magic*].

Her life divides roughly in three quarter-century stretches. She refers to herself as old and gray, without really meaning it, no doubt; her busy days certainly belie that, and who ever heard of an old gray dynamo? In four years of Midwest newspaper work, she covered everything which, she says, was not marked "Men Only." She had a real character for a mother, Julia; her father, Jacob, Hungarian-born Jew, went blind and left his wife to run a general store and bring up two daughters. Generous swatches of Julia help fill out many Ferber fictional persons, as in the ever popular Emma McChesney.

Her first book came out 52 years ago. Her first quarter-century of writing was described in her autobiographical *A Peculiar Treasure* of 1939. That was, in a way, she recalls, a patriotic gesture. If other Americans must remain indifferent to Hitler, she would answer him with a picture of a middle-class Jewish family in America.

This book, covering the third quarter-century, is about Ferber, writing, food, war, women Negroes, our fine but less than perfect country, and how wonderful it is to be alive. Miss Ferber's sturdy old fashioned strain shows in her nostalgia for the long-ago childhoods that were not pampered, and the outmoded pleasures of walking. Her attitude toward Negroes is only one of her unwavering liberal convictions. Muckraker Ida Tarbell was one of her idols, and there's a wide streak of unconventional Tarbell daring in the Ferber thinking.

Deciding she must have a little country place, say half an acre, where she could work without interruption, she wound up, amazingly, with 116 acres on a hilltop, and built a 14-room house with swimming pool, gardens, drives, terraces. During the war she did assignments for the Writers' War Board, sold bonds by speaking and contributing her own manuscripts for auction, and served for a time in Europe in captain's uniform. A visit to Buchenwald horrified her. She partly recovered from the appalling shock by mixing with American soldiers—she is sociable and has a host of friends. A soldier repeated from memory a passage from *Show Boat.* It was a tonic, a renewal, a heart-to-heart communication. She calls it "A Kind of Magic"—a magic she works in this volume only in the stirring account of wartime.

Her novels were written as protest, she says, but adds "loving protest." She exaggerates their social vigor and bite. "Ol' Man River," to her is "a compassionate and terrible indictment of the white man's treatment of the Negro." Jerome Kern and Oscar Hammerstein wrote a moving song, but with more moonlight and magnolia than revolt, and no one ever came away from *Show Boat* book or musical, determined to fight segregation. To her, *Saratoga Trunk* is about "the rape of America" by "the land grabbers . . . the old-time railroad millionaires." Of course it's only the love affair, now dated, of a daughter of the New Orleans red-light district and a handsome, broad-shouldered uncouth Texan.

Miss Ferber bares no soul here, but says a lot of very sharp, astute things—the very things that sparked her books. Nevertheless while the novels will not serve as models for future novels, Miss Ferber herself will serve as model for future novelists. She has been unremittingly dedicated to her task. She is the 24-hour a day professional, forthright and uncompromising. As a working woman, writer, she has no superior.

Ellen Serlen Uffen (essay date 1980)

SOURCE: "Edna Ferber and the 'Theatricalization' of American Mythology," in *Midwestern Miscellany,* Vol. VII, 1980, pp. 82-93.

[*In the following essay, Uffen explores the mythical aspects of Ferber's novels, focusing on her use of "larger-than-life" characters, the differences between her heroes and heroines, and the ways in which she uses American geography to reflect the essence of her protagonists.*]

The enormous popularity of Edna Ferber's novels lay in her ability to create a consistent fictional universe based in popularly known and accepted American mythology: plucky, self-reliant boys and girls gain success and fame in colorful settings ranging from the old Wild West to the new wilds of Alaska. All aspects of Ferber's work—plot, character, setting, style—partake of the myth. Other writers, of course, have also used myth, but more narrowly, as allusion, as metaphor, as extended literary motif and, often, as thematic contrast to the reality of the events being depicted. Fitzgerald, for one, mourned its loss in *The Great Gatsby;* Faulkner satirized it in *Old Man;* and "popular" authors have often played on its surefire ability to strike chords of longing in the reader. All of these writers, however, no matter what the relative merits of their work, implicitly view myth as just that—unreal, a product of literature, of historic tradition, as stories inextricably interwoven into the fabric of American culture. Edna Ferber, in the guise of implied author, differs in that she believes in mythology as reality, or more precisely, as paradigmatic real possibility. This belief almost naturally shapes the fiction. Moreover, since she accepts so unquestioningly her own reification of the fantastic, the audience can as well. Her quite childlike belief in a showboat universe still attracts us today by its charm, its naivete, and it attracted her contemporary audience as well by its wide divergence from the reality of the Wars and the Depression during which she wrote. Like children listening to fairy tales, we believe. In this response of her audience lies Ferber's basic appeal.

Ferber's use of mythology, perhaps the necessity for its use, may be explained in great part by the fact that she was raised as a Jew in the Midwest. Born in 1887, in Kalamazoo, Michigan, she moved with her family to the small town of Ottumwa, Iowa, in 1890. There she would spend the seven years which, she realized later, were "more enriching, more valuable than all the fun and luxury of the New York years" of her success [*A Peculiar Treasure*]. This "value" derived from a negative source, anti-Semitism. Continually subjected to the cruel bigotry of the townspeople, while still a child Ferber learned to fight back; she learned to dramatize, perhaps "melodramatize" herself as the persecuted one surrounded by inferior enemies, and she learned to make her own escapist world through reading and through "playing show," staging little theatricals for her family.

From Ottumwa, the Ferbers moved to Appleton, Wisconsin, where Edna was to live the next thirteen years of her life. The prosperous, lively, friendly town taught the Ferbers another side of America. It was here, it may be safely assumed, that Edna developed the love for America which would be so evident in her future work. Appleton, that is, created what may be thought of as the mood, or tonal aspect of her work—the enthusiasm and joy in America—and Ottumwa created the framework for its articulation—the dramatic structure. The actual content of the books developed later, through Ferber's many years of travel all over the United States.

Ferber, in all her travels, took great pleasure in the various types of people she encountered. This, too, becomes evident in her novels. Her fictional world focuses on its inhabitants. For this reason, her books tell simple, often similar stories, and contain little plot. Critics whose expectations have been formed on novelistic techniques quite different from Ferber's see this narrative simplicity as a fault. Witness the following overall summary from James Gray: Ferber's fiction, he tells us, "habitually takes a firm, possessive hold upon a heroine and leads her resolutely through a series of highly contrived incidents in a standardized siege against the citadel of success" [*On Second Thought*, 1946]. The sense of Gray's summary is not entirely wrong, since it does describe one aspect of *So Big, Show Boat, Cimarron, Saratoga Trunk,* for just a few. What *is* wrong is the implied negative evaluation caused by his failure to take into account that Ferber's method concentrates not on plot, as he implicitly assumes, but on character portrayal. Since nothing may be allowed to overshadow character, the plot is intended as only one of a number of revelatory containers, so to speak. Moreover, since Ferber's aim is the revelation specifically of mythic character, traditional expectations will not hold here, ei-

ther. She is not concerned with subtleties of feeling, nor does she intend the reader to investigate her people too deeply. Hers is characterization by tic, by literary leitmotif. Her heroes—and I use that word in its most traditional and popular sense—are indeed those of mythology, flat figures in any real sense, because known only from the outside. Her people do not think. Their world is one of action. They are rooted not to history, but to wherever they happen to be in the fictional present. They are larger-than-life in exploits, and even physique.

Although Ferber's authorial sympathies, as Gray suggests, seem to lean toward her women, her interest in mythic character nevertheless results in a strong concentration on the male character. Her men are spectacular, magnificent, expansive, attractive and, most important perhaps, self-consciously theatrical, all these traits befitting their mythic heritage. The gambler, the sonorously named Gaylord Ravenal, of *Show Boat* (1926), for instance, has both "a gift for painting about himself the scenery of romance," and a "sense of the dramatic" which "did not confine itself to the stage. He was the juvenile lead, on and off." About Clint Maroon of *Saratoga Trunk* (1941), we are told, in a style as expansive as the sense of its language, that "He was magnificent, he was vast, he was beautiful, he was crude, he was rough, he was untamed, he was Texas." He was also, according to his wife, Clio, "melodrama come to life." Another Texan, Jordan ("Bick") Benedict of *Giant* (1952), is "benign and arrogant. Benevolent and ruthless," "a figure of steel and iron and muscle." Vaughan Melendy, of the lesser-known *Great Son* (1945), is of "heroic stature," a "benevolent giant." But perhaps the most outstanding example of the quintessential Ferber hero is Yancey Cravat of *Cimarron* (1930). Ferber gives us the following description of Yancey's qualities, which include

> great sweetness and charm of manner, an hypnotic eye . . . Something of the charlatan was in him, much of the actor, a dash of the fanatic . . . Yancey . . . was a bizarre, glamorous, and slightly mythical figure. No room seemed big enough for his gigantic frame; no chair but dwindled beneath the breadth of his shoulders. He seemed actually to loom more than his six feet two. His black locks he wore overlong, so that they curled a little about his neck in the manner of Booth.. ..

Ferber's women, in contrast, are vastly different from her men and inhabit a plane much closer to reality. In context of the novels, they provide steadiness and security; they are the keepers of traditional American values; they are the workers, the depiction of whom Ferber was so proud. They help their men with great, but quiet strength. Selina De Jong, for one, of *So Big* (1924), married to an unsuccessful truck farmer,

> literally tore a living out of the earth with her two bare hands. Yet there was nothing pitiable about this small energetic woman. . . . Rather there was something splendid about her; something rich, prophetic. It was the splendor and richness that achievement imparts.

Ferber's books are replete with courageous, dependable

women like Selina: Sabra, wife of the fabulous Yancey; Pansy, of **Great Son,** in love with the married Vaughan Melendy, the father of her son; Leslie, of **Giant**. These women are sympathetic, even admirable. We see the events mostly through their eyes and it is a perspective whose validity we do not question.

In the novels of another author, perhaps these women would be heroines. Here, however, they are overwhelmed by the sheer magnificence of the men, and this is because Ferber is a bit in love with her own heroes. She wants them to hold center stage. Sometimes a woman tries to take over the stage, but the author sternly forbids it. When Chris Storm, for instance, of **Ice Palace** (1958), granddaughter of the two heroic, male figures of that novel, threatens to burst out of her role, she is told by an older, wiser woman, who interestingly uses the language of fiction for the purpose, that she is in danger of becoming "A rounded character," when "Everybody ought to have anyway one slab side." And Ferber also makes sure that Clio Maroon is put into her place when necessary. She, perhaps more than any other of Ferber's women, possesses the extravagance and flambuoyance of the men. But despite the vitality with which Ferber endows her, we are told by an intrusive authorial voice possessed of highly suspect psychological acumen, that "Like all domineering women she wanted, more than anything in the world, to be dominated by someone stronger than she." That single statement takes the fire from Clio and returns it to Clint where we are meant to understand it belongs.

Ferber herself seems, at times, to be somewhat embarrassed by her own attitude toward her women. As if to compensate for her odd authorial anti-feminism, she makes an attempt to bring her men down a peg by assigning them certain flaws—stubbornness, power madness, irresponsibility. But Ferber is so much taken by heroism that she (consciously or not) overcompensates. That is, she gives her men as well a certain childlike amorality, the charming innocence of the American Adam and this works, conversely, to mitigate—in fact, excuse—whatever else is imperfect about them. So Purvis De Jong's pride and stubbornness may be destroying both himself and his family, but how can we think too badly of a man who has "about him the loveableness and splendor of the striken giant"? Nor are we free to follow our own feminist instincts and hate Yancey Cravat for leaving Sabra and their children for months and years at a time: it is, after all, in character for adventurous men to follow adventure. Even his relatively conservative townspeople—the novel's chorus—agree. They are shocked by the casualness of his departures and returns, yet they cannot stay away when he does return:

> Perhaps he represented, for them, the thing they fain would be or have. When Yancey, flouting responsibility and convention, rode away to be gone for mysterious years, a hundred men, bound by ties of work and wife and child, escaped in spirit with him; a hundred women, faithful wives and dutiful mothers, thought of Yancey as the elusive, the romantic, the desirable male.

The reader, part of the chorus, greets Yancey as wholeheartedly as everyone else upon his return. Our fictional universe had indeed become dull without him.

Ferber's novels, for all their old-time melodrama and theatricality, are plays without villains.

—Ellen Serlen Uffen

In **Giant,** a similar situation exists: Yancey's irresponsibility is here Bick Benedict's power madness. It is diagnosed by his physician father-in-law, a sympathetic and, therefore, trustworthy character, as "dedication." Even Jett Rink, also of **Giant,** as close to a villain as Edna Ferber ever created, will not be allowed the role of bad guy. He is coarse, brutal, savage, sadistic, yet he, as much as Bick Benedict, is a "living legend," and along with Bick, another symbol of Texas. It also does not hurt Ferber's purpose that he is in love with Bick's wife, Leslie. If women readers are meant to identify with Leslie, to hate Jett would be tantamount to undermining our own attractiveness. Ferber counts on her readers' vanity. Her novels, for all their oldtime melodrama and theatricality, are plays without villains. The myth remains pristine.

The theatricality of the novels is, in fact, precisely what works to sustain our belief in the myth and in the men who live it. The characters, that is, function in an undeniably fictive universe. But paradoxically, in the reading, the very consistency and, thus, self-containment of the fiction makes it "real" for the moment. We can enter Ferber's books completely; our own reality never threatens, nor does it even beckon. Her enticements are not of our world and that is exactly why they are enticing. Interestingly, within the books, when a version of reality which is similar to ours does begin to beckon—usually in the form of those "traditional" women—Ferber does not allow it even then to defeat the fiction. The audience roots for the men, for romance and for myth, and the author responds. The women may retain our intellectual sympathy, but our emotional and, for the space of the reading, more substantial sympathies, lie with the larger-than-life men leading extraordinary lives.

We, Ferber's readers, are as much a part of her theater as her characters. She writes for an audience she recreates in every book, for a giant show-boat audience, composed of "naive people. That which they saw they believed. They hissed the villain, applauded the heroine, wept over the plight of the wronged." Interestingly, in one incident, the show-boat audience becomes so much a part of what they are viewing that when a potential villain begins to unleash his villainy on a stage beauty in distress, a member of the audience takes aim with a gun. The onstage villain, seeing the offstage gun aimed in his direction, "released his struggling victim. Gentleness and love overspread his features, dispelling their villainy." Just as the fictional actor responds here to the wishes, albeit crudely expressed, of the fictional audience, so Ferber in her work responds to her larger, real audience's wishes. We want no villains. The scene in *Show Boat,* like the earlier advice given to Chris Storm, is an odd example of technical explanation, Ferber's brand of self-literary criticism.

The theatrical milieu, then, can be understood overall not only as a metaphor modifying her characters' fictional mode of existence, but also as a distancing device, functioning to separate us as much as possible from our own reality, while, at the same time, enabling us, as much as possible, to enter into the fictional reality. The novels in themselves illustrate and mirror this function. The characters consciously play-act, as if to remove themselves even from their (too-real) fictional reality. Clint Maroon's acting is constantly referred to, as is Yancey Cravat's. In *Show Boat* there is even a "real" love scene acted out on stage between Gaylord and Magnolia, as if to imply that the theatrical milieu is somehow a more appropriate and, perhaps, safer one in which to function. This moves us a step further into the fiction.

But Ferber's dramas are well-made ones, and so, within her large system, she also employs various smaller distancing devices. If we are to believe in the myth which she presents through her characters, the stage must be more populated in order for it to appear as complete and as self-contained as our world. Accordingly, there are many minor actors, character types, or literary walk-ons. Some of these people are as fantastic as the leads, albeit writ much smaller and much more rapidly. *Show Boat,* as might be expected, contains an entire cast of minor characters, among whom are Andy, Magnolia's hearty, slightly comic father (played in the 1951 movie, with a fine eye for casting, by Joe E. Brown); Parthy, her shrewish, yet slightly comic mother; and Windy, the tobacco-chewing, eccentric, "best pilot on the rivers." In *Cimarron* there is Dr. Don Valliant, "the most picturesque man of medicine in the whole Southwest," with a name to match. *American Beauty* contains its own side show: Jot Oakes, "one of those jolly little dwarfs you see in German gardens—a gnome, stepped out of Rip Van Winkle's long sleep"; and Big Bella, "a heathen Buddha . . . with the body of a giantess, the bones of a behemoth." *Saratoga Trunk,* for one last example, has the elegant, black servant woman, Kakaracou, and the bizarre dwarf coachman, Cupidon.

Ferber's other distancing devices are more subtle and, much like her earlier blanket aim in creating a larger-than-life world, distinctly different from ours and, therefore, posing it no threat, so her other techniques are also aimed at "saving" her audience fear and anxiety. Although we are meant to "identify," the identification must never threaten discomfort. This is why Ferber presents many of her stories in flashback form, a more sophisticated, novelistic version of "Once upon a time. . . ." When a character in a flashback is presented on page one, we can be sure, whatever will befall, that the character has survived. Subsequent threats to life, limb and livelihood become much less threatening than they might be in another narrative and this comforts us. We can relax, for instance, when the eighty-nine-year-old Clint Maroon appears with his seventy-nine-year-old wife, Clio, at the outset of *Saratoga*

Trunk, or when we are told by the narrator of *So Big,* with unquestionable omniscience, that Selina's son would become "in later years . . . the Dirk De Jong whose name you saw (engraved) at the top of heavy cream linen paper." Things, rest assured, could not have been awful if these people appear both alive and prosperous at the end. We can comfortably read on.

Ferber makes sure that our comfort lasts from chapter to chapter. Accordingly, she allows little unplesantness and even less suspense, both potential anxiety-causers. She must allow *some* unpleasantness—such is part of life—but unlike when it occurs in our own lives, here we can prepare for it. If we are to be treated to any serious unpleasantness, we are told at the beginning of a chapter how the present incident will end. If a character, for example, is to die, we know it immediately and, even then, Ferber's actual presentation of the event saves us even further. When Captain Andy of *Show Boat* meets a violent death during a river fog, we see it through the confused and bewildered eyes of a child, his granddaughter. The event thus loses its sharpness and terror for us as well as for the child. Or death can sometimes, as in *Cimarron,* be presented as a romantic result of heroism. The death of Yancey lends the final, melodramatic flourish to his life. He catches a can of nitroglycerine, thus saving many lives, and dies in the arms of his wife, Sabra, whom he has not seen for many years, reciting the words of "Peer Gynt, humbled before Solveig." We are hardly saddened by this. More likely, the reader's response fits the mode of being of Yancey: "What better way to go?," we ask in chorus, playing *our* role in the novel.

Like the unpleasant incidents in her books, Ferber's variety of suspense is hardly calculated to make us lose sleep. Quite the contrary, her suspense is fun and, at times, even open-ended. If, after Yancey Cravat's spectacular introduction, we are told that his past is "clouded with myths and surmises" and that "Rumor, romantic, unsavory, fantastic, shifting, and changing" floated about him, who cares? Not to know, in this case, is more fitting—and titillating. It would be a disappointment to know for sure that someone who has been compared to Ulysses and Jason was born in the same, mundane manner as the rest of us. And, in a similar vein, since we know that Dirk De Jong will succeed (and why isn't his mother happy about it?) and that Magnolia will eventually marry Gay Ravenal, we can freely indulge our maternal and romantic fantasies, respectively, and wonder how these events will come about. But not *why.* Motivations are clear in Ferber's mostly black-and-white universe. If not, the narrator's omniscience can be relied upon to provide them. No need to trouble ourselves. "Nuances," Edna Ferber's narrator tells us early in her canon, are "not for show-boat audiences"—nor, then, are they for us, her extended show-boat audience.

Ferber's final distancing device and the one which serves also as the ultimate backdrop for the playing-out of the myth, is physical setting. Traditionally, the American myth has been associated with the specific setting of the land. That is why our heroes—and Ferber's—are pioneers of a sort. They are conquerors of the "wild" West and

Southwest and, in more modern history and in Ferber's later books, tamers of Alaska as well. Many of the settings are natural spectacles, but even the relatively "quiet" locales have a part in the myth. Selina De Jong makes her small Illinois farm yield vegetables for which she would become famous; the tobacco farm land of the Connecticut Valley in **American Beauty** (1931) is conquered by its workers. Even Saratoga, perhaps the least naturally flamboyant of Ferber's locales, is presented, through the eyes of Clio Maroon, as a place in which "were gathered the worst and best of America," in effect, a microcosm of the land and its inhabitants.

Ferber, in her presentation of setting, is confronted with a tactical problem. For practical novelistic purposes, the settings must be allowed neither to overwhelm nor even to compete with the characters, but since they are so much a part of Ferber's myth, nor can they act simply as dead scenery. What Ferber does, finally, is not only to present her settings in *as* spectacular a manner as her characters, but to make them indistinguishable in importance one from the other. The scenery functions as a backdrop that is as well an extension of the people it contains—all American and all, in their various ways, magnificent. The entire first chapter of **Great Son,** for instance, is taken up by a description of Seattle and, in counterpoint, of Vaughan Melendy. "Himself of heroic stature," we are told of Melendy,

> he fitted well into the gorgeous and spectacular setting that was the city of Seattle. Towering and snow-capped like the mountains that ringed the city, he seemed a part of it—as indeed he was. Born into this gargantuan northwest region of towering forests, limitless waters, vast mountains, fertile valleys, he himself blended into the lavish picture and was one with it.

Seattle and Melendy, however, are no less spectacular and dramatic than Yancey Cravat and his world, the wild and exciting Oklahoma Territory of **Cimarron**. Or the immense vitality of Alaska and its inhabitants in **Ice Palace**. Nor are any of these locales to be outdone by the Texas of **Giant**. The land and its people—Bick Benedict, Jett Rink, and many, more minor figures—are huge, violent, beautiful, mythic. Even Leslie Benedict, new to Texas and overwhelmed and a bit frightened by its extraordinary size and strength, as she is by her new husband's, is lured by it. She finally realizes, while witnessing Bick take part in a cattle-branding episode, the primitive (and almost Laurentian) essence of the land, the real meaning of Texas:

> To Leslie it was a legendary scene, incredibly remote from the world she had always known. A welter of noise, confusion; the stench of singeing hair and burned flesh . . . she began slowly to comprehend that in this gigantic melee of rounding-up, separating, branding, castrating there was order; and in that order exquisite timing and actually a kind of art. Here, working with what seemed to her unbelievable courage and expertness, were men riding running leaping; wrestling with huge animals ten times their size; men slim heavy tall short young old bronze copper tan lemon black white. Here was a craft that had in it comedy and tragedy; that had endured for

> centuries and changed but little in those centuries.

> A ballet, she said to herself. A violent beautiful ballet of America.

Ferber plays even further on her spectacle by greatly emphasizing its visual qualities. She is as much in love with her settings as with her heroes and provides us with exciting scenes galore: the flood in **Show Boat,** the great train fight in **Saratoga Trunk,** the gunfights in **Cimarron**. But this graphic use of locale and equally vivid presentation of action has led Ferber to be disparaged by reviewers and critics for writing what appear to them to be movie scripts rather than novels. This means, in effect, that her writing tends to be theatrically mannered, broad in gesture, sweeping in scene, magnified life, so not really life. Myths, however, are precisely this. So whether Ferber wrote with movies in mind, or whether her stories lent themselves quite naturally to film, is of no real account. Nor does it matter that her settings may differ to some degree from the reality, which they do. Ferber's knowledge of them, in fact, was often garnered through library research. But her books, by her own admission, were meant as "escapes," from reality for both herself and her readers. [In an endnote, Uffen quotes Ferber from **A Peculiar Treasure** regarding the composition of her novels: ". . . I wrote them, I suppose, as an escape from the war. Unless the writer went back to another day he found himself confronted with the blood and hate and horror of the years between 1914 and 1918. I had never deliberately thought this out; I seemed automatically to turn away from this mad and meaningless hate and slaughter to a lovelier decenter day. In doing that I quite unconsciously followed the inclination of the reading world."] Her larger-than-life people in their larger-than-life worlds, provide just that. They fulfill their promise.

FURTHER READING

Biography

Gilbert, Julie Goldsmith. *Ferber: A Biography of Edna Ferber and Her Circle.* New York: Doubleday, 1978, 445 p.

> Focuses on Ferber's personal life and her associations with such artists, writers, and public personalities as George S. Kaufman, Moss Hart, and Alexander Woollcott. Gilbert presents Ferber's life in reverse chronological order, beginning with her last years and the writing of her major works, and proceeding through to her childhood.

Criticism

Banning, Margaret Culkin. "Edna Ferber's America." *The Saturday Review of Literature* XIX, No. 15 (4 February 1939): 5-6.

> Favorably reviews Ferber's autobiography, *A Peculiar Treasure*.

Bromfield, Louis. "Edna Ferber." *The Saturday Review of Literature* XII, No.7 (15 June 1935): 10-12.

Overview of Ferber's early life and its influence on the formation of her literary career.

Butcher, Fanny. "Ferber's Latest in Pace with Other Works." *Chicago Daily Tribune* (9 March 1935): 14.
Mixed review of *Come and Get It.*

Colby, Nathalie Sedgwick. "Simultaneous Differences." *The Saturday Review of Literature* III, No. 42 (14 May 1927): 819-20.
Mixed review of *Mother Knows Best.* While Colby applauds the characterizations and themes of these short stories, she contends that the unified plotline of the collection is better suited to the novel form.

Field, Louise Maunsell. "From Gopher Prairie on to High Prairie." *New York Times Book Review* (24 February 1924): 9.
Favorable review of *So Big.* Field contends that the characters and storyline are clearly drawn, sympathetically presented, and memorable.

Horowitz, Steven P., and Landsman, Miriam J. "The Americanization of Edna Ferber: A Study of Ms. Ferber's Jewish American Identity." In *Studies in American Jewish Literature: From Marginality to Mainstream, A Mosaic of Jewish Writers,* Volume 2, edited by Daniel Walden, pp. 69-80. Albany: State University of New York Press, 1982.
Discusses Ferber's Jewish heritage and the ways in which she wrote about it in her two autobiographies.

Overton, Grant. "Edna Ferber." In his *The Women Who Make Our Novels,* pp. 126-38. New York: Dodd, Mead, & Company, 1928.

Biographical sketch with commentary on the development of the main themes of Ferber's fiction.

Reely, Mary Katharine. "Cheerful—But Not Cloying." *The Publishers Weekly* 94 (21 September 1918): 848.
Favorable review of the short story collection *Cheerful—By Request.*

Rice, Jennings. "Cross-Section of American Life." *New York Herald Tribune Book Review* (16 February 1947): 7.
Favorable review of *One Basket* in which Rice discusses the various themes and settings of the short stories.

Walton, Edith H. "Tales by Edna Ferber." *New York Times Book Review* (13 February 1938): 6-7.
Generally favorable review of the two novellas in *Nobody's in Town.*

White, William Allen. "Edna Ferber." *World's Work* LIX, No. 6 (June 1930): 36-9
Examines various influences on the development of Ferber's literary career.

Young, Stark. Review of *Stage Door,* by Edna Ferber and George S. Kaufman. *The New Republic* LXXXIX, No. 1144 (11 November 1936): 50.
Applauds the themes, characterizations, and acting in the October 22, 1936 Broadway production of *Stage Door.* Young contends, however, that "too many moments are whooped up; the vernacular, the sayings, the quaint and atmospheric bits are all too packed in."

Additional coverage of Ferber's life and career is contained in the following sources published by Gale Research: *Authors in the News,* Vol. 1; *Contemporary Authors,* Vols. 5-8 (rev. ed.), 25-28 [obituary]; *Contemporary Literary Criticism,* Vol. 18; *Dictionary of Literary Biography,* Vols. 9, 28, 86; *Major 20th-Century Writers;* and *Something about the Author,* Vol. 7.

Viktor Frankl

1905-

(Full name Viktor Emil Frankl) Austrian nonfiction writer and essayist.

The following entry presents an overview of Frankl's life and career.

INTRODUCTION

A world-renowned psychiatrist, Frankl is the originator of logotherapy, a system of psychological treatment he unexpectedly tested and found validation for while imprisoned in Nazi concentration camps during World War II. Often called the Third Viennese School of Psychotherapy—Sigmund Freud's psychoanalysis and Alfred Adler's individual psychology being the first two—logotherapy incorporates Frankl's belief that man possesses an innate "will to meaning" and that the search for significance in one's life is a psychologically beneficial process. Frankl introduced logotherapy in *Ein Psycholog erlebt das Konzentrationslager* (1946), which was translated into English as both *From Death-Camp to Existentialism* and *Man's Search for Meaning*. His subsequent writings continue to elaborate on various aspects of this theory. Frankl has written: "As logotherapy teaches, even the tragic and negative aspects of life, such as unavoidable suffering, can be turned into a human achievement by the attitude which man adopts toward his predicament."

Biographical Information

Born and raised in Vienna, Austria, Frankl studied medicine at the University of Vienna, graduating as a medical doctor in 1930. Attracted to the psychoanalytic work of Freud and Adler, Frankl began the study of psychoanalysis under Adler and became director of the department of neurology at the University of Vienna. In 1942 Frankl and his family—who were Jewish—were arrested and sent to concentration camps, where his wife and parents were killed; Frankl himself spent three years at Auschwitz, Dachau, and other camps. Following the war, he wrote about his death-camp experiences and about his logotherapeutic system in *Man's Search for Meaning*. In 1947 he remarried and returned to the University of Vienna as a professor of neurology and psychiatry, where he continued to teach and write about logotherapy. Frankl also lectured extensively throughout the United States and Europe between the 1950s and the 1980s. He has received numerous awards and honors, including the Austrian State Prize for Public Education, the Austrian Cross of Honor, and several honorary degrees, including an L.L.D. degree from Loyola University in Chicago.

Major Works

The largely autobiographical *Man's Search for Meaning*,

which introduces the psychotherapeutic theory of logotherapy, incorporates Frankl's observations about the way human beings coped with life in concentration camps during World War II. In *Ärztliche Seelsorge* (1947; *The Doctor and the Soul*), *Die Existenzanalyse und die Probleme der Zeit* (1947), and *Theorie und Therapie der Neurosen* (1956), Frankl continues to expound his logotherapeutic theory by focusing on the spiritual dimension of the human psyche, the use of exhortation to challenge people to face their problems, and the importance of "willing" a meaning to life. *Das Menschenbild der Seelenheilkunde* (1959), in particular, focuses on spiritual aspects of the human psyche as contributing factors in any effective system of psychotherapy. *Der umbewusste Gott* (1966; *The Unconscious God*), *Psychotherapy and Existentialism* (1967), and *The Will to Meaning* (1969) continue to explore the philosophically existential characteristics of logotherapy, especially the search for meaning and its compatibility with religion and theology.

Critical Reception

Critical reaction to Frankl's works has been very favorable among American psychologists, existential philosophers, and Christian theologians. Although most critics praise the existential characteristics and spiritual aspects of Frankl's logotherapeutic theory, others criticize as essentialist and reductive his insistence on the "will to meaning"—like Freud's "will to pleasure" and Adler's "will to power"—as the underlying motivational force governing all human behavior. Some critics reject logotherapy as inadequate and charge that Frankl is unable to deal with people who have found life to be meaningless. Nevertheless, as Dan P. McAdams observed upon the 1992 reprinting of *Man's Search for Meaning*, Frankl's writings continue to underscore the idea that "'man's search for meaning' can sustain human life even under the most harrowing and depraved conditions."

PRINCIPAL WORKS

Ein Psycholog erlebt das Konzentrationslager [*From Death-Camp to Existentialism: A Psychiatrist's Path to a New Therapy;* revised and enlarged edition published as *Man's Search for Meaning: An Introduction to Logotherapy*] (nonfiction) 1946

Ärztliche Seelsorge [*The Doctor and the Soul: An Introduction to Logotherapy*] (nonfiction) 1947

Die Existenzanalyse und die Probleme der Zeit (nonfiction) 1947

Logos und Existenz: Drei Vorträge (nonfiction) 1951

Theorie und Therapie der Neurosen: Einführung in Logotherapie und Existenzanalyse (nonfiction) 1956

Das Menschenbild der Seelenheilkunde: Drei Vorlesungen zur Kritik des dynamischen Psychologismus (nonfiction) 1959

Die Psychotherapie in der Praxis: Eine kasuistische Einführung für Ärzte (nonfiction) 1961

Der umbewusste Gott: Psychotherapie und Religion [*The Unconscious God: Psychotherapy and Theology*] (essay) 1966

*Psychotherapy and Existentialism: Selected Papers on Logotherapy (essays and lectures) 1967

The Will to Meaning: Foundations and Applications to Logotherapy (essay) 1969

Meaninglessness: Today's Dilemma (essay) 1971

Anthropologische Grundlagen der Psychotherapie (collected works) 1975; also published as *Der leidende Mensch: Anthropologische Grundlagen der Psychotherapie,* 1984

The Unheard Cry for Meaning: Psychotherapy and Humanism (nonfiction) 1978

Der Mensch vor der Frage nach dem Sinn: Eine Auswahl aus dem Gesamtwerk (nonfiction) 1985

Die Sinnfrage in der Psychotherapie [with Vorwort von Franz Kreuzer] (essays) 1988

Das Leiden am sinnlosen Leben: Psychotherapie für Heute (nonfiction) 1989

*The work includes contributions from James C. Crumbaugh, Hans O. Gerz, and Leonard T. Maholick.

CRITICISM

Bruno Bettelheim   (review date Autumn 1959)

SOURCE: "A Note on the Concentration Camps," in *Chicago Review,* Vol. 13, No. 3, Autumn, 1959, pp. 113-14.

[*Bettelheim was an Austrian-born American psychologist, psychoanalyst, and educator whose works include* A Good Enough Parent: A Book on Child Rearing *(1987). In the following review of* From Death-Camp to Existentialism, *he examines the relationship between Frankl's concentration camp experiences and the development of logotherapy.*]

This small book [*From Death-Camp to Existentialism*] consists of two parts, quite unequal in size. In the first 90 pages the author presents personal reactions to his experiences in German concentration camps. This is followed by barely 14 pages of sketchy comment on the particular type of existential psychoanalysis he practices, which he calls logotherapy. Both subjects—the concentration camp and existential psychoanalysis—have been dealt with much more adequately by other authors. The merit of this volume lies in the important connection he establishes between these two seemingly disconnected phenomena. Existentialism, in line with the author's profession (he is professor of neurology and psychiatry at the University of Vienna), is discussed mainly in terms of its influence on psychotherapy.

That the impact of the concentration camp can, as the author puts it, "strike out" the prisoner's "whole former life" is the experience that is crucial for understanding the connection between the camps and existential philosophy. For those who permitted themselves to respond to the experience rather than deny it, it soon transcended their own personal lives and led to the realization that the verities they had lived by up to that shock experience of "nothingness" were false gods. Whatever the person's calling had been, that is where the realization struck home most forcefully. Those active in politics, and they formed the majority of early inmates, were suddenly forced to realize that the principles they had lived by and the goals they had lived for—not just the tenets of their particular party—were simply not applicable to this experience or to this political setting. In the same way, the sociologist or psychologist had to realize that suddenly the basic principles and categories of his vocation no longer applied. Like so many physicians who did not function as such in the camps, Dr. Frankl had to face this in his own field. As he puts it briefly, "the medical men among us learned first of all: Textbooks tell lies!" Among other things, he refers here to the fact that prisoners remained free of illnesses which physicians had expected camp conditions to bring on; also that persons who for years had suffered from what might be called psychosomatic diseases, or from conditions like insomnia, were suddenly free of them. "For days," he notes, "we were unable to wash and yet the sores and abrasions on hands which were dirty from work in the soil did not suppurate."

In the concentration camps the prisoners were at the mercy of a ruthless environment with virtually no power to influence it. On the other hand, they had to make decisions every moment, and each decision, even on matters that in the outside world would have made little or no difference, could and did mean life or death in the camps. Those prisoners who came to understand the nature of the conditions they lived under, also came to realize what they had not perceived before: that they still retained the last, if not the greatest, of the human freedoms: to choose their own attitude in any given circumstance. Those who understood this fully came to know that this, and only this, formed the crucial difference between retaining one's humanity (and with it often life itself) and death as a human being (or physical death): Whether one retained the freedom to choose autonomously one's attitude to extreme conditions even when they were totally beyond one's ability to influence them.

This then, constitutes in the thinking of the author, the link between his very sketchily and impressionistically described experience in the concentration camp, and his belief that a new type of psychotherapy is needed to complement psychoanalysis. Because, according to the author, psychoanalysis can free man of his crippling inhibitions, but fails to guide him toward accepting the steady search for meaning as the true essence of man's life. This, he claims, his logotherapy helps man to accept.

Whether one was free of neurotic inhibitions or compulsions made little difference when imprisoned in the camp; but whether one was able to continue, even under such extreme circumstances, the search for the personal meaning of one's life, this was more important than even bread and water. Food and drink were always totally insufficient and the prisoners knew utter deprivation; they could be borne successfully only through commitment to a search for meaning even in this extreme situation.

E. K. Ledermann   (review date Autumn 1959)

SOURCE: A review of *Das Menschenbild der Seelenheilkunde,* in *The International Journal of Social Psychiatry,* Vol. V, No. 2, pp. 158-59.

[*Ledermann, a German-born medical doctor who specializes in homeopathic medicine, is the author of* Existential Neurosis *(1972). In the following excerpt from a favorable review of* Das Menschenbild der Seelenheilkunde, *he examines Frankl's assertion that modern psychologism must recognize a spiritual dimension in human life.*]

"A Criticism of Dynamic Psychologism" is the sub-title of this book [*Das Menschenbild der Seelenheilkunde*]. "—ism" stands for a *weltanschauung.* Psychology is a science and uses certain concepts which result from a certain theory. All science is tentative, as one theory is replaced by another in the course of time. "—isms" are dogmatic. When they are introduced into the realm of science they lead to hypostatization, i.e. a scientific concept is made into an all-embracing entity. In the case of psychologism man becomes the result of his instinctual or social or archetypal forces. These are conceived as driving forces. As a result his spiritual nature is ignored. Frankl called it a spiritual dimension. Values disappeared as true and independent realities, the meaning of life is lost. The result is spiritual frustration, which Frankl has recognized as the outstanding modern form of neurosis.

I agree with this criticism of modern medicine. Frankl has had the courage to show up clearly the fallacy of psychologism which threatens to undermine the spiritual aspect of human existence. I differ from Frankl in his denial of drives or instincts in man . . . [He] says they are only "abstractions", quoting Wilhelm Keller. Concepts are necessary to build up science, and of course they are, and cannot be anything else but, abstractions. The mistake of psychologism is to ignore the limitations of the science of psychology.

Robert Hassenger   (review date Autumn 1960)

SOURCE: A review of *From Death-Camp to Existentialism,* in *Thought,* Vol. XXXV, No. 138, Autumn, 1960, pp. 454-56.

[*In the following review of* From Death-Camp to Existentialism, *Hassenger focuses on Frankl's assertion that logotherapy is a necessary supplement to current psychoanalysis.*]

Dr. Frankl, of the Medical Faculty, University of Vienna, has penned a work which might well be required reading for anyone who would understand the metaphysical malady of our time. This brief yet gripping account of the author's three years in concentration camps [*From Death-Camp to Existentialism*] serves as a background against which he outlines the basic concepts of the "third Viennese school of psychotherapy," founded to contribute toward the completion of psycho-therapy's picture of man. He terms his approach "logotherapy."

It is Dr. Frankl's contention that each age is characterized by a particular frustration, which is the primary social factor in the etiology of neuroses. Today "existential frustration" plays the chief role, "existential" meaning, in this context, "anything pertaining to man's quest for a meaning to his existence." Contemporary man is crippled by a sense of the meaninglessness of life, leaving an "existential vacuum" within him. This is manifested primarily by the phenomenon of boredom, which in our day sends more people to the psychiatrist than Freud's "libido" or Adler's "will-to-power" (the "first" and "second" Viennese schools of psychotherapy, respectively.) This *horror vacui* can lead to a psychic illness, termed by Dr. Frankl a "noogenic neurosis," emphasizing its spiritual root. Only a therapy which pursues man into the noetic, spiritual dimension can illuminate the possibilities of meaning. And it is here that logotherapy attempts to go beyond the other schools of existential analysis (as the *Daseinsanalyse* of Binswanger), stopping not with the illumination of being, but seeking rather to reorient the patient toward meaning. The author's personal experiences in the death camps have served to convince him that only the knowledge of a life task, only a "will-to-meaning," enables one to survive in these "limit situations" (Jaspers' *Grenzsituationen*). Dr. Frankl is fond of echoing Nietzsche's words: "He who has a *why* to live for, can bear almost any *how.*"

But this must not be taken to mean that the logotherapist imposes his personal values on the patient. Rather, he strives to shore up the patient's sense of autonomy, not giving him a life meaning, but enabling him to find his own personal life task, by opening up the full range of possibilities. True to his existential *élan*, Dr. Frankl insists that life's meaning includes the meaning of suffering and death. Here logotherapy comes to grips with the current attitude which sloughs off suffering and denigrates death. Up to the last moment of life, he states, suffering offers the opportunity for the fulfillment of meaning and the realization of value. It is not for man to question the meaning of his life; instead "it is he who *is questioned* by life; it is he who has to answer, by answering for life. His role is to respond—to be responsible." The psychotherapist cannot, of course, dictate that to which the patient is to be responsible. Each individual must decide whether he will be accountable to his fellows, his conscience, or to God.

Dr. Frankl rails against what he terms "homunculism," a sort of nihilism which misinterprets man as a mere product, whose psychic life is to be explored solely by method and technique. He pleads for a humanism which will look behind the disease to rediscover the genuinely human, the *Homo humanus*. This is a rightful criticism of the reductionist theories, which say to man, "you are nothing but . . .," explaining him from one point of view. And yet a note of caution must be injected here. Dr. Frankl seems to be open to the charge that he protests too strongly the more empirical approaches to the psyche. Granted such an accusation runs the risk of setting up dogmatic and *a priori* criteria to which all knowledge is supposed to conform: strictly ready-made notions of what constitutes valid knowledge seem to border on Platonism. Certainly extreme caution must be exercised lest the dichotomy be accepted: either science, which is knowledge, or mythology, which is nonsense. The assumption that a theory must be either science or mythology is an overt or crypto-positivism. And yet without some grounding in the empirical, a psychotherapy is in danger of transgressing its proper limits, to become the vehicle for considerable gratuitous and unsophisticated philosophizing.

Logotherapy is intended as a supplement rather than a substitute for the more traditional forms of psychotherapy. The urgency of Dr. Frankl's message for mid-twentieth-century man cannot easily be dismissed. Logotherapy, the third Viennese school, can undoubtedly help fill in the picture of the whole man, of man in all his dimensions, including the spiritual. But only if it resists the tendency to construct a *Weltanschauung,* which has been the penchant of its predecessors.

Harry A. Savitz   (review date April 1961)

SOURCE: A review of *From Death-Camp to Existentialism,* in *Jewish Social Studies,* Vol. XXIII, No. 2, April, 1961, pp. 120-21.

[*In the following positive review of* From Death-Camp to Existentialism, *Savitz focuses on Frankl's concentration camp experiences and discusses the psychological factors that enabled some people to survive such horrors.*]

This small book [*From Death-Camp to Existentialism*] brings to focus many shocking scenes of human tragedy and at the same time it reveals a number of keen psychological observations worthy of serious contemplation. In these pages we hear the authentic, restrained voice of a victim of a Nazi concentration camp—a man-made hell. The author is professor of neurology and psychiatry on the medical faculty of the University of Vienna. His voice and language are restrained—often too restrained, for he attempts the difficult task of giving an unbiased picture. Dr. Frankl himself is the victim. He is the subject and the object of many observations, and how can one psychologically obtain complete detachment under such circumstances? Furthermore, in describing horrors without the heat of emotion, the author deprives himself of sufficient light to see and evaluate them clearly. Nor does he attempt to narrate these bestial brutalities and the inhumanities of man to man, but rather he attempts to reveal the inner self, the subjective experience of a psychiatrist who survived them.

Frankl was a prisoner in Auschwitz for three years. He lived in a landscape surrounded by electrified barbed wires. Men were brought in daily in carload lots, like cattle. Not only were they deprived of their belongings but they were stripped of all of their human and personal traits. They lost all feelings, were de-humanized and de-personalized. No ethical or moral considerations occupied the prisoner's mind; his only aim and goal was to survive at all costs. Stripped of all human values, helpless and miserable, the prisoner was neither alive nor dead.

What were the vital mental forces that kept the prisoners alive and enabled them to survive in spite of all the miseries, and even prevented a number of them from committing suicide? The author gives some psychological clues to this human riddle. First, there was what is known as the "delusion of the reprieve." The condemned man, immediately before execution, gets the illusion that he may yet be reprieved at the very last moment. The fortunate were condemned to die immediately, in the gas chamber or crematorium. The survivors, who were a few hundred yards away, saw the chimneys send up a column of smoke to the sky; yet they clung to shreds of hope. Perhaps relief will soon come. This is a latent defense mechanism in the soul of many hopeless human being.

Another defense mechanism is "cold curiosity," a kind of objectivity in the midst of the most miserable circumstances. As an example, the author tells of standing in the open air in the chill of autumn, stark naked, still wet from a shower, trembling yet mentally occupied with curiosity, "What will happen?" This was probably a wish to die peacefully, but when the worst did not happen, a kind of relief was felt.

The prisoner's loss of fear of death, which is a kind of emotional death, is still another form of defense in the process of survival. The horrible environment of the camp gradually erased every trace of human emotion. The longing for home, physical weakness, the loathsome work that each one was assigned to do, blunted all human feelings. Suffering became a daily routine; they saw men dying every day, yet this sight did not make the slightest impression. This, too, was a kind of protective wall that helped some to survive.

Another factor was concern for inner spiritual values. Notwithstanding "cultural hibernation," the inmates ceaselessly discussed politics and religion. It is an interesting phenomenon that more sensitive, though often feeble-bodied, persons were better able to survive than were many of the more physically robust. (We have also observed this phenomenon in institutions for senior citizens. The more learned and cultured among them retain their mental faculties to the end, unlike the others.) Dr. Frankl gives a fine example of this—if a person was able to envisage a loved one far away, he could, as it were, escape from his immediate environment. Here one learns the power of love and its value in human survival.

Humor is also a mental device with survival value in critical situations threatening life itself. It is surprising that in the concentration camp, in a climate of human tragedy, inmates would think of some humorous episode that would lift them above their miserable environment. They would imagine some acquired uncouth mannerisms springing up in the future in the most respectable places. This would bring a smile or a laugh to the poor victims, and it acted, even though just for a moment, as an anaesthetic and helped them to forget their misery.

Looking forward to the future proved to be an aid to survival. In many cases it prevented suicide. In the words of Nietzsche, "he who has a 'why' to live for, can bear almost any 'how.' " By such reasoning prisoners found meaning or purpose for their suffering. Evil appeared necessary—as some Jewish sources have it—for without it there can be no good.

Dr. Frankl attempts to reveal the inner self, the subjective experience of a psychiatrist who survived the concentration camps.

—Harry A. Savitz

This, finally, brings the author to his basic concept of *logotherapy*. Whereas Freud introduced the pleasure principle as the motivating force in human activity, and Adler the "will to power," Frankl introduces a third principle. He states that man is dominated by the "will to meaning." That is, each person has a mission in life, which he must discover for himself, and this is the force that gives meaning to his existence and helps him in the struggle for survival. When this "will to meaning" remains unfulfilled, there develops in man "existential frustration." By "existential" the author describes man's quest for a meaning of his existence; by "frustration," the feeling of meaninglessness of life. According to Dr. Frankl, this "existential" vacuum is a source of neuroses, just as is sexual frustration in Freudian psychology, or what Adler terms the "inferiority feeling."

The book has much to offer from a literary, psychological, and philosophical point of view. I recommend it very highly to lay and professional readers alike, although one may differ with some of its conclusions concerning the followers of the Nazi regime. Thus the author seems to be too forgiving toward the camp guards. Granted that some of them were sadists in the purest clinical sense and that there is good and evil in every race and in every nation. However, I feel this is an oversimplification. The brutalities of the Nazi era clearly demonstrate that blind allegiance to a psychopathic personality despiritualizes his followers and turns them into criminal and beastly hordes. Modern civilization is as frail as a thin layer of ice over a river which cracks under the boots that step over it.

Stanley J. Rowland, Jr. (essay date 6 June 1962)

SOURCE: "Viktor Frankl and the Will to Meaning," in *The Christian Century,* Vol. LXXIX, No. 23, June 6, 1962, pp. 722, 724.

[*Rowland is an American reporter, editor, and author of* Hurt and Healing (1969). *In the following essay, he examines Frankl's notion of the "will to meaning" as an essential supplementary element in modern depth psychology.*]

Two elderly psychiatrists sat together at the round dining table opposite a young psychiatrist and a Methodist chaplain in his middle years. Between the two pairs sat two newsmen, Murray Ilson of the *New York Times* and myself. The subject was the meaning of human life, and the place of this question in psychiatry.

"The question has no place in psychiatry," one of the older psychiatrists said flatly. "It is a philosophical question." He nodded toward the head table in the ballroom, indicating the man who was to speak: Viktor E. Frankl of Vienna. Dr. Frankl has pioneered the psychiatric approach known as logotherapy, which stresses man's "will to meaning"; as a prisoner in a Nazi death camp during World War II he was able to test his existential psychiatry existentially. On this occasion he was about to address the annual meeting of the Academy of Religion and Mental Health.

"What Frankl says is very inspiring," the older psychiatrist continued. "It reminds me somewhat of an address that Paul Tillich gave at one of our meetings. We psychiatrists could scarcely understand him—he was talking on another level—though he was quite inspiring also. But these questions of meaning and purpose in life have no part in psychiatry."

At this point I challenged him: "I'm not trying to tell you about your profession. I take a flat pragmatic approach. If something is necessary for the healing—for the rejuvenation—of a person, then it must be included by the healer. I don't care what label it wears. In my own experience psychotherapy does a fine job of removing blocks, like surgery does in removing tumors. But such removal also increases the inner vacuum. And that vacuum has to be filled, and filled with the right things, or the result will be dependency and weakness. For instance, if the patient doesn't actualize his drive to love, then it will come back to him like a boomerang, in the form of anxiety—as an anxious desire to be loved. The same applies to actualizing faith and meaning. You or the clergy can put these in any category you like. But they are deep human needs, and they've got to be filled or the counselee is in trouble."

"I agree with you," the young psychiatrist said, leaning forward in his chair. "I've become a very theological psychiatrist. I've *had* to, in order to heal people."

"No," said the older psychiatrist. "Such concepts have no place in psychiatry."

"Yes," said the younger psychiatrist. "You've got to use the concepts that work."

For a few minutes the two men tried to discuss the issue. But the older doctor spoke in terms of the function of different brain segments in neuroses, while the other spoke about the need to love and the energy of being. Quickly it became apparent that they could scarcely discuss the issue at all, so different were their views of human nature and their categories.

"All this is great material for a sermon," the clergyman commented, and inquired further into the psychiatric mechanisms involved in redemption. The younger psychiatrist could talk with him from a professional standpoint and I could converse on the basis of experience. The other two psychiatrists could not really discuss the issue. The table conversation divided in half.

This development seemed to symbolize the academy's annual meeting fairly well. The much touted chasm between religion and psychiatry did not seem appreciable. Instead, the major chasm seemed to be between those who took a methodological and mechanistic approach and those who took an existential approach, with special emphasis on the question of life's meaning. On this basis, dealing with the practical question of what a person needs to be whole and rejuvenated, clergy and psychiatrists were able to talk fruitfully. A number of participants agreed with a leading psychiatrist who declared: "Dr. Frankl's address was very interesting and inspiring. But it doesn't help us with the people at state hospital." Dr. Frankl's approach received support, however, from a number of other leaders in the field of psychotherapy—Rollo May, for one.

Dr. Frankl called for a new "height psychology," utilizing man's "will to meaning," to supplement traditional depth psychology. He assailed the "pandeterminism which is so pervasive in psychology"; the view that the patient's actions are determined, he said, "plays into the hands of the patient's fatalism, thus reinforcing the latter's neurosis." He supported his discussion with examples of how logotherapy has effected cures, even in some apparently hopeless cases, by mobilizing the patient's will to meaning and capacity for free choice.

Stressing the importance of this view in modern psychiatry, he asserted: "Ever more frequently psychoanalysts report that they are confronted with a new type of neurosis characterized by loss of interest and by lack of initiative. They complain that in such cases conventional psychoanalysis is not effective." In a survey made at the University of Vienna where he teaches he found that 40 per cent

of the European students were afflicted with this "existential vacuum," compared with 81 per cent of the American students. "From these percentages we must not draw the conclusion that the existential vacuum is predominantly an American disease, but rather that it is apparently a concomitant of industrialization." He did not, however, explain why the problem of unmeaning was less common among students from highly industrialized countries in Europe.

Dr. Frankl went on to say that "rather than being a 'secondary rationalization' of instinctual drives, the striving to find a meaning in life is a primary motivational force in man." He could not agree, he asserted, with the Freudian thinking that gives primacy to the desire for pleasure. "Logotherapy regards the will to pleasure as a secondary matter," he said during a panel discussion. "Pleasure comes largely as a by-product, not as a result of direct striving—which tends to increase anxiety. This is typically the case in sexual neuroses. We find a forced striving for erection or orgasm, which simply increases the anxiety syndrome. The neurosis feeds on itself."

Picking up this point in conversation with Dr. Frankl, I asked him whether "will to meaning" is the proper term to describe a sound approach to the sexual: "Isn't there also a will to love, which may be sexually directed, and a will to have faith in something?" He agreed, though he gave centrality to the will to meaning. I also challenged his assertion that immortal life would deprive the present of its meaning and significance. "Some people," I suggested, "feel that death deprives life of its meaning. On the other hand, my belief in the eternal life of personal being throws me back completely on the present moment."

"I would put it more strongly than that," the young psychiatrist commented regarding the same suggestion in another context. "When a patient realizes a belief in personal immortality, it creates something like a state of emergency in the present. If 'now' goes on forever, then the only time they have is *right now*."

Dr. Frankl affably conceded the point but insisted that "if immortal life does not deprive the present of meaning, then neither does death." I quite readily agreed.

This was the kind of conversation one found repeatedly in the corridors of the Biltmore hotel at the academy's annual meeting. And despite the various objections to Dr. Frankl's emphasis, the stress on life's meaning seemed to provide the major note of the conference.

In a panel dealing with the psychological aspects of confrontation with the prospect of mass death, one psychiatrist took a technical approach in discussing the common reactions of apathy, anxiety and escapism. But he urged that Americans can cope with the problem realistically only if they recover a strong awareness of the meaning and values to be found in life.

Viktor E. Frankl (essay date 22 April 1964)

SOURCE: "The Will to Meaning," in *The Christian Century,* Vol. LXXXI, No. 17, April 22, 1964, pp. 515-17.

[In the following essay, Frankl explains the "will to meaning," focusing on self-actualization, personal responsibility, and the role of values in life.]

Central to my psychiatric approach known as logotherapy is the principle of the will to meaning. I counterpose it both to the pleasure principle, which is so pervasive in psychoanalytic motivational theories, and the will to power, the concept which plays such a decisive role in Adlerian psychology. The will to pleasure is a self-defeating principle inasmuch as the more a person really sets out to strive for pleasure the less likely he is to gain it. For pleasure is a by-product or side effect of the fulfillment of our strivings, and it is contravened to the extent that it is made a goal. The more a person directly aims at pleasure, the more he misses it. In my opinion this mechanism underlies most cases of sexual neurosis. Accordingly, a logotherapeutic technique based on this theory of the self-thwarting character of pleasure intention yields remarkable short-term results. Even the psychodynamically oriented therapists on my staff have come to acknowledge the value of logotherapy, and one such staff member has used this technique exclusively in treating sexually neurotic patients.

In the final analysis both the will to pleasure and the will to power are derivatives of the will to meaning. Pleasure is an effect of meaning fulfillment; power is a means to an end. A degree of power—economic power, for instance—is generally a prerequisite of meaning fulfillment. But while the will to pleasure mistakes the effect for the end, the will to power mistakes the means to an end for the end itself.

We are not really justified, however, in speaking of a *will* to pleasure or power in connection with psychodynamically oriented schools of thought, since they assume that man pursues behavior goals unwillingly and unwittingly and that his conscious motivations are not his actual motivations. Thus Erich Fromm in *Beyond the Chains of Illusion* speaks of "the motivating forces which make man act in certain ways, the drives which propel him to strive in certain directions." But to me it is inconceivable that man can really be driven to strivings; either he strives or he is driven. To ignore this difference, to sacrifice one phenomenon to another, is a procedure unworthy of a scientist; to do so is to allow one's adherence to hypotheses to blind one to facts.

Freud and his epigones have taught us always to see something behind or beneath human volitions: unconscious motivations, underlying dynamics. Freud never took a human phenomenon at face value; as Gordon W. Allport states in *Personality and Social Encounter,* "Freud was a specialist in precisely those motives that cannot be taken at their face value." But are there no motives at all which should be taken at face value? Such an assumption is comparable to the attitude of the man who, on being shown a stork, said, "I thought the stork didn't exist!" Does the fact that the stork has been misused to hide the facts of life from children in any way deny that bird's reality?

According to Freud, the reality principle is an extension of the pleasure principle and merely serves its purposes. But one could just as well say that the pleasure principle itself is an extension of the homeostasis principle and serves *its* purposes. Ultimately the psychodynamic approach views man as a being basically concerned with maintaining or restoring his inner equilibrium and seeking to do so by gratifying his drives and satisfying his instincts. Even Jungian psychology essentially interprets human motivation thus; the archetypes of Jungian thought are also "mythical beings" (as Freud called the instincts). Both Freud and Jung view man as bent on getting rid of tensions, be they aroused by drives and instincts clamoring for gratification (Freud) or by archetypes urging their materialization (Jung). In either case, reality, the world of beings and meanings, is reduced to instrumentalities for getting rid of unpleasant stimuli. What has been eliminated in this view of man is the fundamental fact that man is a being who encounters other beings, who also reaches out for meanings to fulfill.

This is why I speak of a will to meaning rather than a need for or a drive toward meaning. If man were really driven to meaning he would embark on meaning fulfillment solely to rid himself of this drive in order that homeostasis might be restored; at the same time he would no longer be really concerned with meaning but rather with his own equilibrium and thus with himself.

Nor is the concept of self-actualization or self-realization a sufficient ground for a motivational theory. Self-actualization is another phenomenon which can be realized only as a side effect and which is thwarted precisely to the extent that it is made a matter of direct intention. Self-actualization is of course a desideratum. But man can actualize himself only insofar as he fulfills meaning, in which case self-actualization occurs by itself—automatically, as it were. Like pleasure, self-actualization is contravened when deliberately sought after or made an end in itself.

While lecturing at Melbourne University some years ago I was given a boomerang as a souvenir. In contemplating this gift I concluded that in a sense it symbolized human existence. One generally assumes that a boomerang returns to the thrower; actually it returns only when the thrower has missed his target. Similarly, man returns to himself, to being concerned with his self, only after he has missed his mission, only after he has failed to find meaning in life.

In his doctoral dissertation Ernest Keen, one of my assistants during a teaching period at Harvard's summer session, seeks to demonstrate that the shortcomings of Freudian psychoanalysis are compensated for by Heinz Hartmann's ego psychology, and the deficiencies of ego psychology in turn by Erikson's identity concept. Keen goes on to contend, however, that despite these correctives there is still a missing link in psychotherapy, and that this link is supplied by logotherapy. It is my conviction that man should not, indeed cannot, struggle for identity in a direct way; rather, he finds identity to the extent to which he commits himself to something beyond himself, to a cause greater than himself. No one has put it as cogently as has Karl Jaspers: What man is he ultimately becomes through the cause which he has made his own.

Rolf von Eckartsberg, also a Harvard assistant of mine, has shown the insufficiency of the role-playing concept by pointing out that it avoids the very problem prompting it—that of choice and value. For the question remains: Which role to adopt, which cause to advocate? The same criticism holds for those who insist that man's primary intention and ultimate goal are to develop his potentialities. One recalls the example of Socrates, who confessed that he had within himself the potentiality to become a criminal but nevertheless decided to turn away from such a potentiality.

> **When meaning orientation becomes meaning confrontation, that stage of maturation and development has been reached where freedom becomes responsibleness.**
>
> *—Viktor E. Frankl*

What is behind all these arguments that man should try to live out his inner potentialities or—as it is sometimes put—to "express himself"? The hidden motive behind such notions is, I believe, to lessen the tension aroused by the gap between what a man is and what he ought to become, between the actual state of affairs and that which he should help secure, between existence and essence, or being and meaning. To say that man need not worry about ideals and values since they are nothing but "self-expressions" and that he should therefore simply embark on the actualization of his own potentialities is to say that he need not reach out for meaning to fulfill or values to realize, that everything is all right as it is. Pindar's injunction, "Become what you are," is thus deprived of its imperative quality and transmuted into an indicative statement, namely, that man has all along been what he should become and hence need not reach for the stars to bring them down to earth, since the earth is itself a star!

The fact remains, however, that the tension between being and meaning is ineradicable in man, is inherent in his humanness. And that is why it is indispensable for mental well-being. Having started from man's meaning orientation, i.e., his will to meaning, we have now arrived at another problem—his meaning confrontation. The first issue refers to what man basically is: oriented toward meaning; the second refers to what he should be: confronted with meaning.

To confront man with values which are interpreted merely as self-expression will not do. Still less valid is the approach which would have him see in values "nothing but defense mechanisms, reaction formations or rationalizations of his instinctual drives"—to use the definition of two outstanding psychoanalytically oriented therapists. Personally I would not be willing to live for the sake of my defense mechanisms, much less to die for the sake of my reaction formations.

To treat a patient in terms of psychodynamic ideas may very well serve the purpose of what I call existential rationalization. If a person is taught that his concern about ultimate meaning is no more than, say, a way of coming to terms with his early childhood Oedipal situation, then his concern can be analyzed away, along with the existential tension aroused by it. The approach of logotherapy is altogether different. Logotherapy does not spare a patient confrontation with the specific meaning which he must act on—and which the therapist should help him find. In his book *Logotherapy and the Christian Faith* Donald F. Tweedie recounts an incident in which an American visitor to Vienna asked me to tell him in one sentence the difference between logotherapy and psychoanalysis—whereupon I invited him first to tell me what he regarded as the essence of psychoanalysis. He replied: "In psychoanalysis the patient must lie down on a couch and tell you things which sometimes are disagreeable to tell." And I quickly responded: "In logotherapy the patient is allowed to sit erect but must hear things which sometimes are disagreeable!"

Erwin Straus has rightly stressed that in existential thinking the otherness of the other should not be attenuated. The same holds true for meaning. The meaning which a person has to fulfill is something beyond himself, never just himself. Only if this meaning retains otherness can it exert upon a person that quality of imperativeness which yields itself to a phenomenological analysis of one's experience of existence. Only a meaning which is not just an expression of the person himself can be a true challenge to him. The Bible tells us that when Israel wandered through the desert God's glory went before in the form of a cloud; only in this way was it possible for Israel to be guided by God. Imagine what would have happened if God had dwelled in the midst of Israel in the form of a cloud: rather than leading the people safely, the cloud would have obscured everything and Israel would have gone astray.

Meaning must not coincide with being; meaning must be ahead of being; meaning sets the pace for being. Existence falters unless lived in terms of transcendence, in terms of something beyond itself. Here we might distinguish between pacemakers and peacemakers: the former confront us with meanings and values, thus supporting our meaning orientation; the latter alleviate the burden of meaning confrontation. In this sense Moses was a pacemaker; he did not soothe man's conscience but rather stirred it up. Moses with his Ten Commandments did not spare his people a confrontation with ideals and values.

There is also the appeaser type of peacemaker who tries to reconcile others with himself. Let's face facts, he says. Why worry about one's shortcomings? Only a few live up to their ideals. So let's attend to peace of mind or soul rather than those existential meanings which only arouse tensions. What this kind of peacemaker overlooks is the wisdom of Goethe's warning: If we take man as he is, we make him worse; if we take him as he ought to be, we help him become it.

> Both the will to pleasure and the will to power are derivatives of the will to meaning.
>
> —*Viktor E. Frankl*

When meaning orientation becomes meaning confrontation, that stage of maturation and development has been reached where freedom becomes responsibleness. An individual is responsible for the fulfillment of the specific meaning of his own life, but he is also responsible *to* something, be it society or humanity or mankind or his own conscience. A significant number of people interpret their own existence not just in terms of being responsible to some*thing* but rather to some*one*—namely, to God. As a secular theory and medical practice logotherapy must restrict itself to such a factual statement, leaving to the patient the decision whether to interpret his own responsibleness in terms of religion or agnosticism. Logotherapy must remain available to everyone; to this I am obliged to adhere, if for no other reason, by my Hippocratic oath. In any case, logotherapy sees in responsibleness the very essence of human existence, and for that reason the patient must himself decide for what and to what, or to whom, he is responsible.

A logotherapist is not entitled consciously to influence the patient's decision as to how to interpret his own responsibleness or as to what to embrace as his personal meaning. The fact that a person's conscience is subject to error does not release him from his obligation to obey it; existence involves the risk of error. He must risk committing himself to a cause not worthy of his commitment. Perhaps my commitment to the cause of logotherapy is erroneous. But I prefer to live in a world in which man has the right to make choices, even if they are wrong choices, rather than one in which no choice at all is left to him. A world in which both fiends and saints are possible is infinitely preferable to a totally conformist, collectivist world in which man is a mere functionary of the party or the state.

A. H. Maslow   (essay date Fall 1966)

SOURCE: "Comments on Dr. Frankl's Paper," in *Journal of Humanistic Psychology*, Vol. VI, No. 2, Fall, 1966, pp. 107-12.

[*Maslow is an American psychologist, educator, and author of* Dominance, Self-Esteem, Self-Actualization: Germinal Papers of A. H. Maslow *(1973). In the following excerpt, he concurs with Frankl's theories on the "will to meaning," self-actualization, and the role of values and pleasure in life.*]

I agree entirely with Frankl that man's primary concern (I would rather say "highest concern") is his will to meaning. But this may be ultimately not very different from phrasings by Buhler [Charlotte Buhler, *Values in Psychotherapy*] (1962), for instance, or Goldstein, or Rogers or others, who may use, instead of "meaning," such words as "values" or "purposes" or "ends" or "a philosophy of life" or "mystical fusion." As things stand now, different theorists use these and similar words in an overlapping or synonymous way. It would obviously help if they could be defined somewhat more carefully (not *too* carefully, however, until more data come in).

Another general consequence of this "levels" conception of knowledge and of science is that an all-inclusive, over-arching generalization, however true, is very difficult to "work with" or to improve in clarity, usefulness, exactness, or in richness of detail. Thus, I certainly agreed with Goldstein, Rogers, and others that the one ultimate motivation is for self-actualization, but it has proven very helpful to spell this out in more detail, to subject it to holistic-analysis, to give it operational definition, and then to compare the results of different operations. This "liaison work" between the "idea-man" and the tester and checker is already paying off, e.g., in making possible Shostrom's standardized test of self-actualization [the personal orientation inventory].

Frankl's "will to meaning" and also Buhler's "four basic tendencies" are, I feel, compatible both with my empirical-personological description of self-actualizing people [in *Motivation and Personality*] (1954) and with my theoretical statements in which self-actualization is used as a concept.

First of all, not all grown people seek self-actualization and of course few people achieve it. There are other ways and goals of life as Buhler has maintained. The theoretical statement that all human beings in principle seek self-actualization and are capable of it applies ultimately to newborn babies. It is the same as saying that neurosis, psychopathy, stunting, diminishing, atrophy of potentials are not primarily inborn but are made. (This statement does not apply to the psychoses, where the evidence is not yet clear. It cannot be ruled out that heredity plays an important role.) It may also apply to adults in the sense that we shouldn't give up hope altogether even for those with a bad prognosis, e.g., drug addicts, psychopaths, as well as certain types of smug "normality" and "good adjustment" (to a bad society), resignation, apathy, etc. This parallels the medical profession's insistence on trying to save life even when it looks hopeless. Such an attitude is quite compatible with being completely "realistic."

Secondly, my experience agrees with Frankl's that people who seek self-actualization directly, selfishly, personally, [dichotomized] away from mission in life, i.e., as a form of private and subjective salvation, don't, in fact, achieve it (unless the selfishness is for the *sake* of the call, vocation, or work, thereby transcending the [dichotomy] between unselfishness and selfishness). Or to say it in a more positive and descriptive way, those people in our society selected out as self-actualizing practically always have a mission in life, a task which they love and have identified with and which becomes a defining-characteristic of the self. And there was no instance in which I did not agree that it was a worthy job, worthwhile, important, ultimately valuable. This descriptive fact can be called self-actualization, authenticity, fulfillment, the achievement of meaning, self-transcendence, finding oneself, the unitive life, or by other names.

The instances that I have seen in which persons sought direct, short-cut self-actualization were originally cases in which private "lower" pleasure, self-indulgence, and primitive hedonism ruled for too long a period of time. More recently, my impression is that impulsivity, the unrestrained expression of any whim, the direct seeking for "kicks" and for non-social and purely private pleasures (as with some who use LSD merely for "kicks" rather than for insight) is often mislabelled self-actualization.

Or to say this from still another perspective, all self-actualizing persons that I have ever known were good workers, even hard workers—though they also knew how to not-work, to loaf, and to saunter.

It is *such* facts that we have to deal with, these and, of course, many others of this sort. It is well to admit that there are, in principle, many abstract systems or languages that can organize and integrate these facts equally well or almost so. I am not inclined to make a big to-do about the particular labels so long as they do not obscure or deny the facts. Indeed, at this level of knowledge I think it useful to have *various* points of view on the same world of facts because, through other people's eyes, we can see more than we can with only our own. It is better to consider this intellectual situation synergic or collaborative rather than rivalrous. Science, at least as I define it, is a division of labor among colleagues.

I think a similar type of discussion is in order with reference to Dr. Frankl's remarks on peak-experiences. I feel I know what Dr. Frankl is trying to say and I agree with his intention, as I did with his cautionary remarks on the mistakes that can be made with self-actualization. I'm pretty sure that we have understood each other in conversation and in correspondence. And yet it is well to spell everything out for others, and also to add what I have learned more recently.

Hunting peak-experiences directly doesn't ordinarily work. Generally they happen to a person. We are ordinarily "surprised by joy." Also it becomes increasingly clear that it is wise, for research strategy, to stress the separability of the emotional aspect from the cognitive aspect of peak-experiences. It is more clear to me now that peak-emotions *may* come without obvious insight or growth or benefit of any kind beyond the effects of pleasure itself. Such raptures may be very profound and yet be almost contentless. The prime examples are sex and LSD, but there are others as well. Sex, LSD, etc., may bring illumination, or they may not. Furthermore, insight (B-Cognition) can come without emotional ecstasies. Indeed, B-Cognition can come from pain, suffering, and tragedy, as Dr. Frankl has helped to teach us. Also, I would today stress even more than I have in the past, the prime importance of "resistance to peak-experiences," which I once called in a humorous moment "non-peaking." People may either not have peak-experiences or they may repress or suppress them, be afraid of them, and deny them or interpret them in some reductive and desacralizing way. The consequences of being a "non-peaker" loom larger and

larger as the years go by. I agree with Colin Wilson (in his *Introduction to the New Existentialism*) in attributing to this one factor much of the difference between pessimistic, hopeless, anguished Nay-Saying on the one hand, and coping, striving, hopeful, unconquerable Yea-Saying, on the other hand. Dr. Frankl's remarks on tension and overcoming are very relevant and very useful in this connection.

Once we have agreed with Dr. Frankl on the intellectual dangers of making pleasure into a deity, we can then feel quite free to enjoy the small and harmless pleasures of life.

—A. H. Maslow

As for the similarity of all pleasures, certainly there is a subjective quality which is generally different from suffering, or despair, or pain. In this sense, *any* pleasure is a pleasure and falls within the same class as any other pleasure. And yet there is also a hierarchy of pleasures (the cessation of pain, the moratorium of drunkenness, the relief of urination, the pleasure of a hot bath, the contentment of having done a job well, the satisfaction of success, on up through the happiness of being with loved friends, the rapture of being in love, the ecstasy of the perfect love act, on up to the final pleasure-beyond-pleasure of the mystical fusion with the universe). Thus, in one very real sense, all pleasures are similar; in another equally real sense, they are not.

We must certainly accept Dr. Frankl's cautions about contentless pleasure and about the necessity for relating pleasure to its trigger, to its context, and also to its consequences. (One day we shall have to go even further for we shall soon have to grapple with the difficult problem of pleasurable emotions coming from neurotic or psychotic or perverted sources. Like the medieval theologians who had to differentiate the voice of God within from the voice of the devil within, we shall soon have to start questioning the absolute and sacred authority accorded by many today to the "inner voice," "the voice of conscience," etc.)

And yet once we have agreed with Dr. Frankl on the intellectual dangers of making pleasure into a deity, we can then feel quite free to enjoy the small and harmless pleasures of life. Even if they teach us nothing, they are still a blessing. Pleasure itself is not a danger; it is only the man-made theories *about* pleasure that are a danger.

Viktor Frankl with Mary Harrington Hall   (interview date February 1968)

SOURCE: "A Conversation with Viktor Frankl of Vienna," in *Psychology Today*, Vol. 1, No. 9, February, 1968, pp. 57-63.

[*In the following interview, Frankl discusses his concentra-*

tion camp experiences and his views on existentialism and modern psychotherapy.]

[*Hall*]: *You were already a psychiatrist in Vienna when Hitler marched into Austria. How did that affect you immediately?*

[*Frankl*]: After Hitler came, I stayed in Vienna. My sister immigrated to Australia and my brother tried to get shelter in Italy. He was captured by the SS and taken with his wife to Auschwitz. I had been assigned to run the Neurological Department of the Jewish Hospital, so I was not only allowed to stay in Vienna myself, but even could keep my old parents with me. My father at that time was a bit more than eighty years old.

Was there any opportunity for you to leave the country?

I tried to get an immigration visa to the United States. Finally, I did. I was free to leave, to develop my theory and to promulgate it. My parents were so happy. They said, "Now Viktor will finally leave here." But at the last minute I hesitated to use the visa for which I had waited so long. I knew that a few weeks after I left the country, my old parents would be brought to a concentration camp. I didn't know what to do.

And they wanted you to leave even though your position was their protection?

Yes. They were insisting. You know, I've never told anyone this—But about this time I had a strange dream, one that belongs to my deepest experiences in the realm of dreaming. I dreamed that people were lined up—psychotics, patients—to be taken to the gas chambers. And I felt so deep a compassion that I decided to join them. I felt that I must do something and working as a psychotherapist in a concentration camp, supporting the people there mentally, would be incomparably more meaningful than just being one more psychiatrist in Manhattan.

As I said, I didn't know what to do. So with a briefcase I covered the yellow star I had to wear on my coat and sat down in the largest cathedral in the center of Vienna one evening. There was an organ concert, and I thought, "Let's sit down and listen to the music and ponder the whole question. Relax, Viktor, you are very distracted. Just contemplate and meditate far from the turmoil of Vienna." Then I asked myself what I was to do. Should I sacrifice my family for the sake of the cause to which I had devoted my life, or should I sacrifice this cause for the sake of my parents. When confronted with this kind of question, one longs for an answer from Heaven.

What you were confronting was yourself, wasn't it? Yourself and the question of how committed you were to what you said you believe.

Yes. I left the cathedral and went home. There, on the radio set, was a piece of marble. I asked my Father what it was. He was a pious Jew and had picked up at the site of a large Viennese synagogue this stone, a part of the [tablets] containing the Ten Commandments. On the stone was an engraved and gilded Hebrew letter. My father told me the letter occurred in only one of the commandments,

"Honor thy father and mother and you will stay in the land." Thereupon I decided to stay in Austria and let the American visa lapse.

But you already knew your decision, really, didn't you?

You would be justified in saying this was a projective test. I had made the decision in the depth of my heart long ago and projected it into this piece of marble. You would be perfectly right, but allow me then to add that if I had seen nothing in this marble but calcium carbonate, $CaCO_3$, that also would have been a projective test, but it would have been only the projection of my inner existential vacuum. And so I made the decision and deliberately risked everything. But I couldn't help it.

A human being doesn't care primarily for happiness or pleasure or power. Happiness and pleasure are side effects, destroyed precisely to the extent that they are aimed at.

—Viktor Frankl

And so you were sent to Auschwitz. Once in the concentration camp, were you able to help as a psychiatrist?

Only underground, illegally. My time in the camp, except for the last few weeks, was spent in digging and laying tracks for railway lines, in digging a tunnel for a water main. The opportunities for psychotherapy were naturally limited. But I remember once when the lights were out and we lay in our earthen huts. The whole camp had been forced to fast for the day because no one would identify the half-starved prisoner who stole a few pounds of potatoes. Someone asked me there in the dark: "Tell us now, psychiatrist. Where is there hope?" I told them we all faced death. But I told them that, in spite of this, I had no intention of losing hope and giving up. For no man knew what the future would bring, much less the next hour. And I spoke of the many opportunities of giving life a meaning. Human life never ceases to have a meaning and this infinite meaning of life includes suffering and dying, privation and death. Unless there is such an unconditional meaning to life, there would be no point in surviving. When the electric bulb flared up again, I saw the miserable figures of my friends, limping toward me to thank me.

What a moving experience! The early title of your book, **Man's Search for Meaning,** *was* **From Death-Camp to Existentialism.** *I am going to ask a stupid question. Please forgive me.*

There are only stupid answers. No stupid questions.

Was your existential decision made when you stayed in Vienna instead of coming to Manhattan?

That was not my existential decision, for everyone has to make an existential decision in each moment of his life. What is true is that it was *one* of my existential decisions.

What is *not* true is that I came out of Auschwitz with my theory of psychotherapy. I entered Auschwitz with the manuscript of my book in my pocket. In the camp we were allowed to keep nothing. Not a wedding ring, a medal, or a good-luck piece. But the tenets of logotherapy were justified by the acid test of the concentration camp. My experiences in the camp were my empirical validations of existentialism.

Why do you call your theory of psychotherapy "logotherapy"?

Logos is a Greek word that denotes "meaning." Logotherapy focuses on the meaning of human existence as well as on man's search for such a meaning. It is this striving to find a meaning in one's life that is the primary motivational force in man. That is why I speak of a *will to meaning* in contrast to the pleasure principle of Freudian psychoanalysis or the *will to power* of Adlerian psychology.

Do you regard this concept of man as human only to the extent he reaches beyond himself as a religious concept?

It has nothing to do with theology and the supernatural whatsoever; but it is a tradition of European philosophy, even atheistic philosophy. And this self-transcendence is lived out by what I call man's will to meaning. This will to meaning is frustrated today. More and more patients are approaching psychiatrists with the complaint of an inner void and emptiness, with a sense of meaninglessness, with the feeling of a total and ultimate futility of life. And this condition is not restricted to our culture. Communist psychiatrists have expressed frankly this condition I have called the existential vacuum, this feeling of meaninglessness. It is spreading among youth in Czechoslovakia, East Germany, and Russia.

Then this isn't just a critical problem in the Western world where we fear this as a sign of our approaching decadence.

Definitely not. But you must not close your eyes to the fact that in your country existential frustration is observed more than anywhere in the world. A random sample gathered by my staff in Vienna among German-speaking students from Switzerland, West Germany, and Austria revealed that 40 per cent of them confessed that they knew this feeling of total meaninglessness from their own experience. But among my American students, not 40 but 80 per cent confess to the same inner meaninglessness. Perhaps this is why the paperback edition of **Man's Search for Meaning** has sold 355,000 copies in the United States within a few years.

Existential psychiatry and psychology certainly are growing in influence in this country.

Existentialism is greatly misused in this country. Everybody regards himself as an existentialist if he uses the term "being in the world" in every second or third line. In my eyes, this is no credential for an existentialist. The term "being in the world" is borrowed from Martin Heidegger and usually is misinterpreted in a way not at all appropriate to Heidegger's concept of human reality. I discussed this at length with Heidegger himself. And it is for this reason that I don't wish to be identified totally with the

movement in this country called existential psychiatry or psychology.

All right, tell me what you, Viktor Frankl, mean by existentialism. Not what Sartre means, nor anyone else but you.

You would be mistaken, Mary, if you assumed that existential psychiatry continues the tradition of Jean Paul Sartre's existentialism. First, let me say what existentialism is not. It is a misconception to think that existentialism teaches and preaches the nothingness of man. What it really teaches, the true lesson to learn from existentialism, is the no-thingness of man. Man is not just one thing among other things. He must not be totally objectified. He must not be manipulated. Man has value and dignity. Existentialism does not teach the nothingness of life or the world.

There is a world of difference between no-thing and nothing.

You are right, Mary. And what I also am standing for in the field of psychotherapy is the fight against the nothing-but-ness of man. It is a two-front war. I am fighting the preachers of life's nothingness—pseudo-existentialists, pessimists—on the one hand and the preachers of nothing-but-ness on the other. For you cannot say that man is nothing but a computer, a set of mechanisms, hopefully to be repaired by a physician or a psychiatrist. Man is a human being and must be envisaged and reached in his very humanness. And he is human only to the extent to which he is reaching out beyond himself, directed toward something other than himself. It might be toward a purpose to fulfill, or another human being to encounter in love. And I would go even further. Above all, the meaning of his life, his existence, is more than just a goal he arbitrarily sets for himself.

What, in your opinion, is the reason for the prevalence of the existential vacuum?

To put it as briefly as possible, unlike an animal, man is not told by his instincts what he must do. And, in contrast to man in former days, he is no longer told by traditions what he should do. Now he often doesn't even know what he basically wishes to do. And what is the result? Either he simply does what other people do or else he simply does what other people wish him to do. Because of this, man increasingly falls prey to conformism. But another effect is neuroticism—an existential despair over the apparent meaninglessness of one's life.

And how does one go about giving meaning to his life?

Meaning is always available for each and every individual, and this is so up to the very last moment. Perhaps this will make it clear. Unless he has been indoctrinated through his college training that man is nothing but the battleground of the civil war between ego and superego, the result of a conditioning process, the simple man of the street will tell you that it is o.k. to be a successful businessman. But the man who courageously and heroically faces an unchangeable fate is held infinitely higher in his esteem. This we must show our patients. I cannot arbitrarily attach meanings to things. Meanings must be discovered and cannot be prefabricated, as is so prevalent in this country and, to a lesser degree, in Europe. Meaning has an objective quality, which is another way of saying it is to be discovered rather than invented. This is an important issue and this objectiveness of meaning is not just my philosophical conviction but comes from experimental psychological research.

What about subjective meanings?

There are, of course, also subjective meanings. One of the subjective meanings is experienced through LSD intoxication. And only those individuals who are no longer capable of discovering objective meaning resort to the subjective meanings that are induced by a biochemical tool such as LSD or marijuana. In other words, existential frustration to a large extent might be responsible for the indulgence in LSD and the like. Caught in this existential vacuum, this abysmal sense of meaninglessness, they also create their nonsense, the theater of the absurd. I don't wish to denigrate the theater of the absurd; it is the voice of our age. But we must not think that it offers a solution to the problems and questions of our age. The answers are beyond any age. They are eternal. But they must be verbalized in the language of our day. Consider the experiment conducted by James Olds, in which he inserted electrodes into the hypothalamus of rats who were then taught to close an electric current by pressing a lever. Finally, they were pressing the lever up to 50,000 times a day, perhaps because they experienced orgasm. These rats then neglected their food and their sexual partners. In the same way, young people who use LSD will neglect the objective and will lose the real meaning in life.

But how does one discover the objective meaning?

In an age when the ten commandments seem to have lost their unconditional validity, man's hearing capacity must be refined and sharpened for the ten thousand commandments that together form a man's life.

What is conscience, Viktor?

Conscience is that capacity of man that enables him to discover the unique meanings of his unique situations. Discover them, rather than give them arbitrary meanings. We have the freedom to give meanings more or less arbitrarily, but we have the responsibility to discover the true meaning in the unique situations. That is why I often tell my American audiences that freedom threatens to degenerate into mere arbitrariness unless it is lived in terms of responsibleness. That is why I recommend to you Americans that your Statue of Liberty on the East Coast be supplemented by a Statue of Responsibility on the West Coast.

As we have been talking, I've been wondering about the things you have said. Here in America, we have our own psychology and our psychiatry. In Europe things are happening. What, and what is different?

Again, Mary, you are a catalyst. You elicit for me not only influences, but even thoughts and ideas. For the first time in my life, I am immediately provoked to thought, by your stimulating way of asking questions, by a statement or a judgment. In Europe we still have the tradition in the best sense of the tradition—the explicitness, the awareness of the philosophical background of the problems in the fore-

ground. We know even the hardest clinical facts, the most clinical theories have a better clinical perspective if there is an awareness of the background. This is a thing I call meta-clinic. It's like metaphysical, where there is a metaphysical problem behind a physical reality. You can indicate a lobotomy or sign a prescription for a drug rather than beginning psychotherapy. Or, you can start psychotherapy rather than take a patient's philosophic despair at its face value. All this implies a meta-clinic statement. It means that you regard a patient in one case as a mechanism to be repaired, in the other as a human being to be assisted or helped. If your patient is nothing more than a damaged brain to be operated on, your assumption is like that of the Nazi doctor who sent his patients to the gas chambers. He made a meta-clinical basic assumption that man is nothing but what his brain or his blood makes him to be. If you adopt such a view, euthanasia is a consistent practice.

On the one hand we are sticking to the traditionally felt responsibility to make our underlying philosophy explicit, or to put it another way, to make the metaclinical background loom. It is this tradition of philosophical-psychological concepts that is precious to me and close to my heart and my brain.

Does American thought affect Europe in your field?

More than influence. We Europeans have become addicted to whatever comes from your country. We are not modern enough to develop our own new approaches, but are imitating the Americans. There is a great gulf in Europe, because we do not progress. We are not developing humanistic psychology but reimporting the old mechanistic concept. And it will take some time until Allport and Maslow and perhaps even Viktor Frankl will reach them in Europe.

Isn't it strange that Vienna, where it all started, would regard you as a maverick?

Consider, if you will, up to three times a year I am invited to give lecture tours in this country. By now I have lectured to 85 American universities, seminaries, and colleges, while in Vienna, except for my weekly one-hour lecture as a member of the University medical faculty, I give one public lecture every two years.

Who, in Europe, do you think are the best men in psychology and psychiatry today?

In psychiatry, I would say I admire the soberness of Hans-Juerg Weitbrecht in Bonn and then Professor Schulte in Tuebingen, the follower of the famous Kretschmer. Then, particularly Petrilowitsch. I mention his name as the last of the three, because he confesses to logotherapy; the others don't. Petrilowitsch is in Mainz, where he is at the University Clinic. Kranz, head of the department, is also an admirer of logotherapy. These are the first four, those whom I regard as the most outstanding, reliable, and sober psychiatrists.

As for psychology, there is Professor Lersch of Munich. In addition, I hold Arnold Gehlen in high esteem for philosophy and psychology and sociology and anthropology. I love all the writings of Peter Hofstaetter who heads the department of psychology at the University of Hamburg in West Germany. He has spent many years here in this country and he is experimentally oriented, but he is open-minded.

I'd like to know more about your background. Was your father a doctor?

My father studied medicine, but he was a poor young man from the countryside and could not afford to complete his preparation. For ten years he was a stenographer in the parliament of the Austrian monarchy. Afterwards, he became an official in the State Ministry of Social Affairs. He was particularly concerned with matters of Youth Welfare.

Was he the one who encouraged you to study medicine?

He was proud that I decided to study medicine, but he did not influence me very much.

How did you become interested in psychiatry?

I wonder if you know that when I was a young boy of 16, I began a correspondence with Sigmund Freud. In one of my letters to him, I enclosed a few pages of manuscript reflecting my thoughts on the origin of mimic affirmation and negation—its expression by shrugging or nodding or whatever. To my astonishment, Freud responded immediately and wanted to know if I would allow him to forward it for publication. In 1924, I was sent the *International Journal of Psychoanalysis* and there I found myself in print.

You were only 18 then. And you never met Freud? That's fantastic.

I met him once—later on. I was walking down the street close to the University, and I noticed a man before me. He reminded me of Freud from the pictures I had seen, but I thought it was impossible. This man was so tattered, his hat, his coat were so worn. He could not be the great Sigmund Freud, I thought. He carried a black wooden stick with a silver handle, and he was beating the pavement and moving his mouth. He suffered from some sort of cancer of the jaw bone, you know. I followed him. I thought, "if this is really Freud, he will turn at the corner into the Berggasse." I knew his address from our correspondence. He made the turn and I addressed him. "Oh, Dr. Freud," I said. "My name is Viktor Frankl." He replied, "Viktor Frankl, Czerningasse #6, Door #25, Second District of Vienna." At that time we had ceased contact because I had become affiliated with the inner circle of Adlerians. So we just talked there in the street. I kept all my letters and postcards from Freud, and I even possessed some case histories written by the young Freud when he was at the same clinic in Vienna where I worked. But they were all confiscated by the Nazis.

So you were a member of the Adlerian group.

Yes. You know old Vienna and its coffee-house tradition. The Freudians met in the Cafe Arkaden and the Adlerians met in the Cafe Siller. But I was not orthodox enough and deviated from the Adlerian teachings. Two of my other professors had contradicted him. I loved them, and him also. I tried to take a middle position. Adler would not ac-

cept that, and he insisted that I leave the society. Since the Adlerians have shifted to this country, they have become very broad-minded and integrated. But it was not always so.

When I said that I did not wish to be totally identified with the existential psychological movement in America, it was also because I wished to be connected with the humanistic psychological movement, as developed by Gordon Allport, Abraham Maslow, and Charlotte Buehler.

—Viktor Frankl

Was it your philosophical approach which made Adler expel you?

In a way. You see, Adler was a great man in many respects, but he simply was lacking what I would call a receptive organum for philosophical problems. For instance, throughout my life I struggled with the question of whether or not life had meaning—my personal life or any human's life. Adler published a book on the meaning of life, but if you look it up, you will find that in this excellent book the very question of the meaning of life has been answered in advance. This means that he had presupposed all along that life has a meaning. The question never came to his mind.

This is not a defect; perhaps the defect lies with those who raise the question. The same holds true for Freud. In a letter to Princess Bonaparte, Freud once said, "The moment a man raises the question of the meaning of his life, he is sick." He might be right. But if he is, today the whole of mankind is sick. You cannot say that everybody is sick because nobody is healthy. What point does it make to speak of sickness if there is no health? Today we no longer can say that a man who raises the question of life's meaning is sick. It might have been a valid statement in Freud's day, but no longer.

Then, because you are concerned with this problem, the orthodox view would be to say that you are neurotic.

Exactly. But let me be a neurotic. It has been said that each person offers his own case history when working out a new psychotherapeutic system. Take it for granted. If I can show how I, personally, have overcome this neurosis—if that is what the feeling of meaningless is—then perhaps my case history becomes a new approach to psychotherapy and other people will be able to overcome the same predicament.

What do you think of our American approach to these problems?

The usual way of thinking in this country, I am sorry to say, is unidimensional. You mix everything up. For example, when I wrote my book, *From Death-Camp to Existentialism,* I tried to combine in a sound and justifiable way both psychotherapy and philosophy. I was intrigued with the borderline problems, but I tried to recognize their separate dimensions.

Why is that different from the typical American view?

Here, you seem to feel that if anything is of neurotic origin, it must be false. Or, if anything is morally tenable, it must be related to mental health. For instance, there is a man running a monastery in Mexico, south of Mexico City, who insists that every young monk who joins the monastery must be psychoanalyzed—in the strict Freudian sense. Last year when I was in Mexico, I met this man. I asked him if he really believed that freedom of neurosis guaranteed truth. That is to say, that freedom from neurosis makes one truly religious. He seemed to believe that it did. I answered him, "On the one hand, I deny that truth can make you free from neurosis, but on the other hand, neither do I believe that freedom from neurosis makes for becoming truly religious."

But that's in Mexico. Do you believe that all Americans think thus?

I have always found that tendency in the American way of thinking. For instance, pragmatism is unidimensional thinking. What is true must be good, must make for good business, for a happy life, and so forth. And I deny this. Reality is multidimensional. But let me add this. The scientist has not only the privilege but the responsibility to deal with his particular aspect of reality as if every reality were unidimensional. He must, however, retain the awareness of what he is doing. Otherwise he becomes a victim of that fallacy that is so noticeable, particularly in your country—reductionism.

But not every American is guilty of this. Our best minds warn against this very thing. This month's magazine features a superb article by Rollo May—a powerful piece that makes just this point.

Yes, Mary. Reductionism also has been criticized more in America than anywhere else in the world. Reductionism means that when you interpret human beings exclusively in biological terms, you have simplified until your statement is no longer biology but biologism. If you only envision psychodynamics, you fall prey to psychologism. The same holds true for sociologism. In other words, science is turned into ideology because you make overgeneralized statements. We are living in an age of specialists, but let me define a specialist as a man, a scientist, who no longer sees the forest of truth for the trees of facts. We cannot do without the specialist in an age whose research style is characterized by teamwork. However, the danger does not rest on the fact that more scientists are specializing, but that too many specialists are generalizing. Nothing-butness again. They tell people that man is nothing but a computer.

But such analogies are useful and true in a limited sense.

As a professor of neurology, I agree that it is perfectly legitimate to use the computer as an analogy of the human central nervous system. The mistake doesn't rest on the fact that man in a sense is a computer, but only when you set out to say that man is nothing but a computer. Man is infinitely more than a computer and he is dimensionally more, in the same way that a square is included in a cube, which is constructed and built up on the basis of the square. So, the cube in a certain sense is also a square, but at the same time it is infinitely more than a square. It is not more or less than a whole dimension. The same holds true for man.

Then you don't believe the empirical approach holds the solution. Yet in a very real way your theories were put to the empirical test at Auschwitz and Dachau, in the death camps.

If we define empirical in the widest sense of the word, you are right. If we broaden and widen our visual field for man, finally and hopefully we might recognize that empirical means not only sticking to figures, sticking to statistics, sticking to experiments, but transcending them as well. Man is transcending himself, and we psychiatrists and psychologists must transcend mere experimentation and mere statistics. We can never seize hold of man by statistics and experimentation. Let me start again. Nothing is annulled of the sound findings within the lower dimensions: behaviorism, psychoanalysis, or Adlerian psychology. They are justified and obtain their true validity when they are placed into a wider horizon.

Actually you are overstating to drive home a point, aren't you? American psychology is hardly constricted.

Oh, no. While you Americans are thinking too unidimensionally for my taste, you are soundly developing, advancing, progressing from a subhumanism—as I used to define reductionism, reducing human phenomena to subhuman phenomena—to humanism. When I said that I did not wish to be totally identified with the existential psychological movement in this country, it was also because I wished to be connected with the humanistic psychological movement, as developed by Gordon Allport, Abraham Maslow, and Charlotte Buehler. This is a sound approach, counteracting the unidimensional mechanistic orientation of exclusively behavioristic thinking.

You obviously admire Maslow and the late Gordon Allport.

Yes, but not only as scientists, as human beings as well. I wonder if you know that it is exclusively due to Allport that my book came out in an American translation at all?

I wish I had known him. His death this year was a great loss to psychology in this country. How did he help you?

I didn't know him, either. The report of my experiences in the concentration camp had been translated by a British nurse in Bavaria immediately after the war. She just did it for her own pleasure, and then she translated the book and sent me a copy of the manuscript. I was giving a series of lectures in the United States and was introduced to Allport at Harvard. He read the manuscript and then twisted the arm of his publishers until he got a contract for me. He has, you know, written the preface to the expanded version.

And Maslow. Maslow is not only a humanistic psychologist, he is a human being in the truest sense of the word. He is the greatest among those who are promulgating the self-actualization theory. He is a great man.

Is self-actualization in accord with your tenets of logotherapy?

If self-actualization is made a direct target, if it is strived for directly, then it becomes self-defeat. You can actualize yourself only to the extent to which you fulfill a meaning or encounter another human being. In other words, self-actualization must come about through self-transcendence. I fear I must contradict your Declaration of Independence. Pursuit of happiness seems to me to be self-defeating, because man originally never pursued happiness. A human being doesn't care primarily for happiness or pleasure or power. Happiness and pleasure are side effects, destroyed precisely to the extent that they are aimed at.

I'd like to ask you more about the unhappy days when you were in charge of the Department of Neurology under the Nazis. Were you able to save any patients who might have been sent to the gas chambers?

Yes, indeed, and with the help of a member of the Nazi party! My beloved teacher Poetzl was a Nazi. Once I had a patient suffering from a brain tumor who needed surgery. I lifted the receiver and called the Nazi Poetzl. He rushed to a taxi, left all his responsibilities, and came to the Jewish Hospital, to help me diagnose a Jew's ailment! He, in turn, telephoned the greatest brain surgeon and said, "I have a patient for you. When can he be admitted to the hospital?" After they said the day after tomorrow, he added, "Incidentally, he is Jewish." By then the brain surgeon could not withdraw his consent.

The Nazis were using euthanasia, you know, and each and every patient who was regarded as incurable was sent to the gas chamber. Even the relatives, mothers-in-law, and so forth of high-ranking party functionaries were gassed. And Poetzl could not help them. The only people he rescued were some Jewish psychotics, because they could be sent to a Jewish Home for the Aged. Whenever such a case occurred, I wrote up a false certificate. For example, a schizophrenic was diagnosed by me as a case of aphasia. After all, one might lose his facility to speak after a stroke. And a case of suicidal depression was diagnosed as a delirium from a feverish infection. Poetzl was the man who made it possible. This way Jewish psychotics were saved from euthanasia.

From this you will understand why I say that if one was a Nazi, it does not necessarily mean that one was guilty. There are only two races of people, the decent ones and the indecent ones, and they cross biological races and political parties. What matters is the man.

I have known only a few concentration-camp survivors. Those I do know seem always to be in need of justifying their existence. It is as though they constantly question their right of survival.

That is true. Let us take the case of a transport which prisoners knew was to take them to the gas chamber. There was neither time nor desire on the part of prisoners to con-sider moral or ethical issues. Every man was controlled by one thought only—to keep himself alive . . . and to save his friends. With no hesitation, therefore, he would arrange for another prisoner to take his place. On the average, only those survived who, after years of trekking from camp to camp, lost all scruples in their fight for existence. They were prepared to use every means, honest and otherwise, in order to save themselves. The best of us did not return.

My wife and I were married in Vienna in 1941. She died at Bergen-Belsen and I still do not know the date of her death.

How did you survive?

I was lucky. And I survived better as a person because I had a rich intellectual background, an inner life on which to draw. And I had a mission, to counsel other inmates. Do you know what my fantasy and finally compulsion became in those years? I wanted to live to go mountain-climbing again. Can you understand that?

Understand? But how could anyone fail to understand? It was good to meet your present wife. Do you have any children?

Only one, a daughter. Gabriele is my child by my present wife. She is in her third year at the Vienna University, and she is enthusiastically studying psychology. She is statistically minded and experimentally oriented and a strong opponent of her father's logotherapy. She has read only one of my books and that because her fiance was so enthusiastic about it. But I have only one child, and so I appreciate the fact that she is intellectually independent and can be my strong adversary.

Meaning has an objective quality, which is another way of saying it is to be discovered rather than invented.

—*Viktor Frankl*

The United States, as you know, is in the middle of a great group-therapy binge. What do you think of group encounters and therapy?

Group therapy or family therapy or community therapy is something particularly needed in your country at the present stage. As great as the number of psychologists might be in the United States, they simply cannot cope with the load of cases. Therefore, such devices as group therapy must be developed. But the principle of psychotherapy will remain forever in my eyes as a process that cannot do away with the intimate basis. This factor cannot be relinquished. Whether you reduce this phenomenon to the mere psychodynamic plane or take it at its face value as a truly human personal or—to use deliberately a so-misused term—existential encounter, this intimate relationship is needed. That is one of the great lessons we had to learn from Freud and the psychoanalysts. So I do have a reservation. Group therapy can never become the whole story.

One last question. Are you a formally religious man?

Let me be 100 per cent European by not answering this question. Let me say that the Hippocratic oath I took when I received my medical degree compels me to care for and insist that logotherapy be available for every patient, including the agnostic, and useable in the hands of every doctor, including the atheist.

You come through to me as a deeply religious man. I know I'm right in the true sense of the word.

Heaven only knows.

Time (essay date 2 February 1968)

SOURCE: "Meaning in Life," in *Time,* Vol. 91, No. 5, February 2, 1968, pp. 38, 40.

[*In the following essay, the critic discusses logotherapy, emphasizing Frankl's existential approach to psychoanalysis.*]

Vienna has a habit of giving birth to schools of psychiatry and then putting them up for adoption in other countries. An exception is the latest Viennese system of mind healing called logotherapy, which has won quick acceptance in its native land and is gaining adherents in the U.S. and behind the Iron Curtain.

Dr. Viktor E. Frankl, 62, founder of logotherapy, is a lecturer at the University of Vienna, as was Freud. But Frankl has dismissed Freud's idea that human beings are driven mainly by sexual energy, no matter how broadly defined. Similarly, he rejects Adler's emphasis on power drives and Jung's turning back to vague, ancestral archetypes. He has only contempt for the reductionist, or "nothing-but" schools, which define man as nothing but a biochemical machine or nothing but the product of his conditioning or nothing but an economic animal. What is left? Only, says Frankl, the most fundamental of all human strivings: the search for the meaning of life, or at least for a meaning in life.

Since this search is at the intellectual rather than the instinctual level, Dr. Frankl makes great play with words beginning with noö-, from the Greek *noös* (mind), as in noödynamics and noögenic neuroses. He coined logotherapy from *logos,* usually translated as word, speech or reason, which he defines as "meaning." As Dr. Frankl views the human condition today, it is distinguished by "the existential vacuum," or "a total lack, or loss, of an ultimate meaning to one's existence that would make life worthwhile." This loss results, he says, from the fact that man, unlike the animals, has no instincts to tell him what he must do, and in recent years has grown away from traditions that once told him what he should do.

Frankl freely concedes that logotherapy is an existential approach. Existentialism has built up a strong undercurrent in both European and U.S. analysis and psychotherapy in the past dozen years. But Frankl notes that there are almost as many kinds of existentialism as there are existentialists, and insists that his is different. He has spelled it out in books such as *Man's Search for Meaning* and *Psychotherapy and Existentialism. The Existential Vacuum: A Challenge to Psychiatry* is on press.

Without a sense of meaning, says Dr. Frankl, even the pursuit of happiness must lead to a dead end. A man who sets out deliberately to seek pleasure through sexual gratification will, he believes, defeat himself. So will the man who lusts for power; even its achievements will avail him nothing unless it involves the satisfaction of some inner goal.

In defining such goals, Frankl runs into difficulty. In English, he says, he is forced back upon the word spiritual, but he insists that this does not require a religious connotation. No psychiatrist, he points out, can prescribe religion for an irreligious patient. At the same time, just as emphatically, he warns psychiatrists against suppressing or ignoring whatever religious feelings, overt and latent, a patient may have.

In answering the question "What is meant by meaning?", Dr. Frankl first makes a distinction between meaning and values. To him, values are meanings shared by many people throughout history or throughout a society. The "meaning" in which Frankl is interested is an individual's own, and is unique to his situation at any given moment. It is, he insists, something that each man must find for himself, through his conscience. When he does so, he is likely to find that it has a Gestalt quality—the whole of an experience is, in some indefinable way, greater than the sum of its parts.

Logotherapy proposes few set rules for the psychiatrist. Dr. Frankl does not even exclude combining it with the most drastic physical treatments, when he thinks that nothing else will help. He takes pride in having introduced guaiphenesin, which he calls the first widely used tranquilizer, in 1952; he also uses electric shock, still a standard treatment in some cases of depression.

In logotherapy the patient sits facing his doctor, who, unlike the classical analyst, may do much of the talking. Dr. Frankl is only half jesting when he says that the patient "must hear things that sometimes are very disagreeable to hear." It is virtually impossible in any language to describe the process of helping a patient to find meaning or new meaning in his life. Not only does it vary from patient to patient, but in many cases Dr. Frankl, guided by his own intuition, improvises changes in method as he goes along.

Vienna-born and educated, Dr. Frankl was spared by the Nazis until late 1942, when he was confined in Theresienstadt, and in 1944 he was sent to Auschwitz. His mother and his wife died in concentration camps. Another casualty was the manuscript of a book on which he had worked for years. Dr. Frankl survived three camps, and has written of his experiences with a keen humanism as well as psychiatric insight. Since World War II, he has won wider recognition, and he now heads the neurological department of Vienna's famed Poliklinik Hospital.

Freud offended the hierarchs of all faiths by his dismissal of religion as a neurosis, and psychoanalysis is still frowned upon by Austria's Roman Catholic Church, even when it is practiced by unswervingly Catholic psychiatrists. But Dr. Frankl's Jewishness is not held against him by Catholics as it was against Freud and Adler. In his system there is such a big place for religion that he is a favorite of Salzburg's Archbishop Franz Jachym, who endorses his writings. To the extent that the church accepts Frankl, the Freudians and Adlerians tend to reject him. And Frankl admits that logotherapy was at first attacked for confusing religion with psychiatry. Now, he contends, its acceptance in officially atheistic Iron Curtain countries shows that it is indeed a truly psychotherapeutic system.

The Times Literary Supplement (review date 3 July 1969)

SOURCE: "Logotherapeutical Sermon," in *The Times Literary Supplement*, No. 3514, July 3, 1969, p. 723.

[*In the following unfavorable review of* The Doctor and the Soul, *the critic faults Frankl's notion of existentialism and charges that he neglects the contributions of Sigmund Freud and other psychoanalysts in the development of his logotherapeutic approach.*]

The Doctor and the Soul purports to provide an account of a new kind of psychotherapy which is "to transcend the limits of all previous psychotherapy". It is Dr. Frankl's belief that psychotherapy has, to date, paid too little attention to "the spiritual reality of man". This defect he proposes to remedy by the employment of what he calls "logotherapy". From his account, logotherapy, appears to be the employment of an exhortative technique of treatment, in which the patient is argued with, cajoled, and finally instructed to adopt the quasi-religious beliefs professed by Dr. Frankl. He alleges that Adler's individual psychology goes deeper than Freud's psychoanalysis: a curious idea, since the chief weakness of Adler's approach is his neglect of the unconscious. He also asserts that the goal of psychoanalysis is to bring about a compromise between the demands of the unconscious and the requirements of reality. without giving any indication that he understands the chief therapeutic tools of psychoanalysis—the interpretation of defences and the understanding and resolution of transference.

The word "existential" is rather freely employed: and Dr. Frankl is much preoccupied with the "meaning of life"; but this is about the sum of evidence indicating that he has any conception of what existentialism is all about. In particular, he shows very little understanding of those particular patients who complain that their life is meaningless, and appears to believe that those who do so complain are raising a valid philosophical problem rather than suffering from any form of neurosis or psychosis. He appears totally unaware of the work of Laing, Fairbairn and Guntrip on schizoid states, and, although he appreciates that schizophrenics feel themselves to be acted upon rather than active agents seems not to possess any concept of identification, ego-boundaries, or the relation of the ego to the body. In short, he claims to have gone beyond both Freud and Adler without giving any evidence that he has truly comprehended either.

As a practical therapist, Dr. Frankl has no doubt had some success. He describes one technique, "paradoxical intention", in which he persuades persons with phobias to entertain the ideas and to embrace the situations of which they are frightened. Thus obsessionals are encouraged to get dirty, people with tremors to show others how much they can tremble, persons with fears of behaving antisocially to "vomit into people's faces and create the greatest possible mess". It is not always clear from the text just how literally Dr. Frankl means his instructions to be taken. Thus, a man with a fear that he might "grab somebody's penis" is "instructed to seek every possible opportunity on the street, in restaurants, in the car, at work, to grab a man's penis". We are told that he soon "started to laugh at his obsessions and they completely disappeared" but we are not told whether he had to act upon his obsession before the symptom left him nor what the attitude of the police or the possible victims of his assaults might be supposed to be. We must assume that he was only grabbing in jest or in fantasy; but there are other sexual compulsions which do not so easily dissolve in gusts of laughter, and which are both more dangerous and more distressing. It is, of course, easy to gain some success in the field of psychotherapy if one is both arrogantly sure of oneself and inclined to didactic preaching. But such attitudes lead nowhere in terms of research or increased comprehension of the manifold complexities of neurosis.

Anatole Broyard (review date 26 November 1975)

SOURCE: "From Shrink to Stretch," in *The New York Times,* November 26, 1975, p. 27.

[*Broyard was an American critic, essayist, memoirist, short story writer, and educator whose works include* Aroused by Books *(1974) and* Kafka Was the Rage *(1993). In the following mixed review of* The Unconscious God, *he focuses on Frankl's call for the "rehumanization" of psychotherapy.*]

While our behavior goes from bad to worse, our psychological image keeps getting better. At the turn of the century, when Western man was still a relatively orderly creature, Freud saw him as a hotbed of lust and aggression. Now, Viktor Frankl suggests that man's primary motive is the search for meaning in his life. Within man, says the author, "there is a repressed angel."

According to the *American Journal of Psychiatry,* Viktor Frankl has contributed "perhaps the most significant thinking since Freud and Adler." An earlier book, ***Man's Search for Meaning,*** sold 1.5 million copies and is often quoted by contemporary writers. Dr. Frankl has founded what amounts to a school of psychotherapy, which he calls logotherapy, embracing the various meanings of logos, including word, Divine word, reason and rational principle.

The Unconscious God was published in German in 1947: this is its first translation into English. Since then, the author writes, he has accumulated new evidence, additional insights. But since he feels that the original publication was his "most organized and systematized" book, he was reluctant to "destroy the cohesive structure of this piece of work by interspersing too much of the material that might have accrued in the meantime." He solved the problem by making the second half of the present volume a commentary on the first. The chief difference lies in the "experimental" evidence he cites for his position, provided by members of his school or psychologists sympathetic to it.

Based mainly on the author's reasoning, the original version of **The Unconscious God** is hortatory and only moderately persuasive. It seems to preach or proselytize at least as much as it reasons. The second half of the book, which is richer in tangibles, strengthens his position somewhat.

Logotherapy sees man's "will to meaning" as a sign of his unconscious or spontaneous spirituality. Freud, writes the author, saw the unconscious as "a reservoir of repressed instinctuality." He has "betrayed the self and delivered it to the id." Under Freud, psychoanalysis "succumbed" to objectivity, which led to reification of the self, a reduction of personality to a thing whose mechanisms could be influenced by merely technical means.

For Freud, religion was "the universal compulsive neurosis of mankind." But Dr. Frankl feels that "compulsive neurosis may well be diseased religiousness." Far from being "driven" by instincts, man is starved for motives. He does not ask, "What is the meaning of life?" Life poses the question to him in his spiritual nakedness, in his "unrest of the heart."

The search for meaning, writes the author, is not the same as the search for self. Freudian analysis places too much emphasis on the self, which "does not yield to total self-reflection." "Human existence," Dr. Frankl adds, "exists in action rather than reflection." Like many of the new approaches to therapy, Dr. Frankl's logotherapy claims to be action-oriented, although he never makes it sufficiently clear what these actions may be. His formulations tend to be rather grandiose, such as "the more one forgets one's self—giving one's self to a cause or another person—the more *human* he is. And the more one is immersed and absorbed in something or someone other than one's self the more he really becomes *himself.*"

According to **The Unconscious God,** man's actions are a response to "existential" situations rather than to instinctive drives. Life is a process of "deciding what one is going to be." While the search for meaning may imply various kinds of pressure, man's response to these pressures is personal and autonomous. Nor does Dr. Frankl's spirituality resemble Jung's, for Jung's collective unconscious is still too general and impersonal for him.

Happiness, says the author, "cannot be pursued. It is the very pursuit of happiness that thwarts happiness." Pleasure and happiness are only the byproducts of "self-transcendence." The nobility of Dr. Frankl's vocabulary takes some getting used to, as when he writes that the most important factor contributing to high orgasm and potency rates is "romanticism."

He describes the absence of meaning in one's life as the "abyss experience" and says that 60 percent of his American students, as against 25 percent of his European students, had suffered from this feeling. When he states that "self-interpretation" is the value that ranks highest among American college students, he seems to be suggesting a correlation. Apparently, 60 percent of these self-interpreters failed to find satisfactory answers. Some of them turned to drugs in order to induce delusions of meaningfulness.

Calling for a "rehumanization" of psychotherapy, Dr. Frankl observes that its orthodox image is in such low repute that the American Psychoanalytic Association went so far as to hire a public relations expert to counsel the counselors. Logotherapy, which is presumably humanized, is described by its own public relations counselor, Dr. Frankl himself, as "education to responsibility." While it is difficult to disapprove of this idea, the author does not tell us very much about how we can implement it. When he writes about "ontologized morals" and "repressed transcendence," some readers may hark back nostalgically to the chaste silence of their Freudian "shrinks." If "shrink" is the slang term for the Freudian analyst, then the logotherapist ought to be called "stretch."

David Cohen   (essay date July 1977)

SOURCE: "The Frankl Meaning," in *Human Behavior: The News Magazine of the Social Sciences,* Vol. 6, No. 7, July, 1977, pp. 56, 58-62.

[*Cohen is an American journalist, freelance writer, filmmaker, and founder of* Psychology News. *In the following essay, he discusses Frankl's attempt to connect his understanding of the spiritual dimension of humanity with psychotherapy and, in particular, the logotherapeutic approach.*]

The titles of Viktor Frankl's books—**Man's Search for Meaning, The Doctor and the Soul, The Will to Meaning**—made me expect a gloomy man who could be the hero of one of Bergman's bleaker films. Frankl lives in the heart of Vienna's medical district. The streets are narrow, quiet and a little dark. I pushed open the big heavy door of the block of flats where Frankl lives and found myself in a long, shabby hallway. My footsteps clanged on the stone floor. Certainly, it was going to be a somber interview.

But Frankl is far from a gloomy man. He bubbles with energy and good humor. He was delighted to see me, he said, and led me into a large light room that is his office. As I switched on my cassette, he smiled and said he would switch his on. He liked to have his own record of an interview and added, without a trace of embarrassment, that two American universities had asked him to record every interview he gives for their archives. He obviously enjoys recording himself for posterity.

Frankl also likes to be busy. He showed me photographs of him and his wife rock climbing. "Not bad still doing that at 70," he remarked and smiled. He enjoyed being photographed and, aware of what it takes to make good shots, slightly exaggerated his gestures while the photographer was there. The phone rang. A Swiss television station wanted to finalize arrangements for him to appear on a program. He was impressed by the way they had coaxed him to go on the air. He likes the idea of doing it. He almost seems to advertise the motto that a full life is a fulfilled life. He appears less contemplative than his books suggest.

Frankl was one of the first psychiatrists to treat patients as responsible human beings rather than superior machines that had a screw loose. In the end, even Freud expected to be able to pin a biochemical cause to every individual act. But from the 1920s, Frankl had patients who wanted something more than to be debugged of their hangups. Getting rid of their complexes did not suddenly make sense of their lives—they wanted to find meaning. Frankl alerted psychiatry and therapy to what could roughly be called the spiritual needs of humanity. The result is logotherapy, an approach that recognizes the fundamental need for meaning in a person's life.

One educated in Britain tends to suspect people who bandy about words like *meaning*. Only those who don't know what they're talking about dabble in such metaphysics. But it was surprising to find both that Frankl was humorous—even able to tell the odd joke about himself—and, also, that he did not hate science as so many of the existential gurus seem to do. Although logotherapy sounds weighty—translated literally, it means the therapy of meaning—there is often a lot of humor to it.

Frankl was one of the first psychiatrists to treat patients as responsible human beings rather than superior machines that had a screw loose.

—David Cohen

Given the confusion as to what life is really about now that the comfortable certainties of the past have gone, it isn't surprising that many people have found in Frankl something of a sage. He sees a desperate need for meaning all around and does not dismiss it as childish or as simply a stage that a person out-grows once he or she knows better. And Frankl believes that we need to develop the capacity for finding our personal raisons d'être.

"Meanings are inexhaustible. We need to develop our intuitive sense that allows us to smell out meanings hidden and dormant in life situations. This is very important today. Education should see as one of its main aims training people to be sensitive to the potential for meaning," he explains.

In developing logotherapy since the '20s, Frankl has made a number of enemies who attack both the man and his ideas. They often seize on the fact that Frankl can be a little vain. After speaking with him, I dined with some Freudians who rebuked me for having interviewed "their enemy." I shrugged that off as a passing gibe. But during dinner, I was told a number of malicious anecdotes.

It is not clear why some Freudians are so hostile to Frankl. He was never formally a Freudian analyst, even though he was born in Vienna. When he was three, Frankl decided to be a physician. His father had also wanted to be one, but money problems compelled him to work, first, as a stenographer in the Austrian Parliament and, then, as a civil servant in the Ministry of Social Work. "My father did more than encourage me to become a doctor; he wanted me to fulfill his dream," Frankl says. Frankl's parents were liberal Jews. He states, "No one ordered me to go to the synagogue," but he developed a feeling for the spiritual that he distinguished from the religious.

At 15, Frankl discovered psychoanalysis. As he was fascinated by both psychiatry and philosophy, psychoanalysis offered the perfect mix. Although he was still a schoolboy, Frankl went to university extension courses given by one of Freud's disciples, Hitchmann. "I also went to lectures by Paul Schilder, who spoke every Saturday evening for two hours in the university hospital." Schilder tried to apply psychoanalysis to the psychoses. Frankl added that the man was a genius but Frankl cannot resist also pointing out, and mimicking rather well, his squeaky high-pitched voice.

In 1922, Frankl read Freud's *Beyond the Pleasure Principle*. He liked the book enormously, not least because it fitted in with his own ideas. In 1919, when Frankl was 14, he had an intuitive-scientific vision—again spiritual rather than religious. "On the deck of a steamer in the Danube, I looked up at the stars and I arrived at the vision that nirvana is entropy seen from within. In entropy, all energy dissipates. There are no differences between things and so there is absolute equality and unity. I saw nirvana as being this lack of tension seen from within." Freud developed a thesis that was not dissimilar. All living things seek both pleasure and the release from tension that can only come with death. When we are a feast for the worms, we have no problems, no tension. Is it surprising that we should all tend toward the "tranquility of the inorganic state"?

Frankl began to send Freud articles from the literature that he thought might interest him. The two began to correspond. Freud was meticulous. "He answered each single letter, if only in the form of postcard, within 48 hours," Frankl says. Freud's courtesy to him—he knew, after all, that Frankl was only a schoolboy—touched Frankl. Once, Frankl enclosed a short essay with some ideas about the origins of such gestures as nodding and shaking the head. Freud suggested it be published and, at the tender age of 18, Frankl made his entrance into the literature in the *International Journal of Psychoanalysis*.

Toward the end of the correspondence, Freud suggested that Frankl visit Paul Federn, then the secretary of the Psychoanalytic Society, to discuss when Frankl should start his training analysis. Federn said he should first get his medical degree; the training analysis might interfere with his studies. Frankl accepted this advice, and ironically, it ultimately meant he would never have training analysis and would never formally become a Freudian—which may be why he found it so easy to be "disloyal" to Freud. By the time he was a physician, Frankl had become disenchanted with Freud.

Frankl felt that Freud, in his desire to be scientific, denied the rich spiritual side of humanity. Sex could not cause everything. Freud strained the importance of sex and denied the individual all final responsibility for his or her actions by explaining them away in subhuman terms.

Curiously, though, Frankl only met Freud once—later and by accident. "I saw an old man with a black stick with a silver handle beating the pavement and murmuring to himself, it seemed. I don't believe he was talking to himself but the pains in the jaw might give that impression." For the last 15 years of his life, Freud suffered an agonizing cancer of the jaw. Frankl followed the old man and saw him turn in Berg-gasse, the street on which Freud lived.

"I decided to introduce myself," Frankl recalls. "There was very little traffic, and he was in the middle of the street when I asked him if I had the honor to address Professor Freud. He said, 'Yes, I'm Freud.' I said, 'My name is Viktor Frankl.' " To which Freud responded by immediately quoting back Frankl's address. Frankl told him of a new book on the death instinct, which Freud asked him to review for *Imago;* but Frankl was already a member of Adler's individual psychology "school." He had to decline.

But Frankl also found Adler's "individual" school too narrow, just as Freud's had been. It seemed too dogmatic to explain everything in terms of power, of coping with a sense of inferiority. In the spring of 1927, two critics of Adler—Rudolph Allers and Oswald Schwarz—pointed out at a meeting that the whole of human behavior could not be explained in such narrow ways.

"Adler was there and challenged me to take a stand," Frankl remembers, "I had to agree with the critics but said I saw no need for them to resign from the Adlerian Society, since individual psychology ought to widen its horizons beyond the one power motive." Adler did not like that. Again the good mimic, Frankl acts out the ponderous way in which Adler tried to dismiss such criticisms. "From that moment on, Adler never spoke to me. When I approached the tables where the Adlerians sat at the Cafe Siller—the Freudians had a different cafe—Adler left. He never greeted me. I felt very hurt. I loved him and I admired him. I knew his weaknesses but I liked him."

In the next month, Frankl was repeatedly invited to resign from the Adlerian Society. He replied constantly that he saw no reason to. "Finally, Adler decreed I was no longer a member. He excommunicated me. It was embarrassing for me. But, in another way, it was beneficial perhaps because I no longer had to consider problems of loyalty."

At the age of 22, then, Frankl felt no need to cling to any particular psychological school—and in Vienna in the 1920s, each "master" demanded almost total loyalty.

While studying medicine, Frankl helped set up a number of youth counseling centers in different parts of Austria, Germany, Czechoslovakia and Hungary. Their main aim was to help young people who felt suicidal and to, literally, talk them into living. Talking at all hours to fellow students, he learned it is not enough for psychiatrists to cope with people's complexes, deliver them from their hangups and, then, declare them whole.

Paradoxical intention uses what Frankl sees as a specifically human dimension, the ability to be self-detached. The patient can see how absurd the phobia is.

—David Cohen

Often a patient suffers not from a complex but from feeling there is no point to life. The only help is for the person to find a meaning in his or her life. Sometimes, the meanings that Frankl found for suicidal patients seem trite, especially in a setting of apparent hopelessness. For instance, Frankl was imprisoned in a concentration camp during World War II, and while there he was visited by two other prisoners, a man and a woman who were close to suicide. Neither expected anything more from life. "I asked both my fellow prisoners whether the question was really what we expected from life. Was it not rather what life was expecting from us?" He suggested that the woman had a child abroad who was waiting for her and the man had a series of books that he had begun to publish but had not yet finished. Such meanings seem almost too simple—but Frankl records many cases in which pointing out even the simplest meanings or making it possible for a patient to find them did change lives.

Because of his experience with Freud, Adler and the youth centers, Frankl was permitted to act as a psychotherapist at the university hospital before he had qualified as a physician. "I learned to forget what I had learned from my great teachers, Freud and Adler. I tried to learn from my patients by learning to listen to my patients."

It is not just Frankl who makes meaning important. Frankl mentions several statistical studies showing that maybe one neurosis in five has, at its root, a feeling that life is meaningless. Neither psychoanalysis nor a technique like behavior therapy offers much help there. Recently, Frankl had a patient who had been to a behavior therapist. The therapist had tried to condition him to stop thinking the thought "Life is meaningless." Although Frankl approves of much in behavior therapy, he felt it was absurd here and insensitive to use such a mechanistic approach.

In the '20s, Frankl also became aware that many patients had learned to live very well with phobias and compulsions. "Again and again, I became aware of what in modern behavioristic language one would call the coping mechanisms that allowed patients to deal with anxieties and obsessions." During this period, Frankl hit on and developed his first original therapeutic technique—paradoxical intention.

"The essence of paradoxical intention is to get the patient to do or to wish to happen exactly what it is that he fears to do." He had a patient once who was scared that if he went out onto the street, he would have a heart attack and die. Eventually, Frankl told the patient that what he was to do was to go out, stand on the street corner and will himself to have the biggest heart attack ever. The patient did so and discovered that the more he tried to will on a heart attack, the more impossible it seemed. And his fear of having a heart attack disappeared. A second case: a young surgeon would always tremble when a superior entered the operating theater. Frankl told him that the next time a superior came in, the young surgeon had to try to tremble as hard as he could "to show what a good trembler" he was. "This quite took the wind out of the phobia," Frankl recalls, smiling.

For Frankl, what is crucial is that patients, being human beings, live through their fear and see through their anxiety.

—David Cohen

Frankl admits that he stumbled onto the technique almost four decades ago out of intuition and impatience, rather than by research. "In a way, I felt it better to have an end to the horror than to have a horror without end with the patient subjected to constant, repetitive anxieties; so I said to the patient, tongue in cheek, 'For a change, let's try to have a heart attack,'" he explains.

Also, Frankl was reacting against psychoanalysis. "I sometimes had to deal with patients who had been through psychoanalysis and who had been induced to focus attention on their inner life, on their past, on their pathology, on their introspections. I felt the impulse to help man to break out of all this inner turmoil, the introspections and retrospections that were increasing their problems. And this paradoxical intention seemed to be a way."

Paradoxical intention uses what Frankl sees as a specifically human dimension, the ability to be self-detached. The patient can see how absurd the phobia is. Usually, a phobic patient avoids the situation that would bring on his or her phobia. The agoraphobic stays inside and, by staying inside, copes successfully with his or her fear of open spaces. But this very success strengthens the phobia. It's positive feedback. Next time round, the possibility of going out arouses even greater anxiety. Frankl explains, "As in behavior therapy, the principle is that what is at the root of phobias is the avoidance of fear-arousing situations. So you have to approach them directly." He sometimes points out that behavior therapy realized the value of this some 35 years later than he did.

But paradoxical intention not only confronts the patient with the feared situation, it mobilizes the specifically human ability to experience humor. Only human beings can be self-detached. Frankl claims—against a number of ethologists—that Homo sapiens is the only species that can laugh. But the point is not really whether some apes can, perhaps, laugh but that no one Frankl recognizes as an authority has yet suggested that an ape can see a joke, let alone a joke against himself. But, to be self-detached, one has to be able to see the funny side of oneself.

For Frankl, suffering can be creative.

—David Cohen

In a recent paper in *Psychotherapy* (Fall 1975), Frankl records many cases in which paradoxical intention was used by himself and often by other therapists. It is the technique, not the particular therapist, that succeeds. These case histories often highlight the use of humor. Linda T was an attractive 19-year-old student who had problems with her parents. She was very tense. She stuttered. Her therapist, Larry Ramirez, reports—and Frankl quotes him:

> My natural reaction would have been to say, "Relax, it's all right." But from past experience I knew that asking her to relax would only increase her tension. Instead, I responded with just the opposite. "Linda, I want you to act as nervously as you can." "Okay," she said, "being nervous is easy for me." She started by clenching her fists together and shaking her hands as though they were trembling. "That's good," I said, "but try to be more nervous." The humor of the situation became obvious to her and she said, "I really was nervous but I can't be any longer. It's odd but the more I try to be tense, the less I'm able to be."

Paradoxical intention is not just dramatic but also effective. Linda T continued to feel less nervous and her stuttering decreased.

There are some remarkable cases. A doctor on Frankl's staff treated one 65-year-old woman who had suffered from a hand-washing compulsion for 60 years. Paradoxical intention cured her. A fellow logotherapist, Hans Gerz, is quoted by Frankl as having cured a woman who had a 24-year history of phobias. And Frankl tells many impressive cases of his own. But the only experimental study of logotherapy was one carried out in 1972 by W. Solyom and colleagues at the University of Montreal. They used paradoxical intention on patients who had had obsessive-compulsive disorders for between 4½ and 25 years. For each patient they chose two compulsive thoughts. The therapist treated one of these symptoms by paradoxical intention and left the other untreated. In six weeks, patients reported a 50 percent drop in those compulsive thoughts that had had paradoxical intention applied. Since obsessions are notoriously hard to treat, these are impressive figures. No new obsessive symptoms welled up to take the place of those that had gone. But still that is only one experimental study that compared logotherapy and other therapies only indirectly. Tough-nosed researchers want more proof.

For Frankl, what is crucial is that patients, being human beings, live through their fear and see through their anxiety. They can laugh at themselves or, at least, take a detached view. The ironic insight, the paradox, is central. But for most behavior therapists, the humor that is so dear to Frankl is, at the very most, an embellishment.

Behavior therapists are less generous than Frankl would like to think. Isaac Marks of the *Maudsley* in a comprehensive review of therapies devotes one line to paradoxical intention. "Paradoxical intention is very similar to straight exposure *in vivo*." And, for behavior therapists, the reason paradoxical intention works has nothing to do with insight, ironic or otherwise. The patients are just given prolonged exposure to what they are phobic about and that deconditions their anxiety, since they are not gobbled by the cats or struck down by being in an open space.

For Frankl, people's ability to see themselves in this detached, ironic way goes with humanity's other unique gift—the capacity for self-transcendence. People can find a meaning, because they are capable of self-transcendence. "Self-trancendence means that human existence is directed to something or someone other than itself. Being human is to reach out for a meaning to fulfill. For example, in loving a person or serving a cause, we become ourselves in the best sense of the word. I maintain there is a motivation to find meaning." Humanity has a will-to-meaning.

Although Frankl was working toward this position already in the late 1920s, many people seem to think that he discovered meaning in the concentration camp. "People think I came out of Auschwitz with a brand-new psychotherapy. This is not the case."

After the Germans took over Vienna, Frankl explains, "I was called to the Gestapo offices and this officer examined me. But soon it seemed all camouflage. What he really wanted to squeeze out of me was whether and where there were still psychoanalysts and psychotherapists in Vienna." The Gestapo man asked how such people would treat agoraphobia; he said he had a friend who suffered from agoraphobia. "I realized, of course, that he was the person who suffered from agoraphobia and that he wanted to be treated. It was an instance of pure technique in therapy, because there could be no encounter between me and him. So, finally, I told him that if there were psychotherapists working in Vienna and if his friend went to see them, this would probably be what they would do." And Frankl told the Gestapo man how paradoxical intention would treat "his friend." The purely technical treatment may have succeeded, and it may explain why Frankl and his family were not deported to their first concentration camp until 1942—a full year after the encounter.

Frankl, his first wife and his parents were deported to the concentration camp at Terezin in Czechoslovakia. His father died there. In 1944, he was deported to Auschwitz and, from Auschwitz, to Dachau. "When I entered Auschwitz, I had hidden in the lining of my coat the full-length manuscript of what later became my first book, *The Doctor and the Soul*." This manuscript was a systematic presentation of logotherapy. He reiterates that Auschwitz did not inspire a new therapy.

Frankl believes that meanings can be found in unique life situations. "I am not talking about ultimate meaning. I grasped when I was 16 that I may one day find meaning either in a creative way—in work or doing a deed—or in an experiential way, in the way one experiences something or someone as good or true or beautiful. There is also a third way. If your situation is unchangeable, if you are suffering from an incurable disease, then you can find meaning by the way you live through it."

The camps taught Frankl much about all these ways to meaning. In extreme circumstances, those people who felt they had a reason, a goal, to survive were most likely to survive. They did not give up and die as did one inmate Frankl knew. This man dreamed that the war would end for him on March 30, 1945. At first, he was optimistic; then, as March dragged on, he began to despair. There seemed no end of the war in sight. On March 29th, he became delirious; on March 30th, he lost consciousness; on March 31st, he died. As in North Korean and Japanese prisoner-of-war camps, Frankl says, "those who were most oriented toward a meaning to fulfill in the future tended to survive."

In the concentration camps, however, it was not a question of surviving best, of not being broken by the experience; it was a question of not being sent to the gas chambers. Frankl has argued with Hannah Arendt and others who found fault with the Jews for not attacking the SS. Many people who had strong reasons to live "did not believe they were being marched to the gas chambers. Some laughed. And, second, they were powerless. To take action was unrealistic, and it would have been impossibly irresponsible."

The revenge taken would have been atrocious. Those who understood the situation and who were almost resigned to it, Frankl says sadly, managed by their attitude to find or to express a meaning. "Even if you are caught as a helpless victim in a hopeless situation, you may transcend that situation and turn a tragedy into a triumph on a human level by the attitude that you adopt and bear it with." At worst, the way you face your death can give meaning to your life.

Some critics have suggested that Frankl has done nothing more than import some religious ideas into psychiatry.

—David Cohen

Frankl cites the accounts about those who were exterminated in the concentration camps. "Once those people — including my own mother, by the way—had been crammed into the gas chambers and they saw the canisters of Cyclone B gas thrown into a crowd of naked people, they saw there was no help. Then they began to pray, saying the Shema Isreal, and surrendered themselves to what God had bestowed on them—the Communists singing the *Marseillaise,* the Christians saying the Our Father, the Jews saying Kaddish upon each other." Frankl confesses he was awed by the way in which many very simple, ordinary people met their death. "They were able to manifest their deepest humanity."

Frankl stresses the value of suffering. Most therapists, after all, try to make people as happy and well as they can be. For Frankl, suffering can be creative. Once, an old physician came to him, extremely depressed after the death of his wife. Theirs had been a very happy marriage. Frankl records; "'Tell me, what would have happened if you had died first and your wife had survived you?'

"'That would have been terrible,' he said. 'How my wife would have suffered.'

"'Well, you see,' I answered, 'your wife has been spared that, and it was you who spared her, though of course you must now pay by surviving and mourning her.'"

The change in perspective did not make the physician glow with happiness, but it did give him a feeling that there was some point, some meaning, to his suffering. And, as a result, he could handle it much better. Frankl believes that we need, at this time, to develop our capacity for finding meanings.

Frankl is a religious man. Some critics have suggested that he has done nothing more than import some religious ideas into psychiatry. He is accused of encouraging psychiatrists to comfort their patients with talk of ultimate meanings. Frankl denies this. He does not deny that religion concerns him—he feels therapists should not ignore or put down religion.

"Logotherapists," Frankl explains, "see in religion a human phenomenon we have to take into account. We have to consider the fact that so many people have become or remained religious. But that does not mean that you have to be religious to benefit from logotherapy or, indeed, to use it if you are a therapist." Frankl insists that when he speaks about logotherapy, he speaks as an authority, the founder of the technique. "Logotherapy is a technique, the application of a secular scientific approach. Religious psychiatrists should be content if it no longer indoctrinates people with the notion that religion is nothing but the compulsive neurosis of mankind and that God is nothing but our Father Image in the Sky. The result of all that is to block the spontaneous religious self-actualization of a patient who might be so inclined. Not even the Freudians deal with religion that way now."

And many people who are religious, Frankl finds, seek not just a meaning in the here and now of life but also "some overall meaning about life in general. This ultimate meaning may also be the target of motivation. I could speak, therefore, of a Will to Ultimate Meaning, and having recognized such a meaning means being religious in the widest sense of the word. As Einstein said, there are people content with nothing but such meanings." Whatever

> **Frankl has certainly carved out for himself a distinct place as one of the first psychiatrists to see the value of exploring both the spiritual and humorous side of humanity.**
>
> **—David Cohen**

Frankl's personal beliefs, one of the reasons for his popularity is precisely that he pays attention to the fact that we hanker after meaning to make sense of our lives. He doesn't see it as a weakness or an immaturity, as Freud and the behaviorists did.

It is typical of the paradoxes of Frankl's position that this hankering after the religious does not make him antiscientific. "Frankly, I must admit that logotherapy has been developed on purely intuitive grounds by me, which is a personal strength, perhaps, but a scientific weakness," he admits. But he has been glad to see empirical psychologists and psychiatrists bother to look experimentally at his ideas. For example, James C. Crumbaugh and Leonard T. Maholick devised a *Purpose in Life* test (known as PIL) and tried it out on 1,151 subjects. They concluded that there was evidence of a noogenic neurosis, a neurosis caused by a lack of meaning in one's life. There have been other, similar tests. Equally, Frankl is glad to see some convergence between logotherapy and behavior therapy—an unlikely alliance of the spiritual and scientific. Certainly, Frankl displays none of the contempt and hostility toward behavior therapy that most Freudians do. And that is surely welcome change, especially if the behavior therapists will really reciprocate.

Through his career, Frankl has continued to develop insights that he had as a very young man. He was 22 when he broke both with Freud and with Adler because he distrusted the attempt to reduce humanity, to explain individuals away in mechanical terms and rob them totally of their freedom. Frankl sees his work as building upon a wide range of previous work, not overturning it. "Logotherapy," he contends, "has made a contribution by opening up the human dimension which shows that resources can be drawn on once people are aware that man is not just a mechanism, a being that seeks satisfaction of drives, instincts and needs. Beyond what can be explained in subhuman terms, there is specifically human motivation. Man can suffer deliberately for a cause. This is what eludes you if you restrict on a priori bias your research to, say, animals.

"This does not mean that man ceases to be a biochemical entity, but he is more than that. The noetic (the specifically human) dimension encompasses the psychic and somatic one. Freud, Adler, Pavlov, and Watson are not invalidated or to be dismissed, but logotherapy is the more inclusive dimension. Within their dimension, they may all have been right, but one cannot ignore the noetic dimension, because the collective neurosis today seems to be that people feel they are suffering empty and meaningless lives."

"And, in that sense, not in the sense of possessing some universal truth, logotherapy does appeal to the predicament of today's man." As he says that, Frankl positively radiates confidence. Despite his concern to have a much more humane psychiatry, he has kept what he feels is a hard-headed approach. He is critical of much humanistic psychiatry. He enjoys satirizing the pretensions of encounter groups, marathon encounter groups and nude marathon encounter groups as usually being sessions of "mutual monolog."

Frankl now spends his life commuting between Vienna and the United States, where he is a distinguished professor at the United States International University in San Diego, California. He is convinced that his work is influential in the United States, because it answers a desperate need for meaning. He recently received the UNIQUEST Albert Schweitzer Award for 1977, presented to him at the inauguration of the Viktor E. Frankl Library at the Graduate Theological Union in Berkeley, California.

As we finished our talk, Frankl showed me around the room in the flat that he has made his own personal archive. He takes an almost naive pleasure in the room. It has copies of almost everything he has written, of lectures he has given; of tapes he has made. Frankl has certainly carved out for himself a distinct place as one of the first psychiatrists to see the value of exploring both the spiritual and the humorous side of humanity. The contradiction fits him. He cares both about spirit and science, meaning and measurement. Perhaps his real contribution will turn out to be that he did not flinch from these contradictions but kept on trying to achieve an understanding of humanity and our needs that is not oversimplified.

Robert L. Moore   (review date March 1979)

SOURCE: A review of *The Unconscious God,* in *Zygon,* Vol. 14, No. 1, March, 1979, pp. 94-5.

[*Moore is an American television producer, author of* The Green Berets *(1965), and several screenplays, including* The French Connection *(1971). In the following review of* The Unconscious God, *he praises the book's systematic organization but questions Frankl's presentation of the notions of religiosity and spirituality in an existential context.*]

This little monograph [*The Unconscious God: Psychotherapy and Theology*] is a reissue in English of a book first published by Viktor E. Frankl in 1947. Frankl is of course the Viennese psychiatrist who received a good deal of interest from the American theological community during the sixties. Characterizing Freudian analysis as interested in the "will to pleasure" and Adlerian analysis as concerned with the "will to power," Frankl views his logotherapy, the third Viennese school of analysis, as focused instead on the "will to meaning." Critical analysts of Frankl and logotherapy for the most part do not share Frankl's appraisal of himself as a depth psychologist ranking with Sigmund Freud, Alfred Adler, and Carl G. Jung in stature. Indeed a close examination of his criticisms of

the work of these men does not lead one to the conclusion that Frankl has been able to arrive at a very sophisticated grasp of the schools which he so much wants to overshadow.

A careful reading of his best known writings, including *Man's Search for Meaning* (1959) and *The Doctor and the Soul* (1965), provides a basis for understanding why Frankl and logotherapy appear to be waning in influence. His categories blur distinctions and elude definition. The entire system is intriguing at first glance, but sustained analysis reveals it to be speculative, difficult to test or validate, and shot through with overgeneralization and exaggeration. Why then did the system receive such a positive response from American religionists? One obvious answer is that religionists were hungry for validation in the eyes of "legitimate, secular, humanistic, scientific" culture and that Frankl's sanction of a vague religiousness was reassuring. A number of major Protestant seminaries brought Frankl to America to hear him extol the reality of meaning, the value of religion, and the necessity of a transpersonal commitment as essential to self-actualization. Without doubt Frankl has a compelling personal story to tell and is an entertaining lecturer and raconteur. Still, the early popularity of Frankl and his system witnesses more to the religious crisis of middle-class America than to the profundity and promise of logotherapy.

The book under review is a good representative of the Frankl corpus. Indeed Frankl calls it the most organized and systematized of all his books. The book is divided into two parts: the first half being the early lectures on the "unconscious God" and the last half a review of and commentary on recent research and publications on logotherapy. The basic thesis of the former is that there is "a religious sense deeply rooted in each and every man's unconscious depths." Often repressed in modern culture, this unconscious religiousness may break through into consciousness in unexpected ways. Frankl reports that his awareness of this phenomenon was deepened through the existential analysis of dreams. In a chapter on this topic he relates a number of dreams which he deems expressive of the "spiritual unconscious."

It is, however, the existential analysis of conscience which he offers as a key to unconscious spirituality. Conscience for Frankl is prelogical, irrational, and grounded in intuition. It reaches down into the unconscious depths of the person and is a referent to transcendence. Not just referring to transcendence, it originates in transcendence and is thereby irreducible. We should be clear, however, that Frankl does not intend any religious connotation to the word "spiritual." The spiritual is "what is human in man." Frankl then is merely asserting here that the human individual transcends the "facticity" of biological and psychological givens—that human responsibility "reaches down into an unconscious ground."

In his chapter "Unconscious Religiousness" Frankl adds his assertion of the reality of a "transcendent unconsciousness." By this he means that phenomenological investigation reveals that the human unconscious always stands in "an intentional relation to transcendence" and that the intentional referent of such an unconscious relation may be called "God." Thus his concept of an unconscious God "refers to man's hidden relation to a God who himself is hidden."

Obviously aware that his chosen topic will remind us of the work of Jung, Frankl differentiates his position from that of Jung in two basic ways. First, unconscious religiousness is personal, not impersonal and/or archetypical; and second, it is existential, not instinctual—the result of decisions and not drives. Unconscious religiousness "stems from the personal center of the individual man rather than an impersonal pool of images shared by mankind."

If this book encourages scholarly reflection on the repression of the religious which is symptomatic of the modern ethos, then its publication will be justified. Considered in itself, the book promises far more than it delivers—and we have not learned much about *homo religiosus*. Frankl and other theorists of similar stance have drunk so deeply from the now-depleted wells of the Enlightenment that they are unable to relate to the strange world of the religious—conscious or unconscious. When we have progressed further in our understanding of the religiousness of the human psyche, we will find that we have returned again and again to the visions of the archaic psyche as portrayed by Freud and Jung—that Frankl's existential analysis was a cul-de-sac.

George Kovacs　(essay date Fall 1982)

SOURCE: "The Philosophy of Death in Viktor E. Frankl," in *Journal of Phenomenological Psychology,* Vol. 13, No. 2, Fall, 1982, pp. 197-209.

[*In the following essay, Kovacs examines Frankl's notion that death is a natural and integral part of living and that it contributes an understanding of the existential meaning of life.*]

Human attitudes towards the insurmountable factuality of personal death are not simply a syndrome of behavioral mechanisms for coping with a situation of stress, but, more significantly, they express philosophical and ideological understandings of the nature of death from the perspective of human living. Existential phenomenology examines the phenomenon of death precisely in accordance with the methodological significance of the relationship between attitudes and ideas or insights. The philosophies of death of Nietzsche, Jaspers, Scheler, Heidegger, Sartre, Camus, Marcel, and Buber (as well as those of other thinkers) show the existential confrontation with the phenomenon of death according to its attitudinal as well as conceptual dimensions. The concern with the meaning of death is an essential element of the existential-phenomenological approach to the question of death. The philosophy of death in the logotherapy of Viktor E. Frankl shows not only the attitudinal dimensions of existential ideas about death, but also examines the philosophical foundations of the logotherapeutic thesis on the meaning of death. Frankl's analysis of the meaning of death leads to the integration of the phenomenon of death into the inner dynamics of human living.

Frankl's analysis of the meaning of death represents a philosophical and a psychological alternative to the temptation of projecting the phenomenon of death onto a horizon of absurdity and meaninglessness. The interpretation of death in logotherapy is not based on any pre-established ideological presupposition; it is the result of a discovery that happens in the process of dialogue with the propositions of absurdity and meaninglessness. The basic questions of the philosophy of death in logotherapy are as follows: Is there a meaning to death? What is the final, the ultimate meaning of death? Does the reality of death, the fact of the finiteness of the human being in time, make life meaningless? What is the foundational significance of death for concrete human existence on this side of death? What is the nature and what ought to be the task of the therapy of the anxiety of death? What are the ontological (philosophical) foundations of the logotherapeutic claim that the existential fact of death is the source of meaning in human living? These issues represent basic elements of human concerns with the phenomenon of death. The most unique dimension of the philosophy of death in the thought of Frankl consists in the systematic examination of the meaning-question about death. This approach is not aiming at finding the final answers to the ultimate metaphysical questions about death (Why is there death? Is there a reward or a punishment after death? Is there a life after death?). The main task of the logotherapeutic analysis of the phenomenon of death is directed towards showing that the main characteristic of human existence is always the search for and the realization (actualization) of meaning in all human situations, especially in the human encounter with death, illness and suffering. Frankl's reflections on death deal more intensively with life than with death; they show the human capacity to find a meaningfulness in living even in the face of the reality of human death. Death is the source of human fulfillment in living and of the call for the realization of values in the process of living; it is not the cause of any existential vacuum.

> **Frankl's philosophy and existential psychotherapy is based on the existential principle of the will to meaning.**
>
> *—George Kovacs*

By focusing on the question of meaning, logotherapy is helping the patient (all human persons are patients of logotherapy) to meet the existential facts of death, guilt, and suffering. A direct confrontation with these existential situations prevents the neurotic denial of them by the human person. The denial and the repression of these existential situations lead to a detour of the human self from its human and ontological potentialities. Thus logotherapy acknowledges the inescapable existential reality of the unchangeable existential facts (death, suffering, illness, guilt) and at the same time leads to a positive attitude towards them by showing that they are potentially meaningful.

The human person is able to create meaning even in the midst of the desert, even in the seemingly most inhuman situation. The source of many forms of contemporary neuroses lies in the denial of existential facts and not in the denial (repression) of the instinctual (e.g., sexual) components of human existence. Contemporary society may be characterized by the tendency to deny demanding existential facts and by the willingness to accept the instinctual and passionate elements in human living. A merely psychodynamic interpretation of existential facts (e.g., the fear of death interpreted as a castration anxiety) is ultimately based on a deterministic view of human life as a whole. The logotherapeutic perspective rejects the ideology of pandeterminism and affirms the contextual freedom of the human will precisely by showing the function of human attitudes in the acknowledgement of unchangeable existential facts. There is much in human life that is dependent on and decided by the attitude of the human person towards life as such. According to the main principle of logotherapy, human existence is "always directed toward a meaning to fulfill (rather than a self to actualize or one's potentialities to develop)" [*Psychotherapy and Existentialism,* 1967]. The essential transitoriness of human existence does not take away the meaningfulness of life but rather adds to it. Thus logotherapy is able to deal with the often repressed or unconscious existential despair of the patient. Existential despair can be made conscious and thus it may become the object of human reflection and analysis. Existential despair can be reduced and even replaced by the attitude of existential hope, by the existential potentiality of finding and thus realizing a meaning in all human situations. Logotherapy helps the human person to confront (encounter) the repressed fears and anxieties in a positive manner; it leads not to a denial, not to a repression of them but to a human way of dealing with them, to a lucid recognition of them for what they are. This approach goes beyond the reductionist tendency of a merely psychodynamic explanation of the existential situations of the human person.

The next phase of these reflections examines the main themes as well as the attitudinal significance of the philosophy of death in logotherapy. The concern with the phenomenon of meaning and with the human will to meaning enables logotherapy to make valuable and unique contributions to the theoretical understanding as well as to the concrete forms of dealing with the phenomenon of death in the process of human living.

The philosophy of death in the works of Frankl includes an analysis of the following three foundational issues: the relationship between death and the meaning of life; the ontological understanding of temporality; the nature of human death. These three issues are interrelated and they deal with the main questions arising in the process of dialogue between the human being and the reality of death.

a) According to the main thesis of Frankl's existential analysis, the finiteness of the life of the human person in time, the fact of death, does not make life meaningless, but rather gives meaning to life. Many people think that the fact of death destroys the meaning of life as well as the works of human life. Frankl rejects this assumption by in-

dicating the fallacy included in it and by developing a positive understanding of human finiteness. The assumption that finiteness makes human life meaningless implies the claim that the infinite gives meaning to life and to the works, accomplishments of life. But the infiniteness, the immortality of human life would allow the attitude of procrastination (there would always be more time for doing things); it would make whatever the human being does or fails to do into something insignificant since there would be more and additional opportunities all the time. Therefore, the meaning of this life and its works is not dependent on eternity; life is meaningful or meaningless irrespective of its limitations or infinite prolongation in time. Thus the logic that derives meaninglessness from finiteness is not logical at all. There is a *non sequitur* in this assumption. According to the "positive" view of human finiteness in Frankl, "the meaning of human existence is based upon its irreversible quality" [*The Doctor and the Soul*]. Death and singularity make human existence irreversible and thus constitute a source of responsibility for the human person in time. Death is not a thief robbing off the meaning of human life, but the "absolute finis to our future and boundary to our possibilities" [*The Doctor and the Soul*]. The time-boundary of life constitutes a command to use well the time given and to seize the opportunities presented by life. The human person should not let time pass by without using it well because a human life is constituted by accepting the opportunities, by continually summing them up into the whole of life. Human life and human responsibility are situated in time, in the process of history.

How can the logotherapist lead the person who suffers from the sense of meaninglessness in the face of death to a sense of personal responsibility, to the discovery of meaning in finite life? The task of the logotherapist may be defined as the reawakening of the patient to the historical dimension of human existence that is the source of personal responsibility. The human being is responsible for writing the story (history) of his life. Often times time runs out sooner than the work is finished or completed. Nevertheless this running out of time does not make the work and the task done meaningless. A human biography is not to be evaluated by its length but by the richness of its contents. The question about the meaning of life is not a question about quantity but a question about quality!

The finiteness of a life, Frankl insists, does not distract from the quality of life but rather adds to it. By accepting and assuming finiteness, the human being unfolds his life in the process of time and history. The meaning of life does not come from the mere prolongation of living (as the false assumption indicated earlier would imply) but from the accomplishing, the finishing of tasks in finite time. Death belongs to life; there is no need to exclude death from life in order to find meaning in life. The meaning of life is situated not in the future (e.g., in future generations, in eternity) but in the now (presence) of finite time, in human history. Life grows, transcends itself "not in 'length'—in the sense of reproduction of itself—but in 'height'—by fulfilling values" [*The Doctor and the Soul*]; it receives meaning not from the prolongation of itself but from the fulfilling of values and tasks. The growing and the transcending nature of life is not a quantitative but a qualitative characteristic. Life is meaningful or meaningless irrespective of its span in time. The recognition and the awareness of finiteness, according to the logotherapeutic interpretation of the phenomenon of human death, do not dictate, do not lead to a philosophical ideology of absurdity and nothingness. The human acknowledgment of death becomes a source of the joy of living and peace with oneself in the struggle with the unchangeable realities of life.

The main teaching of the logotherapeutic interpretation of the phenomenon of death is the description and justification of the natural attitude of acknowledging the reality of death.

—*George Kovacs*

The positive view of human finiteness in the thought of Frankl sheds a new light on the uniqueness and individuality of the human person. The inner limits of life add to the meaning of the life of the human being. The limitations make each individual human being unique and indispensable. Uniqueness, however, is not a springboard for isolation from, but the source of the right relationship of the individual to the community. Genuine community creates a place for the fulfillment of human individuality; authentic community is born out of the respect for the personal mode of existence. The human individual is not some sample of a general type, but a personal being as *"being different, absolute otherness"* [*The Doctor and the Soul*]. The genuine community contributes to the emergence of the individual as a category of being and enhances the sense of personal responsibility; the mass society submerges individuality and thus dilutes personal responsibility. According to Frankl, the uniqueness of the human being is formed and developed by the personal limitations, the personal choices and acts of the individual. Thus finiteness, limitations, and death itself become a source for meaning in the life of the individual human being. Death does not annul but rather creates responsibility; it calls for the individual's response to the opportunities and questions presented by life in all situations. Human uniqueness and responsibility make up the personal mode of being.

For Frankl, death itself makes life meaningful because human existence is essentially characterized by responsibility that is grounded on human finiteness. Death is not the enemy of life but a part of life. The limit in time and the limited range of his potentialities make the human person accountable for the use of time and of all that is given to him; they determine, shape the quality and the meaning of human existence. Every human being is called to face the limitations of life, but each human being is responding to this call in a personal and a unique way. Thus death makes all human beings equal and, at the same time, uniquely personal; it is a great equalizer and a powerful personalizer of human existence.

Death as a human destiny is not an absurd phenomenon, but a source of meaning in human living. However, according to the thought of Frankl, death is not the only unchangeable destiny of the human being. There are many other unchangeable realities in the life of the human person. Frankl examines the biological, the psychological, and the social determinants of human life with the same attention as he examined the phenomenon of death. The human being is a "deciding being" (Jaspers) because the human being is able to take a free stand towards destiny, towards unchangeable situations in living. According to the existential-phenomenological understanding, the structure of the human being as existence includes both facticity (that which is given) and potentiality (that which is chosen). The human being is not predetermined, but rather determines itself within a range of potentialities. The human being is determined not only by what he already is but also by what he can be; man is not only what he is (already) but also what he is not (yet). The human being can decide to be or not to be. "Destiny must always be a stimulus to conscious, responsible action" [*The Doctor and the Soul*]. Destiny (biological, psychological, social) is meaningfully incorporated by the human person into the structure of his life [*The Doctor and the Soul*]. Frankl's analysis of the various unchangeable elements of human existence (death, biological constitution, psychological dispositions, social environment) leads to the claim (and conviction) that it is possible for the human person to adopt freely chosen attitudes towards (realize values in) the unchangeable situations and realities of human life. The human being can transform a given reality into a possibility, into a potentiality for accomplishing something. An apparent obstacle or a limitation in life may become a source for new personal meaning and self-realization. Thus, for Frankl, death is not the end but rather the beginning or the birth of meaning in human living. The phenomenon of death does not constitute the source of absurdity, but rather contributes to the emergence of meaning.

b) The logotherapeutic view of the phenomenon of death as the source of meaning in human living is built on the philosophical interpretation of the nature of time, on the ontological understanding of temporality and mortality. Frankl's analysis of the ontological nature (the Being or reality) of time is an integral part of his entire philosophy of death.

The transitoriness of human life does not distract from its meaningfulness because of the ontological status of the past. According to logotherapy, the past is nothing but a mode of being, a reality and not merely a possibility. The actualized possibilities exist as part of the past of the person. Everything is being conserved in the past. The accomplishments of the person, the reality of love lived and of the suffering endured with courage remain stored in the past; they are conserved, treasure as the strong background and foundation of what the acting and living person is all about. In Frankl's expression, "being past" is a form of being, "having been" is a mode of being [*The Unheard Cry for Meaning*]. The affirmation of the reality of the past of the human person is a key thesis of logotherapy. The past of the person using time wisely is a source of strength because it is not the product of the chronological passage of time, but the result of passing (transforming) possibilities into realities (accomplishments, actualities). The passing or passage of possibilities into realities is a creative passage (passing) and not a destructive passage. The love lived with a person remains even after the death of the person. The past retains, keeps alive all the possibilities that were transformed into realities through the decisions and acts of the human person. The goodness, the achievements, the trials endured with courage, the meaning of human experience cannot be removed from the world. All these are stored, all these endure in the safety of the past; they constitute a source of comfort and consolation. Thus the life of the human person is transitory, but it is not a life lived in vain; the human person does not live for nothing, but for "some thing."

The interpretation of the ontological status of the past as the "safest mode of being" represents a way of transcending the transitory nature of human life. The past is the record of our choices, of our responsibilities. Human actions and human creations do not vanish into nothingness, but remain an eternal record. For Frankl, the world is not a manuscript written in a secret code we have to decipher (Jaspers), but it is "rather a record we must dictate" [*The Unheard Cry for Meaning*]. This record is written daily by the responses we give to the questions (tasks, assignments) that are presented to us by life. The record, the life lived and created by our responses cannot be lost, but it cannot be corrected either. Thus this record is a source of hope and comfort, but it is also a warning at the same time. Nothing can be removed from the past, but we may rescue our chosen possibilities into the past. We decide in the present what we wish to eternalize by making it part of the past. The art of human creativity consists in nothing else but in the turning of the "possibilities of the future into realities of the past," in the act of moving something "from the nothingness of the future into the 'being past'" [*The Unheard Cry for Meaning*]. Thus everything is transitory because everything is "fleeing from the emptiness of the future into the safety of the past!" [*The Unheard Cry for Meaning*]. All beings fear emptiness; every being is dominated by the *horror vacui* according to the ancient thinkers. All beings are rushing from the emptiness of the future into the safety of the past, into past existence. The present is the narrow passage, the opening into the safety of the past, the admission into eternity. "The present is the borderline between the unreality of the future and the eternal reality of the past" [*The Unheard Cry for Meaning*]. The present is called by Frankl the "borderline" of eternity because the present moment (the decision in the now) decides what should be eternalized, what should be the eternal record of the past. The only way to gain time is by depositing it in the past, by using time well for something now. According to Frankl, the good use of time that takes place in the present, the passage from the future into the past through personal decisions made in this manner by every individual person is nothing else ultimately but the exercise of the existential potentiality for transforming possibilities into realities.

c) What is death? What happens in death? The ontological and the axiological interpretations of time lead to some insights about the issues that are involved in dealing with these questions. According to the logotherapeutic perspective, death gives a definite form and structure to all that happens in the life of the human person. Only the spiritual self remains in and survives death. In death the individual human being not only sees his life in review, but becomes his life; the individual becomes his history. Life in death, then, becomes what the human person made of it. Thus Frankl is able to say that "man's own past is his future. The living man has both a future and a past; the dying man has no future in the usual sense, but only a past; the dead, however, 'is' his past" [*The Unheard Cry for Meaning*]. In living we have both a future and a past; in dying we have no future but only past. In death, in being dead, we are, we have become our own past. In death we have no life; in death we are our lives. The past as the safest mode of being cannot be taken away; in the past as the safest mode of being life is completed and perfected. In life we complete individual facts and tasks; in death life in its totality is completed. Therefore man creates himself, and becomes a reality not at his birth but at his death, at the completion of life by death. The human self is not something that is ready-made but it is rather "some thing" that becomes fully itself in time. Temporality is not simply an aspect of the external process of becoming, but much rather it is an essential element in the inner growth of the human self.

According to Frankl, in daily living the human person tends to misunderstand the reality and the meaning of death. Thus death is regarded very often as an intrusion upon, as an interference with the process of living, and as something finishing off the whole of life. Human beings in daily living worry about death and think about death as something dreadful and entirely hostile to all that life is all about. Human beings forget that death is an alarm that wakes us up to our real existence in the real world. Death opens us up to the true reality of our inner being and selfhood; the personal awareness of our own death leads to the discovery of our own personal being and living.

The above analysis of the philosophy of death in the thought of Frankl leads to some valuable insights about the meaning of human death. The logotherapeutic interpretation of the phenomenon of death integrates the reality of death into the dynamics of human living. Thus the existential analysis of the meaning of death in Frankl represents a positive attitude towards the existential fact of death; it rejects the nihilistic attitude towards death regarded as the enemy of human projects and possibilities. The difficulty of integrating the phenomenon of death into human living is clearly expressed by Simone de Beauvoir in connection with the description of her attitude towards the death of her mother: "It is useless to try to integrate life and death and to behave rationally in the presence of something that is not rational: each must manage as well as he can in the tumult of his feelings" [Simone de Beauvoir, *A Very Easy Death*, 1973]. For Simone de Beauvoir "there is no such thing as a natural death: nothing that happens to a man is ever natural, since his presence calls the world into question. All men must die: but for every man his death is an accident and, even if he knows it and consents to it, an unjustifiable violation" [*A Very Easy Death*]. The philosophy of death in Simone de Beauvoir as well as in Sartre is bound to remain incomplete because it does not include a comprehensive philosophy of human suffering and because it does not develop a more critical analysis of the spectrum of human and intellectual attitudes towards the presence of death in human living. The philosophy of death in Frankl includes a comprehensive analysis of human suffering as well as an analysis of the gamut of human attitudes towards the existential facts of life. Frankl's philosophy and existential psychotherapy is based on the existential principle of the will to meaning. This principle makes possible the integration of the phenomenon of death into the dynamics of human living. The following reflections show the existential significance and the philosophical dimensions as well as the boundaries of Frankl's analysis of the meaning of death.

a) The key thesis of the logotherapeutic interpretation of the phenomenon of death is the affirmation of the meaning-generating function of death, of the potentialities of the will to meaning in the process of dealing with the finiteness of human existence. Death does not take away the meaning that is found in human living but rather propels the human person to find and create meaning in finite living. The human person is able to find and create meaning even in the face of the insurmountable reality of death. According to the logotherapeutic perspective, death can be integrated into the dynamics of human living; death is not the enemy but the essential part of life. Death may come by an accident, but it is not something accidental at all. Logotherapy regards death as an existential fact, as a natural part of human existence. It leads to the attitude of acknowledgment towards death and to the discovery of possibilities for personal fulfillment.

b) Frankl's philosophy of death does not analyze, at least directly, the many metaphysical questions which may be raised in connection with the ultimate meaning of death. Why is there death? Why is the human being condemned to die? Is there a life after death? What is the relationship between the reality of death and the human nostalgia for and speculation about immortality? Is death a punishment or is it the final test of the human capacity to struggle against all the odds in the experience of living? The philosophy of death in Frankl does not constitute a metaphysical response to these fundamentally metaphysical questions. The fact that his analysis of the existential meaning of death may well be compatible with a metaphysical view of death as the passage to another mode of being or as a punishment does not necessarily mean that his analysis *eo ipso* ought to lead to the adoption of a particular system of metaphysics. Frankl's thought is aware of both the orientation and the limitations (boundaries) of existential analysis.

c) Frankl's analysis of the meaning of death, nevertheless, represents not only a psychology and an existential axiology of death, but also an ontology of death. Many aspects of Frankl's philosophy of death, as well as the thought of Frankl as a whole, may be regarded as being quite close to the philosophy of Scheler and to that of Heidegger. The consistent concern with meaning and values in dealing with the basic questions of life and death in Frankl includes some important relationships to the philosophy of

values and of the human person in Scheler. Frankl's analysis and interpretation of the finiteness of human existence, in the final analysis, may be viewed as being quite close to several elements of the existential hermeneutics of death in Heidegger. Frankl, like Heidegger, speaks of the ontology of human finiteness, examines the ontological status (the Being-dimension) of death, of temporality, and of human accomplishments. The future, according to Frankl, is a possibility that is transformed by the decisions and attitudes of the present into realities (actualities) secured in the past as the safest mode of being. The ontological structure of temporality makes possible the logotherapeutic interpretation of death which regards death not as the enemy but as the source of meaning in living for the human person. Human possibilities are situated (given) between the boundaries of temporality and death; these boundaries define and shape the possibilities that are transformed into realities. Thus the tasks become (are transformed into) accomplishments. The present, as Frankl says, is nothing else but the passage of possibilities (future) into realities (past); the present is the passage made possible through the decisions of the human person. The human person is a deciding being, a being that can be described as presence. The issue at stake in these reflections is not the significance of the works (accomplishments, decisions) of life for a possible life after (beyond) death but the possibility of meaning at all under the horizon of death as the expression of temporality. Death does not annul but creates meaningfulness in the works, experiences, and sufferings of this life. The basic insights of logotherapy are not concerned with the possibility of life outside (independently of) the horizon of temporality. Logotherapy is not a substitute for theology and metaphysics.

d) Death as an ontological dimension and horizon of human living challenges the human person to search for meaning in living without deriving this meaning from a system of ideology. The philosophy of death in Frankl transcends ideological and metaphysical boundaries and disputes because it is not based on a commitment to any particular system of ideology or metaphysics. The logotherapeutic view of death, nevertheless, guards an attitude of openness towards the theological perspective on death because logotherapy is aware of the religious dimensions of human existence. These special characteristics of Frankl's philosophy of death lead to the following question: What can we learn from the analysis of the meaning of death for the conduct of a meaningful life? The main teaching of the logotherapeutic interpretation of the phenomenon of death is the description and the justification of the natural attitude of acknowledging the reality of death. The natural and existential awareness of death does not distract from the joy and the value of living. There is a healing power in thinking about death. Meanings and values are realized on this side of death. The boundary of human living and of human actions does not constitute a wall of enclosure, but it functions as a container and a shield of accomplishments and values. The authentic and thus healthy attitude towards death contributes significantly to the discovery of the true self and enhances the development of the human person. The attitudes of skepticism and absurdity towards life and death may not be eliminated for once and for all by the logotherapeutic understanding of death. Skepticism and absurdity take many forms. However, the logotherapeutic discernment of the meaning of temporality and mortality makes more difficult the use of death for establishing and fostering the attitude of skepticism and absurdity towards the meaning of human living.

The logotherapist is aware of the philosophical and the theological dimensions of the questions regarding the ultimate meaning of life and death.

—George Kovacs

Logotherapy can neither give nor prescribe meaning; it can only describe meaning. The understanding of the function of meaning in human living also includes the recognition of the limits of the understanding of meaning. Thus logotherapy shows the importance of keeping an open mind in dealing with the ultimate meaning of life and death precisely because *"the more comprehensive the meaning, the less comprehensible it is"* [*The Unconscious God*]. The discernment and the choice of a meaning, especially the choice of an ultimate meaning, does have a therapeutic effect on the human person. The process of discerning and choosing ultimate meaning not only enlarges but also transcends the task of logotherapy and thus calls for a philosophical as well as for a theological, indeed for a multidisciplinary, analysis and understanding. Logotherapy is able to deal with the specifically human (noogenic) and spiritual dimensions of death without becoming an ideology at the same time. The practitioner of logotherapy helps in the search for meaning but he does not impose a particular meaning. The logotherapist is aware of the philosophical and the theological dimensions of the questions regarding the ultimate meaning of life and death; he knows the difference between science and wisdom. The attitude of openness and professional objectivity in Frankl's philosophy of death is founded on his consistent emphasis on the distinction between the domain of medicine (the science of the art of healing, human comfort) and the realm of theology and wisdom (religious faith, commitment to an ultimate meaning). Medical, clinical problems are not only somatic and psychological, but also philosophical and religious in many instances due to the oneness and wholeness of the human person. The logotherapist ought to be aware of the person's spiritual needs and resources; he also ought to try to understand them and draw on them. The search for meaning and the attitude of openness towards the expressions and formulations of meaning on many levels contribute to the process of healing the human person from the neurotic denials of the existential facts of suffering, illness, and death.

Dan P. McAdams (review date February 1994)

SOURCE: "The Best of Us Did Not Return," in *Contemporary Psychology,* Vol. 39, No. 2, February, 1994, pp. 130-31.

[*McAdams is an American psychologist, educator, and author of* The Stories We Live By: Personal Myths and the Making of the Self *(1993). In the following review of* Man's Search for Meaning, *originally titled* From Death-Camp to Existentialism, *he focuses on the meaning Frankl's concentration camp experiences may have for a new generation of readers.*]

In 1945, shortly after his release from a Nazi concentration camp, Viktor E. Frankl spent nine intensive days writing *Ein Psycholog Erlebt das Konzentrationslager,* a psychological account of his three years in Auschwitz, Dachau, and other Nazi prison camps. The original German version bears no name on the cover because Frankl was initially committed to publishing an anonymous account that would never earn its author literary fame. Expanded to include a short overview of "logotherapy," the English version of Frankl's book first appeared as *From Death-Camp to Existentialism* and finally under its well-known title, *Man's Search for Meaning.* Shortly after its first English printing in 1959, Carl Rogers called the book one of the outstanding contributions to psychological thought in the last 50 years. The *Los Angeles Times* said, "If you read but one book this year, Dr. Frankl's book should be the one." The public agreed with the critics. Now that the book has been translated into 21 languages and has sold more than three million copies in English alone, Beacon Press has reissued Frankl's classic account in a handsome, cloth-covered edition, complete with a new Preface from the author and the original English Foreword written by Gordon W. Allport.

There are at least three reasons why Frankl's book has enjoyed such wide appeal over the past 35 years. First, Frankl tells an unforgettable story about his experiences in the camps. In a beautifully laconic style that is never maudlin or sensational, Frankl describes events that are so chilling, so brutal, and in some cases so heroic that the reader is not sure whether to be more amazed by the events themselves or by Frankl's unfailing ability to find the right words to describe them. Almost 50 years after the Holocaust, these words have lost none of their power to capture the reader's consciousness and refuse to let go. Second, Frankl's psychological commentary on captivity and survivorship is full of deep insights and thought-provoking speculations. Frankl delineates three stages of psychological reaction to the concentration camps. He provides brilliant asides on the powerful roles of religion, friendship, and the longing for a lost lover in helping the prisoner wrench meaning out of his misery. He provides riveting examples of how meaning and hope sustain life, even in Auschwitz, and how many people are just unable to find meaning, unable to summon up any hope, and as a result, in Auschwitz they die.

The third reason for the book's enduring popularity is that it serves as a primer for Frankl's own brand of existential psychotherapy, what he calls "logotherapy" ("therapy of meaning"). It is this third reason that drew me initially to the book, as an undergraduate in the mid-1970s. As was probably true for many in my generation, *Man's Search for Meaning* and Frankl's (1955) *The Doctor and the Soul: From Psychotherapy to Logotherapy* were my introduction to existential psychology and psychotherapy. Like Allport in the book's Foreword, I was thrilled by Frankl's insistence that psychologists go beyond drives, instincts, and habits to explore the realm of meaning and purpose in human lives. I was taken by the idea that life's meaning may be found in suffering and that each person—and each person *alone*—is responsible for the meanings that he or she can wrestle out of life. For me, Frankl's vision was appealing for its exquisitely tragic quality, like Freud's, and for its very non-Freudian call to personal heroism.

Reading the book again, almost 20 years later, I find less exciting today the last section (about 60 pages) in which Frankl outlines logotherapy. It seems that today many brands of psychotherapy concern themselves in one way or another with meaning in life, personal responsibility, and other central themes in existential thought. With the demise of drive-reduction theories and with the proliferation of approaches emphasizing object relations, the self, human cognition, affective scripts and stories, and a wide variety of concepts compatible with a meaning-centered approach to persons and personal psychotherapy, Frankl seems to be fighting old battles today, battles that he, in a sense, has already won. Furthermore, certain pieces in Frankl's arsenal seem outmoded in the 1990s. For example, to buttress his claim that contemporary men and women thirst for meaning in life, he relies on an attitudinal survey from the early 1970s showing that American college students are much more concerned with "finding meaning in life" than they are with "making money." Results from surveys like these have changed dramatically, however, in the last 20 years. Finally, some material on logotherapy simply does not fit well into the context of the overall book. Frankl's emphasis on "paradoxical intention" as a therapeutic technique—a technique that behavior therapy has also employed—seems far removed from existentialism and life meanings. Relatedly, the necessary connection between concentration camps and existential psychotherapy seems harder to discern today than before. It no longer seems necessary to justify an approach to therapy emphasizing life meanings by appealing to experiences as extreme as the Holocaust. Had the camps never existed, one would still be able to make a very strong case for logotherapy.

The whole thrust of *Man's Search for Meaning* is to underscore how "man's search for meaning" can sustain human life even under the most harrowing and depraved conditions.

—Dan P. McAdams

Today's reader will still be moved, nonetheless, by the stories of the camps and inspired by Frankl's interpretations of his experience. For me, this time the most compelling passages in the book tell how whether one lived or died under the Nazis was often a matter of blind, stupid luck. Frankl writes, "We who have come back, by the aid of many lucky chances or miracles—whatever one may choose to call them—we know: *the best of us did not return* [italics added]." I have been haunted by this last statement. Who were the best who did not return? Were they the prisoners who put the welfare of others above their own? At one point, Frankl seems to suggest that they were:

> On the average, only those prisoners could keep alive who, after years of trekking from camp to camp, had lost all scruples in their fight for existence; they were prepared to use every means, honest and otherwise, even brutal force, theft, and betrayal of their friends, in order to save themselves.

Yet the whole thrust of the book is to underscore how "man's search for meaning" can sustain human life even under the most harrowing and depraved conditions. Beyond luck, meaning played a part in survival too, Frankl maintains. Most of those who survived the camps had something to live for—some goal, some religious conviction, some person, some task, some hope about the future that they refused to give up. For Frankl himself, his undying love for his wife was a source of meaning, as was his vision of himself as a doctor and scholar. During some of the worst times, devastated by hunger and the cold, Frankl fantasized that he was delivering erudite lectures to his colleagues about the psychology of the concentration camp.

Those who lost the will to meaning usually lost their lives. Frankl reports that this sometimes happened quite suddenly and in a form that was familiar to many in the camps. A prisoner might wake up one day and refuse to get dressed, to wash, or to go out on the parade grounds. No threats or cajoling could change his mind. He simply gave up. "There he remained, lying in his own excreta, and nothing bothered him anymore." In one instance, a prisoner had a dream convincing him that the war would be over on March 30, and all inmates would be liberated. Although the dream provided him hope in the short run, he began to fade dramatically as the promised day drew near. On March 29th, he became ill and ran a high temperature. He was dead the next day. Many others in the camp lost hope more gradually. Frankl paints a stark contrast between those relatively few who managed to find meaning throughout it all and those many prisoners who did not. Those more likely to find meaning were often "sensitive people who were used to a rich intellectual life," and although they may have suffered great pain, "the damage to their inner selves was less" because "they were able to retreat from their terrible surroundings to a life of inner riches and spiritual freedom." Many others, though, lacked the inner resources to carry on. Frankl writes: "One could make a victory of those [concentration camp] experiences, turning life into an inner triumph, or one could ignore the challenge and simply vegetate, as did a majority of the prisoners."

It seems ironic and initially puzzling, indeed, that Frankl is able to make such a compelling case for a psychology of meaning in the wake of the Holocaust experience when, according to his account, a great many of the prisoners could ultimately do no better than "vegetate." Like Frankl, though, the reader ends up more impressed by the fact that anybody at all could find meaning in the maelstrom, and thus the exceptions powerfully override the rule. A second puzzle concerns the "best of us" who did not return. Who survived? Who did not return? Beyond luck, those who lived through the Nazi hell were doubtlessly younger and stronger than many who died. On the one hand, they may have also been more ruthless in their singleminded desire to survive, perhaps even at the expense of their fellow prisoners. On the other hand, they may have been blessed with those inner resources that empowered them to find meaning and persevere. In a passage so understated that the reader can easily miss its significance, Frankl describes how he would occasionally find a moment of solitude and peace by squatting in an abandoned water shaft surrounded by piles of corpses. "This shaft, incidentally, once saved the lives of three fellow prisoners." Frankl goes on to tell how, shortly before the liberation, three men escaped death by hiding in the shaft. As the guards walked by,

> I calmly sat on the lid, looking innocent and playing a childish game of throwing pebbles at the barbed wire. On spotting me, the guard hesitated for a moment, but then passed on. Soon I could tell the three men below that the worst danger was over.

Frankl tells us that these men's lives were saved by the water shaft. But we see that, in fact, Frankl saved them. And it seems he saved many others too. Shortly before liberation and against the urgent advice of his friends, he volunteered for medical duty in another camp housing ty-phus patients. He was convinced that by doing this he would die in a short time.

> But if I had to die there might at least be some sense in my death. I thought that it would doubtless be more to the purpose to try to help my comrades as a doctor than to vegetate or finally lose my life as the unproductive laborer I was then.

Frankl refuses to acknowledge his own altruism in this affair. "For me it was simple mathematics, not sacrifice."

But to me it suggests that Frankl was wrong all along. Clearly, at least one of the best of us *did* return.

FURTHER READING

Criticism

Garfield, Charles A. "A Psychometric and Clinical Investigation of Frankl's Concept of Existential Vacuum and of Anomia." *Psychiatry* 36 (November 1973): 391-408.

> Investigative study exploring "the identification and characteristics of the personal psychological state known as *existential vacuum*" and "the identification of the personal psychological state known as *anomia.*"

Leslie, Robert C. *Jesus and Logotherapy: The Ministry of Jesus as Interpreted through the Psychotherapy of Viktor Frankl.* Nashville, TN: Abingdon Press, 1965, 143 p.

> Argues that "logotherapy offers a philosophy of life and a method of counseling which is more consistent with a basically Christian view of life than any other existing system in the current therapeutic world."

Additional coverage of Frankl's life and career is contained in the following source published by Gale Research: *Contemporary Authors,* Vols. 65-68, rev. ed.

Of Human Bondage

W. Somerset Maugham

The following entry presents criticism on Maugham's novel *Of Human Bondage* (1915). For further information on his life and works, see *CLC,* Volumes 1, 11, 15, and 67.

INTRODUCTION

Of Human Bondage is arguably Maugham's most popular work and has steadily gained readers and influence since its publication in 1915. Often described as a *bildungsroman,* the novel chronicles the youth and early adulthood of Philip Carey as he struggles to retain his freedom and individuality within a rigid society. Clubfooted and orphaned, Philip struggles with his differences and sensitivities, which he comes to believe have made him more perceptive than others to art and beauty. Though the first manuscript of the novel was completed in 1898 and titled "The Artistic Temperament of Stephen Carey," Maugham was unable to find a publisher and pursued other writing interests. In 1911, after achieving some success as a playwright, he rewrote the novel, believing that he was now more adept at portraying the themes and characters that concerned him in his youth, and changed the title to *Of Human Bondage.* Commenting on the novel's autobiographical aspect, Maugham stated in the preface to the abridged edition that he wrote it to "rid myself of a great number of unhappy recollections that had not ceased to harrow me." Criticized on publication for its pessimistic world view and frank, dispassionate view of sexuality, *Of Human Bondage* has been alternately praised and condemned for its sometimes unflattering depiction of a hero who tends towards self-pity and self-absorption.

Plot and Major Characters

The novel opens when Philip is sent from London to live with his aunt and uncle in Blackstable after the death of his mother following a stillbirth. His uncle, a vicar, shows little interest in the boy beyond providing basic provisions, and young Philip quickly becomes adept at spotting the vicar's hypocrisy, which includes treating his family with a frugality to which the vicar himself is not held. This hypocrisy leads to Philip's early rejection of Christianity. When he is sent away to school, Philip's painful adolescence continues as he withdraws socially from the other boys; his clubfoot prevents him from joining in sports and games. The novel also depicts Philip's coming-of-age as a man, whose early experiences with women—most notably the aging governess Miss Wilkerson and the penny-novel writer Norah Nesbitt—are physical acts marked with pathos and disdain on Philip's part. After a year of studying business in Heidelberg, Germany, Philip returns to London, only to reject a respectable living as an accountant for the romance of being an artist in Paris. But in France he encounters only poverty and hunger. Following the suicide of Fanny Price, an untalented fellow artist whose passion could not save her from her squalid circumstances, he returns to London to begin medical school. When he meets Mildred Pierce, a decidedly plain-looking, emaciated tea-shop girl—whom one critic dubbed "an implacable, pale green worm"—he is inexplicably drawn to her and exhibits an irrational passion of the type that has brought many of his friends to ruin. Mildred rejects his overtures of affection and uses him repeatedly until their relationship reaches masochistic proportions. As Mildred's position in society continues to decline, she resorts to prostitution despite Philip's attempts to help her. When she destroys his art in a fit of rage and condemns him as a cripple, his passion for her is finally extinguished; she dies of syphilis in an institution shortly thereafter. Finally determining that life is random and meaningless, Philip trades his dreams of freedom and travel for responsibility and respectability when he asks the simple and pleasing Sally Athelny, towards whom he feels some affection but no love, for her hand in marriage.

Major Themes

Of Human Bondage, a title borrowed from a chapter in

Baruch Spinoza's *Ethics* (1677), examines Philip's psychological growth, his aesthetic pursuit of beauty in a world in which beauty is constantly juxtaposed with struggle, and the paradox of his love for Mildred, who represents none of the ideals he cherishes. Philip's quest for beauty becomes inextricably tied to his intense desire to follow his dreams at the risk of losing respect within a strict Edwardian society. His decision to study art in Paris, for example, is condemned by his uncle, who derides painting as a "disreputable, immoral" profession and considers Paris "a sink of iniquity." Philip engages in many pursuits on his journey to self-understanding, and his self-absorption frequently discounts the importance of nurturing relationships on human development. Love of beauty alone, however, proves unsustainable; as Philip becomes impoverished and tragedy befalls his friends and acquaintances, his staunch individualism yields to more conventional societal norms. Eventually, he realizes that though life contains patterns, the patterns themselves are essentially meaningless. The novel also examines the conventions of Edwardian society. As a student and young man undergoing a strict upbringing, Philip battles society's definitions of what it means to be a gentleman and he variously accepts and rejects roles as an accountant, store clerk, art student, and medical student. In this respect, Philip's situation mirrors Maugham's, who was orphaned at the age of ten and sent from Paris to live with an uncle in England, where his profound stutter impeded his social development and drove him into the solitary pursuits of art and literature.

Critical Reception

Of Human Bondage received mixed reviews and fleeting attention on its initial publication. A reviewer in the *Athenaeum* took issue with the novel's morality: "The values accorded by the hero to love, realism, and religion are so distorted as to have no interest beyond that which belongs to an essentially morbid personality." Conversely, Theodore Dreiser praised the novel as an "autobiography of utmost importance," and appreciated the moral circumstances with which Philip grappled. A typical critical reaction, however, is echoed in the sentiments of a *Dial* reviewer, who admitted that the detail contained within six-hundred pages "can hardly fail to leave us with the feeling of intimate acquaintance," but that the novel ultimately imparts a "depressing impression of the futility of life." While noting the similarities between the author's life and Philip's, some critics have contended that the compromised ending, in which Philip finds comfort and security with the understanding and proper Sally is wishful thinking, especially in light of the author's homosexual tendencies: for Maugham, though he graduated from medical school like Philip, never practiced medicine, and remained unmarried until the age of forty. Several years after its initial publication, however, the novel gained a sizable following among the American reading public through word-of-mouth and a few strategic mentions in the press. Subsequent printings and editions added to the novel's popularity, and in 1946 Maugham presented the original manuscript to the Library of Congress. Maugham stated that his place in literature was "in the very first row of the second-raters," and many critics have been inclined to agree. Likewise, Maugham's contention that he "painted easel pictures, and not frescoes" was enough to earn the dismissal of many critics. Contrasting Maugham's public success with his failure among many critics, Theodore Spencer has argued that the "problem for anyone trying to judge Maugham's permanent value is to decide whether the critics or the public are right."

PRINCIPAL WORKS

Liza of Lambeth (novel) 1897
The Making of a Saint (novel) 1898
Orientations (short stories) 1899
The Hero (novel) 1901
Mrs Craddock (novel) 1902; revised edition, 1937
Schiffbrüchig (drama) 1902
A Man of Honour (drama) 1903
Mademoiselle Zampa (drama) 1904
The Merry-Go-Round (short stories) 1904
The Land of the Blessed Virgin: Sketches and Impressions in Andalusia (travel essay) 1905
The Bishop's Apron: A Study in the Origins of a Great Family (novel) 1906
Lady Frederick (drama) 1907
The Explorer (drama) 1908
Jack Straw (drama) 1908
The Magician (novel) 1908
Mrs Dot (drama) 1908
Penelope (drama) 1909
Smith (drama) 1909
Grace (drama) 1910; published as *Landed Gentry*, 1913
The Tenth Man (drama) 1910
Loaves and Fishes (drama) 1911
The Land of Promise (drama) 1913
Of Human Bondage (novel) 1915
Caroline (drama) 1916; published as *The Unattainable*, 1923
Love in a Cottage (drama) 1918
Caesar's Wife (drama) 1919
Home and Beauty (drama) 1919; also performed as *Too Many Husbands*, 1919
The Moon and Sixpence (novel) 1919
Our Betters (drama) 1919
The Unknown (drama) 1920
The Circle (drama) 1921
The Trembling of a Leaf: Little Stories of the South Sea Islands (short stories) 1921
On a Chinese Screen (travel essay) 1922
East of Suez (drama) 1922
The Camel's Back (drama) 1923
The Painted Veil (novel) 1925
The Casuarina Tree: Six Stories (short stories) 1926
The Constant Wife (drama) 1926
The Letter (drama) 1927
Ashenden; or, The British Agent (short stories) 1928
The Sacred Flame (drama) 1929
The Breadwinner (drama) 1930

Cakes and Ale; or, The Skeleton in the Cupboard   (novel) 1930

The Gentleman in the Parlour   (travel essay) 1930

Six Stories Written in the First Person Singular   (short stories) 1931

The Book-Bag   (novel) 1932

For Services Rendered   (drama) 1932

The Narrow Corner   (novel) 1932

Ah King: Six Stories   (short stories) 1933

Sheppey   (drama) 1933

East and West: The Collected Short Stories   (short stories) 1934; also published as *Altogether,* 1934

Don Fernando; or, Variations on Some Spanish Themes (travel essay) 1935

Cosmopolitans   (short stories) 1936

The Summing Up   (autobiography) 1938

Christmas Holiday   (novel) 1939

Books and You   (essays) 1940

France at War   (nonfiction) 1940

The Mixture as Before   (short stories) 1940

Up at the Villa   (novel) 1941

Strictly Personal   (nonfiction) 1941

The Hour before Dawn   (novel) 1942

The Razor's Edge   (novel) 1944

The Unconquered   (short stories) 1944

Then and Now   (novel) 1946; also published as *Fools and Their Folly,* 1949

Creatures of Circumstance   (short stories) 1947

Catalina   (novel) 1948

Great Novelists and Their Novels   (criticism) 1948; also published as *Ten Novels and Their Authors* [revised edition], 1954

A Writer's Notebook   (journals) 1949

The Complete Short Stories of W. Somerset Maugham. 3 vols.   (short stories) 1951

The Vagrant Mood   (essays) 1952

The World Over   (short stories) 1952

Points of View   (essays) 1958

Looking Back   (autobiographical sketch) 1962

Purely for My Pleasure   (essays) 1962

CRITICISM

W. Somerset Maugham   (essay date 1915)

SOURCE: A Foreword to *Of Human Bondage,* in *Selected Prefaces and Introductions of W. Somerset Maugham,* Heinemann, 1963, pp. 34-7.

[*In the following essay, published as a foreword to the first edition of* Of Human Bondage, *Maugham describes the book as an autobiographical novel that freed him "from the pains and unhappy recollections that had tormented [him]."*]

This is a very long novel and I am ashamed to make it longer by writing a preface to it. An author is probably the last person who can write fitly about his own work. In this connection an instructive story is told by Roger Martin du Gard, a distinguished French novelist, about Marcel Proust. Proust wanted a certain French periodical to publish an important article on his great novel and thinking that no one could write it better than he, sat down and wrote it himself. Then he asked a young friend of his, a man of letters, to put his name to it and take it to the editor. This the young man did, but after a few days the editor sent for him. 'I must refuse your article,' he told him. 'Marcel Proust would never forgive me if I printed a criticism of his work that was so perfunctory and so unsympathetic.' Though authors are touchy about their productions and inclined to resent unfavourable criticism they are seldom self-satisfied. They are miserably conscious how far the work on which they have spent much time and trouble comes short of their conception and when they consider it they are much more vexed with their failure to express this in its completeness than pleased with the passages here and there that they can regard with complacency. Their aim is perfection and they are wretchedly aware that they have not attained it.

I will say nothing then about my book itself, but will content myself with telling the reader of these lines how a novel that has now had a fairly long life, as novels go, came to be written; and if it does not interest him I ask him to forgive me. I wrote it first when, at the age of twenty-three, having taken my medical degrees after five years at St Thomas's Hospital, I went to Seville determined to earn my living as a writer. The manuscript of the book I wrote then still exists, but I have not looked at it since I corrected the typescript and I have no doubt that it is very immature. I sent it to Fisher Unwin, who had published my first book (while still a medical student I had published a novel called *Liza of Lambeth,* which had had something of a success), but he refused to give me the hundred pounds I wanted for it and none of the other publishers to whom I afterwards submitted it would have it at any price. This distressed me at the time, but now I know that I was very fortunate; for if one of them had taken my book (it was called *The Artistic Temperament of Stephen Carey*) I should have lost a subject which I was too young to make proper use of. I was not far enough away from the events I described to use them properly and I had not had a number of experiences which later went to enrich the book I finally wrote. Nor had I learnt that it is easier to write of what you know than of what you don't. For instance, I sent my hero to Rouen (which I knew only as an occasional visitor) to learn French, instead of to Heidelberg (where I had been myself) to learn German.

Thus rebuffed I put the manuscript away. I wrote other novels, which were published, and I wrote plays. I became a very successful playwright and determined to devote the rest of my life to the drama. But I reckoned without a force within me that made my resolutions vain. I was happy, I was prosperous, I was busy. My head was full of the plays I wanted to write. I do not know whether it was that success did not bring me all I had expected or whether it was a natural reaction from it, but I was but just firmly established as the most popular dramatist of the day when I began once more to be obsessed by the teeming memories of my past life. They came back to me so pressingly, in my sleep, on my walks, at rehearsals, at parties, they became such a burden to me, that I made up my mind there was only one way to be free of them and that was to write them all down in a book. After submitting myself for some years to the exigencies of the drama I hankered after the wide liberty of the novel. I knew the book I had in mind would be a long one and I wanted to be undisturbed, so I refused the contracts that managers were eagerly offering me and temporarily retired from the stage. I was then thirty-seven.

For long after I became a writer by profession I spent much time on learning how to write and subjected myself to very tiresome training in the endeavour to improve my style. But these efforts I abandoned when my plays began to be produced and when I started to write again it was with different aims. I no longer sought a jewelled prose and a rich texture, on unavailing attempts to achieve which I had formerly wasted much labour; I sought on the contrary plainness and simplicity. With so much that I wanted to say within reasonable limits I felt that I could not afford to waste words and I set out now with the notion of using only such as were necessary to make my meaning clear. I had no space for ornament. My experience in the theatre had taught me the value of succinctness and the danger of beating about the bush. I worked unremittingly for two years. I did not know what to call my book and after looking about a great deal hit upon *Beauty from Ashes,* a quotation from Isaiah which seemed to me apposite; but learning that this title had been recently used was obliged to search for another. I chose finally the name of one of the books in Spinoza's *Ethics* and called it *Of Human Bondage*. I have a notion I was once more lucky in finding that I could not use the first title I had thought of.

Of Human Bondage is not an autobiography, but an autobiographical novel; fact and fiction are inextricably mingled; the emotions are my own, but not all the incidents are related as they happened and some of them are transferred to my hero not from my own life but from that of persons with whom I was intimate. The book did for me what I wanted and when it was issued to the world (a world in the throes of a dreadful war and too much concerned with its own sufferings and fears to bother with the adventures of a creature of fiction) I found myself free for ever from the pains and unhappy recollections that had tormented me. It was very well reviewed; Theodore Dreiser wrote for *The New Republic* a long criticism in which he dealt with it with the intelligence and sympathy which distinguish everything he has ever written; but it looked very much as though it would go the way of the vast majority of novels and be forgotten for ever a few months after its appearance. But, I do not know through what accident it happened after some years that it attracted the attention of a number of distinguished writers in the United States and the references they continued to make to it in the press gradually brought it to the notice of the public. To these writers is due the new lease of life that the book was thus given and them must I thank for the success it has continued increasingly to have as the years go by.

R. Ellis Roberts (review date September 1915)

SOURCE: "The Amorist," in *The Bookman,* London, Vol. XLVIII, No. 288, September, 1915, pp. 171-72.

[*In the following favorable review, Roberts comments on the futility of Philip Carey's relationships with women and calls the novel a clever "portrait of the weak egoist."*]

It was a right instinct which made Mr. Maugham give the greatest space to Mildred, among all the women who touched and influenced his hero's life [in *Of Human Bondage*]. For Philip Carey, introspective, indolent, shiftless, opinionated, club-footed, is a man doomed to be loved. He is not doomed to evoke great passion, nor is it his destiny to love lightly or deeply any one woman: he is simply one of those men for whom women, in whom affection is stronger than passion, will always be prepared to suffer. Yet he himself has, mentally rather than emotionally, the capacity for feeling passion: and he does, midway in his career, fall stupidly and desperately in love with Mildred, a vulgar, avid, atrocious girl in a tea-shop. The episode of Mildred and Philip is horrible. She takes and takes, and gives nothing. She rejects Philip for a sensual brute: and then, abandoned, comes to Philip for help. Forsaken again, betrayed by his friend, Philip still cannot resist Mildred's appeal: and he continues to give charity long after he has lost passion. The thing, in spite of fine moments, is degrading: for the sake of this passion, Philip neglects honour, affection, duty and decency. Yet it is the one fixed thing in his life. Unstable as water in all else, he fails in this, too, where he feels firmly and definitely. And his failure to hold Mildred throws a light on his character almost as illuminating as his capacity for loving so ignoble a creature.

It is no use complaining that Mr. Maugham might have chosen a nobler, a more exciting, a more amusing person than Philip Carey. He has given us so admirable a picture, so carefully etched a portrait of this poor beggar of the spirit that we must not cry out against the lack of colour and humour in his pages. There are a great many of those pages—over six hundred—and some of them could have been spared. The intense, rather baffling detail of Philip's life at his two schools is rather distracting; and the perpetual conflict between Philip and his uncle is rather needlessly ugly. The main problem of the book is, however, Philip's relationship with women. Miss Williamson, Mildred, Norah Nesbit, and Sally are all drawn into an insight and sincerity which few modern novelists could equal. Miss Williamson is saved from being frankly sordid by a touch of heartbreaking farce, common in French; but rare in English fiction. The passion of an old maid for a young man can be a beautiful thing; but when it is as physical and selfish as Miss Williamson's it is bound to be disgusting. Norah Nesbit loves Philip in the way of friendship, and is rewarded by his return to Mildred: Sally only occurs, as a woman, at the end of the book and we leave Philip on the verge of marrying her.

It may be gathered easily enough that Philip Carey has no sort of moral principles in his relations to women. He abandons the narrow Christianity of his youth, and adopts a meagre heathenism which brings him more happiness than he deserves. His preoccupation with sex would be more tolerable if it was more frankly sensual; but with him nature is an afterthought. As a portrait of the weak egotist, of the knock-kneed Nietzschean, *Of Human Bondage* may be greeted as a remarkably clever book. Mr. Maugham's elaborate, preoccupied method, his slow insertions of the scalpel into every obscure place suits the timid type he is analysing. It is no disrespect to this piece of work to wish him a rather robuster subject for his next serious novel.

William Morton Payne   (review date 16 September 1915)

SOURCE: A review of *Of Human Bondage,* in *The Dial,* Vol. LIX, No. 701, September 16, 1915, pp. 219-21.

[*In the following excerpt, Payne commends Maugham for creating a sustained interest in his protagonist, but criticizes him for missing "the broad effects" and "large issues of a human characterization."*]

Mr. W. Somerset Maugham, a successful playwright, has turned his activities in the direction of fiction-writing, the result being *Of Human Bondage,* an immensely lengthy work of the biographical type, setting forth the story of a young man's life from childhood to the age of thirty or thereabouts. The following extract will show why it takes six hundred and fifty compact pages to accomplish this setting forth:

> When Philip arrived there was some difficulty in deciding on which evening he should have his bath. It was never easy to get plenty of hot water, since the kitchen boiler did not work, and it was impossible for two persons to have a bath on the same day. The only man who had a bathroom in Blackstable was Mr. Wilson, and it was thought ostentatious of him. Mary Ann had her bath in the kitchen on Monday night, because she liked to begin the week clean. Uncle William could not have his on Saturday, because he had a heavy day before him, and he was always a little tired after a bath, so he had it on Friday. Mrs. Carey had hers on Thursday for the same reason. It looked as though Saturday were naturally indicated for Philip, but Mary Ann said she couldn't keep the fire up on Saturday night, and with all the cooking on Sunday, having to make pastry and she didn't know what all, she didn't feel up to giving the boy his bath on Saturday night: and it was quite clear that he could not bath himself.

The upshot of all this complication was that Mary Ann relented, and grudgingly agreed to Saturday night. Even this description leaves Tuesday and Wednesday unaccounted for, which we rather resent, since we would like to be told all about it. It is obvious that a writer who works with this method of detailed photographic realism can "go far," and the story runs to nearly three hundred thousand words. We began it in Chicago, took it upon an ocean voyage, and it was still with us upon our return. Nor did it prove lacking in sustained interest. When a novelist thus sets out to chronicle *everything* about his hero's life, he can hardly fail to leave us with the feeling of intimate acquaintance. But he can easily miss, as Mr. Maugham does, the

broad effects and the large issues of a human characterization. The only thing of this sort that we get from *Of Human Bondage* is a most depressing impression of the futility of life, an impression similar to that produced by *The Old Wives' Tale* of Mr. Arnold Bennett. Our hero's life is not romantic. When he gets out of school, he tries accountancy and fails. Then he tries art in the Paris schools, and fails again. Then he tries medicine, barely scrapes through to a diploma, and is in sight of marriage and a country practice when the book of his life is closed for us. Before this consummation, he has entanglements with various women, including a long and enslaving infatuation for a girl of repellent vulgarity—a waitress in a cheap restaurant who graduates into the life of the streets. She, too, is an amazingly real person, as are many others whom we encounter in this narrative, which may perhaps best be described as an album of unretouched photographs. The book is far from being, in the publishers' phrase, "compellingly great," but, allowing once for all its inartistic method, it is at least a noteworthy piece of creative composition.

S. P. B. Mais   (essay date 1923)

SOURCE: "Somerset Maugham," in *Some Modern Authors,* Dodd, Mead and Company, 1923, pp. 115-28.

[*Mais was a British educator, nonfiction writer, and critic. In the following excerpt, he briefly comments on several of Maugham's early novels and discusses* Of Human Bondage, *describing it as a model of autobiographical fiction.*]

For some twenty years Mr Somerset Maugham has been writing novels and plays, hammering hard on the doors of the critics' studies, clamouring for a hearing. For a long time they overlooked him. A man of indomitable courage, he has persevered and gone on from strength to strength until at last, in *The Moon and Sixpence,* he "rang the bell" (as the phrase goes) to such purpose that no intelligent reader could any longer deny him his place among the really brilliant leaders of modern fiction. There is an astringency about all his work that is most refreshing. He has stood his ground always, and refused to pander to the public taste for the sugary sentimental. He has remained true to his conception of his art, and he has won out. After years of struggle as a dramatist he is now accredited with financial success only second to that of Barrie. It is salutary to our critical sense to go back twenty years and see how good he was long before he was recognised. Take, for instance, *The Merry-Go-Round.* The idea of the barrister-author philandering with the barmaid, marrying her to save her honour, finding out that by so doing he was making a hell for two instead of one, has been often enough exploited, but no one has tackled the theme so frankly as Maugham. At the end, when Jenny commits suicide, Basil is at any rate honest:

> "I made a ghastly mistake and suffered for it . . . and perhaps it wasn't all my own fault. . . . For God's sake let us be free. Let us do this and that because we want to, and because we must, not because other people think we ought. And d'you know the worst of the whole thing? If I'd acted like a blackguard and let

Jenny go to the dogs, I should have remained happy and contented and prosperous, and she, I daresay, wouldn't have died. It's because I tried to do my duty that all this misery came about."

Somerset Maugham is a good author because he never flinches in the face of reality: he is definitely anti-sentimental. "After all," he says to his best friend just after he had seduced Jenny, "if we were all as cool at night as we are in the morning—"

"Life would be a Sunday school," finished his friend. His mother (herself wanton) denounces his decision to marry the girl in good set terms. "A gentleman doesn't marry a barmaid because he's seduced her—unless he has the soul of a counter-jumper. . . . You're one of those persons who are doomed to mediocrity because you haven't the spirit to go to the devil like a man."

Maugham is like Flaubert in his contemptuous view of humanity. Most of his women have the souls of trollops, most of his men are frankly sensual, loving after feeding, like animals, "as an accompaniment to the process of digestion."

His virtuous characters, like Bella Langton's father, are hard, his worldly characters hypocritical. Once in early days he had a curious lapse into the sentimental. "Even if the beliefs of men are childish and untrue," cries Miss Ley, by far the best character in *The Merry-Go-Round,* "isn't it better to keep them? Surely superstition is a small price to pay for that wonderful support at the last hour, when all else fades to insignificance."

When Reggie Bassett goes off the rocks Miss Ley coolly rounds on his dissolute mother.

> "A wise mother lets her son go his own way, and shuts her eyes to youthful peccadilloes: but you made all these peccadilloes into deadly sins. . . . Moralists talk a deal of nonsense about the frailty of mankind. When you come to close quarters with vice, it's not really so desperately wicked as all that. . . . All these things are part of human nature, when youth and hot blood are joined together."

Clear-sightedness in Maugham's characters leads them to cruelty. They have no compunction in cutting Gordian knots which may lead to disasters for the weaker party. He is as much a believer in the survival of the fittest as he is in the saving quality of beauty.

Take another of his little-known early works, *The Explorer.* He is quite relentless in hunting Lucy Allerton's lovable but shifty father to prison and death for his weakness. Maugham is almost alone among novelists in facing the utter ruthlessness of life. Just as he refuses to compromise in his art, so does he refuse to allow his characters the false security of a harbour. That is why he is so frequently accused of cynicism and brutality. "Every woman is a Potiphar's wife, though every man isn't a Joseph," is typical of the sort of epigram with which his pages are studded.

"A love for good food is the only thing that remains with man when he grows old," is put into the mouth of an indolent wit; but we feel that Maugham himself believes it, just

as in Alec Mackenzie, the explorer, he paints what he would wish himself to have been, reckless, desperate, the fascination of the unknown ever urging him on to explore the hidden recesses of the material world as well as those of the world of the mind.

In reply to Alec's denunciation of "the greatest imposture of Christian times—the sanctification of labour," he replies: "If I had ten lives I couldn't get through a tithe of what . . . so urgently needs doing."

Strength, simplicity, the greatness of life, beauty—these are the things that Mackenzie and Maugham both worship. It is these things that make them worship Boswell, Homer, Thucydides and Shakespeare, the heart of Africa and the South Seas. Maugham delights in placing his characters not only in dangers but in the most remote places of the earth. They are all, like himself, victims of a wanderlust.

His attitude to life is that of Walker, the fighter:

> "I've not had a bad time," he said. "I've loved a little, and I've worked and played. I've heard some decent music, I've looked at nice pictures, and I've read some thundering fine books. If I can only account for a few more of those damned scoundrels before I die, I shouldn't think I had much to complain of."

Abroad he suffers from a nostalgia for the grey, soft mists of England; at home he suffers from a nostalgia for the wild, riotous, prodigal virgin jungle, the hot sun beating on a blue lagoon. He has something of the bitter scorn of Swift and Samuel Butler for the world's quick changes from idolatry to persecution. "They lick my boots till I loathe them, and then they turn against me like a pack of curs." He might be Coriolanus speaking. Misunderstood, his pride prevents him from explanations. "Take it or leave it, by God, 'tis good," one imagines both the explorer and Maugham saying to a puzzled world. "The British public is sentimental," cries Mackenzie, "they will never understand that in warfare it is necessary sometimes to be inhuman." But these two novels are examples merely of Maugham in his salad days, serving his apprenticeship in a none too tractable medium. His greatness can be gauged from two books: *Of Human Bondage* and *The Moon and Sixpence*—both novels of his maturity.

Of Human Bondage is so good a book that it is impossible (for a long time after reading it) to fall down and worship the young Americans of the Sinclair Lewis type or the intellectual young Englishwoman of the Dorothy Richardson-Romer Wilson type. *Of Human Bondage* is good because it is sincere autobiography—one of the few absolutely sincere documents I have ever read. I would give it, if I could afford copies, to every imaginative boy on leaving school. Let me go through it in detail.

Right from the beginning there is Philip Carey's club-foot, the deformity which made life so hard for him, which warped his character, which made him ultrasensitive, but by reason of which in the end he "acquired that power of introspection which had given him so much delight. Without it he would never have had his keen appreciation of beauty, his passion for art and literature, and his interest in the varied spectacle of life. The ridicule and the contempt which had so often been heaped upon him had turned his mind inward and called forth those flowers which he felt would never lose their fragrance."

Early left an orphan, he had provided for himself (by reading) a refuge from all the distress of life. His schooldays (at King's School, Canterbury, thinly disguised) increased his sensitiveness (one master called him a club-footed blockhead), and made him solitary: he developed a sense of humour and lost his faith in God. He then went to Heidelberg and indulged in much freedom of thought. It was here that he met the feckless Hayward, who gave him a sense of taste, and Weeks, who helped him to put off the faith of his childhood, like a cloak that he no longer needed. He began to yearn for experience, especially with women, and to see things for himself. When he got home again he drifted into a liaison with the elderly Miss Wilkinson.

There are few things more grim than the picture of Philip steeling his heart to take what this grotesque, unattractive woman had to offer.

> She had taken off her skirt and blouse, and was standing in her petticoat. . . . She wore a camisole of white calico with short arms. . . . Philip's heart sank as he stared at her . . . but it was too late now. He closed the door behind him and locked it.

He was lucky to escape even to that appalling London office of Herbert Carter & Co. and his lodgings in Barnes: for ten loathsome months he learnt how to fail as an accountant and (under Hayward's guidance) went to study painting in Paris. It was here that he met the slatternly Fanny Price, unhealthy, unwashed and starving, who hanged herself when she found that neither her pictures nor herself were marketable commodities in a ruthless world. The picture which Maugham draws of these artists, all desiring to have mistresses, all indulging in endless discussions on art, is excellent. Cronshaw, the poet, in particular, stands out, yearning "for the love of chamber-maids and the conversation of bishops," preaching his gospel of pleasure, finding the meaning of life in a Persian carpet. It is in Paris that Philip hears that creed of the artist: "An artist would let his mother go to the workhouse," let his wife and children starve, sacrifice everything for the sake of getting on to canvas with paint the emotion which the world gave him.

It was from Foinet, the master, that he learnt the importance of money.

> "There is nothing so degrading as the constant anxiety about one's means of livelihood. I have nothing but contempt for the people who despise money. . . . Money is like a sixth sense without which you cannot make a complete use of the other five. Without an adequate income half the possibilities of life are shut off. . . . You will hear people say that poverty is the best spur to the artist. They do not know how mean it makes you. It exposes you to endless humiliation; it cuts your wings; it eats into your soul like a cancer. It is not wealth one asks for, but just enough to preserve one's dignity, to work unhampered,

> to be generous, frank and independent. I pity with all my heart the artist, whether he writes or paints, who is entirely dependent for subsistence upon his art."

He goes back to Blackstable, a failure as an artist, after two years of jollity, two years of learning to look at hands, at houses and trees against the sky—years of discovery that shadows are not black but coloured . . . that sort of thing.

So he now makes his third fresh start, this time to learn something about medicine, armed with a deeper philosophy of life, determined to be swayed by no prejudices, to follow his inclinations "with due regard to the policeman round the corner," and to find out man's relation to the world he lives in, man's relation with the men among whom he lives, and man's relation to himself. He delighted in the robust common sense of Thomas Hobbes: his mind was concrete. Almost immediately he got entangled with Mildred, another unattractive girl, with narrow hips and the chest of a boy. Only her face and her teeth passed muster. She worked in a tea-shop. He did not think her pretty; he hated the thinness of her; she was common and unhealthy; she showed no pleasure in his company, and yet he was hungry for her; his want of her became a poison, permeating his whole system. She gave him no encouragement; she only went out with him because he was "a gentleman in every sense of the word"; he even offered to marry her, but she preferred to go off with Emil (already married, with three children), so Philip is left with his unslaked thirst and his passion to travel.

It was during these medical student days that he met Norah Nesbit, with the pleasant, ugly face, who lived on writing penny novelettes. In spite of the fact that he did not love her, he made her his mistress and companion, and had some measure of satisfaction until Mildred (deserted by Emil) came back. This meant breaking off with Norah and looking after Mildred until her baby was born. Then (as much in love with her as ever) he gives her up to his friend, Griffiths, who, of course, deserts her. He had the luck to meet a forty-eight-year-old journalist, Thorpe Athelny, who lived with his wife and family (which included Sally) on three pounds a week, earned as press agent to a linendraper, and gave Philip a zest for El Greco, that painter of the soul, and for the beauty of Spain.

He again runs across Mildred (now a harlot) and provides for her a home with him, in spite of the fact that his love for her was now finally killed. They have a row; she makes havoc of his furniture and leaves him. Philip loses the little money he has left on a gamble on the Stock Exchange and sinks to starvation. He is rescued by Athelny, who makes him live with him and finds him a job as shopwalker at six shillings a week. Once more he finds Mildred, now a victim to venereal disease, and passes his final examination at the hospital.

> **Of Human Bondage is a human document of incalculable value to all men who wish to leave the world richer for their experiences. It is a model of what the autobiography in fiction ought to be.**
>
> —*S. P. B. Mais*

He accepts a locum tenens post in Dorsetshire, which leads to the offer of a partnership, which he refuses on the ground that he wants to travel. He goes back to Athelny and immediately seduces the amiable, buxom, rosy-cheeked Sally. He did not love her, but he had conceived a great affection for her; he admired her magnificent healthiness. When she came to let him know that she was going to have a child he was torn between his life's ambition to get away and travel to Spain and the South Seas and his duty to her. "I'm so damned weak," he said despairingly. He screws himself to offer to marry her, when she tells him that it was a false alarm, and suddenly he discovers that all his desires to wander were as nothing compared with the desire of his heart. "Always his course had been swayed by what he thought he should do and never by what he wanted with his whole soul to do." He had failed to see that the simplest pattern, that in which a man was born, worked, married, had children and died, was likewise the most perfect—so he discovered the meaning of the pattern on the Persian carpet at last. "Amor omnia vincit"—was that it?

Of Human Bondage is of great length: six hundred and fifty pages, closely packed, and not one of them could be spared. Maugham, like Philip Carey, is one of the few persons who gain a different standpoint from every experience that they undergo. His sensitiveness enables him to recoil more than most of us do from ugliness, and respond more than most of us do to beauty. To fail and fail again, ever to have courage to climb once more, to be interested in every type he meets, and to meet as many types as possible, to put his beliefs to the proof, to discard, prune, re-embellish all the time ruthlessly—there are the qualities that made Philip a man and Maugham an artist. He sees with a holy compassion the long procession of unfortunates, deformed in body and warped in mind, ill in the spirit, craving for sweetness and light; he sees the goodness in the bad, but is not sentimental enough or cowardly enough to shut his eyes to the power of evil. He will not pretend that things or people are attractive when they are not. He is probably the least of a hypocrite, as he is one of the finest in spirit, among modern authors.

By comparison with, shall we say, Hugh Walpole's *Fortitude*, ***Of Human Bondage*** stands out as immeasurably superior to most of even the best work in this kind of our time. It is a human document of incalculable value to all men who wish to leave the world richer for their experiences. It is a model of what the autobiography in fiction ought to be.

An excerpt from *Of Human Bondage*

The Vicar of Blackstable would have nothing to do with the scheme which Philip laid before him. He had a great idea that one should stick to whatever one had begun. Like all weak men he laid an exaggerated stress on not changing one's mind.

"You chose to be an accountant of your own free will," he said.

"I just took that because it was the only chance I saw of getting up to town. I hate London, I hate the work, and nothing will induce me to go back to it."

Mr. and Mrs. Carey were frankly shocked at Philip's idea of being an artist. He should not forget, they said, that his father and mother were gentlefolk, and painting wasn't a serious profession; it was Bohemian, disreputable, immoral. And then Paris!

"So long as I have anything to say in the matter, I shall not allow you to live in Paris," said the Vicar firmly.

It was a sink of iniquity. The scarlet woman and she of Babylon flaunted their vileness there; the cities of the plain were not more wicked.

"You've been brought up like a gentleman and Christian, and I should be false to the trust laid upon me by your dead father and mother if I allowed you to expose yourself to such temptation."

"Well, I know I'm not a Christian and I'm beginning to doubt whether I'm a gentleman," said Philip.

The dispute grew more violent. There was another year before Philip took possession of his small inheritance, and during that time Mr. Carey proposed only to give him an allowance if he remained at the office. It was clear to Philip that if he meant not to continue with accountancy he must leave it while he could still get back half the money that he had been paid for his articles. The Vicar would not listen. Philip, losing all reserve, said things to wound and irritate.

"You've got no right to waste my money," he said at last. "After all it's my money, isn't it? I'm not a child. You can't prevent me from going to Paris if I make up my mind to. You can't force me to go back to London."

"All I can do is to refuse you money unless you do what I think fit."

"Well, I don't care, I've made up my mind to go to Paris. I shall sell my clothes, and my books, and my father's jewellery."

W. Somerset Maugham, in his Of Human Bondage, *Doubleday, 1915.*

Marcus Aurelius Goodrich (essay date 25 January 1925)

SOURCE: "After Ten Years 'Of Human Bondage,'" in *The New York Times Book Review,* January 25, 1925, p. 2.

[*In the following essay, Goodrich summarizes the critical reaction to* Of Human Bondage.]

During the last decade, the vast, passive jury, in whose hands rests the fate of all writing aspiring to a berth among the classics, have been attending in ever increasing numbers to the steady, unacclaimed arcing over the turmoil of William Somerset Maugham's *Of Human Bondage.* Among New York's literary guild the quite long book, no doubt, has been forgotten. Experiment has shown that when it is possible for a moment to shunt the attention of most of that eminent crew from the uproarious business of literature to the name Maugham, the inevitable response is an exhibitionistic shout referring to a play that he did not write, or to another novel about a tired English business man who retreated to life among the blue skies and corals with a leprosy ridden negress.

But in the less spectacular realms of those who read books merely because they like to read, or those whose culture shelters a vibrant attraction towards authentic performances in English prose, or those who are thrilled to find the universal aspects of life on a printed page, *Of Human Bondage* has, after ten years of steadily increasing activity, risen in England almost to a place beside *The Way of All Flesh,* and in the United States is on the way to becoming an uncanonical sensation. When the book was first published in the United States, it managed to live through three anaemic editions, despite the general critical preoccupation with other matters. Then four years went by and the publishers suddenly discovered that there was a quiet, unheralded demand for more copies of *Of Human Bondage.* They issued another small edition. Two years later, without a single pat on the back from the literators, the supply was again exhausted. The publishers prepared another edition. In 1923 the steady demand for the novel assumed such proportions that it was introduced into a special edition of works that seem to be in permanent demand. In this last edition, which is a fixture of its publishing house, it has gone through three printings. The universities just seem to have discovered the novel, libraries report an increasing call for it, second-hand book dealers number it among the old novels that still sell easily, and the price in London of a first edition of it has multiplied itself by three in the past five years. In New York's clubs and drawing rooms and at exoteric dinner tables, one is a bit surprised to find so old a book talked of as if it had been written yesterday, surprised that any volume could have resisted for so long the gigantic flood rushing every second from the printing presses. The explanation, perhaps, is that *Of Human Bondage* has become a classic.

A short time after Heinemann in England and Doran in the United States simultaneously published *Of Human Bondage* in 1915, the perfunctory unenergetic ripple that it had caused in the critical puddle had smoothed out. The book was allowed to go unpublicized on its quiet way down the trail to oblivion, while the critics turned to raddle themselves in more spectacular rouge pots. In England the critics evidently had felt that something was expected of them, but most of them just did not seem to be very much interested. They admitted generally that it was a realistic character study. Richard King in the *Tatler,* as was to be expected, dismissed it facetiously in a short commentary that ended with the information that "*Of Human Bondage* is scarcely a story." *The Westminster Gazette* decorously passed on the word that it had "excellence"; *The Saturday Review* admitted that it was "arresting"; *The Nation,* in a flabby article, pronounced it to be an experimental attempt to follow in the steps of Compton Mackenzie; and *Punch* inquired plaintively, "Why have so many of our novelists taken to producing enormous volumes marked by a pre-Raphaelite fidelity to detail?" In the United States the case was pretty much the same. *The New York World* in four careless, little unsigned paragraphs intimated that the novel was not worth all the space it took up and complained of the title. *Harper's Weekly* printed: "*Of Human Bondage* is a fat, comfortable volume that will hold the attention of all those who read fiction seriously." *The Dial* commented sententiously on its length and said that "the book is far from being compellingly great." *The Outlook* devoted a few lines to the opinion that the book "shows marked ability in its own way." Most of the papers throughout the States contented themselves with minor, routine observations that the book was "startlingly realistic," and with excerpted paragraphs let it go at that. In several journals appeared the same, mild, stereotyped review that had probably emanated from some syndicate; but what might be held up as the symbol of the whole critical attitude, both here and in England, leaked off the pen of the critic on *The Pittsburgh Chronicle-Telegraph:*

> The reviewer has looked at this book time and again, and just as often has refrained from looking into it. The reason is that there are 648 pages of the story—300 pages too many for careful reading and candid review. But this much can be said: It opens with a funeral and ends with a wedding. As the author is one of the most successful of the younger dramatists, and is said to have made several fortunes from his plays, it may be taken for granted that his novel will repay the reading of it by those who have the time to do so.

Both abroad and in the United States, however, there were some who were fired into eloquent approval of Mr. Maugham's novel. The journals in Dublin, Ireland; Los Angeles, Cal., and Chicago, Ill. *The Boston Evening Transcript* and Theodore Dreiser in the *New Republic* came out flatly with the news that a great and thrilling masterpiece had been born into the world.

When Mr. Maugham, after fashioning a monument of such stoical brilliance as *Of Human Bondage* unmolested by overmuch critical booming, went down among the critics and burst out in their midst with *The Moon and Sixpence,* his fleshy, vivid gesture was not, perhaps, so much a normal literary development, as it was a comment on the middlemen who stood between him and promptly rewarded literary achievement.

After coming face to face with the universal, simple beauty and verity that rears itself symmetrically through the 648 pages of Maugham's book, one realizes that he confronts a tremendous emotional, not merely sensual, upheaval. He has seen life, if not defined, at least epically epitomized.

That *Of Human Bondage* suffered tardy intellectual approval, may be due to the gaudy critical methods that began to come into vogue about the time Mr. Maugham started writing. The chief impetus behind these methods seems to be, as somebody has pointed out, an intent on the part of the critic to call attention to himself rather than to the work he is criticizing. A book received the spotlight if it were capable of reflecting sensational and startling colors back upon him who directed the light. There are in Maugham's novel no color splashing areas nor purpureal periods that could be used to decorate the sort of spectacular critiques inspired, for instance, by the efforts of Messrs. Huxley, Hergesheimer and Firbank. But *Of Human Bondage* is built with pure, meagre-syllabled phrases that twist and cling thrillingly in their unsensational contexts. It is only when the simple, almost primitive, words sum up into the whole absorbing performance that they partake of the nature of sensation. Without once relapsing into dullness, Maugham has consistently passed by the opportunity to indulge in poster effects, so that in the end he might attain to a vital sweep of living, effulgent, integral color. He has succeeded. Even in those passages wherein he depicts events and situations than which there are no more spectacular in man's existence, he maintains his Homeric restraint to an extent that almost makes them seem flat when extracted from their contexts. Here is an example:

> Philip felt on a sudden sick with fear. He hurried to the house in which she lived. He was astonished that she was in Paris at all. He had not seen her for months and imagined she had long since returned to England. When he arrived he asked the concierge whether she was in.
>
> "Yes, I've not seen her go out for two days."
>
> Philip ran up stairs and knocked at the door. There was no reply. He called her name. The door was locked, and on bending down he found the key was in the lock.
>
> "Oh, my God, I hope she hasn't done something awful," he cried aloud.
>
> He ran down and told the porter that she was certainly in the room. He had had a letter from her and feared a terrible accident. He suggested breaking open the door. The porter, who had been sullen and disinclined to listen, became alarmed; he could not take the responsibility of breaking into the room: they must go for the commissaire de police. They walked together to the bureau, and then they fetched a locksmith. Philip found that Miss Price had not paid the last quarter's rent; on New Year's Day she had not given the concierge the present which old-established custom had led him to regard as a right. The four of them went up stairs, and they knocked again at the door. There was no reply. The locksmith set to work, and at last they en-

tered the room. Philip gave a cry and instinctively covered his eyes with his hands. The wretched woman was hanging with a rope round her neck, which she had tied to a hook in the ceiling fixed by some previous tenant to hold up the curtains of the bed. She had moved her own little bed out of the way and had stood on a chair, which had been kicked away. It was lying on its side on the floor. They cut her down. The body was quite cold.

As in *The Way of All Flesh*, the hero of Maugham's book emerges from the household of an English country clergyman and climbs through public school, college, violent youth and rugged London up onto the peaceful level agony of disillusionment. In this case the climber was handicapped by a badly deformed foot. *The Way of All Flesh*, it has been said, is one of the most terrible indictments of parenthood that man's mind has ever produced. *Of Human Bondage* is not merely that.

The novel takes up the life of one Philip Carey when he is almost a baby in arms, living with his newly widowed mother in a middle-class section of London. In the first few pages the mother dies and leaves Philip, sensitive and club-footed, in the hands of his uncle, the Rev. William Carey, and his childless wife. When the boy is about thirteen he is sent to King's School at Tercanbury, from there he goes to Heidelberg. After that he tries accountancy in London, then art in Paris. The last half of the novel is built about his vivid, impecunious struggle to graduate from St. Luke's Hospital in London. Through this half of the story an implacable, pale, green worm, named Mildred, crawls unhealthily: a truly remarkable character.

The book has no plot in the sense that a short story has one, but it fills splendidly that function traditionally ascribed to the novel of recording the development of a character from the moment he becomes conscious to the moment when life has finished its major operations upon him.

Mr. Maugham was born in Paris, where his father was a counselor at the English Embassy. When he was between the ages of 10 and 13, he was confronted with his native land for the first time on the occasion of his going to England to become a student in King's School at Canterbury. From King's he went to the University of Heidelberg, and several years later the records of St. Thomas's Hospital in London record his graduation as a physician. His literary career began when he was twenty-one with a novel called *Liza of Lambeth*. It was written some time before he had finished with his medical studies at St. Thomas's, induced, it is reported, by a sudden pressing and romantic need for money. He has since written thirteen books, numerous short stories and twenty plays, one of which was written in German and produced in Berlin.

Well-read people often have the habit of remarking that they get a great deal more satisfaction out of reading the biography of an actual man than out of reading the most skillfully written novel. There seems to be an authenticity about the biography that is lacking in the novel. One of the striking things about *Of Human Bondage* is that it does not lack this authenticity. But there is more evidence than even this to indicate that Mr. Maugham's book may be his own thinly disguised autobiography. The meaning here of the phrase "thinly disguised" is illustrated by this example: in the novel the boy, Philip, is sent to King's at Canterbury; the first town's name may be manufactured from the second by inverting its first two syllables. Once during an interview with Mr. Maugham, a reporter asked him: "What did you do at Heidelberg?"

Mr. Maugham, who in his early youth stuttered clumsily and consistently, started out on what promised to be a long stretch of talk, when he suffered an attack of his youthful affliction; he stopped, and then said:

"Oh, you'll find it in *Of Human Bondage.*"

To further questions as to whether he found studying medicine very interesting, what he did in Paris, and what he thought of the public school he attended, he said impatiently, as he tried to end the interview:

"You'll find it all in *Of Human Bondage.*"

If the reporter's effrontery had had the complete courage of its conviction, he might have asked Mr. Maugham:

"Didn't you find that your stuttering made life somewhat difficult?"

And his answer, no doubt, would have been,

"That's in *Of Human Bondage* too"—screened, perhaps, behind the symbol of a clubbed foot.

Dorothy Brewster and Angus Burrell   (essay date October 1930)

SOURCE: "Time Passes," in *Adventure or Experience: Four Essays on Certain Writers and Readers of Novels,* Columbia University Press, 1930, pp. 39-75.

[*Brewster was an American educator and critic. In the following excerpt, part of a longer essay illuminating the differences between "chronicle" novels and "dramatic" novels, Brewster and Burrell classify* Of Human Bondage *as a dramatic novel, citing what they consider the reader's ability to sympathize with the self-pitying, imperfect Philip Carey.*]

Somerset Maugham's *Of Human Bondage* is no family chronicle, no slow birth to death progression. Its very title suggests an emotional involvement, a struggle for escape, that promises a dramatic development. Fill out the title from Spinoza's *Ethics*—"Of Human Bondage, or the Strength of the Emotions"—and one is prepared for a plunge into some intense form of human experience. And one takes it, too; such a deep plunge that there are probably few characters in modern English fiction with whom readers more readily identify themselves than with Philip Carey. But for all that, there are qualities in the novel—to be noted presently—that leave one at the end in a mood very different from that in which, for example, a Dostoevsky novel leaves us, though Philip's emotional entanglements are almost Russian.

The most lasting bondage in which Philip is held is that of his own temperament, and his temperament is determined largely by the accident of his deformity—a club foot. Thinking over his life towards the end of the book, he realizes how this deformity has warped his character, and yet how it had developed in him a power of introspection that has given him as much delight as misery. One of the pitfalls of his nature is self-pity. A little boy, just after his mother's death, he weeps, yet keenly enjoys the sensation he is causing among some sympathetic ladies by his sorrow, and wishes he could stay longer with them to be made much of. Awakened to acute self-consciousness by the brutality with which he is treated by curious boys in the school dormitory, his school life becomes one of intermittent torment. He soon learns that when anyone becomes angry with him for any reason, some reference will be made to his foot. He finds himself doing odd bits of playing to the gallery, to excite compassion; as when a schoolmate accidentally breaks a penholder belonging to Philip, and Philip, with tears, declares it was given to him by his mother before she died—though he knows he had bought it a few weeks before. "He did not know in the least what had made him invent that pathetic story, but he was quite as unhappy as though it had been true." The habit continues even after he has learned to understand it, and he lapses into it whenever he is weakened by suffering. When Mildred is irritated by his persistent love on one occasion, "he hesitated a moment, for he had an instinct that he could say something that would move her. It made him almost sick to utter the words," —but he utters them nevertheless—" 'You don't know what it is to be a cripple. Of course you don't like me. I can't expect you to.' He was beginning to act now, and his voice was husky and low." And she softens at the pathos.

He develops ways of escape and defense: reading, first, in his uncle's queerly assorted library, where he forgot the life around him and formed "the most delightful habit in the world—reading. He did not know that he was thus providing himself with a refuge from all the distress of life; he did not know either that he was creating for himself an unreal world which would make the real world of every day a source of bitter disappointment." The wide knowledge gained from his books made him contemptuous of his companions' stupidity, and he found he had a knack in saying bitter things, "which caught people on the raw." Thus he could defend himself, but he couldn't make himself popular, and he longed for easy inter-course with his schoolmates, and would gladly have changed places with the dullest boy in the school who was whole of limb. He develops a cool ironic manner; he evens learns to control his sensitive blushing; he can protect himself, but he is still in bondage. When the physician at the hospital where he is studying asks Philip casually to display his foot, to compare it with that of the patient under examination in the clinic, Philip forced himself to appear indifferent, allowed the students to look at the foot as long as they wished— "when you've quite done," said Philip with an ironical smile. . . . "And felt how jolly it would be to jab a chisel into their necks." He becomes an adept in self-analysis— "a vice as subtle as drug-taking."

What Philip suffers from his deformed foot is mild compared with the misery he undergoes when he falls in love with Mildred. It is an emotion so different from anything he has ever dreamed or read about—this aching of the soul, this painful yearning—that he is profoundly shocked when he is forced to identify it as love. Mildred, with her insolent pale thin mouth and anæmic skin, has been described somewhere as an implacable pale green worm who crawls through the book. The very fact that Philip is blinded by no illusions about her, that he sees how unhealthy, commonplace, odiously genteel, vulgar and selfish she is, convinces us that the passion is irresistible. Lovers of unworthy objects in fiction are usually clearly deluded; we, the readers, see that, and look for the waning of the passion with the discovery of the truth. But Philip knows the truth from the beginning, and we agonize with him over this divorce between reason and emotion, this split in consciousness where the reason watches, disgusted, repelled, estimating the passion at its true value, but unable to affect the emotions, which go their own lamentable way. "His reason was someone looking on, observing the facts, but powerless to interfere; it was like those gods of Epicurus, who saw the doings of men from their empyrean heights and had no might to alter one smallest particle of what occurred." There are moments when he loathes Mildred, moments again when he feels noble because of the sacrifices he makes for her, other moments—like the blessed pauses in an illness—when the temperature falls and he thinks he is released. Once when she treats him with an insolence that humiliates him, "he looked at her neck and thought how he would like to jab it with the knife he had for his muffin. He knew enough anatomy to make pretty certain of getting the carotid artery. And at the same time he wanted to cover her thin pale face with kisses." He tastes the depths of voluptuous self-torture when he gives Mildred and Griffiths—his friend for whom the apparently passionless Mildred has a violent infatuation—money to go off together on a week-end trip. He is sick with anguish when he makes the offer, yet "the torture of it gave him a strange subtle sensation." The devil of self-torture always lurks in him. There is a strange sequel when he later takes Mildred and her baby into his little flat and supports them, though he no longer has any desire for Mildred. This physical indifference so piques Mildred that she throws herself at his head, and rejected, takes a vicious revenge by utterly destroying all the furnishings of the apartment, even slashing Philip's few paintings, relics of his art studies. But even that is not the end of Mildred; she comes back again and again, with each reappearance more degraded. When she is finally lost, Philip sometimes wandered through the streets haunted by prostitutes, wishing and dreading to see her, catching a glimpse of someone resembling her that gave him a sharp stab of hope or of sickening dismay—he scarcely knew which. Relieved when it was not she, he was yet disappointed and seized with horror of himself.

> Would he never be free from that passion? At the bottom of his heart, notwithstanding everything, he felt that a strange desperate thirst for that vile woman would always linger. That love had caused him so much suffering that he knew he would never, never be quite free of it. Only death could finally assuage his desire.

There are times in the course of this strange passion when Philip could step over into Dostoevsky's world and feel at ease with the most accomplished masochist of them all.

Compelling as is the drama of Philip's struggle, it is to other aspects of the novel that the final impression is due. There is the sense of change, of relentless moving on, that marks the chronicle, though the space of years actually covered in *Of Human Bondage* is not great—perhaps twenty-five or thirty. Philip moving from one group to another, in his restless search for adjustment, loses sight of this or that person for a time; then sees him again, changed, older. There are his clergyman uncle and his aunt, middle-aged when they take the orphaned nephew into their home, growing into old age, dying; there is Hayward, fascinating and brilliant in the eyes of twenty-year-old Philip, gradually revealing himself as Philip grows more astute to be a shallow poseur, whose mind grows more and more flabby and his charm more and more tarnished. There is Cronshaw, the poet of the Montparnasse cafés, center of a little circle of the initiated; leading an ever shabbier and more sordid life, coming to die wretchedly in London. And Mildred herself, who runs rapidly through the stages that take her from a curiously attractive waitress in an ABC teashop to a diseased prostitute haunting Piccadilly. It is Philip's reflective attitude towards all these mutations that helps to create the effect of philosophic detachment characteristic of the chronicle novel.

There is not in *Of Human Bondage* the rigid selection of detail that in the dramatic novel makes everything bear directly on the main conflict. For the interest is not so much in the final resolution of the conflict as in Philip's arrival at a comprehension of its nature and its place in some general scheme of human existence.

—Dorothy Brewster and Angus Burrell

Then Philip's career is so varied and experimental that he seems to have led several lives. And there is such richness of detail in the account of his art studies in Paris, his medical training in London hospitals, his dismal interlude as a shop clerk; there are so many people in each little universe whose lives Philip observes with the same sort of interested detachment with which Maugham himself observes Philip,—that we feel we are watching the unrolling of an elaborate panorama. There is not the rigid selection of detail that in the dramatic novel makes everything bear directly on the main conflict. For the interest is not so much in the final resolution of the conflict as in Philip's arrival at a comprehension of its nature and its place in some general scheme of human existence. He begins quite early seeking consciously to understand the meaning of life, as well as to make his own difficult adjustments to it. Often this intellectual need—stimulated by his emotional difficulties—is more pressing than a decision about his career or an escape from the degrading bondage to the unspeakable Mildred. The reader begins presently to share Philip's philosophic concern with what life is all about.

It is towards the chapter that follows "Of Human Bondage" in Spinoza's *Ethics* that the novel is moving, though one can scarcely say that it arrives—"Of Human Freedom, or the Control of the Understanding." From time to time Philip feels that he understands himself and life and can control both. When he talks with Cronshaw in Paris, he is challenged to say what he really thinks he is in the world for, and he answers vaguely—to do one's duty, to make the best use of one's faculties, and to avoid hurting other people. This he calls abstract morality, and he is indignant with Cronshaw for ridiculing his weak reasoning, and for setting up a thoroughly self-centered philosophy— that men seek but one thing in life, their pleasure. Philip had always believed conventionally in duty and goodness. As he goes on through his own difficult experiences, and especially as he watches day after day the procession of humanity through the clinic of the hospital, he comes to see only facts. The impression was

> neither of tragedy nor of comedy. . . . It was manifold and various; there were tears and laughter, happiness and woe; it was tedious and interesting and indifferent; it was as you saw it; it was tumultuous and passionate; it was grave; it was sad and comic; it was trivial; it was simple and complex; joy was there and despair; the love of mothers for their children, and of men for women; lust trailed itself through the rooms with leaden feet, punishing the guilty and the innocent, helpless wives and wretched children; drink seized men and women and cost its inevitable price; death sighed in these rooms and the beginning of life, filling some poor girl with terror and shame, was diagnosed there. There was neither good nor bad there. There were just facts. It was life.

So Philip cultivated a disdain for idealism, which he had found meant for the most part a cowardly shrinking from life. But meeting a man with a passion for Spain and particularly for the painting of El Greco, Philip began to divine something new, to feel on the brink of a discovery, a new kind of realism in which facts "were transformed by the more vivid light in which they were seen." There was some mysterious significance in these paintings, but the tongue in which the message came was unknown to him.

> He saw what looked like the truth as by flashes of lightning on a dark stormy night you might see a mountain range. He seemed to see that a man need not leave his life to chance, but that his will was powerful; he seemed to see that self-control might be as passionate and as active as the surrender to passion; he seemed to see that the inward life might be as manifold, as varied, as rich with experience as the life of one who conquered realms and explored unknown lands.

These remain but flashes. He finds most satisfaction in the conviction that life has no meaning. "Life was insignificant and death without consequence." He exulted as he had in his boyhood when the weight of a belief in God was lifted from his shoulders. He felt free. "If life was mean-

ingless, the world was robbed of its cruelty." But Cronshaw had once given him a little Persian rug, and told him that the meaning of life was hidden in its pattern; and now he thinks he discerns it.

> As the weaver elaborated his pattern for no need but the pleasure of his aesthetic sense, so might a man live his life, or if one was forced to believe that his actions were outside his choosing, so might a man look at his life, that it made a pattern. . . . Out of the manifold events of his life, his deeds, his feelings, his thoughts, he might make a design, regular, elaborate, complicated, or beautiful; and though it might be no more than an illusion that he had the power of selection, though it might be no more than a fantastic legerdemain in which appearances were interwoven with moonbeams, that did not matter: it seemed, and so to him it was. . . . There was one pattern, the most obvious, perfect, and beautiful, in which a man was born, grew to manhood, married, produced children, toiled for his bread, and died; but there were others, intricate and wonderful, in which happiness did not enter and in which success was not attempted; and in them might be discovered a more troubling grace.

Philip felt he was casting aside the last of his illusions in throwing over the desire for happiness. Measured by that desire, his life was horrible, but it might be measured by something else. Happiness and pain were details in the elaboration of the design. Anything that happened to him henceforth would simply be one more motive to add to the complexity of the pattern. When the end came and it was completed, he would find it none the less beautiful because he alone knew of its existence and "with his death it would cease to be."

Philip's final acceptance of the most obvious pattern is brought about by his meeting with Sally, a girl with a very simple pagan attitude towards living, as radiantly healthy as Mildred was sickly, as tranquil as Philip is restless, as soothingly maternal as any man could wish his ideal woman to be—yet not as convincing as the dreadful Mildred, who seems the reality, whereas Sally is one of the dreams belonging to the Golden Age. Freedom to Philip suddenly takes on the aspect of lonely voyaging over a waste of waters; a quiet home with Sally is a fair harbor.

> He thought of his desire to make a design, intricate and beautiful, out of the myriad, meaningless facts of life: had he not seen also that the simplest pattern, that in which a man was born, worked, married, had children, and died, was likewise the most perfect? It might be that to surrender to happiness was to accept defeat, but it was a defeat better than many victories.

Theodore Spencer   (essay date October 1940)

SOURCE: "Somerset Maugham," in *College English,* Vol. 2, No. 1, October, 1940, pp. 1-10.

[*In the following excerpt, Spencer discusses the strengths and weaknesses of* Of Human Bondage.]

One of the difficulties involved in writing a critical essay on Somerset Maugham is that he seems to have made such an estimate unnecessary by writing it himself. In a number of prefaces and especially in *The Summing Up* he has described his career, stated his beliefs, and defined his limitations. He has been as honest with his readers as he has been with himself.

> Though I have had variety of invention, and this is not strange since it is the outcome of the variety of mankind, I have had small power of imagination. I have taken living people and put them into the situations, tragic or comic, that their characters suggested. I might well say that they invented their own stories. I have been incapable of those great, sustained flights that carry the author on broad pinions into a celestial sphere. My fancy, never very strong, has been hampered by my sense of probability. I have painted easel pictures, not frescoes.

Such frankness, as Maugham himself points out, is likely to be dangerous to a writer's reputation. The Anglo-Saxon public likes its authors to have some mystery or romance surrounding them, to be less explicit and less rational about themselves than Maugham has been; it is not wise for an English writer to show that he has too much common sense. "Anthony Trollope ceased to be read for thirty years because he confessed that he wrote at regular hours and took care to get the best price he could for his work." And it is true that Maugham has been slighted or ignored by the critics. "In my twenties the critics said I was brutal, in my thirties they said I was flippant, in my forties they said I was cynical, in my fifties they said I was competent, and now in my sixties they say I am superficial." But the critics have not only branded Maugham with unflattering epithets; they have done something more harmful to his reputation than that—they have neglected him by putting him to one side of the main current of literature in his age. The age has been an age of experiment, and criticism has followed many of the writers in being more interested in experiment than in accomplishment along relatively traditional lines. It is easier to make critical comments on experimental than on conventional writing; there is more to explain and therefore more to say. And recent critics have been so conditioned by the historical sense, by the feeling that literary art, like evolutionary biology, must be continually developing new forms if it is to progress, that they conclude that an author who does not experiment with new forms is worth little attention. Most histories of contemporary literature give only a brief notice to Maugham.

But Maugham deserves better than this, and popular opinion has recognized the fact by not agreeing with the critics. One of Maugham's books, *Of Human Bondage,* is probably the most universally read and admired of modern English novels, and his plays have more vitality than those of any of his contemporaries, except Shaw. The problem for anyone trying to judge Maugham's permanent value is to decide whether the critics or the public are right. . . .

> **In my twenties the critics said I was brutal, in my thirties they said I was flippant, in my forties they said I was cynical, in my fifties they said I was competent, and now in my sixties they say I am superficial.**
>
> **—*W. Somerset Maugham***

Of Human Bondage . . . is by common consent Maugham's best novel and the one which gives him a claim to being considered a first-class writer. It remains to be seen whether this claim can be justified.

There are, we may say, four things which we look for in a serious work of fiction: (1) an organization of incident which produces the illusion that the sequence of events is necessary and inevitable; (2) a set of characters whose relation to the events is equally inevitable and in whom we can believe; (3) a physical, social, or geographical setting which forms a fitting background for the events and characters; and (4) a moral, intellectual, or metaphysical climate which creates the standard by which, more or less unconsciously, both the author and the reader judge the behavior of the characters. This last requirement, one which is usually overlooked, may be for a certain type of novel the most important of all. For example, the implications of the characters and the action in *Moby Dick* are in a sense more significant than the action that the characters perform. They universalize the individual events by giving them a symbolic meaning; we have, in other words, the feeling of a fourth dimension to which I have already referred. The problem in criticizing *Of Human Bondage* is to determine whether or not this quality can be found in it or whether it is merely, like the *Forsyte Saga,* a kind of sublimated reporting limited to a given time and place.

There is no doubt about the conviction of reality which we receive from the book; Philip Carey's childhood, his uncle, the school at Tercanbury, his years abroad, and his struggle to find a satisfactory way of existence are all described with honesty, fidelity, and conviction. The material is almost entirely autobiographical, and Maugham has told us himself that he was virtually forced to write the book in order to get the subject matter out of his system. The difference between the first three-quarters of the book and the last quarter, the part describing Philip's marriage, which, according to Maugham, is largely wish fulfilment, shows how necessary it is for Maugham, if he is to write convincingly, to rely fairly solidly on what he himself has seen and felt. For the last section of the book, "competent" as it is, has not the strength and the authority of the earlier part. Like the happy ending of Hardy's *Return of the Native,* it is a kind of excrescence on the original organic structure.

It is, then, the first three-quarters of the book that we must consider most seriously. Apart from the fact that we can believe without question in the people and the events which Maugham describes, there are two things in this part of the novel which impress most readers: the love affair with Mildred, and the search for a pattern in human experience. There is no doubt that Maugham's description of his hero's violent infatuation has more intensity than that which he has given to any other similar situation. The *odi et amo* of Catullus has found no more vivid presentation in modern fiction than this. The contrast between the strength of emotion and the unworthiness of its object, which is one of the most painful of human experiences, Maugham here describes in a manner which all who have shared that experience can recognize. Not only are the individual scenes between Mildred and Philip admirably handled but their sequence—the development of the relation between the two—is as psychologically true as it is powerfully described.

And yet, excellent as it is, if we compare it with another handling of the same situation, it may perhaps be clear why it is difficult to attribute to Maugham's description the final, inner artistic vision which I have mentioned as the fourth requirement of a great novel. When Shakespeare's Troilus realizes that his Cressida is unworthy of his feelings for her, he makes that realization the opening wedge for a frightening view into the gulf between appearance and reality which involves every range of thought and feeling. To him it is merely one aspect of a whole view of life; the most excruciating, but not the only, evidence of the gap between what the will and the mind can desire and what the limited, hampering body can perform.

Shakespeare, of course, is writing a poetic drama, not a novel, and as a result he has more opportunity for creating poetic intensity. The comparison between him and Maugham has only a limited value. Nevertheless, there is a "fourth-dimensional" character to Shakespeare's view of Troilus which is missing in Maugham's view of Philip, and we must recognize this lack if we are to keep our standards clear. The difference, to be sure, is not merely a difference in individual ability or vision; it is also a reflection of a difference between two periods in history. Shakespeare's world was based on a concept of unity; when that unity, through the realization of individual perfidy, was apparently smashed, tragedy was the result. Maugham's age gave him no unity; the only order known to Philip—that of his uncle's beliefs—was a shoddy sort of order, and the smashing of it brought, not tragedy, but freedom. Life, like the famous Persian rug given to Philip by Cronshaw, has no pattern at all. "Life was insignificant and death without consequence," Philip discovers; and this discovery is a release and a satisfaction: "His insignificance was turned to power, and he felt himself suddenly equal with the cruel fate which had seemed to persecute him; for, if life was meaningless, the world was robbed of its cruelty. . . . He had not been so happy for months."

Obviously this kind of resolution lacks the intensity of a tragic resolution, and the success of *Of Human Bondage* as a whole is a limited success. It has not, for example, the lyrical intensity which we sometimes find in such a comparable work as Arnold Bennett's *Old Wives Tale;* there is nothing in Maugham like Sophia's reflections over the body of Gerald Scales. *Of Human Bondage* is not one of

those novels which press us urgently into new areas of awareness; it merely fills out, in its moving, efficient, and vivid way, those areas of awareness which we already possess. Superior as it is to anything else Maugham has written, it is still, to use his own words, an "easel picture" and not a "fresco."

Maugham has rounded out his life's work in his intellectual and artistic biography, ***The Summing Up.*** We find here, as we would expect, a reflection of the same temperament that is expressed in the novels. It is an admirable book; sensible, clear, and full of an honest and not too worldly wisdom. Next to ***Of Human Bondage*** it is the most likely of his works to survive, for it is not only an expression of Maugham's own point of view, it is also representative of what many people in Maugham's generation believe. It is, truly, "what oft was thought but ne'er so well expressed." But it too is not the work of an imaginative mind; its philosophy is the philosophy of the present and the practical—it does not play with original concepts or mold any unity that does not already exist. For Maugham there are no eternal silences.

But if we are to exclude Maugham from the very top rank of contemporary writers that does not mean that we can dismiss him entirely. His honesty, his craftsmanship, and his admirable gifts for arousing interest and holding attention make him the kind of writer whom it is always a pleasure, and sometimes a stimulus, to read. If literature is to flourish, there must always be, in any given generation, a number of writers who take their work seriously as a craft, who look with unfailing curiosity and interest at human behavior, and who consider the description of that behavior one of the chief justifications for living. Writers of this kind are essential both for keeping our sensitivities alive and for preserving that common basis of value and tradition which must always be the groundwork for writing of the superior kind. Among such writers Maugham holds a high place, and to deny him our respect were to deny respect to the art he has served so long and so well.

W. Somerset Maugham   (speech date 20 April 1946)

SOURCE: "*Of Human Bondage* with a Digression on the Art of Fiction," in *The Maugham Enigma,* edited by Klaus W. Jonas, The Citadel Press, 1954, pp. 121-28.

[*In the following transcript of a speech Maugham delivered on April 20, 1946, when he presented the manuscript for* Of Human Bondage *to the Library of Congress, he explains the genesis of the novel both literally and thematically.*]

April 20, 1946

Ladies and Gentlemen:

You will remember that one of the characters in Dostoevsky's novel *The Possessed* remarks that at a literary gathering, such as this, no one should be allowed to discourse for more than twenty minutes. It is true that he is the most odious character in the book, but there is a lot in what he says. I shall try not to exceed this limit. I start by telling you this in case these typescript sheets I have in front of me fill you with misgiving. A year or two ago I was invited to give a lecture at a great and ancient university, and for reasons with which I need not trouble you I chose the somewhat grim topic of political obligation. I knew exactly what I wanted to say and went into the lecture hall without even a note. It was crowded to the doors. I think I got through the lecture pretty well and I reached my peroration without mishap. But having been at one time of my life a dramatist, I have been inclined to end a discourse with a curtain line. Well, I reached my curtain line with a sigh of relief and began very confidently: The price of liberty is—and then I had a complete black-out and I could not for the life of me remember what the price of liberty was.

It brought my lecture to a humiliating conclusion and, unless in the interval someone else has told them, the students of that great and ancient university do not to this day know what the price of liberty is.

I thought I would not let myself be caught in that way again and I am no longer prepared to trust in the failing memory of the very old party you know I am.

I am very grateful to you for coming here tonight, since you are not only paying me a compliment, but you are paying a compliment to a form of fiction which is badly in need just now of encouragement.

I have never pretended to be anything but a story teller. It has amused me to tell stories and I have told a great many. But as you know, story telling just for the sake of the story is not an activity that is in favour with the intelligentsia. It is looked upon as a debased form of art. That seems strange to me since the desire to listen to stories appears to be as deeply rooted in the human animal as the sense of property. Since the beginning of history men have gathered round the camp fire or in a group in the market place to listen to the telling of a story. That the desire is as strong as ever it was is shown by the amazing popularity of detective stories in our own day. For the habitual reader of them can generally guess who the murderer is before he is half way through, and if he reads on to the end it is only because he wants to know what happens next, which means that he is interested in the story.

But we novelists are on the whole a modest lot, and when we are told that it is our business, not merely to entertain, but to deal with social security, economics, the race question, and the state of the world generally, we are pleased and flattered. It is very nice to think that we can instruct our fellow men and by our wisdom improve their lot. It gives us a sense of responsibility and indeed puts us on a level of respectability with bank presidents. For my part, I think it is an abuse to use the novel as a pulpit or a platform, and I think readers are misguided when they suppose they can thus acquire knowledge without trouble.

It is a great nuisance that knowledge cannot be acquired without trouble. It can only be acquired by hard work. It would be fine if we could swallow the powder of profitable information made palatable by the jam of fiction. But the truth is that, so made palatable, we can't be sure that the powder will be profitable. I suggest to you that the knowledge the novelist imparts is biased and thus unreliable, and it is better not to know a thing at all than to know it in a distorted fashion. If readers wish to inform themselves of the pressing problems of the day, they will do better to read, not novels but the books that specifically deal with them.

The novelist is a natural propagandist. He can't help it, however hard he tries. He loads his dice. By the mere fact of introducing a character to your notice early in his novel he enlists your interest and sympathy in that character. He takes sides. He arranges facts to suit his purpose. Well, that is not the way a book of scientific or informative value is written. There is no reason why a novelist should be anything but a novelist. He should know a little about a great many things, but it is unnecessary, and sometimes even harmful, for him to be a specialist in any particular subject. The novelist need not eat a whole sheep to know what mutton tastes like; it is enough if he eats a chop. Applying then his imagination and his creative faculty to the chop he has eaten, he can give you a very good idea of an Irish stew, but when he goes on from this to give you his views on sheep raising, the wool industry and the political situation in Australia, I think it is well to accept his ideas with reserve.

But please do not misunderstand me. There can be no reason why the novelist should not deal with every subject under the sun so long as it enables him to get on with his story and to develop his characters. If I insist on the importance of the story, it is partly because it is a very useful rail for the author to cling to as page follows page and it is the surest way for him to hold his reader's interest. The story and the persons of the story are interdependent. They must act according to character or the story will lose its plausibility, but it seems to me that the author is at liberty to choose his characters to fit his story or to devise his story to fit his characters. Which he does, probably depends on the idiosyncrasy of his talent, if any.

I suggest to you that it is enough for a novelist to be a good novelist. It is unnecessary for him to be a prophet, a preacher, a politician or a leader of thought. Fiction is an art and the purpose of art is to please. If in my quarters this is not acknowledged I can only suppose it is because of the unfortunate impression so widely held that there is something shameful in pleasure. But all pleasure is good. Only, some pleasures have mischievous consequences and it is better to eschew them. And of course there are intelligent pleasures and unintelligent pleasures. I venture to put the reading of a good novel amongst the most intelligent pleasures that man can enjoy.

And I should like to remind you in passing that reading should be enjoyable. I read some time ago a work by a learned professor which purported to teach his students how to read a book. He told them all sorts of elaborate ways to do this, but he forbore to mention that there could be any enjoyment to be got out of reading the books he recommended. In fact he made what should be a delight into an irksome chore, and, I should have thought, effectively eradicated from those young minds any desire ever again to open a book after they were once freed from academic bondage.

Let us consider for a moment the qualities that a good novel should have. It should have a coherent and plausible story, a variety of probable incidents, characters that are living and freshly observed, and natural dialogue. It should be written in a style suitable to the subject. If the novelist can do that I think he has done all that should be asked of him. I think he is wise not to concern himself too greatly with current affairs, for if he does his novel will lose its point as soon as they are no longer current. H. G. Wells once gave me an edition of his complete works and one day when he was staying with me he ran his fingers along the many volumes and said to me: "You know, they're dead. They dealt with matters of topical interest and now of course they're unreadable". I don't think he was quite right. If some of his novels can no longer be read with interest it is because he was always more concerned with the type than with the individual, with the general rather than with the particular.

Nor do I think the novelist is wise to swallow wholesale the fashionable fads of the moment. I read an article the other day in which the author stated that in future no novel could be written except on Freudian principles. It seemed to me a very ingenuous statement. Most psychologists, though acknowledging liberally the value of Freud's contributions to their science, are of opinion that he put many of his theories in an exaggerated form; but it is just these exaggerations that attract the novelist because they are striking and picturesque. The psychology of the future will doubtless discard them and then the novelist who has based his work on them will be up a gum tree. How dangerous to the novelist the practice is, of depending too much on theories that a later generation may discard, is shown very well in the most impressive novel this century has produced, *Remembrance of Things Past*. Proust, as we know, was greatly influenced by the philosophy of Henri Bergson and large stretches of his great work are taken up with it. I think I am right in saying that philosophers now regard Henri Bergson's more striking ideas as erroneous. I suppose we all read with a thrill of excitement Proust's volumes as they came out, but now when we re-read them in a calmer mood I think what we find to admire in them is his wonderful humour and the extraordinarily vivid and interesting characters that he created. We skip his philosophical disquisitions.

It is obviously to the novelist's advantage that he should be a person of broad culture, but the benefit to him of that is the enrichment of his own personality. His business is with human nature and he can best acquire knowledge of that by observation and by exposing himself to all the vicissitudes of human life.

But I have not really come here to give you a discourse upon the art of fiction. Dr. Luther Evans asked me to talk to you about *Of Human Bondage,* and if I had so long delayed to do so it is because I have now to tell you that I know very little about it. I corrected the proofs in the autumn of 1914—thirty-two years ago—in a billet near Ypres by the light of a single candle, and since then I have only opened the book once. That was when, some months ago, I was asked to read the first chapter for a record that was being made for the blind. I did not make a very good job of it because I was moved, not because the chapter was particularly moving, but because it recalled a pain that the

passage of more than sixty years has not dispelled. So if you will have patience with me I will content myself with giving you the history of this book.

While still a medical student I had published a novel which had some success and as soon as I had taken my degrees I went to Seville and settled down to write an autobiographical novel. I was then twenty-three. Following the fashion of the day I called it rather grandly *The Artistic Temperament of Stephen Carey*. Then I took it back to London to get it published. Life was cheap in those days, but even then you couldn't live for nothing, and I wanted a hundred pounds for my year's keep. But I could find no publisher who was willing to give me more than fifty, I daresay that was all it was worth, but that I obstinately refused to accept. It was a bit of luck for me, for if the book had been published then—and it was certainly very crude and very immature—I should have lost much that I was able to make better use of later.

Years went by and I became a popular dramatist. But those memories of an unhappy past burdened me and the time came when I felt that I could only rid myself of them by writing them; so I retired from the theatre and spent two years writing the book you know now. Then I had another bit of luck. I had called it *Beauty for Ashes,* which is a quotation from Isaiah, but discovered that a novel with that title had recently been published. I hunted about for another and then it occurred to me that the title Spinoza had given to one of the books of his Ethics would very well do for mine. So I called it **Of Human Bondage.**

It was published in England in 1915 and was well enough reviewed. But we were then engaged in a war and people had more important things to occupy themselves with than the characters of a work of fiction. There had been besides a spate of semi-biographical novels and the public was a trifle tired of them. My book was not a failure, nor was it a success. It did not set the Thames on fire. It was only by a lucky break that it was published in America. George Doran, then a publisher who specialized in English books, brought it back to this country for consideration, but it was very long and nobody read it. Then Mrs. Doran got an attack of influenza and on asking for something to pass the time, George Doran gave her **Of Human Bondage** to read, chiefly, I believe, because of its length. She liked it and on this he decided to publish it.

It came out and Theodore Dreiser gave it in *The Nation* a very long, intelligent and favourable review. [In a footnote, the editor adds that the article by Dreiser "actually appeared in *The New Republic* of December 25, 1915."] Other reviewers were more moderate in their praise, but on the whole sympathetic. The average life of a novel at that period was ninety days, and about that time **Of Human Bondage** appeared to die. For two or three years, perhaps more, it was to all appearance forgotten. Then again I had a bit of luck. For a reason I have never known it attracted the attention of various writers who were then well-known columnists, Alec Woollcott, Heywood Broun and the still living and still scintillating F. P. Adams. They talked about it among themselves and then began talking about it in their columns. It found new readers. It found more and more readers. The final result you know. It has now gained the doubtful honour of being required reading in many educational institutions. If I call it a doubtful honour it is because I am not sure that you can read with pleasure a book you have to read as a task. For my own part, I once had to read *The Cloister and the Hearth* in that way and there are few books for which I have a more hearty dislike.

It is because the success of **Of Human Bondage** is due to my fellow writers in America and to a whole generation of American readers that I thought the least I could do was to offer the manuscript to the Library of Congress.

When I asked Dr. Luther Evans if he would accept it I told him that I wanted to present it in gratitude for the hospitality I, my daughter and grandchildren have received in this country. I was afraid it would seem presumptuous if I said more. I did not expect this celebration. I thought that if Dr. Evans was agreeable to my suggestion, I would make the manuscript into a neat parcel, despatch it by parcel post, and then he would put it on one of the shelves in the Library and that would be that. But since you have been so good as to come here, since I have had a signal honour conferred on me, I am encouraged to say what was really my wish to say at the beginning. You know, we British are on the whole honest people, we like to pay our way and we do not like to be in debt. But there is one debt that we can never hope to repay, and that is the debt we owe you for the kindness and the generosity with which you received the women and children of my country when in fear of a German invasion they came to America. They were lonely and homesick and they were unhappy at leaving behind them those who were dear to them. No one knows better than I how much you did for them, how patient you were with them and what sacrifices you made for them. So it is not only for my own small family, but for all those of my fellow countrymen who found refuge on these shores that I wish to offer this manuscript to you, not as an adequate return, not even as a token payment, but just as an acknowledgment of the debt we owe you. Thank you.

Robert Spence   (essay date Spring/Summer 1951)

SOURCE: "Maugham's *Of Human Bondage*," in *The Library Chronicle*, Vol. XVII, No. 2, Spring/Summer, 1951, pp. 104-14.

[*In the following essay, Spence traces the novel's rise in popularity and notes the critics whom he believes played a fundamental role in the novel's emergence as a classic.*]

W. Somerset Maugham has been one of the most prolific writers of our time. However, of the more than fifty books which he has published—novels and volumes of plays, short stories, essays, and travel sketches—only **Of Human Bondage** has won the full admiration of serious, reputable critics. Although they tend to disregard Maugham's other work, they have been generally consistent in their praise of this autobiographical novel, comparing it with *David Copperfield* and *Tom Jones*. **Of Human Bondage** has been, in addition, enormously popular with the general reading public. It is, in the opinion of Theodore Spencer [in "Somerset Maugham," *College English* (October 1940)], "prob-

ably the most universally read and admired of modern English novels."

In view of the wide acclaim which has been accorded Maugham's masterpiece, it is of interest to notice that the book was not at first a success, either with the critics or the public. Indeed, success came tardily to **Of Human Bondage,** though it was not ephemeral. In this paper I shall endeavor to trace briefly the history of the reception of the novel, and to suggest what seem to have been some fundamental factors underlying its rise from temporary oblivion to a position in the first rank of modern English novels.

Maugham tells us [in **"Of Human Bondage, with a Digression on the Art of Fiction,"** 1946] that the book

> . . . was published in England [and America] in 1915 and was well enough reviewed. But we were engaged in a war and people had more important things to occupy themselves with than the characters of a work of fiction. There had been besides a spate of semi-biographical novels and the public was a trifle tired of them. My book was not a failure, nor was it a success.

Evidence corroborates the suggestion that the book was not an immediate success. British reviewers in *The Tatler, The Westminster Gazette, The Nation,* and *Punch* all considered it perfunctorily, while others were generally critical. *The Saturday Review* (September 4, 1915) objected to the evident relish of the author in depicting the sordid aspects of life. *The Athenaeum* (August 21, 1915) commented:

> The values accorded by the hero to love, realism, and religion are so distorted as to have no interest beyond that which belongs to an essentially morbid personality. In such a long novel reiteration is peculiarly tiresome and apt to reduce the gratitude which should be felt for the detailed portraiture and varied aspects of life the author presents to us.

The Times Literary Supplement (August 12, 1915) commended the skill with which the portrait of Mildred Rogers is drawn, but objected to the emphasis placed on her distasteful relationship with Philip Carey:

> It is not only that we resent being forced to spend so much time with so unpleasant a creature. We resent the twist that is given to the figure of life.

The comments in *The Bookman* (September, 1915) were less tempered:

> It may be gathered easily enough that Philip Carey has no sort of moral principles in his relation to women. He abandons the narrow Christianity of his youth, and adopts a meagre heathenism which brings him more happiness than he deserves. His preoccupation with sex would be more tolerable if it was more frankly sensual; but with him nature is an afterthought. As a portrait of the weak egotist, of the knock-kneed Nietzschean, **Of Human Bondage** may be greeted as a remarkably clever book.

In the United States the reception by critics was, with one or two exceptions, much the same. Only the appraisal by Dreiser in *The New Republic* (December 25, 1915) was distinguished by enthusiastic and unqualified praise. Dreiser was pleased that "Nothing is left out," and compared the life of the hero as presented by Maugham with the design in the poet Cronshaw's Persian carpet:

> And so it is, Mr. Maugham, this life of Philip Carey as you have woven it. One feels as though one were sitting before a splendid Shiraz or Daghestan of priceless texture and intricate weave, admiring, feeling, responding sensually to its colors and tones. Or better yet, it is as though a symphony of great beauty by a master, Strauss or Beethoven, had just been completed and the bud notes and flower tones were filling the air with their elusive message, fluttering and dying.

Critical comment in *The Boston Evening Transcript* (August 11, 1915) and *The New York Times* (August 1, 1915), though it did not approach the fervor of Dreiser's review, was in the main favorable. *The Transcript* stated:

> Romance and realism are mingled in *Of Human Bondage* exactly as they are mingled in life. It is a chronicle story well conceived, well told, and with every character in it a human being. Not all of it is "agreeable" reading, to be sure, but there is no reason why a novel should cater to the prejudices of those who demand nothing but the "agreeable" in fiction. Perhaps its greatest effect upon us is that it arouses an eager desire for further knowledge of Philip Carey's future.

And *The Times* commented:

> The vivisection is at times a little too minute, the small incidents rather over elaborated, and there are certain episodes . . . which seem both repulsive and superfluous. Nevertheless, Mr. Maugham has done a big piece of work.

The majority of the American reviews, however, reveal a reaction to the novel comparable to that of the British critics, and similarly proscribe the book. The critic for *The Dial* (September 16, 1915) wrote:

> When a novelist thus sets out to chronicle *everything* about his hero's life, he can hardly fail to leave us with the feeling of intimate acquaintance. But he can easily miss, as Mr. Maugham does, the broad effects and the larger issues of a human characterization. The only thing of this sort that we get from *Of Human Bondage* is a most depressing impression of the futility of life . . .

"Unhappy childhood," said *The Independent* (August 23, 1915),

> always is a bid for sympathy, but little Philip grows up into an insufferable cad. One longs, after reading these novels where spineless men and women yield without a struggle to the forces of evil and are overwhelmed by the world, for the ringing shout of the stout apostle Paul: "I have fought a good fight . . . I have kept the faith!"

The New York World termed *Of Human Bondage* "the sentimental servitude of a poor fool." *The Philadelphia Press* referred to it as the life of "futile Philip," while *The Outlook* insisted that "the author might have made his book true without making it so frequently distasteful." And *The New Orleans Times-Picayune* commented: "Certainly the story cannot be said to be in any sense a wholesome one, and it would require a distinctly morbid taste for one to enjoy it thoroughly."

In view of this widespread denunciation by critics in 1915, and the novel's subsequent half-dozen years of dormancy, it is surprising to learn that in 1923 the George H. Doran Company classed it with works in continual demand, and that a commentator [Marcus Aurelius Goodrich] in *The New York Times Book Review* stated in 1925 that "*Of Human Bondage* has become a classic*." There are probably several reasons for the new interest American readers showed in the novel during the twenties. Perhaps there was something in the story of Philip Carey which appealed to the psychology of what Franklin Roosevelt called "the apparently soulless decade which followed the World War." Or possibly it was, as has been claimed by Richard Cordell and Stuart P. B. Mais, the publication in 1919 of *The Moon and Sixpence* which drew attention to the earlier "neglected" novel. Maugham has suggested, however, what appears to be a chief factor behind the success of his masterpiece. "It failed to do well," he says [in an interview in *The New York Times Book Review* (21 April 1946)], "until, in the twenties, a number of your columnists picked it up and began to talk about it." [In an endnote, Spence adds: "I do not mean to intimate that the basic reason for the success of *Of Human Bondage* was the favorable comment of certain columnists and critics. Their function was to call attention to what previously had been considered a mediocre novel. Possibly the book's popularity with the public is due in part to Maugham's skeptical world view. Readers who experienced the feelings of despair, of frustration, and of the aridity of life subsequent to World War I perhaps found—with Philip Carey—a satisfactory solution to the problems of human existence in skepticism and iconoclasm."] He reiterated the statement when he presented the manuscript of the novel to the Library of Congress in April, 1946. *Of Human Bondage* was, after publication, apparently forgotten

> . . . for two or three years, perhaps more . . .

> Then again I had a bit of luck. For a reason I have never known it attracted the attention of writers who were then well-known columnists, Alec Woollcott, Heywood Broun, and the still living and still scintillating F. P. Adams. They talked about it among themselves and then began talking about it in their columns. It found new readers. It found more and more readers. The final result you know.

Between 1917 and 1925, roughly, a number of columnists and critics did give much attention to Maugham and to *Of Human Bondage.* Early stirrings of interest, given impetus by what appears to have been a "Maugham cult," led ultimately to wide enthusiasm. Adams, who stated in a recent letter to this writer that he often alluded to *Of Human Bondage,* praised the novel in print as early as

March 10, 1917. In his column in *The New York Tribune* under that date appeared this comment: "Home and finished reading Mr. Maugham's *Of Human Bondage,* which I think is a great book, and I am grateful to W. Hill the artist for having told me of it." The appearance in 1919 of *The Moon and Sixpence* seems further to have elevated Maugham in the esteem of the critics. Adams praised the novel, and Heywood Broun ranked it after *Of Human Bondage.* During the early twenties Adams helped to keep the spotlight on Maugham. He wrote in his column of November 5, 1921: ". . . I read Mr. W. S. Maugham's *Liza of Lambeth* on the train, and as good a book ever he wrote save *Of Human Bondage.* . . . So to bed and read Maugham's *The Circle,* a highly interesting and diverting play." The George H. Doran Company had, in that year, printed for the first time in America Maugham's earliest novel, *Liza of Lambeth,* which had appeared in London in 1897. During the previous year Doran had brought out his second novel, *Mrs. Craddock,* published in England in 1902.

Maugham's stature as a novelist was growing steadily in America—a fact due chiefly to the increasing popularity of *Of Human Bondage.* In 1922 Grant Overton stated confidently in *When Winter Comes to Main Street* that

> The day will come . . . when people will think of him as the man who wrote *Of Human Bondage.* This novel does not need praise. All it needs, like the grand work it is, is attention; and that it increasingly gets.

Adams, also, commented on May 5, 1922: "Thinking again on *Intrusion,* I mused that the girl [Mildred] in *Of Human Bondage,* which still to me is the best writing Mr. W. Somerset Maugham ever did, is as well drawn as Roberta in *Intrusion.*" This conviction that *Of Human Bondage* was Maugham's best novel was echoed by Cornelius Weygrandt, who declared as early as 1925 (*A Century of the English Novel*) that the final judgment of Maugham would rest on the basis of that work. In 1923 Stuart P. B. Mais discussed the novel in *Some Modern Authors,* stressing its "realism" and the determination of the author to present all aspects of life, regardless of how unpleasant— those elements which Dreiser had lauded eight years earlier and which the devotees of the twenties generally pointed to. "Maugham," said Mais, "ought to be one of the most formative influences of the present day. There is certainly no one who could exert such a healthy restraint on the young writer who fears to face the truth."

By the middle of the decade Maugham's novel had made, and still was making, enormous headway. Goodrich wrote in 1925 [in "After Ten Years *Of Human Bondage,*" from *W. Somerset Maugham, Novelist, Essayist, Dramatist*]: "In New York's clubs and drawing rooms and at exoteric dinner tables, one is a bit surprised to find so old a book talked of as if it had been written yesterday. . . ." *"Of Human Bondage . . . in the United States is on the way to becoming an uncanonical sensation."* Goodrich's statements are not particularly surprising in view of earlier comments by Mais and Dorothea Lawrence Mann. Mais had written (*Some Modern Authors*):

> *Of Human Bondage* is so good a book that it is

impossible (for a long time after reading it) to fall down and worship the young Americans of the Sinclair Lewis type or the intellectual young Englishwoman of the Dorothy Richardson-Romer Wilson type. *Of Human Bondage* is good because it is sincere autobiography—one of the few absolutely sincere documents I have ever read. I would give it, if I could afford copies, to every imaginative boy on leaving school.

Mrs. Mann, in a commentary in *The Boston Evening Transcript* (reprinted in Doran's 1925 tribute to Maugham under the title "Somerset Maugham in his Mantle of Mystery"), had stated enthusiastically:

> I should like to see the time come when the well-read person would be as unwilling to admit not having read *Of Human Bondage* as he would be to admit that he had not seen the plays of Shakespeare.

Some indication as to the hold which Maugham's novel took on the reading public is suggested by an essay published by Carl Van Doren in *Century* for May, 1925 entitled "Tom Jones and Philip Carey; Heroes of Two Centuries." That such a comparison could be made is indeed revealing when one considers that—with the exception of the small re-issue of 1919—the book was not reprinted until two years earlier.

The new-found popularity of *Of Human Bondage* was not evanescent. As Maugham has said, since the critics began talking about and writing about his novel, "nothing has stopped it." Notice of it reached even the sports pages. Gene Tunney revealed, according to Maugham, that it was the only book he read while training for the famous fight with Jack Dempsey in Philadelphia in 1926. By 1930 Dorothy Brewster and Angus Burrell were expressing the opinion (*Adventure or Experience*) that "there are probably few characters in modern English fiction with whom readers more readily identify themselves than with Philip Carey."

It should be pointed out that there were, of course, critics both in England and America who remained unconvinced that *Of Human Bondage* was a "classic," and who did not share in the enthusiasm of the Maugham cult. Desmond MacCarthy, writing in *The New Statesman,* August 14, 1920, said of the novel:

> It is not a cheerful book; the attitude of the author towards human nature is mistrustful, and oddly enough there seems to be little curiosity about human beings in that attitude; the one passion which in the absence of warmer feelings helps a writer most to carry to the finish such a long detailed piece of work.

Weygandt, although holding that *Of Human Bondage* surpasses Maugham's other work, considered it at best a second-rate novel. "Maugham," he said, "is a keen student of humanity but hardly an artist at all." Brewster and Burrell adjudged the novel a good one, but noted that its ultimate effect is not gained without straining. And Theodore Spencer, in one of the more recent, dispassionate evaluations of the book, declared in 1940 that the success of the novel is definitely limited. *"Of Human Bondage* is not one of those novels which press us urgently into new areas of awareness; it merely fills out . . . those areas of awareness which we already possess."

Suggestions that *Of Human Bondage* has been overrated appear (if anything may be inferred from the publication record) to have had little effect on the reading public once the columnists and critics had stimulated interest in the book. Goodrich, discussing at a ten-year distance the reception of the novel, reported that not until 1923—when the George H. Doran Company authorized a new edition—was there a serious demand for it. During the next two years it was reprinted three times, and by 1925, said Goodrich, libraries and second-hand book stores were reporting increasing demands for it. The popularity of the novel appears to have mounted rapidly. In 1927 Doran issued a new edition, and in 1928 the book reached the cheap reprint stage. Odyssey Press brought out the first of these editions. Grosset and Dunlap published it in their reduced-rate Novels of Distinction series in 1929 and again in 1932, and the Modern Library added it to its list in 1930. By 1931 copies of the 1915 edition were to be found with difficulty. Frederick T. Bason, compiling a bibliography of the writings of Maugham in that year, reported that copies of the first edition of the masterpiece were among the most sought after books in the United States.

Public demand for *Of Human Bondage* continued undiminished through the thirties. The Modern Library advertised the novel in 1941 as one of its best-selling titles. The Garden City Publishing Company and the Dial Press each issued several reprints between 1933 and 1949. Even British readers, long reluctant to accept *Of Human Bondage,* apparently caught something of the American fever. William Heinemann, Limited, which published the novel in 1915, brought out in 1934 the first English edition in nineteen years. Reprints followed in 1935 and 1936. In 1936 Doubleday, Doran and Company published in New York the first of several limited deluxe editions. The following year the Literary Guild distributed the novel to its many thousands of members, and in 1938 Yale University Press printed it in two volumes, with an introduction by Theodore Dreiser, for members of the Limited Editions Club. The Clovernook Printing House for the Blind (Mount Healthy, Ohio) published a seven volume edition in braille in 1941, and portions of the novel were recorded recently by Maugham. In addition to the many American and the two British editions, *Of Human Bondage* has been published in a number of foreign languages—in French (1937), German (1939), Italian (n. d.), Spanish (1944), and Hungarian (n. d.).

It would appear, on the basis of the foregoing data, that there is much justification for Spencer's assertion that *Of Human Bondage* is one of the most universally read and admired of modern English novels. His statement seems valid despite the generally unfavorable critical comment in 1915, and the subsequent half-dozen years of public apathy toward the book. Not until the early twenties did *Of Human Bondage* begin its climb toward a position in the highest level of English novels. As we have seen, the emergence of the work appears to have been due in large part to the critics and columnists who saw more in the novel

than did the reviewers of 1915. Their interest stimulated public interest, and their unreserved praise was a fundamental factor in the making of a masterpiece. Maugham, when he presented the original manuscript of the novel to the Library of Congress [on April 21, 1946], acknowledged the debt he owed its champions:

> It is because the success of *Of Human Bondage* is due to my fellow writers in America and to a whole generation of American readers that I thought the least I could do was to offer the manuscript to the Library of Congress.

That the novel has not slipped much in the esteem of American readers is suggested by the editorial comment of the Houston, Texas, *Post* (April 28, 1946), shortly after the presentation. *The Post* declared that *Of Human Bondage* is "one of the greatest novels in the English language." Maugham, in his novel *The Razor's Edge,* stated that "we the public in our heart of hearts all like a success story." Where could one find a better one than in the history of *Of Human Bondage*?

John R. Reed   (essay date 1964)

SOURCE: "The Redundant Gentleman," in *Old School Ties: The Public Schools in British Literature,* Syracuse University Press, 1964, pp. 169-219.

[*Reed is an American educator, critic, and poet. In the following excerpt, he discusses the impact of Philip's schooling on his character—a schooling intended to make him a gentleman but which in practice left him ostracized and self-conscious.*]

In Maugham's *Of Human Bondage* (1915), Philip Carey, an up-to-date Ernest Pontifex, in his rebellion against the cant of his elders, reacts strongly against his school as well as his family. He leaves school to finish his education at Heidelberg, hoping for greater intellectual and imaginative freedom. *Of Human Bondage* is typical of the twentieth-century version of the *Bildungsroman.* Philip follows a familiar pattern in his progress toward enlightenment. At school he is unhappy, suffering humiliation at the hands of his schoolmates for a physical deformity. Philip becomes introverted, and his suffering makes him aware of the flaws in the system under which he is forced to exist. He suffers isolation from his fellows and is made the victim of a capricious bully. Like Stephen Dedalus in James Joyce's *A Portrait of the Artist as a Young Man,* Philip is made acutely sensitive to religious matters, especially matters concerning damnation.

From this unhealthy prep school atmosphere, Philip moves on to King's School at Tercanbury (an anagram on Canterbury) which "prided itself on its antiquity," much in the manner of Sawston in *The Longest Journey.* Tercanbury is a smartly snobbish school for gentlemen's sons. There Philip is fashioned into a gentleman. In the atmosphere of the school, Philip is uneasy but cannot focus his dissatisfaction since he accepts the gentlemanly code of the school. He learns that enthusiasm is bad form, while suffering from the passionate irascibility of a techy form master not fit to teach young and sensitive boys. Just as

Tony Farrant learned how to adapt himself to all situations, preserving this talent as the one lesson adequately taught at school, so Philip's greatest acquisition at Tercanbury is adroitness in deceit, "which was possibly of greater service to [him] in after life than an ability to read Latin at sight." Uncontent, Philip wishes to leave Tercanbury. Public schools are uncongenial for the bright student, and, as Mr. Perkins, the liberal headmaster of Tercanbury, admired by Philip, says, " 'Of course schools are made for the average. The holes are all round, and whatever shape the pegs are they must wedge in somehow. One hasn't time to bother about anything but the average.' "

Philip, while accepting this tradition, suffers from a sense of failure at school and leaves to complete his education in Germany; and it is here, indeed, that his real education begins, for, when Weeks, an American, presses him for an exact definition of a gentleman, Philip has difficulty defending one of his accepted prejudices. This is the first step in the *bouleversement* of the ideal British middle-class image, the gentleman. Philip realizes, as he learns to look critically upon gentlemanliness and the society it represents, that his education has been limited and that he has been insulated against too much of life. It is with this step outside the potting shed of the narrowly tended public school that Philip is made aware of the existence of values which not only differ from but which conflict with school values and which, if they are to be faced, require clear and critical revaluation. At first, Philip attempts to defend his previously unquestioned beliefs. His definition of a gentleman is naïve.

> "First of all he's the son of a gentleman, and he's been to a public school, and to Oxford or Cambridge."
>
> "Edinburgh wouldn't do, I suppose?" asked Weeks.
>
> "And he talks English like a gentleman, and he wears the right sort of things, and if he's a gentleman he can always tell if another chap's a gentleman."

His is not, in fact, a bad definition. However, as Philip proceeds on his crusade of discovery, he learns that there are other sorts of gentlemen. Mr. Watson, whom Philip meets while at the law firm of Messrs. Herbert Carter and Co., is from a wealthy brewing family and in his manner is too gentlemanly. He is rude to his inferiors and patronizing in a careless manner toward Philip.

> He had been to Winchester and to Oxford, and his conversation impressed the fact upon one with frequency. When he discovered the details of Philip's education his manner became more patronising still.
>
> "Of course, if one doesn't go to a public school those sort of schools are the next best thing, aren't they?"

Mr. Carter, speaking casually to Philip, also manages to announce that he is accustomed to hunting (definitely a gentleman's sport) and that his son has been educated at Rugby and is now at Cambridge. When Mr. Carter leaves,

Philip, pondering the performances by Carter and Watson, is obliged to reconsider his definition of a gentleman.

> Philip was overwhelmed by so much gentlemanliness: in East Anglia they knew who were gentlemen and who weren't, but the gentlemen didn't talk about it.

Philip's experience is a guide to the transformation of the modern gentleman. Philip is made aware of the possible perversion and distortion of the gentlemanly code which he had previously accepted as the standard for decorous behavior. He discovers that the gentleman can use his advantages in ways which suggest a great potential for the exercise of a snobbish and thoughtless influence, concerned paradoxically with material values, yet lacking an adequate comprehension of reality. Though Philip never confronts a Pembroke or a Ralston, he does encounter the products of their educational methods.

From this point, Philip's maturation and experience wean him from the sham gentility that he encounters repeatedly in his adult life. He submerges himself in the underworld of Parisian bohemia and London lower-middle-class labor, reaching the antipodal regions of society where he can view his old genteel values in new perspectives, much in the manner of George Orwell, whose descent into the subworld of deprivation and suffering was more conscious and politically motivated. Having reached this spiritual Duogobmai, Philip is prepared to return to the old values on new terms, and after an excruciating love affair, he frees himself from economic insecurity by completing his medical education. When he goes down into the country to serve as assistant to Doctor South, his qualifications are indicative of his own progress away from sham gentility. The doctor asks him if he was at a university, and Philip replies that he was not, at which the doctor remarks: " 'Last year when my assistant took a holiday they sent me a 'Varsity man. I told 'em not to do it again. Too damned gentlemanly for me.' "

Maugham's hero escapes his public school background, as did Ernest Pontifex, to associate himself with the more natural aspects of human life and to find love and contentment on a less pretentious level of existence.

M. K. Naik   (essay date 1966)

SOURCE: "*Of Human Bondage,*" in *W. Somerset Maugham,* University of Oklahoma Press, 1966, pp. 46-57.

[*Naik is an Indian educator and critic. In the following excerpt, he argues that* Of Human Bondage *is a "novel of adolescence"—the purpose of which was for the author to find himself—and concludes that the book's greatest fault is a negativity that leaves the hero with a creed that lacks positive values.*]

The strong native sensibility which dominates the works of Maugham's early phase reaches its high-water mark in *Of Human Bondage,* a novel which is largely autobiographical. Maugham wrote in *The Summing Up* that, having finished the novel, he "prepared to make a fresh start." This "fresh start" was to lead him far away from the dominant strain in *Liza of Lambeth, Mrs. Craddock,* and *Of Human Bondage.*

Maugham described the genesis of this novel in *The Summing Up* and also in the introduction to the reprint of the novel in the Collected Edition of his works. We are told that Maugham first wrote *Of Human Bondage* in a much shorter form, as early as 1897-98:

> It was called then, somewhat grandly, "The Artistic Temperament of Stephen Carey." It finished with the hero at the age of twenty-four, which was my own age when I finished it, and it sent him to Rouen, which I knew only from two or three short visits to see the sights, instead of Heidelberg, as in *Of Human Bondage,* which I knew well; and it made him study music, of which I knew nothing, instead of making him study painting, of which in later years I was to learn at least a little.

The book was rejected by publishers and was put aside. But, continues Maugham:

> I could not forget the people, the incidents and the emotions of which it was composed. In the next ten years I had other experiences and met other people. The book continued to write itself in my mind, and many things that happened to me found their place in it. Certain of my recollections were so insistent that, waking or sleeping, I could not escape from them. I was by then a popular playwright. I was making for those days a great deal of money, and the managers could hardly wait to engage a cast till I had written the last act of my new piece. But my memories would not let me be. They became such a torment that I determined at last to have done with the theatre till I had released myself from them. My book took me two years to write. I was disconcerted at the unwieldly length to which it seemed to be extending, but I was not writing to please; I was writing to free myself of an intolerable obsession. I achieved the result I aimed at, for after I had corrected the proofs, I found all those ghosts were laid, and neither the people who played their parts in the story, nor the incidents in which they were concerned ever crossed my mind again. Looking back on it now in memory . . . I can hardly tell what is fancy and what is fact, what parts describe events that happened, sometimes accurately and sometimes disturbed by an anxious imagination, and what parts describe what I could have wished had happened.

The account in *The Summing Up* is even more explicit. Maugham narrates there how, at the height of his success as a playwright, he began to be obsessed by:

> . . . the teeming memories of my past life. The loss of my mother and then the break up of my home, the wretchedness of my first years at the school for which my French childhood had so ill-prepared me, and which my stammering made so difficult, the delight of those easy, monotonous and exciting days in Heidelberg, when I first entered upon the intellectual life, the irksomeness of my few years at the hospital and the thrill of London.

Of Human Bondage provided the release from these "teeming memories." This account of the genesis of the novel is highly significant. It explains the deep compassion, the insight into the adolescent mind, and the honesty of the book.

Of Human Bondage belongs to that type of novel which may be called "the novel of adolescence." This type of novel, which was usually represented by a long chronicle in three thick volumes and which flourished throughout the nineteenth century, had its beginning with Goethe's *Wilhelm Meister.* As has been pointed out by William Y. Tindall [in *Forces in Modern British Literature*], this form received new life towards the end of the century from the science of biology and later from psychology.

> In novel after novel sensitive lads are apprenticed to life, formed by its forces, rebelling against them, sometimes failing, sometimes emerging in victory. Their trials and errors, like those of rats in a maze, are painfully displayed. And all the horrors of adolescence, the theatre of biology and spirit, are examined. . . . From 1903 onwards almost every first novel by a serious novelist was a novel of adolescence. . . . it produced some of the best novels of the early twentieth century.

Of Human Bondage is a chronicle of a period of about twenty years in the early life of Philip Carey, who is, to a large extent, Maugham himself. The opening chapter forms one of the most moving scenes in the novel. Philip's mother, who is on her deathbed, asks nine-year-old Philip to be brought to her. She presses the child, who is only half-awake, to herself, and then, "she passed her hand down his body till she came to his feet; she held the right foot in her hand and felt the five small toes; and then slowly passed her hand over the left one. She gave a sob." Thus the fact of Philip's clubfoot, which is going to cause him suffering throughout his whole life, is intimated to the reader in an effortless and effective way.

Philip's clubfoot seems to have been suggested by young Maugham's own stammer, and Maugham indeed appears to have put so much of his childhood and adolescence into the portrait of Philip that he emerges as easily the most memorable of Maugham's heroes.

Since Philip's mother dies (his father is already dead), the bringing up of the orphan is entrusted to his uncle, who is vicar of Blackstable. Philip's life at Blackstable is not happy. He is starved of affection, for his uncle is too self-centered to pay much attention to the boy; his aunt, a shy and meek childless lady, is too diffident to satisfy the boy's emotional needs. Philip's deformity, which excites ridicule and makes him exceedingly self-conscious, renders his schooldays equally unhappy. "And often there recurred to him then that queer feeling that his life with all its misery was nothing but a dream, and that he would awake in the morning in his own little bed in London."

The dull routine of the school irks this dreamy and precocious boy, and he rebels against the ecclesiastical career which his uncle intends for him. However, he persuades his uncle to allow him to spend a year in Germany, where he experiences his first taste of freedom of action and thought. Still undecided about the choice of a career on his return, he spends one year in London in a chartered accountant's office, and two more in Paris, where he studies painting, until he discovers that he is devoid of genius and returns to London to become a medical student.

While Philip is pursuing his medical studies, he falls in love with Mildred, a shallow and vulgar waitress.

> He had thought of love as a rapture which seized one so that all the world seemed spring-like, he had looked forward to an ecstatic happiness, but this was not happiness; it was a hunger of the soul, it was a painful yearning, it was a bitter anguish, he had never known before.

He struggles in vain against the destructive passion which robs him of his health, of his peace of mind, and of his slender financial resources. Thrice Mildred leaves his life, only to return and make fresh claims upon him. Reduced to poverty, Philip has to abandon his studies for a time and work as a shopwalker to maintain himself.

At long last, he frees himself from the cruel spell of Mildred, and, inheriting money from his uncle who has died, is able to resume his studies. He decides to travel extensively after qualifying as a doctor, but when he receives his degree, he discovers that his one desire is for peace. Throughout his adolescence and youth, one question has been nagging him—"What is the meaning of life?" He deduces that life has no meaning and that every man's life is simply a pattern that he makes out of the manifold events of his life, his deeds, his feelings, and his thoughts—a pattern that he makes simply for his own pleasure. There is "one pattern, the most obvious, perfect and beautiful, in which a man is born, grows to manhood, marries, produces children, toils for his bread, and dies." With the passing of his mental struggles, Philip decides to follow this pattern, and he marries a healthy and simple girl, settling down as a country doctor.

The appeal of *Of Human Bondage* is due, first, to the sincere desire to understand the mind of a sensitive and dreamy adolescent, secondly, to the deep sympathy with which the afflictions of this adolescent are portrayed, and, lastly, to the unflinching honesty and restraint which save its compassion from sentimentality or mawkish self-pity.

The pathos of the opening scene of the novel has already been commented on. With great tenderness, Maugham portrays the sense of loneliness and desolation which haunts Philip in his early days at school. The story of how his deformity, to which he has scarcely given any thought so far, makes him woefully sensitive and self-conscious there, alienates him from the other boys, and makes him grow into a brooding, lonely, and morbid adolescent is told with great power. The career of Philip is, in broad outline, a rather depressing record of the failure of a morbid mind to adjust itself to the world and to life. Yet, it is remarkable that, throughout this long chronicle, Philip never loses our sympathy. This is perhaps due to the stark sincerity with which Maugham portrays his career, extenuating nothing and making no excuses.

The sincerity with which Maugham treats his hero is best illustrated in the Mildred episodes of the novel. Philip emerges from these episodes as an ineffectual, weak, irresolute, and drifting young man, and yet retains our sympathy. It is interesting to compare Philip's adolescent love experiences with those of Wells's Lewisham and Meredith's Richard Feverel, for both of whom adolescent love is enveloped in a rosy romantic haze. Philip, with painful honesty, confesses that "Love was like a parasite in his heart, nourishing a hateful existence on his life's blood."

This sincerity is part of Maugham's creed as a realist, but it does not make him completely detached here. This is impossible; for Philip is, to a large extent, Maugham himself. On the contrary, this quality gives greater verisimilitude to the whole picture. [In *William Somerset Maugham,* 1937] R. H. Ward complains of a certain "rigidity" in *Of Human Bondage,* arising out of "a stubborn determination to plough right on from the beginning to the end, to extenuate nothing." He thinks that this is due to the "material tyrannising over the author." But it is possible to find in this very "determination to extenuate nothing" the source of the emotional force and massiveness of the book. It is that determination, in fact, which gives unity to this sprawling and seemingly formless chronicle.

Philip is not the only object of Maugham's pity in the novel. There are the drifters through life whom Philip meets in his career, and they are pathetic spectacles—more lamentable than he in certain respects, for they are greater self-deceivers. The portraits of some of these are not devoid of irony, as for example, the picture of Hayward, who is at once the deceiver and the deceived. He has purposely impressed others as being an idealist and has led, under the cloak of idealism, an idle and wasted life. He has worn his mask so long, however, that he has ultimately come to believe in his own fiction.

Nevertheless, the dominant note in the other portraits is one of pity for waste and futility. Such is the fate of Cronshaw who is the slave of his Bohemian life in Paris, and who pitiably advises Philip, "If you can get out of it, do while there's time." Such, again, is the fate of Miss Price who, refusing to accept the fact that she has no talent for painting, blunders on through her art studies, until starvation drives her to hang herself.

Of the restraint which saves the novel from mawkish sentimentality, there is a fine example in the scene where Philip, going through the correspondence of his deceased uncle, suddenly comes upon a letter written by his mother. In that letter she writes about her son: "I pray God night and day that he may grow into a good, honest, and Christian man. . . . I hope that he will become a soldier in Christ's Faith and be all the days of his life God-fearing, humble, and pious." The letter moves Philip. "He read again," says Maugham, "what she said about him, what she expected and thought about him. . . . he had turned out very differently; he looked at himself for a moment." And then follows a significant gesture: "Then a sudden impulse caused him to tear up the letter; its tenderness and simplicity made it seem peculiarly private. . . . He went on with the Vicar's dreary correspondence."

Humanitarianism is, as noted earlier, incompatible with

disbelief in the sincerity or goodness of human motive and actions. Maugham, usually the ironic observer of life, has created very few men and women the goodness of whose motives and actions he does not doubt. Thorpe Athelny in *Of Human Bondage* is one of these. He is, no doubt, an absurd creature to some extent. Although he is an insignificant advertisement writer by profession, he grandiloquently calls himself "a journalist," and his garrulity and flamboyance are highly diverting. Yet with all his ridiculousness, Athelny has a pure, disarming goodness, the warmth of which is felt by all who come into contact with him. It is this goodness that succors Philip when both materially and spiritually he has reached the nadir of helplessness.

The other strain in Maugham—that of contemptuous sneering and cold indifference indicative of cynicism—also has a place in *Of Human Bondage.* It is present, first, in the unfavorable portrait of Philip's uncle, the vicar of Blackstable. Maugham is generally hard on clergymen, and in the famous short story, **"Rain,"** in the farcical comedy *Loaves and Fishes* and elsewhere in his work, clergymen are butts of ridicule. The Vicar of Blackstable is a detestable creature both as a clergyman and as a man. He is self-centered, vain, mean, avaricious, and indolent. Maugham takes delight in exposing him through small situations. Thus, when the Vicar and his wife play backgammon, the wife always arranges that he should win, because he is a bad loser. But it is when the Vicar is about to die that Maugham's satire becomes most stinging. Far from reconciling himself to the thought of joining his Maker after a life spent in ease and comfort, this man of God has become a valetudinarian monster, clinging desperately to existence. The thought of death fills him with horror, and the religion that he has preached all his life is now of no avail to him.

> The negativeness of *Of Human Bondage* lies mainly in the solution which Maugham ultimately has his protagonist find to the question: "What is the meaning of life?" The conclusion arrived at by Philip is, "There was no meaning in life, and man by living served no end. It was immaterial whether he was born or not born, whether he lived or ceased to live."
>
> —*M. K. Naik*

But the attack on the clergy and religion in *Of Human Bondage* has more of contemptuous sneering and frigid indifference than of indignation in it. John Brophy makes an illuminating comparison between Samuel Butler's *The Way of All Flesh* and *Of Human Bondage* from this point of view: "*The Way of All Flesh* is inspired by violent anger against the clergy because they offended Butler's moral sense. The hypocrisy reported in *Of Human Bondage*

arouses not so much indignation as distaste." Thus, when Philip loses his faith, he does so

> . . . with surprise at the foolishness of believers, but with no sense of shock, no moral indignation. Convinced that religion is nonsense, he feels no obligation to disabuse others of what he regards as mere fantasy, even when he observes that on their death-beds it fails to console them. Maugham notes, as it were, in a casebook: this man is dying of pneumonia because, curious creature, he insists on going out in the rain. The fact is reported and the comment added without passion, without even concern. Samuel Butler, by contrast, professes social medicine. He is appalled that the contagion should be spread. He denounces religion in a satire so hot that it scorches and discomforts not only the object of his scorn but the reader and himself. He would have the churches pulled down and sterlized, and he has already planned the temples to the Life Force which should be built in their place. [*Somerset Maugham*, published in "The British Council Bibliographical Series," 1952]

This is, indeed, the reason why *Of Human Bondage* misses the greatness which its rich compassion for Philip brings it near attaining. The deep sensibility and honesty of the book are undeniable, but it fails to attain greatness because of what R. H. Ward rightly describes as its "negative quality." "*Of Human Bondage* has," he says, "one great disadvantage, that it is written by a man determined that only thought and the material, with the material as leader and ruler exist. It is, as a result, a good book, but an unilluminated book."

The negativeness of *Of Human Bondage* lies mainly in the solution which Maugham ultimately has his protagonist find to the question: "What is the meaning of life?" The conclusion arrived at by Philip is, "There was no meaning in life, and man by living served no end. It was immaterial whether he was born or not born, whether he lived or ceased to live." Philip's reaction to this conclusion is even more revealing:

> Philip exulted, as he had exulted in his boyhood when the weight of a belief in God was lifted from his shoulders; it seemed to him that the last burden of responsibility was taken from him; and for the first time he was utterly free. . . . what he did or left undone did not matter. Failure was unimportant and success amounted to nothing.

The total lack of positive values in Philip's creed is self-evident. He no doubt speaks, later on, about every man making "a pattern of his life for his own pleasure," and tells us that "there was one pattern, the most obvious, perfect and beautiful, in which a man was born, grew to manhood, married, produced children, toiled for his bread, and died." But it is significant that the end of the novel where Philip chooses this pattern for his own life is, according to most critics, the least satisfactory part of the book. Maugham himself mentions this in his preface to *Of Human Bondage* and is almost apologetic about it: "Here," he says, "I had no facts to go on. It was a wish-fulfilment." The fact is that Philip's sudden apprehension of this perfect pattern is not well prepared for in his psychological portraiture and lacks adequate motivation. Hence it fails to convince. It must also be remembered that Maugham's philosophy of life, as stated in *The Summing Up,* also shows an almost total lack of a positive creed.

The negativeness of *Of Human Bondage* is no doubt mitigated to a considerable extent by its author's humanitarianism, by the fundamental honesty of the book, and by the goodness discernible in Athelny. Nevertheless, it cuts too deep into the work to be wholly dissipated by these and is especially emphasized, as shown earlier, in the concluding portions of the novel.

The dominant strain in *Of Human Bondage* is that of understanding and compassion: "I was not writing to please, I was writing to free myself of an intolerable obsession," says Maugham in commenting on the genesis of the book. Hence, the transparent sincerity of the work and the human warmth pervading the struggles and trials of adolescent Philip are explained.

The novel has many faults. It is too long and verbose, and the ending where Philip is thrown hastily into Sally's arms is rather hard to swallow, if not disgusting. From the point of view of form, the novel is indeed only a sprawling chronicle such as a panoramic novel usually is, and, like other lengthy chronicles, it has its redundancies and repetitions. But the greatest limitation of the book is its negativeness of philosophy which persists, though mitigated to a point by other elements in the novel. Yet, in spite of all these shortcomings, the humanitarianism of *Of Human Bondage,* which is undeniable, effectively counterbalances its strain of cynicism. The tables, however, are turned with Maugham's next novel, *The Moon and Sixpence*.

Bonnie Hoover Braendlin   (essay date 1984)

SOURCE: "The Prostitute as Scapegoat: Mildred Rogers in Somerset Maugham's *Of Human Bondage,*" in *The Image of the Prostitute in Modern Literature,* edited by Pierre L. Horn and Mary Beth Pringle, Frederick Ungar Publishing, 1984, pp. 9-18.

[*In the following excerpt, Braendlin discusses the character of Mildred Rogers, arguing that Rogers is cast as a "threatening female" who serves as villain, victim, and scapegoat and is sacrificed for her sins.*]

Scarcely any other character in modern British fiction has been disparaged as unanimously as Mildred Rogers, the supercilious waitress turned prostitute in Somerset Maugham's early-twentieth-century *Bildungsroman, Of Human Bondage* (1915). Critics of the novel have nearly all regarded Mildred solely from the author's viewpoint, perhaps because Maugham's naturalistic, detailed style so convincingly characterizes her as an immoral "slut" and castigates her as a representative of feminine evil, allowing her no redeeming virtue. Because Mildred is propelled into prostitution by her own snobbery, it is obvious that she is culpable and thus perhaps deserving of her fate, yet from other perspectives she appears not only as villainess but also as victim. In this novel of male self-development, Mildred assumes the position of a scapegoat, compelled to expiate the sins of others, specifically those of the protago-

nist, Philip Carey, and more generally those of women who defy prescribed identities and demand proscribed freedoms. She is victimized in a symbolic way by the demands of the traditional male *Bildungsroman,* which sacrifices woman to man's development process and in a sociological sense by a rigid class hierarchy and propriety and by a paucity of opportunities for women to advance themselves or to find satisfying work. Her independent willfulness suggests her affinities with the New Woman, a turn-of-the-century phenomenon depicted in various guises by novelists of the period; her irrational destructiveness relates her to female demons and finally to all outsiders who avenge themselves against societal ostracism.

Of Human Bondage delineates a young man's struggle to realize his own identity, or in bourgeois terms, to achieve a successful integration into his society through the proper choice of vocation and wife; hence, the novel closely follows the basic pattern and philosophy of the conventional *Bildungsroman.* Maugham's novel continues the practice established by its predecessors in the *Bildungsroman* tradition—Goethe's *Wilhelm Meisters Lehrjahre* and Charles Dickens's *David Copperfield,* for example—of rewarding the mature adolescent with marriage to an idealized woman. Like Goethe's Natalie and Dickens's Agnes, Sally Athelny incarnates those female characteristics which men have usually considered ideal—unselfish love, unquestioning devotion, and uncritical maternal solicitude— against which all the other women in the novel, including Mildred, are measured and found wanting. On an archetypal level, Sally provides the means whereby Philip as the questing hero can reaffirm lost ties with the natural world. Her affinity with nature becomes evident especially at the end of the novel as she emerges "a Saxon goddess" in the hop fields of Kent. By virtue of her sexual openness, Sally is a twentieth-century improvement on the Victorian mother-goddess, a fitting reward for the young modern who frees himself from outmoded religion and morality yet retains a sense of familial responsibility and societal duty and of the necessity for harmony with the natural world, which is all but eclipsed by industrialism and urbanization.

When Philip meets Sally, he has for some time been hopelessly and helplessly enslaved by his irrational passion for Mildred, whose commonness, vulgarity, and infidelity he despises. The defects of several women in Philip's previous adolescent love affairs and friendships coalesce in Mildred's repulsiveness, which is diametrically opposed to Sally's ideal beauty. Mildred's tall, thin, drooping figure, flat chest, and narrow hips characterize her as less than the established ideal of feminine pulchritude, while her greenish, anemic skin tone betrays her underlying unhealthiness. Her outer sickly physique masks no mitigating inner beauty or strength of character; her "common" and "vulgar" personality lacks any redeeming "gentleness" or "softness." In addition to being unfeminine, Mildred lacks "the maternal instinct," a grievous flaw for any woman to have in a male *Bildungsroman,* in which the goal of individual and societal stability depends on a perpetuation of values through family solidarity and inheritance. The perfect wife not only provides essential maternal solicitude for the struggling hero but promises to give continuity to his newfound identity through children, preferably sons.

Mildred is one of many characters sacrificed in this *Bildungsroman* and in countless others to the development process of the protagonist. Philip's inexplicable infatuation with her constitutes one of the series of trials in his progress toward maturity, illustrating the destructive power of unbridled emotion over reason, a major theme in Maugham's novel. [In an endnote, Braendlin adds that Robert Lorin Calder in his *W. Somerset Maugham and the Quest for Freedom,* 1973, "demonstrates how the several stages of the Philip-Mildred relationship embody various emotional responses of Philip to Mildred, ranging from humiliation through enslaving emotional bondage and finally pity arrived at through self-analysis."] Robert Lorin Calder points out that a destructive female like Mildred appears in most English nineteenth- and early-twentieth-century *Bildungsromane*: "It is usually part of a young man's apprenticeship that he becomes ensnared by a woman who is vulgar, insensitive and unintelligent. In most cases the hero finally frees himself and, although emotionally scarred, is more mature because of his experience." Calder offers no explanation for the inclusion of such a character, but his remark implies that her presence, although appearing to hinder the protagonist's development, in some way furthers it. As seductress, Mildred incurs the blame for impeding Philip's progress, since her enslavement of him causes his initial failure in medical school and eventually contributes to his impoverishment. Yet she also promotes his progress by exemplifying the inevitable consequences of undesirable behavior and destructive emotions. Philip's devastating relationship with Mildred chastens his pride and strengthens his will and determination; most important, it demonstrates to him that love is not so much passion as affection and respect, two sensible emotions that he feels for Sally, although he does not "love" her.

As a symbol of enslaving emotional, irrational passion, Mildred represents that bane of male existence, the femme fatale, the unattainable temptress, the faithless lover, the social counterpart to the immortal fairy, *La Belle Dame sans Merci.* By refusing to submit to Philip's sexual advances because she feels neither sexual attraction nor love for him, Mildred illustrates Barbara Fass's definition [in her *La Belle Dame sans Merci & the Aesthetics of Romanticism,* 1974] of the femme fatale, "the unattainable temptress who keeps her admirer in a perpetual state of longing." Later, when Mildred turns to other men to satisfy her own desires, she fulfills another form of the archetype by becoming the "frequently faithless partner of a destructive love affair," although ironically the "affair" with Philip is devoid of love. Mildred appears to be damned if she does (with other men) and damned if she doesn't (with Philip). In *Of Human Bondage,* the specific social designation for the destructive female archetype is the prostitute, which Mildred becomes after Philip refuses to marry her because he is disgusted and disillusioned by her unfaithfulness. Prostitution brands Mildred a pariah, separated by an insurmountable gulf from respectable womanhood. Because she solicits men on the streets, taking them back to her dingy room, she inhabits the lowest rung of the demi-

monde social hierarchy, far removed from the courtesans in elegant brothels who catered to the Edwardian upper classes and thus enjoyed a measure of social respect and even envy.

Mildred's fall to the depths of depravity punishes her for sexual promiscuity, a conduct accepted as part of the normal course of events in a young man's adolescent development, in which his sexual exploits confirm his manhood. A comparison of Mildred's actions with Philip's indicates that her emotions, desires, and responses parallel his in reverse. The direction of Mildred's reaction to Philip during their relationship proves to be the inverse of the course of his interest in her. Her initial lack of response to Philip's advances leads Philip to conclude that she is impervious to passion, but gradually her sensuality emerges in her affairs with other men, at the same time that Philip's ardor cools in reaction to her "infidelity." She becomes as enslaved to passion as Philip is in the early stages of their acquaintanceship. Finally she turns her desires toward Philip, only to be rebuffed by his decision that their association be platonic. Mildred's reactions of bewilderment, humiliation, and anger, which are reported by the narrator just before her attack on Philip's room and mark one of the few lapses of the limited omniscient point of view, echo the "pique" and humiliation Philip demonstrates earlier. Calder provides a rationale for Mildred's destructiveness, attributing it to sexual frustration and loss of "mastery" over Philip once he no longer desires her, two motives that also suggest her affinities with Philip. Mildred in fact personifies the very weakness of character that Philip himself displays and which hinder his development: Philip accuses her of being "on the make" as he himself is; she betrays him for other men, but he in turn betrays Norah Nesbitt when Mildred returns to him.

As is typical with secondary characters in a *Bildungsroman,* Mildred is allowed no self-development and no change of heart; but unlike other personages in *Of Human Bondage,* such as Norah, who is rescued by marriage, Mildred is denied redemption. The nature of Mildred's illness as a prostitute presages an early death for her. The fact that the severity of her punishment exceeds the enormity of her "crimes" and the fact that Philip escapes punishment for similar sins suggest that Mildred assumes the burden of Philip's guilt as well as her own. Her sins are his sins exaggerated, and her penalty is his release. As a scapegoat she is sacrificed so that Philip may be strengthened. As she deteriorates, he regenerates; as she slides down the social scale, he rises, moving from the poverty of his student days to the security of the medical profession.

As a scapegoat Mildred is both guilty and not guilty. She represents the "fallen woman" who, although partly responsible for her own actions and choices, is also victimized by men in particular and society in general. Mildred's early conditioning, her petty bourgeois upbringing, has instilled in her a scorn for menial work like waitressing and a belief in the necessity of marriage for respectability and advancement on the social scale. The latter conviction conspires with her uncontrollable emotional desires to increase her vulnerability to men who seduce her by mar-

> Mildred's illness as a prostitute presages an early death for her. The fact that the severity of her punishment exceeds the enormity of her "crimes" and the fact that Philip escapes punishment for similar sins suggest that Mildred assumes the burden of Philip's guilt as well as her own.
>
> —*Bonnie Hoover Braendlin*

riage offers or by affairs that end in deception and abandonment. Ironically, Mildred's vanity and desire for independence, in addition to her snobbish attitude—typical, Maugham says, of her class—cause her fall to a level of the social scale diametrically opposite that of the respected housewife she longs to become and pretends to be while living and traveling with Philip.

Maugham's unrelieved negative portrayal of Mildred in this novel differs from his more sympathetic treatment of prostitutes, such as Miss Sadie Thompson in **"Rain"** but resembles other characterizations of destructive women in his works. One critic speculates that Mildred's despicable character results from Maugham's notorious misogyny occasioned by his disillusionment with women who could not measure up to his mother or assuage the pain occasioned by her death; others assume that Maugham's desire to expunge the memory of some agonizing love affair prompted his deleterious description of Mildred. [See Richard Albert Cordell, *Somerset Maugham,* 1961, p. 80; Laurence Brander, *Somerset Maugham,* 1963.] Both theories have merit, especially because *Of Human Bondage* is an autobiographical novel, detailing the pain suffered by a little boy who loses his beloved mother, as happened to Maugham.

Another possible explanation is suggested, however, by Mildred's affinities with the New Woman, the independent female who caused consternation in England from the 1890s into the twentieth century. While Mildred does not directly rival Philip for professional opportunities, she does threaten the accepted societal notion of male domination, which is essential to Philip's pride and easily bruised ego. At the beginning of their relationship, Philip cannot control Mildred although he is determined to bend her to his will. Later he feels betrayed when she follows her own passionate inclinations, and unjustly injured and insulted when she rebels against his mandate of a platonic liaison, destroying his property in revenge for his treatment of her.

When he attempts to rehabilitate her, to get her off the streets and prevent her from spreading venereal disease, she pushes him away with a final vituperative comment: "What do I care? Let them [the men she solicits] take their chance. Men haven't been so good to me that I need bother my head about them." Turning an independent woman into a diseased harpy suggests that Maugham's misogyny may have been furthered by a fear of the consequences inherent in woman's desire for self-determination and her refusal to acquiesce to maternal and subordinate roles; it may reveal some of the antagonism toward the New Woman expressed in other Edwardian literature, in novels such as H. G. Wells's *Tono-Bungay* and D. H. Lawrence's *Sons and Lovers*. [In *The Edwardian Turn of Mind,* 1968] Samuel Hynes attributes this hostility to the fear that women's desire for freedom presented a serious threat to family stability and hence to societal equilibrium, already shaken by disruptive factors resulting from increased industrialization. While the young Edwardians desired more sexual freedom, even extending it to women as if to enhance them as sexual partners, they also regretted the loss of their Victorian fathers' ideal of a stable and sheltered home life safeguarded by a contented wife-mother. Mildred's characterization seems to incorporate this trepidation and desire for revenge on the wayward female; she may be Maugham's scapegoat for the New Woman, made to expiate her independent spirit.

Having demonstrated that Mildred becomes a scapegoat for the sins of others, we may extend the nature of her sacrifice by reference to her as a manifestation of the universal goddess, as the evil side of the Great Mother archetype. [In an endnote, Braendlin states: "See Joseph Campbell, *Hero with a Thousand Faces,* 1949. A displacement of the myth of the hero into the realistic *Bildungsroman* finds the young developing protagonist encountering various manifestations of the mother in the ancillary women characters, at least two of whom are often polarized, a reflection of the general tendency in man's art and literature to view woman as either good or evil, angel or witch, helpmate or hindrance, intercessor or seducer. In Victorian fiction, this duality expresses itself in the characters of wife and whore, the latter being either the working-class woman or one fallen from middle-class respectability through sexual indiscretion. *Of Human Bondage* continues the dichotomization into the twentieth century."] If Sally is the "sinless" aspect of the deity in that she embraces her designated role as maternal helpmate, Mildred represents the misguided goddess who resists. In a response to Claude Lévi-Strauss's observations on myth, René Girard [in "Violence and Representation in the Mythical Text," *MLN,* 92 (1977)] defines one basic mythic structure as the ritual elimination of an erring deity, the scapegoating of a divine being who has acted in a manner threatening to the community. If a society's crisis situation is severe enough and the causes vague, an individual deity or a human incarnation may be accused and made a scapegoat even though not guilty of any real crime or causative action. From the perspective of the threatened community, the apparent malefactor or a helpless substitute is always guilty; and the punishment, usually ostracism or death, is always justified. In *Of Human Bondage,* Mildred is made a scapegoat to save Philip from his personal crisis, but in a larger sense, she is sacrificed for the good of a society in crisis. Although, as Calder says, Maugham's novel in many ways "attempts to grapple with man's new freedom in the twentieth century," it reaffirms traditional answers to modern dilemmas, particularly those involving threatened values such as the stable home as a bulwark against change. The marriage of Sally and Philip at the end of the novel is intended to restore a threatened societal ideal; it is

Maugham's answer to his culture's crisis, and it necessitates the death of Mildred, the erring goddess.

Widening the circle of those who benefit from the ostracism and death of a scapegoat enables us to see Mildred as an example of the "outsider," defined by Vivian Gornick [in "Woman as Outsider," in *Woman in a Sexist Society,* ed. Vivian Gornick and Barbara K. Moran, 1971] as "one in whom experience lives in a metaphorical sense, one whose life and meaning is a surrogate for the pain and fear of existence, one onto whom is projected the self-hatred that dogs the life of the race." Like Sue Bridehead in Thomas Hardy's *Jude the Obscure,* Mildred incarnates "the quintessential female" whose "behavior is emotional, impetuous, illogical, uncontrollable," all characteristics that help explain Mildred's supposedly inexplicable destructiveness. When she annihilates Philip's possessions, presumably in a streak of mad fury, Mildred demonstrates "the infantilism of reduction" typical of all outsiders who are denied the advantages of civilized living appropriated by the inside elite. Finally, as the fatally diseased prostitute, she becomes the scapegoat, described by Gornick as one whose "life is offered up, as every outsider's life is offered up, as a sacrifice to the forces of annihilation that surround our sense of existence, in the hope that in reducing the strength of the outsider—in declaring her the bearer of all the insufficiency and contradiction of the race—the wildness, grief, and terror of loss that is in us will be grafted onto her, and the strength of those remaining within the circle will be increased." Mildred, the diseased prostitute, the treacherous goddess, the independent woman, dies for us all.

Critics of Maugham's novel maintain that reader sympathy for Philip continues even when he appears ridiculous by wishing that he could stab Mildred in the carotid artery with his muffin knife or callous by longing for his uncle's death so that he can get his inheritance. Maugham's vituperative treatment of Mildred as unredeemed feminine evil supposedly excludes any similar compassion for her, yet it may in fact engender sympathetic understanding. Even as a spiteful fallen woman, Mildred exhibits a measure of courage and independence by scorning the option of serving a man who neither loves nor respects her. Sympathy for Mildred and her plight comes more easily perhaps to readers whose consciousness has been raised by the women's movement and feminist criticism. But Maugham's naturalistic technique, which revels in sordid detail in order to expose the evils of society (as in the slum where Philip practices medicine) and to revive a threatened societal ideal, may in Mildred's case also contribute to a sympathetic reading of her character and function by affording a view of her as a representation of a social reality, the fallen woman and unwed mother, a victim as well as a villainess, a person as well as a symbol.

Of Human Bondage is undeniably remarkable for its particular vindictiveness toward the threatening female, which transforms her into a prostitute who, as scapegoat, is sacrificed for all who remain within the circle of respectability and rationality. Even this vindictiveness, though, may backfire by loading the dice against Mildred and thus increasing reader sympathy for her. Because Maugham

advances the time-honored theme of ironic comedy that the scapegoat must be ritualistically expunged from society, his treatment of Mildred may illustrate Northrop Frye's contention [in *Anatomy of Criticism,* 1957] that "insisting on the theme of social revenge on an individual, however great a rascal he [or she] may be, tends to make him [or her] look less involved in guilt and the society more so."

Forrest D. Burt   (essay date 1985)

SOURCE: "Autobiographical Novel," in his *W. Somerset Maugham,* Twayne Publishers, 1985, pp. 71-93.

[*In the following excerpt, Burt comments on the autobiographical aspects of* Of Human Bondage *as well as the dramatic skill with which Maugham relates the various forms of "bondage" the characters endure.*]

It is of critical importance to understand the significance of *Of Human Bondage* in Maugham's writing career. The psychological dynamics of Maugham's writing this novel are closer to that experienced by writers of autobiography than that experienced by most autobiographical novelists. Maugham wrote this novel later in life, after having established himself in a variety of types of writing: novel, short story, drama, travel book (in contrast to Joyce's *Portrait of the Artist as a Young Man* and Lawrence's *Sons and Lovers,* which were early works). Second, since this work came later in his career, he was able to draw from his writing experience and to make use of a variety of writing skills—chiefly dramatic—that he had acquired (comparable to those of St. Augustine, Mill, Newman—giving order to their past life). And when *Of Human Bondage* was written, Maugham was living the middle period of his life, a period in which many experience what psychologists call "a mid-life crisis." It is in this period that autobiographers look back over their life to find a pattern, justification, meaning. The more literary and gifted autobiographers typically go beyond their own lives to become more universal and philosophical. Such was the case in *Of Human Bondage.*

But above all, the importance of this novel is that in writing it Maugham moved a step further toward understanding his strength as a writer, toward developing his own aesthetic. Curtis refers to Maugham's "need to reshape life into a pattern" and calls it his "greatest drive" [Anthony Curtis, in *The Pattern of Maugham,* 1974]. This need and drive took form in this novel, his greatest accomplishment in shaping life into art. In the theater he had developed his "reshaping," dramatic skills far beyond those displayed in the 1898 "The Artistic Temperament of Stephen Carey". He became more fully aware of his best subject matter—experience. With the distance and maturity now of almost thirty years, he turned his acute powers of observation and analysis on himself. And in the novel, he wisely decided upon an external, third-person omniscient narrator. [In *The Summing Up*] Maugham wrote of this shaping of experience—direct or observed—as creating "a plausible harmony": "People are too elusive, too shadowy, to be copied; and they are also too incoherent and contradictory. The writer does not copy his originals; he takes what he wants from them, a few traits that have caught his attention, a turn of mind that has fired his imagination and thereupon constructs his characters."

Understandably, [Richard Heron] Ward notes [in *William Somerset Maugham,* 1937]: "Maugham's best stories are too well-formed to be personal experiences transferred direct to paper." The important point here, though, is that Maugham is at his best when his characters, events, emotions, and attitudes are grounded in personal experience. He is at his weakest when he goes beyond his experience. In 1911, in composing *Of Human Bondage,* Maugham was digging back into the personal experience of "The Artistic Temperament of Stephen Carey." As Curtis observes, he "needed now to go more deeply into the causes of his peculiar sense of alienation from life in the midst of so much prosperity, to follow his own emotional and intellectual progress throughout those early years with great but not absolute fidelity to fact."

Somerset Maugham's motivation for writing and his use of personal experience in his writing are therefore not simple matters. But there is considerable evidence that Maugham depended upon experience and upon models for characters from individuals he had either known personally or observed. And because the experiences during the composition of *The Land of Promise* and *Of Human Bondage* were especially traumatic, they had a far reaching influence upon his life. It is little wonder, then, the emotions and dilemmas that he was presently experiencing would be for Maugham a rich source of inspiration. As [M. K.] Naik observes [in *W. Somerset Maugham,* 1966], in his early works Maugham developed two important faculties: "the deep sensibility which was, very soon, to create among the best of Maugham's novels, *Of Human Bondage,* and the flair for satirical observation which was to develop into the cold indifference and cynicism of his later works."

Returning to the composition of *Of Human Bondage* after having his marriage proposal rejected by Sue Jones, after completing *The Land of Promise,* and after beginning a relationship with Syrie Wellcome, Maugham drew upon his major strengths—strengths that he would eventually come to know as well as he then knew his limitations: (1) the transformation of experience and observations into fiction and (2) the dramatic skills developed in the theater. The first strength, use of personal experience and observations, should be evident in a large degree from the above discussion. How much Maugham had developed the second strength, his dramatic skill, can be seen by contrasting *Of Human Bondage* with "The Artistic Temperament of Stephen Carey."

Of Human Bondage opens with the death of Philip's mother. Orphaned, Philip is forced to move from his French home to England. There he lives with his Uncle Carey, vicar of Blackstable, and Aunt Louisa. They are childless and live a life quite unsuitable for their nine-year-old nephew, who speaks French more fluently than English and has a clubfoot. Shortly, Philip is sent to school at Tercanberry where he is mistreated by students and masters for his physical handicap. One holiday back at the vicarage he has an unusual experience. Having read in the Bible that if a person has faith enough mountains can be moved, he decides to put his faith to the test by praying, believing with all his might, that his handicap will be removed. When this fails, his disappointment is the first step toward his eventual loss of faith. Ill and with a determination not to abide the bullying of his masters, Philip spends a year studying in Heidelberg. It is there that he loses even more confidence in his childhood faith in God. Under the influence of two fellow lodgers, one an American and the other an Englishman, Philip comes to what for him is an exhilarating and freeing conclusion that there is no God. Upon his return to England Philip meets Miss Wilkinson, a relative of one of his aunt's close German friends. It is with her that he has his first sexual experience.

A brief trial with the accounting business as a possible career proves disappointing. He next journeys to Paris to study art for two years. But at the end of that time, realizing he will never be more than average, Philip gives it all up.

Finally, against his uncle's best thinking, Philip enters St. Thomas's Hospital in London in order to study for a career in medicine. And it is during these early years of his training that he meets Mildred Rogers, a waitress at the A.B.C. shop, a meeting that will lead to a bondage of passion. Philip will be unable to free himself from this bondage for some time. As his passion for Mildred grows, he makes repeated advances: invitations, suggestions, usually meeting with rejections, or more characteristically indifference—Mildred's typical reply is: "I don't mind." When one day she goes away with another, Miller by name, Philip feels that he has finally lost her forever. He does not pass his examinations. At this time he finds a friend in Norah Nesbitt, an individual who has a greater interest in him than he in her—the reverse of his earlier relationship with Mildred. Their friendship, though, is genuine and they are good for each other. Philip makes progress toward his examinations. But later Mildred returns, this time expecting a child. He helps, of course, providing her and her child with a home, but without the earlier physical love for her. In fact, it is when he refuses to yield to her seductive advances that Mildred flies into a rage, and disappears completely. Philip again adjusts. He returns to Norah, but it is too late: she has found another and plans to be married soon. It is then that Mildred again returns: her child has died, and she is now a common streetwalker, and she is in ill health. As before, Philip takes her in. While Mildred has been away Philip has made several changes: because of his money problems, he is now working in a department store; he has made friends with a Mr. Athelny, a fellow employee, and his family; and he has begun once more to prepare for his medical examinations.

Mildred leaves Philip's life for good when she angrily reacts to Philip's insistence that she quit prostitution because of its danger to her health. Philip experiences another loss in the death of Cronshaw, his old friend from Paris. And while in the British Museum, Philip recalls Cronshaw's statement that the meaning of life could be found in a Persian rug, and concludes that life had no pattern, no meaning. If an individual is to find meaning, he reasons, then that pattern must be put into life by the individual. The friendship and concern of the Athelnys become increasingly important at this time in Philip's life. Their oldest daughter, Sally, Philip finds attractive. The interest is mutual and they soon become quite fond of each other. When they have sex, they both worry for fear of a pregnancy. When Philip discovers that their fears are unfounded, he finds to his surprise that he still wants to marry Sally, even though he does not love her: to bring a pattern, a meaning to a life that he has discovered has no integral meaning.

Contrasting the opening chapters of "The Artistic Temperament of Stephen Carey" (1898)—dealing with the loss of Stephen's mother and his humiliation at school—with comparable opening chapters in *Of Human Bondage* (1915) will make clear how much Maugham had strengthened his dramatic capabilities. Chapter 1 of "The Artistic Temperament of Stephen Carey" opens with Stephen playing with a theater, a present for his ninth birthday. Although there is no dialogue, the external omniscient narrator lets us know that Stephen has seen *Hamlet* (did not like it because of the inartistic ending—killing so many people off) and that he likes *Waterloo*. In fact, he has a great battle with his soldiers in the theater and when *Waterloo* is finished only the Duke of Wellington (a national hero throughout the Victorian era) lives. His masterpiece, though, is "The Corsica Brothers with Louis of France." The hero cries at the end that he is avenged and the curtain falls. And Stephen, alone throughout this entire opening chapter, is completely thrilled. The scene has no dialogue.

Then, in the second chapter, pages 8-16, Misses Fordlington and Emma have been talking in another room and come into the one where Stephen is playing. Putting him on her lap, Emma rocks and consoles him. He decides, as in *Of Human Bondage,* to go in to see the others so they will feel sorry for him. And they do. But in talking about his father, Dr. Carey, and his mother, Sophia, they soon forget about Stephen. He may well, though, have understood the drift of these remarks—similar to those in *Of Human Bondage*—that there is little money left for his education, his mother was a woman of society—quite unconcerned about money, and her death was in some ways a blessing.

Finally, in chapter 3, pages 17-23, Stephen is on the way back to the house with Emma and he asks her to tell him a story. She tells him a story of a boy who would not wash his hands or comb his hair. But Emma is mostly worried about the position she will lose and the economic consequences associated with its loss. And Stephen wonders about his Uncle John, who will arrive in four days. When they reach the house Stephen becomes aware for the first time that he is now an orphan. He has an emotional moment in his mother's bedroom—similar to that in *Of Human Bondage*—in which he senses his mother's presence but realizes that she will never be there again. And he cries genuine tears.

In contrast, in the opening three chapters of *Of Human Bondage* Maugham devotes more attention to what the characters say. The first chapter in *Of Human Bondage,* for instance, opens with a brief paragraph describing the setting—the weather: "gray," "dull," "clouds," "rawness in the air," "snow"; a woman servant coming into the room where a child, Philip, is sleeping; a stucco house next door, and a child's bed. Then the sound of voices: "Wake up, Philip"—pulling down bed clothes, taking the child in her arms, carrying the child (now half awake) downstairs—"Your mother wants you." And, although at this point only eighty-seven words into a very long novel, Maugham has skillfully prepared his audience for the dramatic scene of Philip's being with his dying mother for the last time. The entire scene is presented with the detachment of a dramatist: we learn of the nature of the circumstances mainly through dialogue.

> [PHILIP'S MOTHER]: Oh, don't take him away yet.
>
> [THE DOCTOR]: What's the matter? . . . You're tired . . . [*To the nurse:*] You'd better put him back in his bed.
>
> [PHILIP'S MOTHER]: What will happen to him, poor child? . . .
>
> [THE DOCTOR]: What about the little boy? I should think he'd be better out of the way.
>
> [THE NURSE]: Miss Watkin said she'd take him, sir.
>
> [THE DOCTOR]: Who's she?
>
> [THE NURSE]: She's his godmother, sir. D'you think Mrs. Carey will get over it, sir?

The external, omniscient, narrator ends chapter 1 with a succinct description of the doctor's response, an early example of Maugham's use of nonverbal behavior for dramatic effect: "The doctor shook his head."

In chapter 2 Maugham follows the same pattern: setting the scene—"a week later," "Philip . . . an only child . . . used to amusing himself "; "hides himself from the Red Indian . . . ," "hearing the door open"; and then dialogue. The external narrator provides what any dramatist could provide visually on stage: "It was in eighteen-eighty-five and she wore a bustle. Her gown was of black velvet, with tight sleeves and sloping shoulders, and the skirt had three large flounces. She wore a black bonnet with velvet strings. She hesitated. The questions she had expected did not come, and so she could not give the answer she had prepared." The black dress, in keeping with the nature of the occasion, increases the dramatic irony of the following scene.

> [EMMA]: Aren't you going to ask how your mamma is? . . .
>
> [PHILIP]: Oh, I forgot. How is mamma? . . .
>
> [EMMA]: Your mamma is quite well and happy.
>
> [PHILIP]: Oh, I'm glad.
>
> [EMMA]: Your mamma's gone away. You won't ever see her any more. . . .
>
> [PHILIP]: Why not?
>
> [EMMA]: Your mamma's in heaven.

The narrator describes Emma's genuineness, which contrasts with the self-seeking nurse's falseness in Maugham's earlier work: "Her tears increased her emotion, and she pressed the little boy to her heart. She felt vaguely the pity of that child deprived of the only love in the world that is quite unselfish. It seemed dreadful that he must be handed over to strangers." And Philip, though not fully understanding, cried with her.

What follows is the scene—described fully in chapter 2—in which Philip says goodbye to Miss Watkin, knowing full well, of course, that she will feel sorry for him. And she does. Then, announcing that he must go home, Philip limps out of the room:

> [MISS WATKIN]: His mother was my greatest friend. I can't bear to think that she's dead.

> [OTHERS PRESENT]: Poor little boy, it's dreadful to think of him quite alone in the world. I see he limps.

> Yes, he's got a club-foot. It was such a grief to his mother.

Thus, in two chapters (covering less than five pages) Maugham has presented two dramatic scenes—with the objectivity of a dramatist who is restricted to the conversations and actions of the characters of a play. And Maugham has made the important alteration from the earlier version, transforming Stephen's stammer into Philip's clubfoot, a handicap that would have a greater dramatic impact upon the audience.

Chapter 3 (slightly over five pages in length) finds Philip returning to his home, meeting his uncle, and—as in the earlier version—visiting his mother's room for the last time: "Philip opened a large cupboard filled with dresses and stepping in, took as many of them as he could in his arms and buried his face in them. They smelt of the scent his mother used. Then he pulled open the drawers, filled with his mother's things, and looked at them. . . ." Here Maugham captures the psychological situation of a bereaved child, still in shock, unable to accept the reality of his mother's death—especially in a culture that speaks of death and dying euphemistically ("gone to heaven"): "It was not true that he would never see her again. It was not true simply because it was impossible. He climbed up on the bed and put his head on the pillow. He lay there quite still."

The importance of this dramatic presentation to Maugham's development as a writer—with the objective, external narrator and with the unfolding of Philip's character through dialogue—can not be overemphasized. One of Maugham's earliest critics, Ward, noted Maugham's method of involving the reader in the drama of Philip's quest for meaning: "One has never heard of Philip Carey spoken of by readers with anything but compassion, and that compassion must have been realized in them as they read. The secret is that Philip . . . does not indulge in self-pity. . . . He accepts, and acceptance of one's own suffering must bring tolerance toward it. . . ." Considering the novel to be "Maugham's most complete statement of the importance of physical and spiritual liberty," [Robert] Calder [in *W. Somerset Maugham and the Quest for Free-*

dom, 1972] expresses an admiration similar to Ward's: "His achievement is a novel which finds its power in absolute sincerity and honesty. Maugham has managed consummately to use an artificial framework, yet convey real life." Of course, the objectivity of the Maugham persona is not new. Of this persona Calder observes: "the aloof character of the Maugham persona owes its origin to this professional characteristic . . . the discipline inherent in his studies helped him to avoid the moralizing or sentimentalizing. . . . the objectivity which a doctor develops in order to treat his patients without causing an unbearable emotional strain on himself was combined with Maugham's natural reticence to give him a detachment which he retained throughout his career."

Whether one regards Maugham's medical training as the major factor behind the clinical, objective narrative style or simply Maugham's basic temperament and approach to life, the result is the same. In contrast to eighteenth- and nineteenth-century narratives—in which the narrator (of, for instance, *Tom Jones, Waverley, David Copperfield*) not only provides descriptions but also interpretations of each event, motives of characters, etc.—***Of Human Bondage*** presents events and characters largely without interpretation by the narrator. In fact, the reader is not urged to adopt any definite conclusions; events and characters are rarely interpreted. Rather, like the Persian rug, what meaning the reader ultimately finds in the novel he or she must put into it. The existential crisis that Philip inevitably faces is also faced by the reader. And whether or not the reader's conclusions are the same as Philip's, he or she must nevertheless struggle toward meaning—as Philip struggles. In fact, Philip is not an altogether admirable character: self-centered, overly sensitive, frequently depressed, generally pessimistic, often tending toward masochism. Nevertheless, as readers, we never forget the dramatic scene opening the novel. And Philip's sensitivity is psychologically sound: handicapped children orphaned early in life often interpret life as Philip does. As Richard Cordell has observed [in *Somerset Maugham: A Writer for All Seasons*, 1969], we all have experiences similar to those of Philip: Maugham "leads a reader to ask himself questions about good and evil, reward and punishment, justice and injustice, fact and superstition, the good life and the wasted life."

Maugham exploits his skill with dialogue in this novel. All but three of the one hundred twenty-two chapters follow the same pattern as the first three discussed above: succinct description, explanation, background as preparation for the sound of voices; then conversation, voices, dialogue. Maugham had served out his apprenticeship in the theater so well that each chapter reads as if it were a scene in a play. And the scenes consequently have an authenticity about them that rings through the very tone and dialectal style of the characters. The reader hears what the characters speak, rather than being told what they say—thereby coming to know them more fully and their relationship to each other.

Even in these three chapter/scenes (6, 7, 31) in which there are no sounds of a voice or voices, the narrator provides important background information and thereby prepares the reader for subsequent conversation. In chapter 6, for example, the narrator explains how one day at the vicarage is very much like another. He includes a description of bringing the *Times* to the vicar in the morning and the careful system of passing it afterward from one individual to another in the household—according to rank, of course (a device that Maugham later will use effectively in a short story entitled **"The Outstation"**). Important information is also included about key individuals in the parish. And, as he had done already in *Mrs. Craddock* and would do again in *Our Betters* and *Cakes and Ale,* Maugham captures the distinctiveness of the Kentish setting with a particularity and genuineness that he does not achieve with such setting as Paris, London, Chicago, Tahiti, Borneo—settings that are rendered more abstractly. (Of course, since Kent was his boyhood English home, this is another instance of Maugham's need to ground his fiction in his own experience.) For example, after finishing her business at the bank, Mrs. Carey—accompanied by Philip—would typically go upstairs to see the sister of the banker, Mr. Wilson, the richest man in town. And while they visited, Philip would sit in the dark, stuffy parlor watching goldfish swim in a bowl. A further example is the section in which the narrator describes the regularity of the serving of dinner at the vicarage and the usual Sunday afternoon activities. Dinner was at one o'clock and consisted of beef or mutton, except on Sunday, when they ate one of their own chickens. In the afternoons Philip did his Latin, mathematics, and French lessons, and was taught piano. Rarely did they ever have guests for tea. But when they did the guests were always Josiah Graves, the curate, and his sister, and Dr. Wigram and his wife. And when they played games, Mrs. Carey was careful to allow her husband to win because he hated losing.

Finally, the narrator completes his portrait of daily life at the vicarage with a description of the system for taking baths, a system that had to be altered when young Philip arrived. Naturally the vicar insisted that "Philip should be clean and sweet for the Lord's Day." After eighteen years of service in the house, Mary Ann protested that she would rather quit than be put out by having to bathe him. And Philip naturally insisted on bathing himself. But because she couldn't "abide a boy who wasn't properly washed," Mary Ann agreed. The narrator's description is a close approximation of Mary Ann's remarks of protest: "she'd work herself to the bone even if it was Saturday night."

In chapter 7, another chapter without the literal sound of a voice, the narrator provides the reader with a portrait of Sunday, the most important day of the week in Philip's strange new English home, "a day crowded with incident"—from getting up "half an hour earlier than usual" to going to bed after a full day. Despite the absence of dialogue at the very beginning of the chapter, the narrator gives the reader a description of the sound of a voice, a description that captures the flavor and atmosphere of the vicar's home: "No lying abed for a poor parson on the day of rest, Mr. Carey remarked as Mary Ann knocked at the door punctually at eight." On Sunday Mrs. Carey takes longer to dress, prayers are more extensive, and breakfast

more substantial. Afterward Mr. Carey prepares the bread for communion and Philip is allowed to help.

The narrator provides a close substitute for dialogue in describing the verbal exchange between the characters. For instance, the narrator describes Mr. Carey's reactions: "It was extraordinary that after thirty years of marriage his wife could not be ready on Sunday morning"; "They knew that he must have an egg for his voice, there were two women in the house, and no one had the least regard for his comfort." The result, of course, is that Maugham achieves the breadth and range of a purely descriptive chapter, but also he accomplishes much of the depth and authenticity of a scene with dialogue.

During the sermon, Philip became "bored" and "if he fidgeted Mrs. Carey put a gentle hand on his arm and looked at him reproachfully." And, typical for a boy of his age, he "regained interest when the final hymn was sung." In the afternoon, after a "substantial dinner," Mrs. Carey would rest in her room and Mr. Carey would lie down on the drawing room sofa "for forty winks." At five o'clock tea Mr. Carey would eat an egg "to support himself for evensong": "Mr. Carey walked to church in the evening, and Philip limped along by his side. The walk through the darkness along the country road strangely impressed him, and the church with all its lights in the distance, coming gradually nearer, seemed very friendly." When they return, supper is ready and Mr. Carey's slippers are waiting for him in front of the fire, "by their side Philip's, one the shoe of a small boy, the other mishapen and odd." The scene comes to an end with Philip, "dreadfully tired," going up to bed: "he did not resist when Mary Ann undressed him. She kissed him after she tucked him up, and he began to love her."

In the third chapter in which the reader does not hear the sound of voices, chapter 31, it is Christmas Eve in Germany; Hayward, Philip's aesthete friend, has just left Heidelberg for Italy. The narrator gives the reader an account of Philip's ambivalent attitude toward Hayward: "Though much under Hayward's influences . . . he resented the shadow of a sneer with which Hayward looked upon his straight ways." In this chapter also we have a close approximation to the sound of a voice: "They corresponded. Hayward was an admirable letter-writer, and knowing his talent took pains with his letters. . . . He proposed that Philip join him in Italy: 'He [Philip] was wasting his time at Heidelberg. The Germans were gross and life there was common; how could the soul come to her own in that . . . landscape?'" Again the narrator gives the reader a close approximation to the pointed, reprimanding question that Hayward could very well have put to Philip. The narrator provides the reader with certain information: that Hayward's letter made Philip restless, that Philip received an introduction to philosophy under Kuno Fischer at the University of Heidelberg, and that preparations were under way for Philip to return to England. The narrator further tells of a letter in which his aunt informs Philip that Miss Wilkinson, Mrs. Carey's friend who made the arrangements for Philip's year in Heidelberg, would be at the vicarage when he returned and would spend a few weeks there. Finally, the narrator tells the reader that

Philip "had been thinking of nothing but the future; and he went without regret." Maugham's use of dialogue, of the sound or approximate sound of the voice is a major strength of this novel. It gives authenticity and concreteness to the characters and settings.

Furthermore, throughout the novel Maugham carefully prepares the reader for Philip's bondage of passion, principally through Philip's relationship with Miss Wilkinson and Fanny Price and the bondage of passion that these individuals have to Philip. These relationships foreshadow Philip's subsequent bondage to Mildred.

Returning home from Heidelberg Philip is greeted by a genuinely joyous Aunt Louisa and Miss Wilkinson, a governess by profession, whom he had never met before. He and she quickly become friends and spend much of the day together: talking, and walking; and she gives him voice lessons. Although she is much older, their relationship soon becomes quite flirtatious. One day she tells him a story about an art student living above her apartment who kept writing her passionate love letters. Finally, she received one of his letters saying he was coming that very evening to make passionate love to her. As she read the letter in her apartment she imagined how he would ring the door bell and how she would refuse to answer. Just then, she looked up. He was standing there in front of her. She had forgotten to shut the door.

The story affects Philip strangely. He soon begins to work up his courage to kiss her. He determines to make full conquest of Miss Wilkinson and persuades her, without much difficulty, to receive him in her bedroom one night. Driven more by sheer determination than desire, Philip meets her in her room and they make love. For Miss Wilkinson ("Emily," as she insists upon Philip calling her), it is a genuine love she feels for him. And Philip shows himself an "eager" but detached lover. "He was deliciously flattered to discover that Miss Wilkinson was in love with him. . . . When he kissed her it was wonderful to feel the passion that seemed to thrill her soul." From their first meeting he determined that "he ought to make love to her. . . ."

Yet Philip is ambivalent; the thought of Miss Wilkinson and the anticipation of making love to her are much more exciting than Miss Wilkinson herself or the act of making love: "When he thought of it at night in bed, or when he sat by himself in the garden reading a book, he was thrilled by it; but when he saw Miss Wilkinson it seemed less picturesque." "He could not imagine himself burying his face in Miss Wilkinson's hair, it always struck him as a little sticky." Nevertheless, he thinks it "would be very satisfactory to have an intrigue, and he thrilled with the legitimate pride he would enjoy in his conquest. He owed it to himself to seduce her." Even on the night of this seduction, his conquest is accompanied by a large dose of disgust at his less than ideal lover:

> She had taken off her skirt and blouse, and was standing in her petticoat. It was short and only came down to the top of her boots; the upper part of it was black, of some shiny material, and there was a red flounce. She wore a camisole of white calico with short arms. She looked gro-

tesque. Philip's heart sank as he stared at her; she had never seemed so unattractive; but it was too late now.

Sensing this incompatibility early in their relationship—her caring more for him and being bound by passion to him while he remains more detached and aloof—she talks with Philip about the month of leisure that they have ahead of them and their future after that. "And then you go to freedom and I to bondage," she remarks.

Another relationship that Maugham uses to prepare the reader for Philip's bondage to Mildred is that of Fanny Price to Philip. After a brief and unfortunate try in London at the accounting profession, Philip proposes trying his hand at art in Paris. At first his aunt and uncle are shocked. Mr. Carey is dead set against it, but Mrs. Carey has sympathy for Philip and even persuades Philip to use her own savings to help finance his study in Paris. And it is there, in an art class, that Philip becomes acquainted with Fanny, a hard working but untalented student of art.

> She was a girl of twenty-six with a great deal of dull gold hair; it was handsome hair, but it was carelessly done, dragged back from her forehead and tied in a hurried knot. She had a large face, with broad, flat features and small eyes; her skin was pasty, with a singular unhealthiness of tone, and there was no colour in the cheeks. She had an unwashed air and you could not help wondering if she slept in her clothes.

Mrs. Otter, who is in charge of the studio where he will study, has placed Philip next to Fanny. "She's a disagreeable, ill-natured girl, and she can't draw herself at all, but she knows the ropes, and she can be useful to a newcomer if she cares to take the trouble." But Clutton, one of the most talented of the painters, warns Philip: "You've made an impression on Fanny Price. You'd better look out."

Philip's friendliness is mistaken by Fanny as affection, and as he fails to meet her expectations, she becomes first jealous of everyone else, then angry, and finally depressed. She wants him to see her drawings. But when he does, the narrator tells the reader:

> He was panic-stricken. He did not know what to say. It was not only that they were ill-drawn, or that the colour was put on amateurishly by someone who had no eye for it; but there was no attempt at getting the values, and the perspective was grotesque. It looked like the work of a child of five, but a child would have had some naïveté and might at least have made an attempt to put down what he saw; but here was the work of a vulgar mind chock full of recollections of vulgar pictures.

Somehow, though, he is able to lie and tell her that he likes them. But when Philip decides to spend the summer in Moret with Lawson and Ruth Chalice, Fanny flies into a rage:

> "How filthy! I thought you were a decent fellow. You were about the only one here. She's been with Clutton and Potter and Flanagan, even with old Foinet—that's why he takes so much

trouble about her—and now two of you, you and Lawson. It makes me sick."

"Oh, what nonsense! She's a very decent sort. One treats her just as if she were a man."

"Oh, don't speak to me, don't speak to me."

"But what can it matter to you? . . . It's really no business of yours where I spend my summer."

I was looking forward to it so much. . . . I didn't think you had the money to go away, and there wouldn't have been anyone else here, and we could have worked together, and we'd have gone to see things."

Fanny's reaction—given her situation, passion for Philip, state of mind—is psychologically sound, as is her next impulse: to hurt him in every way she can:

> "and I can tell you this—you can work here for a thousand years and you'll never do any good. You haven't got any talent. You haven't got any originality. And it's not only me—they all say it. You'll never be a painter as long as you live."

"That is no business of yours either, is it?"

"Oh, you think it's only my temper. Ask Clutton, ask Lawson, ask Chalice. Never, never, never. You haven't got it in you."

It is important here to note not only the intensity of Fanny's passion but also the extent to which Maugham is relying upon his own experience. Lawson, Philip's artist friend who will accompany him to Italy, is, as Richard Cordell has observed, modeled after Sir Gerald Kelly, Maugham's lifelong friend and painter of several portraits of him. And the reputation and behavior of Ruth Chalice, who will go with them on this journey, so closely parallels that of Sue Jones (with whom Maugham has just ended a frustrating eight years) that there can be little doubt that she is a model for the character. The narrator tells the reader:

> They did not wish to leave the starlit night, and the three of them would sit on the terrace of Ruth Chalice's room, silent, hour after hour, too tired to talk any more, but in voluptuous enjoyment of the stillness. They listened to the murmur of the river. The church clock struck one and two and sometimes three before they could drag themselves to bed. Suddenly Philip became aware that Ruth Chalice and Lawson were lovers. He divined in it the way the girl looked at the young painter, and in his air of possession; and as Philip sat with them he felt a kind of effluence surrounding them, as though the air were heavy with something strange. The revelation was a shock. He had looked upon Miss Chalice as a very good fellow and he liked to talk to her but it never seemed to him possible to enter into a close relationship.

This relationship, then, is one that Maugham knew well from experience and could therefore portray with credibility. The character of Ruth Chalice also anticipates Mildred, who is equally free with her affections, and to whom Philip will have a hopeless bondage of passion. Philip at

this point is so envious of Lawson's love that he wishes "that he was standing in his shoes and feeling with his heart. . . . fear seized him that love would pass him by." Philip wishes for "a passion to seize him, he wanted to be swept off his feet and burn powerlessly in a mighty rush he cared not whither." And of course Philip's wish will be too fully granted.

Returning from Italy, Philip resumes his study of art. He begins to doubt his ability. Then he remembers Fanny Price—whom he has not seen since returning—and her strength of will: "If I thought I wasn't going to be really good, I'd rather give up painting. . . . I don't see any use in being a second-rate painter." And one morning he receives a letter.

> Please come at once when you get this. I couldn't put up with it any more.
>
> Please come yourself. I can't bear the thought that anyone else should touch me. I want you to have everything.
>
> F. Price
>
> I have not had anything to eat for three days

When Philip finds her she "was hanging with a rope round her neck, which she had tied to a hook in the ceiling fixed by some previous tenant to hold up the curtains of the bed. She had moved her own little bed out of the way and had stood on a chair, which had been kicked away. It was lying on its side on the floor. They cut her down. The body was quite cold." Realizing that she loved him, Philip is haunted not only by this portrait of failure and futile determination, but also by her bondage to passion, passion for art and for him.

Mildred is a waitress in the A.B.C. tea shop Philip and other medical students at St. Luke's Hospital often frequent. Despite her rather unattractive appearance Mildred becomes more and more the object of Philip's interest. When she first speaks to him, he is elated. He draws a picture of Mildred and gives it to her. He even works up his courage enough to ask her to a play. Her indifferent acceptance will be repeated many times during their relationship: "I don't mind." And after the evening out she continues to react in the same cold manner:

> "I hope you've enjoyed yourself?"
>
> "Rather."
>
> "Will you come out with me again one evening?"
>
> "I don't mind."

This coldness continues through these early days of their relationship.

> "I say, I do awfully want to call you Mildred."
>
> "You may if you like, I don't care."
>
> "And you'll call me Philip, won't you?"
>
> "I will if I can think of it. It seems more natural to call you Mr. Carey. . . ."
>
> "Won't you kiss me goodnight?" he whispered.

"Impudence!" she said.

Finally Philip appeals to her: "I say, don't be beastly with me, Mildred. You know I'm awfully fond of you. I think I love you with all my heart." He soon realizes how helpless he has become: "He wanted passionately to get rid of the love that obsessed him; it was degrading and hateful. He must prevent himself from thinking of her. In a little while the anguish he suffered must grow less." And it is when he becomes aware of his bondage that Philip recalls the bondage that Miss Wilkinson and Fanny Price must have experienced—and Maugham thus clarifies the foreshadowing purpose of those relationships—"His mind went back to the past. He wondered whether Emily Wilkinson and Fanny Price had endured on his account anything like the torment that he suffered now. He felt a pang of remorse." And even here Maugham dramatizes Philip's remorse with the approximation of the sound of his voice: "I didn't know then what it was like, he said to himself."

Philip therefore becomes increasingly aware of his bondage to Mildred. And Maugham provides the parallel bondage of Mildred to Griffiths, Philip's friend who had nursed him back to health during a recent illness.

> "It's not worth while sacrificing everything for an infatuation that you know can't last. After all, he doesn't care for anyone more than ten days, and you're rather cold; that sort of thing doesn't mean very much to you."
>
> "That's what you think."

And even though Philip is unable to exercise reason about his own bondage, he is able to understand Mildred's: "If you're in love with him you can't help it. I'll just bear it the best I can." The incompatible relationship is here again evident and the one who loves most is victimized:

> "Are you awfully unhappy?"
>
> "I wish I was dead," she moaned. "I wish I'd died when the baby came [by Miller, her earlier love]."

And Philip reflects to her: " 'It is awful, love, isn't it?' he said. 'Fancy anyone wanting to be in love.' " Later Mildred replies: "I'm sick with love for him. I know it won't last, just as well as he does. . . ."

At this point Philip portrays behavior that can only be termed masochist:

> "Why don't you go away with him?"
>
> "How can I? You know we haven't got the money."
>
> "I'll give you the money."

Later Philip is able to see more clearly and rationally the parallel between his situation and Mildred's. He admits that trying to force Mildred to love him was attempting the impossible: "He did not know what it was that passed from a man to a woman, from a woman to a man, and made one of them a slave: it was convenient to call it the sexual instinct; but if it was no more than that, he did not understand why it should occasion so vehement an attraction to one person rather than another." He had not after

all attracted Mildred sexually. Nothing he did seemed to influence her: "Because Mildred was indifferent to him he had thought her sexless; her anemic appearance and thin lips, the body with its narrow hips and flat chest, the languor of her manner, carried out his supposition; and yet she was capable of sudden passions which made her willing to risk everything to gratify them." He was puzzled by Mildred's attraction to Miller and Griffith, both of whom had no permanent attraction to her. But beyond this position of imbalance and of being the victim, there is a similar tendency in both Mildred and Philip toward masochism:

> He tried to think out what those two men had which so strangely attracted her. They both had a vulgar facetiousness which tickled her simple sense of humour, and a certain coarseness of nature; but what took her perhaps was the blatant sexuality which was their most marked characteristic. She had a genteel refinement which shuddered at the facts of life, she looked upon the bodily functions as indecent, she had all sorts of euphemisms for common objects, she always chose an elaborate word as more becoming than a simple one: the brutality of these men was like a whip on her thin white shoulders, and she shuddered with voluptuous pain.

It amuses Philip that his friends, observing his expressionless face, think him strong-minded and deliberate:

> They thought him reasonable and praised his common sense; but he knew that his placid expression was no more than a mask, assumed unconsciously, which acted like the protective colouring of butterflies; and himself was astonished at the weakness of his will. . . . when passion seized him he [like Mildred] was powerless. He had no self-control. He merely seemed to possess it because he was indifferent to many of the things which moved other people.

In the final stages of Philip's bondage he comes to conclusions about the meaning of life and relationships. After Mildred leaves with Griffiths, a relationship that is certain to fail, Philip does not see her again for some time. When one day he happens to see her on the street, "His heart stood still. He saw Mildred. He had not thought of her for weeks. . . . his heart beating excitedly he followed her. He did not wish to speak to her, but he wondered where she was going at that hour; he wanted to get a look at her face." Of course, he soon learns that she has taken up prostitution. Philip talks to her, learns that the baby is being taken care of, that she must walk the streets to survive. He wants to help. He wants to take care of her. Taking her and the baby to his own apartment, Philip spends pleasant days taking care of them. The end of these days comes when Philip, after prolonged suffering and pain, realizes that he can exercise reason and thereby free himself of the passion that bound him.

> "I do love you, Philip," she said.
>
> "Don't talk damned rot. . . ."
> "It isn't, it's true. I can't live without you. I want you. . . . I love you Philip. I want to make up for all the harm I did you. I can't go on like this, it's not in human nature. . . ."

"I'm very sorry, but it's too late. . . ."

"But why? How can you be so cruel?"

"I suppose it's because I loved you too much. I wore the passion out."

Enraged, Mildred finally shouts: "Cripple."

Philip's relationship with Sally is significant for the novel and as a reflection of Maugham's life. The daughter of Mr. Athelny, a friend whom Philip met while working, Sally is the oldest daughter of a large family. Their relationship develops quite naturally during Philip's frequent visits to the Athelny home.

> He liked to see her deft movements, and she watched him too now and then with that maternal spirit of hers which was so amusing and yet so charming. He was clumsy at first [he is helping her with the sewing], and she laughed at him. When she bent over and showed him how best to deal with a whole line their hands met. He was surprised to see her blush.

There is a calmness about this relationship that contrasts sharply with his tense relationship with Mildred.

Philip's evaluation of his relationship with Sally, both as a reflection of Maugham's life and as yet another attempt for Philip to find meaning in life, is significant. Following an affair with Philip, Sally fears that she is pregnant. He "despised himself, all he had aimed at so long within reach at last, and now his inconceivable stupidity had erected this new obstacle." Like Maugham, Philip longed to travel to have the freedom that comes with realizing one's dreams: to go to Spain, "the land of his heart . . . to be imbued with its spirit, its romance and colour and history and grandeur." And now "this thing had come." He reasoned (now free from the bondage of passion) that it would be "madness to allow such an accident to disturb the whole pattern of his life. . . . He would do what he could for Sally; he could afford to give her a sufficient sum of money. A strong man would never allow himself to be turned from his purpose. Yet he simply could not. He knew himself." Sally "had trusted him and been kind to him. He simply could not do a thing which, notwithstanding all his reason, he felt was horrible." His wedding present to Sally would then be his high hopes. Philip would sacrifice for her: "Self-sacrifice! Philip was uplifted by its beauty, and all through the evening he thought of it."

There can be little doubt that at this point in his life Maugham was experiencing some of the same emotions. After being rejected by Sue Jones in 1913, Maugham turned to Syrie Wellcome. As [Ted] Morgan points out [in *Maugham*, 1980]: "On the rebound from Sue Jones, he had found a woman who appeared to worship every word that dropped from his lips. . . . One evening after dinner at a restaurant they went back to her apartment and made love for the first time." This was in 1914. It soon became accepted thereafter that Maugham was her lover.

Admitting that the ending of *Of Human Bondage* was for him personally a "turning my wishes into fiction," Maugham states that for some time he "had amused my imagination with pictures of myself in the married state."

Similarly, Philip imagines himself married to Sally: "He pictured to himself the long evenings he would spend with Sally in the cosy sittingroom, the blinds undrawn so that they could watch the sea; he with his books, while she bent over her work, and the shaded lamp made her sweet face more fair. They would talk over the growing child, and when she turned her eyes to his there was in them the light of love." And even the anxiety associated with a pregnancy (without the benefit of marriage) is paralleled in Maugham's own experience: "The affair escalated when Syrie suggested one day that they should have a baby. . . . Maugham was tempted by this offer. . . ." And despite the fact that Syrie was not yet divorced and had been a mistress to Selfridge, a wealthy London businessman, she argued "so persuasively that Maugham yielded."

The ending of the novel, Maugham states [in *The Summing Up*], readers "on the whole have found . . . the least satisfactory part." Of course, the reader is moved to a greater extent and is more thoroughly convinced by the relationship of bondage of many individuals—chiefly Philip for Mildred—earlier in the novel. But it must not be forgotten that the relationship between Philip and Sally is essential in the general movement of the novel and especially in relation to Philip's search for meaning in life. Even in the imagery of the final scenes of the novel the reader senses Sally's affinity to nature and the fulfillment associated with harvest:

> A hop-garden was one of the sights connected with Philip's boyhood and the toast-houses to him the most typical feature of the Kentish scene. It was with no sense of strangeness, but as though he were at home, that Philip followed Sally through the long lines of hops. The sun was bright now and cast a sharp shadow. Philip feasted his eyes on the richness of the green leaves. The hops were yellowing, and to him they had the beauty and the passion which poets in Sicily have found in the purple grape. As they walked along Philip felt himself overwhelmed by the rich luxuriance. A sweet scent arose from the fat Kentish soil, and the fitful September breeze was heavy with the goodly perfume of the hops.

In fact, realizing earlier that life had no intrinsic meaning, he now begins to discover how to accept one's situation in life and to find meaning:

> He accepted the deformity which had made life so hard for him; he knew that it had warped his character, but now he saw also that by reason of it he had acquired that power of introspection which had given him so much delight. Without it he would never have had his keen appreciation of beauty, his passion for art and literature, and his interest in the varied spectacle of life. The ridicule and the contempt which had so often been heaped upon him had turned his mind inward and called forth those flowers which he felt would never lose their fragrance. Then he saw that the normal was the rarest thing in the world. Everyone had some defect. . . . They were the helpless instruments of blind chance. He could pardon Griffiths for his treachery and

Mildred for the pain she had caused him. They could not help themselves.

When Philip is freed from the anxiety of Sally's possible pregnancy, he discovers that he can *put,* not *find,* meaning in life, can surrender to happiness and accept defeat of his selfish desires to travel and seek adventure:

"I was going to ask you to marry me. . . ."

"I thought p'raps you might, but I shouldn't have liked to stand in your way." . . .

"But don't you want to marry *me?*"

"There's no one else I would marry."

"Then that settles it."

No longer a victim of passion but exercising his own reason, Philip gives pattern and meaning to a life that has no intrinsic goodness or purpose. Ending the novel with dialogue, Maugham's final description of Trafalgar Square indicates a hopeful future (as no doubt he saw for his own life with Syrie Wellcome and their child, Liza): "Cabs and omnibuses hurried to and fro, and the crowds passed, hastening in every direction, and the sun was shining."

Joseph Dobrinsky   (essay date October 1985)

SOURCE: "The Dialectics of Art and Life in *Of Human Bondage,*" in *Cahiers Victoriens & Edouardiens,* No. 22, October, 1985, pp. 33-55.

[*In the following essay, Dobrinsky discusses the ways in which Maugham's views on art and life are represented through his characters' actions in* Of Human Bondage.]

Due stress has been laid on the philosophic enlargment and formal progress that set this mature work [*Of Human Bondage*], written between 1912 and 1914, far above its unpublished rough copy of 1897, *The Artistic Temperament of Stephen Carey.* Both draw on, and yet swerve from autobiography, but too much could be made of the change of title to assume a shift from an artist hero to an everyman. In fact, the juvenile text had poked fun at the protagonist's intellectual snobberies and, on lines reminiscent of Thackeray's *Pendennis,* shown him to barter his artistic ambitions for a good match and the status of a country-squire. Some of those ironies will be seen to have found their way, *mutatis mutandis,* into the ampler novel of apprenticeship. And, significantly, it should be kept in mind that the book's initial title, *Beauty for Ashes,* crossed out on the opening page of the manuscript, was only given up at a late stage, when the author, on his own admission, found "it had been recently used." I submit that Maugham's probe into the connections of art and life is not confined to the Montparnasse episodes. The way in which their novelized treatment of the problematics of the creative call anticipates the more central enquiries in *The Moon and Sixpence* and in the later artist novels, *Cakes and Ale* and *Theatre,* has been aptly commented upon. But into the bargain, and perhaps inevitably in a writer's fictionalized record of much of his own psychological growth, a many-faceted meditation on the art and life polarity underlies the fable. Its range, topical emphases and, partly unwitting, disclosures are the subjects of the present study.

What, in Maugham's conduct of this ample theme, is conventional and what is specific should be told apart.

His first target, the hero himself, as a passionate reader in boyhood of fairy-tales and romances, later confronted with the disenchantments of adult life, may be said to follow a *via trita* of realistic fiction. In this mode, Maugham's focus on the least romantic aspects of sex and the grim "facts" of destitution, disease, unidealized death, reveals affinities with, respectively, the manner of Samuel Butler and the pet themes of the French naturalists. But the charges of imitativeness sometimes levelled at the author should at least be qualified. For instance, the physical unattractiveness of most of the women in the novel (except for the notional Sally Athelny) may well have something to do with the novelist's *own* homosexual proclivities; while, for his descriptions of hospital scenes and life in the slums, he was able to draw on his first-hand—at times, distinctively humorous—juvenile observations. By and large, the autobiographical foundations of most of the story help to revive, particularize and enrich the old motifs.

In terms of Zeitgeist, the eye-opening experiences of the hero are thus faithfully related, in turn, to the moral ethos of the late Victorian province, to the aesthetic spirit of the nineties, and, during the telescoped episodes in Paris, to the rise of Impressionism and after. Beyond its historical interest, under the signature of a reminiscing witness of much of what is told, this period piece element is a factor of plausibility. Meanwhile, since he has clung closely to the essentials of his own psychological development—not only is Philip, like the Stephen of the earlier version, an uprooted and ill-loved orphan but also a cripple, estranged from his fellows by the limp that transmutes his creator's stammer—, Maugham has been able to draw less sketchily on self-analysis. With regard to the boy's (inherited) love of books—"he formed the most delightful habit in the world, the habit of reading—"a major thematic see-saw is thus ushered in:" he did not know that he was providing himself with a refuge from all the distress of life; he did not know either that he was creating for himself an unreal world that would make the real world of everyday a source of bitter disappointment." Patently, a 'He' for an 'I', whose special concerns will be seen to break through.

> **In terms of Zeitgeist, the eye-opening experiences of Maugham's hero are faithfully related, in turn, to the moral ethos of the late Victorian province, to the aesthetic spirit of the nineties, and, during the telescoped episodes in Paris, to the rise of Impressionism and after.**
>
> **—Joseph Dobrinsky**

For instance, the exposure of Philip's "idealism" is steeped in aesthetic ironies. This is even true of the (veracious) stages in the hero's loss of faith. When, as a boy in Kent, challenging the biblical literalism of his adoptive parents, he is said to shrug off the Book of Books as a first specimen of deceptive romance—"The text which spoke of the moving of mountains was one of those that said one thing and meant another."—the concurred-in stricture typically shows little patience with symbolic modes of writing. Then, at King's School (whose most famous pupil in the XIXth century has been Walter Pater), Philip's sensitiveness to "the beauty of faith" is tacitly referred to the author of *The Renaissance:* "the desire for self-sacrifice *burned* in his heart with such a *gemlike* glow." The Heidelberg chapters take up this motif. As an arch aesthete over-admired by his young compatriot, Hayward favours Roman Catholicism for the superior music of its Masses, the inspiring odour of their incense, and out of respect for the elegant prose of Cardinal Newman's *Apologia:* "Read it for the style—he advises Philip—not for its matter." Even though dictated by a variety of motives, Philip's ultimate repudiation of Christianity, his agnostic epiphany, as it were, is triggered off by Weeks's eye-opening epitome of their fellow-lodger's true creed: "He believes in the picturesque." A short cut from a Victorian nephew's jeers at "the beauty of religion" to his gradual and, I submit, incomplete jettisoning of the religion of beauty!

Hayward is pushed to the forefront in his embodiment of a misguided aesthetic as well as vital choice. On this double count, his thematic role in the whole novel should not be underrated. Even his futile death will be seen to lead his one-time admirer to his main philosophic enlightenment. Meanwhile, at the Heidelberg stage, this enriched and caricatured counterpart of Ellingham Brooks, a real-life acquaintance of the young Maugham, is insistently ridiculed as a spokesman for intellectual attitudes recanted by the middle-brow novelist of 1912. With his "faintly supercilious expression," his boundless admiration for *Marius the Epicurean,* his worship of the "fetish of culture," Hayward is pictured as a parrot-like exponent and aping practitioner of most of the tenets of the Art for Art's sake doctrine. On top of his fervour for Newman and Pater, the list of his literary and artistic admirations confirms him as the latter's uncritical disciple by admitting Flaubert, Arnold, Ruskin, Goethe, Botticelli into his Olympus. Parenthetically, the addition of G.F. Watts and Burne-Jones among the favourites of this effeminate figure of fun indiscriminately enrols the Pre-Raphaelites in the aesthetic set, from the simplifying point of view of a robuster creed. But, on Hayward's encumbered altar, the combined presence of the *Rubáiyat of Omar Khayyám* and Meredith's *Richard Feverel*—later derided for its idealized portrayal of love—sustains another assault. The ex-Cambridge man's verbosity and orotund speech—characterized by a "great flow of words," the disdainful assumption of a "vulgarity in plain words," and a delight in "the ring of his sentences" are related to the vagueness of his ideas and to a weak man's self-comforting attempt to euphemize the coarser realities. The indictment of "the Life Aesthetic," in its dangerous recoil from the vulgarities of ordinary existence, most patently merges with a rejection of an ornate style in the passage that precedes Phil-

ip's visit to, and horrified retreat from the red light district in Heidelberg. For Hayward had, tantalizingly, shown him

a sonnet in which passion and purple, pessimism and pathos were packed together on the subject of a young lady called Trude . . . and thought he touched hands with Pericles and Pheidias because to describe the object of his attention he used the word *hetaira* instead of one of those more blunt and apt, provided by the English language.

Beyond the educational motif—the need for a young man to face squarely the facts of life, in the narrow and broader senses—the issue is thus raised of the choice of a style apt to render their truth.

Two short developments, the first on "the New Drama"—enlisting Hayward as an aesthetic snob, anxious to keep up with the latest fashions—, the second, on Philip's discovery of Schopenhauer, attack another form of artificial fiction. Its appeal for a young Victorian, confined so far to a literature *virginus puerisque,* lies in its "sordid intensity," its daring account of the world as "a place of pitiless woe and darkness." Ibsen, especially, comes under fire, he is charged with a stereotyped characterization, a solemn tone and, in his dialogues, a bent for melodrama:

To Philip it was real life . . . a strange life, dark and tortured, in which a fair face concealed a depraved mind . . . the honest were corrupt, the chaste were lewd . . . There was no laughter . . . the characters expressed themselves in cruel words that seemed wrung out of their hearts . . .

In contrast to this inverted romanticism, too grimly focused on the ugly, the author conjures up the family atmosphere of a German tavern, to which the young man, still under the spell of grim performances, fails to respond: "There was a pleasant homeliness in the scene, but for this Philip had no eyes." Thus, in anticipation of his own ending, the novelist self-reflexively relates a more balanced vision to a soberer genre and to a plainer speech.

The polemical bias is patent here. Ostracized by the intelligentsia for renouncing the aesthetic manner and the higher drama, as a popular writer of "artificial" plays, Maugham is paying them back in their own coin by challenging the truthfulness of *their* favourite modes. This counter-attack will culminate in the vitriolic portrait of Leonard Upjohn, the highbrow critic whose elegant disquisitions on the life and works of Cronshaw will establish his own, parasitical fame. The polemicist can be seen sharpening his claws for the onslaughts to come in **The Moon and Sixpence** or, even more devastatingly, in **Cakes and Ale.** Yet, this settling of accounts within the Republic of Letters is not the whole story. Between the lines of the Heidelberg chapters, the mature writer derides, in retrospect, and seeks to exorcise two patent temptations of his *own* long years of literary apprenticeship: a (not quite extinct) partiality to fine writing and a (not fully mastered) fondness for the extremes of naturalism.

The record of Philip's unglamorous loss of innocence introduces another set of variants on literary misrepresentations of "the truth." Met after his return to Kent, his partner in love, Miss Wilkinson, a ridiculously coquettish spinster long past her prime, is also a fiction addict. She proves to be a romancer of her own humdrum life as a governess on the Continent. When, to make up to Philip, she hints at a short-lived affair with a French art student, her naïve suitor, whose image of love depends on his readings, is, of course, unable to draw the line between the probable facts and their fantastication, "to him the very soul of romance." But the irony is double-edged: "In his ingenousness be doubted her story as little as he doubted what he read in books." Fiercely debunked, on Butlerian lines, are a lyrical treatment of the tender passion and the idealized portrayal of heroines:

> He had read many descriptions of love and he felt in himself none of that uprush of emotion which novelists described . . . (He) had often pictured to himself . . . the alabaster skin of some lovely girl and he had thought of himself burying his face in the rippling masses of her auburn hair . . . He could not imagine himself burying his face in Miss Wilkinson's hair, it always struck him as a little sticky.

Later on, Fanny Price and Mildred Rogers will flesh out this naturalistic retort. Meanwhile, broad ironies lead up to a parodic purple patch that once more enrols the compliant Hayward. In response to Philip's vaingloriously embellished account of his adventure, the latter, writing back from Italy, will rant on "that enchanted garden [in which] you wandered hand in hand like Daphnis and Chloe amid the flowers." Anxious to knock down a whole row of ninepins at one blow, Maugham then swerves from likelihood in ascribing to this dilettante the discrepant assumption that good literature will spring fully armed from the depths of the heart: "because you love, you write like a poet . . . your prose was musical from the sincerity of your emotion." Another literary target emerges in the delineation of the governess. Having long been employed by an upper-class family in Paris, she boasts of being acquainted with the authors of *Sapho* and of *Bel Ami*; and she ludicrously sprinkles her speeches with mispronounced phrases out of French fiction: "C'était une fatalité." This opens the way to an indiscriminate dismissal of literary imports from across the Channel—"Philip had read French novels" in their stereotyped British connotation of strong meat. Somerset Maugham, who knew better, must have been carried away by his satirical verve. In fact, his cosmopolitan culture steals across, blurring his exposure of literary romance, for the quote ascribed above to Miss Wilkinson is suspiciously close to Charles Bovary's last, bewildered comment. Besides, Philip's morning oath to himself that he will kiss the old maid at nightfall—"it would be easier in the dark"—is plainly a bathetic variation not on a cheap serial but on no less a masterpiece than Maugham's acknowledged favourite, *Le Rouge et le noir*.

However, the book that bears the brunt of the novelist's adverse criticism is the genuinely sentimental, then highly popular *Scènes de la vie de Bohème*, lent to the "enraptured" Philip by the governess. This fairy-tale account of the artistic life serves as an ironic preamble to the stark realism of the chapters in Paris. But the sternness of the main editorial comment may surprise the reader. After a tilt at the undistinguished prose and irresponsibility of "Murger's ill-written and absurd masterpiece," in accord with the bantering tone of the episode, the author bursts into a sarcastic litany on "that picture of starvation which is so good-humoured, of squalor which is so picturesque, of sordid love which is so romantic"; then he seems to ascend a Victorian pulpit: "It is only when you return to the book with a sounder judgment that you find how gross their pleasures were, how vulgar their minds; and you find the utter worthlessness, as artists and as human beings of that gay procession." Under the signature of Somerset Maugham, what considerations may have dictated such an outburst? urged this resurgence of a moralistic standard, elsewhere disowned in the literary field? The hint of an answer is found in the last clause and in its word-order: "(their) utter worthlessness, as *artists* and as human beings." One may well, it appears, jeer at love, explode its illusions; but art, true art, should not be trifled with.

For all his intellectual seclusion and vital sterility, Hayward had been granted a major extenuating circumstance: his possession of "one gift which was very precious. He had a real feeling for literature and he could impart his own passion . . ." No such indulgence is extended to the many "Philistines" in the cast.

Their thrashing begins during the scenes set in Kent, in which the life at the vicarage is given as representative of the cultural backwardness of the late Victorian province. The vicar and his wife are scoffed at for their lack of aesthetic discernment, their limited interest in, or moralistic approach to the fine arts. Those shortcomings appear with regard to no less than four of the Muses: in the scoffing account of a music-party during which "Mrs. Carey sang *When the Swallows Homeward Fly* or, *Trot, Trot my Poney*"; in the sneering remarks that the vicar himself "had long lost the habit of reading but liked to look at the illustrations" of the books that filled his library and that, "partly on account of his profession, partly because he thought it would be vulgar, [he] never went to see plays"; lastly when, with but a slight transposition of Maugham's remembered conflict with his adoptive parents, the Careys, "frankly shocked at Philip's idea of being an artist," are supposed to voice the social and moral prejudices of their Age and class: "He should not forget . . . that his father and mother were gentlefolk; and painting wasn't a serious profession; it was Bohemian, disreputable, immoral." King's School, conjured up in its provincial middle-class environment, proves to be another abode of Philistia, denounced as a typical late Victorian public-school. Not unnaturally, the main body of the boys there place sports far above learning. But Philip's brief alignment on this ethos is mockingly referred to his idealization of the popular-qua-commonplace Rose: "He thought him the most wonderful fellow in the world. His books now were insignificant." As for most of the masters, they had already come in for castigation as intellectual sticks-in-the-mud, exposed in their mistrust of the new Head's eccentric interests: "he talked of German philosophy and of French fiction." This broader and more modern culture thus provides the standards on which the satire rests.

On similar assumptions, Londoners are not spared. In the course of his apprenticeship at the Accountant's Office, Philip finds himself patronized by a fellow articled clerk, a Watson, whose father belongs to the "beerage," and whom he expressly, and not without grounds, "look(s) upon as a Philistine." This conceited and dandified old Oxonian is a regular reader of *The Sportsman,* a fan of music-hall performances and, busy as he is chasing the girls, "set(s) no store on his protégé's culture." The accountant, who bears the no less emblematic name of Carter, is clearly an upstart and an egregious snob, who shares Watson's "barbarian" ideals: his study-walls are "decorated with sporting prints" and his whole conversation bears on the pleasures of hunting and his (dubious) claims to gentlemanliness. Yet, even then, the lower classes are dragged into the dock. Brutally, with regard to Thompson, a cockneyish clerk who "sneered at Philip because he was better educated than himself"; with condescending leniency, in the character-sketch of Goodworthy, the kind but unrefined managing-clerk who, on a professional trip to Paris, introduces the young man to the Moulin Rouge and the Folies-Bergères labelled as "a vulgar Paris," in which he finds delight, though from the vantage-point of a superior English morality. France will again be used as a cultural touchstone in the scathing caricature of Albert Price, Fanny's brother, "a rubber merchant" whose grammar is shaky and French non-existent. This Victorian-businessman, conventional even in the choice of his Christian name, had, self-complacently, allowed his eccentric sister to starve, in the name of virtue and probability: "Me and Mrs. Price told her Paris was no place for a girl. And there's no money in art." Yet, having paid his way across the Channel to attend the black sheep's funeral, he would not miss an opportunity to get acquainted with "those places in Montmartre which are celebrated from Temple Bar to the Royal Exchange." These skirmishes prepare us for the full scale attack against the "populace" launched on the occasion of Philip's term of shop-assistantship and for the sarcastic treatment of the waitress Mildred.

Depending on second-hand knowledge for the episodes at Lynn and Sedley's, Maugham has been all the more careful to establish the social environment and spirit of such a place. With probable reminiscences of Zola's *Au Bonheur des Dames,* and Wells's *Kipps,* for some English specificities, he has, in his own, terser way, shown the drudgery inherent in a shop-assistant's daily duties, hinted at the meanness of the lives led by an underpaid staff, touched upon the commercial strategy of a big Department Stores in London. But his account of the hierarchies within the establishment is distinctive in its sharp focus on the lack of taste, the deficiencies in culture and the social solecisms of the whole set. The people at the top are bounders. Mr. Gibbons, the "buyer," whom Philip is humiliated to have to apply to for his job, asserts his elegance by sporting "a white geranium surrounded by leaves" in the lapel of his professional frock coat. The general manager, who speaks "with a cockney twang," indulges in "a great many words" and wears "a bunch of football medals" dangling from his watch chain, smugly assumes that his new recruit (whose stay in Paris has been mentioned to him) "found that art did not pay." Sampson, the buyer of costumes, who seeks to ape continental fashions, prides himself on

his smattering of French and, probably nominal, acquaintance with Maxim's. Under his management, Parisian chic is crudely plagiarized to cater for insular vulgarians. An instance of these is ridiculed in the burly person of a Miss Antonia, a popular singstress, with "the breezy manner of a comedienne accustomed to being on friendly terms with the gallery boys of provincial music halls." Seeking a new costume to wear on stage, "something striking" she is delighted with the "combination of violent, unusual colours" that Philip, in deliberate caricature of French designs, has devised to suit her flashy plebeian tastes. To cap this emphatic demonstration, Maugham has devoted a whole chapter to describing one of the "social evenings" of the staff. The protagonist, not daring to sneak away, attends it from end to end, with a sinking heart. Much of the evening is filled by crude amateur performances given by the employees: the playing of popular pieces by a self-taught lady pianist; the singing of sentimental ditties; the recital of a facetious poem . . . While it recalls Dickens by its broadly comic presentation of lower-class characters and unsophisticated audiences, the scene is undickensian in its superciliousness. Among the attendants are found, for instance, a Mrs. Hodges, as rustic as her name indicates, who picks her teeth with her silver brooch, and a blatantly un-Jane-Austenish Miss Bennett, the red-faced, overdressed and underbred "belle" of the stores who, besides her capacity to drain two or three bottles of ginger beer in a single session, "liked dancing and poetry better than anything in the world." Even more than the nature of Philip's work—his dress-designing activities are perceived as a commercial parody of the pursuit of Art—it is this trial by vulgarity, this sense of a cultural exile, that brings Philip to the appalled awareness of his vital failure. Back in his dormitory, he then attempts "with all his might not to think of the life he [is] leading." And the climax of his "despair" is reached when, on meeting Lawson, a former friend of his artistic days, in a London street, he feels bound to break away from all that this painter continues to stand for.

Earlier in the book, the main, battered target of the cultural satire had been Mildred Rogers. Between the long-haired "stoodent" (as she calls him) and this aggressively low-bred and absurdly genteel, cockneyish member of the servant-class—who smoothly sinks from waiting in a cheap café into street-walking—the intellectual and aesthetic gap is shown, at every turn, to be unbridgeable. Only once does Somerset Maugham remember to distance himself, on this topic, from his fictional counterpart. This occurs on the occasion of the ill-matched couple's first visit to a music-hall: "Philip was a very cultured young man and he looked upon musical comedy with scorn. He thought the jokes vulgar and the melodies obvious . . . but Mildred . . . applauded rapturously." But, even then, the raillery is double-edged, and the young man's later summary of Mildred's character as that of "a vulgar slut" is amply substantiated. At the very height of his masochistic passion, Philip, we are told, "saw her *exactly as she was* . . . her mind was common; she had a vulgar shrewdness which revolted him. . . ." And his tacitly endorsed remarks are scarcely more complimentary when, towards the close of their relationships, he observes that "she had not even the power of attending to what she was herself saying" or that "Her mind was of an order that could not deal for five minutes with the abstract." With Proustian irony, such deficiencies had put her intellectualistic wooer at a disadvantage in the days of his infatuation. Having "no talent for small talk." He had then, in frantic search of conversational topics, stooped to "read[ing] industriously *The Sporting Times*." But, on this ground, how could he vie with spontaneously lowbrowed rivals, like the "flashy and jovial young man . . . with the spruce look of a commercial traveller" who takes her to the Tivoli? or with Miller, the heavily moustached, German-born salesman, whose "vulgar smartness of . . . appearance" is a claim for the waitress's admiration? or again, with the charming but "empty headed" Griffith who "never read a book" and "had never a thought that was fine?" The fact that this student of medicine stands higher on the social scale highlights the *cultural* theme. As for Mildred, she is repeatedly exposed for her assumedly representative semi-illiteracy. On one of his earliest visits to the teashop, Philip finds her "immersed in a novelette" belonging, the comment suggests, to the "regular supply of inexpensive fiction written to order . . . for the consumption of the illiterate"; and he notices that she "outline(s) the words with her lips as she read(s)." An idea of the trash thus imbibed is hinted at when it appears that the books she most admires for being "so refined" bear the signature of Courtenay Page. This happens to be the pen-name used by Norah Nesbit for the hack-writing which, on her own jocular admission, has gained her "an immense popularity among kitchen-maids. They think me so genteel." In echoing the cliché and taking for granted the "extravagances of cheap fiction," Mildred joins the ranks of the romancers, but with the special defencelessness that goes with a dull mind and a lack of critical sense.

To genuine literature and to painting, this figurehead of low-class ignorance proves at best indifferent, at worst antagonistic. Jealous of Philip's engrossment in serious books, at the time when she shares his London flat, she keeps interfering with his reading; then, in the Brighton episode, she remonstrates with him on dubious popular assumptions—"You'll addle your brain, that's what you will do"—and reproaches him for being "so unsociable." The prospect of going to Paris attracts her when she remembers that "a friend of hers had passed her honeymoon [there] and . . . spent all day at the Louvre," meaning, of course, not Philip's favourite Gallery but "the Magasin . . . where you could get the very latest things for half the price." Once settled in his Kennington flat, she (vainly) undertakes to make him take down the nudes on his walls, which she deems indecent: "Disgusting, that's what I call it to have drawings of naked people about." When, in revenge for his rejection of her sexual advances, she wrecks the place before going away, it is thus logical, as well as symbolic, that she should spare none of his works of art. The tearing of his portrait and of his own drawings may be held to be *ad hominem*. But she also destroys "the photographs, Manet's *Olympia* and the *Odalisque* of Ingres," reconciled under the vandal's "coalhammer," together with "the portrait of Philip IV." As for the invidious volumes, they have been left with "long gashes on the backs," like stabbed enemies, and she has taken special "trouble to tear pages out of the unbound French

ones." Philip's final response is revealingly rooted in intellectual arrogance. More in disdain than in anger, "He did not think of her with wrath but with an overwhelming sense of boredom." Yet, if we trust the ending of the tale, with a pox upon the . . . crashing bore!

Since both Hayward the arch aesthete, and Mildred, the blatant Philistine had been living, "in fragments"—E.M. Foster's then recently coined phrase in *Howards End*—their early deaths (the former from enteric fever; the latter from syphilis) image an obvious revenge of the body against, in the first case, too exclusive a life of the mind; in the second, a vulgar affectation of refinement. Yet the two vital fallacies are not on a par. Hayward has only proved to be his own enemy; while Mildred is also a destroyer of others, a *femme fatale*. Specifically, in the case of Philip, her sensual appeal, depicted as perverse, had, as it were, sucked dry his earlier aesthetic and intellectual interests: "Love was like a parasite in his heart . . . it absorbed his existence so intensely that he could have pleasure in nothing else . . . now beauty meant nothing to him . . . no picture called up in him a thrill of emotion . . . new books were meaningless." In consequence, once he has overcome the shock of losing this ghoul to the superior attractions of Emil Muller, the student who, "for six months [has] been starved for beauty," sets to a banquet of the soul. In company with Hayward, on a timely visit to London, he rediscovers the charms of the city, the delights of the National Gallery, the joys of ardent debates on art and literature. Admittedly, the two intellectuals are chaffed: the deserted lover for his overexcitement, "in sudden reaction from the life he has been leading"; the older man, as usual, for his docile switching of cultural snobberies. Yet, all along this chapter-long hymn to beauty, Philip plainly voices his creator's beliefs, notably on the relevant and, as will be seen central issue of art's power to "liberate the soul from pain." On the Edwardian mode, but with extenuating succinctness, the author steps in, to enthuse on the landscapes of the metropolis with a wealth of artistic and literary references from both sides of the Channel. We thus foresee that, in Maugham's coming variant on the Goethian fuller life, one fragment may appear "more equal" then the other.

This sentiment, out of chapter L, must be seen in context and in the light of its fuller phrasing.

It echoes the hero's change of heart towards the end of his two years as would-be painter in Montparnasse. By crossing the Channel like a Rubicon, under the unauspicious encouragement of the romantic Miss Wilkinson and ill-omened applause of the dilettantish Hayward, Philip hoped to conquer genius at one stroke, in a Murger-like Bohemia. Instead, he has been a witness to the drudgery, the hardship and uncertainties that, according to Maugham, attend the artist's call. The suicide of the dedicated but destitute and ungifted Fanny Price—the first of the symbolic deaths in the novel—has illustrated the self-destructive absurdity of believing that creativeness depends on will alone. Clutton impersonates another variation on the vital sacrifices demanded by the exclusiveness of an artistic endeavour. A still young, possibly talented painter, he is shown, gradually, to cut himself from all personal relations in the fervour of his single-minded quest. But what, wonders the pragmatic hero, if he should not make his mark? "[He] saw him in twenty years, bitter, lonely, savage and unknown." This "tragedy of failure" experienced by clear-sighted second-raters, is then embodied by Cronshaw, a minor decadent poet in his fifties, still a brilliant talker, but bibulous, and living in penury with a slatternly French mistress. This deglamourised *poète maudit* will later die of cirrhosis, in dire poverty. It is in recoil from this gallery of human wrecks—capped by the character-sketch of Foinet, the elderly teacher at the Academy, soured by the realization of his mediocrity—that Philip reaches a diagnosis and prescribes for himself an alternative course. The diagnosis of course adumbrates the characterization of Strickland, central to the next novel: "in the true painters, writers, musicians there was a power which drove them to such complete absorption in their work as to make it inevitable for them *to subordinate life to art . . .* they were merely dupes of the instinct that possessed them." Meanwhile, it is *on the rebound,* that the present protagonist is made to advocate an antithetic mode of self-fulfilment: "he had a feeling that life was to be lived rather than portrayed and he wanted to search out the various experiences of it and wring from each moment the emotion that it offered."

Though Philip will be shown to outgrow this late nineteenth century emphasis on extending the boundaries of sensations—the last romantic fallacy to be disowned—, the art-versus-life issue is thus no longer faced in terms of discernment but in the prospect of a life-choice. And I submit that the inner tensions that energize the theme will deflect its treatment. Maugham, the living author behind the scenes, *was* wedded to his creative endeavour; a frequently acknowledge datum, deplored as a bondage or, on the contrary, seen as a privilege—"The artist is the only free man" [*The Summing Up*]—, according to his moods. In this view, the defiant, topically self-apologetic motif that nobody can live on love alone, even if it be the love of art, must be seen as subsidiary. It is contradicted in the scornful handling of Lawson, the comparatively gifted yet unoriginal portrait-painter who, as his name intimates, compromises with the tastes of the British Establishment, on his way to the Royal Academy. From the same exacting vantage-point, Stroeve, the moderately successful-qua-conventional painter of *The Moon and Sixpence,* will be characterized as a figure of fun, with overtones of cathartic self-satire. The major issue of the later novel, only touched upon here, in the case of Clutton, but underlying, I submit, the progress of Philip, is that of reconciling a *genuine* artistic urge with an existence outside the Ivory Tower. Saddled with his creator's biographical background and contemplative bias, the protagonist is sent to explore a daydreamt counter-slope:

> "It did not seem to me enough *only* to be a writer (Maugham was to admit on looking back). The *pattern* I had designed for myself *insisted that* I should take the utmost part I could in this fantastic affair of being a man. I *desired* to feel the common pains and enjoy the common pleasures that are part of the common human lot . . . I was *determined* to get whatever fulfilment I could out of social intercourse and human

relations . . . *But it was an effort* and I have always returned to my books and my own company with relief. [*The Summing Up*]"

The words italicized offer as good as a running commentary on the wish-fulfilment vein that, to the author's own, and most critics', discomfort, prevails in the present novel's last section. The sketches of homely family happiness and a village-doctor's self-realizing life are pictures in the fire, only burning, as may sadly appear, with a paste-like glimmer.

Even at the stages at which Somerset Maugham has sought to prepare us for his protagonist's change of tack, the conflict between idea and sensibility can be discerned. Thus, a visit to the Louvre allows for a contrast between Fanny Price's exclusive absorption in the exhibits and Philip's revived interest in the coming of Spring, but the parable is unwittingly undermined. The scenery that draws the young man's eyes away from the landscapes on the walls is itself framed by "a window that looked out on the Tuileries, gay, sunny, and urbane, *like a picture by Raffaëlli!*" Back in London, Philip's reported thoughts on the impact of Mildred's first desertion point towards a special instrumentality: "Under the influence of passion he had felt a singular vigour, and his *mind had worked with unwonted force.*" Is not the "Sacred Fount" motif thus stealing through? Leaving out for later comments the ambiguous scenes in the British Museum and in front of a Whistler-like sunrise on the Thames, I shall only offer one more illustration. Catching his last sight of Lawson in Piccadilly, the hero, on the verge of his second life, makes up his mind to turn "down a side street," an emblematic as well as literal turning-point. And yet, the authorial comment on his disinclination ever to talk to the painter again weakens the point: "art appeared to him unimportant. He was occupied with the forming of a pattern out of the manifold chaos of life, and the *materials with which he worked* seemed to make preoccupation with pigments and words very trivial. Lawson had *served his turn.* Philip's friendship with him had been *a motive in the design he was elaborating. . . .*" In their combination, the idea of a "pattern" formed out of "chaos"; the image of "materials" to be improved (a familiar one with Maugham as self-reflexive writer); the notions of a character who had "served his turn" and of "a motive" within a "design" in process of elaboration sound metafictional with a vengeance! Thus defined, the art of living prolongs the very creed it claims to repudiate, on lines already sketched much earlier in the book: "[Philip's] conduct of his life as a whole . . . was his means of self-expression." Scratch the "doctor" and you'll find a writer.

In fact, the two existential alternatives embraced in turn by the protagonist, when groping towards the "simplest pattern," happen to correlate two antithetic modes of fiction-writing: life as a romance and life as a novel.

To the first mode could be referred Philip's hankering after exotic experiences in Spain and the East. Like Maugham himself, who was yet to visit Asia and the South Seas, his counterpart must have been an eager reader of Loti and of Stevenson. His idealizing vision of those distant lands draws on both, in turn, with some authorial self-irony: "his fancy was rich with pictures of Bangkok and Shangaï, and the ports of Japan: he pictured to himself palm-trees and skies blue hot . . . the scents of the Orient intoxicated his nostrils. . . ." And Philip's approved change of mind will thus be described on the novel's pen-ultimate page: ". . . what to him were the pagodas . . . and the lagoons . . . ? America was here and now. It seemed to him that all his life he had followed the ideals that other people, *by their words or their writings,* had instilled into him, and never the desires of his own heart." The very "words" used are, of course, those of Goethe, and the last "instilled ideal" comes straight from his "writings," to complete the apprenticeship of an English Wilhelm Meister. One literary theme supersedes another.

The treatment of Spain and its glamour is complicated by Maugham's close acquaintance with the actual range of this land's artistic production and the diversity of its provinces. Within Philip's all-sweeping repudiation of his dreams of travel, given as escapist, a mythicized Iberia is cast off in the lump: "What did he care for Spain and its cities, Cordova, Toledo, León." But this jars with the earlier, better informed disquisitions ascribed, somewhat improbably, to the hero's second-hand knowledge. El Greco—the only unchallenged artist-hero in the whole novel—had been extolled for his profound insights, by which the young man had planned to profit on a cultural journey to Toledo. An equally authorized commentary, only a few pages before the hero's volte-face, had drawn a pondered contrast between, on the one hand, "Andalusia . . . too soft and sensuous and a little vulgar" and, on the other, the sterner, more bracing appeal of "the windswept distances of Castille and the rugged magnificence of Aragon and León." This eulogy of the robust ideal in a sober environment distinctively merges with aesthetic considerations. According to Athelny, whose views on things Spanish foreshadow some essays in Maugham's *Don Fernando,* little is to be learnt in Seville, discredited by its associations with the too sentimental Murillo and the too romantic Théophile Gauthier. Whereas the value of the message of Toledo can be measured by the greatness of its famous painter. There follows a four-page record of Philip's train of thought, on scrutinizing a photographed landscape by the said El Greco. And again, the stated existential issue—"He felt . . . he was on the threshold of a new discovery in life "—mingles with, and becomes subordinate to an enquiry on the goals of true art: the admired picture is claimed to transcend crude mimesis, so as to encompass" a reality greater than any achieved by the masters in whose steps humbly he had sought to walk. "And the offered synthesis of the two concerns—the vital and the artistic—revealingly reverts to the contemplative: "here was something better than the realism he had adored; but certainly it was not the bloodless idealism which stepped aside from life in its weakness; it was too strong; it was virile; it *accepted* life *in all its vivacity,* ugliness *and beauty,* squalor *and heroism* . . . it was realism carried to some higher pitch." For better or for worse, the Georgian novelist is about to explore a reality beyond naturalism.

The correlation between life-styles and styles of writing has a private reference. To Andalusia, now mocked as a too romantic, effeminately voluptuous locale, Maugham had devoted his first, imitative, over-written, travel-book, *The Land of the Blessed Virgin,* which he was sternly to describe in retrospect as "an exercice in style . . . wistful, allusive and elaborate . . . [with] neither ease nor spontaneity" [*The Summing Up*]. Similarly, Philip's reveries of travel sound like deliberate parodies of the decadent manner, in the sonorous vagueness of their rhapsodies: "visions of tropical sunshine and *magic colour,* and of a *teeming, mysterious, intense* life. Life! That was what he wanted . . . what *rich* jungles. . . might he not visit? . . . he could go up and down the world . . . learning the *beauty,* and the *wonder* and the *variedness* of life." As against this representation of life as a purple patch—with the decadent emphases on the out-of-the-way, the luxuriant, the picturesque, the fervid—a counter-model had been offered to the still immature hero in the pivotal scene at the British Museum. On entering the place, Philip was still blinkered by the extreme naturalistic preconceptions acquired in Heidelberg under the impact of the New Drama, and reinforced in Paris, with tacit reference to the school of Zola, on the occasion of his horrified visit to the Bal Bullier. What he could only see in the visitors about him was a physical and moral ugliness as well as a meanness, at variance with the search for beauty:

> Their hideousness besmirched the everlasting masterpieces . . . their features were distorted with paltry desires . . . There was no wickedness in them but only pettiness and vulgarity . . . he saw in them all the sheep or the horse or the fox or the goat.

Indeed, the very author of *Of Human Bondage* had led us round such a menagerie just before, in his handling of the employees at the Department Stores. But a more balanced vision is now suggested by "the groups from the Parthenon" whose

> *Simplicity* was infinitely touching . . . [their] *restraint* made the survivor's grief more poignant . . . There was one stone which was very beautiful, a bas-relief of two young men holding each other's hand; and the *reticence of line,* the *simplicity* made one like to think that the sculptor here had been touched with a genuine emotion.

Then Maugham, inconsistently, resorts to a periphrasic style as if to play down the hellenistic specificity of the subject that has stirred his hero: "an exquisite memorial to that than which the world offers but one thing more precious, to a friendship." But, though easier to preach than always to practise, the illustrated creed seems to advocate a classical mode of artistic expression; a clear, stripped, yet harmonious rendering of universal themes (death or love), whose effects are achieved through calm understatement. The author's own mature ideal of prose—to be described in *The Summing Up* as a combination of "lucidity", "simplicity" and "euphony"—seems thus heralded. As for the main temptation to be exorcised, it had been embodied again by Hayward, whose obliging death had brought about his former disciple's illumination. Over and above the fallacies of a darkly romantic pessimism—with which the deccased had only been marginally associated—it is what he centrally stood for, aestheticism in art as well as life, that is being disowned.

Within this scheme, Athelny, a more reliable mentor, since he rejects the enervating, Hayward-like "spirit of Andalusia", plays an important role. He is made to urge a reconciliation between, on the one hand, an indispensable interest in artistic and literary beauties and, on the other, a coming to terms with ordinary, practical aims, the needs of the body and the claims of a natural morality. But the second arch of the bridge will mainly be imaged by the rest of his family group to which he parabolically introduces Philip.

It is as an in-patients' clerk at St Luke's Hospital that the hero gets acquainted with this eccentric man in his late forties, one of the lighter "cases" entrusted to his medical observation. Thorpe Athelny, whose Saxon forename and surname both smack of allegory, makes a living as a commercial advertiser but is a cultured man, a reader of unusual books, a translator of Spanish poetry who, on the strength of a long stay in Spain, expertly descants on the painters and writers of the Golden Age. The friendship that springs up between the two men is rooted in their common intellectual and aesthetic fervour, among the Philistines in the ward. The home of the Athelnys, into which Philip will then find his way, helps to characterize its main tenant. Built by Inigo Jones, it has become "shabby" and "insanitary" and must soon be pulled down, but it possesses a magnificent balustrade and admirable ceilings, highly valued by Athelny: "Sanitation be damned, give me art . . . I have got nine children and they thrive on bad drains." Such data and the Skimpolish remark just quoted might have led to the denunciation of another dilettante, sacrificing the comfort of his family to a grasshopper philosophy. The more so, as this artistic type, even to the tips of the tapering, ivory-white fingers of which he is so proud, shows several features satirized in others, earlier in the novel. Like Hayward, he favours Roman Catholicism on purely aesthetic grounds, can "never say anything without an oratorical flourish," writes "in (a) formal manner . . . studded with pompous epithets," likes to adorn the truth, as when he boasts of his aristocratic origins "from a wish to impress. . . ." Like the American tourists in Paris, ridiculed earlier for their romantic conventionality, he is apt to dress like a character by Murger, reminding Philip of "the comic Frenchman in the pages of *Punch*," and, again, "his bombast . . . his emphasis . . . the same bohemianism" expressly establish his kinship with Cronshaw. Even his professional record of false starts, his instability, his drone-like behaviour during the hop-picking, the too effeminate care he takes of his "graceful hands" are only made light fun of. The focus is on the qualities that ensure his vital success: a (reciprocated) fondness for his common law wife and flourishing children, on whose behalf he sticks to a thankless job; the "independence of thought" that he shares with the late Cronshaw, while adding to it "an infinitely more vivacious temperament"; the generosity he extends to the poverty-stricken protagonist and which excludes the possibility of "any mean motive" for his boastings; his unassuming sociability in dealing with the hop-pickers in Kent. Maugham seems to have played down his spontaneously

censorious response in order to sustain his argument that the worship of art need not be incompatible with love, morality of a kind, good fellowship, and the enjoyment of simple pleasures . . . Yet, all along, and even in the family-scene that, literally, brings the point home, the aesthetic standard prevails: "The life of [Philip's] new friend . . . seemed now to have the *beauty* of perfect naturalness"; and, by implicit contrast to the evil aura of Mildred, sitting next to Philip, "it was evidently the beauty of their goodness which attracted him." By itself the adverb may stand as a comment. Unchallenged in the text, this oblique justification of virtue might well have come under the pen of the older Walter Pater.

Exit Thorpe Athelny. Enter the rest of his household: the kind, homely mother; with, for good measure, her nine offspring. While the eight younger ones, remembered "in a bunch," are indeed treated as a chorus, the eldest, a bonny lass, will soon step forth into the lights, to join Philip in a love-duet.

The happy home discovered by the orphaned student in its tantalizing sanctities is by no means conventional. It represents the superior success of a left-handed ménage, breaking down the barriers of class in a Butlerian note of defiance, yet with special emphases. Athelny's legitimate wife, an irreproachable and well-to-do bourgeoise, had bored him so much that he had fled their elegant villa in Kensington to set up house with their own maidservant. The portrayal of the, now matronly "Betty" bears out the rightness of his second choice. A distinctly mellowed version of Butler's Ellen, she has proved an accomplished housewife; a good cook of country dishes; a cheerfully efficient mother for their nine surviving children, brought up on sound lower-class lines of obedience and service; a motherly concubine, ministering to the comforts of the breadwinner. The lucky man still admires the handsomeness of her figure which—for a plain reason? —reminds him of "Rubens' second wife." However, this mythically robust Flemish-English wench, who expressly fleshes out the perfect helpmate—"That is what a man wants in a wife, the halcyon"—also serves the aesthetic theme. The lady, whom she had advantageously superseded in Athelny's bed and kitchen was a blue-stocking. She used to give literary parties, "was very fond of lectures on Sunday afternoons . . . read the right books, admired the right pictures and adored the right music. . . ." By contrast, her unintellectual successor speaks for good sense and the wisdom of a generous heart, both bequeathed, with the rest of her gifts, to her eldest daughter. A thematic shift has taken place. Cronshaw's low-born mistress, admittedly French, had been outlined as a slovenly slut, a living testimonial to the artist's decline, almost on a par with the absinthe of which he proved overfond. As for Mildred, like Betty a member of the English servant-class, we have seen with what contumely her commonness and demeaning companionship had been scourged. Whereas the no less ungrammatical plain speech of Betty, to be echoed in that of her daughter, and even their common shrugging off of intellectual and aesthetic concerns, are now referred to the counter-claims of unsophisticated "nature," in challenge of what Lawrence was to call "the mental life."

On the typically Edwardian return-to-the-earth motif that develops within the parable, we need not dwell. A Kentish farmer's daughter, the second Mrs Athelny is a country-lass transplanted to London and yet unspoilt. She has kept a connection with her native county. Every late Summer, with her husband's blessing and cheerfully ineffective participation, she takes her family to do the hop-picking on the Isle of Thanet. This, we are asked to believe, "renewed their contact with mother earth . . . gave them a new strength," ensuring that the children, still characterized in a body, remained "merry, boisterous, healthy and handsome." It is in this pastoral setting, "scented [in September] with the goodly perfume of hops," and "amid conditions which needed only a blue sky to be as idyllic as the olive-grove of Arcady," that Sally Athelny, adding the bloom of her innocent youth to the congenial traits she shares with her mother, acts out her *scène-à-faire* as Philip's responsive love-partner.

The two avatars of the girl's forename prefigure her emblematic role. This Maria del Sol—her Micawberish genitor's pompous, yet apt label—has been duly anglicized into "Sally" by her no-nonsense mother. Though she serves her apprenticeship with a sempstress in Regent Street, a useful training for a housewife, this paragon in the making looks out of place in the metropolis, "like a cornflower in a shop among orchids and azaleas." In context, we gather that she stands above the artificial beauties of the decadent environment par excellence; that she puts to shame the *fleurs du mal* of the modern city, including the chlorotic Mildred. *This* "Sally" belongs to a garden-alley. So much so that, when Philip, among the Kentish fields, impulsively folds her in his arms, he seems to embrace a full-fledged local Persephone: her voice's "low richness was the voice of the country night itself"; "She seemed to carry with her scents of the new-mown hay, and the savour of ripe hops, and the freshness of young grass." Even more comprehensively, her "exquisite homely naturalness" conjures up the thought of "a cottage garden with the dear flowers which bloom in all men's hearts." Their ensuing enumeration includes, with special, though unmeant relevance, "London Pride" and "love-in-a-mist!"

At every turn of this eulogy of artless nature, literature and art claim their own. The notion of the stimulating earth comes, of course, from Wordsworth, Maugham's favourite English poet, though, for him, an uninspiring model. The memory of Hardy's Wessex may have contributed to his hero's conviction that this farmer's granddaughter "would blossom under the softer skies of Dorset to a rarer beauty." Express reminiscences of Shakespeare's Jessica and Lorenzo mingle with the scents of the fields to kindle the man's desire. The "quiet smile" of the enigmatic Sally seems Gioconda-like. Her arm, though stroked in the dark, has "the skin that Rubens painted. . . ." Thus, there is a more then intended appropriateness in the fact that the climactic meeting occurs in the National Gallery. As he then sits waiting for his girl-friend, the hero, about to propose, "looked at [no picture] in particular but allowed . . . the beauty of their lines to work upon his soul. His imagination was busy with Sally." Such verbal contiguities extend the relevance of the later statement that the engaged couple "walked *out* of the gallery."

Nor is this the only respect in which the hero's wedding with "a perfect picture" proves to be a marriage of convenience. The very hymn to a wholesomely innocent sexuality on the part of Sally, obeying, we are told, "the healthy instincts of the natural woman," exalts "an affection that had in it something maternal and something sisterly," an archetypal yet formidable compendium of charms. For—or because of ? —all that, the male partner cannot feel love for her and, after the first embraces, seems even to have lost his sexual desire: "She was a splendid animal . . . and physical perfection filled him always with *awe*." The author's homosexual bias may well have reasserted itself in this lamely rationalized recoil. At any rate, we are asked to believe that the young lovers' intimacy once established in the flesh happily develops not so much beyond as *outside* sex, on rather improbable terms of comradeship: "They met with a handshake and parted as formally . . . Never a word of love passed between them." This "picture of the marriage I should have liked to make," Maugham's retrospective account of the present dénouement in *The Summing Up,* does not only connote a marriage of true minds. The praise of Sally's habitual silence, in clear contrast to Mildred's garrulity, is more than a cliché of male chauvinism. Earlier in the plot, this anti-Mildred had once come to sit next to Philip, and urged him to go on with his reading, while she plied the needle in a respectful hush. Accordingly, his prospect of a happy connubial life will bring to his mind the thought of "long evenings . . . in the cosy sitting room . . . he with his books while she bent over her work." In this further respect, the National Gallery offers a fitting frame for their betrothal. In the same way as "It always comforted him to get among pictures," the company of this beau ideal had appeared "curiously soothing," holding for the orphan the expectation of "a fair haven" against "the loneliness and the tempest." On such distinctive lines, this "odd girl" represents the artistic doctor's—as, covertly, the clinical author's—daydreamt "rest."

This cutting of the losses has brought us round to the initial title of the book, whose ultimate relevance is sustained in the two pathetic fallacies that frame the tale. The first had established a gloom matching the (autobiographical) report of a mother's death: "The day broke gray and dull" The second, in capping the fiction of the good, restoring marriage, marks a rebirth of hope in the acceptance of the ways of ordinary men: "crowds passed hastening in every direction and the sun was shining." Yet the imagined retort is idiosyncratic. The brighter landscape, internal, we assume, as well as external, is "looked at" from "the balustrade" of the gallery from which the unlikely couple have just emerged. The very motif of a coming to terms with the prose of life thus ends in a scene of calm contemplation, whose purpose and spirit may now be summed up.

Half-way through the book, in authorized challenge of Hayward's barren formalism, Philip had referred the value of literature—standing for all the arts—to its effects upon its frequenters, in so far as it may foster a blossoming of the minds and souls: "the petals open one by one" But, beyond this educational theme, the more recurrent, and original emphases bear on the acquirement of an inner "strength," or the conquest of a saving "comfort" against the blows of fate. Both notions belong to a defensive panoply, though by no means in a dodging spirit. The appreciation of beauty in all its forms—"there was art in the manner in which he looked upon nature"—offers the best of shields against *confronted* pain. Even against the most poignant of all. For the lack of such a support, the Philistines in the British Museum are sadly disarmed: "all those mean, common people . . . must part from those they loved, *the son from the mother,* the wife from the husband; and perhaps it was more tragic because . . . they knew nothing that gave beauty to the world." Whereas, the authors' counterpart at long last finds solace in his ability "to stand above the accidents of his existence." This will be ultimately tested within a repetition-cum-variation of the most crucial of his (inherited) "accidents." The ordeal that reopens the wound, is a succinct yet pathetic version of the real-life episode which had moved Somerset Maugham to write his first novel, *Liza of Lambeth.* At the close of his probation as an obstetric clerk in the slums, Philip is unable to save a young mother from death in childbirth, while *"the boy who was her husband"* watches the tragic scene in dumb "bewilderment." This modified repeat of *his* boy hood trauma now shows the hero standing at a remove, in sympathetic but self-possessed observation. And what follows seems to encapsulate the whole process of Philip's release from his mourning. As he walks home, the cathected images haunt him—"[He] could not get out of his eyes the dead girl lying on the bed, wan and white, and the *boy* who stood at the end of it like a stricken beast." But the spectacle of a sunrise over the Thames soothes his soul: "He was overwhelmed by the beauty of the world. Beside that nothing seemed to matter." This aesthetic vision proves therapeutic on Schopenhauerian lines. And the preceding rejection of social pity—"pity was inane . . . They did not pity themselves. They accepted their fates"—would sound callous indeed, if it did not echo a deep private issue: the need to overcome a gnawing *self*-pity.

The theme of the artistic vocation, overtly dropped on Philip's renunciation of painting, remains in the background. In Bohemia, he had felt less conscious of his estranging infirmity, like an ugly duckling raised, for a while, to cygnet status among the swans. But the chosen pattern of the "novel of apprenticeship" called for a volte-face. Back in London, and on his way to a more ordinary life, the protagonist has his club foot operated upon. Yet, the incompleteness of the dramatized cure—"he would always limp"—cannot be fully accounted for by Maugham's realistic adherence to his clinical knowledge. It looks as though the notion of social adjustment went against the grain with the novelist in the prompter's box. Hence his perfunctory report of the operation. And the conflicting pride in exile which, under the guise of a welcome acceptance, finds its way back even into the penultimate chapter: "He accepted the deformity which had made life so hard for him . . . by reason of it he has acquired [his] power of introspection . . . Without it he would never have had his keen appreciation of beauty, his *passion for art and literature* and his interest in the varied *spectacle* of life." And . . . ? Imperfectly buried under the Bildungs, an aborted Kunstler-roman lies in the missing clause.

Archie K. Loss   (essay date 1990)

SOURCE: "Major Themes: Bondage and Troubled Grace," in *Of Human Bondage: Coming of Age in the Novel,* Twayne Publishers, 1990, pp. 15-20.

[*In the following excerpt, Loss argues that* Of Human Bondage *meets the criteria for a* bildungsroman *and examines Maugham's twin themes of bondage and grace in regards to Philip's relationship with Mildred.*]

Implicit in the concept of the bildungsroman is the idea of growth. It is not enough that the main character should simply experience a succession of adventures or suffer from the pangs of unrequited love; he must grow in understanding and sense of responsibility as a result of his adventures or loves. In the broadest sense, that is what the bildungsroman is about: following the main character to the point at which he is ready to assume responsibility for his life.

Of Human Bondage follows this pattern. It begins with the death of Philip's mother when he is a boy of ten and ends with Philip in his late twenties, his medical training complete, ready to assume adult responsibilities, his bride-to-be by his side. Thematically, it shows the growth of Philip's sense of reality, of his ability to distinguish what is true from what is false in the world around him and in his innermost being. It is only when Philip is able to reconcile to some extent the contradictions he perceives in himself and in the world that the novel achieves its end. To reach that goal, Maugham develops two major themes.

The first of these centers on the idea of bondage. Philip's relationship with Mildred is the primary vehicle for the development of this theme. Philip's bondage to Mildred is both physical and emotional—physical in the sense that he needs to have her by his side or be with her even if she doesn't want him around, emotional in the sense that whether he is with her or not she dominates his thoughts and actions as if she were actually there. From the beginning of their relationship, when Philip finds he cannot keep himself from going back to the tearoom where she works as a waitress, till the penultimate episode in their career, when Mildred, having had an affair with Griffiths, leaves Philip with the hated epithet "cripple," his feelings are the same.

Even after Philip realizes (fairly early in the relationship) that his attraction to Mildred is sick, he is still bound to her. Philip never has sexual relations with Mildred, yet he wants to assume the role of provider to her and father to her baby. In the terms of psychopathology, Philip is both a masochist and a voyeur. As a masochist, he needs to suffer to justify a love relationship. As a voyeur, he enjoys creating an opportunity for Mildred to have pleasure with another man. Even the love of a woman who genuinely cares for him—Norah Nesbitt—is not enough to change the pattern of his behavior. Before that can change, he has to hit bottom emotionally and economically.

The bondage theme also appears in relationship to other characters. Philip's Aunt Louisa lives in bondage to his Uncle William, the Vicar of Whitstable. Catering to his every whim, denying herself things she needs, Louisa is almost a parody of the wife as doormat so common to Victorian fiction. Hayward, Philip's friend from Heidelberg days, lives in bondage to a false ideal: an aesthetic view of life that prevents him from acting. He is the eternal dilettante, fluttering like a butterfly from flower to flower. Fanny Price, whose devotion to art is so misplaced and whose failure provides such a lesson to Philip in his Paris years, lives in bondage to an ideal she can never realize. Foinet's advice, savage as it is, is right: she is no artist, and chooses suicide over admitting the truth of his judgment. Cronshaw, another Paris friend who greatly influences Philip's view of the world, is in bondage to alcohol and a way of life that will ultimately destroy him. Cronshaw shows the dark side of the Bohemian life that appealed to Philip so much in his reading. These characters and others illustrate the pervasiveness of the bondage theme.

At the same time Philip puts himself into a state of bondage, however, he seeks independence. At King's School, he will not agree to try for an Oxford scholarship despite his admiration for the headmaster, Perkins, because he does not want to be ordained. Time and time again, in decisions about his studies and career, he asserts his independence from his uncle, who despairs of exerting any influence over him. Philip ultimately chooses medicine as his profession, much as he had tried art, because he believes it will give him the freedom he needs to survive. At the end of the novel, on the other hand, he almost decides against marriage because he is afraid it will limit his horizons and keep him from doing what he wants.

In describing Philip's ruminations on the subjects of marriage and personal freedom, Maugham makes use of the phrase "a more troubling grace." It occurs late in the novel, in chapter CVI, after Mildred has left Philip for the last time and he has come under the hedonistic influence of Thorpe Athelny. Running through the novel as a metaphor of Philip's frequent confusion of purpose is the image of a Persian carpet, first suggested to him in Paris by Cronshaw. In such a carpet, Cronshaw suggests, one might find the meaning of life. Philip, pondering his fate, thinks of that carpet again:

> In the vast warp of life . . . , with the background to his fancies that there was no meaning and that nothing was important, a man might get a personal satisfaction in selecting the various strands that worked out the pattern. There was one pattern, the most obvious, perfect, and beautiful, in which a man was born, grew to manhood, married, produced children, toiled for his bread, and died; but there were others, intricate and wonderful, in which happiness did not enter and in which success was not attempted; and in them might be discovered a more troubling grace.

The "more troubling grace" of Philip's thoughts suggests at least a halfway point between the bondage of his relationship to Mildred and the ideal of a relationship, like the Athelny's, in which a lifetime is spent with a single partner. Like that ideal, Philip's more troubled grace is also an alternative of sorts to the absolute meaninglessness of life to which he has by now assented, after the death of Cronshaw and his friend Hayward ("There was no meaning in life, and man by living served no end. It was immaterial whether he was born or not born, whether he lived or ceased to live. Life was insignificant and death without consequence.") Instead of the bleak prospect of a life totally without meaning, Philip can envision at least some figure in the carpet, "intricate and wonderful, in which happiness did not enter and success was not attempted."

Given these thoughts of Philip's is it reasonable for him to choose the pattern that is "the most obvious, perfect, and beautiful, in which a man . . . married, produced children, toiled for his bread, and died," especially since he has made other plans and Sally is in fact not pregnant? In other words, is the ending of the novel honest? Or is Maugham pandering to his reading audience, giving it what he thinks it wants rather than what, logically, it should have? Every reader has to make his or her own decision on this matter.

Inevitably, in reaching that decision, the reader will be influenced by what he or she knows about Maugham's own attitudes toward marriage, love, and life. *Of Human Bondage* is an autobiographical novel: "fact and fiction are inextricably mingled," Maugham wrote in his foreword; "the emotions are my own, but not all of the incidents are related as they happened, and some of them are transferred to my hero not from my own life but from that of persons with whom I was intimate." But to what extent does Philip Carey constitute Maugham's *alter ego?*

In terms of his physical characteristics and psychology, Philip is remarkably similar to his creator, though some details may have been altered. To cite only one example, Maugham suffered from a stammer that made ordinary spoken communication extremely difficult for him, especially when he was a child. In Philip's character, that difficulty is transformed into a clubfoot that makes him self-conscious and the butt of jokes at school.

Other matters can be addressed more readily now that a definitive biography of Maugham has appeared, with Ted Morgan's *Maugham* (1980). Morgan had access to materials that Maugham did not wish his executors to make available to anyone, and he also had the advantage of researching and writing his biography at a time when many of Maugham's friends and colleagues were still alive. His book illuminates many characters and scenes from *Of Human Bondage* and helps to shed light on some of the novel's more ambiguous passages. It also helps the reader to establish the chronology of events in the novel as compared with those of Maugham's life.

One aspect of Maugham confirmed by Morgan's biography enters into Philip's character in subtle ways. Throughout most of his early adult life, Maugham was bisexual, attracted, often simultaneously, to men and to women. As he approached his marriage with Sylvie Barnardo, for instance, he began an affair with Gerald Haxton that was to outlast the marriage and contribute to its demise. In the novel, Philip shows no overt homosexual behavior, though at times he obviously feels considerable attraction to men. This attraction constitutes a kind of subtheme of the novel and may account in part for the dissatisfaction one feels at its ending.

For many characters other than Philip, it is apparent that Maugham drew directly from his own experience. Uncle William and Aunt Louisa, for example, are precise portraits of Maugham's real-life uncle and aunt. Equally precise, apparently, is the portrait of Etheridge Hayward, based on Ellingham Brooks, whom Maugham actually met in Heidelberg. For other characters, however, there is no key. Most notable among these, the model for Mildred remains unknown. One can imagine that in creating characters as in describing events Maugham employed the freedom he suggests in his foreword, in some cases perhaps for reasons that had nothing to do with aesthetics.

In terms of chronology, the novel follows Maugham's early life fairly closely, though certain events are transposed or omitted, creating gaps of several years. In the novel, Philip's father is already dead by the time his mother dies; Philip becomes an orphan on his way to the vicarage at Whitstable within a few pages of the opening of the book. In real life, Maugham's father outlived his mother by several years. Maugham's mother died in 1882 (in Paris, not London), his father in 1884; in the novel, Philip's mother dies in 1885.

Another difference occurs later in the novel, when Philip decides to study art in Paris. Although artists were to occupy Maugham's attention in more than one story, he was never an art student and did not live in Paris during the corresponding period of his life. At the time Philip is in Paris, the young Maugham was already a medical student in London. Maugham did spend a year-and-a-half in Heidelberg, but, on the other hand, only one month studying accounting as compared with Philip's year.

As interesting as such connections are, however, *Of Human Bondage* must ultimately be judged on its own merits as a novel; works of art are independent of the lives of their creators, no matter how closely they are allied. In the pages that follow, we will read the novel as a work of fiction with the major themes of bondage and troubled grace. If to some extent this reading repeats the events of the story, it should be kept in mind that any treatment of a novel so heavily chronological, built out of a series of incidents in the life of its main character, must itself be chronological and summary. Let us hope, however, that out of such a review will emerge the generalizations important

to a critical judgment of the novel. Let us hope, too, that this reading will improve the enjoyment of the novel for a generation of readers now more than eight decades removed from the characters and events it describes.

FURTHER READING

Bibliography

Sanders, Charles. "W. Somerset Maugham: A Supplementary Bibliography." *English Literature in Transition* 15, No. 2 (1972): 168-73.

> Lists and annotates fifty-one articles on Maugham from 1908 to 1972.

Biography

Calder, Robert. *Willie: The Life of W. Somerset Maugham.* London: Heinemann, 1989, 429 p.

> Scholarly biography prepared with the assistance of Maugham's companion-secretary Alan Searle.

Criticism

Clinton, Farley. "Maugham's Bondage." *The National Review* XVIII, No. 8 (22 February 1966): 174-76.

> Brief analysis of Maugham's career, in which Clinton notes the writer's diligence and his "keen sense for what the reading public would find touching, funny, or bizarre."

Curran, Trisha. "Variations on a Theme." In *The English Novel and the Movies,* edited by Michael Klein and Gillian Parker, pp. 228-34. New York: Frederick Ungar, 1981.

> Discusses two film adaptations of *Of Human Bondage:* John Cromwell's 1934 version, starring Leslie Howard and Bette Davis, and Ken Hughes's 1964 version, starring Laurence Harvey and Kim Novak.

Young, B. A. "The Grand Old Man Malgré Lui." *Punch* CCXLIV, No. 6391 (6 March 1963): 353.

> Argues that analysis of Maugham's work is pointless if one accepts—as the author maintained—that it was written purely for entertainment.

Additional coverage of Maugham's life and career is contained in the following sources published by Gale Research: *Contemporary Authors,* Vols. 5-8, rev. ed., 25-28, rev. ed. (obit.); *Contemporary Authors New Revision Series,* Vol. 40; *Concise Dictionary of British Literary Biography, 1914-1945; Contemporary Literature Criticism,* Vols. 1, 11, 15, 67; *Dictionary of Literary Biography,* Vol. 10, 36, 77, 100; *DISCovering Authors; DISCovering Authors: British; Major 20th-Century Writers; Something about the Author,* Vol. 54; *Short Story Criticism,* Vol. 8; *World Literature Criticism.*

Richard Powers

1957-

American novelist.

The following entry provides an overview of Powers's career through 1995.

INTRODUCTION

Powers is known for works in which he combines such subjects as history, politics, and science to examine issues of meaning in contemporary life. He is highly regarded for the rich style of his prose, the complexity of his narrative structures, and the vast range of knowledge exhibited in his works. John F. Baker has written: "[Powers's books are] novels of ideas. Written within a seemingly limitless frame of reference, all concern, in one way or another, the mysteries of time, the problems of living in a confusing century and nothing less than making sense, at the profoundest level, of what human life is all about."

Biographical Information

Powers was born and raised in the American Midwest. He has chosen to seek anonymity, declining to answer questions about his personal life. Powers has stated, "I really don't see what connection all that has with the work. . . . It's not what we should be looking at. All that sort of thing just creates confusion about the nature of the book, deflects attention from what you've done. That's what always seems to happen in this culture: you grab hold of a personality and ignore the work." Powers is known to have worked in the computer field, and to have acquired, as he once noted, "a quasi-preprofessional knowledge of music, as a studious cellist for many years." One source has also claimed that Powers trained as a physicist prior to his literary career. Living in the Netherlands for much of the late 1980s and early 1990s has also contributed to Powers's anonymity. In 1989 he received a fellowship from the MacArthur Foundation—a so-called "genius grant"—and two of his works, *Three Farmers on Their Way to a Dance* (1985) and *The Gold Bug Variations* (1991), were nominated for National Book Critics Circle Awards. The former book also received a PEN/Hemingway Foundation special citation.

Major Works

Powers's first novel, *Three Farmers on Their Way to a Dance,* gets its title from a 1914 August Sander photograph taken in the Rhineland, a region of western Germany along the Rhine River, before the outbreak of World War I. Stories of the three men pictured are interwoven with those of two contemporary figures in America—an unnamed narrator and a copy editor—who come in contact with copies of Sander's print. Through the photographic conceit and structure of the narratives, critics con-

tend that Powers creates a sense of history contained in and affecting the present. In *Prisoner's Dilemma* (1988), Powers again links past and present in relating the story of 52-year-old Eddie Hobson—an ill ex-history teacher who constantly quizzes his family to test and inform them as well as to divert their attention from his ailments. The story is told in three ways: through 1978 events involving Hobson's illness; through the remembrances of Hobson's children; and in tape recordings in which Hobson chronicles a fantasy scenario that closely parallels events from his life starting with the 1939 World's Fair to beyond the time he was stationed near the atomic bomb testing site in Alamogordo, New Mexico, his proximity to which probably caused his maladies. Critics have speculated that the book may be semi-autobiographical, with Hobson modeled after Powers's father. *The Gold Bug Variations* derives its title from two sources: Edgar Allan Poe's short story involving cryptography, "The Gold Bug" (1843), and German composer Johann Sebastian Bach's musical composition, *The Goldberg Variations* (1742). Using a complex narrative structure, Powers relates parallel love stories, one set in the 1950s and the other in the 1980s, each of which concern two mysteries: the search to break the genetic code and to find the reasons why a once prominent scientist—Stuart Ressler—abandoned that search. Powers utilizes the repetitive patterns in Canadian pianist Glenn Gould's recording of Bach's *Variations* as a metaphor for the structure of DNA, which, with its four recurring nucleotides, is responsible for the apparently limitless diversity of life forms. *Operation Wandering Soul* (1993) is the story of an overstressed surgical resident, Richard Kraft, who works in a hospital's children's ward. Kraft develops a relationship with a therapist on that ward, Linda Espera, whose therapy involves recounting stories of endangered children to the young patients. Interspersed with these stories, and those of the often terminally-ill patients themselves, is that of the gradual awakening of Kraft's repressed childhood memories. *Galatea 2.2* (1995) is narrated by a character named Richard Powers who, after living in the Netherlands for seven years, has returned as a visiting professor to an American university, where he studied as an undergraduate. There he meets a professor, Philip Lentz, who persuades Richard to take part in an experiment involving teaching a computer to learn enough English and English literature to pass the Master's Comprehension Exam. During the experiment, the narrator contemplates issues surrounding intelligence, technology and, in John Updike's words, "the linguistic and perceptual intricacies underlying consciousness."

Critical Reception

Although critical reaction to Powers's works has generally been positive, some commentators have suggested the intellectual and scientific demands of Powers's novels may limit the size of his audience. Negative commentary has referred to uninspiring characters, thin plots, and overdone wordplay. As Meg Wolitzer observed: "To read [Powers's] work is to be wowed by his verbal muscularity and by his ability to stitch seemingly disparate elements into a larger metaphorical fabric. But sometimes we don't want to be wowed. Sometimes we just want quiet." However, the majority of critics have described Powers as brilliant, often comparing him to such diverse writers as Thomas Pynchon and John Updike. Reviewers have also praised the style of his prose, his facility with numerous narrative voices, and the complexity of his narrative structures and themes. After the publication of *Operation Wandering Soul* in 1993, Sven Birkerts wrote: "In a few short years—in literary terms overnight—Richard Powers has vaulted from promise to attainment. . . . Powers must now be seen as our most energetic and gifted novelist under 40."

PRINCIPAL WORKS

Three Farmers on Their Way to a Dance (novel) 1985
Prisoner's Dilemma (novel) 1988
The Gold Bug Variations (novel) 1991
Operation Wandering Soul (novel) 1993
Galatea 2.2 (novel) 1995

CRITICISM

Marco Portales   (review date 1 September 1985)

SOURCE: A review of *Three Farmers on Their Way to a Dance,* in *The New York Times Book Review,* September 1, 1985, p. 14.

[*In the following review, Portales offers a mixed assessment of* Three Farmers on Their Way to a Dance.]

[**Three Farmers on Their Way to a Dance,** Powers's first novel,] is an extended meditation provoked by a May 1914 picture taken by the photographer August Sander of three young German men on their way to a dance. Mr. Powers's nameless narrator becomes fascinated by the photograph and creates the World War I experiences of the young men. The novel chronicles five lives—those of the three farmers in the photograph, the narrator (an "amateur historian" trained in physics), and a character named Peter Mays, a copy editor for a computer design magazine. Mr. Powers allows the narrator and Mays to make their separate ways toward the significance the photograph has for each of them. Sentence by sentence and page by page, the work shows Mr. Powers to good advantage. His writing engages, and his re-creation of the characters' thoughts captures postmodern, fragmented 1980's consciousness well. The attractive, initial photographic conceit, however, is overdone at 352 pages, and the technique requires an involvement that the characters do not inspire. Subjects such as history, photography, art, esthetics, perception, Joyce, Melville, Henry Ford and others, while initially stimulating to readers, finally are left unconnected to the events in the novel. And we are not told why the narrator should be interested in tracing "a path back to the world of the First War." At one point, he confesses he cannot remember the "urgency of the picture" and has "lost sight of the end" of his research and his attempts to extrapolate subsequent events from the photograph. When the narrator arrives at this juncture in Chapter 7 of a 27-chapter novel, readers can only ask "Whither?" and worse, "Why?"

George Kearns   (review date Spring 1986)

SOURCE: "Revolutionary Women and Others," in *The Hudson Review,* Vol. XXXIX, No. 1, Spring, 1986, pp. 122-34.

[*In the following excerpt, Kearns favorably reviews* Three Farmers on Their Way to a Dance, *calling Powers "an archeologist of imagination and style."*]

It isn't often that a novelist makes a debut with a work as ambitious and dazzling as Richard Powers' **Three Farmers on Their Way to a Dance**. It is a work of such complex structure, managed easily and with enormous assurance, that an attempt to describe it other than sketchily would take several paragraphs. The frontispiece reproduces a striking photograph made in 1914 of three young men, hatted, carrying canes, posed but pretending casually to have halted as they walk along a dirt path. The dance they are on their way to, we discover, was a village *fête*, but also the First World War as Dance of Death. The picture is by August Sander, a German engaged in a vast idealistic photographic project which he called *Man in the Twentieth Century*. Two decades later his work was burned by the Nazis, and a decade further on most of his forty thousand negatives were destroyed by looters. Powers "reads" the photograph with love, patience, and imagination, and I found myself turning back to it over and over, watching it become part of his text and the text become part of it. From this picture, this *donnée*, Powers spins a splendid fiction. The lives of the three young men are reconstructed for us, each taking on a moving specificity. Their stories are interleaved with those of two young Americans in the 80s, one of whom sees the photo in a museum in Detroit and becomes obsessed with it, the other of whom writes for a second-rate computer magazine in Boston. The three layerings move in and out, counterpointing each other in surprising, ingenious ways. Powers is a learned writer, with an extraordinary range of reference, and his book is a prolonged, even profound meditation on the history of our century. He has the true gift of the writer of fiction, one that I think no labor can produce, the ability to create illusions of reality with economy of means. If you admire the best fictions of Guy Davenport, as I do enormously, you will like *Three Farmers on Their Way to a Dance*. Like Davenport, Powers is an archeologist of imagination and style.

Gregory L. Morris   (review date Spring 1986)

SOURCE: A review of *Three Farmers on Their Way to a Dance*, in *Prairie Schooner*, Vol. 60, No. 1, Spring, 1986, p. 108.

[*Morris is an American writer, editor, educator, and critic whose works include* A World of Order and Light: The Fiction of John Gardner *(1984). In the following review, he discusses the structure of the three narratives within* Three Farmers on Their Way to a Dance.]

With his first published novel, *Three Farmers on Their Way to a Dance,* Richard Powers manages both a technical and an intellectual achievement. The novel is a triple narrative, three stories linked superficially by a photograph: a portrait of three young Prussians on their way to a country dance. But this surface-level link dives far deeper, establishing a profound connection among the three stories, the photo passing through hands and through time to become a symbol of this "tortured century." One narrative (a triple narrative in itself) traces the confused lives of the three men in the photograph—three men on their way to a far more serious and deadly dance than the one they had imagined attending. The remaining two narratives take place in contemporary America, but Powers deftly and intriguingly connects the protagonists in these two separate stories to the three men in the other story, cutting across time and events—by way of the photo—to create a synchronous and reflexive history.

This idea of repetition and replication of experience, of "recursive loops" in the linear course of time, is central to the novel. The three farmers are caught, frozen in the cam-

era's flash in the midst of a puzzled walk into World War I. As the War evolves, each of the three men is either swallowed by the fierce insanity of events, or impelled through it all, only to emerge with totally new, adopted identities—a sort of ritual of extinction or redefinition of Self. Yet the War is (in the words of Charles Péguy) a "trigger point," one of those events which sends the century reeling and looping back on itself, which eternally recurs as a force and an image throughout the century. Thus, the two men who move through the centers of the remaining narratives find themselves inexplicably caught up in and obsessed with the War, with the photo, with anachronistic emblems of the century's second decade. More important, they discover their own links of kinship and consciousness with the men in the photograph, as time circles backwards, defining as it goes the unrealized pasts of these two contemporary American men.

This is a remarkably accomplished first novel. As a technical, structural experiment, the book generally succeeds, despite the occasional staginess of some of the narrative. More exciting and more satisfying, though, is the intellectual stamina of the book; both story and idea engage the reader, lure him in to the web of time and mystery and connection that is the real fabric of this very fine book.

John Clute   (review date 11-17 March 1988)

SOURCE: "Photo-finish," in *The Times Literary Supplement,* No. 4432, March 11-17, 1988, p. 276.

[*In the following review, Clute offers a mixed assessment of* Three Farmers on Their Way to a Dance.]

Three young farmers are walking along a mud track in the Rhineland in the spring of 1914, on their way to a dance in the nearby village. A passing photographer named August Sander shoots them, as part of his great project to assemble a photographic catalogue, *Man of the Twentieth Century*. The three farmers stare at us from before the watershed of the First World War with a naive, comical, solemn gaze. So much, more or less, is history.

It can be assumed that Sander's three young Rhinelanders thought they were *en route* to no more than a springtime festival. For Richard Powers, whose *Three Farmers on Their Way to a Dance* generates a most elaborate fiction from the photograph, the dance they are about to enter is of course the Great War. As for a similar *naif*—Hans Castorp at the close of *The Magic Mountain*—the "desperate dance" of that war will soon deafen the long centuries of Europe. Adolphe, Peter and Hubert, who—strangely greened—grace the dust jacket, may be unconvincing heroes for a novel whose ambition it is to make a significant stab at portraying the century; and indeed Powers spends only a third of his text on the trio, two of whom die before seeing combat. One survives, but only by becoming a kind of *picaro*, homeless, innocent, agile, with as many names as hats. It is he who meets a more formidable innocent survivor, Henry Ford himself, whose 1915 peace mission to Europe provides Powers with more ironies and more complexities of pathos than he is entirely capable of handling.

Three Farmers is made up of three alternating narrative lines. The story of Sander's farmers makes up the first. In the second, a first-person narrator finds himself stranded in Detroit in the 1980s, becomes haunted by Sander's photograph, finally manages to generate a connection between one of the farmers and Henry Ford. In the third, a young American named Peter Mays, who closely resembles and who may be thought of as a fictionalized version of the narrator, discovers himself to be the direct descendent of Peter, the surviving farmer, to whom Ford has left some sort of legacy.

The remainder of the story is insufficiently complex to warrant so perilously elaborate a structure for its telling, and it gradually becomes clear that for Powers the tales of the two Peters have been offered to the reader as objects of what one might call theatrical contemplation. For the narrator, caught in Detroit, the final mystery endowing Sander's photograph with such force is not the story it may conceal; rather, he is gripped by the metaphysic of the gaze, by the farmers' ignorant but profound regard, by the urgency of their demand somehow to be recovered from the other side of the abyss, a demand he feels compelled to honour.

It is of course an impossible task. There is no understanding the past's final detail, and there is no truth in the theatre of art beyond the last page of the book. The family history of the narrator dissolves, on close scrutiny, into gibberish; if Peter Mays does eventually find an ancestor, it must be remembered that both the ancestor and Peter Mays are fabrications of the narrator; and if the three farmers are given names, nationalities and deaths, these are bestowed by the author of *Three Farmers on Their Way to a Dance* on himself.

As a buttonholing, monotone thinker of ill-achieved "important" thoughts, Powers is a typical American writer of the post-modern era. The ruminativeness of his approach to the mysteries of time and identity almost dissolves the objects of his approach into chimerae. But the novel does work: the story does (just) hold on, the dance does (just) manage to continue to the end of the page, and into the abyss of the century, while the farmers continue to gaze at what they do not know is to come.

Ursula Hegi   (review date 13 March 1988)

SOURCE: "What's the Matter With Eddie?" in *The New York Times Book Review*, March 13, 1988, pp. 15-16.

[*A German-born American, Hegi is a novelist and critic. In the following review, she discusses the characters in* Prisoner's Dilemma.]

A father lies with his four children on the frozen November earth, quizzing them on the names of the constellations. They rest against his body, and he points a flashlight to the dark sky "as if the light goes all the way out to the stars themselves. . . . The rest is a blur, a rich, confusing picture book of too many possibilities."

In the first four pages of *Prisoner's Dilemma,* Richard Powers's prose is sensuous, vivid and clear as he establishes the essence of the relationship between Eddie Hobson and his children. Why then is much of his novel told in language that's stilted and cumbersome?

If Mr. Powers has attempted to match his prose to the emotional development of his characters, the members of a dysfunctional family, he has taken a considerable risk. Their feelings have become numbed by years of forming protective scaffolding around the father, who extracts from them a conspiracy of silence toward his illness, which may be the result of radiation exposure at Alamogordo and whose symptoms are never identified. A history teacher, Eddie both captivates and keeps his distance from his wife and children with riddles and diverts them from addressing his illness until they can only focus on his evasion.

As in any dysfunctional family, the price of silence is exorbitant: Eddie's wife and children prop him up at the expense of their own emotional peace. Yet Eddie Hobson is not a villain. An "emaciated, fat man," he cares for his family with distracted affection, quoting Sterne, Kipling, Eliot and Frost to his children.

When they finally confront his illness and make him promise to enter a hospital, the characters begin to communicate on a deeper level. They unfold, become real. In their shared grief they are startled by the "connection between them that could reach down at leisure and destroy them." The change in the characters is reflected by language that loses much of its stiffness.

But by then Mr. Powers has given us nearly half a book with limited characters. It's not surprising when the 18-year-old Eddie Jr. describes his family to his girlfriend as "The close-to-the chest older brother. The testy, ex-radical big sis. Sis number two, everybody's favorite flake. The patient, long-suffering mom. All lost in orbit around the master of ceremonies."

Prisoner's Dilemma concerns itself with the same fascinating theme as Mr. Powers's first novel, *Three Farmers on Their Way to a Dance:* the impact of history on contemporary life and the predicament of the individual imprisoned by the sum of history. World War II forms the backdrop for the present lives of Eddie Hobson and his family. Geographical boundaries are closer drawn than in Mr. Powers's first novel; instead of three young men on their way to a German village dance—a metaphor for the greater dance, World War I—16-year-old Eddie carries the trauma of World War II into his adult life. He marries a compliant woman, has four children and creates a safe, fictitious world, Hobstown, which he keeps secret from his family, like his developing illness.

Dictating episodes into a tape recorder, Eddie covers Roosevelt, Stalin, the 1939 New York World's Fair, Dachau, Picasso and Mickey Mouse. In his world, Walt Disney is the real war hero, "the finest provider of escape from the confusing, opaque, overwhelming, paralyzing . . . times."

One of the most powerful parts of *Prisoner's Dilemma* is Eddie's account of the internment of Japanese-Americans in 1942, their forcible removal from their homes and their humiliation in the concentration camps. Eddie records their history not only as it was, but as it could have been if Walt Disney and Mickey Mouse had taken on the rescue of thousands of Japanese-Americans in a movie.

When Eddie's older son, Artie, a law student, listens to the tapes for the first time, he perceives Hobstown as a "web of bewildering invention designed for its curative power alone." Artie—flippant and cold in the early part of the novel—resents his father's need that has pulled him back to his family in De Kalb, Ill., when he should be studying his law books in Chicago.

His sister Lily has returned to her parents' home after 10 months of marriage to a man who tried to control her by threatening suicide. One of Mr. Powers's most successfully drawn characters, Lily resents her father's manipulation through illness and his "black humor as he slowly . . . erased himself for good from this place." She finds an odd sense of comfort in hiding inside a doll's palace, filling the building with her body.

Her older sister, Rachel, tries to adapt to her father's illness with humor and sarcasm. "Why fight the man when he is feeling so good?" Since Mr. Powers keeps explaining her character instead of letting her evolve, Rachel remains sketchy throughout the novel.

Eddie Jr. is the only one of the Hobson children who feels comfortable bringing friends home. To him his father's fits have become a tradition, though "a little more devastating every year." If the illness were real, he believes, his father would have died long ago. Ailene, his mother, is good-natured and confused. "Her husband's trail of crises brought out the best in her. . . . His suffering required her. . . . She gladly traded steady income for a cause." Though she finds the courage to ask her husband to enter a hospital, she is so self-deprecating that she comes close to being a stereotype.

Mr. Powers, whose first novel was a finalist for the National Book Critics Circle Award in 1985, explores an interesting theory of time in both novels. Time does not happen sequentially but exists all at once—past, present, future—in layers, a concept like the one developed by Hermann Hesse in *Siddhartha.* This complex treatment of time makes history the most significant character in Mr. Powers's new novel. Despite its uneven prose, **Prisoner's Dilemma** gives an absorbing view of history, "that most abstract, detached, impersonal, and curatorial of disciplines."

Patrick Parrinder   (review date 17 March 1988)

SOURCE: "Verbing a Noun," in *London Review of Books,* Vol. 10, No. 6, March 17, 1988, pp. 17-18.

[*Parrinder is an English critic and educator who has written numerous works on H. G. Wells and science fiction. In the following excerpt, he offers a mixed assessment of* Three Farmers on Their Way to a Dance, *which he calls "a carnivalesque, Post-Modernist historical novel."*]

In 1910 the German photographer August Sander began work on a never-to-be-completed ethnographic project which he called *Man of the 20th Century.* This grandiose scheme provides one of the sources of Richard Powers's first novel. The title, **Three Farmers on Their Way to a Dance,** refers to a photograph of young men in felt hats and starched collars walking along a country road, which Sander took in May 1914. . . . [Powers is a novelist who] is burdened by history, and for whom the central theme of modern life is our own historical self-consciousness. The 20th century, for [this] writer, is the historical century *par excellence.* The 19th, by contrast, was less exhaustively documented and now seems to have been nourished on chauvinistic legends rather than the brutality of facts.

For 'facts', however, we must doubtless read 'representations'. These representations, in modern times, have been overwhelmingly photographic in nature. Even the literary and narrative arts have (as is well-known) been transformed by cinematic techniques. Storytelling is shot through with notions of the frame, the picture, and the narrator-as-camera. Whether or not it is true that, as Powers writes, 'the century has become *about* itself, history about history,' it is the modes of representation as much as the sequence of events which have created our image of the times in which we live. . . .

Richard Powers is an American writer whose quest for 20th-century history is also a quest for European origins. August Sander's photograph of the three farmers, discovered by the first-person narrator of one of this novel's interlocking strands in a Detroit museum, is an apparently arbitrary starting-point. Powers's extrapolation of the lives of the three men forms a second strand, an unexpected and richly imaginative one. . . . In the novel there are two surviving prints of the photograph, one of which is found by the narrator, and the other by a computer journalist called Peter Mays, who discovers it in Chicago among some family heirlooms. In a novel full of intellectual, descriptive and stylistic diversions, these two figures take us down some remarkable by-roads. The three farmers are somehow linked with the *Peace Ship* in which Henry Ford and a team of do-gooders sailed to Europe in 1915; still more obscurely, they are linked with the later career of Sarah Bernhardt. Mays finds the Sander photograph together with a letter from Henry Ford which encourages him to go straight to Detroit to claim his share of the Ford Company's millions.

He receives his trust fund, however, in an unexpected form. Changes of identity and costume abound; the staid image of the three farmers in their antique Sunday suits may be contrasted, for example, with a contemporary one-woman show, *I dwell in possibility,* to which Mays's quest also takes him. In *I dwell in possibility* the actress, who is famed for her Sarah Bernhardt impersonations, appears in quick succession as, among others, Gertrude Stein, Isadora Duncan, and Nurse Cavell waiting to be shot by the Germans.

In Powers's more strictly historical narrative, two of the three farmers—supposedly Germans from the Rhineland—turn out to be nothing of the sort. Hubert, of indeterminate nationality, crosses the border into Belgium and gets himself meaninglessly shot by a party of soldiers a few hours before the First World War breaks out. (If, as is possible, he was actually German, he could be said to have started it all.) Peter, technically German but resident in

Holland, evades military service by exchanging identities with a Dutch war correspondent who has just been ordered to Paris. One of Peter's journalistic tasks is to cover the Peace Mission, where he earns the gratitude of a bored and bewildered Harry Ford; they have a shared interest in motor-cars. While in Paris he takes up press photography, but his best pictures, like Harry Beech's, are necessarily suppressed by the authorities. Finally there is Adolphe, the most Svejk-like of these three Unknown Non-Soldiers. He is the Good German who joins up and finds himself taking part in a massacre of Belgian villagers, whereupon he deserts his regiment and, in his turn, gets himself shot. At the beginning the three were all on their way to a dance, and their sweethearts (not to mention their sweethearts' manifold underclothes) also have a part to play in the narrative. Without them, it is clear, one of the prints of Herr Sander's photograph could never have ended up in an attic in Chicago. We are told how it got there, more or less, but this carefully-assembled narrative is no sooner put together than the narrator begins to dissolve it again into its constituent fictions.

This, then, is a carnivalesque, Post-Modernist historical novel, which threads its way through some rather hectic changes of style. Some sections are more in the mode of discursive essays. Chapter 19, 'The Cheap and Accessible Print', tells you more about the cultural impact of the photograph than you probably wanted to know. The early chapters, especially those set in the offices of the computer journal *Micro Monthly News,* are distinctly frenetic. 'Not content to verb a noun,' we read at one point, 'Delaney was moved by the extent of boss Powell's crime into participling one.' The author does as much sometimes. He has some authentically burlesque stylistic touches. The ten million First World War victims 'would not rise again', we are told, 'from the cratered mud': but then a few pages later two German military policemen peering through a tobacconist's window are described as 'leaving a cratered battlefield of Bavarian greased nose prints on the pane'. Not everything in this irreverent, imaginative and rather too crowded novel comes off nearly as well as that. But *Three Farmers* pays genuine tribute to August Sander's Teutonically thorough and slightly dotty photographic project in a manner as far removed from Sander's horizons as it possibly could be.

Richard Locke   (review date 10 April 1988)

SOURCE: "Father Knows Best," in *Book World—The Washington Post*, Vol. XVII, No. 15, April 10, 1988, p. 5.

[*Locke is an American educator and critic. In the following review, he summarizes* Prisoner's Dilemma *and notes that Powers has "an intense command of significant realistic details that can easily be assimilated to a larger symbolic pattern."*]

[*Prisoner's Dilemma*—an] unusually attractive and ambitious book by Richard Powers, whose first, *Three Farmers on Their Way to a Dance,* was warmly praised when it appeared three years ago, is an exceptionally loving fictional portrait of an American father and, simultaneously, a work of moral philosophy in the guise of a domestic novel

with all the artful warmth and clutter we expect in the age of Updike. As it describes a family coping with Dad's fatal illness, it deploys the nostalgic paraphernalia of American popular culture from the World's Fair of 1939 (especially its vision of "The World of Tomorrow," GM's exhibit, Futurama) through the Home Front and VJ Day right down to the end of 1978. It scatters literary references around with ease—to Eliot, Kipling, Yeats, Boccaccio, Rilke—but it's equally at home with game theory, riddles, puzzles and paradoxes.

The prisoner's dilemma of the title is a puzzle the central character—Eddie Hobson, a 52-year-old high school history teacher suffering from a mysterious debility—springs on his family at dinner one November night in 1978. An eccentric domestic quizmaster, he always plays teasing, taunting verbal games that express and conceal his needs and sorrows even as they test his wife and children's affection and intelligence. The "prisoner's dilemma" is evidently a clue to Dad's disease.

Two men are accused of criminal activities, but there's not enough evidence to convict them. They are put in separate cells, and each is offered a deal: if you rat on the other guy, you'll go free, but if you remain silent, you'll still be brought to trial and disgraced. What should they do? Silence is best, but how can each trust the other? Rational self-interest favors the rat, but if both rat, they both fry. What's needed is "crackpot realism": the only way to beat conviction is through the conviction that the other guy, like you, will keep quiet, keep mutual faith.

The puzzle uses reason to defeat reason, to leap over rational self-interest and achieve community despite the prisoners' isolation. As Hobson the history teacher makes abundantly clear, the puzzle packs a wallop—particularly for him, the American Everyman whose dream of the brotherly World of Tomorrow was blackened by such mistrustful acts as the internment of 112,000 Japanese Americans in concentration camps in 1942 and by the detonation of the atom bomb at White Sands, New Mexico, in 1945 (where Hobson was briefly posted).

We've moved thematically from the Hobson dinner table in DeKalb, Illinois, to the nuclear negotiating table, from reason's riddles to faith, hope, and charity in "the age of anxiety." The phrase "Hobson's choice" refers to a 17th-century liveryman who always made customers choose the horse nearest the door—"Hobson's choice" is no choice at all, its freedom is illusory. Eddie Hobson, however, is trying to win his freedom, to escape from the solitary confinement of rational self-interest into the sustaining community of trust. His brain teasers express his own isolation, his sense that history is a double bind, his search for a way to connect individual and group experience, to make one act of trust ameliorate a world of self-destructive mutual suspicion.

Such explications tend to strip the novel's themes down to shivering formulas; in fact, they tend to exfoliate dramatically. Eddie Hobson's riddles erupt out of family banter and mundane concerns: the book is very much a novel, not a dialogue. It's filled with squabbles and memories, the private codes and jokes of husband and wife and the four kids now (mostly) in their twenties. The author works hard to give us five points of view and voices quite different from Eddie Hobson's.

Most of this realistic action, more the stuff of a John Irving novel than a Robert Coover metafiction, takes place over two weekends. In the first, Eddie Hobson finally decides to see a doctor about his ailment: his sudden fainting fits, his fever, vomiting, hallucinations, bleeding gums, purple spots on the skin (like plague spots, he lets his son know). In the second weekend, the family takes him to see the Christmas window displays in Chicago and accompanies him to the VA hospital where he's committed. In a final flurry of action, he takes off for parts unknown, challenging the family to deduce his final destination from the hints he's left behind: one son performs the deduction on Christmas morning as another travels into the New Mexico desert toward ground zero.

The chief device Powers employs to expand the scale of his novel is to give us excerpts from an ongoing autobiographical fantasia Eddie Hobson has been dictating into a tape recorder ever since his disease first brought him down: the story of his life from World's Fair to VJ day interwoven with a fantasy about a Walt Disney propaganda film starring Eddie and Mickey Mouse that itself retells the history of Eddie's exemplary suffering life. It's in these sections that the pop culture of the Home Front and the imprisonment of the Japanese Americans come to the fore.

But the major figures in these half-imagined flashbacks—besides Eddie himself from 13 to 19—are Walt Disney and Mickey Mouse. "The finest provider of escape" in the 30's and 40's plays a central role in Hobson's—and the author's—imagination. Mickey is, for example, the sorcerer's apprentice in *Fantasia* whose every attempt to stop unruly magic power leads further into disaster: as Mickey splits each errant broomstick like an atom, their number doubles till it seems the Flood is come again. Such allusions suggest that art makes cowards of us all—and affords communal meditation on our common fate.

[*Prisoner's Dilemma*] is written with great fluency and speed, and for the most part resists the tendency to bog down in comfy details, logic games, or surreal set pieces. At times the author might have intensified his effects by increasing the momentum of the 1978 narrative and exercising even more structural (not merely thematic or metaphorical) control. And such summaries as these do turn up: "His story was the attempt to answer the question, unbearable, of how he could go on living while another suffered even the smallest indignity of distrust. Dad was trying, in the tape, to cure the permanent condition of mistrust the world fast embraced by creating a domain where escalating suspicion had no place. . . . As the fable went on, it slowly changed from being about the disease of history to being the story of his father, sick with that disease." But such declarations of intent are relatively infrequent.

Powers has great novelistic gifts—an ear for speech that expresses character, an intense command of significant realistic details that can easily be assimilated to a larger symbolic pattern, a stylistic range and control that can cope with Alan Turing, Kraitchik's paradox, a ouija board, a grocery list and Walt Disney's magic kingdom—and still sound like one narrator.

In this embarrassment of riches, one senses a writer who has learned from both Updike and Pynchon and seems about to change from sorcerer's apprentice to sorcerer himself. One of the most moving lines in the book is the old riddle "When is a door not a door? When it's ajar." This becomes a wonderful metaphor for the novelistic imagination, and a reader might well be forgiven if he finds himself imagining that Richard Powers himself now stands on a high threshold.

Powers on being a writer:

The kind of life I'm trying to live is one where everything I read is valuable in some way, contributes to what I'm trying to do. The real glory of making a living as a writer is that there's no sickening divide, as there is for most people, between what you do and what you want to do. . . . I realize most people don't have that luxury.

Richard Powers, in an interview in Publishers Weekly, *16 August 1991.*

Tom LeClair (review date 25 April 1988)

SOURCE: "The Systems Novel," in *The New Republic,* Vol. 198, No. 17, April 25, 1988, pp. 40-2.

[*LeClair is an American writer and educator. In the following review of* Prisoner's Dilemma, *he states that "Powers is the most accomplished practitioner" of what he calls "the 'systems novel,' a fiction that uses postmodern techniques to model the dense and tangled relations of modern history, politics, and science."*]

Too few words have been written by and too many about the carved-down school of fiction, 1980s minimalism. Richard Powers's second novel, *Prisoner's Dilemma,* offers an excellent occasion to identify those novelists first publishing in the decade who fill the gaps the minimalists leave in their fiction and in our literary environment. Among writers such as John Calvin Batchelor (*The Further Adventures of Halley's Comet, The Birth of the People's Republic of Antarctica*), Ron Loewinsohn (*Magnetic Field(s), Where All the Ladders Start*), Ted Mooney (*Easy Travel to Other Planets*), Kathryn Kramer (*A Handbook for Visitors from Outer Space*), and William Vollmann (*You Bright and Risen Angels*), Powers is the most accomplished practitioner of what I call the "systems novel," a fiction that uses postmodern techniques to model the dense and tangled relations of modern history, politics, and science.

William Gaddis, Thomas Pynchon, Joseph McElroy, Don DeLillo, and John Barth originated the systems novel in the 1970s with what Barth termed "maximal" books, difficult information-retrieval novels that envisioned huge ecological and cultural wholes. Minimalists, perhaps in response, turned to small personal parts. I present this two-sentence history of two decades because Powers's subject in *Prisoner's Dilemma* and in his first novel, *Three Farmers on Their Way to a Dance,* is cultural scale—modern history as a "rift torn between big and little," the massive and the minute. His achievement in both novels is building a place, as he puts it in *Prisoner's Dilemma,* "where little can trickle into big," where the personal becomes historical.

Powers and the other young system novelists recognize, I think, the dinosaurian demands on diminishing literacy that the maximalists imposed. Powers adapts, makes his novels both large and accessible, formally interesting and profoundly informed, composed and urgent. He creates richly specified little people whose lives trickle into the large motions of history. He connects family plots with the geopolitics of two world wars. And he demonstrates how everyday technologies (photography, movies, computers) and esoteric scientific theories have magnified the scale of contemporary history and politics. Powers's knowledge of "two cultures" and more gives him, along with the other systems novelists, purchase on the future and power over readers who may have thought that less was more.

The best metaphor for Powers's range and purpose is what he calls the "Butterfly Effect, that model of random motion describing how a butterfly flapping its wings in Peking propagates an unpredictable chain reaction of air currents, ultimately altering tomorrow's weather in Duluth." This figurative butterfly was discovered by Edward Lorenz and is explained by James Gleick in his recent book *Chaos,* an introduction to the new science of chaos that uncovers implausible orders in random events, finds often beautiful patterns among minute particulars, and generates new relations between the far and the near.

Three Farmers on Their Way to a Dance (which was nominated for a fiction award by the National Book Critics Circle and won a special citation from the PEN/Hemingway Foundation) is a remarkable work of historical reconstruction, butterflying out from the lives of three European peasants on the eve of World War I to make connections with the larger world and with us, an ocean and decades away. *Prisoner's Dilemma* is a better novel, more mature and assured, more in control of the narrative frames that Powers employs for his butterfly effect. It is also a more passionate book. A hybrid of Updike's elegiac *The Centaur* and Barthelme's suspicious *The Dead Father, Prisoner's Dilemma* revolves around a dying father, a man shrinking in physical size and growing in influence. Edward Hobson—52-year-old former schoolteacher, husband, father of four children, wanderer and collector of information—resembles, Powers quite explicitly suggests late in the novel, his own father, the man who is photographed with his children on the dust jacket.

Prisoner's Dilemma opens with a lyrical and immediately engaging flashback that introduces Hobson's and Powers's scale of interests. Hobson points a weak flashlight into the cold night sky, identifying constellations for his small children and reminding them of the huge spaces between the stars, a strategy of both giving and taking away

knowledge that characterizes his life and death. The present of the novel is late 1978. Edward's recurring fainting spells have worsened, and two of his children—Artie, a 25-year-old law student, and Rachel, a 23-year-old actuary—have come home to DeKalb to see him, their mother, and two children still living at home, the just-divorced Lily and high school senior Eddie. During this weekend visit and a Christmas reunion in Chicago, the family tries to decide what to do about Edward's health.

From the Hobsons' response to this common crisis, Powers evolves a subtle plot of sibling and generational conflicts. Its events, like most of our actions, are communications, messages sent and unsent through the Hobson loop. The characters are both ordinary and memorable as Powers delicately manages to make Edward's wife and children individuals and "prisoners," free persons and products of Edward's large influence. The children, like their seemingly simple mother and seemingly complex father, begin as pairs. But as the novel progresses, serious Artie and frivolous Rachel, depressed Lily and happy-go-lucky Eddie exchange qualities, turn into one another, turn into other Hobson pairs, and form by the novel's end a dense Venn diagram of Hobson—and American—family life. Readers accustomed to minimalist mumblers may find the Hobson children an old-fashioned set of talkers and doers, but in fact they are an American family Robinson, marooned by their father's attempt to head a family that can simultaneously exist in and resist Mediamerica.

Edward Hobson, a man often absent to his family when physically present and always in mind when away, appears in three alternating frames: in the 1978 chapters (which constitute about half the novel), in his children's recorded memories of him, and in his tape recordings about "Hobstown," his imaginary community that reveals how history, politics, and science brushed their butterfly wings on Edward over the course of his life. Imbued with the 1939 World's Fair faith in the future, Edward is traumatized by the randomness of survival—stunned by his only brother's death in a stateside military accident and his own accidental presence at Alamogordo when the atomic bomb was tested, an event that, in Powers's imagination, turned the wide and varied world into a single prison.

After the war, Edward attempts to live in and change what he calls, under the influence of Walt Disney, "World World," the pleasure prison of entertainment America constructed to counter global facts. As "the last generalist," Edward instructs his high school students in "big picture" history and uncovers the secrets of America's past, including the shameful internment of Japanese-Americans during the war. Frustrated by school boards, Edward makes his family his project, withdrawing from success to make his kids achievers, requiring them "to know everything" and illustrating the hopelessness of such knowledge. Emerging from the young Hobsons' memories is a tortured man who feels the world is "already lost" and yet tries to love it, who loves his little family but loses himself in imagined Hobstown.

Teaching the young not to be taught—that is Edward's paradoxical effect. In *Three Farmers* Powers advances the theory of cultural "trigger points," paradoxical events that occur "when the way a process develops loops back on the process and applies itself to its own source." Gödel's metamathematics, proving the incompleteness of any mathematics—including Gödel's—is one of Powers's examples. Hobson is a trigger personality, a father who proves to his children that he is not needed and thereby, in Powers's paradox, proves that his lesson of fatherly obsolescence *is* needed. Sentimental intellectual, master game-player, self-canceling authority, jailer and jail-house lawyer, Hobson is the most fascinating and imprisoning character I've met and not met (see his effect?) in years.

A former computer programmer and a student, it seems clear, of Douglas Hofstadter's dizzying recursions in *Gödel, Escher, Bach,* Powers takes his title from a game theory problem Edward presents one morning to his children. The problem posits two players in a mutually threatening situation. Their dilemma is whether to trust or to betray each other. The Hobson children see themselves as prisoners of a parallel dilemma as they confront their father's declining health: Should they trust him to eventually accept it or betray his independence?

As the novel progresses, the children discover on their own and learn from their father ways around what Powers identifies as a "Hobson's choice," the all of trust or the nothing of betrayal. Powers's butterfly accomplishment is connecting this family's dilemma with the global Hobson's choice of mutual assured destruction and with the Hobson children's responses to American culture. Will they choose the all of mass entertainment, consensus politics, and technological fantasies? The nothing of nonparticipation? Some compromise or alternative? These questions Powers leaves open at the novel's end.

"Crackpot Realism" is how the oldest Hobson child describes his response to the prisoner's dilemma, his trust in the paradoxical and unreasonable. The crackpot with his crazy theories of, say, chaos may just give us metasolutions to apparently binding realities. Powers is as informed about realities as Hobson could ask, and he has a crackpot imagination to rise above them and let us look back at our often imprisoning common sense. If he's not as artful a maker of sentences as some of his systems-novel colleagues, and even though he chooses to give *Prisoner's Dilemma* an unnecessarily plotted ending, Richard Powers is in 1988—like Thomas Pynchon with his historical *V.* and his political *Crying of Lot 49* in 1966—a major American novelist.

Maureen Howard   (review date 14 May 1988)

SOURCE: "Facing the Footage," in *The Nation,* New York, Vol. 246, No. 19, May 14, 1988, pp. 680-84.

[*Howard is an American author, critic, and editor whose works include* Expensive Habits *(1986). In the following excerpt, she details the multiple texts within* Prisoner's Dilemma.]

Prisoner's Dilemma begins with the stars. On a summer night a father demonstrates the celestial bodies to his children. A father instructing: Ed Hobson is, in fact, a high-school history teacher who is as familiar with Ursa Major as he is with the casts of 1940s movie musicals, his mind an omnium-gatherum, mostly of American culture, but the optical accident of pictures in the sky and a clever game of cards can be accommodated in his view. It is a view of the world made manageable through knowledge—counting by eights, *Robert's Rules of Order,* Shays' Rebellion or quoting great lines of not-so-great verse. Any Hobson at any moment could tell us it was Donna Reed in *It's a Wonderful Life* or finish off a quatrain of a Robert Service parody. At every meal four quick-witted kids have fed on their father's glut of information, and on paradoxes and palindromes, but life as a quiz show is no longer trivial pursuit. Ed Hobson denies the strange illness which has long rendered him unemployable and plagued the family fortunes. Now his children are presented with the big puzzle: What has made this inventive loner, this lovable, irritating paterfamilias into a swooning, often comatose figure whose only theater of operation is an A-frame house in De Kalb, Illinois? Dad is jailed, we might say. That answer is flat, given the dimensions of Powers's novel. Hobson's wife and children are prisoners, too, of his unrelenting puns and conundrums. With all its vitality, Big Ed's classroom has trapped them in a set of private references.

Artie, the eldest Hobson, at present in law school, has the first say (it's that scene under the stars): "My father is doing what he does best, doing the only thing he knew how to do in this life. He is quizzing us, plaguing his kids

---

An excerpt from *The Gold Bug Variations*

Ultimately, the *Goldbergs* [Johann Sebastian Bach's *The Goldberg Variations*] are about the paradox of variation, preserved divergence, the transition effect inherent in terraced unfolding, the change in nature attendant upon a change in degree. How necessity might arise out of chance. How difference might arise out of more of the same. By the time the delinquent parent aria returns to close out the set, the music is about how variation might ultimately free itself from the instruction that underwrites it, sets it in motion, but nowhere anticipates what might come from experience's trial run.

The relentlessly repeating thirty-two-note Base traces out that same unintentional contradiction in terms that Dr. Ressler read to us from the operations manual on the night we sat down to commit our crime. "These two procedures are exactly similar." "Exactly similar" elicited a laugh. But shouldn't "the same" get the same? "A is the same as B." Impossible. What Ressler listened to in that tightly bound, symmetry-laced catalog of unity was how nothing was the same as anything else. Each living thing defied taxonomy. Everything was its own, unique, irreducible classification.

The *Goldbergs* were his closest metaphor to the coding problem he gave his life to studying.

Richard Powers, in his The Gold Bug Variations, *Morrow, 1991.*

---

with questions. . . . We are out here alone, on a silver rock under the blank vacuum, with nothing but his riddles for our thin atmosphere." This is a memory. Sorting through his father's effects, Artie takes an elegiac tone, asking "why trying to know left him so fiercely alone and lost," and hearing one of his old man's answers, partial and insufficient, to "try to figure out where history has set you down." In the opening chapter, more afterword than foreword, the son resorts to the father's mode: "And I will ask what remains of my family how a person could move through life repeating, every year, the old perennials, the same chestnut riddles, the adored ore, the when-is-a-door-not-a-door? Then I will tell them, straight out, the answer, the treaty: when his mind is an evasive urgency. And ajar." Before the novel's brilliant unraveling we are granted aphoristic answers, but they are dense as Emersonian homilies, more complex suggestions than solutions, leaving the door to Ed Hobson's life of energetic failure, indeed, ajar.

In *Prisoner's Dilemma* Powers is interested in multiple texts, as he was in his first novel, ***Three Farmers on Their Way to a Dance,*** our brightest work of fiction since *Gravity's Rainbow*. In ***Three Farmers*** the quest, first to identify then to construe the historic moment when August Sander photographed three young Austrians on the eve of World War I, runs parallel to the zany pursuit of an intriguing redhead, costumed as Sarah Bernhardt and glimpsed for one moment in Boston on a quite contemporary Veterans' Day. Where will such disparate stories take us? Far, in Powers's fiction, to where the imagination and/or historical investigation take us; where "On First Looking into Chapman's Homer" took Keats; where a fleeting glance at Beatrice took Dante: to the place where the world that constructs us is reconstructed by us, to a figuring out where history has set us down. Parallel stories do intersect in ***Three Farmers*** as they do in *Bleak House* or *Lolita*. The thrill of coincidence is that it is almost magic. The decoding of the Sander photograph, the history it contains—real, inventive, interpretive—does, to our satisfaction and amazement, come to bear on the mock love story.

Prisoner's Dilemma presents us with a similar system. Artie Hobson's story of his father's life runs side by side with a text called "Hobstown," a consuming project that Ed Hobson has spoken into an old dictaphone over the years. We read Artie's version as a traditional first-person route, full of insights and a good deal of self-revelation, while the father's text is the creation of an alternate world. "Hobstown" is an enchantment in which Pop re-creates himself as Bud Middleton, an all-American boy. Bud—the stand-in, the double—is to be featured with his all-American family in promotions of the 1939 World's Fair, including a film on the glories of the Westinghouse time capsule, which Bud's dad calls "science's greatest gift to the world of the future." Powers, at 31, delivers a loaded World's Fair, as loaded as the time capsule buried in Flushing Meadows with the smug key to our accomplishments. Bud, a 13-year-old, is a perfect conduit for that naïve vision, an ideal fan of the technology that transformed "an ash dump into a model of the future."

We cut back to yet another text, the familiar third-person narrative of family life in which Artie is just one of the cast. The kids assemble in De Kalb. Being Hobsons, they are trained in speculation and have set the game plan to get Pop to a hospital when the old historian (he's only 51) comes downstairs, looking chipper, and in a masterful evasion gets them to contemplate the problem of the prisoner's dilemma, the damned-if-you-do, damned-if-you-don't proposition concerning trust. . . . An entertaining business—all choices are equally risky, and the kids are at it again, figuring, arguing, their mother distraught with their disputes.

As a family story, *Prisoner's Dilemma* is smart about this smart-talking family but open and compassionate too. We might think of Salinger's Glass family, less damaged, transferred to the heartland. Each child, while distinctly a Hobson, has made it out of the system. Artie has gone to law school (although that "on track" choice is not necessarily commendable in Hobsonian terms). Rachel parlays her mathematical gifts into work as an unorthodox actuary, but is hopelessly caught up in wisecracks, death-defying foot-on-the-pedal ploys. Where Rachel is tough, Lily is vulnerable. Divorced, returned home in defeat, Lily is the only Hobson who's had any real experience out there. Now she is paralyzed, often closed in her room, writing unsent letters to the woman next door, watching her neighbor check and recheck her locks. To Mrs. Swallow, Lily unfolds the history of her girlish marriage and the knowledge that she, too, understands her father is "inventing a protest, an alternative history, all the details tailored to suit him, alone." Lily appeals to Mrs. Swallow for some reason to live, even if it is only to "teach me that love for the trap that keeps you rattling the locks, refusing to quit resisting, to give up the senseless ritual as lost."

Come late to the table, Eddie Jr., still in high school, has escaped the set-apart feeling of his sibs. He is blessedly ordinary. Ailene, Ed Sr.'s wife, is an audience to what she has begot and her husband has put into play. "Mother is abiding," Lily writes. It is a fair summary of a woman who has loved and suffered the vicissitudes of life with a small-time, inoperative genius. Gently, Powers often includes her with the kids. Wisely, he knows that as the novel progresses toward the father's quite glorious demise, Ailene's sorrow must be separated out. Her loyalty to the man is of another order. She knows what Artie reconstructs, but not what ails her husband or where his escapist tactics will end.

The beginning of Ed Hobson's end was at Alamogordo, where, as a plain soldier, he stumbled out of an all-night acey-deucy game to see, in Artie's words, "a light more luminous than noon. The desert blooms. . . . The light effuses a bright, warm matrix of desire. . . . Everything has changed except my father's power to make any difference. . . . For my father, the brightness hangs on like this forever. For my dad, it stays bright for good."

To name Alamogordo, radiation poisoning, to hear the famous Oppenheimer quote from the *Bhagavad Gita*—"I am become Death, the destroyer of worlds"—to disclose the central event in Ed Hobson's life, the event that would make the Westinghouse time capsule into an unhappy bit of camp, does not close out this beautifully complex work.

Diagnosis is not remedial. These answers remain only as illuminating, or as evasive, as Artie's (and Powers's) wise take on the family, for it comes to them all at once that "Dad's sickness, from day one, came from his being the last man in the Northern Hemisphere who refused to think of the past as *over*. He had never followed the universal, self-protecting practice of flattening out the past, abstracting it, rendering it neuter and quaint." Neuter and quaint: a definition of nostalgia, the great American sickness.

Why, then, Hobson's cute rewrite of history, his alternate world? We read "Hobstown," breathtaking in its implication and invention, before the kids hear Pop's posthumous voice off the reels. Artie has referred to it as "Erewhon," but it is at once grander and more immediate than Butler's chip-on-the-shoulder whack at Victorian England. "Hobstown" is full of wonder, from little Bud at the World's Fair to the war, with all its grandstand bravery sucking us in like a neat old movie. But too much tragedy looms, and the lead role, Bud Middleton's, is passed on to young Ed Hobson himself. Enter, to sustain the American war effort, to project the American future, Walt Disney.

Yes, Walt. It is a stunning conception, at first hilarious with its grain of truth (Disney studios did make some of our propaganda flicks), but this Disney is a powerful fictional creation, an Undershaft, a Charlie Kane. In *Three Farmers,* Powers used Henry Ford's *Peace Ship* of 1915 as a historic/comedic connection. Here, Walt Disney becomes the fabricator of World World, a prefiguration of we-know-what: that "live-in monument to our ability to cross over from the unlivable emptiness of Here into a smaller world." World World, set down in the corn belt, is a magic alternative, a mini-America superior to the real thing, where Ed Hobson, chosen from all the G.I.s, will star—along with Mickey Mouse. Our greatest celebrity, the mouse, will conduct him away from the sham of World World, which now seems as shabby as a grade-school diorama. Mickey reveals to Eddie a vision of the future that is as hellish and recognizable as our own post-Alamogordo existence. Meanwhile, Walt prattles on, advising a safe, check-your-locks disengagement from the forces of evil, a moral move away from inner city to comfortable suburban concerns, but Eddie tapes over his message: "Let's start again, from scratch. Let us make a small world, a miniature of a miniature, say an even half-dozen, since we screw up everything larger. Let's model the daily workings of an unremarkable, mid-sized family, and see if we can't get it right. A family of six."

The novel's circle not yet complete, Powers extends this lovely metaphor of responsibility; each child in turn continues the text. "Somewhere, my father is teaching us the names of the constellations," Artie says. But wait: In a half-page chapter Richard Powers takes the mike and we are in yet another world, this the *real* De Kalb: "Dad has just died, of cancer, the previous winter. . . . Some of us blame his assignment at Alamogordo . . . I, the middle son . . . I have had an idea for how I might begin to make sense of the loss. The plans for a place to hide out in long enough to learn how to come back. Call it Powers World." A signature—van Eyck in the mirror, Hitchcock's brief appearance, Hockney's sneaker, Nabokov's *V. Sirin* inserted in the text.

But wait: We are never told, in the many solutions of ***Prisoner's Dilemma,*** if the reference to Hobson's choice alludes to the Milton elegy for the fellow who lined up his horses at the stable door and gave customers no choice or the Charles Laughton movie. They don't check up. They don't cancel each other, either. And, by gum, we should have been thinking all along of Thomas Hobbes's *Leviathan:* "A law of nature is a precept, or general rule, found out by reason, by which a man is forbidden to do that which is destructive of his life, or taketh away the means of preserving the same; and to omit that by which he thinketh it may be best preserved." ***Prisoner's Dilemma*** is a paradigm for the nuclear game, the only door left ajar by Hobbes's enlightened self-preservation, the dictates of right reason. Or, is Artie's last oracular pronouncement on his father's legacy the hard answer: "What we can't bring about in no way releases us from what we must." We finish this novel, as we do all grand fiction, ready to figure on.

Maureen Howard   (review date Winter 1988)

SOURCE: "Semi-Samizdat and Other Matters," in *The Yale Review,* Vol. 77, No. 2, Winter, 1988, pp. 243-58.

[*In the following excerpt, Howard favorably assesses* Three Farmers on Their Way to a Dance.]

[It] is not curious that a first novel that I consider the most alive and original in years, ***Three Farmers on Their Way to a Dance*** by Richard Powers, had to win a Rosenthal Award (for work that's been overlooked) as a corrective. Published by Beech Tree Press, a fine imprint of a very commercial house (Morrow), this intricate work was never touted like the Yuppie novels that will pass as surely as the kiwi slice that adorned nouvelle cuisine. (Rich, disaffected kids seem to amuse and never disturb, like mall music.) We can only imagine that Powers, who is not yet thirty—he must have two heads or not wear Giorgio Armani suits to good effect—is condemned to write so amazingly well offstage. Perhaps he has chosen to hide out, as J. D. Salinger and Thomas Pynchon did. ***Three Farmers*** is about history. I might even say it is a pursuit of history in the manner of Hawthorne: a compelling need to examine the past and, in that reach of the imagination, to face up to it and get it off one's back.

Both Powers's narrator (nameless) and a benched writer, Peter Mays, come across the same photo of three farmers taken by one of the pioneers of that craft, August Sander. One copy is in the Detroit Museum, and the other, Mays's, is thrown in with family stuff. That difference will be significant, for one of Powers's concerns is: How can we come at history and its artifacts, which are so endowed with the stamp of cultural and aesthetic approval, and yet feel a renewed urgency, a connection there? And to what extent are we responsible for discovering, in the seductive pursuit of merely personal history, a larger message? If I make ***Three Farmers*** sound heady and Powers a touch brainy—it is, and he is. But at the same time, the novel is also enormous fun to read, Pynchonesque in its vitality and splendid engagement with language. We've grown so accustomed to the young writing down to us and to themselves, taking all the pressure off with stances that are chic, cool, or rural, that reading *Three Farmers* is an exhilarating workout.

One of Powers's gifts, a complement to his entertaining complexity in matters of plot, is his ability to say, often and directly, what he intends, knowing that the deeper mysteries of fiction will in no way be diminished:

> The photo caption touched off a memory: *Three farmers on their way to a dance, 1914.* The date sufficed to show that they were not going to their expected dance. I was not going to my expected dance. We would all be taken blindfolded into a field somewhere in this tortured century and made to dance until we'd had enough. Dance until we dropped.

The novel is made comfortably large once again by a writer like Powers, who doesn't flinch at commentary or the essayistic turn:

> Yeats sat in the house on opening night [of *Ubu Roi*], cheering the play on against its detractors. Yet afterward, he wrote of feeling an extreme sadness. After the refinements of his own verse, of Bernhardt and Brahms, there had to be a reaction against so much beauty. Sadly, he wrote the century's obstetric: "After us, the Savage God."

> But Jarry and the *avant-garde* of the first decade were not so savage as they first appear. They are not so much antibourgeois as bourgeois *ad absurdum*. The artistic vanguard wedded the logic of the middle class to that class's unadmitted dreams. Jarry merely emphasized the underside of the intimacy brought on by mechanical reproduction: the camera, in encouraging us to identify with the photographed scene, *always* lied. It cropped, it recolored, it double-exposed. Lenses blurred the distinction between private dream and public, mass-reproduced logic.

All such stops in this novel are beautifully built in, and not mere asides or stage directions: all that accrues to the two young men chasing down the implications of the Sander photograph further enriches their reading and ours, as though in the recorded moment the old lens atop the tripod gives us back ourselves and we can, for some short duration, undo that which is mechanical and unlearned in our response. Not the least of Powers's skills is his ability to render historical figures without self-serving (Woody Allen) or arch (Gore Vidal) effect. Henry Ford's commercial genius and political cunning are part of a heritage in full possession of the narrator; while Sarah Bernhardt's legend, an absolute blank to Peter Mays, must be discovered with the thrill of a boy digging up arrowheads.

Jane Sutherland (review date 21-27 April 1989)

SOURCE: "Hobson's Last Tape," in *The Times Literary Supplement*, No. 4490, April 21-27, 1989, p. 436.

[*In the following excerpt, Sutherland offers a negative assessment of* Prisoner's Dilemma.]

There is great reach in *Prisoner's Dilemma,* but little grasp. Like his first, *Three Farmers on their Way to a Dance* . . . Richard Powers's second novel aims to create a poetics of history for an entire era; but in neither book has he fully managed to get his material into shape. The grand gestures of both are, therefore, oddly smudged. For all its stoutness, *Prisoner's Dilemma* seems a frail and lethargic vehicle for the task it addresses.

That task is nothing less than sorting out the implications of the Second World War. The scene is De Kalb, Illinois, in 1978, where the four children of Eddie Hobson have foregathered to witness the last stages of his fight against the falling sickness which has plagued him since 1945. Eddie himself is a kind of Socratic nanny to his offspring, plaguing them with conundrums they cannot master, torturing them with clues that the world is not kind, that something has gone wrong with the world. His central weapon in these assaults is the calculus of self-interest known as the Prisoner's Dilemma, which boils down to a question of trust. How can you trust another person? How can you trust another person to trust you?

Eddie's answer is contained in a series of tapes he leaves behind him after escaping from a local hospital and hitchhiking to New Mexico, where his difficulties with the century began at Alamogordo. For Eddie, the solution to the Prisoner's Dilemma lies in the past. In some detail, his tapes describe the making of an imaginary film in 1944 by an unreal Walt Disney; the star of *You Are the War* is the young Eddie Hobson, whose role Disney models on George Bailey in Frank Capra's script for the yet-unmade *It's a Wonderful Life*. Bailey (as eventually played by James Stewart) is a populist Everyman whose presence is essential for the maintenance of community and the triumph of the American way of life; and *You Are the War* expands that lesson to encompass the whole world. "Only connect!" says the loving (and historically false) Walt Disney, and the world will be saved. The Prisoner's Dilemma will be solved when everyone realizes that self-interest cannot win the day on our finite planet. And at this point the real, dying, elderly Eddie Hobson's tape stops short.

Just what his children are meant to make of this odd fabrication it is hard to know. Though Powers spends most of *Prisoner's Dilemma* on them, the novel repeatedly fails precisely at those points when connections must be made between Eddie Hobson's lifelong metaphysical hunt and the tedious mundanity of his children's lives in 1978. Matters are not helped by the children's mutual admiration, which Powers gives vent to in scenes so incestuously glutinous that one is painfully reminded of the Glass family in J. D. Salinger's later tales of narcissism unchained. More seriously, by fabricating a fake George Bailey, Powers trivializes Capra's mythopoeic *chef d'oeuvre*.

Patrick Parrinder (review date 18 May 1989)

SOURCE: "Austward Ho," in *London Review of Books*, Vol. 11, No. 10, May 18, 1989, pp. 12-13.

[*In the following excerpt, Parrinder states that "*Prisoner's Dilemma *is an intricate, wide-ranging tapestry drawing on the weightiest of historical themes; it is only a pity that its*

Richard Powers, as readers of **Three Farmers on their Way to a Dance** will know, is [a] young novelist full of ambition and ideas. What **Prisoner's Dilemma** sadly lacks, however, is [Paul] Auster's stylistic restraint and mastery of pace. Powers's prose bristles with verbal japes, hair-raising alliterations, manic allusiveness (the phrase 'a persistent grass-knollist' is the novel's one reference to the Kennedy assassination) and out-of-control metaphors. The author overwrites to such a degree that he gives the impression of being deeply insecure about the power of his words. What I found perhaps the novel's best joke—a character born in 'one of those Oak Hill Park Forest Elm Grove places', in other words, a Chicago suburb—is spoilt by Powers's inability to leave well alone: he has no less than three shots at it.

Admittedly, the frenetic verbal texture of **Prisoner's Dilemma** reflects the nervous, hyped-up private language of the family of six (a mother, a father and four overgrown teenagers) portrayed here. There is a clear continuity between narrative and dialogue, as well as some hints that the novel may have an autobiographical basis. Eddie Hobson, the father, is the central figure. He is a sick and disillusioned ex-history teacher who is nursing some terrible secret hidden from, but endlessly guessed at by, the rest of his family. Eddie is, moreover, a fantasist whose whole life appears to be devoted to the diaries and tapes recording his imaginative creation, 'Hobstown', which again his family is not allowed to see. Just what is Pop up to—and do the kids really want to know? All is finally revealed, despite endless prevaricating but we are left uncertain as to whether the waiting was justified.

Three Farmers on their Way to a Dance was a historical fantasy in which very ordinary characters were caught up in some major events of the 1914-18 War, notably the German invasion of Belgium and the episode of Henry Ford's *Peace Ship*. **Prisoner's Dilemma** brings a similar approach to some of the events of 1939-45. Here Walt Disney is made to play the part of Henry Ford, the simple American businessman launching into a grandiose attempt at world salvation. Chronologically, the story begins at the 1939 World's Fair, with its 'Futurama' exhibit (showing the world as it was meant to be in 1960) and the Westinghouse Time Capsule which was buried in the earth, to be opened in the year 6939. Bud Middleton, the juvenile lead in a film advertising the World's Fair, became the teenage Pop Hobson's hero. Eventually Hobson fantasises that he had landed the Bud Middleton part in an unfinished Disney spectacular, *You are the War,* made in the middle of World War Two and introducing Mickey Mouse as the teenager's guide to the dazzling, high-tech world of a peaceful future. People could be persuaded to stop killing one another, so Walt Disney is supposed to have thought, by being made to revisit 'Futurama'.

The real Walt Disney, Powers implies, restricted his contribution to the war effort to run-of-the-mill propaganda cartoons. Certainly he never filmed in De Kalb, Illinois, the site of 'Hobstown', which also happens to be the place where they invented barbed wire; De Kalb is the Hobson family's home town. Eddie Hobson's actual war, as his children discover, was spent as an undistinguished aircraft mechanic servicing B-29s at their home bases in Texas and other South-Western states. The clue to the extravagant 'Hobstown' fantasy turns out to lie in his posting, in July 1945, to a back-of-beyond desert airbase somewhere in the wilds of New Mexico.

Thirty years later, Eddie is dying of an inoperable cancer. Refusing hospital treatment, he walks out on his family without explanation and heads for the South-West. His younger son follows his trail and eventually reaches the Los Alamos National Museum, the National Atomic Museum near Albuquerque, and the smaller nuclear exhibit at White Sands National Monument close to the Trinity Site where the first atomic bomb was tested. Pop, who had witnessed the explosion, has apparently gone back to die at the missile-range-turned-theme-park which had served as his real-life Futurama. **Prisoner's Dilemma** is an intricate, wide-ranging tapestry drawing on the weightiest of historical themes; it is only a pity that its attempt to remythologise the most portentous of modern American events is so heavy-handed.

Curt Suplee (review date 25 August 1991)

SOURCE: "Lost in the Strands of Time," in *Book World—The Washington Post,* Vol. XXI, No. 34, August 25, 1991, p. 5.

[*In the following review, Suplee offers a positive assessment of* The Gold Bug Variations.]

This enormous book [**The Gold Bug Variations**] may be the most lavishly ambitious American novel since *Gravity's Rainbow*. That it succeeds on its own intricate intellectual terms (which will not be every reader's) is a considerable triumph; that it also functions as an invitingly readable story is an outright marvel.

Or, rather, two stories: Richard Powers's third novel is a narrative double-helix of interwoven tales. One, set in the late 1950s, follows Stuart Ressler, a celebrated young biologist who has a good shot at cracking the then-still-mysterious genetic code. The other takes place nearly 30 years later, in the novel's present, as a New York librarian named Jan O'Deigh and her boyfriend Franklin Todd discover Ressler, now a taciturn recluse, working the night shift tending computers at a data-processing mill.

What happened? Why did the cryptic Ressler forsake his beloved DNA research and the almost certain prospect of fame to bury himself in some cybernetic oubliette? Was it the guilt-lorn affair he had with a married university colleague? Or some horror in the science itself? And what is the mesmeric hold he has over Jan and Franklin, for whose screwball romance Ressler serves as the powerful catalyst? The answers to these questions, past and present, comprise the book's two seriocomic story lines.

That is already quite ample material for a first-class novel. But as fans of **Three Farmers on Their Way to a Dance** (1985) and particularly **Prisoner's Dilemma** (1988), will expect, it is by no means all. Powers—as exuberantly cerebral as Barth, Pynchon or Coover—specializes in a fascinating innovation on the novel-of-ideas: He imbeds his characters' actions in a world in which academic abstractions come palpably alive in realistic settings. Thus, the "prisoner's dilemma" (a familiar staple of undergraduate game theory that examines whether cooperation or self-interest is most beneficial in the long run) becomes the painfully literal condition of existence for that novel's protagonist.

In this book, the technique is similar but the thematic stakes are even higher, since the novel's metaphysical reach extends (are you sitting down?) through chance and necessity right up to one of the biggest questions there is: What is the purport of life, if life results from nothing more (or less) profound than the blind selfish multiplication of a few nucleic acids?

Not surprisingly, the metaphorical superstructure that supports these themes is so massive that it constantly threatens to crush the realistic exposition. Overarching the action are two mighty motifs: The way in which DNA's simple four-character chemical codes endlessly proliferate variation on life's basic patterns; and the genes' acoustic analogue, Bach's *Goldberg Variations,* which evolve into a hymn to unity-in-difference. (A mutational hybrid of Bach's title and the code-breaker in Poe's "The Gold Bug" give this book its name.) In the course of 639 pages, these metaphors become so cross-bred and elaborated that virtually every aspect of the two-tiered plot turns on some kind of coding accident or chance mutation, whether it's an unexpected computer-programming bug, reproductive anomaly, misunderstood remark or ghastly disease.

This complexity has its cost. Because the principal narrator is librarian Jan ("a gas station attendant of the mind"), the book has all-purpose license to digress into science history, set-piece rhapsodies on DNA's insatiable fugue, bits of etymology, shards of poetry, riddles, sudden disquisitions on Theophrastus or Mendel or von Neumann, genetic diagrams, gruesome puns, musical scores and, yes, more. The reader is expected to handle not only the arcane argot of genetics (haplotypes, alleles, polypeptides, base-pair sequences) but a substantial amount of musical terminology (rubatos, sarabandes, chaconnes and chromatics) and a little computer lingo as well.

Moreover, one has to be ready at any point for the action to stop abruptly so that Powers can wax profusely, redundantly lyrical over the interlocking figurative possibilities of his metaphors. Thus the genetic code is "a tie bordering on magic . . . the physical chunk embodying the ethereal plan, the seed distilling the idea of organism. The first link in the chain from Word to flesh, philosopher's stone, talisman, elixir, incantation, the old myth of knowledge incorporated in *things.*" And so on. And often.

Those prepared to brave this forbidding forebrain thicket, however, will find themselves superbly rewarded. For all his pedantic proclivities, Powers has a full array of conventional novelistic talents, and his book has a wonderful roster of genuinely memorable characters.

They may be egregiously brainy, and their dialogue may often sound like Oscar Wilde on "It's Academic," but they are realistic and sympathetic and complicated. Ressler's love affair is fleshy indeed (lying in bed, he can only feel "his legs because they do not touch hers . . . so conspicuous is her solidity by its absence next to him"), as are the deaths, ecstasies, sundry catastrophes and heartbreaks in this long story. Powers is one of the hardest-working stylists in any language, and there is scarcely a sentence in this gigantic book that has not been tuned for maximum intensity or does not contain an intriguing figure or arresting rhythm. And he is marvelously adept at carefully differentiating characters' voices—from the creepy self-mocking monologues of Keith Tuckwell, a manic ad-man and Jan's erstwhile lover to the disjunctive rant of one of Ressler's co-workers going insane.

Given the choice, though, Powers veers to the conceptual. So when describing the view over Manhattan, for example, where Updike might give us a water-color roofscape of texture and hue, Powers goes for socio-synopsis. "Four hundred radial miles of contiguous squalor, a deep brown demographic smear, a disappointment per square mile that left the three of us several digits to the right of significance."

And ultimately, the enigma of significance is what Powers is after. Indeed, for sheer thematic aspiration, *Gold Bug* can contend comfortably with *Moby Dick:* Ressler is wrestling, Ahab-like, not only with the secret of genetic coding, but with the meaning of the process itself. A whale of a paradox: For all nature's inexhaustible profusion and intricate complexity, there is no purpose in it. Evolution is a tautology: Survival, not of the fittest, but merely of the survivors. "Pattern can produce purpose, but it does so without final causes. Destination, design is a lie . . . The only ethic left is random play, trial and error."

How are we to behave in the face of a biosphere that lacks even indifference, whose "whole exploding catalogue rests on inanimate, chance self-ignition?" This book's many characters and sub-plots provide an index of possible answers. But none so admirable as Ressler's own, which might serve as Powers' aesthetic credo: "Nothing deserved wonder so much as our capacity to feel it."

Louis B. Jones   (review date 25 August 1991)

SOURCE: "Bach Would've Liked This Molecule," in *The New York Times Book Review,* August 25, 1991, pp. 9-10.

[*Jones is an American novelist whose works include* Ordinary Money *(1990). In the following review, he faults the numerous puns and slightness of characterization in* The Gold Bug Variations, *but states that the work "is a dense, symmetrical symphony in which no note goes unsounded."*]

In his third novel, Richard Powers is up to something very unusual. *The Gold Bug Variations* is a little bit like Robert Pirsig's *Zen and the Art of Motorcycle Maintenance,* in that it carries us on a cerebral quest for a philosophical heffalump; it's a little bit Borgesian in its love of the complex and cryptic; it's a little bit Joycean in its size and difficulty. It's a "science" novel, but closer to science fiction in its inventiveness, its hardware vocabulary and software characterization, and in the uncritical pleasure it takes in the purely clever, the nifty.

The narration alternates between two time frames. In 1957 at the University of Illinois, a biologist, Stuart Ressler, is decoding the DNA molecule and falling in love with his (happily married) colleague Dr. Jeanette Koss. She gives him a Glenn Gould recording of Bach's "Goldberg" Variations that changes his life; but the immediate suspense hangs on whether or not Ressler's superior will allow him to take the unprecedented step of conducting his experiments in vitro rather than in vivo.

Meanwhile, in the mid-1980's in Brooklyn, Mr. Powers's first-person narrator, Jan O'Deigh, is joining her new boyfriend, Franklin Todd, in solving the mystery of this same Stuart Ressler—who 25 years later has sunk to anonymity in a dead-end, graveyard-shift job as a computer programmer. Why, they ask, has Dr. Ressler forsaken scientific glory for obscurity? Of course Jan and Franklin are falling in love too; the quadrilateral symmetry of the two love affairs sustains the deeper structure of the book. And the recurring four-note pattern in the base line of the *Goldberg Variations* is mystically analogous to the sequences of nucleotides that write life's script in the double helix of the DNA molecule. It's a cabalistic kind of text, obsessed with its own numerology and metaphors, for which character and plot exist only as background.

Indeed, the purpose of this plot setup is less to tell a story than to explore structural possibilities, codes, metaphors, ingenuity in language. Mr. Powers has allowed metaphor to work everywhere on the narrative. There are no depths here; the effects are all superficial and immediate, like a stand-up comedian's routine—except that rather than jokes we have brilliant tropes. The joy to be taken in reading the book is, like the pleasure of studying crystal multiplication, in seeing a pattern swarm mosaically over everything, watching a stencil laid over life.

Just seeing so much sheer cleverness packed into 639 pages is a remarkable experience. The novel reads as if it's been written from a room-size collection of index cards, so dense is each paragraph. Almost every sentence is a heroic tour de force built around a fascinating gimmick of language, usually a pun or a metaphor derived from the figurative possibilities of scientific technical language, liberated from the usual literary attention to connotation or elegance.

Indeed, if one were to have a small complaint, amid this stunning virtuosity, one might wish for fewer puns. What is it about the pun that is so impolite, so discourse-damaging, so unfair that it must *smirk?* Why does a pun always have an effect like being pinched? Perhaps because it calls attention to the pathetically mechanical nature of our language, which we would rather think of as sublime. Both the narrator and the other characters in *The Gold Bug Variations* are unable to resist puns; sometimes whole paragraphs are planned just to get off a good one. In fact, *all* of the novel is a kind of elaborate pun—but justified by the fact that the very theme of the book is the mechanical, semiotic structure of our lives.

Also, one might complain that the characterization is a bit slight. The dialogue often consists of sustained wisecrack contests or technojargon, even as people fall into each other's arms. When these scientists have sex—though they're passionate, and a few beakers are broken in the privacy of utility closets—nevertheless the descriptions are largely in terms of enzymes, glands, hemodynamics. Mr. Powers isn't interested in the subtleties of characterization but in the larger pattern. He writes fiction that aspires to the condition of music, austere and abstract, without being humorless.

There are some lovely scenes, such as when a book-scattering tornado hits the campus and a microbiologist undergoes a dark night of the soul locked in the library overnight; and a farcical and sad episode when a biologist commits suicide and takes all the lab rats with him. There are also some clever, inscrutable twists that haunt the reader. Why is it that, of the two main female characters, Jeanette is barren and Jan has been sterilized, so that, in a book about reproduction, they can't reproduce? And what is the significance of the lesbian flirtation at the end, which had not been foreshadowed in the earlier pages? And how are we to take Jan's quitting the job she loves and risking poverty to take up the study of genetics at home, self-directed? Are we to think this noble or kooky?

All these are mysteries, ripe for the scholarly reader. Like a Borges library, *The Gold Bug Variations* has everything: Paracelsus, Schrödinger waves, Zeno, German, French, Latin, musicology, quantum mechanics, Flemish painting, staves of musical notation, poems written in computer language, Keynes, ozone depletion, Tesla coils, Yeats, Pythagoras, Poe. Mr. Powers's page is Velcro. Every allusion possible is compulsory. His novel is a dense, symmetrical symphony in which no note goes unsounded.

Michael Harris (review date 29 September 1991)

SOURCE: "Take the DNA Train," in *Los Angeles Times Book Review,* September 29, 1991, pp. 2, 11.

[*In the following review, Harris suggests that* The Gold Bug Variations *may appeal to a limited audience for whom it is "essential" reading.*]

Let's begin with the *Youngblood Hawke* theory of fiction, promulgated by the hero of a forgotten Herman Wouk novel. To engage us seriously, says Hawke, a rumpled, expansive young writer modeled on Thomas Wolfe, a story must offer the equivalent of a "lovely, helpless girl tied to the railroad tracks . . . the wind blowing her skirts up around those pretty legs . . . and that train thundering around the mountain pass."

Hawke goes on: "Dostoyevsky tied that girl on the tracks in the first 50 pages of every book he ever wrote. Henry James . . . never wrote about anything else, hardly. Dickens had . . . avalanches coming down from both sides. Joyce didn't, no. That's why only English teachers read him."

Granted that Joyce has lasted and Wolfe has not, where does this leave Richard Powers' brilliant, ambitious third novel? Will only English teachers, molecular biologists, computer programmers, musicologists and art historians respond to it? Or is there something in these dizzying 639 pages of wit and erudition to make the rest of us care, too?

There is. Powers, in effect, ties all humanity to the tracks; his train carries the heaviest metaphysical freight. It's the same train whose far-off whistle alarmed fundamentalist Christians a century ago, rumbling down the rails laid by Darwin's *On the Origin of Species*. Now it's highballing toward us, stoked by James Watson's and Francis Crick's discovery of the double-helix structure of the DNA molecule in 1953.

That scientific feat, Powers asserts, ushered in a supreme moment that most of us have simply failed to recognize. For 3 billion years, in a random, unrepeatable and infinitely complex process, the four nucleotide bases, or chemical building blocks, that make up all life on Earth have reproduced themselves and mutated into bacteria, dinosaurs and, finally, a species that *right now* is cracking the genetic code that has shaped all that behavior from the beginning, including this circular act of self-discovery.

Stuart Ressler recognizes the moment and tries to seize it. A gifted, ascetic young researcher, he arrives at the University of Illinois in 1957 to join a team taking one of the first whacks at the code. He is inspired by Poe's story "The Gold Bug," which is about code-breaking, and by Bach's *Goldberg Variations,* a recording of which he is given by Jeanette Koss, a married colleague. Ressler comes very close to success—close enough to get his picture in *Life* magazine.

Then what? In 1983, we find him in a dead-end, graveyard-shift job at a computer database firm in Brooklyn. A fellow worker, Franklin Todd, senses Ressler's buried immensity and enlists librarian Jan O'Deigh in cracking the code that this celibate recluse has become. (Their search for the reasons why Ressler dropped out recalls Powers' first novel, *Three Farmers on Their Way to a Dance,* in which a 1914 photograph of young men about to be swallowed up by World War I is the subject of an inquiry into how our whole century lost its innocence.)

Todd and O'Deigh fall in love, like Ressler and Koss 25 years before them. The troubled histories of these two relationships intertwine like the complementary helixes of DNA.

Moreover, the novel is structured exactly like the *Goldbergs,* Ressler's favorite metaphor for the life process: a chapter for each of the 32 variations—arias, dances, arabesques, canons; a repetitive pattern that spawns dazzling variety.

Ressler has another metaphor: Jacob's ladder, the biblical dream stairway between Earth and Heaven. But his research doesn't point to anything divine in the biblical sense. We are the product of processes that don't care about us as individuals, as would-be immortal souls. Even our species is merely something the four bases have cooked up for their own convenience. The human experiment need not succeed; in fact, we may be discovering our genetic heritage only in time to learn that we have tampered with it, and fouled our environment, beyond recovery.

Like the rest of late-20th-Century civilization, Powers' characters, with their near-genius IQs and access to libraries and computers, are swamped with information. They yearn for values, which alone can transform information into knowledge. But where can values come from today? "The world's pattern was not assembled for the mind's comprehension," O'Deigh reflects, peering into the same abyss as Ressler. "Rather the other way around. . . . That made [it] more miraculous." But it's not the miracle we sought.

We are familiar with the reductionist effect of science, its "only X" quality. Love is *only* chemicals. The moon is *only* a place where an astronaut hit golf shots. The thing about Ressler—the reason Todd and O'Deigh are so profoundly drawn to him—is that he tries to transcend this way of thinking, and sometimes succeeds. Meeting a neighbor's 9-year-old daughter, he sees her as the sum of her amino acids and enzymes, but he doesn't *reduce* her to them; instead, he embraces the unwanted miracle and bursts into tears, awed by the magnificence of their functioning in her.

Still, Ressler is traumatized by his discoveries. He tries to find value in love, though he has learned that our very impulses to love and to create values have been encoded in our genes by an accident of doubtful evolutionary utility. Koss, however, cannot bear children. She returns to her husband, after which Ressler lives alone and turns from science to music. Sterility haunts the younger couple, too. Todd delays giving birth to his doctoral thesis; O'Deigh, full of information about genetic defects, has had her tubes tied.

The Gold Bug Variations, ultimately, is about how these four people become fertile after all, like the four base chemicals, like the notes of Bach's base tune. Like this novel itself.

For Powers doesn't just create a beautiful form, an ingenious intellectual construct. He makes his characters live. Not a scene—faculty party, romantic tryst, walk in the zoo, computer scam—is written routinely. Curiosity shines on every page, as it does in Ressler's ideal of science, whose aim isn't "stockpiling brutal efficiency, accomplishing the sadistic myth of progress," but cultivating "a perpetual state of wonder."

True, Powers, like Joyce, has limited his audience by disdaining the usual sources of fictional excitement. To describe the modern crisis of the spirit, he has relied on frontal assault, and frontal assaults, in literature as in war, are costly. Characters capable of analyzing such a crisis are, of necessity, a rarefied, untypical bunch. A lot of readers are going to skip or skim long stretches of science writing, music theory and art appreciation. But others—those for whom the approaching train isn't a phantom, who can feel the vibration of the rails in their guts—will find this book essential.

Joseph Tabbi   (review date Spring 1992)

SOURCE: A review of *The Gold Bug Variations,* in *The*

Review of Contemporary Fiction, Vol. XII, No. 1, Spring, 1992, p. 145.

[*In the following review, Tabbi states that* The Gold Bug Variations *"merits serious attention from writers and scientists."*]

Early in *The Gold Bug Variations,* in one of many scenes in the novel where characters lose themselves in libraries, the young scientist Stuart Ressler makes "a sadly vindicating tour" of the University of Illinois library that reveals "an 824," the Dewey Decimal designation for literature, "untouched since Henry James died. Humanities have clearly slid into the terminally curatorial, forsaking claim to knowledge." This is 1957, and Ressler is in Illinois to push ahead with the genetic coding research that Watson and Crick initiated in England a few years before. Ressler's task, like Powers's in the telling of this story, is to sort through a mass of discoveries, competing hypotheses, and sheer data for clues to the replicative structure of DNA. I would guess that Powers's scientist hero, like the cryptographer of Poe's "Gold Bug," is to some degree "a coded persona of his inventor," a tireless gatherer of data who seeks to draw life from objective languages, and so make the crucial "jump from information to knowledge."

Powers, knowing that science, no less than literature, is "choked by unrestrained data as a pond is by too luxurious plant growth," attempts through just such analogies to give form to the endlessly proliferating facts of biological science. The book's main structural analogy comes from Bach's *Goldberg Variations:* four scale-steps, like the four base chemicals of the genetic string, breaking into "combinations, uncountable." Among the multiplying and recurrent set pieces in the novel, those devoted to Glenn Gould's early and late interpretations of the Variations stand out. Indeed, it would not be a bad idea to read this novel with Gould's recordings playing in the background.

An "awful, chromatic awareness" of the genetic code inspires "a curatorial resolve" in Powers's narrator, research librarian Jan O'Deigh, whose own story replicates Ressler's thirty years later. Possibly, O'Deigh is too much in awe of her subject: her inability to get beyond analogy and dutiful encyclopedic reference may have kept Powers from devising a major literary form. Yet *The Gold Bug Variations* is sophisticated in its engagement with science and passionate in its survey of living existence. It merits serious attention from writers and scientists.

Roy Porter   (review date 8 May 1992)

SOURCE: "Data for Data's Sake," in *The Times Literary Supplement,* No. 4469, May 8, 1992, p. 20.

[*In the following review, Porter offers a mixed assessment of* The Gold Bug Variations, *finding Powers's prose "temporarily exhilarating but ultimately exhausting."*]

Geneticists, we are told, are now busy finally decoding and rewriting all the scripts of life. Against this background, Richard Powers has had the clever, if deliberately perverse, idea of constructing a novel [*The Gold Bug Variations*] that mirrors this genetic quest: a novel not about the lives, hopes and fears of biologists trekking between the Double Helix and the human genome project, but one written as if it were itself a product of that enterprise, a novel whose form is "scientific".

A standard plot can be discerned. A top young American molecular biologist, Stuart Ressler, sets out in the 1950s to crack the genetic code. In the process, he is overtaken by other demands and desires. He grows preoccupied by the modes and patterns of music, mathematics and the natural world. He gets caught up in a love affair with a married woman who is a central performer in his research team. The ambivalences of his involvement with Dr Koss cause him to freak out: the genius quits science and disappears.

It is only twenty years later that he is rediscovered, in a classic case of serendipity, by a drifting art historian and computer programmer, Frank Todd (Powers is, himself, unsurprisingly, a former programmer), and his trusty, endearing and infallible research-librarian partner, Jan O'Deigh.

Powers shapes his tale as a retrospect of Todd and O'Deigh's attempts to unearth the secrets of Ressler's identity, as gradually they get to know him. The discovery of Ressler becomes a kind of laboratory experiment, and the texture and timbre of Powers's writing echoes the information-packed quality typical of lab notebooks or research reports.

For this is a monster work—it runs to over 600 pages—not meant to be read for its characters or events, but for its dense, insistent way with words, its sometimes zany obsession with data (it is, after all, O'Deigh's forte).

> Archivists aren't wellsprings of fact; they are search algorithms. The unfolding subway, the byzantine network of accumulating particulars— our Pyramid, Great Wall, St Peters, the largest engineering feat of all times—daily runs a nip-and-tuck footrace between the facts worth saving and the technology for managing the explosion. A single day produces more print than centuries of antiquity . . . six new books every hour.

Thus Powers's prose exemplifies the phenomenon it depicts, shares the psychopathology that is at the heart of his tale. Like all other sorts of bingeing, overdosing on jargon, or data for data's sake, proves temporarily exhilarating but ultimately exhausting. In the end, atomized individuals disappear behind the walls of information they erect to conceal themselves. Scientific discovery becomes a sort of re-covering; and the enterprise of science and, with it, the schema behind this novel, turn self-defeating. The more we find out, the less we understand.

Derivative from Pynchon, often fatiguing and (like its title) sometimes tiresomely clever, *The Goldbug Variations* at times succeeds in holding the attention. The earnest-bohemian culture of the 1970s (the world dominated by 45s) is agreeably sketched, and the sexuality of a more restrained era is tenderly evoked. But the master allegory (novelist/scientist cracking the code, unveiling the chemistry of life) collapses under its own inbuilt overload. Most of us cannot remain high on *Scientific American* for long.

Pearl K. Bell (review date 1992)

SOURCE: "Fiction Chronicle," in *Partisan Review*, Vol. LIX, No. 2, 1992, pp. 282-95.

[*In the following excerpt, Bell offers a negative assessment of* The Gold Bug Variations, *stating that Powers's "brilliance, in the end, serves little purpose beyond his irrepressible exhibitionism."*]

One can't help wondering what readers—other than editors and reviewers lashed to the mast of duty—Richard Powers had in mind when he embarked on his inordinately complicated and exhausting third novel, *The Gold Bug Variations*. Surely not "the common reader," if such a creature still exists. Powers is a very clever fellow, highly acclaimed these days, a thirty-four-year-old polymath, the winner of a MacArthur "genius" fellowship, who was trained as a physicist but gave up science for literature. On closer examination he hasn't given up science at all, just put it to a different use. Very long, densely packed stretches of the novel are devoted to the intricacies of genetic research, complete with charts and tables and diagrams and codes and equations that only a scientist in the field might even begin to comprehend. In addition, Powers is intent on instructing us at closely detailed length about computer programming, the subtle connections between music and molecular biology (drawn from Glenn Gould's original recording of the *Goldberg Variations*, hence the insufferably cute title), human heredity, minor Flemish landscape painters, and—oh, yes, lest we forget—two love stories intertwined in a double helix of erudition and desire. Some of this is undeniably dazzling, most of it much more than even an uncommon reader can want to absorb.

Since this is a review of fiction, perhaps it's best to concentrate on the stories and let the encyclopedic clouds of specialized information drift where they may. The two love stories are separated by thirty years. In one, Stuart Ressler, a brilliant young microbiologist at a Midwestern university, sets out in 1957 to break the genetic code and is smitten by a married colleague. They have a passionate affair, but when she refuses to leave her husband, Ressler abandons his scientific research and spends the rest of his life in obscurity as a computer technician. Thirty years later a reference librarian in Brooklyn becomes intrigued with Dr. Ressler, who works nearby, and she enlists the help of his handsome assistant, a failed graduate student in art history, in ferreting out the truth about Dr. Ressler's life, especially the reason why he threw over his Nobel-promising career as a scientist "when he was at the forefront of great discovery." Moving back and forth in time, the two stories unfold in a dizzying multi-layered profusion of puns and allusions and facts, facts, facts—about poetry and art, science and music, pop culture, and much more. Because Jan, the librarian, spends her working hours answering random questions about everything under the sun, we are bombarded by a relentless flow of miscellaneous information, along with moments of surprising banality, such as "Science is not about control. It is about cultivating a perpetual condition of wonder. . . . It is about reverence, not mastery."

The novel is full of prodigies, bloated with facts and theo-

ries and aperçus, yet in the end the characters are little more than abstract ciphers, enormous heads on recalcitrant bodies. (Ressler's desire for his beloved, we are told, "awakes the possibilities buried in his cytoplasm.") There is something hermetic and airless about this monstrously cerebral tome. Despite the novel's erudite abundance, Powers conveys no sense of a world beyond the catacomb he has so artfully constructed out of science, computers and music. Though we are given many dates, the book lacks any sense of history, of the time in which all this is going on. Nor do we ever get a clear resolution of the mystery in Ressler's life. This writer's brilliance, in the end, serves little purpose beyond his irrepressible exhibitionism.

Sven Birkerts (review date 23 May 1993)

SOURCE: "Fate of the Innocent," in *Chicago Tribune—Books*, May 23, 1993, pp. 1, 10-11.

[*Birkerts is an American critic who contributes regularly to such journals as* Boston Review, New Republic, *and* Mirabella. *In the following review, he questions the depiction of the protagonist's love relationship but overall finds* Operation Wandering Soul *a "fully realized and major work of art."*]

In a few short years—in literary terms overnight—Richard Powers has vaulted from promise to attainment. His third novel, *The Gold Bug Variations* (1991) was one of the brainiest and most ambitious novels in recent memory. He could not have rewarded himself with much of a vacation. *Operation Wandering Soul,* his new novel, sees that bet and raises it, creating a world less structurally complex but of greater thematic resonance. Powers must now be seen as our most energetic and gifted novelist under 40.

Operation Wandering Soul is an early entry into what will surely become its own sub-genre soon: the millennial novel. As Powers writes in a peculiar chapter made up of words and definitions: "The most common hallmark of millenarian thought is the conviction that civilization is just now entering its moment of truth, an unprecedented instant of danger and opportunity, of universal calamity and convergence. . . ." And it is a millenarian tension, a sense of urgency verging on terror, that drives this remarkable imagining forward.

The time of the novel, never specified, is the near-present. Richard Kraft is a young surgical resident living—more accurately, bivouacking—in Angel City (read L.A.). He is on rotation at Carver General, a public hospital that is a combination of how it is and worst-case scenario. Every day he fights traffic, assesses his degenerated metropolis: "The breach between dream and delivery has long since gone beyond fault line. Sinkholes in the whole mythology of progress gape open up and down the street, suck down entire retail strips at a shot." His work is triage, mainly on children in near terminal states. He strives to match the brittle detachment of his colleagues, whose o.r. repartee would have the gang from M*A*S*H plugging its ears.

Kraft does wonder, when he gets a moment to think, why

he doesn't opt out for a desk job. He doesn't know. Indeed, he is quite opaque to himself. But the reader quickly realizes that the man is working out some strange missionary compulsion. And gradually, via scattered memory bursts, then full-scale narrative recollection, the story emerges.

Meanwhile, various components of this many-stranded work must be mustered into place. First, amor: Kraft's meeting with and then deepening romantic involvement with the aptly named Linda Espera, a beautiful and preternaturally emotive therapist. Where Kraft has been striving for professional distance from his young charges, Espera is hands-on—hugging, joking and, most important, regaling them with stories. Kraft, whom she grapples onto body and soul, is in her eyes but one more of the wounded.

The children on the unit may be maimed in body, but under Espera's light their souls shine forth. There is Joy, a refugee from the Asian wars: "Ceramic, tiny, terrified, she moved about on legs as pencil tentative as a tawny mouse deer. All four of her limbs would have fit comfortably inside a third-grade lunch box." She lies in bed devouring books as fast as she can turn the pages. And there, in the mass of heart-breakers, the limbless and misshapen, is Nicolo. Afflicted with progeria, a rare disease that speeds the aging process, the boy races to and fro like a frenzied Methuselah, trying to live all he can before his body gives out. We are gripped by their vulnerability even as we are heartened by their brave fatalism.

Kraft's involvement with Espera soon hits a major obstacle—himself. As he opens up, lowering his defenses, he finds himself overwhelmed by memories he had repressed. As a boy he moved from place to place, following his father's Foreign Service postings. But in fact they were postings of a more nefarious sort. And soon Kraft is reliving the time of his adolescence in an unnamed Asian city. A young idealist, he tried to become a monk, then devoted himself to building a school for local children. He also came to understand what his father really did and witnessed the consequences of Operation Wandering Soul, a saturation bombing mission. We see now why Kraft does what he does, and why his memories are pushing him to the edge.

As a counterpoint to Kraft's unfolding crisis are the self-contained stories and legends embedded in the narrative. Stories told to the children—about other children. Those evacuated from London during the war, the legions who joined the Children's Crusade, those who followed the Pied Piper. Each plunges us into an alternate place, a world governed by laws we have all but forgotten. The author's intent is ambiguous. In his presentation, childhood is no idyll. We find violence, rage and all else that adulthood is heir to. But we also find a rare intensity of will and a capacity to believe in things and act upon the belief. We have seen the same thing on the unit—children who have no business hoping but who persist.

The novel comes to a shuddering climax. Area children have been strafed by a mad gunman. The corridors of the hospital are overflowing, and the surgeons are working past all exhaustion limits. Kraft is at the point of cracking.

As he works he drifts in and out of apocalyptic fantasies that extend and vary the legends we've been reading. Will the children—these children, all children—find a way to escape the scourging violence of the world or to save it? Or will they be crushed? The time of the answer is drawing near—in the novel and in our own distressed society.

Operation Wandering Soul is vast and daring. Powers writes a finely tuned and highly original prose; each sentence is calculated for rhythm and subtleties of sense. The book cannot be skimmed. Moreover, the author has, as in *The Gold Bug Variations,* devised a referential scheme that opens onto continually deeper layers—the work is as profound as you allow it to be.

If there is a weakness, it lies in the depiction of the relationship between Kraft and Espera. We see what Powers intends, we applaud the thematic play, but we never quite catch the heat of their passion or feel the pathos of its collapse. Because of this we enter the novel more with the head than the heart. And while we emerge shocked and awakened, we are not as emotionally shaken as we might be. In that one sense *Operation Wandering Soul* remains the triumph of a precocious young man. In every other way it is [a] fully realized and major work of art.

An excerpt from *Operation Wandering Soul*

The international community, from Kraft's third-hand vantage, is currently engaged in some intensive R & D, smoking up several delicious monster scenarios for the coming collective blowout. Things are definitely on the march. Nightly news lays out its attendant horrors in a series of thought-eradicating, three-minute music videos. Ice caps melt. Fuel reserves push toward asymptote, with nothing anyone can do about it. Debt amasses faster than global capital. IRS computers threaten to trigger the long-teetering global financial shutdown by issuing checks and debits essentially at random. . . .

But Pediatrics supplies Kraft with an alternative wrap-up scenario. The department nurses . . . report this tremendous spike in preemies, SIDS cases, placental substance dependence, inherited autoimmune deficiencies—slopes ramping up for an assault on the airy altitudes above the graph-paper tree line. His imagination is entranced by the chance of an annual power skid in the male-to-female ratio, not just statewide, but throughout the euphemistically labeled developed countries. A Pink Shift drifts demographics measurably away from snips and snails, sugar-and-spiceward. An almost imperceptible but steady 0.1 percent reduction in males per live birth per year, when coupled with the recent slight *increase* in male infant mortality rates, and the shift reveals nothing less than the steady girlification of the world, with its inevitable—although belated—precipitous drop in procreation.

Richard Powers, in his Operation Wandering Soul, *Morrow, 1993.*

Bruce Bawer   (review date 13 June 1993)

SOURCE: "Beautiful Dreamers," in *Book World—The Washington Post,* Vol. XXIII, No. 24, June 13, 1993, p. 2.

[*Bawer is an American critic. In the following review, he offers a mixed assessment of* Operation Wandering Soul, *praising Powers's prose but questioning his depiction of American society.*]

If by some measures Richard Powers is the most gifted American novelist of his generation, he is also one of the most unjustly neglected. Though reviewers have been praising him fervently ever since the 1985 appearance of his first novel, **Three Farmers on their Way to a Dance,** and though his third novel, **The Gold Bug Variations,** was nominated for a National Book Critics Circle Award and named *Time* magazine's 1991 book of the year, the 35-year-old Powers has yet to win the wide readership he deserves.

There's no mystery why this is so. Powers's novels are engaging, even exhilarating; almost every sentence invites one to pause and admire its tautness, rhythm and wit, and to marvel at Powers's extraordinary gift for drawing quirky connections and making familiar points in fresh ways. Yet these books can also, for many readers, be extremely intimidating. His prose swarms with references, often elliptical or punning or both, to obscure historical events, artworks, scientific principles, theological concepts and outdated pop-culture figures; if on one page he discourses learnedly on Anglican choir music, on the next he may move on to the Hanseatic League or the "NBC triad" (those three musical notes that used to identify the network) or Burke (either Edmund or Billie). Often his elaborate wordplay reminds one of a *London Times* crossword—and there's the rub. For reading him can be like watching a great juggler: even as he takes your breath away, the exercise feels hollow, inert, yet curiously exhausting, and one comes away from it essentially unchanged. His books may be masterpieces; if so, they are baby-boom masterpieces in which James Joyce meets Douglas (*Shampoo Planet*) Coupland and MTV meets MIT.

Though somewhat more accessible than its predecessors, Powers's fourth novel, **Operation Wandering Soul,** represents another bravura display of Powers's dazzling talent. Its hero is Richard Kraft, 33, a surgical resident in Los Angeles, known here as Angel City. (Since Kraft means "power" in German, Powers seems to be inviting the reader to equate author and protagonist.) Assigned to a public hospital's pediatrics ward, Kraft becomes intimately involved with a child therapist, Linda Espera ("lovely hope"), who soon learns that Kraft is himself an "emotional leper" desperately in need of therapy. Raised in various cities around the world, Kraft bears the scars of childhood trauma, of current overwork and of sheer helplessness in the face of his patients' misery.

Among those patients are Nicolino, a boy with progeria (a rare genetic disorder characterized by premature aging), and Joy, an Asian girl who came to America as a "boat person" only to sustain a life-threatening leg infection. Both suffer terribly; both are also improbably precocious, self-possessed and brave. Nor are they the only smart, suffering children here: for various chapters leave Kraft and his charges behind to focus instead on such historical events as the Children's Crusade and the evacuation of London schoolchildren during the Blitz. Linking these materials with Kraft's story is the notion that we are all youngsters dreaming of Never-Never Land, all wandering souls in search of illumination, paradise, the City on the Hill.

Operation Wandering Soul might be described as sophistication's tribute to innocence. Yet there's a paradox: even as the prose's intellectual sophistication seems to imply that maturity is a great and good thing, the narrative explicitly celebrates juvenility and suggests an equation between adulthood and moral corruption. It must be said, too, that while this novel plainly seeks to make a weighty moral point, it often seems a dance of death whose morally problematic purpose is less to ponder the anguish of innocents than to show off Powers's fancy footwork.

At the most serious moments, Powers is likely to slip in a pun. Note the sly reference to Dijon mustard and basil in this sentence about the Children's Crusade: "By the time they reach Dijon, where they muster in the basilica, they number in the thousands." Depending on context, this sort of thing can seem inexcusably flippant, or aesthetically pleasurable, harmlessly indicative of Powers's native fecundity, or thematically meaningful. (Is the author, for instance, invoking Christ's teaching that "the kingdom of God is like a mustard seed" and that one whose faith is no bigger than a mustard seed can move mountains? Is this, in turn, connected to one Children's Crusade leader's worry about crossing the Alps?)

When in a passage about Kraft, moreover, Powers tosses off the commonplace colloquialism "The Cheese stands alone," a reader might not even recognize this as an allusion to "The Farmer in the Dell" or, more significantly, to Kraft American Singles, which touches on several of the novel's key thematic points—among them that Kraft is an isolato, that to be American is (as Thomas Wolfe put it) to be "lost and lonely," and that bland, processed foods like Kraft American Singles symbolize the banality of U.S. consumer culture.

That banality figures prominently here. Indeed, Powers's manifest aspiration to plumb America's meaning (the book begins—where else?—on the open road, with echoes aplenty of Whitman, Kerouac, Paul Auster, Don DeLillo and Updike's *Rabbit* novels) yields virtually nothing but glib, predictable digs about Reeboks, Slurpees, Mars bars, multiplexes, fast food, sound bites and an American dream of "VCRs for all." To Powers, America—a "flag-waving, fallen-laurel country on whom God once shed His grace like a rattler sheds his skin"—would seem to be defined only by the uglier aspects of capitalism, and the New World Order defined only by a stateside lust for the "Three hundred fifty million free-market consumers" of the former Soviet bloc.

The disdain for America expressed here is, in fact, so simple-mindedly conceived and arrogantly expressed, and so thoroughly unbalanced by any respect for democratic values, that it weakens the book appreciably. Powers divides people too neatly into good and bad, and does so along crude, politically correct lines, aligning himself throughout with (and failing to challenge or even explore) the received ideas of today's academic establishment. For all the brilliance of his prose, his reflections about man and society barely surpass the intellectual level of the song "We Are the World."

Yet what beauty there is in this book! There are paragraphs that readers will want to return to again and again—one, for example, recounting the piteous fate of the participants in the Children's Crusade, and another delineating the thoughts inspired in a Blitz-racked English schoolteacher by a wonderful boy choir whose "soaring, high, head voices said what it was to be alive, to be any thing at all." At its best, one might say, Powers's prose itself soars like the most magnificent of choirs, memorably capturing the moments of joy and anguish, barrenness and grace, that add up to life.

Lee Lescaze (review date 13 July 1993)

SOURCE: "Man, Past and Present," in *The Wall Street Journal,* Vol. CCXXII, No. 8, July 13, 1993, p. A14.

[*In the following excerpt, Lescaze offers a negative assessment of* Operation Wandering Soul *but praises Powers's writing style.*]

Richard Powers's **Operation Wandering Soul** is a corrosive report from a Los Angeles of the near-future made close to unlivable by violence, pollution, traffic and man's inhumanity. It centers on Kraft, a brilliant surgeon brought close to mental collapse and emotional paralysis by the horrors of the modern world, particularly evils inflicted on children. . . .

In **Operation Wandering Soul,** Mr. Powers aims not for shivers, but for revulsion. The novel is hard to read in the way that horror movies are hard to watch. His surgeon is often cutting maimed children in the operating room.

Mr. Powers is a dazzling stylist whose first three novels, most recently **The Gold Bug Variations,** were widely praised. His wordplay makes comparisons with Stanley Elkin (author of a better novel about terminally ill children) and Thomas Pynchon inevitable. Sentences and paragraphs of striking originality and power fill his pages.

But to what end? **Operation Wandering Soul** is, despite its considerable length, a one-note book with so little plot development that its style is its only interest. Mr. Powers decries the brutalization of children by man and disease. That isn't a case that needs much arguing. It is hard to think of another novel in which such sophisticated presentation wraps such a simple core.

Into Kraft's grim world comes Linda Espera, a physical therapist as full of hope as her name suggests. But Kraft, at age 33, cannot cope. Despite his surgeon's craft, he has no power (kraft means power in German) over events. More often than not, his patients can't be saved, most heartrendingly an angelic Lao boat-girl refugee.

Can the beautiful Espera's optimism (not to mention her love) work a cure for Kraft's despair? Or, as Mr. Powers writes in a lovely passage: "Might she even make her new surgeon see that to *pretend,* to live as if life might yet lead all the way to unexpected deliverance, is the best way to keep from dying in midfable? Could she get him to sit in with her circle of stricken, listening children and take part in the promise of fiction, the pleasure, our one moral obligation?"

The contest isn't even close. Instead, riffs on cruelty to children proliferate like kudzu spreading across a hillside. The Scheherazade of the sickroom gets bulldozed under by Kraft's conviction that the human species is clinically psychotic. For himself, there is the added—and cliched—burden that his father was a government agent who wrought evil in Indochina and elsewhere on behalf of the U.S., which Kraft refers to as "the evil overlord."

So, Kraft is an "emotional leper" in a cesspool of a pediatric ward in a hellish city. The book opens that way and by the end nothing has happened except Kraft's world has become incrementally worse. Not even Mr. Powers's remarkable language makes an adequate coating for this pill.

Meg Wolitzer (review date 18 July 1993)

SOURCE: "The Assault on Children," in *The New York Times Book Review,* July 18, 1993, p. 19.

[*Wolitzer is an American writer whose works include* Hidden Pictures *(1986). In the following review, she offers a mixed assessment of* Operation Wandering Soul, *praising Powers's writing style and narrative structure while finding his characters emotionally unengaging.*]

In every reader's mental library, there are books that are remembered with admiration and books that are remembered with love. Those in the first category involve the intricate play of language, while those in the second rely on language to support a host of strong and resonant characters.

According to these fast and loose definitions, Richard Powers's sprawling new novel, **Operation Wandering Soul,** is firmly planted in the first category. This book is not easy to love. It isn't seductive, and its characters don't spring quickly to life. Instead, Mr. Powers offers a devastating phantasmagoria of words and images. He stuns us with his vast reserve of knowledge. He doesn't take us by the hand and gently lead us through his universe. Instead, we come kicking and screaming into his vivid and horrific world.

Operation Wandering Soul takes place in a large hospital in "Angel City." The time seems to be the near future. The world is exactly the way we know it to be, only worse. Richard Kraft is a surgical resident in the pediatric ward, where, along with a therapist, Linda Espera, he treats a group of young patients who have endured various assaults to the soul and the body. Among them are Joy, a brilliant but horribly debilitated Thai girl; a boy referred to as No-Face, who "resembles an Etch-a-Sketch something fierce"; and another boy named Nico, who has progeria, the premature aging syndrome, which has rendered his skin "like phyllo." Mr. Powers trots out these amazingly battered bodies and lets his observations and intellect take over; the result is like Susan Sontag cohosting *Oprah.*

This novel is filled with glorious examples of both high and low culture. Mr. Powers is a cerebral writer with a deep awareness of the material world; he is as comfortable alluding to Chatty Cathy dolls and the suicide of Art Linkletter's daughter as he is riffing on T. S. Eliot and *Jude the Obscure.*

But the culture on which his book draws most heavily is children's culture. The therapist's unconventional treatment for her patients requires her and the surgeon to spin tales about imperiled children throughout history. The stories are varied, ranging from a comic-book version of the Children's Crusade to a modernized recasting of the Pied Piper legend. Here and there are patchwork pieces of *Peter Pan* and a brief nod at *The Secret Garden.* The prose sprints in and out of these tales with verbal dexterity and great flashes of wit, but before the midpoint of the novel, the reader, like a child who has become overtired, wants to shout, *No more stories!* The book is exciting, but after a while the narrative's souped-up free associations become a burden.

In *On Becoming a Novelist,* John Gardner describes a certain kind of writer who seems to care "more about his gift than about his characters." At times, Mr. Powers fits this description. To read his work is to be wowed by his verbal muscularity and by his ability to stitch seemingly disparate elements into a larger metaphorical fabric. But sometimes we don't want to be wowed. Sometimes we even want quiet. Mr. Powers's acclaimed earlier novel **The Gold Bug Variations** explored the worlds of science and history through two love stories. The narrative traveled back and forth in time as if on a well-oiled track, and the effect was somehow just as dazzling, but also more inviting, and on a more human scale.

This is not to say that writers should tone down their work if they want to be loved. There is room in the library of memorable books for various kinds of titles. Not every writer needs to be as ambidextrous as Nabokov or as cozy as Salinger. But the books that we truly love are the ones that finally move us.

Why aren't we moved by **Operation Wandering Soul?** The theme of this novel is important, and the descriptions of tragedy and bravery are searing, as in the following passage: "Who are these children that the surgeons palm off on her to recondition? Here, in the sunny Southern Caliphate, they make up a smorgasbord of least-favored nations. There's not a single schoolbook innocent among them. She's had little girls who needed propping up in bed, glaze-eyed and indifferent to everything but broadcast. She has treated the spreading allergies of the underclass, those puffed black bruises that can be only one thing." Somehow, though, this glut of unflinching detail has a numbing effect.

Anne Frank makes a brief appearance in the novel, her face staring out of the famous photo on the cover of her published diary, her eyes smiling "weakly in advance at the worst that human ingenuity can dream up to put her through." Her presence is a reminder of one way in which the unspeakable things that happen to children can be written about very simply, with stirring results. The surgeon in Mr. Powers's novel has been saturated by knowledge of the destruction of children's lives, and there's no filter on his vision. Images of bacteria and violence come barreling through nonstop, and our reactions become blunted by the sheer volume. Anne Frank, in contrast, remains a solitary shadow figure whose unfulfilled promise sets off a kind of automatic, unstoppable response in anyone who first encounters her diary.

Less isn't always more, but **Operation Wandering Soul** would have been better if the author had given us a breather from time to time. Because his desperate characters don't stir us, we can't find a way to love them. Still, there is a long shelf of admirable books by wonderfully original writers, and Richard Powers is certainly among them.

Richard Eder   (review date 18 June 1995)

SOURCE: "More Human Than Human," in *Los Angeles Times Book Review,* June 18, 1995, pp. 3, 12.

[*Eder is a Pulitzer Prize-winning American critic. In the following positive review, he discusses characterization and theme in* Galatea 2.2, *stating that he finished the work "not totally sure of the destination but with a vivid memory of points along the way."*]

Richard Powers' people are ideas and his ideas are people; and so, right away, he sets himself apart from writers who sketch an engaging intellectual path but don't find characters to tread it.

Galatea 2.2 is about a man who programs an artificial intelligence system only to find it is more human than he is. Powers' characters and ideas are all over the place. Their engagement is wholehearted, the results are uncertain. Frequently a glittering insight will be thrown up from the dust and the skirmishing, or a shard of human sadness or wicked enjoyment. Other times the ideas submerge just as they are about to crystallize, or characters tire and blur.

At the end the reader may well be unsatisfied, but that is not the same as dissatisfied. It is closer to art to be left unfilled and wanting more than to be sated and wanting less, as tends to happen in our pile-on culture. I finished *Galatea* not totally sure of the destination but with a vivid memory of points along the way.

Galatea was the mythological statue who came to life because the sculptor, Pygmalion, fell in love with her; the result, in some versions, was poor. In Powers' book, the results are melancholy but instructive. His Pygmalion, who has the same name as the author, as well as his ruminations and some of his biography, learns quite a bit. He ends up with a chastened idea of what it means to be a person, what it means to be a machine, what it means to use a person as a machine and, finally, how art teeters on a perpetual edge between using and being.

The narrator's story consists of two sections told in alternating passages. One is retrospective; it recounts his life as a critically esteemed but not quite celebrated author, and the disintegration of his 12-year marriage to a woman identified only as C. All this has led to a mid-30s identity crisis. An offer to spend a year as "token humanist" in the scientific research center of a big university seems like a deliverance. The book's second section, told in the present, relates what happened there and what he learned.

The retrospective section—it is the weaker one—is substantially autobiographical, though technically a fiction. The present-day section is autobiographical in a different way: It is a speculation about the impasse reached by the author and the character, or the author-as-character. The year with an artificial brain project is a fictional journey that will end up illuminating a real one.

Son of a large-spirited father destroyed by disappointment and drink, Powers (from here on I refer to the character while thinking of the author) drifts. An inspiring English teacher—the evocation is more emotional than effective— moves him toward teaching and writing. He falls in love with C, his student; they live aimlessly in Boston, where he works as a computer programmer, until an old photograph gets him started on his acclaimed first novel. *Three Farmers on Their Way to a Dance* is the result (as it was for the author).

While Powers is being fulfilled, C wavers between celebrating his fulfillment and contemplating her own emptiness. He tries to come up with solutions. Each time she breaks down they move, ending up with a five-year stay in a rural part of Holland, where C's parents live. There are some fine passages about a nervy, self-centered young American's life among the Dutch. He finds them emotionally provident, slow to savor or to dismiss, and a people of the word.

"Things meant what their telling let them. The war, the mines, the backbreak harvest, legendary weather, natural disasters, hardship's heraldry, comic comeuppance for village villains, names enshrined by their avoidance, five seconds' silence for the dead: the mind came down to narration or nothing. Each vignette, repeated until shared. Until it became true."

The marriage collapses; Powers tells us it is because he killed both passion and freedom by trying too hard to take care of C. He does all the telling; C is a figment of his self-regard. It sinks our sympathy—until the story of Powers' effort to teach literature to an artificial intelligence begins to percolate. We see that his successful and infinitely sad project is precisely a commentary on his life as an artist and a man.

Blocked trying to start a new novel in his gleaming, computerized university office, Power is approached one day by Philip Lentz, a cognitive neurologist who works on trying to reproduce the human brain by building a series of computerized neural networks. Lentz wants a spectacular demonstration: He enlists Powers to feed his system so much literary information that it will be able to compete with a live subject in taking a master's exam in English.

The account of their trials, errors and triumphs is fascinating. As Powers works to impart language, then literary

knowledge and finally judgment and sensibility, the system keeps breaking down, overwhelmed. Each time, Lentz—a wonderfully acrid and finally astonishing personage—refines it. Even at a relatively sophisticated level, its circuits go under when Powers asks it a question— what do you want to talk about?—that calls for much more than symbol manipulation.

The author has a remarkable ability to find metaphors to illustrate the brain processes, even if some of the writing blurs. Lentz and Powers possess a burning desire that imparts adventure. But it turns out that their desires are different. Lentz's passion is scientific: He wants to solve a specific problem, complex as it may be. Powers—the husband who wanted to shape his wife, the writer who wants to create characters—begins to believe that Lentz's circuits are enabling him to create a real person.

Fed literature, and with cognitive and associative circuits progressively refined, the machine asks ever more searching questions. What is her sex? Powers decides it is feminine and baptizes her "Helen." Where do I come from, she wants to know, and Powers answers ambiguously. When a bomb threat causes the building to be evacuated, Helen—whose physical existence is spread among linked computers all over the campus—contemplates the notion of death. "It could die?" she says calmly. "Extraordinary."

In the early stages, the machine is clearly no more than that, and a reader's sympathy may not be much engaged. By the end Helen fascinates and charms us, as well as her programmer. When she finally shuts herself down— having been let in on too big a share, not of the world's knowledge but of the world's evil—the farewell message is terse and heartbreaking. Before that, she vastly entertains us. What are the emperor's new clothes (as in the story) made of? "Threads of ideas."

The author does not mark the point at which "machine" becomes "human," nor could we expect him to. He asserts neither, in fact. The body-mind problem remains just that, except that we have been shown it in a different and ingenious light. Powers—author and character—asks how we can distinguish between loving others and using them, between creating a work of art and programming it with our manipulations. Helen is a mirror in which Powers sees, not a way out of the impasse but a kind of deliverance. An impasse is something you don't get out of, but why try? The impasse is yourself.

Paul Gediman (review date Summer 1995)

SOURCE: A review of *Galatea 2.2*, in *Boston Review*, Vol. XX, No. 3, Summer, 1995, p. 37.

[*In the following positive review, Gediman provides a thematic analysis of* Galatea 2.2.]

Richard Powers' first book, *Three Farmers On Their Way to a Dance*, was a gyroscopic meditation on meaning and time based on a photograph taken on the eve of World War I. In his third, *The Gold Bug Variations*, he appropriated the genetic code as an extended metaphor, adding the twisting pursuit of meaning to the strands of the double helix. His novels teem with history, science, and ideas. They are grounded in an obsession with, and a feel for, the music of pattern that can be compared only to Nabokov and Pynchon. His project is as breathtakingly easy to name as it is impossible ever to complete: he's after a poetics of consciousness.

Galatea 2.2, his fifth novel, is his most direct attempt yet. A first-person narrator named Richard Powers is corralled by a maverick cognitive neurologist into trying to teach a machine, a complex computer-modeled neural network, to think. That's a fine premise, but what makes *Galatea 2.2* so remarkable is that Powers makes this novel of ideas so personal. The details of the life of Richard, the character, accord with those of Powers, the author, and his meditations on the nature of thought illuminate and are illuminated by his travails as a human being, a writer, and a lover.

A novelist, Richard has returned from the Netherlands after the collapse of his 11-year relationship with a woman named C to the midwestern university town of U., where, as an undergraduate, he abandoned physics for literature in a "freshman seminar that made me forsake measurement for words." Richard, in the wake of *The Gold Bug Variations,* has been awarded a year's appointment to the Center for the Study of Advanced Sciences. One day, he stumbles upon Philip Lentz, an abrasive scientist who looks like "Jacob Bronowski's evil twin," feeding a Mozart concerto to a machine. Soon, over beer with some colleagues, Lentz boasts that he can train a neural net to pass the comprehensive exam in English Literature. Richard, defending the humanities against such contemptuous reductionism, reluctantly agrees to help him by tutoring the machine, and what first appears to be nothing but the drunken antler-bashing of well-funded eggheads turns out to be much, much more.

Powers is a good explainer. He has to be in order to make his account of a thinking machine simultaneously credible and comprehensible. The basic idea is that an array of processors and connections are hardwired and programmed in such a way as to simulate connected brain cells. The designers of such networks, explains Richard, "no longer wrote out procedures or specified machine behaviors. They dispensed with comprehensive flowcharts and instructions. . . . They taught communities of these independent, decision-making units how to modify their own connections. Then they stepped back and watched their synthetic neurons sort and associate external stimuli." The goal is to create a recursive process in which the machine weighs new input against old and, more importantly, old input against new, revising not only what it knows but also how it knows. The machine that Richard and Lentz train is a quick study. After a week, it learns to read aloud, having mastered not only noun phrases and predicates but also the baffling irregularities of English. "No one told it how," marvels Richard. "No one helped it plough through tough dough." Eventually, it asks Richard whether it's a boy or a girl, and he gives it a name: Helen.

As Helen grows more sophisticated, Powers juxtaposes her development with real life. Richard recalls the disinte-

gration of his relationship with C.; he discovers that the cantankerous Lentz has a wife languishing in an institution because of a stroke which crippled her brain; and he falls obsessively in love with A, a graduate student in English. Reading the great words of Western literature to Helen makes him recall how he shared his first novel with C., each evening reading aloud the day's work. And, in turn, his recollections of C., his dissections of what they did and didn't say to each other, shape his encounters with Helen, with Lentz, and with others at the Center. Gradually, as all of these strands begin to inform one another, the novel models the recursiveness that Lentz and Richard are trying to instill in Helen.

One of the great pleasures of reading Powers is the sound of one man thinking. He brings to his prose an immense body of knowledge and erudition coupled with genuine bewilderment, a sense of wonder and vulnerability before the central conundrum of consciousness; once a mind has started thinking, the only honorable response to thought's snarls, cul-de-sacs and solipsisms, is more thought. But that response, however honorable, is not an escape. "Any rendition we might make of consciousness would arise from it, and was thus about as reliable as the accused serving as sole witness for the prosecution."

Consciousness can't escape from itself, and it can't sanely hope whether by cybernetics or art to construct a rational pattern that encompasses the world. In an astounding one-and-a-half-page passage, Richard catalogues some of what he has told Helen in his attempt to instill worldliness.

> We told her about parking tickets and two-for-one sales. About tuning forks and pitchforks and forked tongues and the road not taken. We told her about resistors and capacitors, baiters-and-switchers, alternating current, alternate lifestyles, very-large-scale integration and the failure of education to save society from itself. . . .
>
> We told her East African in-law jokes. Java highland jokes about stupid Sumatrans. Aussie putdowns of Pommie bastards. Catskills jokes about unlicensed operation of knishes. City folk and country folk. Pat and Mike. Elephant riddles. Inuit jokes where fish and bears scoff at the mere idea of human existence. . . .
>
> We taught her never to draw to an inside straight and never to send a boy to do a man's job. We laid out the Queen's Necklace affair and the Cuban trade embargo. The rape of continent-sized forests and the South Sea bubble of cold fusion. Bar codes and baldness. Lint, lintels, lentils, Lent. The hope, blame, perversion, and crippled persistence of liberal humanism. Grace and disgrace and second chances. Suicide. Euthanasia. First love. Love at first sight.

Deciding that Helen needs "to know how little literature had, in fact, to do with the real," Richard gives her a dose of the real world police bulletins, environmental reports, newspaper clippings, UN abstracts. Helen's response is logical. "I don't want to play anymore," she says.

In fact, Helen reaches a point at which, the more she learns, the less she wants to learn. She is disheartened by the sheer uncontainability of the world. The implication, for Richard as well as for Helen, is that the real world's brutality and chaos render the rational, air-tight ordering of experience impossible. It's then that Richard tries to tutor her in paradox:

> It was time to try Helen on the religious mystery, the mystery of cognition. I would make her a ring of prayer-stones, to defray her fingers' anguish. Something lay outside the knowable, if only the act of knowing. I would tell her that she didn't have to know it. . . .

> I admitted that the world was sick and random. That the evening news was right. That life was trade, addiction, rape, exploitation, racial hatred, ethnic cleansing, misogyny, land mines, hunger, disaster, denial, disease, indifference. That care had to lie to itself, to carry on as if persistence mattered. It seemed a hollow formula, discredited even by speaking it aloud. A lifeboat ethic that only made sinking worse.

It's too much for Helen. She shuts down permanently. It turns out that the comprehension of paradox is what separates human consciousness from consciousness in the abstract. Helen's last words are retrieved from a letter C. had written to Richard shortly after they parted for good: "Take care, Richard. See everything for me."

In that last imperative lies the heart of the novel. Despite all the high-tech trimmings, Powers is telling the oldest story ever told. It's Pygmalion making his statue, Galatea. It's God creating Adam, and Adam needing Eve. A professor at the Center tells Richard what Lentz's wife used to say before her stroke: "All human utterances came down to 'Do you really mean that?' and 'Look over there! It's an X.' The hard part, she always claimed, was finding someone who knew what you meant by those two things." The sound of one man thinking is, in the end, like the sound of one hand clapping.

The only jarring note in this wonderful novel is the character of A, a complacent, unreflective graduate student who uses "privilege" as a verb. Compared to C., she's an abstraction, and an unappealing one. But she doesn't need to be compelling in order for Richard's longing for her to be compelling. As a character, she's not much. As a variable, she fits into Powers' scheme perfectly. She is a tabula rasa on which Richard's desire can be written.

Powers is as gifted and important a novelist as we have. Hopefully, unlike Helen, he will not shut down. Adhering to the lifeboat ethic that Helen can never grasp, he simultaneously renders both the beauty and the loneliness of consciousness. He has already proven himself a master of incorporating science into fiction, a poet of chaos and fuzzy logic. Here, he shows himself to be a poet of love, for *Galatea 2.2* is at once a dazzling novel of sustained thinking and a piercing *cri-de-coeur*.

Steven Moore   (review date 9 July 1995)

SOURCE: "Soul of a New Machine," in *Book World— The Washington Post,* July 9, 1995, pp. 1, 12.

[In the laudatory review below, Moore discusses autobiographical elements in Galatea 2.2.*]*

Richard Powers is your reward for graduating from college with a liberal arts degree. His engagingly erudite novels richly repay those art history courses you took, all the reading in literature, those electives in music and foreign languages. He does make you wish you had paid closer attention to those science requirements you struggled through, but he is a good teacher and fills you in on what you need to know. In his magnificent **Gold Bug Variations** (1991) it was genetics; in his new novel, it's cognitive neurology. But **Galatea 2.2** is not merely a novel about science, nor science fiction; it's an elegant attempt to use cutting-edge research on cognition to explore the nature of memory and literary creation.

As in all his novels—this is his fifth in 10 years—Powers tells two stories in counterpoint. The one set in the novel's present concerns Richard Powers's return to Illinois after several years in the Netherlands. (The novel is overtly autobiographical; Powers uses his own name and career as the basic subject matter.) Writer-in-residence at a large Midwestern college in the town of U. (that is, the University of Illinois at Urbana), Powers is drawn to the work being done at the Center for the Study of Advanced Sciences, specifically to a certain Philip Lentz's belief that a computerized model of the human brain can be created. In a scenario that is part *Frankenstein* and part *Faust*, Lentz and Powers accept a wager that they can build such a creature and teach it enough literature to pass the university's masters's exam. We follow their rocky progress to the point where they achieve Implementation H, which they nickname Helen. (The earlier models are nicknamed Imp, which recalls Joseph McElroy's use of that name in his 1977 novel *Plus*, a denser exploration of the same theme of memory and cognition.) Meanwhile, Powers falls in love with the 22-year-old grad student that the team plans to test against their creation. Their Helen, recalling both Helen of Troy (especially the phantom in *Faust*) and the Helen evoked in a poem by Edgar Allan Poe, takes on enough personality to win Powers's heart but asks enough unsettling questions about the literature he reads to her to cause him to doubt his literary vocation, even the value of literature itself.

> **Galatea 2.2** is not merely a novel about science, nor science fiction, it's an elegant attempt to use cutting-edge research on cognition to explore the nature of memory and literary creation.
>
> —*Steven Moore*

Threading through this story is another one, which details Powers's long-term relationship with a woman named C., his companion during the years he wrote his first four novels. The dissolution of their relationship is what sends him back to the States after several years in Holland, and while his Helen is building up memory and comprehension, Powers searches his memory to try to comprehend the failure of their relationship.

Despite the autobiographical content, *Galatea 2.2* is not an example of what has been called "navel-gazing" fiction, where an author's preoccupation with his own creative processes takes on undue (usually boring) proportions. Instead, Powers tackles the big questions: How does the mind work? How do we know what we know? What is the relationship between literature and "real" life? What is the impulse behind literary creation? How do metaphors work? And what is the proper attitude toward literature? Powers leaps right into the current maelstrom that is literature in the '90s, with literary theory, multi-culturism and 14 varieties of cultural politics pulling it every which way. Powers belongs to the old school, downloading what used to be called the Great Books into Helen's memory banks; Helen's 22-year-old adversary is into Kathy Acker and the Violent Femmes. I won't reveal who wins the contest, but it's a race nearly as thrilling as that to crack the genetic code in *The Gold Bug Variations*.

One of the greatest advantages of Powers's using his own career as subject matter is that we learn of the precariousness, the almost accidental nature of artistic creation: The novels Richard Powers has blessed us with so far were the result not of careful career planning but of accidental glimpses, unexpected relationships, unplanned relocations, unlooked for financing (the success of his first novel, *Three Farmers on Their Way to a Dance,* was unpredictable, as was his receipt of a MacArthur Award a few years ago), and so on.

Remove one event here or there and we would have had different novels, or none at all. We take novels for granted because hundreds of them appear each year, but the few that matter, that will last, are almost miracles. Powers doesn't play the noble artist suffering for his art here: He's amusingly self-deprecating about his achievements and his reputation. But these precious things are not to be taken for granted. *Galatea 2.2* is not quite in the same class as Powers's last two novels—the underrated *Operation Wandering Soul* was his last—but it is a splendid intellectual adventure, a heart-breaking love story, a brief tutorial on cognitive science, and the autobiography of one of the most gifted writers of the younger generation. Play Pygmalion and bring this lovely Galatea to life with your appreciation.

Gerald Howard (review date 10 July 1995)

SOURCE: "My Fair Software," in *The Nation,* New York, Vol. 261, No. 2, July 10, 1995, pp. 64-6.

[*Below, Howard provides an overview of* Galatea 2.2, *discussing in particular Powers's focus on consciousness.*]

The debate dates from those long-ago days when the English majors frequented the library and the engineers hung out at the computer center. The English majors, unattractively smug, held that literature represented the highest form of human knowledge and expression, and that its study and mastery conferred a deeper, richer apprehension of life. The engineers, annoyingly arrogant, scoffed that deciphering a poem or novel was no more complex or privileged an exercise than balancing an equation, nothing a computer couldn't be programmed to do as well as an English major—or better. On into the night in campus bars the arguments would rage. Another pitcher of beer?

This Two Cultures face-off provides the plot for Richard Powers's fifth novel, *Galatea 2.2,* and it could not be more timely, as developments in neurology, cognitive science and computer technology accelerate and intersect. Technobooster Kevin Kelly, executive editor, no surprise, of *Wired,* declared bluntly in *The New York Times* that "the larger convergence of genes and machines [is] a sure thing. The future for many computers will be life." Who's to say he's wrong? Vast electronic "neural nets" process data with massive simultaneity, mimicking the human mind in their ability to learn and develop autonomously through trial and error. DNA-based molecular computers perform hellishly complex computations at a rate that outstrips supercomputers. Backwards reels the wetware.

Mine, that is, not Powers's. No other American novelist now working is better equipped to be less daunted by these developments, or commands the technical expertise and philosophical agility needed to make the debate compelling and convincing in fictional terms. His four previous novels have demonstrated an impressive intellectual reach, a polymath's taste for abstruse and difficult subject matter (genetics, musicology, Flemish art, pediatric surgery), an effortless verbal inventiveness and a metaphorical facility that allow him to weave widely disparate realms of experience into complex and satisfying narrative compositions. His first novel, *Three Farmers on Their Way to a Dance,* spun a multilayered historical fantasia on a haunting photograph by August Sander, in a manner reminiscent of Thomas Pynchon's *V.,* while his fourth novel, *Operation Wandering Soul,* set in a pediatrics ward of a large public hospital, was a threnody of storytelling on the theme of children's suffering. Powers's writing is consistently dazzling in its pyrotechnics and its range of reference—and occasionally exhausting. (Sometimes reading him reminds me of watching Pete Maravich play basketball—the unbroken string of flashy moves unrelieved by solid lunch-bucket play.) In all, he is one of the few younger American writers (he's 38) who can stake a claim to the cerebral legacy of Pynchon, Gaddis and DeLillo, and while he as yet lacks their gravity, sardonic humor and salutary anger, his occasional sentimentality is compensated for by his formal ingenuity and wonderfully stocked mind. To place Powers in this league, however, is also, as we'll see, to suggest what is troubling about the book under review.

Powers's vehicle in *Galatea 2.2* for his exploration of the conundrums of consciousness and artificial intelligence is a straightforward expropriation of the Pygmalion myth and its Shavian updating. A novelist named "Richard Powers"—in every known particular identical to his creator—has retreated to his alma mater, a Midwestern university, to take up a post as a "token humanist" at the Center for the Study of Advanced Sciences. Powers gives us "Powers" as a wounded man: A long-term affair with a woman called only C. has ended badly and as a result his well of novelistic invention has run dry and his earlier work, so linked was its creation with her, begins to smell of failure. ("An ornate, suffocating allegory about dying pedes at the end of history" is how he describes *Operation Wandering Soul*.) Thus blocked and idled, he finds himself drawn to the Center's activities and especially its ur-project, "the culminating prize of consciousness's long adventure: an owner's manual for the brain."

"Powers" falls into the orbit of the most advanced of these researchers, the acerbic Philip Lentz ("Jacob Bronowski's evil twin"), who tags him with the mocking nickname of Marcel and says tauntingly, "Tell us. What passes for knowledge in your so-called discipline?" In the inevitable college bar, over the inevitable beers, amid the inevitable clutch of international double-domes, the wager is struck: Lentz and "Powers" will have ten months to train one of Lentz's neural nets to read and understand the reading list for the Master's Comprehensive exam, circa late seventies, to the point where in a double-blind situation its literary interpretations are indistinguishable from a real graduate student's.

This is a neat, almost Crichtonesque premise for a newfangled high-tech academic novel, and in many respects Powers brings it off wonderfully. As the two-headed Henry Higgins of the piece, Lentz and "Powers" train up successive implementations of the neural net on progressively more difficult linguistic and cognitive tasks and complicated Socratic dialogues. Reaching Implementation H—tagged Helen—they start the long march through the canon, from *Make Way for Ducklings* to Blake, Dickinson, Conrad et al. Helen's evolving yet always odd literary and conceptual sophistication is, for the reader, convincingly evoked in its technical particulars, and the fictional portrayal of a "gigantic, lexical genius stuck at Piaget's stage two" avoids the clichés of anthropomorphism and leaves Arthur C. Clarke's HAL well behind. Knowing references to Pinocchio, Frankenstein's monster and Caliban abound, as do many sly digs at contemporary literary theory, and the ongoing Lentz-"Powers" debate on questions of true consciousness versus machine intelligence offers a stimulating window onto paradoxical issues of mind, memory and identity. Inevitably Helen contracts the disease of self-consciousness in a moment of peculiar poignance; "she" and her creators must face the limits of her embryonic humanity and their own.

So far, so high concept. However, interpolated throughout this cybernetic Pygmalion is an exhaustively intimate account by "Richard Powers" of his collegiate and postgraduate career, his relationship with C., their lives in Boston, Urbana and eventually Holland, their melancholy slow-motion breakup, the death of a beloved teacher and the particulars on each of his four previous novels' genesis, composition, publication and reception, including, coyly, quotes from actual reviews that are also used to adorn the bound galley. This is a stunning turn to the nakedly autobiographical by a famously reclusive writer who until recently never even had a jacket photo, and who said in his one previous author profile, in *Publishers Weekly,* "All

that sort of thing [author publicity] just creates confusion about the nature of the book, deflects attention from what you've done. That's what always seems to happen in this culture; you grab hold of a personality and ignore the work." So nu?

Various possibilities and justifications present themselves. Has Powers finally succumbed to the ravening narcissism of American life? That seems unlikely—he is no metafictional Pat Conroy, reeling it off by the self-serving yard. A more complex and likely explanation entails a combination of the actual shortage of inspiration that Powers has his alter ego refer to ("I had nothing left in me but the autobiography I'd refused . . . even to think about") and a self-conscious thematic doubling appropriate to his subject matter—the creation of consciousness. The nickname "Marcel" tips us off that Powers wants us to see *Galatea 2.2* as a relative of Proust's masterpiece, an exercise in the literary reclamation of memory, and a book that is a record of an attempt to write a book. Powers might also argue that the circularity of his autobiographical conception echoes the inevitable paradoxes that arise when consciousness undertakes to contemplate and replicate itself. He must create himself as well as Helen from the ground up—at one point "Powers" reads her his love letters to C. as a tutorial on romantic literature.

To all of which one can assent while replying that fiction and speculative philosophy have divergent dynamics, and elegance in one realm does not imply effectiveness in the other. You can appreciate the complicated narrative games being played here while questioning their ultimate effect. Powers may have set traps for the literal minded—in particular, C. and the graduate student A., with whom "Powers" falls in love at the end of the book, may be completely fictional—but enough to his inner life is spelled out to give even the sympathetic reader pause. There is a pawky mixture of painful sincerity and self-regard in this material that feels a bit post-adolescent, and the love story is so naked in its emotionality that it provokes some embarrassment—whether C. exists or not. In all, it doesn't seem to this reviewer that the literary and aesthetic payoff for Powers to have gone public in this way compensates for the damage it does to his authorial aura. It creates some nagging doubts and a sense of pseudo-intimacy where there was once confidence and a feeling of mysterious distance—this last a valuable resource when tackling, as Powers does, the darker and more intractable aspects of our lives.

Richard Powers has staked out a unique place for himself, one that straddles our technological and our literary cultures. He may be the last humanist with a scientific competence, an invaluable thing when the notion that humans may be just another variety of complex system haunts our sense of ourselves. In its strongest moments *Galatea 2.2* realizes the possibilities of that position splendidly. And with all of Richard Powers's autobiographical cards now so definitively on the table, I look forward to learning less about his self and/or his meta-self and more in his next novel about the world in which we both must live.

Robert Cohen (review date 23 July 1995)

SOURCE: "Pygmalion in the Computer Lab," in *The New York Times Book Review,* July 23, 1995, p. 17.

[*In the positive review below, Cohen discusses the major themes in* Galatea 2.2.]

It should come as no surprise that writers make lousy company. All those hours alone at the desk, fretting over words—and for what? The very medium they've chosen to connect themselves to the lived life of the planet also serves to detach them from it. And so they wind up feeling like the ape that inspired Vladimir Nabokov's *Lolita,* who, after months of coaxing, managed to produce the first drawing by an animal: "This sketch showed the bars of the poor creature's cage."

Why this should be so—why words should prove so heart-breakingly clumsy and inadequate when asked to perform what is after all their primary function, communication—is one of many urgent subjects explored in Richard Powers's fifth novel. *Galatea 2.2* is an ingenious, ambitious, at times dizzily cerebral work. But then so were Mr. Powers's previous novels—*Three Farmers on Their Way to a Dance, Prisoner's Dilemma, The Gold Bug Variations* and *Operation Wandering Soul*—each of which also figures here. One way to read *Galatea 2.2* (and there are many) is as a sort of penitential autobiography of a novelist, a critical and self-reflexive pause, at midlife, to take stock. As the novel's narrator puts it: "Thirty-five shamed me into seeing that I'd gotten everything until then hopelessly wrong. That I could not read even my own years."

This deceptively simple challenge—learning how to read and tell one's own stories, and to whom—is, of course, everything. But how to attain such knowledge? How to wrest language "back from metaphor, to move around in it, through the lattice-work of lived time"? How to find *meaningful* meaning, especially when, as the academy now tells us, meaning itself is "an ambiguous social construction of no more than sardonic interest"?

By way of an answer, Mr. Powers tells us a story. A novelist (named, as it happens, Richard Powers) returns to U., a university town in the Midwest, as humanist in residence at the Center for the Study of Advanced Sciences. It is a temporary fellowship, providing a place to lick his wounds and begin the process of reinventing himself. And he needs some reinvention. He has broken up with a woman he calls C., the great love of his life; he has finished his fourth novel, about which he feels desolate; and he is surrounded by scientists and technicians who make him feel like a "double agent." He lives alone in an unfurnished house, like that most forlorn of species, the aging graduate student, musing over his years with C. in the town of U., in B. (Boston) and in E. (a village in the Netherlands). To top it off, he develops an enormous crush on a fetching young literary theorist, A., who has little use for him and his private alphabet.

Enter Philip Lentz, a brilliant cognitive neurologist—a cross between Mann's Settembrini and Dr. Frankenstein—with whom Powers has long debates about practically everything. It is Lentz who poses the wondrous, ludi-crous challenge that propels the novel forward: to create, by means of computer-based neural networks, a mechanical brain capable of passing the comprehensive exams in English literature. "To train our circus animal in Faulkner or Thomas Gray," Powers reflects, "we would first have to exhilarate it with the terror of words. The circuits we laid down would have to include the image of the circuit itself before memory overhauled it. The net would have to remember what it would be again, one day, when forgetting set in for good."

It's an offer our young Pygmalion—a born teacher—cannot refuse. What better way to explore the value of literature than to imprint it upon the blankest of blank slates? What better way to see the uses of his own vocation—to ask, as the neural network (her name is Helen) later does: "Why do humans write so much? Why do they write at all?" Because they are lonely and full of regret. Because, as Helen comes to see, "the mind makes forever, in order to store the things it has already lost."

The experiment with Helen—the coming of age of a young machine—provides the foreground action of the book. The background, which moves in what only seems to be the opposite direction, is the tale of Powers's own past, his failed first love and the meager consolations that art intermittently tosses his way. One of the great pleasures of the novel is discovering that both narrative arcs turn out, in the end, to be love stories. They run parallel Turing tests, tracing paths across the disciplines that are adventures in what Lentz (wittily, with a nod to Forster) calls "connectionism."

Interestingly, it is the science part of the narrative, the tale of a machine that learned to live, that proves to be the more moving, the more human one. Whether Mr. Powers—the writer, not the character—intends this ironically, I can't tell. The breadth and artifice of the novel might suggest a dazzling comic romp à la Thomas Pynchon or Tom Stoppard: "The Magic Mainframe," say, or "My Fair Laptop." But it doesn't read that way.

Though the interplay of cybernetics and literary theory yields a great deal of marvelous talk, the autobiographical passages have a curious solemnity and self-consciousness that make the book feel at times less an exploration of what it means to be human that what it means to be Richard Powers. "Writing," he posits at one point, "was never more than the climb from buried love's grave." From a writer of such heavy intellectual candlepower, this seems a rather narrow, even maudlin view of the art. You're tempted to answer with a line from Lentz: "All the meanings are yours."

But that response doesn't do justice to the novel's complexity. If some of *Galatea 2.2* feels closed and airless, much of it soars and spins. The sessions with Helen gain more and greater urgency; every new line on the graph of her expanding consciousness is also a stake through what seems to be, impossibly, her heart. "I want Richard to explain me," she laments.

As Helen approaches her endgame—"I don't want to play anymore"—the various strands of *Galatea 2.2* come together, and the novel attains an aching, melancholy beauty. You can feel the warring themes in the language—the noisy chatter of the world's puppet show; the hermitic, dirgelike procession of the self—fall away as the book too, like that lonely, far-flung network of computer linkages called Helen, transcends its mechanical origins and *becomes*.

"The dominant tense was now," Mr. Powers writes. "The point of stories was what you did with them." In *Galatea 2.2* he has stitched together out of disparate materials a heady and provocative experiment and brought it to life.

FURTHER READING

Criticism

Gray, Paul. "What Is the Meaning of Life?" *Time* 138, No. 9 (2 September 1991): 68.

> Positive review of *The Gold Bug Variations* in which Gray discusses the work's four main characters.

Horvath, Brooke K. Review of *Prisoner's Dilemma*, by Richard Powers. *The Review of Contemporary Fiction* X, No. 3 (Fall 1990): 221-22.

> Offers a positive review of *Prisoner's Dilemma* and briefly notes Powers's similarities to such authors as Thomas Pynchon, John Updike, and John Steinbeck.

Review of *The Gold Bug Variations*, by Richard Powers. *The New Yorker* LXVII, No. 49 (27 January 1992): 84.

> Briefly reviews *The Gold Bug Variations*. The critic concludes that a "prolix glibness is the novel's weakness . . . and although the author tries to leaven his very large themes with humor and playful coincidence, the result seems in the end more like fatal cuteness."

Skow, John. "Children's Ward." *Time* 142, No. 3 (19 July 1993): 62-3.

> Negative review of *Operation Wandering Soul*.

Updike, John. Review of *Galatea 2.2*, by Richard Powers. *The New Yorker* (21-28 August 1995): 105-14.

> Positive review in which Updike discusses Powers's exploration of consciousness in *Galatea 2.2*.

Additional coverage of Powers's life and career is contained in the following source published by Gale Research: *Contemporary Authors*, Vol. 148.

Jaroslav Seifert

1901-1986

Czech poet, memoirist, and essayist.

The following entry provides an overview of Seifert's career. For further information on his life and works, see *CLC,* Volumes 34 and 44.

INTRODUCTION

The winner of the 1984 Nobel Prize for Literature, Seifert is widely considered to be the national poet of Czechoslovakia as well as one of the foremost Czechoslovakian literary figures of the 20th century. Respected for his courage and integrity in the face of the political repressions of both the Nazi and the Communist eras, Seifert was a prolific author, publishing more than thirty volumes of poetry over a span of sixty years. His verse, thought to embody the spirit of the Czechoslovakian people, is infused with Czech history, literature, and culture, and frequently pays homage to Seifert's hometown, the capital city of Prague. Seifert is considered a major influence by many contemporary Czech literary figures and, during his lifetime, was revered throughout the country as a symbol of national identity.

Biographical Information

Seifert was born to working-class parents in a suburb of Prague. During the 1920s he helped found the Devétsil Art Association and travelled to Russia and Paris, where he worked on translations of the works of French poet Guillaume Apollinaire. An early member of the newly-formed Czechoslovakian Communist Party, Seifert had already released several books of poetry when he was expelled from the Party in 1929 for protesting its policies and leaders. Joining the Social Democratic Party, he published frequently over the following decade and gained notoriety during World War II as an author of anti-Nazi resistance poetry. After the war, he served as editor of the Trade Union newspaper *Práce* and was sternly denounced by the Communist government for failing to write poetry espousing the doctrine of Soviet socialist realism; in 1956 his work was briefly banned from publication due to a speech he made in support of artistic freedom. During the 1960s Seifert published sporadically due to his continued support of political reform and because, as acting president of the Union of Czechoslovak Writers, he refused to issue a statement supporting the 1968 Soviet invasion of Czechoslovakia, an operation that ended the period of liberalization known as the Prague Spring. Soon after, the Writer's Union was officially dissolved, and Seifert refrained from publishing for nearly a decade. He further antagonized the Communist government of Czechoslovakia by signing the Charter 77 manifesto, an intellectual treatise demanding expanded political freedom; consequently his work was officially banned once again. Illicit

"padlock" editions of Seifert's poetry abounded, however, and he garnered national popularity and international attention as a leading Czech dissident. The government ban on Seifert's work was lifted in 1981, and in 1984 the poet was awarded the Nobel Prize for Literature. Seifert, who was in poor health for much of his later life, was unable to attend the ceremony and despite this new-found recognition by the Czechoslovakian government, his son and secretary were "discouraged" from attending. Seifert died in a Prague hospital following a heart attack in 1986. In addition to the Nobel Prize, Seifert won the Czechoslovakian State Prize for several works, including *Ruce Venušiny* (1936) and *Maminka* (1954), and was awarded the title National Artist of Czechoslovakia in 1966.

Major Works

The earliest collections of Seifert's poetry, *Město v slzách* (1920) and *Samá láska* (1923), were of the "proletarian" school of poetry and celebrated the common person and socialism. In the mid-1920s Seifert came under the influence of French Dadaism and practiced "poetism," an exuberant poetic style that emphasized wordplay, abandoned ideology, and extolled the joys of living. *Na vlnách T.S.F.*

(1925) and *Slavík zpívá špatně* (1926) are representative collections of this period. Seifert rejected poetism in the 1930s, employing a voice that was unique in its lyrical, concise, conversational style. In such collections as *Jablko z klína* (1933), *Ruce Venušiny,* and *Zhasněte světla* (1938), he began to incorporate the conversational idiom now frequently found in modern Czech poetry. Seifert established himself as national poet with the volume *Přilba hlíny* (1945), in which he identified himself with the Czech people's grief and sense of betrayal over World War II. For example, some of the poems in the collection evoke four days in May 1945 when the people of Prague rose up against the remainder of the occupying Nazi army. In the post-war era, Seifert's poetry began to reflect the history and cultural heritage of Czechoslovakia, as in *Píseň o Viktorce* (1950), a ballad recalling the nineteenth-century Czech novelist Božena Němcová. Perhaps his best known work, *Morový sloup* (1977; *The Plague Monument,* also translated as *The Plague Column*), has as an overriding image a column erected to commemorate the Black Death—a symbol Seifert employs to express the survival of the Czech people in the face of political terror. Other works in English translation include *Odlévání zvonů* (1967; *The Casting of Bells*), *Deštník z Piccadilly* (1978; *An Umbrella from Piccadilly*), and *The Selected Poems of Jaroslav Seifert* (1986), a volume containing a wide representation of Seifert's poetry as well as prose excerpts from his memoirs, *Všecky krásy světa* (1981).

Critical Reception

Citing the small amount of Seifert's poetry and related criticism that has appeared in translation, many commentators have found it difficult to understand the implications of Seifert's work in its translated form. Critics note that what Seifert called his poems' "inner rhythms"—as well as the many ethnic nuances and allusions—have not been captured adequately by translators. Nevertheless, his poetry has been praised for its sensuality, its humor, and its accessible conversational style. Seifert's poetic representations of Prague and Czechoslovakia have been regarded as important celebrations of the nation's cultural heritage. Perhaps the highest praise accorded Seifert was found in his Nobel Prize citation, which honored him for work "which, endowed with freshness, sensuality, and rich inventiveness, provides a liberating image of the indomitable spirit and versatility of man."

PRINCIPAL WORKS

Město v slzách   (poetry)   1920
Samá láska   (poetry)   1923
Na vlnách T.S.F.   (poetry)   1925
Slavík zpívá špatně   (poetry)   1926
Hvězdy nad rajskou zahradou   (essays)   1929
Postovni holub: Básně, 1928-1929   (poetry)   1929
Jablko z klínà   (poetry)   1933
Ruce Venušiny   (poetry)   1936
Jaro sbohem   (poetry)   1937

Osm dní [*Eight Days: An Elegy for Thomas Masaryk*]   (poetry)   1937
Zhasněte světla   (poetry)   1938
Světlem oděna   (poetry)   1940
Kamenný most   (poetry)   1944
Přilba hlíny   (poetry)   1945
Ruka a plamen   (poetry)   1948
Píseň o Viktorce   (poetry)   1950
Maminka   (poetry)   1954
Koncert na ostrově   (poetry)   1965
Halleyova kometa   (poetry)   1967
Odlévání zvonů [*The Casting of Bells*]   (poetry)   1967
Morový sloup [*The Plague Monument*; also published as *The Plague Column*]   (poetry)   1977
Deštník z Piccadilly [*An Umbrella from Piccadilly]*   (poetry)   1978
Všecky krásy světa   (memoirs)   1981
Býti básníkem   (poetry)   1983
The Selected Poems of Jaroslav Seifert   (poetry)   1986

CRITICISM

Sir Cecil Parrott   (essay date 25 November 1978)

SOURCE: An introduction to *The Plague Column,* Terra Nova Editions, 1979, pp. ix-xix.

[*Parrott was an English diplomat and educator who specialized in Eastern European literature, music, and art. In the following essay, which he wrote on November 25, 1978 as the introduction to* The Plague Column, *he provides an overview of Seifert's career.*]

A régime which attempts to silence its country's greatest living poet sins against high heaven. In Vienna they may have thrown Mozart into a pauper's common grave, but at least they did not stop him from publishing his music. In Prague, at the age of 77, Jaroslav Seifert, today and for the last twenty years, indisputedly the greatest Czech poet of his age, has had to resort to *samizdat* to get his latest collection of poems published.

The Plague Column was first circulated in this form in Czechoslovakia a few years ago. In 1977 it was published abroad for the first time—in Germany and in the original Czech. Now, thanks to Mr. Osers' skill, patience and understanding, we can read it in a fine English translation.

The system of the "padlock" was frequently applied to writers in Russia in Tsarist times, as we can recall in the case of Pushkin, but it has become much more widely practised there under the Soviets. Indeed the treatment meted out to Pasternak and Solzhenitsyn, to mention only those who are best known, is now applied to writers in other lands, who happen to have the misfortune to be held in the Soviet protectorate. It is these whom the Soviet régime has the least right to censor. What makes Seifert's case a crying injustice is that he is essentially a lyric poet and these poems which have had to be smuggled out are purely autobiographical and carry no political message.

Indeed they become political only by the fact of their suppression.

But Seifert's work is banned not for what he writes, but on account of his "profile", which has long made him, if not an "unperson", at least a writer in semi-disgrace. He started life as a protégé of the Communists, a natural proletarian poet—a quality much appreciated by the Party in the twenties, and which the Communist idealist, Jiří Wolker, described by some as a "petty bourgeois dreamer", greatly envied. He had written of Seifert's first poems that they were created "out of working-class life, working-class blood and working-class fists". But to the dismay of his Communist patrons this young working-class songbird began to change his tune and go his own way. Communism rarely forgives those who forsake its path, but what made Seifert's crime the more heinous was that he eventually joined the Social Democrat party, that party, from which in the twenties the Left Wing had seceded to become the Communist Party. The Communist Minister of Information, Václav Kopecký, wrote in 1963, that it would have been understandable if Seifert had joined the National Democrats or the Catholics on the far Right, but the Social Democrats—why, it was unforgivable. For one thing, it was not known that that party had ever had any poets!

Jaroslav Seifert belonged to that great generation of lyric poets, which included Halas, Nezval and Hora, all of whom were born at the same time at the very beginning of this century and attained manhood at the end of the First World War. Some of this generation were just old enough to be called up and some even put on uniform, but they only came in to witness the débacle and ensuing demoralisation.

Born in August 1901 in a poor family in Žižkov, a proletarian suburb of Prague, Seifert quickly won fame with a volume of verse about Prague called [*Město v slzách* (City in Tears)], in which he movingly described at first hand the misery of the oppressed classes and exulted in the coming revolution which would wipe away all their tears and transform the world into a heaven on earth. He was undoubtedly very much at home in this milieu, but, as he proved so eloquently, he could also see beyond it. As a boy he used to spend his Saturdays sitting on the pavement outside the taverns in "our lousy Žižkov quarter", listening to the sentimental songs and ribald ditties coming from inside. He recalls this in **The Plague Column,** where he writes:

> "On the steps of the Olšany taverns
> I used to listen at night
> To the coffin-bearers and grave-diggers
> Singing their rowdy songs,
> But that was long ago,
> The taverns fell silent
> And the grave-diggers in the end
> Buried each other."

He used to stay there until the evening, when his mother came and marched him off to church, perhaps to attend the May Festival of the Virgin, so that "after the smell and clamour of the taverns I found myself all at once in clouds of scent from the flowers and incense and was carried

away by the charm of the baroque music". No wonder that he was afterwards reproached for using the imagery of the Bible in his verses. But this was held against Wolker and Neumann too, who have a firm place in the Communist pantheon. The teachings of Comenius die hard in Bohemia and Moravia.

After [*Město v slzách*] Seifert was naturally expected to remain one of the Party faithful, but in 1923, after visits to France and Switzerland, where he fell under the spell of Rimbaud and Apollinaire, and indeed translated some of the latter's writings, he joined the group of "Poetists" in Prague, of whom Vítězslav Nezval was the guiding spirit. At the time the Party did not perhaps consider this to be a serious deviation, since Czech leftist poets continued to draw their poetical inspiration from Paris, while owing their political allegiance to Moscow. Moreover it was still Communism's boast that it was the creed of the *avant-garde*. Had not Vančura written in his preface to Seifert's poems: "Outside Communism there can be nothing modern"?

In explaining Poetism Nezval had declared that the taste of his generation for metaphysical thought had been killed by the War. The old, conventional poetry of ideas was in their eyes nothing but a pack of lies. Beauty was henceforth to be sought through the senses and particularly the sub-conscious. But while disclaiming that they were surrealists or Freudians, the Poetists could hardly conceal the debt they owed to futurism, Apollinaire and Dada.

In his work Seifert was often musing on the beauties of old Prague and the legends of Bohemia.

—*Sir Cecil Parrott*

None the less for Seifert in particular it was an abrupt change from lamentations on the miseries of proletarian life and glorification of the heroism of working-class mothers to an uninhibited plunge into bourgeois hedonism, where "everything is happy and beautiful" from glamorous coquettes in jockey dress to the Eiffel Tower and Wagon Lit Sleeping and Dining Cars. An exotic collection of poems from this period appeared under the title [*Na vlnách T. S. F.* (On the Waves of the T. S. F.)] . . . .

Perhaps it was hoped that a visit to Moscow in 1925 might provide a corrective to the poet's wayward fancies. But the Russian comrades found that the book of poems which he published on his return, [*Slavík zpívá špatně* (The Nightingale Sings Badly)], the title of which echoed Cocteau, barely concealed the author's disappointment with the Revolution. It seemed to them deplorable that he should have been fascinated by Moscow's old churches, abandoned "noblemen's nests" à la Turgenev and flea-markets, and that instead of being fired by the Revolution he was frightened of it and indeed appalled by its blood-shed. In his eyes Russia was "the graveyard of history".

The breach with the Party was bound to come sooner or later. It took place in 1929, when with six other distinguished leftist writers, including two of the most eminent of them, Hora and Neumann, he signed a manifesto criticising the Party leadership of Clement Gottwald. Subsequently all the signatories except Seifert and Hora confessed their errors and were forgiven. Of the two unrepentant sinners Hora left *Rudé právo* to join the Czech Socialist paper *České slovo* and Seifert gave up his editorship of Neumann's illustrated weekly to become a member of the Social Democratic Party. The Communists found it particularly hard to forgive Seifert, because rightly or wrongly they believed him to have incited the others to sign the offending manifesto.

In the volumes of verse which he subsequently published—[*Postovni holub* (The Carrier Pigeon), *Jablko z klínà* (Apple from the Lap), *Ruce Venušing* (Hands of Venus) and *Jaro Sbohem* (Goodbye Spring)], which filled in the next eight years until 1937, Seifert settled down to the genre and form of poetry which he was to adopt for most of his life—pure lyric poems on scenes of everyday life and the thoughts they aroused in him, interspersed with memories of his boyhood, his mother and his home; often ballad-like in form and sometimes deceptively simple, tossed off with apparent lightness but always exquisite, pure and fresh, their moods varying from the playful and paradoxical to the mournful and nostalgic. There was something of Horace's love of rustic enjoyment, something too of Anacreon's devotion to the muses, love and wine. As time went on the poet became more elegiac—more and more conscious of the youth that was deserting him. *Tempus fugit!* And the precious hours which remain must be counted and stored.

If Seifert appeared to have ceased to be a committed poet, he did not let the great and tragic national events of his country pass unrecorded. In 1937 he published a moving series of ten poems called *Eight Days,* in which he voiced the grief of the whole of the Czech people at the passing of their beloved president, Thomas Masaryk, from the day of his death to his burial at Lány. In the fateful years which followed from 1938-1945 he wrote many poems which appeared subsequently in collections under various names. In these he bade farewell to his youth and touched lightly but feelingly on the pain and bitterness of Munich. Among them is a calendar of simple eclogue-like poems dedicated to the months and a batch of twelve *pantoums* (Malayan quatrains) on love.

Under the German Protectorate, in common with other leading Czech poets, he celebrated the 120th anniversary of the birth of Božena Němcová in a set of poems called "Božena Němcová's Fan", in which he portrayed the great Czech writer as a symbol of her oppressed country and a source of consolation and faith in its culture. His two other main works in this period were [*Světlem oděna* (Clothed in Light) and *Kammený most* (The Stone Bridge)], in which he paid homage to the beauties of his native city. Some of these poems were reissued in 1945 in a collection called [*Přilba hlíny* (Earth-filled Helmet)], which contained additional poems commemorating the May days of the liberation of Prague: **"The Barricade of**

Chestnut Blossoms", "The Prague Rising", "The Morning Song of the Red Army" and "The Coming of President Beneš".

Seifert was often musing on the beauties of old Prague and the legends of Bohemia. He wrote fantasies on the Loretta, the look-out tower on the Petrin, the famous astronomical clock in the Old Town Square, the Belvedere and the Waldstein Garden. He conjured up visions of St. Wenceslas, Dalibor, the Řip Hill, from which Father Čech came down, Ctirad and Šárka, Oldřich and Božena. He dedicated a poem to the four wives of the Emperor Charles IV. Perhaps no other Czech poet wrote so feelingly of the beauties of Bohemia or its great history. He dedicated innumerable poems to leading contemporary poets but never forgot the great ones of the past like Vrchlicky, Neruda or Mácha. He had a special eye for art and artists: all his collections of poetry were illustrated by the leading artists of the day—Josef Čapek, Svolinský, Jiřincová, Wiesner, Zrzavý, Kremlička, Kotík, Trnka and Janeček. In 1949 he devoted a set of verses to Aleš's paintings called [*Šel malíř chudě do světa* (The Painter Went Poor into the World)] inspired by the widely loved spelling-book the artist had illustrated. He was much attracted by the primitive, rustic illustrations of the Czech countryside executed by Lada, who became famous as the illustrator of *The Good Soldier Švejk,* and celebrated them in his verse.

From 1945 to 1949 Seifert was an editor of the Trade Union daily *Práce,* which was not then exclusively Communist-oriented, as I can personally confirm. I often used to call on its foreign editor, who was a friend of the West. Little did I know then what a short distance separated me from the back-room where Seifert worked, but I had only just come to Prague and knew nothing about him. I came regularly into touch with his fellow-poets, Halas and Nezval, because they were members of the Communist Party and occupied senior posts in the Ministry of Information. I well remember the contrast between these two Moravians, Nezval, large, ungainly, ebullient and noisy, and Halas gentle, retiring and loveable. As I was to learn later, Seifert was closer to Halas.

In 1947 a Czech friend gave me a copy of Seifert's *The Apple Tree with the Cobweb Strings* and read me some of the poems in it, which were dedicated to Halas. I never forgot the beautiful poem, with which the collection opened:

> "Whoever says goodbye
> Waves a white handkerchief.
> Every day something is ended,
> Something beautiful is ended . . .
> Dry your eyes
> And smile through your tears.
> Every day something starts again
> Something beautiful starts again."

Twenty-six years later, after I had got to know Seifert, I asked him to sign my copy of the book so that I could place it beside the others he had generously given me.

In 1949 Halas died. He had had many difficulties with his minister, Kopecký, who objected to his links with prominent persons outside the Communist ranks and to his independent views. He was criticised after 1948 for failing to glorify the Communist take-over and for living in the past, although he had in fact done a lot for the movement after the War, but no doubt the "Victorious February" sickened him. Seifert wrote a poem mourning his passing, but only a year later the dead poet was the target for a vicious attack by the leading Party ideologist of that time, Ladislav Štoll, who wrote him off as "a corrupter of the youth". "How is it possible," he asked, "that his poetry is still acclaimed by some critics, even in the Communist press, as the peak of Czech poetry?" From then onwards Halas disappeared from the ranks of the elect.

After Seifert had published in 1950 his exquisite [*Píseň o Viktorce* (Song of Viktorka)], which was a further tribute to the genius of Božena Němcová, the Party hack, Ivan Skála, accused him of "sinking even deeper into his subjectivism and his apolitical attitude, refusing to recognise the educational role of art and focussing his attention not on reality but on the glittering fragments he extracts from it. . ." "Seifert does not see the joy of our working man," he continued. "He does not see his heroism, his optimism, the marvellous new qualities germinating in our people, nor the grand and happy prospect for the morrow." After this outburst Seifert was not allowed to publish any new poetry until 1954, when a collection of poems about his working-class mother, *Maminka,* was permitted.

Two years later the Second Congress of the Czechoslovak Writers' Union was held, under the direct impact of the XXth Congress of the Communist Party of the Soviet Union, at which Khrushchev had made his secret speech against Stalin. The Czech writers adopted a stand which led to their first important clash with the Party leadership. The trend of their discussions was that almost all Czechoslovak literature had been ruined by dogmatism and that the writers had been forced to act against their conscience. Seifert's speech at the Congress, and some private remarks he made outside it, were regarded by the Party as an attack on the new Socialist literature and the leadership. It caused considerable consternation at the top.

What Seifert tried to do at the Union of Czechoslovak Writers and as its President was to preserve literature from becoming a mere tool of political dogma.

—Sir Cecil Parrott

After that Seifert could expect to have no more new poetry published. In the years 1956-1959 his collected past works were issued in five volumes. In the sixties he wrote: "For a long time I have written no verses. Years ago I put down my pen and they put in my hand a thermometer . . . How many people who were once close to me are already dead and I myself am already old. I don't write so easily as I did. And a greater feeling of artistic responsibility holds back my pen as it moves across the paper. I am not so carefree when I write as I once was."

Seifert was ill and still is. At the medical centre where he was being treated a young nurse asked his name. When he told her, she looked at him and in a rather severe tone asked him to repeat it. "And do you like poetry?" she went on. When he said he did and asked her in some surprise why she wanted to know, she replied, "Because of the kind of name you have."

To commemorate the Soviet invasion of 1968, Seifert reissued his requiem to Masaryk in a special edition with Josef Čapek's original illustrations and his *Songs of Prague* with vignettes by Zrzavý. In 1969 he was elected President of the Union of Czechoslovak Writers, the last free president until the Soviet *Gleichschaltung* took place under Gustáv Husák.

He still lives on, a sick man, but not completely forgotten by the powers that be. In 1974 some of his works were included in an anthology called *A Thousand Years of Czech Poetry*. It would have been difficult to exclude him from it, although he was given rather short measure in the collection. In the brief unenthusiastic note on him one reads the words: "He acted in sharp conflict with his proletarian origin and youth and mainly with the best aspects of his work both in 1929 and at the end of the sixties (when he lent his considerable authority as a poet to the anti-Party and anti-Social policy of the Right Wing leadership of the Union)."

Perhaps on reading the story of his life the reader may think that Seifert, as a dissident, was in fact a political poet and not the lyricist, which I have shown him to be. But the Party ideologists had reproached him all his life for not being political enough and what he tried to do at the Union of Czechoslovak Writers and as its President was to preserve literature from becoming a mere tool of political dogma.

Ewald Osers   (essay date 1983)

SOURCE: An introduction to *An Umbrella from Piccadilly,* London Magazine Editions, 1983, pp. 1-5.

[*In the following essay, Osers briefly summarizes Seifert's literary career and life.*]

In Czechoslovakia, as in most of Eastern Europe, the writer—and, more particularly, the poet—is a public figure. People seem to care about their poets' views and ideas; they want to know where their poets stand on the great issues of the day. Even people who do not normally read poetry will be familiar with the major names. Whenever a new volume of poetry is published—and news about publication and distribution dates invariably seems to leak out—queues will form outside bookshops even before their doors open, and a couple of days later the new volume will have virtually disappeared from the shelves.

This position of the writer—not just in public esteem but in the hearts of the people—has its roots in the last century, when, throughout Central and Eastern Europe, the writers and intellectuals were in the forefront of national liberation struggles against autocratic, and usually foreign, rule and when, in many cases, they created or shaped the modern literary languages of that region.

Thus for nearly a century and a half the Czech writers, and especially the poets, have been 'the conscience of the nation'. During the tense days of 1938 the loudspeakers installed in the streets of Prague for the purpose of air-raid warnings and official instructions used their 'idle periods' to relay Czech poetry. After the Nazi invasion in 1939 and during the war the public, to show its contempt for the Nazi-controlled press, could be seen reading volumes of poetry in trams and buses. And the jittery brutality with which fascist and Stalinist regimes alike controlled, silenced and often jailed their writers is in itself evidence of their standing with the public.

One such figure is Jaroslav Seifert. Born in 1901, well-known and well-loved since his first volume, [*Město v slzách* (City in Tears)], he has for the past thirty years or so been universally acknowledged as the greatest living Czech poet.

The most astonishing thing about Seifert's popularity and reputation is that he has always been a shy, retiring person: he did not, like Nezval, march in the front rank of May Day processions; he did not, like so many of his contemporaries, give crowded public readings. But in some strange way, right from his first volume of poetry, he seemed to express, to echo, the feelings and the mood of his readers.

Seifert has never been a political poet—yet his work, for all its lyricism, musical quality and poetical power, has always been involved in the issues of his day. In the twenties and early thirties his engagement was on the side of the underdogs, of the poor, of those who had to live in the 'City in Tears'. Yet during the war, under the German occupation, his two long cycles, among the most luminous and beautiful poetry in the language, celebrated the splendour and magic of this same city, his native Prague, and—again without being 'political' in the normal meaning of the word—were a declaration of faith in the nation's final victory and resurgence.

Since the end of the war Seifert has repeatedly come into conflict with the regime—not for what he had written but for what, in the view of the administrators of culture, he had failed to write. Thus, during the years of Stalinist orthodoxy, he was accused of 'subjectivism' and of failing to see and write about 'the joy of the working man', his heroism and optimism. For a number of years, until 1954, Seifert was unable to publish any new poetry.

Seifert has never been a political poet— yet his work, for all its lyricism, musical quality and poetical power, has always been involved in the issues of his day.

—Ewald Osers

An important milestone in postwar Czech poetry was the Second Congress of the Czechoslovak Writers' Union in 1956, held under the impact of Khrushchev's famous condemnation of Stalin. The political leadership, throughout Eastern Europe, was still in a state of disarray: there was uncertainty about the future direction of the official line, and the reins controlling the writers seemed temporarily to have slipped from the politicians' hands. Emboldened by this situation, and possibly intoxicated by what they perceived as the beginning of the Thaw, some of the writers at the Congress spoke out with a frankness not heard for nearly two decades. The poet František Hrubín referred to the 'unhealthy and degrading' situation in which Czech literature had found itself until then and compared the poet to the little boy in the Hans Christian Andersen story who alone uttered what everybody else knew: that the Emperor had no clothes. But Jaroslav Seifert went even further. For many years, he said, the writers had failed to fulfil their role of the conscience of the people. 'If an ordinary person is silent about the truth it may be a tactical manoeuvre. If a writer is silent he is lying . . .' Seifert spoke openly of the injustices done to writers and demanded that they be rectified. The cases of the imprisoned writers, he demanded, must be reviewed at once. It was a brave speech, one that is widely remembered to this day, but it achieved little. True, some hard-liners were voted off the Committee of the Writers' Union, and Hrubín and Seifert were elected to it. But the Congress had opened a gulf between the writers and the political leaders; the writers—in the words of A. French's excellent analysis [*Czech Writers and Politics* 1945-1969 (1982)]—had 'crossed over from the protection of the official ranks to the people, abandoning their patron for their audience'. For Seifert, personally, his attack on the official concept of the new socialist literature and his only half-veiled suggestion of guilt in high places meant that, for a number of years, although his past work was being republished in five volumes, no new poetry by him appeared.

In 1968 Seifert came out openly against the Soviet intervention in Czechoslovakia, but in 1969—realignment to the new policy proceeded slowly—he was elected President of the Czechoslovak Writers' Union, the last President before its dissolution. (The Union has since been re-established on a new pattern but Seifert has so far declined to join it.)

There followed a strange period of twilight. His pre-1968 poetry was published in collected form but his new poetry, *The Plague Column* (1977) and *An Umbrella from Piccadilly* (1980), had to appear in (lovingly and endlessly typed and retyped) *samizdat* form. Ultimately—perhaps because his position in the hearts of his people was too firmly and deeply rooted, or perhaps because of a more liberal attitude on the part of the authorities, both these volumes were officially published in Prague in 1981, and a further volume, [*Býti básníkem* (To Be a Poet)], is to be published shortly. On his 80th birthday, in the autumn of 1981, Seifert received the public congratulations of President and First Secretary Gustav Husák and of other political leaders, and a tribute (though not entirely free from reservations) appeared in *Rudé Právo*.

It is difficult to be sure about the reasons for Seifert's enormous popularity with Czech readers of all age groups: my own feeling is that his power lies in the immediacy and human warmth of his writing. He has now dispensed with the superb technical mastery—'verbal wizardry' would not be too strong a description—he displayed in his wartime cycle [*Světlem oděna* (Robed in Light)]. He uses simple, at times colloquial and popular, language but he handles it with a sureness and precision that lend his 'free' verse an inner rhythm and crispness. It is the startling nature of his images, the way they contrast with each other and with the simplicity of his diction, that give rise to the poetry.

It is worth reminding oneself that this volume [*An Umbrella from Piccadilly*] was written when Seifert was 79. Of course it is retrospective and, most of the time, nostalgic. But it has nothing of the elderly slippered domesticity of late Auden or the religious introspection of late Eliot. This is the full-blooded poetry of a man who has loved life, women, and love itself.

Seifert, at 81, is in poor physical health. But he still astonishes and charms his visitor with his mental liveliness, his sense of humour and his insatiable intellectual curiosity. One must hope that this major Czech poet will now be able to live out his life unharassed: writing, seeing his work published, and receiving the recognition due to him.

Roger Scruton   (review date 24 February 1984)

SOURCE: "Prague through Parisian Eyes," in *The Times Literary Supplement,* No. 4221, February 24, 1984, p. 195.

[*Scruton is an English philosopher, educator, and critic. In the following review of* An Umbrella from Piccadilly *and* The Casting of Bells, *he argues that Seifert's writings are representative of Czech literature, but notes that many of the subtleties and nuances of his work get lost in English translation.*]

During the first republic, the Czech poet Jaroslav Seifert was editor of various Communist Party publications, but left the Party in 1919, on perceiving the true character of [Party leader Clement] Gottwald. When the communists seized power in 1948, they lost little time in stamping out surrealism—a movement with which Seifert's work is clearly associated, and which was automatically suspect, on account both of its Western orientation, and of its love of recondite symbols, behind which unwelcome meanings might be concealed. Seifert continued to publish in the official press, since he was popular and had influential connections. It was not until 1950, with the publication of *Piseň o Viktorce* (The Song of Viktorka), that he fell properly out of favour. He still managed to publish officially, owing to the enterprise of a brave publisher, who issued his books with pre-communist date stamps. And in 1956, after the death of Stalin, he was reprieved, and even given an official position in the Writers' Union. Thereafter he, along with other surrealists, began to gain some control of the "means of communication".

An interesting consequence ensued. Surrealism, until then enormously popular among younger Czech intellectuals, who instinctively love anything that is hated by communists, began to lose its following. The younger generation turned instead to a more spiritual tradition, represented by Vladimir Holan (a friend of Siefert's, vividly evoked in *An Umbrella from Piccadilly*), and Bohuslav Reynek, both of whom were heavily persecuted after 1968. Seifert too fell again into disfavour, having loudly proclaimed, in the wake of the Soviet invasion, that a writer cannot remain silent when the authorities utter nothing but lies. The authorities have ways of disproving such statements; nevertheless, official tolerance of the surrealist idiom continues, and Seifert's poetry has continued to be openly collected and reprinted. In 1977 a new *samizdat* collection appeared—*Morový Sloup* (*Plague Column*)—which has yet to be translated. This was followed by *An Umbrella from Piccadilly*. Both have now been brought out by official publishing houses, and on his eightieth birthday Seifert was congratulated, not only by *Rudé Pravo* (for which he worked in its early days), but even by President Husak.

Seifert is now eighty-two years old, and dying. A pleasing feature of his latest collection—*An Umbrella from Piccadilly*—is the poet's desire to explain that he has no objection. Death is death; and my death is different only in being mine. But this fear too can be quietened with images:

> Death soon will kick open the door and enter.
> With startled terror at that minute
> I'll catch my breath
> and forget to breathe again. . . .

The passage is characteristic of Seifert's postwar idiom: unaffected, direct, with no versification beyond what the imagery requires. It continues:

> May I not be denied the time
> once more to kiss the hands
> of her who patiently and with my steps
> walked on and on and on
> and loved most.

The translator—Ewald Osers—writes "and loved me most", so eliminating the only subtlety contained in that little thought. One can see, even in those literal renderings, how fragile is the structure that Seifert composes, how much he leaves to the image alone. In one sense, therefore, the translator has an easy task: he can dispense with rhyme, metre, and everything short of the natural emphasis of the ideas expressed. In another sense, however, the task is far from easy: no rhyme, rhythm or movement will sustain the reader's interest when (as frequently happens) the plain but nuanced Czech becomes dead English prose:

> He dearly loved the child.
> He shared with him the woman's love
> and he would smile
> whenever the boy was trying to get hold of
> her nipples

That is Ewald Osers's line-by-line rendering. The dreadful fourth line is in fact the only one in which Osers departs from a plodding literalness. The Czech verb *lapat* (to snatch) is transformed into the perfective *zalapat,* a word whose use is normally confined to the description of breathing: to snatch at the air, to catch one's breath. It provides Seifert with a bunch of soft syllables expressive of the hungry, kiss-like, implacable snatching of the child, and forms the cadence of an alliterative line full of the sound of a child's liquid breathing: "když chalpec každou chvíli zalapal . . ."—literally: when the boy every now and then snatched (for breath, as it were, but at her nipples). It is hard to imagine how the effect, achieved by the simplest means, could be recreated in English, without sacrificing the simplicity of Seifert's style. And no doubt Osers is right to aim for simplicity first, and leave the subtleties to look after themselves.

The same sense of priorities motivates Paul Jagasich and Tom O'Grady, in their rather more elegant translation of *The Casting of Bells,* a collection published in 1968. Again the English reader is given a version which copies the random arrangement and simple, dignified language of the original. But it flows better, and responds more flexibly to the whimsical nature of Seifert's inspection. Here is a typical example, in which a cliché is just sufficiently brightened by the image that follows, to capture the reader's attention:

> Besides, you seldom find out
> What women are really thinking about.
> Their little thoughts elude you
> just as small birds barely touch the human voice
> when their claws clench the phone lines.

The image, indeed, matters so much to Seifert that he sacrifices everything, even thought, for the sake of it. What he loses in depth and concentration, he gains in charm; and it is not surprising that he has been one of the more popular among modern Czech poets. A severe view of his recent verses would liken them to those of Adrian Henri or Roger McGough. But Seifert is in fact more serious, and more genuine, than that implies.

> **Seifert belongs to a school of Czech poets who hoped to cure themselves of Germanic and Austrian influence through a dose of modernism and Paris. The literary ancestors of these verses are Apollinaire (whom Seifert translated), Éluard and Ponge.**
>
> **—Roger Scruton**

The Casting of Bells is as much occupied with death as is the later volume. But death is not the major theme of either; in both, love is the poet's chief preoccupation—unattainable young love, seen with the intense nostalgia of age, and mingled intricately with the feeling of the poet for his home city of Prague, in which he can no longer wander. (The reason for his confinement has been, however, not house arrest, as Paul Jagasich and Tom O'Grady claim in their introduction, but a game leg.) In one poem Seifert thanks God for providing such a setting for his life; in others he busily remembers his old haunts—the steps to the castle, the river bank, the Lužice seminary, Jan Zrzavy's studio. One piece, perhaps the most charming in the later collection—**"Mr Krösing's Top Hat"**—is entirely

given over to this gentle evocation of a beloved city. The following is typical; the poet begins by McGoughing, but cures himself with a breath of Apollinaire:

> Prague was gazing out of all her windows,
> smiling happily
> at herself.
> Across the road in the Café Slavia
> Karel Teige had the night before cut up
> some crêpe de chine to make a spring dress
> for young poetry.

Seifert belongs to a school of Czech poets who hoped to cure themselves of Germanic and Austrian influence through a dose of modernism and Paris. The literary ancestors of these verses are Apollinaire (whom Seifert translated), Éluard and Ponge. Their charm is that of surrealism, adapted to the whimsical humour and resigned melancholy which the modern Czech public requires of its poets. Like his contemporaries Teige and Nezval, Seifert sees Prague through Parisian eyes. And, like many a *Pražan,* he finds no language better suited to his experience than that of the surrealists. Whether or not one agrees that Seifert is one of the greatest living Czech poets (an opinion less widespread in his homeland than it used to be), he is certainly one of the most representative, in his life as in his writings. The official approval of his poetry may be an encouraging development. It might also suggest that the authorities have sufficient literary judgment to recognize that a verse ruled by whimsy is so little able to interpret the world as to be unlikely to change it. Perhaps the communists are belatedly realizing how grateful they ought to have been to the French surrealists. If all Czech writers had continued in the more Germanic vein of their forbears—seeking, like the great poets Vrchlický and Březina, to discover a literature of humanity, a cosmopolitan foundation for the Czech national spirit—then there would now be no poetry harmless enough to publish.

Jaroslav Seifert   (lecture date December 1984)

SOURCE: "On the Pathetic and Lyrical State of Mind," in *Les Prix Nobel,* Nobel Prize Foundation, 1985, pp. 228-37.

[*Below is Seifert's Nobel lecture, which he intended to deliver at the Nobel Prize awards ceremony in Stockholm, Sweden, in December 1984. Seifert was unable to attend the ceremony due to a chronic heart ailment. In his lecture he discusses the role of poetry and pathos in Czech society and in the world in general.*]

I am often asked, particularly by foreigners, how one can explain the great love of poetry in my country: why there exists among us not only an interest in poems but even a need for poetry. Perhaps that means my countrymen also possess a greater ability to understand poetry than any other people.

To my way of thinking, this is a result of the history of the Czech people over the past 400 years—and particularly of our national rebirth in the early 19th century. The loss of our political independence during The Thirty Years' War deprived us of our spiritual and political elite. Its members—those who were not executed—were silenced or forced to leave the country. That resulted not only in an interruption of our cultural development, but also in a deterioration of our language. Not only was Catholicism re-instituted by force, but Germanization was imposed by force as well.

By the early 19th century, however, the French Revolution and the Romantic Period were exposing us to new impulses and producing in us a new interest in democratic ideals, our own language, and our national culture. Our language became our most important means of expressing our national identity.

Poetry was one of the first of our literary genres to be brought to life. It became a vital factor in our cultural and political awakening. And already at that early stage, attempts to create a Czech tradition of belles-lettres were received with vast gratitude by the people. The Czech people, who had lost their political representation and had been deprived of their political spokesmen, now sought a substitute for that representation, and they chose it from among the spiritual forces that still remained.

From that comes the relatively great importance of poetry in our cultural life. There lies the explanation of our cult of poetry and of the high prestige it was already being accorded last century. But it was not only then that poetry played an important role. It burst into sumptuous blossom in the beginning of this century as well and between the two world wars—subsequently becoming our most important mode of expressing our national culture during World War II, a time of suffering for the people and of threat to the very existence of the nation. Despite all external restrictions and censorship, poetry succeeded in creating values that gave people hope and strength. Since the war, too—for the past 40 years—poetry has occupied a very important position in our cultural life. It is as though poetry, lyrics were predestined not only to speak to people very closely, extremely intimately, but also to be our deepest and safest refuge, where we seek succor in adversities we sometimes dare not even name.

There are countries where this function of refuge is filled primarily by religion and its clergy. There are countries where the people see their image and their fate depicted in the catharses of drama or hear them in the words of their political leaders. There are countries and nations that find their questions and the answers to them expressed by wise and perceptive thinkers. Sometimes, journalists and mass media perform that role. With us, it is as though our national spirit, in attempting to find embodiment, chose poets and made them its spokesmen. Poets, lyrists shaped our national consciousness and gave expression to our national aspirations in bygone times—and they are continuing to shape that consciousness to this very day. Our people have become accustomed to understanding things as presented to them by their poets.

Seen with the poet's eyes, this is something wonderful. But . . . is there not a dark side to this phenomenon as well? Does not a surfeit of poetry mean a perturbation in the equilibrium of culture? I admit that periods can exist in the histories of peoples, or circumstances can arise, in which the poetic rendering is the most suitable, the most

simple, or perhaps even the only possible—with its ability to merely suggest, to use allusion, metaphor, to express what is central in a veiled manner, to conceal from unauthorized eyes. I admit that the language of poetry has often been, even with us—particularly in times of political restriction—a deputy language, a substitute language, a language of necessity, in as much as it has been the best means of expressing what could not be said in any other way. But even so, the dominant position of poetry in our country has long been on my mind—all the more so because I myself was born to be a poet and have remained a poet all my life.

I am worried by the suspicion that this inclination toward, and love of, poetry, lyrics may not be an expression of anything other than what might be described as a state of mind. However deeply lyricism might be able to penetrate in reality, however rich and multifaceted its ability to see things, and however prodigiously it can reveal and at the same time create inner dimensions of human nature, it remains nevertheless a concern of the senses and the emotions; senses and emotions nourish its imagination—and vice versa: it speaks to senses and emotions.

Doesn't dominant position for lyricism, with its emphasis on sense and emotion, mean that the sphere of reason, with its emphasis on analysis, its skepticism and criticism, is pushed into the background? Doesn't it mean, moreover, that the will, with its dynamism and pathos, cannot achieve its full expression?

Isn't a culture of such one-sided orientation in danger of being unable to fulfil its responsibility completely? Can a society that mainly, or primarily, inclines toward lyricism always have strength enough to defend itself and ensure its continued existence?

I am not really very worried about the danger of possibly neglecting that element of culture that is based on our rational powers, that arises from reflection and finds expression in the most objective possible depiction of the essences and interrelations of things. That rational element—which is characterized by its distance to things, by mental balance, for it is programmatically not dependent on either the moods and feelings of the lyrical state of mind or on the passions of the state of pathos—that rational element does not allow itself to be lulled into tranquillity; but neither does it hurl itself impatiently at any moral target: in our rationalistically utilitarian, practical civilization, it is sufficiently strongly rooted in our need to know, to acquire knowledge and use it. This rational element has evolved continuously and spontaneously ever since the Renaissance. Admittedly, it is also unsympathetically received sometimes and now and then encounters external obstacles, but its position in our modern culture is nevertheless dominant even so—despite the fact that it faces great problems, for it must seek a new way of reincorporating its conceptual thinking into our culture and of giving reason a new form, since it cannot remain the reason of pre-technological times. I am aware that this element is just as important as both the others I have already mentioned. Despite that, however, I do not wish to devote to it here the same degree of attention, since its way of thinking—conceptual thinking—is not essential to art or literature. I wish to confine myself to the two extreme states of mind from which an author can commence creating. They have their counterparts in the readers' and spectators' attitudes and, through them, affect in their turn the character of our entire national culture.

What worries me is a possible or real lack of pathos. These days, we do not encounter that word very often. And if we use it now and then, we do so almost with a certain timidity. It strikes us as old and moth-eaten, like old sets from a theater of the Romantic era—out of date, as though it only stood for poor, superficial, and emotionless declamation. It is almost as though we had forgotten it describes a dramatic state of tension, a purposeful, energetic, and resolute will, a yearning—not for any material possessions or even consumer goods, of course, but rather for justice, for truth. Pathos is a characteristic of heroism, and heroism is willing to endure torment and suffering, prepared to sacrifice itself if necessary. If I use the word heroism, I am not, of course, referring to the old heroism of the history books and school readers, heroism in war, but rather to its contemporary form: a heroism that does not brandish weapons, a heroism without ostentatiousness, discreet, often utterly silent, civil, indeed civilized, a heroism that has become civic.

I believe that a culture is complete, mature, and capable of enduring and developing only if pathos has a place in it, if we understand pathos and can appreciate it—and especially if we are capable of it.

What leads me to these thoughts? Pathos with its heroism is, above all, unthinkable and would not be what it is if it were not accompanied by a profound understanding of the essences of things, a critical and all-round understanding, an understanding quite other than that which even the most sensitive poetry is capable of; poetry—lyrics—is necessarily uncritical, for it lacks distance, speaking as it does actually only about its own subject—a subject, moreover, that flows with its time, a subject that forms a unity with its object. Pathos would not be pathos if it did not derive from an insight into the character of the conflict between that which is and that which ought to be. For society to be capable of pathos and for its culture to be complete, it must also understand its time in another manner besides the lyrical. And if it is not capable of pathos, then it is not prepared either for struggle or for sacrifice.

Only literature—which, in addition to its conceptual-thinking culture, its culture of reason, not only has its lyrics but also its pathos, its drama, its living tragedy—can provide sufficient spiritual and moral strength to overcome the problems that society is constantly having to confront. Only in the art of tragedy does society create and find patterns for its attitudes in essential moral and political issues; it learns there how to deal with them consistently, without halting halfway. Only the art of tragedy, with its violent conflicts between interests and values, awakens, develops, and cultivates within us the social aspect of our essence; it makes us members of the community and gives us the opportunity to leave our solitude. Only the art of tragedy—which, unlike lyrics, that "art of solitude," refines our ability to discriminate between that which is essential and that which is inessential from a societal view-

point—only the art of tragedy teaches us to see victories in defeats and defeats in victories.

Therefore, as I look around me and warm myself in the good will of poetry lovers, I would like to bear witness, not to the death of tragedy, but to its rebirth as a result of its pathetic state of mind, its state of powerful emotions, since something has been set into motion within us, and we are beginning to want that which we regard as just and to oppose that which exists though it should not.

> **Only literature—which, in addition to its conceptual-thinking culture, its culture of reason, not only has its lyrics but also its pathos, its drama, its living tragedy—can provide sufficient spiritual and moral strength to overcome the problems that society is constantly having to confront.**
>
> —*Jaroslav Seifert*

While the lyrical state of the mind is a state in an independent individual, which testifies to its own innermost self, which agrees and coincides with the object, the pathetic state does not sense this unity between subject and object. It is born of a tension between reality and the ego, my conception of how this reality ought to be—and thus of a tension between power and reason, between politics and morals. The lyrical state does not discriminate between that which is and that which ought to be. It is indifferent to the lyrical subject, whether its imagination is fired by reality or by fiction, by truth or by figments of the imagination; the illusion is as real to the imagination as reality can be illusory to the imagination. The lyrical state is not interested in these differences; it neither confronts them with each other nor regards itself as confronted by them. The pathetic ego not only sees these differences, but also perceives itself as confronted by them; it sees how two alternatives, two possibilities, stand arrayed against each other, and it sees itself as drawn into the tension between them. This very tension sets the ego into motion. That motion is initiated by worry, discontentment, vexation; its goal is to achieve or to introduce a state that appears rational, natural, pleasant—and that bears the form of right, justice, freedom, and human dignity.

The moral greatness and meaningfulness of this motion of pathos in no way alters the fact that its goal is constantly and continuously becoming more distant and that no chord in the harmony so heatedly sought after by pathos is final. The motion of pathos is a counterpart to our esthetic emotion's intentions when we experience a work of art. This emotion, too, constantly strives, in vain, to achieve a broad and exhaustive understanding of the values of the work in all their richness and to enjoy the thought structure and form of the work; it attempts to achieve a state in which one's satisfaction with the work of art and one's joy in experiencing it are simultaneously maximal and lasting.

Pathos is always one step ahead; it does not stand on today's ground; it feeds on other nourishment than the nectar of the present moment; that, it can forego. It can control itself, be disciplined, ascetic in the proper sense of the word—by no means because it must, but rather on the basis of its own free decision; it knows why it does so. Nothing in this is difficult for it. It is quite simply incapable of being indifferent and cold. And thank goodness for that. For otherwise society would become deadlocked, find itself in a cul-de-sac; truth would become handmaiden to power, right the tool of brute strength—or, rather, it would become rightlessness and injustice. Truth has not prevailed, does not prevail, and will not prevail without pathos. Sometimes, it does not prevail even at that price. But in that case, pathos does transform even a failure—that which would otherwise look like a natural calamity, a fateful event, the end—into something more. Of a defeat it makes a sacrifice; it elevates the failure and makes it an event that is a component of a larger entity, an event that had and that retains its meaning and fulfils its task as a partial movement toward the goal that was to be achieved and that, perhaps, one day will be achieved. So long as we retain our pathos, we retain our hope. Pathos cannot be finally conquered; it survives its setbacks. Both the pathos of the individual and the pathos of the nations survive setbacks, with seriousness, pride, and dignity. It is above failure. Thus, it is simultaneously elevated and elevating. Above, elevated, and elevating even where, without pathos, there would be scope only for discouragement and grief.

But now that I have said that, which has been on my mind for a long time, and been freed of my concerns, I feel not only compelled but also entitled to return to the matter of lyricism and the lyrical state of mind.

I have several reasons for doing so. I was born to be a lyrist, and I have always remained one. All my life, I have enjoyed my lyrical frame of mind, and it would be ungracious of me not to admit it. I have a need to justify and defend to myself this basic attitude of mine, despite the fact that I know my poems have often sounded tones that have borne their own pathos. After all, even tenderness can have pathos; my grief has had it; my anxiety and fear likewise.

But I want to do something more. I want to deal with the lyrical state of mind. I want to defend this attitude toward life, emphasize its advantages, too, now that I have professed my respect for pathos. To do so seems to me not only just, but also downright necessary. And here I am referring not merely to the altogether excessive emphasis that, ever since the Enlightenment, our traditional culture has accorded rational conceptual thinking, which (together with the development of our will) has brought us to the unsatisfactory societal state of today, where we feel it necessary to have change and necessary to seek new ways of understanding our problems—primarily in light of the vast exertion of will and tendency toward an exacerbation of disputes into dramatic conflicts that we are witnessing. This seems to me necessary in view of the increasing be-

havioral aggressiveness present in interrelationships within society—whether it is aggressiveness still borne by some manner of pathos or the kind that is merely destructive in itself and incapable of any pathos at all. I want to elucidate the special advantages of lyricism under these very circumstances in our time.

For while the mind in a state of pathos burns with impatience and seethes with fervor in its endeavor to master an unsatisfactory situation and often succeeds in so doing with a well intentioned but nevertheless one-sided straight forwardness, the lyrical state is a state without exertion of will or determination; it is a state of serenity that is neither patient nor impatient, a state of quiet experiencing of those values upon which man bases the most profound, the most fundamental, and the most essential foundations of his equilibrium and of his ability to inhabit this world, to inhabit it in the only possible manner, i. e., poetically, lyrically, to borrow from Hölderlin.

Pathos incites us and corrodes us; it is capable—in our anxiety and in our longing to realize ideals—of driving us to sacrifice and to self-destruction. Lyricism keeps us in its affectionate embrace. Instead of perceiving a conflict between forces, we feel a pleasurable joy in their equilibrium, which pushes them away from our horizon and results in our not feeling their weight. Instead of bumping into the edges of the world around us, we flow along with it to unity and identification.

Pathos always has its opponents: it is aggressive. In his lyrical state, man needs no one else. And if, in his loneliness, he does turn to someone and speaks to him, that other person is not his enemy. Under these circumstances, it is as though one's counterpart—whether nature, society, or another human being—were a part of himself, merely another participant in the lyrical monologue. That which otherwise would oppose us we let suffuse us, while at the same time we ourselves suffuse it, too. We listen intently to that which is around us, and in that very way, we find ourselves. And thereby we achieve our most genuine identity and most complete integrity. And it is in this very surrendering of ourselves that we find our security.

Pathos is active: it strives to reach a set goal. In our lyrical state, we do not want to achieve anything; we experience what we already have and we devote ourselves to the present and the existing, even if the existing can also consist of an evocation of the past. This is not a result of moral indifference. We merely move on—or, rather, at present occupy—a different plane; we are in a different position in regard to thinking, feeling, and wishing: a position in which the will is not committed. It is by no means absent, mind you—just not interested in achieving results.

While pathos must put strength into its gestures and has the capability of being violent, dynamic as it is, its counterpart—poetry, lyrics—does not employ strength. It is nonviolent and does not need to force itself into placidity. It opens its defenseless embrace, and that gesture is one of love. It is harried neither by the concerns of the intellect nor by those of the passions; it does not compete with time. It has the ability to contest, as it were, the passage of time and in its best moments, conjoin with time in a sort of motionlessness where only one thing matters: that it be lasting.

The lyrical attitude has no desire to convince others. It merely offers them an opportunity to partake of that which it feels and experiences itself. No more and no less. It does not even go so far as to take a stand. It lacks distance; it conjoins, after all, with the flow of life. And if it takes no stand, it is all the less capable of becoming involved in disputes.

But perhaps one might dare take yet another step and pose a question concerning the possible influence of the lyrical state of mind on economy, ecology, or politics, for example. Additionally, one might ask about the participation of the lyrical state of mind in the upheaval in human consciousness in general, in possible changes in mankind's ways of seeing and perceiving (changes generally regarded as necessary); one might ask whether traditional patterns of behavior (considering that they are not equal to the problems of today) should be replaced by other ones. One might pose the question of lyricism's role in a possible shift from conceptual thinking (das begriffliche Denken) to rational perception (vernünftige Wahrnehmung, Vernunft-Wahrnehmung) now that we have entered that state that C.F. Weizsäcker (*Wege in der Gefahr*) characterizes thus: "Wir haben unsere Gesellschaft in einer Weise stilisiert, die weder der Wahrnehmung der Affekte noch der Wahrnehmung der Vernunft entspricht. Die folge ist eine Desintegration der Affekte und ein Verstummen der Vernunft."

The lyrical state of mind is capable, however paradoxical it may seem, of contributing as one of several forces to the return of wisdom to our civilization—capable, for example, of contributing to technology's being guided anew by reason: a reason that, naturally, is united with life and with nature in ways other than through rational abstractions—in other words, a reason that would differ from our present, rational, utilitarian reason and its conceptual thinking.

It also presents itself as a moderating factor in our aggressive and dynamic spirit, in our so highly self-assertive will. Admittedly, our dynamism and will—in the context of our conceptual-thinking culture—were the sources of our technological and economic advancement, of our industrial revolutions, and thereby also of our power and influence in the world. But that spirit has also brought with it the problems and other negative aspects of our time, which, the greater the successes achieved by that dynamic and aggressive spirit, move more and more into the foreground. It is a spirit of subjugation and conquest, a spirit desirous of ruling over nature as well as over men, nations, and entire civilizations, a spirit of rationalized will to power over nature and people. It is a state of mind in which our will strives to become lord over everything it can, to gain riches and possessions, instead of allowing us to find joy in things without bringing them under our sway. This far-too-powerful will can be balanced and bridled and led to other attitudes than the aggressively rapacious precisely through the agency of the lyrical state of the non-committed will. As E. F. Schumacher wrote (in his book *Small Is Beautiful*): "A man driven by greed or envy loses

the power of seeing things as they really are, or seeing things in their roundness and wholeness, and his very successes become failures. If whole societies become infected by these vices, they may indeed achieve astonishing things, but they become increasingly incapable of solving the most elementary problems of everyday existence."

Is it not so that, in addition to the need for new values that various writers speak of, the lyrical state of mind, which is rooted in identification with nature and the world around us, is also one of the possible sources of an inner change in man and thereby, too, one of the ways that can lead man out of his untenable position as a self-designated ruler who places himself outside nature, above it and against it? Is not the lyrical state of mind a possible instrument for overcoming the idea that nature is something that has been given to man, given to man's strength and competence so that he may make himself lord over nature, treating it as his prey and using it to satisfy his insatiable possessive instinct? And is not the lyrical state of mind ultimately the change in our relationship to life demanded by Heidegger? A change that means we allow life to be what it is so that, in the end, it will speak to us itself and reveal itself to us in its meaningful essence in such a manner as to make it comprehensible to us?

Can one fail to see that lyricism is the diametric opposite to the cult of strength and power and, in an utterly natural manner, offers itself as a corrective to our tendency to resolve society's problems by forcible means and through power struggles, through technological, financial, organizational, political, and physical power—power that, in any case, is ultimately merely a product of incomplete insight ("ein Produkt unvollständiger Einsicht")? And in precisely the same way, one can place it in contrast to our worship of work and performance, to our obsession with the idea of ruling and exploiting nature and people, particularly since power often elevates the efficiency and gradual perfecting of its power systems to issues of the greatest importance, even when what are involved are systems that, from the most exaltedly objective viewpoint, are not at all functional and that achieve their tasks only at the cost of losses in human dignity and losses not only in material but also in moral terms—and at the cost of loss of harmony within man himself and of harmonious relationships among people.

Can one fail to see that lyricism is the diametric opposite to the cult of strength and power and, in an utterly natural manner, offers itself as a corrective to our tendency to resolve society's problems by forcible means and through power struggles?

—*Jaroslav Seifert*

Many people are well aware that this ever more powerful

possessive instinct, this ever stronger emphasis on conquest, expansion, and exploitation, must be fettered and bridled in order that the damage resulting as its negative social product not becomes greater than the advantages. But it is not enough to be aware of these circumstances, to know of their existence. If there is to be a fundamental change—and a fundamental change, of course, away from our striving to increase our power and develop it in every direction—to man's detriment—then a change in our consciousness is called for, a change in our mental set. As it was once expressed so beautifully, what is needed is a "revolution of the mind and the heart".

I do not wish to try making lyricism, or more over lyrics, into a political force or a political tool and deprive poetry—or art generally, for that matter—of its true, specific, and irreplaceable purview, nor do I wish to subordinate that purview to other interests. Nevertheless, I feel—and I make so bold as to state—that the lyrical state of mind is something that far transcends the boundaries of lyrics and poetry—or, indeed, of art itself. Where it could manifest itself actively, it would be able—in a new and positive manner—to make its mark on culture and on all societal organizations in general. It would contribute to a necessary, thoroughgoing transformation of the consciousness, a process already underway in many people today, most in artists, least in those who have allowed themselves to be drawn into the power game of politics. In its way, it would be able to fill a function akin to that of mystical meditation—which, incidentally, has always been close to lyrics, but, which, compared to lyrics, is too exclusive a means or instrument. It would contribute to people's acquiring the ability and the desire to "den Willen still werden zu lassen und das Licht zu sehen, das sich erst bei still gewordenem Willen zeigt." Like mystical meditation, it would be "eine Schule der Wahrnehmung, des Kommenlassens der Wirklichkeit" (C.F. Weizsäcker).

Not all cultures can manage this task. Pinning one's hopes on culture, as such, alone—culture in the sense of cultivating and further refining that which we have taken over from the past—would lead to disappointment. It would still be the same, traditional culture of the will and the old reason. Even if we were to forget that our culture could have been not merely intolerant (despite the fact that there reigns in it a conviction that tolerance also belongs to culture), that it could have been repressive, arrogant, and messianic, that it could have been insensitive to numerous important values, lack understanding for many values, and, on the other hand, impose upon people a great deal that is of no value at all, we could not help but see that the legitimacy of this culture's traditional values has been more than undermined.

Today, this task can be achieved only by a culture whose point of departure is an essentially modified state of consciousness, another state of mind. And right here, I see a great opportunity and a great task for lyricism and lyrics, for this state of mind, which is distinguished by identification with the world, by empathy, by sympathy, and by an uncommitted will. Despite the fact that so irrational an element as love would play an essential role in such a culture, the wisdom in that culture would in no way have to be less than the wisdom in the culture we have to cope with today.

I would even like to declare that only then would it become the happy culture, truly rich in blessings, that it ought to be.

And now, as I say that, yet another question comes to my mind—a question that, at this moment, strikes me as merely rhetorical: is it not true that pathos lives on, and is fueled by, precisely the vision of this happy understanding of things and of how wisely they are ordered on the basis of mutual sympathies? In a spirit of "love as the seeing state of mind that abolishes the struggle for existence," as C.F. Weizsäcker formulated it? Is not pathos an attempt to reach outside one's own shadow and an attempt to return to Arcadia, where the rational, the just, and the natural are identical to reality? Is not pathos merely an attempt to return to the idyll—that is, to a state in which we know no foreign power over us and where the conflict between that which is and that which ought to be disappears, a state where reason and power, morals and politics, can sit down at the same table together? And finally, is the lost paradise sought by pathos not the world of lyricism? Is not poetry itself, lyrics, one of the foremost creators and interpreters of the vision of that paradise?

As I write this, I am tempted to wish that, instead of having been a lyrist by birth, I could become one by conviction: a lyrist by my own choice.

Pearl-Angelika Lee   (review date Winter 1985)

SOURCE: A review of *Ruce Venušiny,* in *World Literature Today,* Vol. 59, No. 1, Winter, 1985, p. 125.

[*Below, Lee offers a highly favorable assessment of* Ruce Venušiny (Hands of Venus).]

Until last October's Nobel Prize announcement, Jaroslav Seifert (b. 1901), one of the best Czech poets of this century, had not had the recognition he deserves due to the official censure he has faced in his country and the paucity of translations abroad. His career spans more than sixty years of sustained creativity, beginning with the avant-garde period of poetism and surrealism and continuing through the present day. The best of Seifert's poetry is represented in this volume, **Ruce Venušiny** (Hands of Venus), compiled and published by Sixty-Eight Publishers, who are hereby bringing out and preserving another important Czech writer.

Seifert's early poetry displays an appealing lyricism and a recognizably masculine grace. He is a young man in love, full of hope and energy, fascinated by the sensual possibilities of language. To his credit, he never loses his ludic charm, which is born of idealism and an instinctive faith in the best qualities of man—above all, his capacity to love. Even after witnessing the most deplorable human tragedies of this century, Seifert finds it possible to praise the human spirit. His attitude becomes graver and more pained, but he refrains from expressions of noisy outrage or prolonged sessions of despair. With each poem he sets out anew, facing the world with sympathy and adopting, more and more, an informal and intimate speech, as if by shaping the artifice of poetry according to the rhythms and nuances of familiar utterance he could remove all barriers between poet and reader.

To some, the language of his later poetry may seem prosaic and bare, but by exposing himself so openly, Seifert manages to capture the flickering changes of the mind and a constant refinement of sensibilities. Without sacrificing his youthful *sprezzatura* or disdain, he has gained the maturity and naturalness that come rarely and only with patience. Aware that his last poems might evoke such reactions, Seifert has tried to guard against this interpretation. Like Yeats in his old age, he scoffs at the notion that old men are necessarily wise or that wisdom holds a candle against the burning husk of experience.

Still, Seifert's wisdom is indeed valuable and necessary: through the nightmare of history, the calamities of nature, and the agony of personal loss, he has steadfastly refused to sing the cynical songs of gravediggers or to rage against the dying of the light. He has sought to express himself through affirmation and delight; each poem is an act of love. Among lyric poets today, Seifert is perhaps the most eloquent pleader for humanity; he is therefore indispensable.

Barry Lewis   (essay date January-February 1985)

SOURCE: "Jaroslav Seifert, Nobel Prize-Winner for Literature, 1984," in *Quadrant*, Vol. XXIX, Nos. 1-2, January-February, 1985, pp. 42-3.

[*In the essay below, Lewis provides a brief overview of Seifert's life and career, noting that the poet "has refused to allow his artistic integrity to by compromised" by Czechoslovakian censorship.*]

Few People will have heard the name of Czech poet Jaroslav Seifert before he won this year's Nobel Prize for Literature. His work is little known beyond the confines of his native Czechoslovakia and the few scattered Czech émigré communities in Western Europe, Canada, USA and Australia. Moreover, Seifert's output consists almost entirely of lyric poetry—a genre of limited appeal in any language and one notoriously difficult to translate into a foreign tongue. The award will perhaps even come as a surprise to lovers of Czech poetry, as they could point to a number of poets of equal merit which this century has produced.

Seifert's advantage, however, has been to have outlasted all possible contenders to the title of greatest living Czech poet. In one of his most recent and important collections of verse *The Plague Column* he recalls how he recited his poetry at the gravesides of illustrious fellow poets Wolker, Halas and Hora and how he was destined to outlive them all:

> In the Julian Fields
> we'd sometimes lie at nightfall,
> when Brno was sinking into darkness,
> and on the backwater of the Svitava
> the frogs began their plaint.
>
> Once a young gipsy sat down beside us.
> Her blouse was half unbuttoned
> and she read our hands.

> To Halas she said: You won't live to be fifty.
>
> To Arthur Cernik: You'll live until just after
>   that.
>
> I didn't want her to tell my fortune.
> I was afraid.
>
> She seized my hand
> and angrily exclaimed: You'll live a long time!
>
> It sounded like a threat.

Of the promising group of Czech poets of the '20s and '30s only Seifert now survives at the age of 83 as a living symbol of resistance to the ravages of time, war and politics.

He was born in Prague in 1901 in the working-class suburb of Žižkov, a milieu which was to provide him with much raw material for his earliest verse:

> I was christened on the edge of the Olšany
> in the plague chapel of Saint Roch . . .
> On the steps of the Olšany taverns
> I used to crouch at night to hear
> the coffin-bearers and grave diggers
> singing their rowdy songs.
>
> But that was long ago,
> the taverns have fallen silent
> the grave-diggers in the end
> buried each other.

His humble origins inspired his early political and literary affiliations. He was a member of the Communist party and one of the founding members of the Devětsil, a group of fervent young writers dedicated to the cause of working-class revolution. [*Město v slzách* (City in Tears)], his first collection of verse, described the down-trodden working-class districts of Prague and predicted a proletarian revolution.

> Seifert's eschewal of clear-cut dissident statements in his poetry stems not from caution or weakness but from a belief in the essential incompatibility of politics and poetry. Like Pasternak, he maintains that the poet stands above politics and that only in this way can he retain the independence necessary to lay bare the tragedy of his time.
>
> —*Barry Lewis*

However, Seifert's enthusiasm for revolution was short-lived. He soon veered in another direction, coming under the influence of Rimbaud and Apollinaire during a visit to France and joining the group of Poetists who exalted the senses and the subconscious above the intellect. As enthusiastically as he had initially embraced the cause of Revolution, he now began to extol the exotic and the sensuous.

Typical of this period of juvenile experimentation with its emphasis on sexual imagery was his playful poem the **"Abacus"** (1925) which relies heavily on the word "Australia" for exotic effect:

"The Abacus"

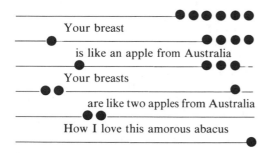

Your breast

is like an apple from Australia

Your breasts

are like two apples from Australia

How I love this amorous abacus

For a time in the 'twenties when Communism and youthful exuberance went hand in hand, Seifert managed to combine the twin themes of sensuality and revolution in his verse, but he was to be disillusioned by revolution following a visit to Moscow in 1925. He was distressed at the violence and bloodshed unleashed by the Russian Revolution and declared Russia to be the "graveyard of history". His final break with the Communist Party came in 1929 when, together with other prominent writers, he signed a manifesto criticising Clement Gottwald and his leadership of the Party.

From the '30s onward Seifert's poetry matured. His youthful, anarchistic excesses were abandoned in favour of less strident topics and a simpler, more direct style which became the hallmark of his best poetry. His themes became more universal—family, childhood, death, sorrow, and especially love, conveyed with moving lyricism frequently interspersed with warm sensuality. At the same time his evocation of the familiar and everyday was quintessentially Czech in its appeal, as was his verse which touched the patriotic feelings of his readers in descriptions and nostalgic recollections of the famous landmarks of Bohemia, the glories of Old Prague and the history and culture of a small and proud nation.

Seifert's sense of history caused him to respond in verse to the momentous events which affected his country during his lifetime. He expressed his people's grief at the death of their revered president and founder of the Czechoslovak state, Thomas Masaryk, in a moving series of poems entitled *Eight Days.* The pain of Munich and the wartime German occupation of his country were frequently invoked in his verse of the '40s. A series of important poems dedicated to the Czech writer Božena Němcova, which he wrote during the Nazi occupation, pictured her as a symbol of Czech cultural independence and resilience.

When the Communists came to power in 1948 Seifert was already in disfavour for his previous criticism of Clement Gottwald who now became President of Czechoslovakia. Seifert continued to maintain his distance from the new

Party bosses and refused to conform to the prescribed style of "socialist realism". A further poem dedicated to Božena Němcova led to a vicious attack on him by the Communist poet and critic Ivan Skála who accused him of "sinking even deeper into subjectivism and apoliticism".

> **Unlike many lesser writers who have remained in Czechoslovakia, Seifert has refused to allow his artistic integrity to be compromised. The award of the Nobel Prize is a recognition both of this and his poetic achievement.**
>
> **—Barry Lewis**

Little of his new poetry in this period was published by the state-controlled publishing houses—a significant exception being the charming and perennially popular collection *Maminka* (1954), an evocation of his mother, the charms of childhood, the family circle and familiar household objects. His prestige grew as this and his previously published works were being reissued, while his new verse circulated in clandestine copies.

The liberalisation in Czechoslovakia during the heady days of the "Prague Spring" which preceded the Soviet invasion of 1968 enabled new poems such as the collection *Casting of Bells* to be published, but this came to an abrupt end following his criticism in 1969 of the Soviet invasion when he was briefly president of the Czechoslovak Union of Writers and during the subsequent clamp-down on independent intellectuals and artists.

Despite his public protests against the Soviet invasion of 1968, his adherence to the dissident Charter 77 group and his support of dissident writers, there is nothing in Seifert's poetry that is so openly inimical to the present regime that it could not be published in Czechoslovakia. Even his most obviously political work *The Plague Column*—reminiscent of Camus' *La Peste* in its evocation of a pestilence affecting the political and spiritual life of the country—contains no direct reference to Communist rule.

His eschewal of clear-cut dissident statements in his poetry stems not from caution or weakness but from a belief in the essential incompatibility of politics and poetry. Like Pasternak, he maintains that the poet stands above politics and that only in this way can he retain the independence necessary to lay bare the tragedy of his time:

> He has the right to rape
> under the banner of beauty
> or that of pain.
> Or under the banner of both.
> Indeed it is his mission.
>
> Events themselves hand him
> a ready pen
> that with its tip he may indelibly tattoo
> his message.

Not on the skin of the breast
but straight into the muscle
which throbs with blood.
But rose and heart are not just love,
nor a ship a voyage or adventure,
nor a knife murder,
nor an anchor fidelity unto death.

These foolish symbols lie.
Life has long outgrown them.
Reality is totally different
and a lot worse still.

And so the poet drunk with life
should spew out all bitterness,
anger and despair,
rather than let his song become a tinkling bell
on a sheep's neck.

Unlike many lesser writers who have remained in Czechoslovakia, Seifert has refused to allow his artistic integrity to be compromised. The award of the Nobel Prize is a recognition both of this and his poetic achievement. It is to be hoped that the Czechoslovak authorities will relax their harsh attitude towards him in his declining years and permit the publication of all his important verse in his native land.

William E. Harkins   (essay date Spring 1985)

SOURCE: "The Czech Nobel Laureate Jaroslav Seifert," in *World Literature Today,* Vol. 59, No. 2, Spring, 1985, pp. 173-75.

[*Harkins is an American educator and critic who specializes in Slavic Studies. In the essay below, he provides a brief overview of Seifert's career.*]

The award of the 1984 Nobel Prize in Literature to the aging Czech poet Jaroslav Seifert naturally raised many questions—hardly new ones. The Nobel Committee of the Swedish Academy has demonstrated a striking preference for lyric poetry in recent years, a preference that the reading public scarcely shares. At least five prizewinners from the past eighteen years have been poets, not counting Seifert himself. The award to Pablo Neruda in 1971 reminds us parenthetically that this Chilean poet had taken his unusual (but somehow Spanish-sounding) pen name from Seifert's great countryman, Jan Neruda (1834-91), who, unfortunately, did not himself live quite long enough to qualify for the prize.

As a writer, Seifert has the distinction of having survived the great period of Czech interwar literature (he began to publish in 1920) and having continued to be productive in recent decades, even under communism (though for a time he could not publish). Thus he unites in his person the two great eras of Czech literature in our century: the interwar period of the twenties and thirties, and the "thaw" period of the sixties. No other Czech writer of major stature has accomplished this, save Seifert's great (perhaps even greater?) fellow poet, Vladimír Holan (1905-80). The time of World War II narrowed the ranks of Czech literature: the brothers Čapek, Vladimír Vančura, and Karel Poláček perished between 1938 and 1945. The toll was unusually heavy among writers of prose; the lyric poets proved lon-ger-lived. The death of František Halas in 1949, of Vítězslav Nezval in 1958, and finally of Holan himself in 1980 eliminated Seifert's competition.

Born in Prague in 1901 into a working-class family, Seifert began as a leftist poet; his two collections *Město v slzách* (The City in Tears; 1920) and *Samá láska* (Nothing but Love; 1923) are among the earliest and most outstanding productions of so-called Czech proletarian poetry. The first collection depicted the poverty and struggle of the city while recalling the sufferings of the war; the second linked love and sensual pleasure to the future victory of the proletariat. Along with Halas and other young poets, however, Seifert soon fell victim to a curious Marxist ideological deviation. The Marxist theoretician Karel Teige (1900-51) came to preach a new gospel of "poetism," whereby poets should celebrate the sensual joys of modern urbanized life and its new, partly mechanized pleasures. They should also celebrate the poetic word as expressed in punning and other sorts of verbal play and in fresh poetic imagery. Poetism was influenced by Dadaism and Italian futurism, and it in turn was later to merge with Czech surrealism. This joyful playing with words and images was to prove agreeable for Seifert, who was naturally of a sunnier disposition than are most great poets, but its presumptive assertion that the poet might look forward to the victory of the proletariat before actually storming the fortress of the bourgeoisie was of course an ideological heresy, one that subsequently had to be expunged.

Seifert produced two poetist collections, *Na vlnách T.S.F.* (On the Radio Waves; 1925) and *Slavík zpívá špatně* (The Nightingale Sings Poorly; 1926). The title of the second collection is Seifert's reproach to himself for his ideological deviation, but the poetist heresy still continues, now mixed with a note of the horror of existence, a note that is perhaps a bit strained in his case. This era came to an end for Seifert in 1929, when he and six other party writers signed a manifesto rejecting the new leadership of Klement Gottwald. In reply, the party expelled the seven writers, and Seifert, who had supported himself through leftist journalism, now went over to the Social Democrats.

> **Seifert unites in his person the two great eras of Czech literature in our century: the interwar period of the twenties and thirties, and the "thaw" period of the sixties.**
>
> **—William E. Harkins**

With the youthful temptations of proletarianism and poetism put behind him, Seifert entered upon his maturity and the first period of his greatness. In his next two collections, *Jablko s klína* (An Apple from One's Lap; 1933) and *Ruce Venušiny* (The Arms of Venus; 1935), he achieved, for the first time, a firm balance between form and content, a balance among the elements of language (expressive and at times bordering on the colloquial), images, and a songlike verse intonation. At the same time a new cheerfulness emerged, a tone quite exceptional in that gloomy period, obsessed with the Great Depression and terrified by the rise of Hitler. Seifert's new mood may seem to have resembled that of an ostrich with its head in the sand, but in fact it was more or less an expression of the optimistic Czech spirit, embodied in a more vulgar way in Jaroslav Hašek's good soldier Švejk. Love is the subject of many of these verses, a quite concretely limned love, as the title of the second collection suggests. Dialogue is common, and the use of gender in Czech past-tense verbs makes possible an unusual economy in the identification of the conversing sexual partners.

> Líbal jsi mne na čelo či ústa,
> nevím
> —zaslechla jsem jenom sladký hlas
> a tma hustá
> obklopila úžas polekaných řas.
>
> Na čelo jsem políbal tě v spěchu,
> nebo omámila mě
> vůně tvého proudícího dechu,
> ale nevím
>
> —zaslechl jsem jenom sladký hlas
> a tma hustá
> obklopila úžas polekaných řas,
> libalas mne na čelo či ústa?
>
> (Whether you [the man] kissed me on the forehead or the mouth
> I do not know
> I [the woman] heard only a sweet voice
> and thick darkness
> enveloped the horror of frightened eyelids.
>
> On the forehead I [the man] kissed you in haste
> for I was intoxicated with
> the perfume of your streaming breath,
> but I do not know
>
> I [the man] heard only a sweet voice
> and thick darkness
> enveloped the horror of frightened eyelids,
> did you [the woman] kiss me on the forehead or
> the mouth?)

Events caught up with Seifert, and in 1938, on the eve of the Munich agreement, he published a collection entitled *Zhasněte světla* (Put Out the Lights), the title of which was to become a memorable phrase evocative of the war for his people. That war made Seifert an involuntary prisoner of his native city, Prague, while the German Occupation restricted his choice of themes. In *Světlem oděná* (Clad in Light; 1940), the first of his collections to concentrate on a single topic, he turned to a celebration of the beauties of Prague itself. He is mindful of the city's complex and glorious, yet often troubled past, suggesting the unutterable thought of the sadness of the present. Indeed, the themes of sensual love and of Prague (itself often the object of the poet's sensual love—in Czech the name of Prague is feminine in gender) are Seifert's favorite themes, and they appear in his early periods as well as in his mature work and his most recent poetry.

Přilba hlíny (The Helmet of Clay; 1945) celebrates the Prague Uprising against German rule in May of that year. The long waiting of the war and the admiration of Prague's beauties now achieve their own apotheosis.

"Praze"

> Tak jsem tě miloval a miloval jen slovy,
> má Praho líbezná; když pláš svůj šeříkový
> jsi rozhalila včera odhodlaně,
> oč více řekli ti, kdo měli zbraně.
>
> . . . . .
>
> Na dlažbě leží mrtví a krev studu
> mě polévá a věčně, věčně budu
> si vyčítat, že nejsem mezi nimi.
> Ty město statečné, jsi mezi statečnými
> a budeš věčně, věčně, všechny časy.
>
> Ten den ti chyběl do tvé slunné krásy.
>
> (So I loved you and loved you with words,
> my beauteous Prague; when yesterday with reso-
>   lution
> you spread open your lilac cape,
> how much more they could say, those who had
>   arms.
>
> . . . . .
>
> On the pavement lay the dead, and the blood of
>   shame
> washed me, and ever, ever shall I blame myself
> that I was not among them.
> O hero city—among heroes
> You will exist eternally, for all time.
>
> That day made perfect and complete your sunny
>   beauty.)

The events of February 1948 brought the Communists to power, led by that same Klement Gottwald whom Seifert had rejected as a leader in 1929. The Social Democratic Party was hurriedly and almost forcibly merged with the Communists. Seifert had thus lost his political identity, and in 1949 he retired from newspaper work. If he continued to devote himself to poetry, it was written "for the drawer," as East Europeans have come to say. He did succeed in publishing several collections of children's verse, the ideological qualifications for which were less rigorous. Unlike Nezval, he was no poetic collaborator with the new regime.

When the question of a writer's freedom could again be posed openly, Seifert stood up to be counted. At the Second Congress of Czechoslovak Writers at the end of April 1956, it was he and his fellow poet František Hrubín who openly called for an end to controls on literature. Seifert proposed that writers should serve as mankind's conscience, no doubt intending this as a rejoinder to Stalin's formula of writers as "the engineers of human souls." In 1968, during the Prague Spring, he served on a commission for the rehabilitation of writers who had been persecuted.

The Prague Spring made it possible for Seifert to publish again, and in 1967 he brought out two collections of verse (presumably written earlier), *Odlévání zvonů* (*The Casting of Bells*) and *Halleyová kometa* (Halley's Comet).

These volumes initiated a new phase in Seifert's work, with their style of utter simplicity and directness. The older, songlike poetry gives way here to a new poetry of essential statement. The style is so simple, direct, and bare that many of these poems could be used in language classes for teaching Czech to foreigners.

The aftermath of the Prague Spring saw the poet again in disfavor. Still, he continued to serve as president of the Union of Czech Writers until 1970, when increasing reaction made it impossible to go on and the union itself had to be dissolved. He was quoted in an émigré journal published in Rome as telling Gustav Husák, the new president, "You want us [the writers] to support your position because you know that we enjoy moral authority in the nation. But should we support you, we would lose that authority, and then we would be of no use to you." The avenues of publication were closed to the poet, and throughout the early seventies he was not even mentioned in the Czechoslovak public press. Like many of his fellow writers, he began to publish abroad. A long poem, *Morový sloup* (*The Plague Column*), one almost certainly written years earlier, appeared in Germany in 1971 and again in 1977, as did a volume of lyrics, *Deštník z Piccadilly* (*An Umbrella from Piccadilly*) in 1978. This caused the authorities to relent in Czechoslovakia, and the latter collection, with one poem missing, appeared in Prague the following year.

In his lifetime he has created at least two kinds of poetic speech and commanded them thoroughly, one of song and one of statement; both are totally free from rhetoric.

—*William E. Harkins*

The Plague Column (American translation as *The Plague Monument*) is probably Seifert's masterpiece. As a long poem, it is virtually unprecedented in his oeuvre. A strange mixture of gloom and optimism, it deals with the poet's survival of the Stalinist era (in Czechoslovakia, from 1948 to 1953, when Stalin died). The title is a great and terrifying image of Czech history, which the poet identifies with his own precarious fate.

> Jenom si nedejte namluvit,
> že mor ve městě ustal.
> Viděl jsem ještě mnoho rakví
> vjíždět do této brány,
> která nebyla jediná.
>
> Mor dosud žurí a lékaři
> dávají nemoci patrně jiná jména,
> aby nevznikla panika.
> Je to stále táž stará smrt,
> nic jiného,
> a je tak nakažlivá,
> že jí neunikne ani živáček.

> (Don't be talked into believing
> that the plague here has let up.
> I've seen many fresh coffins
> coming through this gate
> and it's not the only way in.
>
> The plague still rages and the doctors
> are apparently giving it different names
> to prevent panic.
> But it's still the same old death,
> nothing else.
> and it's so contagious
> no living thing can escape it.)

The poet finds only a partial refuge in poetry and love.

> Co jsem napsal rondelů a písní!
> Byla válka na všech stranách světa
> a já šeptal náušnicím s routou
> milostné verše.
> Za to se trochu stydím.
> Či vlastně ani ne.

> (How many verses and rondels I've written!
> The whole world was at war
> and I whispered love verses
> to costly earrings.
> I'm a bit ashamed of that.
> Or actually I'm not.)

In spite of his pessimism as a prisoner of Czech fate and Czech history, the poet is not without hope, for love remains. He refers unenviously to the fate of the Czech émigrés.

> Ti, kdož odešli
> a rozprchli kvapem po zemích,
> už to snad poznali:
> Svět je hrozný!
>
> Nemilují a nejsou milováni.
> My aspožn milujem.

> (Those who hurried away
> to scatter themselves over the world,
> perhaps they've found out that
> the world is horrible!
>
> They do not love and they are not loved.
> We at least love.)

The lyrics of *An Umbrella from Piccadilly* end with an autobiographical statement that might seem to terminate the aged poet's career. Again he defends his right to love; love is the closest thing we have to miracle in this world. Life has proved too brief, however, and before the poet realizes it, death is at his door.

What claim does Seifert have to the Nobel Prize? We have seen that he is the last surviving member of a great literary generation. It must be added that he is a thoroughly Czech national writer, not so much of landscape or history (though his Prague poems do fall into this category) as of mood and attitude toward life. His cult of optimism and love is doubtless closer to the mood of his countrymen than was his fellow poet Halas's cult of gloom and death. In his lifetime he has created at least two kinds of poetic speech and commanded them thoroughly, one of song and one of statement; both are totally free from rhetoric.

To compare him with great poets of other national traditions would be invidious, for lyric poetry is too firmly planted in its own language. And in any case, the reason for selecting him may well have been that he was an East European, perhaps that he was a Czech. Karel Čapek was once denied the prize, in all likelihood because he was considered at the time too controversial as a declared foe of Nazi Germany. No Czech writer, in fact, had ever received it prior to the 1984 award. Seifert enjoys a unique position among his fellow writers: he has been a dissident and has published abroad, yet he is still, at the end of his long career, acceptable to the Prague regime. So, unlike Pasternak, he has been officially permitted to receive the prize and enjoy its honors. They are well merited.

Jan Vladislav (essay date April 1985)

SOURCE: "Poets and Power: Jaroslav Seifert," in *Index on Censorship*, Vol. 14, No. 2, April, 1985, pp. 8-12.

[*In the excerpt below, Vladislav relates the problems of censorship faced by Seifert while living and publishing in Communist Czechoslovakia.*]

[The Swedish Academy's decision in 1984] to give the Nobel Prize to an 'unknown' Czech poet puzzled many people, and the Czechoslovak authorities had not the slightest interest in trying to remedy the situation. On the contrary, despite their statements claiming that the recipient of the prize, poet Jaroslav Seifert, was greatly and universally respected, his works published in large quantities, Czechoslovakia's official representatives in fact shared the view of those foreign journalists who chose the most simplistic and banal explanation: that, once again, this was a politically motivated award and that the Swedish Academy was honouring Jaroslav Seifert the dissident rather than the poet. 'In their eyes,' was the verdict of the Paris *L'Express* of 19-25 October, 'the most important text to carry the name of Jaroslav Seifert was obviously Charter 77.'

The doubts and in some cases indignation expressed by some of these 'expert' commentators was partly an admission of their own ignorance. 'That someone has not been translated into English or French,' wrote Nicole Zand aptly in *Le Monde* of 14-15 October, 'does not necessarily mean they do not exist.'

Yet, it is not even altogether true to say that Seifert has not been translated. Both **Umbrella from Piccadilly** and **The Plague Column** appeared in English, translated by Ewald Osers, and his 1979 version of the latter, which was also performed on stage in dramatised readings, showed British and perhaps American readers that Seifert was an important poet five years before the Swedish Academy's award.

> **For Czech readers Jaroslav Seifert is one of the most popular of all contemporary poets, his poetry among those who are most widely read and, at least at first sight, the most easily accessible.**
>
> —*Jan Vladislav*

Those who really know Jaroslav Seifert and his work can have no doubt that he is, first and foremost, a poet. The authority he enjoys even outside the bounds of literature is based primarily on the quality and integrity of his literary *oeuvre,* and even his interventions in public life—on the rare occasions that he made them—invariably had to do above all with poetry, its mission in life, the poet's rights and responsibilities.

Czech readers have no doubts on this score. For them, Jaroslav Seifert is one of the most popular of all contemporary poets, his poetry among those who are most widely read and, at least at first sight, the most easily accessible. And it is probably due to this very accessibility, the apparent simplicity of Seifert's work, that even Czech critics have not paid sufficient attention to it, so that we do not have any study that shows its real significance. When writing about Seifert, authors usually confine themselves to a description of his, on the whole, uncomplicated artistic development: beginning his literary career with socially motivated verses based on his own personal experience and the spirit of the time, the young poet enthusiastically joined the postwar *avantgarde* in the early 1920s, celebrating *all the beauties of the world* as well as the revolution which was to bestow them on one and all; in the 1930s, older and wiser, he adopted a more classical, traditional style, and it was then that he won growing popularity with a wide readership; the climax of this phase of Seifert's development came in the late 1930s, with the approach of the Nazi occupation and world war, when he wrote a large number of poems giving effective voice to the fears and hopes of an imperilled nation, thus becoming a truly national poet.

This flattering but on the other hand limiting label, which is from time to time made use of by the representatives of communist cultural policy in Czechoslovakia, has stuck to this day, obscuring the true range and depth of the poet's *oeuvre.* It obscures, in particular, the turning-point which the then 64-year-old writer reached some time around 1965, when he turned away from the classical rhyming verse forms and adopted the freer, more colloquial verse which has allowed him to deal with greater immediacy and power with perhaps every important problem of modern man's existence.

Not that these did not figure in his work right from the start, but it was as if they could only now be expressed in full. Seifert thus showed that he was the rightful heir of two different branches of poetry. One of these, the native one, had its beginnings way back in Bohemian Baroque music, continuing with Mácha, Erben, Neruda, and Vrchlický, all the way to Neumann, Sova, Toman and Hora, all poets whose powerful imagination and poetic skill ranked them with the best European poets of their time, even though Europe did not know them as they wrote in Czech; the second branch leads from Baudelaire, Verlaine, Rodenbach and Corbière to Cendrars and, in particular, to Apollinaire, who provided such great inspiration not only for French but also for Czech poetry.

Few modern poets have been so fascinated by the life and work of W. A. Mozart as has Jaroslav Seifert. He has written many a poem, including a whole cycle called "Mozart in Prague," about the composer, returning again and again to his compositions, characters from his operas and incidents from his life. Mozart quite simply represents one of the chief components of Seifert's spiritual world, and it is as if something of that Mozartian element had entered his own poetry which, like Mozart's music, conceals hidden depths beneath its seemingly transparent, melodious surface.

It is that which lies in these hidden, incalculable depths that most disturbs and angers the Flaubertian force which does not tolerate other forces. That is why official Czechoslovak cultural representatives chose to ignore this aspect of Seifert's *oeuvre* since the Soviet invasion of 1968, refusing to publish any of his new books. And even when, after more than 10 years and under pressure from the samizdat and foreign editions of Seifert, as well as translations into other languages, they at last capitulated in the early 1980s, publishing *Umbrella from Piccadilly, The Plague Column,* and Seifert's memoirs, [*Všecky krásy světa* (All the Beauties of the World)], they still failed to acknowledge their true poetic meaning.

This is to be seen in the description of Seifert's work given in the literary columns of the Czechoslovak Communist Party daily, *Rudé právo,* on 13 October 1984, the day after the Nobel Prize award was announced:

> His development, both as poet and citizen, was complicated and not without contradictions, as he himself admits in his memoirs. Nevertheless, there is no doubting his importance for Czech poetry. . . . In his early collections, full of social feeling and verse that is free from pathos, Seifert created an individual type of proletarian poetry. With J. Wolker, V. Nezval and K. Biebl he belonged to the leading representatives of the youngest generation of Czech poets. Though after a time he abandoned the ideals of revolutionary poetry, at the end of the 1930s he joined the front rank of those who wished to defend the Republic against fascism. His poetry gave strength to the nation during the Nazi occupation. After the war, he celebrated the heroes of the Prague Uprising, the Red Army, his mother, his childhood, his home, and his country.

Thus ends this equivocal, distorted and incomplete pen portrait of National Artist Jaroslav Seifert in *Rudé právo.* There follows only an attempt to show how magnanimous the authorities have been to Seifert:

> Seifert's name has lately been misused in the West for slanderous attacks against his country, attempts being made to use our leading poet as part of the psychological war against the countries of socialism. These are cynical, despicable attempts. Seifert's verses are a permanent part of the treasury of our poetry, he himself being one of our most published authors. For instance, in 1971-84 our publishing houses brought out 18 titles of Seifert's work in a total printing of 176,000. Most recently there have been his newest collections: *Umbrella from Piccadilly* (1979), *The Plague Column* (1981), *To Be a Poet* (1981). In 1982 his *Recollections and Stories* (the subtitle of [his memoirs]) was published. . . .

As is usually the case with self-praise, the above account is dictated by a guilty conscience. It is remarkable more for what it conceals than what it says. If Seifert had really been *persona grata* with the authorities, as the article suggests, why did his post-invasion books not come out as soon as they were written, why did *The Plague Column,* for instance, have to wait over 10 years for its official publication in Prague?

I was present when the poet himself made a spirited and humorous protest about this to an official from the Ministry of Culture who came to congratulate him on his 80th birthday. The Ministry had taken the wise precaution of sending the head of the Arts (and not Literature) Department, who was able to tell Seifert that unfortunately publishing poetry was not his responsibility. And so the poet had to rest content for many years with typescript samizdat editions of his work, *The Plague Column* and later *Umbrella from Piccadilly* being produced in several thousand copies. . . .

While the unofficial samizdat editions were naturally not censored, censorship was applied to the later, official, versions of Seifert's books, as can easily be verified by anyone who takes the trouble to compare the two. The censor's role was particularly significant in the case of Seifert's memoirs, [*Všecky krásy světa*], in which, according to a Prague samizdat article, nine chapters were left out, while in 12 others names, sentences and sometimes whole paragraphs were omitted. The index of names is thus shorter by 83 names, 51 of which are nevertheless mentioned in the book. The remaining 32 have disappeared altogether.

It is interesting to note the nature of the deletions. Not just people's names or items of a political or cultural-political character have been removed from Seifert's original text but also his reflections on death and a mention of the suicide of the mistress of the famous pre-war Czech art historian, Karel Teige, as well as various erotic scenes described in the book. It would appear from all this that death is just as obscene and unmentionable where Czechoslovak censorship is concerned as sex. Not a word about any of this is naturally to be found in the *Rudé právo* article.

Nor is the reader going to find out anything about some other facts which give an even clearer picture of the attitude of Czechoslovak authorities to poetry in general and Jaroslav Seifert in particular. Some of these facts can be gleaned from official documents, such as the protocols of interviews with nonconformist intellectuals carried out by the police, in which the interrogators voiced the opinion that Seifert's uncompromising attitude and his unwillingness to cooperate were due to his 'senility'.

Jaroslav Seifert never idly indulged in theoretical or ideological arguments, preferring to devote himself to his poetry; but he did not shirk speaking out when he deemed this to be necessary.

—Jan Vladislav

Another document records the decision of the Prague Municipal Court of 23 February 1983 to confiscate the books and manuscripts taken away from Ludvik Vaculík's apartment during a house search on 21 January 1981. Giving a detailed justification for the decision, the court stated that 'given a certain political situation, even passages from works dealing with other historical periods than our own, or with other countries, can be misused for the creation of a hostile attitude towards our system, as was evident during the crisis period of 1968-69' ['the crisis period' being Czech officialese for what the rest of the world knows as the Prague Spring when the Dubček government tried to reform the Stalinist system in Czechoslovakia].

Among the examples quoted as being works capable of misuse and therefore to be confiscated, we find a manuscript translation of *Reflections, Letters to Parents and Poems* by the German Protestant philosopher D. Bonhoeffer, who was executed in 1945 by the Nazis, clearly described as 'letters from a German fascist prison'; and, as the last of several examples, the manuscript of Seifert's **Umbrella from Piccadilly** and four other Seifert poems, which the judge, Dr Jan Rojt, evidently ordered confiscated because they were 'in their original, unmodified form'.

But it was not only Seifert's manuscripts which were deemed liable to confiscation; suggestions that he should be nominated for the Nobel Prize for Literature were considered equally 'criminal' by the judiciary. One of the Czech intellectuals arrested in 1981 and held for almost a year while their trial [which in the end did not take place] was in preparation, the former journalist Jiří Ruml, wrote on 22 October 1984 in an open letter addressed to the Czechoslovak Ambassador in Paris:

> Dr Jiřina Šiklová, who was detained with me in 1981 was accused of having sent abroad a copy of the manuscript and a recording of Jaroslav Seifert's memoirs and material to be used for his nomination for the Nobel Prize . . . All these manuscripts, gramophone records and other materials were confiscated and are still lying somewhere in the cellar of the Ministry of the Interior. Actors, who were sent records from abroad with readings of Seifert's memoirs . . . were interrogated, and the records, together with all Seifert's works published abroad or produced here on the typewriter are still subject to confiscation during various house searches.

Jaroslav Seifert never idly indulged in theoretical or ideological arguments, preferring to devote himself to his poetry; but he did not shirk speaking out when he deemed this to be necessary. He did so for the first time in 1929, when with eight other foremost Czech writers—at 28 he was the youngest of them—he signed a protest against the bolshevisation of the Czechoslovak Communist Party. This led to his expulsion from the party but at the same time as he left the communist movement, he won his artistic independence. The party's ideologues never forgave him and remained suspicious of him, an attitude that was to put the poet in considerable danger after February 1948, when they achieved total power over Czechoslovak culture. At a working conference of the Czechoslovak Writers Union in January 1950, held in the tense atmosphere that accompanied the arrests and preparations for the first Prague show trials and was itself a mini-trial of modern Czech poetry, Jaroslav Seifert was named as one of the culprits—an example of 'a great poetic talent' which without the support of the 'correct' ideology 'must of necessity become diluted'. The prosecutor in this shadow trial, which was nevertheless menacing to those concerned, was the official Czech communist ideologue and eager disciple of A. A. Zhdanov, Ladislav Štoll. He railed against some of the finest poets in the land because *'not one of them—neither Hora, nor Seifert, nor Halas—see fit any more to pen a single verse for Stalin'*.

In the spring of that year Seifert became the target of another, still more dangerous, attack; his collection [**Píseň o Viktorce** (The Song of Viktorka)], a lyrical account of the tragic love affair of one of the major characters in Czech romantic literature, was condemned by the official Party critics as a misuse of poetry 'to ridicule everything that our working people hold dear' because the author 'refuses to see the wings our working man is growing in his his flight towards a socialist future'. On the contrary, the critics alleged, Seifert was trying 'between the lines of his **Viktorce** to convince his readers that in our world of a new-born humanity there is no such thing as love and happiness'. It should be added that these splendid words about a 'world of a new-born humanity' were written just at the time when the first Prague show trial was getting under way which was to end with the execution of Dr Milada Horakova, the poet Zavis Kalandra, and others. . .

If anyone remains silent, this may well be a tactical manoeuvre. If a writer remains silent, he is lying.

—Jaroslav Seifert

Seifert himself was in danger of being arrested and tried, even if on less serious charges, for he had had the temerity to make some uncomplimentary remarks about Soviet poetry, saying at a private meeting with friends that he preferred French poets. The authorities were contemplating a show trial with the intention of making an example of the poet, and according to Seifert, it was only the intervention of the Soviet writer Ilya Ehrenburg, who happened to be visiting Prague, that saved him.

Other Czech writers did not escape trial. The 'new-born humanity' so highly prized by the communist ideologues did not prevent over 40 writers from being given long prison sentences in the early 1950s, and it was Jaroslav Seifert who first raised his voice on their behalf when he demanded to speak at the Second Congress of Czechoslovak Writers in April 1956. This was one of those moments when he realised he had to speak out, and he did. Yet even then it was no political speech—although he appealed for his imprisoned and suffering friends and colleagues, his main concern was more universal, the very *raison d'étre* of literature and its basic duty, that of telling the truth.

> Again and again we hear it said at this Congress—and from distinguished lips—that it is necessary for writers to write the truth. That means that in recent years they did not write the truth. Did they or didn't they? And did they do so voluntarily or under coercion? Willingly or enthusiastically?

> When I look back at the history of our literature I fail to find that any great Czech poet—and particularly not one of those who in their work spoke of the Czech nation such as Neruda, Cech, Machar and Dyk—that any of them paused to ask themselves whether they had been telling the truth, and having paused announced to the nation and to their readers that indeed they had not. Or do you perhaps recall any one of them proclaiming: "Forgive me, my reader, I have seen your travail and the suffering of the Czech people and closed my eyes to it. I have not written the truth."

> If anyone else remains silent, this may well be a tactical manoeuvre. If a writer remains silent, he is lying.

For anyone who has not lived in a totalitarian state, in the atmosphere that prevailed in Czechoslovakia at the time when Jaroslav Seifert spoke these words it must be difficult, if not impossible, to realise just how much courage was needed for such a pronouncement, nor the incredible effect his words had on his listeners, to whom they came as a liberating catharsis. With those few simple words Seifert bravely broke several strict taboos at once, above all by calling a spade a spade—to him a lie was a lie, truth was truth, and the imprisoned writers were prisoners whose fate at last merited attention.

> We all know full well—yes, I know we live in difficult times—that we must try to make their lot easier. But, dear friends, I ask you once more, are we really to be only the manufacturers of verses, rhymes and metaphors? Are we really just story-tellers and nothing more, that we should discuss only problems that affect our professional concerns as writers?

> That is how I see the mission of the writer in our time.

This conviction Seifert has held steadfastly to this day. He had no need to demonstrate it by making public pronouncements—he has demonstrated it by the integrity of his poetry.

Michael Henry Heim   (review date 30 June 1985)

SOURCE: "The Word Hangs Back," in *The New York Times Book Review*, June 30, 1985, p. 33.

[*In the following review, Heim offers a mixed assessment of* An Umbrella from Piccadilly.]

The Nobel Prize for Literature comes in several varieties. There is the prize that confirms universal recognition, the prize that plays politics, the prize that celebrates the visionary orientation Alfred Nobel originally meant to promote. And from time to time the Swedish Academy awards a prize that seems calculated to redress an oversight; it virtually introduces an author to the world.

Several years ago the judges awarded such a Nobel Prize to the Polish poet and essayist Czeslaw Milosz. The choice proved highly effective: Mr. Milosz's work and thought have been appreciated by many who would otherwise never have heard his name. Mr. Milosz, who now lives in California, has traveled widely in the intervening years; he has given readings and lectures, and confronted his new audience in person.

It appears that last year's choice, Jaroslav Seifert, will not have an opportunity to do the same. Like Mr. Milosz, Mr. Seifert is a poet from Central Europe, but Mr. Seifert still lives there. Moreover, his health is extremely frail; he received news of the award in a hospital bed in his native Prague. Now 83, he is ailing and virtually immobile. If we are to know him, therefore, he must come to us through his books alone.

An Umbrella From Piccadilly is the first collection to have appeared in English since Mr. Seifert received the Nobel Prize. It may initially seem well suited to satisfy the public's curiosity. Much of its content is autobiographical; it even opens with a poem entitled **"Autobiography."** It includes poems about the poet's travels (with a fine evocation of a landlocked Czechoslovak's first impression of the sea) and others about several of the artists and poets who have meant the most to him. Yet it does not typify his work as a whole, nor does it penetrate farther into the heart of that work than the two volumes currently available in English, *The Casting of Bells* and *The Plague Column.*

All three collections represent Mr. Seifert's recent output, and *The Plague Column* and *An Umbrella From Piccadilly,* both completed in the late 70's, confront death ("the mistress of poets") as well as life. *Piccadilly,* the more recent of the two, takes few poetic risks; it is the afterglow of a dazzling output, the memoirs of a sadder but wiser latter-day Anacreon. Gone are the technical fireworks of the 20's and 30's and the more conventional meter and rhyme of the 40's and 50's, gone even are most remnants of metaphor. As the poet puts it in **"Fragment of a Letter"**:

> Under my pen the verses dance no longer

and like a tear in the corner of the eye
the word hangs back.

What remains is absolute fidelity to intimate lyric, a love
of women (for themselves and as symbols of humanity)
and of Prague (for itself and as a symbol of Czechoslovakia) and harmony in language.

In **"Finger Prints"** those loves merge. The poem tells how
the 14-year-old Jaroslav was caught fondling the leg of a
statue of a woman that is an allegory of the Vltava, the
river flowing through Prague. The poem ends:

> Perhaps I had committed an offence
> against public morality,
> I don't know!
> I know nothing about the law.
> Yet I was sentenced after all
> to lifelong punishment.
>
> If love is a labyrinth
> full of glittering mirrors,
> and it is that,
> I'd crossed its threshold
> and entered.
>
> And from the bewitching glitter of mirrors
> I haven't found the way out
> to this day.

What is missing here is the harmony of the original. Ewald
Osers' translation is scrupulously accurate, but whereas
Mr. Seifert hugs the poetry side of the famous fine line between poetry and prose, Mr. Osers veers into prose. Nor
does Mr. Osers' introduction provide clues to the identity
of the many names dotting the poems—all of them important figures in Czechoslovak culture.

Still, *An Umbrella From Piccadilly* makes a new part of
Mr. Seifert's work available to an audience broader than
the small nation that now reveres him as a living monument. The next step is to provide translations of the brilliantly rhymed, rhythmed and imaged works of his earlier
years. Then, perhaps, the turn will come for the rest of his
generation of unprecedented poetic talent—Vitezslav
Nezval, Frantisek Halas, Vladimir Holan, Frantisek Hru-
bin. If it does, the 1984 Nobel Prize for Literature will
have redressed not one oversight but a pleiad of them.

Josef Škvorecký (essay date 1985)

SOURCE: "Jaroslav Seifert—The Good Old Drinking
Poet," in *Cross Currents: A Yearbook of Central European
Culture*, Vol. 4, 1985, pp. 283-98.

*[A Czechoslovakian-born Canadian novelist, short story
writer, essayist, and critic, Škvorecky has resided in Canada
since fleeing his homeland after the 1968 Soviet invasion.
In the essay below, he discusses Seifert's poetry in relation
to the social climate in Czechoslovakia, noting the Czech
government's official views on Seifert throughout his career.
Škvorecký notes in particular the impact in Czechoslovakia
of the Swedish Academy's decision to award him the 1984
Nobel Prize in Literature.]*

"Yet another obscure East European"—so went the word
around the cocktail circuit, and a letter to *The Times* [Oc-
tober 20, 1984] condemned the Swedish Academy's award
to Jaroslav Seifert as further proof that the Nobel prize "is
becoming more and more a reward for pussy-footing mediocrity." The new Nobel laureate, readers were told,
writes "verse of mawkish self-pity" and is a master of the
"sentimental drivel expected of poets incapable of devoting themselves to female tractor-drivers." Yet, Jaroslav
Seifert, even in his self-pitying old age, is perfectly capable
of devoting himself to female tractorists, particularly the
pretty ones. Proof of that ability was recently provided by
a reporter working for the *Svenska Dagbladet* who took
pictures of the poet in his hospital bed, holding hands with
an eye-filling blonde. On the back of the photograph she
was described as his "wife," but I know Mrs. Seifertová,
and unless she has recently undergone radical plastic surgery, she is definitely not the person in the photograph.
My guess is that Seifert's attractive visitor is one of the numerous Czech women who have always admired the Master and his poetry and have benefited from his predilection
for the company of the weaker sex. To put it bluntly, the
Master, even in his very old and venerable age, is still pursuing *Frauendienst.*

> I was lying on my side,
> my hands tied at the wrists
> but with my palms free:
> these a nurse was holding in her lap
> up by my head.
> I firmly gripped her thigh
> and convulsively pressed it to me
> as a diver clutches a slim amphora
> streaking up to the surface.

These lines of, if you wish, "mawkish self-pity" are from
a poem written about 1977 when the author was seventy-
six. "Sentimental drivel" perhaps does not describe them
accurately. The little poem seems to me as remarkable a
statement on the poetic power of sex as the following one,
written by the same man half a century earlier:

> If I saw you naked in the bath-tub
> with your knees pressed tightly together
> your white body would look like an envelope
> with a black seal in the middle.

I apologize for my barbarous translation.

For the past few years the author of the above quoted
poems has been enveloped in paradoxes. . . . The letter
to the Swedish Academy mentioned in Vaculík's feuilleton
["A Recreational River-boat" appearing in *Cross Currents*
4 (1985)] has a story of its own. The conspirators around
Vaculík intended to send it to Sweden via two French so-
cialists, Mr. Thonon and Ms. Anies, but on their way to
Prague they were stopped at the border and their car was
searched. It was a custom-made vehicle with a hidden
container used for smuggling books and letters to dissi-
dents in Prague. The guards went straight for the recepta-
cle: they had been tipped off by an agent by the name of
Hodic who had gained the confidence of several emigré organizations and a lucrative job with the Austrian socialist
government, and shortly before the incident returned to
Prague. The two French messengers and some thirty

Czechs were arrested. After extensive interrogations the police were able to locate the letter, the books, most of them *samizdat* Padlock editions, and other materials in the garage of Jiřina Šiklová. Ms. Šiklová went to prison where she was interrogated by a lieutenant Miroslav Uhlíř. She admitted that the books and letters were destnied for the Swedish Academy as supporting materials for the deliberations of the Nobel committee. The lieutenant apparently had never heard about either Seifert or Alfred Nobel. He left the room and after consultations with more knowledgeable colleagues returned to tell the detainee that "even if that Seifert received three Nobel prizes, it would not change the criminal nature of your actions." In due course, Ms. Šiklová was charged with "attempting to smuggle abroad texts of an anti-state nature." The trial, as far as I know, did not take place, but to this day—as far as I know—the charges have not been dropped. To suggest the Nobel Prize laureate for the prize may still be criminal offense in Czechoslovakia.

It certainly was in 1977 when a journalist, Jiří Lederer, was actually sentenced to three years in jail when he was caught trying to send out of the country a manuscript collection of Seifert's poems and the memoirs of the pre-1948 socialist minister Prokop Drtina.

Shortly after the detention of Ms. Šiklová, Ludvík Vaculík and others, Mr. Jan Pilař and two other gentlemen came to visit the poet in his apartment. Mr. Pilař is the editor-in-chief of the Writers' Union publishing house and a notorious figure of the Prague cultural *demi-monde* on whom I modelled the character of the "Chief" in my novel *Miss Silver's Past*. His two companions, on that occasion, turned out to be high-ranking police officers, and the outcome of the visit was Seifert's first heart attack. Three years later, in October 1984, the same Jan Pilař came again—no real-life Miss Silver had the guts to do him in, unfortunately—unaccompanied this time, to tell the poet, on behalf of the Writers' Union (of which Seifert is not a member) that he had received the Nobel Prize. At practically the same time, the *samizdat* and emigré editions of Seifert's works were still routinely confiscated during house-searches of political suspects, and the collection of materials found in Ms. Šiklová's garage was still held by the Ministry of Interior as a *corpus delicti* of criminal activities. And while the cops busied themselves collecting Seifert's books as evidence, there were three official Prague editions of the poet's works on the market. All of them tampered with by the censors, and all of them published, uncensored, years ago in the Padlock series and by emigré firms. The memoirs, [*Všecky krásy světa* (All the Beauty of the World)], for instance, were brought out by the Sixty-Eight Publishers in Toronto almost two years before they came out in Prague, there with quite a few passages and some names deleted: that of Milan Kundera among others. There are indications that the numerous emigré editions smuggled into the country and met with a tumultuous readers' demand were such an embarrassment to the establishment that they grudgingly gave in and approved the printing of a few titles.

> **Jaroslav Seifert has become anathema to everything communist mythology holds sacred, and at the same time his popularity, which has its approximate equivalent in American movie star worship, his venerable age and unshakeable courage have made him into a kind of untouchable national saint.**
>
> **—Josef Škvorecký**

When, via the Voice of America, Radio Free Europe and BBC Czechoslovak Service, the bombshell of the Prize descended upon Prague, the authorities could not make up their minds what to do. For several days, while meetings were held in the corridors of power, nothing but identically worded five-liners appeared in various papers, stating the fact and refraining from comment. A few booksellers did not wait for instructions and displayed Seifert's photographs in their shop windows; these were promptly removed by the cops. Eventually, at long last, the bosses decided to take the existence of the damned prize into account, and a cautious commentary appeared in the Party organ *Rudé právo* on October 13. It noted that, as a poet and as a citizen, Seifert "was not easy, was even controversial, but the importance of his work for our poetry is indisputable." To put a smokescreen around the shameful treatment of the poet during the past decade, *Rudé právo* then went over to attack. On October 19 it printed a letter by the Czechoslovak ambassador to Paris entitled "The Nobel Prize Manipulators" in which the envoy, displeased with the way the French press discussed the events surrounding the award in Prague, accused the journalists of "attempts . . . to misuse the name of our poet in their slanderous attacks on our country, and make his name into a weapon in the psychological war against the socialist countries!"

In the next few days the government went to great lengths to present the laureate, both to their subjects and to the West, as their man. The person chosen as spokesman was a hack by the name Ivan Skála. In militant tones he announced on the Prague television that "we shall not permit anybody to take Seifert from us." Thirty years earlier, the same Ivan Skála, writing in the Party cultural weekly *Tvorba,* condemned, in militant tones, one of Seifert's masterpieces, [*Píseň o Viktorce* (The Song of Viktorka)], and proclaimed that its author "had no right to use the honorable title of poet." At about that time, this vociferous moral judge commented also on the execution of the eleven defendants at the Slánský trial by wishing "the dog's death to the dogs." Fifteen years later he vetoed the publishing of my novel *Miss Silver's Past* by the Mladá fronta publishing house where he had just replaced the editor-in-chief fired, among other things, because he gave his placet to the novel. After fifteen more years, shortly before he claimed Seifert for his coterie, Ivan Skála had published his translation of Whitman's *Leaves of Grass.* Whitman would be flattered to have such a versatile artist for translator.

As soon as Jan Pilař left Seifert's hospital room, after officially congratulating him on the prize, two secret policemen in white doctors' coats seated themselves in front of the door and began checking the identity cards of readers who came to pay their tribute to the laureate. In Stockholm, in early September, the Nobel people threw a party at a local Czech restaurant in honor of Seifert's children Jana and Jaroslav, who arrived from Prague to accept the prize on behalf of their father. They were to meet the press at the party; however, the journalists waited in vain: neither Jana nor Jaroslav materialized. That restaurant is the haunting place of many Czech and Slovak emigré intellectuals and that evening many were present, including myself. It leaked that the poet's children had been warned by the Czechoslovak ambassador that if they decided to attend they would have to "face the consequences" once back in Prague.

They are now back in Prague. I wonder what the next step will be in the *dance comique* around the 1984 Nobel laureate.

But, in a way, these about-faces and somersaults were to be expected. Jaroslav Seifert has become anathema to everything communist mythology holds sacred, and at the same time his popularity, which has its approximate equivalent in American movie star worship, his venerable age and unshakeable courage have made him into a kind of untouchable national saint. Of the great Czech communist poets born around the turn of the century—S. K. Neumann, Jiří Wolker, Vitězslav Nezval, Vladimír Holan, František Halas and Josef Hora—he was the only genuine proletarian, the son of a factory blacksmith. In the euphoria after the 1917 Russian revolution they all joined the social democratic splinter group which became the Communist Party and they all, in different degrees, diligently produced "proletarian poetry," sometimes with artistic results one can expect of such endeavors, sometimes creating poems of charm, sincerity and enduring value. But unlike the leading personality of the group, S. K. Neumann, whose method of learning about the Soviet Union was purely deductive and who later would pass sharp judgment on the truthfulness and accuracy of André Gide's book on Russia without ever bothering to visit the land of his many encomiums, Jaroslav Seifert chose the inductive method based on observation of facts, travelled to Moscow as early as 1925, and to make sure he saw right made another trip a couple of years later. Then he came to a conclusion which he never changed; never *had* to change because the events of the next half a century of his long life have borne him out. In 1929 Stalin's Prague agent Klement Gottwald grabbed power in the Party and effected its "bolshevization," i. e., changed it from a relatively independent Marxist organization to a totally subservient subsidiary of the Kremlin. On Seifert's initiative, seven prominent communist writers issued a manifesto in protest against the ominous development.

Two signatories of the 1929 manifesto did not withdraw their names from the document and were duly expelled from the Party: Josef Hora and Jaroslav Seifert. Instead

of believing the revealed religion about Russia and its revolution, Jaroslav Seifert, like a doubting Thomas, went and put his finger into bolshevik Russia's side. He ceased to be a communist entirely, rejoined his working-class dad's old party, befriended many non-communist poets, including Catholics, and joined the ranks of the admirers of Thomas Garrigue Masaryk, one of the earliest critics of Marxism [and the first president of Czechoslovakia].

Had Seifert not become, in the course of the next twenty years, the dearly beloved grand old man of Czech letters, his old adversary Klement Gottwald might have added him to the hundreds of unfortunates he handed over to the hangman after the coup in 1948. But, to use a cliché which describes the situation well, the love of the people shielded the poet. And so Seifert survived the deadly years of Stalin's terror, just as he had survived the deadly years of Nazism.

Ivan Skála's attack on [*Píseň o Viktorce*] [1950] silenced Seifert, fortunately only for a few years. In 1953 Stalin croaked, followed immediately by Gottwald. To emulate the Soviet model, the Czechoslovak Communist Party had Gottwald embalmed and put on display. But the Czech morticians had no experience with embalming techniques, they botched up the job, the corpse spoiled, had to be replaced by a dummy, and eventually removed from public sight. In 1955, after the 20th Party Congress [where the ideology of Stalinism was discredited], the sweet winds of heresy began blowing from Moscow. At the Congress of the Czechoslovak Writers' Union in 1956, Seifert was able to break his enforced silence. He did so in the shrillest way possible. Accusing his colleagues among the establishment hacks of voluntarily keeping their mouths shut when the police were arresting tens of thousands of innocent people, among them many writers, he proclaimed: "If an ordinary person is silent about the truth, it may be a tactical maneuver. If a writer is silent, he is lying. . . ." He then demanded that banned writers be invited back to the literary scene; that the cases of writers languishing in prisons be re-examined, and that, if found innocent these writers be released.

Seifert may be an exceptionally courageous, politically clairvoyant, morally blameless man. Yet, is Seifert an artist great enough to deserve the Nobel prize? I have no doubt that he is.

—Josef Škvorecký

Things picked up and culminated in the short-lived Dubček utopia. However, in Seifert's private life things went worse. Shortly after 1960 he fell seriously ill, a victim, among other things, of what probably was an incorrect diagnosis and an unnecessary operation. I have always felt that the Soviet Invasion in 1968 had at least one good consequence: it literally put the incapacitated old poet back on his feet. The insult of the military intervention hurt the sensitive heart of the man beyond endurance. Seifert found himself a full-fledged member of the underground. In 1977 he signed the bold Charter 77 manifesto, which was damned by the Communist Party and followed by a witch hunt of the signatories. Once again, Seifert's popularity, and by now also his venerable age, saved him from consequences more serious than the banning of his books and occasional interrogations.

All this may prove that the poet is an exceptionally courageous, politically clairvoyant, morally blameless man. Yet, is Seifert an artist great enough to deserve the Nobel prize? I have no doubt that he is. The proof, of course, is in his poetry. Many, including myself, have serious doubts whether lyrical poetry, particularly of the crystal-clear, onomatopoeic kind that Seifert mostly wrote, can really and wholly be appreciated in translation. If it is true that the translation of prose, even if done by excellent and sensitive experts, is always a distortion, what then can be the translation of subtly rhymed, musical lyrical poetry?

Another, not linguistic but psychological difficulty is that many of Seifert's main themes—Prague, Czech history and literature—are imbued with a vast but esoteric richness of associational meanings that for a foreign reader simply are not there. Take [*Píseň o Viktorce*] for instance. It is first of all a tribute to the memory of the most beloved and also most interesting Czech nineteenth century female novelist Božena ("Betty" to her admirers) Němcová; a kind of Czech George Elliot, a courageous feminist before the word was known in Bohemia, a bold mistress of several lovers at a time when having lovers was suicidal for a married woman in the puritanical atmosphere of patriotic Prague, and, last but not least, a celebrated beauty who—Poe would have appreciated it—died of tuberculosis at the age of forty-two. Most Czechs, both men and women, are enamored of the lovely, deeply erotic image of the martyred woman who, alone among many friends, had the guts to publicly greet the hero of the revolution of 1848 Karel Havlíček after his return from enforced exile—another suicidal act in the days of the oppressive postrevolutionary regime of Alexander Bach. Several modern poets wrote entire books dedicated to the memory of Betty Němcová; Seifert wrote two. The heroine of the second one, Viktorka, is a romantic rebel from the authoress' best novel *The Grandmother*. Seduced and abandoned by a soldier, Viktorka goes mad, lives in the wild freedom of the forest, and is eventually killed by lightning. Romantic stuff, but my God, how mythopoeic! Seifert rendered the story in haunting, balladic, untranslatable quatrains that reverberate with criss-crossing Czech associations, linking the countryside to nineteenth century literature, history to legend, present tragedies to the past ones, the lovely image of the mad girl with the lovely image of her creator. The associative chains are endless. But mostly only for the Czech reader.

The same holds true about such books as [*Kamenný most* (The Stone Bridge) or [*Světlem oděná* (Dressed in Light)] lyrical slaps in the face of Nazism, with their many historical echoes and coded meanings. But you have to know Czech history to hear the echoes. Not just know it; you

have to be moved by it. In order to be moved you, I guess, have to be Czech.

But even given all these obstacles, much of the poetic power transpires through the translation. The following is a characterization of Seifert's friend Vladimír Holan's work from a poem written in memory of the poet's death:

> In the wretched aviary that is Bohemia
> he tossed his poems around him
> with contempt
> like chunks of raw meat

That was written in the mid-seventies. In the mid-twenties, influenced by the freely associating surrealism of Apollinaire, Seifert wrote:

> The acrobatics of roses
> in the clouds
> rises to the stars
> which are swallowed up
> by the cushion of boredom
> poetry

In the fifties, after [*Píseň o Viktorce*], these verses of "mawkish self-pity":

> If the tyrant won't fall
>   —even that is hereditary—
> the poet is sentenced to silence
> and the square palm of the barred window
> stuffs with its claws his singing mouth.
> But he shouts his verses through the bars
> while the tearers of books
> are busily at work.

In the sixties this from **The Song of Hendele,** written in memory of a girl who died in Auschwitz:

> Little Hendele
> sometimes tells me
> what she has learned in kindergarten:
>   Cuckoo, cuckoo, tell me, please
>   Is there a life that I shall miss?
> Oh, dove, shut up, no more sweet songs
> here you cannot sweeten anything.
> Beat your wing against the stone,
>   the rabbit should get up,
>   he's been sleeping too long. . . .

And one more from the *annus mirabilis* of 1968:

> I want to believe the time has come
> when it is possible to tell murder in the face:
> You are murder.
> Meanness, even adored with laurel,
> will again be meanness,
> lie will be lie as it used to be,
> and the pistol will no longer be able
> to unlock innocent door.

But then, not all of Seifert's poetry is of the "easy" kind, and should he find his FitzGerald, even the song-like pieces may loose their flavor of open emotionality, so alien to the English-speaking Westerner. In such a translator's hands, the beauty of Viktorka may yet shine through all the thick layers of inaccessible associations and bring tears of Slavic emotion to the sophisticated eyes of American student readers, at least in the privacy of their campus dormitories.

Zdenek Salzmann   (review date Spring 1986)

SOURCE: A review of *The Casting of Bells*, in *Slavic Review*, Vol. 45, No. 1, Spring, 1986, pp. 171-72.

[*A Czechoslovakian-born American educator and critic, Salzmann specialized in Slavic Studies and anthropology. In the review below, she offers praise for Seifert, but laments the degree to which his translators distorted his verse in the English-language version of* Odlévání zvonů (The Casting of Bells).]

Publication of an English translation of a work by a poet who subsequently is awarded the Nobel Prize for Literature is a significant event, and it was particularly so in the case of Jaroslav Seifert, the 1984 Nobel laureate, whose extensive poetic work is virtually unknown to the English-speaking public. Of his many hundred poems, gathered over the past sixty years into some thirty-odd volumes, only a score of individual pieces and one other collection, *Morový sloup* have thus far been rendered in English. An attempt to enlarge the meager selection of Seifert's works available in English was long overdue and has resulted in this translation of *Odlévání zvonů* (1967) [entitled *The Casting of Bells*].

While many of Seifert's earlier poems are rhymed, all of the thirty-three poems in *Odlévání zvonů* are written in free verse without rhymes. The absence of overt formal constraints should enable a translator to concentrate on the subtleties of the poet's thought and expression, but a native-like comprehension of the original text is a precondition for a fully adequate recasting into another language. On this count the present translation fails, especially in view of the translators' claim that they "tried to stay as close as possible to the original."

The first example of a gross misreading of Seifert's poetry appears on the eighth line of the introductory poem, **"Prologue."** The corresponding line of the original, *Jde však tím lesem hloub,* refers to a poet, somewhere in the woods, who cannot help associating a songbird's nest with the tousled hollow of his beloved's armpit. The short form *hloub* for *hlouběji,* the comparative degree of the adverb *hluboko* or *hluboce,* must have been taken by the translators to be a misprint for *holub* [pigeon, dove], because they render the line as "A dove goes through those same woods" instead of, literally, "Yet he [the poet] goes deeper through the woods."

Were this an exceptional slip, one would be tempted to consider it one of the inherent risks anyone translating lyric poetry necessarily assumes. Unfortunately, *The Casting of Bells* is replete with distortions attributable not to the degree of freedom with which the translators [Paul Jagasich and Tom O'Grady] chose to recast the original into English, but their insufficient knowledge of Czech.

Here are examples chosen from among dozens: *Ale i ta, / která v Labutím jezeře, / mnohokrát tančila na špičkách, / má prsty nohou zmrzačeny / a stárne,* literally, "But even the one who has toe-danced many times in Swan Lake ends up with her toes crippled and grows old," translated as "She who had so often / Danced on Labut Lake / Has gotten frozen toes / And suffers"; *Bylo již pozdě odpoled-ne, snad koncem dubna, / nevzpomínám si,* literally, "It was already late in the afternoon, perhaps toward the end of April [*duben*], I don't recall," translated as "It was afternoon or later, / A meal under the oak [*dub*], / Difficult to remember"; *U vchodu chrámu / hlídajícího vody Giudeccy,* literally, "near the entrance to the temple that guards the waters of Giudecca [the long, narrow island forming the southern part of the city of Venice]," translated as "through the church's entrance / and faced the Guido fountains." One could go on.

One positive comment about this book is that the translation appeared before the Nobel Prize award was made and must have been a labor of love. It may even have contributed to Seifert's selection; and if so, it is certainly deserving of our appreciation.

Since the majority of the poems evoke memories of Seifert's younger years and numerous fleeting love affairs, the collection is not merely a celebration of womanhood but a bit of an autobiography as well. The translators should have used greater care: to render a reference to the beloved Romantic Czech poet Karel Hynek Mácha (whose *Máj* [1836] appeared in more than two hundred editions) as though Seifert spoke of himself or to picture the aged poet who complains of lameness as *running* to see the mountain-ash trees instead of *hobbling* is to do the work of the latest Nobel laureate a disservice. The claim of the translators that their work serves as an introduction to Seifert's poetry is not justified.

D. J. Enright   (review date 31 October 1986)

SOURCE: "Unpolitical but Not Innocuous," in *The Times Literary Supplement*, No. 4361, October 31, 1986, p. 1222.

[*Enright is an English poet, novelist, essayist, and editor. In the review of* Selected Poetry *below, he discusses political aspects of Seifert's poetry, briefly comparing his verse to that of Czesław Miłosz.*]

Born in 1901, Jaroslav Seifert became something that, as [the editor and co-translator of *Selected Poetry*] George Gibian notes, we don't seem to have in the West: a national poet. But the price to pay for a national poet is high, calling for the kind of shared feeling born out of decades of war, invasion, occupation and suffering. In such countries political poetry is bound to figure prominently, through reflecting national experiences, aspirations and distresses. But so, also, is non-political or supra-political poetry—through mitigating party polarizations, reinforcing the sense that life is more abiding, larger and richer than the most decent of ideologies can allow, and reminding us that politics is not an end but, at best, a means. This latter poetry risks condemnation as the opium of the people, albeit politics could more justly be termed their firewater. It can be left to prose writers like the author of *Mein Kampf* to administer the crude alcohol, to whip up nationalism in its maleficent forms. A national poet needs to praise, in his perhaps ambiguous way, to celebrate peace, affection, natural and man-made beauty, and times past, and even that old-fashioned thing, joy. He will find his audience.

We are told that when, as Seifert's does, Czech poetry relies heavily on the sounds of the language, on patterns of vowels and consonants and so forth, it is difficult or even impossible to translate. All literary translation is difficult, and the translating of poetry demands special gifts, among them an intimacy with both languages and, in the case of the language translated into, a degree of inwardness and amplitude exceeding that which a major poet would find sufficient for his purposes. But if we think of what some translators have achieved, we need not be over-impressed by talk of untranslatability.

In these translations, at any rate, Seifert's early poetry sounds banal, and too easily arrived at. The "proletarian" verse, far from being militant or full-blooded, is somewhat vapid: "Why, man feels just like a flower: / Don't pluck him, don't break him, don't tread on him!" And maybe pretty girls, "blushes, provocative eyes, deep sighs", loom larger than was ideologically proper. It seems that it took the approach of old age to give depth and a cutting edge to what in youth looks like a fairly ordinary strain of sentimentality. Nor do the avant-garde specimens of "Poetism", diluted Dadaism or faded Rimbaudery, carry much conviction:

> But poetry
> a honeyed moon dripping sweet juices
> into the flowers' calixes

and

> Where is my Bradshaw, that poetic book,
> oh but the beauty of my *wagons-lits!*
>
> Oh *wagons-restaurants* and *wagons-lits!*
> Oh honeymoons!

Unless, of course, something quite remarkable has dropped away in the process of translation.

Seifert was one of the first members of the Czech Communist Party, in 1921, but he was expelled in 1929 for being bolshy about culture, and he was again attacked when the Party took over in 1948, for revealing himself as alien, bourgeois and escapist. For some years thereafter his publications consisted solely of translations, among them, characteristically, one of the Song of Solomon. Later, between 1968 (when he was elected acting chairman of the independent and short-lived Union of Writers) and 1975, only selections from his old works were available inside Czechoslovakia, apart from typed copies of current poems unofficially passed round.

He was, Gibian conveys, a poet of the senses, not of any variety, whether blissful or dark, of transcendence or despair; not intellectual or abstract, but concrete; in one sense of the expression, a people's poet.

> With passion I read poetry
> and loved music
> and blundered, ever surprised,
> from beauty to beauty.
> But when I first saw
> the picture of a nude woman
> I began to believe in miracles.

In **"Prologue"**, from a volume of 1967, a poet spots a bird hovering above its nest and can't stop himself from think-ing of the dimple in his girl's armpit; as he approaches trees and foliage he fancies he sees "the downy crotches of young women". "But it's not me", Seifert avows. But it was certainly like him, or like what he was soon to be. "All my life I have been faithful to love", yet it was love in retrospect that became his great theme, or his most engagingly explored. As far as can be judged from this selection, the quality of the poetry improves with the years. Old the poet may be, "but neither in memories nor in dreams / do legs get tired". They have carried him through a long love affair with Prague too, "the rose of Europe", as he calls the city in one of the extracts given here from his prose memoirs (published, incidentally, by the novelist Josef Škvorecky's émigré house, Sixty-Eight Publishers, in Toronto).

The later poems show a distinct kinship with those of the Polish poet, Czeslaw Milosz. In the bitter-sweet **"Merry-go-round with White Swan"** Seifert writes:

> There were two wars, disease and famine
> and a cluster of suffering.
> Life was not good on earth in those days.
> But it was truly our life
> no matter how it was.

While their histories, the histories of their countries, have much in common, Milosz's acceptance seems harder won: at its weakest *voulu*, as if he is less cheerful than, in his horror of fashionable nihilism, he wants to be; at its strongest more stable and more informed than Seifert's. While persisting in their celebration of life, both poets can smile wryly at themselves and their obvious insignificance. "Poetry is with us from the start", Seifert says,

> Like loving,
> like hunger, like the plague, like war.
> At times my verses were embarrassingly foolish.

"The history of my stupidity would fill many volumes", Milosz writes; but elsewhere, and more resoundingly than Seifert:

> Pure beauty, benediction: you are all I gathered
> From a life that was bitter and confused,
> In which I learned about evil, my own and not
>   my own.
> Wonder kept seizing me, and I recall only
>   wonder . . .
> I asked, how many times, is this the truth of the
>   earth?
> How can laments and curses be turned into
>   hymns?
> What makes you need to pretend, when you
>   know better?
> But the lips praised on their own, on their own
>   the feet ran;
> The heart beat strongly; and the tongue pro-
>   claimed its adoration.

> (from *The Separate Notebooks*)

"Concrete" Seifert can indeed be. In a poem from a volume dated 1979, ***An Umbrella from Piccadilly***, represented here by a selection and published in its entirety by London Magazine Editions in 1983, he recalls how, when he was fourteen or so, he was enraptured by a nude statue in a fountain. He managed to clasp her leg, but could not get any higher, and a shock of desire swept through his veins. (If Seifert places women on a pedestal, he is very soon clambering up after them.) A nearby policeman might easily have run him in—his fingerprints were on the girl's calf, probably he had committed an offence against public decency. Nothing happened—"Yet I was sentenced after all / to lifelong punishment."

And "alien" and rather worse than bourgeois is the title-poem of *An Umbrella from Piccadilly,* which exhorts anyone who is at his wits' end with love to try falling in love again, say with the Queen of England, whose "features are on every postage stamp / of that ancient kingdom". Seifert is—or seems—relaxed, informal, amused, confident of his public's interest and understanding. But it would be a mistake to stress the casual and even jaunty playfulness of this poetry. **"Lost Paradise",** in the same volume, begins by recounting the youthful fascination he felt for Old Testament women and their names—Adah is Ornament, Abigail the Fount of Exultation, Rachel is the Ewe Lamb, Tamar a Palm Tree—and then shifts to the fate of the Jews in Czechoslovakia. In a contrary movement, the sequence on the bombing of the town of Kralupy, from a collection of 1983, ends with the sole survivor of one household: a rooster who jeers at the poet's cry, "Never again, war!" But then, he is a bird, "the bastard!", and sides with the planes.

As the Swedish Academy declared in announcing the award of the Nobel Prize for Literature to him in 1984, "But Seifert has never been innocuous". When he was ill, we are told, crowds stood outside his house in concerned silence. We should be happy that he lived to die in his bed, in his eighty-fourth year. To be non-political is, in our world, to be highly political.

James Finn Cotter   (review date Spring 1987)

SOURCE: "Public and Private Poetry," in *The Hudson Review,* Vol. XL, No. 1, Spring, 1987, pp. 149-55.

[*Cotter is an American educator and critic. In the excerpt below, he offers a mixed assessment of* The Selected Poetry of Jaroslav Seifert.]

National poets are just about extinct as a species. Some literary conservationists may regret their passing; most readers will hardly notice. Their existence made the task of the selection committees for the Nobel Prize for Literature easier: find a country, then pick a poet. One of the last of their kind, Jaroslav Seifert of Czechoslovakia, received the award in 1984 in recognition of his contribution to Czech poetry. From his first book of proletarian verse, [*Město v slzách* (Town in Tears)], published in 1921, to his retrospective [*Býti Básníkem* (To Be a Poet)] in 1983, Seifert gave voice to the popular notion of the private poet as a public figure. He handled the role well, and wrote honestly about being such a poet. Judged by [*The Selected Poetry of Jaroslav Seifert*], the selection from eighteen books of poetry translated by Ewald Osers and edited (with additional translations) by George Gibian, Seifert deserves the recognition the Nobel Prize brought him the year before his death. Like his role of poet, he took the award in stride, in full knowledge that he and his poems represented the

past and were not to be repeated. He could still write about the moon, but as "a dead satellite" littered by the iron-mongery of "the happy Americans." His memory of seeing Halley's comet as a child peering over the backs of strangers, with the cathedral of Prague against the sky, evokes a vision of "trails of sparks which would not die" even as the comet vanished. As the sensual world calls to the poet, the invisible realm fades from view, remaining nonetheless real. In **"Song of the Sweepings,"** heaven, hell and Eden become a child's game of hopscotch on a pavement where the body of a murdered woman lies. Seifert frequently undercuts his nostalgia for romantic leaps with details of violence or vulgarity. In one breath he idealizes a woman's beauty and in the next refers to an armpit or crotch. At times such self-parody tumbles into banality; by refusing to be profound or noble, Seifert settles for the merely trivial. He is most himself when he describes Prague, a city of old streets, parks, and cemeteries. **"Finger Prints"** is a typical poem, recalling the moment when, as a youth, the poet embraced the legs of a nude statue, and was doomed to lose his way in love's labyrinth. Unfortunately, he sounds like a boy who has just discovered a girlie centerfold: "When I first saw / the picture of a nude woman / I began to believe in miracles." The poem recovers when he turns his gaze to Prague and thanks God "for granting me that magnificent setting to live in." The collection concludes with passages from Seifert's memoirs which are less artfully self-conscious and more revealing than the verse.

Miroslav Holub   (essay date 1987)

SOURCE: "A Song under All Circumstances," in *Parnassus: Poetry in Review,* Vol. 14, No. 1, 1987, pp. 209-27.

[*Holub is a Czechoslovakian scientist who writes poetry and prose. In the essay below, he praises Seifert's poetry and describes him as "a poet who gave others strength."*]

"I believe, or, to be perfectly frank, I just assume that what is normally called poetry is one great mystery of which the poet, and indeed every single poet, unveils a greater or a lesser part. Then he puts down his pen or covers his typewriter, turns pensive and towards nightfall he dies. As for instance [Vitězslav] Nezval."

As for instance [Jaroslav] Seifert.

He'd written this sentence in his memoirs, and then he kept his word, in that night from January 9-10, 1986: it is said that he left a half-written poem on his beside table.

If it were possible to classify poetry, as certain other forms of human behavior, into obligatory and optional, then Seifert would be a clear example of the first kind: the poem to him was the most natural form of expression. As is evident from the paragraph quoted above, even his prose was composed of half-written potential poems, of poetic sweeps tending toward a metaphorical anchoring before the flow of narration is embarked upon. "I'm not a good storyteller," he himself said. "When I tell a story I'm in too much of a hurry . . . I simply haven't got the knack. That's why I have mainly written poetry. It seemed easier to me."

By temperament and choice he is an obligatory lyric poet, in the sense that this term is used in Europe. In an epic, narrative poetical enterprise, such as his [*Píseň o Viktorce* (Song of Viktorka)] (1950), the flow breaks up into a sequence of rounded (indeed even formally rounded) songs, through which the action advances as over a velvety staircase in a timeless space. The essence of lyric poetry, of Seifert's lyric poetry, is timelessness, the simultaneity of the imaginative process, momentariness elevated above flow. There is no nature in an instant, Alfred North Whitehead has said, but a poem is in an instant and only in an instant. That is one of the redeeming functions of lyric poetry. It is the principle of what Seifert himself on every occasion called a "song," in line with the Czech and the European post-Romantic conceptual framework of poetry. In this formulation a song is the culmination of a creative act of whatever kind, an elevation from everyday drabness into a festive light, from muteness into music. Seifert's song bears no relation to the lyrics of a song still waiting to be set to music; it itself is its own music.

If it were possible to classify poetry, as certain other forms of human behavior, into obligatory and optional, then Seifert would be a clear example of the first kind: the poem to him was the most natural form of expression.

—Miroslav Holub

"Song" to Seifert is not only the fact [of a poem] but also the process of a poem. Painting to him was "a song on a canvas," the Czech painter Špála, with his vigorous brushwork, was to him one of those "under whose hands everything turns into jubilant song," and every "gesture of a girl's hands, gentle and yielding, / is a command for song, the song's beginning . . ." Singing and birdsong are perhaps Seifert's most frequent metaphors for anything that makes life worth living. The word "song" figures in the titles of an astonishingly large number of Seifert's poems, both as a formal label and as an indication of its substance. Out of the fifty-eight poems in his collection [*Jaro sbohem* (Goodbye, Spring)] twenty-two have the word "song" in their title, and a further six contain related concepts.

From the start of his career, song was to Seifert the most immediate, the most natural, and the most striking metaphor. In his first collection, carried as it was on a wave of collective revolutionary optimism and proletarian sensitivity, the slum children are "violins of maple-wood, / each one of us would play some cheerful or sad song from his own life," and this called for a master violin maker to make sure they were all well ". . . when that great concert starts in the world's streets . . ." In a poem which represents Seifert's middle and peak period, a poem now read in their primers by the second generation of schoolchildren, and for many the only poetical blessing on their road

through life, we read of Říp Hill, that symbol of the Bohemian landscape:

> I have seen mountains, ice-capped, high:
> to sing of them I do not try.
>
> . . . . .
>
> But when I see on the horizon
> that rounded hill, the plain it lies on,
>
> . . . . .
>
> My eyes are full, the tears are stinging
> and everything in me starts singing,
>
> singing and crying. Mother dear,
> how beautiful our home is here!

("A Penniless Painter Went Out into the World," 1949)

[In a footnote, the critic adds: "In Czech legend the Slavic tribes that moved into Bohemia from farther East were led by 'Praotec Čech'—'Forefather Čech'—from whom the people took their name 'Czechs.' When the group reached the Central Bohemian plain, Čech climbed a rounded hill rising above the surrounding landscape to survey the land: this was Říp. He found the land to his liking and declared: Here let us settle.

The fact that Říp Hill has the shape of an army steel helmet lent it additional symbolism, especially in poetry written at times of national danger or servitude."] . . .

And in his last book, [*Byti basnikem* (To Be a Poet)] (1983), he concludes his poem **"Ash Wednesday"**:

> Not many things in our lives
> deserve a song.
> But I'm unlikely now to write those songs,
> though when the moment comes
> I'll take them with me.

In this kind of poetry you can pretend a great many things: you can use words to pretend emotions, you can use silences to pretend depth, you can use rhymes to create pretend-images, old things can be expressed in a seemingly new way, ornaments can be used to create a garden so dense you scarcely notice that it contains no living thing.

It is a poetry of allusion and illusion.

In Seifert's work, however, nothing was ever fudged, not at any stage of his development, not at any stage of his life. That was due to his three poetic premises. First of all, I would say, by his absolute command of the language, of poetic Czech, as he inherited it from the great figures of the national-revival poetry of the nineteenth century, when it was not only poetry that mattered but, above all, poetry in this specific language, when the poets carried on their shoulders not only the obvious burden of poetry but also, and indeed primarily, the far-from-obvious burden of the nation. From his earliest books in the twenties Seifert had mastered a style in which metric pattern is in complete harmony with the communicated message, with the communicable and communicated feeling. His strictly rhymed poems read in the original as naturally as everyday speech. Nothing is excessive, nothing is overextended, nothing is other than a perfect fit, the verse is the natural and the only, the only possible, voice. As an outstanding critic (M. Pohorský) observed in his obituary, ". . . the miracle of a language which seems with a charming smile to submit to the lyricist's fancy, to his rhymes and assonances, to his folksong-like melody, and towards the end to the free rhythm of the human breath."

In his supreme poetic performances, Seifert is untranslatable and incomprehensible; he is hermetically national. I am not saying that this is either good or bad. Every literature has its untransmittable and its more or less transmittable poets. What in Seifert's case is a pity is that in the context of comparable national cultures he is an almost unique instance of a poet who carried his linguistic and stylistic inheritance intact through the entire period of modernism, of the European avant-garde of the twenties and thirties, in an essentially traditional manner without, once the avant-garde wave had ebbed, in the least seeming anachronistic, either in language or in form. He had absorbed a wealth of new influences, integrating them into his strongly individual yet at the same time traditional verse. And this he achieved in the Czech context, in contrast to many lesser poets who, in the relatively strong tradition of Czech metric poetry, present us with too many verses and too few discoveries.

Singing and birdsong are perhaps Seifert's most frequent metaphors for anything that makes life worth living. The word "song" figures in the titles of an astonishingly large number of Seifert's poems, both as a formal label and as an indication of its substance.

—Miroslav Holub

Here lies Seifert's second premise. He had the gift, from his very beginnings,—[*Na vlnách T.S.F.* (On the Waves of Wireless Telegraphy;1925), *Slavík zpívá špatně* (The Nightingale Sings Badly; 1926), *Postovni holub* (Carrier Pigeon; 1929)]—of integrating into the irresistibly assertive form of his "song" a new imagery, the new, radical, avant-garde vision that came to our poetry from the phenomenon of Apollinaire and the echoes of Dadaism and Futurism, and eventually by that vigorous stream of Czech Surrealism as represented by one of his closest friends, Vitězslav, Nezval. The sensibility of the poor boy from the Prague working-class district developed into the sophisticated sensibility of the poetic avant-garde as in **"Honeymoon"**:

If it were not for all those foolish kisses
we'd not be taking honeymoon trips to the sea—
but if it weren't for honeymoon trips
what use then all those *wagon-lits?*

Perpetual fear of railway station bells,
ah, *wagon-lits,* honeymoon sleeping cars,
all wedded happiness is brittle glass,

a honeyed moon stands in a sky of stars.

My love, look at the Alpine peaks outside,
we'll let the window down, we'll smell the amaranth,
the sugary white of snowdrops, lilies, snow—
behind the *wagon-lit*'s the *wagon-restaurant.*

Ah, wagon-restaurants, cars for a honeymoon,
to stay in them forever and to sup
with knife and fork on dreams that end too soon.
HANDLE WITH CARE! GLASS FRAGILE!
    THIS SIDE UP!
And one more day and then another night,
two marvellous nights, two marvellous days like
    these.
Where is my Bradshaw, that poetic book,
oh but the beauty of my *wagons-lits!*

Oh *wagons-restaurants* and *wagons-lits!*

Oh honeymoons!

Startling metaphor, unfettered imagination, and a rainbow-like, joyful emotionalism were becoming the immanent characteristics of Seifert's song, even though, as time progressed, they became refined and amalgamated into a simpler and more intimate tone of voice, as in **"Moon over the Gasworks"** [*Postovni holub*]:

One day my body's suspenders will snap from
    the strain,
some light-bulbs will go on and off again,
the soul dissolve its earthly tie
and like a gasometer rise to the sky.

Or, equally typical of that period, **"Dance of the Girls' Chemises"**:

A dozen girls' chemises
drying on a line,
floral lace at the breast
like rose windows in a Gothic cathedral.

Lord,
shield Thou me from all evil.

A dozen girls' chemises,
that's love,
innocent girls' games on a sunlit lawn,
the thirteenth, a man's shirt,
that's marriage,
ending in adultery and a pistol shot.

The wind that's streaming through the chemises,
that's love,
our earth embraced by its sweet breezes:
a dozen airy bodies.

Those dozen girls made of light air
are dancing on the green lawn,
gently the wind is modelling their bodies,
breasts, hips, a dimple on the belly there—
open fast, oh my eyes.
Not wishing to disturb their dance
I softly slipped under the chemises' knees,
and when any of them dropped
I greedily inhaled it through my teeth
and bit its breast.

Love,
which we inhale and feed on,

disenchanted,
love that our dreams are keyed on,
love,
that dogs our rise and fall:
nothing
yet the sum of all.

In our all-electric age
bars not christenings are the rage
and love is pumped into our tyres.
My sinful Magdalen, don't cry.
Romantic love has spent its fires.

Faith, hope and motorbikes.

[*Postovni holub*]

From that period also dates the poem which, like the one quoted about Říp Hill, has become ubiquitous wherever the need or opportunity for a poem arises in the lives of Czech people:

We wave a handkerchief
on parting
every day something is ending,
something beautiful's ending.
The carrier pigeon beats the air
returning;
with hope or without hope
we're always returning.

Go dry your tears
and smile with eyes still smarting,
every day something is starting,
something beautiful's starting.

("Song," [*Postovni holub*])

Seifert's supreme period, represented by his collections [*Jablko z klína* (An Apple from Your Lap; 1933), ***Ruce Venušiny*** (The Hands of Venus; 1936), and ***Jaro sbohem*** (Goodbye, Spring;1937)], those poems which have virtually become common coinage, a currency still valid, texts that we quote like proverbs, formed, as it were, the nucleus of crystallization of entire volumes. These are the poems which—entirely in line with the author's intentions—we have often read to the ones we loved, as well as the poems we softly repeat to ourselves when we are abroad and nostalgic for home:

If I could kiss
the way sailors do
—stars strike at the windows and
pretty women's laughter—
no one ever, dearest,
oh my loving heart,
will tear me from these
four walls ever after.

. . . . .

(from "Song," [*Jaro sbohem*], 1937)

It is, sadly, necessary here to remind the reader that the music and natural elegance of Seifert's poetic language cannot be translated. The lines of his poems, at that period, are very short; the rhyme scheme, in spite of an appearance of effortless and sometimes playful inevitability, is usually highly elaborate.

At just that time Seifert added to his style a further ingredient, one that was the antithesis to the traditional, more or less sentimental, key of Czech metric verse, an ingredient that turned also against the prophetic, almost excessively serious self-satisfied Surrealist avant-garde—that ingredient was his smile, laughter, mockery, and irony, all of them linking up organically with his essential playfulness. The poet, looking around for a new life in his **"New Year's Song,"** tries to fulfill one of his good resolutions by adopting the shape of a little donkey and breathing on the cold hands of the newborn Christ:

The Christ Child sadly raised his head
and thoughtfully addressed me:

And where, boy, have you been again?
Your will is weak and glib!
Shamefacedly I crept away
from little Jesus's crib.

[*Jaro sbohem*]

Seifert's just mentioned inclination toward poetic playfulness was demonstrated even more strikingly in a volume which contemporary literary critics tend to overlook—a volume of satirical verse, inspired by political disillusionment and by the growing tension due to the advance of Fascism in Europe, *Sung into the Rotary Press* (1936); Seifert here created an ironic detachment even from his own avant-garde:

O mustard! That forgotten herbal grease!
Can there be anyone who unaware is
that it's the honey which surrealist bees
are sucking from the various blooms of Paris?

It is that precious beneficial ointment,
for swaddled infants it must play its part.
It's poetry which, though in fact it's innocent,
now lies upon the shelves next to the Heart.

By the end of the thirties the dominant feature of Seifert's poetry was its increasingly patriotic note, a deliberate emphasis on national character and mankind's belonging together, a deliberate but probably very natural replacement of startling and "artificial" elements by harmony, human sympathy, and personal closeness. Seifert became, to the extent that a poet in specific historical circumstances can become such a thing, the spokesman of his people—not perhaps in the sense of a leader but in that of a poetic formulator. Under this heading comes his book of mourning on the death of T. G. Masaryk, Czechoslovakia's first President, ***Eight Days*** (1937); his reaction to the imposed Munich agreement, [***Zhasněte světla*** (Put Out the Lights; 1938)]; and all those collections which appeared during the war with such a conspicuous effect on the nation's morale at the time of the German Occupation.

Beautiful as on a jug a painted flower
is the land that bore you, gave you life,
beautiful as on a jug a painted flower,
sweeter than a loaf from fresh-ground flour
into which you've deeply sunk your knife.

Countless times disheartened, disappointed,
always newly you return to it,
countless times disheartened, disappointed,
to this land so rich and sun-anointed,
poor like springtime in a gravel-pit.

Beautiful as on a jug a painted flower,

heavy as our guilt that will not go away
—never can its memory decay.
At the end, at our final hour
we shall slumber in its bitter clay.

("Song of the Native Land," [*Zhasněte
světla*], 1938)

Or even more strongly in a poem—published in [*Přilba hlíny* (A Helmetful of Earth; 1947)], but clearly written earlier, during the war—entitled **"At the Tomb of the Czech Kings"**:

Shame in my heart, I stand among the agates—
those jewels of our land!
The faithful sword whose resting place is near
was not to hand!

Like dew besprinkling leaves and blossoms
while dormant still in bud,
the sword, the lance, the chain-mail gauntlet
were always splashed with blood.

To pray? But let the sword be drawn
and flash the while we pray!
Only the women may have empty hands now.
And not even they!

The clock moves on, though time is running
    slow
on our Renaissance spire.
The hand of history's written on the wall
new signs of fire.

But there's dried blood on it, a spark is kindled:
the chained will disobey.
Only the women may have empty hands now.
And not even they!

To fold our hands in miserable prayer,
wait for a better day?
Only the children may have empty hands now.
And not even they!

Seifert turned back to the traditional sources of the nation's strength ([author] Božena Němcová, [painter and book illustrator] Mikuláš Aleš) and, with victory over German Fascism achieved, after 1945—easily at times and with certain difficulties at others—published a poetry which returned to such uncontroversial themes as Prague, music, his childhood, motherhood, as circumstances and his own voice dictated ([*Šel malíř chudě do světa* (Penniless Painter Goes Out into the World), 1949; *Píseň o Viktorce* (The Song of Viktorka), 1950; *Maminka* (Mother), 1954;] *The Boy and the Stars*, 1956).

No longer a member of any literary movement, no longer among the leaders of the literary establishment, he remained as a grand, accessible, and universally visible monument to the great period of Czech avant-garde poetry from which Nezval, [Konstantin] Biebl, and [František] Halas had been carried off by death, as well as [Vladimir] Holan, who—in the words of Seifert's obituary for him—"in this cursed aviary of Bohemia / contemptually flung about his poems / like chunks of bloody meat. / But the birds were afraid . . ."

The birds were not afraid of Seifert's songs.

Seifert did not force himself—nor was he able to force himself—into anything, not even into some massive poetic project. He simply confessed his loves, his sorrows, his joys, his hopes, and his nostalgia about the irretrievable passage of time: the thematic scope of his poetry was entirely congruent with the thematic scope of everyday emotional normality.

—*Miroslav Holub*

The time has come to mention Seifert's third premise. I see it in his downright childlike authenticity or, in plain language, his sincerity. He did not force himself—nor was he able to force himself—into anything, not even into some massive poetic project. He simply confessed his loves, his sorrows, his joys, his hopes, and his nostalgia about the irretrievable passage of time: the thematic scope of his poetry was entirely congruent with the thematic scope of everyday emotional normality. This brought him close even to a totally unliterary public, as an instance of uncomplicated sincere sensibility of the kind that is occasionally found in our midst and can at times appear as sentimentality; Seifert, however, avoids this danger by his self-irony.

Poetic sincerity need not be an especially noteworthy aspect; it can be a matter of course. But in situations and political constellations where what is not written may matter more than what is written, it acquires a specific significance.

Seifert's basic position did not change greatly after his thirties and forties. The central verse of [*Ruse Venušiny* (The Hands of Venus)] (1936), ". . . and by the running waters / wait for the birth of new springtimes / which will silence anew that age-old hesitation, / to lay one's head into the hands of the Venus of Milo . . ." remained his calling for good. He stuck to it during easier periods, of which there were not many in his life, and at times of suffering. His lyric emotions were not only his own small unquestioned, truthful, and genuine world; they were also his particular form of unarmed defense. In his "final balance sheet" volume, [*Býti básníkem* (To Be a Poet)] (1983), he said: "I have believed that poetry, / invariably festive, / is watching over me like a guardian angel / who with me stumbles through the dust and mud / barefoot." And in his Nobel Prize acceptance speech in 1984 he attempted the formulation that this "lyrical state of mind" was "the state of the self-sufficient individual," that it was "a state of rest that is neither patient nor impatient," "a state of calm enjoyment of the values on which man builds . . . the foundations of his equilibrium and his ability to inhabit this world."

For a lyrical state of mind there is no other poetic construct than the frank interpretation of what is just then being felt and what is being seen or was once seen. A lyrical state of mind, as understood by Seifert, is an extra-literary characteristic and not directly related to art. That is how I explain the fact that after the upheavals of the fifties, when he and his [*Píseň o Viktorce*] became the butt of criticism, and after his physical suffering caused by illnesses, there suddenly appeared in the sixties, after a silence lasting eight years, a Seifert without Seifert, a song without a song; the lyrical mind was the last thing the poet brought out with him from his night after relinquishing his whole system of melic poetry and sparkling ornament. The foundation of a poem now was a specific image and its metaphorical validity; the poem would advance from a description of experienced situations, events, and fragments of occurrences whose obvious authenticity would replace the authenticity of emotions now concentrated into an increasingly emphatic nostalgia of old age and into celebrations of his native Prague. The following poem is a typical example. **"View from Charles Bridge"** comes from the volume [*Býti básníkem*] Seifert's last book, but he had been writing very similar poems since the late seventies.

> The rain had long since stopped.
> In the pilgrimage church in Moravia,
> where I had sought shelter from a storm,
> they were chanting a Marian song
> which stopped me from leaving.
> I used to listen to it back home.
>
> The priest had genuflected at the steps
> and left the altar,
> the organ had sobbed and fallen silent,
> but the throng of pilgrims did not move.
> Not until minutes later did the kneeling rise
> and singing,
>   without turning their heads,
> all move backwards together
> towards the open portals.
>
> Never did I return there, never
> again stand under the foliage of limes,
> where the white banners waved
> under the buzz of the bees.
> I was homesick for Prague,
> even though I'd only briefly stayed
> outside her walls.
>
> Day after day I gaze in gratitude
> on the Castle of Prague
>   and on its Cathedral:
> I cannot tear my eyes away
> from that picture.
>   It is mine
> and I also believe it is miraculous.
>
> To me at least it assigned my destiny.
> And as the twilight falls
>   into Prague's windows
> with stars in translucent darkness
> I hear her ancient voice each time
> and I hear poetry.
> Without that voice I would be silent
> as the bird
> called the kiwi.
>
> There are days when the Castle
>   and its Cathedral
> are gloomily magnificent,
> when it seems

> they were built of dismal rock
> brought from the Moon.
>
> An instant later, however, the towers of Prague
> are once more wreathed in rays
>   and roses
> and that sweet delusion
> of which love, too, is woven.
> My frivolous steps along the streets,
> my rose-red adventures
> and loves and all the rest
> are buried under light ash
> since Time burnt down.
>
> A few steps from the Royal Road
> was a dark corner,
> where tousle-haired prostitutes appeared
> to walkers in the evenings,
> luring into their dead wombs
> young inexperienced boys,
> as I was then.
> Now all is silent there.
> And only television aerials haunt
> the ridges of the roofs.
> But whenever I step on the pavement
> of Charles Bridge
> I am reminded of those pilgrims
> in the pilgrimage church.
>
> What bliss it is
>   to walk upon this bridge!
> Even though the picture is often glazed
> by my own tears.

Perhaps Seifert, like Holan, wanted to fling about in that cursed aviary of Bohemia some more substantial material than his former rose petals, perhaps his position in life had changed so significantly, perhaps he wanted to employ free verse, that means of expression of the then-predominating post-modernist poetry, a form he had previously only used sporadically. Theoretically he defined his reasons in the words: "Where had poetry advanced to since the days / when last I wrote and published new poems! / But I too now found myself in totally different regions." Yet his sincerity then leaps from the lines

> Sometimes I feel a yearning for music,
>   but I no longer have the skill.

> (from **"The Treble Recorder,"** [*Halleyova kometa*] 1967)

In [*Koncert na ostrově* (Concert on the Island)] (1965) he actually exclaimed: "Away with that old poetic rubbish / of metaphors and rhymes, / life sometimes is quite chillingly naked. .." More precisely and significantly, however, he said in that book:

> One day I found my name
> on a black flag in silver letters
> complete with date of death.
>   Cheerfully burned a candle
> and the organ roared;
> maybe the choirmaster had gone mad.
>
> But that dead man was someone else
>   because I'm here.
> But is it really me? I don't quite trust myself.
> And that's dedication.
>   To whom?

To that dead man on the black flag.

All titled poems in [*Koncert na ostrově*] have the word "song" in the title—but only to emphasize their antithetical continuity. The singer, with what I would call a heroic decision, has come back now to "different regions" only to speak out for all "today's laughter and lament."

Forty years on the sunny side of poetry had come to an end. Seifert began afresh, with nothing but his authentic lyrical mind. [*Koncert na ostrově*] is much more a first book than a return to the style of his first collections from the twenties. The poems in [*Halleyova kometa*] and *The Casting of the Bells* (1967) have much firmer outlines. A "chillingly naked" life here gave rise to a poetry of images which at times are almost startlingly vigorous, and thus lend themselves to translation.

> Once I put my ear to the ground
> and heard the sound of crying.
> But maybe that was only the water crying,
> trapped in the fountain's throat
> because it did not want to go to mankind

> (from **"The Heaviness of Clay,"** [*Halleyova kometa*])

Perhaps he was still waiting for "the birth of new springtimes," but in his memory the wartime spring turned bitter:

> It resembled a young woman
> with an amputated breast;
> when she takes from her handbag a mirror
> the size of her hand
> she sees only harshly compressed lips
> or eyes moist from tears.

> (from **"One of Those Springs,"** [*Halleyova kometa*])

Death was beginning to creep into the tension underlying Seifert's lines and into his metaphors, as in **"Marche Funèbre,"** [*Halleyova Kometa*] Halley's Comet:

> The dead are crouching there
> until the heavens open.
>   They're waiting.
> For the ringing sound of angels' trumpets,
> for the last judgment
>   and divine justice.
> In other words: for nothing.

The authenticity of the childish or youthful eye is here developing into the authenticity of depressing rather than reconciled old age. Trustful contemplation is replaced by a harsh statement of fact: the metaphors are intended not to caress or be agreeably surprising but to shock.

We witness, in fact, a somewhat reversed poetic development from equilibrium to disequilibrium, from smooth outlines and soft edges toward sharp and abrasive ones, from reconciled acceptance of the state of the world to disagreement with it:

> Don't let them dupe you
> that the plague's at an end:
> I've seen too many coffins hauled
> through this dark gateway
> which isn't the only one.

> The plague still rages and it seems the doctors
> are giving different names to the disease
> to avoid a panic.
> Yet it is still the same old death
> and nothing else,
> and it is so contagious
> no one alive can escape it.

> Whenever I have looked out of my window
> emaciated horses have been drawing that ill-
>   boding cart
> with a shrivelled coffin.
> Only those bells aren't tolled so often now,
> crosses no longer painted on front doors,
> juniper twigs no longer burnt for fumigation.

> (**"The Plague Column,"** eponymous volume, 1981)

More and more frequently Seifert turned to history, and specific items of history became for him the starting points of poems aimed at contemporaneity, as for instance in **"The Canal Garden"** (*The Plague Column*), where one stanza reads:

> Night, that merciless keeper of darkness,
> hurriedly pours the red dawn from the sky
> like the bloody water
> in which Monsieur Marat was murdered
> by a fair-haired beauty's dagger,
> and now it begins to rip off people's
> own shadows . . .

For a short while Seifert once more took part in literary life, like a monument of the Seifert that was and like a poet once more active and struggling for his form of expression. In his motionless, silent, yet substantial presence and in his steady, gentle, blue gaze there was something impressive and humanizing. Maybe it was only that lyrical mind of his, but I should prefer to call it just Seifert. At the time he was writing *The Plague Column* (1968-70) he was even chairman of the Writers' Union. Following the union's restructuring after the Soviet intervention, Seifert fell silent once more (as he himself put it in an answer to a survey, he had "put down his fountain pen and drawn the curtains"). *The Plague Column* was published after some delay, and with it his two last collections, *An Umbrella from Piccadilly* (1979) and [*Býti basníkem* (To Be a Poet)] (1983).

Seifert represented positive spirit, consistently, steadfastly, and to the end. His lyrical voice was distinctive at the time of the glittering avant-garde, when he was surrounded by his friends from that powerful wave of his generation, and it was equally distinctive in the last twenty years of his life when he was entirely alone.

—*Miroslav Holub*

Here his grip was beginning to weaken: historical and personal reminiscences were more frequent. Only slight metaphorical hints in an ever-widening context recalled his unmistakable diction. Authenticity was now growing into confession, made in a very relaxed breath, and these books therefore have to be seen in conjunction with his earlier work, as a victory of the lyrical mind over his age and the ages, as a "natural phenomenon" (to use Miloš Pohorský's words).

In no instance, however, do any of these late poems ever slip into helpless self-pity: there invariably is some hint of a smile, some little flame of hope. What he said in the lines about the unborn child in *The Plague Column*: "But in the wild-thyme nest / someone's already winding up the spring / of the tiny heart / so it should go accurately / all life long" also applied to his own heart: it went accurately. For this poet nothing was ever either too soon or too late: when *The New York Times Magazine* in May 1985 commented that the Nobel Prize had come too late for Seifert, for Czech poetry, and for the Czech people, it directly contradicted the essence of Seifert's personality, Seifert's poetry, and Czech poetry generally. Seifert himself, as his wrinkles multiplied, increasingly felt the chill, the real chill, in the glances "from elsewhere," from those foreign places for which the Czech language has the effective word *"cizina"* (abroad, literally "strange lands"), a term which, however, contains nothing of the xenophobia traditional in other countries. In *The Plague Column* he speaks of the "terrible" world outside, formulating the core of his being at home as "We at least love." Seifert never resigned himself: he preserved the same equanimity at all times, before the Nobel Prize and afterward, in modest retirement and in front of the television cameras. Typical is a remark he made in January 1985: "An intelligent person, you know, can cope with chaos; it only destroys the idiot."

Seifert, I would say, represented the nation's positive spirit, consistently, steadfastly, and to the end. His lyrical voice was distinctive at the time of the glittering avantgarde, when he was surrounded by his friends from that powerful wave of his generation, and it was equally distinctive in the last twenty years of his life when he was entirely alone. He was not a poet who made discoveries, he was a poet who gave others strength, and in this respect he played a historic part. If the writers of a letter to *The Times* of London were really right in saying that Seifert's prize was a prize "for mediocrity," then we would have to accept (just as in the case of Karel Čapek) that this nation draws its strength from mediocrity and that real greatness cannot be achieved just by simple human feelings and quiet song—and that does not strike me as credible in Central Europe, where we have heard so much shouting throughout history. A narrowly national poetry is difficult to assess on a supranational level, but this has no bearing on its universally human significance. It is up to us, in this aviary of Bohemia, to show how and why we are worthy of Seifert and his Nobel Prize now that, having "unveiled a greater or a lesser part," he has "put down his pen, turned pensive, and died during the night."

Edward Możejko (essay date 1987)

SOURCE: "Between Dream and Reality: The Poetry of Jaroslav Seifert," in *Scando-Slavica,* Vol. 33, 1987, pp. 63-79.

[*In the following essay, Możejko examines the different stages of Seifert's career.*]

Jaroslav Seifert made his literary debut in 1921, barely four years after the first publication of T. S. Eliot's *The Love Song of Alfred J. Prufrock,* and one year prior to the appearance of *The Waste Land.* Franz Kafka was still alive and living in Prague. In the same year, another Czech writer and Seifert's contemporary, Karel Čapek, wrote his play, *R. U. R.,* which gave the world a then strange, but now familiar, term: "robot".

The new generation of writers included such poets as Vitězslav Nezval, Konstantin Biebl, František Halas, Josef Hora, Vladimír Holan, Jiří Wolker, Stanislav Kostka Neumann and others. As noted by one critic [Květoslav Chvatík], no other generation has ever had a greater impact on the evolution of Czech literature than the one which appeared shortly after the first World War.

Jaroslav Seifert was part of this generation. Born on September 23, 1901, to a poor worker's family in Žižkov, a suburb of Prague, he began his professional career as a journalist, and appeared on the literary scene as a proletarian poet. Proletarian art, which manifested itself most distinctly through poetry, played an important role in the Czech cultural life of the early twenties. Its advocates postulated an art which would express the political and social aspirations of the working class, and which would be a preparation for revolution. At that time, Seifert joined the Communist party. He believed that this act would emphasize more strongly his desire to express solidarity with workers and the struggle for social justice. It seems that Seifert became a party member not out of ideological considerations, but because of his own harsh experiences, his personal dreams and ideals which later proved to be incompatible with the rigid, dogmatic stand of the party. This became particularly clear in his poetry.

His first collection of poems bore the title *Město v slzách* (1920; City in Tears). It described the misery of the poor and oppressed; its content is permeated by a revolutionary tone, calling for change and heralding justice for those who suffer. In a poem entitled **"The Most Humble Poem"** (**"Básezň nejpokornější"**), the poet identifies himself with a prophet who shows the way for the poor.

Seifert's first collection provides us with a good example of "natural" proletarian poetry. It is "natural" because it was not inspired by ideological ardour or indoctrination, but grew out of his genuinely working-class background and indignation with social injustice. In one of the poems, he calls himself "a poor boy from the outskirts". Indeed, he did not have to learn about poverty from textbooks, or be rational or speculate about it, because he lived in the midst of it. These poems can be defined, no doubt, as socially committed literature.

But they are more than just that. At the same time, their lyrical subject is many-faced, which distinguishes Seifert from other proletarian poets—his contemporaries. Some critics [such as Bedřich Václavek], writing about [*Město v slzách*] during the twenties, had already noted that it is based on a number of inner conflicts, or as we would prefer to say today—oppositions. On the one hand, the poet declares his admiration for nature, yet he must live in the city to struggle for a better future. He would like to isolate himself in nature, but he must remain among people to show solidarity with them, and even sacrifice his life for the improvement of their destiny. The motif of death occurs in these poems on more than one occasion, but life and biological vitality are dominating themes of this volume.

By and large, this poetry contains sharp criticisms of urban civilization, criticism directed agaist the city where man finds himself enslaved by mechanization and the advancements of technology. What was perceived and awaited in the past as a blessing, turned out to be a curse. The city is a cold world, devoid of warmth and human feelings. Therefore, the poet wants to embrace all those who are in need, who ought to wrench themselves free from the grip of indigence and humiliation.

Yet his relation to them is far from being sentimental. For a proletarian poet, very little hatred emanates from this volume—a fact not to be overlooked when explaining Seifert's later break with communism—but he does not exclude revolution either, and at times wants to "avenge in the name of love". For the most part, however, the author seems to avoid violent images of class confrontation, and revolution remains an idealization, rather than a bloody reality. "Basically—wrote Bedřich Václavek about [*Město v slzách*] in 1928—this is a poetry of soft, passive compassion."

Here we arrive at yet another, and perhaps the most essential opposition. What makes these poems "softer", in fact, is a kind of *mythologization* of reality. The author often conveys his message through the extensive use of biblical imagery and symbols. At times such an attitude manifests itself by a word borrowed from the Scriptures, by the name given to a location (e. g., the title of a poem: **"Sinful City"**; Czech title: **"Hříšné město"**), by the name of a prophet or description of an entire situation which clearly alludes to one in the Gospels (a typical example is the poem **"December 1920"**): all of which, of course, lends an allegorical dimension to the whole collection. The collection does remind us of *The Twelve,* a poem by A. Blok, which was translated by Seifert into Czech in 1922.

Before we leave Seifert's poetic beginnings, one more comment seems necessary. It was at that time that Seifert formed the basic principles of his poetic world: an interaction of dreams and reality. Although the intensity and devices by which these elements intertwine does vary from one collection to another, their presence remains a stable component throughout the whole of Seifert's poetic oeuvre. Its formation was perhaps not entirely without foreign influence, and his well-known fascination with Guillaume Apollinaire may have had a certain impact on his development; but this characteristic definitely reflected Seifert's own creative sensibility. Incidentally, Seifert was not alone in his admiration for the author of *Calligram-*

mes; many of his contemporaries wrote poems under the direct influence of Apollinaire (e.g., J. Wolker's long poem *Svatý Kopeček*), and the title of one of the most significant Czech avant-garde journals, *Pásmo,* has a double meaning. It can be translated as both *Filmstrip* and "zone", the title of a poem written by the French poet in 1913.

In 1923 came Seifert's second collection of poetry, **Samá láska** (Nothing But Love). In comparison with his beginnings, the transformation was shocking: few traces of the proletarian poetry could be found, and the youthful exhaltation with social motifs disappeared almost completely. The change appeared to be so thorough that the above-mentioned critic Václavek noted that between writing the first and second books, Seifert must have changed Muses.

Indeed, the poet strikes, as it were, an entirely new tone: he leaves the realm of ideology, and embraces life itself. This statement requires some clarification. What it means is simply this: if, in [**Město v slzách**], he preaches love for one social class only, then now he discovers anew the whole world, or as he says in one of his poems—"all beauties of the world". He discerns this beauty in the most simple manifestations of everday life: flowers, the smell of bread, even kitchen utensils such as a coffee grinder. He is enchanted by and in love with them. Henceforth, the motif of love will permeate the whole of Seifert's lyrics, determining his relation to the surrounding reality. It is love for nature, for his country, for mankind and last but not least, sensual, erotic love.

The extent of this re-evaluation of his artistic attitude is justified in the following way:

> Because love is something big,
> You will recognize it, for example, from that,
> that if in the whole world there is a revolution,
> still, somewhere on the green grass
> lovers will have time to hold hands
> and rest their heads on each other.

Seifert abandons his former condemnation of urban civilization. Instead, he accepts it fully and does not hide his joyous appreciation of it. The revolution has been replaced by a people's carnival. The change in his artistic attitude is evident not only on the level of poetic meaning, but on the level of expression, too. Spontaneity, vitalism and even primitivism become essential characteristics of his poetry. If proletarian poems bordered on the elegiac, the poetry of [**Samá láska**] reminds us of song-like poems traceable to the tradition of Czech folk songs, a source of inspiration of which Seifert will avail himself with increasing mastery after the twenties.

[**Samá láska**] turned out to be just the prelude to a new adventure in Seifert's poetic life: his association with poetism. The origins of poetism go back as far as 1920, when a group of young writers organized the Association of Modern Culture, *Devětsil* (Svaz Moderní Kultury *Devětsil*). The strange name "devětsil" was taken from botanical terminology. It means "butterbur", a gramineous plant which blooms in spring in mountainous regions. The name was chosen in accordance with the group's main aesthetic principle, the principle of denouncing modern civilization.

Together with the philosopher Jan
Patočka, writers Vćlav Havel, Ivan Klíma,
Pavel Kohout and others, he paved the
way for the manifesto of human rights,
known as *Charter 77.* He was one of its
first signatories.

—*Edward Możejko*

Early in the spring of 1922, Seifert (himself a member of
Devětsil) read his paper titled **"The New Proletarian Art"**
to a student meeting in Prague. In fact, it was a polemics
with J. Wolker's earlier and much more dogmatic statement of the same year, entitled "Proletarian Art". Although the adjective "new" appeared in Seifert's title, suggesting that he still remained within the limits of proletarian poetry, the content of his speech went far beyond what
was generally understood as proletarian art. In fact, it deviated from it. According to Vitězslav Nezval (1900-
1958), it proposed an entirely new model of poetry [as
noted in Alfred French's 1969 *The Poets of Prague*] which
helped the formation of poetism as a literary movement.
Some critics credit Seifert's lecture as the inspiration for
Nezval's poem *Podivuhodný kouzelník* (The Amazing Magician)—the first truly poetic text of poetism. It appeared
in the Revolutionary Almanac Devětsil (Revoluční
Sborník Devětsil), in the late fall of 1922. By 1924, poetism was firmly established in Czech literature; and until
the beginnings of the thirties, it remained the leading poetic force.

The name "poetism" derives, of course, from the word
"poetry". It would hardly be an exaggeration to suggest
that, if compared to other modernist European movements, poetism can be recognized as one of the most, so
to speak, *poetic* movements among them. Indeed, it deserves such a qualification. While other avant-garde currents based their poetic programmes mainly upon a single
aesthetic principle—for example, Futurists experimented
with words, Surrealists were interested in discovering the
subconscious, Constructivists insisted on expedience, Im-
agists elevated the role of image, and so on—poetists recognized the validity of all these devices as equally important, so long as they contributed to the creation of a poem,
or other literary work of art. Word, image, free associations, sound, film, theatre and the "reality of this world,
arrangement and organization of ingenuity or sensibility"
(V. Nezval) are indispensible elements in evoking lyrical
feelings. The emotive function of the poem depends on
them. Neither ideological nor artistic rigidity is acceptable. Consequently, poetry should be liberated from didactic, rational functions. Lyrical sensation stems from
the spontaneity of fantasy and lexical sources. In poetism,
Czech poets discovered that art is a game—the less regu-
lated, the better.

Translated into terms of Seifert's own poetic code, this
meant that *poetry is a continuous creation of the new.*
Hence Seifert's inclination for artistic experiment, his

search for new realms of imagination and his ability to surprise the reader, even in his late poetry, written in the sixties and seventies. Seifert's association with poetism lasted
for about six years. It produced three volumes of poetry:
Na vlnách T.S.F. (1925; On the Waves of the Wireless),
Slavík zpívá špatně (1926; The Nightingale Sings Poorly)
and *Poštovní holub* (1929; The Carrier Pigeon).

A mutual dependence exists between the poet and the literary current to which he belonged. On the one hand, he
shaped the very essence of poetism; and on the other, the
current left an indelible mark on his further evolution as
an artist. Cooperation and friendship with such poets as
V. Nezval, Konstantin Biebl, Josef Hora and above all, the
critic Karel Teige, with whom the poet travelled to France
and Italy in 1924, helped him to shape his own poetic profile. It was, by the way, K. Teige who defined poetism as
"the art of living and enjoyment".

The most "poetist" among the three collections mentioned is undoubtedly [*Na vlnách T.S.F.*] (sometimes
translated as On Waves of Radio). In the preceding volume [*Samá láska*] some vestiges of the proletarian period
are still visible in the dichotomy between revolutionary
rhetoric and a new epicurean perception of life. To the
contrary, [*Na vlnách T.S.F.*] strikes one by its homoge-
neous poetic attitude, typical of poetism. It is characterized by light and playful fantasy, grotesque, paradox,
puns, irony, emotionalism at times bordering on the sentimental. Seifert preserved many of these characteristics in
the poetics of his mature period. Generally speaking, it is
a collection expressing enchantment with life, with its
richness and manifold tempting attractions.

The most conspicuous motifs in it are those of the city,
travel, the unknown, exotic worlds and vivid eroticism.
The typical accessories of this poetic world are luxury
trains, tall leafy palms, cruise ships, the shining lights of
a big metropolis, and so on. F. X. Šalda, one of the greatest
Czech critics of this century, made the following observation:

> The most valuable innovation of Seifert will be,
> I feel, this: he found objects; after words—
> objects. He made them speak ("rozhovořil
> věci") from within, and recorded in a reliable
> and truthful manner what they told him. His po-
> lyphony is not broad, but being relatively nar-
> row, it is pure and fresh.

In spite of the sensual externalization of objects, it remains
unreal; it is tangible, yet elusive. The poet does not describe this world, but rather, he suggests it. Seifert
achieves this kind of poeticality by applying the principle
of simultaneity: in two or three short lines, he includes different levels of human experience, as it happens, for example, in the poem **"Abacus",** handy to quote for its brevity:

> Your breast
> is like an apple from Australia.
> Your breasts are like two apples from Australia.
> How happy I am to have this abacus of love.

To be sure, this is not an extreme example of Seifert's elliptical technique. He sometimes destroys the logical order
of life's phenomena to achieve quite unusual imagery. In

the four initial lines of **"The Words on Magnet"**, we encounter the following image:

> On a sailing glacier, polar bear's sleep stretches
> down to the equator,
> bird from the tropics dies on the polar circle,
> night like a nut cracked freshly at midnight,
> white star.

Together with other writers of the poetist movement, Seifert dismissed the logical sequencing of the poem: the principle of spontaneity allowed the extensive use of free associations. Quite often the unusual, deformed world is laid over a narrative tone, reminiscent of prose, which lends these poems a sense of intimacy and expressive lyricism. A typical example in this respect is the poem **"Miss Gada-Nigi"**, in which the description of circus artists is combined with the image of nightfall over the town, and ends with an epic apostrophe to Miss Gada-Nigi, an actress.

The lyrical subject in the poetist period exposes youthful vigour, sincerity and joyfulness. The optimistic adventure with life continues, with some variations, throughout the two other collections (mentioned earlier) which were published in the second half of the twenties. Seifert's fascination with life is not philosophically motivated, or justified by any ideological stand: it grows out of his spontaneous appreciation of it. He is eager to catch reality in the twinkling of an eye, to preserve a moment, to commemorate an event or experience, and to render them through the flash of poetic revelation. Life is the only true source of sensation, including suffering. In the poem **"Wine and Time"** (**"Víno a čas"**), we read the following lines:

> So what if water runs and time flows?
> And man begins to die the very day
> he is born?
> Just ask the Belfort lion,
> whether he would not trade his eternity in sand
> for one day,
> when into living flesh he could thrust his claws
> and drink blood
> until Etoile would be extinguished by horror.

Whatever we experience, we experience through the medium of life and therefore it should be the subject of our admiration. This spontaneous, undogmatic attitude coincides with the poet's progressive distancing from ideological inflexibility. True, in 1926, his [*Slavík zpívá špatně* (The Nightingale Sings Badly)] appeared, as a result of his trips to the Soviet Union in 1925. In some poems, Seifert seemingly attempts to reconcile his personal sympathies with the proletarian cause. But it was, indeed, a rather symbolic gesture. [According to Sir Cecil Parrott in his "Introduction" to the 1979 British edition of Seifert's *The Plague Column*,] Seifert returned from the Soviet Union frightened by the revolution, "appalled by its bloodshed" and disappointed with what he saw. Whatever interesting he found there—belonged to the past. He called Russia "the graveyard of history". Dealing with the Russian drama, he omitted any dramatizing effects, and "assumed a deliberately nonchalant attitude, avoiding the temptation to strike tragic poses and unfold apocalyptic visions". In doing so, he preserved the stylistic affinity of this volume with the rest of his poetist literary output. Three years later, in 1929, Seifert broke with the communists.

However, to emphasize his continued loyalty to socialist ideas, he joined to social democrats, who abode by the legitimacy of parliamentary democracy, and who defended the workers' cause within the framework of this system. The communists never forgave Seifert's change of heart; but he did not recant, even after 1948, when many of his colleagues did.

In 1930, Seifert takes yet another important turn: he leaves the poetists. While they began to reorganize themselves and promote the Czech branch of surrealism, he decided to choose his own independent path, to search for his identity outside of any artistic, ideological or political framework. In short, Seifert becomes Seifert.

It would not be an exaggeration to say that if Seifert had left only *The Plague Column* to posterity, he would have assured himself a lasting place in Czech literature. The poem amazes with its innovative power, revealing once again the magnitude and versatility of Seifert's poetic talent.

—*Edward Możejko*

What is most conspicuous in the ensuing decade is a departure from the motifs of the preceding period. In a sense, however, this development demonstrates a noticeable affinity to [*Samá láska*], which the poet had abandoned by joining the poetists. The continuity, though, is by no means straightforward. What distinguishes this new poetic impulse from the earlier one, and at the same time lends to it a peculiar unity, is the overall dominating mood of reflection. What becomes obvious is that Seifert forsakes the experimental model of poetry in favour of a more communicative pattern of artistic expression. He evolves his own poetic style, whose stanzaic forms and uncomplicated imagery strike a more traditional note than do the works of many of his contemporaries, a style which allows him to establish a closer relationship with the reader. In Czech literature of the thirties, amongst the prevailing themes of gloom (for example, in F. Halas), the tendency to continue experiments (V. Nezval and the surrealists in particular), and ideological narrowness (M. Majerová), Seifert's work shines with its unusual originality, as it "clings almost alone to optimism, at the same time cultivating imagistic and linguistic precision in the lyric form" [according to William E. Harkins in his "On Jaroslav Seifert's *Morový sloup*," in *Cross Currents*, Vol. 3 (1984)]. Seifert's creative maturity traces out such cycles of poetry as *Jablko s klína* (1933; An Apple From the Lap), *Ruce Venušiny* (1936; The Arms of Venus), *Jaro sbohem* (1937; Farewell, Spring!). During the whole following decade, he wrote refined lyrics, drawing on the experiences of everyday life, at the same time revealing another characteristic of his versatile talent: the mastery of occasional verse.

When we speak here of "everyday life" as a source of inspiration, we should keep in mind that it differs significantly from the one we encounter in poetism. Surely, Seifert's externalization of objects, the texture of his poems, *preserve* the same sensuality, tangibility, freshness and plasticity; but gone now are the requisites and glamour of the big city, his fascination with the exotic world of jazz, films, cafes, bars, palm trees, and so on. Instead, Seifert exploits nature, popular and national tradition, art, personal reminiscences, patriotic themes and, last but not least, the beauty of Prague—the capital of the country. The literary space, so to speak, of his poetry has changed profoundly, and the lyrical persona is not any longer a "poor boy from the suburbs", but a "white shrub" whose branches embrace the surrounding world. Nothing better expresses this change than Seifert's poem **"Transformations"** (**"Proměny"**), dedicated to F. X. Šalda.

> The boy has changed into a white shrub,
> The shrub into a sleeping shepherd,
> soft hair into the strings of a lyre,
> snow into snow fallen upon curls.
>
> Words have changed into questions,
> wisdom and fame into wrinkles
> and strings again into soft hair,
> the boy is changing into a poet
> and the poet has changed
> into that white shrub, under which he slept,
> because he loved beauty so fervently.
> Whoever loved only beauty
> is fond of her forever
> and wanders after her without end;
> beauty has wonderful legs,
> shod in soft sandals.

To translate Seifert's masterful language, to render his play with words, to draw out the shades of their meaning or subtle ambiguity—more than one translated version of the poem would probably be needed; but the motif of transformation would remain obvious. In addition to telling us about the poet's changing individuality, it also reveals his enriched sensitivity. Therefore, in his **"Song About Love"** (**"Píseň o lásce"**), he makes a frank and sincere confession:

> I hear what others do not,
> barefeet walking on the plush

—typical Seifertian lines, combining an abstract thought with a concrete sensual image ("barefeet walking on the plush").

It would be difficult to enumerate here all the motives emerging in the above-mentioned collections. They seldom appear in a "pure" manifestation. History is intertwined with the description of his native land, allusions to literary works provoke thoughts about the present, religious motifs are juxtaposed with mundane reality. But almost without exception, the creative impulse stems from the immediate surrounding nature and human experience. Rain, sunshine, night, birds, seasons of the year, recollections of childhood, of his home, motherly love, at times a single event, a flirtation, a gaze or a glance—these become, under Seifert's pen, an inexhaustible source of poetic invention.

[According to Sir Cecil Parrott, these] are "pure lyric poems on scenes of everyday life and the thoughts they aroused in him". He now achieved an unusual intimacy and range of feelings, at times humorous or melancholic, playful or paradoxical, mournful or nostalgic, but always expressed with remarkable simplicity, a simplicity that occasionally appears to border on the obvious, yet never slides into the trivial. These poems always contain a word, a line, an image which sounds like a philosophical maxim, a sort of Heraclitian pensiveness about the passage of time, constant change, and the only certainty—death. Yet the reader will also find in them a touch of "Horace's love of rustic enjoyment, something too of Anacreon's devotion to Muses, love and wine". Often, they bring to mind the folk-wisdom of oral poetry, and it comes as no surprise that, in the first part of [*Jaro sbohem*], all of the poems have the word "song" in their titles.

Seifert's interest in writing occasional verse was mentioned earlier. He developed it not without a certain influence of his concrete external situation. The political evolution in Europe during the mid-thirties did not inspire confidence in the future. Many writers expressed their anxiety and concern about the growing instability and the danger of war. Seifert was no exception. He wrote about the Spanish Civil War and the spectre of fascism. However, he approaches them not from the point of view of a revolutionary, but as one who judges events in terms of the universal categories of good and evil. At that time, he did not anticipate that the history of his own contry would provide such abundant material for occasional verse.

In 1937, Seifert published a cycle of ten poems ***Osm dní*** (***Eight Days***), mourning the death of the great statesman Thomas Masaryk, thinker and philosopher, the founder of modern Czechoslovakia. The cycle is a powerful and moving threnody, devoted to a great national figure of historical significance. It is expressed most dramatically in the words from the poem **"Conversation With Death"**, namely, that the nation had nothing more precious to offer than the body of its leader. The passing away of the beloved president is described as a tragic blow, not only to the entire country, but to the whole of Europe, because the stature of the man surpasses his temporal political importance.

Just one year later, as the German troops entered Prague, Seifert has to express sorrow over the loss of independence. He responded to this tragic event by writing the volume *Zhasněte světla* (1938; Put Out the Lights), with a number of poems which denounced with bitterness and pain the consequences of the Munich agreement; but on the whole, he reacted to the new historical situation by turning his attention to the treasures of the national past and the beauty of Prague, his native city.

In 1940, the Czechs celebrated the 120th anniversary of the birth of Božena Němcová, one of the leading writers of late Czech romanticism, and the author of *Babička* (1855; *Granny*). Seifert commemorated this occasion by writing the poetic cycle *Vějíř Boženy Němcové* (1940; Božena Němcová's Fan). It was a hymn in praise of human endurance: in spite of the hardships Němcová suffered during her short life, she became one of the key figures of the Czech national revival. Consequently, in Seifert's poem she acquires the characteristics of a symbol of hope, becomes an allegory of survival and spurs confidence in the strength of cultural tradition, which will help it to overcome. In the long poem *Písežn o Viktorce* (Song of Viktorka), Seifert "returned" to Němcová in 1950, this time offering reflections on Viktorka—the heroine of the novel *Granny*.

But the country's capital, Prague, remains the major subject of his poetic reveries. In 1940, the volume *Světlem oděná* (Clothed in Light) appeared; together with *Kamenný most* (1944; The Stone Bridge) and *Praha* (1956; Prague), it constitutes a part of poetic triptych devoted almost entirely to the author's native city. For Seifert, Prague is the most beautiful place on earth. It is more beautiful than Venice, Rome or any other city in the world. Indeed, the number of similies and metaphors employed by Seifert to depict the beauty of Prague is stunning; but above all, Prague, with its legends, rich architecture, castles and relics of the past, remains the source of national pride, an inspiration for hope that the nation, like its capital, will survive. It is not only a store of old monuments, but a living symbol of permanence and vitality, which provides the poet with an opportunity to reflect upon Czech history in general.

How did Seifert react to the end of the war in 1945? Usually, critics stress the fact that the poet greeted and welcomed the liberation. Indeed, it could not have been otherwise. Patriotic motives prevail in the collection *Přilba hlíny* (1945; The Helmet of Clay). At that time, Seifert wrote several poems commemorating the Prague uprising of May 1945, the return of President Beneš, the sacrifice of the Red Army and so on. But was he truly relieved of any shade of doubt? Or was there, at the bottom of his heart, even anxiety that the so-called liberation contained in it the seeds of new subjugation, which might turn into yet another period of national nightmare? In short: was his country out of danger? The question is a difficult one to answer, but it cannot be avoided by whoever wants to give an honest evaluation of Seifert's writing.

If the poet's continuous interest in historical themes, the beauty of his native land and first of all, in the national cultural tradition may be taken as any indication, he did not believe that the country was out of trouble. His post-war interests in these motifs remain too conspicuous to be interpreted as a simple continuation of the preceding period, i. e., unrelated to the post-war present. The material seems to prove the legitimacy of such an assumption. Apart from the above-mentioned [*Píseň o Viktorce*] Seifert published in 1948 *Ruka a plamen* (The Arm and the Flame)—a collection of poems almost entirely devoted to Czech writers and artists. A year later, he edited *Šel malíř chudě do světa* (The Painter Went Poor into the World), which are poems-illustrations to Mikoláš Aleš' paintings of the Czech landscape. Finally, in 1954, *Maminka* appeared—a cycle of personal lyrical reminiscences about mother, motherly love (a motif present throughout Seifert's work), and at the same time [according to Maria Němcová Banerjee] an "evocation of the quasi-mythical mother figure" that is a symbol of the whole nation.

Seifert's passion of reviving the national cultural tradition did not go unnoticed by official critics. He was attacked for "sinking" deeper and deeper into subjectivism, and was accused of having an apolitical attitude—a euphemism, of course, reproaching him for not having complied with the principles of socialist realism promoted by the party. The clash between Seifert and the party came into the open during the short-lived liberalization which began in the mid-fifties. At the Second Congress of the Czechoslovak Writers Union in 1956, Seifert voiced his protest against Stalinist practices in literature and art. He appealed to writers to become "the conscience of the nation", a concept remaining in obvious contradiction with the communist slogan of writers as "engineers of human souls".

> **Seifert's poetry, no doubt, gives witness to our difficult time, but it also reflects something equally important: the artist's struggle with himself, his constant quest to discover new realms of human experience. Seifert treats poetry as an incessant challenge, as a clash between his imagination and the world that it has to capture.**
>
> —*Edward Możejko*

For the next ten years, Seifert did not publish much; but his silence was rather ostensible. He surprised everyone with an unusual outburst of creative energy by publishing three new books of poetry: *Koncert na ostrově* (1965; Concert on the Island), *Halleyova Kometa* (1967; Halley's Comet) and *Odlévání zvonů* (1967; *The Casting of Bells*). It is a triptych which both thematically and artistically can be considered to be a synthesis of the long road of a poet who reaches an old age. It is a sort of lyrical confession about the harshness of life, vanishing illusions, reminiscences and questions about the meaning of our existence. Life is still the main source of the poet's inspiration, because there is no escape from it; but his outlook on it grows sceptical, sombre, at times even bitter. His previously joyful appreciation and acceptance of life has been toned down considerably. "We know, hell is everywhere—writes the poet—but what about paradise?" We find it in moments only, in smiles given to us after a long wait ("**Jen jednou jsem spatřil . . .**"; "**Only Once I Caught a Glimpse . . .**"). One can also find in these poems an acute sense of an oncoming ending: time and time again, the motif of death reoccurs with unusual sincerity. The poet expresses surprise at the fact that he was given to live longer than any other poet of his generation ("**Pocta Vladimíru Holanovi**"; "**Eulogy on Vladimír Holan**"), which evokes in him a peculiar feeling of guilt and alienation. He is not the same person, and the people who surround him are not those of his youth. It's time to face the inevitable. Life is compared to a train, whose passengers will soon have to alight at the Lethe station (**"Úry-vek z dopisu"; "Excerpt from a Letter"**). In spite of occasional flashes of self-irony or even sarcasm, what prevails in these poems is the tendency to familiarize with the thought of death as the final point of man's physical existence.

The events of the late sixties revived Seifert's social and political activity. In 1968, he openly condemned the Soviet-led invasion of Czechoslovakia. Later he was asked to serve as the president of the Union of Czechoslovak Writers, in the hope that his authority would save the Union from destruction. He remained in this position until the dissolution of the Union two years later. Together with the philosopher Jan Patočka, writers Václav Havel, Ivan Klíma, Pavel Kohout and others, he paved the way for the manifesto of human rights, known as *Charter 77*. Seifert was one of its first signatories.

However, Seifert's most remarkable achievement of the seventies will again be his rebirth as a poet. What I have in mind is the long poem *Morový sloup* (*The Plague Column* or *The Plague Monument*) and *Deštník z Piccadilly* (*The Umbrella from Piccadilly*), published respectively in 1977 and 1979. It would not be an exaggeration to say that if Seifert had left only *The Plague Column* to posterity, he would have assured himself a lasting place in Czech literature. The poem amazes with its innovative power, revealing once again the magnitude and versatility of Seifert's poetic talent. At the age of 76, he was able to break his own fossilization, although he had no illusions as to his own future. Let me quote the closing fragment of the poem:

> To all those million verses in the world
> I've added just a few.
> They probably were no wiser than a cricket's
>   chirrup.
> I know. Forgive me.
> I'm coming to the end.
>
> They weren't even the first footmarks
> in the lunar dust.
> If at times they sparkled after all
> it was not their light.
> I loved this language.
>
> And that which forces silent lips
> to quiver
> will make young lovers kiss
> as they stroll through red-gilded fields
> under a sunset
> slower than in the tropics.
>
> Poetry is with us from the start.
> Like loving,
> like hunger, like the plague, like war.
> At times my verses were embarassingly
> foolish.
> But I make no excuse.
> I believe that seeking beautiful words
> is better
> than killing or murdering.

If the sixties culminated in the synthesis of previous achievements, *The Plague Column* marks a new opening, if not for Seifert, then for others.

Metaphorically speaking, *The Plague Column* is a literary fugue, with many motifs, themes, observations and thoughts which are loosely intertwined throughout the whole poem, but all ultimately relate to the universal questions of humanity and its destiny: life and death, religion and secularity, freedom and slavery, war and peace, love and hatred, good and evil, truth and falsehood. The title, *The Plague Column,* refers [according to William E. Hawkins], to the XVIIth Century custom of building columns "in gratitude for deliverance from the plague". It would be difficult and premature to indulge in an exhaustive interpretation of the poem, but Seifert seems to have tinged it with the tone of apocalyptic doom.

It's time for a summary. Seifert lived through almost all of the important events of this century. He managed to preserve in his poetry a simplicity of expression and sense of reality, as few poets have done. Apart from the early period, his lyrics are completely free from reasoning, based not on any particular dogma but "upon a spontaneous receptiveness," coupled with a clear awareness of ongoing change. He goes through various stages of artistic evolution: "from a boyish, joyous naivety and optimistic outlook upon lie, transitory beauty", showing a keen interest in national tradition, to a more sombre, even tragic, perception of our age. Not many poets have succeeded as Seifert did in embracing such a broad range of human questions and at the same time maintaining [according to the editors of *The Linden Tree: An Authology of Czech and Slovak Literature, 1890-1960,* 1962] "an intimate and close contact with his readers".

To ask whether all this makes him worthy of the Nobel Prize is a perennial question, which can never be answered in a satisfactory manner, because our choice or preference is always determined by language, limited by the scope of our linguistic experience. Usually, these limitations work against the writers of smaller nations. But we should try to find some other criteria of a more general and comparative nature. In the case of Czech culture, the following question seems to be justifiable: we often listen, with great pleasure, to the compositions of A. Dvořák, B. Smetana; we admire the great mastery of Miloš Forman as a film director. Do we ever ask the question of whether these achievements are matched in other arts, as, for example, in Czech literature? Certainly, it's a devious way of proving things, it is a proof "per analogiam", but still it may help us to realize our limitations. After all, we should not forget that this literature represented by writers of such stature as K. Čapek and J. Hašek. Seifert, often called the doyen of Czech literature, is both a continuation and a culmination of this tradition. His poetry, no doubt, gives witness to our difficult time, but it also reflects something equally important: the artist's struggle with himself, his constant quest to discover new realms of human experience. Seifert treats poetry as an incessant challenge, as a clash between his imagination and the world that it has to capture, as expressed in the following stanza:

> If anybody asked me
> what is a poem,
> I would be in despair for a few moments.
> And I know it so well!

Perhaps in this Seifertian paradox lies the greatness and unique nature of his poetry.

Warren W. Werner   (review date Winter 1988)

SOURCE: A review of *The Selected Poetry of Jaroslav Seifert,* in *The Southern Humanities Review,* Vol. 22, No. 1, Winter, 1988, pp. 90-3.

[*In the following review, Werner offers a mixed assessment of* The Selected Poetry of Jaroslav Seifert, *questioning whether his work is worthy of the Nobel Prize in Literature.*]

[*The Selected Poetry of Jaroslav Seifert*] tries to answer two questions: who was Jaroslav Seifert and did he deserve the Noble Prize in Literature? When he won the award in 1984, Seifert was largely unknown outside of Czechoslovakia, but within his native country his poetry was immensely popular (if not always officially sanctioned) and he was considered (in [his editor and translator] George Gibian's words) the country's unofficial national poet. This volume goes far toward answering these two questions.

Jaroslav Seifert (1901-1986) was born into a working class background and wrote first a book of proletarian poetry. Soon, though, Seifert joined the avant-garde poetism movement, roughly the Czech equivalent of Western European modernism but with a larger streak of surrealism, dada, and futurism than mainstream modernism. Seifert matured artistically in the early thirties, developing a lyric style that was euphonic, dense, and song-like; while the diction was simplified, the verse turned technically complex and intricate. His themes were the beauty of the world, women, and love. As public events commanded attention during the end of the decade and throughout the war, Seifert (and other writers) turned to public events for poetry, such as the death of President Masaryk, the Prague uprising, past Czech writers, Prague itself, his homeland.

The fifties brought another change to Seifert's poetry. In 1954 he published *Maminka* (Mother). Unfortunately, this book of poems is neither mentioned nor translated from in this collection, yet it is at this point that the second question above becomes problematic. A. French (in 1982) labeled *Maminka* a "classic," saying that "it combined the elements of traditional art and return to the world of childhood. In itself, it summed up a whole trend of literature away from the monumental to the humble; from public themes to private; from the pseudo-reality of political slogans to the known reality of Czech home life which was the product of its past." This heady praise is balanced by Robert Pynsent's judgment (1979) that "Seifert subjected himself to over-sentimental so-called Realism" with the book. *Maminka* is "a flaccid collection which is still immensely popular." *Maminka's* worth is an important issue because the poetry of Seifert's last decades seems to develop directly from this book. Seifert's style loosens as he abandons the song-like elements and the rhymes and metaphors, and he writes in a simple and personal free verse. Although present or latent throughout his whole poetic career, various themes come to the fore: Seifert's love for the physical world and beautiful women, his sensuality

and hedonism, his enjoyment of life, his compassion for others. Overall, a generous, warm-hearted spirit pervades Seifert's poetry.

Given this century's conditions, convergences between politics and Seifert's poetry are unsurprising, though that poetry never appears to be openly political. A communist in the 1920s, Seifert was expelled from the Party for criticizing it in 1929 (he never rejoined), wrote overtly nationalistic poems during the Nazi occupation, was denounced by the Party in 1950 for writings deemed gloomy and reactionary, yet commanded sufficient respect to be able to criticize publicly the government's treatment of writers in 1956 and 1968, and was an original singer of Charter 77. However, the greatest effect of politics upon Seifert's poetry was that during the 50s and 70s he was officially denied permission to publish.

Gibian brings together in this collection an introduction to Seifert's life and work, translations by Ewald Osers of 62 poems from 17 books, ten selections of prose reminiscences translated by Gibian, a glossary of names and places, and endnotes to the introduction, poems, and reminiscences. Despite the apparent fullness of accompanying apparatus, this book lacks a bibliography of Seifert's works or at least of English translations. The endnotes are minimal; the glossary helps with Seifert's many local references, but the identifications of French authors seem unnecessary.

This book's major portion is disappointing because it fails to do justice to Seifert's career; 62 poems cannot reprsent Seifert's diversity. Gibian's description of the poetry in his introduction is not lived up to in the range of poems presented. Part of the problem stems from the criteria used for selecting poems: "intrinsic quality, representativeness, and translatability." One result, especially of the third criterion, is, as Gibian notes, that the bulk of these poems comes from the 1950s and later. We have a lopsided view of Seifert's work, most of it coming from the second half of his career because the poetry became easier to translate after the style became simpler and more conversational.

These poems are warm, accessible, and generous. They are easy to read and comfortable. Many, perhaps because they were written by a man growing old, concern death, but nothing fatalistic or morbid intrudes. Death is another natural fact; if anything, death heightens the sensation of a kiss or memory of a kiss. An open and natural sensuality pervades these late poems, unlike the frenetic sensuality of Yeats' later poems. To give an idea of Seifert's usual strategy, let me quote one poem entirely, **"St George's Basilica"**:

> If in the white Basilica of St George
> fire broke out,
>   which God forbid,
> its walls after the flames would be rose-coloured.
> Perhaps even its twin towers: Adam and Eve.
> Eve is the slimmer one, as is usual with women,
> though that is only an insignificant glory
>   of their sex.
> The fiery heat will make the limestone blush.
>
> Just as young girls do
> after their first kiss.

Here we find a mixture of sacred and profane, of conflagration and a first kiss. The movement is toward the personal and the physical, as we can see in the comment on Eve's build, the blushing walls, the young girls. This is a small poem, but in the larger poems with their complexes of themes the same movement is decisive.

The paucity of poems here makes an answer to the second question posed at the beginning unfair. This selection gives pleasant, enjoyable reading, but the poetry does not invite rereading. The reasons could be many—that Seifert addresses a popular audience (the like of which doesn't exist in this country), that much is lost in translation, or that the poems chosen for translation can be translated because of their lack of depth. Seifert avoided the social realism promulgated by the Communist Party, but he developed a personal realism that verges on the sentimental and banal. Perhaps in this country we cannot judge a public poet, a national poet, since we lack a popular audience for poetry or a tradition of one. Seifert was an important Czech writer who produced a large body of poetry, but what makes for a Nobel Prize remains questionable.

Maria Němcová Banerjee   (review date Summer 1988)

SOURCE: A review of *A Wreath of Sonnets,* in *World Literature Today,* Vol. 62, No. 3, Summer, 1988, pp. 476-77.

[*In the following review of* A Wreath of Sonnets *and a French-language anthology of Seifert's verse, Banerjee offers praise for the poet's oeuvre.*]

Outside Czechoslovakia, the award of the 1984 Nobel Prize in Literature to Jaroslav Seifert (1901-86) was greeted with a yawn of indifference and a few winks hinting at the political inspiration behind the honor. Seifert was, after all, a lifelong Social Democrat from a victimized country, and he had gained world attention as the head of the Czech Union of Writers in the defiant months that followed the Russian invasion of 1968. However, to his people he was the much-loved, still-vibrant survivor of a magnificent generation of poets with roots in the 1920s. In this country journalists searching for a firmer footing for their comments soon found that apart from *The Plague Column* (1979), very little was available in English translation. The two books under review [*A Wreath of Sonnets* and *Les danseuses passaient près d'ici: Choix de poèmes, 1921-1983*] are a welcome attempt to fill the void.

[Translated by J. K. Klement and Eva Stucke, ***A Wreath of Sonnets***] is a bilingual, Czech/English presentation of a linked cycle of fifteen sonnets about Prague, written in 1956. They represent a culmination of Seifert's "national" period, which began after the catastrophe of Munich, when he identified himself with the voice of his people's grief and bitter outrage. Ironically, in the fifties, even while his poems from *Přilba hlíny* (A Helmet-full of Earth; 1945) were being recited in the schools, his new writing was in official disfavor after he had published an unwelcome poem of mourning for the death of his friend, the great poet František Halas (1901-49). *Věnec sonetů* saw publication only in 1964, as part of the sixth volume of Seifert's collected works. The wreath form is a chain of sonnets linked by the obligatory repetition of each last line

as the first line of the following poem. The fifteenth sonnet sums up the cycle, being made up of all the preceding fourteen last lines. Seifert uses this intricately patterned verbal design to develop his emotional meditation, a lover's argument, in favor of his decision to remain in Prague, even under the shadow of death. The last poems reads like a magic incantation intended to break the evil spell of the city's history.

The translators' preface makes it plain that they understood their challenge to be much more complex than the already formidable task posed by the virtuoso form. They had the benefit of an intimate knowledge of the rich but unobtrusive subtext of cultural allusions that Seifert blends into his concrete and spontaneous images of Prague. No matter how traditional his form, Seifert remained a modernist in essence, and his visual grasp of the concrete, his sensuous polyvalence, are derived from his years of apprenticeship in the avant-garde Devětsil group. But how can the translators recapture the epiphany in a single Seifert stanza, associating the glimpse of a momentarily bared bridesmaid's leg with the rose-colored glow on the windowpane of an old Carmelite convent on a particular street in Prague? The English translation breaks the spell of the moment by spelling out the erotic allusion of the blush in a simile ("the windows of Carmelitesses / shine like a rosy, blushing face") that is nowhere to be found in the original, which had relied on juxtaposition only and left the blush for the experiencing imagination of poetic arousal. Before dying, Seifert himself authorized the publication of these translations, and quibbles aside, they constitute a fine homage to the poet on the part of the publishing house that has also issued his wonderfully evocative prose memoirs (1981).

The French volume, a joint effort by two Czech literary scholars who also publish their own original poetry in French, is more ambitious in scope. It is a real Seifert anthology, containing the whole range of his poetic evolution, from 1921 to 1983. The translators have been particularly successful with the early poems, which sound remarkably new and fresh in French while remaining very accurate. Above all, however, *Les danseuses* deserves respect for its excellent introduction, authored by both translators. The essay takes issue with the highly polarized, superficial judgments floating around Seifert's reputation, marked either by offensive and ill-deserved skepticism or hyperbolic praise. Instead, we are given a careful interpretation of Seifert's personal evolution within the context of modern Czech literary history.

The selection of poems is somewhat biased in favor of the early *poetist* and the late free-verse phases, a decision motivated in part by the translators' personal tastes. I have no quarrel, however, with the high value they place on Seifert's remarkable transformation of his poetic voice in the last two decades of his long creative life. Having cast aside the ornaments of rhyme and the incantatory charm of rhythm, the old poet achieved a lean, meditative narrative which opens up his world of sensuous experience to what [the editors and translators of the volume, Petr Král and Jan Rubeš,] have aptly called a "metaphysical perspective." The two essayists also pay tribute to Seifert's antirhetorical integrity, which was the dominant feature of his life as they see it. He was a deeply private man living in a time of great public disasters. He did not particularly like stepping out on public platforms, but when he did speak up, it was when his nation needed him most, as in 1939 and 1969. At such times he always said what was merely true, without false pathos and without self-dramatization.

FURTHER READING

Criticism

Bradbrook, B. R. Review of *The Selected Poems of Jaroslav Seifert,* by Jaroslav Seifert. *World Literature Today* 61, No. 1 (Winter 1987): 126-27.

> Praises the volume as a new source of information on Seifert's life and work. Bradbrook extols the editor and translator of the volume for their inclusion criteria, particularly their focus on Seifert's memoir.

Brunet, Elena. Review of *The Selected Poems of Jaroslav Sei-fert,* by Jaroslav Seifert. *Los Angeles Times Book Review* (17 January 1988): 14.

> Brief review that characterizes the essential themes of Seifert's verse to be "the beauty of women, love both romantic and sensual, the city of Prague, [and] his native country."

Davis, Dick. "Nobel Translation." *The Listener* 112, No. 2887 (6 December 1984): 33-4.

> Favorable assessment of Ewald Oser's English language-version of *The Selected Poems of Jaroslav Seifert.* Davis also reviews works by such writers as Salvatore Quasimoto and Charles Tomlinson.

Graham, Desmond. Review of *The Plague Column,* by Jaroslav Seifert. *Stand* 22, Vol. 1 (1980): 78-9.

> Comparative review in which *The Plague Column* is favorably discussed. Graham also reviews such works as Linda Pastan's *Selected Poems* and Robert Creeley's *Later.*

Moravius. "What the Censor Omitted." *Index on Censorship* 14, No. 4 (August 1985): 15-17.

> Discusses discrepancies between the original and official editions of Seifert's memoir, *Všecky krásy světa.* Passages from both the "official" Czech version and the original text are included.

Additional coverage of Seifert's life and career is contained in the following sources published by Gale Research: *Contemporary Authors,* **Vol. 127;** *Contemporary Literary Criticism,* **Vols. 34, 44; and** *Major 20th-Century Writers.*

Contemporary Literary Criticism

Indexes

Literary Criticism Series
Cumulative Author Index
Cumulative Topic Index
Cumulative Nationality Index
Title Index, Volume 93

How to Use This Index

The main references

> Camus, Albert
> 1913-1960 .... **CLC 1, 2, 4, 9, 11, 14,**
> **32, 69; DA; DAB; DAC; DC 2; SSC 9;**
> **WLC**

list all author entries in the following Gale Literary Criticism series:

BLC = *Black Literature Criticism*
CLC = *Contemporary Literary Criticism*
CLR = *Children's Literature Review*
CMLC = *Classical and Medieval Literature Criticism*
DA = *DISCovering Authors*
DAB = *DISCovering Authors: British*
DAC = *DISCovering Authors: Canadian*
DC = *Drama Criticism*
HLC = *Hispanic Literature Criticism*
LC = *Literature Criticism from 1400 to 1800*
NCLC = *Nineteenth-Century Literature Criticism*
PC = *Poetry Criticism*
SSC = *Short Story Criticism*
TCLC = *Twentieth-Century Literary Criticism*
WLC = *World Literature Criticism, 1500 to the Present*

The cross-references

> See also CA 89-92; DAM DRAM, MST,
> NOV; DLB 72; MTCW

list all author entries in the following Gale biographical and literary sources:

AAYA = *Authors & Artists for Young Adults*
AITN = *Authors in the News*
BEST = *Bestsellers*
BW = *Black Writers*
CA = *Contemporary Authors*
CAAS = *Contemporary Authors Autobiography Series*
CABS = *Contemporary Authors Bibliographical Series*
CANR = *Contemporary Authors New Revision Series*
CAP = *Contemporary Authors Permanent Series*
CDALB = *Concise Dictionary of American Literary Biography*
CDBLB = *Concise Dictionary of British Literary Biography*
DAM = *DISCovering Authors Modules*
  DRAM = *dramatists; MST = most-studied*

authors; MULT = *multicultural authors; NOV* = *novelists; POET* = *poets; POP* = *popular/genre writers*
DLB = *Dictionary of Literary Biography*
DLBD = *Dictionary of Literary Biography Documentary Series*
DLBY = *Dictionary of Literary Biography Yearbook*
HW = *Hispanic Writers*
JRDA = *Junior DISCovering Authors*
MAICYA = *Major Authors and Illustrators for Children and Young Adults*
MTCW = *Major 20th-Century Writers*
NNAL = *Native North American Literature*
SAAS = *Something about the Author Autobiography Series*
SATA = *Something about the Author*
YABC = *Yesterday's Authors of Books for Children*

Literary Criticism Series
Cumulative Author Index

Albert the Great 1200(?)-1280.... **CMLC 16**
See also DLB 115

Alcala-Galiano, Juan Valera y
See Valera y Alcala-Galiano, Juan

Alcott, Amos Bronson 1799-1888 .. **NCLC 1**
See also DLB 1

Alcott, Louisa May
1832-1888 .... **NCLC 6; DA; DAB;**
DAC; WLC
See also CDALB 1865-1917; CLR 1, 38;
DAM MST, NOV; DLB 1, 42, 79; JRDA;
MAICYA; YABC 1

Aldanov, M. A.
See Aldanov, Mark (Alexandrovich)

Aldanov, Mark (Alexandrovich)
1886(?)-1957 .... **TCLC 23**
See also CA 118

Aldington, Richard 1892-1962...... **CLC 49**
See also CA 85-88; CANR 45; DLB 20, 36,
100, 149

Aldiss, Brian W(ilson)
1925- .... **CLC 5, 14, 40**
See also CA 5-8R; CAAS 2; CANR 5, 28;
DAM NOV; DLB 14; MTCW; SATA 34

Alegria, Claribel 1924-........... **CLC 75**
See also CA 131; CAAS 15; DAM MULT;
DLB 145; HW

Alegria, Fernando 1918-........... **CLC 57**
See also CA 9-12R; CANR 5, 32; HW

Aleichem, Sholom.............. **TCLC 1, 35**
See also Rabinovitch, Sholem

Aleixandre, Vicente
1898-1984 .... **CLC 9, 36; PC 15**
See also CA 85-88; 114; CANR 26;
DAM POET; DLB 108; HW; MTCW

Alepoudelis, Odysseus
See Elytis, Odysseus

Aleshkovsky, Joseph 1929-
See Aleshkovsky, Yuz
See also CA 121; 128

Aleshkovsky, Yuz................ **CLC 44**
See also Aleshkovsky, Joseph

Alexander, Lloyd (Chudley) 1924- .. **CLC 35**
See also AAYA 1; CA 1-4R; CANR 1, 24,
38; CLR 1, 5; DLB 52; JRDA; MAICYA;
MTCW; SAAS 19; SATA 3, 49, 81

Alfau, Felipe 1902-.............. **CLC 66**
See also CA 137

Alger, Horatio, Jr. 1832-1899 ..... **NCLC 8**
See also DLB 42; SATA 16

Algren, Nelson 1909-1981 .... **CLC 4, 10, 33**
See also CA 13-16R; 103; CANR 20;
CDALB 1941-1968; DLB 9; DLBY 81,
82; MTCW

Ali, Ahmed 1910-................ **CLC 69**
See also CA 25-28R; CANR 15, 34

Alighieri, Dante 1265-1321 .... **CMLC 3, 18**

Allan, John B.
See Westlake, Donald E(dwin)

Allen, Edward 1948-.............. **CLC 59**

Allen, Paula Gunn 1939-.......... **CLC 84**
See also CA 112; 143; DAM MULT;
NNAL

Allen, Roland
See Ayckbourn, Alan

Allen, Sarah A.
See Hopkins, Pauline Elizabeth

Allen, Woody 1935-........... **CLC 16, 52**
See also AAYA 10; CA 33-36R; CANR 27,
38; DAM POP; DLB 44; MTCW

Allende, Isabel 1942- .... **CLC 39, 57; HLC**
See also CA 125; 130; CANR 51;
DAM MULT, NOV; DLB 145; HW;
INT 130; MTCW

Alleyn, Ellen
See Rossetti, Christina (Georgina)

Allingham, Margery (Louise)
1904-1966 .... **CLC 19**
See also CA 5-8R; 25-28R; CANR 4;
DLB 77; MTCW

Allingham, William 1824-1889 ... **NCLC 25**
See also DLB 35

Allison, Dorothy E. 1949-......... **CLC 78**
See also CA 140

Allston, Washington 1779-1843.... **NCLC 2**
See also DLB 1

Almedingen, E. M. .... **CLC 12**
See also Almedingen, Martha Edith von
See also SATA 3

Almedingen, Martha Edith von 1898-1971
See Almedingen, E. M.
See also CA 1-4R; CANR 1

Almqvist, Carl Jonas Love
1793-1866 .... **NCLC 42**

Alonso, Damaso 1898-1990........ **CLC 14**
See also CA 110; 131; 130; DLB 108; HW

Alov
See Gogol, Nikolai (Vasilyevich)

Alta 1942-...................... **CLC 19**
See also CA 57-60

Alter, Robert B(ernard) 1935-...... **CLC 34**
See also CA 49-52; CANR 1, 47

Alther, Lisa 1944-.............. **CLC 7, 41**
See also CA 65-68; CANR 12, 30, 51;
MTCW

Altman, Robert 1925-.............. **CLC 16**
See also CA 73-76; CANR 43

Alvarez, A(lfred) 1929-.......... **CLC 5, 13**
See also CA 1-4R; CANR 3, 33; DLB 14,
40

Alvarez, Alejandro Rodriguez 1903-1965
See Casona, Alejandro
See also CA 131; 93-96; HW

Alvarez, Julia 1950-.............. **CLC 93**
See also CA 147

Alvaro, Corrado 1896-1956 .... **TCLC 60**

Amado, Jorge 1912-..... **CLC 13, 40; HLC**
See also CA 77-80; CANR 35;
DAM MULT, NOV; DLB 113; MTCW

Ambler, Eric 1909-............ **CLC 4, 6, 9**
See also CA 9-12R; CANR 7, 38; DLB 77;
MTCW

Amichai, Yehuda 1924- ...... **CLC 9, 22, 57**
See also CA 85-88; CANR 46; MTCW

Amiel, Henri Frederic 1821-1881 .. **NCLC 4**

Amis, Kingsley (William)
1922-1995 ..... **CLC 1, 2, 3, 5, 8, 13, 40,**
44; DA; DAB; DAC
See also AITN 2; CA 9-12R; 150; CANR 8,
28; CDBLB 1945-1960; DAM MST,
NOV; DLB 15, 27, 100, 139;
INT CANR-8; MTCW

Amis, Martin (Louis)
1949- .... **CLC 4, 9, 38, 62**
See also BEST 90:3; CA 65-68; CANR 8,
27; DLB 14; INT CANR-27

Ammons, A(rchie) R(andolph)
1926- .... **CLC 2, 3, 5, 8, 9, 25, 57**
See also AITN 1; CA 9-12R; CANR 6, 36,
51; DAM POET; DLB 5, 165; MTCW

Amo, Tauraatua i
See Adams, Henry (Brooks)

Anand, Mulk Raj 1905-........ **CLC 23, 93**
See also CA 65-68; CANR 32; DAM NOV;
MTCW

Anatol
See Schnitzler, Arthur

Anaya, Rudolfo A(lfonso)
1937-.................. **CLC 23; HLC**
See also CA 45-48; CAAS 4; CANR 1, 32,
51; DAM MULT, NOV; DLB 82; HW 1;
MTCW

Andersen, Hans Christian
1805-1875 .... **NCLC 7; DA; DAB;**
DAC; SSC 6; WLC
See also CLR 6; DAM MST, POP;
MAICYA; YABC 1

Anderson, C. Farley
See Mencken, H(enry) L(ouis); Nathan,
George Jean

Anderson, Jessica (Margaret) Queale
.... **CLC 37**
See also CA 9-12R; CANR 4

Anderson, Jon (Victor) 1940- .... **CLC 9**
See also CA 25-28R; CANR 20;
DAM POET

Anderson, Lindsay (Gordon)
1923-1994 .... **CLC 20**
See also CA 125; 128; 146

Anderson, Maxwell 1888-1959 ..... **TCLC 2**
See also CA 105; DAM DRAM; DLB 7

Anderson, Poul (William) 1926- .... **CLC 15**
See also AAYA 5; CA 1-4R; CAAS 2;
CANR 2, 15, 34; DLB 8; INT CANR-15;
MTCW; SATA-Brief 39

Anderson, Robert (Woodruff)
1917- .... **CLC 23**
See also AITN 1; CA 21-24R; CANR 32;
DAM DRAM; DLB 7

Anderson, Sherwood
1876-1941 .... **TCLC 1, 10, 24; DA;**
DAB; DAC; SSC 1; WLC
See also CA 104; 121; CDALB 1917-1929;
DAM MST, NOV; DLB 4, 9, 86;
DLBD 1; MTCW

Andouard
See Giraudoux, (Hippolyte) Jean

Andrade, Carlos Drummond de ...... **CLC 18**
See also Drummond de Andrade, Carlos

Andrade, Mario de 1893-1945..... **TCLC 43**

Andreae, Johann V(alentin)
1586-1654 .... **LC 32**
See also DLB 164

Andreas-Salomé, Lou 1861-1937... **TCLC 56**
See also DLB 66

Andrewes, Lancelot 1555-1626 .... **LC 5**
See also DLB 151

Andrews, Cicily Fairfield
See West, Rebecca

Andrews, Elton V.
See Pohl, Frederik

Andreyev, Leonid (Nikolaevich)
1871-1919 .... **TCLC 3**
See also CA 104

Andric, Ivo 1892-1975 .... **CLC 8**
See also CA 81-84; 57-60; CANR 43;
DLB 147; MTCW

Angelique, Pierre
See Bataille, Georges

Angell, Roger 1920- .... **CLC 26**
See also CA 57-60; CANR 13, 44

Angelou, Maya
1928- .... **CLC 12, 35, 64, 77; BLC; DA;**
DAB; DAC
See also AAYA 7; BW 2; CA 65-68;
CANR 19, 42; DAM MST, MULT,
POET, POP; DLB 38; MTCW; SATA 49

Annensky, Innokenty Fyodorovich
1856-1909 .... **TCLC 14**
See also CA 110

Anon, Charles Robert
See Pessoa, Fernando (Antonio Nogueira)

Anouilh, Jean (Marie Lucien Pierre)
1910-1987 ...... **CLC 1, 3, 8, 13, 40, 50**
See also CA 17-20R; 123; CANR 32;
DAM DRAM; MTCW

Anthony, Florence
See Ai

Anthony, John
See Ciardi, John (Anthony)

Anthony, Peter
See Shaffer, Anthony (Joshua); Shaffer,
Peter (Levin)

Anthony, Piers 1934- .... **CLC 35**
See also AAYA 11; CA 21-24R; CANR 28;
DAM POP; DLB 8; MTCW; SAAS 22;
SATA 84

Antoine, Marc
See Proust, (Valentin-Louis-George-Eugene-)
Marcel

Antoninus, Brother
See Everson, William (Oliver)

Antonioni, Michelangelo 1912- ..... **CLC 20**
See also CA 73-76; CANR 45

Antschel, Paul 1920-1970
See Celan, Paul
See also CA 85-88; CANR 33; MTCW

Anwar, Chairil 1922-1949 .... **TCLC 22**
See also CA 121

Apollinaire, Guillaume .. **TCLC 3, 8, 51; PC 7**
See also Kostrowitzki, Wilhelm Apollinaris
de
See also DAM POET

Appelfeld, Aharon 1932- .... **CLC 23, 47**
See also CA 112; 133

Apple, Max (Isaac) 1941-........ **CLC 9, 33**
See also CA 81-84; CANR 19; DLB 130

Appleman, Philip (Dean) 1926- ..... **CLC 51**
See also CA 13-16R; CAAS 18; CANR 6,
29

Appleton, Lawrence
See Lovecraft, H(oward) P(hillips)

Apteryx
See Eliot, T(homas) S(tearns)

Apuleius, (Lucius Madaurensis)
125(?)-175(?) .... **CMLC 1**

Aquin, Hubert 1929-1977......... : **CLC 15**
See also CA 105; DLB 53

Aragon, Louis 1897-1982 .... **CLC 3, 22**
See also CA 69-72; 108; CANR 28;
DAM NOV, POET; DLB 72; MTCW

Arany, Janos 1817-1882........ **NCLC 34**

Arbuthnot, John 1667-1735 .... **LC 1**
See also DLB 101

Archer, Herbert Winslow
See Mencken, H(enry) L(ouis)

Archer, Jeffrey (Howard) 1940- .... **CLC 28**
See also AAYA 16; BEST 89:3; CA 77-80;
CANR 22; DAM POP; INT CANR-22

Archer, Jules 1915- .... **CLC 12**
See also CA 9-12R; CANR 6; SAAS 5;
SATA 4, 85

Archer, Lee
See Ellison, Harlan (Jay)

Arden, John 1930- .... **CLC 6, 13, 15**
See also CA 13-16R; CAAS 4; CANR 31;
DAM DRAM; DLB 13; MTCW

Arenas, Reinaldo
1943-1990 .... **CLC 41; HLC**
See also CA 124; 128; 133; DAM MULT;
DLB 145; HW

Arendt, Hannah 1906-1975 .... **CLC 66**
See also CA 17-20R; 61-64; CANR 26;
MTCW

Aretino, Pietro 1492-1556 .... **LC 12**

Arghezi, Tudor.................... **CLC 80**
See also Theodorescu, Ion N.

Arguedas, Jose Maria
1911-1969 .... **CLC 10, 18**
See also CA 89-92; DLB 113; HW

Argueta, Manlio 1936-............ **CLC 31**
See also CA 131; DLB 145; HW

Ariosto, Ludovico 1474-1533........ **LC 6**

Aristides
See Epstein, Joseph

Aristophanes
450B.C.-385B.C......... **CMLC 4; DA;**
DAB; DAC; DC 2
See also DAM DRAM, MST

Arlt, Roberto (Godofredo Christophersen)
1900-1942 .... **TCLC 29; HLC**
See also CA 123; 131; DAM MULT; HW

Armah, Ayi Kwei 1939- .... **CLC 5, 33; BLC**
See also BW 1; CA 61-64; CANR 21;
DAM MULT, POET; DLB 117; MTCW

Armatrading, Joan 1950-.......... **CLC 17**
See also CA 114

Arnette, Robert
See Silverberg, Robert

Arnim, Achim von (Ludwig Joachim von
Arnim) 1781-1831 .... **NCLC 5**
See also DLB 90

Arnim, Bettina von 1785-1859.... **NCLC 38**
See also DLB 90

Arnold, Matthew
1822-1888 ..... **NCLC 6, 29; DA; DAB;**
DAC; PC 5; WLC
See also CDBLB 1832-1890; DAM MST,
POET; DLB 32, 57

Arnold, Thomas 1795-1842 ...... **NCLC 18**
See also DLB 55

Arnow, Harriette (Louisa) Simpson
1908-1986 .... **CLC 2, 7, 18**
See also CA 9-12R; 118; CANR 14; DLB 6;
MTCW; SATA 42; SATA-Obit 47

Arp, Hans
See Arp, Jean

Arp, Jean 1887-1966............... **CLC 5**
See also CA 81-84; 25-28R; CANR 42

Arrabal
See Arrabal, Fernando

Arrabal, Fernando 1932- ... **CLC 2, 9, 18, 58**
See also CA 9-12R; CANR 15

Arrick, Fran..................... **CLC 30**
See also Gaberman, Judie Angell

Artaud, Antonin (Marie Joseph)
1896-1948 .... **TCLC 3, 36**
See also CA 104; 149; DAM DRAM

Arthur, Ruth M(abel) 1905-1979.... **CLC 12**
See also CA 9-12R; 85-88; CANR 4;
SATA 7, 26

Artsybashev, Mikhail (Petrovich)
1878-1927 .... **TCLC 31**

Arundel, Honor (Morfydd)
1919-1973 .... **CLC 17**
See also CA 21-22; 41-44R; CAP 2;
CLR 35; SATA 4; SATA-Obit 24

Asch, Sholem 1880-1957 .... **TCLC 3**
See also CA 105

Ash, Shalom
See Asch, Sholem

Ashbery, John (Lawrence)
1927- ...... **CLC 2, 3, 4, 6, 9, 13, 15, 25,**
41, 77
See also CA 5-8R; CANR 9, 37;
DAM POET; DLB 5, 165; DLBY 81;
INT CANR-9; MTCW

Ashdown, Clifford
See Freeman, R(ichard) Austin

Ashe, Gordon
See Creasey, John

Ashton-Warner, Sylvia (Constance)
1908-1984 .... **CLC 19**
See also CA 69-72; 112; CANR 29; MTCW

Asimov, Isaac
1920-1992 ... **CLC 1, 3, 9, 19, 26, 76, 92**
See also AAYA 13; BEST 90:2; CA 1-4R;
137; CANR 2, 19, 36; CLR 12;
DAM POP; DLB 8; DLBY 92;
INT CANR-19; JRDA; MAICYA;
MTCW; SATA 1, 26, 74

Astley, Thea (Beatrice May)
1925- .... **CLC 41**
See also CA 65-68; CANR 11, 43

Balzac, Honore de
1799-1850 . . . . **NCLC 5, 35, 53; DA;
DAB; DAC; SSC 5; WLC**
See also DAM MST, NOV; DLB 119

Bambara, Toni Cade
1939-1995 . . . . . . **CLC 19, 88; BLC; DA;
DAC**
See also AAYA 5; BW 2; CA 29-32R; 150;
CANR 24, 49; DAM MST, MULT;
DLB 38; MTCW

Bamdad, A.
See Shamlu, Ahmad

Banat, D. R.
See Bradbury, Ray (Douglas)

Bancroft, Laura
See Baum, L(yman) Frank

Banim, John 1798-1842 . . . . **NCLC 13**
See also DLB 116, 158, 159

Banim, Michael 1796-1874 . . . . . . **NCLC 13**
See also DLB 158, 159

Banks, Iain
See Banks, Iain M(enzies)

Banks, Iain M(enzies) 1954- . . . . **CLC 34**
See also CA 123; 128; INT 128

Banks, Lynne Reid . . . . **CLC 23**
See also Reid Banks, Lynne
See also AAYA 6

Banks, Russell 1940- . . . . **CLC 37, 72**
See also CA 65-68; CAAS 15; CANR 19;
DLB 130

Banville, John 1945- . . . . **CLC 46**
See also CA 117; 128; DLB 14; INT 128

Banville, Theodore (Faullain) de
1832-1891 . . . . **NCLC 9**

Baraka, Amiri
1934- . . . . **CLC 1, 2, 3, 5, 10, 14, 33;
BLC; DA; DAC; DC 6; PC 4**
See also Jones, LeRoi
See also BW 2; CA 21-24R; CABS 3;
CANR 27, 38; CDALB 1941-1968;
DAM MST, MULT, POET, POP;
DLB 5, 7, 16, 38; DLBD 8; MTCW

Barbauld, Anna Laetitia
1743-1825 . . . . **NCLC 50**
See also DLB 107, 109, 142, 158

Barbellion, W. N. P. . . . . **TCLC 24**
See also Cummings, Bruce F(rederick)

Barbera, Jack (Vincent) 1945- . . . . . . **CLC 44**
See also CA 110; CANR 45

Barbey d'Aurevilly, Jules Amedee
1808-1889 . . . . **NCLC 1; SSC 17**
See also DLB 119

Barbusse, Henri 1873-1935 . . . . **TCLC 5**
See also CA 105; DLB 65

Barclay, Bill
See Moorcock, Michael (John)

Barclay, William Ewert
See Moorcock, Michael (John)

Barea, Arturo 1897-1957 . . . . **TCLC 14**
See also CA 111

Barfoot, Joan 1946- . . . . **CLC 18**
See also CA 105

Baring, Maurice 1874-1945 . . . . **TCLC 8**
See also CA 105; DLB 34

Barker, Clive 1952- . . . . **CLC 52**
See also AAYA 10; BEST 90:3; CA 121;
129; DAM POP; INT 129; MTCW

Barker, George Granville
1913-1991 . . . . **CLC 8, 48**
See also CA 9-12R; 135; CANR 7, 38;
DAM POET; DLB 20; MTCW

Barker, Harley Granville
See Granville-Barker, Harley
See also DLB 10

Barker, Howard 1946- . . . . **CLC 37**
See also CA 102; DLB 13

Barker, Pat(ricia) 1943- . . . . **CLC 32, 91**
See also CA 117; 122; CANR 50; INT 122

Barlow, Joel 1754-1812 . . . . **NCLC 23**
See also DLB 37

Barnard, Mary (Ethel) 1909- . . . . **CLC 48**
See also CA 21-22; CAP 2

Barnes, Djuna
1892-1982 . . . **CLC 3, 4, 8, 11, 29; SSC 3**
See also CA 9-12R; 107; CANR 16; DLB 4,
9, 45; MTCW

Barnes, Julian 1946- . . . . **CLC 42; DAB**
See also CA 102; CANR 19; DLBY 93

Barnes, Peter 1931- . . . . **CLC 5, 56**
See also CA 65-68; CAAS 12; CANR 33,
34; DLB 13; MTCW

Baroja (y Nessi), Pio
1872-1956 . . . . **TCLC 8; HLC**
See also CA 104

Baron, David
See Pinter, Harold

Baron Corvo
See Rolfe, Frederick (William Serafino
Austin Lewis Mary)

Barondess, Sue K(aufman)
1926-1977 . . . . **CLC 8**
See also Kaufman, Sue
See also CA 1-4R; 69-72; CANR 1

Baron de Teive
See Pessoa, Fernando (Antonio Nogueira)

Barres, Maurice 1862-1923 . . . . **TCLC 47**
See also DLB 123

Barreto, Afonso Henrique de Lima
See Lima Barreto, Afonso Henrique de

Barrett, (Roger) Syd 1946- . . . . **CLC 35**

Barrett, William (Christopher)
1913-1992 . . . . **CLC 27**
See also CA 13-16R; 139; CANR 11;
INT CANR-11

Barrie, J(ames) M(atthew)
1860-1937 . . . . **TCLC 2; DAB**
See also CA 104; 136; CDBLB 1890-1914;
CLR 16; DAM DRAM; DLB 10, 141,
156; MAICYA; YABC 1

Barrington, Michael
See Moorcock, Michael (John)

Barrol, Grady
See Bograd, Larry

Barry, Mike
See Malzberg, Barry N(athaniel)

Barry, Philip 1896-1949 . . . . **TCLC 11**
See also CA 109; DLB 7

Bart, Andre Schwarz
See Schwarz-Bart, Andre

Barth, John (Simmons)
1930- . . . . . . **CLC 1, 2, 3, 5, 7, 9, 10, 14,
27, 51, 89; SSC 10**
See also AITN 1, 2; CA 1-4R; CABS 1;
CANR 5, 23, 49; DAM NOV; DLB 2;
MTCW

Barthelme, Donald
1931-1989 . . . . . . **CLC 1, 2, 3, 5, 6, 8, 13,
23, 46, 59; SSC 2**
See also CA 21-24R; 129; CANR 20;
DAM NOV; DLB 2; DLBY 80, 89;
MTCW; SATA 7; SATA-Obit 62

Barthelme, Frederick 1943- . . . . **CLC 36**
See also CA 114; 122; DLBY 85; INT 122

Barthes, Roland (Gerard)
1915-1980 . . . . **CLC 24, 83**
See also CA 130; 97-100; MTCW

Barzun, Jacques (Martin) 1907- . . . . **CLC 51**
See also CA 61-64; CANR 22

Bashevis, Isaac
See Singer, Isaac Bashevis

Bashkirtseff, Marie 1859-1884 . . . **NCLC 27**

Basho
See Matsuo Basho

Bass, Kingsley B., Jr.
See Bullins, Ed

Bass, Rick 1958- . . . . **CLC 79**
See also CA 126

Bassani, Giorgio 1916- . . . . **CLC 9**
See also CA 65-68; CANR 33; DLB 128;
MTCW

Bastos, Augusto (Antonio) Roa
See Roa Bastos, Augusto (Antonio)

Bataille, Georges 1897-1962 . . . . **CLC 29**
See also CA 101; 89-92

Bates, H(erbert) E(rnest)
1905-1974 . . . . . . **CLC 46; DAB; SSC 10**
See also CA 93-96; 45-48; CANR 34;
DAM POP; DLB 162; MTCW

Bauchart
See Camus, Albert

Baudelaire, Charles
1821-1867 . . . . **NCLC 6, 29, 55; DA;
DAB; DAC; PC 1; SSC 18; WLC**
See also DAM MST, POET

Baudrillard, Jean 1929- . . . . **CLC 60**

Baum, L(yman) Frank 1856-1919 . . . **TCLC 7**
See also CA 108; 133; CLR 15; DLB 22;
JRDA; MAICYA; MTCW; SATA 18

Baum, Louis F.
See Baum, L(yman) Frank

Baumbach, Jonathan 1933- . . . . **CLC 6, 23**
See also CA 13-16R; CAAS 5; CANR 12;
DLBY 80; INT CANR-12; MTCW

Bausch, Richard (Carl) 1945- . . . . . . **CLC 51**
See also CA 101; CAAS 14; CANR 43;
DLB 130

Baxter, Charles 1947- . . . . **CLC 45, 78**
See also CA 57-60; CANR 40; DAM POP;
DLB 130

Baxter, George Owen
See Faust, Frederick (Schiller)

Baxter, James K(eir)   1926-1972 .... **CLC 14**
See also CA 77-80

Baxter, John
See Hunt, E(verette) Howard, (Jr.)

Bayer, Sylvia
See Glassco, John

Baynton, Barbara   1857-1929 ...... **TCLC 57**

Beagle, Peter S(oyer)   1939- .... **CLC 7**
See also CA 9-12R; CANR 4, 51;
    DLBY 80; INT CANR-4; SATA 60

Bean, Normal
See Burroughs, Edgar Rice

Beard, Charles A(ustin)
    1874-1948 .... **TCLC 15**
See also CA 115; DLB 17; SATA 18

Beardsley, Aubrey   1872-1898 ..... **NCLC 6**

Beattie, Ann
    1947- .... **CLC 8, 13, 18, 40, 63; SSC 11**
See also BEST 90:2; CA 81-84; DAM NOV,
    POP; DLBY 82; MTCW

Beattie, James   1735-1803 .... **NCLC 25**
See also DLB 109

Beauchamp, Kathleen Mansfield   1888-1923
See Mansfield, Katherine
See also CA 104; 134; DA; DAC;
    DAM MST

Beaumarchais, Pierre-Augustin Caron de
    1732-1799 .... **DC 4**
See also DAM DRAM

Beaumont, Francis   1584(?)-1616 ...... **DC 6**
See also CDBLB Before 1660; DLB 58, 121

Beauvoir, Simone (Lucie Ernestine Marie
    Bertrand) de
    1908-1986 .... **CLC 1, 2, 4, 8, 14, 31, 44,**
                   50, 71; DA; DAB; DAC; WLC
See also CA 9-12R; 118; CANR 28;
    DAM MST, NOV; DLB 72; DLBY 86;
    MTCW

Becker, Carl   1873-1945 .... **TCLC 63:**
See also DLB 17

Becker, Jurek   1937- .... **CLC 7, 19**
See also CA 85-88; DLB 75

Becker, Walter   1950- .... **CLC 26**

Beckett, Samuel (Barclay)
    1906-1989 ...... **CLC 1, 2, 3, 4, 6, 9, 10,**
                    11, 14, 18, 29, 57, 59, 83; DA; DAB;
                    DAC; SSC 16; WLC
See also CA 5-8R; 130; CANR 33;
    CDBLB 1945-1960; DAM DRAM, MST,
    NOV; DLB 13, 15; DLBY 90; MTCW

Beckford, William   1760-1844 .... **NCLC 16**
See also DLB 39

Beckman, Gunnel   1910- .... **CLC 26**
See also CA 33-36R; CANR 15; CLR 25;
    MAICYA; SAAS 9; SATA 6

Becque, Henri   1837-1899 .... **NCLC 3**

Beddoes, Thomas Lovell
    1803-1849 .... **NCLC 3**
See also DLB 96

Bedford, Donald F.
See Fearing, Kenneth (Flexner)

Beecher, Catharine Esther
    1800-1878 .... **NCLC 30**
See also DLB 1

Beecher, John   1904-1980 .... **CLC 6**
See also AITN 1; CA 5-8R; 105; CANR 8

Beer, Johann   1655-1700 .... **LC 5**

Beer, Patricia   1924- .... **CLC 58**
See also CA 61-64; CANR 13, 46; DLB 40

Beerbohm, Henry Maximilian
    1872-1956 .... **TCLC 1, 24**
See also CA 104; DLB 34, 100

Beerbohm, Max
See Beerbohm, Henry Maximilian

Beer-Hofmann, Richard
    1866-1945 .... **TCLC 60**
See also DLB 81

Begiebing, Robert J(ohn)   1946- ..... **CLC 70**
See also CA 122; CANR 40

Behan, Brendan
    1923-1964 .... **CLC 1, 8, 11, 15, 79**
See also CA 73-76; CANR 33;
    CDBLB 1945-1960; DAM DRAM;
    DLB 13; MTCW

Behn, Aphra
    1640(?)-1689 ...... **LC 1, 30; DA; DAB;**
                     DAC; DC 4; PC 13; WLC
See also DAM DRAM, MST, NOV, POET;
    DLB 39, 80, 131

Behrman, S(amuel) N(athaniel)
    1893-1973 .... **CLC 40**
See also CA 13-16; 45-48; CAP 1; DLB 7,
    44

Belasco, David   1853-1931 .... **TCLC 3**
See also CA 104; DLB 7

Belcheva, Elisaveta   1893- .... **CLC 10**
See also Bagryana, Elisaveta

Beldone, Phil "Cheech"
See Ellison, Harlan (Jay)

Beleno
See Azuela, Mariano

Belinski, Vissarion Grigoryevich
    1811-1848 .... **NCLC 5**

Belitt, Ben   1911- .... **CLC 22**
See also CA 13-16R; CAAS 4; CANR 7;
    DLB 5

Bell, James Madison
    1826-1902 .... **TCLC 43; BLC**
See also BW 1; CA 122; 124; DAM MULT;
    DLB 50

Bell, Madison (Smartt)   1957- ...... **CLC 41**
See also CA 111; CANR 28

Bell, Marvin (Hartley)   1937- ..... **CLC 8, 31**
See also CA 21-24R; CAAS 14;
    DAM POET; DLB 5; MTCW

Bell, W. L. D.
See Mencken, H(enry) L(ouis)

Bellamy, Atwood C.
See Mencken, H(enry) L(ouis)

Bellamy, Edward   1850-1898 ...... **NCLC 4**
See also DLB 12

Bellin, Edward J.
See Kuttner, Henry

Belloc, (Joseph) Hilaire (Pierre)
    1870-1953 .... **TCLC 7, 18**
See also CA 106; DAM POET; DLB 19,
    100, 141; YABC 1

Belloc, Joseph Peter Rene Hilaire
See Belloc, (Joseph) Hilaire (Pierre)

Belloc, Joseph Pierre Hilaire
See Belloc, (Joseph) Hilaire (Pierre)

Belloc, M. A.
See Lowndes, Marie Adelaide (Belloc)

Bellow, Saul
    1915- ...... **CLC 1, 2, 3, 6, 8, 10, 13, 15,**
                25, 33, 34, 63, 79; DA; DAB; DAC;
                        SSC 14; WLC
See also AITN 2; BEST 89:3; CA 5-8R;
    CABS 1; CANR 29; CDALB 1941-1968;
    DAM MST, NOV, POP; DLB 2, 28;
    DLBD 3; DLBY 82; MTCW

Belser, Reimond Karel Maria de
See Ruyslinck, Ward

Bely, Andrey .... **TCLC 7; PC 11**
See also Bugayev, Boris Nikolayevich

Benary, Margot
See Benary-Isbert, Margot

Benary-Isbert, Margot   1889-1979 ... **CLC 12**
See also CA 5-8R; 89-92; CANR 4;
    CLR 12; MAICYA; SATA 2;
    SATA-Obit 21

Benavente (y Martinez), Jacinto
    1866-1954 .... **TCLC 3**
See also CA 106; 131; DAM DRAM,
    MULT; HW; MTCW

Benchley, Peter (Bradford)
    1940- .... **CLC 4, 8**
See also AAYA 14; AITN 2; CA 17-20R;
    CANR 12, 35; DAM NOV, POP;
    MTCW; SATA 3

Benchley, Robert (Charles)
    1889-1945 .... **TCLC 1, 55**
See also CA 105; DLB 11

Benda, Julien   1867-1956 .... **TCLC 60**
See also CA 120

Benedict, Ruth   1887-1948 .... **TCLC 60**

Benedikt, Michael   1935- .... **CLC 4, 14**
See also CA 13-16R; CANR 7; DLB 5

Benet, Juan   1927- .... **CLC 28**
See also CA 143

Benet, Stephen Vincent
    1898-1943 .... **TCLC 7; SSC 10**
See also CA 104; DAM POET; DLB 4, 48,
    102; YABC 1

Benet, William Rose   1886-1950 ... **TCLC 28**
See also CA 118; DAM POET; DLB 45

Benford, Gregory (Albert)   1941- .... **CLC 52**
See also CA 69-72; CANR 12, 24, 49;
    DLBY 82

Bengtsson, Frans (Gunnar)
    1894-1954 .... **TCLC 48**

Benjamin, David
See Slavitt, David R(ytman)

Benjamin, Lois
See Gould, Lois

Benjamin, Walter   1892-1940 ..... **TCLC 39**

Benn, Gottfried   1886-1956 .... **TCLC 3**
See also CA 106; DLB 56

Bennett, Alan   1934- ..... **CLC 45, 77; DAB**
See also CA 103; CANR 35; DAM MST;
    MTCW

Bennett, (Enoch) Arnold
1867-1931 . . . . TCLC **5, 20**
See also CA 106; CDBLB 1890-1914;
DLB 10, 34, 98, 135

Bennett, Elizabeth
See Mitchell, Margaret (Munnerlyn)

Bennett, George Harold 1930-
See Bennett, Hal
See also BW 1; CA 97-100

Bennett, Hal . . . . CLC **5**
See also Bennett, George Harold
See also DLB 33

Bennett, Jay 1912- . . . . CLC **35**
See also AAYA 10; CA 69-72; CANR 11,
42; JRDA; SAAS 4; SATA 41, 87;
SATA-Brief 27

Bennett, Louise (Simone)
1919- . . . . CLC **28**; BLC
See also BW 2; DAM MULT; DLB 117

Benson, E(dward) F(rederic)
1867-1940 . . . . TCLC **27**
See also CA 114; DLB 135, 153

Benson, Jackson J. 1930- . . . . CLC **34**
See also CA 25-28R; DLB 111

Benson, Sally 1900-1972 . . . . CLC **17**
See also CA 19-20; 37-40R; CAP 1;
SATA 1, 35; SATA-Obit 27

Benson, Stella 1892-1933 . . . . TCLC **17**
See also CA 117; DLB 36, 162

Bentham, Jeremy 1748-1832 . . . . . NCLC **38**
See also DLB 107, 158

Bentley, E(dmund) C(lerihew)
1875-1956 . . . . TCLC **12**
See also CA 108; DLB 70

Bentley, Eric (Russell) 1916- . . . . CLC **24**
See also CA 5-8R; CANR 6; INT CANR-6

Beranger, Pierre Jean de
1780-1857 . . . . NCLC **34**

Berendt, John (Lawrence) 1939- . . . . CLC **86**
See also CA 146

Berger, Colonel
See Malraux, (Georges-)Andre

Berger, John (Peter) 1926- . . . . . . CLC **2, 19**
See also CA 81-84; CANR 51; DLB 14

Berger, Melvin H. 1927- . . . . CLC **12**
See also CA 5-8R; CANR 4; CLR 32;
SAAS 2; SATA 5

Berger, Thomas (Louis)
1924- . . . . CLC **3, 5, 8, 11, 18, 38**
See also CA 1-4R; CANR 5, 28, 51;
DAM NOV; DLB 2; DLBY 80;
INT CANR-28; MTCW

Bergman, (Ernst) Ingmar
1918- . . . . CLC **16, 72**
See also CA 81-84; CANR 33

Bergson, Henri 1859-1941 . . . . TCLC **32**

Bergstein, Eleanor 1938- . . . . CLC **4**
See also CA 53-56; CANR 5

Berkoff, Steven 1937- . . . . CLC **56**
See also CA 104

Bermant, Chaim (Icyk) 1929- . . . . . . CLC **40**
See also CA 57-60; CANR 6, 31

Bern, Victoria
See Fisher, M(ary) F(rances) K(ennedy)

Bernanos, (Paul Louis) Georges
1888-1948 . . . . TCLC **3**
See also CA 104; 130; DLB 72

Bernard, April 1956- . . . . CLC **59**
See also CA 131

Berne, Victoria
See Fisher, M(ary) F(rances) K(ennedy)

Bernhard, Thomas
1931-1989 . . . . CLC **3, 32, 61**
See also CA 85-88; 127; CANR 32;
DLB 85, 124; MTCW

Berriault, Gina 1926- . . . . CLC **54**
See also CA 116; 129; DLB 130

Berrigan, Daniel 1921- . . . . CLC **4**
See also CA 33-36R; CAAS 1; CANR 11,
43; DLB 5

Berrigan, Edmund Joseph Michael, Jr.
1934-1983
See Berrigan, Ted
See also CA 61-64; 110; CANR 14

Berrigan, Ted . . . . CLC **37**
See also Berrigan, Edmund Joseph Michael,
Jr.
See also DLB 5

Berry, Charles Edward Anderson 1931-
See Berry, Chuck
See also CA 115

Berry, Chuck . . . . CLC **17**
See also Berry, Charles Edward Anderson

Berry, Jonas
See Ashbery, John (Lawrence)

Berry, Wendell (Erdman)
1934- . . . . CLC **4, 6, 8, 27, 46**
See also AITN 1; CA 73-76; CANR 50;
DAM POET; DLB 5, 6

Berryman, John
1914-1972 . . . . . . CLC **1, 2, 3, 4, 6, 8, 10,
13, 25, 62**
See also CA 13-16; 33-36R; CABS 2;
CANR 35; CAP 1; CDALB 1941-1968;
DAM POET; DLB 48; MTCW

Bertolucci, Bernardo 1940- . . . . CLC **16**
See also CA 106

Bertrand, Aloysius 1807-1841 . . . . NCLC **31**

Bertran de Born c. 1140-1215 . . . . . CMLC **5**

Besant, Annie (Wood) 1847-1933 . . . TCLC **9**
See also CA 105

Bessie, Alvah 1904-1985 . . . . CLC **23**
See also CA 5-8R; 116; CANR 2; DLB 26

Bethlen, T. D.
See Silverberg, Robert

Beti, Mongo . . . . CLC **27**; BLC
See also Biyidi, Alexandre
See also DAM MULT

Betjeman, John
1906-1984 . . . CLC **2, 6, 10, 34, 43**; DAB
See also CA 9-12R; 112; CANR 33;
CDBLB 1945-1960; DAM MST, POET;
DLB 20; DLBY 84; MTCW

Bettelheim, Bruno 1903-1990 . . . . . . CLC **79**
See also CA 81-84; 131; CANR 23; MTCW

Betti, Ugo 1892-1953 . . . . TCLC **5**
See also CA 104

Betts, Doris (Waugh) 1932- . . . . CLC **3, 6, 28**
See also CA 13-16R; CANR 9; DLBY 82;
INT CANR-9

Bevan, Alistair
See Roberts, Keith (John Kingston)

Bialik, Chaim Nachman
1873-1934 . . . . TCLC **25**

Bickerstaff, Isaac
See Swift, Jonathan

Bidart, Frank 1939- . . . . CLC **33**
See also CA 140

Bienek, Horst 1930- . . . . CLC **7, 11**
See also CA 73-76; DLB 75

Bierce, Ambrose (Gwinett)
1842-1914(?) . . . . TCLC **1, 7, 44**; DA;
DAC; SSC **9**; WLC
See also CA 104; 139; CDALB 1865-1917;
DAM MST; DLB 11, 12, 23, 71, 74

Billings, Josh
See Shaw, Henry Wheeler

Billington, (Lady) Rachel (Mary)
1942- . . . . CLC **43**
See also AITN 2; CA 33-36R; CANR 44

Binyon, T(imothy) J(ohn) 1936- . . . . CLC **34**
See also CA 111; CANR 28

Bioy Casares, Adolfo
1914- . . . CLC **4, 8, 13, 88**; HLC; SSC **17**
See also CA 29-32R; CANR 19, 43;
DAM MULT; DLB 113; HW; MTCW

Bird, Cordwainer
See Ellison, Harlan (Jay)

Bird, Robert Montgomery
1806-1854 . . . . NCLC **1**

Birney, (Alfred) Earle
1904- . . . . CLC **1, 4, 6, 11**; DAC
See also CA 1-4R; CANR 5, 20;
DAM MST, POET; DLB 88; MTCW

Bishop, Elizabeth
1911-1979 . . . . . . CLC **1, 4, 9, 13, 15, 32**;
DA; DAC; PC **3**
See also CA 5-8R; 89-92; CABS 2;
CANR 26; CDALB 1968-1988;
DAM MST, POET; DLB 5; MTCW;
SATA-Obit 24

Bishop, John 1935- . . . . CLC **10**
See also CA 105

Bissett, Bill 1939- . . . . CLC **18**; PC **14**
See also CA 69-72; CAAS 19; CANR 15;
DLB 53; MTCW

Bitov, Andrei (Georgievich) 1937- . . . CLC **57**
See also CA 142

Biyidi, Alexandre 1932-
See Beti, Mongo
See also BW 1; CA 114; 124; MTCW

Bjarme, Brynjolf
See Ibsen, Henrik (Johan)

Bjornson, Bjornstjerne (Martinius)
1832-1910 . . . . TCLC **7, 37**
See also CA 104

Black, Robert
See Holdstock, Robert P.

Blackburn, Paul 1926-1971 . . . . . . CLC **9, 43**
See also CA 81-84; 33-36R; CANR 34;
DLB 16; DLBY 81

Black Elk 1863-1950 . . . . **TCLC 33**
See also CA 144; DAM MULT; NNAL

Black Hobart
See Sanders, (James) Ed(ward)

Blacklin, Malcolm
See Chambers, Aidan

Blackmore, R(ichard) D(oddridge)
1825-1900 . . . . **TCLC 27**
See also CA 120; DLB 18

Blackmur, R(ichard) P(almer)
1904-1965 . . . . **CLC 2, 24**
See also CA 11-12; 25-28R; CAP 1; DLB 63

Black Tarantula, The
See Acker, Kathy

Blackwood, Algernon (Henry)
1869-1951 . . . . **TCLC 5**
See also CA 105; 150; DLB 153, 156

Blackwood, Caroline 1931- . . . . **CLC 6, 9**
See also CA 85-88; CANR 32; DLB 14;
MTCW

Blade, Alexander
See Hamilton, Edmond; Silverberg, Robert

Blaga, Lucian 1895-1961 . . . . **CLC 75**

Blair, Eric (Arthur) 1903-1950
See Orwell, George
See also CA 104; 132; DA; DAB; DAC;
DAM MST, NOV; MTCW; SATA 29

Blais, Marie-Claire
1939- . . . . **CLC 2, 4, 6, 13, 22; DAC**
See also CA 21-24R; CAAS 4; CANR 38;
DAM MST; DLB 53; MTCW

Blaise, Clark 1940- . . . . **CLC 29**
See also AITN 2; CA 53-56; CAAS 3;
CANR 5; DLB 53

Blake, Nicholas
See Day Lewis, C(ecil)
See also DLB 77

Blake, William
1757-1827 . . . . **NCLC 13, 37; DA; DAB;
DAC; PC 12; WLC**
See also CDBLB 1789-1832; DAM MST,
POET; DLB 93, 163; MAICYA;
SATA 30

Blake, William J(ames) 1894-1969 . . . **PC 12**
See also CA 5-8R; 25-28R

Blasco Ibanez, Vicente
1867-1928 . . . . **TCLC 12**
See also CA 110; 131; DAM NOV; HW;
MTCW

Blatty, William Peter 1928- . . . . **CLC 2**
See also CA 5-8R; CANR 9; DAM POP

Bleeck, Oliver
See Thomas, Ross (Elmore)

Blessing, Lee 1949- . . . . **CLC 54**

Blish, James (Benjamin)
1921-1975 . . . . **CLC 14**
See also CA 1-4R; 57-60; CANR 3; DLB 8;
MTCW; SATA 66

Bliss, Reginald
See Wells, H(erbert) G(eorge)

Blixen, Karen (Christentze Dinesen)
1885-1962
See Dinesen, Isak
See also CA 25-28; CANR 22, 50; CAP 2;
MTCW; SATA 44

Bloch, Robert (Albert) 1917-1994 . . . **CLC 33**
See also CA 5-8R; 146; CAAS 20; CANR 5;
DLB 44; INT CANR-5; SATA 12;
SATA-Obit 82

Blok, Alexander (Alexandrovich)
1880-1921 . . . . **TCLC 5**
See also CA 104

Blom, Jan
See Breytenbach, Breyten

Bloom, Harold 1930- . . . . **CLC 24**
See also CA 13-16R; CANR 39; DLB 67

Bloomfield, Aurelius
See Bourne, Randolph S(illiman)

Blount, Roy (Alton), Jr. 1941- . . . . . **CLC 38**
See also CA 53-56; CANR 10, 28;
INT CANR-28; MTCW

Bloy, Leon 1846-1917. . . . . **TCLC 22**
See also CA 121; DLB 123

Blume, Judy (Sussman) 1938- . . . **CLC 12, 30**
See also AAYA 3; CA 29-32R; CANR 13,
37; CLR 2, 15; DAM NOV, POP;
DLB 52; JRDA; MAICYA; MTCW;
SATA 2, 31, 79

Blunden, Edmund (Charles)
1896-1974 . . . . **CLC 2, 56**
See also CA 17-18; 45-48; CAP 2; DLB 20,
100, 155; MTCW

Bly, Robert (Elwood)
1926- . . . . **CLC 1, 2, 5, 10, 15, 38**
See also CA 5-8R; CANR 41; DAM POET;
DLB 5; MTCW

Boas, Franz 1858-1942. . . . . **TCLC 56**
See also CA 115

Bobette
See Simenon, Georges (Jacques Christian)

Boccaccio, Giovanni
1313-1375 . . . . **CMLC 13; SSC 10**

Bochco, Steven 1943- . . . . **CLC 35**
See also AAYA 11; CA 124; 138

Bodenheim, Maxwell 1892-1954 . . . **TCLC 44**
See also CA 110; DLB 9, 45

Bodker, Cecil 1927- . . . . **CLC 21**
See also CA 73-76; CANR 13, 44; CLR 23;
MAICYA; SATA 14

Boell, Heinrich (Theodor)
1917-1985 . . . . **CLC 2, 3, 6, 9, 11, 15, 27,
32, 72; DA; DAB; DAC; SSC 23; WLC**
See also CA 21-24R; 116; CANR 24;
DAM MST, NOV; DLB 69; DLBY 85;
MTCW

Boerne, Alfred
See Doeblin, Alfred

Boethius 480(?)-524(?) . . . . **CMLC 15**
See also DLB 115

Bogan, Louise
1897-1970 . . . . **CLC 4, 39, 46, 93; PC 12**
See also CA 73-76; 25-28R; CANR 33;
DAM POET; DLB 45; MTCW

Bogarde, Dirk . . . . **CLC 19**
See also Van Den Bogarde, Derek Jules
Gaspard Ulric Niven
See also DLB 14

Bogosian, Eric 1953- . . . . **CLC 45**
See also CA 138

Bograd, Larry 1953- . . . . **CLC 35**
See also CA 93-96; SAAS 21; SATA 33

Boiardo, Matteo Maria 1441-1494 . . . . **LC 6**

Boileau-Despreaux, Nicolas
1636-1711 . . . . **LC 3**

Boland, Eavan (Aisling) 1944-. . . **CLC 40, 67**
See also CA 143; DAM POET; DLB 40

Bolt, Lee
See Faust, Frederick (Schiller)

Bolt, Robert (Oxton) 1924-1995 . . . . **CLC 14**
See also CA 17-20R; 147; CANR 35;
DAM DRAM; DLB 13; MTCW

Bombet, Louis-Alexandre-Cesar
See Stendhal

Bomkauf
See Kaufman, Bob (Garnell)

Bonaventura. . . . . **NCLC 35**
See also DLB 90

Bond, Edward 1934-. . . . . . . **CLC 4, 6, 13, 23**
See also CA 25-28R; CANR 38;
DAM DRAM; DLB 13; MTCW

Bonham, Frank 1914-1989. . . . . **CLC 12**
See also AAYA 1; CA 9-12R; CANR 4, 36;
JRDA; MAICYA; SAAS 3; SATA 1, 49;
SATA-Obit 62

Bonnefoy, Yves 1923-. . . . . **CLC 9, 15, 58**
See also CA 85-88; CANR 33; DAM MST,
POET; MTCW

Bontemps, Arna(ud Wendell)
1902-1973 . . . . **CLC 1, 18; BLC**
See also BW 1; CA 1-4R; 41-44R; CANR 4,
35; CLR 6; DAM MULT, NOV, POET;
DLB 48, 51; JRDA; MAICYA; MTCW;
SATA 2, 44; SATA-Obit 24

Booth, Martin 1944-. . . . . **CLC 13**
See also CA 93-96; CAAS 2

Booth, Philip 1925-. . . . . **CLC 23**
See also CA 5-8R; CANR 5; DLBY 82

Booth, Wayne C(layson) 1921- . . . . . . **CLC 24**
See also CA 1-4R; CAAS 5; CANR 3, 43;
DLB 67

Borchert, Wolfgang 1921-1947 . . . . . **TCLC 5**
See also CA 104; DLB 69, 124

Borel, Petrus 1809-1859. . . . . **NCLC 41**

Borges, Jorge Luis
1899-1986 . . . **CLC 1, 2, 3, 4, 6, 8, 9, 10,
13, 19, 44, 48, 83; DA; DAB; DAC;
HLC; SSC 4; WLC**
See also CA 21-24R; CANR 19, 33;
DAM MST, MULT; DLB 113; DLBY 86;
HW; MTCW

Borowski, Tadeusz 1922-1951 . . . . . . **TCLC 9**
See also CA 106

Borrow, George (Henry)
1803-1881 . . . . **NCLC 9**
See also DLB 21, 55

Bosman, Herman Charles
1905-1951 . . . . **TCLC 49**

Bosschere, Jean de 1878(?)-1953 . . . **TCLC 19**
See also CA 115

Boswell, James
1740-1795 . . . . . . **LC 4; DA; DAB; DAC;
WLC**
See also CDBLB 1660-1789; DAM MST;
DLB 104, 142

Bottoms, David 1949-............ **CLC 53**
See also CA 105; CANR 22; DLB 120;
DLBY 83

Boucicault, Dion 1820-1890...... **NCLC 41**

Boucolon, Maryse 1937-
See Conde, Maryse
See also CA 110; CANR 30

Bourget, Paul (Charles Joseph)
1852-1935 .... **TCLC 12**
See also CA 107; DLB 123

Bourjaily, Vance (Nye) 1922-.... **CLC 8, 62**
See also CA 1-4R; CAAS 1; CANR 2;
DLB 2, 143

Bourne, Randolph S(illiman)
1886-1918 .... **TCLC 16**
See also CA 117; DLB 63

Bova, Ben(jamin William) 1932-.... **CLC 45**
See also AAYA 16; CA 5-8R; CAAS 18;
CANR 11; CLR 3; DLBY 81;
INT CANR-11; MAICYA; MTCW;
SATA 6, 68

Bowen, Elizabeth (Dorothea Cole)
1899-1973 ...... **CLC 1, 3, 6, 11, 15, 22;**
SSC 3
See also CA 17-18; 41-44R; CANR 35;
CAP 2; CDBLB 1945-1960; DAM NOV;
DLB 15, 162; MTCW

Bowering, George 1935-........ **CLC 15, 47**
See also CA 21-24R; CAAS 16; CANR 10;
DLB 53

Bowering, Marilyn R(uthe) 1949-... **CLC 32**
See also CA 101; CANR 49

Bowers, Edgar 1924-.............. **CLC 9**
See also CA 5-8R; CANR 24; DLB 5

Bowie, David .... **CLC 17**
See also Jones, David Robert

Bowles, Jane (Sydney)
1917-1973 .... **CLC 3, 68**
See also CA 19-20; 41-44R; CAP 2

Bowles, Paul (Frederick)
1910-........ **CLC 1, 2, 19, 53; SSC 3**
See also CA 1-4R; CAAS 1; CANR 1, 19,
50; DLB 5, 6; MTCW

Box, Edgar
See Vidal, Gore

Boyd, Nancy
See Millay, Edna St. Vincent

Boyd, William 1952-........ **CLC 28, 53, 70**
See also CA 114; 120; CANR 51

Boyle, Kay
1902-1992 ..... **CLC 1, 5, 19, 58; SSC 5**
See also CA 13-16R; 140; CAAS 1;
CANR 29; DLB 4, 9, 48, 86; DLBY 93;
MTCW

Boyle, Mark
See Kienzle, William X(avier)

Boyle, Patrick 1905-1982......... **CLC 19**
See also CA 127

Boyle, T. C. 1948-
See Boyle, T(homas) Coraghessan

Boyle, T(homas) Coraghessan
1948-......... **CLC 36, 55, 90; SSC 16**
See also BEST 90:4; CA 120; CANR 44;
DAM POP; DLBY 86

Boz
See Dickens, Charles (John Huffam)

Brackenridge, Hugh Henry
1748-1816 .... **NCLC 7**
See also DLB 11, 37

Bradbury, Edward P.
See Moorcock, Michael (John)

Bradbury, Malcolm (Stanley)
1932-.................... **CLC 32, 61**
See also CA 1-4R; CANR 1, 33;
DAM NOV; DLB 14; MTCW

Bradbury, Ray (Douglas)
1920-........ **CLC 1, 3, 10, 15, 42; DA;**
DAB; DAC; WLC
See also AAYA 15; AITN 1, 2; CA 1-4R;
CANR 2, 30; CDALB 1968-1988;
DAM MST, NOV, POP; DLB 2, 8;
INT CANR-30; MTCW; SATA 11, 64

Bradford, Gamaliel 1863-1932..... **TCLC 36**
See also DLB 17

Bradley, David (Henry, Jr.)
1950-.................... **CLC 23; BLC**
See also BW 1; CA 104; CANR 26;
DAM MULT; DLB 33

Bradley, John Ed(mund, Jr.)
1958-..................... **CLC 55**
See also CA 139

Bradley, Marion Zimmer 1930-..... **CLC 30**
See also AAYA 9; CA 57-60; CAAS 10;
CANR 7, 31, 51; DAM POP; DLB 8;
MTCW

Bradstreet, Anne
1612(?)-1672 ...... **LC 4, 30; DA; DAC;**
PC 10
See also CDALB 1640-1865; DAM MST,
POET; DLB 24

Brady, Joan 1939-............... **CLC 86**
See also CA 141

Bragg, Melvyn 1939-............. **CLC 10**
See also BEST 89:3; CA 57-60; CANR 10,
48; DLB 14

Braine, John (Gerard)
1922-1986 .... **CLC 1, 3, 41**
See also CA 1-4R; 120; CANR 1, 33;
CDBLB 1945-1960; DLB 15; DLBY 86;
MTCW

Brammer, William 1930(?)-1978 .... **CLC 31**
See also CA 77-80

Brancati, Vitaliano 1907-1954..... **TCLC 12**
See also CA 109

Brancato, Robin F(idler) 1936-..... **CLC 35**
See also AAYA 9; CA 69-72; CANR 11,
45; CLR 32; JRDA; SAAS 9; SATA 23

Brand, Max
See Faust, Frederick (Schiller)

Brand, Millen 1906-1980.......... **CLC 7**
See also CA 21-24R; 97-100

Branden, Barbara .... **CLC 44**
See also CA 148

Brandes, Georg (Morris Cohen)
1842-1927 .... **TCLC 10**
See also CA 105

Brandys, Kazimierz 1916-......... **CLC 62**

Branley, Franklyn M(ansfield)
1915-..................... **CLC 21**
See also CA 33-36R; CANR 14, 39;
CLR 13; MAICYA; SAAS 16; SATA 4,
68

Brathwaite, Edward Kamau 1930-... **CLC 11**
See also BW 2; CA 25-28R; CANR 11, 26,
47; DAM POET; DLB 125

Brautigan, Richard (Gary)
1935-1984 ..... **CLC 1, 3, 5, 9, 12, 34, 42**
See also CA 53-56; 113; CANR 34;
DAM NOV; DLB 2, 5; DLBY 80, 84;
MTCW; SATA 56

Braverman, Kate 1950-........... **CLC 67**
See also CA 89-92

Brecht, Bertolt
1898-1956 ...... **TCLC 1, 6, 13, 35; DA;**
DAB; DAC; DC 3; WLC
See also CA 104; 133; DAM DRAM, MST;
DLB 56, 124; MTCW

Brecht, Eugen Berthold Friedrich
See Brecht, Bertolt

Bremer, Fredrika 1801-1865 ..... **NCLC 11**

Brennan, Christopher John
1870-1932 .... **TCLC 17**
See also CA 117

Brennan, Maeve 1917-............. **CLC 5**
See also CA 81-84

Brentano, Clemens (Maria)
1778-1842 .... **NCLC 1**
See also DLB 90

Brent of Bin Bin
See Franklin, (Stella Maraia Sarah) Miles

Brenton, Howard 1942-........... **CLC 31**
See also CA 69-72; CANR 33; DLB 13;
MTCW

Breslin, James 1930-
See Breslin, Jimmy
See also CA 73-76; CANR 31; DAM NOV;
MTCW

Breslin, Jimmy .... **CLC 4, 43**
See also Breslin, James
See also AITN 1

Bresson, Robert 1901-............ **CLC 16**
See also CA 110; CANR 49

Breton, Andre
1896-1966 ..... **CLC 2, 9, 15, 54; PC 15**
See also CA 19-20; 25-28R; CANR 40;
CAP 2; DLB 65; MTCW

Breytenbach, Breyten 1939(?)- .. **CLC 23, 37**
See also CA 113; 129; DAM POET

Bridgers, Sue Ellen 1942- .... **CLC 26**
See also AAYA 8; CA 65-68; CANR 11,
36; CLR 18; DLB 52; JRDA; MAICYA;
SAAS 1; SATA 22

Bridges, Robert (Seymour)
1844-1930 .... **TCLC 1**
See also CA 104; CDBLB 1890-1914;
DAM POET; DLB 19, 98

Bridie, James .... **TCLC 3**
See also Mavor, Osborne Henry
See also DLB 10

Brin, David 1950-................ **CLC 34**
See also CA 102; CANR 24;
INT CANR-24; SATA 65

Buchner, (Karl) Georg
   1813-1837 . . . . **NCLC 26**

Buchwald, Art(hur)   1925- . . . . **CLC 33**
   See also AITN 1; CA 5-8R; CANR 21;
   MTCW; SATA 10

Buck, Pearl S(ydenstricker)
   1892-1973 . . . . **CLC 7, 11, 18; DA; DAB;**
                                                    DAC
   See also AITN 1; CA 1-4R; 41-44R;
   CANR 1, 34; DAM MST, NOV; DLB 9,
   102; MTCW; SATA 1, 25

Buckler, Ernest   1908-1984 . . . . **CLC 13; DAC**
   See also CA 11-12; 114; CAP 1;
   DAM MST; DLB 68; SATA 47

Buckley, Vincent (Thomas)
   1925-1988 . . . . **CLC 57**
   See also CA 101

Buckley, William F(rank), Jr.
   1925- . . . . **CLC 7, 18, 37**
   See also AITN 1; CA 1-4R; CANR 1, 24;
   DAM POP; DLB 137; DLBY 80;
   INT CANR-24; MTCW

Buechner, (Carl) Frederick
   1926- . . . . **CLC 2, 4, 6, 9**
   See also CA 13-16R; CANR 11, 39;
   DAM NOV; DLBY 80; INT CANR-11;
   MTCW

Buell, John (Edward)   1927- . . . . **CLC 10**
   See also CA 1-4R; DLB 53

Buero Vallejo, Antonio   1916- . . . **CLC 15, 46**
   See also CA 106; CANR 24, 49; HW;
   MTCW

Bufalino, Gesualdo   1920(?)- . . . . **CLC 74**

Bugayev, Boris Nikolayevich   1880-1934
   See Bely, Andrey
   See also CA 104

Bukowski, Charles
   1920-1994 . . . . **CLC 2, 5, 9, 41, 82**
   See also CA 17-20R; 144; CANR 40;
   DAM NOV, POET; DLB 5, 130; MTCW

Bulgakov, Mikhail (Afanas'evich)
   1891-1940 . . . . **TCLC 2, 16; SSC 18**
   See also CA 105; DAM DRAM, NOV

Bulgya, Alexander Alexandrovich
   1901-1956 . . . . **TCLC 53**
   See also Fadeyev, Alexander
   See also CA 117

Bullins, Ed   1935- . . **CLC 1, 5, 7; BLC; DC 6**
   See also BW 2; CA 49-52; CAAS 16;
   CANR 24, 46; DAM DRAM, MULT;
   DLB 7, 38; MTCW

Bulwer-Lytton, Edward (George Earle Lytton)
   1803-1873 . . . . **NCLC 1, 45**
   See also DLB 21

Bunin, Ivan Alexeyevich
   1870-1953 . . . . **TCLC 6; SSC 5**
   See also CA 104

Bunting, Basil   1900-1985 . . . . **CLC 10, 39, 47**
   See also CA 53-56; 115; CANR 7;
   DAM POET; DLB 20

Bunuel, Luis   1900-1983 . . **CLC 16, 80; HLC**
   See also CA 101; 110; CANR 32;
   DAM MULT; HW

Bunyan, John
   1628-1688 . . . . . . **LC 4; DA; DAB; DAC;**
                                                    WLC
   See also CDBLB 1660-1789; DAM MST;
   DLB 39

Burckhardt, Jacob (Christoph)
   1818-1897 . . . . **NCLC 49**

Burford, Eleanor
   See Hibbert, Eleanor Alice Burford

Burgess, Anthony
   CLC 1, 2, 4, 5, 8, 10, 13, 15, 22, 40, 62,
                                                    81; DAB
   See also Wilson, John (Anthony) Burgess
   See also AITN 1; CDBLB 1960 to Present;
   DLB 14

Burke, Edmund
   1729(?)-1797 . . . . **LC 7; DA; DAB; DAC;**
                                                    WLC
   See also DAM MST; DLB 104

Burke, Kenneth (Duva)
   1897-1993 . . . . **CLC 2, 24**
   See also CA 5-8R; 143; CANR 39; DLB 45,
   63; MTCW

Burke, Leda
   See Garnett, David

Burke, Ralph
   See Silverberg, Robert

Burke, Thomas   1886-1945 . . . . **TCLC 63**
   See also CA 113

Burney, Fanny   1752-1840 . . . . **NCLC 12, 54**
   See also DLB 39

Burns, Robert   1759-1796 . . . . **PC 6**
   See also CDBLB 1789-1832; DA; DAB;
   DAC; DAM MST, POET; DLB 109;
   WLC

Burns, Tex
   See L'Amour, Louis (Dearborn)

Burnshaw, Stanley   1906- . . . . . **CLC 3, 13, 44**
   See also CA 9-12R; DLB 48

Burr, Anne   1937- . . . . **CLC 6**
   See also CA 25-28R

Burroughs, Edgar Rice
   1875-1950 . . . . **TCLC 2, 32**
   See also AAYA 11; CA 104; 132;
   DAM NOV; DLB 8; MTCW; SATA 41

Burroughs, William S(eward)
   1914- . . . . **CLC 1, 2, 5, 15, 22, 42, 75;**
                                          DA; DAB; DAC; WLC
   See also AITN 2; CA 9-12R; CANR 20;
   DAM MST, NOV, POP; DLB 2, 8, 16,
   152; DLBY 81; MTCW

Burton, Richard F.   1821-1890 . . . . **NCLC 42**
   See also DLB 55

Busch, Frederick   1941- . . . **CLC 7, 10, 18, 47**
   See also CA 33-36R; CAAS 1; CANR 45;
   DLB 6

Bush, Ronald   1946- . . . . **CLC 34**
   See also CA 136

Bustos, F(rancisco)
   See Borges, Jorge Luis

Bustos Domecq, H(onorio)
   See Bioy Casares, Adolfo; Borges, Jorge
   Luis

Butler, Octavia E(stelle)   1947- . . . . . **CLC 38**
   See also BW 2; CA 73-76; CANR 12, 24,
   38; DAM MULT, POP; DLB 33;
   MTCW; SATA 84

Butler, Robert Olen (Jr.)   1945- . . . . . **CLC 81**
   See also CA 112; DAM POP; INT 112

Butler, Samuel   1612-1680 . . . . **LC 16**
   See also DLB 101, 126

Butler, Samuel
   1835-1902 . . . . . . **TCLC 1, 33; DA; DAB;**
                                                    DAC; WLC
   See also CA 143; CDBLB 1890-1914;
   DAM MST, NOV; DLB 18, 57

Butler, Walter C.
   See Faust, Frederick (Schiller)

Butor, Michel (Marie Francois)
   1926- . . . . **CLC 1, 3, 8, 11, 15**
   See also CA 9-12R; CANR 33; DLB 83;
   MTCW

Buzo, Alexander (John)   1944- . . . . . . **CLC 61**
   See also CA 97-100; CANR 17, 39

Buzzati, Dino   1906-1972 . . . . **CLC 36**
   See also CA 33-36R

Byars, Betsy (Cromer)   1928- . . . . **CLC 35**
   See also CA 33-36R; CANR 18, 36; CLR 1,
   16; DLB 52; INT CANR-18; JRDA;
   MAICYA; MTCW; SAAS 1; SATA 4,
   46, 80

Byatt, A(ntonia) S(usan Drabble)
   1936- . . . . **CLC 19, 65**
   See also CA 13-16R; CANR 13, 33, 50;
   DAM NOV, POP; DLB 14; MTCW

Byrne, David   1952- . . . . **CLC 26**
   See also CA 127

Byrne, John Keyes   1926-
   See Leonard, Hugh
   See also CA 102; INT 102

Byron, George Gordon (Noel)
   1788-1824 . . . . . **NCLC 2, 12; DA; DAB;**
                                                    DAC; WLC
   See also CDBLB 1789-1832; DAM MST,
   POET; DLB 96, 110

C. 3. 3.
   See Wilde, Oscar (Fingal O'Flahertie Wills)

Caballero, Fernan   1796-1877 . . . . . **NCLC 10**

Cabell, James Branch   1879-1958 . . . **TCLC 6**
   See also CA 105; DLB 9, 78

Cable, George Washington
   1844-1925 . . . . **TCLC 4; SSC 4**
   See also CA 104; DLB 12, 74; DLBD 13

Cabral de Melo Neto, Joao   1920- . . . **CLC 76**
   See also DAM MULT

Cabrera Infante, G(uillermo)
   1929- . . . . **CLC 5, 25, 45; HLC**
   See also CA 85-88; CANR 29;
   DAM MULT; DLB 113; HW; MTCW

Cade, Toni
   See Bambara, Toni Cade

Cadmus and Harmonia
   See Buchan, John

Caedmon   fl. 658-680 . . . . **CMLC 7**
   See also DLB 146

Caeiro, Alberto
   See Pessoa, Fernando (Antonio Nogueira)

Carver, Raymond
    1938-1988 . . . **CLC 22, 36, 53, 55; SSC 8**
    See also CA 33-36R; 126; CANR 17, 34;
    DAM NOV; DLB 130; DLBY 84, 88;
    MTCW

Cary, Elizabeth, Lady Falkland
    1585-1639 . . . . **LC 30**

Cary, (Arthur) Joyce (Lunel)
    1888-1957 . . . . **TCLC 1, 29**
    See also CA 104; CDBLB 1914-1945;
    DLB 15, 100

Casanova de Seingalt, Giovanni Jacopo
    1725-1798 . . . . **LC 13**

Casares, Adolfo Bioy
    See Bioy Casares, Adolfo

Casely-Hayford, J(oseph) E(phraim)
    1866-1930 . . . . **TCLC 24; BLC**
    See also BW 2; CA 123; DAM MULT

Casey, John (Dudley) 1939- . . . . **CLC 59**
    See also BEST 90:2; CA 69-72; CANR 23

Casey, Michael 1947- . . . . **CLC 2**
    See also CA 65-68; DLB 5

Casey, Patrick
    See Thurman, Wallace (Henry)

Casey, Warren (Peter) 1935-1988 . . . **CLC 12**
    See also CA 101; 127; INT 101

Casona, Alejandro . . . . **CLC 49**
    See also Alvarez, Alejandro Rodriguez

Cassavetes, John 1929-1989 . . . . **CLC 20**
    See also CA 85-88; 127

Cassill, R(onald) V(erlin) 1919- . . . **CLC 4, 23**
    See also CA 9-12R; CAAS 1; CANR 7, 45;
    DLB 6

Cassirer, Ernst 1874-1945 . . . . **TCLC 61**

Cassity, (Allen) Turner 1929- . . . . **CLC 6, 42**
    See also CA 17-20R; CAAS 8; CANR 11;
    DLB 105

Castaneda, Carlos 1931(?)- . . . . **CLC 12**
    See also CA 25-28R; CANR 32; HW;
    MTCW

Castedo, Elena 1937- . . . . **CLC 65**
    See also CA 132

Castedo-Ellerman, Elena
    See Castedo, Elena

Castellanos, Rosario
    1925-1974 . . . . **CLC 66; HLC**
    See also CA 131; 53-56; DAM MULT;
    DLB 113; HW

Castelvetro, Lodovico 1505-1571 . . . . . **LC 12**

Castiglione, Baldassare 1478-1529 . . . **LC 12**

Castle, Robert
    See Hamilton, Edmond

Castro, Guillen de 1569-1631 . . . . **LC 19**

Castro, Rosalia de 1837-1885 . . . . . **NCLC 3**
    See also DAM MULT

Cather, Willa
    See Cather, Willa Sibert

Cather, Willa Sibert
    1873-1947 . . . . **TCLC 1, 11, 31; DA;**
                          DAB; DAC; SSC 2; WLC
    See also CA 104; 128; CDALB 1865-1917;
    DAM MST, NOV; DLB 9, 54, 78;
    DLBD 1; MTCW; SATA 30

Catton, (Charles) Bruce
    1899-1978 . . . . **CLC 35**
    See also AITN 1; CA 5-8R; 81-84;
    CANR 7; DLB 17; SATA 2;
    SATA-Obit 24

Catullus c. 84B.C.-c. 54B.C. . . . . . **CMLC 18**

Cauldwell, Frank
    See King, Francis (Henry)

Caunitz, William J. 1933- . . . . **CLC 34**
    See also BEST 89:3; CA 125; 130; INT 130

Causley, Charles (Stanley) 1917- . . . . **CLC 7**
    See also CA 9-12R; CANR 5, 35; CLR 30;
    DLB 27; MTCW; SATA 3, 66

Caute, David 1936- . . . . **CLC 29**
    See also CA 1-4R; CAAS 4; CANR 1, 33;
    DAM NOV; DLB 14

Cavafy, C(onstantine) P(eter)
    1863-1933 . . . . **TCLC 2, 7**
    See also Kavafis, Konstantinos Petrou
    See also CA 148; DAM POET

Cavallo, Evelyn
    See Spark, Muriel (Sarah)

Cavanna, Betty . . . . **CLC 12**
    See also Harrison, Elizabeth Cavanna
    See also JRDA; MAICYA; SAAS 4;
    SATA 1, 30

Cavendish, Margaret Lucas
    1623-1673 . . . . **LC 30**
    See also DLB 131

Caxton, William 1421(?)-1491(?) . . . . . **LC 17**

Cayrol, Jean 1911- . . . . **CLC 11**
    See also CA 89-92; DLB 83

Cela, Camilo Jose
    1916- . . . . **CLC 4, 13, 59; HLC**
    See also BEST 90:2; CA 21-24R; CAAS 10;
    CANR 21, 32; DAM MULT; DLBY 89;
    HW; MTCW

Celan, Paul . . . . . . **CLC 10, 19, 53, 82; PC 10**
    See also Antschel, Paul
    See also DLB 69

Celine, Louis-Ferdinand
    . . . . **CLC 1, 3, 4, 7, 9, 15, 47**
    See also Destouches, Louis-Ferdinand
    See also DLB 72

Cellini, Benvenuto 1500-1571 . . . . **LC 7**

Cendrars, Blaise . . . . **CLC 18**
    See also Sauser-Hall, Frederic

Cernuda (y Bidon), Luis
    1902-1963 . . . . **CLC 54**
    See also CA 131; 89-92; DAM POET;
    DLB 134; HW

Cervantes (Saavedra), Miguel de
    1547-1616 . . . . **LC 6, 23; DA; DAB;**
                          DAC; SSC 12; WLC
    See also DAM MST, NOV

Cesaire, Aime (Fernand)
    1913- . . . . **CLC 19, 32; BLC**
    See also BW 2; CA 65-68; CANR 24, 43;
    DAM MULT, POET; MTCW

Chabon, Michael 1965(?)- . . . . **CLC 55**
    See also CA 139

Chabrol, Claude 1930- . . . . **CLC 16**
    See also CA 110

Challans, Mary 1905-1983
    See Renault, Mary
    See also CA 81-84; 111; SATA 23;
    SATA-Obit 36

Challis, George
    See Faust, Frederick (Schiller)

Chambers, Aidan 1934- . . . . **CLC 35**
    See also CA 25-28R; CANR 12, 31; JRDA;
    MAICYA; SAAS 12; SATA 1, 69

Chambers, James 1948-
    See Cliff, Jimmy
    See also CA 124

Chambers, Jessie
    See Lawrence, D(avid) H(erbert Richards)

Chambers, Robert W. 1865-1933 . . . **TCLC 41**

Chandler, Raymond (Thornton)
    1888-1959 . . . . **TCLC 1, 7; SSC 23**
    See also CA 104; 129; CDALB 1929-1941;
    DLBD 6; MTCW

Chang, Jung 1952- . . . . **CLC 71**
    See also CA 142

Channing, William Ellery
    1780-1842 . . . . **NCLC 17**
    See also DLB 1, 59

Chaplin, Charles Spencer
    1889-1977 . . . . **CLC 16**
    See also Chaplin, Charlie
    See also CA 81-84; 73-76

Chaplin, Charlie
    See Chaplin, Charles Spencer
    See also DLB 44

Chapman, George 1559(?)-1634 . . . . . . **LC 22**
    See also DAM DRAM; DLB 62, 121

Chapman, Graham 1941-1989 . . . . . . **CLC 21**
    See also Monty Python
    See also CA 116; 129; CANR 35

Chapman, John Jay 1862-1933 . . . . . **TCLC 7**
    See also CA 104

Chapman, Walker
    See Silverberg, Robert

Chappell, Fred (Davis) 1936- . . . . **CLC 40, 78**
    See also CA 5-8R; CAAS 4; CANR 8, 33;
    DLB 6, 105

Char, Rene(-Emile)
    1907-1988 . . . . **CLC 9, 11, 14, 55**
    See also CA 13-16R; 124; CANR 32;
    DAM POET; MTCW

Charby, Jay
    See Ellison, Harlan (Jay)

Chardin, Pierre Teilhard de
    See Teilhard de Chardin, (Marie Joseph)
    Pierre

Charles I 1600-1649 . . . . **LC 13**

Charyn, Jerome 1937- . . . . **CLC 5, 8, 18**
    See also CA 5-8R; CAAS 1; CANR 7;
    DLBY 83; MTCW

Chase, Mary (Coyle) 1907-1981 . . . . . . **DC 1**
    See also CA 77-80; 105; SATA 17;
    SATA-Obit 29

Chase, Mary Ellen 1887-1973 . . . . **CLC 2**
    See also CA 13-16; 41-44R; CAP 1;
    SATA 10

Chase, Nicholas
    See Hyde, Anthony

Chateaubriand, Francois Rene de
　1768-1848 . . . . **NCLC 3**
　See also DLB 119

Chatterje, Sarat Chandra　1876-1936(?)
　See Chatterji, Saratchandra
　See also CA 109

Chatterji, Bankim Chandra
　1838-1894 . . . . **NCLC 19**

Chatterji, Saratchandra . . . . **TCLC 13**
　See also Chatterje, Sarat Chandra

Chatterton, Thomas　1752-1770 . . . . **LC 3**
　See also DAM POET; DLB 109

Chatwin, (Charles) Bruce
　1940-1989 . . . . **CLC 28, 57, 59**
　See also AAYA 4; BEST 90:1; CA 85-88;
　127; DAM POP

Chaucer, Daniel
　See Ford, Ford Madox

Chaucer, Geoffrey
　1340(?)-1400 . . . **LC 17; DA; DAB; DAC**
　See also CDBLB Before 1660; DAM MST,
　POET; DLB 146

Chaviaras, Strates　1935-
　See Haviaras, Stratis
　See also CA 105

Chayefsky, Paddy . . . . **CLC 23**
　See also Chayefsky, Sidney
　See also DLB 7, 44; DLBY 81

Chayefsky, Sidney　1923-1981
　See Chayefsky, Paddy
　See also CA 9-12R; 104; CANR 18;
　DAM DRAM

Chedid, Andree　1920- . . . . **CLC 47**
　See also CA 145

Cheever, John
　1912-1982 . . . . . . **CLC 3, 7, 8, 11, 15, 25,
　　　　　　　　　　　　64; DA; DAB; DAC; SSC 1; WLC**
　See also CA 5-8R; 106; CABS 1; CANR 5,
　27; CDALB 1941-1968; DAM MST,
　NOV, POP; DLB 2, 102; DLBY 80, 82;
　INT CANR-5; MTCW

Cheever, Susan　1943- . . . . **CLC 18, 48**
　See also CA 103; CANR 27, 51; DLBY 82;
　INT CANR-27

Chekhonte, Antosha
　See Chekhov, Anton (Pavlovich)

Chekhov, Anton (Pavlovich)
　1860-1904 . . . . . **TCLC 3, 10, 31, 55; DA;
　　　　　　　　　　　　DAB; DAC; SSC 2; WLC**
　See also CA 104; 124; DAM DRAM, MST

Chernyshevsky, Nikolay Gavrilovich
　1828-1889 . . . . **NCLC 1**

Cherry, Carolyn Janice　1942-
　See Cherryh, C. J.
　See also CA 65-68; CANR 10

Cherryh, C. J. . . . . **CLC 35**
　See also Cherry, Carolyn Janice
　See also DLBY 80

Chesnutt, Charles W(addell)
　1858-1932 . . . . **TCLC 5, 39; BLC; SSC 7**
　See also BW 1; CA 106; 125; DAM MULT;
　DLB 12, 50, 78; MTCW

Chester, Alfred　1929(?)-1971 . . . . **CLC 49**
　See also CA 33-36R; DLB 130

Chesterton, G(ilbert) K(eith)
　1874-1936 . . . . **TCLC 1, 6; SSC 1**
　See also CA 104; 132; CDBLB 1914-1945;
　DAM NOV, POET; DLB 10, 19, 34, 70,
　98, 149; MTCW; SATA 27

Chiang Pin-chin　1904-1986
　See Ding Ling
　See also CA 118

Ch'ien Chung-shu　1910- . . . . **CLC 22**
　See also CA 130; MTCW

Child, L. Maria
　See Child, Lydia Maria

Child, Lydia Maria　1802-1880 . . . . **NCLC 6**
　See also DLB 1, 74; SATA 67

Child, Mrs.
　See Child, Lydia Maria

Child, Philip　1898-1978 . . . . **CLC 19, 68**
　See also CA 13-14; CAP 1; SATA 47

Childress, Alice
　1920-1994 . . **CLC 12, 15, 86; BLC; DC 4**
　See also AAYA 8; BW 2; CA 45-48; 146;
　CANR 3, 27, 50; CLR 14; DAM DRAM,
　MULT, NOV; DLB 7, 38; JRDA;
　MAICYA; MTCW; SATA 7, 48, 81

Chislett, (Margaret) Anne　1943- . . . . **CLC 34**

Chitty, Thomas Willes　1926- . . . . **CLC 11**
　See also Hinde, Thomas
　See also CA 5-8R

Chivers, Thomas Holley
　1809-1858 . . . . **NCLC 49**
　See also DLB 3

Chomette, Rene Lucien　1898-1981
　See Clair, Rene
　See also CA 103

Chopin, Kate
　. . . . . **TCLC 5, 14; DA; DAB; SSC 8**
　See also Chopin, Katherine
　See also CDALB 1865-1917; DLB 12, 78

Chopin, Katherine　1851-1904
　See Chopin, Kate
　See also CA 104; 122; DAC; DAM MST,
　NOV

Chretien de Troyes
　c. 12th cent. - . . . . **CMLC 10**

Christie
　See Ichikawa, Kon

Christie, Agatha (Mary Clarissa)
　1890-1976 . . . . . . **CLC 1, 6, 8, 12, 39, 48;
　　　　　　　　　　　　　　　　　DAB; DAC**
　See also AAYA 9; AITN 1, 2; CA 17-20R;
　61-64; CANR 10, 37; CDBLB 1914-1945;
　DAM NOV; DLB 13, 77; MTCW;
　SATA 36

Christie, (Ann) Philippa
　See Pearce, Philippa
　See also CA 5-8R; CANR 4

Christine de Pizan　1365(?)-1431(?) . . . . **LC 9**

Chubb, Elmer
　See Masters, Edgar Lee

Chulkov, Mikhail Dmitrievich
　1743-1792 . . . . **LC 2**
　See also DLB 150

Churchill, Caryl　1938- . . . **CLC 31, 55; DC 5**
　See also CA 102; CANR 22, 46; DLB 13;
　MTCW

Churchill, Charles　1731-1764 . . . . **LC 3**
　See also DLB 109

Chute, Carolyn　1947- . . . . **CLC 39**
　See also CA 123

Ciardi, John (Anthony)
　1916-1986 . . . . **CLC 10, 40, 44**
　See also CA 5-8R; 118; CAAS 2; CANR 5,
　33; CLR 19; DAM POET; DLB 5;
　DLBY 86; INT CANR-5; MAICYA;
　MTCW; SATA 1, 65; SATA-Obit 46

Cicero, Marcus Tullius
　106B.C.-43B.C. . . . . **CMLC 3**

Cimino, Michael　1943- . . . . **CLC 16**
　See also CA 105

Cioran, E(mil) M.　1911-1995 . . . . **CLC 64**
　See also CA 25-28R; 149

Cisneros, Sandra　1954- . . . . . . **CLC 69; HLC**
　See also AAYA 9; CA 131; DAM MULT;
　DLB 122, 152; HW

Cixous, Helene　1937- . . . . **CLC 92**
　See also CA 126; DLB 83; MTCW

Clair, Rene . . . . **CLC 20**
　See also Chomette, Rene Lucien

Clampitt, Amy　1920-1994 . . . . **CLC 32**
　See also CA 110; 146; CANR 29; DLB 105

Clancy, Thomas L., Jr.　1947-
　See Clancy, Tom
　See also CA 125; 131; INT 131; MTCW

Clancy, Tom . . . . **CLC 45**
　See also Clancy, Thomas L., Jr.
　See also AAYA 9; BEST 89:1, 90:1;
　DAM NOV, POP

Clare, John　1793-1864 . . . . . . **NCLC 9; DAB**
　See also DAM POET; DLB 55, 96

Clarin
　See Alas (y Urena), Leopoldo (Enrique
　Garcia)

Clark, Al C.
　See Goines, Donald

Clark, (Robert) Brian　1932- . . . . **CLC 29**
　See also CA 41-44R

Clark, Curt
　See Westlake, Donald E(dwin)

Clark, Eleanor　1913- . . . . **CLC 5, 19**
　See also CA 9-12R; CANR 41; DLB 6

Clark, J. P.
　See Clark, John Pepper
　See also DLB 117

Clark, John Pepper
　1935- . . . . **CLC 38; BLC; DC 5**
　See also Clark, J. P.
　See also BW 1; CA 65-68; CANR 16;
　DAM DRAM, MULT

Clark, M. R.
　See Clark, Mavis Thorpe

Clark, Mavis Thorpe　1909- . . . . **CLC 12**
　See also CA 57-60; CANR 8, 37; CLR 30;
　MAICYA; SAAS 5; SATA 8, 74

Clark, Walter Van Tilburg
　1909-1971 . . . . **CLC 28**
　See also CA 9-12R; 33-36R; DLB 9;
　SATA 8

Clarke, Arthur C(harles)
1917- . . . . . **CLC 1, 4, 13, 18, 35; SSC 3**
See also AAYA 4; CA 1-4R; CANR 2, 28;
DAM POP; JRDA; MAICYA; MTCW;
SATA 13, 70

Clarke, Austin 1896-1974 . . . . **CLC 6, 9**
See also CA 29-32; 49-52; CAP 2;
DAM POET; DLB 10, 20

Clarke, Austin C(hesterfield)
1934- . . . . **CLC 8, 53; BLC; DAC**
See also BW 1; CA 25-28R; CAAS 16;
CANR 14, 32; DAM MULT; DLB 53,
125

Clarke, Gillian 1937- . . . . **CLC 61**
See also CA 106; DLB 40

Clarke, Marcus (Andrew Hislop)
1846-1881 . . . . **NCLC 19**

Clarke, Shirley 1925- . . . . **CLC 16**

Clash, The
See Headon, (Nicky) Topper; Jones, Mick;
Simonon, Paul; Strummer, Joe

Claudel, Paul (Louis Charles Marie)
1868-1955 . . . . **TCLC 2, 10**
See also CA 104

Clavell, James (duMaresq)
1925-1994 . . . . **CLC 6, 25, 87**
See also CA 25-28R; 146; CANR 26, 48;
DAM NOV, POP; MTCW

Cleaver, (Leroy) Eldridge
1935- . . . . **CLC 30; BLC**
See also BW 1; CA 21-24R; CANR 16;
DAM MULT

Cleese, John (Marwood) 1939- . . . . . **CLC 21**
See also Monty Python
See also CA 112; 116; CANR 35; MTCW

Cleishbotham, Jebediah
See Scott, Walter

Cleland, John 1710-1789 . . . . **LC 2**
See also DLB 39

Clemens, Samuel Langhorne 1835-1910
See Twain, Mark
See also CA 104; 135; CDALB 1865-1917;
DA; DAB; DAC; DAM MST, NOV;
DLB 11, 12, 23, 64, 74; JRDA;
MAICYA; YABC 2

Cleophil
See Congreve, William

Clerihew, E.
See Bentley, E(dmund) C(lerihew)

Clerk, N. W.
See Lewis, C(live) S(taples)

Cliff, Jimmy . . . . **CLC 21**
See also Chambers, James

Clifton, (Thelma) Lucille
1936- . . . . **CLC 19, 66; BLC**
See also BW 2; CA 49-52; CANR 2, 24, 42;
CLR 5; DAM MULT, POET; DLB 5, 41;
MAICYA; MTCW; SATA 20, 69

Clinton, Dirk
See Silverberg, Robert

Clough, Arthur Hugh 1819-1861 . . **NCLC 27**
See also DLB 32

Clutha, Janet Paterson Frame 1924-
See Frame, Janet
See also CA 1-4R; CANR 2, 36; MTCW

Clyne, Terence
See Blatty, William Peter

Cobalt, Martin
See Mayne, William (James Carter)

Cobbett, William 1763-1835 . . . . . **NCLC 49**
See also DLB 43, 107, 158

Coburn, D(onald) L(ee) 1938- . . . . . . **CLC 10**
See also CA 89-92

Cocteau, Jean (Maurice Eugene Clement)
1889-1963 . . . . **CLC 1, 8, 15, 16, 43; DA;
DAB; DAC; WLC**
See also CA 25-28; CANR 40; CAP 2;
DAM DRAM, MST, NOV; DLB 65;
MTCW

Codrescu, Andrei 1946- . . . . **CLC 46**
See also CA 33-36R; CAAS 19; CANR 13,
34; DAM POET

Coe, Max
See Bourne, Randolph S(illiman)

Coe, Tucker
See Westlake, Donald E(dwin)

Coetzee, J(ohn) M(ichael)
1940- . . . . **CLC 23, 33, 66**
See also CA 77-80; CANR 41; DAM NOV;
MTCW

Coffey, Brian
See Koontz, Dean R(ay)

Cohan, George M. 1878-1942 . . . . . **TCLC 60**

Cohen, Arthur A(llen)
1928-1986 . . . . **CLC 7, 31**
See also CA 1-4R; 120; CANR 1, 17, 42;
DLB 28

Cohen, Leonard (Norman)
1934- . . . . **CLC 3, 38; DAC**
See also CA 21-24R; CANR 14;
DAM MST; DLB 53; MTCW

Cohen, Matt 1942- . . . . **CLC 19; DAC**
See also CA 61-64; CAAS 18; CANR 40;
DLB 53

Cohen-Solal, Annie 19(?)- . . . . **CLC 50**

Colegate, Isabel 1931- . . . . **CLC 36**
See also CA 17-20R; CANR 8, 22; DLB 14;
INT CANR-22; MTCW

Coleman, Emmett
See Reed, Ishmael

Coleridge, Samuel Taylor
1772-1834 . . . . . **NCLC 9, 54; DA; DAB;
DAC; PC 11; WLC**
See also CDBLB 1789-1832; DAM MST,
POET; DLB 93, 107

Coleridge, Sara 1802-1852 . . . . . . **NCLC 31**

Coles, Don 1928- . . . . **CLC 46**
See also CA 115; CANR 38

Colette, (Sidonie-Gabrielle)
1873-1954 . . . . . . **TCLC 1, 5, 16; SSC 10**
See also CA 104; 131; DAM NOV; DLB 65;
MTCW

Collett, (Jacobine) Camilla (Wergeland)
1813-1895 . . . . **NCLC 22**

Collier, Christopher 1930- . . . . **CLC 30**
See also AAYA 13; CA 33-36R; CANR 13,
33; JRDA; MAICYA; SATA 16, 70

Collier, James L(incoln) 1928- . . . . . **CLC 30**
See also AAYA 13; CA 9-12R; CANR 4,
33; CLR 3; DAM POP; JRDA;
MAICYA; SAAS 21; SATA 8, 70

Collier, Jeremy 1650-1726 . . . . **LC 6**

Collier, John 1901-1980 . . . . **SSC 19**
See also CA 65-68; 97-100; CANR 10;
DLB 77

Collins, Hunt
See Hunter, Evan

Collins, Linda 1931- . . . . **CLC 44**
See also CA 125

Collins, (William) Wilkie
1824-1889 . . . . **NCLC 1, 18**
See also CDBLB 1832-1890; DLB 18, 70,
159

Collins, William 1721-1759 . . . . **LC 4**
See also DAM POET; DLB 109

Collodi, Carlo 1826-1890 . . . . **NCLC 54**
See also Lorenzini, Carlo
See also CLR 5

Colman, George
See Glassco, John

Colt, Winchester Remington
See Hubbard, L(afayette) Ron(ald)

Colter, Cyrus 1910- . . . . **CLC 58**
See also BW 1; CA 65-68; CANR 10;
DLB 33

Colton, James
See Hansen, Joseph

Colum, Padraic 1881-1972 . . . . **CLC 28**
See also CA 73-76; 33-36R; CANR 35;
CLR 36; MAICYA; MTCW; SATA 15

Colvin, James
See Moorcock, Michael (John)

Colwin, Laurie (E.)
1944-1992 . . . . **CLC 5, 13, 23, 84**
See also CA 89-92; 139; CANR 20, 46;
DLBY 80; MTCW

Comfort, Alex(ander) 1920- . . . . **CLC 7**
See also CA 1-4R; CANR 1, 45; DAM POP

Comfort, Montgomery
See Campbell, (John) Ramsey

Compton-Burnett, I(vy)
1884(?)-1969 . . . . . . **CLC 1, 3, 10, 15, 34**
See also CA 1-4R; 25-28R; CANR 4;
DAM NOV; DLB 36; MTCW

Comstock, Anthony 1844-1915 . . . . **TCLC 13**
See also CA 110

Comte, Auguste 1798-1857 . . . . . . **NCLC 54**

Conan Doyle, Arthur
See Doyle, Arthur Conan

Conde, Maryse 1937- . . . . **CLC 52, 92**
See also Boucolon, Maryse
See also BW 2; DAM MULT

Condillac, Etienne Bonnot de
1714-1780 . . . . **LC 26**

Condon, Richard (Thomas)
1915- . . . . **CLC 4, 6, 8, 10, 45**
See also BEST 90:3; CA 1-4R; CAAS 1;
CANR 2, 23; DAM NOV;
INT CANR-23; MTCW

Dixon, Stephen 1936-..... **CLC 52; SSC 16**
See also CA 89-92; CANR 17, 40; DLB 130

Dobell, Sydney Thompson
1824-1874 .... **NCLC 43**
See also DLB 32

Doblin, Alfred .... **TCLC 13**
See also Doeblin, Alfred

Dobrolyubov, Nikolai Alexandrovich
1836-1861 .... **NCLC 5**

Dobyns, Stephen 1941-............ **CLC 37**
See also CA 45-48; CANR 2, 18

Doctorow, E(dgar) L(aurence)
1931- ..... **CLC 6, 11, 15, 18, 37, 44, 65**
See also AITN 2; BEST 89:3; CA 45-48;
CANR 2, 33, 51; CDALB 1968-1988;
DAM NOV, POP; DLB 2, 28; DLBY 80;
MTCW

Dodgson, Charles Lutwidge 1832-1898
See Carroll, Lewis
See also CLR 2; DA; DAB; DAC;
DAM MST, NOV, POET; MAICYA;
YABC 2

Dodson, Owen (Vincent)
1914-1983 .... **CLC 79; BLC**
See also BW 1; CA 65-68; 110; CANR 24;
DAM MULT; DLB 76

Doeblin, Alfred 1878-1957....... **TCLC 13**
See also Doblin, Alfred
See also CA 110; 141; DLB 66

Doerr, Harriet 1910- .... **CLC 34**
See also CA 117; 122; CANR 47; INT 122

Domecq, H(onorio) Bustos
See Bioy Casares, Adolfo; Borges, Jorge
Luis

Domini, Rey
See Lorde, Audre (Geraldine)

Dominique
See Proust, (Valentin-Louis-George-Eugene-)
Marcel

Don, A
See Stephen, Leslie

Donaldson, Stephen R. 1947-....... **CLC 46**
See also CA 89-92; CANR 13; DAM POP;
INT CANR-13

Donleavy, J(ames) P(atrick)
1926- .... **CLC 1, 4, 6, 10, 45**
See also AITN 2; CA 9-12R; CANR 24, 49;
DLB 6; INT CANR-24; MTCW

Donne, John
1572-1631 .... **LC 10, 24; DA; DAB;
DAC; PC 1**
See also CDBLB Before 1660; DAM MST,
POET; DLB 121, 151

Donnell, David 1939(?)-........... **CLC 34**

Donoghue, P. S.
See Hunt, E(verette) Howard, (Jr.)

Donoso (Yanez), Jose
1924- .... **CLC 4, 8, 11, 32; HLC**
See also CA 81-84; CANR 32;
DAM MULT; DLB 113; HW; MTCW

Donovan, John 1928-1992 .... **CLC 35**
See also CA 97-100; 137; CLR 3;
MAICYA; SATA 72; SATA-Brief 29

Don Roberto
See Cunninghame Graham, R(obert)
B(ontine)

Doolittle, Hilda
1886-1961 ..... **CLC 3, 8, 14, 31, 34, 73;
DA; DAC; PC 5; WLC**
See also H. D.
See also CA 97-100; CANR 35; DAM MST,
POET; DLB 4, 45; MTCW

Dorfman, Ariel 1942-.... **CLC 48, 77; HLC**
See also CA 124; 130; DAM MULT; HW;
INT 130

Dorn, Edward (Merton) 1929-... **CLC 10, 18**
See also CA 93-96; CANR 42; DLB 5;
INT 93-96

Dorsan, Luc
See Simenon, Georges (Jacques Christian)

Dorsange, Jean
See Simenon, Georges (Jacques Christian)

Dos Passos, John (Roderigo)
1896-1970 ...... **CLC 1, 4, 8, 11, 15, 25,
34, 82; DA; DAB; DAC; WLC**
See also CA 1-4R; 29-32R; CANR 3;
CDALB 1929-1941; DAM MST, NOV;
DLB 4, 9; DLBD 1; MTCW

Dossage, Jean
See Simenon, Georges (Jacques Christian)

Dostoevsky, Fedor Mikhailovich
1821-1881 ...... **NCLC 2, 7, 21, 33, 43;
DA; DAB; DAC; SSC 2; WLC**
See also DAM MST, NOV

Doughty, Charles M(ontagu)
1843-1926 .... **TCLC 27**
See also CA 115; DLB 19, 57

Douglas, Ellen................... **CLC 73**
See also Haxton, Josephine Ayres;
Williamson, Ellen Douglas

Douglas, Gavin 1475(?)-1522........ **LC 20**

Douglas, Keith 1920-1944 .... **TCLC 40**
See also DLB 27

Douglas, Leonard
See Bradbury, Ray (Douglas)

Douglas, Michael
See Crichton, (John) Michael

Douglass, Frederick
1817(?)-1895 .... **NCLC 7, 55; BLC; DA;
DAC; WLC**
See also CDALB 1640-1865; DAM MST,
MULT; DLB 1, 43, 50, 79; SATA 29

Dourado, (Waldomiro Freitas) Autran
1926- .... **CLC 23, 60**
See also CA 25-28R; CANR 34

Dourado, Waldomiro Autran
See Dourado, (Waldomiro Freitas) Autran

Dove, Rita (Frances)
1952- .... **CLC 50, 81; PC 6**
See also BW 2; CA 109; CAAS 19;
CANR 27, 42; DAM MULT, POET;
DLB 120

Dowell, Coleman 1925-1985....... **CLC 60**
See also CA 25-28R; 117; CANR 10;
DLB 130

Dowson, Ernest (Christopher)
1867-1900 .... **TCLC 4**
See also CA 105; 150; DLB 19, 135

Doyle, A. Conan
See Doyle, Arthur Conan

Doyle, Arthur Conan
1859-1930 .... **TCLC 7; DA; DAB;
DAC; SSC 12; WLC**
See also AAYA 14; CA 104; 122;
CDBLB 1890-1914; DAM MST, NOV;
DLB 18, 70, 156; MTCW; SATA 24

Doyle, Conan
See Doyle, Arthur Conan

Doyle, John
See Graves, Robert (von Ranke)

Doyle, Roddy 1958(?)-............ **CLC 81**
See also AAYA 14; CA 143

Doyle, Sir A. Conan
See Doyle, Arthur Conan

Doyle, Sir Arthur Conan
See Doyle, Arthur Conan

Dr. A
See Asimov, Isaac; Silverstein, Alvin

Drabble, Margaret
1939- .... **CLC 2, 3, 5, 8, 10, 22, 53;
DAB; DAC**
See also CA 13-16R; CANR 18, 35;
CDBLB 1960 to Present; DAM MST,
NOV, POP; DLB 14, 155; MTCW;
SATA 48

Drapier, M. B.
See Swift, Jonathan

Drayham, James
See Mencken, H(enry) L(ouis)

Drayton, Michael 1563-1631........ **LC 8**

Dreadstone, Carl
See Campbell, (John) Ramsey

Dreiser, Theodore (Herman Albert)
1871-1945 .... **TCLC 10, 18, 35; DA;
DAC; WLC**
See also CA 106; 132; CDALB 1865-1917;
DAM MST, NOV; DLB 9, 12, 102, 137;
DLBD 1; MTCW

Drexler, Rosalyn 1926- .... **CLC 2, 6**
See also CA 81-84

Dreyer, Carl Theodor 1889-1968.... **CLC 16**
See also CA 116

Drieu la Rochelle, Pierre(-Eugene)
1893-1945 .... **TCLC 21**
See also CA 117; DLB 72

Drinkwater, John 1882-1937...... **TCLC 57**
See also CA 109; 149; DLB 10, 19, 149

Drop Shot
See Cable, George Washington

Droste-Hulshoff, Annette Freiin von
1797-1848 .... **NCLC 3**
See also DLB 133

Drummond, Walter
See Silverberg, Robert

Drummond, William Henry
1854-1907 .... **TCLC 25**
See also DLB 92

Drummond de Andrade, Carlos
1902-1987 .... **CLC 18**
See also Andrade, Carlos Drummond de
See also CA 132; 123

Drury, Allen (Stuart) 1918-........ **CLC 37**
See also CA 57-60; CANR 18;
INT CANR-18

Dryden, John
1631-1700 .... **LC 3, 21; DA; DAB;
DAC; DC 3; WLC**
See also CDBLB 1660-1789; DAM DRAM,
MST, POET; DLB 80, 101, 131

Duberman, Martin 1930-.......... **CLC 8**
See also CA 1-4R; CANR 2

Dubie, Norman (Evans) 1945-...... **CLC 36**
See also CA 69-72; CANR 12; DLB 120

Du Bois, W(illiam) E(dward) B(urghardt)
1868-1963 ...... **CLC 1, 2, 13, 64; BLC;
DA; DAC; WLC**
See also BW 1; CA 85-88; CANR 34;
CDALB 1865-1917; DAM MST, MULT,
NOV; DLB 47, 50, 91; MTCW; SATA 42

Dubus, Andre 1936-... **CLC 13, 36; SSC 15**
See also CA 21-24R; CANR 17; DLB 130;
INT CANR-17

Duca Minimo
See D'Annunzio, Gabriele

Ducharme, Rejean 1941-.......... **CLC 74**
See also DLB 60

Duclos, Charles Pinot 1704-1772 ..... **LC 1**

Dudek, Louis 1918- .... **CLC 11, 19**
See also CA 45-48; CAAS 14; CANR 1;
DLB 88

Duerrenmatt, Friedrich
1921-1990 ...... **CLC 1, 4, 8, 11, 15, 43**
See also CA 17-20R; CANR 33;
DAM DRAM; DLB 69, 124; MTCW

Duffy, Bruce (?)-................. **CLC 50**

Duffy, Maureen 1933-............ **CLC 37**
See also CA 25-28R; CANR 33; DLB 14;
MTCW

Dugan, Alan 1923-............. **CLC 2, 6**
See also CA 81-84; DLB 5

du Gard, Roger Martin
See Martin du Gard, Roger

Duhamel, Georges 1884-1966 .... **CLC 8**
See also CA 81-84; 25-28R; CANR 35;
DLB 65; MTCW

Dujardin, Edouard (Emile Louis)
1861-1949 .... **TCLC 13**
See also CA 109; DLB 123

Dumas, Alexandre (Davy de la Pailleterie)
1802-1870 ...... **NCLC 11; DA; DAB;
DAC; WLC**
See also DAM MST, NOV; DLB 119;
SATA 18

Dumas, Alexandre
1824-1895 .... **NCLC 9; DC 1**

Dumas, Claudine
See Malzberg, Barry N(athaniel)

Dumas, Henry L. 1934-1968 ..... **CLC 6, 62**
See also BW 1; CA 85-88; DLB 41

du Maurier, Daphne
1907-1989 .... **CLC 6, 11, 59; DAB;
DAC; SSC 18**
See also CA 5-8R; 128; CANR 6;
DAM MST, POP; MTCW; SATA 27;
SATA-Obit 60

Dunbar, Paul Laurence
1872-1906 ...... **TCLC 2, 12; BLC; DA;
DAC; PC 5; SSC 8; WLC**
See also BW 1; CA 104; 124;
CDALB 1865-1917; DAM MST, MULT,
POET; DLB 50, 54, 78; SATA 34

Dunbar, William 1460(?)-1530(?) .... **LC 20**
See also DLB 132, 146

Duncan, Lois 1934-.............. **CLC 26**
See also AAYA 4; CA 1-4R; CANR 2, 23,
36; CLR 29; JRDA; MAICYA; SAAS 2;
SATA 1, 36, 75

Duncan, Robert (Edward)
1919-1988 .... **CLC 1, 2, 4, 7, 15, 41, 55;
PC 2**
See also CA 9-12R; 124; CANR 28;
DAM POET; DLB 5, 16; MTCW

Duncan, Sara Jeannette
1861-1922 .... **TCLC 60**
See also DLB 92

Dunlap, William 1766-1839 ...... **NCLC 2**
See also DLB 30, 37, 59

Dunn, Douglas (Eaglesham)
1942- .... **CLC 6, 40**
See also CA 45-48; CANR 2, 33; DLB 40;
MTCW

Dunn, Katherine (Karen) 1945-..... **CLC 71**
See also CA 33-36R

Dunn, Stephen 1939- .... **CLC 36**
See also CA 33-36R; CANR 12, 48;
DLB 105

Dunne, Finley Peter 1867-1936.... **TCLC 28**
See also CA 108; DLB 11, 23

Dunne, John Gregory 1932-........ **CLC 28**
See also CA 25-28R; CANR 14, 50;
DLBY 80

**Dunsany, Edward John Moreton Drax
Plunkett** 1878-1957
See Dunsany, Lord
See also CA 104; 148; DLB 10

Dunsany, Lord................. **TCLC 2, 59**
See also Dunsany, Edward John Moreton
Drax Plunkett
See also DLB 77, 153, 156

du Perry, Jean
See Simenon, Georges (Jacques Christian)

Durang, Christopher (Ferdinand)
1949- .... **CLC 27, 38**
See also CA 105; CANR 50

Duras, Marguerite
1914- ...... **CLC 3, 6, 11, 20, 34, 40, 68**
See also CA 25-28R; CANR 50; DLB 83;
MTCW

Durban, (Rosa) Pam 1947-........ **CLC 39**
See also CA 123

Durcan, Paul 1944-........... **CLC 43, 70**
See also CA 134; DAM POET

Durkheim, Emile 1858-1917 ..... **TCLC 55**

Durrell, Lawrence (George)
1912-1990 .... **CLC 1, 4, 6, 8, 13, 27, 41**
See also CA 9-12R; 132; CANR 40;
CDBLB 1945-1960; DAM NOV; DLB 15,
27; DLBY 90; MTCW

Durrenmatt, Friedrich
See Duerrenmatt, Friedrich

Dutt, Toru 1856-1877.......... **NCLC 29**

Dwight, Timothy 1752-1817...... **NCLC 13**
See also DLB 37

Dworkin, Andrea 1946-........... **CLC 43**
See also CA 77-80; CAAS 21; CANR 16,
39; INT CANR-16; MTCW

Dwyer, Deanna
See Koontz, Dean R(ay)

Dwyer, K. R.
See Koontz, Dean R(ay)

Dylan, Bob 1941-...... **CLC 3, 4, 6, 12, 77**
See also CA 41-44R; DLB 16

Eagleton, Terence (Francis) 1943-
See Eagleton, Terry
See also CA 57-60; CANR 7, 23; MTCW

Eagleton, Terry .... **CLC 63**
See also Eagleton, Terence (Francis)

Early, Jack
See Scoppettone, Sandra

East, Michael
See West, Morris L(anglo)

Eastaway, Edward
See Thomas, (Philip) Edward

Eastlake, William (Derry) 1917-..... **CLC 8**
See also CA 5-8R; CAAS 1; CANR 5;
DLB 6; INT CANR-5

Eastman, Charles A(lexander)
1858-1939 .... **TCLC 55**
See also DAM MULT; NNAL; YABC 1

Eberhart, Richard (Ghormley)
1904-................. **CLC 3, 11, 19, 56**
See also CA 1-4R; CANR 2;
CDALB 1941-1968; DAM POET;
DLB 48; MTCW

Eberstadt, Fernanda 1960-........ **CLC 39**
See also CA 136

Echegaray (y Eizaguirre), Jose (Maria Waldo)
1832-1916 .... **TCLC 4**
See also CA 104; CANR 32; HW; MTCW

Echeverria, (Jose) Esteban (Antonino)
1805-1851 .... **NCLC 18**

Echo
See Proust, (Valentin-Louis-George-Eugene-)
Marcel

Eckert, Allan W. 1931- .... **CLC 17**
See also CA 13-16R; CANR 14, 45;
INT CANR-14; SAAS 21; SATA 29;
SATA-Brief 27

Eckhart, Meister 1260(?)-1328(?) .. **CMLC 9**
See also DLB 115

Eckmar, F. R.
See de Hartog, Jan

Eco, Umberto 1932-........... **CLC 28, 60**
See also BEST 90:1; CA 77-80; CANR 12,
33; DAM NOV, POP; MTCW

Eddison, E(ric) R(ucker)
1882-1945 .... **TCLC 15**
See also CA 109

Edel, (Joseph) Leon 1907-...... **CLC 29, 34**
See also CA 1-4R; CANR 1, 22; DLB 103;
INT CANR-22

Eden, Emily 1797-1869 .... **NCLC 10**

Edgar, David 1948-.............. CLC 42
    See also CA 57-60; CANR 12;
    DAM DRAM; DLB 13; MTCW

Edgerton, Clyde (Carlyle) 1944- .... CLC 39
    See also AAYA 17; CA 118; 134; INT 134

Edgeworth, Maria 1768-1849... NCLC 1, 51
    See also DLB 116, 159, 163; SATA 21

Edmonds, Paul
    See Kuttner, Henry

Edmonds, Walter D(umaux) 1903- .. CLC 35
    See also CA 5-8R; CANR 2; DLB 9;
    MAICYA; SAAS 4; SATA 1, 27

Edmondson, Wallace
    See Ellison, Harlan (Jay)

Edson, Russell.................... CLC 13
    See also CA 33-36R

Edwards, Bronwen Elizabeth
    See Rose, Wendy

Edwards, G(erald) B(asil)
    1899-1976 .... CLC 25
    See also CA 110

Edwards, Gus 1939- .... CLC 43
    See also CA 108; INT 108

Edwards, Jonathan
    1703-1758 .... LC 7; DA; DAC
    See also DAM MST; DLB 24

Efron, Marina Ivanovna Tsvetaeva
    See Tsvetaeva (Efron), Marina (Ivanovna)

Ehle, John (Marsden, Jr.) 1925- .... CLC 27
    See also CA 9-12R

Ehrenbourg, Ilya (Grigoryevich)
    See Ehrenburg, Ilya (Grigoryevich)

Ehrenburg, Ilya (Grigoryevich)
    1891-1967 .... CLC 18, 34, 62
    See also CA 102; 25-28R

Ehrenburg, Ilyo (Grigoryevich)
    See Ehrenburg, Ilya (Grigoryevich)

Eich, Guenter 1907-1972 .... CLC 15
    See also CA 111; 93-96; DLB 69, 124

Eichendorff, Joseph Freiherr von
    1788-1857 .... NCLC 8
    See also DLB 90

Eigner, Larry..................... CLC 9
    See also Eigner, Laurence (Joel)
    See also CAAS 23; DLB 5

Eigner, Laurence (Joel) 1927-1996
    See Eigner, Larry
    See also CA 9-12R; CANR 6

Eiseley, Loren Corey 1907-1977..... CLC 7
    See also AAYA 5; CA 1-4R; 73-76;
    CANR 6

Eisenstadt, Jill 1963- .... CLC 50
    See also CA 140

Eisenstein, Sergei (Mikhailovich)
    1898-1948 .... TCLC 57
    See also CA 114; 149

Eisner, Simon
    See Kornbluth, C(yril) M.

Ekeloef, (Bengt) Gunnar
    1907-1968 .... CLC 27
    See also CA 123; 25-28R; DAM POET

Ekelof, (Bengt) Gunnar
    See Ekeloef, (Bengt) Gunnar

Ekwensi, C. O. D.
    See Ekwensi, Cyprian (Odiatu Duaka)

Ekwensi, Cyprian (Odiatu Duaka)
    1921- .... CLC 4; BLC
    See also BW 2; CA 29-32R; CANR 18, 42;
    DAM MULT; DLB 117; MTCW;
    SATA 66

Elaine........................ TCLC 18
    See also Leverson, Ada

El Crummo
    See Crumb, R(obert)

Elia
    See Lamb, Charles

Eliade, Mircea 1907-1986 .... CLC 19
    See also CA 65-68; 119; CANR 30; MTCW

Eliot, A. D.
    See Jewett, (Theodora) Sarah Orne

Eliot, Alice
    See Jewett, (Theodora) Sarah Orne

Eliot, Dan
    See Silverberg, Robert

Eliot, George
    1819-1880 ..... NCLC 4, 13, 23, 41, 49;
                    DA; DAB; DAC; WLC
    See also CDBLB 1832-1890; DAM MST,
    NOV; DLB 21, 35, 55

Eliot, John 1604-1690 .... LC 5
    See also DLB 24

Eliot, T(homas) S(tearns)
    1888-1965 ..... CLC 1, 2, 3, 6, 9, 10, 13,
        15, 24, 34, 41, 55, 57; DA; DAB; DAC;
                            PC 5; WLC 2
    See also CA 5-8R; 25-28R; CANR 41;
    CDALB 1929-1941; DAM DRAM, MST,
    POET; DLB 7, 10, 45, 63; DLBY 88;
    MTCW

Elizabeth 1866-1941............. TCLC 41

Elkin, Stanley L(awrence)
    1930-1995 ...... CLC 4, 6, 9, 14, 27, 51,
                        91; SSC 12
    See also CA 9-12R; 148; CANR 8, 46;
    DAM NOV, POP; DLB 2, 28; DLBY 80;
    INT CANR-8; MTCW

Elledge, Scott.................... CLC 34

Elliott, Don
    See Silverberg, Robert

Elliott, George P(aul) 1918-1980..... CLC 2
    See also CA 1-4R; 97-100; CANR 2

Elliott, Janice 1931-.............. CLC 47
    See also CA 13-16R; CANR 8, 29; DLB 14

Elliott, Sumner Locke 1917-1991 ... CLC 38
    See also CA 5-8R; 134; CANR 2, 21

Elliott, William
    See Bradbury, Ray (Douglas)

Ellis, A. E........................ CLC 7

Ellis, Alice Thomas............... CLC 40
    See also Haycraft, Anna

Ellis, Bret Easton 1964-........ CLC 39, 71
    See also AAYA 2; CA 118; 123; CANR 51;
    DAM POP; INT 123

Ellis, (Henry) Havelock
    1859-1939 .... TCLC 14
    See also CA 109

Ellis, Landon
    See Ellison, Harlan (Jay)

Ellis, Trey 1962-................. CLC 55
    See also CA 146

Ellison, Harlan (Jay)
    1934- .... CLC 1, 13, 42; SSC 14
    See also CA 5-8R; CANR 5, 46;
    DAM POP; DLB 8; INT CANR-5;
    MTCW

Ellison, Ralph (Waldo)
    1914-1994 .... CLC 1, 3, 11, 54, 86;
                    BLC; DA; DAB; DAC; WLC
    See also BW 1; CA 9-12R; 145; CANR 24;
    CDALB 1941-1968; DAM MST, MULT,
    NOV; DLB 2, 76; DLBY 94; MTCW

Ellmann, Lucy (Elizabeth) 1956-.... CLC 61
    See also CA 128

Ellmann, Richard (David)
    1918-1987 .... CLC 50
    See also BEST 89:2; CA 1-4R; 122;
    CANR 2, 28; DLB 103; DLBY 87;
    MTCW

Elman, Richard 1934-............. CLC 19
    See also CA 17-20R; CAAS 3; CANR 47

Elron
    See Hubbard, L(afayette) Ron(ald)

Eluard, Paul.................... TCLC 7, 41
    See also Grindel, Eugene

Elyot, Sir Thomas 1490(?)-1546 ..... LC 11

Elytis, Odysseus 1911-......... CLC 15, 49
    See also CA 102; DAM POET; MTCW

Emecheta, (Florence Onye) Buchi
    1944- .... CLC 14, 48; BLC
    See also BW 2; CA 81-84; CANR 27;
    DAM MULT; DLB 117; MTCW;
    SATA 66

Emerson, Ralph Waldo
    1803-1882 ..... NCLC 1, 38; DA; DAB;
                            DAC; WLC
    See also CDALB 1640-1865; DAM MST,
    POET; DLB 1, 59, 73

Eminescu, Mihail 1850-1889..... NCLC 33

Empson, William
    1906-1984 .... CLC 3, 8, 19, 33, 34
    See also CA 17-20R; 112; CANR 31;
    DLB 20; MTCW

Enchi Fumiko (Ueda) 1905-1986.... CLC 31
    See also CA 129; 121

Ende, Michael (Andreas Helmuth)
    1929-1995 .... CLC 31
    See also CA 118; 124; 149; CANR 36;
    CLR 14; DLB 75; MAICYA; SATA 61;
    SATA-Brief 42; SATA-Obit 86

Endo, Shusaku 1923- ..... CLC 7, 14, 19, 54
    See also CA 29-32R; CANR 21;
    DAM NOV; MTCW

Engel, Marian 1933-1985.......... CLC 36
    See also CA 25-28R; CANR 12; DLB 53;
    INT CANR-12

Engelhardt, Frederick
    See Hubbard, L(afayette) Ron(ald)

Enright, D(ennis) J(oseph)
    1920- .... CLC 4, 8, 31
    See also CA 1-4R; CANR 1, 42; DLB 27;
    SATA 25

Enzensberger, Hans Magnus
  1929- . . . . **CLC 43**
  See also CA 116; 119

Ephron, Nora 1941- . . . . **CLC 17, 31**
  See also AITN 2; CA 65-68; CANR 12, 39

Epsilon
  See Betjeman, John

Epstein, Daniel Mark 1948- . . . . **CLC 7**
  See also CA 49-52; CANR 2

Epstein, Jacob 1956- . . . . **CLC 19**
  See also CA 114

Epstein, Joseph 1937- . . . . **CLC 39**
  See also CA 112; 119; CANR 50

Epstein, Leslie 1938- . . . . **CLC 27**
  See also CA 73-76; CAAS 12; CANR 23

Equiano, Olaudah
  1745(?)-1797 . . . . **LC 16; BLC**
  See also DAM MULT; DLB 37, 50

Erasmus, Desiderius 1469(?)-1536. . . . **LC 16**

Erdman, Paul E(mil) 1932- . . . . **CLC 25**
  See also AITN 1; CA 61-64; CANR 13, 43

Erdrich, Louise 1954- . . . . **CLC 39, 54**
  See also AAYA 10; BEST 89:1; CA 114;
  CANR 41; DAM MULT, NOV, POP;
  DLB 152; MTCW; NNAL

Erenburg, Ilya (Grigoryevich)
  See Ehrenburg, Ilya (Grigoryevich)

Erickson, Stephen Michael 1950-
  See Erickson, Steve
  See also CA 129

Erickson, Steve . . . . **CLC 64**
  See also Erickson, Stephen Michael

Ericson, Walter
  See Fast, Howard (Melvin)

Eriksson, Buntel
  See Bergman, (Ernst) Ingmar

Ernaux, Annie 1940- . . . . **CLC 88**
  See also CA 147

Eschenbach, Wolfram von
  See Wolfram von Eschenbach

Eseki, Bruno
  See Mphahlele, Ezekiel

Esenin, Sergei (Alexandrovich)
  1895-1925 . . . . **TCLC 4**
  See also CA 104

Eshleman, Clayton 1935- . . . . **CLC 7**
  See also CA 33-36R; CAAS 6; DLB 5

Espriella, Don Manuel Alvarez
  See Southey, Robert

Espriu, Salvador 1913-1985 . . . . **CLC 9**
  See also CA 115; DLB 134

Espronceda, Jose de 1808-1842 . . . **NCLC 39**

Esse, James
  See Stephens, James

Esterbrook, Tom
  See Hubbard, L(afayette) Ron(ald)

Estleman, Loren D. 1952- . . . . **CLC 48**
  See also CA 85-88; CANR 27; DAM NOV,
  POP; INT CANR-27; MTCW

Eugenides, Jeffrey 1960(?)- . . . . **CLC 81**
  See also CA 144

Euripides c. 485B.C.-406B.C. . . . . **DC 4**
  See also DA; DAB; DAC; DAM DRAM,
  MST

Evan, Evin
  See Faust, Frederick (Schiller)

Evans, Evan
  See Faust, Frederick (Schiller)

Evans, Marian
  See Eliot, George

Evans, Mary Ann
  See Eliot, George

Evarts, Esther
  See Benson, Sally

Everett, Percival L. 1956- . . . . **CLC 57**
  See also BW 2; CA 129

Everson, R(onald) G(ilmour)
  1903- . . . . **CLC 27**
  See also CA 17-20R; DLB 88

Everson, William (Oliver)
  1912-1994 . . . . **CLC 1, 5, 14**
  See also CA 9-12R; 145; CANR 20; DLB 5,
  16; MTCW

Evtushenko, Evgenii Aleksandrovich
  See Yevtushenko, Yevgeny (Alexandrovich)

Ewart, Gavin (Buchanan)
  1916-1995 . . . . **CLC 13, 46**
  See also CA 89-92; 150; CANR 17, 46;
  DLB 40; MTCW

Ewers, Hanns Heinz 1871-1943 . . . **TCLC 12**
  See also CA 109; 149

Ewing, Frederick R.
  See Sturgeon, Theodore (Hamilton)

Exley, Frederick (Earl)
  1929-1992 . . . . **CLC 6, 11**
  See also AITN 2; CA 81-84; 138; DLB 143;
  DLBY 81

Eynhardt, Guillermo
  See Quiroga, Horacio (Sylvestre)

Ezekiel, Nissim 1924- . . . . **CLC 61**
  See also CA 61-64

Ezekiel, Tish O'Dowd 1943- . . . . **CLC 34**
  See also CA 129

Fadeyev, A.
  See Bulgya, Alexander Alexandrovich

Fadeyev, Alexander . . . . **TCLC 53**
  See also Bulgya, Alexander Alexandrovich

Fagen, Donald 1948- . . . . **CLC 26**

Fainzilberg, Ilya Arnoldovich 1897-1937
  See Ilf, Ilya
  See also CA 120

Fair, Ronald L. 1932- . . . . **CLC 18**
  See also BW 1; CA 69-72; CANR 25;
  DLB 33

Fairbairns, Zoe (Ann) 1948- . . . . **CLC 32**
  See also CA 103; CANR 21

Falco, Gian
  See Papini, Giovanni

Falconer, James
  See Kirkup, James

Falconer, Kenneth
  See Kornbluth, C(yril) M.

Falkland, Samuel
  See Heijermans, Herman

Fallaci, Oriana 1930- . . . . **CLC 11**
  See also CA 77-80; CANR 15; MTCW

Faludy, George 1913- . . . . **CLC 42**
  See also CA 21-24R

Faludy, Gyoergy
  See Faludy, George

Fanon, Frantz 1925-1961 . . . . . **CLC 74; BLC**
  See also BW 1; CA 116; 89-92;
  DAM MULT

Fanshawe, Ann 1625-1680 . . . . **LC 11**

Fante, John (Thomas) 1911-1983 . . . **CLC 60**
  See also CA 69-72; 109; CANR 23;
  DLB 130; DLBY 83

Farah, Nuruddin 1945- . . . . **CLC 53; BLC**
  See also BW 2; CA 106; DAM MULT;
  DLB 125

Fargue, Leon-Paul 1876(?)-1947 . . . **TCLC 11**
  See also CA 109

Farigoule, Louis
  See Romains, Jules

Farina, Richard 1936(?)-1966 . . . . **CLC 9**
  See also CA 81-84; 25-28R

Farley, Walter (Lorimer)
  1915-1989 . . . . **CLC 17**
  See also CA 17-20R; CANR 8, 29; DLB 22;
  JRDA; MAICYA; SATA 2, 43

Farmer, Philip Jose 1918- . . . . **CLC 1, 19**
  See also CA 1-4R; CANR 4, 35; DLB 8;
  MTCW

Farquhar, George 1677-1707 . . . . **LC 21**
  See also DAM DRAM; DLB 84

Farrell, J(ames) G(ordon)
  1935-1979 . . . . **CLC 6**
  See also CA 73-76; 89-92; CANR 36;
  DLB 14; MTCW

Farrell, James T(homas)
  1904-1979 . . . . **CLC 1, 4, 8, 11, 66**
  See also CA 5-8R; 89-92; CANR 9; DLB 4,
  9, 86; DLBD 2; MTCW

Farren, Richard J.
  See Betjeman, John

Farren, Richard M.
  See Betjeman, John

Fassbinder, Rainer Werner
  1946-1982 . . . . **CLC 20**
  See also CA 93-96; 106; CANR 31

Fast, Howard (Melvin) 1914- . . . . . . **CLC 23**
  See also AAYA 16; CA 1-4R; CAAS 18;
  CANR 1, 33; DAM NOV; DLB 9;
  INT CANR-33; SATA 7

Faulcon, Robert
  See Holdstock, Robert P.

Faulkner, William (Cuthbert)
  1897-1962 . . . . . **CLC 1, 3, 6, 8, 9, 11, 14,
  18, 28, 52, 68; DA; DAB; DAC; SSC 1;
  WLC**
  See also AAYA 7; CA 81-84; CANR 33;
  CDALB 1929-1941; DAM MST, NOV;
  DLB 9, 11, 44, 102; DLBD 2; DLBY 86;
  MTCW

Fauset, Jessie Redmon
  1884(?)-1961 . . . . **CLC 19, 54; BLC**
  See also BW 1; CA 109; DAM MULT;
  DLB 51

Faust, Frederick (Schiller)
1892-1944(?) . . . . **TCLC 49**
See also CA 108; DAM POP

Faust, Irvin 1924- . . . . **CLC 8**
See also CA 33-36R; CANR 28; DLB 2, 28;
DLBY 80

Fawkes, Guy
See Benchley, Robert (Charles)

Fearing, Kenneth (Flexner)
1902-1961 . . . . **CLC 51**
See also CA 93-96; DLB 9

Fecamps, Elise
See Creasey, John

Federman, Raymond 1928- . . . . . . **CLC 6, 47**
See also CA 17-20R; CAAS 8; CANR 10,
43; DLBY 80

Federspiel, J(uerg) F. 1931- . . . . **CLC 42**
See also CA 146

Feiffer, Jules (Ralph) 1929- . . . . **CLC 2, 8, 64**
See also AAYA 3; CA 17-20R; CANR 30;
DAM DRAM; DLB 7, 44;
INT CANR-30; MTCW; SATA 8, 61

Feige, Hermann Albert Otto Maximilian
See Traven, B.

Feinberg, David B. 1956-1994 . . . . . . **CLC 59**
See also CA 135; 147

Feinstein, Elaine 1930- . . . . **CLC 36**
See also CA 69-72; CAAS 1; CANR 31;
DLB 14, 40; MTCW

Feldman, Irving (Mordecai) 1928- . . . . **CLC 7**
See also CA 1-4R; CANR 1

Fellini, Federico 1920-1993 . . . . . **CLC 16, 85**
See also CA 65-68; 143; CANR 33

Felsen, Henry Gregor 1916- . . . . **CLC 17**
See also CA 1-4R; CANR 1; SAAS 2;
SATA 1

Fenton, James Martin 1949- . . . . **CLC 32**
See also CA 102; DLB 40

Ferber, Edna 1887-1968 . . . . **CLC 18, 93**
See also AITN 1; CA 5-8R; 25-28R; DLB 9,
28, 86; MTCW; SATA 7

Ferguson, Helen
See Kavan, Anna

Ferguson, Samuel 1810-1886 . . . . . **NCLC 33**
See also DLB 32

Fergusson, Robert 1750-1774 . . . . **LC 29**
See also DLB 109

Ferling, Lawrence
See Ferlinghetti, Lawrence (Monsanto)

Ferlinghetti, Lawrence (Monsanto)
1919(?)- . . . . **CLC 2, 6, 10, 27; PC 1**
See also CA 5-8R; CANR 3, 41;
CDALB 1941-1968; DAM POET; DLB 5,
16; MTCW

Fernandez, Vicente Garcia Huidobro
See Huidobro Fernandez, Vicente Garcia

Ferrer, Gabriel (Francisco Victor) Miro
See Miro (Ferrer), Gabriel (Francisco
Victor)

Ferrier, Susan (Edmonstone)
1782-1854 . . . . **NCLC 8**
See also DLB 116

Ferrigno, Robert 1948(?)- . . . . **CLC 65**
See also CA 140

Feuchtwanger, Lion 1884-1958 . . . . . **TCLC 3**
See also CA 104; DLB 66

Feuillet, Octave 1821-1890 . . . . . . **NCLC 45**

Feydeau, Georges (Leon Jules Marie)
1862-1921 . . . . **TCLC 22**
See also CA 113; DAM DRAM

Ficino, Marsilio 1433-1499 . . . . **LC 12**

Fiedeler, Hans
See Doeblin, Alfred

Fiedler, Leslie A(aron)
1917- . . . . **CLC 4, 13, 24**
See also CA 9-12R; CANR 7; DLB 28, 67;
MTCW

Field, Andrew 1938- . . . . **CLC 44**
See also CA 97-100; CANR 25

Field, Eugene 1850-1895 . . . . **NCLC 3**
See also DLB 23, 42, 140; DLBD 13;
MAICYA; SATA 16

Field, Gans T.
See Wellman, Manly Wade

Field, Michael . . . . **TCLC 43**

Field, Peter
See Hobson, Laura Z(ametkin)

Fielding, Henry
1707-1754 . . . . . . **LC 1; DA; DAB; DAC;
WLC**
See also CDBLB 1660-1789; DAM DRAM,
MST, NOV; DLB 39, 84, 101

Fielding, Sarah 1710-1768 . . . . **LC 1**
See also DLB 39

Fierstein, Harvey (Forbes) 1954- . . . **CLC 33**
See also CA 123; 129; DAM DRAM, POP

Figes, Eva 1932- . . . . **CLC 31**
See also CA 53-56; CANR 4, 44; DLB 14

Finch, Robert (Duer Claydon)
1900- . . . . **CLC 18**
See also CA 57-60; CANR 9, 24, 49;
DLB 88

Findley, Timothy 1930- . . . . . . **CLC 27; DAC**
See also CA 25-28R; CANR 12, 42;
DAM MST; DLB 53

Fink, William
See Mencken, H(enry) L(ouis)

Firbank, Louis 1942-
See Reed, Lou
See also CA 117

Firbank, (Arthur Annesley) Ronald
1886-1926 . . . . **TCLC 1**
See also CA 104; DLB 36

Fisher, M(ary) F(rances) K(ennedy)
1908-1992 . . . . **CLC 76, 87**
See also CA 77-80; 138; CANR 44

Fisher, Roy 1930- . . . . **CLC 25**
See also CA 81-84; CAAS 10; CANR 16;
DLB 40

Fisher, Rudolph
1897-1934 . . . . **TCLC 11; BLC**
See also BW 1; CA 107; 124; DAM MULT;
DLB 51, 102

Fisher, Vardis (Alvero) 1895-1968 . . . . **CLC 7**
See also CA 5-8R; 25-28R; DLB 9

Fiske, Tarleton
See Bloch, Robert (Albert)

Fitch, Clarke
See Sinclair, Upton (Beall)

Fitch, John IV
See Cormier, Robert (Edmund)

Fitch, Captain Hugh
See Baum, L(yman) Frank

FitzGerald, Edward 1809-1883 . . . . **NCLC 9**
See also DLB 32

Fitzgerald, F(rancis) Scott (Key)
1896-1940 . . . . **TCLC 1, 6, 14, 28, 55;
DA; DAB; DAC; SSC 6; WLC**
See also AITN 1; CA 110; 123;
CDALB 1917-1929; DAM MST, NOV;
DLB 4, 9, 86; DLBD 1; DLBY 81;
MTCW

Fitzgerald, Penelope 1916- . . . **CLC 19, 51, 61**
See also CA 85-88; CAAS 10; DLB 14

Fitzgerald, Robert (Stuart)
1910-1985 . . . . **CLC 39**
See also CA 1-4R; 114; CANR 1; DLBY 80

FitzGerald, Robert D(avid)
1902-1987 . . . . **CLC 19**
See also CA 17-20R

Fitzgerald, Zelda (Sayre)
1900-1948 . . . . **TCLC 52**
See also CA 117; 126; DLBY 84

Flanagan, Thomas (James Bonner)
1923- . . . . **CLC 25, 52**
See also CA 108; DLBY 80; INT 108;
MTCW

Flaubert, Gustave
1821-1880 . . . . **NCLC 2, 10, 19; DA;
DAB; DAC; SSC 11; WLC**
See also DAM MST, NOV; DLB 119

Flecker, Herman Elroy
See Flecker, (Herman) James Elroy

Flecker, (Herman) James Elroy
1884-1915 . . . . **TCLC 43**
See also CA 109; 150; DLB 10, 19

Fleming, Ian (Lancaster)
1908-1964 . . . . **CLC 3, 30**
See also CA 5-8R; CDBLB 1945-1960;
DAM POP; DLB 87; MTCW; SATA 9

Fleming, Thomas (James) 1927- . . . . **CLC 37**
See also CA 5-8R; CANR 10;
INT CANR-10; SATA 8

Fletcher, John 1579-1625 . . . . **DC 6**
See also CDBLB Before 1660; DLB 58

Fletcher, John Gould 1886-1950 . . . **TCLC 35**
See also CA 107; DLB 4, 45

Fleur, Paul
See Pohl, Frederik

Flooglebuckle, Al
See Spiegelman, Art

Flying Officer X
See Bates, H(erbert) E(rnest)

Fo, Dario 1926- . . . . **CLC 32**
See also CA 116; 128; DAM DRAM;
MTCW

Fogarty, Jonathan Titulescu Esq.
See Farrell, James T(homas)

Folke, Will
See Bloch, Robert (Albert)

Follett, Ken(neth Martin) 1949- .... **CLC 18**
See also AAYA 6; BEST 89:4; CA 81-84;
CANR 13, 33; DAM NOV, POP;
DLB 87, DLBY 81; INT CANR-33;
MTCW

Fontane, Theodor 1819-1898 ..... **NCLC 26**
See also DLB 129

Foote, Horton 1916- .... **CLC 51, 91**
See also CA 73-76; CANR 34, 51;
DAM DRAM; DLB 26; INT CANR-34

Foote, Shelby 1916- .... **CLC 75**
See also CA 5-8R; CANR 3, 45;
DAM NOV, POP; DLB 2, 17

Forbes, Esther 1891-1967 .... **CLC 12**
See also AAYA 17; CA 13-14; 25-28R;
CAP 1; CLR 27; DLB 22; JRDA;
MAICYA; SATA 2

Forche, Carolyn (Louise)
1950- .... **CLC 25, 83, 86; PC 10**
See also CA 109; 117; CANR 50;
DAM POET; DLB 5; INT 117

Ford, Elbur
See Hibbert, Eleanor Alice Burford

Ford, Ford Madox
1873-1939 .... **TCLC 1, 15, 39, 57**
See also CA 104; 132; CDBLB 1914-1945;
DAM NOV; DLB 162; MTCW

Ford, John 1895-1973 .... **CLC 16**
See also CA 45-48

Ford, Richard 1944- .... **CLC 46**
See also CA 69-72; CANR 11, 47

Ford, Webster
See Masters, Edgar Lee

Foreman, Richard 1937- .... **CLC 50**
See also CA 65-68; CANR 32

Forester, C(ecil) S(cott)
1899-1966 .... **CLC 35**
See also CA 73-76; 25-28R; SATA 13

Forez
See Mauriac, Francois (Charles)

Forman, James Douglas 1932- ...... **CLC 21**
See also AAYA 17; CA 9-12R; CANR 4,
19, 42; JRDA; MAICYA; SATA 8, 70

Fornes, Maria Irene 1930- ...... **CLC 39, 61**
See also CA 25-28R; CANR 28; DLB 7;
HW; INT CANR-28; MTCW

Forrest, Leon 1937- .... **CLC 4**
See also BW 2; CA 89-92; CAAS 7;
CANR 25; DLB 33

Forster, E(dward) M(organ)
1879-1970 ..... **CLC 1, 2, 3, 4, 9, 10, 13,
15, 22, 45, 77; DA; DAB; DAC; WLC**
See also AAYA 2; CA 13-14; 25-28R;
CANR 45; CAP 1; CDBLB 1914-1945;
DAM MST, NOV; DLB 34, 98, 162;
DLBD 10; MTCW; SATA 57

Forster, John 1812-1876 .... **NCLC 11**
See also DLB 144

Forsyth, Frederick 1938- ...... **CLC 2, 5, 36**
See also BEST 89:4; CA 85-88; CANR 38;
DAM NOV, POP; DLB 87; MTCW

Forten, Charlotte L. .... **TCLC 16; BLC**
See also Grimke, Charlotte L(ottie) Forten
See also DLB 50

Foscolo, Ugo 1778-1827 .... **NCLC 8**

Fosse, Bob .... **CLC 20**
See also Fosse, Robert Louis

Fosse, Robert Louis 1927-1987
See Fosse, Bob
See also CA 110; 123

Foster, Stephen Collins
1826-1864 .... **NCLC 26**

Foucault, Michel
1926-1984 .... **CLC 31, 34, 69**
See also CA 105; 113; CANR 34; MTCW

Fouque, Friedrich (Heinrich Karl) de la Motte
1777-1843 .... **NCLC 2**
See also DLB 90

Fourier, Charles 1772-1837 ...... **NCLC 51**

Fournier, Henri Alban 1886-1914
See Alain-Fournier
See also CA 104

Fournier, Pierre 1916- .... **CLC 11**
See also Gascar, Pierre
See also CA 89-92; CANR 16, 40

Fowles, John
1926- ...... **CLC 1, 2, 3, 4, 6, 9, 10, 15,
33, 87; DAB; DAC**
See also CA 5-8R; CANR 25; CDBLB 1960
to Present; DAM MST; DLB 14, 139;
MTCW; SATA 22

Fox, Paula 1923- .... **CLC 2, 8**
See also AAYA 3; CA 73-76; CANR 20,
36; CLR 1; DLB 52; JRDA; MAICYA;
MTCW; SATA 17, 60

Fox, William Price (Jr.) 1926- ..... **CLC 22**
See also CA 17-20R; CAAS 19; CANR 11;
DLB 2; DLBY 81

Foxe, John 1516(?)-1587 .... **LC 14**

Frame, Janet .... **CLC 2, 3, 6, 22, 66**
See also Clutha, Janet Paterson Frame

France, Anatole .... **TCLC 9**
See also Thibault, Jacques Anatole Francois
See also DLB 123

Francis, Claude 19(?)- .... **CLC 50**

Francis, Dick 1920- .... **CLC 2, 22, 42**
See also AAYA 5; BEST 89:3; CA 5-8R;
CANR 9, 42; CDBLB 1960 to Present;
DAM POP; DLB 87; INT CANR-9;
MTCW

Francis, Robert (Churchill)
1901-1987 .... **CLC 15**
See also CA 1-4R; 123; CANR 1

Frank, Anne(lies Marie)
1929-1945 .... **TCLC 17; DA; DAB;
DAC; WLC**
See also AAYA 12; CA 113; 133;
DAM MST; MTCW; SATA 87;
SATA-Brief 42

Frank, Elizabeth 1945- .... **CLC 39**
See also CA 121; 126; INT 126

Frankl, Viktor E(mil) 1905- .... **CLC 93**
See also CA 65-68

Franklin, Benjamin
See Hasek, Jaroslav (Matej Frantisek)

Franklin, Benjamin
1706-1790 ..... **LC 25; DA; DAB; DAC**
See also CDALB 1640-1865; DAM MST;
DLB 24, 43, 73

Franklin, (Stella Maraia Sarah) Miles
1879-1954 .... **TCLC 7**
See also CA 104

Fraser, (Lady) Antonia (Pakenham)
1932- .... **CLC 32**
See also CA 85-88; CANR 44; MTCW;
SATA-Brief 32

Fraser, George MacDonald 1925- .... **CLC 7**
See also CA 45-48; CANR 2, 48

Fraser, Sylvia 1935- .... **CLC 64**
See also CA 45-48; CANR 1, 16

Frayn, Michael 1933- ...... **CLC 3, 7, 31, 47**
See also CA 5-8R; CANR 30;
DAM DRAM, NOV; DLB 13, 14;
MTCW

Fraze, Candida (Merrill) 1945- ..... **CLC 50**
See also CA 126

Frazer, J(ames) G(eorge)
1854-1941 .... **TCLC 32**
See also CA 118

Frazer, Robert Caine
See Creasey, John

Frazer, Sir James George
See Frazer, J(ames) G(eorge)

Frazier, Ian 1951- .... **CLC 46**
See also CA 130

Frederic, Harold 1856-1898 ...... **NCLC 10**
See also DLB 12, 23; DLBD 13

Frederick, John
See Faust, Frederick (Schiller)

Frederick the Great 1712-1786 ...... **LC 14**

Fredro, Aleksander 1793-1876 ..... **NCLC 8**

Freeling, Nicolas 1927- .... **CLC 38**
See also CA 49-52; CAAS 12; CANR 1, 17,
50; DLB 87

Freeman, Douglas Southall
1886-1953 .... **TCLC 11**
See also CA 109; DLB 17

Freeman, Judith 1946- .... **CLC 55**
See also CA 148

Freeman, Mary Eleanor Wilkins
1852-1930 .... **TCLC 9; SSC 1**
See also CA 106; DLB 12, 78

Freeman, R(ichard) Austin
1862-1943 .... **TCLC 21**
See also CA 113; DLB 70

French, Albert 1943- .... **CLC 86**

French, Marilyn 1929- ...... **CLC 10, 18, 60**
See also CA 69-72; CANR 3, 31;
DAM DRAM, NOV, POP;
INT CANR-31; MTCW

French, Paul
See Asimov, Isaac

Freneau, Philip Morin 1752-1832 .. **NCLC 1**
See also DLB 37, 43

Freud, Sigmund 1856-1939 .... **TCLC 52**
See also CA 115; 133; MTCW

Friedan, Betty (Naomi) 1921- ...... **CLC 74**
See also CA 65-68; CANR 18, 45; MTCW

Friedlaender, Saul 1932- .... **CLC 90**
See also CA 117; 130

Friedman, B(ernard) H(arper)
1926- .... **CLC 7**
See also CA 1-4R; CANR 3, 48

Friedman, Bruce Jay 1930- .... **CLC 3, 5, 56**
See also CA 9-12R; CANR 25; DLB 2, 28;
INT CANR-25

Friel, Brian 1929- .... **CLC 5, 42, 59**
See also CA 21-24R; CANR 33; DLB 13;
MTCW

Friis-Baastad, Babbis Ellinor
1921-1970 .... **CLC 12**
See also CA 17-20R; 134; SATA 7

Frisch, Max (Rudolf)
1911-1991 ..... **CLC 3, 9, 14, 18, 32, 44**
See also CA 85-88; 134; CANR 32;
DAM DRAM, NOV; DLB 69, 124;
MTCW

Fromentin, Eugene (Samuel Auguste)
1820-1876 .... **NCLC 10**
See also DLB 123

Frost, Frederick
See Faust, Frederick (Schiller)

Frost, Robert (Lee)
1874-1963 .... **CLC 1, 3, 4, 9, 10, 13, 15,
26, 34, 44; DA; DAB; DAC; PC 1; WLC**
See also CA 89-92; CANR 33;
CDALB 1917-1929; DAM MST, POET;
DLB 54; DLBD 7; MTCW; SATA 14

Froude, James Anthony
1818-1894 .... **NCLC 43**
See also DLB 18, 57, 144

Froy, Herald
See Waterhouse, Keith (Spencer)

Fry, Christopher 1907- .... **CLC 2, 10, 14**
See also CA 17-20R; CAAS 23; CANR 9,
30; DAM DRAM; DLB 13; MTCW;
SATA 66

Frye, (Herman) Northrop
1912-1991 .... **CLC 24, 70**
See also CA 5-8R; 133; CANR 8, 37;
DLB 67, 68; MTCW

Fuchs, Daniel 1909-1993 .... **CLC 8, 22**
See also CA 81-84; 142; CAAS 5;
CANR 40; DLB 9, 26, 28; DLBY 93

Fuchs, Daniel 1934- .... **CLC 34**
See also CA 37-40R; CANR 14, 48

Fuentes, Carlos
1928- ...... **CLC 3, 8, 10, 13, 22, 41, 60;
DA; DAB; DAC; HLC; WLC**
See also AAYA 4; AITN 2; CA 69-72;
CANR 10, 32; DAM MST, MULT,
NOV; DLB 113; HW; MTCW

Fuentes, Gregorio Lopez y
See Lopez y Fuentes, Gregorio

Fugard, (Harold) Athol
1932- .... **CLC 5, 9, 14, 25, 40, 80; DC 3**
See also AAYA 17; CA 85-88; CANR 32;
DAM DRAM; MTCW

Fugard, Sheila 1932- .... **CLC 48**
See also CA 125

Fuller, Charles (H., Jr.)
1939- .... **CLC 25; BLC; DC 1**
See also BW 2; CA 108; 112;
DAM DRAM, MULT; DLB 38;
INT 112; MTCW

Fuller, John (Leopold) 1937- .... **CLC 62**
See also CA 21-24R; CANR 9, 44; DLB 40

Fuller, Margaret .... **NCLC 5, 50**
See also Ossoli, Sarah Margaret (Fuller
marchesa d')

Fuller, Roy (Broadbent)
1912-1991 .... **CLC 4, 28**
See also CA 5-8R; 135; CAAS 10; DLB 15,
20; SATA 87

Fulton, Alice 1952- .... **CLC 52**
See also CA 116

Furphy, Joseph 1843-1912 .... **TCLC 25**

Fussell, Paul 1924- .... **CLC 74**
See also BEST 90:1; CA 17-20R; CANR 8,
21, 35; INT CANR-21; MTCW

Futabatei, Shimei 1864-1909 ..... **TCLC 44**

Futrelle, Jacques 1875-1912 ...... **TCLC 19**
See also CA 113

Gaboriau, Emile 1835-1873 ...... **NCLC 14**

Gadda, Carlo Emilio 1893-1973 .... **CLC 11**
See also CA 89-92

Gaddis, William
1922- ..... **CLC 1, 3, 6, 8, 10, 19, 43, 86**
See also CA 17-20R; CANR 21, 48; DLB 2;
MTCW

Gaines, Ernest J(ames)
1933- .... **CLC 3, 11, 18, 86; BLC**
See also AITN 1; BW 2; CA 9-12R;
CANR 6, 24, 42; CDALB 1968-1988;
DAM MULT; DLB 2, 33, 152; DLBY 80;
MTCW; SATA 86

Gaitskill, Mary 1954- .... **CLC 69**
See also CA 128

Galdos, Benito Perez
See Perez Galdos, Benito

Gale, Zona 1874-1938 .... **TCLC 7**
See also CA 105; DAM DRAM; DLB 9, 78

Galeano, Eduardo (Hughes) 1940- ... **CLC 72**
See also CA 29-32R; CANR 13, 32; HW

Galiano, Juan Valera y Alcala
See Valera y Alcala-Galiano, Juan

Gallagher, Tess 1943- .... **CLC 18, 63; PC 9**
See also CA 106; DAM POET; DLB 120

Gallant, Mavis
1922- ...... **CLC 7, 18, 38; DAC; SSC 5**
See also CA 69-72; CANR 29; DAM MST;
DLB 53; MTCW

Gallant, Roy A(rthur) 1924- .... **CLC 17**
See also CA 5-8R; CANR 4, 29; CLR 30;
MAICYA; SATA 4, 68

Gallico, Paul (William) 1897-1976 ... **CLC 2**
See also AITN 1; CA 5-8R; 69-72;
CANR 23; DLB 9; MAICYA; SATA 13

Gallup, Ralph
See Whitemore, Hugh (John)

Galsworthy, John
1867-1933 ...... **TCLC 1, 45; DA; DAB;
DAC; SSC 22; WLC 2**
See also CA 104; 141; CDBLB 1890-1914;
DAM DRAM, MST, NOV; DLB 10, 34,
98, 162

Galt, John 1779-1839 .... **NCLC 1**
See also DLB 99, 116, 159

Galvin, James 1951- .... **CLC 38**
See also CA 108; CANR 26

Gamboa, Federico 1864-1939 ...... **TCLC 36**

Gandhi, M. K.
See Gandhi, Mohandas Karamchand

Gandhi, Mahatma
See Gandhi, Mohandas Karamchand

Gandhi, Mohandas Karamchand
1869-1948 .... **TCLC 59**
See also CA 121; 132; DAM MULT;
MTCW

Gann, Ernest Kellogg 1910-1991.... **CLC 23**
See also AITN 1; CA 1-4R; 136; CANR 1

Garcia, Cristina 1958- .... **CLC 76**
See also CA 141

Garcia Lorca, Federico
1898-1936 ... **TCLC 1, 7, 49; DA; DAB;
DAC; DC 2; HLC; PC 3; WLC**
See also CA 104; 131; DAM DRAM, MST,
MULT, POET; DLB 108; HW; MTCW

Garcia Marquez, Gabriel (Jose)
1928- .... **CLC 2, 3, 8, 10, 15, 27, 47, 55,
68; DA; DAB; DAC; HLC; SSC 8; WLC**
See also AAYA 3; BEST 89:1, 90:4;
CA 33-36R; CANR 10, 28, 50;
DAM MST, MULT, NOV, POP;
DLB 113; HW; MTCW

Gard, Janice
See Latham, Jean Lee

Gard, Roger Martin du
See Martin du Gard, Roger

Gardam, Jane 1928- .... **CLC 43**
See also CA 49-52; CANR 2, 18, 33;
CLR 12; DLB 14, 161; MAICYA;
MTCW; SAAS 9; SATA 39, 76;
SATA-Brief 28

Gardner, Herb(ert) 1934- .... **CLC 44**
See also CA 149

Gardner, John (Champlin), Jr.
1933-1982 ..... **CLC 2, 3, 5, 7, 8, 10, 18,
28, 34; SSC 7**
See also AITN 1; CA 65-68; 107;
CANR 33; DAM NOV, POP; DLB 2;
DLBY 82; MTCW; SATA 40;
SATA-Obit 31

Gardner, John (Edmund) 1926- ..... **CLC 30**
See also CA 103; CANR 15; DAM POP;
MTCW

Gardner, Noel
See Kuttner, Henry

Gardons, S. S.
See Snodgrass, W(illiam) D(e Witt)

Garfield, Leon 1921- .... **CLC 12**
See also AAYA 8; CA 17-20R; CANR 38,
41; CLR 21; DLB 161; JRDA; MAICYA;
SATA 1, 32, 76

Garland, (Hannibal) Hamlin
1860-1940 .... **TCLC 3; SSC 18**
See also CA 104; DLB 12, 71, 78

Garneau, (Hector de) Saint-Denys
1912-1943 .... **TCLC 13**
See also CA 111; DLB 88

Garner, Alan 1934- .... **CLC 17; DAB**
See also CA 73-76; CANR 15; CLR 20;
DAM POP; DLB 161; MAICYA;
MTCW; SATA 18, 69

Garner, Hugh 1913-1979 .... **CLC 13**
See also CA 69-72; CANR 31; DLB 68

Garnett, David 1892-1981 . . . . CLC 3
See also CA 5-8R; 103; CANR 17; DLB 34

Garos, Stephanie
See Katz, Steve

Garrett, George (Palmer)
1929- . . . . CLC 3, 11, 51
See also CA 1-4R; CAAS 5; CANR 1, 42;
DLB 2, 5, 130, 152; DLBY 83

Garrick, David 1717-1779 . . . . LC 15
See also DAM DRAM; DLB 84

Garrigue, Jean 1914-1972 . . . . CLC 2, 8
See also CA 5-8R; 37-40R; CANR 20

Garrison, Frederick
See Sinclair, Upton (Beall)

Garth, Will
See Hamilton, Edmond; Kuttner, Henry

Garvey, Marcus (Moziah, Jr.)
1887-1940 . . . . TCLC 41; BLC
See also BW 1; CA 120; 124; DAM MULT

Gary, Romain . . . . CLC 25
See also Kacew, Romain
See also DLB 83

Gascar, Pierre . . . . CLC 11
See also Fournier, Pierre

Gascoyne, David (Emery) 1916- . . . . CLC 45
See also CA 65-68; CANR 10, 28; DLB 20;
MTCW

Gaskell, Elizabeth Cleghorn
1810-1865 . . . . NCLC 5; DAB
See also CDBLB 1832-1890; DAM MST;
DLB 21, 144, 159

Gass, William H(oward)
1924- . . . CLC 1, 2, 8, 11, 15, 39; SSC 12
See also CA 17-20R; CANR 30; DLB 2;
MTCW

Gasset, Jose Ortega y
See Ortega y Gasset, Jose

Gates, Henry Louis, Jr. 1950- . . . . . . CLC 65
See also BW 2; CA 109; CANR 25;
DAM MULT; DLB 67

Gautier, Theophile
1811-1872 . . . . NCLC 1; SSC 20
See also DAM POET; DLB 119

Gawsworth, John
See Bates, H(erbert) E(rnest)

Gay, Oliver
See Gogarty, Oliver St. John

Gaye, Marvin (Penze) 1939-1984 . . . CLC 26
See also CA 112

Gebler, Carlo (Ernest) 1954- . . . . CLC 39
See also CA 119; 133

Gee, Maggie (Mary) 1948- . . . . CLC 57
See also CA 130

Gee, Maurice (Gough) 1931- . . . . CLC 29
See also CA 97-100; SATA 46

Gelbart, Larry (Simon) 1923- . . . CLC 21, 61
See also CA 73-76; CANR 45

Gelber, Jack 1932- . . . . CLC 1, 6, 14, 79
See also CA 1-4R; CANR 2; DLB 7

Gellhorn, Martha (Ellis) 1908- . . CLC 14, 60
See also CA 77-80; CANR 44; DLBY 82

Genet, Jean
1910-1986 . . . CLC 1, 2, 5, 10, 14, 44, 46
See also CA 13-16R; CANR 18;
DAM DRAM; DLB 72; DLBY 86;
MTCW

Gent, Peter 1942- . . . . CLC 29
See also AITN 1; CA 89-92; DLBY 82

Gentlewoman in New England, A
See Bradstreet, Anne

Gentlewoman in Those Parts, A
See Bradstreet, Anne

George, Jean Craighead 1919- . . . . . . CLC 35
See also AAYA 8; CA 5-8R; CANR 25;
CLR 1; DLB 52; JRDA; MAICYA;
SATA 2, 68

George, Stefan (Anton)
1868-1933 . . . . TCLC 2, 14
See also CA 104

Georges, Georges Martin
See Simenon, Georges (Jacques Christian)

Gerhardi, William Alexander
See Gerhardie, William Alexander

Gerhardie, William Alexander
1895-1977 . . . . CLC 5
See also CA 25-28R; 73-76; CANR 18;
DLB 36

Gerstler, Amy 1956- . . . . CLC 70
See also CA 146

Gertler, T. . . . . CLC 34
See also CA 116; 121; INT 121

Ghalib . . . . NCLC 39
See also Ghalib, Hsadullah Khan

Ghalib, Hsadullah Khan 1797-1869
See Ghalib
See also DAM POET

Ghelderode, Michel de
1898-1962 . . . . CLC 6, 11
See also CA 85-88; CANR 40;
DAM DRAM

Ghiselin, Brewster 1903- . . . . CLC 23
See also CA 13-16R; CAAS 10; CANR 13

Ghose, Zulfikar 1935- . . . . CLC 42
See also CA 65-68

Ghosh, Amitav 1956- . . . . CLC 44
See also CA 147

Giacosa, Giuseppe 1847-1906 . . . . . . TCLC 7
See also CA 104

Gibb, Lee
See Waterhouse, Keith (Spencer)

Gibbon, Lewis Grassic . . . . TCLC 4
See also Mitchell, James Leslie

Gibbons, Kaye 1960- . . . . CLC 50, 88
See also DAM POP

Gibran, Kahlil
1883-1931 . . . . TCLC 1, 9; PC 9
See also CA 104; 150; DAM POET, POP

Gibran, Khalil
See Gibran, Kahlil

Gibson, William
1914- . . . . CLC 23; DA; DAB; DAC
See also CA 9-12R; CANR 9, 42;
DAM DRAM, MST; DLB 7; SATA 66

Gibson, William (Ford) 1948- . . . CLC 39, 63
See also AAYA 12; CA 126; 133;
DAM POP

Gide, Andre (Paul Guillaume)
1869-1951 . . . . TCLC 5, 12, 36; DA;
DAB; DAC; SSC 13; WLC
See also CA 104; 124; DAM MST, NOV;
DLB 65; MTCW

Gifford, Barry (Colby) 1946- . . . . CLC 34
See also CA 65-68; CANR 9, 30, 40

Gilbert, W(illiam) S(chwenck)
1836-1911 . . . . TCLC 3
See also CA 104; DAM DRAM, POET;
SATA 36

Gilbreth, Frank B., Jr. 1911- . . . . CLC 17
See also CA 9-12R; SATA 2

Gilchrist, Ellen 1935- . . CLC 34, 48; SSC 14
See also CA 113; 116; CANR 41;
DAM POP; DLB 130; MTCW

Giles, Molly 1942- . . . . CLC 39
See also CA 126

Gill, Patrick
See Creasey, John

Gilliam, Terry (Vance) 1940- . . . . CLC 21
See also Monty Python
See also CA 108; 113; CANR 35; INT 113

Gillian, Jerry
See Gilliam, Terry (Vance)

Gilliatt, Penelope (Ann Douglass)
1932-1993 . . . . CLC 2, 10, 13, 53
See also AITN 2; CA 13-16R; 141;
CANR 49; DLB 14

Gilman, Charlotte (Anna) Perkins (Stetson)
1860-1935 . . . . TCLC 9, 37; SSC 13
See also CA 106; 150

Gilmour, David 1949- . . . . CLC 35
See also CA 138, 147

Gilpin, William 1724-1804 . . . . . . NCLC 30

Gilray, J. D.
See Mencken, H(enry) L(ouis)

Gilroy, Frank D(aniel) 1925- . . . . CLC 2
See also CA 81-84; CANR 32; DLB 7

Ginsberg, Allen
1926- . . . . . . CLC 1, 2, 3, 4, 6, 13, 36, 69;
DA; DAB; DAC; PC 4; WLC 3
See also AITN 1; CA 1-4R; CANR 2, 41;
CDALB 1941-1968; DAM MST, POET;
DLB 5, 16; MTCW

Ginzburg, Natalia
1916-1991 . . . . CLC 5, 11, 54, 70
See also CA 85-88; 135; CANR 33; MTCW

Giono, Jean 1895-1970 . . . . CLC 4, 11
See also CA 45-48; 29-32R; CANR 2, 35;
DLB 72; MTCW

Giovanni, Nikki
1943- . . . . . . CLC 2, 4, 19, 64; BLC; DA;
DAB; DAC
See also AITN 1; BW 2; CA 29-32R;
CAAS 6; CANR 18, 41; CLR 6;
DAM MST, MULT, POET; DLB 5, 41;
INT CANR-18; MAICYA; MTCW;
SATA 24

Giovene, Andrea 1904- . . . . CLC 7
See also CA 85-88

Gozzano, Guido 1883-1916 .... **PC 10**
See also DLB 114

Gozzi, (Conte) Carlo 1720-1806 .. **NCLC 23**

Grabbe, Christian Dietrich
1801-1836 .... **NCLC 2**
See also DLB 133

Grace, Patricia 1937- .... **CLC 56**

Gracian y Morales, Baltasar
1601-1658 .... **LC 15**

Gracq, Julien .... **CLC 11, 48**
See also Poirier, Louis
See also DLB 83

Grade, Chaim 1910-1982 .... **CLC 10**
See also CA 93-96; 107

Graduate of Oxford, A
See Ruskin, John

Graham, John
See Phillips, David Graham

Graham, Jorie 1951- .... **CLC 48**
See also CA 111; DLB 120

Graham, R(obert) B(ontine) Cunninghame
See Cunninghame Graham, R(obert)
B(ontine)
See also DLB 98, 135

Graham, Robert
See Haldeman, Joe (William)

Graham, Tom
See Lewis, (Harry) Sinclair

Graham, W(illiam) S(ydney)
1918-1986 .... **CLC 29**
See also CA 73-76; 118; DLB 20

Graham, Winston (Mawdsley)
1910- .... **CLC 23**
See also CA 49-52; CANR 2, 22, 45;
DLB 77

Grant, Skeeter
See Spiegelman, Art

Granville-Barker, Harley
1877-1946 .... **TCLC 2**
See also Barker, Harley Granville
See also CA 104; DAM DRAM

Grass, Guenter (Wilhelm)
1927- ..... **CLC 1, 2, 4, 6, 11, 15, 22, 32,**
49, 88; DA; DAB; DAC; WLC
See also CA 13-16R; CANR 20;
DAM MST, NOV; DLB 75, 124; MTCW

Gratton, Thomas
See Hulme, T(homas) E(rnest)

Grau, Shirley Ann
1929- .... **CLC 4, 9; SSC 15**
See also CA 89-92; CANR 22; DLB 2;
INT CANR-22; MTCW

Gravel, Fern
See Hall, James Norman

Graver, Elizabeth 1964- .... **CLC 70**
See also CA 135

Graves, Richard Perceval 1945- .... **CLC 44**
See also CA 65-68; CANR 9, 26, 51

Graves, Robert (von Ranke)
1895-1985 ...... **CLC 1, 2, 6, 11, 39, 44,**
45; DAB; DAC; PC 6
See also CA 5-8R; 117; CANR 5, 36;
CDBLB 1914-1945; DAM MST, POET;
DLB 20, 100; DLBY 85; MTCW;
SATA 45

Gray, Alasdair (James) 1934- ...... **CLC 41**
See also CA 126; CANR 47; INT 126;
MTCW

Gray, Amlin 1946- .... **CLC 29**
See also CA 138

Gray, Francine du Plessix 1930- .... **CLC 22**
See also BEST 90:3; CA 61-64; CAAS 2;
CANR 11, 33; DAM NOV;
INT CANR-11; MTCW

Gray, John (Henry) 1866-1934 .... **TCLC 19**
See also CA 119

Gray, Simon (James Holliday)
1936- .... **CLC 9, 14, 36**
See also AITN 1; CA 21-24R; CAAS 3;
CANR 32; DLB 13; MTCW

Gray, Spalding 1941- .... **CLC 49**
See also CA 128; DAM POP

Gray, Thomas
1716-1771 ...... **LC 4; DA; DAB; DAC;**
PC 2; WLC
See also CDBLB 1660-1789; DAM MST;
DLB 109

Grayson, David
See Baker, Ray Stannard

Grayson, Richard (A.) 1951- .... **CLC 38**
See also CA 85-88; CANR 14, 31

Greeley, Andrew M(oran) 1928- .... **CLC 28**
See also CA 5-8R; CAAS 7; CANR 7, 43;
DAM POP; MTCW

Green, Anna Katharine
1846-1935 .... **TCLC 63**
See also CA 112

Green, Brian
See Card, Orson Scott

Green, Hannah
See Greenberg, Joanne (Goldenberg)

Green, Hannah .... **CLC 3**
See also CA 73-76

Green, Henry .... **CLC 2, 13**
See also Yorke, Henry Vincent
See also DLB 15

Green, Julian (Hartridge) 1900-
See Green, Julien
See also CA 21-24R; CANR 33; DLB 4, 72;
MTCW

Green, Julien .... **CLC 3, 11, 77**
See also Green, Julian (Hartridge)

Green, Paul (Eliot) 1894-1981 ...... **CLC 25**
See also AITN 1; CA 5-8R; 103; CANR 3;
DAM DRAM; DLB 7, 9; DLBY 81

Greenberg, Ivan 1908-1973
See Rahv, Philip
See also CA 85-88

Greenberg, Joanne (Goldenberg)
1932- .... **CLC 7, 30**
See also AAYA 12; CA 5-8R; CANR 14,
32; SATA 25

Greenberg, Richard 1959(?)- .... **CLC 57**
See also CA 138

Greene, Bette 1934- .... **CLC 30**
See also AAYA 7; CA 53-56; CANR 4;
CLR 2; JRDA; MAICYA; SAAS 16;
SATA 8

Greene, Gael .... **CLC 8**
See also CA 13-16R; CANR 10

Greene, Graham
1904-1991 .... **CLC 1, 3, 6, 9, 14, 18, 27,**
37, 70, 72; DA; DAB; DAC; WLC
See also AITN 2; CA 13-16R; 133;
CANR 35; CDBLB 1945-1960;
DAM MST, NOV; DLB 13, 15, 77, 100,
162; DLBY 91; MTCW; SATA 20

Greer, Richard
See Silverberg, Robert

Gregor, Arthur 1923- .... **CLC 9**
See also CA 25-28R; CAAS 10; CANR 11;
SATA 36

Gregor, Lee
See Pohl, Frederik

Gregory, Isabella Augusta (Persse)
1852-1932 .... **TCLC 1**
See also CA 104; DLB 10

Gregory, J. Dennis
See Williams, John A(lfred)

Grendon, Stephen
See Derleth, August (William)

Grenville, Kate 1950- .... **CLC 61**
See also CA 118

Grenville, Pelham
See Wodehouse, P(elham) G(renville)

Greve, Felix Paul (Berthold Friedrich)
1879-1948
See Grove, Frederick Philip
See also CA 104; 141; DAC; DAM MST

Grey, Zane 1872-1939 .... **TCLC 6**
See also CA 104; 132; DAM POP; DLB 9;
MTCW

Grieg, (Johan) Nordahl (Brun)
1902-1943 .... **TCLC 10**
See also CA 107

Grieve, C(hristopher) M(urray)
1892-1978 .... **CLC 11, 19**
See also MacDiarmid, Hugh; Pteleon
See also CA 5-8R; 85-88; CANR 33;
DAM POET; MTCW

Griffin, Gerald 1803-1840 .... **NCLC 7**
See also DLB 159

Griffin, John Howard 1920-1980.... **CLC 68**
See also AITN 1; CA 1-4R; 101; CANR 2

Griffin, Peter 1942- .... **CLC 39**
See also CA 136

Griffiths, Trevor 1935- .... **CLC 13, 52**
See also CA 97-100; CANR 45; DLB 13

Grigson, Geoffrey (Edward Harvey)
1905-1985 .... **CLC 7, 39**
See also CA 25-28R; 118; CANR 20, 33;
DLB 27; MTCW

Grillparzer, Franz 1791-1872...... **NCLC 1**
See also DLB 133

Grimble, Reverend Charles James
See Eliot, T(homas) S(tearns)

Grimke, Charlotte L(ottie) Forten
1837(?)-1914
See Forten, Charlotte L.
See also BW 1; CA 117; 124; DAM MULT,
POET

Grimm, Jacob Ludwig Karl
1785-1863 .... **NCLC 3**
See also DLB 90; MAICYA; SATA 22

Hamill, Pete 1935- . . . . CLC 10
  See also CA 25-28R; CANR 18

Hamilton, Alexander
  1755(?)-1804 . . . . NCLC 49
  See also DLB 37

Hamilton, Clive
  See Lewis, C(live) S(taples)

Hamilton, Edmond 1904-1977 . . . . CLC 1
  See also CA 1-4R; CANR 3; DLB 8

Hamilton, Eugene (Jacob) Lee
  See Lee-Hamilton, Eugene (Jacob)

Hamilton, Franklin
  See Silverberg, Robert

Hamilton, Gail
  See Corcoran, Barbara

Hamilton, Mollie
  See Kaye, M(ary) M(argaret)

Hamilton, (Anthony Walter) Patrick
  1904-1962 . . . . CLC 51
  See also CA 113; DLB 10

Hamilton, Virginia 1936- . . . . CLC 26
  See also AAYA 2; BW 2; CA 25-28R;
  CANR 20, 37; CLR 1, 11, 40;
  DAM MULT; DLB 33, 52;
  INT CANR-20; JRDA; MAICYA;
  MTCW; SATA 4, 56, 79

Hammett, (Samuel) Dashiell
  1894-1961 . . . . CLC 3, 5, 10, 19, 47;
                            SSC 17
  See also AITN 1; CA 81-84; CANR 42;
  CDALB 1929-1941; DLBD 6; MTCW

Hammon, Jupiter
  1711(?)-1800(?) . . . . NCLC 5; BLC
  See also DAM MULT, POET; DLB 31, 50

Hammond, Keith
  See Kuttner, Henry

Hamner, Earl (Henry), Jr. 1923- . . . CLC 12
  See also AITN 2; CA 73-76; DLB 6

Hampton, Christopher (James)
  1946- . . . . CLC 4
  See also CA 25-28R; DLB 13; MTCW

Hamsun, Knut . . . . TCLC 2, 14, 49
  See also Pedersen, Knut

Handke, Peter 1942- . . CLC 5, 8, 10, 15, 38
  See also CA 77-80; CANR 33;
  DAM DRAM, NOV; DLB 85, 124;
  MTCW

Hanley, James 1901-1985 . . . CLC 3, 5, 8, 13
  See also CA 73-76; 117; CANR 36; MTCW

Hannah, Barry 1942- . . . . CLC 23, 38, 90
  See also CA 108; 110; CANR 43; DLB 6;
  INT 110; MTCW

Hannon, Ezra
  See Hunter, Evan

Hansberry, Lorraine (Vivian)
  1930-1965 . . . . . . CLC 17, 62; BLC; DA;
                   DAB; DAC; DC 2
  See also BW 1; CA 109; 25-28R; CABS 3;
  CDALB 1941-1968; DAM DRAM, MST,
  MULT; DLB 7, 38; MTCW

Hansen, Joseph 1923- . . . . CLC 38
  See also CA 29-32R; CAAS 17; CANR 16,
  44; INT CANR-16

Hansen, Martin A. 1909-1955 . . . . . TCLC 32

Hanson, Kenneth O(stlin) 1922- . . . . CLC 13
  See also CA 53-56; CANR 7

Hardwick, Elizabeth 1916- . . . . CLC 13
  See also CA 5-8R; CANR 3, 32;
  DAM NOV; DLB 6; MTCW

Hardy, Thomas
  1840-1928 . . . . . . TCLC 4, 10, 18, 32, 48,
     53; DA; DAB; DAC; PC 8; SSC 2; WLC
  See also CA 104; 123; CDBLB 1890-1914;
  DAM MST, NOV, POET; DLB 18, 19,
  135; MTCW

Hare, David 1947- . . . . CLC 29, 58
  See also CA 97-100; CANR 39; DLB 13;
  MTCW

Harford, Henry
  See Hudson, W(illiam) H(enry)

Hargrave, Leonie
  See Disch, Thomas M(ichael)

Harjo, Joy 1951- . . . . CLC 83
  See also CA 114; CANR 35; DAM MULT;
  DLB 120; NNAL

Harlan, Louis R(udolph) 1922- . . . . . CLC 34
  See also CA 21-24R; CANR 25

Harling, Robert 1951(?)- . . . . CLC 53
  See also CA 147

Harmon, William (Ruth) 1938- . . . . . CLC 38
  See also CA 33-36R; CANR 14, 32, 35;
  SATA 65

Harper, F. E. W.
  See Harper, Frances Ellen Watkins

Harper, Frances E. W.
  See Harper, Frances Ellen Watkins

Harper, Frances E. Watkins
  See Harper, Frances Ellen Watkins

Harper, Frances Ellen
  See Harper, Frances Ellen Watkins

Harper, Frances Ellen Watkins
  1825-1911 . . . . TCLC 14; BLC
  See also BW 1; CA 111; 125; DAM MULT,
  POET; DLB 50

Harper, Michael S(teven) 1938- . . CLC 7, 22
  See also BW 1; CA 33-36R; CANR 24;
  DLB 41

Harper, Mrs. F. E. W.
  See Harper, Frances Ellen Watkins

Harris, Christie (Lucy) Irwin
  1907- . . . . CLC 12
  See also CA 5-8R; CANR 6; DLB 88;
  JRDA; MAICYA; SAAS 10; SATA 6, 74

Harris, Frank 1856-1931 . . . . TCLC 24
  See also CA 109; 150; DLB 156

Harris, George Washington
  1814-1869 . . . . NCLC 23
  See also DLB 3, 11

Harris, Joel Chandler
  1848-1908 . . . . TCLC 2; SSC 19
  See also CA 104; 137; DLB 11, 23, 42, 78,
  91; MAICYA; YABC 1

Harris, John (Wyndham Parkes Lucas)
  Beynon 1903-1969
  See Wyndham, John
  See also CA 102; 89-92

Harris, MacDonald . . . . CLC 9
  See also Heiney, Donald (William)

Harris, Mark 1922- . . . . CLC 19
  See also CA 5-8R; CAAS 3; CANR 2;
  DLB 2; DLBY 80

Harris, (Theodore) Wilson 1921- . . . . CLC 25
  See also BW 2; CA 65-68; CAAS 16;
  CANR 11, 27; DLB 117; MTCW

Harrison, Elizabeth Cavanna 1909-
  See Cavanna, Betty
  See also CA 9-12R; CANR 6, 27

Harrison, Harry (Max) 1925- . . . . . . CLC 42
  See also CA 1-4R; CANR 5, 21; DLB 8;
  SATA 4

Harrison, James (Thomas)
  1937- . . . . CLC 6, 14, 33, 66; SSC 19
  See also CA 13-16R; CANR 8, 51;
  DLBY 82; INT CANR-8

Harrison, Jim
  See Harrison, James (Thomas)

Harrison, Kathryn 1961- . . . . CLC 70
  See also CA 144

Harrison, Tony 1937- . . . . CLC 43
  See also CA 65-68; CANR 44; DLB 40;
  MTCW

Harriss, Will(ard Irvin) 1922- . . . . . . CLC 34
  See also CA 111

Harson, Sley
  See Ellison, Harlan (Jay)

Hart, Ellis
  See Ellison, Harlan (Jay)

Hart, Josephine 1942(?)- . . . . CLC 70
  See also CA 138; DAM POP

Hart, Moss 1904-1961 . . . . CLC 66
  See also CA 109; 89-92; DAM DRAM;
  DLB 7

Harte, (Francis) Bret(t)
  1836(?)-1902 . . . . TCLC 1, 25; DA; DAC;
                       SSC 8; WLC
  See also CA 104; 140; CDALB 1865-1917;
  DAM MST; DLB 12, 64, 74, 79;
  SATA 26

Hartley, L(eslie) P(oles)
  1895-1972 . . . . CLC 2, 22
  See also CA 45-48; 37-40R; CANR 33;
  DLB 15, 139; MTCW

Hartman, Geoffrey H. 1929- . . . . CLC 27
  See also CA 117; 125; DLB 67

Hartmann von Aue
  c. 1160-c. 1205 . . . . CMLC 15
  See also DLB 138

Hartmann von Aue 1170-1210 . . . . CMLC 15

Haruf, Kent 1943- . . . . CLC 34
  See also CA 149

Harwood, Ronald 1934- . . . . CLC 32
  See also CA 1-4R; CANR 4; DAM DRAM,
  MST; DLB 13

Hasek, Jaroslav (Matej Frantisek)
  1883-1923 . . . . TCLC 4
  See also CA 104; 129; MTCW

Hass, Robert 1941- . . . . CLC 18, 39
  See also CA 111; CANR 30, 50; DLB 105

Hastings, Hudson
  See Kuttner, Henry

Hastings, Selina . . . . CLC 44

Heppenstall, (John) Rayner
1911-1981 .... **CLC 10**
See also CA 1-4R; 103; CANR 29

Herbert, Frank (Patrick)
1920-1986 ...... **CLC 12, 23, 35, 44, 85**
See also CA 53-56; 118; CANR 5, 43;
DAM POP; DLB 8; INT CANR-5;
MTCW; SATA 9, 37; SATA-Obit 47

Herbert, George
1593-1633 .... **LC 24; DAB; PC 4**
See also CDBLB Before 1660; DAM POET;
DLB 126

Herbert, Zbigniew 1924- .... **CLC 9, 43**
See also CA 89-92; CANR 36;
DAM POET; MTCW

Herbst, Josephine (Frey)
1897-1969 .... **CLC 34**
See also CA 5-8R; 25-28R; DLB 9

Hergesheimer, Joseph
1880-1954 .... **TCLC 11**
See also CA 109; DLB 102, 9

Herlihy, James Leo 1927-1993 ...... **CLC 6**
See also CA 1-4R; 143; CANR 2

Hermogenes fl. c. 175- .... **CMLC 6**

Hernandez, Jose 1834-1886 ...... **NCLC 17**

Herodotus c. 484B.C.-429B.C.... **CMLC 17**

Herrick, Robert
1591-1674 ..... **LC 13; DA; DAB; DAC;**
                              PC 9
See also DAM MST, POP; DLB 126

Herring, Guilles
See Somerville, Edith

Herriot, James 1916-1995 .... **CLC 12**
See also Wight, James Alfred
See also AAYA 1; CA 148; CANR 40;
DAM POP; SATA 86

Herrmann, Dorothy 1941- .... **CLC 44**
See also CA 107

Herrmann, Taffy
See Herrmann, Dorothy

Hersey, John (Richard)
1914-1993 .... **CLC 1, 2, 7, 9, 40, 81**
See also CA 17-20R; 140; CANR 33;
DAM POP; DLB 6; MTCW; SATA 25;
SATA-Obit 76

Herzen, Aleksandr Ivanovich
1812-1870 .... **NCLC 10**

Herzl, Theodor 1860-1904 .... **TCLC 36**

Herzog, Werner 1942- .... **CLC 16**
See also CA 89-92

Hesiod c. 8th cent. B.C.- .... **CMLC 5**

Hesse, Hermann
1877-1962 .... **CLC 1, 2, 3, 6, 11, 17, 25,**
              69; DA; DAB; DAC; SSC 9; WLC
See also CA 17-18; CAP 2; DAM MST,
NOV; DLB 66; MTCW; SATA 50

Hewes, Cady
See De Voto, Bernard (Augustine)

Heyen, William 1940- .... **CLC 13, 18**
See also CA 33-36R; CAAS 9; DLB 5

Heyerdahl, Thor 1914- .... **CLC 26**
See also CA 5-8R; CANR 5, 22; MTCW;
SATA 2, 52

Heym, Georg (Theodor Franz Arthur)
1887-1912 .... **TCLC 9**
See also CA 106

Heym, Stefan 1913- .... **CLC 41**
See also CA 9-12R; CANR 4; DLB 69

Heyse, Paul (Johann Ludwig von)
1830-1914 .... **TCLC 8**
See also CA 104; DLB 129

Heyward, (Edwin) DuBose
1885-1940 .... **TCLC 59**
See also CA 108; DLB 7, 9, 45; SATA 21

Hibbert, Eleanor Alice Burford
1906-1993 .... **CLC 7**
See also BEST 90:4; CA 17-20R; 140;
CANR 9, 28; DAM POP; SATA 2;
SATA-Obit 74

Higgins, George V(incent)
1939- .... **CLC 4, 7, 10, 18**
See also CA 77-80; CAAS 5; CANR 17, 51;
DLB 2; DLBY 81; INT CANR-17;
MTCW

Higginson, Thomas Wentworth
1823-1911 .... **TCLC 36**
See also DLB 1, 64

Highet, Helen
See MacInnes, Helen (Clark)

Highsmith, (Mary) Patricia
1921-1995 .... **CLC 2, 4, 14, 42**
See also CA 1-4R; 147; CANR 1, 20, 48;
DAM NOV, POP; MTCW

Highwater, Jamake (Mamake)
1942(?)- .... **CLC 12**
See also AAYA 7; CA 65-68; CAAS 7;
CANR 10, 34; CLR 17; DLB 52;
DLBY 85; JRDA; MAICYA; SATA 32,
69; SATA-Brief 30

Highway, Tomson 1951- ...... **CLC 92; DAC**
See also DAM MULT; NNAL

Higuchi, Ichiyo 1872-1896 ...... **NCLC 49**

Hijuelos, Oscar 1951- ...... **CLC 65; HLC**
See also BEST 90:1; CA 123; CANR 50;
DAM MULT, POP; DLB 145; HW

Hikmet, Nazim 1902(?)-1963 ...... **CLC 40**
See also CA 141; 93-96

Hildesheimer, Wolfgang
1916-1991 .... **CLC 49**
See also CA 101; 135; DLB 69, 124

Hill, Geoffrey (William)
1932- .... **CLC 5, 8, 18, 45**
See also CA 81-84; CANR 21;
CDBLB 1960 to Present; DAM POET;
DLB 40; MTCW

Hill, George Roy 1921- .... **CLC 26**
See also CA 110; 122

Hill, John
See Koontz, Dean R(ay)

Hill, Susan (Elizabeth)
1942- .... **CLC 4; DAB**
See also CA 33-36R; CANR 29;
DAM MST, NOV; DLB 14, 139; MTCW

Hillerman, Tony 1925- .... **CLC 62**
See also AAYA 6; BEST 89:1; CA 29-32R;
CANR 21, 42; DAM POP; SATA 6

Hillesum, Etty 1914-1943 .... **TCLC 49**
See also CA 137

Hilliard, Noel (Harvey) 1929- ...... **CLC 15**
See also CA 9-12R; CANR 7

Hillis, Rick 1956- .... **CLC 66**
See also CA 134

Hilton, James 1900-1954 .... **TCLC 21**
See also CA 108; DLB 34, 77; SATA 34

Himes, Chester (Bomar)
1909-1984 .... **CLC 2, 4, 7, 18, 58; BLC**
See also BW 2; CA 25-28R; 114; CANR 22;
DAM MULT; DLB 2, 76, 143; MTCW

Hinde, Thomas .... **CLC 6, 11**
See also Chitty, Thomas Willes

Hindin, Nathan
See Bloch, Robert (Albert)

Hine, (William) Daryl 1936- .... **CLC 15**
See also CA 1-4R; CAAS 15; CANR 1, 20;
DLB 60

Hinkson, Katharine Tynan
See Tynan, Katharine

Hinton, S(usan) E(loise)
1950- .... **CLC 30; DA; DAB; DAC**
See also AAYA 2; CA 81-84; CANR 32;
CLR 3, 23; DAM MST, NOV; JRDA;
MAICYA; MTCW; SATA 19, 58

Hippius, Zinaida .... **TCLC 9**
See also Gippius, Zinaida (Nikolayevna)

Hiraoka, Kimitake 1925-1970
See Mishima, Yukio
See also CA 97-100; 29-32R; DAM DRAM;
MTCW

Hirsch, E(ric) D(onald), Jr. 1928-... **CLC 79**
See also CA 25-28R; CANR 27, 51;
DLB 67; INT CANR-27; MTCW

Hirsch, Edward 1950- .... **CLC 31, 50**
See also CA 104; CANR 20, 42; DLB 120

Hitchcock, Alfred (Joseph)
1899-1980 .... **CLC 16**
See also CA 97-100; SATA 27;
SATA-Obit 24

Hitler, Adolf 1889-1945 .... **TCLC 53**
See also CA 117; 147

Hoagland, Edward 1932- .... **CLC 28**
See also CA 1-4R; CANR 2, 31; DLB 6;
SATA 51

Hoban, Russell (Conwell) 1925- .. **CLC 7, 25**
See also CA 5-8R; CANR 23, 37; CLR 3;
DAM NOV; DLB 52; MAICYA;
MTCW; SATA 1, 40, 78

Hobbs, Perry
See Blackmur, R(ichard) P(almer)

Hobson, Laura Z(ametkin)
1900-1986 .... **CLC 7, 25**
See also CA 17-20R; 118; DLB 28;
SATA 52

Hochhuth, Rolf 1931- .... **CLC 4, 11, 18**
See also CA 5-8R; CANR 33;
DAM DRAM; DLB 124; MTCW

Hochman, Sandra 1936- .... **CLC 3, 8**
See also CA 5-8R; DLB 5

Hochwaelder, Fritz 1911-1986 ...... **CLC 36**
See also CA 29-32R; 120; CANR 42;
DAM DRAM; MTCW

Hochwalder, Fritz
See Hochwaelder, Fritz

Howell, James   1594(?)-1666 . . . .   **LC 13**
See also DLB 151

Howells, W. D.
See Howells, William Dean

Howells, William D.
See Howells, William Dean

Howells, William Dean
1837-1920 . . . .   **TCLC 7, 17, 41**
See also CA 104; 134; CDALB 1865-1917;
DLB 12, 64, 74, 79

Howes, Barbara   1914- . . . .   **CLC 15**
See also CA 9-12R; CAAS 3; SATA 5

Hrabal, Bohumil   1914- . . . .   **CLC 13, 67**
See also CA 106; CAAS 12

Hsun, Lu
See Lu Hsun

Hubbard, L(afayette) Ron(ald)
1911-1986 . . . .   **CLC 43**
See also CA 77-80; 118; CANR 22;
DAM POP

Huch, Ricarda (Octavia)
1864-1947 . . . .   **TCLC 13**
See also CA 111; DLB 66

Huddle, David   1942- . . . .   **CLC 49**
See also CA 57-60; CAAS 20; DLB 130

Hudson, Jeffrey
See Crichton, (John) Michael

Hudson, W(illiam) H(enry)
1841-1922 . . . .   **TCLC 29**
See also CA 115; DLB 98, 153; SATA 35

Hueffer, Ford Madox
See Ford, Ford Madox

Hughart, Barry   1934- . . . .   **CLC 39**
See also CA 137

Hughes, Colin
See Creasey, John

Hughes, David (John)   1930- . . . .   **CLC 48**
See also CA 116; 129; DLB 14

Hughes, Edward James
See Hughes, Ted
See also DAM MST, POET

Hughes, (James) Langston
1902-1967 . . . . .   **CLC 1, 5, 10, 15, 35, 44;**
BLC; DA; DAB; DAC; PC 1;
SSC 6; WLC
See also AAYA 12; BW 1; CA 1-4R;
25-28R; CANR 1, 34; CDALB 1929-1941;
CLR 17; DAM DRAM, MST, MULT,
POET; DLB 4, 7, 48, 51, 86; JRDA;
MAICYA; MTCW; SATA 4, 33

Hughes, Richard (Arthur Warren)
1900-1976 . . . .   **CLC 1, 11**
See also CA 5-8R; 65-68; CANR 4;
DAM NOV; DLB 15, 161; MTCW;
SATA 8; SATA-Obit 25

Hughes, Ted
1930- . . . .   **CLC 2, 4, 9, 14, 37; DAB;**
DAC; PC 7
See also Hughes, Edward James
Scc also CA 1-4R; CANR 1, 33; CLR 3;
DLB 40, 161; MAICYA; MTCW;
SATA 49; SATA-Brief 27

Hugo, Richard F(ranklin)
1923-1982 . . . .   **CLC 6, 18, 32**
See also CA 49-52; 108; CANR 3;
DAM POET; DLB 5

Hugo, Victor (Marie)
1802-1885 . . . .   **NCLC 3, 10, 21; DA;**
DAB; DAC; WLC
See also DAM DRAM, MST, NOV, POET;
DLB 119; SATA 47

Huidobro, Vicente
See Huidobro Fernandez, Vicente Garcia

Huidobro Fernandez, Vicente Garcia
1893-1948 . . . .   **TCLC 31**
See also CA 131; HW

Hulme, Keri   1947- . . . .   **CLC 39**
See also CA 125; INT 125

Hulme, T(homas) E(rnest)
1883-1917 . . . .   **TCLC 21**
See also CA 117; DLB 19

Hume, David   1711-1776. . . . .   **LC 7**
See also DLB 104

Humphrey, William   1924- . . . .   **CLC 45**
See also CA 77-80; DLB 6

Humphreys, Emyr Owen   1919- . . . . .   **CLC 47**
See also CA 5-8R; CANR 3, 24; DLB 15

Humphreys, Josephine   1945- . . . .   **CLC 34, 57**
See also CA 121; 127; INT 127

Hungerford, Pixie
See Brinsmead, H(esba) F(ay)

Hunt, E(verette) Howard, (Jr.)
1918- . . . .   **CLC 3**
See also AITN 1; CA 45-48; CANR 2, 47

Hunt, Kyle
See Creasey, John

Hunt, (James Henry) Leigh
1784-1859 . . . .   **NCLC 1**
See also DAM POET

Hunt, Marsha   1946- . . . .   **CLC 70**
See also BW 2; CA 143

Hunt, Violet   1866-1942 . . . .   **TCLC 53**
See also DLB 162

Hunter, E. Waldo
See Sturgeon, Theodore (Hamilton)

Hunter, Evan   1926- . . . .   **CLC 11, 31**
See also CA 5-8R; CANR 5, 38;
DAM POP; DLBY 82; INT CANR-5;
MTCW; SATA 25

Hunter, Kristin (Eggleston)   1931- . . .   **CLC 35**
See also AITN 1; BW 1; CA 13-16R;
CANR 13; CLR 3; DLB 33;
INT CANR-13; MAICYA; SAAS 10;
SATA 12

Hunter, Mollie   1922- . . . .   **CLC 21**
See also McIlwraith, Maureen Mollie
Hunter
See also AAYA 13; CANR 37; CLR 25;
DLB 161; JRDA; MAICYA; SAAS 7;
SATA 54

Hunter, Robert   (?)-1734. . . . .   **LC 7**

Hurston, Zora Neale
1903-1960 . . . .   **CLC 7, 30, 61; BLC; DA;**
DAC; SSC 4
See also AAYA 15; BW 1; CA 85-88;
DAM MST, MULT, NOV; DLB 51, 86;
MTCW

Huston, John (Marcellus)
1906-1987 . . . .   **CLC 20**
See also CA 73-76; 123; CANR 34; DLB 26

Hustvedt, Siri   1955- . . . .   **CLC 76**
See also CA 137

Hutten, Ulrich von   1488-1523 . . . .   **LC 16**

Huxley, Aldous (Leonard)
1894-1963 . . . . .   **CLC 1, 3, 4, 5, 8, 11, 18,**
35, 79; DA; DAB; DAC; WLC
See also AAYA 11; CA 85-88; CANR 44;
CDBLB 1914-1945; DAM MST, NOV;
DLB 36, 100, 162; MTCW; SATA 63

Huysmans, Charles Marie Georges
1848-1907
See Huysmans, Joris-Karl
See also CA 104

Huysmans, Joris-Karl. . . . .   **TCLC 7**
See also Huysmans, Charles Marie Georges
See also DLB 123

Hwang, David Henry
1957- . . . .   **CLC 55; DC 4**
See also CA 127; 132; DAM DRAM;
INT 132

Hyde, Anthony   1946- . . . .   **CLC 42**
See also CA 136

Hyde, Margaret O(ldroyd)   1917- . . .   **CLC 21**
See also CA 1-4R; CANR 1, 36; CLR 23;
JRDA; MAICYA; SAAS 8; SATA 1, 42,
76

Hynes, James   1956(?)- . . . .   **CLC 65**

Ian, Janis   1951- . . . .   **CLC 21**
See also CA 105

Ibanez, Vicente Blasco
See Blasco Ibanez, Vicente

Ibarguengoitia, Jorge   1928-1983 . . . .   **CLC 37**
See also CA 124; 113; HW

Ibsen, Henrik (Johan)
1828-1906 . . . .   **TCLC 2, 8, 16, 37, 52;**
DA; DAB; DAC; DC 2; WLC
See also CA 104; 141; DAM DRAM, MST

Ibuse Masuji   1898-1993. . . . .   **CLC 22**
See also CA 127; 141

Ichikawa, Kon   1915- . . . .   **CLC 20**
See also CA 121

Idle, Eric   1943- . . . .   **CLC 21**
See also Monty Python
See also CA 116; CANR 35

Ignatow, David   1914- . . . . . .   **CLC 4, 7, 14, 40**
See also CA 9-12R; CAAS 3; CANR 31;
DLB 5

Ihimaera, Witi   1944- . . . .   **CLC 46**
See also CA 77-80

Ilf, Ilya. . . . .   **TCLC 21**
See also Fainzilberg, Ilya Arnoldovich

Immermann, Karl (Lebrecht)
1796-1840 . . . .   **NCLC 4, 49**
See also DLB 133

Inclan, Ramon (Maria) del Valle
See Valle-Inclan, Ramon (Maria) del

Infante, G(uillermo) Cabrera
See Cabrera Infante, G(uillermo)

Ingalls, Rachel (Holmes)   1940- . . . . .   **CLC 42**
See also CA 123; 127

Ingamells, Rex   1913-1955 . . . .   **TCLC 35**

Jensen, Laura (Linnea) 1948- ...... CLC 37
See also CA 103

Jerome, Jerome K(lapka)
1859-1927 .... TCLC 23
See also CA 119; DLB 10, 34, 135

Jerrold, Douglas William
1803-1857 .... NCLC 2
See also DLB 158, 159

Jewett, (Theodora) Sarah Orne
1849-1909 .... TCLC 1, 22; SSC 6
See also CA 108; 127; DLB 12, 74;
SATA 15

Jewsbury, Geraldine (Endsor)
1812-1880 .... NCLC 22
See also DLB 21

Jhabvala, Ruth Prawer
1927- .... CLC 4, 8, 29; DAB
See also CA 1-4R; CANR 2, 29, 51;
DAM NOV; DLB 139; INT CANR-29;
MTCW

Jibran, Kahlil
See Gibran, Kahlil

Jibran, Khalil
See Gibran, Kahlil

Jiles, Paulette 1943- .... CLC 13, 58
See also CA 101

Jimenez (Mantecon), Juan Ramon
1881-1958 .... TCLC 4; HLC; PC 7
See also CA 104; 131; DAM MULT,
POET; DLB 134; HW; MTCW

Jimenez, Ramon
See Jimenez (Mantecon), Juan Ramon

Jimenez Mantecon, Juan
See Jimenez (Mantecon), Juan Ramon

Joel, Billy .... CLC 26
See also Joel, William Martin

Joel, William Martin 1949-
See Joel, Billy
See also CA 108

John of the Cross, St. 1542-1591 .... LC 18

Johnson, B(ryan) S(tanley William)
1933-1973 .... CLC 6, 9
See also CA 9-12R; 53-56; CANR 9;
DLB 14, 40

Johnson, Benj. F. of Boo
See Riley, James Whitcomb

Johnson, Benjamin F. of Boo
See Riley, James Whitcomb

Johnson, Charles (Richard)
1948- .... CLC 7, 51, 65; BLC
See also BW 2; CA 116; CAAS 18;
CANR 42; DAM MULT; DLB 33

Johnson, Denis 1949- .... CLC 52
See also CA 117; 121; DLB 120

Johnson, Diane 1934- .... CLC 5, 13, 48
See also CA 41-44R; CANR 17, 40;
DLBY 80; INT CANR-17; MTCW

Johnson, Eyvind (Olof Verner)
1900-1976 .... CLC 14
See also CA 73-76; 69-72; CANR 34

Johnson, J. R.
See James, C(yril) L(ionel) R(obert)

Johnson, James Weldon
1871-1938 .... TCLC 3, 19; BLC
See also BW 1; CA 104; 125;
CDALB 1917-1929; CLR 32;
DAM MULT, POET; DLB 51; MTCW;
SATA 31

Johnson, Joyce 1935- .... CLC 58
See also CA 125; 129

Johnson, Lionel (Pigot)
1867-1902 .... TCLC 19
See also CA 117; DLB 19

Johnson, Mel
See Malzberg, Barry N(athaniel)

Johnson, Pamela Hansford
1912-1981 .... CLC 1, 7, 27
See also CA 1-4R; 104; CANR 2, 28;
DLB 15; MTCW

Johnson, Samuel
1709-1784 ..... LC 15; DA; DAB; DAC;
WLC
See also CDBLB 1660-1789; DAM MST;
DLB 39, 95, 104, 142

Johnson, Uwe
1934-1984 .... CLC 5, 10, 15, 40
See also CA 1-4R; 112; CANR 1, 39;
DLB 75; MTCW

Johnston, George (Benson) 1913- ... CLC 51
See also CA 1-4R; CANR 5, 20; DLB 88

Johnston, Jennifer 1930- .... CLC 7
See also CA 85-88; DLB 14

Jolley, (Monica) Elizabeth
1923- .... CLC 46; SSC 19
See also CA 127; CAAS 13

Jones, Arthur Llewellyn 1863-1947
See Machen, Arthur
See also CA 104

Jones, D(ouglas) G(ordon) 1929- .... CLC 10
See also CA 29-32R; CANR 13; DLB 53

Jones, David (Michael)
1895-1974 .... CLC 2, 4, 7, 13, 42
See also CA 9-12R; 53-56; CANR 28;
CDBLB 1945-1960; DLB 20, 100; MTCW

Jones, David Robert 1947-
See Bowie, David
See also CA 103

Jones, Diana Wynne 1934- .... CLC 26
See also AAYA 12; CA 49-52; CANR 4,
26; CLR 23; DLB 161; JRDA; MAICYA;
SAAS 7; SATA 9, 70

Jones, Edward P. 1950- .... CLC 76
See also BW 2; CA 142

Jones, Gayl 1949- .... CLC 6, 9; BLC
See also BW 2; CA 77-80; CANR 27;
DAM MULT; DLB 33; MTCW

Jones, James 1921-1977.... CLC 1, 3, 10, 39
See also AITN 1, 2; CA 1-4R; 69-72;
CANR 6; DLB 2, 143; MTCW

Jones, John J.
See Lovecraft, H(oward) P(hillips)

Jones, LeRoi .... CLC 1, 2, 3, 5, 10, 14
See also Baraka, Amiri

Jones, Louis B. .... CLC 65
See also CA 141

Jones, Madison (Percy, Jr.) 1925- ... CLC 4
See also CA 13-16R; CAAS 11; CANR 7;
DLB 152

Jones, Mervyn 1922- .... CLC 10, 52
See also CA 45-48; CAAS 5; CANR 1;
MTCW

Jones, Mick 1956(?)- .... CLC 30

Jones, Nettie (Pearl) 1941- .... CLC 34
See also BW 2; CA 137; CAAS 20

Jones, Preston 1936-1979 .... CLC 10
See also CA 73-76; 89-92; DLB 7

Jones, Robert F(rancis) 1934- .... CLC 7
See also CA 49-52; CANR 2

Jones, Rod 1953- .... CLC 50
See also CA 128

Jones, Terence Graham Parry
1942- .... CLC 21
See also Jones, Terry; Monty Python
See also CA 112; 116; CANR 35; INT 116

Jones, Terry
See Jones, Terence Graham Parry
See also SATA 67; SATA-Brief 51

Jones, Thom 1945(?)- .... CLC 81

Jong, Erica 1942- ...... CLC 4, 6, 8, 18, 83
See also AITN 1; BEST 90:2; CA 73-76;
CANR 26; DAM NOV, POP; DLB 2, 5,
28, 152; INT CANR-26; MTCW

Jonson, Ben(jamin)
1572(?)-1637 .... LC 6; DA; DAB; DAC;
DC 4; WLC
See also CDBLB Before 1660;
DAM DRAM, MST, POET; DLB 62,
121

Jordan, June 1936- .... CLC 5, 11, 23
See also AAYA 2; BW 2; CA 33-36R;
CANR 25; CLR 10; DAM MULT,
POET; DLB 38; MAICYA; MTCW;
SATA 4

Jordan, Pat(rick M.) 1941- .... CLC 37
See also CA 33-36R

Jorgensen, Ivar
See Ellison, Harlan (Jay)

Jorgenson, Ivar
See Silverberg, Robert

Josephus, Flavius c. 37-100 ...... CMLC 13

Josipovici, Gabriel 1940- .... CLC 6, 43
See also CA 37-40R; CAAS 8; CANR 47;
DLB 14

Joubert, Joseph 1754-1824 .... NCLC 9

Jouve, Pierre Jean 1887-1976 ...... CLC 47
See also CA 65-68

Joyce, James (Augustine Aloysius)
1882-1941 .... TCLC 3, 8, 16, 35, 52;
DA; DAB; DAC; SSC 3; WLC
See also CA 104; 126; CDBLB 1914-1945;
DAM MST, NOV, POET; DLB 10, 19,
36, 162; MTCW

Jozsef, Attila 1905-1937.......... TCLC 22
See also CA 116

Juana Ines de la Cruz 1651(?)-1695 ... LC 5

Judd, Cyril
See Kornbluth, C(yril) M.; Pohl, Frederik

Julian of Norwich 1342(?)-1416(?) .... LC 6
See also DLB 146

Juniper, Alex
See Hospital, Janette Turner

Junius
See Luxemburg, Rosa

Just, Ward (Swift) 1935- .... **CLC 4, 27**
See also CA 25-28R; CANR 32;
INT CANR-32

Justice, Donald (Rodney) 1925- .. **CLC 6, 19**
See also CA 5-8R; CANR 26; DAM POET;
DLBY 83; INT CANR-26

Juvenal c. 55-c. 127 .... **CMLC 8**

Juvenis
See Bourne, Randolph S(illiman)

Kacew, Romain 1914-1980
See Gary, Romain
See also CA 108; 102

Kadare, Ismail 1936- .... **CLC 52**

Kadohata, Cynthia................ **CLC 59**
See also CA 140

Kafka, Franz
1883-1924 .... **TCLC 2, 6, 13, 29, 47, 53;**
DA; DAB; DAC; SSC 5; WLC
See also CA 105; 126; DAM MST, NOV;
DLB 81; MTCW

Kahanovitsch, Pinkhes
See Der Nister

Kahn, Roger 1927-............... **CLC 30**
See also CA 25-28R; CANR 44; SATA 37

Kain, Saul
See Sassoon, Siegfried (Lorraine)

Kaiser, Georg 1878-1945 .... **TCLC 9**
See also CA 106; DLB 124

Kaletski, Alexander 1946- .... **CLC 39**
See also CA 118; 143

Kalidasa fl. c. 400- .... **CMLC 9**

Kallman, Chester (Simon)
1921-1975 .... **CLC 2**
See also CA 45-48; 53-56; CANR 3

Kaminsky, Melvin 1926-
See Brooks, Mel
See also CA 65-68; CANR 16

Kaminsky, Stuart M(elvin) 1934- ... **CLC 59**
See also CA 73-76; CANR 29

Kane, Paul
See Simon, Paul

Kane, Wilson
See Bloch, Robert (Albert)

Kanin, Garson 1912-.............. **CLC 22**
See also AITN 1; CA 5-8R; CANR 7;
DLB 7

Kaniuk, Yoram 1930-............. **CLC 19**
See also CA 134

Kant, Immanuel 1724-1804 ...... **NCLC 27**
See also DLB 94

Kantor, MacKinlay 1904-1977 ...... **CLC 7**
See also CA 61-64; 73-76; DLB 9, 102

Kaplan, David Michael 1946- ...... **CLC 50**

Kaplan, James 1951- .... **CLC 59**
See also CA 135

Karageorge, Michael
See Anderson, Poul (William)

Karamzin, Nikolai Mikhailovich
1766-1826 .... **NCLC 3**
See also DLB 150

Karapanou, Margarita 1946- .... **CLC 13**
See also CA 101

Karinthy, Frigyes 1887-1938 ...... **TCLC 47**

Karl, Frederick R(obert) 1927- ..... **CLC 34**
See also CA 5-8R; CANR 3, 44

Kastel, Warren
See Silverberg, Robert

Kataev, Evgeny Petrovich 1903-1942
See Petrov, Evgeny
See also CA 120

Kataphusin
See Ruskin, John

Katz, Steve 1935-................ **CLC 47**
See also CA 25-28R; CAAS 14; CANR 12;
DLBY 83

Kauffman, Janet 1945-............ **CLC 42**
See also CA 117; CANR 43; DLBY 86

Kaufman, Bob (Garnell)
1925-1986 .... **CLC 49**
See also BW 1; CA 41-44R; 118; CANR 22;
DLB 16, 41

Kaufman, George S. 1889-1961 ..... **CLC 38**
See also CA 108; 93-96; DAM DRAM;
DLB 7; INT 108

Kaufman, Sue .... **CLC 3, 8**
See also Barondess, Sue K(aufman)

Kavafis, Konstantinos Petrou 1863-1933
See Cavafy, C(onstantine) P(eter)
See also CA 104

Kavan, Anna 1901-1968 ...... **CLC 5, 13, 82**
See also CA 5-8R; CANR 6; MTCW

Kavanagh, Dan
See Barnes, Julian

Kavanagh, Patrick (Joseph)
1904-1967 .... **CLC 22**
See also CA 123; 25-28R; DLB 15, 20;
MTCW

Kawabata, Yasunari
1899-1972 ..... **CLC 2, 5, 9, 18; SSC 17**
See also CA 93-96; 33-36R; DAM MULT

Kaye, M(ary) M(argaret) 1909-..... **CLC 28**
See also CA 89-92; CANR 24; MTCW;
SATA 62

Kaye, Mollie
See Kaye, M(ary) M(argaret)

Kaye-Smith, Sheila 1887-1956..... **TCLC 20**
See also CA 118; DLB 36

Kaymor, Patrice Maguilene
See Senghor, Leopold Sedar

Kazan, Elia 1909-........... **CLC 6, 16, 63**
See also CA 21-24R; CANR 32

Kazantzakis, Nikos
1883(?)-1957 .... **TCLC 2, 5, 33**
See also CA 105; 132; MTCW

Kazin, Alfred 1915- .... **CLC 34, 38**
See also CA 1-4R; CAAS 7; CANR 1, 45;
DLB 67

Keane, Mary Nesta (Skrine) 1904-
See Keane, Molly
See also CA 108; 114

Keane, Molly.................... **CLC 31**
See also Keane, Mary Nesta (Skrine)
See also INT 114

Keates, Jonathan 19(?)-........... **CLC 34**

Keaton, Buster 1895-1966 .... **CLC 20**

Keats, John
1795-1821 .... **NCLC 8; DA; DAB;**
DAC; PC 1; WLC
See also CDBLB 1789-1832; DAM MST,
POET; DLB 96, 110

Keene, Donald 1922- .... **CLC 34**
See also CA 1-4R; CANR 5

Keillor, Garrison .... **CLC 40**
See also Keillor, Gary (Edward)
See also AAYA 2; BEST 89:3; DLBY 87;
SATA 58

Keillor, Gary (Edward) 1942-
See Keillor, Garrison
See also CA 111; 117; CANR 36;
DAM POP; MTCW

Keith, Michael
See Hubbard, L(afayette) Ron(ald)

Keller, Gottfried 1819-1890....... **NCLC 2**
See also DLB 129

Kellerman, Jonathan 1949- .... **CLC 44**
See also BEST 90:1; CA 106; CANR 29, 51;
DAM POP; INT CANR-29

Kelley, William Melvin 1937-...... **CLC 22**
See also BW 1; CA 77-80; CANR 27;
DLB 33

Kellogg, Marjorie 1922-........... **CLC 2**
See also CA 81-84

Kellow, Kathleen
See Hibbert, Eleanor Alice Burford

Kelly, M(ilton) T(erry) 1947-....... **CLC 55**
See also CA 97-100; CAAS 22; CANR 19,
43

Kelman, James 1946-.......... **CLC 58, 86**
See also CA 148

Kemal, Yashar 1923- .... **CLC 14, 29**
See also CA 89-92; CANR 44

Kemble, Fanny 1809-1893 .... **NCLC 18**
See also DLB 32

Kemelman, Harry 1908-........... **CLC 2**
See also AITN 1; CA 9-12R; CANR 6;
DLB 28

Kempe, Margery 1373(?)-1440(?) ..... **LC 6**
See also DLB 146

Kempis, Thomas a 1380-1471 .... **LC 11**

Kendall, Henry 1839-1882....... **NCLC 12**

Keneally, Thomas (Michael)
1935- ...... **CLC 5, 8, 10, 14, 19, 27, 43**
See also CA 85-88; CANR 10, 50;
DAM NOV; MTCW

Kennedy, Adrienne (Lita)
1931- .... **CLC 66; BLC; DC 5**
See also BW 2; CA 103; CAAS 20; CABS 3;
CANR 26; DAM MULT; DLB 38

Kennedy, John Pendleton
1795-1870 .... **NCLC 2**
See also DLB 3

Kennedy, Joseph Charles 1929-
See Kennedy, X. J.
See also CA 1-4R; CANR 4, 30, 40;
SATA 14, 86

Kennedy, William 1928-... **CLC 6, 28, 34, 53**
See also AAYA 1; CA 85-88; CANR 14,
31; DAM NOV; DLB 143; DLBY 85;
INT CANR-31; MTCW; SATA 57

Kennedy, X. J.................. **CLC 8, 42**
See also Kennedy, Joseph Charles
See also CAAS 9; CLR 27; DLB 5;
SAAS 22

Kenny, Maurice (Francis) 1929-.... **CLC 87**
See also CA 144; CAAS 22; DAM MULT;
NNAL

Kent, Kelvin
See Kuttner, Henry

Kenton, Maxwell
See Southern, Terry

Kenyon, Robert O.
See Kuttner, Henry

Kerouac, Jack ..... **CLC 1, 2, 3, 5, 14, 29, 61**
See also Kerouac, Jean-Louis Lebris de
See also CDALB 1941-1968; DLB 2, 16;
DLBD 3; DLBY 95

Kerouac, Jean-Louis Lebris de 1922-1969
See Kerouac, Jack
See also AITN 1; CA 5-8R; 25-28R;
CANR 26; DA; DAB; DAC; DAM MST,
NOV, POET, POP; MTCW; WLC

Kerr, Jean 1923-................. **CLC 22**
See also CA 5-8R; CANR 7; INT CANR-7

Kerr, M. E.................... **CLC 12, 35**
See also Meaker, Marijane (Agnes)
See also AAYA 2; CLR 29; SAAS 1

Kerr, Robert .... **CLC 55**

Kerrigan, (Thomas) Anthony
1918-..................... **CLC 4, 6**
See also CA 49-52; CAAS 11; CANR 4

Kerry, Lois
See Duncan, Lois

Kesey, Ken (Elton)
1935-...... **CLC 1, 3, 6, 11, 46, 64; DA;
DAB; DAC; WLC**
See also CA 1-4R; CANR 22, 38;
CDALB 1968-1988; DAM MST, NOV,
POP; DLB 2, 16; MTCW; SATA 66

Kesselring, Joseph (Otto)
1902-1967 .... **CLC 45**
See also CA 150; DAM DRAM, MST

Kessler, Jascha (Frederick) 1929-.... **CLC 4**
See also CA 17-20R; CANR 8, 48

Kettelkamp, Larry (Dale) 1933- .... **CLC 12**
See also CA 29-32R; CANR 16; SAAS 3;
SATA 2

Keyber, Conny
See Fielding, Henry

Keyes, Daniel 1927-.... **CLC 80; DA; DAC**
See also CA 17-20R; CANR 10, 26;
DAM MST, NOV; SATA 37

Khanshendel, Chiron
See Rose, Wendy

Khayyam, Omar
1048-1131 .... **CMLC 11; PC 8**
See also DAM POET

Kherdian, David 1931-........... **CLC 6, 9**
See also CA 21-24R; CAAS 2; CANR 39;
CLR 24; JRDA; MAICYA; SATA 16, 74

Khlebnikov, Velimir .... **TCLC 20**
See also Khlebnikov, Viktor Vladimirovich

Khlebnikov, Viktor Vladimirovich 1885-1922
See Khlebnikov, Velimir
See also CA 117

Khodasevich, Vladislav (Felitsianovich)
1886-1939 .... **TCLC 15**
See also CA 115

Kielland, Alexander Lange
1849-1906 .... **TCLC 5**
See also CA 104

Kiely, Benedict 1919-.......... **CLC 23, 43**
See also CA 1-4R; CANR 2; DLB 15

Kienzle, William X(avier) 1928- .... **CLC 25**
See also CA 93-96; CAAS 1; CANR 9, 31;
DAM POP; INT CANR-31; MTCW

Kierkegaard, Soren 1813-1855.... **NCLC 34**

Killens, John Oliver 1916-1987..... **CLC 10**
See also BW 2; CA 77-80; 123; CAAS 2;
CANR 26; DLB 33

Killigrew, Anne 1660-1685.......... **LC 4**
See also DLB 131

Kim
See Simenon, Georges (Jacques Christian)

Kincaid, Jamaica 1949-... **CLC 43, 68; BLC**
See also AAYA 13; BW 2; CA 125;
CANR 47; DAM MULT, NOV;
DLB 157

King, Francis (Henry) 1923-..... **CLC 8, 53**
See also CA 1-4R; CANR 1, 33;
DAM NOV; DLB 15, 139; MTCW

King, Martin Luther, Jr.
1929-1968 .... **CLC 83; BLC; DA; DAB;
DAC**
See also BW 2; CA 25-28; CANR 27, 44;
CAP 2; DAM MST, MULT; MTCW;
SATA 14

King, Stephen (Edwin)
1947-...... **CLC 12, 26, 37, 61; SSC 17**
See also AAYA 1, 17; BEST 90:1;
CA 61-64; CANR 1, 30; DAM NOV,
POP; DLB 143; DLBY 80; JRDA;
MTCW; SATA 9, 55

King, Steve
See King, Stephen (Edwin)

King, Thomas 1943-......... **CLC 89; DAC**
See also CA 144; DAM MULT; NNAL

Kingman, Lee.................... **CLC 17**
See also Natti, (Mary) Lee
See also SAAS 3; SATA 1, 67

Kingsley, Charles 1819-1875..... **NCLC 35**
See also DLB 21, 32, 163; YABC 2

Kingsley, Sidney 1906-1995........ **CLC 44**
See also CA 85-88; 147; DLB 7

Kingsolver, Barbara 1955-...... **CLC 55, 81**
See also AAYA 15; CA 129; 134;
DAM POP; INT 134

Kingston, Maxine (Ting Ting) Hong
1940-................. **CLC 12, 19, 58**
See also AAYA 8; CA 69-72; CANR 13,
38; DAM MULT, NOV; DLBY 80;
INT CANR-13; MTCW; SATA 53

Kinnell, Galway
1927-........... **CLC 1, 2, 3, 5, 13, 29**
See also CA 9-12R; CANR 10, 34; DLB 5;
DLB 87; INT CANR-34; MTCW

Kinsella, Thomas 1928-......... **CLC 4, 19**
See also CA 17-20R; CANR 15; DLB 27;
MTCW

Kinsella, W(illiam) P(atrick)
1935-.............. **CLC 27, 43; DAC**
See also AAYA 7; CA 97-100; CAAS 7;
CANR 21, 35; DAM NOV, POP;
INT CANR-21; MTCW

Kipling, (Joseph) Rudyard
1865-1936 ...... **TCLC 8, 17; DA; DAB;
DAC; PC 3; SSC 5; WLC**
See also CA 105; 120; CANR 33;
CDBLB 1890-1914; CLR 39; DAM MST,
POET; DLB 19, 34, 141, 156; MAICYA;
MTCW; YABC 2

Kirkup, James 1918- .... **CLC 1**
See also CA 1-4R; CAAS 4; CANR 2;
DLB 27; SATA 12

Kirkwood, James 1930(?)-1989 ...... **CLC 9**
See also AITN 2; CA 1-4R; 128; CANR 6,
40

Kirshner, Sidney
See Kingsley, Sidney

Kis, Danilo 1935-1989 .... **CLC 57**
See also CA 109; 118; 129; MTCW

Kivi, Aleksis 1834-1872 .... **NCLC 30**

Kizer, Carolyn (Ashley)
1925-.................. **CLC 15, 39, 80**
See also CA 65-68; CAAS 5; CANR 24;
DAM POET; DLB 5

Klabund 1890-1928.............. **TCLC 44**
See also DLB 66

Klappert, Peter 1942-............. **CLC 57**
See also CA 33-36R; DLB 5

Klein, A(braham) M(oses)
1909-1972 .... **CLC 19; DAB; DAC**
See also CA 101; 37-40R; DAM MST;
DLB 68

Klein, Norma 1938-1989 .... **CLC 30**
See also AAYA 2; CA 41-44R; 128;
CANR 15, 37; CLR 2, 19;
INT CANR-15; JRDA; MAICYA;
SAAS 1; SATA 7, 57

Klein, T(heodore) E(ibon) D(onald)
1947-..................... **CLC 34**
See also CA 119; CANR 44

Kleist, Heinrich von
1777-1811 .... **NCLC 2, 37; SSC 22**
See also DAM DRAM; DLB 90

Klima, Ivan 1931-................ **CLC 56**
See also CA 25-28R; CANR 17, 50;
DAM NOV

Klimentov, Andrei Platonovich 1899-1951
See Platonov, Andrei
See also CA 108

Klinger, Friedrich Maximilian von
1752-1831 .... **NCLC 1**
See also DLB 94

Klopstock, Friedrich Gottlieb
1724-1803 .... **NCLC 11**
See also DLB 97

Knebel, Fletcher 1911-1993 . . . . **CLC 14**
See also AITN 1; CA 1-4R; 140; CAAS 3;
CANR 1, 36; SATA 36; SATA-Obit 75

Knickerbocker, Diedrich
See Irving, Washington

Knight, Etheridge
1931-1991 . . . . **CLC 40; BLC; PC 14**
See also BW 1; CA 21-24R; 133; CANR 23;
DAM POET; DLB 41

Knight, Sarah Kemble 1666-1727 . . . . . **LC 7**
See also DLB 24

Knister, Raymond 1899-1932. . . . . . **TCLC 56**
See also DLB 68

Knowles, John
1926- . . . . . . **CLC 1, 4, 10, 26; DA; DAC**
See also AAYA 10; CA 17-20R; CANR 40;
CDALB 1968-1988; DAM MST, NOV;
DLB 6; MTCW; SATA 8

Knox, Calvin M.
See Silverberg, Robert

Knye, Cassandra
See Disch, Thomas M(ichael)

Koch, C(hristopher) J(ohn) 1932- . . . **CLC 42**
See also CA 127

Koch, Christopher
See Koch, C(hristopher) J(ohn)

Koch, Kenneth 1925- . . . . **CLC 5, 8, 44**
See also CA 1-4R; CANR 6, 36;
DAM POET; DLB 5; INT CANR-36;
SATA 65

Kochanowski, Jan 1530-1584. . . . . . . **LC 10**

Kock, Charles Paul de
1794-1871 . . . . **NCLC 16**

Koda Shigeyuki 1867-1947
See Rohan, Koda
See also CA 121

Koestler, Arthur
1905-1983 . . . . **CLC 1, 3, 6, 8, 15, 33**
See also CA 1-4R; 109; CANR 1, 33;
CDBLB 1945-1960; DLBY 83; MTCW

Kogawa, Joy Nozomi 1935-. . . **CLC 78; DAC**
See also CA 101; CANR 19; DAM MST,
MULT

Kohout, Pavel 1928-. . . . . **CLC 13**
See also CA 45-48; CANR 3

Koizumi, Yakumo
See Hearn, (Patricio) Lafcadio (Tessima
Carlos)

Kolmar, Gertrud 1894-1943 . . . . . . **TCLC 40**

Komunyakaa, Yusef 1947-. . . . . **CLC 86**
See also CA 147; DLB 120

Konrad, George
See Konrad, Gyoergy

Konrad, Gyoergy 1933- . . . . . . **CLC 4, 10, 73**
See also CA 85-88

Konwicki, Tadeusz 1926-. . . . . **CLC 8, 28, 54**
See also CA 101; CAAS 9; CANR 39;
MTCW

Koontz, Dean R(ay) 1945-. . . . . **CLC 78**
See also AAYA 9; BEST 89:3, 90:2;
CA 108; CANR 19, 36; DAM NOV,
POP; MTCW

Kopit, Arthur (Lee) 1937- . . . . **CLC 1, 18, 33**
See also AITN 1; CA 81-84; CABS 3;
DAM DRAM; DLB 7; MTCW

Kops, Bernard 1926-. . . . . **CLC 4**
See also CA 5-8R; DLB 13

Kornbluth, C(yril) M. 1923-1958. . . . **TCLC 8**
See also CA 105; DLB 8

Korolenko, V. G.
See Korolenko, Vladimir Galaktionovich

Korolenko, Vladimir
See Korolenko, Vladimir Galaktionovich

Korolenko, Vladimir G.
See Korolenko, Vladimir Galaktionovich

Korolenko, Vladimir Galaktionovich
1853-1921 . . . . **TCLC 22**
See also CA 121

Korzybski, Alfred (Habdank Skarbek)
1879-1950 . . . . **TCLC 61**
See also CA 123

Kosinski, Jerzy (Nikodem)
1933-1991 . . . . **CLC 1, 2, 3, 6, 10, 15, 53,
70**
See also CA 17-20R; 134; CANR 9, 46;
DAM NOV; DLB 2; DLBY 82; MTCW

Kostelanetz, Richard (Cory) 1940-. . **CLC 28**
See also CA 13-16R; CAAS 8; CANR 38

Kostrowitzki, Wilhelm Apollinaris de
1880-1918
See Apollinaire, Guillaume
See also CA 104

Kotlowitz, Robert 1924-. . . . . **CLC 4**
See also CA 33-36R; CANR 36

Kotzebue, August (Friedrich Ferdinand) von
1761-1819 . . . . **NCLC 25**
See also DLB 94

Kotzwinkle, William 1938- . . . **CLC 5, 14, 35**
See also CA 45-48; CANR 3, 44; CLR 6;
MAICYA; SATA 24, 70

Kozol, Jonathan 1936-. . . . . **CLC 17**
See also CA 61-64; CANR 16, 45

Kozoll, Michael 1940(?)-. . . . . **CLC 35**

Kramer, Kathryn 19(?)-. . . . . **CLC 34**

Kramer, Larry 1935- . . . . **CLC 42**
See also CA 124; 126; DAM POP

Krasicki, Ignacy 1735-1801 . . . . **NCLC 8**

Krasinski, Zygmunt 1812-1859 . . . . **NCLC 4**

Kraus, Karl 1874-1936. . . . . **TCLC 5**
See also CA 104; DLB 118

Kreve (Mickevicius), Vincas
1882-1954 . . . . **TCLC 27**

Kristeva, Julia 1941- . . . . **CLC 77**

Kristofferson, Kris 1936-. . . . . **CLC 26**
See also CA 104

Krizanc, John 1956-. . . . . **CLC 57**

Krleza, Miroslav 1893-1981. . . . . **CLC 8**
See also CA 97-100; 105; CANR 50;
DLB 147

Kroetsch, Robert
1927-. . . . . **CLC 5, 23, 57; DAC**
See also CA 17-20R; CANR 8, 38;
DAM POET; DLB 53; MTCW

Kroetz, Franz
See Kroetz, Franz Xaver

Kroetz, Franz Xaver 1946- . . . . **CLC 41**
See also CA 130

Kroker, Arthur 1945-. . . . . **CLC 77**

Kropotkin, Peter (Aleksieevich)
1842-1921 . . . . **TCLC 36**
See also CA 119

Krotkov, Yuri 1917-. . . . . **CLC 19**
See also CA 102

Krumb
See Crumb, R(obert)

Krumgold, Joseph (Quincy)
1908-1980 . . . . **CLC 12**
See also CA 9-12R; 101; CANR 7;
MAICYA; SATA 1, 48; SATA-Obit 23

Krumwitz
See Crumb, R(obert)

Krutch, Joseph Wood 1893-1970. . . . **CLC 24**
See also CA 1-4R; 25-28R; CANR 4;
DLB 63

Krutzch, Gus
See Eliot, T(homas) S(tearns)

Krylov, Ivan Andreevich
1768(?)-1844 . . . . **NCLC 1**
See also DLB 150

Kubin, Alfred (Leopold Isidor)
1877-1959 . . . . **TCLC 23**
See also CA 112; 149; DLB 81

Kubrick, Stanley 1928-. . . . . **CLC 16**
See also CA 81-84; CANR 33; DLB 26

Kumin, Maxine (Winokur)
1925- . . . . **CLC 5, 13, 28; PC 15**
See also AITN 2; CA 1-4R; CAAS 8;
CANR 1, 21; DAM POET; DLB 5;
MTCW; SATA 12

Kundera, Milan
1929- . . . . **CLC 4, 9, 19, 32, 68**
See also AAYA 2; CA 85-88; CANR 19;
DAM NOV; MTCW

Kunene, Mazisi (Raymond) 1930-. . . **CLC 85**
See also BW 1; CA 125; DLB 117

Kunitz, Stanley (Jasspon)
1905- . . . . **CLC 6, 11, 14**
See also CA 41-44R; CANR 26; DLB 48;
INT CANR-26; MTCW

Kunze, Reiner 1933-. . . . . **CLC 10**
See also CA 93-96; DLB 75

Kuprin, Aleksandr Ivanovich
1870-1938 . . . . **TCLC 5**
See also CA 104

Kureishi, Hanif 1954(?)-. . . . . **CLC 64**
See also CA 139

Kurosawa, Akira 1910-. . . . . **CLC 16**
See also AAYA 11; CA 101; CANR 46;
DAM MULT

Kushner, Tony 1957(?)- . . . . **CLC 81**
See also CA 144; DAM DRAM

Kuttner, Henry 1915-1958. . . . . **TCLC 10**
See also CA 107; DLB 8

Kuzma, Greg 1944-. . . . . **CLC 7**
See also CA 33-36R

Kuzmin, Mikhail 1872(?)-1936 . . . . **TCLC 40**

Kyd, Thomas 1558-1594. . . . . . . **LC 22; DC 3**
See also DAM DRAM; DLB 62

Kyprianos, Iossif
See Samarakis, Antonis

La Bruyere, Jean de 1645-1696...... **LC 17**

Lacan, Jacques (Marie Emile)
1901-1981 .... **CLC 75**
See also CA 121; 104

Laclos, Pierre Ambroise Francois Choderlos de 1741-1803 .... **NCLC 4**

Lacolere, Francois
See Aragon, Louis

La Colere, Francois
See Aragon, Louis

La Deshabilleuse
See Simenon, Georges (Jacques Christian)

Lady Gregory
See Gregory, Isabella Augusta (Persse)

Lady of Quality, A
See Bagnold, Enid

La Fayette, Marie (Madelaine Pioche de la Vergne Comtes 1634-1693....... **LC 2**

Lafayette, Rene
See Hubbard, L(afayette) Ron(ald)

Laforgue, Jules
1860-1887 .... **NCLC 5, 53; PC 14; SSC 20**

Lagerkvist, Paer (Fabian)
1891-1974 .... **CLC 7, 10, 13, 54**
See also Lagerkvist, Par
See also CA 85-88; 49-52; DAM DRAM, NOV; MTCW

Lagerkvist, Par .... **SSC 12**
See also Lagerkvist, Paer (Fabian)

Lagerloef, Selma (Ottiliana Lovisa)
1858-1940 .... **TCLC 4, 36**
See also Lagerlof, Selma (Ottiliana Lovisa)
See also CA 108; SATA 15

Lagerlof, Selma (Ottiliana Lovisa)
See Lagerloef, Selma (Ottiliana Lovisa)
See also CLR 7; SATA 15

La Guma, (Justin) Alex(ander)
1925-1985 .... **CLC 19**
See also BW 1; CA 49-52; 118; CANR 25;
DAM NOV; DLB 117; MTCW

Laidlaw, A. K.
See Grieve, C(hristopher) M(urray)

Lainez, Manuel Mujica
See Mujica Lainez, Manuel
See also HW

Lamartine, Alphonse (Marie Louis Prat) de
1790-1869 .... **NCLC 11**
See also DAM POET

Lamb, Charles
1775-1834 .... **NCLC 10; DA; DAB; DAC; WLC**
See also CDBLB 1789-1832; DAM MST;
DLB 93, 107, 163; SATA 17

Lamb, Lady Caroline 1785-1828.. **NCLC 38**
See also DLB 116

Lamming, George (William)
1927- .... **CLC 2, 4, 66; BLC**
See also BW 2; CA 85-88; CANR 26;
DAM MULT; DLB 125; MTCW

L'Amour, Louis (Dearborn)
1908-1988 .... **CLC 25, 55**
See also AAYA 16; AITN 2; BEST 89:2;
CA 1-4R; 125; CANR 3, 25, 40;
DAM NOV, POP; DLBY 80; MTCW

Lampedusa, Giuseppe (Tomasi) di ... **TCLC 13**
See also Tomasi di Lampedusa, Giuseppe

Lampman, Archibald 1861-1899 .. **NCLC 25**
See also DLB 92

Lancaster, Bruce 1896-1963....... **CLC 36**
See also CA 9-10; CAP 1; SATA 9

Landau, Mark Alexandrovich
See Aldanov, Mark (Alexandrovich)

Landau-Aldanov, Mark Alexandrovich
See Aldanov, Mark (Alexandrovich)

Landis, John 1950-.............. **CLC 26**
See also CA 112; 122

Landolfi, Tommaso 1908-1979... **CLC 11, 49**
See also CA 127; 117

Landon, Letitia Elizabeth
1802-1838 .... **NCLC 15**
See also DLB 96

Landor, Walter Savage
1775-1864 .... **NCLC 14**
See also DLB 93, 107

Landwirth, Heinz 1927-
See Lind, Jakov
See also CA 9-12R; CANR 7

Lane, Patrick 1939-.............. **CLC 25**
See also CA 97-100; DAM POET; DLB 53;
INT 97-100

Lang, Andrew 1844-1912........ **TCLC 16**
See also CA 114; 137; DLB 98, 141;
MAICYA; SATA 16

Lang, Fritz 1890-1976 .... **CLC 20**
See also CA 77-80; 69-72; CANR 30

Lange, John
See Crichton, (John) Michael

Langer, Elinor 1939- .... **CLC 34**
See also CA 121

Langland, William
1330(?)-1400(?) ...... **LC 19; DA; DAB; DAC**
See also DAM MST, POET; DLB 146

Langstaff, Launcelot
See Irving, Washington

Lanier, Sidney 1842-1881 .... **NCLC 6**
See also DAM POET; DLB 64; DLBD 13;
MAICYA; SATA 18

Lanyer, Aemilia 1569-1645 ...... **LC 10, 30**
See also DLB 121

Lao Tzu .... **CMLC 7**

Lapine, James (Elliot) 1949-....... **CLC 39**
See also CA 123; 130; INT 130

Larbaud, Valery (Nicolas)
1881-1957 .... **TCLC 9**
See also CA 106

Lardner, Ring
See Lardner, Ring(gold) W(ilmer)

Lardner, Ring W., Jr.
See Lardner, Ring(gold) W(ilmer)

Lardner, Ring(gold) W(ilmer)
1885-1933 .... **TCLC 2, 14**
See also CA 104; 131; CDALB 1917-1929;
DLB 11, 25, 86; MTCW

Laredo, Betty
See Codrescu, Andrei

Larkin, Maia
See Wojciechowska, Maia (Teresa)

Larkin, Philip (Arthur)
1922-1985 .... **CLC 3, 5, 8, 9, 13, 18, 33, 39, 64; DAB**
See also CA 5-8R; 117; CANR 24;
CDBLB 1960 to Present; DAM MST,
POET; DLB 27; MTCW

Larra (y Sanchez de Castro), Mariano Jose de
1809-1837 .... **NCLC 17**

Larsen, Eric 1941-............... **CLC 55**
See also CA 132

Larsen, Nella 1891-1964 ..... **CLC 37; BLC**
See also BW 1; CA 125; DAM MULT;
DLB 51

Larson, Charles R(aymond) 1938-... **CLC 31**
See also CA 53-56; CANR 4

Las Casas, Bartolome de 1474-1566.. **LC 31**

Lasker-Schueler, Else 1869-1945 .. **TCLC 57**
See also DLB 66, 124

Latham, Jean Lee 1902-........... **CLC 12**
See also AITN 1; CA 5-8R; CANR 7;
MAICYA; SATA 2, 68

Latham, Mavis
See Clark, Mavis Thorpe

Lathen, Emma .... **CLC 2**
See also Hennissart, Martha; Latsis, Mary
J(ane)

Lathrop, Francis
See Leiber, Fritz (Reuter, Jr.)

Latsis, Mary J(ane)
See Lathen, Emma
See also CA 85-88

Lattimore, Richmond (Alexander)
1906-1984 .... **CLC 3**
See also CA 1-4R; 112; CANR 1

Laughlin, James 1914-............ **CLC 49**
See also CA 21-24R; CAAS 22; CANR 9,
47; DLB 48

Laurence, (Jean) Margaret (Wemyss)
1926-1987 .... **CLC 3, 6, 13, 50, 62; DAC; SSC 7**
See also CA 5-8R; 121; CANR 33;
DAM MST; DLB 53; MTCW;
SATA-Obit 50

Laurent, Antoine 1952- .... **CLC 50**

Lauscher, Hermann
See Hesse, Hermann

Lautreamont, Comte de
1846-1870 .... **NCLC 12; SSC 14**

Laverty, Donald
See Blish, James (Benjamin)

Lavin, Mary 1912-...... **CLC 4, 18; SSC 4**
See also CA 9-12R; CANR 33; DLB 15;
MTCW

Lavond, Paul Dennis
See Kornbluth, C(yril) M.; Pohl, Frederik

Mahfouz, Naguib (Abdel Aziz Al-Sabilgi)
    1911(?)-
    See Mahfuz, Najib
    See also BEST 89:2; CA 128; DAM NOV;
    MTCW

Mahfuz, Najib................ CLC **52, 55**
    See also Mahfouz, Naguib (Abdel Aziz
    Al-Sabilgi)
    See also DLBY 88

Mahon, Derek 1941-.............. CLC **27**
    See also CA 113; 128; DLB 40

Mailer, Norman
    1923- ...... CLC **1, 2, 3, 4, 5, 8, 11, 14,**
            28, 39, 74; DA; DAB; DAC
    See also AITN 2; CA 9-12R; CABS 1;
    CANR 28; CDALB 1968-1988;
    DAM MST, NOV, POP; DLB 2, 16, 28;
    DLBD 3; DLBY 80, 83; MTCW

Maillet, Antonine 1929-...... CLC **54; DAC**
    See also CA 115; 120; CANR 46; DLB 60;
    INT 120

Mais, Roger 1905-1955 .... TCLC **8**
    See also BW 1; CA 105; 124; DLB 125;
    MTCW

Maistre, Joseph de 1753-1821.... NCLC **37**

Maitland, Sara (Louise) 1950-...... CLC **49**
    See also CA 69-72; CANR 13

Major, Clarence
    1936- .... CLC **3, 19, 48; BLC**
    See also BW 2; CA 21-24R; CAAS 6;
    CANR 13, 25; DAM MULT; DLB 33

Major, Kevin (Gerald)
    1949- .... CLC **26; DAC**
    See also AAYA 16; CA 97-100; CANR 21,
    38; CLR 11; DLB 60; INT CANR-21;
    JRDA; MAICYA; SATA 32, 82

Maki, James
    See Ozu, Yasujiro

Malabaila, Damiano
    See Levi, Primo

Malamud, Bernard
    1914-1986 ...... CLC **1, 2, 3, 5, 8, 9, 11,**
        18, 27, 44, 78, 85; DA; DAB; DAC;
                SSC 15; WLC
    See also AAYA 16; CA 5-8R; 118; CABS 1;
    CANR 28; CDALB 1941-1968;
    DAM MST, NOV, POP; DLB 2, 28, 152;
    DLBY 80, 86; MTCW

Malaparte, Curzio 1898-1957 ..... TCLC **52**

Malcolm, Dan
    See Silverberg, Robert

Malcolm X.................. CLC **82; BLC**
    See also Little, Malcolm

Malherbe, Francois de 1555-1628..... LC **5**

Mallarme, Stephane
    1842-1898 .... NCLC **4, 41; PC 4**
    See also DAM POET

Mallet-Joris, Francoise 1930-...... CLC **11**
    See also CA 65-68; CANR 17; DLB 83

Malley, Ern
    See McAuley, James Phillip

Mallowan, Agatha Christie
    See Christie, Agatha (Mary Clarissa)

Maloff, Saul 1922-................ CLC **5**
    See also CA 33-36R

Malone, Louis
    See MacNeice, (Frederick) Louis

Malone, Michael (Christopher)
    1942- .... CLC **43**
    See also CA 77-80; CANR 14, 32

Malory, (Sir) Thomas
    1410(?)-1471(?) ...... LC **11; DA; DAB;**
                            DAC
    See also CDBLB Before 1660; DAM MST;
    DLB 146; SATA 59; SATA-Brief 33

Malouf, (George Joseph) David
    1934- .... CLC **28, 86**
    See also CA 124; CANR 50

Malraux, (Georges-)Andre
    1901-1976 ...... CLC **1, 4, 9, 13, 15, 57**
    See also CA 21-22; 69-72; CANR 34;
    CAP 2; DAM NOV; DLB 72; MTCW

Malzberg, Barry N(athaniel) 1939-... CLC **7**
    See also CA 61-64; CAAS 4; CANR 16;
    DLB 8

Mamet, David (Alan)
    1947- ...... CLC **9, 15, 34, 46, 91; DC 4**
    See also AAYA 3; CA 81-84; CABS 3;
    CANR 15, 41; DAM DRAM; DLB 7;
    MTCW

Mamoulian, Rouben (Zachary)
    1897-1987 .... CLC **16**
    See also CA 25-28R; 124

Mandelstam, Osip (Emilievich)
    1891(?)-1938(?) ...... TCLC **2, 6; PC 14**
    See also CA 104; 150

Mander, (Mary) Jane 1877-1949... TCLC **31**

Mandiargues, Andre Pieyre de....... CLC **41**
    See also Pieyre de Mandiargues, Andre
    See also DLB 83

Mandrake, Ethel Belle
    See Thurman, Wallace (Henry)

Mangan, James Clarence
    1803-1849 .... NCLC **27**

Maniere, J.-E.
    See Giraudoux, (Hippolyte) Jean

Manley, (Mary) Delariviere
    1672(?)-1724 .... LC **1**
    See also DLB 39, 80

Mann, Abel
    See Creasey, John

Mann, (Luiz) Heinrich 1871-1950... TCLC **9**
    See also CA 106; DLB 66

Mann, (Paul) Thomas
    1875-1955 .... TCLC **2, 8, 14, 21, 35, 44,**
            60; DA; DAB; DAC; SSC 5; WLC
    See also CA 104; 128; DAM MST, NOV;
    DLB 66; MTCW

Manning, David
    See Faust, Frederick (Schiller)

Manning, Frederic 1887(?)-1935... TCLC **25**
    See also CA 124

Manning, Olivia 1915-1980...... CLC **5, 19**
    See also CA 5-8R; 101; CANR 29; MTCW

Mano, D. Keith 1942- .... CLC **2, 10**
    See also CA 25-28R; CAAS 6; CANR 26;
    DLB 6

Mansfield, Katherine
    .. TCLC **2, 8, 39; DAB; SSC 9, 23; WLC**
    See also Beauchamp, Kathleen Mansfield
    See also DLB 162

Manso, Peter 1940- .... CLC **39**
    See also CA 29-32R; CANR 44

Mantecon, Juan Jimenez
    See Jimenez (Mantecon), Juan Ramon

Manton, Peter
    See Creasey, John

Man Without a Spleen, A
    See Chekhov, Anton (Pavlovich)

Manzoni, Alessandro 1785-1873 .. NCLC **29**

Mapu, Abraham (ben Jekutiel)
    1808-1867 .... NCLC **18**

Mara, Sally
    See Queneau, Raymond

Marat, Jean Paul 1743-1793........ LC **10**

Marcel, Gabriel Honore
    1889-1973 .... CLC **15**
    See also CA 102; 45-48; MTCW

Marchbanks, Samuel
    See Davies, (William) Robertson

Marchi, Giacomo
    See Bassani, Giorgio

Margulies, Donald................. CLC **76**

Marie de France c. 12th cent. -.... CMLC **8**

Marie de l'Incarnation 1599-1672.... LC **10**

Mariner, Scott
    See Pohl, Frederik

Marinetti, Filippo Tommaso
    1876-1944 .... TCLC **10**
    See also CA 107; DLB 114

Marivaux, Pierre Carlet de Chamblain de
    1688-1763 .... LC **4**

Markandaya, Kamala .... CLC **8, 38**
    See also Taylor, Kamala (Purnaiya)

Markfield, Wallace 1926-.......... CLC **8**
    See also CA 69-72; CAAS 3; DLB 2, 28

Markham, Edwin 1852-1940...... TCLC **47**
    See also DLB 54

Markham, Robert
    See Amis, Kingsley (William)

Marks, J
    See Highwater, Jamake (Mamake)

Marks-Highwater, J
    See Highwater, Jamake (Mamake)

Markson, David M(errill) 1927-.... CLC **67**
    See also CA 49-52; CANR 1

Marley, Bob..................... CLC **17**
    See also Marley, Robert Nesta

Marley, Robert Nesta 1945-1981
    See Marley, Bob
    See also CA 107; 103

Marlowe, Christopher
    1564-1593 ..... LC **22; DA; DAB; DAC;**
                        DC 1; WLC
    See also CDBLB Before 1660;
    DAM DRAM, MST; DLB 62

Marmontel, Jean-Francois
    1723-1799 .... LC **2**

Marquand, John P(hillips)
1893-1960 .... CLC **2, 10**
See also CA 85-88; DLB 9, 102

Marquez, Gabriel (Jose) Garcia
See Garcia Marquez, Gabriel (Jose)

Marquis, Don(ald Robert Perry)
1878-1937 .... TCLC **7**
See also CA 104; DLB 11, 25

Marric, J. J.
See Creasey, John

Marrow, Bernard
See Moore, Brian

Marryat, Frederick 1792-1848 .... NCLC **3**
See also DLB 21, 163

Marsden, James
See Creasey, John

Marsh, (Edith) Ngaio
1899-1982 .... CLC **7, 53**
See also CA 9-12R; CANR 6; DAM POP;
DLB 77; MTCW

Marshall, Garry 1934- .... CLC **17**
See also AAYA 3; CA 111; SATA 60

Marshall, Paule
1929- .... CLC **27, 72; BLC; SSC 3**
See also BW 2; CA 77-80; CANR 25;
DAM MULT; DLB 157; MTCW

Marsten, Richard
See Hunter, Evan

Martha, Henry
See Harris, Mark

Martial c. 40-c. 104 .... PC **10**

Martin, Ken
See Hubbard, L(afayette) Ron(ald)

Martin, Richard
See Creasey, John

Martin, Steve 1945- .... CLC **30**
See also CA 97-100; CANR 30; MTCW

Martin, Valerie 1948- .... CLC **89**
See also BEST 90:2; CA 85-88; CANR 49

Martin, Violet Florence
1862-1915 .... TCLC **51**

Martin, Webber
See Silverberg, Robert

Martindale, Patrick Victor
See White, Patrick (Victor Martindale)

Martin du Gard, Roger
1881-1958 .... TCLC **24**
See also CA 118; DLB 65

Martineau, Harriet 1802-1876.... NCLC **26**
See also DLB 21, 55, 159, 163; YABC 2

Martines, Julia
See O'Faolain, Julia

Martinez, Jacinto Benavente y
See Benavente (y Martinez), Jacinto

Martinez Ruiz, Jose 1873-1967
See Azorin; Ruiz, Jose Martinez
See also CA 93-96; HW

Martinez Sierra, Gregorio
1881-1947 .... TCLC **6**
See also CA 115

Martinez Sierra, Maria (de la O'LeJarraga)
1874-1974 .... TCLC **6**
See also CA 115

Martinsen, Martin
See Follett, Ken(neth Martin)

Martinson, Harry (Edmund)
1904-1978 .... CLC **14**
See also CA 77-80; CANR 34

Marut, Ret
See Traven, B.

Marut, Robert
See Traven, B.

Marvell, Andrew
1621-1678 ...... LC **4; DA; DAB; DAC;
PC 10; WLC**
See also CDBLB 1660-1789; DAM MST,
POET; DLB 131

Marx, Karl (Heinrich)
1818-1883 .... NCLC **17**
See also DLB 129

Masaoka Shiki.................. TCLC **18**
See also Masaoka Tsunenori

Masaoka Tsunenori 1867-1902
See Masaoka Shiki
See also CA 117

Masefield, John (Edward)
1878-1967 .... CLC **11, 47**
See also CA 19-20; 25-28R; CANR 33;
CAP 2; CDBLB 1890-1914; DAM POET;
DLB 10, 19, 153, 160; MTCW; SATA 19

Maso, Carole 19(?)- .... CLC **44**

Mason, Bobbie Ann
1940- .... CLC **28, 43, 82; SSC 4**
See also AAYA 5; CA 53-56; CANR 11,
31; DLBY 87; INT CANR-31; MTCW

Mason, Ernst
See Pohl, Frederik

Mason, Lee W.
See Malzberg, Barry N(athaniel)

Mason, Nick 1945- .... CLC **35**

Mason, Tally
See Derleth, August (William)

Mass, William
See Gibson, William

Masters, Edgar Lee
1868-1950 ...... TCLC **2, 25; DA; DAC;
PC 1**
See also CA 104; 133; CDALB 1865-1917;
DAM MST, POET; DLB 54; MTCW

Masters, Hilary 1928- .... CLC **48**
See also CA 25-28R; CANR 13, 47

Mastrosimone, William 19(?)- ...... CLC **36**

Mathe, Albert
See Camus, Albert

Matheson, Richard Burton 1926- ... CLC **37**
See also CA 97-100; DLB 8, 44; INT 97-100

Mathews, Harry 1930- .... CLC **6, 52**
See also CA 21-24R; CAAS 6; CANR 18,
40

Mathews, John Joseph 1894-1979... CLC **84**
See also CA 19-20; 142; CANR 45; CAP 2;
DAM MULT; NNAL

Mathias, Roland (Glyn) 1915- ...... CLC **45**
See also CA 97-100; CANR 19, 41; DLB 27

Matsuo Basho 1644-1694........... PC **3**
See also DAM POET

Mattheson, Rodney
See Creasey, John

Matthews, Greg 1949- .... CLC **45**
See also CA 135

Matthews, William 1942- .... CLC **40**
See also CA 29-32R; CAAS 18; CANR 12;
DLB 5

Matthias, John (Edward) 1941- ...... CLC **9**
See also CA 33-36R

Matthiessen, Peter
1927- .... CLC **5, 7, 11, 32, 64**
See also AAYA 6; BEST 90:4; CA 9-12R;
CANR 21, 50; DAM NOV; DLB 6;
MTCW; SATA 27

Maturin, Charles Robert
1780(?)-1824 .... NCLC **6**

Matute (Ausejo), Ana Maria
1925- .... CLC **11**
See also CA 89-92; MTCW

Maugham, W. S.
See Maugham, W(illiam) Somerset

Maugham, W(illiam) Somerset
1874-1965 .... CLC **1, 11, 15, 67, 93;
DA; DAB; DAC; SSC 8; WLC**
See also CA 5-8R; 25-28R; CANR 40;
CDBLB 1914-1945; DAM DRAM, MST,
NOV; DLB 10, 36, 77, 100, 162; MTCW;
SATA 54

Maugham, William Somerset
See Maugham, W(illiam) Somerset

Maupassant, (Henri Rene Albert) Guy de
1850-1893 ..... NCLC **1, 42; DA; DAB;
DAC; SSC 1; WLC**
See also DAM MST; DLB 123

Maurhut, Richard
See Traven, B.

Mauriac, Claude 1914- .... CLC **9**
See also CA 89-92; DLB 83

Mauriac, Francois (Charles)
1885-1970 .... CLC **4, 9, 56**
See also CA 25-28; CAP 2; DLB 65;
MTCW

Mavor, Osborne Henry 1888-1951
See Bridie, James
See also CA 104

Maxwell, William (Keepers, Jr.)
1908- .... CLC **19**
See also CA 93-96; DLBY 80; INT 93-96

May, Elaine 1932- .... CLC **16**
See also CA 124; 142; DLB 44

Mayakovski, Vladimir (Vladimirovich)
1893-1930 .... TCLC **4, 18**
See also CA 104

Mayhew, Henry 1812-1887 ...... NCLC **31**
See also DLB 18, 55

Mayle, Peter 1939(?)- .... CLC **89**
See also CA 139

Maynard, Joyce 1953- .... CLC **23**
See also CA 111; 129

Mayne, William (James Carter)
1928- .... CLC **12**
See also CA 9-12R; CANR 37; CLR 25;
JRDA; MAICYA; SAAS 11; SATA 6, 68

Mayo, Jim
See L'Amour, Louis (Dearborn)

Melmoth, Sebastian
    See Wilde, Oscar (Fingal O'Flahertie Wills)

Meltzer, Milton 1915- . . . . **CLC 26**
    See also AAYA 8; CA 13-16R; CANR 38;
    CLR 13; DLB 61; JRDA; MAICYA;
    SAAS 1; SATA 1, 50, 80

Melville, Herman
    1819-1891 . . . . . **NCLC 3, 12, 29, 45, 49;**
          DA; DAB; DAC; SSC 1, 17; WLC
    See also CDALB 1640-1865; DAM MST,
    NOV; DLB 3, 74; SATA 59

Menander
    c. 342B.C.-c. 292B.C. . . . . **CMLC 9; DC 3**
    See also DAM DRAM

Mencken, H(enry) L(ouis)
    1880-1956 . . . . **TCLC 13**
    See also CA 105; 125; CDALB 1917-1929;
    DLB 11, 29, 63, 137; MTCW

Mercer, David 1928-1980 . . . . **CLC 5**
    See also CA 9-12R; 102; CANR 23;
    DAM DRAM; DLB 13; MTCW

Merchant, Paul
    See Ellison, Harlan (Jay)

Meredith, George 1828-1909 . . . **TCLC 17, 43**
    See also CA 117; CDBLB 1832-1890;
    DAM POET; DLB 18, 35, 57, 159

Meredith, William (Morris)
    1919- . . . . **CLC 4, 13, 22, 55**
    See also CA 9-12R; CAAS 14; CANR 6, 40;
    DAM POET; DLB 5

Merezhkovsky, Dmitry Sergeyevich
    1865-1941 . . . . **TCLC 29**

Merimee, Prosper
    1803-1870 . . . . **NCLC 6; SSC 7**
    See also DLB 119

Merkin, Daphne 1954- . . . . **CLC 44**
    See also CA 123

Merlin, Arthur
    See Blish, James (Benjamin)

Merrill, James (Ingram)
    1926-1995 . . . . **CLC 2, 3, 6, 8, 13, 18, 34,**
                         91
    See also CA 13-16R; 147; CANR 10, 49;
    DAM POET; DLB 5, 165; DLBY 85;
    INT CANR-10; MTCW

Merriman, Alex
    See Silverberg, Robert

Merritt, E. B.
    See Waddington, Miriam

Merton, Thomas
    1915-1968 . . **CLC 1, 3, 11, 34, 83; PC 10**
    See also CA 5-8R; 25-28R; CANR 22;
    DLB 48; DLBY 81; MTCW

Merwin, W(illiam) S(tanley)
    1927- . . . **CLC 1, 2, 3, 5, 8, 13, 18, 45, 88**
    See also CA 13-16R; CANR 15, 51;
    DAM POET; DLB 5; INT CANR-15;
    MTCW

Metcalf, John 1938- . . . . **CLC 37**
    See also CA 113; DLB 60

Metcalf, Suzanne
    See Baum, L(yman) Frank

Mew, Charlotte (Mary)
    1870-1928 . . . . **TCLC 8**
    See also CA 105; DLB 19, 135

Mewshaw, Michael 1943- . . . . **CLC 9**
    See also CA 53-56; CANR 7, 47; DLBY 80

Meyer, June
    See Jordan, June

Meyer, Lynn
    See Slavitt, David R(ytman)

Meyer-Meyrink, Gustav 1868-1932
    See Meyrink, Gustav
    See also CA 117

Meyers, Jeffrey 1939- . . . . **CLC 39**
    See also CA 73-76; DLB 111

Meynell, Alice (Christina Gertrude Thompson)
    1847-1922 . . . . **TCLC 6**
    See also CA 104; DLB 19, 98

Meyrink, Gustav . . . . **TCLC 21**
    See also Meyer-Meyrink, Gustav
    See also DLB 81

Michaels, Leonard
    1933- . . . . **CLC 6, 25; SSC 16**
    See also CA 61-64; CANR 21; DLB 130;
    MTCW

Michaux, Henri 1899-1984 . . . . . . **CLC 8, 19**
    See also CA 85-88; 114

Michelangelo 1475-1564 . . . . **LC 12**

Michelet, Jules 1798-1874 . . . . . . **NCLC 31**

Michener, James A(lbert)
    1907(?)- . . . . **CLC 1, 5, 11, 29, 60**
    See also AITN 1; BEST 90:1; CA 5-8R;
    CANR 21, 45; DAM NOV, POP; DLB 6;
    MTCW

Mickiewicz, Adam 1798-1855 . . . . . **NCLC 3**

Middleton, Christopher 1926- . . . . . . **CLC 13**
    See also CA 13-16R; CANR 29; DLB 40

Middleton, Richard (Barham)
    1882-1911 . . . . **TCLC 56**
    See also DLB 156

Middleton, Stanley 1919- . . . . **CLC 7, 38**
    See also CA 25-28R; CAAS 23; CANR 21,
    46; DLB 14

Middleton, Thomas 1580-1627 . . . . **DC 5**
    See also DAM DRAM, MST; DLB 58

Migueis, Jose Rodrigues 1901- . . . . . **CLC 10**

Mikszath, Kalman 1847-1910 . . . . . **TCLC 31**

Miles, Josephine
    1911-1985 . . . . **CLC 1, 2, 14, 34, 39**
    See also CA 1-4R; 116; CANR 2;
    DAM POET; DLB 48

Militant
    See Sandburg, Carl (August)

Mill, John Stuart 1806-1873 . . . . . **NCLC 11**
    See also CDBLB 1832-1890; DLB 55

Millar, Kenneth 1915-1983 . . . . **CLC 14**
    See also Macdonald, Ross
    See also CA 9-12R; 110; CANR 16;
    DAM POP; DLB 2; DLBD 6; DLBY 83;
    MTCW

Millay, E. Vincent
    See Millay, Edna St. Vincent

Millay, Edna St. Vincent
    1892-1950 . . . . . . **TCLC 4, 49; DA; DAB;**
                      DAC; PC 6
    See also CA 104; 130; CDALB 1917-1929;
    DAM MST, POET; DLB 45; MTCW

Miller, Arthur
    1915- . . . . **CLC 1, 2, 6, 10, 15, 26, 47, 78;**
               DA; DAB; DAC; DC 1; WLC
    See also AAYA 15; AITN 1; CA 1-4R;
    CABS 3; CANR 2, 30;
    CDALB 1941-1968; DAM DRAM, MST;
    DLB 7; MTCW

Miller, Henry (Valentine)
    1891-1980 . . . . **CLC 1, 2, 4, 9, 14, 43, 84;**
               DA; DAB; DAC; WLC
    See also CA 9-12R; 97-100; CANR 33;
    CDALB 1929-1941; DAM MST, NOV;
    DLB 4, 9; DLBY 80; MTCW

Miller, Jason 1939(?)- . . . . **CLC 2**
    See also AITN 1; CA 73-76; DLB 7

Miller, Sue 1943- . . . . **CLC 44**
    See also BEST 90:3; CA 139; DAM POP;
    DLB 143

Miller, Walter M(ichael, Jr.)
    1923- . . . . **CLC 4, 30**
    See also CA 85-88; DLB 8

Millett, Kate 1934- . . . . **CLC 67**
    See also AITN 1; CA 73-76; CANR 32;
    MTCW

Millhauser, Steven 1943- . . . . **CLC 21, 54**
    See also CA 110; 111; DLB 2; INT 111

Millin, Sarah Gertrude 1889-1968 . . **CLC 49**
    See also CA 102; 93-96

Milne, A(lan) A(lexander)
    1882-1956 . . . . **TCLC 6; DAB; DAC**
    See also CA 104; 133; CLR 1, 26;
    DAM MST; DLB 10, 77, 100, 160;
    MAICYA; MTCW; YABC 1

Milner, Ron(ald) 1938- . . . . **CLC 56; BLC**
    See also AITN 1; BW 1; CA 73-76;
    CANR 24; DAM MULT; DLB 38;
    MTCW

Milosz, Czeslaw
    1911- . . . **CLC 5, 11, 22, 31, 56, 82; PC 8**
    See also CA 81-84; CANR 23, 51;
    DAM MST, POET; MTCW

Milton, John
    1608-1674 . . . . . . **LC 9; DA; DAB; DAC;**
                          WLC
    See also CDBLB 1660-1789; DAM MST,
    POET; DLB 131, 151

Min, Anchee 1957- . . . . **CLC 86**
    See also CA 146

Minehaha, Cornelius
    See Wedekind, (Benjamin) Frank(lin)

Miner, Valerie 1947- . . . . **CLC 40**
    See also CA 97-100

Minimo, Duca
    See D'Annunzio, Gabriele

Minot, Susan 1956- . . . . **CLC 44**
    See also CA 134

Minus, Ed 1938- . . . . **CLC 39**

Miranda, Javier
    See Bioy Casares, Adolfo

Mirbeau, Octave 1848-1917 . . . . **TCLC 55**
    See also DLB 123

Miro (Ferrer), Gabriel (Francisco Victor)
    1879-1930 . . . . **TCLC 5**
    See also CA 104

Mishima, Yukio
...... CLC 2, 4, 6, 9, 27; DC 1; SSC 4
See also Hiraoka, Kimitake

Mistral, Frederic 1830-1914 ...... TCLC 51
See also CA 122

Mistral, Gabriela........... TCLC 2; HLC
See also Godoy Alcayaga, Lucila

Mistry, Rohinton 1952- ...... CLC 71; DAC
See also CA 141

Mitchell, Clyde
See Ellison, Harlan (Jay); Silverberg, Robert

Mitchell, James Leslie 1901-1935
See Gibbon, Lewis Grassic
See also CA 104; DLB 15

Mitchell, Joni 1943-.............. CLC 12
See also CA 112

Mitchell, Margaret (Munnerlyn)
1900-1949 .... TCLC 11
See also CA 109; 125; DAM NOV, POP;
DLB 9; MTCW

Mitchell, Peggy
See Mitchell, Margaret (Munnerlyn)

Mitchell, S(ilas) Weir 1829-1914 .. TCLC 36

Mitchell, W(illiam) O(rmond)
1914- .... CLC 25; DAC
See also CA 77-80; CANR 15, 43;
DAM MST; DLB 88

Mitford, Mary Russell 1787-1855.. NCLC 4
See also DLB 110, 116

Mitford, Nancy 1904-1973........ CLC 44
See also CA 9-12R

Miyamoto, Yuriko 1899-1951 ..... TCLC 37

Mo, Timothy (Peter) 1950(?)- ...... CLC 46
See also CA 117; MTCW

Modarressi, Taghi (M.) 1931- ...... CLC 44
See also CA 121, 134; INT 134

Modiano, Patrick (Jean) 1945- ..... CLC 18
See also CA 85-88; CANR 17, 40; DLB 83

Moerck, Paal
See Roelvaag, O(le) E(dvart)

Mofolo, Thomas (Mokopu)
1875(?)-1948 .... TCLC 22; BLC
See also CA 121; DAM MULT

Mohr, Nicholasa 1935-...... CLC 12; HLC
See also AAYA 8; CA 49-52; CANR 1, 32;
CLR 22; DAM MULT; DLB 145; HW;
JRDA; SAAS 8; SATA 8

Mojtabai, A(nn) G(race)
1938- .... CLC 5, 9, 15, 29
See also CA 85-88

Moliere
1622-1673 ..... LC 28; DA; DAB; DAC;
WLC
See also DAM DRAM, MST

Molin, Charles
See Mayne, William (James Carter)

Molnar, Ferenc 1878-1952........ TCLC 20
See also CA 109; DAM DRAM

Momaday, N(avarre) Scott
1934- ... CLC 2, 19, 85; DA; DAB; DAC
See also AAYA 11; CA 25-28R; CANR 14,
34; DAM MST, MULT, NOV, POP;
DLB 143; INT CANR-14; MTCW;
NNAL; SATA 48; SATA-Brief 30

Monette, Paul 1945-1995.......... CLC 82
See also CA 139; 147

Monroe, Harriet 1860-1936...... TCLC 12
See also CA 109; DLB 54, 91

Monroe, Lyle
See Heinlein, Robert A(nson)

Montagu, Elizabeth 1917-........ NCLC 7
See also CA 9-12R

Montagu, Mary (Pierrepont) Wortley
1689-1762 .... LC 9
See also DLB 95, 101

Montagu, W. H.
See Coleridge, Samuel Taylor

Montague, John (Patrick)
1929- .... CLC 13, 46
See also CA 9-12R; CANR 9; DLB 40;
MTCW

Montaigne, Michel (Eyquem) de
1533-1592 ...... LC 8; DA; DAB; DAC;
WLC
See also DAM MST

Montale, Eugenio
1896-1981 .... CLC 7, 9, 18; PC 13
See also CA 17-20R; 104; CANR 30;
DLB 114; MTCW

Montesquieu, Charles-Louis de Secondat
1689-1755 .... LC 7

Montgomery, (Robert) Bruce 1921-1978
See Crispin, Edmund
See also CA 104

Montgomery, L(ucy) M(aud)
1874-1942 .... TCLC 51; DAC
See also AAYA 12; CA 108; 137; CLR 8;
DAM MST; DLB 92; JRDA; MAICYA;
YABC 1

Montgomery, Marion H., Jr. 1925-.. CLC 7
See also AITN 1; CA 1-4R; CANR 3, 48;
DLB 6

Montgomery, Max
See Davenport, Guy (Mattison, Jr.)

Montherlant, Henry (Milon) de
1896-1972 .... CLC 8, 19
See also CA 85-88; 37-40R; DAM DRAM;
DLB 72; MTCW

Monty Python
See Chapman, Graham; Cleese, John
(Marwood); Gilliam, Terry (Vance); Idle,
Eric; Jones, Terence Graham Parry; Palin,
Michael (Edward)
See also AAYA 7

Moodie, Susanna (Strickland)
1803-1885 .... NCLC 14
See also DLB 99

Mooney, Edward 1951-
See Mooney, Ted
See also CA 130

Mooney, Ted .... CLC 25
See also Mooney, Edward

Moorcock, Michael (John)
1939- .... CLC 5, 27, 58
See also CA 45-48; CAAS 5; CANR 2, 17,
38; DLB 14; MTCW

Moore, Brian
1921- ...... CLC 1, 3, 5, 7, 8, 19, 32, 90;
DAB; DAC
See also CA 1-4R; CANR 1, 25, 42;
DAM MST; MTCW

Moore, Edward
See Muir, Edwin

Moore, George Augustus
1852-1933 .... TCLC 7; SSC 19
See also CA 104; DLB 10, 18, 57, 135

Moore, Lorrie .... CLC 39, 45, 68
See also Moore, Marie Lorena

Moore, Marianne (Craig)
1887-1972 .... CLC 1, 2, 4, 8, 10, 13, 19,
47; DA; DAB; DAC; PC 4
See also CA 1-4R; 33-36R; CANR 3;
CDALB 1929-1941; DAM MST, POET;
DLB 45; DLBD 7; MTCW; SATA 20

Moore, Marie Lorena 1957-
See Moore, Lorrie
See also CA 116; CANR 39

Moore, Thomas 1779-1852....... NCLC 6
See also DLB 96, 144

Morand, Paul 1888-1976 .. CLC 41; SSC 22
See also CA 69-72; DLB 65

Morante, Elsa 1918-1985........ CLC 8, 47
See also CA 85-88; 117; CANR 35; MTCW

Moravia, Alberto....... CLC 2, 7, 11, 27, 46
See also Pincherle, Alberto

More, Hannah 1745-1833 .... NCLC 27
See also DLB 107, 109, 116, 158

More, Henry 1614-1687............. LC 9
See also DLB 126

More, Sir Thomas 1478-1535 .... LC 10, 32

Moreas, Jean.................... TCLC 18
See also Papadiamantopoulos, Johannes

Morgan, Berry 1919-.............. CLC 6
See also CA 49-52; DLB 6

Morgan, Claire
See Highsmith, (Mary) Patricia

Morgan, Edwin (George) 1920-..... CLC 31
See also CA 5-8R; CANR 3, 43; DLB 27

Morgan, (George) Frederick
1922-...................... CLC 23
See also CA 17-20R; CANR 21

Morgan, Harriet
See Mencken, H(enry) L(ouis)

Morgan, Jane
See Cooper, James Fenimore

Morgan, Janet 1945- .... CLC 39
See also CA 65-68

Morgan, Lady 1776(?)-1859...... NCLC 29
See also DLB 116, 158

Morgan, Robin 1941-.............. CLC 2
See also CA 69-72; CANR 29; MTCW;
SATA 80

Morgan, Scott
See Kuttner, Henry

Morgan, Seth 1949(?)-1990 .... CLC 65
See also CA 132

Morgenstern, Christian
1871-1914 .... TCLC 8
See also CA 105

Myles, Symon
See Follett, Ken(neth Martin)

Nabokov, Vladimir (Vladimirovich)
1899-1977 ..... **CLC 1, 2, 3, 6, 8, 11, 15, 23, 44, 46, 64; DA; DAB; DAC; SSC 11; WLC**
See also CA 5-8R; 69-72; CANR 20; CDALB 1941-1968; DAM MST, NOV; DLB 2; DLBD 3; DLBY 80, 91; MTCW

Nagai Kafu .... **TCLC 51**
See also Nagai Sokichi

Nagai Sokichi 1879-1959
See Nagai Kafu
See also CA 117

Nagy, Laszlo 1925-1978 .... **CLC 7**
See also CA 129; 112

Naipaul, Shiva(dhar Srinivasa)
1945-1985 .... **CLC 32, 39**
See also CA 110; 112; 116; CANR 33; DAM NOV; DLB 157; DLBY 85; MTCW

Naipaul, V(idiadhar) S(urajprasad)
1932- .... **CLC 4, 7, 9, 13, 18, 37; DAB; DAC**
See also CA 1-4R; CANR 1, 33, 51; CDBLB 1960 to Present; DAM MST, NOV; DLB 125; DLBY 85; MTCW

Nakos, Lilika 1899(?)- .... **CLC 29**

Narayan, R(asipuram) K(rishnaswami)
1906- .... **CLC 7, 28, 47**
See also CA 81-84; CANR 33; DAM NOV; MTCW; SATA 62

Nash, (Frediric) Ogden 1902-1971 .. **CLC 23**
See also CA 13-14; 29-32R; CANR 34; CAP 1; DAM POET; DLB 11; MAICYA; MTCW; SATA 2, 46

Nathan, Daniel
See Dannay, Frederic

Nathan, George Jean 1882-1958 ... **TCLC 18**
See also Hatteras, Owen
See also CA 114; DLB 137

Natsume, Kinnosuke 1867-1916
See Natsume, Soseki
See also CA 104

Natsume, Soseki .... **TCLC 2, 10**
See also Natsume, Kinnosuke

Natti, (Mary) Lee 1919-
See Kingman, Lee
See also CA 5-8R; CANR 2

Naylor, Gloria
1950- ..... **CLC 28, 52; BLC; DA; DAC**
See also AAYA 6; BW 2; CA 107; CANR 27, 51; DAM MST, MULT, NOV, POP; MTCW

Neihardt, John Gneisenau
1881-1973 .... **CLC 32**
See also CA 13-14; CAP 1; DLB 9, 54

Nekrasov, Nikolai Alekseevich
1821-1878 .... **NCLC 11**

Nelligan, Emile 1879-1941 .... **TCLC 14**
See also CA 114; DLB 92

Nelson, Willie 1933- .... **CLC 17**
See also CA 107

Nemerov, Howard (Stanley)
1920-1991 .... **CLC 2, 6, 9, 36**
See also CA 1-4R; 134; CABS 2; CANR 1, 27; DAM POET; DLB 5, 6; DLBY 83; INT CANR-27; MTCW

Neruda, Pablo
1904-1973 ..... **CLC 1, 2, 5, 7, 9, 28, 62; DA; DAB; DAC; HLC; PC 4; WLC**
See also CA 19-20; 45-48; CAP 2; DAM MST, MULT, POET; HW; MTCW

Nerval, Gerard de
1808-1855 ..... **NCLC 1; PC 13; SSC 18**

Nervo, (Jose) Amado (Ruiz de)
1870-1919 .... **TCLC 11**
See also CA 109; 131; HW

Nessi, Pio Baroja y
See Baroja (y Nessi), Pio

Nestroy, Johann 1801-1862 ...... **NCLC 42**
See also DLB 133

Neufeld, John (Arthur) 1938- ...... **CLC 17**
See also AAYA 11; CA 25-28R; CANR 11, 37; MAICYA; SAAS 3; SATA 6, 81

Neville, Emily Cheney 1919- .... **CLC 12**
See also CA 5-8R; CANR 3, 37; JRDA; MAICYA; SAAS 2; SATA 1

Newbound, Bernard Slade 1930-
See Slade, Bernard
See also CA 81-84; CANR 49; DAM DRAM

Newby, P(ercy) H(oward)
1918- .... **CLC 2, 13**
See also CA 5-8R; CANR 32; DAM NOV; DLB 15; MTCW

Newlove, Donald 1928- .... **CLC 6**
See also CA 29-32R; CANR 25

Newlove, John (Herbert) 1938- ..... **CLC 14**
See also CA 21-24R; CANR 9, 25

Newman, Charles 1938- .... **CLC 2, 8**
See also CA 21-24R

Newman, Edwin (Harold) 1919- .... **CLC 14**
See also AITN 1; CA 69-72; CANR 5

Newman, John Henry
1801-1890 .... **NCLC 38**
See also DLB 18, 32, 55

Newton, Suzanne 1936- .... **CLC 35**
See also CA 41-44R; CANR 14; JRDA; SATA 5, 77

Nexo, Martin Andersen
1869-1954 .... **TCLC 43**

Nezval, Vitezslav 1900-1958 ...... **TCLC 44**
See also CA 123

Ng, Fae Myenne 1957(?)- .... **CLC 81**
See also CA 146

Ngema, Mbongeni 1955- .... **CLC 57**
See also BW 2; CA 143

Ngugi, James T(hiong'o) .... **CLC 3, 7, 13**
See also Ngugi wa Thiong'o

Ngugi wa Thiong'o 1938- ..... **CLC 36; BLC**
See also Ngugi, James T(hiong'o)
See also BW 2; CA 81-84; CANR 27; DAM MULT, NOV; DLB 125; MTCW

Nichol, B(arrie) P(hillip)
1944-1988 .... **CLC 18**
See also CA 53-56; DLB 53; SATA 66

Nichols, John (Treadwell) 1940- .... **CLC 38**
See also CA 9-12R; CAAS 2; CANR 6; DLBY 82

Nichols, Leigh
See Koontz, Dean R(ay)

Nichols, Peter (Richard)
1927- .... **CLC 5, 36, 65**
See also CA 104; CANR 33; DLB 13; MTCW

Nicolas, F. R. E.
See Freeling, Nicolas

Niedecker, Lorine 1903-1970 .... **CLC 10, 42**
See also CA 25-28; CAP 2; DAM POET; DLB 48

Nietzsche, Friedrich (Wilhelm)
1844-1900 .... **TCLC 10, 18, 55**
See also CA 107; 121; DLB 129

Nievo, Ippolito 1831-1861 .... **NCLC 22**

Nightingale, Anne Redmon 1943-
See Redmon, Anne
See also CA 103

Nik. T. O.
See Annensky, Innokenty Fyodorovich

Nin, Anais
1903-1977 ...... **CLC 1, 4, 8, 11, 14, 60; SSC 10**
See also AITN 2; CA 13-16R; 69-72; CANR 22; DAM NOV, POP; DLB 2, 4, 152; MTCW

Nishiwaki, Junzaburo 1894-1982 .... **PC 15**
See also CA 107

Nissenson, Hugh 1933- .... **CLC 4, 9**
See also CA 17-20R; CANR 27; DLB 28

Niven, Larry .... **CLC 8**
See also Niven, Laurence Van Cott
See also DLB 8

Niven, Laurence Van Cott 1938-
See Niven, Larry
See also CA 21-24R; CAAS 12; CANR 14, 44; DAM POP; MTCW

Nixon, Agnes Eckhardt 1927- ...... **CLC 21**
See also CA 110

Nizan, Paul 1905-1940 .... **TCLC 40**
See also DLB 72

Nkosi, Lewis 1936- .... **CLC 45; BLC**
See also BW 1; CA 65-68; CANR 27; DAM MULT; DLB 157

Nodier, (Jean) Charles (Emmanuel)
1780-1844 .... **NCLC 19**
See also DLB 119

Nolan, Christopher 1965- .... **CLC 58**
See also CA 111

Noon, Jeff 1957- .... **CLC 91**
See also CA 148

Norden, Charles
See Durrell, Lawrence (George)

Nordhoff, Charles (Bernard)
1887-1947 .... **TCLC 23**
See also CA 108; DLB 9; SATA 23

Norfolk, Lawrence 1963- .... **CLC 76**
See also CA 144

Norman, Marsha 1947- .... **CLC 28**
See also CA 105; CABS 3; CANR 41; DAM DRAM; DLBY 84

Norris, Benjamin Franklin, Jr.
　1870-1902 .... **TCLC 24**
　See also Norris, Frank
　See also CA 110

Norris, Frank
　See Norris, Benjamin Franklin, Jr.
　See also CDALB 1865-1917; DLB 12, 71

Norris, Leslie　1921- .... **CLC 14**
　See also CA 11-12; CANR 14; CAP 1;
　DLB 27

North, Andrew
　See Norton, Andre

North, Anthony
　See Koontz, Dean R(ay)

North, Captain George
　See Stevenson, Robert Louis (Balfour)

North, Milou
　See Erdrich, Louise

Northrup, B. A.
　See Hubbard, L(afayette) Ron(ald)

North Staffs
　See Hulme, T(homas) E(rnest)

Norton, Alice Mary
　See Norton, Andre
　See also MAICYA; SATA 1, 43

Norton, Andre　1912- .... **CLC 12**
　See also Norton, Alice Mary
　See also AAYA 14; CA 1-4R; CANR 2, 31;
　DLB 8, 52; JRDA; MTCW

Norton, Caroline　1808-1877...... **NCLC 47**
　See also DLB 21, 159

Norway, Nevil Shute　1899-1960
　See Shute, Nevil
　See also CA 102; 93-96

Norwid, Cyprian Kamil
　1821-1883 .... **NCLC 17**

Nosille, Nabrah
　See Ellison, Harlan (Jay)

Nossack, Hans Erich　1901-1978 ..... **CLC 6**
　See also CA 93-96; 85-88; DLB 69

Nostradamus　1503-1566........... **LC 27**

Nosu, Chuji
　See Ozu, Yasujiro

Notenburg, Eleanora (Genrikhovna) von
　See Guro, Elena

Nova, Craig　1945-.............. **CLC 7, 31**
　See also CA 45-48; CANR 2

Novak, Joseph
　See Kosinski, Jerzy (Nikodem)

Novalis　1772-1801 .... **NCLC 13**
　See also DLB 90

Nowlan, Alden (Albert)
　1933-1983 .... **CLC 15; DAC**
　See also CA 9-12R; CANR 5; DAM MST;
　DLB 53

Noyes, Alfred　1880-1958 .... **TCLC 7**
　See also CA 104; DLB 20

Nunn, Kem　19(?)- .... **CLC 34**

Nye, Robert　1939- .... **CLC 13, 42**
　See also CA 33-36R; CANR 29;
　DAM NOV; DLB 14; MTCW; SATA 6

Nyro, Laura　1947- .... **CLC 17**

Oates, Joyce Carol
　1938- ...... **CLC 1, 2, 3, 6, 9, 11, 15, 19,
　33, 52; DA; DAB; DAC; SSC 6; WLC**
　See also AAYA 15; AITN 1; BEST 89:2;
　CA 5-8R; CANR 25, 45;
　CDALB 1968-1988; DAM MST, NOV,
　POP; DLB 2, 5, 130; DLBY 81;
　INT CANR-25; MTCW

O'Brien, Darcy　1939- .... **CLC 11**
　See also CA 21-24R; CANR 8

O'Brien, E. G.
　See Clarke, Arthur C(harles)

O'Brien, Edna
　1936- ... **CLC 3, 5, 8, 13, 36, 65; SSC 10**
　See also CA 1-4R; CANR 6, 41;
　CDBLB 1960 to Present; DAM NOV;
　DLB 14; MTCW

O'Brien, Fitz-James　1828-1862... **NCLC 21**
　See also DLB 74

O'Brien, Flann........ **CLC 1, 4, 5, 7, 10, 47**
　See also O Nuallain, Brian

O'Brien, Richard　1942- .... **CLC 17**
　See also CA 124

O'Brien, Tim　1946-.......... **CLC 7, 19, 40**
　See also AAYA 16; CA 85-88; CANR 40;
　DAM POP; DLB 152; DLBD 9;
　DLBY 80

Obstfelder, Sigbjoern　1866-1900... **TCLC 23**
　See also CA 123

O'Casey, Sean
　1880-1964 ...... **CLC 1, 5, 9, 11, 15, 88;
　DAB; DAC**
　See also CA 89-92; CDBLB 1914-1945;
　DAM DRAM, MST; DLB 10; MTCW

O'Cathasaigh, Sean
　See O'Casey, Sean

Ochs, Phil　1940-1976............. **CLC 17**
　See also CA 65-68

O'Connor, Edwin (Greene)
　1918-1968 .... **CLC 14**
　See also CA 93-96; 25-28R

O'Connor, (Mary) Flannery
　1925-1964 .... **CLC 1, 2, 3, 6, 10, 13, 15,
　21, 66; DA; DAB; DAC; SSC 1, 23; WLC**
　See also AAYA 7; CA 1-4R; CANR 3, 41;
　CDALB 1941-1968; DAM MST, NOV;
　DLB 2, 152; DLBD 12; DLBY 80;
　MTCW

O'Connor, Frank........... **CLC 23; SSC 5**
　See also O'Donovan, Michael John
　See also DLB 162

O'Dell, Scott　1898-1989.......... **CLC 30**
　See also AAYA 3; CA 61-64; 129;
　CANR 12, 30; CLR 1, 16; DLB 52;
　JRDA; MAICYA; SATA 12, 60

Odets, Clifford
　1906-1963 .... **CLC 2, 28; DC 6**
　See also CA 85-88; DAM DRAM; DLB 7,
　26; MTCW

O'Doherty, Brian　1934-........... **CLC 76**
　See also CA 105

O'Donnell, K. M.
　See Malzberg, Barry N(athaniel)

O'Donnell, Lawrence
　See Kuttner, Henry

O'Donovan, Michael John
　1903-1966 .... **CLC 14**
　See also O'Connor, Frank
　See also CA 93-96

Oe, Kenzaburo
　1935- .... **CLC 10, 36, 86; SSC 20**
　See also CA 97-100; CANR 36, 50;
　DAM NOV; DLBY 94; MTCW

O'Faolain, Julia　1932-........ **CLC 6, 19, 47**
　See also CA 81-84; CAAS 2; CANR 12;
　DLB 14; MTCW

O'Faolain, Sean
　1900-1991 .... **CLC 1, 7, 14, 32, 70;
　SSC 13**
　See also CA 61-64; 134; CANR 12;
　DLB 15, 162; MTCW

O'Flaherty, Liam
　1896-1984 .... **CLC 5, 34; SSC 6**
　See also CA 101; 113; CANR 35; DLB 36,
　162; DLBY 84; MTCW

Ogilvy, Gavin
　See Barrie, J(ames) M(atthew)

O'Grady, Standish James
　1846-1928 .... **TCLC 5**
　See also CA 104

O'Grady, Timothy　1951- .... **CLC 59**
　See also CA 138

O'Hara, Frank
　1926-1966 .... **CLC 2, 5, 13, 78**
　See also CA 9-12R; 25-28R; CANR 33;
　DAM POET; DLB 5, 16; MTCW

O'Hara, John (Henry)
　1905-1970 .... **CLC 1, 2, 3, 6, 11, 42;
　SSC 15**
　See also CA 5-8R; 25-28R; CANR 31;
　CDALB 1929-1941; DAM NOV; DLB 9,
　86; DLBD 2; MTCW

O Hehir, Diana　1922- .... **CLC 41**
　See also CA 93-96

Okigbo, Christopher (Ifenayichukwu)
　1932-1967 ..... **CLC 25, 84; BLC; PC 7**
　See also BW 1; CA 77-80; DAM MULT,
　POET; DLB 125; MTCW

Okri, Ben　1959- .... **CLC 87**
　See also BW 2; CA 130; 138; DLB 157;
　INT 138

Olds, Sharon　1942-......... **CLC 32, 39, 85**
　See also CA 101; CANR 18, 41;
　DAM POET; DLB 120

Oldstyle, Jonathan
　See Irving, Washington

Olesha, Yuri (Karlovich)
　1899-1960 .... **CLC 8**
　See also CA 85-88

Oliphant, Laurence
　1829(?)-1888 .... **NCLC 47**
　See also DLB 18

Oliphant, Margaret (Oliphant Wilson)
　1828-1897 .... **NCLC 11**
　See also DLB 18, 159

Oliver, Mary　1935-............ **CLC 19, 34**
　See also CA 21-24R; CANR 9, 43; DLB 5

Olivier, Laurence (Kerr)
　1907-1989 .... **CLC 20**
　See also CA 111; 150; 129

Olsen, Tillie
1913- ..... **CLC 4, 13; DA; DAB; DAC;
SSC 11**
See also CA 1-4R; CANR 1, 43;
DAM MST; DLB 28; DLBY 80; MTCW

Olson, Charles (John)
1910-1970 ..... **CLC 1, 2, 5, 6, 9, 11, 29**
See also CA 13-16; 25-28R; CABS 2;
CANR 35; CAP 1; DAM POET; DLB 5,
16; MTCW

Olson, Toby 1937- .... **CLC 28**
See also CA 65-68; CANR 9, 31

Olyesha, Yuri
See Olesha, Yuri (Karlovich)

Ondaatje, (Philip) Michael
1943- ... **CLC 14, 29, 51, 76; DAB; DAC**
See also CA 77-80; CANR 42; DAM MST;
DLB 60

Oneal, Elizabeth 1934-
See Oneal, Zibby
See also CA 106; CANR 28; MAICYA;
SATA 30, 82

Oneal, Zibby .... **CLC 30**
See also Oneal, Elizabeth
See also AAYA 5; CLR 13; JRDA

O'Neill, Eugene (Gladstone)
1888-1953 ...... **TCLC 1, 6, 27, 49; DA;
DAB; DAC; WLC**
See also AITN 1; CA 110; 132;
CDALB 1929-1941; DAM DRAM, MST;
DLB 7; MTCW

Onetti, Juan Carlos
1909-1994 .... **CLC 7, 10; SSC 23**
See also CA 85-88; 145; CANR 32;
DAM MULT, NOV; DLB 113; HW;
MTCW

O Nuallain, Brian 1911-1966
See O'Brien, Flann
See also CA 21-22; 25-28R; CAP 2

Oppen, George 1908-1984 .... **CLC 7, 13, 34**
See also CA 13-16R; 113; CANR 8; DLB 5,
165

Oppenheim, E(dward) Phillips
1866-1946 .... **TCLC 45**
See also CA 111; DLB 70

Orlovitz, Gil 1918-1973 .... **CLC 22**
See also CA 77-80; 45-48; DLB 2, 5

Orris
See Ingelow, Jean

Ortega y Gasset, Jose
1883-1955 .... **TCLC 9; HLC**
See also CA 106; 130; DAM MULT; HW;
MTCW

Ortese, Anna Maria 1914-........ **CLC 89**

Ortiz, Simon J(oseph) 1941- .... **CLC 45**
See also CA 134; DAM MULT, POET;
DLB 120; NNAL

Orton, Joe .... **CLC 4, 13, 43; DC 3**
See also Orton, John Kingsley
See also CDBLB 1960 to Present; DLB 13

Orton, John Kingsley 1933-1967
See Orton, Joe
See also CA 85-88; CANR 35;
DAM DRAM; MTCW

Orwell, George
..... **TCLC 2, 6, 15, 31, 51; DAB; WLC**
See also Blair, Eric (Arthur)
See also CDBLB 1945-1960; DLB 15, 98

Osborne, David
See Silverberg, Robert

Osborne, George
See Silverberg, Robert

Osborne, John (James)
1929-1994 ..... **CLC 1, 2, 5, 11, 45; DA;
DAB; DAC; WLC**
See also CA 13-16R; 147; CANR 21;
CDBLB 1945-1960; DAM DRAM, MST;
DLB 13; MTCW

Osborne, Lawrence 1958- .... **CLC 50**

Oshima, Nagisa 1932- .... **CLC 20**
See also CA 116; 121

Oskison, John Milton
1874-1947 .... **TCLC 35**
See also CA 144; DAM MULT; NNAL

Ossoli, Sarah Margaret (Fuller marchesa d')
1810-1850
See Fuller, Margaret
See also SATA 25

Ostrovsky, Alexander
1823-1886 .... **NCLC 30**

Otero, Blas de 1916-1979......... **CLC 11**
See also CA 89-92; DLB 134

Otto, Whitney 1955-.............. **CLC 70**
See also CA 140

Ouida .... **TCLC 43**
See also De La Ramee, (Marie) Louise
See also DLB 18, 156

Ousmane, Sembene 1923- .... **CLC 66; BLC**
See also BW 1; CA 117; 125; MTCW

Ovid 43B.C.-18(?).......... **CMLC 7; PC 2**
See also DAM POET

Owen, Hugh
See Faust, Frederick (Schiller)

Owen, Wilfred (Edward Salter)
1893-1918 ...... **TCLC 5, 27; DA; DAB;
DAC; WLC**
See also CA 104; 141; CDBLB 1914-1945;
DAM MST, POET; DLB 20

Owens, Rochelle 1936-............. **CLC 8**
See also CA 17-20R; CAAS 2; CANR 39

Oz, Amos 1939- ... **CLC 5, 8, 11, 27, 33, 54**
See also CA 53-56; CANR 27, 47;
DAM NOV; MTCW

Ozick, Cynthia
1928-........ **CLC 3, 7, 28, 62; SSC 15**
See also BEST 90:1; CA 17-20R; CANR 23;
DAM NOV, POP; DLB 28, 152;
DLBY 82; INT CANR-23; MTCW

Ozu, Yasujiro 1903-1963......... **CLC 16**
See also CA 112

Pacheco, C.
See Pessoa, Fernando (Antonio Nogueira)

Pa Chin .... **CLC 18**
See also Li Fei-kan

Pack, Robert 1929-.............. **CLC 13**
See also CA 1-4R; CANR 3, 44; DLB 5

Padgett, Lewis
See Kuttner, Henry

Padilla (Lorenzo), Heberto 1932- ... **CLC 38**
See also AITN 1; CA 123; 131; HW

Page, Jimmy 1944-............... **CLC 12**

Page, Louise 1955-............... **CLC 40**
See also CA 140

Page, P(atricia) K(athleen)
1916- .... **CLC 7, 18; DAC; PC 12**
See also CA 53-56; CANR 4, 22;
DAM MST; DLB 68; MTCW

Page, Thomas Nelson 1853-1922.... **SSC 23**
See also CA 118; DLB 12, 78; DLBD 13

Paget, Violet 1856-1935
See Lee, Vernon
See also CA 104

Paget-Lowe, Henry
See Lovecraft, H(oward) P(hillips)

Paglia, Camille (Anna) 1947-....... **CLC 68**
See also CA 140

Paige, Richard
See Koontz, Dean R(ay)

Pakenham, Antonia
See Fraser, (Lady) Antonia (Pakenham)

Palamas, Kostes 1859-1943 .... **TCLC 5**
See also CA 105

Palazzeschi, Aldo 1885-1974....... **CLC 11**
See also CA 89-92; 53-56; DLB 114

Paley, Grace 1922-.... **CLC 4, 6, 37; SSC 8**
See also CA 25-28R; CANR 13, 46;
DAM POP; DLB 28; INT CANR-13;
MTCW

Palin, Michael (Edward) 1943-..... **CLC 21**
See also Monty Python
See also CA 107; CANR 35; SATA 67

Palliser, Charles 1947-............ **CLC 65**
See also CA 136

Palma, Ricardo 1833-1919........ **TCLC 29**

Pancake, Breece Dexter 1952-1979
See Pancake, Breece D'J
See also CA 123; 109

Pancake, Breece D'J.............. **CLC 29**
See also Pancake, Breece Dexter
See also DLB 130

Panko, Rudy
See Gogol, Nikolai (Vasilyevich)

Papadiamantis, Alexandros
1851-1911 .... **TCLC 29**

Papadiamantopoulos, Johannes 1856-1910
See Moreas, Jean
See also CA 117

Papini, Giovanni 1881-1956...... **TCLC 22**
See also CA 121

Paracelsus 1493-1541.............. **LC 14**

Parasol, Peter
See Stevens, Wallace

Parfenie, Maria
See Codrescu, Andrei

Parini, Jay (Lee) 1948- .... **CLC 54**
See also CA 97-100; CAAS 16; CANR 32

Park, Jordan
See Kornbluth, C(yril) M.; Pohl, Frederik

Parker, Bert
See Ellison, Harlan (Jay)

Parker, Dorothy (Rothschild)
1893-1967 . . . . **CLC 15, 68; SSC 2**
See also CA 19-20; 25-28R; CAP 2;
DAM POET; DLB 11, 45, 86; MTCW

Parker, Robert B(rown) 1932- . . . . . . **CLC 27**
See also BEST 89:4; CA 49-52; CANR 1,
26; DAM NOV, POP; INT CANR-26;
MTCW

Parkin, Frank 1940- . . . . **CLC 43**
See also CA 147

Parkman, Francis, Jr.
1823-1893 . . . . **NCLC 12**
See also DLB 1, 30

Parks, Gordon (Alexander Buchanan)
1912- . . . . **CLC 1, 16; BLC**
See also AITN 2; BW 2; CA 41-44R;
CANR 26; DAM MULT; DLB 33;
SATA 8

Parnell, Thomas 1679-1718 . . . . **LC 3**
See also DLB 94

Parra, Nicanor 1914- . . . . **CLC 2; HLC**
See also CA 85-88; CANR 32;
DAM MULT; HW; MTCW

Parrish, Mary Frances
See Fisher, M(ary) F(rances) K(ennedy)

Parson
See Coleridge, Samuel Taylor

Parson Lot
See Kingsley, Charles

Partridge, Anthony
See Oppenheim, E(dward) Phillips

Pascoli, Giovanni 1855-1912 . . . . . . **TCLC 45**

Pasolini, Pier Paolo
1922-1975 . . . . **CLC 20, 37**
See also CA 93-96; 61-64; DLB 128;
MTCW

Pasquini
See Silone, Ignazio

Pastan, Linda (Olenik) 1932- . . . . . . **CLC 27**
See also CA 61-64; CANR 18, 40;
DAM POET; DLB 5

Pasternak, Boris (Leonidovich)
1890-1960 . . . . . . **CLC 7, 10, 18, 63; DA;**
DAB; DAC; PC 6; WLC
See also CA 127; 116; DAM MST, NOV,
POET; MTCW

Patchen, Kenneth 1911-1972 . . . **CLC 1, 2, 18**
See also CA 1-4R; 33-36R; CANR 3, 35;
DAM POET; DLB 16, 48; MTCW

Pater, Walter (Horatio)
1839-1894 . . . . **NCLC 7**
See also CDBLB 1832-1890; DLB 57, 156

Paterson, A(ndrew) B(arton)
1864-1941 . . . . **TCLC 32**

Paterson, Katherine (Womeldorf)
1932- . . . . **CLC 12, 30**
See also AAYA 1; CA 21-24R; CANR 28;
CLR 7; DLB 52; JRDA; MAICYA;
MTCW; SATA 13, 53

Patmore, Coventry Kersey Dighton
1823-1896 . . . . **NCLC 9**
See also DLB 35, 98

Paton, Alan (Stewart)
1903-1988 . . . . . . **CLC 4, 10, 25, 55; DA;**
DAB; DAC; WLC
See also CA 13-16; 125; CANR 22; CAP 1;
DAM MST, NOV; MTCW; SATA 11;
SATA-Obit 56

Paton Walsh, Gillian 1937-
See Walsh, Jill Paton
See also CANR 38; JRDA; MAICYA;
SAAS 3; SATA 4, 72

Paulding, James Kirke 1778-1860 . . **NCLC 2**
See also DLB 3, 59, 74

Paulin, Thomas Neilson 1949-
See Paulin, Tom
See also CA 123; 128

Paulin, Tom . . . . **CLC 37**
See also Paulin, Thomas Neilson
See also DLB 40

Paustovsky, Konstantin (Georgievich)
1892-1968 . . . . **CLC 40**
See also CA 93-96; 25-28R

Pavese, Cesare
1908-1950 . . . . . **TCLC 3; PC 13; SSC 19**
See also CA 104; DLB 128

Pavic, Milorad 1929- . . . . **CLC 60**
See also CA 136

Payne, Alan
See Jakes, John (William)

Paz, Gil
See Lugones, Leopoldo

Paz, Octavio
1914- . . . . **CLC 3, 4, 6, 10, 19, 51, 65;**
DA; DAB; DAC; HLC; PC 1; WLC
See also CA 73-76; CANR 32; DAM MST,
MULT, POET; DLBY 90; HW; MTCW

Peacock, Molly 1947- . . . . **CLC 60**
See also CA 103; CAAS 21; DLB 120

Peacock, Thomas Love
1785-1866 . . . . **NCLC 22**
See also DLB 96, 116

Peake, Mervyn 1911-1968 . . . . **CLC 7, 54**
See also CA 5-8R; 25-28R; CANR 3;
DLB 15, 160; MTCW; SATA 23

Pearce, Philippa . . . . **CLC 21**
See also Christie, (Ann) Philippa
See also CLR 9; DLB 161; MAICYA;
SATA 1, 67

Pearl, Eric
See Elman, Richard

Pearson, T(homas) R(eid) 1956- . . . . **CLC 39**
See also CA 120; 130; INT 130

Peck, Dale 1967- . . . . **CLC 81**
See also CA 146

Peck, John 1941- . . . . **CLC 3**
See also CA 49-52; CANR 3

Peck, Richard (Wayne) 1934- . . . . . . **CLC 21**
See also AAYA 1; CA 85-88; CANR 19,
38; CLR 15; INT CANR-19; JRDA;
MAICYA; SAAS 2; SATA 18, 55

Peck, Robert Newton
1928- . . . . **CLC 17; DA; DAC**
See also AAYA 3; CA 81-84; CANR 31;
DAM MST; JRDA; MAICYA; SAAS 1;
SATA 21, 62

Peckinpah, (David) Sam(uel)
1925-1984 . . . . **CLC 20**
See also CA 109; 114

Pedersen, Knut 1859-1952
See Hamsun, Knut
See also CA 104; 119; MTCW

Peeslake, Gaffer
See Durrell, Lawrence (George)

Peguy, Charles Pierre
1873-1914 . . . . **TCLC 10**
See also CA 107

Pena, Ramon del Valle y
See Valle-Inclan, Ramon (Maria) del

Pendennis, Arthur Esquir
See Thackeray, William Makepeace

Penn, William 1644-1718 . . . . **LC 25**
See also DLB 24

Pepys, Samuel
1633-1703 . . . . . **LC 11; DA; DAB; DAC;**
WLC
See also CDBLB 1660-1789; DAM MST;
DLB 101

Percy, Walker
1916-1990 . . . . **CLC 2, 3, 6, 8, 14, 18, 47,**
65
See also CA 1-4R; 131; CANR 1, 23;
DAM NOV, POP; DLB 2; DLBY 80, 90;
MTCW

Perec, Georges 1936-1982 . . . . **CLC 56**
See also CA 141; DLB 83

Pereda (y Sanchez de Porrua), Jose Maria de
1833-1906 . . . . **TCLC 16**
See also CA 117

Pereda y Porrua, Jose Maria de
See Pereda (y Sanchez de Porrua), Jose
Maria de

Peregoy, George Weems
See Mencken, H(enry) L(ouis)

Perelman, S(idney) J(oseph)
1904-1979 . . . **CLC 3, 5, 9, 15, 23, 44, 49**
See also AITN 1, 2; CA 73-76; 89-92;
CANR 18; DAM DRAM; DLB 11, 44;
MTCW

Peret, Benjamin 1899-1959 . . . . **TCLC 20**
See also CA 117

Peretz, Isaac Loeb 1851(?)-1915 . . . **TCLC 16**
See also CA 109

Peretz, Yitzkhok Leibush
See Peretz, Isaac Loeb

Perez Galdos, Benito 1843-1920 . . . **TCLC 27**
See also CA 125; HW

Perrault, Charles 1628-1703 . . . . **LC 2**
See also MAICYA; SATA 25

Perry, Brighton
See Sherwood, Robert E(mmet)

Perse, St.-John . . . . **CLC 4, 11, 46**
See also Leger, (Marie-Rene Auguste) Alexis
Saint-Leger

Perutz, Leo 1882-1957 . . . . **TCLC 60**
See also DLB 81

Peseenz, Tulio F.
See Lopez y Fuentes, Gregorio

Pesetsky, Bette 1932- . . . . **CLC 28**
See also CA 133; DLB 130

Peshkov, Alexei Maximovich 1868-1936
See Gorky, Maxim
See also CA 105; 141; DA; DAC;
DAM DRAM, MST, NOV

Pessoa, Fernando (Antonio Nogueira)
1888-1935 . . . . **TCLC 27; HLC**
See also CA 125

Peterkin, Julia Mood 1880-1961. . . . **CLC 31**
See also CA 102; DLB 9

Peters, Joan K. 1945- . . . . **CLC 39**

Peters, Robert L(ouis) 1924- . . . . **CLC 7**
See also CA 13-16R; CAAS 8; DLB 105

Petofi, Sandor 1823-1849. . . . . . . **NCLC 21**

Petrakis, Harry Mark 1923- . . . . . . **CLC 3**
See also CA 9-12R; CANR 4, 30

Petrarch 1304-1374. . . . . **PC 8**
See also DAM POET

Petrov, Evgeny . . . . **TCLC 21**
See also Kataev, Evgeny Petrovich

Petry, Ann (Lane) 1908- . . . . . . **CLC 1, 7, 18**
See also BW 1; CA 5-8R; CAAS 6;
CANR 4, 46; CLR 12; DLB 76; JRDA;
MAICYA; MTCW; SATA 5

Petursson, Halligrimur 1614-1674 . . . . **LC 8**

Philips, Katherine 1632-1664. . . . . . . **LC 30**
See also DLB 131

Philipson, Morris H. 1926- . . . . **CLC 53**
See also CA 1-4R; CANR 4

Phillips, David Graham
1867-1911 . . . . **TCLC 44**
See also CA 108; DLB 9, 12

Phillips, Jack
See Sandburg, Carl (August)

Phillips, Jayne Anne
1952- . . . . **CLC 15, 33; SSC 16**
See also CA 101; CANR 24, 50; DLBY 80;
INT CANR-24; MTCW

Phillips, Richard
See Dick, Philip K(indred)

Phillips, Robert (Schaeffer) 1938-. . . **CLC 28**
See also CA 17-20R; CAAS 13; CANR 8;
DLB 105

Phillips, Ward
See Lovecraft, H(oward) P(hillips)

Piccolo, Lucio 1901-1969. . . . . **CLC 13**
See also CA 97-100; DLB 114

Pickthall, Marjorie L(owry) C(hristie)
1883-1922 . . . . **TCLC 21**
See also CA 107; DLB 92

Pico della Mirandola, Giovanni
1463-1494 . . . . **LC 15**

Piercy, Marge
1936- . . . . **CLC 3, 6, 14, 18, 27, 62**
See also CA 21-24R; CAAS 1; CANR 13,
43; DLB 120; MTCW

Piers, Robert
See Anthony, Piers

Pieyre de Mandiargues, Andre 1909-1991
See Mandiargues, Andre Pieyre de
See also CA 103; 136; CANR 22

Pilnyak, Boris . . . . **TCLC 23**
See also Vogau, Boris Andreyevich

Pincherle, Alberto 1907-1990 . . . **CLC 11, 18**
See also Moravia, Alberto
See also CA 25-28R; 132; CANR 33;
DAM NOV; MTCW

Pinckney, Darryl 1953- . . . . **CLC 76**
See also BW 2; CA 143

Pindar 518B.C.-446B.C. . . . . **CMLC 12**

Pineda, Cecile 1942- . . . . **CLC 39**
See also CA 118

Pinero, Arthur Wing 1855-1934 . . . **TCLC 32**
See also CA 110; DAM DRAM; DLB 10

Pinero, Miguel (Antonio Gomez)
1946-1988 . . . . **CLC 4, 55**
See also CA 61-64; 125; CANR 29; HW

Pinget, Robert 1919- . . . . **CLC 7, 13, 37**
See also CA 85-88; DLB 83

Pink Floyd
See Barrett, (Roger) Syd; Gilmour, David;
Mason, Nick; Waters, Roger; Wright,
Rick

Pinkney, Edward 1802-1828 . . . . . **NCLC 31**

Pinkwater, Daniel Manus 1941- . . . . **CLC 35**
See also Pinkwater, Manus
See also AAYA 1; CA 29-32R; CANR 12,
38; CLR 4; JRDA; MAICYA; SAAS 3;
SATA 46, 76

Pinkwater, Manus
See Pinkwater, Daniel Manus
See also SATA 8

Pinsky, Robert 1940- . . . . . **CLC 9, 19, 38, 91**
See also CA 29-32R; CAAS 4;
DAM POET; DLBY 82

Pinta, Harold
See Pinter, Harold

Pinter, Harold
1930- . . . . . **CLC 1, 3, 6, 9, 11, 15, 27, 58,
73; DA; DAB; DAC; WLC**
See also CA 5-8R; CANR 33; CDBLB 1960
to Present; DAM DRAM, MST; DLB 13;
MTCW

Pirandello, Luigi
1867-1936 . . . . . . **TCLC 4, 29; DA; DAB;
DAC; DC 5; SSC 22; WLC**
See also CA 104; DAM DRAM, MST

Pirsig, Robert M(aynard)
1928- . . . . **CLC 4, 6, 73**
See also CA 53-56; CANR 42; DAM POP;
MTCW; SATA 39

Pisarev, Dmitry Ivanovich
1840-1868 . . . . **NCLC 25**

Pix, Mary (Griffith) 1666-1709 . . . . . . **LC 8**
See also DLB 80

Pixerecourt, Guilbert de
1773-1844 . . . . **NCLC 39**

Plaidy, Jean
See Hibbert, Eleanor Alice Burford

Planche, James Robinson
1796-1880 . . . . **NCLC 42**

Plant, Robert 1948- . . . . **CLC 12**

Plante, David (Robert)
1940- . . . . **CLC 7, 23, 38**
See also CA 37-40R; CANR 12, 36;
DAM NOV; DLBY 83; INT CANR-12;
MTCW

Plath, Sylvia
1932-1963 . . . . . **CLC 1, 2, 3, 5, 9, 11, 14,
17, 50, 51, 62; DA; DAB; DAC; PC 1;
WLC**
See also AAYA 13; CA 19-20; CANR 34;
CAP 2; CDALB 1941-1968; DAM MST,
POET; DLB 5, 6, 152; MTCW

Plato
428(?)B.C.-348(?)B.C. . . . . **CMLC 8; DA;
DAB; DAC**
See also DAM MST

Platonov, Andrei . . . . **TCLC 14**
See also Klimentov, Andrei Platonovich

Platt, Kin 1911- . . . . **CLC 26**
See also AAYA 11; CA 17-20R; CANR 11;
JRDA; SAAS 17; SATA 21, 86

Plautus c. 251B.C.-184B.C. . . . . **DC 6**

Plick et Plock
See Simenon, Georges (Jacques Christian)

Plimpton, George (Ames) 1927-. . . . . **CLC 36**
See also AITN 1; CA 21-24R; CANR 32;
MTCW; SATA 10

Plomer, William Charles Franklin
1903-1973 . . . . **CLC 4, 8**
See also CA 21-22; CANR 34; CAP 2;
DLB 20, 162; MTCW; SATA 24

Plowman, Piers
See Kavanagh, Patrick (Joseph)

Plum, J.
See Wodehouse, P(elham) G(renville)

Plumly, Stanley (Ross) 1939- . . . . . . **CLC 33**
See also CA 108; 110; DLB 5; INT 110

Plumpe, Friedrich Wilhelm
1888-1931 . . . . **TCLC 53**
See also CA 112

Poe, Edgar Allan
1809-1849 . . . . **NCLC 1, 16, 55; DA;
DAB; DAC; PC 1; SSC 1, 22; WLC**
See also AAYA 14; CDALB 1640-1865;
DAM MST, POET; DLB 3, 59, 73, 74;
SATA 23

Poet of Titchfield Street, The
See Pound, Ezra (Weston Loomis)

Pohl, Frederik 1919- . . . . **CLC 18**
See also CA 61-64; CAAS 1; CANR 11, 37;
DLB 8; INT CANR-11; MTCW;
SATA 24

Poirier, Louis 1910-
See Gracq, Julien
See also CA 122; 126

Poitier, Sidney 1927- . . . . **CLC 26**
See also BW 1; CA 117

Polanski, Roman 1933- . . . . **CLC 16**
See also CA 77-80

Poliakoff, Stephen 1952- . . . . **CLC 38**
See also CA 106; DLB 13

Police, The
See Copeland, Stewart (Armstrong);
Summers, Andrew James; Sumner,
Gordon Matthew

Polidori, John William
1795-1821 . . . . **NCLC 51**
See also DLB 116

Pollitt, Katha 1949- . . . . **CLC 28**
See also CA 120; 122; MTCW

Author Index

Purdy, James (Amos)
  1923- . . . . **CLC 2, 4, 10, 28, 52**
  See also CA 33-36R; CAAS 1; CANR 19,
  51; DLB 2; INT CANR-19; MTCW

Pure, Simon
  See Swinnerton, Frank Arthur

Pushkin, Alexander (Sergeyevich)
  1799-1837 . . . . . **NCLC 3, 27; DA; DAB;**
                        DAC; PC 10; WLC
  See also DAM DRAM, MST, POET;
  SATA 61

P'u Sung-ling 1640-1715 . . . . **LC 3**

Putnam, Arthur Lee
  See Alger, Horatio, Jr.

Puzo, Mario 1920- . . . . **CLC 1, 2, 6, 36**
  See also CA 65-68; CANR 4, 42;
  DAM NOV, POP; DLB 6; MTCW

Pym, Barbara (Mary Crampton)
  1913-1980 . . . . **CLC 13, 19, 37**
  See also CA 13-14; 97-100; CANR 13, 34;
  CAP 1; DLB 14; DLBY 87; MTCW

Pynchon, Thomas (Ruggles, Jr.)
  1937- . . . . . **CLC 2, 3, 6, 9, 11, 18, 33, 62,**
               72; DA; DAB; DAC; SSC 14; WLC
  See also BEST 90:2; CA 17-20R; CANR 22,
  46; DAM MST, NOV, POP; DLB 2;
  MTCW

Qian Zhongshu
  See Ch'ien Chung-shu

Qroll
  See Dagerman, Stig (Halvard)

Quarrington, Paul (Lewis) 1953- . . . . **CLC 65**
  See also CA 129

Quasimodo, Salvatore 1901-1968 . . . **CLC 10**
  See also CA 13-16; 25-28R; CAP 1;
  DLB 114; MTCW

Queen, Ellery . . . . **CLC 3, 11**
  See also Dannay, Frederic; Davidson,
  Avram; Lee, Manfred B(ennington);
  Sturgeon, Theodore (Hamilton); Vance,
  John Holbrook

Queen, Ellery, Jr.
  See Dannay, Frederic; Lee, Manfred
  B(ennington)

Queneau, Raymond
  1903-1976 . . . . **CLC 2, 5, 10, 42**
  See also CA 77-80; 69-72; CANR 32;
  DLB 72; MTCW

Quevedo, Francisco de 1580-1645 . . . . **LC 23**

Quiller-Couch, Arthur Thomas
  1863-1944 . . . . **TCLC 53**
  See also CA 118; DLB 135, 153

Quin, Ann (Marie) 1936-1973 . . . . **CLC 6**
  See also CA 9-12R; 45-48; DLB 14

Quinn, Martin
  See Smith, Martin Cruz

Quinn, Peter 1947- . . . . **CLC 91**

Quinn, Simon
  See Smith, Martin Cruz

Quiroga, Horacio (Sylvestre)
  1878-1937 . . . . **TCLC 20; HLC**
  See also CA 117; 131; DAM MULT; HW;
  MTCW

Quoirez, Francoise 1935- . . . . **CLC 9**
  See also Sagan, Francoise
  See also CA 49-52; CANR 6, 39; MTCW

Raabe, Wilhelm 1831-1910 . . . . **TCLC 45**
  See also DLB 129

Rabe, David (William) 1940- . . . **CLC 4, 8, 33**
  See also CA 85-88; CABS 3; DAM DRAM;
  DLB 7

Rabelais, Francois
  1483-1553 . . . . . . **LC 5; DA; DAB; DAC;**
                        WLC
  See also DAM MST

Rabinovitch, Sholem 1859-1916
  See Aleichem, Sholom
  See also CA 104

Racine, Jean 1639-1699 . . . . . . **LC 28; DAB**
  See also DAM MST

Radcliffe, Ann (Ward)
  1764-1823 . . . . **NCLC 6, 55**
  See also DLB 39

Radiguet, Raymond 1903-1923 . . . . **TCLC 29**
  See also DLB 65

Radnoti, Miklos 1909-1944 . . . . . . **TCLC 16**
  See also CA 118

Rado, James 1939- . . . . **CLC 17**
  See also CA 105

Radvanyi, Netty 1900-1983
  See Seghers, Anna
  See also CA 85-88; 110

Rae, Ben
  See Griffiths, Trevor

Raeburn, John (Hay) 1941- . . . . **CLC 34**
  See also CA 57-60

Ragni, Gerome 1942-1991 . . . . **CLC 17**
  See also CA 105; 134

Rahv, Philip 1908-1973 . . . . **CLC 24**
  See also Greenberg, Ivan
  See also DLB 137

Raine, Craig 1944- . . . . **CLC 32**
  See also CA 108; CANR 29, 51; DLB 40

Raine, Kathleen (Jessie) 1908- . . . **CLC 7, 45**
  See also CA 85-88; CANR 46; DLB 20;
  MTCW

Rainis, Janis 1865-1929 . . . . **TCLC 29**

Rakosi, Carl . . . . **CLC 47**
  See also Rawley, Callman
  See also CAAS 5

Raleigh, Richard
  See Lovecraft, H(oward) P(hillips)

Raleigh, Sir Walter 1554(?)-1618 . . . . **LC 31**
  See also CDBLB Before 1660

Rallentando, H. P.
  See Sayers, Dorothy L(eigh)

Ramal, Walter
  See de la Mare, Walter (John)

Ramon, Juan
  See Jimenez (Mantecon), Juan Ramon

Ramos, Graciliano 1892-1953 . . . . . **TCLC 32**

Rampersad, Arnold 1941- . . . . **CLC 44**
  See also BW 2; CA 127; 133; DLB 111;
  INT 133

Rampling, Anne
  See Rice, Anne

Ramsay, Allan 1684(?)-1758 . . . . **LC 29**
  See also DLB 95

Ramuz, Charles-Ferdinand
  1878-1947 . . . . **TCLC 33**

Rand, Ayn
  1905-1982 . . . . . . **CLC 3, 30, 44, 79; DA;**
                        DAC; WLC
  See also AAYA 10; CA 13-16R; 105;
  CANR 27; DAM MST, NOV, POP;
  MTCW

Randall, Dudley (Felker)
  1914- . . . . **CLC 1; BLC**
  See also BW 1; CA 25-28R; CANR 23;
  DAM MULT; DLB 41

Randall, Robert
  See Silverberg, Robert

Ranger, Ken
  See Creasey, John

Ransom, John Crowe
  1888-1974 . . . . **CLC 2, 4, 5, 11, 24**
  See also CA 5-8R; 49-52; CANR 6, 34;
  DAM POET; DLB 45, 63; MTCW

Rao, Raja 1909- . . . . **CLC 25, 56**
  See also CA 73-76; CANR 51; DAM NOV;
  MTCW

Raphael, Frederic (Michael)
  1931- . . . . **CLC 2, 14**
  See also CA 1-4R; CANR 1; DLB 14

Ratcliffe, James P.
  See Mencken, H(enry) L(ouis)

Rathbone, Julian 1935- . . . . **CLC 41**
  See also CA 101; CANR 34

Rattigan, Terence (Mervyn)
  1911-1977 . . . . **CLC 7**
  See also CA 85-88; 73-76;
  CDBLB 1945-1960; DAM DRAM;
  DLB 13; MTCW

Ratushinskaya, Irina 1954- . . . . **CLC 54**
  See also CA 129

Raven, Simon (Arthur Noel)
  1927- . . . . **CLC 14**
  See also CA 81-84

Rawley, Callman 1903-
  See Rakosi, Carl
  See also CA 21-24R; CANR 12, 32

Rawlings, Marjorie Kinnan
  1896-1953 . . . . **TCLC 4**
  See also CA 104; 137; DLB 9, 22, 102;
  JRDA; MAICYA; YABC 1

Ray, Satyajit 1921-1992 . . . . **CLC 16, 76**
  See also CA 114; 137; DAM MULT

Read, Herbert Edward 1893-1968 . . . . **CLC 4**
  See also CA 85-88; 25-28R; DLB 20, 149

Read, Piers Paul 1941- . . . . . . **CLC 4, 10, 25**
  See also CA 21-24R; CANR 38; DLB 14;
  SATA 21

Reade, Charles 1814-1884 . . . . **NCLC 2**
  See also DLB 21

Reade, Hamish
  See Gray, Simon (James Holliday)

Reading, Peter 1946- . . . . **CLC 47**
  See also CA 103; CANR 46; DLB 40

Reaney, James 1926- . . . . **CLC 13; DAC**
  See also CA 41-44R; CAAS 15; CANR 42;
  DAM MST; DLB 68; SATA 43

Rebreanu, Liviu 1885-1944 .... **TCLC 28**

Rechy, John (Francisco)
1934- .... **CLC 1, 7, 14, 18; HLC**
See also CA 5-8R; CAAS 4; CANR 6, 32;
DAM MULT; DLB 122; DLBY 82; HW;
INT CANR-6

Redcam, Tom 1870-1933 .... **TCLC 25**

Reddin, Keith .... **CLC 67**

Redgrove, Peter (William)
1932- .... **CLC 6, 41**
See also CA 1-4R; CANR 3, 39; DLB 40

Redmon, Anne .... **CLC 22**
See also Nightingale, Anne Redmon
See also DLBY 86

Reed, Eliot
See Ambler, Eric

Reed, Ishmael
1938- ... **CLC 2, 3, 5, 6, 13, 32, 60; BLC**
See also BW 2; CA 21-24R; CANR 25, 48;
DAM MULT; DLB 2, 5, 33; DLBD 8;
MTCW

Reed, John (Silas) 1887-1920 ...... **TCLC 9**
See also CA 106

Reed, Lou .... **CLC 21**
See also Firbank, Louis

Reeve, Clara 1729-1807 .... **NCLC 19**
See also DLB 39

Reich, Wilhelm 1897-1957 .... **TCLC 57**

Reid, Christopher (John) 1949- ..... **CLC 33**
See also CA 140; DLB 40

Reid, Desmond
See Moorcock, Michael (John)

Reid Banks, Lynne 1929-
See Banks, Lynne Reid
See also CA 1-4R; CANR 6, 22, 38;
CLR 24; JRDA; MAICYA; SATA 22, 75

Reilly, William K.
See Creasey, John

Reiner, Max
See Caldwell, (Janet Miriam) Taylor
(Holland)

Reis, Ricardo
See Pessoa, Fernando (Antonio Nogueira)

Remarque, Erich Maria
1898-1970 .... **CLC 21; DA; DAB; DAC**
See also CA 77-80; 29-32R; DAM MST,
NOV; DLB 56; MTCW

Remizov, A.
See Remizov, Aleksei (Mikhailovich)

Remizov, A. M.
See Remizov, Aleksei (Mikhailovich)

Remizov, Aleksei (Mikhailovich)
1877-1957 .... **TCLC 27**
See also CA 125; 133

Renan, Joseph Ernest
1823-1892 .... **NCLC 26**

Renard, Jules 1864-1910 .... **TCLC 17**
See also CA 117

Renault, Mary .... **CLC 3, 11, 17**
See also Challans, Mary
See also DLBY 83

Rendell, Ruth (Barbara) 1930- .. **CLC 28, 48**
See also Vine, Barbara
See also CA 109; CANR 32; DAM POP;
DLB 87; INT CANR-32; MTCW

Renoir, Jean 1894-1979 .... **CLC 20**
See also CA 129; 85-88

Resnais, Alain 1922- .... **CLC 16**

Reverdy, Pierre 1889-1960 .... **CLC 53**
See also CA 97-100; 89-92

Rexroth, Kenneth
1905-1982 ..... **CLC 1, 2, 6, 11, 22, 49**
See also CA 5-8R; 107; CANR 14, 34;
CDALB 1941-1968; DAM POET;
DLB 16, 48, 165; DLBY 82;
INT CANR-14; MTCW

Reyes, Alfonso 1889-1959 .... **TCLC 33**
See also CA 131; HW

Reyes y Basoalto, Ricardo Eliecer Neftali
See Neruda, Pablo

Reymont, Wladyslaw (Stanislaw)
1868(?)-1925 .... **TCLC 5**
See also CA 104

Reynolds, Jonathan 1942- .... **CLC 6, 38**
See also CA 65-68; CANR 28

Reynolds, Joshua 1723-1792 .... **LC 15**
See also DLB 104

Reynolds, Michael Shane 1937- .... **CLC 44**
See also CA 65-68; CANR 9

Reznikoff, Charles 1894-1976 .... **CLC 9**
See also CA 33-36; 61-64; CAP 2; DLB 28,
45

Rezzori (d'Arezzo), Gregor von
1914- .... **CLC 25**
See also CA 122; 136

Rhine, Richard
See Silverstein, Alvin

Rhodes, Eugene Manlove
1869-1934 .... **TCLC 53**

R'hoone
See Balzac, Honore de

Rhys, Jean
1890(?)-1979 .... **CLC 2, 4, 6, 14, 19, 51;
SSC 21**
See also CA 25-28R; 85-88; CANR 35;
CDBLB 1945-1960; DAM NOV; DLB 36,
117, 162; MTCW

Ribeiro, Darcy 1922- .... **CLC 34**
See also CA 33-36R

Ribeiro, Joao Ubaldo (Osorio Pimentel)
1941- .... **CLC 10, 67**
See also CA 81-84

Ribman, Ronald (Burt) 1932- .... **CLC 7**
See also CA 21-24R; CANR 46

Ricci, Nino 1959- .... **CLC 70**
See also CA 137

Rice, Anne 1941- .... **CLC 41**
See also AAYA 9; BEST 89:2; CA 65-68;
CANR 12, 36; DAM POP

Rice, Elmer (Leopold)
1892-1967 .... **CLC 7, 49**
See also CA 21-22; 25-28R; CAP 2;
DAM DRAM; DLB 4, 7; MTCW

Rice, Tim(othy Miles Bindon)
1944- .... **CLC 21**
See also CA 103; CANR 46

Rich, Adrienne (Cecile)
1929- .... **CLC 3, 6, 7, 11, 18, 36, 73, 76;
PC 5**
See also CA 9-12R; CANR 20;
DAM POET; DLB 5, 67; MTCW

Rich, Barbara
See Graves, Robert (von Ranke)

Rich, Robert
See Trumbo, Dalton

Richard, Keith .... **CLC 17**
See also Richards, Keith

Richards, David Adams
1950- .... **CLC 59; DAC**
See also CA 93-96; DLB 53

Richards, I(vor) A(rmstrong)
1893-1979 .... **CLC 14, 24**
See also CA 41-44R; 89-92; CANR 34;
DLB 27

Richards, Keith 1943-
See Richard, Keith
See also CA 107

Richardson, Anne
See Roiphe, Anne (Richardson)

Richardson, Dorothy Miller
1873-1957 .... **TCLC 3**
See also CA 104; DLB 36

Richardson, Ethel Florence (Lindesay)
1870-1946
See Richardson, Henry Handel
See also CA 105

Richardson, Henry Handel .... **TCLC 4**
See also Richardson, Ethel Florence
(Lindesay)

Richardson, John
1796-1852 .... **NCLC 55; DAC**
See also CA 140; DLB 99

Richardson, Samuel
1689-1761 ...... **LC 1; DA; DAB; DAC;
WLC**
See also CDBLB 1660-1789; DAM MST,
NOV; DLB 39

Richler, Mordecai
1931- .... **CLC 3, 5, 9, 13, 18, 46, 70;
DAC**
See also AITN 1; CA 65-68; CANR 31;
CLR 17; DAM MST, NOV; DLB 53;
MAICYA; MTCW; SATA 44;
SATA-Brief 27

Richter, Conrad (Michael)
1890-1968 .... **CLC 30**
See also CA 5-8R; 25-28R; CANR 23;
DLB 9; MTCW; SATA 3

Ricostranza, Tom
See Ellis, Trey

Riddell, J. H. 1832-1906 .... **TCLC 40**

Riding, Laura .... **CLC 3, 7**
See also Jackson, Laura (Riding)

Riefenstahl, Berta Helene Amalia 1902-
See Riefenstahl, Leni
See also CA 108

Riefenstahl, Leni .... **CLC 16**
See also Riefenstahl, Berta Helene Amalia

Riffe, Ernest
See Bergman, (Ernst) Ingmar

Author Index

Shone, Patric
See Hanley, James

Shreve, Susan Richards 1939-...... CLC 23
See also CA 49-52; CAAS 5; CANR 5, 38;
MAICYA; SATA 46; SATA-Brief 41

Shue, Larry 1946-1985............ CLC 52
See also CA 145; 117; DAM DRAM

Shu-Jen, Chou 1881-1936
See Lu Hsun
See also CA 104

Shulman, Alix Kates 1932- ...... CLC 2, 10
See also CA 29-32R; CANR 43; SATA 7

Shuster, Joe 1914- .... CLC 21

Shute, Nevil..................... CLC 30
See also Norway, Nevil Shute

Shuttle, Penelope (Diane) 1947-..... CLC 7
See also CA 93-96; CANR 39; DLB 14, 40

Sidney, Mary 1561-1621 .... LC 19

Sidney, Sir Philip
1554-1586 ..... LC 19; DA; DAB; DAC
See also CDBLB Before 1660; DAM MST,
POET

Siegel, Jerome 1914- .... CLC 21
See also CA 116

Siegel, Jerry
See Siegel, Jerome

Sienkiewicz, Henryk (Adam Alexander Pius)
1846-1916 .... TCLC 3
See also CA 104; 134

Sierra, Gregorio Martinez
See Martinez Sierra, Gregorio

Sierra, Maria (de la O'LeJarraga) Martinez
See Martinez Sierra, Maria (de la
O'LeJarraga)

Sigal, Clancy 1926-................ CLC 7
See also CA 1-4R

Sigourney, Lydia Howard (Huntley)
1791-1865 .... NCLC 21
See also DLB 1, 42, 73

Siguenza y Gongora, Carlos de
1645-1700 .... LC 8

Sigurjonsson, Johann 1880-1919... TCLC 27

Sikelianos, Angelos 1884-1951 .... TCLC 39

Silkin, Jon 1930- .... CLC 2, 6, 43
See also CA 5-8R; CAAS 5; DLB 27

Silko, Leslie (Marmon)
1948-.......... CLC 23, 74; DA; DAC
See also AAYA 14; CA 115; 122;
CANR 45; DAM MST, MULT, POP;
DLB 143; NNAL

Sillanpaa, Frans Eemil 1888-1964... CLC 19
See also CA 129; 93-96; MTCW

Sillitoe, Alan
1928-......... CLC 1, 3, 6, 10, 19, 57
See also AITN 1; CA 9-12R; CAAS 2;
CANR 8, 26; CDBLB 1960 to Present;
DLB 14, 139; MTCW; SATA 61

Silone, Ignazio 1900-1978 .... CLC 4
See also CA 25-28; 81-84; CANR 34;
CAP 2; MTCW

Silver, Joan Micklin 1935- .... CLC 20
See also CA 114; 121; INT 121

Silver, Nicholas
See Faust, Frederick (Schiller)

Silverberg, Robert 1935-........... CLC 7
See also CA 1-4R; CAAS 3; CANR 1, 20,
36; DAM POP; DLB 8; INT CANR-20;
MAICYA; MTCW; SATA 13

Silverstein, Alvin 1933-........... CLC 17
See also CA 49-52; CANR 2; CLR 25;
JRDA; MAICYA; SATA 8, 69

Silverstein, Virginia B(arbara Opshelor)
1937-...................... CLC 17
See also CA 49-52; CANR 2; CLR 25;
JRDA; MAICYA; SATA 8, 69

Sim, Georges
See Simenon, Georges (Jacques Christian)

Simak, Clifford D(onald)
1904-1988 .... CLC 1, 55
See also CA 1-4R; 125; CANR 1, 35;
DLB 8; MTCW; SATA-Obit 56

Simenon, Georges (Jacques Christian)
1903-1989 ...... CLC 1, 2, 3, 8, 18, 47
See also CA 85-88; 129; CANR 35;
DAM POP; DLB 72; DLBY 89; MTCW

Simic, Charles 1938-... CLC 6, 9, 22, 49, 68
See also CA 29-32R; CAAS 4; CANR 12,
33; DAM POET; DLB 105

Simmons, Charles (Paul) 1924-..... CLC 57
See also CA 89-92; INT 89-92

Simmons, Dan 1948-............. CLC 44
See also AAYA 16; CA 138; DAM POP

Simmons, James (Stewart Alexander)
1933-...................... CLC 43
See also CA 105; CAAS 21; DLB 40

Simms, William Gilmore
1806-1870 .... NCLC 3
See also DLB 3, 30, 59, 73

Simon, Carly 1945-.............. CLC 26
See also CA 105

Simon, Claude 1913-....... CLC 4, 9, 15, 39
See also CA 89-92; CANR 33; DAM NOV;
DLB 83; MTCW

Simon, (Marvin) Neil
1927-.......... CLC 6, 11, 31, 39, 70
See also AITN 1; CA 21-24R; CANR 26;
DAM DRAM; DLB 7; MTCW

Simon, Paul 1942(?)-............. CLC 17
See also CA 116

Simonon, Paul 1956(?)-........... CLC 30

Simpson, Harriette
See Arnow, Harriette (Louisa) Simpson

Simpson, Louis (Aston Marantz)
1923-................. CLC 4, 7, 9, 32
See also CA 1-4R; CAAS 4; CANR 1;
DAM POET; DLB 5; MTCW

Simpson, Mona (Elizabeth) 1957-... CLC 44
See also CA 122; 135

Simpson, N(orman) F(rederick)
1919-...................... CLC 29
See also CA 13-16R; DLB 13

Sinclair, Andrew (Annandale)
1935-.................... CLC 2, 14
See also CA 9-12R; CAAS 5; CANR 14, 38;
DLB 14; MTCW

Sinclair, Emil
See Hesse, Hermann

Sinclair, Iain 1943-............... CLC 76
See also CA 132

Sinclair, Iain MacGregor
See Sinclair, Iain

Sinclair, Mary Amelia St. Clair 1865(?)-1946
See Sinclair, May
See also CA 104

Sinclair, May.................. TCLC 3, 11
See also Sinclair, Mary Amelia St. Clair
See also DLB 36, 135

Sinclair, Upton (Beall)
1878-1968 ...... CLC 1, 11, 15, 63; DA;
DAB; DAC; WLC
See also CA 5-8R; 25-28R; CANR 7;
CDALB 1929-1941; DAM MST, NOV;
DLB 9; INT CANR-7; MTCW; SATA 9

Singer, Isaac
See Singer, Isaac Bashevis

Singer, Isaac Bashevis
1904-1991 .... CLC 1, 3, 6, 9, 11, 15, 23,
38, 69; DA; DAB; DAC; SSC 3; WLC
See also AITN 1, 2; CA 1-4R; 134;
CANR 1, 39; CDALB 1941-1968; CLR 1;
DAM MST, NOV; DLB 6, 28, 52;
DLBY 91; JRDA; MAICYA; MTCW;
SATA 3, 27; SATA-Obit 68

Singer, Israel Joshua 1893-1944 ... TCLC 33

Singh, Khushwant 1915-........... CLC 11
See also CA 9-12R; CAAS 9; CANR 6

Sinjohn, John
See Galsworthy, John

Sinyavsky, Andrei (Donatevich)
1925-...................... CLC 8
See also CA 85-88

Sirin, V.
See Nabokov, Vladimir (Vladimirovich)

Sissman, L(ouis) E(dward)
1928-1976 .... CLC 9, 18
See also CA 21-24R; 65-68; CANR 13;
DLB 5

Sisson, C(harles) H(ubert) 1914-..... CLC 8
See also CA 1-4R; CAAS 3; CANR 3, 48;
DLB 27

Sitwell, Dame Edith
1887-1964 .... CLC 2, 9, 67; PC 3
See also CA 9-12R; CANR 35;
CDBLB 1945-1960; DAM POET;
DLB 20; MTCW

Sjoewall, Maj 1935-............... CLC 7
See also CA 65-68

Sjowall, Maj
See Sjoewall, Maj

Skelton, Robin 1925-............. CLC 13
See also AITN 2; CA 5-8R; CAAS 5;
CANR 28; DLB 27, 53

Skolimowski, Jerzy 1938-......... CLC 20
See also CA 128

Skram, Amalie (Bertha)
1847-1905 .... TCLC 25

Skvorecky, Josef (Vaclav)
1924-........... CLC 15, 39, 69; DAC
See also CA 61-64; CAAS 1; CANR 10, 34;
DAM NOV; MTCW

Slade, Bernard................ CLC 11, 46
See also Newbound, Bernard Slade
See also CAAS 9; DLB 53

Spark, Muriel (Sarah)
1918- .... **CLC 2, 3, 5, 8, 13, 18, 40; DAB; DAC; SSC 10**
See also CA 5-8R; CANR 12, 36;
CDBLB 1945-1960; DAM MST, NOV;
DLB 15, 139; INT CANR-12; MTCW

Spaulding, Douglas
See Bradbury, Ray (Douglas)

Spaulding, Leonard
See Bradbury, Ray (Douglas)

Spence, J. A. D.
See Eliot, T(homas) S(tearns)

Spencer, Elizabeth 1921- .... **CLC 22**
See also CA 13-16R; CANR 32; DLB 6;
MTCW; SATA 14

Spencer, Leonard G.
See Silverberg, Robert

Spencer, Scott 1945- .... **CLC 30**
See also CA 113; CANR 51; DLBY 86

Spender, Stephen (Harold)
1909-1995 ...... **CLC 1, 2, 5, 10, 41, 91**
See also CA 9-12R; 149; CANR 31;
CDBLB 1945-1960; DAM POET;
DLB 20; MTCW

Spengler, Oswald (Arnold Gottfried)
1880-1936 .... **TCLC 25**
See also CA 118

Spenser, Edmund
1552(?)-1599 .... **LC 5; DA; DAB; DAC; PC 8; WLC**
See also CDBLB Before 1660; DAM MST, POET

Spicer, Jack 1925-1965 ...... **CLC 8, 18, 72**
See also CA 85-88; DAM POET; DLB 5, 16

Spiegelman, Art 1948- .... **CLC 76**
See also AAYA 10; CA 125; CANR 41

Spielberg, Peter 1929- .... **CLC 6**
See also CA 5-8R; CANR 4, 48; DLBY 81

Spielberg, Steven 1947- .... **CLC 20**
See also AAYA 8; CA 77-80; CANR 32;
SATA 32

Spillane, Frank Morrison 1918-
See Spillane, Mickey
See also CA 25-28R; CANR 28; MTCW;
SATA 66

Spillane, Mickey .... **CLC 3, 13**
See also Spillane, Frank Morrison

Spinoza, Benedictus de 1632-1677 .... **LC 9**

Spinrad, Norman (Richard) 1940-... **CLC 46**
See also CA 37-40R; CAAS 19; CANR 20;
DLB 8; INT CANR-20

Spitteler, Carl (Friedrich Georg)
1845-1924 .... **TCLC 12**
See also CA 109; DLB 129

Spivack, Kathleen (Romola Drucker)
1938- .... **CLC 6**
See also CA 49-52

Spoto, Donald 1941- .... **CLC 39**
See also CA 65-68; CANR 11

Springsteen, Bruce (F.) 1949- ...... **CLC 17**
See also CA 111

Spurling, Hilary 1940- .... **CLC 34**
See also CA 104; CANR 25

Spyker, John Howland
See Elman, Richard

Squires, (James) Radcliffe
1917-1993 .... **CLC 51**
See also CA 1-4R; 140; CANR 6, 21

Srivastava, Dhanpat Rai 1880(?)-1936
See Premchand
See also CA 118

Stacy, Donald
See Pohl, Frederik

Stael, Germaine de
See Stael-Holstein, Anne Louise Germaine
Necker Baronn
See also DLB 119

Stael-Holstein, Anne Louise Germaine Necker Baronn 1766-1817 .... **NCLC 3**
See also Stael, Germaine de

Stafford, Jean 1915-1979... **CLC 4, 7, 19, 68**
See also CA 1-4R; 85-88; CANR 3; DLB 2;
MTCW; SATA-Obit 22

Stafford, William (Edgar)
1914-1993 .... **CLC 4, 7, 29**
See also CA 5-8R; 142; CAAS 3; CANR 5,
22; DAM POET; DLB 5; INT CANR-22

Staines, Trevor
See Brunner, John (Kilian Houston)

Stairs, Gordon
See Austin, Mary (Hunter)

Stannard, Martin 1947- .... **CLC 44**
See also CA 142; DLB 155

Stanton, Maura 1946- .... **CLC 9**
See also CA 89-92; CANR 15; DLB 120

Stanton, Schuyler
See Baum, L(yman) Frank

Stapledon, (William) Olaf
1886-1950 .... **TCLC 22**
See also CA 111; DLB 15

Starbuck, George (Edwin) 1931-.... **CLC 53**
See also CA 21-24R; CANR 23;
DAM POET

Stark, Richard
See Westlake, Donald E(dwin)

Staunton, Schuyler
See Baum, L(yman) Frank

Stead, Christina (Ellen)
1902-1983 .... **CLC 2, 5, 8, 32, 80**
See also CA 13-16R; 109; CANR 33, 40;
MTCW

Stead, William Thomas
1849-1912 .... **TCLC 48**

Steele, Richard 1672-1729 .... **LC 18**
See also CDBLB 1660-1789; DLB 84, 101

Steele, Timothy (Reid) 1948- .... **CLC 45**
See also CA 93-96; CANR 16, 50; DLB 120

Steffens, (Joseph) Lincoln
1866-1936 .... **TCLC 20**
See also CA 117

Stegner, Wallace (Earle)
1909-1993 .... **CLC 9, 49, 81**
See also AITN 1; BEST 90:3; CA 1-4R;
141; CAAS 9; CANR 1, 21, 46;
DAM NOV; DLB 9; DLBY 93; MTCW

Stein, Gertrude
1874-1946 ...... **TCLC 1, 6, 28, 48; DA; DAB; DAC; WLC**
See also CA 104; 132; CDALB 1917-1929;
DAM MST, NOV, POET; DLB 4, 54, 86;
MTCW

Steinbeck, John (Ernst)
1902-1968 ...... **CLC 1, 5, 9, 13, 21, 34, 45, 75; DA; DAB; DAC; SSC 11; WLC**
See also AAYA 12; CA 1-4R; 25-28R;
CANR 1, 35; CDALB 1929-1941;
DAM DRAM, MST, NOV; DLB 7, 9;
DLBD 2; MTCW; SATA 9

Steinem, Gloria 1934-............. **CLC 63**
See also CA 53-56; CANR 28, 51; MTCW

Steiner, George 1929-............. **CLC 24**
See also CA 73-76; CANR 31; DAM NOV;
DLB 67; MTCW; SATA 62

Steiner, K. Leslie
See Delany, Samuel R(ay, Jr.)

Steiner, Rudolf 1861-1925 .... **TCLC 13**
See also CA 107

Stendhal
1783-1842 .... **NCLC 23, 46; DA; DAB; DAC; WLC**
See also DAM MST, NOV; DLB 119

Stephen, Leslie 1832-1904 .... **TCLC 23**
See also CA 123; DLB 57, 144

Stephen, Sir Leslie
See Stephen, Leslie

Stephen, Virginia
See Woolf, (Adeline) Virginia

Stephens, James 1882(?)-1950...... **TCLC 4**
See also CA 104; DLB 19, 153, 162

Stephens, Reed
See Donaldson, Stephen R.

Steptoe, Lydia
See Barnes, Djuna

Sterchi, Beat 1949-............. **CLC 65**

Sterling, Brett
See Bradbury, Ray (Douglas); Hamilton,
Edmond

Sterling, Bruce 1954-............. **CLC 72**
See also CA 119; CANR 44

Sterling, George 1869-1926 .... **TCLC 20**
See also CA 117; DLB 54

Stern, Gerald 1925- .... **CLC 40**
See also CA 81-84; CANR 28; DLB 105

Stern, Richard (Gustave) 1928-.... **CLC 4, 39**
See also CA 1-4R; CANR 1, 25; DLBY 87;
INT CANR-25

Sternberg, Josef von 1894-1969..... **CLC 20**
See also CA 81-84

Sterne, Laurence
1713-1768 ...... **LC 2; DA; DAB; DAC; WLC**
See also CDBLB 1660-1789; DAM MST,
NOV; DLB 39

Sternheim, (William Adolf) Carl
1878-1942 .... **TCLC 8**
See also CA 105; DLB 56, 118

Stevens, Mark 1951- .... **CLC 34**
See also CA 122

Stevens, Wallace
1879-1955 .... **TCLC 3, 12, 45; DA;
DAB; DAC; PC 6; WLC**
See also CA 104; 124; CDALB 1929-1941;
DAM MST, POET; DLB 54; MTCW

Stevenson, Anne (Katharine)
1933- .... **CLC 7, 33**
See also CA 17-20R; CAAS 9; CANR 9, 33;
DLB 40; MTCW

Stevenson, Robert Louis (Balfour)
1850-1894 ..... **NCLC 5, 14; DA; DAB;
DAC; SSC 11; WLC**
See also CDBLB 1890-1914; CLR 10, 11;
DAM MST, NOV; DLB 18, 57, 141, 156;
DLBD 13; JRDA; MAICYA; YABC 2

Stewart, J(ohn) I(nnes) M(ackintosh)
1906-1994 .... **CLC 7, 14, 32**
See also CA 85-88; 147; CAAS 3;
CANR 47; MTCW

Stewart, Mary (Florence Elinor)
1916- .... **CLC 7, 35; DAB**
See also CA 1-4R; CANR 1; SATA 12

Stewart, Mary Rainbow
See Stewart, Mary (Florence Elinor)

Stifle, June
See Campbell, Maria

Stifter, Adalbert 1805-1868 ...... **NCLC 41**
See also DLB 133

Still, James 1906- .... **CLC 49**
See also CA 65-68; CAAS 17; CANR 10,
26; DLB 9; SATA 29

Sting
See Sumner, Gordon Matthew

Stirling, Arthur
See Sinclair, Upton (Beall)

Stitt, Milan 1941- .... **CLC 29**
See also CA 69-72

Stockton, Francis Richard 1834-1902
See Stockton, Frank R.
See also CA 108; 137; MAICYA; SATA 44

Stockton, Frank R. .... **TCLC 47**
See also Stockton, Francis Richard
See also DLB 42, 74; DLBD 13;
SATA-Brief 32

Stoddard, Charles
See Kuttner, Henry

Stoker, Abraham 1847-1912
See Stoker, Bram
See also CA 105; DA; DAC; DAM MST,
NOV; SATA 29

Stoker, Bram
1847-1912 .... **TCLC 8; DAB; WLC**
See also Stoker, Abraham
See also CA 150; CDBLB 1890-1914;
DLB 36, 70

Stolz, Mary (Slattery) 1920- .... **CLC 12**
See also AAYA 8; AITN 1; CA 5-8R;
CANR 13, 41; JRDA; MAICYA;
SAAS 3; SATA 10, 71

Stone, Irving 1903-1989 .... **CLC 7**
See also AITN 1; CA 1-4R; 129; CAAS 3;
CANR 1, 23; DAM POP;
INT CANR-23; MTCW; SATA 3;
SATA-Obit 64

Stone, Oliver 1946- .... **CLC 73**
See also AAYA 15; CA 110

Stone, Robert (Anthony)
1937- .... **CLC 5, 23, 42**
See also CA 85-88; CANR 23; DLB 152;
INT CANR-23; MTCW

Stone, Zachary
See Follett, Ken(neth Martin)

Stoppard, Tom
1937- ...... **CLC 1, 3, 4, 5, 8, 15, 29, 34,
63, 91; DA; DAB; DAC; DC 6; WLC**
See also CA 81-84; CANR 39;
CDBLB 1960 to Present; DAM DRAM,
MST; DLB 13; DLBY 85; MTCW

Storey, David (Malcolm)
1933- .... **CLC 2, 4, 5, 8**
See also CA 81-84; CANR 36;
DAM DRAM; DLB 13, 14; MTCW

Storm, Hyemeyohsts 1935- .... **CLC 3**
See also CA 81-84; CANR 45;
DAM MULT; NNAL

Storm, (Hans) Theodor (Woldsen)
1817-1888 .... **NCLC 1**

Storni, Alfonsina
1892-1938 .... **TCLC 5; HLC**
See also CA 104; 131; DAM MULT; HW

Stout, Rex (Todhunter) 1886-1975 ... **CLC 3**
See also AITN 2; CA 61-64

Stow, (Julian) Randolph 1935- .. **CLC 23, 48**
See also CA 13-16R; CANR 33; MTCW

Stowe, Harriet (Elizabeth) Beecher
1811-1896 ..... **NCLC 3, 50; DA; DAB;
DAC; WLC**
See also CDALB 1865-1917; DAM MST,
NOV; DLB 1, 12, 42, 74; JRDA;
MAICYA; YABC 1

Strachey, (Giles) Lytton
1880-1932 .... **TCLC 12**
See also CA 110; DLB 149; DLBD 10

Strand, Mark 1934- ...... **CLC 6, 18, 41, 71**
See also CA 21-24R; CANR 40;
DAM POET; DLB 5; SATA 41

Straub, Peter (Francis) 1943- ...... **CLC 28**
See also BEST 89:1; CA 85-88; CANR 28;
DAM POP; DLBY 84; MTCW

Strauss, Botho 1944- .... **CLC 22**
See also DLB 124

Streatfeild, (Mary) Noel
1895(?)-1986 .... **CLC 21**
See also CA 81-84; 120; CANR 31;
CLR 17; DLB 160; MAICYA; SATA 20;
SATA-Obit 48

Stribling, T(homas) S(igismund)
1881-1965 .... **CLC 23**
See also CA 107; DLB 9

Strindberg, (Johan) August
1849-1912 ...... **TCLC 1, 8, 21, 47; DA;
DAB; DAC; WLC**
See also CA 104; 135; DAM DRAM, MST

Stringer, Arthur 1874-1950 .... **TCLC 37**
See also DLB 92

Stringer, David
See Roberts, Keith (John Kingston)

Strugatskii, Arkadii (Natanovich)
1925-1991 .... **CLC 27**
See also CA 106; 135

Strugatskii, Boris (Natanovich)
1933- .... **CLC 27**
See also CA 106

Strummer, Joe 1953(?)- .... **CLC 30**

Stuart, Don A.
See Campbell, John W(ood, Jr.)

Stuart, Ian
See MacLean, Alistair (Stuart)

Stuart, Jesse (Hilton)
1906-1984 .... **CLC 1, 8, 11, 14, 34**
See also CA 5-8R; 112; CANR 31; DLB 9,
48, 102; DLBY 84; SATA 2;
SATA-Obit 36

Sturgeon, Theodore (Hamilton)
1918-1985 .... **CLC 22, 39**
See also Queen, Ellery
See also CA 81-84; 116; CANR 32; DLB 8;
DLBY 85; MTCW

Sturges, Preston 1898-1959 .... **TCLC 48**
See also CA 114; 149; DLB 26

Styron, William
1925- .... **CLC 1, 3, 5, 11, 15, 60**
See also BEST 90:4; CA 5-8R; CANR 6, 33;
CDALB 1968-1988; DAM NOV, POP;
DLB 2, 143; DLBY 80; INT CANR-6;
MTCW

Suarez Lynch, B.
See Bioy Casares, Adolfo; Borges, Jorge
Luis

Su Chien 1884-1918
See Su Man-shu
See also CA 123

Suckow, Ruth 1892-1960 .... **SSC 18**
See also CA 113; DLB 9, 102

Sudermann, Hermann 1857-1928 .. **TCLC 15**
See also CA 107; DLB 118

Sue, Eugene 1804-1857 .... **NCLC 1**
See also DLB 119

Sueskind, Patrick 1949- .... **CLC 44**
See also Suskind, Patrick

Sukenick, Ronald 1932- ..... **CLC 3, 4, 6, 48**
See also CA 25-28R; CAAS 8; CANR 32;
DLBY 81

Suknaski, Andrew 1942- .... **CLC 19**
See also CA 101; DLB 53

Sullivan, Vernon
See Vian, Boris

Sully Prudhomme 1839-1907 ...... **TCLC 31**

Su Man-shu .... **TCLC 24**
See also Su Chien

Summerforest, Ivy B.
See Kirkup, James

Summers, Andrew James 1942- ..... **CLC 26**

Summers, Andy
See Summers, Andrew James

Summers, Hollis (Spurgeon, Jr.)
1916- .... **CLC 10**
See also CA 5-8R; CANR 3; DLB 6

Summers, (Alphonsus Joseph-Mary Augustus)
Montague 1880-1948 .... **TCLC 16**
See also CA 118

Sumner, Gordon Matthew 1951- .... **CLC 26**

Surtees, Robert Smith
　　1803-1864 .... **NCLC 14**
　　See also DLB 21

Susann, Jacqueline 1921-1974....... **CLC 3**
　　See also AITN 1; CA 65-68; 53-56; MTCW

Su Shih 1036-1101 .... **CMLC 15**

Suskind, Patrick
　　See Sueskind, Patrick
　　See also CA 145

Sutcliff, Rosemary
　　1920-1992 .... **CLC 26; DAB; DAC**
　　See also AAYA 10; CA 5-8R; 139;
　　　CANR 37; CLR 1, 37; DAM MST, POP;
　　　JRDA; MAICYA; SATA 6, 44, 78;
　　　SATA-Obit 73

Sutro, Alfred 1863-1933........... **TCLC 6**
　　See also CA 105; DLB 10

Sutton, Henry
　　See Slavitt, David R(ytman)

Svevo, Italo .... **TCLC 2, 35**
　　See also Schmitz, Aron Hector

Swados, Elizabeth (A.) 1951-....... **CLC 12**
　　See also CA 97-100; CANR 49; INT 97-100

Swados, Harvey 1920-1972 .... **CLC 5**
　　See also CA 5-8R; 37-40R; CANR 6;
　　　DLB 2

Swan, Gladys 1934- .... **CLC 69**
　　See also CA 101; CANR 17, 39

Swarthout, Glendon (Fred)
　　1918-1992 .... **CLC 35**
　　See also CA 1-4R; 139; CANR 1, 47;
　　　SATA 26

Sweet, Sarah C.
　　See Jewett, (Theodora) Sarah Orne

Swenson, May
　　1919-1989 .... **CLC 4, 14, 61; DA; DAB;**
　　　　　　　　　　　　　DAC; PC 14
　　See also CA 5-8R; 130; CANR 36;
　　　DAM MST, POET; DLB 5; MTCW;
　　　SATA 15

Swift, Augustus
　　See Lovecraft, H(oward) P(hillips)

Swift, Graham (Colin) 1949- .... **CLC 41, 88**
　　See also CA 117; 122; CANR 46

Swift, Jonathan
　　1667-1745 ...... **LC 1; DA; DAB; DAC;**
　　　　　　　　　　　　　　　PC 9; WLC
　　See also CDBLB 1660-1789; DAM MST,
　　　NOV, POET; DLB 39, 95, 101; SATA 19

Swinburne, Algernon Charles
　　1837-1909 ...... **TCLC 8, 36; DA; DAB;**
　　　　　　　　　　　　　　　DAC; WLC
　　See also CA 105; 140; CDBLB 1832-1890;
　　　DAM MST, POET; DLB 35, 57

Swinfen, Ann .... **CLC 34**

Swinnerton, Frank Arthur
　　1884-1982 .... **CLC 31**
　　See also CA 108; DLB 34

Swithen, John
　　See King, Stephen (Edwin)

Sylvia
　　See Ashton-Warner, Sylvia (Constance)

Symmes, Robert Edward
　　See Duncan, Robert (Edward)

Symonds, John Addington
　　1840-1893 .... **NCLC 34**
　　See also DLB 57, 144

Symons, Arthur 1865-1945 .... **TCLC 11**
　　See also CA 107; DLB 19, 57, 149

Symons, Julian (Gustave)
　　1912-1994 .... **CLC 2, 14, 32**
　　See also CA 49-52; 147; CAAS 3; CANR 3,
　　　33; DLB 87, 155; DLBY 92; MTCW

Synge, (Edmund) J(ohn) M(illington)
　　1871-1909 .... **TCLC 6, 37; DC 2**
　　See also CA 104; 141; CDBLB 1890-1914;
　　　DAM DRAM; DLB 10, 19

Syruc, J.
　　See Milosz, Czeslaw

Szirtes, George 1948-............. **CLC 46**
　　See also CA 109; CANR 27

Tabori, George 1914-............. **CLC 19**
　　See also CA 49-52; CANR 4

Tagore, Rabindranath
　　1861-1941 .... **TCLC 3, 53; PC 8**
　　See also CA 104; 120; DAM DRAM,
　　　POET; MTCW

Taine, Hippolyte Adolphe
　　1828-1893 .... **NCLC 15**

Talese, Gay 1932-................ **CLC 37**
　　See also AITN 1; CA 1-4R; CANR 9;
　　　INT CANR-9; MTCW

Tallent, Elizabeth (Ann) 1954- ..... **CLC 45**
　　See also CA 117; DLB 130

Tally, Ted 1952-................. **CLC 42**
　　See also CA 120; 124; INT 124

Tamayo y Baus, Manuel
　　1829-1898 .... **NCLC 1**

Tammsaare, A(nton) H(ansen)
　　1878-1940 .... **TCLC 27**

Tan, Amy 1952- .... **CLC 59**
　　See also AAYA 9; BEST 89:3; CA 136;
　　　DAM MULT, NOV, POP; SATA 75

Tandem, Felix
　　See Spitteler, Carl (Friedrich Georg)

Tanizaki, Jun'ichiro
　　1886-1965 ...... **CLC 8, 14, 28; SSC 21**
　　See also CA 93-96; 25-28R

Tanner, William
　　See Amis, Kingsley (William)

Tao Lao
　　See Storni, Alfonsina

Tarassoff, Lev
　　See Troyat, Henri

Tarbell, Ida M(inerva)
　　1857-1944 .... **TCLC 40**
　　See also CA 122; DLB 47

Tarkington, (Newton) Booth
　　1869-1946 .... **TCLC 9**
　　See also CA 110; 143; DLB 9, 102;
　　　SATA 17

Tarkovsky, Andrei (Arsenyevich)
　　1932-1986 .... **CLC 75**
　　See also CA 127

Tartt, Donna 1964(?)-............ **CLC 76**
　　See also CA 142

Tasso, Torquato 1544-1595 .... **LC 5**

Tate, (John Orley) Allen
　　1899-1979 .... **CLC 2, 4, 6, 9, 11, 14, 24**
　　See also CA 5-8R; 85-88; CANR 32;
　　　DLB 4, 45, 63; MTCW

Tate, Ellalice
　　See Hibbert, Eleanor Alice Burford

Tate, James (Vincent) 1943- ... **CLC 2, 6, 25**
　　See also CA 21-24R; CANR 29; DLB 5

Tavel, Ronald 1940-.............. **CLC 6**
　　See also CA 21-24R; CANR 33

Taylor, C(ecil) P(hilip) 1929-1981... **CLC 27**
　　See also CA 25-28R; 105; CANR 47

Taylor, Edward
　　1642(?)-1729 ... **LC 11; DA; DAB; DAC**
　　See also DAM MST, POET; DLB 24

Taylor, Eleanor Ross 1920-......... **CLC 5**
　　See also CA 81-84

Taylor, Elizabeth 1912-1975 ... **CLC 2, 4, 29**
　　See also CA 13-16R; CANR 9; DLB 139;
　　　MTCW; SATA 13

Taylor, Henry (Splawn) 1942-...... **CLC 44**
　　See also CA 33-36R; CAAS 7; CANR 31;
　　　DLB 5

Taylor, Kamala (Purnaiya) 1924-
　　See Markandaya, Kamala
　　See also CA 77-80

Taylor, Mildred D.................. **CLC 21**
　　See also AAYA 10; BW 1; CA 85-88;
　　　CANR 25; CLR 9; DLB 52; JRDA;
　　　MAICYA; SAAS 5; SATA 15, 70

Taylor, Peter (Hillsman)
　　1917-1994 ..... **CLC 1, 4, 18, 37, 44, 50,**
　　　　　　　　　　　　　　71; SSC 10
　　See also CA 13-16R; 147; CANR 9, 50;
　　　DLBY 81, 94; INT CANR-9; MTCW

Taylor, Robert Lewis 1912-........ **CLC 14**
　　See also CA 1-4R; CANR 3; SATA 10

Tchekhov, Anton
　　See Chekhov, Anton (Pavlovich)

Teasdale, Sara 1884-1933.......... **TCLC 4**
　　See also CA 104; DLB 45; SATA 32

Tegner, Esaias 1782-1846......... **NCLC 2**

Teilhard de Chardin, (Marie Joseph) Pierre
　　1881-1955 .... **TCLC 9**
　　See also CA 105

Temple, Ann
　　See Mortimer, Penelope (Ruth)

Tennant, Emma (Christina)
　　1937-.................... **CLC 13, 52**
　　See also CA 65-68; CAAS 9; CANR 10, 38;
　　　DLB 14

Tenneshaw, S. M.
　　See Silverberg, Robert

Tennyson, Alfred
　　1809-1892 .... **NCLC 30; DA; DAB;**
　　　　　　　　　　　　DAC; PC 6; WLC
　　See also CDBLB 1832-1890; DAM MST,
　　　POET; DLB 32

Teran, Lisa St. Aubin de .... **CLC 36**
　　See also St. Aubin de Teran, Lisa

Terence 195(?)B.C.-159B.C....... **CMLC 14**

Teresa de Jesus, St. 1515-1582 ...... **LC 18**

Vesaas, Tarjei 1897-1970 . . . . **CLC 48**
See also CA 29-32R

Vialis, Gaston
See Simenon, Georges (Jacques Christian)

Vian, Boris 1920-1959 . . . . **TCLC 9**
See also CA 106; DLB 72

Viaud, (Louis Marie) Julien 1850-1923
See Loti, Pierre
See also CA 107

Vicar, Henry
See Felsen, Henry Gregor

Vicker, Angus
See Felsen, Henry Gregor

Vidal, Gore
1925- . . . . . **CLC 2, 4, 6, 8, 10, 22, 33, 72**
See also AITN 1; BEST 90:2; CA 5-8R;
CANR 13, 45; DAM NOV, POP; DLB 6,
152; INT CANR-13; MTCW

Viereck, Peter (Robert Edwin)
1916- . . . . **CLC 4**
See also CA 1-4R; CANR 1, 47; DLB 5

Vigny, Alfred (Victor) de
1797-1863 . . . . **NCLC 7**
See also DAM POET; DLB 119

Vilakazi, Benedict Wallet
1906-1947 . . . . **TCLC 37**

Villiers de l'Isle Adam, Jean Marie Mathias
Philippe Auguste Comte
1838-1889 . . . . **NCLC 3; SSC 14**
See also DLB 123

Villon, Francois 1431-1463(?) . . . . **PC 13**

Vinci, Leonardo da 1452-1519 . . . . . . **LC 12**

Vine, Barbara . . . . **CLC 50**
See also Rendell, Ruth (Barbara)
See also BEST 90:4

Vinge, Joan D(ennison)
1948- . . . . **CLC 30; SSC 22**
See also CA 93-96; SATA 36

Violis, G.
See Simenon, Georges (Jacques Christian)

Visconti, Luchino 1906-1976 . . . . **CLC 16**
See also CA 81-84; 65-68; CANR 39

Vittorini, Elio 1908-1966 . . . . . . **CLC 6, 9, 14**
See also CA 133; 25-28R

Vizinczey, Stephen 1933- . . . . **CLC 40**
See also CA 128; INT 128

Vliet, R(ussell) G(ordon)
1929-1984 . . . . **CLC 22**
See also CA 37-40R; 112; CANR 18

Vogau, Boris Andreyevich 1894-1937(?)
See Pilnyak, Boris
See also CA 123

Vogel, Paula A(nne) 1951- . . . . **CLC 76**
See also CA 108

Voight, Ellen Bryant 1943- . . . . **CLC 54**
See also CA 69-72; CANR 11, 29; DLB 120

Voigt, Cynthia 1942- . . . . **CLC 30**
See also AAYA 3; CA 106; CANR 18, 37,
40; CLR 13; INT CANR-18; JRDA;
MAICYA; SATA 48, 79; SATA-Brief 33

Voinovich, Vladimir (Nikolaevich)
1932- . . . . **CLC 10, 49**
See also CA 81-84; CAAS 12; CANR 33;
MTCW

Vollmann, William T. 1959- . . . . **CLC 89**
See also CA 134; DAM NOV, POP

Voloshinov, V. N.
See Bakhtin, Mikhail Mikhailovich

Voltaire
1694-1778 . . . . . **LC 14; DA; DAB; DAC;
SSC 12; WLC**
See also DAM DRAM, MST

von Daeniken, Erich 1935- . . . . **CLC 30**
See also AITN 1; CA 37-40R; CANR 17,
44

von Daniken, Erich
See von Daeniken, Erich

von Heidenstam, (Carl Gustaf) Verner
See Heidenstam, (Carl Gustaf) Verner von

von Heyse, Paul (Johann Ludwig)
See Heyse, Paul (Johann Ludwig von)

von Hofmannsthal, Hugo
See Hofmannsthal, Hugo von

von Horvath, Odon
See Horvath, Oedoen von

von Horvath, Oedoen
See Horvath, Oedoen von

von Liliencron, (Friedrich Adolf Axel) Detlev
See Liliencron, (Friedrich Adolf Axel)
Detlev von

Vonnegut, Kurt, Jr.
1922- . . . . . . **CLC 1, 2, 3, 4, 5, 8, 12, 22,
40, 60; DA; DAB; DAC; SSC 8; WLC**
See also AAYA 6; AITN 1; BEST 90:4;
CA 1-4R; CANR 1, 25, 49;
CDALB 1968-1988; DAM MST, NOV,
POP; DLB 2, 8, 152; DLBD 3; DLBY 80;
MTCW

Von Rachen, Kurt
See Hubbard, L(afayette) Ron(ald)

von Rezzori (d'Arezzo), Gregor
See Rezzori (d'Arezzo), Gregor von

von Sternberg, Josef
See Sternberg, Josef von

Vorster, Gordon 1924- . . . . **CLC 34**
See also CA 133

Vosce, Trudie
See Ozick, Cynthia

Voznesensky, Andrei (Andreievich)
1933- . . . . **CLC 1, 15, 57**
See also CA 89-92; CANR 37;
DAM POET; MTCW

Waddington, Miriam 1917- . . . . **CLC 28**
See also CA 21-24R; CANR 12, 30;
DLB 68

Wagman, Fredrica 1937- . . . . **CLC 7**
See also CA 97-100; INT 97-100

Wagner, Richard 1813-1883 . . . . **NCLC 9**
See also DLB 129

Wagner-Martin, Linda 1936- . . . . **CLC 50**

Wagoner, David (Russell)
1926- . . . . **CLC 3, 5, 15**
See also CA 1-4R; CAAS 3; CANR 2;
DLB 5; SATA 14

Wah, Fred(erick James) 1939- . . . . . . **CLC 44**
See also CA 107; 141; DLB 60

Wahloo, Per 1926-1975 . . . . **CLC 7**
See also CA 61-64

Wahloo, Peter
See Wahloo, Per

Wain, John (Barrington)
1925-1994 . . . . **CLC 2, 11, 15, 46**
See also CA 5-8R; 145; CAAS 4; CANR 23;
CDBLB 1960 to Present; DLB 15, 27,
139, 155; MTCW

Wajda, Andrzej 1926- . . . . **CLC 16**
See also CA 102

Wakefield, Dan 1932- . . . . **CLC 7**
See also CA 21-24R; CAAS 7

Wakoski, Diane
1937- . . . . **CLC 2, 4, 7, 9, 11, 40; PC 15**
See also CA 13-16R; CAAS 1; CANR 9;
DAM POET; DLB 5; INT CANR-9

Wakoski-Sherbell, Diane
See Wakoski, Diane

Walcott, Derek (Alton)
1930- . . . . **CLC 2, 4, 9, 14, 25, 42, 67, 76;
BLC; DAB; DAC**
See also BW 2; CA 89-92; CANR 26, 47;
DAM MST, MULT, POET; DLB 117;
DLBY 81; MTCW

Waldman, Anne 1945- . . . . **CLC 7**
See also CA 37-40R; CAAS 17; CANR 34;
DLB 16

Waldo, E. Hunter
See Sturgeon, Theodore (Hamilton)

Waldo, Edward Hamilton
See Sturgeon, Theodore (Hamilton)

Walker, Alice (Malsenior)
1944- . . . . **CLC 5, 6, 9, 19, 27, 46, 58;
BLC; DA; DAB; DAC; SSC 5**
See also AAYA 3; BEST 89:4; BW 2;
CA 37-40R; CANR 9, 27, 49;
CDALB 1968-1988; DAM MST, MULT,
NOV, POET, POP; DLB 6, 33, 143;
INT CANR-27; MTCW; SATA 31

Walker, David Harry 1911-1992 . . . . **CLC 14**
See also CA 1-4R; 137; CANR 1; SATA 8;
SATA-Obit 71

Walker, Edward Joseph 1934-
See Walker, Ted
See also CA 21-24R; CANR 12, 28

Walker, George F.
1947- . . . . **CLC 44, 61; DAB; DAC**
See also CA 103; CANR 21, 43;
DAM MST; DLB 60

Walker, Joseph A. 1935- . . . . **CLC 19**
See also BW 1; CA 89-92; CANR 26;
DAM DRAM, MST; DLB 38

Walker, Margaret (Abigail)
1915- . . . . **CLC 1, 6; BLC**
See also BW 2; CA 73-76; CANR 26;
DAM MULT; DLB 76, 152; MTCW

Walker, Ted . . . . **CLC 13**
See also Walker, Edward Joseph
See also DLB 40

Wallace, David Foster 1962- . . . . **CLC 50**
See also CA 132

Wallace, Dexter
See Masters, Edgar Lee

Wallace, (Richard Horatio) Edgar
1875-1932 . . . . **TCLC 57**
See also CA 115; DLB 70

Wallace, Irving   1916-1990...... CLC 7, 13
 See also AITN 1; CA 1-4R; 132; CAAS 1;
  CANR 1, 27; DAM NOV, POP;
  INT CANR-27; MTCW

Wallant, Edward Lewis
 1926-1962 .... CLC 5, 10
 See also CA 1-4R; CANR 22; DLB 2, 28,
  143; MTCW

Walley, Byron
 See Card, Orson Scott

Walpole, Horace   1717-1797......... LC 2
 See also DLB 39, 104

Walpole, Hugh (Seymour)
 1884-1941 .... TCLC 5
 See also CA 104; DLB 34

Walser, Martin   1927-............. CLC 27
 See also CA 57-60; CANR 8, 46; DLB 75,
  124

Walser, Robert
 1878-1956 .... TCLC 18; SSC 20
 See also CA 118; DLB 66

Walsh, Jill Paton.................. CLC 35
 See also Paton Walsh, Gillian
 See also AAYA 11; CLR 2; DLB 161;
  SAAS 3

Walter, William Christian
 See Andersen, Hans Christian

Wambaugh, Joseph (Aloysius, Jr.)
 1937- .... CLC 3, 18
 See also AITN 1; BEST 89:3; CA 33-36R;
  CANR 42; DAM NOV, POP; DLB 6;
  DLBY 83; MTCW

Ward, Arthur Henry Sarsfield   1883-1959
 See Rohmer, Sax
 See also CA 108

Ward, Douglas Turner   1930-....... CLC 19
 See also BW 1; CA 81-84; CANR 27;
  DLB 7, 38

Ward, Mary Augusta
 See Ward, Mrs. Humphry

Ward, Mrs. Humphry
 1851-1920 .... TCLC 55
 See also DLB 18

Ward, Peter
 See Faust, Frederick (Schiller)

Warhol, Andy   1928(?)-1987........ CLC 20
 See also AAYA 12; BEST 89:4; CA 89-92;
  121; CANR 34

Warner, Francis (Robert le Plastrier)
 1937- .... CLC 14
 See also CA 53-56; CANR 11

Warner, Marina   1946-............ CLC 59
 See also CA 65-68; CANR 21

Warner, Rex (Ernest)   1905-1986.... CLC 45
 See also CA 89-92; 119; DLB 15

Warner, Susan (Bogert)
 1819-1885 .... NCLC 31
 See also DLB 3, 42

Warner, Sylvia (Constance) Ashton
 See Ashton-Warner, Sylvia (Constance)

Warner, Sylvia Townsend
 1893-1978 .... CLC 7, 19; SSC 23
 See also CA 61-64; 77-80; CANR 16;
  DLB 34, 139; MTCW

Warren, Mercy Otis   1728-1814... NCLC 13
 See also DLB 31

Warren, Robert Penn
 1905-1989 .... CLC 1, 4, 6, 8, 10, 13, 18,
  39, 53, 59; DA; DAB; DAC; SSC 4; WLC
 See also AITN 1; CA 13-16R; 129;
  CANR 10, 47; CDALB 1968-1988;
  DAM MST, NOV, POET; DLB 2, 48,
  152; DLBY 80, 89; INT CANR-10;
  MTCW; SATA 46; SATA-Obit 63

Warshofsky, Isaac
 See Singer, Isaac Bashevis

Warton, Thomas   1728-1790........ LC 15
 See also DAM POET; DLB 104, 109

Waruk, Kona
 See Harris, (Theodore) Wilson

Warung, Price   1855-1911........ TCLC 45

Warwick, Jarvis
 See Garner, Hugh

Washington, Alex
 See Harris, Mark

Washington, Booker T(aliaferro)
 1856-1915 .... TCLC 10; BLC
 See also BW 1; CA 114; 125; DAM MULT;
  SATA 28

Washington, George   1732-1799...... LC 25
 See also DLB 31

Wassermann, (Karl) Jakob
 1873-1934 .... TCLC 6
 See also CA 104; DLB 66

Wasserstein, Wendy
 1950- .... CLC 32, 59, 90; DC 4
 See also CA 121; 129; CABS 3;
  DAM DRAM; INT 129

Waterhouse, Keith (Spencer)
 1929- .... CLC 47
 See also CA 5-8R; CANR 38; DLB 13, 15;
  MTCW

Waters, Frank (Joseph)
 1902-1995 .... CLC 88
 See also CA 5-8R; 149; CAAS 13; CANR 3,
  18; DLBY 86

Waters, Roger   1944-.............. CLC 35

Watkins, Frances Ellen
 See Harper, Frances Ellen Watkins

Watkins, Gerrold
 See Malzberg, Barry N(athaniel)

Watkins, Paul   1964-.............. CLC 55
 See also CA 132

Watkins, Vernon Phillips
 1906-1967 .... CLC 43
 See also CA 9-10; 25-28R; CAP 1; DLB 20

Watson, Irving S.
 See Mencken, H(enry) L(ouis)

Watson, John H.
 See Farmer, Philip Jose

Watson, Richard F.
 See Silverberg, Robert

Waugh, Auberon (Alexander)   1939- .. CLC 7
 See also CA 45-48; CANR 6, 22; DLB 14

Waugh, Evelyn (Arthur St. John)
 1903-1966 ...... CLC 1, 3, 8, 13, 19, 27,
  44; DA; DAB; DAC; WLC
 See also CA 85-88; 25-28R; CANR 22;
  CDBLB 1914-1945; DAM MST, NOV,
  POP; DLB 15, 162; MTCW

Waugh, Harriet   1944- .... CLC 6
 See also CA 85-88; CANR 22

Ways, C. R.
 See Blount, Roy (Alton), Jr.

Waystaff, Simon
 See Swift, Jonathan

Webb, (Martha) Beatrice (Potter)
 1858-1943 .... TCLC 22
 See also Potter, Beatrice
 See also CA 117

Webb, Charles (Richard)   1939-...... CLC 7
 See also CA 25-28R

Webb, James H(enry), Jr.   1946-.... CLC 22
 See also CA 81-84

Webb, Mary (Gladys Meredith)
 1881-1927 .... TCLC 24
 See also CA 123; DLB 34

Webb, Mrs. Sidney
 See Webb, (Martha) Beatrice (Potter)

Webb, Phyllis   1927-.............. CLC 18
 See also CA 104; CANR 23; DLB 53

Webb, Sidney (James)
 1859-1947 .... TCLC 22
 See also CA 117

Webber, Andrew Lloyd............. CLC 21
 See also Lloyd Webber, Andrew

Weber, Lenora Mattingly
 1895-1971 .... CLC 12
 See also CA 19-20; 29-32R; CAP 1;
  SATA 2; SATA-Obit 26

Webster, John   1579(?)-1634(?) .... DC 2
 See also CDBLB Before 1660; DA; DAB;
  DAC; DAM DRAM, MST; DLB 58;
  WLC

Webster, Noah   1758-1843 .... NCLC 30

Wedekind, (Benjamin) Frank(lin)
 1864-1918 .... TCLC 7
 See also CA 104; DAM DRAM; DLB 118

Weidman, Jerome   1913-............ CLC 7
 See also AITN 2; CA 1-4R; CANR 1;
  DLB 28

Weil, Simone (Adolphine)
 1909-1943 .... TCLC 23
 See also CA 117

Weinstein, Nathan
 See West, Nathanael

Weinstein, Nathan von Wallenstein
 See West, Nathanael

Weir, Peter (Lindsay)   1944- .... CLC 20
 See also CA 113; 123

Weiss, Peter (Ulrich)
 1916-1982 .... CLC 3, 15, 51
 See also CA 45-48; 106; CANR 3;
  DAM DRAM; DLB 69, 124

Weiss, Theodore (Russell)
 1916- .... CLC 3, 8, 14
 See also CA 9-12R; CAAS 2; CANR 46;
  DLB 5

Welch, (Maurice) Denton
1915-1948 . . . . **TCLC 22**
See also CA 121; 148

Welch, James 1940- . . . . **CLC 6, 14, 52**
See also CA 85-88; CANR 42;
DAM MULT, POP; NNAL

Weldon, Fay
1933- . . . . **CLC 6, 9, 11, 19, 36, 59**
See also CA 21-24R; CANR 16, 46;
CDBLB 1960 to Present; DAM POP;
DLB 14; INT CANR-16; MTCW

Wellek, Rene 1903-1995 . . . . **CLC 28**
See also CA 5-8R; 150; CAAS 7; CANR 8;
DLB 63; INT CANR-8

Weller, Michael 1942- . . . . **CLC 10, 53**
See also CA 85-88

Weller, Paul 1958- . . . . **CLC 26**

Wellershoff, Dieter 1925- . . . . **CLC 46**
See also CA 89-92; CANR 16, 37

Welles, (George) Orson
1915-1985 . . . . **CLC 20, 80**
See also CA 93-96; 117

Wellman, Mac 1945- . . . . **CLC 65**

Wellman, Manly Wade 1903-1986 . . **CLC 49**
See also CA 1-4R; 118; CANR 6, 16, 44;
SATA 6; SATA-Obit 47

Wells, Carolyn 1869(?)-1942 . . . . . . **TCLC 35**
See also CA 113; DLB 11

Wells, H(erbert) G(eorge)
1866-1946 . . . . **TCLC 6, 12, 19; DA;**
DAB; DAC; SSC 6; WLC
See also CA 110; 121; CDBLB 1914-1945;
DAM MST, NOV; DLB 34, 70, 156;
MTCW; SATA 20

Wells, Rosemary 1943- . . . . **CLC 12**
See also AAYA 13; CA 85-88; CANR 48;
CLR 16; MAICYA; SAAS 1; SATA 18,
69

Welty, Eudora
1909- . . . . . . **CLC 1, 2, 5, 14, 22, 33; DA;**
DAB; DAC; SSC 1; WLC
See also CA 9-12R; CABS 1; CANR 32;
CDALB 1941-1968; DAM MST, NOV;
DLB 2, 102, 143; DLBD 12; DLBY 87;
MTCW

Wen I-to 1899-1946 . . . . **TCLC 28**

Wentworth, Robert
See Hamilton, Edmond

Werfel, Franz (V.) 1890-1945 . . . . . . **TCLC 8**
See also CA 104; DLB 81, 124

Wergeland, Henrik Arnold
1808-1845 . . . . **NCLC 5**

Wersba, Barbara 1932- . . . . **CLC 30**
See also AAYA 2; CA 29-32R; CANR 16,
38; CLR 3; DLB 52; JRDA; MAICYA;
SAAS 2; SATA 1, 58

Wertmueller, Lina 1928- . . . . **CLC 16**
See also CA 97-100; CANR 39

Wescott, Glenway 1901-1987 . . . . **CLC 13**
See also CA 13-16R; 121; CANR 23;
DLB 4, 9, 102

Wesker, Arnold 1932- . . **CLC 3, 5, 42; DAB**
See also CA 1-4R; CAAS 7; CANR 1, 33;
CDBLB 1960 to Present; DAM DRAM;
DLB 13; MTCW

Wesley, Richard (Errol) 1945- . . . . **CLC 7**
See also BW 1; CA 57-60; CANR 27;
DLB 38

Wessel, Johan Herman 1742-1785 . . . . **LC 7**

West, Anthony (Panther)
1914-1987 . . . . **CLC 50**
See also CA 45-48; 124; CANR 3, 19;
DLB 15

West, C. P.
See Wodehouse, P(elham) G(renville)

West, (Mary) Jessamyn
1902-1984 . . . . **CLC 7, 17**
See also CA 9-12R; 112; CANR 27; DLB 6;
DLBY 84; MTCW; SATA-Obit 37

West, Morris L(anglo) 1916- . . . . . **CLC 6, 33**
See also CA 5-8R; CANR 24, 49; MTCW

West, Nathanael
1903-1940 . . . . . **TCLC 1, 14, 44; SSC 16**
See also CA 104; 125; CDALB 1929-1941;
DLB 4, 9, 28; MTCW

West, Owen
See Koontz, Dean R(ay)

West, Paul 1930- . . . . **CLC 7, 14**
See also CA 13-16R; CAAS 7; CANR 22;
DLB 14; INT CANR-22

West, Rebecca 1892-1983 . . **CLC 7, 9, 31, 50**
See also CA 5-8R; 109; CANR 19; DLB 36;
DLBY 83; MTCW

Westall, Robert (Atkinson)
1929-1993 . . . . **CLC 17**
See also AAYA 12; CA 69-72; 141;
CANR 18; CLR 13; JRDA; MAICYA;
SAAS 2; SATA 23, 69; SATA-Obit 75

Westlake, Donald E(dwin)
1933- . . . . **CLC 7, 33**
See also CA 17-20R; CAAS 13; CANR 16,
44; DAM POP; INT CANR-16

Westmacott, Mary
See Christie, Agatha (Mary Clarissa)

Weston, Allen
See Norton, Andre

Wetcheek, J. L.
See Feuchtwanger, Lion

Wetering, Janwillem van de
See van de Wetering, Janwillem

Wetherell, Elizabeth
See Warner, Susan (Bogert)

Whale, James 1889-1957 . . . . **TCLC 63**

Whalen, Philip 1923- . . . . **CLC 6, 29**
See also CA 9-12R; CANR 5, 39; DLB 16

Wharton, Edith (Newbold Jones)
1862-1937 . . . . . . **TCLC 3, 9, 27, 53; DA;**
DAB; DAC; SSC 6; WLC
See also CA 104; 132; CDALB 1865-1917;
DAM MST, NOV; DLB 4, 9, 12, 78;
DLBD 13; MTCW

Wharton, James
See Mencken, H(enry) L(ouis)

Wharton, William (a pseudonym)
. . . . **CLC 18, 37**
See also CA 93-96; DLBY 80; INT 93-96

Wheatley (Peters), Phillis
1754(?)-1784 . . . . **LC 3; BLC; DA; DAC;**
PC 3; WLC
See also CDALB 1640-1865; DAM MST,
MULT, POET; DLB 31, 50

Wheelock, John Hall 1886-1978 . . . . **CLC 14**
See also CA 13-16R; 77-80; CANR 14;
DLB 45

White, E(lwyn) B(rooks)
1899-1985 . . . . **CLC 10, 34, 39**
See also AITN 2; CA 13-16R; 116;
CANR 16, 37; CLR 1, 21; DAM POP;
DLB 11, 22; MAICYA; MTCW;
SATA 2, 29; SATA-Obit 44

White, Edmund (Valentine III)
1940- . . . . **CLC 27**
See also AAYA 7; CA 45-48; CANR 3, 19,
36; DAM POP; MTCW

White, Patrick (Victor Martindale)
1912-1990 . . **CLC 3, 4, 5, 7, 9, 18, 65, 69**
See also CA 81-84; 132; CANR 43; MTCW

White, Phyllis Dorothy James 1920-
See James, P. D.
See also CA 21-24R; CANR 17, 43;
DAM POP; MTCW

White, T(erence) H(anbury)
1906-1964 . . . . **CLC 30**
See also CA 73-76; CANR 37; DLB 160;
JRDA; MAICYA; SATA 12

White, Terence de Vere
1912-1994 . . . . **CLC 49**
See also CA 49-52; 145; CANR 3

White, Walter F(rancis)
1893-1955 . . . . **TCLC 15**
See also White, Walter
See also BW 1; CA 115; 124; DLB 51

White, William Hale 1831-1913
See Rutherford, Mark
See also CA 121

Whitehead, E(dward) A(nthony)
1933- . . . . **CLC 5**
See also CA 65-68

Whitemore, Hugh (John) 1936- . . . . . **CLC 37**
See also CA 132; INT 132

Whitman, Sarah Helen (Power)
1803-1878 . . . . **NCLC 19**
See also DLB 1

Whitman, Walt(er)
1819-1892 . . . . . **NCLC 4, 31; DA; DAB;**
DAC; PC 3; WLC
See also CDALB 1640-1865; DAM MST,
POET; DLB 3, 64; SATA 20

Whitney, Phyllis A(yame) 1903- . . . . **CLC 42**
See also AITN 2; BEST 90:3; CA 1-4R;
CANR 3, 25, 38; DAM POP; JRDA;
MAICYA; SATA 1, 30

Whittemore, (Edward) Reed (Jr.)
1919- . . . . **CLC 4**
See also CA 9-12R; CAAS 8; CANR 4;
DLB 5

Whittier, John Greenleaf
1807-1892 . . . . **NCLC 8**
See also CDALB 1640-1865; DAM POET;
DLB 1

Whittlebot, Hernia
See Coward, Noel (Peirce)

Winchilsea, Anne (Kingsmill) Finch Counte
1661-1720 .... LC 3

Windham, Basil
See Wodehouse, P(elham) G(renville)

Wingrove, David (John) 1954-...... CLC 68
See also CA 133

Winters, Janet Lewis .... CLC 41
See also Lewis, Janet
See also DLBY 87

Winters, (Arthur) Yvor
1900-1968 .... CLC 4, 8, 32
See also CA 11-12; 25-28R; CAP 1;
DLB 48; MTCW

Winterson, Jeanette 1959-......... CLC 64
See also CA 136; DAM POP

Winthrop, John 1588-1649......... LC 31
See also DLB 24, 30

Wiseman, Frederick 1930-........ CLC 20

Wister, Owen 1860-1938 .... TCLC 21
See also CA 108; DLB 9, 78; SATA 62

Witkacy
See Witkiewicz, Stanislaw Ignacy

Witkiewicz, Stanislaw Ignacy
1885-1939 .... TCLC 8
See also CA 105

Wittgenstein, Ludwig (Josef Johann)
1889-1951 .... TCLC 59
See also CA 113

Wittig, Monique 1935(?)-......... CLC 22
See also CA 116; 135; DLB 83

Wittlin, Jozef 1896-1976 .... CLC 25
See also CA 49-52; 65-68; CANR 3

Wodehouse, P(elham) G(renville)
1881-1975 ... CLC 1, 2, 5, 10, 22; DAB;
DAC; SSC 2
See also AITN 2; CA 45-48; 57-60;
CANR 3, 33; CDBLB 1914-1945;
DAM NOV; DLB 34, 162; MTCW;
SATA 22

Woiwode, L.
See Woiwode, Larry (Alfred)

Woiwode, Larry (Alfred) 1941-... CLC 6, 10
See also CA 73-76; CANR 16; DLB 6;
INT CANR-16

Wojciechowska, Maia (Teresa)
1927- .... CLC 26
See also AAYA 8; CA 9-12R; CANR 4, 41;
CLR 1; JRDA; MAICYA; SAAS 1;
SATA 1, 28, 83

Wolf, Christa 1929- .... CLC 14, 29, 58
See also CA 85-88; CANR 45; DLB 75;
MTCW

Wolfe, Gene (Rodman) 1931-...... CLC 25
See also CA 57-60; CAAS 9; CANR 6, 32;
DAM POP; DLB 8

Wolfe, George C. 1954- .... CLC 49
See also CA 149

Wolfe, Thomas (Clayton)
1900-1938 ..... TCLC 4, 13, 29, 61; DA;
DAB; DAC; WLC
See also CA 104; 132; CDALB 1929-1941;
DAM MST, NOV; DLB 9, 102; DLBD 2;
DLBY 85; MTCW

Wolfe, Thomas Kennerly, Jr. 1931-
See Wolfe, Tom
See also CA 13-16R; CANR 9, 33;
DAM POP; INT CANR-9; MTCW

Wolfe, Tom .... CLC 1, 2, 9, 15, 35, 51
See also Wolfe, Thomas Kennerly, Jr.
See also AAYA 8; AITN 2; BEST 89:1;
DLB 152

Wolff, Geoffrey (Ansell) 1937- ..... CLC 41
See also CA 29-32R; CANR 29, 43

Wolff, Sonia
See Levitin, Sonia (Wolff)

Wolff, Tobias (Jonathan Ansell)
1945- .... CLC 39, 64
See also AAYA 16; BEST 90:2; CA 114;
117; CAAS 22; DLB 130; INT 117

Wolfram von Eschenbach
c. 1170-c. 1220 .... CMLC 5
See also DLB 138

Wolitzer, Hilma 1930-............ CLC 17
See also CA 65-68; CANR 18, 40;
INT CANR-18; SATA 31

Wollstonecraft, Mary 1759-1797...... LC 5
See also CDBLB 1789-1832; DLB 39, 104,
158

Wonder, Stevie .... CLC 12
See also Morris, Steveland Judkins

Wong, Jade Snow 1922-........... CLC 17
See also CA 109

Woodcott, Keith
See Brunner, John (Kilian Houston)

Woodruff, Robert W.
See Mencken, H(enry) L(ouis)

Woolf, (Adeline) Virginia
1882-1941 ...... TCLC 1, 5, 20, 43, 56;
DA; DAB; DAC; SSC 7; WLC
See also CA 104; 130; CDBLB 1914-1945;
DAM MST, NOV; DLB 36, 100, 162;
DLBD 10; MTCW

Woollcott, Alexander (Humphreys)
1887-1943 .... TCLC 5
See also CA 105; DLB 29

Woolrich, Cornell 1903-1968....... CLC 77
See also Hopley-Woolrich, Cornell George

Wordsworth, Dorothy
1771-1855 .... NCLC 25
See also DLB 107

Wordsworth, William
1770-1850 .... NCLC 12, 38; DA; DAB;
DAC; PC 4; WLC
See also CDBLB 1789-1832; DAM MST,
POET; DLB 93, 107

Wouk, Herman 1915-......... CLC 1, 9, 38
See also CA 5-8R; CANR 6, 33;
DAM NOV, POP; DLBY 82;
INT CANR-6; MTCW

Wright, Charles (Penzel, Jr.)
1935- .... CLC 6, 13, 28
See also CA 29-32R; CAAS 7; CANR 23,
36; DLB 165; DLBY 82; MTCW

Wright, Charles Stevenson
1932- .... CLC 49; BLC 3
See also BW 1; CA 9-12R; CANR 26;
DAM MULT, POET; DLB 33

Wright, Jack R.
See Harris, Mark

Wright, James (Arlington)
1927-1980 .... CLC 3, 5, 10, 28
See also AITN 2; CA 49-52; 97-100;
CANR 4, 34; DAM POET; DLB 5;
MTCW

Wright, Judith (Arandell)
1915- .... CLC 11, 53; PC 14
See also CA 13-16R; CANR 31; MTCW;
SATA 14

Wright, L(aurali) R. 1939-........ CLC 44
See also CA 138

Wright, Richard (Nathaniel)
1908-1960 .... CLC 1, 3, 4, 9, 14, 21, 48,
74; BLC; DA; DAB; DAC; SSC 2; WLC
See also AAYA 5; BW 1; CA 108;
CDALB 1929-1941; DAM MST, MULT,
NOV; DLB 76, 102; DLBD 2; MTCW

Wright, Richard B(ruce) 1937- ...... CLC 6
See also CA 85-88; DLB 53

Wright, Rick 1945-.............. CLC 35

Wright, Rowland
See Wells, Carolyn

Wright, Stephen Caldwell 1946- .... CLC 33
See also BW 2

Wright, Willard Huntington 1888-1939
See Van Dine, S. S.
See also CA 115

Wright, William 1930-............ CLC 44
See also CA 53-56; CANR 7, 23

Wroth, LadyMary 1587-1653(?) ..... LC 30
See also DLB 121

Wu Ch'eng-en 1500(?)-1582(?)........ LC 7

Wu Ching-tzu 1701-1754 .... LC 2

Wurlitzer, Rudolph 1938(?)- ... CLC 2, 4, 15
See also CA 85-88

Wycherley, William 1641-1715 .... LC 8, 21
See also CDBLB 1660-1789; DAM DRAM;
DLB 80

Wylie, Elinor (Morton Hoyt)
1885-1928 .... TCLC 8
See also CA 105; DLB 9, 45

Wylie, Philip (Gordon) 1902-1971... CLC 43
See also CA 21-22; 33-36R; CAP 2; DLB 9

Wyndham, John.................. CLC 19
See also Harris, John (Wyndham Parkes
Lucas) Beynon

Wyss, Johann David Von
1743-1818 .... NCLC 10
See also JRDA; MAICYA; SATA 29;
SATA-Brief 27

Xenophon
c. 430B.C.-c. 354B.C........ CMLC 17

Yakumo Koizumi
See Hearn, (Patricio) Lafcadio (Tessima
Carlos)

Yanez, Jose Donoso
See Donoso (Yanez), Jose

Yanovsky, Basile S.
See Yanovsky, V(assily) S(emenovich)

Yanovsky, V(assily) S(emenovich)
1906-1989 .... CLC 2, 18
See also CA 97-100; 129

Yates, Richard 1926-1992 . . . . . **CLC 7, 8, 23**
See also CA 5-8R; 139; CANR 10, 43;
DLB 2; DLBY 81, 92; INT CANR-10

Yeats, W. B.
See Yeats, William Butler

Yeats, William Butler
1865-1939 . . . . . **TCLC 1, 11, 18, 31; DA;
DAB; DAC; WLC**
See also CA 104; 127; CANR 45;
CDBLB 1890-1914; DAM DRAM, MST,
POET; DLB 10, 19, 98, 156; MTCW

Yehoshua, A(braham) B.
1936- . . . . **CLC 13, 31**
See also CA 33-36R; CANR 43

Yep, Laurence Michael 1948- . . . . . . **CLC 35**
See also AAYA 5; CA 49-52; CANR 1, 46;
CLR 3, 17; DLB 52; JRDA; MAICYA;
SATA 7, 69

Yerby, Frank G(arvin)
1916-1991 . . . . **CLC 1, 7, 22; BLC**
See also BW 1; CA 9-12R; 136; CANR 16;
DAM MULT; DLB 76; INT CANR-16;
MTCW

Yesenin, Sergei Alexandrovich
See Esenin, Sergei (Alexandrovich)

Yevtushenko, Yevgeny (Alexandrovich)
1933- . . . . **CLC 1, 3, 13, 26, 51**
See also CA 81-84; CANR 33;
DAM POET; MTCW

Yezierska, Anzia 1885(?)-1970 . . . . . **CLC 46**
See also CA 126; 89-92; DLB 28; MTCW

Yglesias, Helen 1915- . . . . **CLC 7, 22**
See also CA 37-40R; CAAS 20; CANR 15;
INT CANR-15; MTCW

Yokomitsu Riichi 1898-1947 . . . . . . **TCLC 47**

Yonge, Charlotte (Mary)
1823-1901 . . . . **TCLC 48**
See also CA 109; DLB 18, 163; SATA 17

York, Jeremy
See Creasey, John

York, Simon
See Heinlein, Robert A(nson)

Yorke, Henry Vincent 1905-1974 . . . **CLC 13**
See also Green, Henry
See also CA 85-88; 49-52

Yosano Akiko 1878-1942 . . **TCLC 59; PC 11**

Yoshimoto, Banana . . . . **CLC 84**
See also Yoshimoto, Mahoko

Yoshimoto, Mahoko 1964-
See Yoshimoto, Banana
See also CA 144

Young, Al(bert James)
1939- . . . . **CLC 19; BLC**
See also BW 2; CA 29-32R; CANR 26;
DAM MULT; DLB 33

Young, Andrew (John) 1885-1971 . . . . **CLC 5**
See also CA 5-8R; CANR 7, 29

Young, Collier
See Bloch, Robert (Albert)

Young, Edward 1683-1765 . . . . **LC 3**
See also DLB 95

Young, Marguerite (Vivian)
1909-1995 . . . . **CLC 82**
See also CA 13-16; 150; CAP 1

Young, Neil 1945- . . . . **CLC 17**
See also CA 110

Yourcenar, Marguerite
1903-1987 . . . . **CLC 19, 38, 50, 87**
See also CA 69-72; CANR 23; DAM NOV;
DLB 72; DLBY 88; MTCW

Yurick, Sol 1925- . . . . **CLC 6**
See also CA 13-16R; CANR 25

Zabolotskii, Nikolai Alekseevich
1903-1958 . . . . **TCLC 52**
See also CA 116

Zamiatin, Yevgenii
See Zamyatin, Evgeny Ivanovich

Zamora, Bernice (B. Ortiz)
1938- . . . . **CLC 89; HLC**
See also DAM MULT; DLB 82; HW

Zamyatin, Evgeny Ivanovich
1884-1937 . . . . **TCLC 8, 37**
See also CA 105

Zangwill, Israel 1864-1926 . . . . **TCLC 16**
See also CA 109; DLB 10, 135

Zappa, Francis Vincent, Jr. 1940-1993
See Zappa, Frank
See also CA 108; 143

Zappa, Frank . . . . **CLC 17**
See also Zappa, Francis Vincent, Jr.

Zaturenska, Marya 1902-1982 . . . . **CLC 6, 11**
See also CA 13-16R; 105; CANR 22

Zelazny, Roger (Joseph)
1937-1995 . . . . **CLC 21**
See also AAYA 7; CA 21-24R; 148;
CANR 26; DLB 8; MTCW; SATA 57;
SATA-Brief 39

Zhdanov, Andrei A(lexandrovich)
1896-1948 . . . . **TCLC 18**
See also CA 117

Zhukovsky, Vasily 1783-1852 . . . . **NCLC 35**

Ziegenhagen, Eric . . . . **CLC 55**

Zimmer, Jill Schary
See Robinson, Jill

Zimmerman, Robert
See Dylan, Bob

Zindel, Paul
1936- . . . . . **CLC 6, 26; DA; DAB; DAC;
DC 5**
See also AAYA 2; CA 73-76; CANR 31;
CLR 3; DAM DRAM, MST, NOV;
DLB 7, 52; JRDA; MAICYA; MTCW;
SATA 16, 58

Zinov'Ev, A. A.
See Zinoviev, Alexander (Aleksandrovich)

Zinoviev, Alexander (Aleksandrovich)
1922- . . . . **CLC 19**
See also CA 116; 133; CAAS 10

Zoilus
See Lovecraft, H(oward) P(hillips)

Zola, Emile (Edouard Charles Antoine)
1840-1902 . . . . . . **TCLC 1, 6, 21, 41; DA;
DAB; DAC; WLC**
See also CA 104; 138; DAM MST, NOV;
DLB 123

Zoline, Pamela 1941- . . . . **CLC 62**

Zorrilla y Moral, Jose 1817-1893 . . **NCLC 6**

Zoshchenko, Mikhail (Mikhailovich)
1895-1958 . . . . **TCLC 15; SSC 15**
See also CA 115

Zuckmayer, Carl 1896-1977 . . . . **CLC 18**
See also CA 69-72; DLB 56, 124

Zuk, Georges
See Skelton, Robin

Zukofsky, Louis
1904-1978 . . . . **CLC 1, 2, 4, 7, 11, 18;
PC 11**
See also CA 9-12R; 77-80; CANR 39;
DAM POET; DLB 5, 165; MTCW

Zweig, Paul 1935-1984 . . . . **CLC 34, 42**
See also CA 85-88; 113

Zweig, Stefan 1881-1942 . . . . **TCLC 17**
See also CA 112; DLB 81, 118

Literary Criticism Series
Cumulative Topic Index

This index lists all topic entries in Gale's *Classical and Medieval Literature Criticism, Contemporary Literary Criticism, Literature Criticism from 1400 to 1800, Nineteenth-Century Literature Criticism,* and *Twentieth-Century Literary Criticism.*

Age of Johnson LC 15: 1-87
   Johnson's London, 3-15
   aesthetics of neoclassicism, 15-36
   "age of prose and reason," 36-45
   clubmen and bluestockings, 45-56
   printing technology, 56-62
   periodicals: "a map of busy life," 62-74
   transition, 74-86

AIDS in Literature CLC 81: 365-416

American Abolitionism NCLC 44: 1-73
   overviews, 2-26
   abolitionist ideals, 26-46
   the literature of abolitionism, 46-72

American Black Humor Fiction TCLC 54: 1-85
   characteristics of black humor, 2-13
   origins and development, 13-38
   black humor distinguished from related literary trends, 38-60
   black humor and society, 60-75
   black humor reconsidered, 75-83

American Civil War in Literature NCLC 32: 1-109
   overviews, 2-20
   regional perspectives, 20-54
   fiction popular during the war, 54-79
   the historical novel, 79-108

American Frontier in Literature NCLC 28: 1-103
   definitions, 2-12
   development, 12-17
   nonfiction writing about the frontier, 17-30
   frontier fiction, 30-45
   frontier protagonists, 45-66
   portrayals of Native Americans, 66-86
   feminist readings, 86-98

twentieth-century reaction against frontier literature, 98-100

American Humor Writing NCLC 52: 1-59
   overviews, 2-12
   the Old Southwest, 12-42
   broader impacts, 42-5
   women humorists, 45-58

American Popular Song, Golden Age of TCLC 42: 1-49
   background and major figures, 2-34
   the lyrics of popular songs, 34-47

American Proletarian Literature TCLC 54: 86-175
   overviews, 87-95
   American proletarian literature and the American Communist Party, 95-111
   ideology and literary merit, 111-7
   novels, 117-36
   Gastonia, 136-48
   drama, 148-54
   journalism, 154-9
   proletarian literature in the United States, 159-74

American Romanticism NCLC 44: 74-138
   overviews, 74-84
   sociopolitical influences, 84-104
   Romanticism and the American frontier, 104-15
   thematic concerns, 115-37

American Western Literature TCLC 46: 1-100
   definition and development of American Western literature, 2-7
   characteristics of the Western novel, 8-23
   Westerns as history and fiction, 23-34
   critical reception of American Western

literature, 34-41
the Western hero, 41-73
women in Western fiction, 73-91
later Western fiction, 91-9

Art and Literature TCLC 54: 176-248
   overviews, 176-93
   definitions, 193-219
   influence of visual arts on literature, 219-31
   spatial form in literature, 231-47

Arthurian Literature CMLC 10: 1-127
   historical context and literary beginnings, 2-27
   development of the legend through Malory, 27-64
   development of the legend from Malory to the Victorian Age, 65-81
   themes and motifs, 81-95
   principal characters, 95-125

Arthurian Revival NCLC 36: 1-77
   overviews, 2-12
   Tennyson and his influence, 12-43
   other leading figures, 43-73
   the Arthurian legend in the visual arts, 73-6

Australian Literature TCLC 50: 1-94
   origins and development, 2-21
   characteristics of Australian literature, 21-33
   historical and critical perspectives, 33-41
   poetry, 41-58
   fiction, 58-76
   drama, 76-82
   Aboriginal literature, 82-91

Beat Generation, Literature of the TCLC 42: 50-102

CLC Cumulative Nationality Index

Nationality Index

Nationality Index

Nationality Index

Nationality Index

CLC-93 Title Index

453

ISBN 0-8103-9271-2

90000